Praise for the Reformation Commentary on Scripture

"Protestant reformers were fundamentally exegetes as much as theologians, yet (except for figures like Luther and Calvin) their commentaries and sermons have been neglected because these writings are not available in modern editions or languages. That makes this new series of Reformation Commentary on Scripture most welcome as a way to provide access to some of the wealth of biblical exposition of the sixteenth and seventeenth centuries. The editor's introduction explains the nature of the sources and the selection process; the intended audience of modern pastors and students of the Bible has led to a focus on theological and practical comments. Although it will be of use to students of the Reformation, this series is far from being an esoteric study of largely forgotten voices; this collection of reforming comments, comprehending every verse and provided with topical headings, will serve contemporary pastors and preachers very well."

Elsie Anne McKee, *Retired Archibald Alexander Professor of Reformation Studies and the History of Worship, Princeton Theological Seminary*

"This series provides an excellent introduction to the history of biblical exegesis in the Reformation period. The introductions are accurate, clear and informative, and the passages intelligently chosen to give the reader a good idea of methods deployed and issues at stake. It puts precritical exegesis in its context and so presents it in its correct light. Highly recommended as reference book, course book and general reading for students and all interested lay and clerical readers."

Irena Backus, *Professeure Ordinaire, Institut d'histoire de la Réformation, Université de Genève*†

"The Reformation Commentary on Scripture is a major publishing event—for those with historical interest in the founding convictions of Protestantism, but even more for those who care about understanding the Bible. As with IVP Academic's earlier Ancient Christian Commentary on Scripture, this effort brings flesh and blood to 'the communion of saints' by letting believers of our day look over the shoulders of giants from the past. By connecting the past with the present, and by doing so with the Bible at the center, the editors of this series perform a great service for the church. The series deserves the widest possible support."

Mark A. Noll, *Professor Emeritus, University of Notre Dame*

"For those who preach and teach Scripture in the church, the Reformation Commentary on Scripture is a significant publishing event. Pastors and other church leaders will find delightful surprises, challenging enigmas and edifying insights in this series, as many Reformational voices are newly translated into English. The lively conversation in these pages can ignite today's pastoral imagination for fresh and faithful expositions of Scripture."

J. Todd Billings, *Gordon H. Girod Research Professor of Reformed Theology, Western Theological Seminary*

"The reformers discerned rightly what the church desperately needed in the sixteenth century—the bold proclamation of the Word based on careful study of the sacred Scriptures. We need not only to hear that same call again for our own day but also to learn from the Reformation how to do it. This commentary series is a godsend!"

Richard J. Mouw, *President Emeritus and Senior Professor of Faith and Public Life, Fuller Theological Seminary*

"Like the Ancient Christian Commentary on Scripture, the Reformation Commentary on Scripture does a masterful job of offering excellent selections from well-known and not-so-well-known exegetes. The editor's introductory survey is, by itself, worth the price of the book. It is easy to forget that there were more hands, hearts and minds involved in the Reformation than Luther and Calvin. Furthermore, encounters even with these figures are often limited to familiar quotes on familiar topics. However, the Reformation Commentary helps us to recognize the breadth and depth of exegetical interests and skill that fueled and continue to fuel faithful meditation on God's Word. I heartily recommend this series as a tremendous resource not only for ministry but for personal edification."

Michael S. Horton, *J. Gresham Machen Professor of Systematic Theology and Apologetics, Westminster Seminary, California*

"The Reformation was ignited by a fresh reading of Scripture. In this series of commentaries, we contemporary interpreters are allowed to feel some of the excitement, surprise and wonder of our spiritual forebears. Luther, Calvin and their fellow revolutionaries were masterful interpreters of the Word. Now, in this remarkable series, some of our very best Reformation scholars open up the riches of the Reformation's reading of the Scripture."

William H. Willimon, *Professor of the Practice of Christian Ministry, Duke Divinity School*

"The Reformation Scripture principle set the entirety of Christian life and thought under the governance of the divine Word, and pressed the church to renew its exegetical labors. This series promises to place before the contemporary church the fruit of those labors, and so to exemplify life under the Word."

John Webster, *Professor of Divinity, University of St. Andrews*†

"Since Gerhard Ebeling's pioneering work on Luther's exegesis seventy years ago, the history of biblical interpretation has occupied many Reformation scholars and become a vital part of study of the period. The Reformation Commentary on Scripture provides fresh materials for students of Reformation-era biblical interpretation and for twenty-first-century preachers to mine the rich stores of insights from leading reformers of the sixteenth century into both the text of Scripture itself and its application in sixteenth-century contexts. This series will strengthen our understanding of the period of the Reformation and enable us to apply its insights to our own days and its challenges to the church."

Robert Kolb, *Professor Emeritus, Concordia Theological Seminary*

"The multivolume Ancient Christian Commentary on Scripture is a valuable resource for those who wish to know how the Fathers interpreted a passage of Scripture but who lack the time or the opportunity to search through the many individual works. This new Reformation Commentary on Scripture will do the same for the reformers and is to be warmly welcomed. It will provide much easier access to the exegetical treasures of the Reformation and will hopefully encourage readers to go back to some of the original works themselves."

Anthony N. S. Lane, *Professor of Historical Doctrine, Lecturer in Doctrine, London School of Theology*

"This volume of the RCS project is an invaluable source for pastors and the historically/biblically interested that provides unparalleled access not only to commentaries of the leading Protestant reformers but also to a host of nowadays unknown commentaters on Galatians and Ephesians. The RCS is sure to enhance and enliven contemporary exegesis. With its wide scope, the collection will enrich our understanding of the variety of Reformation thought and biblical exegesis."

Sigrun Haude, *Associate Professor of Reformation and Early Modern European History, University of Cincinnati*

"This grand project sets before scholars, pastors, teachers, students and growing Christians an experience that can only be likened to stumbling into a group Bible study only to discover that your fellow participants include some of the most significant Christians of the Reformation and post-Reformation (for that matter, of any) era. Here the Word of God is explained in a variety of accents: German, Swiss, French, Dutch, English, Scottish and more. Each one vibrates with a thrilling sense of the living nature of God's Word and its power to transform individuals, churches and even whole communities. Here is a series to anticipate, enjoy and treasure."

Sinclair Ferguson, *Professor of Systematic Theology, Reformed Theological Seminary*

"I strongly endorse the Reformation Commentary on Scripture. Introducing how the Bible was interpreted during the age of the Reformation, these volumes will not only renew contemporary preaching, but they will also help us understand more fully how reading and meditating on Scripture can, in fact, change our lives!"

Lois Malcolm, *Professor and Olin and Amanda Fjelstad Registad Chair for Systematic Theology, Luther Seminary*

"Discerning the true significance of movements in theology requires acquaintance with their biblical exegesis. This is supremely so with the Reformation, which was essentially a biblical revival. The Reformation Commentary on Scripture will fill a yawning gap, just as the Ancient Christian Commentary did before it, and the first volume gets the series off to a fine start, whetting the appetite for more. Most heartily do I welcome and commend this long overdue project."

J. I. Packer, *Board of Governors' Professor of Theology, Regent College*[†]

"There is no telling the benefits to emerge from the publication of this magnificent Reformation Commentary on Scripture series! Now exegetical and theological treasures from Reformation era commentators will be at our fingertips, providing new insights from old sources to give light for the present and future. This series is a gift to scholars and to the church; a wonderful resource to enhance our study of the written Word of God for generations to come!"

Donald K. McKim, *Executive Editor of Theology and Reference, Westminster John Knox Press*

"Why was this not done before? The publication of the Reformation Commentary on Scripture should be greeted with enthusiasm by every believing Christian—but especially by those who will preach and teach the Word of God. This commentary series brings the very best of the Reformation heritage to the task of exegesis and exposition, and each volume in this series represents a veritable feast that takes us back to the sixteenth century to enrich the preaching and teaching of God's Word in our own time."

R. Albert Mohler Jr., *President, The Southern Baptist Theological Seminary*

"Today more than ever, the Christian past is the church's future. InterVarsity Press has already brought the voice of the ancients to our ears. Now, in the Reformation Commentary on Scripture, we hear a timely word from the first Protestants as well."

Bryan Litfin, *Moody Publishers*

"I am delighted to see the Reformation Commentary on Scripture. The editors of this series have done us all a service by gleaning from these rich fields of biblical reflection. May God use this new life for these old words to give him glory and to build his church."

Mark Dever, *Senior Pastor, Capitol Hill Baptist Church, and President of 9Marks Ministries*

"Monumental and magisterial, the Reformation Commentary on Scripture, edited by Timothy George, is a remarkably bold and visionary undertaking. Bringing together a wealth of resources, these volumes will provide historians, theologians, biblical scholars, pastors and students with a fresh look at the exegetical insights of those who shaped and influenced the sixteenth-century Reformation. With this marvelous publication, InterVarsity Press has reached yet another plateau of excellence. We pray that this superb series will be used of God to strengthen both church and academy."

David S. Dockery, *President of the International Alliance for Christian Education*

"Detached from her roots, the church cannot reach the world as God intends. While every generation must steward the scriptural insights God grants it, only arrogance or ignorance causes leaders to ignore the contributions of those faithful leaders before us. The Reformation Commentary on Scripture roots our thought in great insights of faithful leaders of the Reformation to further biblical preaching and teaching in this generation."

Bryan Chapell, *President Emeritus, Covenant Theological Seminary*

"After reading several volumes of the Reformation Commentary on Scripture, I exclaimed, 'Hey, this is just what the doctor ordered—I mean Doctor Martinus Lutherus!' The church of today bearing his name needs a strong dose of the medicine this doctor prescribed for the ailing church of the sixteenth century. The reforming fire of Christ-centered preaching that Luther ignited is the only hope to reclaim the impact of the gospel to keep the Reformation going, not for its own sake but to further the renewal of the worldwide church of Christ today. This series of commentaries will equip preachers to step into their pulpits with confidence in the same living Word that inspired the witness of Luther and Calvin and many other lesser-known reformers."

Carl E. Braaten, *Cofounder of the Center for Catholic and Evangelical Theology*

"As a pastor, how does one cultivate a knowledge of the history of interpretation? That's where IVP's Reformation Commentary on Scripture and its forerunner, the Ancient Christian Commentary on Scripture, come in. They do an excellent job in helping pastors become more aware of the history of exegesis for the benefit of their congregations. Every pastor should have access to a set of each."

Carl R. Trueman, *Professor of Biblical and Religious Studies, Grove City College*

Reformation Commentary on Scripture

New Testament

IXb

2 Corinthians

Edited by
Scott M. Manetsch

General Editor
Timothy George

Associate General Editor
Scott M. Manetsch

IVP Academic
An imprint of InterVarsity Press
Downers Grove, Illinois

InterVarsity Press
P.O. Box 1400 | Downers Grove, IL 60515-1426
ivpress.com | email@ivpress.com

InterVarsity Press® is the book-publishing division of InterVarsity Christian Fellowship/USA®. For information, visit intervarsity.org.

Design: Cindy Kiple

ISBN 978-0-8308-2487-8 (print) | ISBN 978-1-5140-0477-7 (digital)

Printed in the United States of America ♾

Library of Congress Cataloging-in-Publication Data
A catalog record for this book is available from the Library of Congress.

26 25 24 23 22 | 6 5 4 3 2 1

Dedicated to Doug Sweeney, trusted colleague and cherished friend

Reformation Commentary on Scripture
Project Staff

Project Editor
David W. McNutt

Managing Editor
Elissa Schauer

Assistant Managing Editor
Zachary Gordon

Copyeditor
Jeffrey A. Reimer

Assistant Project Editor
Travis Ables

Editorial and Research Assistants
David J. Hooper
Ashley Davila
April Ponto

Assistants to the General Editors
Evan Musgraves
Bryan Just
Christopher Gow

Design
Cindy Kiple

Proofreader
Gerard Cruz

InterVarsity Press

President & Publisher
Terumi Echols

Divisional Vice President, Editorial
Cindy Bunch

Associate Publisher and Academic Editorial Director
Jon Boyd

Director of Production
Benjamin M. McCoy

CONTENTS

ACKNOWLEDGMENTS

There are many people who deserve my heartfelt gratitude for their encouragement and practical assistance in the completion of this volume. In particular, I wish to thank friends and faculty colleagues John Woodbridge, Eckhard Schnabel, D. A. Carson, Graham Cole, David Luy, Kevin Vanhoozer, Eric Tully, Te-Li Lau, Steve Bryan, and Timothy George for their enthusiasm for this project and their support over these many years. Their friendship and partnership in Christian ministry mean so much to me. In addition, I am grateful for my excellent graduate assistants at Trinity Evangelical Divinity School who have lent a hand in this project by tracking down sources and reading drafts of my work, including Taylor Sexton, Caleb Jenkins, Thomas Parfitt, Bryan Just, and Christopher Gow. I am especially indebted to Thomas Parfitt for his significant contribution in translating German sources, particularly Cyriacus Spangenberg's *Die ander Epistel Pauli an die Corinthier*. My thanks also to the administration of Trinity Evangelical Divinity School for granting me a sabbatical in the spring of 2021, which allowed me to devote focused time to completing this commentary. Over the past decade and a half, it has been a special pleasure to work closely with the excellent editorial team at InterVarsity Press responsible for the Reformation Commentary on Scripture series. Dan Reid, Brannon Ellis, Andre Gazal, Todd Hains, David Hooper, Scott Prather, Travis Ables, and especially David McNutt: thank you for your professionalism, your hard work, and your sustained support and encouragement that have made this volume possible.

In addition, I would like to say a special thank-you to my family. I am so very grateful for the gracious support and love that my dear wife, Catherine, and my daughters, Hannah and Melissa, have shared with me during the course of this writing project. Thank you so much—each one of you is so precious to me.

This commentary is dedicated to Douglas Sweeney, who has been a cherished friend and trusted colleague for more than two decades. Doug, the countless hours we have spent discussing historical topics together, teaching together, praying together, and sharing family life together have been one of God's singular gifts in my life. I am deeply grateful for your friendship and partnership in Christian ministry over these many years.

Scott M. Manetsch

ABBREVIATIONS

ANF	*The Ante-Nicene Fathers.* 10 vols. Edited by Alexander Roberts and James Donaldson. Buffalo, NY: Christian Literature, 1885–1896. Available online at www.ccel.org.
BC	Kolb, Robert, and Timothy J. Wengert, eds. *The Book of Concord: The Confessions of the Evangelical Lutheran Church.* Translated by Charles Arand, Etic Gritsch, Robert Kolb, William Russell, James Schaff, Jane Stohl, and Timothy Wengert. Minneapolis: Fortress, 2000.
CO	*Ioannis Calvini Opera quae supersunt omnia.* 59 vols. Corpus Reformatorum 29-88. Edited by G. Baum, E. Cunitz, and E. Reuss. Berlin: C. A. Schwetschke, 1863–1900. Digital copies online at archive-ouverte.unige.ch/unige:650.
CPMB	*Common Places of Martin Bucer.* Edited by David F. Wright. The Courtenay Library of Reformation Classics 4. Berkshire, UK: Sutton Courtenay Press, 1972.
CR	*Corpus Reformatorum.* Edited by C. G. Bretschneider. Halle, 1834–1860.
CRR	Classics of the Radical Reformation. 12 vols. Waterloo, ON and Scottdale, PA: Herald Press, 1973–2018. Reprint, Walden, NY: Plough Publishing House, 2019–.
CTS	Calvin Translation Society edition of Calvin's commentaries. 46 vols. Edinburgh, 1843–1855. Several reprints, but variously bound; volume numbers (when cited) are relative to specific commentaries and not to the entire set. Available online at www.ccel.org.
CWE	*Collected Works of Erasmus.* 86 vols. planned. Toronto: University of Toronto Press, 1969–.
CWMS	*The Complete Writings of Menno Simons, c. 1496–1561.* Edited by J. C. Wenger. Scottdale, PA: Herald Press, 1984.
CWRS	*The Complete Works of Richard Sibbes.* Edited by Alexander B. Grosart. 7 vols. Edinburgh: James Nichol, 1862–1864.
LCL	Loeb Classical Library. Edited by Jeffrey Henderson. Cambridge, MA: Harvard University Press, 1911–. Digital copy online at www.loebclassics.com.
LW	*Luther's Works* [= "American Edition"]. 82 vols. planned. St. Louis: Concordia; Philadelphia: Fortress, 1955–1986; 2009–.
NPNF	*A Select Library of the Nicene and Post-Nicene Fathers of the Christian Church.* 28 vols. in two series, denoted as NPNF^1 and NPNF^2. Edited by Philip Schaff et al.

	Buffalo, NY: Christian Literature, 1887–1894. Several reprints; also available online at www.ccel.org.
OER	Hillerbrand, Hans, ed. *The Oxford Encyclopedia of the Reformation*. 4 vols. New York: Oxford University Press, 1996.
PG	*Patrologia cursus completus. Series Graeca*. 161 vols. Edited by J.-P. Migne. Paris, 1857–1866. Digital copies online at books.google.com.
PL	*Patrologia cursus completus. Series Latina*. 221 vols. Edited by J.-P. Migne. Paris: Migne, 1844–1864. Digital copies online at books.google.com.
SWHD	*Selected Writings of Hans Denck, 1500–1527*. Edited and translated by Edward J. Furcha. Texts and Studies in Religion Series. Lewiston, NY: Edwin Mellen, 1989.
WA	*D. Martin Luthers Werke, Kritische Gesamtausgabe: [Schriften]*. 73 vols. Weimar: Hermann Böhlaus Nachfolger, 1883–2009. Digital copies online at archive.org.
WABR	*D. Martin Luthers Werke, Kritische Gesamtausgabe. Briefwechsel*. 18 vols. Weimar, 1930–1985.
WTG	*The Works of Thomas Goodwin*. 12 vols. Edinburgh: James Nichol, 1861–1866.

A GUIDE TO USING THIS COMMENTARY

Several features have been incorporated into the design of this commentary. The following comments are intended to assist readers in making full use of this volume.

Pericopes of Scripture

The scriptural text has been divided into pericopes, or passages, usually several verses in length. Each of these pericopes is given a heading, which appears at the beginning of the pericope. For example, the first section in this commentary is 2 Corinthians 1:1-2, "Greeting." This heading is followed by the Scripture passage quoted in the English Standard Version (ESV). The Scripture passage is provided for the convenience of readers, but it is also in keeping with Reformation-era commentaries, which often followed the patristic and medieval commentary tradition, in which the citations of the reformers were arranged according to the text of Scripture.

Overviews

Following each pericope of text is an overview of the Reformation authors' comments on that pericope. The format of this overview varies among the volumes of this series, depending on the requirements of the specific book(s) of Scripture. The function of the overview is to identify succinctly the key exegetical, theological, and pastoral concerns of the Reformation writers arising from the pericope, providing the reader with an orientation to Reformation-era approaches and emphases. It tracks a reasonably cohesive thread of argument among reformers' comments, even though they are derived from diverse sources and generations. Thus, the summaries do not proceed chronologically or by verse sequence. Rather, they seek to rehearse the overall course of the reformers' comments on that pericope.

We do not assume that the commentators themselves anticipated or expressed a formally received cohesive argument but rather that the various arguments tend to flow in a plausible, recognizable pattern. Modern readers can thus glimpse aspects of continuity in the flow of diverse exegetical traditions representing various generations and geographical locations.

Topical Headings

An abundance of varied Reformation-era comment is available for each pericope. For this reason we have broken the pericopes into two levels. First is the verse with its topical heading.

The reformers' comments are then focused on aspects of each verse, with topical headings summarizing the essence of the individual comment by evoking a key phrase, metaphor, or idea. This feature provides a bridge by which modern readers can enter into the heart of the Reformation-era comment.

Identifying the Reformation Authors, Texts, and Events

Following the topical heading of each section of comment, the name of the Reformation commentator is given. An English translation (where needed) of the reformer's comment is then provided. This is immediately followed by the title of the original work rendered in English.

Readers who wish to pursue a deeper investigation of the reformers' works cited in this commentary will find full bibliographic detail for each Reformation title provided in the bibliography at the back of the volume. Information on English translations (where available) and standard original-language editions and critical editions of the works cited is found in the bibliography. The Biographical Sketches section provides brief overviews of the life and work of each commentator, and each confession or collaborative work, appearing in the present volume (as well as in any previous volumes). Finally, a Timeline of the Reformation offers broader context for people, places, and events relevant to the commentators and their works.

Footnotes and Back Matter

To aid the reader in exploring the background and texts in further detail, this commentary utilizes footnotes. The use and content of footnotes may vary among the volumes in this series. Where footnotes appear, a footnote number directs the reader to a note at the bottom of the page, where one will find annotations (clarifications or biblical cross references), information on English translations (where available) or standard original-language editions of the work cited.

Where original-language texts have remained untranslated into English, we provide new translations. Where there is any serious ambiguity or textual problem in the selection, we have tried to reflect the best available textual tradition. Wherever current English translations are already well rendered, they are utilized, but where necessary they are stylistically updated. A single asterisk (*) indicates that a previous English translation has been updated to modern English or amended for easier reading. We have standardized spellings and made grammatical variables uniform so that our English references will not reflect the linguistic oddities of the older English translations. For ease of reading we have in some cases removed superfluous conjunctions.

GENERAL INTRODUCTION

The Reformation Commentary on Scripture (RCS) is a twenty-eight-volume series of exegetical comment covering the entire Bible and gathered from the writings of sixteenth-century preachers, scholars and reformers. The RCS is intended as a sequel to the highly acclaimed Ancient Christian Commentary on Scripture (ACCS), and as such its overall concept, method, format, and audience are similar to the earlier series. Both series are committed to the renewal of the church through careful study and meditative reflection on the Old and New Testaments, the charter documents of Christianity, read in the context of the worshiping, believing community of faith across the centuries. However, the patristic and Reformation eras are separated by nearly a millennium, and the challenges of reading Scripture with the reformers require special attention to their context, resources and assumptions. The purpose of this general introduction is to present an overview of the context and process of biblical interpretation in the age of the Reformation.

Goals

The Reformation Commentary on Scripture seeks to introduce its readers to the depth and richness of exegetical ferment that defined the Reformation era. The RCS has four goals: the enrichment of contemporary biblical interpretation through exposure to Reformation-era biblical exegesis; the renewal of contemporary preaching through exposure to the biblical insights of the Reformation writers; a deeper understanding of the Reformation itself and the breadth of perspectives represented within it; and a recovery of the profound integration of the life of faith and the life of the mind that should characterize Christian scholarship. Each of these goals requires a brief comment.

Renewing contemporary biblical interpretation. During the past half-century, biblical hermeneutics has become a major growth industry in the academic world. One of the consequences of the historical-critical hegemony of biblical studies has been the privileging of contemporary philosophies and ideologies at the expense of a commitment to the Christian church as the primary reading community within which and for which biblical exegesis is done. Reading Scripture with the church fathers and the reformers is a corrective to all such imperialism of the present. One of the greatest skills required for a fruitful interpretation of the Bible is the ability to listen. We rightly emphasize the importance of listening to the voices of contextual theologies today, but in doing so we often marginalize or ignore another crucial context—the community of believing Christians through the centuries. The serious study of Scripture requires more than the latest

Bible translation in one hand and the latest commentary (or niche study Bible) in the other. John L. Thompson has called on Christians today to practice the art of "reading the Bible with the dead."[1] The RCS presents carefully selected comments from the extant commentaries of the Reformation as an encouragement to more in-depth study of this important epoch in the history of biblical interpretation.

Strengthening contemporary preaching. The Protestant reformers identified the public preaching of the Word of God as an indispensible means of grace and a sure sign of the true church. Through the words of the preacher, the living voice of the gospel (*viva vox evangelii*) is heard. Luther famously said that the church is not a "pen house" but a "mouth house."[2] The Reformation in Switzerland began when Huldrych Zwingli entered the pulpit of the Grossmünster in Zurich on January 1, 1519, and began to preach a series of expositional sermons chapter by chapter from the Gospel of Matthew. In the following years he extended this homiletical approach to other books of the Old and New Testaments. Calvin followed a similar pattern in Geneva. Many of the commentaries represented in this series were either originally presented as sermons or were written to support the regular preaching ministry of local church pastors. Luther said that the preacher should be a *bonus textualis*—a good one with a text—well-versed in the Scriptures. Preachers in the Reformation traditions preached not only about the Bible but also from it, and this required more than a passing acquaintance with its contents. Those who have been charged with the office of preaching in the church today can find wisdom and insight—and fresh perspectives—in the sermons of the Reformation and the biblical commentaries read and studied by preachers of the sixteenth century.

Deepening understanding of the Reformation. Some scholars of the sixteenth century prefer to speak of the period they study in the plural, the European Reformations, to indicate that many-diverse impulses for reform were at work in this turbulent age of transition from medieval to modern times.[3] While this point is well taken, the RCS follows the time-honored tradition of using *Reformation* in the singular form to indicate not only a major moment in the history of Christianity in the West but also, as Hans J. Hillerbrand has put it, "an essential cohesiveness in the heterogeneous pursuits of religious reform in the sixteenth century."[4] At the same time, in developing guidelines to assist the volume editors in making judicious selections from the vast amount of commentary material available in this period, we have stressed the multifaceted character of the Reformation across many confessions, theological orientations, and political settings.

Advancing Christian scholarship. By assembling and disseminating numerous voices from such a signal period as the Reformation, the RCS aims to make a significant contribution to the ever-growing stream of Christian scholarship. The post-Enlightenment split between the study of the Bible as an academic discipline and the reading of the Bible as spiritual nurture was foreign

[1]John L. Thompson, *Reading the Bible with the Dead* (Grand Rapids: Eerdmans, 2007).

[2]WA 10,2:48.

[3]See Carter Lindberg, *The European Reformations*, 2nd ed. (Malden, MA: Wiley-Blackwell, 2010).

[4]Hans J. Hillerbrand, *The Division of Christendom* (Louisville, KY: Westminster John Knox, 2007), x. Hillerbrand has also edited the standard reference work in Reformation studies, *OER*. See also Diarmaid MacCulloch, *The Reformation* (New York: Viking, 2003), and Patrick Collinson, *The Reformation: A History* (New York: Random House, 2004).

to the reformers. For them the study of the Bible was transformative at the most basic level of the human person: *coram deo.*

The reformers all repudiated the idea that the Bible could be studied and understood with dispassionate objectivity, as a cold artifact from antiquity. Luther's famous Reformation breakthrough triggered by his laborious study of the Psalms and Paul's letter to the Romans is well known, but the experience of Cambridge scholar Thomas Bilney was perhaps more typical. When Erasmus's critical edition of the Greek New Testament was published in 1516, it was accompanied by a new translation in elegant Latin. Attracted by the classical beauty of Erasmus's Latin, Bilney came across this statement in 1 Timothy 1:15: "Christ Jesus came into the world to save sinners." In the Greek this sentence is described as *pistos ho logos,* which the Vulgate had rendered *fidelis sermo,* "a faithful saying." Erasmus chose a different word for the Greek *pistos—certus,* "sure, certain." When Bilney grasped the meaning of this word applied to the announcement of salvation in Christ, he tells us that "immediately, I felt a marvellous comfort and quietness, insomuch as 'my bruised bones leaped for joy.'"[5]

Luther described the way the Bible was meant to function in the minds and hearts of believers when he reproached himself and others for studying the nativity narrative with such cool unconcern:

> I hate myself because when I see Christ laid in the manger or in the lap of his mother and hear the angels sing, my heart does not leap into flame. With what good reason should we all despise ourselves that we remain so cold when this word is spoken to us, over which everyone should dance and leap and burn for joy! We act as though it were a frigid historical fact that does not smite our hearts, as if someone were merely relating that the sultan has a crown of gold.[6]

It was a core conviction of the Reformation that the careful study and meditative listening to the Scriptures, what the monks called *lectio divina,* could yield transformative results for *all* of life. The value of such a rich commentary, therefore, lies not only in the impressive volume of Reformation-era voices that are presented throughout the course of the series but in the many particular fields for which their respective lives and ministries are relevant. The Reformation is consequential for historical studies, both church as well as secular history. Biblical and theological studies, to say nothing of pastoral and spiritual studies, also stand to benefit and progress immensely from renewed engagement today, as mediated through the RCS, with the reformers of yesteryear.

Perspectives

In setting forth the perspectives and parameters of the RCS, the following considerations have proved helpful.

Chronology. When did the Reformation begin, and how long did it last? In some traditional accounts, the answer was clear: the Reformation began with the posting of Luther's Ninety-five

[5]John Foxe, *The Acts and Monuments of John Foxe: A New and Complete Edition,* 8 vols., ed. Stephen Reed Cattley (London: R. B. Seeley & W. Burnside, 1837), 4:635; quoting Ps 51:8; cited in A. G. Dickens, *The English Reformation,* 2nd ed. (University Park, PA: The Pennsylvannia State University Press, 1991), 102.

[6]WA 49:176-77, quoted in Roland Bainton, "The Bible in the Reformation," in *CHB,* 3:23.

Theses at Wittenberg in 1517 and ended with the death of Calvin in Geneva in 1564. Apart from reducing the Reformation to a largely German event with a side trip to Switzerland, this perspective fails to do justice to the important events that led up to Luther's break with Rome and its many reverberations throughout Europe and beyond. In choosing commentary selections for the RCS, we have adopted the concept of the long sixteenth century, say, from the late 1400s to the mid-seventeenth century. Thus we have included commentary selections from early or pre-Reformation writers such as John Colet and Jacques Lefèvre d'Étaples to seventeenth-century figures such as Henry Ainsworth and Johann Gerhard.

Confession. The RCS concentrates primarily, though not exclusively, on the exegetical writings of the Protestant reformers. While the ACCS provided a compendium of key consensual exegetes of the early Christian centuries, the Catholic/Protestant confessional divide in the sixteenth century tested the very idea of consensus, especially with reference to ecclesiology and soteriology. While many able and worthy exegetes faithful to the Roman Catholic Church were active during this period, this project has chosen to include primarily those figures that represent perspectives within the Protestant Reformation. For this reason we have not included comments on the apocryphal or deuterocanonical writings.

We recognize that "Protestant" and "Catholic" as contradistinctive labels are anachronistic terms for the early decades of the sixteenth century before the hardening of confessional identities surrounding the Council of Trent (1545–1563). Protestant figures such as Philipp Melanchthon, Johannes Oecolampadius and John Calvin were all products of the revival of sacred letters known as biblical humanism. They shared an approach to biblical interpretation that owed much to Desiderius Erasmus and other scholars who remained loyal to the Church of Rome. Careful comparative studies of Protestant and Catholic exegesis in the sixteenth century have shown surprising areas of agreement when the focus was the study of a particular biblical text rather than the standard confessional debates.

At the same time, exegetical differences among the various Protestant groups could become strident and church-dividing. The most famous example of this is the interpretive impasse between Luther and Zwingli over the meaning of "This is my body" (Mt 26:26) in the words of institution. Their disagreement at the Colloquy of Marburg in 1529 had important christological and pastoral implications, as well as social and political consequences. Luther refused fellowship with Zwingli and his party at the end of the colloquy; in no small measure this bitter division led to the separate trajectories pursued by Lutheran and Reformed Protestantism to this day. In Elizabethan England, Puritans and Anglicans agreed that "Holy Scripture containeth all things necessary to salvation: so that whatsoever is not read therein, nor may be proved thereby, is not to be required of any man" (article 6 of the Thirty-Nine Articles of Religion), yet on the basis of their differing interpretations of the Bible they fought bitterly over the structures of the church, the clothing of the clergy and the ways of worship. On the matter of infant baptism, Catholics and Protestants alike agreed on its propriety, though there were various theories as to how a practice not mentioned in the Bible could be justified biblically. The Anabaptists were outliers on this subject. They rejected infant baptism altogether. They appealed to the example of the baptism of Jesus and to his final words as recorded in the Gospel of Matthew (Mt 28:19-20): "Go therefore, and make disciples of all nations, baptizing them in the name of the Father, and of the Son, and of the Holy Spirit, teaching them to observe all that I have commanded you." New Testament Christians, they argued, are to follow not only the commands of Jesus in the Great Commission, but also the exact order in which they were given: evangelize, baptize, catechize.

These and many other differences of interpretation among the various Protestant groups are reflected in their many sermons, commentaries and public disputations. In the RCS, the volume editors' introduction to each volume is intended to help the reader understand the nature and significance of doctrinal conversations and disputes that resulted in particular, and frequently clashing, interpretations. Footnotes throughout the text will be provided to explain obscure references, unusual expressions and other matters that require special comment. Volume editors have chosen comments on the Bible across a wide range of sixteenth-century confessions and schools of interpretation: biblical humanists, Lutheran, Reformed, Anglican, Puritan, and Anabaptist. We have not pursued passages from post-Tridentine Catholic authors or from radical spiritualists and antitrinitarian writers, though sufficient material is available from these sources to justify another series.

Format. The design of the RCS is intended to offer reader-friendly access to these classic texts. The availability of digital resources has given access to a huge residual database of sixteenth-century exegetical comment hitherto available only in major research universities and rare book collections. The RCS has benefited greatly from online databases such as Alexander Street Press's Digital Library of Classical Protestant Texts (DLCPT) and Early English Books Online as well as freely accessible databases like the Post-Reformation Digital Library (prdl.org). Through the help of RCS editorial advisor Herman Selderhuis, we have also had access to the special Reformation collections of the Johannes a Lasco Bibliothek in Emden, Germany. In addition, modern critical editions and translations of Reformation sources have been published over the past generation. Original translations of Reformation sources are given unless an acceptable translation already exists.

Each volume in the RCS will include an introduction by the volume editor placing that portion of the canon within the historical context of the Protestant Reformation and presenting a summary of the theological themes, interpretive issues and reception of the particular book(s). The commentary itself consists of particular pericopes identified by a pericope heading; the biblical text in the English Standard Version (ESV), with significant textual variants registered in the footnotes; an overview of the pericope in which principal exegetical and theological concerns of the Reformation writers are succinctly noted; and excerpts from the Reformation writers identified by name according to the conventions of the *Oxford Encyclopedia of the Reformation*. Each volume will also include a bibliography of sources cited, as well as an appendix of authors and source works.

The Reformation era was a time of verbal as well as physical violence, and this fact has presented a challenge for this project. Without unduly sanitizing the texts, where they contain anti-Semitic, sexist or inordinately polemical rhetoric, we have not felt obliged to parade such comments either. We have noted the abridgement of texts with ellipses and an explanatory footnote.

While this procedure would not be valid in the critical edition of such a text, we have deemed it appropriate in a series whose primary purpose is pastoral and devotional. When translating *homo* or similar terms that refer to the human race as a whole or to individual persons without reference to gender, we have used alternative English expressions to the word *man* (or derivative constructions that formerly were used generically to signify humanity at large), whenever such substitutions can be made without producing an awkward or artificial construction.

As is true in the ACCS, we have made a special effort where possible to include the voices of women, though we acknowledge the difficulty of doing so for the early modern period when for a variety of social and cultural reasons few theological and biblical works were published by women. However, recent scholarship has focused on a number of female leaders whose literary remains show us how they understood and interpreted the Bible. Women who made significant contributions to the Reformation include Marguerite d'Angoulême, sister of King Francis I, who supported French reformist evangelicals including Calvin and who published a religious poem influenced by Luther's theology, *The Mirror of the Sinful Soul;* Argula von Grumbach, a Bavarian noblewoman who defended the teachings of Luther and Melanchthon before the theologians of the University of Ingolstadt; Katharina Schütz Zell, the wife of a former priest, Matthias Zell, and a remarkable reformer in her own right—she conducted funerals, compiled hymnbooks, defended the downtrodden, and published a defense of clerical marriage as well as composing works of consolation on divine comfort and pleas for the toleration of Anabaptists and Catholics alike; and Anne Askew, a Protestant martyr put to death in 1546 after demonstrating remarkable biblical prowess in her examinations by church officials. Other echoes of faithful women in the age of the Reformation are found in their letters, translations, poems, hymns, court depositions, and martyr records.

Lay culture, learned culture. In recent decades, much attention has been given to what is called "reforming from below," that is, the expressions of religious beliefs and churchly life that characterized the popular culture of the majority of the population in the era of the Reformation. Social historians have taught us to examine the diverse pieties of townspeople and city folk, of rural religion and village life, the emergence of lay theologies, and the experiences of women in the religious tumults of Reformation Europe.[7] Formal commentaries by their nature are artifacts of learned culture. Almost all of them were written in Latin, the lingua franca of learned discourse well past the age of the Reformation. Biblical commentaries were certainly not the primary means by which the Protestant Reformation spread so rapidly across wide sectors of sixteenth-century society. Small pamphlets and broadsheets, later called *Flugschriften* ("flying writings"), with their graphic woodcuts and cartoon-like depictions of Reformation personalities and events, became the means of choice for mass communication in the early age of printing. Sermons and works of devotion were also printed with appealing visual aids. Luther's early writings were often accompanied by drawings and sketches from Lucas Cranach and other artists. This was done "above all for the sake of children and simple folk," as Luther

[7]See Peter Matheson, ed., *Reformation Christianity* (Minneapolis: Fortress, 2007).

put it, "who are more easily moved by pictures and images to recall divine history than through mere words or doctrines."[8]

We should be cautious, however, in drawing too sharp a distinction between learned and lay culture in this period. The phenomenon of preaching was a kind of verbal bridge between scholars at their desks and the thousands of illiterate or semiliterate listeners whose views were shaped by the results of Reformation exegesis. According to contemporary witness, more than one thousand people were crowding into Geneva to hear Calvin expound the Scriptures every day.[9] An example of how learned theological works by Reformation scholars were received across divisions of class and social status comes from Lazare Drilhon, an apothecary of Toulon. He was accused of heresy in May 1545 when a cache of prohibited books was found hidden in his garden shed. In addition to devotional works, the French New Testament and a copy of Calvin's Genevan liturgy, there was found a series of biblical commentaries, translated from the Latin into French: Martin Bucer's on Matthew, François Lambert's on the Apocalypse and one by Oecolampadius on 1 John.[10] Biblical exegesis in the sixteenth century was not limited to the kind of full-length commentaries found in Drilhon's shed. Citations from the Bible and expositions of its meaning permeate the extant literature of sermons, letters, court depositions, doctrinal treatises, records of public disputations and even last wills and testaments. While most of the selections in the RCS will be drawn from formal commentary literature, other sources of biblical reflection will also be considered.

Historical Context

The medieval legacy. On October 18, 1512, the degree *Doctor in Biblia* was conferred on Martin Luther, and he began his career as a professor in the University of Wittenberg. As is well known, Luther was also a monk who had taken solemn vows in the Augustinian Order of Hermits at Erfurt. These two settings—the university and the monastery—both deeply rooted in the Middle Ages, form the background not only for Luther's personal vocation as a reformer but also for the history of the biblical commentary in the age of the Reformation. Since the time of the Venerable Bede (d. 735), sometimes called "the last of the Fathers," serious study of the Bible had taken place primarily in the context of cloistered monasteries. The Rule of St. Benedict brought together *lectio* and *meditatio*, the knowledge of letters and the life of prayer. The liturgy was the medium through which the daily reading of the Bible, especially the Psalms, and the sayings of the church fathers came together in the spiritual formation of the monks.[11] Essential to this understanding was a belief in the unity of the people of God throughout time as well as space, and an awareness that life in this world was a preparation for the beatific vision in the next.

[8]Martin Luther, "Personal Prayer Book," LW 43:42-43* (WA 10,2:458); quoted in R. W. Scribner, *For the Sake of Simple Folk: Popular Propaganda for the German Reformation* (Cambridge: Cambridge University Press, 1981), xi.

[9]Letter of De Beaulieu to Guillaume Farel (1561) in *Theodor Beza nach handschriftlichen und anderen gleichzeitigen Quellen*, ed. J. W. Baum (Leipzig: Weidmann, 1851), 2:92.

[10]Francis Higman, "A Heretic's Library: The Drilhon Inventory" (1545), in Francis Higman, *Lire et Découvire: la circulation des idées au temps de la Réforme* (Geneva: Droz, 1998), 65-85.

[11]See the classic study by Jean Leclercq, *The Love of Learning and the Desire for God* (New York: Fordham University Press, 1961).

The source of theology was the study of the sacred page *(sacra pagina)*; its object was the accumulation of knowledge not for its own sake but for the obtaining of eternal life. For these monks, the Bible had God for its author, salvation for its end and unadulterated truth for its matter, though they would not have expressed it in such an Aristotelian way. The medieval method of interpreting the Bible owed much to Augustine's *On Christian Doctrine*. In addition to setting forth a series of rules (drawn from an earlier work by Tyconius), Augustine stressed the importance of distinguishing the literal and spiritual or allegorical senses of Scripture. While the literal sense was not disparaged, the allegorical was valued because it enabled the believer to obtain spiritual benefit from the obscure places in the Bible, especially in the Old Testament. For Augustine, as for the monks who followed him, the goal of scriptural exegesis was freighted with eschatological meaning; its purpose was to induce faith, hope, and love and so to advance in one's pilgrimage toward that city with foundations (see Heb 11:10).

Building on the work of Augustine and other church fathers going back to Origen, medieval exegetes came to understand Scripture as possessed of four possible meanings, the famous *quadriga*. The literal meaning was retained, of course, but the spiritual meaning was now subdivided into three senses: the allegorical, the moral, and the anagogical. Medieval exegetes often referred to the four meanings of Scripture in a popular rhyme:

> The letter shows us what God and our fathers did;
> The allegory shows us where our faith is hid;
> The moral meaning gives us rules of daily life;
> The anagogy shows us where we end our strife.[12]

In this schema, the three spiritual meanings of the text correspond to the three theological virtues: faith (allegory), hope (anagogy), and love (the moral meaning). It should be noted that this way of approaching the Bible assumed a high doctrine of scriptural inspiration: the multiple meanings inherent in the text had been placed there by the Holy Spirit for the benefit of the people of God. The biblical justification for this method went back to the apostle Paul, who had used the words *allegory* and *type* when applying Old Testament events to believers in Christ (Gal 4:21-31; 1 Cor 10:1-11). The problem with this approach was knowing how to relate each of the four senses to one another and how to prevent Scripture from becoming a nose of wax turned this way and that by various interpreters. As G. R. Evans explains, "Any interpretation which could be put upon the text and was in keeping with the faith and edifying, had the warrant of God himself, for no human reader had the ingenuity to find more than God had put there."[13]

With the rise of the universities in the eleventh century, theology and the study of Scripture moved from the cloister into the classroom. Scripture and the Fathers were still important, but they came to function more as footnotes to the theological questions debated in the schools and brought together in an impressive systematic way in works such as Peter Lombard's *Books of Sentences* (the standard theology textbook of the Middle Ages) and the great scholastic *summae* of the thirteenth

[12]Robert M. Grant, *A Short History of the Interpretation of the Bible* (New York: Macmillan, 1963), 119. A translation of the well-known Latin quatrain: *Littera gesta docet/Quid credas allegoria/Moralis quid agas/Quo tendas anagogia.*

[13]G. R. Evans, *The Language and Logic of the Bible: The Road to Reformation* (Cambridge: Cambridge University Press, 1985), 42.

century. Indispensible to the study of the Bible in the later Middle Ages was the *Glossa ordinaria*, a collection of exegetical opinions by the church fathers and other commentators. Heiko Oberman summarized the transition from devotion to dialectic this way: "When, due to the scientific revolution of the twelfth century, Scripture became the *object* of study rather than the *subject* through which God speaks to the student, the difference between the two modes of speaking was investigated in terms of the texts themselves rather than in their relation to the recipients."[14] It was possible, of course, to be both a scholastic theologian and a master of the spiritual life. Meister Eckhart, for example, wrote commentaries on the Old Testament in Latin and works of mystical theology in German, reflecting what had come to be seen as a division of labor between the two.

An increasing focus on the text of Scripture led to a revival of interest in its literal sense. The two key figures in this development were Thomas Aquinas (d. 1274) and Nicholas of Lyra (d. 1340). Thomas is best remembered for his *Summa Theologiae*, but he was also a prolific commentator on the Bible. Thomas did not abandon the multiple senses of Scripture but declared that all the senses were founded on one—the literal—and this sense eclipsed allegory as the basis of sacred doctrine. Nicholas of Lyra was a Franciscan scholar who made use of the Hebrew text of the Old Testament and quoted liberally from works of Jewish scholars, especially the learned French rabbi Salomon Rashi (d. 1105). After Aquinas, Lyra was the strongest defender of the literal, historical meaning of Scripture as the primary basis of theological disputation. His *Postilla*, as his notes were called—the abbreviated form of *post illa verba textus*, meaning "after these words from Scripture"—were widely circulated in the late Middle Ages and became the first biblical commentary to be printed in the fifteenth century. More than any other commentator from the period of high scholasticism, Lyra and his work were greatly valued by the early reformers. According to an old Latin pun, *Nisi Lyra lyrasset, Lutherus non saltasset*, "If Lyra had not played his lyre, Luther would not have danced."[15] While Luther was never an uncritical disciple of any teacher, he did praise Lyra as a good Hebraist and quoted him more than one hundred times in his lectures on Genesis, where he declared, "I prefer him to almost all other interpreters of Scripture."[16]

Sacred philology. The sixteenth century has been called a golden age of biblical interpretation, and it is a fact that the age of the Reformation witnessed an explosion of commentary writing unparalleled in the history of the Christian church. Kenneth Hagen has cataloged forty-five commentaries on Hebrews between 1516 (Erasmus) and 1598 (Beza).[17] During the sixteenth century, more than seventy new commentaries on Romans were published, five of them by Melanchthon alone, and nearly one hundred commentaries on the Bible's prayer book, the Psalms.[18] There were two developments in the fifteenth century that presaged this development and without which it

[14]Heiko Oberman, *Forerunners of the Reformation* (Philadelphia: Fortress, 1966), 284.

[15]Nicholas of Lyra, *The Postilla of Nicolas of Lyra on the Song of Songs*, trans. and ed. James George Kiecker (Milwaukee: Marquette University Press, 1998), 19.

[16]LW 2:164 (WA 42:377).

[17]Kenneth Hagen, *Hebrews Commenting from Erasmus to Bèze, 1516–1598* (Tübingen: Mohr, 1981).

[18]R. Gerald Hobbs, "Biblical Commentaries," *OER* 1:167-71. See in general David C. Steinmetz, ed., *The Bible in the Sixteenth Century* (Durham: Duke University Press, 1990).

could not have taken place: the invention of printing and the rediscovery of a vast store of ancient learning hitherto unknown or unavailable to scholars in the West.

It is now commonplace to say that what the computer has become in our generation, the printing press was to the world of Erasmus, Luther, and other leaders of the Reformation. Johannes Gutenberg, a goldsmith by trade, developed a metal alloy suitable for type and a machine that would allow printed characters to be cast with relative ease, placed in even lines of composition and then manipulated again and again, making possible the mass production of an unbelievable number of texts. In 1455, the Gutenberg Bible, the masterpiece of the typographical revolution, was published at Mainz in double columns in gothic type. Forty-seven copies of the beautiful Gutenberg Bible are still extant, each consisting of more than one thousand colorfully illuminated and impeccably printed pages. What began at Gutenberg's print shop in Mainz on the Rhine River soon spread, like McDonald's or Starbucks in our day, into every nook and cranny of the known world. Printing presses sprang up in Rome (1464), Venice (1469), Paris (1470), the Netherlands (1471), Switzerland (1472), Spain (1474), England (1476), Sweden (1483), and Constantinople (1490). By 1500, these and other presses across Europe had published some twenty-seven thousand titles, most of them in Latin. Erasmus once compared himself with an obscure preacher whose sermons were heard by only a few people in one or two churches while his books were read in every country in the world. Erasmus was not known for his humility, but in this case he was simply telling the truth.[19]

The Italian humanist Lorenzo Valla (d. 1457) died in the early dawn of the age of printing, but his critical and philological studies would be taken up by others who believed that genuine reform in church and society could come about only by returning to the wellsprings of ancient learning and wisdom—*ad fontes,* "back to the sources!" Valla is best remembered for undermining a major claim made by defenders of the papacy when he proved by philological research that the so-called Donation of Constantine, which had bolstered papal assertions of temporal sovereignty, was a forgery. But it was Valla's *Collatio Novi Testamenti* of 1444 that would have such a great effect on the renewal of biblical studies in the next century. Erasmus discovered the manuscript of this work while rummaging through an old library in Belgium and published it at Paris in 1505. In the preface to his edition of Valla, Erasmus gave the rationale that would guide his own labors in textual criticism. Just as Jerome had translated the Latin Vulgate from older versions and copies of the Scriptures in his day, so now Jerome's own text must be subjected to careful scrutiny and correction. Erasmus would be *Hieronymus redivivus,* a new Jerome come back to life to advance the cause of sacred philology. The restoration of the Scriptures and the writings of the church fathers would usher in what Erasmus believed would be a golden age of peace and learning. In 1516, the Basel publisher Froben brought out Erasmus's *Novum Instrumentum,* the first published edition of the Greek New Testament. Erasmus's Greek New Testament would go through five editions in his lifetime, each one with new emendations to the text and a growing section of annotations that expanded to include not only technical notes about the text but also theological comment. The influence of Erasmus's Greek New

[19]E. Harris Harbison, *The Christian Scholar in the Age of the Reformation* (New York: Charles Scribner's Sons, 1956), 80.

Testament was enormous. It formed the basis for Robert Estienne's *Novum Testamentum Graece* of 1550, which in turn was used to establish the Greek *Textus Receptus* for a number of late Reformation translations including the King James Version of 1611.

For all his expertise in Greek, Erasmus was a poor student of Hebrew and only published commentaries on several of the psalms. However, the renaissance of Hebrew letters was part of the wider program of biblical humanism as reflected in the establishment of trilingual colleges devoted to the study of Hebrew, Greek and Latin (the three languages written on the *titulus* of Jesus' cross [Jn 19:20]) at Alcalá in Spain, Wittenberg in Germany, Louvain in Belgium, and Paris in France. While it is true that some medieval commentators, especially Nicholas of Lyra, had been informed by the study of Hebrew and rabbinics in their biblical work, it was the publication of Johannes Reuchlin's *De rudimentis hebraicis* (1506), a combined grammar and dictionary, that led to the recovery of *veritas Hebraica,* as Jerome had referred to the true voice of the Hebrew Scriptures. The pursuit of Hebrew studies was carried forward in the Reformation by two great scholars, Konrad Pellikan and Sebastian Münster. Pellikan was a former Franciscan friar who embraced the Protestant cause and played a major role in the Zurich reformation. He had published a Hebrew grammar even prior to Reuchlin and produced a commentary on nearly the entire Bible that appeared in seven volumes between 1532 and 1539. Münster was Pellikan's student and taught Hebrew at the University of Heidelberg before taking up a similar position in Basel. Like his mentor, Münster was a great collector of Hebraica and published a series of excellent grammars, dictionaries and rabbinic texts. Münster did for the Hebrew Old Testament what Erasmus had done for the Greek New Testament. His *Hebraica Biblia* offered a fresh Latin translation of the Old Testament with annotations from medieval rabbinic exegesis.

Luther first learned Hebrew with Reuchlin's grammar in hand but took advantage of other published resources, such as the four-volume Hebrew Bible published at Venice by Daniel Bomberg in 1516 to 1517. He also gathered his own circle of Hebrew experts, his *sanhedrin* he called it, who helped him with his German translation of the Old Testament. We do not know where William Tyndale learned Hebrew, though perhaps it was in Worms, where there was a thriving rabbinical school during his stay there. In any event, he had sufficiently mastered the language to bring out a freshly translated Pentateuch that was published at Antwerp in 1530. By the time the English separatist scholar Henry Ainsworth published his prolix commentaries on the Pentateuch in 1616, the knowledge of Hebrew, as well as Greek, was taken for granted by every serious scholar of the Bible. In the preface to his commentary on Genesis, Ainsworth explained that "the literal sense of Moses's Hebrew (which is the tongue wherein he wrote the law), is the ground of all interpretation, and that language hath figures and properties of speech, different from ours: These therefore in the first place are to be opened that the natural meaning of the Scripture, being known, the mysteries of godliness therein implied, may be better discerned."[20]

The restoration of the biblical text in the original languages made possible the revival of scriptural exposition reflected in the floodtide of sermon literature and commentary work. Of even

[20]Henry Ainsworth, *Annotations upon the First Book of Moses Called Genesis* (Amsterdam, 1616), preface (unpaginated).

more far-reaching import was the steady stream of vernacular Bibles in the sixteenth century. In the introduction to his 1516 edition of the New Testament, Erasmus had expressed his desire that the Scriptures be translated into all languages so that "the lowliest women" could read the Gospels and the Pauline epistles and "the farmer sing some portion of them at the plow, the weaver hum some parts of them to the movement of his shuttle, the traveler lighten the weariness of the journey with stories of this kind."[21] Like Erasmus, Tyndale wanted the Bible to be available in the language of the common people. He once said to a learned divine that if God spared his life he would cause the boy who drives the plow to know more of the Scriptures than he did![22] The project of allowing the Bible to speak in the language of the mother in the house, the children in the street and the cheesemonger in the marketplace was met with stiff opposition by certain Catholic polemists such as Johann Eck, Luther's antagonist at the Leipzig Debate of 1519. In his *Enchiridion* (1525), Eck derided the "inky theologians" whose translations paraded the Bible before "the untutored crowd" and subjected it to the judgment of "laymen and crazy old women."[23] In fact, some fourteen German Bibles had already been published prior to Luther's September Testament of 1522, which he translated from Erasmus's Greek New Testament in less than three months' time while sequestered in the Wartburg. Luther's German New Testament became the first best-seller in the world, appearing in forty-three distinct editions between 1522 and 1525 with upward of one hundred thousand copies issued in these three years. It is estimated that 5 percent of the German population may have been literate at this time, but this rate increased as the century wore on due in no small part to the unmitigated success of vernacular Bibles.[24]

Luther's German Bible (inclusive of the Old Testament from 1534) was the most successful venture of its kind, but it was not alone in the field. Hans Denck and Ludwig Hätzer, leaders in the early Anabaptist movement, translated the prophetic books of the Old Testament from Hebrew into German in 1527. This work influenced the Swiss-German Bible of 1531 published by Leo Jud and other pastors in Zurich. Tyndale's influence on the English language rivaled that of Luther on German. At a time when English was regarded as "that obscure and remote dialect of German spoken in an off-shore island," Tyndale, with his remarkable linguistic ability (he was fluent in eight languages), "made a language for England," as his modern editor David Daniell has put it.[25] Tyndale was imprisoned and executed near Brussels in 1536, but the influence of his biblical work among the common people of England was already being felt. There is no reason to doubt the authenticity of John Foxe's recollection of how Tyndale's New Testament was received in England during the 1520s and 1530s:

[21]John C. Olin, *Christian Humanism and the Reformation* (New York: Fordham University Press, 1987), 101.

[22]This famous statement of Tyndale was quoted by John Foxe in his *Acts and Monuments of Matters Happening in the Church* (London, 1563). See Henry Wansbrough, "Tyndale," in *The Bible in the Renaissance*, ed. Richard Griffith (Aldershot, UK: Ashgate, 2001), 124.

[23]John Eck, *Enchiridion of Commonplaces*, trans. Ford Lewis Battles (Grand Rapids: Baker, 1979), 47-49.

[24]The effect of printing on the spread of the Reformation has been much debated. See the classic study by Elizabeth L. Eisenstein, *The Printing Press as an Agent of Change* (Cambridge: Cambridge University Press, 1979). More recent studies include Mark U. Edwards Jr., *Printing, Propaganda and Martin Luther* (Minneapolis: Fortress, 1994), and Andrew Pettegree and Matthew Hall, "The Reformation and the Book: A Reconsideration," *Historical Journal* 47 (2004): 1-24.

[25]David Daniell, *William Tyndale: A Biography* (New Haven: Yale University Press, 1994), 3.

> The fervent zeal of those Christian days seemed much superior to these our days and times; as manifestly may appear by their sitting up all night in reading and hearing; also by their expenses and charges in buying of books in English, of whom some gave five marks, some more, some less, for a book: some gave a load of hay for a few chapters of St. James, or of St. Paul in English.[26]

Calvin helped to revise and contributed three prefaces to the French Bible translated by his cousin Pierre Robert Olivétan and originally published at Neuchâtel in 1535. Clément Marot and Beza provided a fresh translation of the Psalms with each psalm rendered in poetic form and accompanied by monophonic musical settings for congregational singing. The Bay Psalter, the first book printed in America, was an English adaptation of this work. Geneva also provided the provenance of the most influential Italian Bible published by Giovanni Diodati in 1607. The flowering of biblical humanism in vernacular Bibles resulted in new translations in all of the major language groups of Europe: Spanish (1569), Portuguese (1681), Dutch (New Testament, 1523; Old Testament, 1527), Danish (1550), Czech (1579–1593/94), Hungarian (New Testament, 1541; complete Bible, 1590), Polish (1563), Swedish (1541), and even Arabic (1591).[27]

Patterns of Reformation

Once the text of the Bible had been placed in the hands of the people, in cheap and easily available editions, what further need was there of published expositions such as commentaries? Given the Protestant doctrine of the priesthood of all believers, was there any longer a need for learned clergy and their bookish religion? Some radical reformers thought not. Sebastian Franck searched for the true church of the Spirit "scattered among the heathen and the weeds" but could not find it in any of the institutional structures of his time. *Veritas non potest scribi, aut exprimi*, he said, "truth can neither be spoken nor written."[28] Kaspar von Schwenckfeld so emphasized religious inwardness that he suspended external observance of the Lord's Supper and downplayed the readable, audible Scriptures in favor of the Word within. This trajectory would lead to the rise of the Quakers in the next century, but it was pursued neither by the mainline reformers nor by most of the Anabaptists. Article 7 of the Augsburg Confession (1530) declared the one holy Christian church to be "the assembly of all believers among whom the Gospel is purely preached and the holy sacraments are administered according to the Gospel."[29]

Historians of the nineteenth century referred to the material and formal principles of the Reformation. In this construal, the matter at stake was the meaning of the Christian gospel: the liberating insight that helpless sinners are graciously justified by the gift of faith alone, apart from any works or merits of their own, entirely on the basis of Christ's atoning work on the cross. For Luther especially, justification by faith alone became the criterion by which all other doctrines and

[26]Foxe, *Acts and Monuments*, 4:218.

[27]On vernacular translations of the Bible, see *CHB* 3:94-140 and Jaroslav Pelikan, *The Reformation of the Bible/The Bible of the Reformation* (New Haven: Yale University Press, 1996), 41-62.

[28]Sebastian Franck, *280 Paradoxes or Wondrous Sayings*, trans. E. J. Furcha (Lewiston, NY: Edwin Mellen Press, 1986), 10, 212.

[29]BoC 42 (BSLK 61).

practices of the church were to be judged. The cross proves everything, he said at the Heidelberg disputation in 1518. The distinction between law and gospel thus became the primary hermeneutical key that unlocked the true meaning of Scripture.

The formal principle of the Reformation, *sola Scriptura*, was closely bound up with proper distinctions between Scripture and tradition. "Scripture alone," said Luther, "is the true lord and master of all writings and doctrine on earth. If that is not granted, what is Scripture good for? The more we reject it, the more we become satisfied with human books and human teachers."[30] On the basis of this principle, the reformers challenged the structures and institutions of the medieval Catholic Church. Even a simple layperson, they asserted, armed with Scripture should be believed above a pope or a council without it. But, however boldly asserted, the doctrine of the primacy of Scripture did not absolve the reformers from dealing with a host of hermeneutical issues that became matters of contention both between Rome and the Reformation and within each of these two communities: the extent of the biblical canon, the validity of critical study of the Bible, the perspicuity of Scripture and its relation to preaching, and the retention of devotional and liturgical practices such as holy days, incense, the burning of candles, the sprinkling of holy water, church art, and musical instruments. Zwingli, the Puritans, and the radicals dismissed such things as a rubbish heap of ceremonials that amounted to nothing but tomfoolery, while Lutherans and Anglicans retained most of them as consonant with Scripture and valuable aids to worship.

It is important to note that while the mainline reformers differed among themselves on many matters, overwhelmingly they saw themselves as part of the ongoing Catholic tradition, indeed as the legitimate bearers of it. This was seen in numerous ways including their sense of continuity with the church of the preceding centuries; their embrace of the ecumenical orthodoxy of the early church; and their desire to read the Bible in dialogue with the exegetical tradition of the church.

In their biblical commentaries, the reformers of the sixteenth century revealed a close familiarity with the preceding exegetical tradition, and they used it respectfully as well as critically in their own expositions of the sacred text. For them, *sola Scriptura* was not *nuda Scriptura*. Rather, the Scriptures were seen as the book given to the church, gathered and guided by the Holy Spirit. In his restatement of the Vincentian canon, Calvin defined the church as "a society of all the saints, a society which, spread over the whole world, and existing in all ages, and bound together by the one doctrine and the one spirit of Christ, cultivates and observes unity of faith and brotherly concord. With this church we deny that we have any disagreement. Nay, rather, as we revere her as our mother, so we desire to remain in her bosom." Defined thus, the church has a real, albeit relative and circumscribed, authority since, as Calvin admits, "We cannot fly without wings."[31] While the reformers could not agree with the Council of Trent (though some recent Catholic theologians have challenged this interpretation) that Scripture and tradition were two separate and equal sources of divine revelation,

[30]LW 32:11-12* (WA 7:317).

[31]John C. Olin, ed., *John Calvin and Jacopo Sadoleto: A Reformation Debate* (New York: Harper Torchbooks, 1966), 61-62, 77.

they did believe in the coinherence of Scripture and tradition. This conviction shaped the way they read and interpreted the Bible.[32]

Schools of Exegesis

The reformers were passionate about biblical exegesis, but they showed little concern for hermeneutics as a separate field of inquiry. Niels Hemmingsen, a Lutheran theologian in Denmark, did write a treatise, *De methodis* (1555), in which he offered a philosophical and theological framework for the interpretation of Scripture. This was followed by the *Clavis Scripturae Sacrae* (1567) of Matthias Flacius Illyricus, which contains some fifty rules for studying the Bible drawn from Scripture itself.[33] However, hermeneutics as we know it came of age only in the Enlightenment and should not be backloaded into the Reformation. It is also true that the word *commentary* did not mean in the sixteenth century what it means for us today. Erasmus provided both annotations and paraphrases on the New Testament, the former a series of critical notes on the text but also containing points of doctrinal substance, the latter a theological overview and brief exposition. Most of Calvin's commentaries began as sermons or lectures presented in the course of his pastoral ministry. In the dedication to his 1519 study of Galatians, Luther declared that his work was "not so much a commentary as a testimony of my faith in Christ."[34] The exegetical work of the reformers was embodied in a wide variety of forms and genres, and the RCS has worked with this broader concept in setting the guidelines for this compendium.

The Protestant reformers shared in common a number of key interpretive principles such as the priority of the grammatical-historical sense of Scripture and the christological centeredness of the entire Bible, but they also developed a number of distinct approaches and schools of exegesis.[35] For the purposes of the RCS, we note the following key figures and families of interpretation in this period.

Biblical humanism. The key figure is Erasmus, whose importance is hard to exaggerate for Catholic and Protestant exegetes alike. His annotated Greek New Testament and fresh Latin translation challenged the hegemony of the Vulgate tradition and was doubtless a factor in the decision of the Council of Trent to establish the Vulgate edition as authentic and normative. Erasmus believed that the wide distribution of the Scriptures would contribute to personal spiritual renewal and the reform of society. In 1547, the English translation of Erasmus's *Paraphrases* was ordered to be placed in every parish church in England. John Colet first encouraged Erasmus

[32]See Timothy George, "An Evangelical Reflection on Scripture and Tradition," *Pro Ecclesia* 9 (2000): 184-207.

[33]See Kenneth G. Hagen, "'*De Exegetica Methodo*': Niels Hemmingsen's *De Methodis* (1555)," in *The Bible in the Sixteenth Century*, ed. David C. Steinmetz (Durham: Duke University Press, 1990), 181-96.

[34]LW 27:159 (WA 2:449). See Kenneth Hagen, "What Did the Term *Commentarius* Mean to Sixteenth-Century Theologians?" in *Théorie et pratique de l'exégèse*, eds. Irena Backus and Francis M. Higman (Geneva: Droz, 1990), 13-38.

[35]I follow here the sketch of Irena Backus, "Biblical Hermeneutics and Exegesis," *OER* 1:152-58. In this work, Backus confines herself to Continental developments, whereas we have noted the exegetical contribution of the English Reformation as well. For more comprehensive listings of sixteenth-century commentators, see Gerald Bray, *Biblical Interpretation* (Downers Grove, IL: InterVarsity Press, 1996), 165-212; and Richard A. Muller, "Biblical Interpretation in the Sixteenth and Seventeenth Centuries," *DMBI* 22-44.

to learn Greek, though he never took up the language himself. Colet's lectures on Paul's epistles at Oxford are reflected in his commentaries on Romans and 1 Corinthians.

Jacques Lefèvre d'Étaples has been called the "French Erasmus" because of his great learning and support for early reform movements in his native land. He published a major edition of the Psalter, as well as commentaries on the Pauline Epistles (1512), the Gospels (1522), and the General Epistles (1527). Guillaume Farel, the early reformer of Geneva, was a disciple of Lefèvre, and the young Calvin also came within his sphere of influence.

Among pre-Tridentine Catholic reformers, special attention should be given to Thomas de Vio, better known as Cajetan. He is best remembered for confronting Martin Luther on behalf of the pope in 1518, but his biblical commentaries (on nearly every book of the Bible) are virtually free of polemic. Like Erasmus, he dared to criticize the Vulgate on linguistic grounds. His commentary on Romans supported the doctrine of justification by grace applied by faith based on the "alien righteousness" of God in Christ. Jared Wicks sums up Cajetan's significance in this way: "Cajetan's combination of passion for pristine biblical meaning with his fully developed theological horizon of understanding indicates, in an intriguing manner, something of the breadth of possibilities open to Roman Catholics before a more restrictive settlement came to exercise its hold on many Catholic interpreters in the wake of the Council of Trent."[36] Girolamo Seripando, like Cajetan, was a cardinal in the Catholic Church, though he belonged to the Augustinian rather than the Dominican order. He was an outstanding classical scholar and published commentaries on Romans and Galatians. Also important is Jacopo Sadoleto, another cardinal, best known for his 1539 letter to the people of Geneva beseeching them to return to the Church of Rome, to which Calvin replied with a manifesto of his own. Sadoleto published a commentary on Romans in 1535. Bucer once commended Sadoleto's teaching on justification as approximating that of the reformers, while others saw him tilting away from the Augustinian tradition toward Pelagianism.[37]

Luther and the Wittenberg School. It was in the name of the Word of God, and specifically as a doctor of Scripture, that Luther challenged the church of his day and inaugurated the Reformation. Though Luther renounced his monastic vows, he never lost that sense of intimacy with *sacra pagina* he first acquired as a young monk. Luther provided three rules for reading the Bible: prayer, meditation, and struggle *(tentatio)*. His exegetical output was enormous. In the American edition of Luther's works, thirty out of the fifty-five volumes are devoted to his biblical studies, and additional translations are planned. Many of his commentaries originated as sermons or lecture notes presented to his students at the university and to his parishioners at Wittenberg's parish church of St. Mary. Luther referred to Galatians as his bride: "The Epistle to the Galatians is my dear epistle. I have betrothed myself to it. It is my Käthe von Bora."[38] He considered his 1535 commentary on Galatians his greatest exegetical work, although his massive commentary on Genesis

[36]Jared Wicks, "Tommaso de Vio Cajetan (1469-1534)," *DMBI* 283-87, here 286.

[37]See the discussion by Bernard Roussel, "Martin Bucer et Jacques Sadolet: la concorde possible," *Bulletin de la Société de l'histoire de protestantisme français* (1976): 525-50, and T. H. L. Parker, *Commentaries on the Epistle to the Romans, 1532–1542* (Edinburgh: T&T Clark, 1986), 25-34.

[38]WATR 1:69 no. 146; cf. LW 54:20 no. 146. I have followed Rörer's variant on Dietrich's notes.

(eight volumes in LW), which he worked on for ten years (1535–1545), must be considered his crowning work. Luther's principles of biblical interpretation are found in his *Open Letter on Translating* and in the prefaces he wrote to all the books of the Bible.

Philipp Melanchthon was brought to Wittenberg to teach Greek in 1518 and proved to be an able associate to Luther in the reform of the church. A set of his lecture notes on Romans was published without his knowledge in 1522. This was revised and expanded many times until his large commentary of 1556. Melanchthon also commented on other New Testament books including Matthew, John, Galatians, and the Petrine epistles, as well as Proverbs, Daniel, and Ecclesiastes. Though he was well trained in the humanist disciplines, Melanchthon devoted little attention to critical and textual matters in his commentaries. Rather, he followed the primary argument of the biblical writer and gathered from this exposition a series of doctrinal topics for special consideration. This method lay behind Melanchthon's *Loci communes* (1521), the first Protestant theology textbook to be published. Another Wittenberger was Johannes Bugenhagen of Pomerania, a prolific commentator on both the Old and New Testaments. His commentary on the Psalms (1524), translated into German by Bucer, applied Luther's teaching on justification to the Psalter. He also wrote a commentary on Job and annotations on many of the books in the Bible. The Lutheran exegetical tradition was shaped by many other scholar-reformers including Andreas Osiander, Johannes Brenz, Caspar Cruciger, Erasmus Sarcerius, Georg Maior, Jacob Andreae, Nikolaus Selnecker, and Johann Gerhard.

The Strasbourg-Basel tradition. Bucer, the son of a shoemaker in Alsace, became the leader of the Reformation in Strasbourg. A former Dominican, he was early on influenced by Erasmus and continued to share his passion for Christian unity. Bucer was the most ecumenical of the Protestant reformers seeking rapprochement with Catholics on justification and an armistice between Luther and Zwingli in their strife over the Lord's Supper. Bucer also had a decisive influence on Calvin, though the latter characterized his biblical commentaries as longwinded and repetitious.[39] In his exegetical work, Bucer made ample use of patristic and medieval sources, though he criticized the abuse and overuse of allegory as "the most blatant insult to the Holy Spirit."[40] He declared that the purpose of his commentaries was "to help inexperienced brethren [perhaps like the apothecary Drilhon, who owned a French translation of Bucer's *Commentary on Matthew*] to understand each of the words and actions of Christ, and in their proper order as far as possible, and to retain an explanation of them in their natural meaning, so that they will not distort God's Word through age-old aberrations or by inept interpretation, but rather with a faithful comprehension of everything as written by the Spirit of God, they may expound to all the churches in their firm upbuilding in faith and love."[41] In addition to writing commentaries on all four Gospels, Bucer published commentaries on Judges, the Psalms, Zephaniah, Romans, and Ephesians. In the early years of the Reformation, there was a great deal of back and forth between Strasbourg and Basel, and both

[39]CNTC 8:3 (CO 10:404).

[40]*DMBI* 249; P. Scherding and F. Wendel, eds., "Un Traité d'exégèse pratique de Bucer," *Revue d'histoire et de philosophie religieuses* 26 (1946): 32-75, here 56.

[41]Martin Bucer, *Enarrationes perpetuae in sacra quatuor evangelia*, 2nd ed. (Strasbourg: Georg Ulrich Andlanus, 1530), 10r; quoted in D. F. Wright, "Martin Bucer," *DMBI* 290.

were centers of a lively publishing trade. Wolfgang Capito, Bucer's associate at Strasbourg, was a notable Hebraist and composed commentaries on Hosea (1529) and Habakkuk (1527).

At Basel, the great Sebastian Münster defended the use of Jewish sources in the Christian study of the Old Testament and published, in addition to his famous Hebrew grammar, an annotated version of the Gospel of Matthew translated from Greek into Hebrew. Oecolampadius, Basel's chief reformer, had been a proofreader in Froben's publishing house and worked with Erasmus on his Greek New Testament and his critical edition of Jerome. From 1523 he was both a preacher and professor of Holy Scripture at Basel. He defended Zwingli's eucharistic theology at the Colloquy of Marburg and published commentaries on 1 John (1524), Romans (1525), and Haggai–Malachi (1525). Oecolampadius was succeeded by Simon Grynaeus, a classical scholar who taught Greek and supported Bucer's efforts to bring Lutherans and Zwinglians together. More in line with Erasmus was Sebastian Castellio, who came to Basel after his expulsion from Geneva in 1545. He is best remembered for questioning the canonicity of the Song of Songs and for his annotations and French translation of the Bible.

The Zurich group. Biblical exegesis in Zurich was centered on the distinctive institution of the *Prophezei,* which began on June 19, 1525. On five days a week, at seven o'clock in the morning, all of the ministers and theological students in Zurich gathered into the choir of the Grossmünster to engage in a period of intense exegesis and interpretation of Scripture. After Zwingli had opened the meeting with prayer, the text of the day was read in Latin, Greek, and Hebrew, followed by appropriate textual or exegetical comments. One of the ministers then delivered a sermon on the passage in German that was heard by many of Zurich's citizens who stopped by the cathedral on their way to work. This institute for advanced biblical studies had an enormous influence as a model for Reformed academies and seminaries throughout Europe. It was also the seedbed for sermon series in Zurich's churches and the extensive exegetical publications of Zwingli, Leo Jud, Konrad Pellikan, Heinrich Bullinger, Oswald Myconius, and Rudolf Gwalther. Zwingli had memorized in Greek all of the Pauline epistles, and this bore fruit in his powerful expository preaching and biblical exegesis. He took seriously the role of grammar, rhetoric, and historical research in explaining the biblical text. For example, he disagreed with Bucer on the value of the Septuagint, regarding it as a trustworthy witness to a proto-Hebrew version earlier than the Masoretic text.

Zwingli's work was carried forward by his successor Bullinger, one of the most formidable scholars and networkers among the reformers. He composed commentaries on Daniel (1565), the Gospels (1542–1546), the Epistles (1537), Acts (1533), and Revelation (1557). He collaborated with Calvin to produce the *Consensus Tigurinus* (1549), a Reformed accord on the nature of the Lord's Supper, and produced a series of fifty sermons on Christian doctrine, known as *Decades,* which became required reading in Elizabethan England. As the *Antistes* ("overseer") of the Zurich church for forty-four years, Bullinger faced opposition from nascent Anabaptism on the one hand and resurgent Catholicism on the other. The need for a well-trained clergy and scholarly resources, including Scripture commentaries, arose from the fact that the Bible was "difficult or obscure to the unlearned, unskillful, unexercised, and malicious or corrupted wills." While forswearing papal claims to infallibility, Bullinger and other leaders of the magisterial Reformation saw the need for a kind of Protestant magisterium as a check against the tendency to read the Bible in "such sense as everyone shall be persuaded in himself to be most convenient."[42]

Two other commentators can be treated in connection with the Zurich group, though each of them had a wide-ranging ministry across the Reformation fronts. A former Benedictine monk, Wolfgang Musculus, embraced the Reformation in the 1520s and served briefly as the secretary to Bucer in Strasbourg. He shared Bucer's desire for Protestant unity and served for seventeen years (1531–1548) as a pastor and reformer in Augsburg. After a brief time in Zurich, where he came under the influence of Bullinger, Musculus was called to Bern, where he taught the Scriptures and published commentaries on the Psalms, the Decalogue, Genesis, Romans, Isaiah, 1 and 2 Corinthians, Galatians and Ephesians, Philippians, Colossians, 1 and 2 Thessalonians, and 1 Timothy. Drawing on his exegetical writings, Musculus also produced a compendium of Protestant theology that was translated into English in 1563 as *Commonplaces of Christian Religion*.

Peter Martyr Vermigli was a Florentine-born scholar and Augustinian friar who embraced the Reformation and fled to Switzerland in 1542. Over the next twenty years, he would gain an international reputation as a prolific scholar and leading theologian within the Reformed community. He lectured on the Old Testament at Strasbourg, was made regius professor at Oxford, corresponded with the Italian refugee church in Geneva and spent the last years of his life as professor of Hebrew at Zurich. Vermigli published commentaries on 1 Corinthians, Romans, and Judges during his lifetime. His biblical lectures on Genesis, Lamentations, 1 and 2 Samuel, and 1 and 2 Kings were published posthumously. The most influential of his writings was the *Loci communes (Commonplaces)*, a theological compendium drawn from his exegetical writings.

The Genevan reformers. What Zwingli and Bullinger were to Zurich, Calvin and Beza were to Geneva. Calvin has been called "the father of modern biblical scholarship," and his exegetical work is without parallel in the Reformation. Because of the success of his *Institutes of the Christian Religion* Calvin has sometimes been thought of as a man of one book, but he always intended the *Institutes*, which went through eight editions in Latin and five in French during his lifetime, to serve as a guide to the study of the Bible, to show the reader "what he ought especially to seek in Scripture and to what end he ought to relate its contents." Jacob Arminius, who modified several principles of Calvin's theology, recommended his commentaries next to the Bible, for, as he said, Calvin "is incomparable in the interpretation of Scripture."[43] Drawing on his superb knowledge of Greek and Hebrew and his thorough training in humanist rhetoric, Calvin produced commentaries on all of the New Testament books except 2 and 3 John and Revelation. Calvin's Old Testament commentaries originated as sermon and lecture series and include Genesis, Psalms, Hosea, Isaiah, minor prophets, Daniel, Jeremiah and Lamentations, a harmony of the last four books of Moses,

[42]Euan Cameron, *The European Reformation* (Oxford: Oxford University Press, 1991), 120.

[43]Letter to Sebastian Egbert (May 3, 1607), in *Praestantium ac eruditorum virorum epistolae ecclesiasticae et theologicae varii argumenti*, ed. Christiaan Hartsoeker (Amsterdam: Henricus Dendrinus, 1660), 236-37. Quoted in A. M. Hunter, *The Teaching of Calvin* (London: James Clarke, 1950), 20.

Ezekiel 1–20, and Joshua. Calvin sought for brevity and clarity in all of his exegetical work. He emphasized the illumination of the Holy Spirit as essential to a proper understanding of the text. Calvin underscored the continuity between the two Testaments (one covenant in two dispensations) and sought to apply the plain or natural sense of the text to the church of his day. In the preface to his own influential commentary on Romans, Karl Barth described how Calvin worked to recover the mind of Paul and make the apostle's message relevant to his day:

> How energetically Calvin goes to work, first scientifically establishing the text ("what stands there?"), then following along the footsteps of its thought; that is to say, he conducts a discussion with it until the wall between the first and the sixteenth centuries becomes transparent, and until there in the first century Paul speaks and here the man of the sixteenth century hears, until indeed the conversation between document and reader becomes concentrated upon the substance (which must be the same now as then).[44]

Beza was elected moderator of Geneva's Company of Pastors after Calvin's death in 1564 and guided the Genevan Reformation over the next four decades. His annotated Latin translation of the Greek New Testament (1556) and his further revisions of the Greek text established his reputation as the leading textual critic of the sixteenth century after Erasmus. Beza completed the translation of Marot's metrical Psalter, which became a centerpiece of Huguenot piety and Reformed church life. Though known for his polemical writings on grace, free will, and predestination, Beza's work is marked by a strong pastoral orientation and concern for a Scripture-based spirituality.

Robert Estienne (Stephanus) was a printer-scholar who had served the royal household in Paris. After his conversion to Protestantism, in 1550 he moved to Geneva, where he published a series of notable editions and translations of the Bible. He also produced sermons and commentaries on Job, Ecclesiastes, the Song of Songs, Romans and Hebrews, as well as dictionaries, concordances, and a thesaurus of biblical terms. He also published the first editions of the Bible with chapters divided into verses, an innovation that quickly became universally accepted.

The British Reformation. Commentary writing in England and Scotland lagged behind the continental Reformation for several reasons. In 1500, there were only three publishing houses in England compared with more than two hundred on the Continent. A 1408 statute against publishing or reading the Bible in English, stemming from the days of Lollardy, stifled the free flow of ideas, as was seen in the fate of Tyndale. Moreover, the nature of the English Reformation from Henry through Elizabeth provided little stability for the flourishing of biblical scholarship. In the sixteenth century, many "hot-gospel" Protestants in England were edified by the English translations of commentaries and theological writings by the Continental reformers. The influence of Calvin and Beza was felt especially in the Geneva Bible with its "Protestant glosses" of theological notes and references.

During the later Elizabethan and Stuart church, however, the indigenous English commentary came into its own. Both Anglicans and Puritans contributed to this outpouring of biblical studies.

[44]Karl Barth, *Die Römerbrief* (Zurich: TVZ, 1940), 11, translated by T. H. L. Parker as the epigraph to *Calvin's New Testament Commentaries*, 2nd ed. (Louisville, KY: Westminster John Knox, 1993).

The sermons of Lancelot Andrewes and John Donne are replete with exegetical insights based on a close study of the Greek and Hebrew texts. Among the Reformed authors in England, none was more influential than William Perkins, the greatest of the early Puritan theologians, who published commentaries on Galatians, Jude, Revelation, and the Sermon on the Mount (Mt 5–7). John Cotton, one of his students, wrote commentaries on the Song of Songs, Ecclesiastes, and Revelation before departing for New England in 1633. The separatist pastor Henry Ainsworth was an outstanding scholar of Hebrew and wrote major commentaries on the Pentateuch, the Psalms, and the Song of Songs. In Scotland, Robert Rollock, the first principal of Edinburgh University (1585), wrote numerous commentaries including those on the Psalms, Ephesians, Daniel, Romans, 1 and 2 Thessalonians, John, Colossians, and Hebrews. Joseph Mede and Thomas Brightman were leading authorities on Revelation and contributed to the apocalyptic thought of the seventeenth century. Mention should also be made of Archbishop James Ussher, whose *Annals of the Old Testament* was published in 1650. Ussher developed a keen interest in biblical chronology and calculated that the creation of the world had taken place on October 26, 4004 B.C. As late as 1945, the Scofield Reference Bible still retained this date next to Genesis 1:1, but later editions omitted it because of the lack of evidence on which to fix such dates.[45]

Anabaptism. Irena Backus has noted that there was no school of "dissident" exegesis during the Reformation, and the reasons are not hard to find. The radical Reformation was an ill-defined movement that existed on the margins of official church life in the sixteenth century. The denial of infant baptism and the refusal to swear an oath marked radicals as a seditious element in society, and they were persecuted by Protestants and Catholics alike. However, in the RCS we have made an attempt to include some voices of the radical Reformation, especially among the Anabaptists. While the Anabaptists published few commentaries in the sixteenth century, they were avid readers and quoters of the Bible. Numerous exegetical gems can be found in their letters, treatises, martyr acts (especially *The Martyrs' Mirror*), hymns, and histories. They placed a strong emphasis on the memorizing of Scripture and quoted liberally from vernacular translations of the Bible. George H. Williams has noted that "many an Anabaptist theological tract was really a beautiful mosaic of Scripture texts."[46] In general, most Anabaptists accepted the apocryphal books as canonical, contrasted outer word and inner spirit with relative degrees of strictness and saw the New Testament as normative for church life and social ethics (witness their pacifism, nonswearing, emphasis on believers' baptism and congregational discipline).

We have noted the Old Testament translation of Ludwig Hätzer, who became an antitrinitarian, and Hans Denck that they published at Worms in 1527. Denck also wrote a notable commentary on Micah. Conrad Grebel belonged to a Greek reading circle in Zurich and came to his Anabaptist convictions while poring over the text of Erasmus's New Testament. The only Anabaptist leader with university credentials was Balthasar Hubmaier, who was made a doctor of theology (Ingolstadt, 1512) in the same year as Luther. His reflections on the Bible are found in his numerous

[45]*The New Scofield Reference Bible* (New York: Oxford University Press, 1967), vi.
[46]George H. Williams, *The Radical Reformation*, 3rd ed. (Kirksville, MO: Sixteenth Century Journal Publishers, 1992), 1247.

writings, which include the first catechism of the Reformation (1526), a two-part treatise on the freedom of the will and a major work *(On the Sword)* setting forth positive attitudes toward the role of government and the Christian's place in society. Melchior Hoffman was an apocalyptic seer who wrote commentaries on Romans, Revelation, and Daniel 12. He predicted that Christ would return in 1533. More temperate was Pilgram Marpeck, a mining engineer who embraced Anabaptism and traveled widely throughout Switzerland and south Germany, from Strasbourg to Augsburg. His "Admonition of 1542" is the longest published defense of Anabaptist views on baptism and the Lord's Supper. He also wrote many letters that functioned as theological tracts for the congregations he had founded dealing with topics such as the fruits of repentance, the lowliness of Christ, and the unity of the church. Menno Simons, a former Catholic priest, became the most outstanding leader of the Dutch Anabaptist movement. His masterpiece was the *Foundation of Christian Doctrine* published in 1540. His other writings include *Meditation on the Twenty-fifth Psalm* (1537); *A Personal Exegesis of Psalm Twenty-five* modeled on the style of Augustine's *Confessions; Confession of the Triune God* (1550), directed against Adam Pastor, a former disciple of Menno who came to doubt the divinity of Christ; *Meditations and Prayers for Mealtime* (1557); and the *Cross of the Saints* (1554), an exhortation to faithfulness in the face of persecution. Like many other Anabaptists, Menno emphasized the centrality of discipleship *(Nachfolge)* as a deliberate repudiation of the old life and a radical commitment to follow Jesus as Lord.

Reading Scripture with the Reformers

In 1947, Gerhard Ebeling set forth his thesis that the history of the Christian church is the history of the interpretation of Scripture. Since that time, the place of the Bible in the story of the church has been investigated from many angles. A better understanding of the history of exegesis has been aided by new critical editions and scholarly discussions of the primary sources. The *Cambridge History of the Bible*, published in three volumes (1963–1970), remains a standard reference work in the field. The ACCS built on, and itself contributed to, the recovery of patristic biblical wisdom of both East and West. Beryl Smalley's *The Study of the Bible in the Middle Ages* (1940) and Henri de Lubac's *Medieval Exegesis: The Four Senses of Scripture* (1959) are essential reading for understanding the monastic and scholastic settings of commentary work between Augustine and Luther. The Reformation took place during what has been called "le grand siècle de la Bible."[47] Aided by the tools of Renaissance humanism and the dynamic impetus of Reformation theology (including permutations and reactions against it), the sixteenth century produced an unprecedented number of commentaries on every book in the Bible. Drawing from this vast storehouse of exegetical treasures, the RCS allows us to read Scripture along with the reformers. In doing so, it serves as a practical homiletic and devotional guide to some of the greatest masters of biblical interpretation in the history of the church.

The RCS gladly acknowledges its affinity with and dependence on recent scholarly investigations of Reformation-era exegesis. Between 1976 and 1990, three international colloquia on the

[47]J-R. Aarmogathe, ed., *Bible de tous les temps*, 8 vols.; vol. 6, *Le grand siècle de la Bible* (Paris: Beauchesne, 1989).

history of biblical exegesis in the sixteenth century took place in Geneva and in Durham, North Carolina.[48] Among those participating in these three gatherings were a number of scholars who have produced groundbreaking works in the study of biblical interpretation in the Reformation. These include Elsie McKee, Irena Backus, Kenneth Hagen, Scott H. Hendrix, Richard A. Muller, Guy Bedouelle, Gerald Hobbs, John B. Payne, Bernard Roussel, Pierre Fraenkel, and David C. Steinmetz (1936–2015). Among other scholars whose works are indispensible for the study of this field are Heinrich Bornkamm, Jaroslav Pelikan, Heiko A. Oberman, James S. Preus, T. H. L. Parker, David F. Wright, Tony Lane, John L. Thompson, Frank A. James, and Timothy J. Wengert.[49] Among these scholars no one has had a greater influence on the study of Reformation exegesis than David C. Steinmetz. A student of Oberman, he emphasized the importance of understanding the Reformation in medieval perspective. In addition to important studies on Luther and Staupitz, he pioneered the method of comparative exegesis showing both continuity and discontinuity between major Reformation figures and the preceding exegetical traditions (see his *Luther in Context* and *Calvin in Context*). From his base at Duke University, he spawned what might be called a Steinmetz school, a cadre of students and scholars whose work on the Bible in the Reformation era continues to shape the field. Steinmetz served on the RCS Board of Editorial Advisors, and a number of our volume editors pursued doctoral studies under his supervision.

In 1980, Steinmetz published "The Superiority of Pre-critical Exegesis," a seminal essay that not only placed Reformation exegesis in the context of the preceding fifteen centuries of the church's study of the Bible but also challenged certain assumptions underlying the hegemony of historical-critical exegesis of the post-Enlightenment academy.[50] Steinmetz helps us to approach the reformers and other precritical interpreters of the Bible on their own terms as faithful witnesses to the church's apostolic tradition. For them, a specific book or pericope had to be understood within the scope of the consensus of the canon. Thus the reformers, no less than the Fathers and the schoolmen, interpreted the hymn of the Johannine prologue about the preexistent Christ in consonance with the creation narrative of Genesis 1. In the same way, Psalm 22, Isaiah 53, and Daniel 7 are seen as part of an overarching storyline that finds ultimate fulfillment in Jesus Christ. Reading the Bible with the resources of the new learning, the reformers challenged the exegetical conclusions of their medieval predecessors at many points. However, unlike Alexander Campbell in the nineteenth century, their aim was not to "open the New Testament as if mortal man had never seen it before."[51]

[48]Olivier Fatio and Pierre Fraenkel, eds., *Histoire de l'exégèse au XVIe siècle: texts du colloque international tenu à Genève en 1976* (Geneva: Droz, 1978); David C. Steinmetz, ed., *The Bible in the Sixteenth Century* [Second International Colloquy on the History of Biblical Exegesis in the Sixteenth Century] (Durham: Duke University Press, 1990); Irena Backus and Francis M. Higman, eds., *Théorie et pratique de l'exégèse. Actes du troisième colloque international sur l'histoire de l'exégèse biblique au XVIe siècle, Genève, 31 août–2 septembre 1988* (Geneva: Droz, 1990); see also Guy Bedouelle and Bernard Roussel, eds., *Bible de tous les temps*, 8 vols.; vol. 5, *Le temps des Réformes et la Bible* (Paris: Beauchesne, 1989).

[49]For bibliographical references and evaluation of these and other contributors to the scholarly study of Reformation-era exegesis, see Richard A. Muller, "Biblical Interpretation in the Era of the Reformation: The View From the Middle Ages," in *Biblical Interpretation in the Era of the Reformation: Essays Presented to David C. Steinmetz in Honor of His Sixtieth Birthday*, ed. Richard A. Muller and John L. Thompson (Grand Rapids: Eerdmans, 1996), 3-22.

[50]David C. Steinmetz, "The Superiority of Pre-Critical Exegesis," *Theology Today* 37 (1980): 27-38.

[51]Alexander Campbell, *Memoirs of Alexander Campbell*, ed. Robert Richardson (Cincinnati: Standard Publishing Company, 1872), 97.

Rather, they wanted to do their biblical work as part of an interpretive conversation within the family of the people of God. In the reformers' emphatic turn to the literal sense, which prompted their many blasts against the unrestrained use of allegory, their work was an extension of a similar impulse made by Thomas Aquinas and Nicholas of Lyra.

This is not to discount the radically new insights gained by the reformers in their dynamic engagement with the text of Scripture; nor should we dismiss in a reactionary way the light shed on the meaning of the Bible by the scholarly accomplishments of the past two centuries. However, it is to acknowledge that the church's exegetical tradition is an indispensible aid for the proper interpretation of Scripture. And this means, as Richard Muller has said, that "while it is often appropriate to recognize that traditionary readings of the text are erroneous on the grounds offered by the historical-critical method, we ought also to recognize that the conclusions offered by historical-critical exegesis may themselves be quite erroneous on the grounds provided by the exegesis of the patristic, medieval, and reformation periods."[52] The RCS wishes to commend the exegetical work of the Reformation era as a program of retrieval for the sake of renewal—spiritual réssourcement for believers committed to the life of faith today.

George Herbert was an English pastor and poet who reaped the benefits of the renewal of biblical studies in the age of the Reformation. He referred to the Scriptures as a book of infinite sweetness, "a mass of strange delights," a book with secrets to make the life of anyone good. In describing the various means pastors require to be fully furnished in the work of their calling, Herbert provided a rationale for the history of exegesis and for the Reformation Commentary on Scripture:

> The fourth means are commenters and Fathers, who have handled the places controverted, which the parson by no means refuseth. As he doth not so study others as to neglect the grace of God in himself and what the Holy Spirit teacheth him, so doth he assure himself that God in all ages hath had his servants to whom he hath revealed his Truth, as well as to him; and that as one country doth not bear all things that there may be a commerce, so neither hath God opened or will open all to one, that there may be a traffic in knowledge between the servants of God for the planting both of love and humility. Wherefore he hath one comment[ary] at least upon every book of Scripture, and ploughing with this, and his own meditations, he enters into the secrets of God treasured in the holy Scripture.[53]

Timothy George
General Editor

[52]Richard A. Muller and John L. Thompson, "The Significance of Precritical Exegesis: Retrospect and Prospect," in *Biblical Interpretation in the Era of the Reformation: Essays Presented to David C. Steinmetz in Honor of His Sixtieth Birthday*, ed. Richard A. Muller and John L. Thompson (Grand Rapids: Eerdmans, 1996), 342.
[53]George Herbert, *The Complete English Poems* (London: Penguin, 1991), 205.

INTRODUCTION TO 2 CORINTHIANS

The biblical books of 1 and 2 Corinthians were situated along the fault line of theological controversy and religious change in sixteenth-century Europe. The seismic impact of the message of these apostolic letters is illustrated in two poignant scenes from the Reformation era. One of these scenes is well-remembered; the other is almost entirely forgotten. One scene set the trajectory of early modern religious history; the other decisively altered the course of one man's life.

The first scene occurred in the autumn of 1529, in the castle of the Landgrave of Hesse in the German city of Marburg. From October 1 to 3, leading Protestant theologians from Germany and Switzerland met in Marburg to debate the nature of Christ's presence in the Eucharist, in hopes of achieving theological consensus that would foster a united political front against the Catholic emperor. The Lutheran delegation, represented by such luminaries as Martin Luther, Philipp Melanchthon, Justus Jonas, and Caspar Cruciger, insisted that Scripture taught the real presence of Christ's body in the sacramental elements. On the other side of the table, the Reformed delegation, represented by Huldrych Zwingli, Johannes Oecolampadius, Martin Bucer, and Caspar Hedio, rejected this Lutheran interpretation and insisted instead that Christ's resurrected body remained in heaven and that the bread and wine were ordinary elements that symbolized Christ's death for sinners. During this protracted debate, Luther repeatedly pushed Zwingli to consider the full import of Jesus' words of consecration, recorded in 1 Corinthians 11. To make his point, he inscribed with chalk on the conference table the words *Hoc est corpus meum* ("This is my body"; 1 Cor 11:24) as biblical proof of the doctrine of real presence. In the end, the religious parties were unable to find common ground on this contested point, and Luther refused to accept Zwingli's offer of the right hand of Christian fellowship. Their disagreement over four biblical words—*Hoc est corpus meum*—was decisive in formalizing a theological rupture that remains to this day.[1]

The second scene occurred twelve years later in Naples and involved the religious conversion of Galeazzo Caracciolo, the Marquis of Vico. Caracciolo was born in 1517 to one of the most powerful and influential Catholic families in Italy, related (through his mother) to archbishops and cardinals, including Gian-Pietro Carafa, the future Pope Paul IV. As a young man, Caracciolo was sent to the imperial court to serve as a page and cupbearer to Emperor Charles V. At age twenty, he contracted a brilliant marriage to Vittoria Carafa, the daughter of the Duke of Naecera, with whom he lived happily for fourteen years and fathered four sons and two daughters.

[1] See Martin Brecht, *Martin Luther: Shaping and Defining the Reformation, 1521–1532*, trans. James Schaaf (Minneapolis: Fortress, 1994), 325-39; W. P. Stephens, *The Theology of Huldrych Zwingli* (Oxford: Clarendon, 1986), 218-59.

Despite the trappings of wealth, prestige, and power, the Marquis of Vico, while still in his early twenties, experienced deep spiritual restlessness that moved him to join a circle of Catholic reformers in Naples known as the *Spirituali*, who were committed to the pursuit of religious truth and personal holiness. As a member of this circle, Caracciolo attended in late 1541 a memorable sermon on 1 and 2 Corinthians preached by the humanist Peter Martyr Vermigli. The message of this sermon proved to be life-changing for Caracciolo, who quietly resolved to disavow the world and its pleasures and embrace the evangelical faith. A decade later, at the age of thirty-four, Caracciolo renounced the Catholic religion and departed Naples, leaving behind his wife, six children, possessions, and aristocratic titles, and immigrated to the Reformed city of Geneva, where he spent the rest of his life for the sake of the Christian gospel.[2] For Caracciolo, the message of 1 and 2 Corinthians spoke to his spiritual hunger and was instrumental in his religious conversion.

Reformation and Sacred Scripture

Historians have sometimes compared the Protestant Reformation of the sixteenth century to a religious and social revolution. And there is something to that. The Reformation brought about vast, fundamental, and lasting changes in church and society in Europe that are still recognizable to this day. The Reformation divided Western Christendom by challenging the Roman Church's dominance in the West. It awakened German nationalism and permanently shaped German language and culture. It introduced new conceptions of vocation, family life, and divorce that became commonplace in the modern world. It challenged traditional Catholic piety and devotional practices, promoting instead a more simplified, Word-centered spirituality. It created rival confessional churches that, unwittingly, contributed to the rise of Europe's modern nation states.[3]

It would be wrong, however, to think of Protestant leaders such as Martin Luther (1483–1546), Huldrych Zwingli (1484–1531), Philipp Melanchthon (1497–1560), and John Calvin (1509–1564) primarily as religious agitators or social revolutionaries. For though they attacked the medieval church and rejected many of its institutions and teachings, their chief concern was not to dismantle the Christian church but to repair or reform it according to the Word of God. In other words, the Protestant reformers were *not* attempting to create a new church; they were attempting to restore to pristine condition the one, holy, universal church. Calvin emphasized this very point in his letter to the Catholic bishop Jacob Sadoleto in 1539: "Our agreement with antiquity is far closer than yours. . . . In all these points, the ancient church is clearly on our side."[4]

The Protestant reformers agreed that true spiritual reformation would occur only as the church submitted to the authority of Scripture. They insisted that the Scripture, as God's holy Word,

[2]For Caracciolo and his conversion, see Benedetto Croce, *Galéas Caracciolo, Marquis de Vico* (Geneva: Droz, 1965), 12-13. Robert Kingdon's study *Adultery and Divorce in Calvin's Geneva* (Cambridge, MA: Harvard University Press, 1995) devotes a chapter to Caracciolo's prolonged (and successful) efforts to divorce his Catholic wife on the grounds of abandonment.

[3]For considerations of the Reformation's long-term impact, see Steven Ozment, *Protestants: The Birth of a Revolution* (New York: Doubleday, 1993); Heinz Schilling, "Confessional Europe," in *Handbook of European History 1400–1600*, ed. Thomas Brady, Heiko A. Oberman, and James Tracy (Leiden: Brill, 1994), 1:641-81.

[4]Calvin, "Reply to Sadoleto," in *A Reformation Debate: John Calvin and Jacopo Sadoleto*, ed. John Olin (repr.; Grand Rapids, MI: Baker, 1987), 62, 74.

must be the *norma normans*—the ruling authority for Christian faith and practice. As Luther stated in 1519, "The church is captive to the authority of Scripture and does not teach anything but the Word of God."[5] It is important to remember that for first-generation reformers such as Luther and Zwingli, this conviction was not an abstract commitment to biblical authority but reflected their own personal encounter with Scripture. Zwingli's career as a reformer commenced when, as the newly appointed people's priest at Grossmünster Church in Zurich on January 1, 1519, he began to preach verse by verse through the Gospel of Matthew. Over the next six years, Zwingli's daily expositions of Scripture served as a kind of wrecking ball that demolished the Catholic institutions and traditional beliefs of the city church. The Word of God, Zwingli once wrote, "will as surely have its way as the Rhine [River], which you can stem for a while, but not stop." With good reason a biographer of Zwingli has claimed that "the Bible was at the heart of Zwingli's reformation."[6] The same can be said of Luther, who discovered the Christian gospel—and found peace for his tormented conscience—as he took up the doctor's cap at the University of Wittenberg and began lecturing in 1513 through the books of Psalms, Romans, and Galatians. As he studied and taught Scripture, as he unleashed the Word of God, the evangelical message spread like wildfire throughout the German empire and beyond. With only a bit of hubris, Luther remembered it this way: "I simply taught, preached, and wrote God's Word; otherwise I did nothing. And then while I slept or drank Wittenberg beer with my friends Philipp and Amsdorf, the Word so greatly weakened the papacy that never a prince or emperor did such damage to it. I did nothing. The Word did it all."[7]

Protestant biblical scholarship in the sixteenth century was in large part the beneficiary of a pedagogical program known as northern humanism, which prioritized the mastery of the humane letters (*studia humanitatis*), the cultivation of eloquence, the recovery of ancient texts, and the careful study of the Christian Scriptures in their original languages of Hebrew and Greek. During the late fifteenth and early sixteenth centuries, Catholic humanist scholars such as Lorenzo Valla, Johannes Reuchlin, Jacques Lefèvre d'Étaples (c. 1455–1536), and Desiderius Erasmus (c. 1466–1536) forged new paths as they undertook rigorous philological study of the Bible in its original languages and produced essential study tools such as Greek and Hebrew grammars and lexicons, commentaries on Scripture, and improved Latin translations of the Greek and Hebrew text. Protestant reformers such as Luther, Zwingli, Melanchthon, Martin Bucer (1491–1551), and Calvin were heirs of this humanist intellectual tradition. They believed that the careful study of the Christian Scriptures in their original languages was necessary for recovering the Christian gospel and achieving the reformation of the church. As Luther put it famously, "Let us be sure of this: we will not long preserve the gospel without the languages."[8] Like their humanist predecessors, the reformers produced a variety of exegetical aids, concordances,

[5]LW 10:29. For development of this theme in Luther's writings, see Mark Thompson, *A Sure Ground on Which to Stand: The Relation of Authority and Interpretive Method in Luther's Approach to Scripture* (Eugene, OR: Wipf & Stock, 2006), 276-82.
[6]W. P. Stephens, *Zwingli: An Introduction to His Thought* (Oxford: Oxford University Press, 2001).
[7]LW 51:77*.
[8]LW 45:360.

commentaries, and dictionaries to elucidate the meaning of the sacred text. So too they promoted curricular reforms at the University of Wittenberg and other Protestant gymnasia, academies, and universities that gave priority to the study of sacred philology and the biblical languages. Within a generation or so, Protestant pastors were expected to be *homines trilinguarum*—knowledgeable in Latin, Hebrew, and Greek—to ensure that they rightly handled God's Word in their preaching and teaching.[9] The Protestants were also committed to making God's Word more accessible to the laity through Bible translation. During the sixteenth century, Protestant scholars produced new (and improved) versions of the Bible in Arabic, Czech, Dutch, English, French, German, Italian, Latin, Portuguese, and Spanish.[10] Around two hundred thousand copies of Luther's German Bible (1534) were printed in Wittenberg before 1620.[11] Similarly, more than eighty editions of the French Bible were produced in Geneva alone between 1550 and 1600.[12]

The priority that Protestant leaders gave to sacred philology and intensive Scripture study is illustrated in the career of a long-forgotten professor named Jean Ribit, who taught theology at the Reformed Academy of Lausanne from 1547 to 1559. In 1549, Ribit drafted his weekly schedule (*studiorum ratio*), which included this Scripture-saturated program of study for Tuesdays:

- Rise at 4:00 a.m. Give thanks to God for his protection through the night and solicit his continued strength for the new day. Prepare the morning's theological lecture and memorize relevant biblical texts.
- At 5:00 a.m., commit theological and biblical insights to writing.
- At 6:00 a.m., attend the daily sermon in Lausanne's church. Following the sermon, make final preparations for the morning lecture.
- At 9:00 a.m., present theological lecture at the Academy. The class session will proceed as follows: recite introductory prayer; read aloud the biblical text in Hebrew or Greek, followed by the French translation; provide a careful exposition of the biblical passage, explaining the words or clauses that are unclear and examining textual variants; introduce the exegetical judgments of ancient and modern commentators; present a detailed discussion of the theological topics found in the biblical text as well as principal points of application. The goal is to "explain as carefully as possible . . . the mind of the [biblical] author," for in doing so one "instructs the church both in private and public."
- At 10:00 a.m., eat lunch and spend time in prayer.
- At 11:00 a.m., attend to domestic duties; write personal correspondence; or attend student sermons at the Academy.

[9]There was, of course, significant difference between the ideal and the reality. In his study of Protestant clergy in the Palatinate between 1555 and 1619, Bernard Vogler concludes that by the end of the sixteenth century almost all the ministers knew Latin, two-thirds knew Greek, but only a few had facility reading Hebrew. See Vogler, *Le Clergé Protestant Rhénan au Siècle de la Réforme, 1555–1619* (Paris: Editions Ophrys, 1976), 228.

[10]Jaroslav Pelikan, *The Reformation of the Bible, the Bible of the Reformation* (New Haven, CT: Yale University Press, 1996), 49-62.

[11]M. H. Black, "The Printed Bible," in *The Cambridge History of the Bible*, vol. 3, *The West from the Reformation to the Present Day*, ed. S. L. Greenslade (Cambridge: Cambridge University Press, 1963), 432.

[12]Bettye Thomas Chambers, *Bibliography of French Bibles: Fifteenth- and Sixteenth-Century French-Language Editions of the Scriptures* (Geneva: Droz, 1983).

- At noon, study the Hebrew text of Scripture, page through a Hebrew dictionary, and recite the Psalms and Proverbs.
- At 1:00 p.m., listen to wife read the Bible and follow along in either the Greek or Hebrew text.
- At 2:00 p.m., read three chapters of the Bible and commit parts of it to memory.
- At 3:00 p.m., study the passage of Scripture that will be examined in the *Congregation* of the city pastors the following day. Consult relevant commentaries, including those of Nicholas of Lyra, Augustine Steuchus, Jerome, Sebastian Münster, Augustine, Huldrych Zwingli, Origen, Basil the Great, and Ambrose. Spend time meditating on the passage for personal edification.
- At 5:00 p.m., read three chapters of the New Testament.
- At 6:00 p.m., eat dinner.
- At 7:00 p.m., assist children with their schoolwork and oversee their catechism lessons.
- At 8:00 p.m., lead household through family prayers and confession of sins.

Ribit concludes that one must "never omit" these household prayers if "God would show his favor on our leadership."[13]

Obviously, most Protestant ministers and laity in the sixteenth century did not possess the educational background, the time, or the motivation to devote such careful attention to the biblical languages and interpretation as did the theologian Jean Ribit. Nevertheless, Ribit's example points to the Protestants' conviction that the renewal of the Christian church was closely tied to the recovery, study, and exposition of God's Word. For reformers such as Luther, Calvin, and Ribit, biblical scholarship was not an end in itself; rather, it was intended to equip preachers to proclaim God's gospel through sermons, sacraments, and catechisms. It is with good reason, then, that historian Irena Backus has argued that biblical exegesis became "the chief purveyor" of Protestant doctrine—and, we might add, a crucial agent of religious change.[14]

Commentaries, Commentators, and Paul's Corinthian Correspondence

One of the primary ways that humanistic biblical scholarship was transmitted to evangelical pulpits was through biblical commentaries. This could happen in several ways. First, professors in Protestant universities and academies relied on biblical commentaries as they trained future pastors in Bible and theology. This was illustrated in the teaching ministry of Jean Ribit. It was also witnessed in the career of the reformer Wolfgang Musculus (1497–1563), whose biblical lectures to students at the municipal secondary school (*Hohe Schule*) in Bern drew extensively from both ancient and modern biblical commentaries.[15] Second, parish ministers also depended on biblical commentaries as

[13]This text is found in Henri Meylan, "Professeurs et Étudiants, Questions d'Horaires et de Leçons," in *La Réforme et l'éducation*, ed. Jean Boisset (Toulouse: Privat, 1974), 70-71.

[14]Irena Backus, "Bible: Biblical Hermeneutics and Exegesis," in *OER* 1:154.

[15]See Scott Manetsch, "(Re)constructing the Pastoral Office: Wolfgang Musculus's Commentaries on 1 and 2 Corinthians," in *On the Writing of New Testament Commentaries*, ed. Stanley Porter and Eckhard Schnabel (Leiden: Brill, 2013), 253-66.

essential tools in preparing sermons and catechetical lessons. Thus, for example, an inventory of the personal libraries of Reformed and Lutheran pastors in the Palatinate from 1580 to 1585 reveals that 12.2 percent of the books were devoted to Old Testament exegesis and 17.4 percent treated New Testament exegesis.[16] Another example is seen in the personal library of a rural pastor from Geneva named Jean de Brunes. At his death in 1603, de Brunes's library contained 549 titles, including the Hebrew Bible; the Greek New Testament; Greek and Hebrew dictionaries, grammars, and concordances; harmonies of the Gospels; and commentaries on every book of the Bible.[17]

A minor episode from Calvin's career illustrates the strategic importance of commentaries in Protestant religious culture.[18] When Calvin returned to Geneva from Strasbourg in 1541, he had recently completed his commentary on Romans and had begun commenting on 1 and 2 Corinthians. Unfortunately, the demands of pastoral ministry, along with incessant polemical battles, made it impossible for Calvin to make progress on his exegetical writing—and his friends became increasingly worried and impatient. When Guillaume Farel urged his colleague to return to his commentaries, Calvin responded, "I only wish I had more time and better health."[19] In November 1545, Calvin received a long, urgent letter from his friend Valeran Pullain:

> All the learned, whenever they meet, ask me when those commentaries will finally be ready. Let me tell you something: You are not being very wise when you allow Satan to draw you away to other projects which, although they are not to be despised, are nevertheless not as useful as the treatment of Scripture. . . . Look, my father, I am speaking in this fashion because I am convinced that it is for the glory of Christ and the up building of his church. For, Calvin, I wish that you would resolve once for all never to rest until you have written commentaries on all the epistles of Paul, then on the prophets, then on the rest of the sacred books. Gracious God! How they would help the church! How much they would do for the glory of Christ![20]

The long-awaited commentary on 1 Corinthians finally appeared in January 1546, to the delight of Calvin's friends in Strasbourg. John Hooper, the future bishop of Gloucester, was less enthusiastic, however. In a letter to Martin Bucer, he complained that "Calvin's commentary on 1 Corinthians displeased me exceedingly"—no doubt due to Calvin's explanation of the Lord's Supper in his comments on 1 Corinthians 11.[21] As this vignette indicates, biblical commentaries were highly valued by early Protestants, who depended on them for edification, biblical understanding, and polemical advantage.

[16]Vogler, *Le Clergé Protestant Rhénan*, 254.

[17]M. Puyroche, "La bibliothèque d'un Pasteur à la fin du XVIe siècle," *Bulletin de la société de l'histoire du Protestantisme français* 21 (1872): 327-37. Jean de Brunes served the Genevan church from 1598 to 1601 and then transferred to the Reformed church in Lyon, where he died in 1603. Lutheran pastors' libraries also contained a substantial number of volumes devoted to biblical exegesis. See, for example, Gerald Strauss, "The Mental World of a Saxon Pastor," in *Reformation Principle and Practice: Essays in Honour of Arthur Geoffrey Dickens*, ed. Peter Newman Brooks (London: Scholar Press, 1980), 161-70.

[18]This incident is reported in T. H. Parker, *Calvin's New Testament Commentaries* (Louisville, KY: Westminster John Knox, 1993), which I follow closely. Translations from Calvin's correspondence are mine.

[19]Farel to Calvin, October 1546, in CO 12:391.

[20]Pullain to Calvin, November 1545, CO 12:216.

[21]Cited in Parker, *Calvin's New Testament Commentaries*, 19.

Calvin was in no way unique among the reformers in writing commentaries. During the sixteenth and early seventeenth centuries, Protestant and Catholic scholars produced hundreds of biblical commentaries interpreting every verse of the Scripture canon. These commentaries were not intended to supplant the authority of holy writ; rather, their purpose was to clarify the meaning of the biblical text, usually in conversation with Christian interpreters both ancient and modern. Commentaries during the Reformation era appeared in a variety of literary forms and genres, spanning a continuum from brief philological comments with little theological content to extensive theological reflection with minimal attention paid to grammar or syntax. Exegetical treatments of Scripture were variously titled commentaries (*commentarii*), paraphrases (*paraphrases*), annotations (*annotationes, annotatiunculae*), explanations (*enarrationes, explicationes*), expositions (*expositiones*), sermons (*sermones*), and homilies or sermon outlines (*postille*)—though as we shall see shortly such nomenclature never constituted hard-and-fast literary categories in the sixteenth century.[22]

Reformation commentaries on 1 and 2 Corinthians illustrate the variety and versatility of these literary genres. More than fifty different Protestant and pre-Tridentine Catholic authors wrote commentaries on 1 Corinthians before 1660. Another forty-five commentaries were produced on 2 Corinthians during the same period.[23] Pre-Tridentine Catholic commentators on 1 and 2 Corinthians included the brilliant biblical scholar Jacques Lefèvre d'Étaples; the Dominican theologian, and Luther's opponent at the Diet of Augsburg, Cardinal Thomas de Vio Cajetan (1469–1534); and the Dutch humanist Desiderius Erasmus. John Colet (1467–1519), the dean of St. Paul's Church in London, also produced a manuscript copy of a commentary on 1 Corinthians.

A significant number of Lutheran churchmen also published sustained interpretations of 1 and 2 Corinthians, whether in the form of commentaries, annotations, sermon collections, or sermon outlines. Chief among these interpreters were the Wittenberg humanist and reformer Philipp Melanchthon; the Wittenberg preacher and pastor Johannes Bugenhagen (1485–1558); the pastor of Nordhausen and Eisleben Johann Spangenberg (1484–1550) and his son Cyriacus Spangenberg (1528–1604); the Gnesio-Lutheran theologians Tilemann Hesshus (1527–1588) and David Chytraeus (1531–1600); and the Danish theologian Niels Hemmingsen (1513–1600). Martin Luther never produced a comprehensive study of either 1 Corinthians or 2 Corinthians, but he did publish brief expositions of 1 Corinthians 7 and 1 Corinthians 15 as well as postils on select passages from the Corinthian correspondence.

In a similar fashion, Reformed authors on the Continent and in England found Paul's Corinthian correspondence to be rich soil for interpretation and comment. During the sixteenth and early seventeenth centuries, noteworthy studies of 1 and 2 Corinthians were produced by the Zurich theologian Huldrych Zwingli and his successor Heinrich Bullinger (1504–1575). Peter Martyr Vermigli's massive study of 1 Corinthians became the gold standard for Reformed

[22]See Kenneth Hagen, "What Did the Term *Commentarius* Mean to Sixteenth-Century Theologians?," in *Théorie et pratique de l'exégèse: Actes du troisième colloque international sur l'histoire de l'exégèse biblique au XVI siècle*, ed. Irena Backus and Francis Higman (Geneva: Droz, 1990), 13-38. Backus, "Bible: Biblical Hermeneutics and Exegesis," 1:158.

[23]These figures include commentaries on the entire Bible, commentaries on the New Testament, commentaries on the Pauline epistles, and discrete commentaries on 1 and 2 Corinthians.

commentaries on that epistle. In Geneva, the reformer John Calvin, his colleague Theodore Beza (1519–1605), and their successor Jean Diodati (1576–1649) all wrote commentaries or annotations on 1 and 2 Corinthians—as did the Bernese biblical scholar Wolfgang Musculus and the Dutch theologian Andreas Hyperius (1511–1564). In addition, the Strasbourg reformer Martin Bucer and Genevan pastor Simon Goulart (1543–1628) penned theological discourses that included extensive comment on select passages from these Pauline letters. A generation later, Reformed Protestants or "Puritans" in England also published popular exegetical studies on 1 and 2 Corinthians, as seen in the commentaries of David Dickson (c. 1583–1663), John Trapp (1601–1669), and Edward Leigh (1602–1671); the sermons of John Donne (1572–1631); and the marginal notes that appeared in the *English Annotations* (1645).

What is missing from this impressive inventory of commentators, however, are so-called Radical Protestant and Anabaptist authors. As has frequently been noted, few Radical and Anabaptist leaders had either the humanistic training or the unhurried leisure and physical safety to produce substantial exegetical works. Nevertheless, in their polemical and catechetical writings, Anabaptist and Radical church leaders such as Balthasar Hubmaier (1480/1485–1528), Andreas Bodenstein von Karlstadt (1486–1541), Hans Denck (c. 1500–1527), Dirk Philips (1504–1568), and Menno Simons (c. 1496–1561) offered occasional comments on passages in 1 and 2 Corinthians that related to their particular theological or practical concerns, such as believers' baptism, pacifism, the Lord's Supper, and free-church ecclesiology.

As noted above, Reformation commentaries on 1 and 2 Corinthians appeared in a variety of literary genres and styles. Four major categories of exegetical commentaries were especially popular. Biblical commentaries known as *paraphrases* were made famous by Erasmus, who published his *Paraphrases* on the New Testament from 1517 to 1524. In Erasmus's hands, the paraphrase provided a continuous exposition and explanation of the New Testament intended to simplify and clarify its meaning for ordinary readers. Paraphrasing was "the art of saying things differently, without saying different things."[24] When his opponents accused him of tampering with Scripture, Erasmus defended his work by insisting that he had elucidated Paul's meaning by "bridging gaps, smoothing rough passages, bringing order out of confusion and simplicity out of complication, untying knots, [and] throwing light on dark places."[25] In the century after their publication, Erasmus's *Paraphrases* were translated into several vernacular languages for use in local parish ministry.[26]

Annotations were a second popular form of Reformation commentary, although this classification allowed for diverse styles that signaled different theological purposes. Of all Erasmus's publications, the *Novum Instrumentum* (1516) was arguably his greatest achievement. In this work, Erasmus presented his reader with the Greek text of the New Testament (drawn from the best available Greek manuscripts), a fresh Latin translation from the Greek text, and extensive

[24]Cited in Cornelis Augustijn, *Erasmus: His Life, Works, and Influence*, trans. J. C. Grayson (Toronto: University of Toronto Press, 1991), 101.

[25]CWE 42:xv. Erasmus is speaking specifically of his *Paraphrases* on Paul's letter to the Romans.

[26]Augustijn, *Erasmus*, 101. In England, for example, it was mandated in 1547 that every parish church possess a copy of Erasmus's *Paraphrases*.

exegetical notes or annotations to justify his new translation. In subsequent editions, these annotations were expanded considerably, creating a full-blown philological and exegetical commentary on the New Testament; hence, the work thereafter became known as the *Annotationes.* In the decades that followed, Protestant exegetes such as Theodore Beza and Jean Diodati produced their own annotations, which provided extensive philological notations on the Greek text—often in conversation with Erasmus—in defense of a Protestant reading of the New Testament.[27] And yet, not all commentaries bearing the title *annotations* were studies in philology and textual criticism. Melanchthon's *Annotationes* on 1 and 2 Corinthians (1522), for example, paid virtually no attention to Greek grammar or syntax, adopting instead a rhetorical approach that explained the meaning of select passages or topics that were of theological and pastoral concern for early evangelicals. Passages that did not contribute to Melanchthon's theological purpose were treated cursorily, or even ignored.[28] Most examples of Protestant annotations, however, fell somewhere in between the divergent approaches adopted by Erasmus and Melanchthon. Thus, for example, the *English Annotations,* commissioned by the English Parliament in the early 1640s, presented its readers with detailed exegetical and doctrinal notes on nearly every verse in 1 and 2 Corinthians so as to confirm the Reformed theological perspective on display at the Westminster Assembly.[29]

Not surprisingly, many Reformation commentaries on 1 and 2 Corinthians bore the title *commentarius* (sometimes called *explicationes,* or *expositiones*), but once again, this classification allowed for different interpretive styles. John Calvin's commentaries on the Corinthian correspondence were characterized by lucid brevity (*perspicua brevitate*) as he provided a concise philological and theological exposition of each verse of the biblical text. Calvin intended that longer, more detailed theological topics (*loci communes*) be treated in his *Institutes of the Christian Religion.*[30] Musculus's commentaries on 1 and 2 Corinthians, by contrast, were far more detailed as they interpreted each biblical pericope in successive steps that included a fresh Latin translation, general remarks on the passage, philological analysis of key terms, and, finally, moral and dogmatic "observations" on the passage.[31] Vermigli's massive commentary on 1 Corinthians adopted this same approach, though it contained more extensive interaction with early Christian commentators and provided the reader with lengthy theological excurses on topics such as marriage and divorce, the *imago Dei,* faith and works, Christian freedom, purgatory, and soul sleep. A very different style of

[27]See Jan Krans, *Beyond What Is Written: Erasmus and Beza as Conjectural Critics of the New Testament* (Leiden: Brill, 2006).

[28]Thus, Melanchthon devotes only a couple of pages of his *Annotations* to 1 Corinthians 7–8, and entirely ignores 1 Corinthians 16. See Melanchthon, *Annotations on the First Epistle to the Corinthians,* ed. and trans. John Patrick Donnelly (Milwaukee: Marquette University Press, 1995), 16-17. For more on Melanchthon's rhetorical method, see Timothy Wengert, "Philip Melanchthon's 1522 Annotations on Romans and the Lutheran Origins of Rhetorical Criticism," in *Biblical Interpretation in the Era of the Reformation,* ed. Richard Muller and John Thompson (Grand Rapids, MI: Eerdmans, 1996), 124-38.

[29]See Randall Pederson, *Unity in Diversity: English Puritans and the Puritan Reformation, 1603–1689* (Leiden: Brill, 2014), 120-23. The first edition of the *English Annotations* was for the most part a revision and update of the notes from the *Genevan Bible* (1560). Subsequent editions in 1651 and 1657–1658 witnessed a significant augmentation of the textual notes.

[30]For Calvin's exegetical method, see especially John L. Thompson, "Calvin as a Biblical Interpreter," in *The Cambridge Companion to John Calvin,* ed. Donald K. McKim (Cambridge: Cambridge University Press, 2004), 58-73.

[31]See Craig Farmer, *The Gospel of John in the Sixteenth Century: The Johannine Exegesis of Wolfgang Musculus* (New York: Oxford University Press, 1997), and Farmer, "Wolfgang Musculus," in *Dictionary of Major Biblical Interpreters,* ed. Donald McKim (Downers Grove, IL: IVP Academic, 2007), 765-69. Hereafter cited as DMBI.

commentary writing is seen in John Colet's manuscript on 1 Corinthians, which exposited the biblical text chapter by chapter, examining select passages that were especially conducive to his Neoplatonic vision for moral improvement and union with God.[32] Yet another approach is found in John Trapp's *A Commentary or Exposition* (1656), which presented a pastiche of terse commentary, moral exempla, and memorable quotations, drawn from the writings of several dozen Reformation authors, including Beza, Calvin, John Foxe, Luther, Melanchthon, Oecolampadius, Richard Sibbes, Jerome Zanchi, and Zwingli.

A fourth popular style of commentary literature on 1 and 2 Corinthians during the Reformation era was the postils (*postille*). The postils were different from other Reformation commentaries in that most of them were compiled by Lutheran or Catholic churchmen, most were written in German (rather than Latin), and most followed closely the calendar of liturgical readings.[33] In the sixteenth century, Lutheran postils could take different forms: some were expositions of Scripture in the form of brief homilies, while others functioned more as sermon outlines, providing brief summaries and exegetical notes on the text. The postils of prominent Lutheran pastors such as Johann Spangenberg, Veit Dietrich, and David Chytraeus were widely read, but Luther's postils were far and away the most popular, appearing in ten separate sermon collections during the sixteenth century. When his *Sommerpostille* appeared in 1544 (thanks to the careful editorial work of his friend Caspar Cruciger), Luther enthused, "In these the epistle and Gospel readings throughout the year are clearly and merrily handed to us, or, as I would say, are chewed for us as a mother chews mash for her little baby."[34] So popular were these postils that laypeople in the countryside sometimes requested that they be read aloud in place of their pastor's Sunday sermon.[35] Long neglected, historians now recognize this postil literature to have been crucial in the dissemination of religious ideas in Germany during the age of the Reformation.[36]

A Guide to Reading 2 Corinthians

Efforts to reconstruct the historical background underlying Paul's correspondence with the Corinthian church has vexed biblical scholars for several centuries. Today, many interpreters believe that Paul wrote no fewer than five letters to the Corinthians: the "previous" letter mentioned in 1 Corinthians 5:9; 1 Corinthians itself; a "severe" letter suggested by 2 Corinthians 2:3-4 (no longer extant); a fourth letter comprising 2 Corinthians 1–9; and a fifth letter consisting of 2 Corinthians 10–13.[37] Scholars have justified this reconstruction by pointing to apparent discontinuities

[32]J. Arnold, "John Colet," in *DMBI* 321-24.

[33]See John Frymire, *The Primacy of the Postils: Catholics, Protestants, and the Dissemination of Ideas in Early Modern Germany* (Leiden: Brill, 2010); and Todd Hains, "Luther and Bound Conscience in his German Church Postils" (MA thesis, Trinity Evangelical Divinity School, 2007), 47-62. Because postils usually followed the liturgical cycle, only a handful of the postils treat passages from 1 and 2 Corinthians.

[34]Cited in Hains, "Luther and Bound Conscience in his German Church Postils," 60. For a modern edition of Luther's Summer Postils, see LW 78.

[35]Strauss, "Mental World of a Saxon Pastor," 163.

[36]Frymire argues this point in *The Primacy of the Postils*, 1.

[37]See C. K. Barrett, *A Commentary on the Second Epistle to the Corinthians* (New York: Harper & Row, 1973), 5-11; Colin Kruse, *2 Corinthians*, Tyndale New Testament Commentaries (Grand Rapids, MI: Eerdmans, 1997), 25-35.

in argument, tone, and content between 2 Corinthians 1–9 and 2 Corinthians 10–13. By contrast, Reformation commentators (along with some modern interpreters[38]) affirmed the essential unity of this letter and understood Paul's mention of a "severe" letter in 2 Corinthians 2:3-4 as a reference to the epistle of 1 Corinthians. Hence, early modern commentators like John Calvin, John Downame, and Wolfgang Musculus concluded that Paul penned only three (known) letters to the Corinthian church: the "previous" letter, 1 Corinthians, and 2 Corinthians. This abbreviated epistolary record inevitably influenced the way the reformers understood Paul's turbulent relationship with the Corinthian church and the pastoral strategies he adopted in response.

In 1 Corinthians, the apostle Paul had sharply rebuked the believers at Corinth for their numerous vices, including their fractious spirit, their abuse of Christian liberty, their sexual misconduct, their disputes over spiritual gifts, and their tolerance of a brother guilty of incest. This "painful" letter had its intended effect in that the believers subsequently reformed their behavior and excommunicated the incestuous member from their assembly. But Paul's letter also offended many Corinthians, who now questioned the apostle's authority and began to throw their support behind false teachers who were preaching salvation through the law rather than by the gospel of grace. For Reformation commentators, then, this was the historical context that informed Paul's second letter to the Corinthians, which he wrote in Macedonia and dispatched through Titus and a second (unnamed) brother. In this second letter, Paul defended his apostolic authority, extolled the beauty of the Christian gospel, and expressed his deep pastoral concern for his Christian flock—while at the same time making final arrangements for a financial collection in support of the impoverished church in Jerusalem.

Modern readers will no doubt encounter material in this present volume that is insightful, edifying, surprising, and sometimes mystifying. Here we briefly explore five themes that receive special treatment in Reformation commentaries on 2 Corinthians.

Pastoral formation and leadership. As noted earlier in this introduction, early modern biblical commentaries were frequently written *by* Christian ministers and intended *for* Christian ministers. The fact that many commentaries had their genesis in university lecture halls, where they served to prepare ministerial candidates for future ministry, goes far in explaining why many of these commentaries read like pastoral handbooks, offering detailed advice regarding the character of the Christian minister and the nature of the pastoral office. Paul's second letter to the Corinthians provided Reformation exegetes a particularly rich reservoir of pastoralia, given his sustained defense of his apostolic credentials and pastoral activities in response to attacks from the so-called false apostles. Reformation commentators extolled the apostle Paul as a kind of model pastor. They called attention to his mature, godly character, his zealous faith, his humble and generous spirit, his passion for God's glory, and his burning love for God's people. These personal qualities found tangible expression in Paul's public ministry as an apostle and Christian pastor. Reformation commentators shared Paul's conviction that the proclamation of the Christian

[38]See Philip Edgcumbe Hughes, *Paul's Second Epistle to the Corinthians*, New International Commentary on the New Testament (Grand Rapids, MI: Eerdmans, 1973), xv-xxxv.

gospel should stand at the center of a minister's vocation, for it was through the agency of preaching that God imparted to men and women his righteousness, grace, the Holy Spirit, and eternal life. In their sermons, preachers must avoid the contrived rhetoric of the schools, but instead should proclaim God's Word in a clear, straightforward, and humble manner that allows the Spirit to work in power. The ministry of the Word always occurs *coram Deo*—in the presence of God. As Cyriacus Spangenberg reminded his readers, "God goes to all sermons and hears how and what we preach. . . . It is no small thing to be a preacher."[39] But preaching was not the only item listed on the minister's job description. Christian pastors must also show concern for the welfare of God's people, leaving no stone unturned in protecting the weak of conscience, disciplining the rebellious, refuting false teachers, and instructing the faithful in biblical doctrine. This pastoral job description would inevitably involve sacrifice, danger, and intense suffering—a point Reformation exegetes made forcefully and frequently as they treated Paul's litany of hardships listed in 2 Corinthians 6, 2 Corinthians 11, and 2 Corinthians 12. Like Paul, pastors must be prepared to live and die for their people, to endure exiles, persecutions, hunger, doubts, slanderous attacks, and temptations from Satan and his minions. In addition, faithful ministers would experience the daily burden of caring for the spiritual well-being of the men and women under their charge. For good reason, then, Martin Luther listed three qualifications required for faithful Christian ministers: reading Scripture, praying, and temptation (*lectio*, *oratio*, and *tentatio*).[40]

Penance and discipline. Whereas Paul's first letter to the Corinthians devoted significant space to the subject of the Lord's Supper, his second epistle deals more extensively with the subject of penance. In this present letter, Paul demands that the incestuous brother who has repented of his sin be restored as a forgiven and welcomed member of the Christian community. Reformation commentators drew a variety of important conclusions from Paul's pastoral example: ministers must avoid excessive severity when caring for the souls of hardened sinners; restoration should be based on the depth of remorse rather than the enormity of the offense; church leaders who practice ecclesiastical discipline must do so with genuine sorrow for their wayward members. Bucer opined that it would be better to achieve weak penance and meager reformation than to have none at all.[41] Corrective pastoral discipline should always be practiced in a spirit of gentleness and love—seeking the restoration of the sinner while protecting the spiritual health of the congregation. Christian ministers must not grow discouraged by their people's sin, apathy, and contentiousness, but find their hope and reward in God's ultimate approval. As they made the case for restorative church discipline, many Protestant commentators criticized models of discipline and penance that they viewed as unbiblical and overly harsh. Some, like Bullinger, raised questions about the intrusive network of discipline practiced by Calvin's Consistory in Geneva. Others condemned Anabaptist communities for their practice of strict separation, their use of the ban,

[39]Spangenberg, *Die ander Epistel Pauli an die Corinthier*, 48v (see his comments at 2 Cor 2:17).

[40]Cited by Trapp, *A Commentary or Exposition*, 706 (see his comments at 2 Cor 2:4). Luther thus revised the medieval *lectio divina*, which had prioritized *lectio*, *oratio* (or *meditatio*), and *contemplatio*.

[41]Bucer, *Concerning the True Care of Souls*, 124.

and their doctrine of perfectionism. Most frequently, Protestant exegetes leveled criticisms against the Catholic sacrament of penance for the distinction it drew between guilt and punishment, and its commitment to priestly absolution, the treasury of merits, and the remission of punishment through works of satisfaction. Here, Protestant commentators spoke with a single voice: Christ's sacrificial death on the cross is a complete and sufficient atonement for the sins of those who trust in him. Penance should be voluntary, heartfelt, and found in Christ alone.

Law versus gospel. Paul's famous statement in 2 Corinthians 3:6—"the letter kills, but the Spirit gives life"—had for centuries been used as a prooftext to justify allegorical interpretations of Scripture that privileged spiritual over literal readings of the sacred text.[42] Protestant commentators interpreted this passage differently, believing that Paul was here asserting the superior power of the new covenant of the gospel over the old covenant of the law. As Hemmingsen succinctly noted, "The terms 'Letter' and 'Spirit' must not be understood to refer to interpretation, but to efficacy."[43] The old covenant with its endless regulations could only coerce people to right behavior; it had no power to change hearts. By contrast, the new covenant of the gospel brings about the forgiveness of sins and spiritual life through the power of the Spirit. The law given through Moses was temporary, addressed to one nation, and could only threaten and kill condemned sinners. The gospel that comes through Jesus Christ is eternal, addressed to all people, and (through the Spirit) is powerful to justify sinners and impart consolation, joy, and eternal life. Protestant interpreters believed that many of Scripture's most precious doctrines are made visible in Paul's sharp contrast between law and gospel: here one finds the glorious message that guilty sinners receive free justification by grace alone through faith alone. Moreover, in the new covenant the Holy Spirit is continually at work to bestow new birth, kindle righteousness, and impart everlasting life to God's people.[44] The apostle Paul's strong defense of his ministry, founded on the new covenant, reminds the Corinthian church—and indeed all believers—that salvation is found neither in the Mosaic law nor in works righteousness, but in the gospel of Jesus Christ alone.

Christian generosity. One of Paul's primary concerns in writing his second letter to the Corinthians was to remind the believers to complete the financial collection that they had begun on behalf of the impoverished church in Jerusalem. Reformation commentators gleaned much practical wisdom from the apostle's exhortation for Christian generosity in 2 Corinthians 8–9. Issues of wealth and poverty, of generosity and avarice, were fiercely debated in the Reformation age as they became enmeshed in controversies surrounding the communal ownership of goods, the spiritual value of almsgiving, the legitimacy of mendicancy (especially as practiced by religious orders such as the Franciscans and Dominicans), and the economic power of the institutional church in Rome.[45] Protestant commentators were unrelenting in their criticism of professional beggars, lazy

[42]For several examples, see *1 and 2 Corinthians*, ACCS 7 NT, ed. Gerald Bray (Downers Grove, IL: InterVarsity Press, 1999), 216-18.
[43]Hemmingsen, *Commentaria in Omnes Epistolas Apostolorum*, 263.
[44]David Chytraeus, *A Postil of Certeine Epistles*, 314-15.
[45]On this see Carter Lindberg, *Beyond Charity: Reformation Initiatives for the Poor* (Minneapolis: Fortress, 1993); Sigrun Kahl, "The Religious Roots of Modern Poverty Policy: Catholic, Lutheran, and Reformed Protestant Traditions Compared," *European Journal of Sociology* 46, no. 1 (2005): 91-126; and Lee Palmer Wandel, "Social Welfare," in *OER* 4:77-83.

mendicant monks, avaricious priests, and money-hungry pontiffs whose acquisitiveness (they believed) continued to undermine the spiritual mission of the church. Instead, the reformers emphasized that charitable giving must be voluntary rather than mandated and should flow from a generous and cheerful heart that was motivated by love for God and neighbor. The recipients of the church's generosity should be the deserving poor—not professional beggars—including persecuted Christians, the elderly, widows, orphans, the sick, and the mentally unstable. Though almsgiving is a fruit of Christian obedience and is pleasing to God, it is not a good work that merits salvation. The reformers recognized that raising money for charitable purposes invited abuse and misunderstanding. Hence, following Paul's lead, they emphasized that church leaders and laymen who administered poor relief must be people of good reputation, zealous for God's work, and careful to avoid all appearance of evil. Throughout their treatment of these passages, Reformation commentators pointed readers to the person of Jesus Christ, who, though he was spiritually rich, experienced abject physical poverty on earth so that he might share the riches of heaven with his blood-bought people. The example of Jesus reminds all believers that their true treasure is not pecuniary but the abundant spiritual blessings that God pours out on those who trust in him.

Paul's boasting and suffering. As Paul responds to the unfair accusations of the false apostles, he frequently resorts to boasting about his vocation and ministry activities—a strategic move that raised questions about Paul's humility. Reformation commentators spilled much ink providing justification for Paul's boasting and detailing the nature of his humble service. Unlike the self-promotion and vainglory of the false teachers of Corinth, Paul's defense of his ministry was truthful, within the bounds of his vocation, and motivated by concerns to protect the purity of the gospel of Jesus Christ and promote God's glory alone. Paul's red-hot jealousy for the Corinthian church and his commitment to present her as a spotless bride to her bridegroom, Christ, should characterize all Christian ministers as they protect the church from the pompous assertions and fake wisdom of false teachers. Protestant exegetes found particularly intriguing Paul's argument in 2 Corinthians 11–12, where he refutes the arrogance of the false apostles in a "fool's speech" that enumerates the multitude of trials and hardships he has endured as a gospel minister. And what a list: repeated imprisonments, beatings, and shipwrecks; continual hunger, thirst, and sleeplessness; relentless anxiety and spiritual warfare! "The whole life of the apostle was full of worries and sorrow, concerns and troubles," Hesshus observed.[46] Of course, suffering does not prove that one is a faithful Christian leader; but, in Paul's case, these hardships displayed God's mighty strength in the apostle's utter weakness. The pinnacle of Paul's "fool's speech" appears in 2 Corinthians 12 where he defends his apostolic credentials by speaking (in the third person) of a heavenly vision where he was caught up into paradise. But lest he become proud, God afflicted him with a thorn in the flesh that continues to torment him fourteen years later. Reformation commentators did not agree as to the precise nature of Paul's "thorn in the flesh," although they

[46]Hesshus, *Explicatio Secundae Epistolae Pauli ad Corinthios* (Helmstadt: Jacob Lucius, 1580), 266v.

offered a long list of possible candidates drawn from the Christian tradition: frequent headaches, a stomach disease, human opponents, satanic temptations, a speech impediment, the terrors of demons, even lust. Paul's example teaches believers of every age that suffering is a normal part of the Christian life; God uses various hardships to vitiate our pride, teach us humility, and strengthen our faith. As John Trapp noted, "Our extremity is [God's] opportunity."[47] The cross that godly people endure is not a sign of an angry judge but the testimony of a loving father.

For early modern exegetes, Paul's second letter to the Corinthians offered readers a rich deposit of theological insight and practical wisdom. Paul's instruction on such topics as pastoral leadership, sin and repentance, law-gospel, almsgiving, and Christian suffering made this epistle relevant for believers of every age as they navigated the difficulties of church life and the demands of daily discipleship. For Reformation commentators, however, these were not merely the collected sayings of a first-century Christian sage; rather, they were a divine "storeroom of celestial treasure," communicated by God to his church through the agency of the apostle Paul. As Hemmingsen noted in the introduction to his commentary: "We know that all things which are found in this epistle and in Paul's other writings have God's authority so that whether establishing and confirming doctrine, or refuting error, they have no less weight than if they were the very voice of the Son of God." Indeed, since Paul is "speaking to us with the voice of Christ" and "conveys heavenly doctrine," there is "nothing of error mixed with his teaching" and all that he commands must be obeyed.[48] The divine authority that the reformers attributed to Paul's epistles added greater weight and special urgency to their study and exposition of holy Scripture. Indeed, for all Christians, the careful study of God's Word required not only understanding but also faithful obedience, devotion, and worship—disciplines of the mind *and* heart. This twofold response to God's Word was captured beautifully in a prayer at the conclusion of Hesshus's commentary on 2 Corinthians:

> O holy and all-powerful God, increase within me the knowledge of you and your will; strengthen my faith; inflame my heart with love for Jesus Christ our redeemer; show to me your saving plans; direct me by your Word and Spirit in all my activity; allow me to be a useful instrument in your church. Grant me a happy and peaceful end to this life, in faith and invocation of Jesus Christ, so that I might worship you, eternal Father, you, only begotten Son, and you, Holy Spirit for all eternity. Amen.[49]

[47]Trapp, *A Commentary or Exposition*, 706.
[48]Hemmingsen, *Commentaria in Omnes Epistolas Apostolorum*, 248-49.
[49]Hesshus, *Explicatio Secundae Epistolae Pauli ad Corinthios*, 309v-310r.

COMMENTARY ON 2 CORINTHIANS

Overview: Paul's first letter to the Corinthians had been a painful one as the apostle was forced to rebuke the immature Corinthian believers for their quarrelsomeness, their spiritual pride, their shocking immorality, and their disordered public assemblies. Though this sorry state of affairs serves as necessary background, Reformation scholars commenting on 2 Corinthians are quick to point out that Paul has not given up on the struggling church. Indeed, there is clear evidence in this present epistle that Paul's strong words have achieved their intended purpose in godly sorrow and renewed obedience. The apostle's extraordinary goodwill and deep pastoral concern are evident throughout this second epistle, notwithstanding the slander he continues to endure from some false apostles at Corinth. In their introductions to 2 Corinthians, Reformation commentators praise the lofty and important matters that it treats, the beauty of the gospel it presents, and the intimate picture of Paul's life and ministry that it portrays. One writer compares Paul's teaching here in 2 Corinthians to a veritable "storehouse of celestial treasure." Several commentators employ the categories of classical rhetoric to classify the central message of the letter; though all agree that its governing genre is apologetic or judicial, some see prominent elements of exhortation and deliberation in it as well. The Lutheran commentator Cyriacus Spangenberg in particular praises Paul's rhetorical style as superior even to that of the great classical orators Isocrates and Cicero.

Prolegomena: Introduction to 2 Corinthians

The Correct Reading of Paul's Epistles. Jacques Lefèvre d'Étaples: The human mind in itself is sterile; if it believes itself able to function by itself it is presumptuous; anything it brings forth will be sterile, ponderous, obscure, and detrimental to the mind, rather than being its true sustenance furthering the life of the soul. . . . Therefore, one ought not give his attention to the mind itself, to the human agent (or whoever might finally be commissioned by God as his instrument), but one ought to attend above all to the heavenly gift and to the divine Giver himself. And therefore you, most humane Father,[†] and all you who are about to read the epistles of God's spokesman, Paul, gathered in this volume, I would pray and beseech you not to pay attention so much to Paul himself as to the grace of Paul and the giver of this grace. This applies all the more to expository sections of mine which might be read: If readers would find traces of food for the spiritual life of the soul, they should not concentrate on the human authors themselves, but they should realize that this power to bear fruit is a gift from above and should recognize the true author and follow him with all their might in purity and piety. . . .

Those who understand these epistles and the comments thereupon to be gifts of God shall profit from them. They owe such profit not to themselves but to grace. But those who attend to the worldly agent—yes, even to St. Paul himself who is more than worldly—as if these epistles were his work and not the work of a higher energy working in a divine fashion in him, and come with their own understanding, they will receive little fruit from it. . . . Let Christ, the author of divine gifts, be present to give grace to all, to preserve and increase it in order that no one should presume to interpret by their own sense. For Paul is only an instrument. INTRODUCTION TO COMMENTARIES ON PAUL'S LETTERS.[1]

SUMMARY OF THE EPISTLE. MARTIN LUTHER: In the first epistle, St. Paul rebuked the Corinthians severely for many things, and poured sharp wine into the wounds, and terrified them. But an apostle should be a preacher of comfort, to raise up terrified and fearful consciences, rather than to frighten them. Therefore, in this epistle, he praises them once more, and pours oil into their wounds, and shows himself wonderfully kind to them, and bids them receive the sinner back with love.

In chapters 1 and 2, he shows his love toward them, how all that he said, did, and suffered was for their profit and good, and how they ought to trust him for the best.

After that, he praises the office of the gospel, which is the highest and most comforting of all works and is for the profit and good of men and women's consciences. He shows how it is nobler than the office of the law, and how it is persecuted and yet increases among believers, and produces through the cross a hope of eternal glory. But with all this he touches the false apostles, who were concerned with the law rather than the gospel and taught mere outward holiness, which is hypocrisy and allows the inner shame of unbelief to continue. This he does in chapters 3, 4, and 5.

In chapters 6 and 7, he exhorts them to obey his preaching with works and sufferings and concludes by praising them so that he may incite them to go forward in it. In chapters 8 and 9, he exhorts them to contribute temporal support and help in a time of scarcity to the saints in Jerusalem, who, at the beginning, had given up all their goods. In chapters 10, 11, and 12, he deals with the false apostles. In chapter 13, he threatens those who had sinned and not reformed. PREFACE TO THE SECOND EPISTLE TO THE CORINTHIANS.[2]

THE APOSTLE PAUL'S DIVINE AUTHORITY. NIELS HEMMINGSEN: Although I have spoken at length in my discussion of the letter to the Romans about the apostle Paul, who is the author of this present letter, nevertheless, because it is often useful to repeat the same thing and many people are like novices, I wish briefly to enumerate here a number of things that will be useful for readers to keep in mind as they take up reading Paul. Who and how great was this apostle of God and teacher of the Gentiles? His message gives testimony concerning the one of whom it was said: "This is my beloved Son. . . ." Now this eternal Son of God called Paul his chosen instrument to bear his name before the Gentiles and before the kings and children of Israel. His violent conversion gives testimony. His teaching gives testimony, drawn from the preaching of Moses, the prophets, and Christ. His passion and zeal in teaching give testimony, such that the one man Paul worked harder than almost all the other apostles, as he himself confesses in chapter 11 of this epistle. The many dangers he faced give testimony, which he did not hesitate to endure for the sake of spreading the truth and glory of God. And finally, his blood gives testimony, by which he at last confirmed his doctrine at the command of Nero. The testimony of the apostle Peter agrees with all this, along with the judgment of the whole church of Christ. In the meantime, I pass over in silence the power of his spirit, the wonders, the divine miracles by which Christ testified that he had spoken through Paul. Whence, Paul himself states in Romans 15: "I will not dare to speak of anything except what Christ has accomplished through me to bring the Gentiles to obedience—by word and deed, by the power of signs and wonders, in the power of the Spirit of Christ." So, too, in chapter 12 of this present letter: "The signs of an apostle were performed among you, with patience, with signs and wonders and with mighty works." All these things are said about Paul,

[1]Oberman, *Forerunners of the Reformation*, 302-4. †A reference to Cardinal Guillaume Briçonnet, to whom his volume is dedicated.

[2]Luther, *Works of Martin Luther*, 6:465-66.

so that the Christian readers might recognize how great is the authority of this man; how certain his doctrine; and with what great reverence it is necessary to take up his teaching and instruction in this storeroom of celestial treasure. For otherwise, they are not accepting that which the Spirit of Christ promises here through this chosen instrument to the Gentiles, that is our apostle; and they are not accepting the heavenly message, which the Father uttered from heaven. Wherefore we know that all things which are found in this epistle and in Paul's other writings have God's authority so that whether establishing and confirming doctrine or refuting error, they have no less weight than if they were the very voice of the Son of God, whom Paul served as his apostle and ambassador. Therefore, the apostolic title reminds us, first of all, that Paul is speaking to us with the voice of Christ. Second, that Paul conveys heavenly doctrine. Then, that there is nothing of error mixed with his teaching. Moreover, that his teaching should be believed as the voice of God. Finally, that if anyone teaches a doctrine that is opposed to the doctrine of the apostle—even if it were an angel from heaven—we should consider it as a plague to our salvation and, as Paul himself states, condemn it as accursed, however they might arrogantly boast concerning apostolic succession.

Now, concerning the person of Paul, it should also be known that he had a very forceful nature and that his heroic passion increased his vehemence for proclaiming the gospel and restraining the false apostles. I mention this because it is from this that the sting of his disputations, his frequent arguments, and piercing refutations might be more easily understood. For with a singular wisdom and holy vehemence he examines everything that he says, and he anticipates carefully whatever can be contradicted by enemies or friends so as to deprive them the opportunity of making false accusations and free them from error. Commentary on the Argument of 2 Corinthians.[3]

Main Topics Addressed in the Letter. Philipp Melanchthon: In his first epistle, Paul severely rebuked the Corinthians because, though they were justified, they were lifeless and had no spiritual passion and were gradually returning to the desires of their flesh. For they were practicing rivalry among themselves; like little children, they were self-satisfied on account of their gifts; they supported in their midst an incestuous fornicator. Paul's rebuke had greatly upset the Corinthians, in a manner akin to when pious children are distressed when their father corrects them. It was this sadness among the Corinthians that prompted Paul to write this second epistle, for it was fitting that a pious father should console his children whom he had punished. . . . Paul's rhetorical style is not primarily didactic; rather, since many different topics from the previous epistle are repeated, the character of this present letter is more in the style of an epistolary sermon. We will point out the order of the sermon in the course of this exposition. The prominent themes [*loci*] in this letter are: Penance, since that incestuous fornicator, who had previously been excluded, was now to be received following his repentance. Second, the difference between the old and new covenants, between the law and gospel. Third, the example of the generosity of the churches of Achaia. Fourth, the nature of bishops. In addition to these subjects, Paul mentions in passing many things that happened to him and what kinds of afflictions he endured in various places. Annotations on 2 Corinthians.[4]

Paul's Purpose in Writing. John Calvin: As much as the context of this letter allows us to conclude, it seems that Paul's first letter was not without some benefit among the Corinthians, yet it was not as successful as it could have been. Moreover, some wicked people, who despised Paul's authority, persisted in their defiance. For the fact that he devotes so much effort to proclaiming his trustworthiness and maintaining the dignity of his

[3]Hemmingsen, *Commentaria in Omnes Epistolas Apostolorum*, 248-49; citing Acts 9; Gal 1–2; Rom 15:18-19; 2 Cor 12:12.

[4]*Melanchthons Werke*, 4:85.

office indicates that they had not yet been fully convinced. Now Paul himself complains in express words that there were some people who ridiculed his former letter more than they derived benefit from it. Therefore, since he understood this to be the situation of the church among them, and being occupied with other matters so that he would be slower in coming to them than he originally planned, he wrote this letter from Macedonia. We now know the purpose he had in mind for writing this letter—namely, so that he might complete what he had already begun, in order that, when he came, he might find everything well-ordered. Argument of 2 Corinthians.[5]

Historical Background of the Letter. Andreas Hyperius: The general consensus is that this letter was sent from the city of Philippi in Macedonia, and indeed through Titus. Whether Luke also played a role, as certain Greek copies indicate, is uncertain. Now, even if it is stated in the eighth chapter of this letter that a brother accompanied Titus, who is "famous for preaching the gospel throughout the churches," nevertheless it does not follow that Luke must be understood as that person—as we have noted in that chapter. Even so, this is nothing that we should squabble about. Commentary on 2 Corinthians 13:14.[6]

Summary of 2 Corinthians. Tilemann Hesshus: This letter of the apostle is intended for comfort. Now, Paul's first letter to the Corinthians was written differently and more gravely in that it rebuked them sharply. By means of his apostolic authority, Paul reproached them for their many vices, because they were zealous in creating factions; they were filled with pride; they polluted themselves with sexual lusts; they tolerated scandals in the church; they abused Christian liberty; they participated in sacrifices to idols; they profaned the sacred assemblies; they fought over the display of tongues and spiritual gifts; they falsified the doctrine concerning the resurrection of the flesh. Great sadness had been aroused among other churches, not only because the Corinthians had offended the apostle, but also the divine majesty. The man who committed incest with his stepmother was thrown into the greatest distress when he was handed over to Satan by the apostle and excommunicated by the church—and he exhibited hope of improvement. But some people, offended by the sharpness of Paul's correction, became more hostile toward the apostle; others persisted in their defiance. And it happened that false apostles, who disparaged Paul's authority, scoffed in their writings at his vehemence, as if he were blaming them for more than was right.

Therefore, this letter to the Corinthian church heals these wounds. Paul encourages with great comfort those who had been aggrieved by the scandal. He commands that the incestuous man, who was now repentant, should be received into the bosom of the church. He demonstrates that he has not attacked them from a bitter heart but out of apostolic authority and paternal concern and goodwill. He shows them the source of true comfort in the midst of such grief.

Next, he draws a comparison between the old and new covenants and reveals how much more exalted the glory of gospel ministry is compared to the whole Mosaic system and law, and at the same time he explains the greatness of the benefits of Christ's spiritual kingdom. So he bestows real comfort upon terrified consciences. Then, since some people, imbued with Jewish opinions, were anticipating the external glory of the old covenant and the earthly kingdom of the Messiah, and were thus offended by the afflictions and pitiful condition of the apostles and the church—Paul refutes and instructs these people correctly regarding the gospel. But lest the Corinthians should be sluggish in their zeal for good works and their practice of piety, Paul urges them to persevere in the faith and the fear of God, and to prove their obedience to God in every kind of virtue. They should separate themselves from participating in defiled practices;

[5]CO 50:5 (CTS 40:102).

[6]Hyperius, *Commentarii . . . in Epistolam D. Pauli ad Romanos, et Utramque ad Corinthios*, 418.

instead, they should exhibit reverence and sincere love toward the ministry.

Next, because great poverty was afflicting the saints in Jerusalem and Palestine, Paul urges them to make a contribution of alms. Finally, Paul refutes the false apostles' empty boasting and the perverse scoffing by which they were railing at Paul's authority and the apostolic office, and were attempting to render him suspicious to the church. He defends the dignity and certainty of his office; he mentions the divine revelation shown him in the third heaven. Paul threatens by means of his apostolic authority those ferocious and careless people who were not allowing themselves to be moved by either reproofs, consolations, revelations, or demonstrations of the truth. And he lets them know that he will come to see them soon. ARGUMENT OF 2 CORINTHIANS.[7]

PAUL'S ELOQUENCE. CYRIACUS SPANGENBERG: But this epistle is more artful and charming in words, although it deals with great and lofty matters. They slander Paul as not especially eloquent, but in this epistle one sees it clearly, because as far as the charm of words and the embellishment of speech according to the art of rhetoric are concerned, in this epistle Paul is far ahead of Isocrates, Cicero, and all others. FIRST SERMON.[8]

THE ARGUMENT OF THE EPISTLE. HEINRICH BULLINGER: Paul's second letter to the Corinthians is almost completely apologetic, written in the judicial genre, sharp, argumentative, and energetic—a style still used in the law courts, but adapted to the situation. For Paul is responding to both the objections and calumnies of the false apostles. . . . In addition to bringing up his inconsistency and lying, they were also accusing him of tyranny and ambition, as if he were striving for dominion when he ordered in such an authoritative manner that the fornicator be handed over to Satan. So too they now desired to raise suspicions regarding the ministry of his gospel, accusing him of both unfaithfulness and impurity. Paul responds to all these things in the first chapter of this epistle, beginning with praise for his affliction, and explaining what happened in Asia and how God had been favorable toward him at just the right moment. He adds that he was not lying, even if he had not come when he said he would come in his previous letter. Moreover, he explains the reason why he ordered that the fornicator be handed over to Satan, to show that those who accused him of tyranny were wronging him. So too he proves here that he has faithfully performed his duty of purely delivering the truth to them (which he continues to do) when he strenuously opposes the Nazarenes, who were trying to lead them into legalism. Therefore, Paul shows how excellent the gospel is, and how weak the law is; at the same time, he shows with what purity and diligence he has preached the gospel (and with how much success)—a gospel ministry that in truth owes more to divine power than to human power, though it is not without trouble. And so, Paul discusses many things here concerning hope and perseverance, as well as consolation amid suffering. Next, he exhorts them by his example to hope and good works, especially that they not associate themselves with impure things. Paul identifies this part of his letter as belonging to the genre of advice-giving [*deliberativum*]. Having addressed these matters, Paul returns to that subject with which he began, concerning the adulterer, which he completes in chapter 7.

In chapters 8 and 9, Paul employs a wonderful argument to encourage generosity, weaving together an exceptional discussion on this matter—an argument that is ascribed to the deliberative [*deliberativum*] genre. Finally, he openly defends his authority for the sake of his ministry, ascribing praise to himself in a way that may seem excessive to many people. But this was necessary lest the truth be jeopardized by that faction. Therefore, he compares himself to those false apostles, and shows by that comparison both his innocence and his

[7]Hesshus, *Explicatio Secundae Epistolae Pauli ad Corinthios*, 19v-21r.
[8]C. Spangenberg, *Die ander Epistel Pauli an die Corinthier*, 3r.

opponents' deceit. At the end of the letter, having established his authority, he threatens that he will come with authority—although he concludes by softening this harshness and wishing them farewell. Argument for 2 Corinthians.[9]

Paul's Apologetic Purpose. David Dickson: The first epistle did not fail in its effect among many of the Corinthians, yet there were some people, especially vain-talking teachers, who persevered in their rebelliousness and not only challenged the apostle's authority but also dared publicly to compare themselves with him, and to prefer themselves to him, while diminishing the authority of the apostle among the people, with no small detriment and prejudice to the gospel. That he might restrain these people, and find all things better ordered when he visited the church of Corinth, Paul wrote this second epistle that is entirely apologetic. Besides an exordium and conclusion, there are three parts to the epistle. In the first part, having removed the scandal of the cross that was laid on him, and the suspicion of his alienated mind from the Corinthians (chapters 1–2), he defends his ministry (chapters 2–3), and thereby proves his constancy and fidelity (chapters 4–5). He exhorts them to bring forth the fruits of his ministry (chapter 6) and to be persuaded of his goodwill toward them (chapter 7). In the second part of the epistle, Paul exhorts them to make a collection for the poor brethren, the afflicted Jews (chapters 8–9). In the third part he vindicates his authority from contempt, and the aspersions of false teachers who labored to render the apostle vile among the Corinthians (chapter 10), and boasts in a holy fashion against them (chapters 11–12), endeavoring to render his authority formidable and also amicable to the Corinthians (chapter 13). Exposition of 2 Corinthians.[10]

Paul's Argument in 2 Corinthians. The English Annotations: The occasion for writing this second epistle was to vindicate his ministry from contempt and his person from various accusations laid upon him by the false apostles. To this end, Paul professes his sincere affection to the Corinthians, and his faithful behavior in the whole course of his ministry. And being thereby compelled, he relates in detail both his sufferings for Christ and the visions and revelations he received from Christ. The epistle consists of the following: (1) Paul gives an excuse for himself not coming to them according to his promise (chapter 1). (2) Paul deprecates the incestuous person who had been excommunicated that he might be restored again to the church (chapter 2). (3) Paul offers a justification for his ministry against the calumnies of false teachers (chapters 3–5). (4) Paul offers an exhortation to Christian duties in general (chapter 7) and, in particular, to a generous contribution to the poor saints in Jerusalem (chapters 8–9). (5) Paul provides a disputation against his combative adversaries and rehearses his manifold trials and the happy result of them (chapters 10–12). (6) Paul denounces severity and defends the power of his apostleship against obstinate sinners (chapter 13). Introduction to Annotations on 2 Corinthians.[11]

Ministry Labors Are Not in Vain. Richard Sibbes: Our blessed apostle had written a sharp epistle to the Corinthians, especially reproving them for tolerating an incestuous person. His first epistle was at least partly effective (though not as much as he desired) in that it prompted them to excommunicate the incestuous person and, likewise, reform various other abuses. Yet, even so, since Corinth was a proud, factious, and rich city where there was a confluence of many nations and an excellent port and marketplace, there were many proud, insolent teachers there who thought poorly of St. Paul. Thus, he writes this second epistle, whose scope is partly apologetic and partly hortatory. . . .

[9]Bullinger, *In Posteriorem D. Pauli ad Corinthios Epistolam Commentarius*, 265.
[10]Dickson, *An Exposition of All St. Paul's Epistles*, 72*.
[11]Downame, ed., *English Annotations*, FF2r*.

The general scope of this letter is to show that the ministerial labor is "not in vain in the Lord," for the fruit of the first epistle to the Corinthians is seen in this second epistle—the first epistle had its effect. Therefore, we should not be discouraged, whether we are ministers of the church or ministers of our own families (as every man should be). Do not be discouraged at unlikelihood. There will always be some success to encourage us, though not so much as we look for in this world, because we deal with a reprobate generation that is always raising trivial objections and opposing us. Yet there will be some success, as we see here. Commentary on 2 Corinthians.[12]

[12]CWRS 3:7*; citing 1 Cor 15:58.

1:1-2 GREETING

Paul, an apostle of Christ Jesus by the will of God, and Timothy our brother,

To the church of God that is at Corinth, with all the saints who are in the whole of Achaia:

2 *Grace to you and peace from God our Father and the Lord Jesus Christ.*

OVERVIEW: In his customary fashion, the apostle Paul begins his letter by greeting the church in Corinth and extending to them God's grace and peace. Reformation commentators recognize that Paul has good reasons to assert his apostolic authority at the outset, given the accusations of the false teachers in Corinth who ridicule Paul's person and dismiss his gospel message. Paul has been faithful in executing the duties of his apostolic office that he received from Christ—something these false apostles cannot claim for themselves. The fact that Paul addresses the Corinthian church with its many problems as "the church of God" also invites comment from several Protestant exegetes, who note that (contrary to the claims of some Anabaptists) Christ's church in this world will never be perfect, free from all error and sin. And yet, Christian believers continue to receive the abundant riches of God's grace and peace, the two most illustrious benefits of the gospel that come from God the Father and the Lord Jesus Christ.

PAUL, TIMOTHY, AND THE CORINTHIANS. DESIDERIUS ERASMUS: Paul, a missionary in the name of Christ Jesus by the authority of God the Father, and Timothy, our brother in religious fellowship and colleague in ministry: to the Christian flock who lives in Corinth—and not only in Corinth—but also to all the saints who serve Christ through the whole of Achaia, whose capital city is Corinth. We pray for you grace, peace, and harmony, which are bestowed by the Lord Jesus Christ and God his Father, with whom we share the same Father. PARAPHRASES ON 2 CORINTHIANS 1.[1]

[1]Erasmus, *Paraphrases*, 355.

THE SIGNIFICANCE OF THE NAME PAUL. CYRIACUS SPANGENBERG: Some (such as St. Jerome[†]) say that the name Paul is Hebrew and means as much as *mirabilis*, wonderful. Others make it half-Hebrew and half-Greek, meaning "the mouth of the trumpets." The third group says that it is from the Greek word *pauomai* and means *quietus*, calm, quiet. The fourth group allows it to be Latin, *Paulus*, that is, *modicus*, small, little. Let that be as it will, Paul was indeed a wonderful man, with whom it went wonderfully in his apostleship and who was wonderfully sustained, protected, and led by God, as he himself shows in this epistle, and whose voice was over all like a trumpet. His sound has gone out through every land and is also still heard in all Christian congregations, such that one might well say that God has fulfilled through him the prophecy of Zechariah 9: "The Lord, the LORD, will sound the trumpets and will march in like the storms of the South."

But he directed all such sound so that the people received keen, calm, and clear consciences through faith in his Word, and he did it in such humility that he lorded it over no believer, but humbled himself as the very smallest of all, although he did not want to and must not allow himself to be despised by the godless. As then the word *Paul* in Latin is a name of humility and lowness, on the other hand the word *apostle* is a name of exaltation and worth, with which he lifts high and praises his office, which was highly necessary with respect to the Corinthians. FIRST SERMON.[2]

[2]C. Spangenberg, *Die ander Epistel Pauli an die Corinthier*, 5r; citing Zech 9:14. [†] Jerome, *Liber interpretationis hebraicorum nominum*, PL 23:851-52.

PROOFS OF APOSTLESHIP. JOHN CALVIN: None are to be listened to except those who have been sent by God and who speak from his mouth. And accordingly, there are two things required for persons to have authority: a calling and fidelity in the execution of their office of those people called. Paul claims he has both of these. The false apostles also do the same, but as they usurp a title that does not belong to them, they do not make headway among the sons and daughters of God, who find it easy to convict them of impertinence. Hence the name apostle alone is not adequate, unless that reality is also present, so that those who allege that they are apostles must also give evidence by their works. COMMENTARY ON 2 CORINTHIANS 1:1.[3]

PAUL ESTABLISHES HIS APOSTOLIC AUTHORITY. WOLFGANG MUSCULUS: "Paul, an apostle of Jesus Christ." Because Paul places this title at the very beginning, I think he had to establish his apostolic authority. He does this in all of his letters, as do James and Peter. They wish to be humble, as when a private person who writes to his superior places his title under the inscription of his name. For he always emphasizes his apostleship, calling himself an apostle of Jesus Christ, not rashly out of a spirit of boasting, but because it was completely necessary. For he knew that his apostleship was not recognized by many people due to the fact that he was not among the twelve chosen disciples who had lived with the Lord when he was in the flesh. Whereby, since the false apostles disparaged his apostleship everywhere, he himself emphasized it everywhere, not for the sake of his own glory, but for this one reason, that he might serve his Lord Christ both faithfully and fruitfully.

True and faithful ministers of Christ should consider what to imitate here. They should not only faithfully perform their office but also defend valiantly the authority and esteem of their ministry against reprobate and factious persons, lest they give a foothold to Satan by their negligence and carelessness. For Satan plots with the greatest diligence to destroy the fruit of ministry, and to this end he undermines the esteem of ministers as much as he can through his imposters. Meanwhile the false apostles, false teachers, and pseudo-bishops extol their titles of rank and preeminence, and with their false presumed authority they oppress the ignorant common people under the yoke of their domination. How much more right is it that true ministers of Christ guard the legitimate titles of their ministry against the enemies of the truth to the end that they might be able to perform more effectively their ministries in the church of God? COMMENTARY ON 2 CORINTHIANS 1:1.[4]

TIMOTHY, OUR BROTHER. CARDINAL CAJETAN: This is the Timothy to whom Paul later wrote two letters and whom Paul remembered to praise at the end of his previous letter to the Corinthians.

According to some books, this Timothy was one of those men by whom Paul sent his first letter to the Corinthians from Philippi. And after having spent a certain amount of time in the Corinthian church, Timothy reported to Paul (as we rightly conjecture) the obedience of the Corinthians with regard to that incestuous man; and the complaint that Paul had not come personally to the Corinthians as he had promised; and examples of how certain Jewish teachers were extolling the old covenant among the Corinthians; and the vehement opposition toward Paul (and even the Christian faith) that the Jewish teachers were sowing—and, in brief, all that was happening among the Corinthians. And since Timothy was not only an informant but also their instructor, he is named here in the beginning [of the letter]. And he is called "brother" because of his brotherly service, his care and interest shown to the Corinthians, so that they might be more fully instructed through this letter. COMMENTARY ON 2 CORINTHIANS 1:1.[5]

[3]CO 50:9 (CTS 40:109-10).

[4]Musculus, *Commentarius . . . in posteriorem epistolam Pauli ad Corinthios*, 3-4.

[5]Cajetan, *In Posteriorem Pauli Epistolam ad Corinthios Commentarii*, 151.

Paul's Authority Came from God. Wolfgang Musculus: It should be observed that when he said "Paul, an apostle of Christ Jesus," he did not qualify it with the phrase "according to his will," but "according to the will of God." He had been chosen as an apostle by Christ himself. For this reason, he could have said "according to the will of Christ." But, instead, he attributed the authority to the will of God because Christ himself is seen to have done this in several passages. For the entire sum and origin of the longed-for dispensation was dependent on God's will. Moreover, since only believers recognized the name of Jesus Christ, while even unbelievers acknowledged God, Paul preferred to say, "by the will of God" rather than "by the will of Christ" so as to make clear that he performed his apostleship by no human authority but was undergirded entirely by divine authority. This is not to say that the name of Christ somehow lacks divine authority; but what believers accept as so weighty, unbelievers disregard completely. Commentary on 2 Corinthians 1:1.[6]

This Letter Written to Laity, Not Only to Priests. Cyriacus Spangenberg: The address or title is, then, as follows: "To the congregation of God in Corinth, together with all the holy ones in all Achaia." From this it is known and obvious that this epistle is not written to the priesthood alone, but to the whole congregation, that is, written to the laypeople also. If this is the case, as no one can deny, then the first epistle is also written to the laypeople as well as to the clergy. See, then, on what grounds the papists dare to prove from the same that the sacrament should be given to the laypeople only in one kind.

Paul is especially advised in not setting the title down badly, "to the congregation in Corinth," but says expressly, "to the congregation of God in Corinth," because the devil also had his congregation and church there, of false teachers and heretics, as is the case everywhere, just as the proverb says, "Where our Lord God builds a church, the devil builds a chapel next door." First Sermon.[7]

The Church Existed in Corinth. John Calvin: It should always be observed that Paul recognizes a church where there was such a wicked mixture of evils. For the faults of certain persons do not prevent there being a church where true tokens of religion are present. But what does he mean by the expression, "with all the saints"? Were those saints outside of the church? I answer that this phrase refers to believers who were spread here and there throughout various corners of the province. For it is likely that, in that turbulent time, when the enemies of Christ were raging furiously, that many were scattered abroad, who were not at all able to gather together in sacred assemblies. Commentary on 2 Corinthians 1:2.[8]

Local Churches Make Up the Universal Church. Martin Bucer: In Romans, Corinthians, and Ephesians, "churches" is the description given to the assemblies of people in particular regions, cities, parishes, families, and houses, who by the same faith call upon and worship the same God. These gatherings, though separated by distance, by virtue of their common faith constitute the one universal church. They possess the ministry and the dispensing of the Word and sacraments, and of every aspect of religion, out of the supply and direction of the Spirit according to the Word; and the same Spirit implants in these ministers the requisite gifts. On the Church.[9]

The True Church on Earth Is Not a Perfect Church. Tilemann Hesshus: Paul addresses the church of God and the saints, whom he had nevertheless severely rebuked in his previous letter for its many vices and errors. In this way, Paul testifies that one should not imagine a Platonic ideal of the church in this life, free from sins, scandals, and errors, for such perfection and

[6]Musculus, *Commentarius . . . in posteriorem epistolam Pauli ad Corinthios*, 4.

[7]C. Spangenberg, *Die ander Epistel Pauli an die Corinthier*, 5v.

[8]CO 50:9 (CTS 40:110).

[9]CPMB 203.

complete happiness is reserved for the next life. The elect and holy church of God is the one in which the doctrine of Christ shines and the sacraments are administered—even if there are many people in it who have serious weakness. And even if scandals appear and errors sneak into it, and even if some men and women are subject to great failures, nevertheless God truly dwells in that church. God is powerful in it for the salvation of many people; truly he sanctifies the disciples with his Word through the Holy Spirit and establishes them as heirs of eternal life. Therefore, we disapprove of the craziness of the Anabaptists and similar fanatics who imagine a kind of church in this life that is free from all sin and immune from the fog of error. Explication of 2 Corinthians 1:1.[10]

To the Saints. The English Annotations: [The saints are] all who embrace the holy profession of Christians, who were admitted into the church, which is the communion of saints, who attend upon the holy ordinances of God and follow after peace and holiness, without which no one shall see God. Annotations on 2 Corinthians 1:1.[11]

The Fountain and Conduit of Divine Blessing. John Trapp: The Father is the fountain, the Son the conduit, whereby all good things are derived to us. Commentary on 2 Corinthians 1:2.[12]

Grace and Peace. Cyriacus Spangenberg: Now Paul wishes for them the two highest goods, between and in which all other goods are comprehended, since the beginning of all good and all salvation is God's grace. Where God's grace is absent, there is no happiness, no salvation, no well-being or anything good or virtuous with humankind; if, however, something good is to be or to begin, God must arouse it with and through his grace; and it is called grace because it is not earned.

After this, peace is the final good. All things are directed to it, that one might gladly be content. If a regent or sovereign has brought about in his country that there is peace everywhere, that he himself and everyone is content, he may concern himself with nothing else; if the human heart is at peace with God, it longs for nothing else; now when we come from this restless world into the heavenly country, into eternal peace, where there is no fear, no worry, no hoping, but God will be all in all, then we will long for nothing else. So peace is everywhere the end of all good, such that Paul can wish for nothing more than when he says, "Grace and peace be with you." Grace is God's good and kind will, his fatherly, faithful, benevolent heart toward us poor men and women, by which he desires our good and loved us even when we were still his enemies. Peace is God's blessing, all happiness and well-being, and everything good beyond the forgiveness of sins, which he allows to happen to human beings. First Sermon.[13]

Grace and Peace Are Joined Together. Andreas Hyperius: Paul always prays on behalf of the pious for two most illustrious benefits, which are joined one after the other. One is the cause of the other. Unless grace is present, peace does not follow, because peace is a result of grace. On the other hand, if peace is not present—especially that spiritual peace in the conscience—this is evidence that grace is not present. Now since these blessings are spiritual, they cannot be obtained or preserved by human strength. And so, Paul adds "from God our Father and the Lord Jesus Christ," for both the power and the goodwill [of the Father and the Son] are adequate for us. . . . The Father gives for the sake of the Son; the Son gives because he has received all power and all judgment from the Father. Commentary on 2 Corinthians 1:2.[14]

[10]Hesshus, *Explicatio Secundae Epistolae Pauli ad Corinthios*, 24r-v.
[11]Downame, ed., *English Annotations*, FF2r*.
[12]Trapp, *A Commentary or Exposition*, 705*.
[13]C. Spangenberg, *Die ander Epistel Pauli an die Corinthier*, 5v-6r.
[14]Hyperius, *Commentarii . . . in Epistolam D. Pauli ad Romanos, et Utramque ad Corinthios*, 338.

God Is Our Father in a Conditional Sense. Philipp Melanchthon: "Father" is not God's personal name, but his conditional name. For it is the title that finds expression in those who believe. The law did not call God "Father"; rather, it was the gospel that called God "Father" and made us children of God. As John 1 states: "He gave to them power to become children of God." And in the Lord's Prayer: "Our Father . . ." Since Paul here adds the phrase "of our Lord Jesus Christ," he thereby testifies concerning the grace of God, as if he were to say: "I wish for you God's grace and peace, and you can be certain that you will experience it, for look here, it is granted through Christ who has given you all things!" Annotations on 2 Corinthians 1:2.[15]

Humans Are Made to Praise God. Cyriacus Spangenberg: Praise be God, that is praise, honor, and worship be to God. Praise is and belongs properly to God and also remains his eternally; even though no human being were to praise him, he nonetheless has praise in and from himself, and he is therefore also praiseworthy; and what he does not praise is not deserving of praise, no matter how highly all human beings might exalt and prize it. Therefore, we should also not praise what he does not want to be praised, as we sing, "Do not praise right or good, except what God himself says and does."

But now he wants the angels and all creatures and especially human beings to praise him. He made them for this, and he therefore bestows all kinds of good things on them, as Moses also says, "that the people of Israel must praise the Lord their God for the good land that he had given them."

Therefore, we must praise and bless God, for all benefactions. This happens when we recognize his benefaction, that he has given it to us without our merit, from pure grace, love, and goodness, and we thank him for this. Second Sermon.[16]

[15]*Melanchthons Werke* 4:86; citing Jn 1:12.

[16]C. Spangenberg, *Die ander Epistel Pauli an die Corinthier*, 6v-7r; citing Deut 8:10.

1:3-11 God of All Comfort

3 Blessed be the God and Father of our Lord Jesus Christ,
the Father of mercies and God of all comfort, 4 who
comforts us in all our affliction, so that we may be able to
comfort those who are in any affliction, with the comfort
with which we ourselves are comforted by God. 5 For as we
share abundantly in Christ's sufferings, so through Christ
we share abundantly in comfort too.[a] *6 If we are afflicted, it*
is for your comfort and salvation; and if we are comforted,
it is for your comfort, which you experience when you
patiently endure the same sufferings that we suffer. 7 Our
hope for you is unshaken, for we know that as you share
in our sufferings, you will also share in our comfort.

8 For we do not want you to be unaware, broth-
ers,[b] *of the affliction we experienced in Asia. For we*
were so utterly burdened beyond our strength that
we despaired of life itself. 9 Indeed, we felt that we
had received the sentence of death. But that was to
make us rely not on ourselves but on God who raises
the dead. 10 He delivered us from such a deadly peril,
and he will deliver us. On him we have set our hope
that he will deliver us again. 11 You also must help us
by prayer, so that many will give thanks on our
behalf for the blessing granted us through the
prayers of many.

a Or *For as the sufferings of Christ abound for us, so also our comfort abounds through Christ* **b** Or *brothers and sisters*. In New Testament usage, depending on the context, the plural Greek word *adelphoi* (translated "brothers") may refer either to *brothers* or to *brothers and sisters*

Overview: Paul begins the substantive part of his letter by praising God as the source of all comfort and mercy who provides help and deliverance to his people in their every difficulty—something that Paul himself has experienced during his recent missionary journey to Asia. Reformation commentators excavate this beautiful passage to discover rich lessons for the Christian life. Paul's opening encomium serves as an important reminder that the chief duty of human beings is to praise and thank God for his lavish grace and kindness shown them in Jesus Christ. As Christians suffer for the sake of the gospel, they both share in Christ's suffering and experience his immense comfort, which they must in turn share with other people facing similar afflictions. Protestant commentators make clear that "sharing in Christ's sufferings" in no way detracts from Christ's unique, sacrificial death on the cross. Christ's expiatory death alone is meritorious before God and salvific for the human race. Nevertheless, as Christian men and women encounter sorrow and various afflictions, they find Christ to be their faithful traveling companion and ever-present comfort and help. Reformation exegetes do not entirely agree as to the precise historical occasion behind Paul's "sentence of death" in Asia, but they do agree that the apostle's personal account provides important insight into the usefulness and fruitfulness of Christian suffering. Suffering humbles us; it forces us to flee to God for help; it prompts us to pray; it assures us of God's deliverance; ultimately, it elicits our thanksgiving. As the Anglican minister John Trapp comments, "Our extremity is God's opportunity."

1:3-7 *Sharing Both Suffering and Comfort*

Celebrating God's Goodness and Kindness. Tilemann Hesshus: We ought to celebrate continually God's goodness and kindness, for this is the chief end of human beings. For God has created us and blessed us with immense and countless blessings. Truly, this not only serves the glory of God but also advances the salvation of the church; among other things, it incites faith, works hope, and confirms patience in affliction. Paul therefore begins this comforting letter with thanksgiving, in which he proclaims the immense goodness and mercy of God, who will supply his powerful and solid comfort to that person in every trial. Explication of 2 Corinthians 1:3.[1]

God and Father of Jesus Christ. Andreas Hyperius: The apostle says, God should be blessed—that is, the name of God should be praised, recommended, and magnified. Now he says, "God and Father of Christ," with respect clearly to the different natures in Christ. For he is called his Father with respect to Christ's divine nature; and he is called his God according to Christ's human nature. Nevertheless, the apostle in no way detracts from the glory of Christ's divinity, which is the reason that Paul here calls Christ "Lord," a title which signifies divinity and is used for Christ in various passages of Scripture. Thus, in Psalm 110: "The Lord said to my Lord, sit at my right hand"—where it is clear that heeding the Lord's voice refers as much to Christ as to the Father. Commentary on 2 Corinthians 1:3.[2]

Father of Christ. Huldrych Zwingli: Paul indicates here the divine nature of Christ. For the Father and the Son are of the same substance, essence, and nature. But when he says, "Father of compassion," this is an exchange (*alloeosis*[†]) of deity and person. For the title "Father" expresses the divine essence, not the divine person. For who is the source of all consolation, if not God? Therefore, he has jumped from essence to person—"Father of compassion, that is God of compassion"—because the divine persons are one God. Annotations on 2 Corinthians 1:3.[3]

Paul Praises God's Mercy and Comfort. Wolfgang Musculus: "Who is the Father of mercies and the God of all comforts." The person who gives praise without any reason yields more to his emotions than to the truth, and his praise serves more to engender deep mistrust rather than true praise. But our apostle, however much he was inclined to praise God with burning zeal when he praised him, he declared publicly those things concerning God that words of praise could never adequately express. Thus, after he had said, "Blessed be the God and Father of our Lord Jesus Christ," he next explained why he called him blessed, saying, "He who is the Father of mercies and the God of all comforts." Many glorious and wonderful things have been done, and are being done by God every day, and his many graces should be celebrated in heaven and on earth by angels, human beings, and all kinds of animals. Nevertheless, I do not know of any more illustrious and brilliant occasion that comes to mind for proclaiming God's praise everywhere than the goodness, comfort, and mercy of God, which has no measure, or number, or end. The apostle's eulogy speaks of this when he calls God the Father of all mercies and the God of all comforts. . . .

"Father of mercies." Why is it that Paul does not use the singular "Father of mercy," but the plural "Father of mercies"? Do we conclude that there is not a single goodness, by which God is good in himself, and a single mercy, by which God is merciful in himself? I answer: One looks for the quality of mercy in faith itself, by which we are rendered merciful. That faith is altogether single in itself, just as the hardness of heart is single which renders us heartless and unmerciful. But when we refer not simply to the disposition of mercy, but to the works and appearance of it, then we rightly speak about mercies and comforts. For although the quality of mercy is single in itself, there are nevertheless many or rather

---

[1]Hesshus, *Explicatio Secundae Epistolae Pauli ad Corinthios*, 25v.
[2]Hyperius, *Commentarii . . . in Epistolam D. Pauli ad Romanos, et Utramque ad Corinthios*, 339; citing Ps 110:1.
[3]Zwingli, *Annotatiunculae . . . ex ore Zvinglij*, 145. [†]Zwingli's use of the rhetorical figure of *alloeosis* (meaning interchange or exchange) is characteristic of his Christology and theology of the Lord's Supper. According to Zwingli, it is proper to refer to one nature of Christ (his humanity or deity) when speaking of the other nature. See Richard Muller, *Dictionary of Latin and Greek Theological Terms* (Grand Rapids: Baker, 1985), 30-31.

innumerable expressions of its functions, especially in God, in whom alone is the infinite and inexhaustible fullness of this quality. Therefore, as the troubles that we face as human beings are innumerable and of various kinds, the merciful God has pity on all of them, for his nature is always to show concern and mercy. And so, God very consistently displays to us expressions of all kinds of mercies in all situations so that, whenever we are in trouble, we know that we have our merciful Father in heaven. . . .

"And God of all comfort," he says. The Vulgate reads "the God of complete comfort," as if the apostle Paul were commending to us the wholeness and completeness of God's comfort. But in the Greek text one does not find the word *olēs*, that is, "complete," but the word *pasēs*, that is, "all," which is the same as saying "all kinds of comfort." For in the midst of the variety of afflictions that exercise both the body and spirit, various comfort of all sorts are furnished to us in God, for which reason he is called here the God of all comfort, that is, the God who consoles us in afflictions of every kind. This praise of God is hidden from carnal human beings, who see God more as the God of all affliction rather than the God of all comfort, especially when they consider the troubles that exercise the saints in this age and see the many afflictions of the righteous. But the apostle is writing this, not to carnal people, but to the faithful in Christ, who gladly embrace, with true faith, the praise of God's goodness. Commentary on 2 Corinthians 1:3.[4]

Father of All Mercies. The English Annotations: Although judgments as well as mercies proceed from God, yet he is not anywhere in Scripture called the Father of judgments, as he is here called the Father of mercies, because mercy and compassion arise merely from himself, and he delights in it, but our sins are the reason he inflicts any judgment on us. And it is further to be noted here, for the comfort of all those that groan under any heavy cross or who suffer conflicts with desperation itself, that the Father of our Lord Jesus Christ is the Father also of mercy, and not of mercy only in the singular number, but of *mercies* in the plural, and what is more, is also the God of all comforts. Annotations on 2 Corinthians 1:3.[5]

God's Mercy Is Never Exhausted. Huldrych Zwingli: "Father of mercies." The mercy of God is singular; however, he grants his mercy to many people. For this reason, therefore, Paul speaks of "mercies." God is the one who is merciful to all and who grants his comfort to all. From him alone, therefore, we should seek all mercy and comfort. However much we drink from this fountain, it is never diminished, it is never exhausted. The Hebrews make use of the plural noun when they wish to emphasize and extol something. That is why they address God in the plural. Annotations on 2 Corinthians 1:3.[6]

Comforted by God. Martin Luther: I have passed through unspeakable trials—trials in which no creature was able to counsel me. . . . I have passed through trials of such a nature that I thought no one on earth had them before. . . . I have at times thought . . . that I endured temptations just as great, just as grievous, and just as manifold as did St. Paul. There would never have been any remedy and advice for difficulties so great, for temptations so grievous, if Christ had not come to open the Bible to me and to advise and comfort me with his Word. Thus God (as Paul says . . .) comforts us in all our tribulations so that we are able to comfort those who are in affliction. Description of Isaiah 9:5.[7]

Christians Rejoice in Their Afflictions. Jacques Lefèvre d'Étaples: We imitate Christ, our God and king, in two ways. First, in enduring sufferings (that is, affliction and tribulations) for

[4]Musculus, *Commentarius . . . in posteriorem epistolam Pauli ad Corinthios*, 9-11.

[5]Downame, ed., *English Annotations*, FF2r*; citing Mic 7:18.
[6]Zwingli, *Annotatiunculae . . . ex ore Zvinglij*, 144-45.
[7]WA 40/3:672-73. This selection comes from Plass, *What Luther Says*, 1380-81.

the sake of his name, and even doing so with joy. Otherwise, we won't be imitating the one who "for the joy set before him endured the cross, [and] despised the shame." Second, when we are freed from these afflictions or they are no longer present, we will offer complete devotion of heart to him who liberates and consoles us, not failing in our duty when hardships and troubles are present, nor despising them when they are not present; rejoicing that our afflictions work for the salvation of others who are strengthened by the example of our patience; rejoicing also that our liberation and consolation provide consolation to other people. Yes, indeed, not only should we rejoice in our afflictions and consolations from God, but we should also rejoice in the afflictions of the saints who patiently imitate the sufferings of our Lord. Knowing that the saints receive consolation from God, I say, we ought to rejoice for their future consolation. Commentary on 2 Corinthians 1:4.[8]

The Assurance of God's Comfort. Wolfgang Musculus: "Who comforts us." Paul does not say that God "is able to comfort us," but that God "comforts us." This gives great comfort to those enduring afflictions because they believe and recognize that it is God himself who keeps them, who is able to comfort them in all things when they are bothered with troubles. And so truly . . . we will proclaim not only what God can do, but what he actually does, and so along with Paul we will meditate on this subject to praise not only his power but also his goodness and mercy. For in his work of comfort God joins together both the power to act and the mercy that prompts the action. Commentary on 2 Corinthians 1:4.[9]

The God Who Comforts Us. Cyriacus Spangenberg: Who is the one who comforts in this way? St. Paul has already said it: "the God of all comfort," he is able to comfort and no one else, the Father of our Lord Jesus Christ, the Father of mercy, and Jesus Christ our Lord, together with the Holy Spirit, the one and eternal God, whom we also invoke: "You greatest comforter in all need, you holy fount of sweet comfort, now help us happily and comforted to remain steady in this service. Let distress not lead us astray. O Lord, by your might prepare us and strengthen the weakness of our flesh, that we might valiantly struggle here, to come through death and life." So note well who the comforter is, and in whom we must seek comfort, namely, in God alone. Second Sermon.[10]

The Nature of God's Comfort. Edward Leigh: [God provides] all sorts and degrees of comfort, who has all comfort at his disposal. The passage suggests (1) that no comfort can be found anywhere else. He has the sole gift of it. (2) [God provides] not only some but all comfort; no imaginable comfort is lacking in him, nor is found outside of him. (3) All degrees of comfort are to be found in him. Annotations on 2 Corinthians 1:3.[11]

God Is a Father of Mercy and Comfort. John Donne: The duty required of a Christian is blessing, praise, and thanksgiving. To whom? To God, to God only, to the only God. There is but one God. But this one God is like a tree that has various boughs to shadow and refresh you, diverse branches to shed fruit upon you, diverse limbs to spread out to reach and embrace you. And here he visits you as a Father: from all eternity a Father of Christ Jesus, and now your Father in him, in that which you need the most. He is a Father of mercy when you are in misery, and a God of comfort when you can find no comfort in this world. And a God of *all* comfort providing even spiritual comfort in the anguishes and distresses of your conscience. Blessed be God, who is also the Father! Sermon on Trinity Sunday (1621).[12]

[8]Lefèvre, *Commentariorum in Epistolas Beati Pauli . . . Liber Tertius*, 130; citing Heb 12:2.

[9]Musculus, *Commentarius . . . in posteriorem epistolam Pauli ad Corinthios*, 12.

[10]C. Spangenberg, *Die ander Epistel Pauli an die Corinthier*, 7v-8r.

[11]Leigh, *Annotations upon all the New Testament*, 256*.

[12]Donne, *Sermons*, 3:258.

God's Blessings Should Not Be Hoarded but Shared. John Calvin: As the apostle was not living for himself, but for the church, so he reckoned that whatever gifts God had given to him were not given to him alone, but so that he might have greater capacity to assist other people. And certainly, when the Lord confers a blessing upon us, he in a manner invites us by his example to be generous to our neighbors. The riches of the Spirit, therefore, should not be hoarded, but whatever we receive should be shared with others. This, indeed, should especially be true among ministers of the Word; nevertheless, it pertains to everyone according to the capacity of each one. Thus Paul acknowledges here that just as he was being sustained by God's comfort, so it was necessary that he comfort others. Commentary on 2 Corinthians 1:4.[13]

Ministers of Comfort. John Trapp: How fortifying are right words, especially when they are uttered from the heart rather than the brain, and from our own experience. This is what made even Christ himself a more compassionate high priest. This is also what made Luther such a heart-affecting preacher, because from his tender years he was much beaten and afflicted with spiritual conflicts, as Melanchthon testifies. Luther often said that three things make a preacher: reading, prayer, and temptation. Reading makes a person full; prayer makes a person holy; and temptation makes a person experienced. Commentary on 2 Corinthians 1:4.[14]

How We Can Comfort Others. Katharina Schütz Zell: We ought to exercise and practice toward each other our office (commended to us by God), the office of care and love, as also the Lord Christ will say at the last judgment, "You have visited and comforted me in sickness and in prison, enter into the kingdom of my Father." . . . He speaks in another place, "The Father of mercy, a God of all comfort, comforts us in all trouble, so that we may also be able to comfort those who are in all kinds of trouble, with the comfort with which God has comforted us." For, just as much suffering comes upon us because of Christ, so also much comfort comes to us through Christ. Yes, the whole holy Scripture teaches us to love and serve our neighbors as the members of one body help each other bear evil. But the head must sway all the members and give the whole body life, force, strength, and everything. So also the Spirit of God must come to help our speaking, praying, comforting, and everything, to give force, breath, and life, if our actions are to serve and be useful to people. Letter to Felix Armbruster.[15]

Why Does God Comfort Us? Cyriacus Spangenberg: To what end or why does God comfort us? So that we can also comfort those who are in all kinds of distress. One reason that God comforts us is that he cannot avoid the fact that it is his nature and character to comfort those whom he finds laden with distress in the cross and misery, because he is a God of comfort. The second reason is so that we will not be left without comfort to despair under the cross. The third reason is that we will learn from his comfort how we are to comfort others who are in similar or different distress, because God does not give us comfort so that we should only use it for ourselves, but he wants us also to serve others with it.

In the same way that he does not give the sun light and brightness so that it might be beautiful and light for itself alone, but rather that it might also serve human beings and other creatures, it is done with all God's gifts. Whatever they may be called, God does not give them with the intention that the one who received them should enjoy them alone, but that with them he should also serve and give advantage to others. Let everyone ponder this.

If someone has wisdom, understanding, knowledge, skill, comfort, hope, strength, confidence, or whatever other similar gifts may be, let

[13]CO 50:10 (CTS 40:111-12).
[14]Trapp, *A Commentary or Exposition*, 706*.
[15]Zell, *Church Mother*, 132; citing Mt 25:36, 34; 2 Cor 1:3-5.

them apply them well, so that they may not load on themselves God's wrath or disgrace through neglect or misuse of the same. And of physical goods, riches, health, power, respect, rule, or whatever it may be, exactly the same is true, that we must serve, help and give advantage to others with them. Second Sermon.[16]

Sharing God's Comfort with Others. John Trapp: Mr. Knox, a little before his death, rose out of his bed. And when asked why he wanted to arise given how sick he was, he answered that he had enjoyed sweet meditations of the resurrection of Jesus Christ the previous night, and now he would go into the pulpit and impart to others the comforts that he felt in his soul. Commentary on 2 Corinthians 1:4.[17]

The Sufferings of Christ. Wolfgang Musculus: We need to study this statement carefully, where the afflictions that we suffer on account of Christ are called the sufferings of Christ. Strictly speaking, the sufferings of Christ are only those that he once endured in his flesh because of our sins. Nevertheless, these afflictions that believers endure because of him are also said to be his. There are two reasons for this. The first reason is that Christ is the cause for these sufferings. For this world persecutes him if, indeed, he is in us. If we were from the world and did not belong to Christ, then the world would not persecute us, but love us. But since Christ himself has chosen us out of this world and separated us from the dregs of the wicked, the world hates us, not because we are human sinners, but because we are Christians. The second reason is that Christ is our head, and we are his members, and so by this affinity our sufferings are his, of whom we are members. These two reasons are applicable not only for those afflictions that are borne because of Christ but also for those strivings and good works that believers do for the sake of Christ. Thus, all the works of brotherly love, by which we provide for the needs of one brother or another, are the works of Christ because they are performed for the sake of Christ and as members of Christ. It is for this reason that Scripture says, "I was hungry and you gave me food." And "what you have done for one of the least, you have done for me." And "Saul, Saul, why are you persecuting me?" It is impossible to describe how such a meditation, if we continually rest our minds on it, is effective for both performing and enduring all things that must either be performed or endured for the name of Christ. And although we should expect no reward for enduring afflictions for the sake of Christ, nevertheless those who love Christ can be abundantly revived when they are afflicted for the name of Christ. Thus Christ's apostles rejoiced because they were considered worthy to suffer insult from the council of priests because of the name of Christ. Commentary on 2 Corinthians 1:5.[18]

Hope for Suffering Christians. Cyriacus Spangenberg: Who would not wish gladly to suffer with Christ and for Christ's sake? And although it seems great to us, in the same way there will be much more comfort. Therefore, he says, "Just as we have much of the suffering of Christ" (he does not say, "some of it," "a little," but "much"), "we will also be richly" (not "sparingly," "meagerly" or "somewhat," but "richly") "comforted through Christ." This is indeed a glorious fruit and appreciable help, a great boast and a splendid honor for all suffering Christians.

Oh, what faithful companionship we have in him, what a desired traveling companion he is on the narrow way. He will indeed make the time short for us. And what could be heavy for us, if we know that we have a gracious God and that we suffer with Christ, who cannot perish and who wants to give abundant comfort? Their manifold cross and suffering did not come with laughter to the holy patriarch Abraham, and indeed to dear

[16]C. Spangenberg, *Die ander Epistel Pauli an die Corinthier*, 8r-v.
[17]Trapp, *A Commentary or Exposition*, 706*.
[18]Musculus, *Commentarius . . . in posteriorem epistolam Pauli ad Corinthios*, 17; citing Mt 25:35, 40; Acts 9:4; Acts 5:41.

Jacob, but they nevertheless rejoice in the Lord and know that they will be abundantly comforted through Christ the promised Messiah. The apostle also overcame all suffering, of which he had very much, with such comfort. In the same way holy Job, who suffered especially, endures it all, and brings use from it, in that he is abundantly comforted. Second Sermon.[19]

Sufferings Are a Form of Martyrdom. David Dickson: [Paul says that] afflictions are a part of martyrdom and, whether for the gospel or for Christ, they are afflicted on me with honor, that they may be called the afflictions of Christ by way of participation. For those things that are inflicted upon the martyrs, Christ takes upon himself, as is clear from Acts 9, "Saul, Saul, why do you persecute me?" . . . Christ gave testimony from his superabundant and seasonable consolations toward me, and in the midst of my afflictions, that the miseries which I suffer are inflicted upon me for the defense of the gospel. Exposition of 2 Corinthians 1:5.[20]

Suffering Promotes the Constancy of Believers. Wolfgang Musculus: Let the observant reader note that the apostle says that his afflictions were profitable for the Corinthian believers in that they were encouraged to endure evil in a similar fashion. Thus it happened that the more Satan raged against the followers of the Christian religion, the more they were stirred up to the same steadfastness of faith. Tertullian† saw this when he wrote that the blood of Christians is the seed. Julian the Apostate also saw this, and so he abstained from cruelty and gave the appearance of being somewhat more compassionate toward Christians than the enemies of Christ had been before him; not that he showed mercy to them, but he did not attack Christianity as in the earlier years it grew stronger and stronger the more Christians suffered. . . . And in our own day we see this same thing in those territories and kingdoms where princes rage against Christians with persecutions, chains, harsh laws, confiscation of property, the sword, the hangman's noose, and fire on account of the truth of the gospel of God and because they have abandoned the Antichrist [i.e., the Roman Church]. For as they intensify this brutality more and more, the number of believers grows more and more so that it is evident that those tyrants have become alarmed by the great number of them. It is clear, then, that the constancy by which true Christians bravely endure every evil for the truth of Christ is useful for the consolation and salvation of other people and it also frustrates the plans of the wicked. For while the wicked imagine that the truth of God can be undermined when they brutally spill the blood of believers, this only serves as the occasion to fortify, rather than diminish, the constancy of believers. Commentary on 2 Corinthians 1:6.[21]

The Nature of Paul's Afflictions and Comfort. John Calvin: It should be noted . . . that the word "afflicted" here refers not only to outward distress but also to that distress of the mind, so that it corresponds with the opposite term "comforted" (*parakaleisthai*). Thus it refers to when a person's mind is weighed down with anxiety on account of a sense of distress. What we translate as comfort (*consolatio*) in Greek is *paraklēsis*—a word that can also mean encouragement. You will understand Paul's meaning, however, if you understand that kind of comfort whereby a person's mind is lightened of grief. Take Paul for an example: he was weighed down with so many afflictions that he would have almost fallen down dead, had not God encouraged him by lifting him up and restoring him to a healthy mind. So, too, the Corinthians derive strength and fortitude from his sufferings, while they find comfort from his example. Commentary 2 Corinthians 1:6.[22]

[19]C. Spangenberg, *Die ander Epistel Pauli an die Corinthier*, 9v.
[20]Dickson, *An Exposition of All St. Paul's Epistles*, 72*; citing Acts 9:4.
[21]Musculus, *Commentarius . . . in posteriorem epistolam Pauli ad Corinthios*, 21-22. †Tertullian's statement "Semen est sanguis Christianorum" is found in his *Apology* 50.3 (see ANF 3:55).
[22]CO 50:12 (CTS 40:114-15).

FRUIT BORNE BY THE AFFLICTIONS OF THE GODLY. TILEMANN HESSHUS: Paul repeats the ultimate purpose for the afflictions of godly people (and especially of the well-instructed): God exercises us in calamities and consoles us in our hardships for this purpose, that we might encourage others in their trials. The mind can barely be convinced that such hardships contribute to the advantage and salvation of the church; rather, the mind is afraid that these hardships will destroy both us and the whole church and will turn many people away from the teaching of the gospel. The Holy Spirit therefore explains and repeats the plan of God so as to impress these matters in the depths of our hearts. Paul also adds several purposes when he says: the salvation of the church was achieved in the endurance of their suffering. For he reminds them that hardships produce an abundant harvest of fruit when they are borne with hope and endurance. Our reason flees all hardships and thinks they will destroy us. But the Holy Spirit testifies that they work for our salvation—that is, as the godly face hardships, a great light bursts forth through the Holy Spirit so that godly men and women see more clearly the teaching of the gospel and understand more fully the benefits of Christ's kingdom. . . . In hardships, the faith of godly people is not only demonstrated but also exercised, increased, and confirmed. In that light, [our] faith learns to find its rest in the Word alone; it turns away from all creatures and fixes its eyes on the all-powerful God. Dangers stir up our prayers, teach us patience, call us back to modesty, extinguish the affections of our flesh, arouse our desire for spiritual things. Hence, our salvation—namely, genuine piety, the spiritual apprehension of Christ, the sure hope of eternal life—is achieved as we endure Christ's sufferings. Therefore, there is enormous fruit in the afflictions of the godly. EXPLICATION OF 2 CORINTHIANS 1:6.[23]

SHARING IN CHRIST'S SUFFERING. NIELS HEMMINGSEN: Because the false apostles challenged Paul by holding his suffering in contempt, the apostle, by contrast, announces that he boasts in his suffering and shows the usefulness that comes to those Corinthians by his cross. He does this to refute the calumnies of the false apostles and call the weak in the church away from manifest error back to fruitfulness. Now there are three sections in this passage: (1) he speaks about the cross; (2) he speaks about comfort; (3) he speaks about sharing in the cross and comfort. . . . In the third section: Paul wants the Corinthians to know that "just as you are partners in suffering, so you will also be partners in comfort. For God wants you to become conformed to the image of his Son, in the cross as well as in comfort and glorious freedom, as is seen in those holy patriarchs, the Lord's apostles, and indeed in all godly people." That is why, when the godly are stationed under the cross by God's decree, they ought to focus upon the examples of God's Son and the saints, and remain steadfast, for they not only share in the cross with Christ and the apostles, but they will also be partners with them of comfort and glorious freedom, as the apostle Paul also stated in Romans 8: "We suffer together with him so that we might also be glorified with him." But lest anyone think that the difficulties of this life are in themselves salvific and merit eternal life (as the false monks assert), we must remember what it means to suffer with Christ. For, as people often say, it is not the death, but the reason, that makes a martyr. We must insist upon this when considering Christ's suffering, therefore, that there are two general reasons why Christ suffered: the first to obey his Father, and the second to conquer and condemn our sins. That is why we also are said to suffer with Christ when we faithfully obey God under the cross, and conquer and condemn our sins—not by expiating them, since Christ is the only priest, but by mortifying them. COMMENTARY ON 2 CORINTHIANS 1:6-7.[24]

SHARING IN SUFFERING AND COMFORT. CARDINAL CAJETAN: Behold, this is the firm

[23]Hesshus, *Explicatio Secundae Epistolae Pauli ad Corinthios*, 30r-v.

[24]Hemmingsen, *Commentaria in Omnes Epistolas Apostolorum*, 251-52; citing Rom 8:17.

foundation of our hope for you: the certainty (not the conjecture) that just as you share in our suffering, so you will also be a willing participant in our comfort. We are certain that just as our overflowing comfort accompanies our overflowing afflictions, so your mutual comfort will accompany your mutual suffering. This statement pertains to our present spiritual comfort. Commentary on 2 Corinthians 1:7.[25]

1:8-11 *Paul's Deadly Peril in Asia*

The Weight of Paul's Afflictions. Desiderius Erasmus: You will rejoice all the more if you know fully how great was the hurricane of evils by which we were blasted in Asia. There we were oppressed to an amazing extent by a weight of afflictions absolutely too heavy for our strength. It had come to the point that we were despairing of life too, truly no match for so many and so great evils that had to be endured. So great was the violence of the persecutions that not only did others despair of our ability to stand firm, but in our own mind, despairing of its strength, we had nothing but death before our eyes; we had no presentiment of anything but final ruin. God suffered us to be reduced to this point, so that we might not trust at all in our own strength, but in his support, which, as a general rule, is most available when human supports most forsake us. Paraphrase on 2 Corinthians 1.[26]

Affliction and Hope. Huldrych Zwingli: "We do not want you to be ignorant about our affliction." Paul demonstrates this from the example of what he had stated earlier, describing what happened to him in Asia and how God delivered him from all harm. You can read about this in Acts 19, where, through the agitation of Demetrius, such a great commotion and uproar took place and Paul was so harshly attacked that he was certain that his death was imminent. Now this happened for a purpose, Paul says, so that once stripped of all hope in himself, he might cast himself upon God. Therefore, as Romans 5 states, afflictions produce endurance and hope. Commentary on 2 Corinthians 1:8.[27]

Paul's Transparency Reflects His Love. The English Annotations: It is not certain whether Paul means by this affliction the great opposition he found by those many adversaries mentioned by him in 1 Corinthians 16:9, or the great tumult at Ephesus by Demetrius and his fellow craftsmen in Acts 19, or some very dangerous sickness wherewith he was visited. But here he thought it important to acquaint them with it, partly to show his great love for them since he concealed nothing from them which befell him, partly to stir them up to give God thanks for his great deliverance. Annotations on 2 Corinthians 1:8.[28]

Paul's Crushing Burden. John Calvin: Paul reports to have been weighed down beyond measure by this affliction—that is, so bereft of strength that he was not able to bear the burden. For it is a metaphor taken from those people who stagger under the weight of a heavy load, or from ships, which sink from being too overloaded. That does not mean that Paul actually succumbed, but he felt that his strength would have failed him if the Lord had not given him fresh strength. Commentary on 2 Corinthians 1:8.[29]

Our Extremity Is God's Opportunity. John Trapp: God is often better to us than our hopes. . . . He comes in the nick of time, and our extremity is his opportunity. Commentary on 2 Corinthians 1:8.[30]

[25]Cajetan, *In Posteriorem Pauli Epistolam ad Corinthios Commentarii*, 153.
[26]CWE 43:207.
[27]Zwingli, *Annotatiunculae . . . ex ore Zvinglij*, 146; citing Rom 5:3-4.
[28]Downame, ed., *English Annotations*, FF2r*.
[29]CO 50:13 (CTS 40:117).
[30]Trapp, *A Commentary or Exposition*, 706*.

Paul's Sentence of Death. Wolfgang Musculus: "We felt that we had received the sentence of death." In what sense did Paul receive the sentence of death in himself? He had not received this sentence from God, for otherwise he would have been dead. Nor had the magistrate proclaimed a death sentence against him. Therefore, what he means here is nothing other than that he considered his grievous affliction as equal to the judgment of death, as if he had already received the sentence of death from either God or the magistrate—so great was the despair of life that afflicted him. Therefore, when saints have been determined by God to experience danger, they are misled as long as they, being ignorant of the divine sentence, suppose that they have been appointed to death according to the perspective of the outward affliction. Many testimonies of this sort are found in the Psalms of David who, as happened here to Paul, endured this experience multiple times. So it was that when David remembers the time that he was surrounded by Saul, besieged from all sides (as we read in 1 Samuel 23), it seems that he was already captured. As he wrote in this passage: "The cords of death were encompassing me, and the floods of Belial were overwhelming me. The cords of the grave encircled me, the snares of death were overtaking me." Commentary on 2 Corinthians 1:9.[31]

God Uses Hardships to Humble Us. Cyriacus Spangenberg: For this is the wicked and harmful vice of our corrupt nature, that people do not rely on anything as much as on themselves and pay heed to nothing as much as to themselves and believe that nothing could fail them. As they plan something, so must it happen. Especially where they find a little wisdom, reason, understanding, ability, power, strength, and such things in themselves, false confidence does not stay away. And if people puff themselves up, become proud and bold and cannot come to see their own weakness, they are forced to recognize it and are humbled by God, which happens when he allows them to come into extreme danger, so that they are burdened beyond measure and all might and must despair of their lives. In this way one becomes aware first of all that we are unable to do anything on our own. And such fragility attaches itself not only to the common people but also to the greatest saints. For this reason, God the Lord also often strikes them hard so that they do not become haughty but learn to be humble. This vice of false confidence lies so deep in human nature that even the very holiest people cannot be completely rid of it, unless God sets death before their eyes and allows them to wrestle with the same. Third Sermon.[32]

Paul's Confidence Was in God. Wolfgang Musculus: "We were not relying on ourselves." The person who relies on himself does so with respect either to his own wisdom, or power, or wealth, or strength of character, or righteousness, or any other virtue or gift of God. When Paul preached the gospel of Christ, he could not rely on his own power because he was not powerful by the world's standards. Nor could he rely on his wealth because he possessed none and earned his sustenance by the labor of his hands. Nor could he rely on the strength of his body that was not able to endure so many dangers. For this reason, there was no danger that he would rely on himself with respect to these three things. There remained, therefore, dangers of relying on various other things, such as his own righteousness, wisdom, strength of character, and unique revelations. . . .

Although the apostle was endowed with so many splendid gifts of the Spirit (I pass over in silence the greatness of his revelations), there was no danger that he would rely on himself with respect to any of them. For he says later in chapter 12: "So that I did not exalt myself because of the greatness of my revelations, God gave to me a thorn." . . . Certainly, this difficulty was given him

[31]Musculus, *Commentarius . . . in posteriorem epistolam Pauli ad Corinthios*, 29; citing Ps 18:4-5.

[32]C. Spangenberg, *Die ander Epistel Pauli an die Corinthier*, 13r.

so that he might be despised, not by the common people, but by the more exceptional people, so that, even though he was gifted with many and important virtues, he would be more inclined to this thorn than to rely on himself. That is why it is necessary for those people who are distinguished to be humbled from time to time and be brought to an awareness and recognition of their own weakness.

But the evil of relying on ourselves, which is harmful and must be avoided, is quite multifaceted so that the types of its deception and wickedness cannot be numbered. It blinds our minds so that we are incapable of seeing that we are vain and altogether nothing in ourselves. It ascribes to creatures what pertains to God alone. It fashions idols from the gifts that have been received from God. It makes us secure, where there is no security, and it makes us great despisers of the divine will. And finally, it throws us headlong into the abyss of hell. It is for this reason, therefore, that the prophet said: "Cursed is the man who trusts in man and makes his flesh his strength." Commentary on 2 Corinthians 1:9.[33]

Even Paul Could Be Tempted by False Confidence. John Calvin: Now we must especially pay attention to the final clause that Paul adds: that he had been reduced to this extremity so that he might not trust in himself. Now, I do not agree with what Chrysostom[†] says—that the apostle was not in need of such a remedy, but offers himself to others as a kind of fictional example. For Paul was a man who was exposed to the common passions that afflict all people—not only to cold and heat but to false confidence, foolish behavior, and other such things. I'm not saying that he was controlled by such vices, but that he could be tempted by them. And so, this was the remedy God put in place at the opportune moment, lest they gain entrance into his mind. Commentary on 2 Corinthians 1:9.[34]

God's Purpose in Our Suffering. Giovanni Diodati: God's goal in reducing his children to these extremities is to teach them to renounce all their presumption and all confidence in human resources and to put all their faith in him alone, for whom no deliverance—not even death itself—is impossible. Annotations on 2 Corinthians 1:9.[35]

Ways That Suffering Is Useful. Andreas Hyperius: The first way that suffering is useful is that, by being humbled, we recognize our unworthiness and are forced to flee to God to beg for his help. There is no greater evil than for a person to trust in their own strength and know nothing about themselves. On the other hand, there is no greater good than when a person is acquainted with himself and places all his trust in God. . . .

The second way that suffering is useful is adduced from the antecedent reason. When God has rescued us previously, we are moved by this to conclude that God will always rescue us. That suffering produces this hope in us. Whence, Romans 5 states: "Suffering produces patience, patience hope, and hope does not make us ashamed"—that is, it doesn't disappoint us, but perfects us. Commentary on 2 Corinthians 1:9-10.[36]

God's Daily Deliverance Reminds Us of Future Resurrection. Cyriacus Spangenberg: He is so powerful and almighty that he can not only deliver someone from the danger of death, but in the case that someone were even dead, he can make them live again. And as God daily helps people out of captivity, sickness, and other danger, it is a picture of the future raising of the dead, and God wants to remind us by these things that we are to believe firmly that as he helps us out of daily danger, in the same way he will also certainly raise us from the dead. Our proverb also comes from this: when someone suffers a heavy assault or a

[33]Musculus, *Commentarius . . . in posteriorem epistolam Pauli ad Corinthios*, 30-31; citing 2 Cor 12:7; Jer 17:5.
[34]CO 50:14 (CTS 40:119). [†]For Chrysostom's interpretation, see PG 61:393 (NPNF[1] 12:279).
[35]Diodati, *La Seconde Epistre de l'Apostre S. Paul aux Corinthiens*, 134.
[36]Hyperius, *Commentarii . . . in Epistolam D. Pauli ad Romanos, et Utramque ad Corinthios*, 342; citing Rom 5:3-5.

hard situation but comes through it, we say, "He has just risen from the dead." Now because God can raise the dead, in every danger we put our confidence fully in him. Third Sermon.[37]

The Church's Special Consolation. Tilemann Hesshus: This is the church's special consolation, that it recognizes and trusts that God's wisdom and power have no limits, that he can easily offer assistance, even if no secondary causes are visible. Even if all creatures desert us and it appears that there is no possibility that we will be preserved, nevertheless, God is able to find a way—since he can call us back to life from death itself. He is the one "who kills and brings to life, who leads down to Sheol and back"; "who lifts me up from the gates of death," "that he might deliver their souls from death and nourish them in their hunger." "Our God is a God of salvation, and the Lord is the Lord who delivers from death." Jonah, in the belly of a whale, was stuck in the jaws of death, and yet the Lord restored him to life. Therefore, people should not despair of their salvation, regardless of the calamities that press upon them, even if it seems that they have been deserted by all creatures. Explication of 2 Corinthians 1:10.[38]

The Prayers of the Church. Wolfgang Musculus: Paul indicates very appropriately three things with this utterance. First, that it was the custom of the churches that they should pour out their prayers to the Lord for the apostles and ministers who were afflicted and endangered because of the work of the Lord. Thus, prayers to God were also made by the church for Peter when he was in chains. Second, that the Corinthian church should pray not only for itself but for others as well. That is why Paul does not simply say, *hypourgountōn* but *synypourgountōn*, that is, "cooperating with one another." Third, that prayers of this type are not worthless before the Lord. For when God delivered the apostle, even though the principal cause of the deliverance was divine mercy, nevertheless, the eagerness of the believers and their harmonious prayer whereby they were praying humbly and diligently among themselves for the apostle was pleasing to God. That is partly why he gives thanks to them, because [as they prayed] so earnestly, he was providentially delivered from all affliction. Chrysostom† notes on this passage that even though the Lord has decided to run to the aid of those who are suffering, nevertheless the prayers of believers play an important role in this matter, especially if they are offered up in harmony. God is merciful, good, and faithful, and consequently he is the chief cause of all goodness, mercy, and kindness. In like manner, those who love him pray to him from a heart of sincere faith; again, those who love him pray to him harmoniously for one another, out of a heart of brother love. That is why it is appropriate for the church to be provoked to pour out diligently prayers of this kind before the Lord. Commentary on 2 Corinthians 1:11.[39]

More Ways That Suffering Is Useful. Andreas Hyperius: The third way that suffering is useful is this: that faith will be aroused and the works of faith be produced by it, especially the work of prayer. When persecution comes, the saints pray to God, as is seen in Acts 4 and 12, where prayer was undertaken by the church for Peter, who had been imprisoned by Herod. Therefore, the apostle encourages them with these words to welcome the exercise of faith, namely, through prayer, so that they might reap some fruit and benefit from their sufferings. And he demonstrates here the great value and efficacy of prayer, namely, because by it the godly are liberated from dangers. That is the reason why this is the surest way for regaining safety when we are endangered,

[37]C. Spangenberg, *Die ander Epistel Pauli an die Corinthier*, 13v.
[38]Hesshus, *Explicatio Secundae Epistolae Pauli ad Corinthios*, 32v; citing 1 Sam 2:6; Ps 9:13; Ps 33:19; Ps 68:20.
[39]Musculus, *Commentarius . . . in posteriorem epistolam Pauli ad Corinthios*, 34-35; citing Acts 12:5. †For Chrysostom's interpretation, see PG 61:399-404 (NPNF[1] 12:281-85).

namely, by praying continually to God, a practice often seen in Scripture. By no action do we demonstrate more love for our neighbor than when we pray for a brother or sister. Whence, in various passages, the apostle requests prayer for himself. . . .

The fourth way that suffering is useful is this, namely, that when anyone is freed from dangers, they are greatly encouraged to give thanks to God and thereafter greatly extol God's glory. . . . In the same way that freedom came about through the intercession of many people, so many people were compelled to give thanks [to God]. Commentary on 2 Corinthians 1:11.[40]

[40]Hyperius, *Commentarii . . . in Epistolam D. Pauli ad Romanos, et Utramque ad Corinthios*, 342-343; citing Rom 15:30-31; Col 4:3-4.

1:12–2:4 PAUL'S CHANGE OF PLANS

12For our boast is this, the testimony of our conscience, that we behaved in the world with simplicity[a] *and godly sincerity, not by earthly wisdom but by the grace of God, and supremely so toward you. 13For we are not writing to you anything other than what you read and understand and I hope you will fully understand— 14just as you did partially understand us—that on the day of our Lord Jesus you will boast of us as we will boast of you.*

15Because I was sure of this, I wanted to come to you first, so that you might have a second experience of grace. 16I wanted to visit you on my way to Macedonia, and to come back to you from Macedonia and have you send me on my way to Judea. 17Was I vacillating when I wanted to do this? Do I make my plans according to the flesh, ready to say "Yes, yes" and "No, no" at the same time? 18As surely as God is faithful, our word to you has not been Yes and No. 19For the Son of God, Jesus Christ, whom we proclaimed among you, Silvanus and Timothy and I, was not Yes and No, but in him it is always Yes. 20For all the promises of God find their Yes in him. That is why it is through him that we utter our Amen to God for his glory. 21And it is God who establishes us with you in Christ, and has anointed us, 22and who has also put his seal on us and given us his Spirit in our hearts as a guarantee.[b]

23But I call God to witness against me—it was to spare you that I refrained from coming again to Corinth. 24Not that we lord it over your faith, but we work with you for your joy, for you stand firm in your faith.

2 *For I made up my mind not to make another painful visit to you. 2For if I cause you pain, who is there to make me glad but the one whom I have pained? 3And I wrote as I did, so that when I came I might not suffer pain from those who should have made me rejoice, for I felt sure of all of you, that my joy would be the joy of you all. 4For I wrote to you out of much affliction and anguish of heart and with many tears, not to cause you pain but to let you know the abundant love that I have for you.*

a Some manuscripts *holiness* **b** Or *down payment*

Overview: Because the false apostles were questioning the credibility of Paul's person and dismissing the truthfulness of his message, the apostle here responds by providing justification for his decision to delay coming to Corinth and demonstrating that his doctrine is trustworthy and sincere, founded upon Christ's infallible teaching, whose promises never change. At the outset, Protestant commentators make clear that Paul's boasting is unlike the self-promotion so common among false teachers and Catholic bishops, for his boasting comes from a pure conscience intent on God's glory alone. For several exegetes, Paul's statement in 2 Corinthians 1:19-20 constitutes a succinct summary of the Christian gospel: God says yes to sinful men and women who trust in the great salvation achieved by Jesus Christ, the Son of God. Throughout their comments, Reformation scholars present Paul as a worthy model for Christian ministers to emulate, praising his simple and honest style of teaching; his fatherly affection for his spiritual children; his clear and sincere proclamation of the gospel; his commitment to serve, not dominate, the church; and his courage to correct sinners with love and moderation. Though early modern commentators differ as to whether Paul's appeal to God as his witness in 2 Corinthians 1:23 actually constitutes oath-giving (a practice Anabaptists explicitly rejected), all agree that Paul's vigorous defense of his ministry provides a compelling picture of the apostle's extraordinary love for the Corinthian Christians.

1:12-14 *The Content of Paul's Boast*

Heartened by a Pure Conscience. Martin Luther: As for me, Martin Luther, unless God had closed for me the eyes of reason, I would long ago have stopped preaching and have despaired. Now a boldness, or certainty, comes to my aid. "Yet surely my right is with the Lord," although it seems empty and vain. It is nevertheless God's work, even though I am deserted by brethren and attacked by tyrants. Yet this consolation and the witness of our conscience heartens us, as Paul says in 2 Corinthians 1:12. Lectures on Isaiah.[1]

The Beauty of a Pure Conscience. Andreas Hyperius: Another reason why Paul is not sad because of his suffering and why he hopes that he is always going to be delivered is because of the innocent life that he maintains, in equity, or in the sincerity of his teaching. And this is his conclusion, that the adverse experiences that we suffer (whenever we suffer unjustly) are not able to shame us when we have the faithful testimony of our conscience. Because of this we can even boast, since we maintain a cause which is in itself just and we are acting in good faith. It is a great thing to have the testimony of one's own conscience when, as Romans 8 states, "the Spirit testifies together with our spirit that we are the children of God." When people suffer unjustly, they ought to boast rather than be filled with shame. And it is truly a great reason to boast when we are very conscious of an innocent life. And it should not be doubted that God wishes people to maintain their innocence when they are undeservedly attacked. He calls simplicity and sincerity "of God" because he wants it known that it is from God, and thus not at all fictitious. For among hypocrites, there also seems to be some simplicity and sincerity—but not in the sight of God, who sees the filthy and phony hearts of those people, whom they cannot deceive.

"Not in earthly wisdom." Paul did not teach nor did he live by employing deceitful or deceptive methods, and he was not liberated from the vile trickery of worldly wisdom by force of law, but by the grace of God alone, whose command has established life and doctrine in the same way throughout the earth. . . . Now it appears that the false apostles are subtly mentioned here, for they were not teaching simply and sincerely, but were forcing their law and traditions upon the gospel and employing carnal wisdom to deceive other people and counsel them for their personal advantage. Commentary on 2 Corinthians 1:12.[2]

The Nature of Paul's Boasting. Wolfgang Musculus: "For our boast is this, the testimony of our conscience." Here we need to inquire in what way the apostle boasts about his conscience when he says elsewhere, "Let him who boasts, boast in the Lord." Can a person boast in the Lord who also boasts in his conscience? I answer: The apostle reports here his motivations for boasting concerning his conscience. The one who boasts according to the flesh, seeks the glory of the flesh, and has arrogantly exalted his own strength. If the apostle boasted in this fashion, he was not boasting in the Lord. But that Paul was not boasting according to his flesh is made abundantly clear from the fact that he had proclaimed with such an extraordinary doxology the mercy of God toward him and had ascribed the whole of his salvation to him. That is why when he says here, "For our boast is this, the testimony of our conscience," he does not say this to make any boast in his flesh, but to counteract the wickedness of the false apostles, through whom Satan was busily holding back the progress of the gospel of God. And in this way, Paul desires more to bring about the glory of God than his own glory. Thus, being animated by motives that were not only blameless, but both pious and useful, Paul boasts in the testimony of his conscience against the apostles of Satan. Commentary on 2 Corinthians 1:12.[3]

[1]LW 17:173-74 (WA 31/II:397); citing Is 49:5.

[2]Hyperius, *Commentarii . . . in Epistolam D. Pauli ad Romanos, et Utramque ad Corinthios*, 343; citing Rom 8:16.

[3]Musculus, *Commentarius . . . in posteriorem epistolam Pauli ad Corinthios*, 37-38; citing 2 Cor 10:17.

Three Characteristics of Godly Boasting. John Calvin: How is Paul's boasting in his sincerity (*integritas*) consistent with that statement "Let him who boasts, boast in the Lord"? And who is so upright that they dare to boast before God? First of all, Paul does not compare himself to God, as if he had anything that was his own or was from himself. Second, he does not place the foundation for his salvation in that sincerity which he ascribes to himself, nor does he rely on such confidence. Third, he does not boast in God's gifts without at the same time rendering all the glory to him as their sole author and ascribing all things to him. These three exceptions are what every godly person freely does who boasts in all God's benefits; while the wicked are unable even to boast in God without doing so falsely and wrongly. Therefore, let it be acknowledged first of all that whatever good we do, we do through God alone, laying claim to nothing from ourselves. Second, let us hold onto this foundation—that our confidence in our salvation resides in the mercy of God alone. Third, let us find our rest in the sole author of every blessing. Then there will be godly boasting in every kind of blessing. Commentary on 2 Corinthians 1:12.[4]

The Testimony of Our Conscience. Wolfgang Musculus: You will ask: Is a person therefore justified by the testimony of his own conscience? Why then does 1 Corinthians 4 say, "My conscience is clear of guilt, but I am not justified by this. It is the Lord who judges me"? If he cannot be justified by the testimony of his own conscience, why does he appeal to it here in defending his own innocence? I respond: there are three courts of judgment in which our life is either accused or excused. The first judgment is internal, which we carry around in our individual consciences and are in no way able to deceive or escape. The second judgment is outside of us, and human, by which people judge our actions, whether the judges are private or public. The third judgment is divine, supreme, and ultimate. As far as the first judgment was concerned, the apostle pronounced it concerning himself in the matter of his apostolic conduct. And he laid bare this testimony in the courtroom of the second, namely, human judgment. Whatever people judged about him in regard to his apostleship was to no effect, [since] Paul was relying on the testimony of his conscience. This is what he said about this matter: "It is of little concern to me if I am judged by you or by human judgment." And then he added: "Indeed, I do not judge myself. For my conscience is clear, but I am not justified in this." Paul looks to the courtroom of the judgment of God, where, he says, he is not justified by his conscience, though he is conscious of no evil in himself. For if, in fact, mercy is not granted, then God would judge the most secret places of our hearts, hidden even to our consciences. Now, as far as the present passage is concerned, he appeals to the testimony of his conscience, not at all because he justifies himself before God, but so that he might vigorously defend his innocence against that second judgment, namely, the court of human judgment, in which he was attacked by the calumnies of the false apostles. Therefore, he counsels us in this present passage how we ought to make use of the testimony of our conscience. Clearly, through our consciences we defend our innocence against the calumnies of the wicked, but we do not justify ourselves in the sight of God by that testimony. Commentary on 2 Corinthians 1:12.[5]

Paul Also Appeals to the Judgment of the Corinthians. Tilemann Hesshus: It is not enough for Paul to boast according to the testimony of his own conscience, but he also appeals to the conscience and testimony of the Corinthians and he designates that church as his judge. It is as if he were saying, "You can be the best witnesses that I have behaved in good faith, in sincerity, and in the fear of the Lord both in this

[4]CO 50:17 (CTS 40:125-126); citing 2 Cor 10:17.

[5]Musculus, *Commentarius . . . in posteriorem epistolam Pauli ad Corinthios*, 38-39; citing 1 Cor 4:3-4.

world and among you. Examine your consciences in what a trustworthy and godly manner I have set before you the teaching of the gospel and have encouraged your salvation. You will no doubt recognize privately that what I write is true." When Paul says, "I trust that you will acknowledge this to the end," he shows that he does not trust in their moral virtue or strength, but wholly in grace from the Holy Spirit, with whose help he promises that he will constantly conquer in purity of spirit. Explication of 2 Corinthians 1:13.[6]

Paul Commends Clear and Honest Speech. Niels Hemmingsen: [Paul offers] a compelling proof of his simplicity and sincerity. For when he says that he is not writing anything other than what the Corinthians read and understand, he indicates that he is writing clearly, honestly, and without any deceit. For, as those who employ concealed and deceitful eloquence are with good reason said to write something different than what is read, so those who employ simple and sincere speech are said to write the same thing that is read. Paul also corroborates this with their own testimony, when he says, "you also understand," namely, "that what I am saying is true and sincere." In this passage, even as candor and simplicity in speaking and teaching are commended to us, so too all deceitfulness and confusing rhetoric are condemned as unworthy of godly people. Commentary on 2 Corinthians 1:13.[7]

The Mutual Boasting of Paul and the Corinthians. Cardinal Cajetan: Paul's sense is this: "I hope that you will recognize this fact (i.e., that we are boasting in you even as you are boasting in us) all the way to the very end—not to the end of a human's lifetime, but to the day of the Lord Jesus. Or, to put it differently, not to the day of human knowledge and clarity, but to the day of the knowledge and clarity of the Lord Jesus. You will recognize this on that day, I say, just as you already recognize it, though not now completely but only partially." Now, Paul and others like him are the object of the Corinthians boasting because, as they were appointed ministers of the gospel, so they were necessary for the Corinthians' salvation and eternal glory. And the Corinthians are the source of the boasting of Paul, Apollos, and Timothy as the Corinthians show themselves to be teachable disciples of the gospel. And Paul adds this statement not only to amass evidence of his own innocence and holy behavior but also to show the fruit that has come to himself and the Corinthians from this mutual boasting. Commentary on 2 Corinthians 1:14.[8]

Boasting in the Day of the Lord. Wolfgang Musculus: Paul adds "on the day of the Lord Jesus." In saying this, he indicates that he is speaking about boasting that is not connected to the worthless and vain world in itself. For this world is surely nothing and transient and will soon come to an end. But there will come a world, true and solid, that will endure, and on that day the Lord will judge. Now Paul secretly refers here to the false apostles who were constantly insulting his apostleship. It was as if Paul were saying, "Whatever your teachers think about me, I am your apostle, and thus I behaved toward you in such a manner that I am your boasting, and you are mine. And this will be revealed in day of the Lord Jesus, when all secret things will come to light and each person will receive according to what he has done in this life."

Today, bishops boast if they have large dioceses, if they are connected to the noble, wealthy, and powerful people of this world. And miserable and bewitched churches boast about bishops of this sort in a manner hardly different than the remaining inhabitants of Shechem and Israel boasted about their king Abimelech in Judges 9. . . . How much happier are the churches of Christ if they are able to boast about legitimate

[6]Hesshus, *Explicatio Secundae Epistolae Pauli ad Corinthios*, 36r-v.
[7]Hemmingsen, *Commentaria in Omnes Epistolas Apostolorum*, 254.
[8]Cajetan, *In Posteriorem Pauli Epistolam ad Corinthios Commentarii*, 154.

and faithful bishops and pastors, and how much better to be administered by bishops if they establish churches in such a way that they can boast about them, not before this present world, but on the day of the Lord Jesus when they will give an account of their oversight? The glory of the shepherd is his flock, if it is well cared for. And the glory of the flock is its shepherd, if he is genuine. Now when the wolves boast about the sheep, and the sheep are transformed by the wolves, what else should we expect than that both will be humbled and destroyed on the day of the Lord Jesus, when the true shepherds boast about their true sheep, and the true sheep boast truthfully and firmly about their true shepherds. Commentary on 2 Corinthians 1:14.[9]

Christians Boast in One Another. Cyriacus Spangenberg: Oh, that God would grant that we also should have such boasting in you on the day of the Lord Jesus, that is, on the last day. But I do not doubt that some people will be the cause for our boasting, of whom we will confess before God that they followed our teaching faithfully and diligently. And we will also be the boasting of some of you. When you bear witness to our faithful and diligent teaching—that will be enduring praise. When one extols and boasts in someone here, it does not endure but often changes. But that boasting remains. May God grant all of us such boasting with one another, for the sake of his dear Son, Jesus Christ. Amen. Third Sermon.[10]

1:15-22 *The Reason for Paul's First Change of Plans*

Paul Wanted to Come to Them First. Cardinal Cajetan: I do not know when or how (by word or writing) Paul had determined these things written here. Nevertheless, I would guess that this resolution [to visit the Corinthians] was before he wrote his first epistle. For at the end of the first epistle he states, "I will visit you after passing through Macedonia, I do not want to see you now just in passing. . . ." Now, it seems that he said these things because he had previously promised that he would return here, namely, to cross over into Macedonia through Corinth. . . . "So that you might have a second grace"—that is, the grace of a second visit and personal preaching. Commentary on 2 Corinthians 1:15.[11]

Paul's Intentions to Visit Were Sincere. Huldrych Zwingli: [Paul is saying:] No one should accuse me of being fickle, for I resolved to visit you according to the Spirit, not rashly or thoughtlessly, nor was I driven to this intention by some fleshly affection. Nevertheless, it was not at all in my own power to do this, as I told you: I keep my word, but in the Lord, who guides our paths according to his will. It is God alone who neither deceives nor is deceived. For he alone is unwavering and unchanging. Truly, God is faithful in this, whom I call as a witness against my conscience, that what I proclaimed was not "yes" and "no," that is, what I proclaimed was in fact the truth. . . . For Christ, whom I proclaimed among you, is not "yes" and "no," that is, he is not wavering, but steady and faithful. But though I promised that I would come to you, but have not yet done so, nonetheless, what I said depends on him. Obviously, his providence determined that it was better to prevent my coming. Nevertheless, I did not lie, for I made this promise without deceit, evil intent, or fraud. Therefore, what I promise concerning these matters, whether they take place or not, will happen as it seems good to him. Annotations on 2 Corinthians 1:15.[12]

Paul Wanted to Visit to Strengthen the Corinthians' Faith. Cyriacus Spangenberg: The second benefit that he wanted to confer on them in his return was this: he wanted to

[9]Musculus, *Commentarius . . . in posteriorem epistolam Pauli ad Corinthios*, 43-44.
[10]C. Spangenberg, *Die ander Epistel Pauli an die Corinthier*, 16r.
[11]Cajetan, *In Posteriorem Pauli Epistolam ad Corinthios Commentarii*, 154; citing 1 Cor 16:5, 7.
[12]Zwingli, *Annotatiunculae . . . ex ore Zvinglij*, 148-49.

strengthen them in their nascent faith with the Word, to warn them about apostasy and false teachers and to exhort them to grow in faith and all virtues. All pious Christians know how necessary this is. And this is also the reason that one always preaches daily and exhorts with the Word, so that anew and always you might receive one benefit upon another. You should recognize this and thank God for it. If one reminds people today of their vows, which they made in baptism, and punishes them because of sin, and earnestly exhorts them to good, they do not recognize such things as benefits, but take it badly, interpret it most angrily, and malign their preachers and pastoral caregivers for it, and do not want to receive it from them. Today's world is thus perverted. May God grant improvement. Fourth Sermon.[13]

A Second Grace. Niels Hemmingsen: [Paul is saying that] since we boast in you, even as you boast in us, I wanted to visit you on my way to Macedonia, and afterward to pass from Macedonia on to Judea, and then to pass again through your region, so that upon our return you might receive a second grace, that is, that you might reap a second benefit by hearing more frequently the teaching of your apostle. Thus the word "grace" is understood as a metonym for "gift" or "benefit." It is also possible that the word "grace" has been placed in this passage as a metalepsis[†] for "joy," which is gleaned from this benefit, so that the "second grace" would be the second joy that is gained from Paul's presence. This passage shows the sort of affection that ought to exist between ministers of the gospel and their hearers, having mutual goodwill for one another. Commentary on 2 Corinthians 1:15-16.[14]

Making Plans in the Flesh. John Calvin: Paul says, "I have not capriciously broken the promise I made." He also insists that he has been free from rashness and shameful self-confidence—for thus I interpret the phrase "making plans according to the flesh." For, as I have said, it is the common practice of men and women to decide what they will do in a rash and arrogant manner, as though they were not dependent on the providence of God or subject to his will. Now God, so as to punish this arrogance, frustrates the success of their plans and often exposes them to derision. It is true that the phrase "according to the flesh" can be interpreted more loosely to mean all wicked schemes and plans that are not directed to the right purpose, such as those that are governed by ambition, greed, or any other depraved affection. But Paul, in my judgment, did not intend here to refer to anything of this sort, but merely to reprove that rashness which is only too familiar and seen daily in human decision-making. Therefore, to "plan according to the flesh" is to not consider God as the one who controls us, but instead, to be seized by a rash presumption which God will afterward justly scorn and punish. Commentary on 2 Corinthians 1:17.[15]

The Dangers of Oaths and Promises. Hans Denck: Oaths and swearing should not be done because no human has power to keep them. What friends of God know to be right should simply be done, so far as they are able, without oaths and promises. They might ask the Lord to help them accomplish something. But they should not make presumptuous promises, as if the Lord were obligated to do what they want the Lord to do. Humans do not have power over a single hair! Therefore, if someone swears that they are able to do something, they either act brazenly without understanding, or if they do understand, then they act as a hypocrite—that is, they say something which in their heart they know is not true. As Scripture says, "You cannot make even one hair white or black," and "Do not fall into hypocrisy. . . ."

[13]C. Spangenberg, *Die ander Epistel Pauli an die Corinthier*, 17r.
[14]Hemmingsen, *Commentaria in Omnes Epistolas Apostolorum*, 254. [†]A metalepsis is a rhetorical figure of speech consisting in the metonymical substitution of one word for another, which is itself a metonym.

[15]CO 50:20 (CTS 40:132).

You should not be too quick to say yes or no. For if you say yes as a guarantee or assurance, this is really a kind of oath, in that by doing this one expects what was promised to be fulfilled as God's will. Then you must break your word if you cannot keep it. If you do right, this will not happen—as Paul did when he apologized before God to the Corinthians that despite his promise he was not able to visit them. CONCERNING THE TRUE LOVE.[16]

PAUL'S INTEGRITY. THE ENGLISH ANNOTATIONS: Christ commands in Matthew 5:37 that our communication should be "yes-yes," and "no-no," and Paul does not contradict this rule here. Paul's meaning is that, with him, he did not say, "yes" and "no" concerning the same thing; he was not careless and inconstant with his words, as those who affirm and deny with the same breath, promising and not performing, and changing their purpose at every turn. . . . Paul's "yes" was always "yes," and his "no" always "no"; his "yes" was not "yes" now but "no" at a later time, nor was his "no" "yes." ANNOTATIONS ON 2 CORINTHIANS 1:17.[17]

PAUL DEFENDS HIS DOCTRINE. DAVID DICKSON: Because Paul's doctrine was the Word of God, it must of necessity be true. Because God is faithful and true, Paul taught only God's dictates and commands among them, not sometimes affirming, sometimes denying, as those that are not constant in themselves are often guilty of doing. Therefore, the Corinthians were to have no doubt about the truth of his doctrine. EXPOSITION OF 2 CORINTHIANS 1.[18]

PAUL'S PREACHING WAS TRUE AND EFFECTIVE. PHILIPP MELANCHTHON: Paul draws the first defense of his character from antecedent proofs: "If my preaching was erroneous, then I would also be seen as erroneous. But if my preaching was true (as it was), why is my trustworthiness questioned? For if my preaching was true, it was true not from my own strength, but from God, who made my words efficacious. For Christ was efficacious in you: he justified and sanctified you. It is through Christ that these promises are efficacious to the glory of God. These are the promises that we proclaimed, and we are true because they were sealed by the Spirit of God." ANNOTATIONS ON 2 CORINTHIANS 1:18.[19]

PAUL'S TEACHING WAS INFALLIBLE. TILEMANN HESSHUS: The scoffing concerning the change in Paul's plan to visit was also extended to his doctrine, as if it too was doubtful. As often happens in this world, when even a hint of suspicion is raised against a doctor of the church soon the whole of his teaching is disparaged. Therefore, Paul first defends the infallible certainty of his doctrine. "God," he says, "who is the author of my teaching, is faithful so that he will not allow my gospel, which I have announced to you and which you have accepted, to be called into doubt. This truth, which I taught among you, is firm and immoveable. It is wrong to allow any doubt concerning it." EXPLICATION OF 2 CORINTHIANS 1:18.[20]

THE ESSENCE OF PAUL'S MESSAGE. WOLFGANG MUSCULUS: "For the Son of God, Jesus Christ, whom we proclaimed among you." Let us note here what Paul preached to the Corinthians, namely, "Christ the Son of God." This preaching consisted of three things: First, it treated the divinity of Christ; second, it treated his humanity; third, it treated the defense of the administration of our salvation. The divinity of Christ is shown because Paul calls him the "Son of God." The humanity of Christ is shown because Paul calls him "Jesus," which was the name given to him at his physical circumcision. The defense of the administration of our salvation is shown because Paul calls him the "Christ." Thus the apostles proclaimed Christ as true God and true man, and as our true Lord and

[16]Liechty, ed., *Early Anabaptist Spirituality*, 119*; citing Mt 5:26.
[17]Downame, ed., *English Annotations*, FF2v*.
[18]Dickson, *An Exposition of All St. Paul's Epistles*, 74*.
[19]*Melanchthons Werke*, 4:93.
[20]Hesshus, *Explicatio Secundae Epistolae Pauli ad Corinthios*, 38.

Savior. The preaching of the gospel consists in these three chief points. This is our Christian faith and confession, as Peter expressed it in Matthew 16: "We believe and have known that you are the Christ, the Son of the living God." . . .

Paul asserts [furthermore] that his teaching and preaching concerning the Christ was not empty and false because the Christ that he proclaimed as the Son of God, Jesus Christ, was not "yes and no," that is, vain and untrue, but "yes," namely, the Christ, the true Son of God—the very one that Paul preached among the Corinthians. This is what I think Paul means when he says that it "was not 'yes' and 'no,' but in him it was 'yes.'" So too Christ was not "yes" in our preaching and "no" in fact; rather, what we preached was faithful to Christ himself. The Roman pontiff whom Catholics proclaim to be the vicar of Christ and the head of the church, he is "yes" and "no." For he is "yes" in what they proclaim about him but "no" in that his person does not accord with what is proclaimed about him. [In a similar fashion], Muhammad who is proclaimed among the Turks is "yes" and "no." For he is "yes" in that they proclaim him to be the prophet of God, but "no" in that he is not the prophet of God but a seducer and prophet of Satan. But Christians proclaim that Jesus Christ is the Son of God, affirming what is true, namely, that he is both the true Christ and the true Son of God. Commentary on 2 Corinthians 1:19.[21]

Christian Preaching Is God's Word. Cyriacus Spangenberg: A preacher must be so certain of his teaching when he goes to the pulpit to proclaim God's Word that he knows and has good reasons for knowing this, that his teaching may so scarcely be thrown down as God himself. For God's Word remains forever, and our preaching is God's Word, as we take it from the writings of the prophets and the apostles and bring it before you. Therefore, we may boldly say, "If we or someone else, indeed even an angel from heaven, should preach a different gospel to you, different from the one we have preached to you until now, let him be cursed."

Who would wish to be so bold about himself, and even about the angels, to pass such a sentence, if he were not completely sure of the thing and did not have good reasons for it? "God," who elected and called us to this office, "is faithful, and there is no falsehood in him." He thus promised also to his church, "I will give you shepherds after my own heart, who will pasture you with teaching and wisdom." Thus, it becomes teachers and preachers to be found at all times with and in the truth, and their listeners should not provide themselves with anything in addition to them.

That Paul raises [the preaching office] so high and says, "O such a faithful God, that our word to you was not 'yes' and 'no'": he does this for the comfort of the Corinthians, that they should comfort themselves all the more against every attack against his true sermons, in which he had promised them so much good about God. Fourth Sermon.[22]

Christ Is the Sole Object of Paul's Preaching. Giovanni Diodati: Christ, who is the unique object of our preaching, has been taught by us without any variation or contradiction, but with perfect agreement and constant uniformity—both by me and these companions of mine, as well as by all those who share our doctrine. And the foundation of this consensus is in Christ himself and in the substance of his gospel, which is very pure, absolute and eternal truth, and in the power of the revelation of his Spirit. Annotations on 2 Corinthians 1:19.[23]

The Identity of Timothy and Sylvanus. Andreas Hyperius: Some people think that Sylvanus is the same person who is called Silas in Acts 18. Certainly, the apostle mentions the names

[21]Musculus, *Commentarius . . . in posteriorem epistolam Pauli ad Corinthios*, 51-52; citing Mt 16:16.

[22]C. Spangenberg, *Die ander Epistel Pauli an die Corinthier*, 18r-v; citing Gal 1:8-9; Deut 32:34; Jer 3:15.

[23]Diodati, *La Seconde Epistre de . . . S. Paul aux Corinthiens*, 135.

of these two men in the inscriptions to both letters to the Thessalonians, so that it is clear that they were faithful companions everywhere Paul went and sincere ministers of the gospel. Commentary on 2 Corinthians 1:19.[24]

The Certainty of God's Promises in Christ. Niels Hemmingsen: Paul proves again how constant and immoveable the doctrine of the gospel is which he delivered to the Corinthians. . . . Now this is the sum of his argument: Since God's promises are founded in Christ, who is always the same in himself and unchanging, it is impossible for these promises *not* to be completely certain and trustworthy. That is why, since the gospel is nothing other than the promulgation and announcement of divine promises, it must of necessity be firm, fixed, and constant. Now since this statement of Paul is one of the most important foundations of our religion, it would be worthwhile to explore and tease out the many doctrines that are contained in it. Thus, this statement contains four brief aphorisms: (1) It shows the foundation of salvation. (2) It recalls the promises of God. (3) It demonstrates what belongs to the ministry of the Word. (4) It explains the purpose for all these things. [First,] it teaches that the foundation of salvation is Christ. For it is clear that without Christ, we have no access to God, for our sin excludes us from God. And so, through him, God has been favorably disposed toward us, having pardoned our sins. The promises are testimonies of God's favor; one ought to consider in them their particular variety, their breadth, their guarantee, and their ratification. Note the *particular variety* of the promise, because some laws hold out the promise of either a reward or salvation apart from the gospel. But because Paul here testifies that all God's promises are founded in Christ, it is impossible that legal promises should be intended here since we apprehend Christ by faith and since legal promises are regarded as certain even if the beginning of obedience is more sluggish. Note the *breadth* of these promises, which are extended not simply to certain men and women, but to the whole human race. For just as we have all sinned in Adam, so Christ has been given by God as reconciler to all people, so that everyone who believes in him will not perish, but have eternal life. The *guarantee* of these promises rests on a solid foundation. For they are founded on Christ and have been granted through him. That is what Paul is saying here: the promises of God are "yes" in him. Now the particle *to nai* in Greek means to affirm and give a guarantee. That is why when we think over the divine promises, it comes to mind that the guarantee of those promises have a solid foundation, namely, the Lord Christ. Consequently, persons who are outside of Christ know that the divine promises in no way pertain to them until they are converted and come to their senses. Finally, note the *ratification* of these same promises rests not on our worthiness and merit, but on Christ. From this our faith draws enormous comfort, since it recognizes that not only the guarantee of our salvation but also the ratification of the same rests on such a solid and trustworthy foundation. This is what Paul says: "the promises are Amen in Christ."

Moreover, the ministry of the gospel is entrusted with proclaiming these promises, which the apostle indicates when he says: "through us," namely, through ministers of the gospel—for he has entrusted to gospel ministers the responsibility of distributing the treasure of these promises. Last of all, even though the purposes for giving the promise are multiple, nevertheless, only this chief one is mentioned here, to which the remaining purposes are subordinate. For the chief purpose is the proclamation of the glory of God, which will finally be complete when, once the kingdom of Satan has been overturned and destroyed, the godly will be granted eternal salvation. Since the ministry of the Word has been appointed for this purpose, we give thanks to God, who preserves that ministry in the church and gives to his church godly ministers, who are public announcers of

[24]Hyperius, *Commentarii . . . in Epistolam D. Pauli ad Romanos, et Utramque ad Corinthios*, 345; citing Acts 18:5.

these divine promises. By their voice many people are called out from the kingdom of Satan and made citizens and heirs of eternal life. COMMENTARY ON 2 CORINTHIANS 1:20.[25]

FAITH IS FOUNDED IN GOD'S FAVOR. MARTIN CHEMNITZ: From this the correct meaning is confirmed that even when faith is concerned with external objects, yet in order that the promise may be sure and the confidence of our hope firm, that faith which relies on the promise of mercy for the sake of Christ must always shine forth. For unless faith first establishes that God is favorable toward us and has been reconciled, no peace of conscience can be sought or aid be expected. . . . This explanation is confirmed by the brilliant statement of Paul in 2 Corinthians 1:20: "All the promises of God in Christ are yea and amen, to the glory of God through us." That is, the promises concerning other objects of faith have only then been ratified for us when by faith in Christ we are reconciled with God. The promises have been made valid on the condition that they must give glory to God through us. Therefore, faith in Christ both causes the promises to be made certain and governs them. For Paul uses two words, *nai* and *amen*; one of these pertains to the assertion that the promises have been ratified. See Matthew 5:37: "Let your word be yes [*nai*]." . . . The second word [*amen*] refers to an expectation in sure confidence, as we have said about the word "Amen." LOCI THEOLOGICI.[26]

THE PROMISES OF GOD ARE CERTAIN. DAVID DICKSON: All the promises of God in and through Christ are firm, unchangeable, and complete, in part because he is the Son of God, by whom all things are made, in part because he is the mediator, the God-man, who achieved for us our redemption, and procured it by his merit, so that the good things promised might be given us. And Christ really applies them to us. Therefore [Paul says], our preaching which contains nothing other than this, is necessarily certain, and no one should doubt it. . . .

As the promises of God are "yes" and "amen" in Christ—that is, really and truly ratified and complete, as they are acknowledged and preached by us—this leads to the glory of God, who will not have his promises fulfilled in anyone but Christ. Therefore [Paul says] our preaching is so sure and firm. For as the purpose of God is in glorifying himself in his Son, neither must you doubt anything in the matter. EXPOSITION OF 2 CORINTHIANS 1:20.[27]

CHRIST IS AT THE HEART OF CHRISTIAN PREACHING. CYRIACUS SPANGENBERG: Now if someone would know where the sum of all Paul's sermons is to be found, let them hear this here: it was all concerned with the one Christ, with whom indeed the whole gospel has to do. And whoever does not diligently pursue Christ is not a true preacher, however great the wisdom he propounds may be. But one must teach about him rightly, not this way today, that way tomorrow, as one finds some, who say to doubt God's grace, like monks and the Council of Trent, who teach that there is "yes" and "no" in Christ. Likewise, those who say that he only made satisfaction for original sin, and that each must himself remove and atone for their actual sins. . . .

See again here what a high and noble matter this is in our preaching office. For this reason, one should hold it in honor and be glad of it and comfort oneself with it. For in it is shown to us that God, for Christ's sake, forgives us our sins. Whoever believes this can comfort themselves and take up all the other promises of God, for this is the highest and most noble promise, that "the woman's seed shall crush the serpent's head," so that "all who believe in him will not perish but have eternal life." FOURTH SERMON.[28]

[25]Hemmingsen, *Commentaria in Omnes Epistolas Apostolorum*, 255; citing Jn 3:16; Gen 3:15.
[26]Chemnitz, *Loci Theologici*, 2:495.
[27]Dickson, *An Exposition of All St. Paul's Epistles*, 74*.
[28]C. Spangenberg, *Die ander Epistel Pauli an die Corinthier*, 19r; citing Gen 3:15; Jn 3:16.

What of God's Promises Before Christ's Incarnation? John Calvin: Some might ask whether [the promises] were feeble or ineffectual before the coming of Christ, for Paul here seems to be speaking of Christ manifested in the flesh. I answer that whatever promises were given to the faithful from the beginning of the world were founded upon Christ. Hence Moses and the prophets, whenever they discuss reconciliation with God, the hope of salvation, or any other [divine] grace, make mention of him, and at the same time address the matter of his coming and his kingdom. I say again that the promises under the old covenant were fulfilled for the godly, insofar as was profitable for their salvation; and yet, it is no less true that they were in a sense suspended, until Christ's coming, through whom they achieved their true completion. Truly, believers themselves were resting on the promises in such a way that, nevertheless, they referred their true fulfillment to the appearing of a mediator and suspended their hope until that time. Commentary on 2 Corinthians 1:20.[29]

Anointing and the Spirit's Power. Philipp Melanchthon: Paul's second defense of his person, by which he proves that he has neither failed nor acted in a carnal manner toward the Corinthians, is that he was anointed by the Holy Spirit. The anointing of kings and priests was fulfilled in Christ—the sign and pledge they signified. The Holy Spirit is a testimony and pledge of God: that God accepts us as righteous, as Romans 8 states: "The Spirit himself testifies with our spirit that we are the children of God." Certainly, it is the work of the Spirit, "when we cry, Abba, Father!" He is powerful to guide us, to lead us, and to change us into different persons. Annotations on 2 Corinthians 1:21.[30]

The Spirit's Anointing. Wolfgang Musculus: Through the metaphor of anointing, Paul understands the grace of sanctification, drawing a comparison with the kings, prophets, and priests who were set apart by the oil of consecration. For just as with that external oil, so we are anointed with that internal oil, which is the Spirit, even as Christ the Son of God was anointed and consecrated as king and priest, not with external oil, but with the internal anointing of the Holy Spirit. Christ's anointing is no different from ours, even if it is of a superior measure, for we also receive our anointing and sanctifying through the measure of the Spirit. Commentary on 2 Corinthians 1:21.[31]

The Ways God Upholds His People. Tilemann Hesshus: This second argument by which Paul demonstrates the certainty of his doctrine is adduced from the efficient cause.[†] God himself, the creator of heaven and earth, is not uncertain or inconsistent, but is unshakeable truth itself. "I, God," he says, "do not change"—therefore, those things that proceed from him cannot be uncertain. If either a human or an angel appeared to be the author of this doctrine, then we could have doubts about it. But in fact it is God himself who upholds us and anoints us with his Spirit. Now God upholds us in many ways, as in the creation and preservation of the material world; in the wondrous works of his divine majesty alone; in the certainty of prophecy; in gladness and calmness of conscience; in bringing the dead back to life and the creation of new life; in the wondrous government and protection of the church; in the glorious defeat of the enemy; in the perpetual preservation of teaching; and in the countless blessings that are stored up for us in heaven. It is therefore wrong to doubt the certainty of this heavenly teaching. Explication of 2 Corinthians 1:21.[32]

---

[29]CO 50:23 (CTS 40:138).

[30]*Melanchthons Werke*, 4:94; citing Rom 8:15-16.

[31]Musculus, *Commentarius . . . in posteriorem epistolam Pauli ad Corinthios*, 55.

[32]Hesshus, *Explicatio Secundae Epistolae Pauli ad Corinthios*, 40v-41r. †Following Aristotle and the medieval scholastics, Hesshus here is employing a fourfold scheme of causality, which includes the efficient cause, the material cause, the formal cause,

The Holy Spirit as Seal and Guarantee. Heinrich Bullinger: This passage is also intended to confirm the indubitable certainty of the truth and true piety. Moreover, the choice of words Paul uses is amazing. First, he says, God confirms that we are ministers of the Word, even as you who have professed the Christian religion are godly hearers in Christ. Now God is the one who builds you and me upon the solid rock, that is Christ. He confirms this through anointing, that is, the inspiration and instruction of the Holy Spirit. The apostle John writes about this anointing in 1 John 2. He seems to be alluding to the anointing of priests and kings in the Old Testament. Second, Paul explains the word "anointing" by substituting a figure that is clearer, saying, "Who has placed his seal on us." . . . Now this signifies the indubitable certainty of a thing. The metaphor is employed by those who seal a document; they give their word by signet rings and pledge themselves to do that which they are sealing. There follows a third statement which is both more efficacious and clearer than the previous two, which, indeed, explains both of them: "And he gave us the Spirit in our hearts as a guarantee." He would have explained himself if he had said only "He has given the Spirit in our hearts," for this is understood by the reference to anointing and sealing. But now, when he adds the phrase "He gave the Spirit as a guarantee," he has said more than previously. For a "guarantee" (*arrabōna*), in the strict sense, is part of a payment made that provides assurance that the whole sum will be paid in full, in other words, a pledge. Hence the author of the *Paraphrases*[†] states, "In fact, Paul says that God's Spirit enters into our hearts as a guarantee and pledge of the promise of happiness for the future. Therefore, this word holds great benefit because of this allusion." Commentary on 2 Corinthians 1:21-22.[33]

Baptism as a Seal. Wolfgang Musculus: This passage can be understood as referring to the seal of baptism. For baptism is the seal by which, as it were, we are sealed in the sheepfold and possession of God. Paul attributes this seal to God, because he regards it more the work of the Spirit than the work of the minister who performs the baptism. Concerning Simon Magus, I would not say that he was sealed by God when he was baptized, since the work of the Spirit was absent from his baptism. The Lord knows who are his. He seals his own people, but in no way other people. Thus, using the metaphor of a seal for baptism is altogether appropriate.

"And he gave the pledge of the Spirit in our hearts." Unless God gives this pledge to those who are baptized, the minister seals them in vain. And so, Paul was able to say simply, "he has given his Spirit in our hearts." Now, Paul speaks here of the Spirit's infusion. Indeed, the metaphor of a pledge seems proper, as he expresses it, by which there ought to be evidence for us given by God and infused into our heart by the Holy Spirit. Clearly, the evidence is a pledge. Now the pledge is a guarantee by which the person who gives as well as the person who receives are bound together. When God gives his Spirit in our hearts, by this pledge he binds himself to us that he does not wish to desert us, but to know us forever, and we him. When we accept this pledge, we promise to be his possession and rightful property in so far as we never wish to withdraw ourselves from his rightful ownership. And in making the pledge, we are spurred on to fulfill it. Commentary on 2 Corinthians 1:22.[34]

The Spirit's Testimony. Tilemann Hesshus: The third argument by which Paul proves the certainty of his doctrine is drawn from the special office and testimony of the Holy Spirit. Now the Holy Spirit, who has been conferred upon our heart by God, testifies that we know the true God from

and the final cause. According to Muller, the efficient cause "is the agent productive of the motion or mutation in any sequence of causes and effects." See Richard Muller, *Dictionary of Latin and Greek Theological Terms* (Grand Rapids: Baker, 1985), 61. See Aristotle, *Physics* 2.3; *Metaphysics* 5.2.

[33]Bullinger, *In Posteriorem D. Pauli ad Corinthios Epistolam Commentarius*, 268; citing Mt 16:18; 1 Jn 2:20. [†]Here, as in many other places, Bullinger quotes approvingly from Erasmus's *Paraphrases*.

[34]Musculus, *Commentarius . . . in posteriorem epistolam Pauli ad Corinthios*, 55; citing Acts 8:13.

the Word; that we have been reconciled to God through Christ; that our prayers in urgent times are surely heard; that we have surely been reckoned as heirs of eternal life; that the divine promises are not empty words, but comprise heavenly and eternal realities. And so, truly, the Holy Spirit is a sure pledge and guarantee that the promises of God are completely certain. Now, "the same Spirit bears witness with our spirit that we are children of God." And since the Spirit of God unites us with God, he communicates to us the light, life, and joy of God. He gives living testimony that the doctrine concerning the mediator Jesus Christ is altogether true and certain. For this reason, the saints have such great certainty, such effusive joy, so much constant eagerness, not only in the midst of great troubles and dangers, but even in death itself. Explication of 2 Corinthians 1:22.[35]

The Seal of the Holy Spirit. Katharina Schütz Zell: Grant in this way we may be assured of your grace and kingdom through the pledge and seal of your Spirit, who also assures our spirit that we are your children, fed and satisfied by you, that no other food may give us joy than your Christ, grace, and eternal heir. Grant that we also may no longer hunger or thirst for the inconstant, unsatisfying world, with all its goods, joys, and honors, which are all a delusion and evil in comparison with your wisdom, but that we may only hunger for your wisdom, righteousness, sanctification, and redemption, hunger that you also will satisfy in Christ alone. Letter to Felix Armbruster.[36]

The Indwelling Spirit Assures Believers of Grace Through Christ. Pilgram Marpeck: As a clear sign of grace, Christ has been nailed to the cross on our behalf. The Holy Spirit, who has been poured out in our hearts, through Christ, to all true believers, comes as the guarantee of the assurance of such grace. Such a covenant or sign of the grace of God has been given to us, and is not at all tied to baptism or any other element or work; such a sign is received only by believers through faith or through the Holy Spirit. The Admonition of 1542.[37]

1:23–2:4 *The Reason for Paul's Second Change of Plans*

Swearing Oaths Is Permitted of Christians. Martin Luther: It is permitted to swear oaths, especially in court and at trials, to bear witness to the truth; for this is nothing else than calling upon God. Thus Paul says in 2 Corinthians 1:23, "I call God to witness against me." Lectures on Genesis.[38]

An Oath Is a Corroborating Witness. Martin Chemnitz: It is clear from the above that the doctrine of oath-taking pertains to the second commandment, for it is said in Deuteronomy 6:13, "You shall swear by his name." Second Corinthians 1:23, "Upon my soul, I call upon God as a witness." In the Old Testament there was never any doubt that in a proper, just, and necessary cause it was permissible to swear by the name of God. But in the New Testament because Christ says, "Swear not at all," Matthew 5:34 (and James 5:12 repeats the same idea), this subject has been under dispute in different ways at all times. For many of the martyrs around AD 200 refused to give the oath demanded by the government, and then contended that it was not permitted to Christians to swear under any circumstances. The Manichaeans rejected the Old Testament because it both used and approved of taking oaths, which they imagined was totally forbidden. Within recent memory there was a controversy with the Anabaptists on this same question. . . .

The strongest argument [that oaths are permissible] is that there is no doubt that Christ

[35]Hesshus, *Explicatio Secundae Epistolae Pauli ad Corinthios*, 41r-v; citing Rom 8:16.
[36]Zell, *Church Mother*, 165.

[37]CRR 2:190.
[38]LW 7:248-49 (WA 44:484).

and the apostles correctly understood the statement "Swear not at all." Christ repeatedly uses the expression, "Verily, verily, I say to you," and it is manifest from Hebrew 6:13-14 that this is a formula for an oath. . . . The evidence is very clear that Paul is using the words of Christ when he says in 2 Corinthians 1:17, ". . . that with me there should be yea, yea and nay, nay." He goes on to add an oath in verses 22-23 and says that he "has been sealed by the Holy Spirit in his heart." Thus, this does not come out of evil. It is unfortunate that the Anabaptists say that a Christian can certainly call on God against their soul as a witness to their words but cannot take an oath; for an oath is nothing else than this kind of corroborating witness. Loci Theologici.[39]

The Nature of Legitimate Oaths. John Calvin: Paul also swears an oath, lest he seem to have contrived something to suit the occasion. For the matter in itself was of no small consequence, and it was very important that he should be entirely free from all suspicion of falsehood and deceit. Now, there are two things that make an oath legitimate and godly: the situation and the disposition. The *situation* I refer to is when an oath is not made rashly, that is, in frivolous matters, or even in matters of small importance, but only when it is worthwhile. The *disposition* I refer to is when a person is not interested in personal advantage so much as zealous for God's honor and the good of one's neighbor. For this end must always be kept in view, that our oaths should promote the glory of God and the advantage of our neighbors in matters that are right.

The form of the oath must also be noted: first, that one call God as witness, and second, that one swears "on my soul." For in matters that are doubtful and obscure, where human understanding fails, we flee to God so that he, who alone is the truth, might render testimony to the truth. But the person who appeals to God as witness is at the same time calling upon the one who is the avenger of perjury, if that person should be deceptive. Commentary on 2 Corinthians 1:23.[40]

Christians Must Not Swear Oaths. Michael Sattler: The oath is a confirmation among those who are quarreling or making promises. And it has been ordained in the [Mosaic] law that it should take place truthfully and not falsely, in the name of God alone. Christ, who teaches the perfection of the law, forbids his followers all swearing, either truthfully or falsely, either in the name of heaven or of earth or of Jerusalem or by our own head. And he does this for the reason which he gives afterward: "For you are not able to make a single hair white or black." Notice this! All swearing has been forbidden because we cannot fulfill what is promised in swearing. For we are not able to alter the slightest thing about ourselves. . . .

Some say further, "Why is it now unjust to use God as a witness to the truth, when the apostles Peter and Paul have sworn?" Our answer is that Peter and Paul testify only to that which God promised Abraham through the oath. And they themselves promised nothing, as the examples clearly show. For testifying and swearing are two different things. When a person swears, in the first place they make a promise about future things as Christ—whom we received a long time later—was promised to Abraham. But when a person testifies, they are testifying about the present, where it is good or evil, as Simon spoke to Mary about Christ and testified to her. Christ has also taught us this same thing when he said, "Your speech should be 'yea' or 'nay' for anything else comes from evil." Christ says, "Your speech or words should be 'yea' or 'nay,' so that none can understand it in the sense that he has permitted swearing." Christ is simply "yea" and "nay" and all who seek him in simplicity will understand his Word. Amen. Schleitheim Articles.[41]

[39]Chemnitz, *Loci Theologici*, 2:382-83.

[40]CO 50:25 (CTS 40:142-43).

[41]Baylor, ed., *The Radical Reformation*, 178-79; citing Mt 5:34, 36; Lk 2:34; Mt 5:37.

Calling on God as Witness. Hans Denck: This is all that needs to be said concerning swearing about future events. As for testimony concerning things past, according to the Lord's teaching we should do it simply, using as few words as possible—yes or no. For we must answer to God for anything we say. One might call on God as a witness that what he says is true, as Paul did. But do not forget never to use God's name frivolously. This is forbidden in the law and also in the New Testament, where we are forbidden to swear at all. It is not wrong to use God's name in itself. In fact, love requires all her children to do so that God might be known and alone be eternally loved and praised. Concerning True Love.[42]

Paul Defends His Teaching with an Oath. Niels Hemmingsen: [The Corinthians] were accusing Paul of capriciousness, since he did not come to Corinth as promised. Because of this the false apostles had falsely attacked the rest of his teaching. But since it was of greater importance to defend the purity of his teaching than to explain why he had not come at the prescribed time, Paul first asserts the solidity of his teaching, to which he adds the reason why he did not come, no doubt so that it might be evident to them that voluntary repentance was expected of them. Now, in order that they might believe this to be the truth, Paul makes an oath by which he invokes God as his witness and defender, swearing on "his soul"—that is at the peril of his life and salvation—if it fails. Commentary on 2 Corinthians 1:23.[43]

Paul's Sense of Apostolic Duty. Huldrych Zwingli: [Paul is saying:] "I say these things, not out of a desire to dominate you or to be the lord of your faith (that is, of your worship), but out of a sense of the duty of my office. For since I proclaimed the gospel to you, I am by no means the least in rank in your church. If I had come, I would have come with a whip so as to drive out that fornicator. For, given my office, the shameless scandal of this person required such a response." Annotations on 2 Corinthians 1:24.[44]

Paul's Fatherly Love. Wolfgang Musculus: [Paul writes:] "not that we lord it over your faith, but that we work with you for your joy." That is, not that we delight to exercise dominion in your faith, but that we greatly delight to show fatherly kindness and love toward you whereupon you are not saddened but filled with joy. . . . Note here the apostolic and paternal heart. Earthly lords have the character that they would prefer to be feared than loved. They say, "The people will only fear those they hate." They do not delight in the joy of their subjects, and thus they do not work for their joy. Instead, they find delight in slavishly oppressing souls with anxiety and trembling in all things, with their subjects speaking submissive words filled with lies and flattery, slavishly acting out humble gestures, and performing duties that reek of nothing but servitude. These are the things that delight the great lords and characterize the way they govern, as if they were born to this dominion and were no longer men but a kind of god, so that they might exercise dominion over men as over beasts. But one can see in this passage that the apostle of Christ was motivated altogether differently. He did not delight in dominion, nor in the sadness and pain of believers, but he delighted in fatherly love and in the joy of those whom he had birthed in Christ. He displays that he was working for this joy, as far as he was able to do. Therefore, he shows mercy even to sinners, in the hope that they will return to their senses, and for that reason he had not yet come to Corinth, lest he inflict sadness and pain on those whom he wished to be joyful. Commentary on 2 Corinthians 1:24.[45]

Faith Recognizes God's Dominion Alone. David Dickson: Paul here answers another

[42]Liechty, ed., *Early Anabaptist Spirituality*, 119-21.
[43]Hemmingsen, *Commentaria in Omnes Epistolas Apostolorum*, 256.
[44]Zwingli, *Annotatiunculae . . . ex ore Zvinglij*, 150.
[45]Musculus, *Commentarius . . . in posteriorem epistolam Pauli ad Corinthios*, 61-62.

objection [from the Corinthians]: "Therefore, you make yourself the lord of our faith, as if you could punish us when you wished." Paul answers by denying any mastery and affirming the power of his ministry, which was employed for the benefit of the church, so that timely censures in keeping with the will of Christ might be used in such a way that the Corinthians might repent and finally rejoice. Paul gives an account of why he denied any dominion over their faith, because faith is the bond of conjunction with Christ, and it is by this faith that we stand fast in the grace of God, in right and title to Christ, in the possession of things in the present, and in the hope of good things for the future. Therefore, faith allows no Lord other than God; it allows men and women to be only ministers and helpers. Exposition of 2 Corinthians 1:24.[46]

Faithful Preachers Are Often Accused of Lording Over Their People. Cyriacus Spangenberg: As today we still find many people, if we chastise them earnestly with the Word of God and threaten them with excommunication or withholding the sacrament unless they repent; again, when we admonish them to Christian conduct and discipline, preach to them, prompt them and prescribe for them how they must conduct themselves outwardly before others in piety and blamelessness, then they come against us and say that we dare to lord it over them. "Look," they say, "the preachers are daring to rule a lot, are taking on a lot of power that doesn't become them and would like to force their way into the worldly regime and be in authority everywhere. . . ." And they construe it in the most malicious way. And those for whom it is serious must endure and suffer much evil slander, and this is how it was for St. Paul also.

But he answers for this and says that he is not looking for any kind of rule, as people might measure it to him, and this would not become him. But his office requires at the same time that he be earnest toward them, and earnestly direct them how they should behave (by God), and this is truly not from tyrannical intent but from fatherly care and love for them. Because upright servants of the Word are not to be blamed for their seriousness and their zeal, it should not be turned back on them in malice or construed as if they were wanting to gain for themselves worldly authority, and it is indeed a foolish and completely absurd suspicion when examined in the light of day. But we have reached the point where the common people says that if we punish sin and vice earnestly and heavily, we want to lord it over and rule over somebody. Eighth Sermon.[47]

True Ministers Do Not Claim Dominion over the Church. Tilemann Hesshus: In this passage, the Holy Spirit very gravely warns bishops and pastors of the church that they should beware lest they assume for themselves dominion in the church, which the Son of God redeemed by his very own blood. It should be enough for us that we have the delight of being ministers of the saints and that the joy of the Holy Spirit is aroused in the hearts of godly people by our preaching. The Roman Antichrist is worthy of a curse, who has set himself up as a tyrant of people's consciences; who continually creates new laws; who has established and changed articles of faith; who has absolved from sin whomever he wishes; who has arbitrarily bound others in sin without a word. Therefore, he truly displays himself to be Satan, not a minister of Christ. Explication of 2 Corinthians 1:24.[48]

The Christian Is a Citizen of Two Kingdoms. Cyriacus Spangenberg: Unbelieving persons must suffer the worldly authorities to be lord over them in all things. But believers are double persons: spiritual for God and fleshly for the world. As for their spiritual standing before God they are called a Christian and live by faith; in this no one can persuade them and they do not

[46]Dickson, *An Exposition of All St. Paul's Epistles*, 74*.

[47]C. Spangenberg, *Die ander Epistel Pauli an die Corinthier*, 24r.

[48]Hesshus, *Explicatio Secundae Epistolae Pauli ad Corinthios*, 44r-v.

allow themselves to be ordered to do anything but depend freely on the Word. But as for their outward life, they are subject to the authorities and all worldly and human orders as any other person, and do whatever they are commanded and ordered, to the extent that it is not expressly against God's clear Word. Eighth Sermon.[49]

The Reason for Paul's Delay. John Calvin: Whoever it was who divided the chapter made here a foolish division. For now at last the apostle explains how he had spared them. "I had determined," he says, "not to come to you any more in sorrow"—that is, "to cause you sorrow by my coming." For Paul had come the first time by means of his epistle, which had severely wounded them. And so, since they had not repented, he was not wanting to come to them, lest he be forced to aggrieve them again when he was with them, for Paul preferred to give them a longer space of time to repent. Commentary on 2 Corinthians 2:1.[50]

The Corinthians Heeded Paul's Warning. Niels Hemmingsen: At the end of the first chapter, the apostle began to defend himself for not coming to Corinth as promised. Now, Paul brings together several reasons for this same excuse. . . . "I did not come to you," he says, "lest I should come to you again with sorrow, which would certainly have happened, if I had discovered that you, still pleased with yourselves, had not punished that incestuous brother." Now, in the meantime, while the apostle postponed his coming, the Corinthians, warned by his writing, had repented and excommunicated the incestuous man until he displayed true repentance. The Corinthians no longer delighted in others' sins. We learn two things from this: First, the whole church should take part in calling a lapsed sinner back to the right path, for unless it does this, the sinner remains bound. Second, the censure of ministers of the Word should be moderate, focused on the repentance of the offender. Commentary on 2 Corinthians 2:1.[51]

Paul's Grief and Love. Desiderius Erasmus: Nothing would be sadder for me than to see in you what is unworthy of your profession; nothing more gladdening than to perceive that there is nothing in you that can be censured. And so, as I was upset beyond measure by the disgrace of the great outrage discovered in your midst, I am writing you this letter in terrible torment of mind and anxiety of heart and with many tears—not in order to sadden you but so that you may understand my love and affection toward you. If anyone has given cause for distress, they have saddened not only me, but to some extent at least, they will have saddened all of you along with me. Paraphrase 2 Corinthians 2.[52]

Paul's Fatherly Care for the Corinthians. Huldrych Zwingli: [Paul is saying:] "Those 'apostles' of yours, who rule over you and oppress you and afflict you with sadness, gladden their own hearts and stuff their own bellies. I do not at all approve of this. For although I am sometimes forced to use the medicine of bitter rebuke because of those who are shameful and thus afflict others with sadness, nevertheless I myself am no less moved with anguish and sadness. Nor can I experience gladness (unless you who have begun to be grieved should set aside your sadness), that is, unless you should derive joy from those who have been corrected. For just as a father, with a pained and tormented soul, is wounded by his son's wrongdoing and made deeply sorrowful; and again, just as a father receives the greatest joy once he has chastised and reformed his son; so also, whenever I am saddened and provoked by your evil deeds, I am forced to deal all the more severely with you. I am not able to find consolation and comfort until I have chastised and corrected those who are hurling you and me into sorrow." Annotations on 2 Corinthians 2:2.[53]

[49]C. Spangenberg, *Die ander Epistel Pauli an die Corinthier*, 24v*.
[50]CO 50:26 (CTS 40:145).
[51]Hemmingsen, *Commentaria in Omnes Epistolas Apostolorum*, 257.
[52]CWE 43:212.
[53]Zwingli, *Annotatiunculae . . . ex ore Zvinglij*, 150-51.

Paul Was Aggrieved by the Corinthians' Grief. Niels Hemmingsen: The cause for his not coming, Paul said, was that he did not want to move the Corinthians to sadness. Now he provides the reason for this cause, adduced from his own person, namely, lest he experience grief by afflicting them with sorrow and correcting them because of their misdeed. The character of a godly pastor is revealed here, who, when he corrects others, is himself affected by sadness. He does not cheerfully gloat over persons who have fallen because they will receive their deserved punishment, but instead, with a fatherly heart, he calls the wandering back to the right path with a holy censure. Therefore, note in this passage the proper attitude that a minister of God must have when he undertakes the correction of those who wander. Commentary on 2 Corinthians 2:2.[54]

Godly Grief. Cyriacus Spangenberg: It is a good sign in a congregation, when one punishes sin and vice, that they do not throw such things to the wind, nor mock, but take it earnestly to heart and submit to such punishment themselves and feel that they themselves are indeed concerned by it, and do not become worse, more stubborn, more wicked, or disobedient, but sad and distressed. It is also a particular grace of God with a preacher by which God honors a whole congregation when he is thus able to punish sin and vice and do it so ardently that it touches hearts and immediately gives rise to fear. Eighth Sermon.[55]

Sadness and Joy. Wolfgang Musculus: In this passage where Paul says, "lest when I came to you I would suffer sadness from those who should have made me rejoice," we should understand how painful and distressing is the kind of sadness where those who love are aggrieved, indeed aggrieved by the people whom they loved at high cost and from whom they expected joy rather than pain. There are many different kinds of sadness. As far as those cases where we are aggrieved, there is no more painful kind of sadness than that which is born in us by friends and those whom we love. It is a minor thing if our enemies aggrieve us, for we expected nothing from them except sorrow; we can easily overcome this kind of sadness. But if we are aggrieved by friends, as happened to David by his father-in-law Saul and Christ by his disciple, or close friends, which happened to the apostle by many of the Corinthians, this kind of sadness that is inflamed by the zeal of love . . . most acutely pierces the heart of those who love. . . .

In a similar fashion, all the churches of Christ should consider how this relates to their apostles, bishops, ministers, and pastors. What sorts of things cause them joy? Clearly, the apostle speaks here about the joy of the spirit, not the joy of the flesh. Nowadays, one discovers that bishops (especially if they are fat) rejoice hardly at all in the people of the churches that they govern. Thus these bishops find their joy in fat riches and make little of salvation. For true bishops, joy is found not in seeking their own benefit but in seeking that which benefits Christ. Commentary on 2 Corinthians 2:3.[56]

The Mutual Love of Pastors and Their People. Tilemann Hesshus: Since the apostles and pastors bathe their listeners with explanations regarding the blessings of the heavenly mediator and the joys of the spiritual life, it is appropriate that the listeners should respond with a sincere confession of the gospel, a holy zeal of piety, and a true spirit of godliness, so as to encourage their pastors and avoid afflicting them with sadness. Paul now demonstrates that he is confident that the Corinthians will respond this way, because they had been so touched by him that they delighted in the apostle's joy no less than their own. Here is portrayed for us a picture of the mutual love that ought to exist between pastors and their congregations. Pastors ought to be touched no differently by

[54]Hemmingsen, *Commentaria in Omnes Epistolas Apostolorum*, 257.
[55]C. Spangenberg, *Die ander Epistel Pauli an die Corinthier*, 25v.
[56]Musculus, *Commentarius . . . in posteriorem epistolam Pauli ad Corinthios*, 65-66.

the happiness and joy of the church than by their own. And in turn, pastors' joy ought to be most pleasing to the church, just as the parents' joy ought to bring great delight to their children. Explication of 2 Corinthians 2:3.[57]

True Pastors Do Not Overlook Sin. Heinrich Bullinger: Paul explains more fully the mindset with which he wrote his previous letter, since it appeared to be tyrannical and completely inappropriate. The sense of Paul's words is plain. "It was very different," Paul says, "because I reaped nothing of joy but only more sorrow from that correction and your grief. Moreover, I announced very painful words against that fornicator not to agitate him, but to help him and show my heartfelt love for you, for the one who loves you the most earnestly is the one who overlooks your guilt the least. Furthermore, if you were stricken with grief, remember that you were not the only ones disturbed, for I too experienced great sorrow, not only because of the fornicator, but also for the reputation of all of you, because I saw that all of you were turning a blind eye to such brazen wickedness. Consequently, so as not finally to be forced to rebuke all of you more severely, I wrote more sharply against the fornicator, lest I burden all of you." (This passage is a somewhat obscure because of the confusing order of the words.) For pastors who truly love the common people reproach those sinning, whereas pastors who turn a blind eye to shameful behavior are those who hate and ruin them. Paul also shows that wicked people serve somewhat as an example by which the rest of the multitude is filled with fear, which provides the entire church an opportunity to refrain from sinning. Commentary on 2 Corinthians 2:4.[58]

Paul's Tears. Wolfgang Musculus: "For I wrote to you out of much affliction and anguish of heart and with many tears." Let us observe here how to distinguish between masters of churches and fathers of churches. It is possible for masters, prelates, and lords to be enraged with sinners, taking hold of them harshly, and condemning them in their hearts. Indeed, they are not aggrieved or anguished of heart, nor do they pour out tears for the sake of sinners. For what they do they do not do out of love (which is alien to them), but out of either pharisaical righteousness full of disdain or hypocrisy, or zeal for personal gain. Now since fathers are moved with paternal love when they see one of their own children sinning, they are troubled and anguished of heart, and they cry copiously. And in this way they take hold of their children—with vigor as well as love—and they intermingle more tears than reproaches. . . .

But wasn't Paul in this way acting like a woman? Certainly, he was no Stoic, since he not only wept but wept a lot. I answer that Christ and the apostles more quickly wept in the fashion of women than remained hardened like the Stoics, because they were more quickly aggrieved by the ruin of humankind than were the Stoics. Now they were more quickly aggrieved because they loved men and women more than the Stoics. And they loved them more because they were partakers of divine goodness more than the Stoics. Christ and the apostles did not share in the harshness of the Pharisees and Stoics, nor in the silliness of Democritus Gelasius;[†] but they had more in common with Heraclitus as they cried when they saw the misery of humankind. Commentary on 2 Corinthians 2:4.[59]

Paul's Many Tears. John Trapp: Johannes Lorinus[†] states, "St. Paul's epistles were written with tears rather than ink." Commentary on 2 Corinthians 2:4.[60]

[57]Hesshus, *Explicatio Secundae Epistolae Pauli ad Corinthios*, 45r-v.
[58]Bullinger, *In Posteriorem D. Pauli ad Corinthios Epistolam Commentarius*, 270.

[59]Musculus, *Commentarius . . . in posteriorem epistolam Pauli ad Corinthios*, 67. [†]The Greek philosopher Democritus of Abdera (born c. 460–457 BC), also known as Gelasius, was famous for his ethical ideal of cheerfulness. See N. G. L. Hammond and H. H. Scullard, eds., *The Oxford Classical Dictionary*, 2nd ed. (Oxford: Clarendon, 1970), 327-28.
[60]Trapp, *A Commentary or Exposition*, 708*. [†]Johannes Lorinus (1559–1634) was a Jesuit author who wrote a commentary on the Bible. This quotation is taken from his comment on Acts 22:19.

GODLY SORROW ENDS IN JOY. THE ENGLISH ANNOTATIONS: The apostle reproves the Corinthians sharply, even though this would certainly cause them sadness. This was not his intent though, for he desired to express his affectionate love for them and his care for their salvation, so that by sorrowing in a godly manner they might receive spiritual consolation. For as worldly joy ends in sorrow, godly sorrow ends in joy. As St. Jerome once exhorted a penitent: "Let him grieve, and rejoice for such grief."[†] ANNOTATIONS ON 2 CORINTHIANS 2:4.[61]

[61]Downame, ed., *English Annotations*, FF2v*. [†]While likely not the intended reference, Jerome makes a similar exhortation in his letter to Heliodorus, NPNF[2] 6:126.

2:5-11 FORGIVE THE SINNER

[5]Now if anyone has caused pain, he has caused it not to me, but in some measure—not to put it too severely—to all of you. [6]For such a one, this punishment by the majority is enough, [7]so you should rather turn to forgive and comfort him, or he may be overwhelmed by excessive sorrow. [8]So I beg you to reaffirm your love for him. [9]For this is why I wrote, that I might test you and know whether you are obedient in everything. [10]Anyone whom you forgive, I also forgive. Indeed, what I have forgiven, if I have forgiven anything, has been for your sake in the presence of Christ, [11]so that we would not be outwitted by Satan; for we are not ignorant of his designs.

Overview: Having defended his apostleship, Paul now exhorts the Corinthians to forgive, comfort, and receive back into fellowship the repentant sinner whom they had previously excommunicated for committing incest with his stepmother. For Reformation commentators, this brief passage provides specific, normative guidelines for treating sin and repentance in their Christian congregations. Many of their comments reflect deep psychological sensitivity and intense pastoral concern. They particularly warn against the dangers of excessive severity in handling repentant sinners. Discipline must always be adapted to particular persons and circumstances. Restoration should be based, not on the enormity of the sin, but on the depth of remorse. Pastors need to beware lest overly harsh discipline causes sinners to leave the church, feign hypocritical contrition, or fall into despair. Martin Bucer comments, "Better weak penance and meager reformation than none at all." Hence, pastoral zeal for congregational discipline must always be tempered by mercy, goodness, and love—and an acute awareness that it is practiced "in the presence of Christ." As they hold up the godly example of Paul, Protestant commentators are confident that their pastors and churches are recovering a biblical model for discipline and soul care that had long been neglected by the medieval church.

2:5-8 *Forgiveness Brings Comfort*

God Wants Sinners to Be Humbled, Not to Perish. Martin Luther: After Paul, in the first epistle to the Corinthians, had reproved the man who had married his stepmother with great offense to the church, Paul shows his care and solicitude in the second epistle, lest perhaps he had sinned because of excessive vehemence, although he had done nothing incompatible with his office and did not find fault with his previous reproof. But he orders him to be buoyed up again and to be strengthened, lest he be overwhelmed by sorrow.

But not enough can be said to hard and unreasonable people to bruise and humble them, because they do not fear the divine wrath, even if God sends his thunderbolts. Thus the pope and the cardinals are not moved by menacing threats. But if anyone is ever struck by God's thunderbolt, they will feel that a conscience destitute of all solace is in serious trouble and finds no easy remedy. Therefore, one must take consolation from the Word and come to the aid of those consciences. It is not God's will that one of these little ones should perish. Thus, Christ commands Peter, "When you have turned again, strengthen your brethren." God wants you to be humbled, not to perish. He is not angry with you. Nor has he hurled this thunderbolt against you in his rage. No, it has been his purpose to lead you to a knowledge of your sins and to buoy you up and strengthen you when you have been humbled. This could not have been done if your heart had not been smitten by terror and fear. Lectures on Genesis.[1]

Three Kinds of Confession. Philipp Melanchthon: The first kind of confession is public, which is described in Matthew 18, where the person whose sin was committed in public should be accused publicly before the church. Those who listened to the church were to be absolved; those who did not repent were excommunicated. This is what happened in Corinth: the offender was cast out by the agreement of the entire church, and afterward, when he repented, he was received back again. And indeed, in that place, confession did not require punishment if they repented of those sins for which they were accused.

The second kind of confession is also public: it involves private confession but public penance, which was practiced at first in the ancient church. Both Cyprian, in his *De lapsis*,[†] and Tertullian, in his *Historia triparti*,[‡] recall this kind of confession. Those who committed disgraceful deeds were to confess to one of the elders alone, who had been appointed in the church. This elder proclaimed a punishment for them, which the offenders were then to undergo in public in the presence of the church. The offenders were not allowed to participate in the table of the Lord unless they had performed their punishment. An example of this sort of confession still exists among us today in the punishment of murderers, [although] in the Greek church this too has been laid aside.

The third kind of confession is private confession, of the sort where people were free to confess to whomever and whenever they wished. People confessed whenever their consciences were in distress; they consulted holy people and heard from them God's absolution and judgment. Basil recalls this kind of confession in his book *De institutis monachorum*.[§] The words of James, "Confess your sins one to another," seems to pertain here as well. Annotations on 2 Corinthians 2:5-11.[2]

Six Reasons for Restoring the Sinner. David Dickson: That [Paul] might show his meekness toward the penitent incestuous person, he advises that the Corinthians should again receive him into favor for these six reasons. Reason 1 [v. 7]. Because they are bound to forgive the penitent man and to comfort him, no less than they were bound to excommunicate him when he was impenitent. . . . Reason 2 [v. 7]. Because otherwise it would be dangerous, lest the penitent man should be swallowed up with too much sorrow if they did not receive him into favor again. . . . Reason 3 [v. 8]. Because (especially since the apostle desired it so greatly) they are bound to testify their love toward the penitent man, that is, by demonstrating that the reason they excommunicated him was not to destroy him, but that, by repentance, they might save him. . . . Reason 4 [v. 9]. Because by this means they were about to show themselves obedient to the command of the apostle in all things, as before in excommunicating him, so now also, by absolving him from the bond of excommunication by which they proved their obedience to the apostle. . . . Reason 5 [v. 10]. Because the apostle, for the sake of the Corinthians, had granted the man pardon, and was about to forgive him. Therefore, it was proper that they should also forgive this man, for the apostle's sake. . . . Reason 6 [v. 11]. Lest through the craftiness of Satan, the church should suffer harm, unless they now forgive the penitent man. For by too much severity sinners are brought into desperation, or leave the church, because Satan, whose arts and deceits do harm and are well-known to the church. Exposition of 2 Corinthians 2:7-11.[3]

"If Anyone Has Caused Me Pain." Cardinal Cajetan: Paul is speaking concerning the

[1]LW 8:26-27* (WA 44:598); citing 1 Cor 5:1; Mt 18:14; Lk 22:32.

[2]*Melanchthons Werke*, 4:96-97; citing Jas 5:16. [†]Cyprian, *De lapsis*; [‡]Tertullian, *On Repentance*, see ANF 3.657-66; [§]Basil, *Regulae fusius tractatae* 26, PG 31:985.

[3]Dickson, *An Exposition of All St. Paul's Epistles*, 75*.

incestuous man, who had produced an occasion for sadness, namely, by his crime. "Not that he caused me sorrow, but in part"—that is, "he not only produced sadness in me, but also in many of you; and in this way, he produced part of the sadness in me, and part in you. So that I might not burden all of you." Paul gives the reason why he said, "but in part," namely, "so that I might not exempt you from sharing in the sorrow"—because it was weighing their hearts down. "For I knew what happened was displeasing to many of them, causing them grief." Commentary on 2 Corinthians 2:5.[4]

Paul and the Corinthians Shared a Common Grief. John Calvin: "But if anyone." This is the third reason for alleviating the offense—that Paul shared a common grief with them, and its cause originated from a different source. "We have been alike grieved," he says, "and another person is to blame for it." At the same time, he speaks about that person rather gently, when he says, "If anyone"—not asserting the matter, but rather, holding it in suspense. Furthermore, this passage is interpreted by some people as if Paul wished to say, "That person who caused me grief has also offended you; for you ought to have been equally aggrieved, yet I have been left almost alone in my grief. But I do not wish to say this frankly, lest I place blame on all of you." And so, in this interpretation, the second statement corrects the first. But the interpretation of Chrysostom[†] is much more suitable, for he reads it as one continuous sentence: "That person has not grieved me alone, but pretty much all of you. And when I say, 'in part' [*ex parte*], I do so in order that I may not burden him too much." I disagree with Chrysostom[†] only in his translation of "in part" (*ex parte*), for I understand it to mean "in some measure." I know that Ambrose[‡] renders this phrase as "part of the saints" since the Corinthian church was divided; but that interpretation is more ingenious than solid. Commentary on 2 Corinthians 2:5.[5]

Moderation Required in Punishing Sinners. Wolfgang Musculus: Paul begins here to prescribe the manner of restoring the sinner. First of all, he indicates that the rebuke of the offender that was made by the majority (that is, the church) is enough. Paul does not want the sinner's exclusion to exceed moderation. For he judges that the offender should be admitted not by the size or degree of the crime, which Paul wanted to be considered in his first epistle when the sentence was being applied, but by the moral quality of the person who has sinned, and by the gravity of the rebuke that he has endured from the church. When describing the moral quality of the person, Paul does not simply say, "for him it is enough," but "for this kind of man it is enough." In saying this, undoubtedly, he wished to suggest either that some infirmity in the man should be considered that justified showing him mercy, or that he was overwhelmed by some exceptional grief when he was rejected by the church. Noting the gravity of the rebuke, Paul did not simply say, "for this kind of man the rebuke that he received is enough," but "this rebuke that was made by the majority." For it is easier to be rebuked by one person, separately and outside of the knowledge of the multitude, than for it to happen openly, in the presence of a crowd of people gathered together in one company. Not only must this shame be applied to the sinner in public in the sight of all, but also the most severe agitations and trembling of conscience must be sustained night and day for the sinner to feel the judgment of condemnation by the majority.

And so we are warned in this passage of the diligence that must be practiced by all those to whom the care of the souls of believers is committed lest in the correction and punishment of sinners they exceed moderation. We are inclined by the nature of our flesh to exercise harshness against those who are sinning just as we find it difficult to be satisfied with them no matter how harsh and extensive the punishment. Yes, indeed, the more severely we treat sinners, the more righteous in this we wish to be seen. And so it is that we are inclined

[4]Cajetan, *In Posteriorem Pauli Epistolam ad Corinthios Commentarii*, 156.
[5]CO 50:23 (CTS 40: 148-49). [†]For Chrysostom's interpretation, see PG 61:421-22 (NPNF[1] 12:296). [‡]For Ambrose's argument, see PL 17:297.

to exceed moderation, beyond which all discipline and punishment is not only useless but even harmful. Therefore, all ministers of Christ have their hands full to discern what is *ikanon*, that is, "enough," and to adjust and guide all things to its standard. Those who are wise discern adequately what is harmful in a case, not only in religion but also in other human affairs, because there are few people who know, or even desire to know what is "enough." . . . To be sure, as an unskilled physician does more harm than good [to a patient] when he does not know the proper remedy—the sort who heals more according to the rule of Hippocrates and Galen than according to the quality of the patient—so also is the unskilled minister of Christ who, not taking into account the person he is caring for but only focusing on the gravity of the offense, serves Satan more than Christ because he loses more people than he saves. COMMENTARY ON 2 CORINTHIANS 2:6[6]

THREE WAYS PENANCE IS ABUSED. MARTIN BUCER: There are three ways in which penance can do harm: first, when the severity of the penance causes people to leave the church completely and reject its discipline altogether, when by more gentle penance they might be brought to proper regret and sorrow for their sins and true reformation: better weak penance and meager reformation than none at all. . . .

The second problem with penance, and almost the most dangerous of all, is when it is misused and made into a hypocritical outward ceremony and not used in the right way as God has ordered and commanded his church to exercise it: that is, to introduce the person to a deeper, but believing contemplation of their evil and what it means in terms of serious offense to God's goodness and their own undoing, in order that they might become the more avid for the grace of God and the more hostile to sins, submit themselves the more heartily and entirely to God, and love him more ardently, the more that they recognize that they have been forgiven; and that they might crucify and put to death in themselves all evil lusts and desires, and awaken and ignite all zeal for the will and pleasure of God.

The third problem with penance is when it is made so severe that the penitents sink into too great sadness and despair, as it does to everything that is useful and necessary, great diligence and true spiritual wisdom and astuteness are necessary in order to impose and moderate penance in such a way that people are caused, moved, brought, and encouraged to exercise genuine, childlike faith and amendment of life in accordance with true faith; and that no one should either be driven completely away from the church, which is the first danger with penance, nor taught to play the hypocrite by an outward show of penance, which is the second danger, nor plunge into despair, which is the third danger. TRUE CARE OF SOULS.[7]

GOD FORGIVES THE REPENTANT SINNER—AND SO SHOULD WE. JACQUES LEFÈVRE D'ÉTAPLES: It is an indication of the great goodness of Paul, as well as of the Holy Spirit (who is both merciful and extraordinarily gracious) who indwelt him, that he pleads on behalf of the man who had caused him sadness and who had scandalized the community, that is, the church of the Corinthians. Paul pleads, I say, that everyone might forgive the offender so that he might find relief in such consolation; otherwise, if the church were too scrupulous, he might kill himself from excessive sorrow or out of desperation. Due to the man's repentance, Paul displays an outpouring of love toward him. Paul covers over the man's sin on the grounds that it had been blotted out before God. And the fact that Paul does not identify the sin by name is instructive for us in that we must show charity toward those who have repented of their wrongdoing. For why, you miserable person, burdened by the chains of your own sin—why will

[6]Musculus, *Commentarius . . . in posteriorem epistolam Pauli ad Corinthios*, 69-70.

[7]Bucer, *Concerning the True Care of Souls*, 124, 127-28 (*Von der waren Seelsorge*, 177, 179-80).

you disclose, remember, and condemn those sins that God says he has pardoned, buried, and destroyed and remembers them no more? COMMENTARY ON 2 CORINTHIANS 2:7.[8]

PUNISHMENT AND PARDON. WOLFGANG MUSCULUS: "And so you should rather turn to forgive and comfort him." After Paul has warned that the excommunication of the sinner should be ended, he adds that pardon and consolation should be imparted to him. Now he wishes that [the Corinthians] be more favorably inclined toward consolation than to prolong the severity of excommunication. And thus he does not simply say, "so you should forgive and comfort him," but "so you should rather turn to forgive and comfort him" than prolong this excommunication any further.

It should be observed in this passage how appropriately and suitably he makes use of these two words "forgive" and "comfort." The Corinthians seemed to be more inclined to punish than to pardon [the sinner], and as a result they were more inclined to afflict than to comfort him. Paul therefore urges they that should be more concerned to forgive the offense and comfort the downhearted than to pass judgment any longer. COMMENTARY ON 2 CORINTHIANS 2:7.[9]

ABSOLUTION SHOULD BE GIVEN TO ALL WHO REPENT. TILEMANN HESSHUS: Paul here prescribes that the incestuous man—who had taken his stepmother as his wife and whom, in Paul's previous letter, he had excommunicated and handed over to Satan—should be graciously received and supported with comfort. It should be gathered from this that the incestuous man had displayed signs of repentance. Truly, this clear example plainly refutes the ragings of the Cathars and Novatians[†] who sullied the mercy of God by closing off the womb of the church and refusing penance to people who had fallen after baptism. Paul does not at all want the incestuous man to grieve and fall into ruin; rather, he commands that the duties of love be extended to him, and that he be encouraged with comfort. Therefore, according to the command of Christ, people who fall into sin after their conversion, when they are repentant and give evidence of their sorrow, should be received back: "I do not say seven times, but seventy-seven times." Aaron, Judah, and David—having fallen most grievously after their conversion to God—obtained the remission of their sins and were reconciled to God. Therefore, absolution ought to be denied to no one who repents. For, where sin abounds, there grace abounds all the more. EXPLICATION OF 2 CORINTHIANS 2:6-7.[10]

UNDUE SEVERITY MUST BE AVOIDED IN DISCIPLINE. CYRIACUS SPANGENBERG: One must use such harsh severity against such blatant sin. But if they then recognize their sin and are deeply distressed by their being cut off from Christian fellowship, are sorry for their sins and humbly plead with God and the congregation or the church for forgiveness of the same together with their offense, one should then (when one sees that they are earnest) without further hesitation take them back into grace again and comfort them by the divine Scripture with the forgiveness of their sins, and not burden them anymore.

In this the former bishops did a little too much in their church sentences, because in the past they used to impose on some three years' and on others seven years' penance before they could be fully received back into the fellowship of the churches. Indeed, some could not experience grace again before they lay on their deathbed. Thus, in this they truly did a little too much.

If God himself will thus take sinners back in grace in the very hour in which they repent, that is, when they do right penance, acknowledge their

[8]Lefèvre, *Commentariorum in Epistolas Beati Pauli . . . Liber Tertius*, 131r-v.

[9]Musculus, *Commentarius . . . in posteriorem epistolam Pauli ad Corinthios*, 70-71.

[10]Hesshus, *Explicatio Secundae Epistolae Pauli ad Corinthios*, 47v-48r; citing Mt 18:22; Rom 5:20. [†]The Novatians, a Christian sect in the third century, and the Cathars (or Albigensians), a heretical group in the Middle Ages, refused readmission to their communities of members who had lapsed after baptism.

sins, fear the wrath of God, and through faith in Christ yearn for forgiveness. Then we shall also behave in the same way toward excommunicated sinners. If they acknowledge their sin, we must forgive them and comfort them. Ninth Sermon.[11]

Excessive Sorrow Can Be Sinful. John Trapp: Some holy men have desired to see their sin in its most ugly colors, and God has heard them; yet his hand was so heavy upon them that they went constantly mourning to their graves. . . . It was a saying of Augustine, "Let a man grieve for his sin, and then rejoice in his grief."[†] Sorrow for sin, if it is so excessive that thereby we are unable to discharge our duties, is a sinful sorrow—even if it is for sin. Commentary on 2 Corinthians 2:7.[12]

How to Restore the Sinner. Wolfgang Musculus: "Wherefore I beg of you that you confirm your love for him." It is as if Paul said, "Seeing that [the sinner] is filled with sadness and mourning to the point that it is to be feared that he might be completely overwhelmed with this excessive sorrow, receive him with love into the fellowship of your church so that his spirit might be revived." Confirm, he says, your love for him. . . . The Greek word *kyrōsai* means to decide, establish, or confirm something either by vote or by some other legitimate authority, and to render it as authentic and settled. Paul's desire is that the Corinthians in their sacred assembly decide and confirm by common vote that the penitent and sorrowful sinner should be received back into the church in love, just as they had previously excommunicated him by common vote. He does not command, rather he begs them to do this, because he does not want them to act reluctantly but rather willingly so that the work of love might be fully perfected by their spontaneity. . . .

Therefore, we find in this passage the method for receiving back excommunicated persons, when and how they ought to be restored into the fellowship of the church. Clearly, when it is feared that persons are being overwhelmed with excessive sorrow, they ought to be restored to the church. Second, those who commit gross sin ought to be restored by the common vote of believers in the same way that they were also excommunicated. Third, this reconciliation ought to be done through brotherly love. Commentary on 2 Corinthians 2:8.[13]

2:9-10 *Restoration of the Sinner*

Paul Has Not Capriciously Changed His Mind. John Calvin: Paul anticipates an objection that [the Corinthians] might make: "What, then, did you mean when you were so indignant because we had not punished him? From being so stern a judge to suddenly becoming his advocate, is this not the sign of a man who wavers between conflicting passions?" This way of thinking could detract greatly from Paul's authority. But he answers that he has achieved what he was seeking and was therefore satisfied so that he must now make way for mercy. For since they had corrected their slowness [in disciplining him], nothing now stood in the way from them lifting up with their gentleness the man who was humbled and downcast. Commentary on 2 Corinthians 2:9.[14]

Restoring the Sinner. Balthasar Hubmaier:

Leonhart: What are the causes for excommunication?

Hans: Refusal to be reconciled to the brother or to desist from sin.

Leonhart: Why is one excommunicated?

Hans: Not for petty offenses as our papists have been doing, but for an offensive sin; and it is

[11]C. Spangenberg, *Die ander Epistel Pauli an die Corinthier*, 38v-39r.
[12]Trapp, *A Commentary or Exposition*, 708*. [†]Trapp may be referring to Augustine, *City of God*, 14:9, NPNF[1] 268-69. Or perhaps he intends to refer to Jerome; see 45n61 above.

[13]Musculus, *Commentarius . . . in posteriorem epistolam Pauli ad Corinthios*, 71-72.
[14]CO 50:30 (CTS 40:151).

done for the good of the sinner, that he may examine himself, know himself, and desist from the sin.

Leonhart: If he desists from his sin, avoids the ways and paths that might cause him to fall again, and reforms, what attitude does the church take toward him?

Hans: She receives him again with joy, as the father did his prodigal son, and as Paul did the Corinthians. She opens the door to heaven for him and lets him return to the communion of the Lord's Supper.

In sum: Where water baptism in accord with Christ's institution is not reestablished and practiced one does not know who is a brother or sister, there is no church, no brotherly discipline or reproof, no ban, no Supper, nor anything that resembles the Christian stance and nature. God lives. So it must be, or heaven and earth must shatter. A Christian Catechism.[15]

Sinners Must Be Reconciled to the Congregation. Cyriacus Spangenberg: The congregation shall not declare any public sinner righteous who is recognized by the teachers, through God's Word, as deserving excommunication. Also again a preacher shall admit no public sinner to the fellowship unless he has been reconciled with the congregation and the same is again satisfied with him. Thereby all shall be beautifully unanimous in such public affairs. But the church does not judge secret cases, as the rule says: *De occultis non iudicat ecclesia* [the church does not judge secret cases]. Ninth Sermon.[16]

The Importance of Caring for Sinners. Wolfgang Musculus: The phrase "in the sight of Christ" is interpreted variously because different interpretations are possible. Some render it "in the face of Christ"; others "with respect to Christ"; others "in the presence of Christ"; and still others "in the person and place of Christ." I think that this is the correct meaning: "If I [Paul] have pardoned him of anything, I have pardoned him in the sight of Christ, not in the sight of the assembly of the church. Hence, I beg that you forgive him so that this pardon might also take place in the assembly of your church. And I do this also for your sake, so that we might not be afflicted by Satan." Someone will say, "If therefore Paul and the Corinthians had not pardoned the penitent sinner, would the church then have been afflicted by Satan? I see how the sinner himself would be swallowed up in despair, but I do not see how for that reason Satan would afflict Paul and the church."

I answer: First, believers ought to show sympathy in the church of Christ inasmuch as others are to be reckoned in jeopardy when one is in danger. For this reason, when Satan afflicts one member of the church, it is correct to say that he afflicts the whole church, just as it is correct to say that the body of a person is wounded when one of its members is injured. Second, when a pastor does not have concern for the salvation of his sheep, and when the sheep do not care for the salvation of one another, but instead are concerned only with themselves, is it not to be feared that false pastors and wolves will afflict them? Clearly, the apostle thinks the same thing pertains to the church in which there is no concern shown to protecting those who are in jeopardy and where even believers themselves are not concerned . . . with the salvation of their brothers and sisters. In such a case, clearly, all should be afraid lest Satan afflict them. I entreat you to consider this: if there was cause to fear that Satan would afflict the Corinthian church that had been planted and was being watched over by the apostle, should one not be afraid for all the rest of the churches where pastors either slumber or exercise dominion for the sake of their own pleasure? Commentary on 2 Corinthians 2:10.[17]

In the Presence of Christ. Tilemann Hesshus: Paul adds "in the presence of Christ," in

[15]CRR 10:353-54*; citing Lk 15:20; 2 Cor 2:10.
[16]C. Spangenberg, *Die ander Epistel Pauli an die Corinthier*, 40v.
[17]Musculus, *Commentarius . . . in posteriorem epistolam Pauli ad Corinthios*, 74.

order to testify that, in his ministry, he does everything with a good conscience and in the fear of the Lord. Thus, all godly people, and especially pastors of churches, ought to consider Christ Jesus in every decision and action; and because of his presence among them, they should determine to attempt or take up nothing except what Christ approves. Explication of 2 Corinthians 2:10.[18]

2:11 *Against the Schemes of Satan*

Misplaced Zeal. Jacques Lefèvre d'Étaples: By the cunning of the devil, the passion for good and holy things can sometimes encourage in some people more zeal than is proper, with the result that those who have the appearance of being zealous for good actually hinder charity, which is a superior good and more rigorously prescribed to us. Now zeal is good when it comprises mercy, goodness, and love—emulating divine zeal. But zeal is evil when, persevering to the end, it does not imitate God's readiness to forgive. By zeal of this sort, the cunning of Satan traps many people, who think that they are pleasing God in this way when they are not. Commentary on 2 Corinthians 2:11.[19]

Satan's Outward and Inward Attacks. Martin Luther: Now that is the least of our troubles, that the world hates us and persecutes us. Even Satan is not satisfied with that; he plans to exercise his malice within our own ranks. If outwardly we are too strong for his stooges, the papists, he will rend and destroy us inwardly through ourselves. May God our Father prevent him from doing this. Amen. So henceforth we must have regard to ourselves rather than to our enemies from without. As St. Paul says in 2 Corinthians 2, we know well what he has in mind. Now that he sees he cannot subdue us from the left side, he rushes over to the right side. Formerly he made us too papistic; now he wants to make us too evangelical.† But God has commanded us many times in the Scriptures to keep on the straight path and not to turn either to the right or to the left. Receiving Both Kinds in the Sacrament.[20]

Satan's Subtle Tricks. Huldrych Zwingli: "So that we would not be tricked or outsmarted." . . . [Paul is saying,] "I am tested by Satan's cunning who seeks to attack, seduce, and cast us down not only from the right, that is, through pleasure and success, but also from the left, that is, in sadness and despair. At first, you were too merciful when I myself was more severe. And now, there are some among you who are very harsh when I am lenient." Either being too merciful or too harsh—both of these extremes are sinful. We ought to observe the method and rule of love. Annotations on 2 Corinthians 2:11.[21]

Immoderate Rigor in Discipline Must Be Avoided. The English Annotations: "Lest Satan overreach us." The Greek word *pleonekteō* signifies to have more than belongs to one, and it is commonly used of a covetous person. The comparison is taken from the greedy merchant who seeks and takes all opportunities to beguile and deceive others. The meaning then is that we should not give Satan an occasion by our immoderate rigor to snatch away from us, or ruin any member of the church, to make thereby the gospel ministry more hateful, and so pervert the holy use of discipline, which consists in the temper of charity, and has no other end than the salvation of the sinner. Annotations on 2 Corinthians 2:11.[22]

Satan's Wiles Against the Church. Tilemann Hesshus: It is quite clear to us that

[18]Hesshus, *Explicatio Secundae Epistolae Pauli ad Corinthios*, 49v-50r.

[19]Lefèvre, *Commentariorum in Epistolas Beati Pauli . . . Liber Tertius*, 131v.

[20]LW 36:237 (WA 10/II:11–12). †Luther here is referring to the "evangelical" excesses of Andreas Bodenstein von Karlstadt and his allies, who, in Luther's absence, had radicalized the reformation in Wittenberg in late 1521 and early 1522.

[21]Zwingli, *Annotatiunculae . . . ex ore Zvinglij*, 153.

[22]Downame, ed., *English Annotations*, FF2v*.

[Satan] is constantly setting traps against us, and he directs all his stratagems to the end that he might block the progress of the gospel; hurl darts against consciences; alienate listeners from their pastors; overwhelm with despair people who are crushed with terrors; inflame pastors with the lust for power; fill minds with false suspicions; stir up hideous scandals in the church; and, in various ways, create opportunities both for God's name to be blasphemed and the salvation of men and women to be undermined. These snares of Satan ought to be guarded against, therefore, with faith, godliness, modesty, moderation, patience, gentleness, wisdom, and prayer. Explication of 2 Corinthians 2:11.[23]

We Are Not Ignorant of Satan's Designs. John Trapp: They are but Christians in name only who have no personal experience of Satan's stratagems, his set and composed machinations, his artificially crafted methods, his plots, his darts, his depths, whereby he outwitted our first parents and continues to deceive us as he sees opportunity. Commentary on 2 Corinthians 2:11.[24]

[23]Hesshus, *Explicatio Secundae Epistolae Pauli ad Corinthios*, 50v.
[24]Trapp, *A Commentary or Exposition*, 708*.

2:12-17 Triumph in Christ

[12]*When I came to Troas to preach the gospel of Christ, even though a door was opened for me in the Lord,* [13]*my spirit was not at rest because I did not find my brother Titus there. So I took leave of them and went on to Macedonia.*

[14]*But thanks be to God, who in Christ always leads us in triumphal procession, and through us spreads the fragrance of the knowledge of him everywhere.* [15]*For we are the aroma of Christ to God among those who are being saved and among those who are perishing,* [16]*to one a fragrance from death to death, to the other a fragrance from life to life. Who is sufficient for these things?* [17]*For we are not, like so many, peddlers of God's word, but as men of sincerity, as commissioned by God, in the sight of God we speak in Christ.*

Overview: After briefly describing his recent visit to Troas and Macedonia, the apostle Paul shifts his discourse to the present, reminding the Corinthians that he is a faithful and sincere minister, commissioned by God, whose gospel message spreads the fragrance of Christ to believers and unbelievers alike. For Reformation commentators, Paul's description of his gospel labors provides clear guidelines and lessons for Christian ministers in every age. Like Paul, they must be zealous in proclaiming Christ; they must care deeply for the spiritual welfare of their people; they must teach God's Word with sincerity and purity, avoiding all hypocrisy and deception. The commentators expect that all faithful pastors will encounter obstacles, various kinds of suffering, and "closed doors" in their ministries. The beautiful aroma of God's gospel that they announce will be, for some people, a sweet fragrance of life, while for others it will become the stench of judgment and death. Despite these many hardships, Christian ministers who persevere in the truth and faith of God are sure to participate in Christ's glorious triumph over Satan and his minions. Even so, as Cyriacus Spangenberg comments, Christian preachers must never forget the gravity of the office to which they have been called, for "God goes to all sermons and hears how and what we preach." Indeed, "it is no small thing to be a preacher."

2:12-13 *Paul's Mission Itinerary*

Paul's Journeys. Heinrich Bullinger: Thus far, Paul has vindicated himself from the charge of tyranny, informing the Corinthians that he did not seek dominion under the pretext of the faith, nor could it be concluded that he had commanded them to hand the fornicator over to Satan. He says much more about this in chapter 7. Now, he moves on to show that he had sincerely taught the Corinthians the truth—the same truth he successfully taught to other Gentiles with fruitfulness. For the false apostles were accusing Paul falsely of being an imposter. Paul here mentions to them a "door" for the same reason, reporting briefly that it had been completely open. It seems that he was speaking about that departure that Luke records in Acts 20, for I think that the apostle, having departed from Ephesus, immediately came to Troas, from whence he straightaway set sail for Macedonia—for he had not discovered Titus [in Troas] as he had hoped, who was still in Corinth, as is clear from chapter 7 of this epistle. Now while Paul was sailing on to Macedonia, he intercepted Titus who was coming from Achaia. . . . And then Paul sent Titus away to Corinth in Achaia to recommend that they prepare the customary collection, and Paul added this letter, making a sacred promise at the end of it that he himself would immediately follow. COMMENTARY ON 2 CORINTHIANS 2:12-13.[1]

FROM TROAS TO MACEDONIA. NIELS HEMMINGSEN: This brief account of Paul's departure is given so that the apostle might show his zeal in proclaiming Christ and explain the reason for his delay, since he had not come to Corinth as promised. Now, when he says that he was quite worried because he did not find his brother Titus in Troas, and so he immediately abandoned Troas and went onto Macedonia—he does this to make clear his apostolic concern for the Corinthians. For he diligently looked for Titus so that he might learn about the condition of the Corinthians. This apostolic concern is given to us as an example that we should care for the church with exceptional zeal and be especially concerned for those whose care has been chiefly entrusted to us. Now, that proverbial saying "opened door" is easily understood as a metaphor, for an opened door gives easy access into a room, while, on the other hand, we are shut out by a "closed door." Therefore, just as access into a house is through an open door, so too ministers of the Word easily go forth to announce the gospel when God's will provides the opportunity; on the other hand, another route must be taken when there is a closed door. And so, when no gospel fruit is produced, the Lord should be asked to open a door by his hand. COMMENTARY ON 2 CORINTHIANS 2:12-13.[2]

GOD ALONE OPENS THE DOOR TO GOSPEL LABORS. TILEMANN HESSHUS: So great is the power of Satan in the world, and so great the wickedness of men and women, that there would otherwise be no place for the gospel of Christ in the whole world except that the Lord Jesus, who sits at the right hand of God, opens doors to his apostles and pastors. To be sure, princes and kings are commanded to open doors for the glorious king Christ, but most of them apply all their strength to outlaw the gospel of Christ from their territories. The world is able to endure all sorts of religions, cults, idolatries, blasphemies, errors, ragings, orgies, and similar things; only the light of the gospel the world cannot endure, because it shows that the works of the world are evil. It is the work and blessing of the all-powerful God alone when the world—either willingly or unwillingly—considers allowing the preaching of the gospel, grants hospitality to godly pastors, and furnishes them with sustenance. The world was hostile to Paul, yet nevertheless, he spread the light of the gospel and gathered the church of Christ in many places. The pope has inflamed the Roman emperor, kings, and princes to crush the doctrine of the gospel, but the Lord from heaven opened the door to Luther and his allies and has gloriously gathered and preserved the church. Now, the world hates us and there are countless enemies who are attempting not only to hinder our progress but even to destroy it from within. But the Lord Jesus from heaven protects us under the shadow of his hand. He grants us hospitality and peace, and he miraculously supplies freedom for propagating the knowledge of him in the world and for gathering the church. Therefore, let us give thanks with our whole hearts to this most holy and compassionate God! And let us not neglect this opportunity to spread widely the light of the gospel! EXPLICATION OF 2 CORINTHIANS 2:12.[3]

THE PASTOR'S PARTICULAR ASSIGNMENT. CYRIACUS SPANGENBERG: Our case is virtually the same: we are obliged to serve all Christians in the whole world with teaching and writing, as we see that there is opportunity, but nevertheless most of all and particularly you, this church, in which God has particularly called us and put us as preachers, pastors, and ministers. Therefore, Paul also says, "Although I found such a fine and good opportunity in Troas, I had no rest in my spirit,

[1]Bullinger, *In posteriorem D. Pauli ad Corinthios Epistolam Commentarius*, 272; citing Acts 20:1-2.
[2]Hemmingsen, *Commentaria in Omnes Epistolas Apostolorum*, 259.
[3]Hesshus, *Explicatio Secundae Epistolae Pauli ad Corinthios*, 51r-52r.

because I did not find Titus my brother." Tenth Sermon.[4]

Paul's Great Concern for the Corinthians. Wolfgang Musculus: "My spirit was not at rest because I did not find my brother Titus there." If it had been inconsequential for the Corinthians to know this, he would not have written it. But it was very important, for Paul had sent Titus to them so he might learn from him about the condition of their church. And thus, Paul had hoped that he would find him in Troas. When he did not find him there, Paul's spirit was troubled by his longing for the arrival of Titus, through whom Paul was later revived, as he writes in chapter 7. Therefore, Paul shows them that their welfare was so important to him that his spirit would experience no peace unless he heard the best report about them. That is why he says, "my spirit had no relaxation or rest because I did not find my brother Titus there." We should not understand this passage the way some people explain it, as if Paul were inadequate to fulfill by himself the double responsibility, namely, of preaching to those who wished to hear him and opposing the heretics and unbelievers, and he did not find Titus to whom he wanted to entrust the responsibility of preaching. . . . This interpretation is very childish. And it would not be a reason for the apostle to write such a thing to the Corinthians.

Let us consider here how the spirit of the apostle was burdened with persistent fatigue. For if he was afflicted with concern and worry for one church, in such a way that his spirit would not find rest unless he heard the best report about it, can one imagine how great was the mountain of concerns for the remaining churches that exhausted him so many days and nights? And I say nothing about the incessant trouble of persecutions and afflictions.

Second, we also see here that Paul was subject to human emotions just as we are. He hoped and desired to find Titus when he came to Troas. But he hoped in vain, for he did not find Titus when he came to that city. Therefore, his hope was frustrated just as it often happens in human affairs. For this reason, when he did not find Titus at Troas as he had hoped, his spirit was troubled and he had no rest. And in this, Paul was like other humans. For in a similar way, we also are agitated and troubled when our hope is frustrated. These are common experiences to all mortals. Nevertheless, Paul acted in a pious and apostolic fashion because he endured this out of his concern for the churches of Christ. Commentary on 2 Corinthians 2:13.[5]

2:14-17 *The Aroma of Christ*

The Triumph of Christ's Name. Desiderius Erasmus: I give thanks to God, who always through us spreads abroad the triumph of the Christian name and [through us] renders the triumph more illustrious as day by day the glory of the gospel shines more widely. Everywhere on earth he disseminates knowledge of himself through our proclamation, using us, so to speak, in the place of sweetly smelling incense. For in preaching the glory of the gospel everywhere in the world, what else are we doing but scattering the fragrance of Christ, pleasing even of itself and salvific for all, but for many, through their own fault, deadly? It is salvific for those who believe in the gospel and attain salvation, but death-dealing to those who reject it and double the condemnation of death upon themselves by adding to their former outrages the offense of ingratitude and stubbornness. Paraphrases on 2 Corinthians 2.[6]

Paul Extols the Fruitfulness of God's Ministry Through Him. John Calvin: Here Paul again boasts in the success of his ministry and asserts that he has not been idle in the various places he has visited. But so as to do this without causing envy, he begins by giving thanks, which he

[4]C. Spangenberg, *Die ander Epistel Pauli an die Corinthier*, 43r.

[5]Musculus, *Commentarius . . . in posteriorem epistolam Pauli ad Corinthios*, 75-76.

[6]CWE 43:213-14.

again repeats afterward. Now he does not extol his own accomplishments out of a spirit of ambition, that his name might be extolled, nor does he give thanks to God by way of pretense (like the Pharisees), while being inflated with haughtiness and ambition. Instead of this, his heartfelt desire is that whatever is worthy of praise, should be recognized as the work of God alone so that his power alone might be extolled. And he recounts his own praises for the good of the Corinthians, so that when they hear that he has served the Lord with such great fruit in other places, they might not allow his labors to be unproductive among themselves and may learn to respect his ministry which God made everywhere so glorious and fruitful. Commentary on 2 Corinthians 2:14.[7]

God Gives Victory to the Weak and Miserable. Martin Luther: So our king is the defender and savior of the miserable, abounding in comfort toward the humble and distressed, completely victorious over his stubborn enemies. And we are really sure of victory if we hold fast to this king. What kind of kingdom would that be if we had to live continually surrounded by enemies, exposed to everyone's plots and weapons, always suffering and hard pressed? There must be some change, and those who have borne with so much must someday gain the victory. Victory is certain if only we persevere, as Paul says in 2 Corinthians 2:14: "I thank God who always causes us to triumph in Christ Jesus." Christians do not succumb to despair and lack of trust, they do not turn from the Word, they do not deny Christ. They persevere in teaching and confessing him—at times strongly, but at other times feebly. For he is a conquering king and a king of the miserable. He can raise us up even though at times we are weak. Commentary on Psalm 45:5.[8]

Gospel Ministers Share in Christ's Victory. John Calvin: Now Paul means that he was also a participant in the triumph that God accomplished, because it had been achieved through his exertions, just as lieutenants escorted on horseback the chariot of the chief general as sharers in the honor. Therefore, just as all ministers of the gospel fight under God's command, so they also win for him the victory and the honor of triumph. But at the same time, he honors each of them with a share in the triumph according to the military rank he has assigned to them, and the diligence performed by each of them. And so, they enjoy as it were a triumph, but it is God's rather than theirs. Paul adds the phrase "in Christ"—the person through whom God himself triumphs—inasmuch as he has conferred on him all the glory of authority. Commentary on 2 Corinthians 2:14.[9]

Victory Is in Christ. Wolfgang Musculus: Why does Paul not say, "who always gives us the victory in the world," but rather "who always gives us the victory in Christ"? The victor who was marching forth in Christ was, as it were, the conquered one who was afflicted in the world. This is the sort of victory that Christians experience: they encounter extreme suffering as far as the world is concerned, and while they seem to be conquered in the world, they are in fact victorious over both Satan and the world. Yes, indeed, they are victorious while they keep their souls intact and undefeated through all sorts of tribulations by virtue of patience in the faith of Christ. Thus, the tyrannical murderers of believers are defeated, and those who were murdered are victorious. The tyrant shouts "No! No!" The confessor of Christ says, "I recognize that vengeance is inappropriate, but I will confess that I am a Christian to my last breath." And when the final article of victory is proclaimed, he calls upon Christ his Deliverer, and commends his spirit to the one whom the impious, defeated, and bewildered tyrant blasphemes. The battle is not of this present and momentary life. But you acknowledge and confess as Lord either

[7]CO 50:32 (CTS 40:156-57).
[8]LW 12:229.
[9]CO 50:33 (CTS 40:157-58).

Christ or Satan. You align yourself either to the truth with the elect of God, or to lies with the reprobate of Satan. And you either live and experience salvation in eternity with Christ and all his saints, or you perish forever with the devil and all the wicked. The person who is victorious in this battle is not the one who kills, but the person who perseveres unconquered in the truth and faith of God. Commentary on 2 Corinthians 2:14.[10]

The Sweet Fragrance of Divine Knowledge. Cardinal Cajetan: Paul describes the second divine benefit from true ministers of the gospel. Not only does [God] triumph over demons through us by using us in the battle against the world to bring it under subjection, but he also reveals through us not only his knowledge but also the fragrance of his knowledge. There is a difference between good and wicked preachers of the gospel, because wicked preachers only hand over the knowledge of God, while good preachers also reveal the fragrance of divine knowledge, that is, sweetness, desirability, and delight. Now the sweetness of divine knowledge consists in works conforming to knowledge, and to this is [added] desirability and delight. Those who speak without action only reveal the teaching of faith. But those who both speak with action reveal in themselves the sweetest fragrance of knowledge that they have from God. Commentary on 2 Corinthians 2:14.[11]

The Fragrance of the Gospel Is Sweet to Some People, Fetid to Others. Huldrych Zwingli: It sometimes happens that a minister of the Word is forced into exile. This is so that God might make known his gospel in other places so that the fragrance of his Word might be poured out everywhere. This charming metaphor is drawn from things with sweet fragrances; some such fragrances revive, others kill. Sweet and fragrant is that gospel balm which is spread about by us—though it is from God, not us. Indeed, it brings death to some people, and life to others; some people are pleased with it and approve it, others reject and curse it. Simeon also testified to this fact when he said that the Christ had been appointed for the resurrection of some but the fall of others. And these things are spoken to comfort those who faithfully preach the Word of God, who defend truth and righteousness. For no matter how faithfully they preach the Word, it is inevitable that they should be hated by some, and their message judged fetid by others. Annotations on 2 Corinthians 2:14.[12]

Paul Compares His Teaching to Old Testament Sacrifices. Tilemann Hesshus: Paul commends his teaching with a striking metaphor drawn from sacrifices. Scripture says concerning Noah's sacrifice, "The Lord smelled the pleasing aroma." And Moses afterward repeats in Leviticus that "the aroma was pleasing to the Lord." Paul applies this phrase to his sermons, as if to say, "God has witnessed in the law that he delights in the aroma of sacrifices and incense, especially if they are offered by a faithful mediator. Now, the sufferings that I endure in proclaiming the gospel, are the sacrifice of the new covenant, and I know that God is more pleased with my sermons and struggles (like a burned sacrifice) than with all the incense and sacrifices of the Jews, who reject the appearing of the Messiah." When Paul says, "We are the aroma of Christ," he shows that Christ is the high priest who satisfies the wrath of the eternal Father by his sacrifice; and that the entirety of his doctrine proclaims only the death and resurrection of Jesus Christ, who became a sacrificial victim for the sins of the world. This message concerning the crucified and resurrected Christ that resounds in the world is a most fragrant aroma to God. By this message is announced the immeasurable wisdom and goodness

[10]Musculus, *Commentarius . . . in posteriorem epistolam Pauli ad Corinthios*, 78.

[11]Cajetan, *In Posteriorem Pauli Epistolam ad Corinthios Commentarii*, 157.

[12]Zwingli, *Annotatiunculae . . . ex ore Zvinglij*, 153-54; citing Lk 2:34.

of God, and his eternal justice and compassion. By this message the lies of Satan are refuted and the kingdom of hell destroyed. By this message the holy church is gathered to live with God for all eternity. Paul makes known this extraordinary and most delightful consolation when he says that the suffering that comes with teaching the gospel is a "pleasant aroma of Christ to God," in which God especially delights. Therefore, God will preserve the ministry; he will watch over the teaching and learning of the assembly; and he will compensate pastors' struggles and sufferings with abundant rewards. EXPLICATION OF 2 CORINTHIANS 2:15.[13]

THE GOSPEL AS THE FRAGRANCE OF GOD'S KNOWLEDGE. CYRIACUS SPANGENBERG: What is occurring through the preachers of the gospel is actually the work of Christ. He is the true high priest and stands continually before his heavenly Father and makes an incense offering—that is, he spreads through his mouth and preaching the beloved and holy gospel of the divine knowledge in all the world. And it is not inappropriate that the gospel is called a fragrance of the knowledge of God. For in the same way that one will always smell the fragrance of something which smells well and strong before one sees it, we also first understand from the preaching of the gospel what God and his will are, and how he is inclined toward us, and what we are to perform for him, before we see him. And just as a good fragrance gives desire and strength, the gospel also does the same.

He does not call the gospel the "knowledge of God" (says Chrysostom[†]) but a "fragrance of the divine knowledge" for this reason, that in the gospel is made known to us that there is a God and that the same is gracious, good, almighty, true, and merciful. Whoever has this knowledge and trusts in it, he has great knowledge indeed, and such knowledge is sufficient for him for blessedness. However, we do not yet see or know God according to his being; our mind is much too small for that. TENTH SERMON.[14]

THE PREACHING OF THE GOSPEL SAVES AND CONDEMNS. THE ENGLISH ANNOTATIONS: The gospel is preached indifferently to all manner of persons, but it works in a very different manner. For when it is received by the faithful, it produces in them life and salvation, containing all the causes thereof in itself. But when it is rejected by unbelievers, it becomes in them the occasion of a greater condemnation and makes their perdition inevitable. As the same light of the sun, says Chrysostom,[†] offends those of weak eyes but re-creates and comforts the clear of sight, and as the same star is to some a morning star bringing the light of day and to others an evening star bringing darkness and night, so the gospel is a comfort to some and a terror to others. It brings eternal life and salvation to some, but (indirectly) everlasting darkness and damnation to others, as is seen in the prophecy of Simeon in Luke 2:34: "Behold, this child is set for the fall and rising of many in Israel." ANNOTATIONS ON 2 CORINTHIANS 2:15.[15]

THE SWEET AROMA OF CHRIST. JOHN TRAPP: The church is the mortar; preaching, the pestle; the promises are the sweet spices, which once ground, yield a heavenly and supernatural aroma in the souls of godly hearers. COMMENTARY ON 2 CORINTHIANS 2:15.[16]

THE SAME SAVOR MAKES SOME ALERT AND OTHERS DROWSY. EDWARD LEIGH: *Beneolentia* [sweet savor] is one word in the Greek. . . . Gregory in his *Morals* states that this word is like the planet Venus, which for some is Lucifer, a bright morning star, arising in their hearts, by which they are roused up and stirred from iniquity. But for others,

[13]Hesshus, *Explicatio Secundae Epistolae Pauli ad Corinthios*, 53v-54r; citing Gen 8:21; Lev 8:28.

[14]C. Spangenberg, *Die ander Epistel Pauli an die Corinthier*, 44v. [†]For Chrysostom's interpretation, see PG 61:430 (NPNF[1] 12:302).

[15]Downame, ed., *English Annotations*, FF3*. [†]For Chrysostom's interpretation, see PG 61:430 (NPNF[1] 12:302).

[16]Trapp, *A Commentary or Exposition*, 708*.

it is Hesperus, an evening star, by which they are brought to bed and put asleep in impiety—like those who send out a sweet savor from themselves. Annotations on 2 Corinthians 2:15.[17]

Faithful Ministry Is Fruitful Before God. John Calvin: Let us now learn by the example of the prophet [Jeremiah], that whenever Satan or our flesh raises an objection and says that we ought to desist from preaching celestial truth because it doesn't produce its proper and legitimate fruits, it is nevertheless a good odor before God, though fatal to the ungodly. Though then the truth of the gospel proves the savor of death to many, yet our labor is not on that account of no value before God; for we know that we offer to God an acceptable sacrifice; and though our labor is useless to others, it is yet fruitful as to the glory of God; and while we are the odor of death unto death to those who perish, yet to God, even in this respect, our labor is acceptable. Lecture on Jeremiah 20:9.[18]

The Gospel of Christ Is Both an Aroma of Life and of Death. Wolfgang Musculus: Wherever Paul was preaching the gospel of Christ and spreading its beautiful fragrance, he encountered different outcomes. Some people approved his message and embraced it by faith. These were the elect and those predestined for eternal life. Others disapproved of his message and rejected it. These were the reprobate and those perishing. Yet the aroma of Christ was intrinsically pleasant and, by the initiative of God, it was spread to the entire world through the preaching of the gospel, although to some it was the aroma of life to life, but for others is was the aroma of death to death. In the former, the fragrance by its intrinsic power was bringing about life; in the latter, because of their own sin and guilt, the fragrance was bringing about death.

Now it should not seem surprising that Paul calls the fragrance of Christ "good" not only for those who were saved by the good aroma of life but also for the reprobate who were perishing by the aroma of death, since Christ did not come into this world for either judgment or death. For it is also very common in human affairs that the same object, which is good and useful in itself, serves as good for some and evil for others; and in some affairs, a different and contrary result is intrinsically obtained. Love believes all things, hopes all things, trusts everyone, and is gentle, compassionate, and kind to everyone. . . And nevertheless, love is employed well by some and badly by others; it provokes some people to do good and gives other people an excuse for contempt and apathy. Medicine is good in itself, but still it is rendered useful for some people and harmful for others on account of the difference of the patients. Human knowledge, which is a singular gift of God, renders some people useful, but other people haughty and dangerous. So too wealth, which is a sign of divine favor, renders some people generous and others proud. The splendor of the sun illuminates some and blinds others. A beautiful fragrance, as one finds in a storeroom of spices and perfumes, refreshes some people and renders others depressed. So also Christ himself came bringing resurrection to some and ruin to others. Commentary on 2 Corinthians 2:16.[19]

The Gospel Both Judges and Blesses. Cyriacus Spangenberg: The sun gives light that is useful and good, but its light is repugnant to anyone who has bad eyes. Honey is sweet, but it nevertheless tastes very bitter to some sick people. Thus, the gospel is also good and precious. That it does not smell or taste good to all people is because of their wickedness. Inasmuch as the gospel judges these same people, its power comes to light just as much as when it makes others blessed.

In the same way then the gospel is today already an odor of death to death for all stubborn papists and enemies of the gospel. They might die for

[17]Leigh, *Annotations upon all the New Testament*, 257*.
[18]CTS 19:34* (CO 38:346).
[19]Musculus, *Commentarius . . . in posteriorem epistolam Pauli ad Corinthios*, 80.

wickedness, because we will not allow them their flea market, but attribute instead the righteousness of man before God as to faith alone in Jesus Christ. Eleventh Sermon.[20]

Scripture Is Full of Gospel Commendations Like This. Philipp Melanchthon: "Who is suitable for these things?" This here is the fourth passage in this letter concerning the ministry of the gospel. The opportunity presents itself when Paul begins speaking about ministers, saying "Who is suitable for these things?" Now this is a most excellent commendation of gospel ministry through which he teaches both from whence the power of ministry comes, and how it differs from the law. Commendations of gospel ministry of this sort are necessary for confirming the faith and strengthening consciences in courage, not only because the gospel is so novel and foreign to the flesh, but also because when consciences are afflicted one cannot magnify grace enough. The human mind always conceives God's mercy as a thing smaller and more restricted than it should. Hence, the prophets are full of gospel commendations of this sort: Isaiah 2, "Come, let us walk in the light of our God"; and Isaiah 52, "The Lord has bared his holy arm," that is, his Word, "before the eyes of all nations, and all the ends of the earth will see the salvation of our God"; and Psalm 68, "You will shed rain willingly upon your inheritance." Annotations on 2 Corinthians 2:16.[21]

Who Is Sufficient for These Things? John Trapp: And yet now, who does not think themselves sufficient for that sacred and terrifying function of the ministry? Moses said, "Who am I?" Our modern upstart says, "Who am I not?" It was with great difficulty that Bradford was persuaded to become a preacher. Latimer leapt in the air when he laid down his bishopric, since he had been discharged, as he said, of so heavy a burden. Luther used to say that if he were again to choose his calling, he would dig or do anything other than take upon himself the office of a minister. Commentary on 2 Corinthians 2:16.[22]

Gospel Doctrine Is Corrupted in Two Ways. John Calvin: I do not think it likely . . . that those people whom Paul here reproached openly preached doctrines that were wicked and false. Rather, I think that they corrupted the right use of doctrine for the sake of either gain or ambition, so as completely to deprive it of effectiveness. This Paul calls "adulterating." Erasmus prefers to call it "huckstering" (*cauponari*). The Greek word *kapēleuein* is drawn from retailers or tavern keepers, who falsify their wares so as to fetch a higher price. . . . For the doctrine of God is corrupted in two ways. It is corrupted *directly* when it is mixed up with falsehood and lies, so that it is no longer the pure and genuine doctrine of God, though it is commended with this false title. It is corrupted *indirectly* when, although it retains its purity, it is nevertheless twisted in different directions to please people and is disfigured by shameful flattery so as to chase after favor. Thus, some people are found whose doctrine is not impious, but either because they hunt after the world's applause by making a display of their cleverness or eloquence, or because they are ambitious for some position or pant after filthy lucre, or because they desire to gain power in some way—they thereby corrupt the doctrine itself by wrongly abusing it, or by making it subservient to their depraved desires. Commentary on 2 Corinthians 2:17.[23]

Four Conditions of a Suitable Minister. Philipp Melanchthon: There are . . . four conditions of a suitable apostle: First, [he speaks] "with sincerity," that is, he does not pervert the Word of God. Second, [he speaks] "from God," that

[20]C. Spangenberg, *Die ander Epistel Pauli an die Corinthier*, 47v.

[21]*Melanchthons Werke*, 4:99-100; citing Is 2:5; Is 52:10; Ps 68:9 (Vg. 67:10).

[22]Trapp, *A Commentary or Exposition*, 709*; citing Ex 3:11. Hugh Latimer* was an Anglican bishop critical of Catholic practices and social injustices. John Bradford* was an evangelical preacher and chaplain to Edward VI*. Both were martyred during the reign of Mary I*.

[23]CO 50:35 (CTS 40:162-63).

is, proclaiming the Word of God with as much certainty as other prophets. Hence, Jeremiah 5, "I am placing my word in your mouth"; and, Matthew 10, "It is not you yourself who speak." . . . Third, "in the sight of God," that is, I am not seeking to please people or focusing upon the judgment of human beings, but the judgment of God, as that passage in Galatians states: "If I were pleasing human beings, I would not be a servant of Christ." Fourth, "in Christ," that is, through the spirit and power of Christ. Here, Paul ascribes efficaciousness to the Word, as is also seen in that passage, "I will give you a mouth and wisdom that no one will be able to oppose"; and Isaiah 51: "I have put my words in your mouth, so that you might establish the heavens and lay the foundations of the earth" (which happens in the new creation); and Psalm 107: "He sent out his Word, and he healed them." Annotations on 2 Corinthians 2:17.[24]

Five Marks of Legitimate Ministry. Wolfgang Musculus: We find here . . . five sure marks of the legitimate ministry of a true minister of Christ. The first mark is found where Paul says, "we speak." Hence, those silent and false bishops who rule rather than preach are excluded. Paul expresses the second mark when he says, "in Christ." Every kind of teaching that does not relate to the subject of Christ is excluded. The third mark is found where Paul says, "as men of sincerity." . . . The one who preaches Christ purely and sincerely is he who mixes nothing foreign with the teaching of Christ. Every kind of admixture is excluded, whether it consists in human traditions, or the observance of the law, or the cunning of human wisdom. For who can count all the kinds of mixing with which the pure teaching of Christ has been vitiated from the times of the apostles until now? The fourth mark relates to Paul's words "but as men [commissioned] by God." That the true minister of Christ is established by divine rather than human authority is required, therefore, so that when he speaks in the church of God, it is as if he speaks the Words and oracles of God. Paul expresses the fifth mark when he says, "in the sight of God." Some things are spoken in the sight of and with regard to human beings. Other things are spoken in the sight of and with regard to God himself, who is everywhere present and who sees and hears everything we do and say. In the sight of human beings there is room for hypocrisy, deception, and bargaining—but not at all in the sight of God. When these marks are missing, we do not acknowledge that there is a minister of Christ. Commentary on 2 Corinthians 2:17.[25]

Preaching Is No Small Thing. Cyriacus Spangenberg: Faithful, upright teachers speak before God, that is, they know that God, Father, Son and Holy Spirit are always present when they speak of God or preach. Therefore, they also speak of God in the way they hope to answer to him at the last judgment. They teach in the way that they know God would have it, that they may stand before him. For God goes to all sermons and hears how and what we teach about him. Preachers should reflect on this. Therefore, it is no small thing to be a preacher. Eleventh Sermon.[26]

Against the Greed of Catholic Theologians. Argula von Grumbach:

> What you so long have plied
> God will no more abide;
> Deceiving rich and poor alike
> No one can possibly be your like:
> You wheel and deal, you strut around
> Affluence in your life abounds
> Yet dare to claim a spiritual name
> When all we see is greed and shame.
> And hypocritically market
> God's Word like some cheap trinket.
> Hear this! Paul boasts it's true,
> In Second Corinthians chapter two:

[24]*Melanchthons Werke*, 4:100; citing Jer 5:14; Mt 10:20; Gal 1:10; Lk 21:15; Is 51:6; Ps 107:20 (Vg. 106:20).

[25]Musculus, *Commentarius . . . in posteriorem epistolam Pauli ad Corinthios*, 82; citing 1 Pet 4:11.

[26]C. Spangenberg, *Die ander Epistel Pauli an die Corinthier*, 48v.

That Christians resembled not the many
Who aim in life to grab each penny.
In Christ, from God, he speaks;
Nothing he does is done for greed.
Speaks each word with honesty
Before God's face talks truthfully.
If the same thing you could do
Right joyously we'd follow you.
But you would lead us all astray;
Let the stones cry out today!
While you oppress God's Word and—Shame!
Consign souls to the devil's game
I cannot and I will not cease
To speak at home and on the street.
As long as God will give me grace
I'll tell my neighbor, face-to-face.
For Paul has not forbidden me,
Where God's Word cannot yet run free,
As sadly is the case with us.

An Answer in Verse to Johannes of Lanzhut.[27]

[27]Grumbach, *Argula von Grumbach*, 181-82. In this poem, Argula responds to a scurrilous poem published in 1524 by a theologian at the University of Ingolstadt named Johannes of Lanzhut, which had attacked her Protestant convictions and her outspoken defense of the evangelical message.

3:1-6 MINISTERS OF THE NEW COVENANT

Are we beginning to commend ourselves again? Or do we need, as some do, letters of recommendation to you, or from you? [2]You yourselves are our letter of recommendation, written on our[a] hearts, to be known and read by all. [3]And you show that you are a letter from Christ delivered by us, written not with ink but with the Spirit of the living God, not on tablets of stone but on tablets of human hearts.[b]

[4]Such is the confidence that we have through Christ toward God. [5]Not that we are sufficient in ourselves to claim anything as coming from us, but our sufficiency is from God, [6]who has made us sufficient to be ministers of a new covenant, not of the letter but of the Spirit. For the letter kills, but the Spirit gives life.

a Some manuscripts *your* b Greek *fleshly hearts*

Overview: Paul continues to defend his apostolic ministry by appealing to the example of the Corinthian believers themselves, whose lives have been transformed by the life-giving power of the Holy Spirit at work through the apostle's message of the new covenant. The Protestant reformers agree that Paul's primary concern in these verses is to extol the superiority of the new covenant of grace (written on human hearts by the Holy Spirit) over the old covenant of law (written on stone tablets with delible ink). The old covenant, with its countless regulations, could only coerce and compel men and women to right behavior, but it was powerless to change their hearts. By contrast, the new covenant of grace, of which Paul is a minister, brings about forgiveness of sins and spiritual life through God's powerful Spirit. In this regard, several Reformation exegetes rehearse the decisive role that the Holy Spirit plays in illumining the minds and transforming the hearts of sinners, thereby restoring God's image within them. Moreover, Paul's words in 2 Corinthians 3:5—"not that we are sufficient in ourselves"—is a clear reminder that the glorious salvation achieved through the new covenant is by God's grace alone, not by human ability or free will. So, too, it reminds Christian preachers that the ultimate effectiveness of their ministries does not come from their learning or eloquence, but through the power of God.

Finally, Paul's statement that "the letter kills, but the Spirit gives life" (2 Cor 3:6) prompts extensive and vigorous comment from Protestant interpreters. They uniformly reject the opinion of Origen and most medieval exegetes, who taught that this verse established the primary rule for interpreting Scripture, namely, to prioritize the spiritual or allegorical sense of the text ("the spirit") over the plain and literal meaning of the text ("the letter"). Instead, Protestant commentators insist that in 2 Corinthians 3:6 Paul is restating his previous argument regarding the superiority of the new covenant to the old. Whereas the old covenant of law was unable to change hearts, but could only "kill" sinners, the new covenant of grace imparted new life to men and women through the agency of the Holy Spirit.

Summary of Chapter 3. John Calvin: Now having made mention here of his journey to Macedonia, [Paul] begins to discuss the glory of his ministry. Nevertheless, because those frivolous "apostles" (who were attempting to disparage him) had easily prevailed over him by trumpeting their own praises, so that he might have nothing in common with them and at the same time might refute their foolish boasting, he declares that he obtains commendation from the work itself and does not derive it from human beings. In the same passage he extols in magnificent terms the efficacy of his preaching and magnifies the dignity of his apostleship by comparing the gospel to the law. However, first of all, he claims nothing as his own, but attributes everything, whatever it might be, to have come forth from God. Argument of 2 Corinthians 3.[1]

The Argument of Chapter 3. Wolfgang Musculus: In order to subdue the wickedness of the false apostles, who were becoming proud about many things related to the Mosaic law and defiling the purity of the gospel of Christ, [Paul] extolls his apostolic office inasmuch as the ministry of the new covenant is above the ministry of the law. Argument of Chapter 3.[2]

The Splendor of Gospel Preaching. Giovanni Diodati: St. Paul protests to the Corinthians that what he said in praise of his ministry was in no way intended to exalt himself, nor to seek the favor of other people, since his ministry had sufficient approval by the divine power of his apostleship, especially in the case of their church. And he recognizes that all this comes completely from God. But, given the fact that God wished to glorify by a divine light the preaching of the gospel—above that of the law—he did not wish, nor could he, suppress this splendor, which, although it was unknown to the Jews, was displayed by him with all clarity for the illumination, regeneration, and salvation of the children of God. Annotations on 2 Corinthians 3.[3]

The Ministry of the Holy Spirit. Argula von Grumbach:

> Only God's Spirit, extolled by Paul,
> In these words instructs us all:
> The Holy Spirit we received
> Out of this world did not proceed;
> Rather the Spirit God has sent
> That we might not stay ignorant;
> Clearly the Spirit to us explains
> What by God's gift we have gained.
> In chapter 3 we are acclaimed,
> The temple of the Lord we're named.
> "God's Spirit is within you" read.
> Is woman shut out, there, indeed?

An Answer in Verse to Johannes of Lanzhut.[4]

3:1-3 *Paul's Recommendation Letter*

Paul Was Not Promoting Himself. Jacques Lefèvre d'Étaples: Now, when Paul says that "we are not peddlers of the Word of God" as many are, "but as much as we speak with sincerity, we speak in Christ in the sight of God and on behalf of God," someone might perhaps conclude that, in saying this, Paul is beginning to commend, praise, and promote himself. This is by no means the case. Rather, he is speaking the truth openly and sincerely, attributing honor not to himself but to God, yes indeed, God, who was working through him and his followers. . . . Paul was not ignorant of the Corinthians, nor the Corinthians of Paul, for Paul had written them so many heartfelt letters. Thus, he was pursuing them with a strong and intimate love of heart and was inscribing upon their minds the teaching of the Holy Spirit; and (as he commended himself to them) he was not seeking the approval of other people. Commentary on 2 Corinthians 3:1.[5]

The Superiority of Paul's Gospel Ministry. Tilemann Hesshus: Although Satan's deceits and deceptions are innumerable (by which

[1]CO 50:6 (CTS 40:104).
[2]Musculus, *Commentarius . . . in posteriorem epistolam Pauli ad Corinthios*, 81.
[3]Diodati, *La Seconde Epistre de . . . S. Paul aux Corinthiens*, 139.
[4]Grumbach, *Argula von Grumbach*, 178; citing 1 Cor 3:16. In this poem, Argula responds to a scurrilous poem published in 1524 by a theologian at the University of Ingolstadt named Johannes of Lanzhut, which had attacked her Protestant convictions and her outspoken defense of the evangelical message.
[5]Lefèvre, *Commentariorum in Epistolas Beati Pauli . . . Liber Tertius*, 132.

he constantly plots against human salvation in every way), nevertheless, these schemes are very common, persistent, and very familiar: to defile with insults; to sow mistrust with lies; to make offensive the pure and godly proclamation of the Word by calumnies. For Satan knows that the world delights in these "treats" and through the person of ministers he attacks Christ and his doctrine. Once Satan has disparaged the reputation and authority of the minister's word by means of calumnies, then it is not difficult for him to instill in the hearers contempt and hatred for the minister's teaching. When he has succeeded in sowing such deception, he has no difficulty in hindering the salvation of men and women and filling them with errors and indignation. To counter this, therefore, apostles and godly pastors should endeavor with as much zeal as they can to commend to their listeners the glory, effectiveness, usefulness, and splendor of the ministry, and to imbue them with love and reverence for it. For all of our salvation depends upon the Word of God. In the Word God reveals himself. Through the Word, God works in us. By means of the Word we are strengthened against Satan's tricks and insults. By the Word and Spirit, God confers upon us life and salvation. . . .

This is the reason why Paul so extensively commends the character of his ministry. The false apostles were not only maligning the person of the apostle but also disparaging Paul's ministry. By contrast, they were extolling with much acclaim the ministry of the law and the old covenant. And they were employing a very plausible argument: Moses had displayed the glory of the law and the old covenant with many miracles; the law had been announced with wondrous spectacles; God had provided the people of Israel with many victories; God had often revealed to the people his glory in the desert; the prophets' authority and wisdom had been great; a powerful kingdom had been established in the old covenant. But Paul, who was abrogating the law and proclaiming only Christ, was not very glorious; there was hardly anyone in the world more ill-starred than he was, and his teaching was accompanied by disgrace, dangers, and afflictions. In response to this scoffing, therefore, Paul presents an extraordinary rebuttal. Concerning his personal modesty, he responds that he has not praised his ministry from ambition or pride, for he freely acknowledges his weakness; in fact, he ascribes all things to God. But nevertheless, his faithfulness in ministry is so apparent that he does not need to be commended by the Corinthians, nor to them. He rejoices in his conscience concerning the fruit of his ministry and he appeals to the whole church to acknowledge it as well. Now, he commends the glory, power, and effectiveness of his apostolic service so much because he prefers it by far to the ministry of the law and the whole old covenant. For this reason, he lowers himself, finally, to explain the difference between the new and old covenant. Explication of 2 Corinthians 3.[6]

The Value of a Recommendation. Wolfgang Musculus: Now in saying this, Paul is not condemning the use of recommendation, which was always useful and is still useful in the church as long as the practice is preserved in a healthy and legitimate manner. Paul himself needed a recommendation at first, following his conversion, so that he might be commended to the brothers, and this was done by Barnabas. Paul also, as much as it was in him, in his letters to the churches recommended his friends, especially men such as Timothy and Titus whom he considered to be his fellow workers. But once Paul had gained authority among all the churches, and once those whom he had recommended were rightly accepted as such, then he attempted neither to commend himself by letter, nor to seek a recommendation from others. In general, for a person that is unknown, letters of recommendation serve as proof, at least to those to whom one is recommended. Commentary on 2 Corinthians 3:1.[7]

[6]Hesshus, *Explicatio Secundae Epistolae Pauli ad Corinthios*, 57v-58r, 58v-59v.

[7]Musculus, *Commentarius . . . in posteriorem epistolam Pauli ad Corinthios*, 84.

Paul's Ministry in Corinth Serves as His Commendation. Huldrych Zwingli: Some false apostles were arguing in this manner: "Don't you see that Paul is doing nothing but commending himself? Why does he write so many letters, if not to make himself great among you?" Paul responds to these words, saying, "Am I commending myself again, as your apostles assert, as if we really needed letters of recommendation to you (as some say), or to be commended by your letters to others? We do not need letters of this sort, since the labor that we have performed is what commends us." The city of Corinth was filled with all kinds of wickedness and sin, engulfed with all kinds of delights and sinful pleasures. "Through the preaching of the gospel, I snatched you out of the jaws of the devil and converted you to Christ; I led you from a life of impurity to a life of purity and innocence. Those of you who had previously served idols and demons, I brought to the true worship of the one true God. And so, those who were previously far from the knowledge of God, have now been made rich in every word and knowledge so that their faith now draws others to the knowledge of God. These are the letters that I produce and point to for my recommendation when it is necessary. Your faith and piety—which all people everywhere can see and observe—adequately demonstrate that I am no less an apostle." With these words (which serve as a shameful reproach), Paul discretely stirs up and stimulates their faith. Annotations on 2 Corinthians 3:1.[8]

Paul's Letter of Recommendation. Desiderius Erasmus: We are so confident about your attitude toward us that, self-recommended by our exercise of duty, we do not stand in need of letters of recommendation from people, so long as you show by sincerity of faith and evangelical life that you are the epistle of Christ, written by him indeed, but through our ministry. . . . Your minds, on which we imprinted evangelical doctrine, served as parchment for us, our tongue as pen, but Christ himself dictated through his Spirit what we were to write. Paraphrases on 2 Corinthians 3.[9]

Paul's Ministry Was the Pencil in the Spirit's Hand. Martin Luther: Inasmuch as Paul's activity among them is his testimonial, and they themselves are aware that through his ministerial office he has constituted them a church, he calls them an epistle written by himself; not with ink and in paragraphs, not on paper or wood, nor engraved upon hard rock as the Ten Commandments written upon tables of stone, which Moses placed before the people, but written by the Holy Spirit upon fleshly tables—hearts of tender flesh. The Spirit is the ink or the inscription, yes, even the writer himself; but the pencil or pen and the hand of the writer is the ministry of Paul. Sermon on the Twelfth Sunday After Trinity.[10]

The Corinthians Were Paul's "Letter." Wolfgang Musculus: Paul gives the reason why he did not provide a letter of recommendation. He says, "because you yourselves serve amply as a letter by which I might recommend myself." Now how were the Corinthians a letter for Paul? Not insofar as they were human beings; nor because they were people who were rich, poor, or wise. . . . But insofar as they were Christians, regenerated by the Word of the gospel in Christ, to this extent they were his letter of recommendation. For through Paul's apostleship they had become Christians. Thus, it is for each and every bishop, that the product of his labor in the church of Christ is the letter by which he will be either commended or declared guilty. This manner of life, this building up or destroying of the church declares a more certain word about a bishop than any letter. The book of deeds is clearer than the book of words and letters.

Paul [next] develops and explains the metaphor of the letter. Now it had to be explained with what

[8]Zwingli, *Annotatiunculae . . . ex ore Zvinglij*, 155-56.

[9]CWE 43:215.

[10]Luther, *Sermons of Martin Luther*, 8:225.

sort of papyrus or writing tablet, with what ink, and by what kind of writing instrument the letter was written; and then for what purpose and from whom this letter was delivered, and how it should be read and understood. To explain these things, Paul says, "Written on our hearts," which in Greek reads *en tais kardiais hēmōn*, that is, written on *our* hearts. This is a clear error in that the single letter *upsilon* [υ] has been replaced by the letter *eta* [η]. For this passage ought to be read *en tais kardiais hymōn* [written on *your* hearts]. I realize that Chrysostom† and other interpreters read and explain the phrase as "on our [*hēmōn*] hearts," with some believing it refers to those who were with Paul, and others believing it referred to both the Corinthians and to Paul. But it is more likely that the apostle is speaking about the hearts of the Corinthians, especially if the flow of his argument is considered. . . . By a "letter," Paul understands Christian faith, attitude, and piety. This was written on their hearts, like a writing tablet, and Paul was commending his work as an apostle among them, by whom they had become Christians. Commentary on 2 Corinthians 3:2.[11]

The Fruit of Paul's Apostolic Service. Tilemann Hesshus: Paul says, "because you were converted to Christ through my ministry and your faith is celebrated all over among the churches, that fact alone fully recommends my teaching and labors." By means of a clear figure of speech, he says that the Corinthian church, which had been gathered by Paul's preaching, is a letter written on Paul's heart—which, nevertheless, is being read by all people. Now, he indicates that he is not looking for personal acclaim, nor is he seeking to flit about for some praise from the mouth of men and women. Rather, he is content with the testimony of his conscience, which rejoices in the fruit of his apostolic service. For, by his labors, he has gathered a holy church for Christ, in which the knowledge of God shines forth, and which is going to be victorious with God for eternity. He not only appeals to the testimony of his conscience, but he also rejoices in the fruit of their labors which is seen by the whole church. For, since the Corinthians' faith in Christ was proclaimed everywhere, the whole church saw that Paul was executing his apostolic office with great fruit. Explication of 2 Corinthians 3:2.[12]

Read by All. Cardinal Cajetan: [Here we see] the extraordinary and most impressive characteristic of this commendation letter of Paul. Certainly, it is greatly superior to other letters. For no letter, whether written in Hebrew, or Greek, or Latin, is understood and read by everyone, but only by those who recognize the characters and the language. But this present letter is read and understood by all people. Commentary on 2 Corinthians 3:2.[13]

The Preacher's Testimonial. John Trapp: The fruitfulness of the people is the preacher's testimonial; as the profiting of the student is the teacher's commendation. Commentary on 2 Corinthians 3:2.[14]

Paul's Ministry Witnessed the Life-Giving Spirit. Philipp Melanchthon: "Not with ink, but with the Spirit of the living God." By the word "ink" (which below Paul expresses with the word "letter"), Paul means not only human traditions, but also divine law and clearly all doctrine insofar as it is heard, learned, and practiced by human calculation without the life-giving Spirit. Paul therefore includes this sentence: "you yourself are a letter," that is, "you are witnesses to the fact that you are receiving from my ministry not only doctrine, but also the Holy Spirit; and you are being made righteous. You are

[11]Musculus, *Commentarius . . . in posteriorem epistolam Pauli ad Corinthios*, 85. †For Chrysostom's interpretation, see PG 62:436-37 (NPNF[1] 12:306).

[12]Hesshus, *Explicatio Secundae Epistolae Pauli ad Corinthios*, 60v-61r.

[13]Cajetan, *In posteriorem Pauli Epistolam ad Corinthios Commentarii*, 158.

[14]Trapp, *A Commentary or Exposition*, 709*.

our recommendation letter that my ministry among you was effective—and truly it was from God." And just as Paul contrasts ink and Spirit, so he also contrasts stone tablets and fleshly tablets. Tablets of stone are human strength without the life-giving Spirit of God. . . . Tablets of the heart of flesh are living receptacles of the Holy Spirit, infused with the strength of heart and invigorating all human strength. Paul's discussion is dependent on Ezekiel 11. Here is the summary of his argument: Because my ministry was effective in you, you are my letter of recommendation; that is, you are witnesses that my word is true and is from God. Annotations on 2 Corinthians 3:3.[15]

Christians Are to Be a Public Letter. Wolfgang Musculus: Paul explains how his letter is to be read and understood by everyone. He does not say, "you are a letter from Christ," but "you demonstrate that you are a letter from Christ"; that is, "you demonstrate before the eyes of all that you are a Christian by your profession of faith and the manner of your life." Here not only the Christians' internal faith of heart but also the entire manner of their life and public profession of religion is praised by the apostle, and he calls it a letter from Christ, which is read and understood by all people, not only believers, but also every other person. That is why the Christian is compared to a letter from Christ. This letter is not written with imaginary or invisible letters, but with letters that are entirely distinct and visible, so that it can be read and understood by all. But today one finds Christians who imagine that it is enough to be Christians in the heart, and so their writing cannot be read and is hidden from the understanding of all other people, and it is known only by God. But Paul writes otherwise concerning the letter from Christ. . . . This letter from Christ must be demonstrated, not hidden, for it is light not darkness. Commentary on 2 Corinthians 3:3.[16]

Tablets of Stone and Tablets of Flesh. Cyriacus Spangenberg: He shows on what, or in what, the letter of Christ is written. "Not on stone tablets, but on tablets of flesh." Here he begins to differentiate the preaching of the old and new covenants. The old covenant is all that drives, necessitates, and compels, all that creates aversion and reluctance. This is why it says, "I command, forbid and curse. . . ." But the new covenant is all that is done with desire and will, uncoerced, unforced. The former he now calls stone tablets, and the latter tablets of flesh. Stone tablets are human capacities without the Spirit, ink written on stone and wood; they are human thoughts, hypocrisy, false trust in our own works. Writing on stone is useless. The ink does not remain. Human capacities are worth little in the things of God.

Tablets of the flesh written on through the Spirit are living vessels of the Holy Spirit, true Christians, in whom the Holy Spirit lives by faith and brings to life all their thoughts, words, and work, and gives them the will and desire to keep what God has commanded them. This is then called the letter of Christ. Twelfth Sermon.[17]

The Spirit's Ministry Is Superior to Philosophy and the Mosaic Law. Tilemann Hesshus: When Paul says, "not with ink," he announces what a great difference there is between philosophy, discipline, doctrine, and human custom on the one hand, and the ministry of the Spirit on the other. Even if philosophy and human custom teach virtue, prevent wickedness, and train men and women for respectable manners, nevertheless they do not impart new light; they do not show who God is; they do not convert the minds of men and women; they do not produce new life—they are just like a dead letter, written in ink. Even if Plato, Themistocles, Laelius, and Scipio strove for virtue through their great character, their excellent teaching, and the greatest zeal, nevertheless they were foreign to the true knowledge of God and devoid of spiritual

[15]*Melanchthons Werke*, 4:101; citing Ezek 11:19-21.

[16]Musculus, *Commentarius . . . in posteriorem epistolam Pauli ad Corinthios*, 86.

[17]C. Spangenberg, *Die ander Epistel Pauli an die Corinthier*, 51v-52r.

life—just like a letter written in ink.† By contrast, the Corinthians were a letter written by the Spirit of the living God. For the Holy Spirit himself is powerful in the message of the gospel; he illumines the mind with the true knowledge of God; he has restored men and women lost through sin; he creates spiritual life anew; he bathes men and women with heavenly joy and transforms them into God's image. Paul has no doubt reflected upon the passage in Jeremiah 31: "This is the covenant that I will make with the house of Israel after those days: I will put my law within them, and I will write it on their hearts. And I will be their God, and they shall be my people." But Paul adds, "not on tablets of stone," to indicate that the ministry of the Spirit must be distinguished not only from human philosophy and teachings, but even from the old covenant and the law itself. The law promulgated on Mount Sinai explained the will of God and taught virtue even more perfectly than any philosophy. Nevertheless, it did not restore God's image to us, nor did it confer life and the Spirit; rather, it abandoned us to death. For the law is written on tablets of stone, that is, our depraved hearts were hardened to God's voice, just like stones. But through the ministry of the gospel, the Holy Spirit removes the heart of stone, as it says in Ezekiel [*sic*, Jeremiah], and gives a heart of flesh, that is, makes it soft and pliant for obeying God's voice. Paul indicates, therefore, how powerful and glorious the ministry of the gospel is, because it creates completely new men and women, just as if it transformed statues into living and thinking human beings. EXPLICATION OF 2 CORINTHIANS 3:3.[18]

THE SPIRIT AND MINISTERS WORK DIFFERENTLY. HEINRICH BULLINGER: We must diligently put a difference between the work of the Spirit and the work of man or of the minister. The minister does not take on himself the honor of God and the work of the Spirit, but his own work, that is to say, the minister. Paul preaches and writes with ink, but the Spirit of God moves the heart; and with his grace, or anointing, he writes on the very heart; so he works together with God, Paul working his proper work, and the Spirit working his work. DECADES.[19]

A LETTER OF FLESH. WOLFGANG MUSCULUS: "Not on tablets of stone but on tablets of fleshly hearts." Paul begins to address the difference between the old and new covenants for the purpose of extolling his apostleship against the false apostles [and] the superiority of his ministry to the Mosaic law. The law of Moses, which was most beneficial in its function, was written on tablets of stone. But the gospel of Christ was inscribed, not on tablets of stone, but on hearts, which are tablets of flesh. Paul uses the word "fleshly" to distinguish them from stones. Therefore, he subtly criticizes the false apostles at this point because they were making the ministry of the Mosaic law so important that they thought that they needed to oppose the ministry of the gospel of Christ. It is as if Paul were saying, "Your teachers wish to be known as zealous imitators of the law and they are impassioned by its name. But they are blind so that they cannot see that you are a living letter, written on your hearts by the Spirit of the living God." This writing is more effective than the law of Moses that was once carved into stone tablets, as the prophet has written: "This is the covenant that I will make with the house of Israel. After that time, declares the Lord, I will give my law in their midst and I will write it on their hearts. I will be their God and they will be my people." COMMENTARY ON 2 CORINTHIANS 3:3.[20]

[18]Hesshus, *Explicatio Secundae Epistolae Pauli ad Corinthios*, 62r-63r; citing Jer 31:33. †Plato (c. 428 BC–c. 348 BC) was an Athenian philosopher. Themistocles (c. 524 BC–c. 460 BC) was an Athenian politician. Gaius Laelius (c. 235 BC–c. 160 BC) was a Roman politician and military leader. Publius Cornelius Scipio Africanus (c. 236 BC–183 BC) was a Roman general and consul.

[19]Bullinger, *Decades*, 2:100*.

[20]Musculus, *Commentarius . . . in posteriorem epistolam Pauli ad Corinthios*, 87-88; citing Jer 31:33.

3:4-5 *Sufficient Ministers of the New Covenant*

TRUE PREACHERS ARE COMMISSIONED BY GOD. MARTIN LUTHER: These words are blows and thrusts for the false apostles and preachers. Paul is a mortal enemy to the blockheads who make great boast, pretending to what they do not possess and to what they cannot do; who boast of having the Spirit in great measure; who are ready to counsel and aid the whole world; who pride themselves on the ability to invent something new. It is to be a surpassingly precious and heavenly thing they are to spin out of their heads, as the dreams of pope and monks have been in time past.

"We do not do this," says Paul. "We do not rely upon ourselves or our wisdom and ability. We preach not what we have ourselves invented. But this is our boast and trust in Christ before God, that we have made of you a divine epistle; have written upon your hearts, not our thoughts, but the Word of God. We are not, however, glorifying our own power, but the works and the power of him who has called and equipped us for such an office; from whom proceeds all you have heard and believed."

It is a glory which every preacher may claim, to be able to say with full confidence of heart: "This trust have I toward God in Christ, that what I teach and preach is truly the Word of God." Likewise, when he performs other official duties in the church—baptizes a child, absolves and comforts a sinner—it must be done in the same firm conviction that such is the command of Christ. SERMON ON THE TWELFTH SUNDAY AFTER TRINITY.[21]

OUR SUFFICIENCY COMES FROM GOD ALONE. JOHN CALVIN: For inasmuch as we are corrupted by original sin, we are like a dry and barren ground that cannot produce any good fruit. For our judgment is perverse; our will is rebellious against God, inclined and given to evil: in sum, our entire nature is vicious. Being such, not only do we not have the power to apply ourselves to good, but, what is more, as St. Paul says, we are incapable of conceiving of a single good thought, rather all our sufficiency must come from him. . . . It is he who illumines us that we might come to his knowledge; it is he who pulls us up; it is he who creates new hearts in us, softening our hardness; it is he who inspires us to pray; it is he who gives us the grace and the strength to resist all of Satan's temptations; it is he who causes us to walk in his commandments. TREATISE AGAINST THE SPIRITUAL LIBERTINES.[22]

SALVATION COMES FROM GOD'S POWER, NOT HUMAN POWER. DAVID CHYTRAEUS: It is not by human power that the preaching of the gospel works for salvation to everyone who believes; nor is it due to the worthiness and power of the ministers or preachers that the true knowledge of God, righteousness, and eternal life are wrought in the hearts of the hearers by the word of the gospel. Rather, it is by the working of God himself who, through the ministry and preaching of his Word, kindles godly thoughts, or the light of the true knowledge of Christ, which is faith, and quickens or transforms our hearts and minds into the same likeness, that they may be made partakers of the light and life of God. And therefore Paul says, "Such is the confidence we have through Christ toward God, not that we are sufficient in ourselves to claim anything as coming from us, but our sufficiency comes from God." It is as if Paul were saying, "Whereas I confess that you Corinthians, having been converted by my preaching, bear witness of my faithfulness and disprove the slanders of the false apostles, I say this, not trusting in my own strength, but only in God, who worked mightily through my preaching." And particularly, this statement of Paul teaches us the weakness of human free will or self-power, which is so poisoned, weakened, and condemned with the venom of sin that of its own strength it can neither perform the

[21]Luther, *Sermons of Martin Luther*, 8:226-27*.

[22]CO 7:190-91; citing 2 Cor 3:5; Ezek 36:27.

righteousness that God desires nor attain forgiveness of sins and salvation, nor conceive of anything that pleases God or may be helpful in converting or justifying oneself. . . . As Paul also says in 1 Corinthians 2, "The natural person does not perceive the things that are of God's Spirit." Postil on the Twelfth Sunday After Trinity.[23]

No Room Is Left for Free Will. Cyriacus Spangenberg: Here nothing at all is left to humans or to free will, which they could do well from themselves. For the least of all good works is a good thought or a good urge. Again, St. Paul says that humans cannot have such good thoughts or urges from themselves, as the Pelagians[†] wish to affirm, and the teachers who lay before others that humans can prepare themselves for grace from their own abilities and free will make themselves capable of the same and accept it when they wish; again, that humans can begin to become pious, but God must bring the same to completion. But as Paul says, "We are not competent in ourselves to claim anything." How then could we oppose him? And Philippians 1: "God, who has begun his good work in you, will also bring it to completion." And Philippians 2: "It is God who works in you both to will and to do according to his good pleasure." And Isaiah 26: "All that we accomplish, Lord, you have granted to us." Twelfth Sermon.[24]

The Ancient Church Rejected Free Will. Heinrich Bullinger: All our power is from God, who also works in us. This is a choice and effective passage against those people who attribute justification to human strength, who defend free will to this end and place human effort above grace. The Synod of Milventana rightly decreed the following from this passage of Paul: "If anyone thinks that through natural strength a person can do a good work (as pertains to salvation to eternal life) that is useful either to elect or to save, that is, if anyone affirms that it is possible to agree to evangelical proclamation without the illumination and inspiration of the Holy Spirit (who gives to all the goodness for consenting to and believing the truth), they are deceived by a heretical spirit, and do not recognize God's voice in the gospel, saying 'Without me you can do nothing,' and that passage of the apostle, 'Not that we are sufficient in ourselves to claim anything as coming from us, but our sufficiency is from God.'"[†] Commentary on 2 Corinthians 3:5.[25]

Our Sufficiency Comes from God Alone. Wolfgang Musculus: "But if in anything we are sufficient, it is from God." In saying this, Paul gave credit to God for every capacity that enabled him to accomplish those things about which he wrote. He did not say, "but if in so many great and considerable things we are sufficient," but rather, "but if in *anything* we are sufficient." It was as if he were saying, "However minute, it is from God not from ourselves." What then remains for Paul to boast about in his strength when he clearly says: if we are able to do anything, it is not from ourselves but from God? Absolutely nothing. . . .

This is one of those passages that refutes the supposition of free will. For if the apostle, who had been trained in the law of the Lord from childhood and, through the strictest discipline of the sect of the Pharisees, had been nourished in a respectable manner of life to the point that he was hostile to all spiritual and heavenly things; if this apostle did not think that any of those things were sufficient in themselves, how will we grant to other people the capacity of free will to do good out of the strength of human nature? Now that which Paul said concerning his apostleship, we appropriately apply to ourselves regarding true piety, faith, hope, love,

[23]Chytraeus, *A Postil of Certeine Epistles*, 313*; citing 1 Cor 2:14.
[24]C. Spangenberg, *Die ander Epistel Pauli an die Corinthier*, 52v; citing Phil 1:6, 2:13; Is 26:12. [†]Pelagians were followers of the British monk Pelagius (born c. 360), who was confronted by Augustine and condemned by the Synod of Carthage (418) for rejecting the doctrine of original sin and affirming instead that human beings possess unhindered free will and are able to achieve salvation without God's grace.

[25]Bullinger, *In posteriorem d. Pauli ad Corinthios epistolam commentarius*, 275; citing Jn 15:5. [†]Bullinger appears to be referring to canon 7 from the Council of Orange (529).

the fear of God, obedience, and the sanctity of life, and so on. . . .

Let us first be reminded from this passage who it is that makes the minister of the divine Word sufficient. It is God, of course, who calls them and also sends them. Those whom he does not make sufficient will never be sufficient no matter how well-learned and eloquent they might be. Paul was learned in the law, having been instructed at the feet of Gamaliel, and at the same time he had an extraordinary zeal for God. Nevertheless, he would not have been sufficient to be a minister of the new covenant if God had not graciously made him sufficient for this out of his kindness. Now if learning and eloquence do not make a minister of the church sufficient, how will an illiterate and uncultured man be sufficient? (Which is not to say that they are lazy men.) Learning [in itself] is vain. That person is sufficient whom God makes sufficient. Even so, education is of value. For, even after his calling, this same apostle did not belittle his training, and he urged Timothy to devote himself to the reading of the sacred writings. It is inappropriate, therefore, for laziness and stupidity to defend the necessity of heavenly grace, just as it is inappropriate for learning and knowledge to dismiss the necessity of God's grace. Commentary on 2 Corinthians 3:5.[26]

The Apostles Depended on God to Impart His Message. Martin Bucer: It is certainly true that prophets under the impulse of God's Spirit and later apostles moved by the same Spirit were commissioned and sent to us as interpreters of the divine will before anything was contained in writing. They themselves in fact gave us writings, so that in some sense the church, of which they were members, can be said to be prior to Scripture. But as Paul himself bears witness in 2 Corinthians 3, however great their holiness as interpreters and messengers of God, they never even imagined that they were sufficient of themselves to effect in the elect their recognition of their messages as the oracles of God or unquestioning assent to them. On Faith.[27]

Ministers Must Pray and Preach. John Trapp: "Our sufficiency is from God." Do ministers then not need to pray? "To pray well is to study well," said Luther. "I cannot say whether ministers do more good to others by their prayers or by their preaching," says a reverend writer, "but they shall certainly by their prayers reap more comfort for themselves." To this I add that unless they pray for their hearers, as well as preach to them, they may preach to as little purpose as did Bede when he preached to a heap of stones.† So, too, if people do not pray for their ministers . . . they may thank themselves for their ministers' insufficiency, and their own non-proficiency. Commentary on 2 Corinthians 3:5.[28]

3:6 *The New Covenant, the Letter, and the Spirit*

The Old and New Covenants. Desiderius Erasmus: If we were or are in any way sufficient, our sufficiency comes from the kindness of God who is working within us. And he has appointed us to this office of dispensing the new covenant that we might impart to you, not the old covenant which is broken and located in the letter whose administration was assigned to Moses, but the new covenant, which is spiritual and heavenly, located in the heart not in ceremonies. Now the author who appointed [us] is not different; rather, it is the apostolic function that is different and far superior. For the letter, with its prescribed laws,

[26]Musculus, *Commentarius . . . in posteriorem epistolam Pauli ad Corinthios*, 89-90.

[27]CPMB 187.

[28]Trapp, *A Commentary or Exposition*, 710*. †The thirteenth-century author Jacobus de Voragine described in the seventh book of his *Golden Legend* an incident where St. Bede, blind in old age, was led by his servant to a field of huge boulders. Bede preached so powerfully to these rocks that, at the end of his sermon, they answered in unison "Amen." See Jacobus de Voragine, *Golden Legend* 7, Medieval Sourcebook, Fordham University, sourcebooks.fordham.edu/basis/goldenlegend/GoldenLegend-Volume7.asp (accessed October 5, 2021).

which was entrusted to Moses, plunged [humanity] into death, since it provokes the desire for sinning, and punishes the sinner with capital punishment. By contrast, the Spirit, which is conferred through the gospel message, provides life by pardoning all the sins committed in our previous life which merited death. Paraphrase on 2 Corinthians 3:5-6.[29]

Ministers of the New Covenant. John Calvin: There is no doubt that by the term "letter" Paul means the old covenant, as by the term "spirit" he means the gospel. For, since he has called himself a minister of the new covenant, he immediately adds by way of explanation, that he is a minister of the spirit, and contrasts the letter to the spirit. We must now inquire into the reason for this designation. That explanation contrived by Origen has predominated, that by the "letter" we ought to understand the grammatical and genuine sense of Scripture (which they call the letter), and by the "spirit" is meant the allegorical meaning, which is commonly considered the spiritual meaning.[†] Accordingly, during several centuries, nothing was more commonly said or more generally received than this, that Paul provides here the key for explaining Scripture by means of allegory—which, nevertheless, is completely foreign to his intentions. For by the term "letter" he means the outward proclamation which does not touch the heart; and by the term "spirit" he means living doctrine which powerfully affects the minds of men and women through the grace of the Spirit. By the term "letter," therefore, he means the preaching of the letter, that is, preaching that is dead and ineffectual, which is only comprehended by the ear. But the term "spirit" means spiritual doctrine, that is, what is not only uttered with the mouth but powerfully penetrates the souls of men and women with a lively feeling. . . . For this reason, Paul gives to the law the name "letter," because it is in itself dead preaching; and he gives to the gospel the name "spirit," because its ministry is living, indeed, life-giving. Commentary on 2 Corinthians 3:6.[30]

Paul Was a Minister of the New Covenant. Huldrych Zwingli: It is possible that someone might say, "Really? God has established another covenant?" Paul responds, "I called myself a minister of a new covenant, not to suggest that God has acted differently or established a different covenant. Rather, the old covenant was nothing other than the letter by which we were put to death—so that you might not strive after it. Christ, however, revivifies the hearts of believers by his Spirit." Now since humans are filled with fleshly lusts, they cannot help but be terrified and completely lose heart when they hear this command: "Do not lust." But when they have been given the Spirit of the heavenly Father, who awakens them spiritually, revives them, and gives them new life, then they see and experience the mercy of God which has been promised and presented to us in his beloved Son Christ. For this is the gospel that restores and makes glad despairing consciences. Paul says that he is a minister of this covenant in the same way that Moses was a minister of the killing letter. Annotations on 2 Corinthians 3:6.[31]

Spirit and Letter. Martin Luther: This passage relative to spirit and letter has in the past been wholly strange language to us. Indeed, to such extent has people's nonsensical interpretation perverted and weakened it that I, though a learned doctor of the holy Scriptures, failed to understand it altogether, and I could find no one to teach me. And to this day it is unintelligible to all popedom. In fact, even the old teachers—Origen, Jerome, and others—have not caught Paul's thought. And no

[29]Erasmus, *Paraphrases*, 367-68.

[30]CO 50:39, 40 (CTS 40:172, 173). [†]For Origen's hermeneutical principles, see *De Principiis* 4 and Henri de Lubac, *History and Spirit: The Understanding of Scripture According to Origen*, trans. Anne Englund Nash (San Francisco: Ignatius Press, 1997). For Origen's influence on medieval interpretation, see de Lubac, *Medieval Exegesis*, trans. Matt Sebanc and E. M. Macierowski, 3 vols. (Grand Rapids: Eerdmans, 1998–2009).

[31]Zwingli, *Annotatiunculae . . . ex ore Zvinglij*, 157-58.

wonder, truly! For it is essentially a doctrine far beyond the power of human intelligence to comprehend. When human reason meddles with it, it becomes perplexed. The doctrine is wholly unintelligible to it, for human thought goes no farther than the law and the Ten Commandments. Laying hold upon these it confines itself to them. It does not attempt to do more, being governed by the principle that unto him who fulfills the demands of the law or commandments, God is gracious. Reason knows nothing about the wretchedness of depraved nature. It does not recognize the fact that no one is able to keep God's commandments; that all are under sin and condemnation; and that the only way whereby help could be received was for God to give his Son for the world, ordaining another ministration, one through which grace and reconciliation might be proclaimed to us. Now, he who does not understand the sublime subject to which Paul speaks cannot but miss the true meaning of his words. How much more did we invite this fate when we threw the Scriptures and St. Paul's epistles under the bench, and, like swine in the husks, wallowed in human nonsense. Therefore, we must submit to correction and learn to understand the apostle's utterance aright. Sermon on the Twelfth Sunday After Trinity.[32]

Slain by the Letter. Argula von Grumbach:

> In Second Corinthians chapter 3,
> Paul shows in our humanity
> We're slain by the letter of the law,
> Unless the Spirit in us lives.
> In this chapter, he let us know
> The Lord is Spirit, he tells us so.
> That none of us God ever sees
> Unless the Father draws us nigh.
> To whom I, too, have had to fly.
> We must be taught by God alone
> As Christ to me has clearly shown.
> It's in John 6 and furthermore,
> It's in Isaiah 54.

An Answer in Verse to Johannes of Lanzhut.[33]

The Ancient Church Misunderstood This Passage. Martin Luther: "Letter" and "spirit" have been understood to mean, according to Origen and Jerome, the obvious sense of the written Word. St. Augustine, it must be admitted, has got an inkling of the truth. Now, the position of the former teachers would perhaps not be quite incorrect did they correctly explain the words. By "literal sense" they signify the meaning of a Scripture narrative according to the ordinary interpretation of the words. By "spiritual sense" they signify the secondary, hidden sense found in the words.

For instance: The Scripture narrative in Genesis 3 records how the serpent persuaded the woman to eat of the forbidden fruit and to give it to her husband, who also ate. This narrative in its simplest meaning represents what they understand by "letter." "Spirit," however, they understand to mean the spiritual interpretation, which is thus: The serpent signifies the evil temptation which lures to sin. The woman represents the sensual state, or the sphere in which such enticements and temptations make themselves felt. Adam, the man, stands for reason, which is called man's highest endowment. Now, when reason does not yield to the allurements of external sense, all is well; but when it permits itself to waver and consent, the fall has taken place.

Origen was the first to trifle thus with the holy Scriptures, and many others followed, until now it is thought to be the sign of great cleverness for the church to be filled with such quibblings. The aim is to imitate Paul, who in Galatians 4:22-24 figuratively interprets the story of Abraham's two sons, the one by the free woman, or the mistress of the

[32]Luther, *Sermons of Martin Luther*, 8:230-31*.

[33]Grumbach, *Argula von Grumbach*, 178. In this poem, Argula responds to a scurrilous poem published in 1524 by a theologian at the University of Ingolstadt named Johannes of Lanzhut, which had attacked her Protestant convictions and her outspoken defense of the evangelical message.

house, and the other by the handmaid. The two women, Paul says, represent the two covenants: one covenant makes only bondservants . . . the other leads to liberty. . . . True, this is an interpretation not directly suggested by the narrative and the text. Paul himself calls it an allegory, that is, a mystic narrative, or a story with a hidden meaning. But he does not say that the literal text is necessarily the letter that kills, and the allegory, or hidden meaning, the spirit. But the false teachers assert of all Scripture that the text, or record itself, is but a dead "letter," its interpretation being "the spirit." Yet they have not pushed interpretation further than the teaching of the law: and it is precisely the law which Paul means when he speaks of "the letter." Sermon on the Twelfth Sunday After Trinity[34]

The Meaning of Letter and Spirit. Wolfgang Musculus: When Paul says that he has been made a minister of the new covenant, not of the letter, but of the Spirit, he does not ascribe to the new covenant both letter and spirit, as if he understood by "letter" the doctrine articulated in writing, and by "spirit" the doctrine revealed by oral proclamation and the Spirit; as if he said, "I did not write with letters of ink, but I proclaimed the gospel." For if he said this—thereby making a distinction between his written doctrine and his oral proclamation—this would have condemned every part of his doctrine that he sent to the churches, especially that which was communicated in letters written with ink. The importance of this insight is sizeable, even for today, when it is taught that oral preaching comes forth from the Holy Spirit no less than written doctrine. That is why [Johann] Eck[†] erroneously cites this passage of the apostle when he extols the authority of the Roman Church above the sacred Scripture. For Paul is not making a distinction here between the sacred Scripture and the oral proclamation of preaching.

The opinion of those interpreters who conclude that by the "letter" one should understand the literal sense . . . and by the "spirit" one should understand the hidden and mystical sense is not correct either. For although on many occasions one finds passages in sacred Scripture where the plain letter should not be accepted, but rather the meaning that is hidden beneath it, nevertheless, this difference does not pertain to the material distinction between the Old and New Testaments, nor to the distinction between the apostolic ministry and the law. For there are many things written in the Old Testament that can be interpreted in no other fashion than according to the plain sense of the letter, and there are not a few things in the New Testament where, if one follows the literal sense, one is forced to accept an absurd interpretation. In the words spoken by our Savior, there are many things figurative and parabolic; so, too, apostolic doctrine is packed with many metaphors and similitudes. On the other hand, in the Old Testament many things are expressed in figures, and in the New Testament many things are expressed with plain and clear speech. That is why this interpretation cannot be accepted.

When the apostle says that he has been made a minister, not of the letter but of the Spirit, he means nothing other than that he is a minister not of the law of Moses, although he was born and raised in it, but that he is a minister of the gracious and efficacious Spirit. Thus, he calls the one Spirit and the other law. And Paul distinguishes between the old and new covenants by giving the term "letter" to one, and "Spirit" to the other, and by these two words he expresses the condition of both, namely, the weakness of the former and the excellence and efficacy of the other. Moreover, he is not speaking about that letter of the law, which contains figures and shadows, but about that law, contained in the clear precepts of the Ten Commandments, written on tablets of stone, as Paul explains in what follows. And to the new covenant, that is, to the gospel of the kingdom of God, he gives the word "spirit," not to dismiss the usefulness of letters and human words, but to express the excellence and efficacy of that superior dispensation of grace. Commentary on 2 Corinthians 3:6.[35]

[34]Luther, *Sermons of Martin Luther*, 8:231-32.

[35]Musculus, *Commentarius . . . in posteriorem epistolam Pauli ad Corinthios*, 91. [†]At the Leipzig debate of 1519, the Catholic

Not of the Letter but of the Spirit. Niels Hemmingsen: So that the apostle might extol the dignity of his ministry, he makes a comparison between ministers of the law and ministers of the gospel, describing the former as ministers of the letter, but the latter as ministers of the spirit—a figure of speech by which he adorns the gospel ministry with the greatest of praises. The reason why he here plainly calls the law "letter" and the gospel "spirit" must be sought in the naming of these things, since the letter carved into stone (for he is alluding to the stone tablets of Moses) is void of all power, but the spirit moves within the heart and is effective. Thus, the law has no more strength than a simple letter devoid of all power in itself, except among those with whom it can be displayed and understood. But the gospel, whose spirit is Christ, is life-giving, so that it effects life, salvation, and peace in the hearts of those who hear it. Therefore, the terms "letter" and "spirit" must not be understood to refer to interpretation but to efficacy. Given this, let us consider the special effect of the law and its minister Moses to the special nature of the gospel and its author Christ. For this reason, as the nature of the law is only to teach people liberally, so the effect of the gospel is to teach people spiritually and with power, so that doctrine might penetrate to the very heart, having been made softer. But whenever the sound of this gospel is not heard, there is no gospel, but one will hear guilt rather than the gospel, and thus all doctrine remains the letter. Commentary on 2 Corinthians 3:6.[36]

Meaning of the Letter and the Spirit. David Chytraeus: The "new covenant" signifies the same thing as the "gospel," or the promise concerning the Son of God, our Lord and Redeemer Jesus Christ, and God's grace, remission of sins and everlasting salvation which are given freely for Christ's sake alone to those who believe. It is through the promise of this new covenant that the Holy Spirit works, kindling new light, new righteousness, and everlasting life in our hearts.

The "letter" signifies both the ceremonial and moral law of Moses, written with letters in tablets of stone, and all obedience to or endeavor to perform the ceremonial or moral works of the law without the Holy Spirit or without true faith kindled by the Holy Spirit.

The "spirit" signifies Christ himself, or the Holy Spirit of Christ, who by the preaching of that gospel kindles true light of the knowledge of God, true comfort, righteousness, and life in human hearts, as it says in 1 John 5: "This is the testimony of the gospel, that God gives us eternal life as a free gift, and this life is in his Son. Whoever has the Son has life; whoever does not have the Son of God, does not have life." Therefore, the spirit and life of all the doctrine delivered by God in both covenants, yes, and all good works, ceremonies, and good intentions, are only in Christ. Therefore, Paul says that God made him a minister of the new covenant or of the gospel, and not of the letter or the law only . . . but of Christ's spirit which works by the gospel. Postil on the Twelfth Sunday After Trinity.[37]

The Ministry of the Gospel Compared to the Law. The English Annotations: Paul amplifies his ministry, that is, the ministry of the gospel, by comparing it with the ministry of the law. He considers the law in the person of Moses, by whom the law was given, against which he compares Christ the author of the gospel. Now the comparison is taken from the very substance of the ministry. The law, as it were, is a written document that is dead in itself and without efficacy, but the gospel is a new covenant, the very power of God in renewing, justifying, and saving human beings. The law propounds death, accusing all people of unrighteousness; the gospel offers and gives

theologian Johann Eck defended papal authority and attacked Luther's assertion that the teachings of Scripture have ultimate authority over the church. Eck defended the Catholic view in several later writings, including *On the Primacy of Peter* (1520) and the *Enchiridion* (1525).

[36]Hemmingsen, *Commentaria in Omnes Epistolas Apostolorum*, 263.

[37]Chytraeus, *Postil of Certeine Epistles*, 314-15*; citing 1 Jn 5:11-12.

righteousness and life. The governance of the law served for a limited time; the gospel remains to the end of the world. What then is the glory of the law in comparison to the majesty of the gospel? ANNOTATIONS ON 2 CORINTHIANS 3:6.[38]

THE PROPER USE OF ALLEGORIES. MARTIN LUTHER: I have often spoken of the sort of theology that prevailed when I began to study the subject. The theologians of that time said: "The letter kills." That is why I disliked [Nicholas of] Lyra[†] more than all other interpreters: he followed the literal meaning so carefully. But now I prefer him for this very reason to all interpreters of Scripture. And I advise you as emphatically as I can carefully to note and to appreciate the histories of the Bible. But whenever you wish to use allegories, see to it that you follow the analogy of faith, that is, make your allegories fit Christ, the church, faith, the ministry of the Word. When patterned in this way, allegories will not depart from the faith, even though they may not fit in every respect. LECTURES ON MOSES.[39]

ORIGEN AND OTHERS TWISTED PAUL'S MEANING. JOHN CALVIN: "For the letter kills." This passage was mistakenly perverted, first by Origen, and then by others, into a debased meaning. From this followed a very pernicious error that imagined the reading of Scripture was not only useless, but even harmful, unless it were drawn out into allegories. This error was the source of many evils. For not only did this give people freedom to adulterate the true sense of Scripture, but the more audacious one was in this sort of interpretation, the more excellent of an interpreter of Scripture they were considered to be. And so, many of the ancients recklessly played with the sacred Word of God, as if it were a ball to be tossed to and fro. And from this, heretics were also given the opportunity to trouble the church, for since it became a common practice to make any passage mean anything that one might choose, there was no crazy interpretation so absurd and careless that it couldn't be introduced under some pretext of allegory. Even good men and women were carried away so that they imagined many mistaken opinions, led astray through the charm of allegories.

But the meaning of this passage is this, that the Word of God, if it is only declared with the mouth, is the occasion for death; and it is life-giving, when it is received in the heart. The terms "letter" and "spirit," therefore, do not refer to the exposition of the Word, but to its power and fruit. COMMENTARY ON 2 CORINTHIANS 3:6.[40]

THE LETTER OF THE LAW KILLS. TILEMANN HESSHUS: The law and the old covenant provide no consolation and do not impart life to us since they accuse us of our filthiness, announce to us God's wrath against our smoldering sin, and confine the whole human race as in a prison (since we are deprived of perfect obedience). Instead, the law and the old covenant produce weighty terrors and, by their curse and condemnation, cause us to die. For the awareness of God's wrath plunges men and women into ruin, unless through Christ they are rescued from death and given life. . . . In this way, the letter, that is, the law and the old covenant, in no way confers life and the spirit, but only death. Not even Moses, the chief legislator, perceived life from the law; rather he craved for protection: "I will place you," God said, "in the cleft of the rock and with my hand I will protect you." Paul speaks of this in Galatians 3: "If the law had been given that could bring life, then righteousness would be from the law." And also in Romans 7: "The commandment that was given to me for life, handed me over to death." By "the letter," Paul did not mean only the external preaching of the law, but the spiritual judgment of the whole law because it cannot bring life since it is enfeebled by

[38]Downame, ed., *English Annotations*, FF3r*.

[39]WA 42:377. [†]Nicholas of Lyra (1270–1349) was a Franciscan teacher and one of the foremost biblical exegetes of the Middle Ages.

[40]CO 50:40-41 (CTS 40:174-175).

the flesh, but only produces death. Explication of 2 Corinthians 3:6.[41]

Is God Cruel in Giving a Law That Kills? Wolfgang Musculus: You ask: "Why did God give such a law to his people when he knew that it would not bring life but kill them?" I answer: We must not call into question the wisdom of God. For he granted to his people a special privilege among the nations, in this especially, that he made known to them his judgments. He did not act in this manner among all the nations, the prophet says. But if it happens that this kindness brings about our ruin, we should not for that reason blame God. God gave a law that was good, righteous, and holy, whose extraordinary usefulness pious people have recognized, as one sees in Psalm 19. When the letter of the law kills, it does so because of the perversity of the human heart, not from its own nature. Commentary on 2 Corinthians 3:6.[42]

The Ministry of the Holy Spirit. Tilemann Hesshus: The Spirit here signifies the Holy Spirit himself, the eternal God, who is not given through the letter of the law but through the promise of the gospel and received by faith. This Spirit does not terrify; he does not accuse; he does not disturb the heart; he does not produce death (as does the letter of the law), but instead, having destroyed the spirit of the law with his lightning bolts, he most pleasantly recreates, comforts, encourages, vivifies, and bathes us with joy. For he reveals to us God's most compassionate will: that the only-begotten Son was made a ransom for the sins of the world. He explains to us the Father's eternal plan: that through a mediator, his Son, he wished to snatch us from the tyranny of Satan, sin, and death. He speaks and confirms within our spirits this comfort: that the eternal Father freely wishes to give us sinners all things on account of his Son and receive us into his grace; that he imputes to us the righteousness of his Son; that he makes us temples of God and designates us heirs of eternal life. This very same Holy Spirit gives testimony to our spirit, that we are sons and daughters of God, and he inflames our hearts so that we cry out "Abba Father!" Explication of 2 Corinthians 3:6.[43]

The Spirit Makes Alive. Wolfgang Musculus: Inasmuch as killing is to take away someone's life, so making alive is to liberate someone from death. Therefore, the Spirit makes us alive when he liberates us from death and sin. Now the Spirit liberates not only those whom the letter of the law kills but also all those remaining people who are made participants with him. Now however many people believe in Christ are made participants with the Spirit, as Jesus says in John 7: "If anyone is thirsty, let him come to me and drink. Whoever believes in me, as the Scripture says, out of his heart will flow rivers of living water. Now this," the Gospel writer adds, "he said about the Spirit, whom those who believed in him were to receive." God formerly promised his life-giving Spirit through his prophets for the times of the New Testament, and which shone brightly through the ministries of the apostles. The apostle [Paul] looks back at this when he says that he was made sufficient to be a minister of the new covenant, not of the letter, but of the spirit. "For the letter kills, but the Spirit gives life." Commentary on Second Corinthians 3:6.[44]

The Spirit Shows Christ's Work for Us. Cyriacus Spangenberg: Now we also want to see what St. Paul names "Spirit." He calls "Spirit" the proclamation of the gospel of the merit of Jesus Christ, accepted through faith and confirmed in our heart by the Spirit of God. This is a different teaching and proclamation from the

[41]Hesshus, *Explicatio Secundae Epistolae Pauli ad Corinthios*, 67v-68r, 68v-69r; citing Ex 33:22; Gal 3:21; Rom 7:10.
[42]Musculus, *Commentarius . . . in posteriorem epistolam Pauli ad Corinthios*, 94.
[43]Hesshus, *Explicatio Secundae Epistolae Pauli ad Corinthios*, 69r-v.
[44]Musculus, *Commentarius . . . in posteriorem epistolam Pauli ad Corinthios*, 95; citing Jn 7:37-39.

proclamation of the law, and St. Paul gives this proclamation a title, so that he calls it "the ministry of the new covenant," the ministry of the Spirit, which does not teach what you should do, because you have heard that before. Rather it shows you what God wants to do for you and give to you, indeed has already done and given, in that he gave his Son Jesus Christ for us to this end when we were still enemies and, because of our disobedience to the law (which no human being can fulfil), under the wrath of God, and belonged in damnation, that his Son might help us out of this, paid for our sins, propitiated God, and gave us his righteousness. Here we hear nothing of what we do, but only of Christ's works for us. THIRTEENTH SERMON.[45]

[45] C. Spangenberg, *Die ander Epistel Pauli an die Corinthier*, 56r.

3:7-18 The Greater Glory of the New Covenant

7 Now if the ministry of death, carved in letters on
stone, came with such glory that the Israelites could
not gaze at Moses' face because of its glory, which was
being brought to an end, 8 will not the ministry of the
Spirit have even more glory? 9 For if there was glory in
the ministry of condemnation, the ministry of
righteousness must far exceed it in glory. 10 Indeed, in
this case, what once had glory has come to have no
glory at all, because of the glory that surpasses it. 11 For
if what was being brought to an end came with glory,
much more will what is permanent have glory.
12 Since we have such a hope, we are very bold, 13 not
like Moses, who would put a veil over his face so that
the Israelites might not gaze at the outcome of what
was being brought to an end. 14 But their minds were
hardened. For to this day, when they read the old
covenant, that same veil remains unlifted, because
only through Christ is it taken away. 15 Yes, to this day
whenever Moses is read a veil lies over their hearts.
16 But when one[a] turns to the Lord, the veil is removed.
17 Now the Lord[b] is the Spirit, and where the Spirit of
the Lord is, there is freedom. 18 And we all, with
unveiled face, beholding the glory of the Lord,[c] are
being transformed into the same image from one
degree of glory to another.[d] For this comes from the
Lord who is the Spirit.

a Greek *he* **b** Or *this Lord* **c** Or *reflecting the glory of the Lord* **d** Greek *from glory to glory*

Overview: Having demonstrated the superiority of the new covenant of grace to the old covenant of law, Paul now appeals to the biblical account of Moses to show that the glory of the new covenant far surpasses, and indeed has made obsolete, the glory that accompanied the giving of the Ten Commandments at Mount Sinai. Reformation authors find in these verses sharp contrasts between the glory of the Jewish law and the glory of the Christian gospel. Whereas the law, which God gave to Israel through Moses, was temporary, was addressed to one particular nation, and was effective only to threaten and condemn the consciences of sinners, the gospel of Jesus Christ that the Spirit mediates is eternal, is addressed to all peoples, and is powerful to justify sinners and impart to them consolation, joy, and eternal life. Compared to the old covenant law, the glory of the gospel is like the brilliance of the sun that overshadows the waning light of the moon. And because the gospel is so glorious, Christian ministers must follow Paul's example by proclaiming it with great boldness.

Paul's allegory of the veil in verses 13-16 raises a number of difficult interpretive questions for Reformation commentators. Why did Moses cover his face with a veil? What did the veil symbolize? In what sense does the veil still cover the hearts of those who read the Mosaic law today? For most early modern Protestant exegetes, Moses' veil was evidence of the evanescence and relative powerlessness of the law; it also constituted a prophecy of the future blindness of the Jews, who refuse to acknowledge Jesus Christ as the fulfillment of the Old Testament law. It is only through spiritual conversion that the veil is lifted so that men and women can see Christ as the purpose and end of the law. Moreover, Christian conversion brings with it freedom (from God's wrath, sin, death, and Satan's power) and spiritual transformation. As Tilemann Hesshus makes clear, this transformation is not one of substance but a qualitative change whereby believers' minds are enlightened, their wills made right, and their hearts purified through the all-powerful divine Spirit.

3:7-11 *The Example of Moses and His Ministry*

The Glory of the Law Can Never Justify Sinners. Martin Luther: Paul is in an ecstasy of delight, and his heart overflows in words of praise for the gospel. Again he handles the law severely, calling it a ministration, or doctrine, of death and condemnation. What term signifying greater abomination could he apply to God's law than to call it a doctrine of death and hell? And again, he calls it a "minister (or preacher) of sin"; and the message which proclaims a curse, saying, "As many as are of the works of the law are under a curse." Absolute, then, is the conclusion that law and works are powerless to justify before God; for how can a doctrine proclaiming only sin, death, and condemnation justify and save?

Paul is compelled to speak thus, as we said above, because of the infamous presumption of both teachers and pupils, in that they permit flesh and blood to coquet with the law and make their own works which they bring before God their boast. Yet, nothing is effected but self-deception and destruction. For, when the law is viewed in its true light, when its "glory," as Paul has it, is revealed, it is found to do nothing more than to kill men and women and sink them into condemnation.

Therefore, Christians will do well to learn this text of Paul and have an armor against the boasting of false teachers, and the torments and trials of the devil when he urges the law and induces men and women to seek righteousness in their own works, tormenting their heart with the thought that salvation is dependent upon the achievements of the individual. Christians will do well to learn this text, I say, so that in such conflicts they may take the devil's own sword, saying, "Why do you annoy me with talk of the law and my works? What is the law after all, however much you may preach it to me, but that which makes me feel the weight of sin, death, and condemnation? Why should I seek therein righteousness before God?" Sermon on the Twelfth Sunday After Trinity.[1]

The Efficacy of Law and Gospel. Philipp Melanchthon: Previously, Paul discussed the offices pertaining to the law and Spirit. Now he discusses the offices and efficacy of the gospel and law, and his preference for the former. Glory signifies power. In the first place, therefore, he argues thusly: if the law was so powerful that it confounded the Israelites, the gospel will also be able to bring life, especially since the power of the law is the glory of God outside of our heart, whereas the gospel is the power of the Spirit of God within our heart. Now, if the power outside the heart was able to kill, why would the power within our heart not bring life? The greatest glory of the law is this: the power to kill. The greatest glory of the gospel is this: the power to bring life. The sons of Israel fled from the light radiating from the face of Moses; by contrast, Peter on the mountain said, "Lord, it is good for us to be here." The splendor of the law is judgment and wrath, and this is why we flee from the face of God, according to that passage: "Let all flesh be silent before the face of God." The splendor of the gospel is grace and mercy, and this is why we can stand before God. This, indeed, is the highest degree of glory. Annotations on 2 Corinthians 3:7.[2]

How Does Paul Distinguish the Law and Gospel? Johann Spangenberg: What does St. Paul say about the distinction between law and gospel? He praises the evangelical office and shows how it is nobler than the law's office, how it follows the same and even grows in believers and creates hope through the cross to eternal glory. By this he touches on the false apostles who promote the law against the gospel, and pure external holiness. That is, they teach hypocrisy, and leave unpunished the internal guilt of unbelief. How does he distinguish the law and gospel? By three

[1] Luther, *Sermons of Martin Luther*, 8:244-45*; citing Gal 2:17, 3:10.
[2] *Melanchthons Werke*, 4:104; citing Mt 17:4; Zech 2:13.

sure distinctions—namely, first, by their offering and provision; second, on account of their office or duty; third, on account of their fruits.

How [are the law and gospel distinguished] by their provision? When God gave the law on Mount Sinai, we saw nothing but storm, dark clouds, torrential downpour, fiery smoke, and steam. We heard nothing but thunder, lightning, great tumult, and whirlwind. And we became completely fearful and terrified, so the children of Israel asked if Moses would speak to them, not God—otherwise they must die. But when the gospel came and Christ transfigured himself on Mount Tabor, we saw nothing but pure light and clarity. We heard nothing but only friendly, lovely words, and there was pure joy and glory. Thus, out of pure joy, St. Peter said, "Lord, it is good to be here, if you want, we will make three huts: one for you, one for Moses, and one for Elijah." So we saw on Pentecost—when the Holy Spirit was given and the gospel was fully revealed—nothing other on the disciples than fiery cloven tongues. And we heard nothing other than that they spoke in all sorts of tongues and languages about the great deeds of God. They preached repentance and the forgiveness of sins in the name of Jesus and promised salvation and eternal life to every believer in Christ. What do these histories show us? They show us the nature and character of the law and the gospel. The law frightens sinners in their conscience, holds their past sins before their eyes, threatens them with curse and eternal death. The gospel, on the other hand, consoles frightened consciences and shows them the One who takes their sin, curse, and eternal death from them.

How [are law and gospel distinguished] on account of their office or duty? The law's office is to command, forbid, drive, coerce, compel, and spur dullness, impatience, wrath, sorrow, and resentment in human beings. As St. Paul says, "The law brings wrath." On what is the law written? Stone tablets. What are the stone tablets? Human strength without God's Spirit. It's hard to write on stone; ink hardly adheres. So, too, human strength accomplishes little in God's matters.

What is the gospel's office? The gospel consoles, pleads, implores, exhorts, uses only friendly words. It gives the Holy Spirit, makes human beings joyous, willing, and ready to do all God's commandments—and finally saves them. As St. Paul says, "The gospel is the power of God that saves all who believe in it." On what should the gospel be written? The hearts of believers in Christ—on fleshly hearts. What are fleshly hearts? True Christians and living vessels of the Holy Spirit, whom God's Spirit guides and governs to everything that is godly and Christian.

What was Moses' office? He preached the law to the Jews and presented them with more than six hundred commandments. In short, he said: "Cursed are those who do not do *all* that stands written in the law." That was a harsh sermon. After this sermon every person must have despaired, for they found that they could not uphold a single commandment from the heart. He held before them a severe mirror so that they could see themselves in it: recognize their weakness and brokenness, become Spirit-hungry and mercy-thirsty, yearn for God's lovingkindness, and then approach Christ's mercy seat and cast their sin on the guiltless Lamb of God.

What is Christ's office? He preaches the gospel. He does not direct us to many commands but instead says with brief words: "Love God above all other things and serve your neighbor as yourself; that is the law and all the prophets."

What is the old covenant? Everything that drives, coerces, compels, and curses and goes no farther. What is the new covenant? Everything that happens with desire, love, and [free] will—uncoerced and uncompelled—out of God's mercy and the Holy Spirit. What is the letter? Everything that is written—law, gospel, all teaching and preaching, words and works—which happen without the Spirit and do not live in the heart. What is the spirit? The life and work of the Holy Spirit in our hearts. . . . Yes, every bishop and preacher are to preach the law and the gospel, repentance and forgiveness of sins in the name of Jesus.

Why does the letter kill? Because it is taught without Spirit and faith. I hear well enough that I should not commit adultery, should not steal, and should not murder. But since I do not have the Spirit and faith so that I am able to keep such commands, it kills me and only accomplishes pure wrath in me. Why does the gospel bring life? Because it is the sort of teaching that brings the Spirit and faith with it. The Spirit alone is the one who leads me to the only Christ and unites me with him, so that he remains in me and I in him.

How [are the law and gospel] distinguished on account of their fruits? The fruits of the law are fear and terror, God's wrath, a bad conscience, curse, and condemnation. The fruits of the gospel are joy and consolation, God's favor, a good conscience, the forgiveness of sins, and eternal life. The law demonstrates well what a person should do and not do, but grants neither help nor the Spirit with it. It commands and forbids, it terrifies and threatens, curses and afflicts. There it remains. No one will become better or more devout from laws, but rather more troubled. The law demonstrates sins well but is not able to help us out of sin. It lets the old Adam remain. The gospel demonstrates what a person should do and not do, but also gives with it strength and power, the Spirit and grace. It forms new people who love and want to do God's commands. And they do it without coercion and compulsion—yes, with joy they do what God wants to have from them. This spirit we cannot capture in letters. Nor does it let itself be written with ink in books; instead it is a living Scripture of the Holy Spirit, written in the hearts of believers. Postil on Epistle for the Twelfth Sunday in Trinity.[3]

Moses' Shining Face. Niels Hemmingsen: Paul summarizes the worth of the gospel by means of comparisons. The law, which is the ministry of death, is glorious. How much more glorious is the gospel which is the ministry of the spirit and life. Now, the law is called "the ministry of death" because it reveals sin, for which the just punishment is death. The gospel is called "the ministry of the spirit" because through it God offers the spirit and life, and thus salvation itself. Now, the fact that he says the ministry of death is carved in stone ought to be understood as the antithesis to the gospel, which is engraved in human hearts by the finger of God. Moreover, the splendor of Moses' face was a symbol of the glory of the law, about which one reads in Exodus 34. When the law was read, Moses' face shone forth with brilliant brightness, so that the sons of Israel were afraid to come near him. By the splendor of Moses' face is signified the intolerable awareness of divine judgment. For no one can endure that frightening splendor of the law which accuses and condemns with fire. The opposite is the splendor of Christ's face, in which loving grace shines forth and by which we are liberated from the damnation of the law. Commentary on 2 Corinthians 3:7.[4]

The Glory of Moses and the Glory of Christ. Heinrich Bullinger: Paul now compares gospel preaching to the law, speaking about the law in the manner we demonstrated above. By the term "ministry of death" he understands the law, for the law kills, as is explained in Romans. Therefore, the gospel is better than the law, first of all, because the ministry of the spirit and life is better than the ministry of death. Second, the law is disfigured, that is, it has been carved onto tablets of stone, while the gospel is engraved in human hearts. The conclusion that he has proved now follows: if the law, which was carved into tablets, was waning in glory, how much greater will be the glory of the eternal gospel, engraved on hearts. Moreover, Paul demonstrates the glory that the law had when he states that the face of Moses shone forth with dignity and majesty, so that the sons of Israel were not able to focus their eyes on the radiance. In these ways, Paul also demonstrates the dignity of the lawgiver, whence it

[3]J. Spangenberg, *Postilla Teütsch*, 4:78v-81r; citing Lk 9:33; Acts 2; Rom 4:15; Rom 1:16; Mt 22:37-40; Lk 24:47.

[4]Hemmingsen, *Commentaria in Omnes Epistolas Apostolorum*, 263.

is easy to gather that the glory of Christ is greater in as much as the son of God is greater than Moses. Now, Matthew shows how great the glory of Christ was when he transfigured himself. The story of Moses is read in Exodus 34. Commentary on 2 Corinthians 3:7.[5]

The Glories of the New Covenant. Tilemann Hesshus: Up to this point Paul has described the effect, purpose, and characteristics of the old covenant. Now he shares with them the characteristics of the ministry of the new covenant, summarizing them with the single word "Spirit." He says, "Will the ministry of the Spirit not have all the more glory?" This term "Spirit" covers a wide field. For the word is opposed to death, letters, stones, infirmity, and passing away. And the word covers all the benefits of the Mediator, for where the Spirit is, there is life, righteousness, joy, freedom, and eternal happiness. Paul therefore insists firmly on this. Through the ministry of the new covenant, we are liberated from the power of Satan, from sins, death, and hell. We are given the remission of all our sins and reconciled with the eternal Father. We are born anew through the Holy Spirit and given life. The new and heavenly light of the true knowledge of God is ignited in us. The power of free will, once lost, is now restored to us. We are united to the Son and made heirs of eternal life. We are filled with joy and gladness in God because he will not leave us. These heavenly, spiritual, and eternal blessings are much better by far than the polity of Moses, the flourishing kingdom of Solomon, the glorious deliverance of Hezekiah, and the whole land of Canaan with all the happiness of the Israelites. How great and wonderful was the glory in the new covenant, seeing Christ resurrected from the dead, victorious over sin, death, Satan, and hell. Explication of 2 Corinthians 3:8.[6]

The Glorious Ministry. John Trapp: Let this passage comfort ministers of the gospel, as they encounter the contempt that the mad world casts upon them, for the world is always beside itself in the matter of salvation. Commentary on 2 Corinthians 3:8.[7]

The Gospel of the New Covenant Brings Perfect Righteousness. Jacques Lefèvre d'Étaples: Now the old covenant is described by the word "letter," and the new covenant is understood by the word "spirit," which is not at all illogical. For letters, unless they are instructed by the spirit—that is, by speaking—are empty and useless; they are powerless. But the spirit and speech give letters all their power. And so, unless the old covenant is made alive by the spirit of Christ, unless it is informed by the gospel, it is empty and useless. Therefore, the old covenant has only as much power as the gospel gives it. The old covenant is also called a ministry of death, and this is especially true now, even though it was never able to supply perfect righteousness, but only gave the shadow of righteousness inasmuch as before the time of the gospel all people were descending to hell. What is this if not a certain kind of death or image of death? But the new covenant supplies perfect righteousness, since by it any person flies immediately to heaven. And so the new covenant is rightly called the ministry of the spirit and righteousness. So, too, the old covenant is rightly called the ministry of condemnation, because everyone who lived according to it alone were condemned to descend to hell, whence the Lord Christ wished to draw out many of those who were held captive there. And as the magnificent conqueror, he led the captives out of their captivity. Commentary on 2 Corinthians 3:9-10.[8]

The Ministry of Righteousness. Wolfgang Musculus: That term "ministry of righteousness" can be taken in two different ways,

[5]Bullinger, *In Posteriorem D. Pauli ad Corinthios Epistolam Commentarius*, 277; citing Mt 17:1-13.

[6]Hesshus, *Explicatio Secundae Epistolae Pauli ad Corinthios*, 76v-77r.

[7]Trapp, *A Commentary or Exposition*, 710*.

[8]Lefèvre, *Commentariorum in Epistolas Beati Pauli . . . Liber Tertius*, 132.

either as the ministry of justification, which is by faith in Christ, or the righteousness of life of those who receive the Spirit of God, who no longer live according to the flesh but according to the Spirit. In Greek, the word is *dikaiosynē*, which can be translated in the sense of justification, as the word appears in Romans 4, Romans 8, and Romans 10. The principle of opposition seems to require this translation, reading the verse as "ministry of justification." For the word *justification*, which is freedom and absolution from guilt and condemnation, is more correctly contrasted to condemnation, than is the term *righteousness of life*, which is contrasted more to unrighteousness than to condemnation. . . .

But either way we read it, either as "ministry of justification" or "ministry of righteousness," they both are truly attributed to and in conformity with the gospel of Christ. This is the fundamental argument of the apostle. For just as it is more glorious to liberate defendants from condemnation and death through the intervention of royal pardon than to condemn them through judicial sentence and kill them by the executioner's sword, so the ministry of justification and righteousness is altogether more glorious than the ministry of condemnation. Commentary on 2 Corinthians 3:9.[9]

The Superiority of the Gospel. Martin Luther: The meaning here is this: When the glory and holiness of Christ, revealed through the preaching of the gospel, is rightly perceived, then the glory of the law—which is but a feeble and transitory glory—is seen to be not really glorious. It is mere dark clouds in contrast to the light of Christ shining to lead us out of sin, death and hell unto God and eternal life. Sermon on the Twelfth Sunday After Trinity.[10]

God Promises to Preserve His Church. Martin Chemnitz: If the civil structure which was going to perish was the ministration of glory, "how much more glorious will be this ministration of eternal salvation"; that is, it will be efficacious in those who receive the gospel, and it will be preserved in marvelous ways. We suffer in our hearts in the midst of so many tumults of human affairs; we are anxious for the church, for its doctrine, and the destruction of its learning. These dangers instruct us that the church is not preserved by human plans but by divine actions among the great overthrow and ruination of kingdoms. God wants us to consider these things and he wants us to seek his protection so that we are not torn apart in our hearts. He gives us the promise that his church shall remain on earth to the end of time, as Christ clearly says in Matthew 28: "Lo, I am with you always, even unto the end of the age." Now, since the church will remain, the gospel must be glorious, that is, efficacious; the church must be protected by the marvelous works of God; the study of theological literature must remain even if in this last age of the world all things are weaker and more out of shape. We must comfort ourselves with these thoughts and continue in prayer. Loci Theologici.[11]

The Superior Glory of the Spirit's Ministry. Wolfgang Musculus: This is the meaning. In the same way that the ministry of the Spirit and righteousness excelled the ministry of death and condemnation, so too that glory which Moses radiated, if it is compared to that glory of the new covenant, is no glory at all, but completely evanescent on account of the surpassing glory of the new covenant. Thus, when Paul says, "what had glory in its place," ought to be understood as referring to the place of the old covenant and the glory that radiated from the face of Moses. He does not simply say that the old covenant had no glory, but that it had no glory in comparison to the far superior glory of the new covenant. It is as if someone were to deny that the splendor of the moon was bright, not when simply considered in

[9]Musculus, *Commentarius . . . in posteriorem epistolam Pauli ad Corinthios*, 99-100.
[10]Luther, *Sermons of Martin Luther*, 8:247*.

[11]Chemnitz, *Loci Theologici*, 2:654-55*; citing 2 Cor 3:9; Mt 28:20.

itself, but when compared to the splendor of the sun on account of its enormous superiority. And in fact, what else was the letter of the law in the old covenant than what the brightness of the moon is in the night? But if it is compared to the glory of the new covenant, does not Christ, the sun of righteousness, illuminate with his superior brightness not only the recesses of one nation but also of the whole world?

And this same superior glory of the new covenant, by which the glory of the old covenant is obscured, will in a similar fashion be overshadowed by that infinite glory of the future life in which not only the apostles will be glorious but also all believers will begin to shine like the appearance of the sun. The Spirit and righteousness will no longer be ministering (much less the law), but God himself will present himself face-to-face, and he will be all things to everyone. Thus, the glory of the divine dispensation rises and gradually swells into an enormous flood as it distributes salvation to the human race in clear and definite steps, before the law, during the law, after the law and, finally, in the world to come. Commentary on 2 Corinthians 3:10.[12]

The Gospel Outshines the Law. The English Annotations: [The law] had no glory in this respect, that is, it had no glory in a comparative sense; just as silver is not precious in comparison to gold, nor precious stones bright in comparison to the stars, nor the light of the moon bright in comparison to the sun. As Oecumenius[†] says, "The light of a candle seems brightest in the night, but in the midday it is so obscured that it does not deserve to be called light. Thus, the light of the law is so obscured by the light of the gospel that it seems to have no light or glory at all." Annotations on 2 Corinthians 3:10.[13]

The Glory of the Law Is Only Temporary. Andreas Hyperius: This argument concerning the superiority of the gospel is adduced from its eternity, and from that preceding statement, where he says that its glory is coming to an end. For how the law is coming to an end and is only temporary, while the gospel is eternal, see Galatians 4, Hebrews 10, Ephesians 2, Acts 15. However, when the apostle in this way praises the gospel and renders powerless the letter or external works, he is doubtlessly reproaching all the teaching of the false apostles who were constantly pressing the law, which was vanishing and worthless. And so it ought to be carefully noted from this passage that the ceremonial law has been abolished. They are free from some civil laws, as the magistrates deem appropriate. The moral law remains, especially the Decalogue, for they are the perpetual law of nature. But the law does not have power to condemn us, just as it cannot justify us, which is derived only from the gospel. Commentary on 2 Corinthians 3:11.[14]

The Ministry of the Law Will Cease. Cyriacus Spangenberg: The ceasing of the law is not tied to a particular fixed year or time, but to the gracious will of our Lord God. The law shall and must be preached to sinners, and they must be accused, judged, and condemned to death through the same, as long as the world endures. By which is not meant that it should continuously be over them, but as quickly and as often as they recognize their sin and accept by faith the proclamations of the gospel of the forgiveness of their sins. Thus the law shall and must cease, and no longer accuse them, much less damn them. Rather the gospel, Christ, and his grace, then begin and remain eternally over the faithful.

This is a particularly comforting word when he says that the ministry of the law is the kind of ministry that then ceases. For if this did not occur, nothing would remain over humankind but eternal

[12]Musculus, *Commentarius . . . in posteriorem epistolam Pauli ad Corinthios*, 100-101.

[13]Downame, ed., *English Annotations*, FF3r*. [†]Oecumenius is believed to have been a biblical scholar in Asia Minor in the sixth or seventh century who wrote several exegetical works, including commentaries on Paul's letters and the Apocalypse.

[14]Hyperius, *Commentarii . . . in Epistolam D. Pauli ad Romanos, et utramque ad Corinthios*, 358.

condemnation. But this ceasing does occur when the proclamation of the gospel of Christ begins. Before him Moses must retreat and leave all room for him, so that he no longer strikes his fear in the conscience of believers. Rather when the conscience feels the glory of Moses and then trembles and fears before God's wrath, thus is it then time for Christ's glory to shine into the heart with its sweet comforting light. Then we can cope with Moses and Elijah. Fifteenth Sermon.[15]

Eight Comparisons Between the Old and New Covenants. David Dickson: Because [Paul's] ministry is the ministry of the new covenant, not of the law and covenant of works, he confirms this argument with a sevenfold [*sic*, eightfold] comparison of the ministry of both covenants. . . .

Comparison 1 [v. 6]. The ministry of the law, or the covenant of works, is only the letter written or spoken, without efficacy, without all spiritual virtue to perform that which it commands. But the ministry of the gospel, or the covenant of grace through Christ, is the ministry of the Spirit, because according to, and by that, the Holy Ghost is administered, whereby the hearer is quickened and strengthened to embrace that which it propounds. . . .

Comparison 2 [v. 6]. Confirming the former [comparison]. The ministry of the law of works, or the written letter only convinces of sin, and kills the sinner, by pronouncing to him the sentence of death. But the ministry of the gospel, or grace in the new covenant shows liberty from sin, absolves the sinner, and so brings life. . . .

Comparison 3 [vv. 7-8]. The law of works, which only administers death (for according to this covenant no one obtains righteousness or life), was engraved in stones to signify that the heart by it cannot be mollified nor renewed, but remains dead. But the gospel of grace is written in the fleshly tables of the heart, that is, in hearts, by the power of the Holy Ghost, quickened and mollified. [And] it is so imprinted that the virtue of divine grace may be discerned in all the expressions of the heart. . . .

Comparison 4 [v. 8]. The ministry of the covenant of works, which is the ministry of death to all who have sinned, was truly glorious, as it appeared in Moses (for justice is glorious in punishing sin). But the ministry of the new covenant, which is the ministry of the quickening Spirit, is more glorious. For as in Moses pronouncing the curse of the law against sinners, his bodily glory shone. But oh, how much spiritual glory shines in the face of Christ, setting sinners at liberty by his grace! . . .

Comparison 5 [v. 9]. The ministry of the law, or the old covenant of works, is a ministry of condemnation for sin, therefore indeed glorious. But the ministry of the gospel, or the new covenant, is the ministry of the righteousness of Christ, and absolution from sin; and therefore it is so much the more glorious, as absolution and justification excel condemnation and sin. Because by the covenant of works we are all accused of sin, we are all condemned, and made obnoxious to death. Therefore, its ministry is called the ministry of sin, condemnation, and death. . . .

Comparison 6 [v. 10]. The ministry of the law, although it was glorious, was exceedingly excelled by the glory of the ministry of the gospel, or of grace, so that it does not deserve to be called glorious. Rather, let [the ministry of the law] vanish in comparison, as the glory of the stars, when the sun appears, is obscured. But the ministry of the gospel is simply glorious in the manner of its excellence.

Comparison 7 [v. 11]. The ministry of the covenant of works, in respect to the annexed ceremonies, has only the glory of temporal dispensation, because so long as it endured, while men in the infancy of the church, convicted of sins, and of their own impotency to deliver themselves, were taught to fly to Christ, and as it were by the hand of a schoolmaster might be led to him. This manner of instruction is abolished as unprofitable since the church is now at its full grown and

[15]C. Spangenberg, *Die ander Epistel Pauli an die Corinthier*, 63r-v.

continues under the brightness of the revealed gospel. But the ministry of the new covenant has permanent glory, until the glorious coming of Christ.

Comparison 8 [vv. 12-13]. The ministry of the new covenant is plain and perspicuous, so that the ministers thereof can plainly and confidently preach the way of salvation, with Christ now revealed, who in times past was a promise hoped for. But the ministry of the law, as it appeared in the type of the Mosaic ministration, was obscure and wrapped up in types. Exposition of 2 Corinthians 3.[16]

3:12-18 *The Veil of Spiritual Blindness*

Christ Is the Spirit for Reading Scripture. Jacques Lefèvre d'Étaples: Because the sons of Israel were not able to look upon Moses' shining face, the fading light which signified the end of the old law—though its end was the ancestral light of Christ—for that reason Moses covered his face with a veil. And the Jews wore this veil for a long time, as if concealing their mind's eye from the clarity and light of the truth when they were reading the books of the old law, as long as they did not fix their mind's eye upon Christ in faith. For Christ is the light of the books of their law. And because the Spirit is the light for all those reading and no one is able to read without the light, so nothing is vivified without life. And so, Christ is the spirit for reading the old Scriptures; without him no one is able to understand them. He is the light. He is the spirit. He is the life for understanding them. Now those who contemplate Christ with illuminating faith, their faces are unveiled and revealed, as in a mirror, so that they drink purely that glory, that light, and that spirit, and are formed into the same image of Christ, that is, marked with the seal and knowledge of the Son of God. Commentary on 2 Corinthians 3:12.[17]

[16]Dickson, *An Exposition of All St. Paul's Epistles*, 76-77*.
[17]Lefèvre, *Commentariorum in Epistolas Beati Pauli . . . Liber Secundus*, r.iiii v.

A Ministry of Boldness. Wolfgang Musculus: We are reminded here not only of what boldness of speech and confidence is appropriate for ministers of Christ, but also where it comes from. We use, Paul writes, great boldness of speech. This boldness is appropriate for the teaching of the truth. A person dishonors the truth of God when they speak in a manner cryptically, timidly, or hesitantly. The person who speaks concerning lies and doubtful opinions should do so in a manner obscure, embarrassed, inconsistent, doubtful, and secretive. [But] it is appropriate that the person who teaches the truth speak with great boldness. . . .

Those people who are powerful in the world say what they want without restraint and, since they wish to be heard, all of their words are like claps of thunder. Those who are learned and wise according to this world say everything with confidence because they think that they alone are wise. The minister of Christ also speaks with confidence and boldness, but neither from any power or from an inflated opinion of his own erudition and wisdom, but from a sure persuasion of the truth. And concerning this hope of his, the apostle is mindful that boldness of speech is received as a divine gift. The reason for the apostle's hope is very clear when he says: If what was coming to an end was glorious, how much more glorious will that be which remains. The ministry of the gospel was foolishness to the Gentiles and offensive to the Jews; moreover, it was attacked with the harshest of persecutions so that the ministers of the gospel were like those driven out from this world. As a result, a great temptation was planted in the consciences of weak people, and this temptation was stirred up all the more by the unfair accusations of the false apostles. Paul objects to this by saying, far be it that he wants to conceal or withhold anything from the doctrine of his gospel, which is everywhere dishonored with reproaches and lies. Rather, he employs great boldness in defending the gospel, strengthened by the hope that as glorious as the teaching of the law once was (although its glory is now fading), the ministry of the gospel will be all the more glorious and permanent and will never fade. The minister of Christ today should think about this in a similar fashion. If he finds in this age that this glory, though mixed, was worthy of so much boasting, how much more deserving of praise will that glory be when it is completely glorious, even if now it is condemned by reprehensible heresies and disgraced by every sort of dishonor? Relying on this hope, the minister acts boldly and with great confidence in his ministry, which the Lord gives to him. Commentary on 2 Corinthians 3:12.[18]

Jewish Interpreters Are Unreliable. Martin Luther: No one should be surprised if here [i.e., Psalm 65:8] and in similar passages we occasionally differ from the rabbis and grammarians. For we followed the rule that wherever the words could have given or tolerated an improved meaning, there we did not allow ourselves to be forced by the artificial Hebrew of the rabbis into accepting a different inferior meaning. For this is what all schoolmasters teach, that words are to serve and follow the meaning, and not the meaning the words. We know this too, and St. Paul informs us in 2 Corinthians 4 [*sic*, 3:13-15] that the face of Moses is hidden from the Jews and that they seldom catch the meaning of the Scriptures, especially in the prophets. Defense of Translation of Psalms.[19]

The Veil of Moses. Heinrich Bullinger: Having demonstrated the glory of the gospel and the weakness of the law, the apostle now suggests that since these matters entail such great boldness, we use much freedom in speaking; that is, having neglected types and laws, we preach Christ alone and his grace. In the meantime, he also harps against the false apostles for teaching the law. And he says that "we did not act in the way that Moses himself predicted that many were going to do." For Moses, by covering his face with a veil, predicted that in the future some of the Jews, having neglected the purpose of the law, were going to admire only that appearance or type. That is what people do today, who fail to preach that Christ alone is the end and perfection of the law but follow instead those types and laws—what I call a shadow. Therefore, the veil is the letter, indeed, that dullness of mind, disbelief, and ignorance of Christ. Next is the statement, "lest the sons of Israel gaze upon his face." Now Moses did not spread the veil over his face so as to gain their attention, but to predict that in the future many people would despise that goal of the law, namely, Christ, and cling to the dead letter and clear types, which nevertheless are said to be abolished in this passage, since they are fulfilled through Christ. Certainly, this passage is exceptional and worthy of much sacred reflection. Commentary on 2 Corinthians 3:12-13.[20]

The Glory of Moses and the Law Could Not Make People Righteous. Philipp Melanchthon: Moses was covering his face because it was shining forth a glory that was powerless for making people righteous. And so it happens that our hearts hide and cover up that brightness; that is, when we read the law, our hearts are frightened. For since our hearts want to delight in themselves, they present the appearance of external good works and think that they are forgiven by hypocritical works. And though the purpose of the law is the righteousness of heart, our hearts do not experience this reality in it. This is why Paul says that we have hope for glorification in the gospel. We are confident. Why? Because we preach a powerful Word that brings righteousness before God, whereas Moses was preaching a powerless word that did not bring righteousness before God. And so, Paul is saying nothing different than what he said earlier: "We are ministers of the Spirit, not the letter." We preach a

[18]Musculus, *Commentarius . . . in posteriorem epistolam Pauli ad Corinthios*, 103.
[19]LW 35:213 (WA 38:11).
[20]Bullinger, *In Posteriorem D. Pauli ad Corinthios Epistolam Commentarius*, 277.

message more powerful than the word of Moses. Annotations on 2 Corinthians 3:13.[21]

Spiritual Blindness and Sight. Desiderius Erasmus: Therefore, when [the Jews] read the Old Testament in such a way that they are not willing to embrace the New promised in it, that Mosaic veil even now remains upon them, does it not? Since the veil has not been removed by faith, they do not perceive that the wrapping of that law is abolished by Christ. They still cling tenaciously to their Moses although the one has come whom Moses bade them heed. They read him in their synagogues, but they read dully, looking for nothing but corporeal things, although the law is spiritual if anyone brings to it keen-sighted eyes. A veil spreads over their hearts, hinders them right up to the present day; it is lifted by evangelical faith. But when they, too, having given up the insensitivity of their mind and embraced the faith we share, turn to the Lord, then the veil will be removed, so that they may perceive what is perceived only by the wholly purified eyes of faith. Paraphrases on 2 Corinthians 3.[22]

The Blindness of the Jewish People. Tilemann Hesshus: The apostle now applies the allegory of the veil to the utter blindness of the Jewish people. He says that a veil has been placed over the reading of the old covenant, for the people of Israel did not embrace Christ Jesus, who is the object and end of all the prophets and of the whole old covenant, but they were not understanding the sense of the Scripture. They read the law; they served the Sabbath; they offered sacrifices; they listened to the prophets' sermons. But they understood nothing concerning the spiritual kingdom of Christ, true penitence, the remission of sins, righteousness, or the passion, death, and resurrection of Christ. They interpreted everything as relating to a worldly kingdom, to the preservation and expansion of the political order, to civil discipline and external sacrifices, as if the whole of salvation was located in these things. Therefore, this veil was thick, namely, it was thick with ignorance and blindness of mind. Certainly, the Scripture is plain and clear, but since their minds were not illumined by the Holy Spirit, they perceived nothing in these spiritual things—such is God's wondrous judgment. Although the words of the Holy Spirit were as clear as the noonday sun, they were not able to perceive, unless the Holy Spirit opened their eyes and minds.

The apostles heard Christ say many times: "Behold, we are going up to Jerusalem, and behold, the Son of Man will be handed over to the Gentiles, and he will be mocked, beaten, and spit upon, and after they have beaten him and killed him, on the third day he will arise." And yet the biblical text goes on to say, "and they understood nothing of these things and this message was hidden from them—they did not understand what was meant." It is utterly astounding that a word so clear and so plain—a word so appropriate and familiar that even children understood it—was not understood by the apostles. But this was because a veil had been placed over their hearts, and they were bewitched by the belief in a worldly messianic kingdom. Thus, although Moses was read daily in the synagogues, and although Moses was a prophet concerning the kingdom of Christ and his death and resurrection, nevertheless they understood nothing because they did not embrace Christ. . . .

Truly, we see here how great is the blindness and hardness of the human heart: even if God's Word is perfectly clear, it is not understood, unless the Holy Spirit illumines the mind. Here also we see how great is Satan's power, who distracts the mind and eyes with his lies so evil that they are unable to discern the light of truth. Therefore, there are not three concurrent causes in human conversion, as the synergists have imagined: the Holy Spirit, the Word of God, and the cooperating mind and will. Rather, there is only one *efficient* cause, namely, the Holy Spirit illuminating the mind with the Word; and the *instrumental* cause is the will bending to God's Word.† The mind and

[21]*Melanchthons Werke*, 4:107-8; citing 2 Cor 3:6.
[22]CWE 43:219.

will are only responsive agents. For this reason, the prophet says, "Convert me, O Lord, and I will be converted." The Lord must be earnestly begged to illumine our eyes so that we might perceive his will in the Word. "Open my eyes," says David, "that I might see wondrous things in your law." Explication of 2 Corinthians 3:14.[23]

The Veil Has Been Lifted for Christians. Huldrych Zwingli: The veil over Moses' face symbolized Christ before he was revealed. Still today the covering remains and [the new covenant] has not been disclosed to the Jews, even though it was revealed through Christ. And this is true not only of the Jews but also of those who boast in Christ's name but place their confidence in Jewish ceremonies and external things. Such people are not Christians but obviously Jews. Those who recognize Christ as the true light, for them the darkness is dispelled and the veil is pulled back. Everyone will err if they do not apply Christ when reading the old covenant. Whoever truly knows Christ will never depart from walking in the faith, even if some things appear dark and concealed. Annotations on 2 Corinthians 3:14.[24]

Without Christ, There Is No Light in the Law or Scripture. John Calvin: Paul gives a reason why they are so long blind in the midst of the light. For the law in itself is bright, but it is only when Christ appears to us in the law that we enjoy its splendor. The Jews turn their eyes away from Christ as much as they can. Thus, it is no wonder if they see nothing since they do not wish to gaze upon the sun. This blindness of the elect people of God, especially given how long it has lasted, is a warning to us not to be lifted up with pride, depending on the benefits that have been conferred on us by God. This subject is treated in Romans 11:20. However, let the reason for this blindness deter us from contempt of Christ, which God so severely punishes. In the meantime, let us learn that without Christ, the sun of righteousness, there is no light even in the law, or the whole Word of God. Commentary on 2 Corinthians 3:14.[25]

The Spiritual Blindness of the Jews. Giovanni Diodati: [Paul's use of the word] "but" is a response to a tacit objection: how does it happen that the people of the Jews at present do not at all believe in the disclosure of the law, which has been made by the gospel, and see nothing there? The apostle answers that the veil does not cover the gospel, but their hearts. And this comes from a willful and malicious blindness, and by a just punishment of God. As some people say, "The light shines forth, but those who ought to see it have their eyes closed." Annotations on 2 Corinthians 3:14.[26]

God Must Give Both Sight and Light. John Trapp: Unless God gives sight as well as light, and enlightens both organ and object, we can see nothing. Commentary on 2 Corinthians 3:14.[27]

Only Christ Can Illumine Human Hearts. Philipp Melanchthon: The veil is never lifted until Christ has illumined hearts by his Spirit, for he himself is light and life. And so, when Moses was speaking to the people, he remained veiled, because the brightness of the law does not illumine hearts, for it is the letter. And so the people's hearts were blinded. On the other hand, when Moses was speaking to the Lord, he lifted the veil, because he

[23]Hesshus, *Explicatio Secundae Epistolae Pauli ad Corinthios*, 83r-84v; citing Lk 18:31-34; Jer 31:8; Ps 119:18. †Following Aristotle and the medieval scholastics, Hesshus here is employing a fourfold scheme of causality, which includes the efficient cause, the material cause, the formal cause, and the final cause. According to Muller, the efficient cause "is the agent productive of the motion or mutation in any sequence of causes and effects." See Richard Muller, *Dictionary of Latin and Greek Theological Terms* (Grand Rapids: Baker, 1985), 61. See Aristotle, *Physics* 2.3; *Metaphysics* 5.2.

[24]Zwingli, *Annotatiunculae . . . ex ore Zvinglij*, 160.

[25]CO 50:45 (CTS 40:183).

[26]Diodati, *La Seconde Epistre de . . . S. Paul aux Corinthiens*, 141; citing Jn 9:39; 12:40; Rom 11:7, 25.

[27]Trapp, *A Commentary or Exposition*, 710*.

was illumined by God's glory, not by the letter. And so, those of us who are converted to Christ are illumined by the glory of God, that is, by the Holy Spirit by grace. And so, because we are of flesh, the veil remains. But those who are converted to the Lord necessarily become spiritual. For "God is spirit"; "For the flesh sets its mind on fleshly things, only the spirit is spiritual." Annotations on 2 Corinthians 3:15.[28]

Lifting the Veil. Wolfgang Musculus: See how careful Paul is to avoid accusing the law of being obscure. Therefore, he assigns all the guilt to those Jews, whose minds have been blinded, saying that a veil has been laid over their hearts when they interpret Moses in the pages of the Old Testament. For this veil can only be removed by Christ. We give the same answer today to all those who contend that the sacred writings of both the Old and New Testaments are obscure, for they are like blind people who contend that the sun is obscure and dark. Covered with a veil, their hearts are altogether dull, bound not by one but a variety of things, including the fetter of human wisdom, respect for great men, and the longstanding Catholic customs of so many centuries—to say nothing about their self-love, personal gain, and devotion to fame and their hungry stomachs. With their minds covered by these "scales," they are not able—and will never be able—to discern the light of the truth shining forth in the sacred Scriptures, unless they receive the simple, plain Christ, who alone can raise all the different kinds of coverings from the hearts of human beings. Commentary on 2 Corinthians 3:15.[29]

The Blindness of Unbelieving Jews. David Dickson: The apostle observes that now blindness may also be perceived in the Jews, who while they read the Old Testament see nothing besides the veil of ceremonies, because the veil of ignorance and infidelity remains upon their minds. This veil, which is represented by the type of the external veil covering Moses' face, is taken away by Christ from all the faithful, for righteousness, life, and virtue. Moreover, all grace and glory are published and communicated to the faithful in Christ. But hitherto this veil remains upon the hearts of the unbelieving Jews. Exposition of 2 Corinthians 3:15.[30]

When We Return to Christ, the Veil Is Removed. Cyriacus Spangenberg: The law is surely bright enough, but nobody enjoys its light and lives, except the one who recognizes Christ in it. Thus, the Jews do not want Christ, therefore the Old Testament also remains veiled for them. Let this be a warning to us, that we not despise Christ and his Word, so that God be not caused to punish us with the same blindness as the Jews. "For up to the present day, when Moses is read, the veil covers their hearts." This is double blindness.

The veil covers the Old Testament, whose light they should see, and then it covers their hearts, with which they should recognize such light. There is no other cure than that they return. "But when it returns" (understand the hearts of the Jews, or the Jewish people) "when it returns to the Lord, then the veil is removed," just as it was removed from Moses' face, when he turned from the people and went in to speak with the Lord. Sixteenth Sermon.[31]

Spiritual Conversion Necessary for True Understanding of the Law. Niels Hemmingsen: Paul explains how long the veil remains covering the heart, and at the same time shows how it is removed. But because this passage is a little less clear—both because the comparison is not complete, and because the character of the analogy has not been added—let us render the clearer meaning in this fashion: When Moses was turning away from God to the people, he had a veil

[28] *Melanchthons Werke*, 4:108; citing Jn 4:24; Rom 8:5.

[29] Musculus, *Commentarius . . . in posteriorem epistolam Pauli ad Corinthios*, 105-6.

[30] Dickson, *An Exposition of All St. Paul's Epistles*, 77*.

[31] C. Spangenberg, *Die ander Epistel Pauli an die Corinthier*, 66r.

over his face; and when he was turning his attention again to the Lord, he removed the veil. And so it is with the human heart: when it has turned away from the Lord, it has a veil placed over it, but as soon as it has been converted to the Lord, the veil is removed, that is, they now have understanding of the carnal law and recognize that Christ is the end of the law. Those people who have been regenerated by the Spirit begin to exhibit spiritual obedience to God. The passage ought to be considered for it teaches us that no one can come to spiritual understanding of the law without first being converted to the Lord Christ. Commentary on 2 Corinthians 3:16.[32]

Christ Gives Life to the Law. John Calvin: "The Lord is Spirit." This passage has also been misinterpreted, as if Paul had meant to say that Christ is a spiritual essence. For they conjoin this passage with that one in John, "God is Spirit." But the passage before us says nothing about Christ's essence, but only about his office, for it connects with what has come before, where we observed that the teaching of the law is the literal, not merely dead, but even the occasion for death. By contrast, he now calls Christ its spirit, meaning by this that it will finally be living and life-giving only if it has been inspired by Christ. Let the soul be connected to the body and it becomes a living human being, endowed with intelligence and feeling, suitable for all vital functions. Let the soul be removed from the body, and it will remain a useless cadaver, totally devoid of feeling.

This passage is worthy of special notice, for it teaches us how to reconcile those encomiums that David employs to commend the law—"The law of the Lord converts souls, illumines the eyes, imparts wisdom to infants," and other like passages—with those statements of Paul, which appear to disagree with them—that [the law] is a ministry of sin and death, a letter which does nothing but kill. For when it is animated by Christ, those things which David mentions are rightly applicable to it. If Christ is taken away, it is entirely as Paul described it. Therefore, Christ is the life of the law.

"Where the Lord is Spirit." Paul now describes the mode by which Christ gives life to the law, namely, by giving us his Spirit. The name "Spirit" here has a different meaning than in the previous clause. There it denoted the soul and it was ascribed metaphorically to Christ. But here it signifies the Holy Spirit, whom Christ himself gives to his people. But Christ, by regenerating us, gives life to the law, and shows himself to be a fountain of life, as all the vital functions proceed from the soul of a human being. Commentary on 2 Corinthians 3:17.[33]

The Meaning of "The Lord Is Spirit." Wolfgang Musculus: Paul explains this by adding the words: "Now the Lord is that spirit." He does not simply write "the Lord is spirit," but he adds the article, "the Lord is *that* spirit." Now Paul says earlier [in v. 6] that he is a minister of the Spirit, and that the Spirit gives life. It is as if he said, "Now the Lord whom I preach, and whom I serve as minister and apostle, is not letter, but spirit, that spirit of the new covenant, that life-giving spirit. The dispensation of the new covenant in the Lord Christ is being perfected, not in the letter that is fading, but through the life-giving spirit." In saying this, Paul is not describing the essence of Christ, that is, that he is Spirit, as some heretics understood this passage (and unfortunately, even today some people propose to us the same thing); rather, he is describing the dispensation and ministry of the new covenant, which is in Christ and by the Lord Christ. For just as Paul is referring to the office and law of Moses when he writes the words "when Moses is read," so too when he writes here "the Lord is that spirit," he is not so much referring to the *person* of Christ, the second hypostasis of the holy Trinity, as to his dispensation, by which

[32]Hemmingsen, *Commentaria in Omnes Epistolas Apostolorum*, 265.

[33]CO 50:45-46 (CTS 40:184-85); citing Jn 4:24; Ps 19:8; 2 Cor 3:6-7.

the new covenant is administered and directed. Commentary on 2 Corinthians 3:17.[34]

The Spirit Is God. Martin Chemnitz: Eudoxius, Eunomius, and many other followers of Macedonius,[†] who under a general heading are called "Spirit fighters" (*pneumatomachoi*), imagined that the Holy Spirit is more outstanding in powers than the angels, to be sure, but is not God or Lord. Others said that they wished to remain neutral as to whether he is God or a created being, since Scripture clearly takes a neutral position. And . . . Paul of Samosata denied that the Son is a person. Later on, Arius, seeing that this position could not hold water, conceded that he is indeed a person, but he denied that the person is by nature God. In the same way Macedonius at first plainly denied that the Spirit is a person. . . . For the refutation of this blasphemy we should note first the testimonies indicated above, which affirm that not only is he the Spirit of God but he is very God himself; not only is he the Spirit of the Lord but he is the Lord himself. For because there is one Lord, and because "the Spirit is Lord," therefore he is the unique and true God. Loci Theologici.[35]

The Glory and Power of the Gospel. Andreas Hyperius: The efficient cause of so great a glory received through the gospel is that Spirit of the Lord, by whom we have been made free, and from whom we draw freedom.[†] For having been unclothed from the letter of the law, we grasp ahold of the spirit and end of the law, namely, Christ, whose spirit enlivens the hearts of everyone so that what results redounds to and corresponds with God's glory. Now very appropriately, these things are brought up to compare the gospel with the law and demonstrate the effect of the most powerful gospel. And in conclusion, Paul boasts with good reason that he is a minister of the new covenant and the spirit, in contrast to his opponents, who promote the law and impart nothing else than the dead letter. Commentary on 2 Corinthians 3:17.[36]

Where the Spirit Is, There Is Liberty. Tilemann Hesshus: After we have been converted, we are no longer confined in servitude; we are not burdened with the veil; we are not killed by the letter, but we enjoy freedom. The Holy Spirit is the one who imparts those true and heavenly blessings of the kingdom of Christ. Whatever Christ, the Son of God, has merited by his suffering and death for us, this the Holy Spirit confers upon and applies to us, which we receive in conversion through faith. Without the Spirit, we are like slaves, bound in chains, we are oppressed in darkness, we are entangled in the veil of ignorance, we are without God and are trapped in death. But when the Holy Spirit is poured into our hearts through faith at our conversion, then we are made alive and liberated. With the word "liberty," Paul sums up the kingdom of Jesus Christ and all its benefits, namely, freedom from the wrath of God, from the curse of the law, from sin, from death and the power of Satan. It includes being born anew and renewal, the imputation of righteousness, the communion in the light and heavenly joy, and fellowship with God. This is the enormous goodness of the spiritual freedom, by which we are established as lords of this world and heirs of the heavenly kingdom through faith in Christ. Explication of 2 Corinthians 3:17.[37]

---

[34]Musculus, *Commentarius . . . in posteriorem epistolam Pauli ad Corinthios*, 108.

[35]Chemnitz, *Loci Theologici*, 1:139*; citing 1 Cor 8:6; 12:5; 2 Cor 3:17. [†]This list of ancient heretics includes those who denied the deity of the Holy Spirit (Eudoxius, Eunomius, and Macedonius); those who believed that Jesus was a mere human being infused with the divine Logos at his baptism (Paul of Samosata); and those who denied that the Son was of the same divine substance and coeternal with the Father (Arius).

[36]Hyperius, *Commentarii . . . in Epistolam D. Pauli ad Romanos, et utramque ad Corinthios*, 361. [†]Following Aristotle and the medieval scholastics, Hyperius here is employing a fourfold scheme of causality, which includes the efficient cause, the material cause, the formal cause, and the final cause. According to Muller, the efficient cause "is the agent productive of the motion or mutation in any sequence of causes and effects." See Muller, *Dictionary of Latin and Greek Theological Terms*, 61. See Aristotle, *Physics* 2.3; *Metaphysics* 5.2.

[37]Hesshus, *Explicatio Secundae Epistolae Pauli ad Corinthios*, 87v-88r; citing Jn 3:16-17.

Reasons Why the Lord's Spirit Gives Liberty. David Dickson: The reason for this is given, because (1) Christ is the spirit, or the soul of all ceremonies, which signified a spiritual thing. (2) Christ is also the spirit, or the soul of the moral law, because he fulfilled the law, in whom alone the perfect righteousness of the law is to be found. (3) Christ is the spirit, because he quickens those who believe to new obedience and everlasting life, and he also delivers them from sin and misery. For when Paul says, "Where the Spirit of Christ the Lord is," or "where Christ is, there is liberty," the liberty is to be understood, not from the obedience of the commandments, but from the ceremonial yoke, from the bondage of sin, from the yoke of the legal covenant and all the evils which follow from its violation. Liberty, I say, was given to believers by the spirit of the gospel, and this belongs to them by right, although it is not always evident to their senses, nor do they possess it in full before the end of life. For although the Spirit proclaims with a loud voice that there is a gate opened to us, that we may go out of prison, yet we by reason of the weakness of our faith go forth slowly. Exposition of 2 Corinthians 3:17.[38]

Christians Are Bathed in New Light. Huldrych Zwingli: This metaphor is taken from a mirror, as Paul demonstrates [his point] by anagogy, moving from a mirror to the glory of God.[†] This is the sense: when we meditate on God through sincere faith, by the radiance of his light, we are transformed into the same glory, we are clothed in a different spirit and illuminated with a different glory. Indeed, whoever has correctly and carefully considered God's immeasurable goodness and compassion with which he has demonstrated us to be his very own children is bathed with new light. Annotations on 2 Corinthians 3:18.[39]

The Glory of the Lord. Tilemann Hesshus: In this way [Paul] invokes the majesty of Christ's kingdom and God's immense wisdom, mercy, goodness, and kindness revealed in the gospel, by which we are saved and admitted into fellowship with God. Nicodemus contemplated the glory of the Lord as in a mirror when he heard from Christ's voice the sweetest sermon that was ever heard on earth: that "God loved the world so much that he gave his only-begotten Son, so that all who believe in him will not perish but have eternal life. For God did not send his son into the world to judge the world, but so that the world might be saved through him." Explication of 2 Corinthians 3:18.[40]

Humans Are Made Up of Body, Soul, and Spirit. Balthasar Hubmaier: Whether now such a power for willing what is right and good is in us, it is not in us as if it were from us, for it is originally from God and his image, in which he created us originally, which the old serpent almost blackened out and darkened through sin. Nevertheless, it was not possible to extinguish entirely this breath of God in us, and it still cannot be done, for God lets no one be more seriously tempted beyond that which he can bear. But God can extinguish it as a punishment so that a person can have eyes, ears, and heart and still not see, hear, nor understand. . . .

Here one sees truly how the flesh after the fall can do wholly and completely nothing; and how, as far as good is concerned, it is completely unprofitable and dead, in all its powers, incapable of doing good, and is impotent, and enemy of the law, to whom it does not want to be subservient even unto the grave. . . . The spiritual person, however, judges all things and is judged by no one. Here you note again, dear Christian, the wholeness of the spirit in the human being that rightly judges all things and the wounds of the soul, which in itself is of no value for judging. Both flesh and soul are damaged and seriously wounded. Only the spirit has retained its original righteousness in which it was

[38]Dickson, *An Exposition of All St. Paul's Epistles*, 77*.

[39]Zwingli, *Annotatiunculae . . . ex ore Zvinglij*, 161. [†]An anagogical interpretation moves from earthly to heavenly realities, particularly as they relate to the world to come.

[40]Hesshus, *Explicatio Secundae Epistolae Pauli ad Corinthios*, 89r-v; citing Jn 3:16-17.

first created. This is the way things are among the three substances in the human being before and after the transgression of Adam, our first father, whatever the scholastics say about the upper and lower parts of the human being. Aristotle, the pagan, seduced them because he knew and ascribed nothing to the human being, save body and soul. The spirit was too heavenly for him. He was not able to grasp this breath of the living God with his natural and pagan understanding. Freedom of the Will.[41]

Christians Are Being Transformed into Christ's Image. Wolfgang Musculus: "We are being transformed into the same image." By this Paul means that we together are being changed into the image that we observe in Christ. The image of the old person is found in the body of sin, whose members are earthly and worldly, characterized by fornication, impurity, weakness, evil lust, and all kinds of impiety toward God and wickedness toward other people. The new person, who is from the spirit of Christ, is formed into the knowledge and likeness of the one who made him, namely, Christ, whose members are heavenly, characterized by all piety, truth, justice, and sanctity of the new life. True believers hold before their eyes and contemplate this image of Christ not only in Christ himself, but they also display and reflect this image in themselves, each one according to the measure of the donation of Christ. That is why those people are entirely foolish who do not think they see Christ unless they have a wooden crucifix before their eyes, which they worship and adore, when, in the meantime, they have no care (or rather, are ignorant) of Christ's living image into which they are being transformed. Commentary on 2 Corinthians 3:18.[42]

The Holy Spirit Effects Spiritual Transformation. Tilemann Hesshus: We are being transformed, that is, renewed, restored, and re-created. Now that restoration of new light and spiritual life is no less a work than that creation of human beings [in the Garden of Eden]. For this reason, David says, "Create in me a clean heart, O God, and renew a right spirit within my inmost parts." And Christ says in John 3, "Unless one has been born anew from water and spirit, they will not enter the kingdom of heaven." Matthias Illyricus† attempted to conclude from this phrase "we are being transformed" that the image of God in a man or woman was that human substance, and when humans are transformed into the image of God, then a new substance is imparted to them. And he wanted to argue from his monstrous error that the origin of sin was in that substance of human beings. But the Holy Spirit mounts an assault against Illyricus's assertion. For "being transformed" does not mean that a new substance is imparted to humans, but that the corrupt and depraved substance of men and women is renewed and restored. The substance remains, but is changed qualitatively; that is, the mind is enlightened, the will is made right, the heart is purified, integrity and freedom are restored—the creation is restored anew and transformed. . . . When the apostle Paul testifies that we are transformed and refashioned by the Holy Spirit and that the image of God is restored to us, he demonstrates the enormous power of the Holy Spirit and that all boasting of creation is rightly ascribed to him. . . . Therefore, this passage is a very convincing testimony of the eternal and all-powerful divinity of the Holy Spirit. Explication of 2 Corinthians 3:18.[43]

Understanding and Belief Must Precede Renewal. Dirk Philips: Since then new believers

[41]CRR 5:438-39; citing Gen 1:27; Gen 3:1-19; 1 Cor 10:13.

[42]Musculus, *Commentarius . . . in posteriorem epistolam Pauli ad Corinthios*, 111.

[43]Hesshus, *Explicatio Secundae Epistolae Pauli ad Corinthios*, 90v-91r; citing Ps 51:10; Jn 3:5. †Hesshus here is attacking the Croatian theologian and Gnesio-Lutheran Matthias Flacius Illyricus (1520–1575) who, in his effort to defend Luther's doctrine of the bondage of the will, argued that unconverted human beings bear the image of Satan and that the substance of their humanness is sinful. See *OER* 2:110-11. Flacius's anthropology was condemned by the Lutheran Book of Concord (1580), see BC 488.

are born of God and baptism is a bath of this new birth, and young children have not come to this new birth so long as they still lack understanding and do not believe, baptism does not apply to them. For baptism belongs to no one and may not be given rightly to anyone except the born-again children of God, that is, to believers who have been renewed after the image and likeness of God, to those forsaking the old Adam so that the new person, yes, Christ lives and works in them through faith. The Baptism of Our Lord Jesus Christ.[44]

From Glory to Glory. Tilemann Hesshus: Basil and those who followed his interpretation explained the phrase "from glory and splendor" to mean that our glory and light is derivative from Christ's light, as if Christ illumines us with his light.[†] This interpretation is very elegant and accords with the analogy of faith. But a simpler interpretation which is more fitting to the text is "from more obscure glory to clearer glory." For at the initial moment of our conversion, we are not immediately filled with the complete light of divinity, but we are bestowed with certain beginnings of light, righteousness, light, and joyfulness which begin to grow day by day and are entered into gradually as we undertake the reading of holy Scripture, preaching and the exercise of penance. Paul says, "Stir up the gift which is in you by the imposition of my hands." And Christ says, "How much more will your Father give the Holy Spirit to those who ask him." . . . Thus, we are transformed from glory to glory when the knowledge of God, faith in the Lord Jesus, righteousness, love of truth, humility, patience, gratitude, joyfulness in God, and desire for eternal life grow in us, while the image of God is perfected in us through our rebirth from the dead. Explication of 2 Corinthians 3:18.[45]

The Gospel Shines Forth God's Glory. The English Annotations: Going forward in the allegory of the covering, Paul compares the gospel to a mirror, which though it is most bright and radiant, yet it does not only dazzle the eyes of those who look on it, as the law did, but also transforms them with its beams so that they are also partakers of the glory and shine forth the light to others. As Christ said to his disciples, "You are the light of the world." . . .

Now instead of the veil of those Mosaic figures, God has given to his church the clear mirror of the gospel. Thus, all the faithful freely behold in it by faith the glorious light of his mercy, truth, and the rest of his divine attributes; and by means thereof they are made like him in the glory of his holiness and in newness of life. Moses lay aside the veil that hung over his face when he appeared before the Lord, and as he beheld God his face shone forth with beams of light. As for us, we now have free access to God by the gospel, which is not like a dark veil, but a pure resplendent mirror wherein we see the glorious countenance of God and we are thereby renewed and glorified in our minds according to the same image of God. Annotations on 2 Corinthians 3:18.[46]

Transformed in God's Image. Edward Leigh: That is, seeing by means of God's grace, the veil is removed, so that we may see the face of God clearly. Now, by means of this knowledge, we must be transformed into his image. That image in which we were created must daily be renewed, and by degrees further restored in us—that is the apostle's meaning of "from glory to glory." As Adam was created in the image of God, so must every believer be renewed into that blessed condition. Annotations on 2 Corinthians 3:18.[47]

[44]CRR 6:80; citing Titus 3:5; Col 3:10; Eph 4:24; Mt 16:10.
[45]Hesshus, *Explicatio Secundae Epistolae Pauli ad Corinthios*, 91v-92r; citing 2 Tim 1:6; Lk 11:13. [†]Basil aligns the believer's reflection of the Lord's light and glory with both Christ (Letter VIII to the Caesareans, NPNF[2] 8:119) and the Holy Spirit (*On the Holy Spirit* XXI.52, NPNF[2] 8:33-34).
[46]Downame, ed., *English Annotations*, FF3v*; citing Mt 5:14.
[47]Leigh, *Annotations upon all the New Testament*, 258*.

4:1-6 THE LIGHT OF THE GOSPEL

Therefore, having this ministry by the mercy of God,[a]
we do not lose heart. 2But we have renounced
disgraceful, underhanded ways. We refuse to practice[b]
cunning or to tamper with God's word, but by the
open statement of the truth we would commend
ourselves to everyone's conscience in the sight of God.
3And even if our gospel is veiled, it is veiled to those
who are perishing. 4In their case the god of this world
has blinded the minds of the unbelievers, to keep
them from seeing the light of the gospel of the glory of
Christ, who is the image of God. 5For what we
proclaim is not ourselves, but Jesus Christ as Lord,
with ourselves as your servants[c] *for Jesus' sake. 6For*
God, who said, "Let light shine out of darkness," has
shone in our hearts to give the light of the knowledge
of the glory of God in the face of Jesus Christ.

a Greek *having this ministry as we have received mercy* **b** Greek *to walk in* **c** Or *slaves*

Overview: Having described the superior splendor of the ministry of the new covenant, Paul now defends his conduct as a minister of the gospel and demonstrates how, through the gospel message he proclaims, God continues to display his glory through Jesus Christ and to impart spiritual life and wisdom to his people. Reformation commentators draw important lessons from these verses that are especially relevant for Christian ministers.

First, they observe that Paul's gospel ministry—indeed all Christian ministry—is a gracious gift and sacred trust bestowed by God. The Christian faithful should therefore hold the preaching office in high esteem since through it God grants to believers abundant blessings, including righteousness, grace, the Holy Spirit, and eternal life. Moreover, Paul's example highlights important qualities that faithful Christian ministers should possess: they must preach Jesus Christ as Lord and seek his glory alone; they must serve the body of Christ with all humility and sincerity; they must announce the truth of salvation clearly, without cunning or vain conceit. Protestant interpreters are quick to point out how far Catholic clergymen, including popes, bishops, and monks, have departed from Paul's standard in their unquenchable thirst for honor, money, and power. Another issue that stimulates extensive comment is why so few people receive the gospel—or, to use the apostle's language, why the gospel is "veiled" to so many. Certainly, this is not because the gospel is impotent! Rather, unbelief results from hard hearts and the wiles of Satan ("the god of this world"), who is ever deceiving and confusing women and men. Some commentators, including Calvin, go further to insist that God himself is the primary sovereign agent who not only permits but also commands Satan to blind the minds of the reprobate.

Finally, early modern interpreters show special interest in the christological themes found in this pericope. Jesus Christ, the eternal Word, bears God's image as he shares the splendor of God's divinity, wisdom, power, will, and grace. Christians must seek God, not in his unsearchable essence, but as he reveals himself in his Son, Jesus Christ. Just as God once created light from darkness through his powerful Word, so God now graciously re-creates and redeems men and women through the light of the gospel as it shines forth in the person of Jesus Christ. As Hesshus notes, it is in the gospel that one sees God's "infinite wisdom, eternal justice, unshakeable truth, inexhaustible goodness, and immeasurable power."

Summary of Chapter. John Calvin: Paul reviews again with what faith and integrity he has discharged the office entrusted to him, by which he reproves those who were wickedly railing against him. In fact, rising still higher in holy confidence, he declares that all who do not perceive the splendor of the gospel have been blinded by the devil. Perceiving, however, that the humbleness of his person (which was seen as despicable) detracted a lot from the respect due his apostleship, he not only takes the opportunity to remove the reason for the offense, but turns it in the opposite direction by saying that the excellence of God's grace shines forth in him all the more brightly just as valuable treasure discovered in clay jars. Thus, he turns to his own praise those things that the wicked were accustomed to hurl against him as invective because being oppressed by so many difficulties, nevertheless, he is always raised up as the victor, like a palm tree. He treats this topic all the way to the middle of the fourth chapter. Since, however, the true glory of Christians is outside this world, he reminds us that we must, through contempt for this present life and mortifying the outward person, eagerly continue with our whole mind to meditate on the blessed immortality. Commentary on 2 Corinthians.[1]

Explanation of Chapter. Tilemann Hesshus: There are three parts to this chapter. In the first part, the apostle commends his ministry and demonstrates that he truly believes those things about which he boasts, and he sets forth an example of faithfulness in teaching. Then he answers the objection concerning the blindness of the wicked and shows the reasons for their blindness and the reasons for light among the godly.

In the second part, he addresses the temptation concerning the scandal of the cross and the suffering that accompanies the preaching of the gospel. And Paul teaches by his example how in these dangers and troubles it is necessary to shine forth our confession and ministry.

In the third part, Paul demonstrates the extraordinary comforts with which the pious mind can sustain itself, as the Spirit with great strength despises and vanquishes all troubles, dangers, and adversities. Explication of 2 Corinthians 4.[2]

Preaching in Light of Eternal Glory. Giovanni Diodati: Paul continues to declare his faithfulness in preaching the gospel with all frankness and spiritual proof, in such a way that he can only be ignored by those who are guilty of willful unbelief. And for this purpose, God had illumined in him the full knowledge of Christ and had displayed in him and by him his power, notwithstanding his weaknesses, miseries, and afflictions. Amid these troubles, he strengthens himself by faith in the lively contemplation and apprehension of life and eternal glory. Annotations on 2 Corinthians 4.[3]

4:1-3 *Paul Commends His Gospel Ministry*

Paul's Faithful Gospel Witness. Desiderius Erasmus: Since the compassion of God willed us to be ministers and heralds of such exceptional felicity, through the apostolic task delegated to us, we do not take up our commission in a lackadaisical manner. Instead, just as we proclaim what is truly glorious, so we have rejected the wrappings that suit disgrace, not glory. We do not live our life under the crafty subtleties of human learning, but openly, frankly, and without disguise, we expose to everyone's view the whole truth unadorned and veiled by no cloud. In this service, we behave in such a way that our life itself, apart from human commendation, commends us before all people, the witnesses and confidants of our sincerity; commends us, indeed, not only before humans, who can be deceived, but also before God, who misses nothing. Paraphrases on 2 Corinthians 4.[4]

The Integrity of Paul's Ministry. Jacques Lefèvre d'Étaples: Just as the face of Moses was shining from the glory of God, so the mind of Paul

[1]CO 50:6-7 (CTS 40:104-5).

[2]Hesshus, *Explicatio Secundae Epistolae Pauli ad Corinthios*, 95v-96r.

[3]Diodati, *La Seconde Epistre de l'Apostre S. Paul aux Corinthiens*, 141.

[4]CWE 43:221.

and of his fellow helpers was filled with the light of truth from the glory of Christ, so that they might grasp a clear, sincere, and unobstructed understanding of the law. They received this understanding by the mercy of God in order to minister to other people. Thus, they were not wavering, they were not yielding to any evil thing, they were neither wishing nor contemplating evil for anyone; because they had acquired this mercy from God, they had nothing to do with all hidden wickedness of the heart and all shameful secrets of a cloaked conscience. They were walking in simplicity, leading no one slyly away from the Word of God, but instead making known the pure truth. And so, they presented themselves as approved before the conscience of all people and blameless before God. Commentary on 2 Corinthians 4:1-2.[5]

The Supremacy of Gospel Ministry Is No Cause for Pride. Wolfgang Musculus: "We do not fall" (*degeneramus*). In Greek, the phrase is *ouk enkakoumen*. Older interpreters rendered it "We do not faint," a reading that some more recent interpreters also follow; Erasmus himself does not disapprove of this translation, although he will render the phrase "We do not fall." Let the minister of Christ observe here for what benefit the supremacy of the gospel ministry ought to be regarded. Whenever the apostle thought about the excellence of his apostleship, his heart was not puffed with pride, nor did it cause him to become more arrogant, but he was stimulated to pursue a more excellent ministry so that he behaved more faithfully in this and was energized by it. Following Paul's example, whenever the minister of Christ considers the dignity of his ministry, he should not be moved to arrogance, but to careful attention to persevere and continue in faith and purity, which is required of a faithful minister. The person to whom much is entrusted, much will be required. The person who breaks faith in great matters is guilty of especially great faithlessness. The person who is employed in lofty affairs, if he should fall, his fall is more perilous since he falls from a higher place. These and similar matters ought to be considered; they rightly make a minister of the gospel of God careful and cautious. Commentary on 2 Corinthians 4:1.[6]

The Glories of the Christian Ministry. Tilemann Hesshus: Paul testifies that he has not been boasting with empty words concerning the supreme blessedness of the new covenant, but that he experiences it truly and from the heart, having a confident hope for these good things. . . . The apostle teaches us here what attitude the godly pastor and preacher of the Word ought to have. He should understand and, with all sincerity, ponder the importance of the ministry to which God has called him, so that prayers, zeal, and diligence might be aroused in him. This responsibility that the Holy Spirit has entrusted to pastors is the highest known to humans, for it has been acquired through the precious blood of the Son of God. Through it God gathers a church out of the human race. The ministry defends God's glory among men and women; it arouses knowledge of him; it calls men and women to repentance; it cleanses them of their sins; it confers to them peace of conscience; and it performs salvation among them. All these things are not accomplished by the power or majesty of emperors, but by the ministry of the Spirit. Therefore, we should not be sluggish in this so important ministry; we should not be disturbed by abuse; we should not become weary in our labors; we should not be disheartened by troubles; we should not be frightened by dangers. So, too, we should not be careless or proud, but in the fear of the Lord be eager for God's glory and call continually upon the Lord that, through his Spirit, he might be present with us, illuminate us with his teaching, fortify us with his strength, and grant us success. Explication of 2 Corinthians 4:1.[7]

---

[5]Lefèvre, *Commentariorum in Epistolas Beati Pauli . . . Liber Tertius*, 133.

[6]Musculus, *Commentarius . . . in posteriorem epistolam Pauli ad Corinthios*, 113.

[7]Hesshus, *Explicatio Secundae Epistolae Pauli ad Corinthios*, 96r-v.

Christian Preaching Should Be Held in High Esteem. Cyriacus Spangenberg: There is no other ministry through which people can be saved from sin, death, the devil, and hell, or attain righteousness, grace, the Holy Spirit, peace, joy, and eternal life. Both preachers and their listeners should consider this and therefore hold the preaching ministry in high esteem and prove themselves to be diligent, upright, and faithful in it. This is one thing that they should reflect on.

They should remember that they have not been placed in such a ministry because of their worthiness or skillfulness; they should not think that God has called them to it before others because they have been so learned, so eloquent, so wise and intelligent. "O no," says Paul, "we have such a ministry after mercy has come to us. I have not earned it from God, nor have I been worthy of his making me a preacher of the gospel. That I have become a preacher comes rather from his graciously having had mercy on me, a sinner, and his entrusting such a high ministry. Therefore, I thank his mercy alone that he has used me, unworthy, for such high matters." Such consideration produces in gospel preachers true fear of God and humility, so that they do not become proud or arrogant, or exalt themselves over others because of their ministry. Seventeenth Sermon.[8]

The High Privilege of Gospel Ministry. John Trapp: Since we have been so freely called to the ministry of sheer mercy, we show forth therein all diligence and sincerity. "When I was born," said that French king, "a thousand others were born besides myself. Now what have I done to God more than they that I should be a king, and not they?" . . . So may ministers say, "What are we that God should call us to so high an office?" Commentary on 2 Corinthians 4:1.[9]

The Importance of a Good Reputation. Martin Luther: But it is true, nonetheless, that we must have a good name and reputation, and everyone ought so to live that nobody can say anything evil of them, and that they give offense to nobody, as St. Paul says in Romans 12, "We should be zealous to do good, not only before God but also before all people." And 2 Corinthians 4, "We walk so honestly that no man knows anything against us." But there must be great diligence and care lest such a reputation puff up the heart and make a person self-satisfied. Here the saying of Solomon holds: "As fire in the furnace proves gold, so a person is proved by the mouth of those who praise them." Those people must be few and very highly spiritual who through honor and praise alike remain indifferent and unchanged, so that they do not care for it or take pride and pleasure in it, but remain utterly free and unconcerned, ascribe all their honor and good name to God alone, offer it to him alone, and use it to no purpose other than the glory of God and the benefit of their neighbors and in no way to their own benefit or advantage. Treatise on Good Works.[10]

The Disgraceful Deceptions of the False Apostles. John Calvin: While Paul commends his own sincerity, he by contrast reproves the false apostles who, even though they have corrupted the innate power of the gospel by their ambition, were nevertheless desiring to be preeminent. And so, the faults from which Paul declares himself exempt, he indirectly imputes on them. Some interpreters understand the terms "hidden things of disgrace" or "concealments" as referring to the shadow of the Mosaic law. Chrysostom† understands the expression to mean the vain display by which they were trying to promote themselves. I take it to mean all the disguises by which they were adulterating the pure and native beauty of the gospel. For just as chaste and virtuous women, content with the elegance of natural beauty, do not resort to artificial adornments, while prostitutes never consider themselves well adorned unless they have corrupted nature, so Paul boasts that he has

[8]C. Spangenberg, *Die ander Epistel Pauli an die Corinthier*, 68v-69r.
[9]Trapp, *A Commentary or Exposition*, 711*.
[10]LW 44:44-45 (WA 6:221); citing Rom 12:17; Prov 27:21.

announced the pure gospel, while his opponents were setting forth one that was disguised and covered over with shameful additions. For since they were ashamed of the simplicity of Christ, or at least because they were not able to excel the true virtue of the apostles, they were fabricating a new gospel, not unlike a profane philosophy, puffed up with a lot of bombast, which was devoid of the efficacy of the Spirit. Such counterfeit ornaments of this sort, by which the gospel is deformed, Paul calls the "concealments of disgrace," because the nakedness of those who take refuge in concealments and disguises must necessarily be dishonorable and disgraceful. Commentary on 2 Corinthians 4:2.[11]

Paul Defends His Ministry. Niels Hemmingsen: From those matters that Paul discussed in chapter 3 about the ministry of the gospel, he now mentions with what faith and diligence he has conducted himself in that same ministry. And first of all, he credits all things to the grace and mercy of God, lest it appear that he was praising himself for the excellence of the ministry—which is an example that should be imitated by all godly ministers of the gospel. Second, Paul defends himself from two disgraceful accusations that the false apostles were hurling at him, and, of course, he makes unfavorable mention of the false apostles. The first accusation was that he was failing in and degrading the ministry of the gospel, and that he was seeking hidden and disgraceful things that were not appropriate for those to whom such a glorious ministry had been entrusted. The other accusation was that he was falsifying the Word of God with skillful cunning and was using human cleverness for the sake of his own security and praise. The apostle denies that these disgraceful accusations apply to him, but rather that he had committed himself to make the truth known to all people, and in the sight of God he appeals to their consciences of this fact. Such sacred boasting is never appropriate for those who, enslaved to empty pride and their stomachs, accommodate their message to the ears of the people. But it is only appropriate among those who apply their lives to reading, teaching, and preaching with holy piety; who seek the glory of God and the salvation of their hearers; who do not degrade the ministry with wicked deeds out of personal weakness, but rather, who are stirred by the example of the cross to do strenuous military service in the camp of the Lord. Commentary on 2 Corinthians 4:1-2.[12]

The Cunning of the Roman Church. Wolfgang Musculus: Now I ask you whether those who "practice cunning and treat the Word of God in a deceitful manner" are not those who conduct business in the church of God with insincere words, seeking their advantage now in pontifical power, now through the patronage of the saints, now in the fire of purgatory, now in the sacrifice of the Mass for the sins of the living and the dead, now in the privileges of their orders, now in papal indulgences? And they disguise their advantage with innumerable other shameful inventions. Commentary on 2 Corinthians 4:2.[13]

Examples of Those Who Treat the Word with Cunning. Tilemann Hesshus: People who treat the Word of God with cunning are those who know the truth of God, and yet, out of fear of danger, or love of wealth, or out of ambition, or stubbornness, either spread false opinions among the people, or excuse it or defend it. Thus, people who treat the Word of God with cunning are those who ascribe foreign meanings to statements of Scripture; or who violently abuse the witness of Scripture by twisting it for the purpose of establishing error; or who put forward interpretations with ambiguous words in such a way that they can be understood to mean multiple things. The

[11]CO 50:48 (CTS 40:189-90). †For Chrysostom's interpretation, see PG 61:433-34 (NPNF[1] 12:317-18).

[12]Hemmingsen, *Commentaria in Omnes Epistolas Apostolorum*, 266.

[13]Musculus, *Commentarius . . . in posteriorem epistolam Pauli ad Corinthios*, 114.

Arians treated the Word of God with cunning, for they spread their wicked teachings and corrupted the statements of Scripture and deceived with ambiguous words. Pelagius, by construing the term "grace" in Paul from the nature and revelation of the law, and by claiming that there was no original sin in humankind, was treating the Word of God with cunning. Various popes treat the Word of God with cunning when they ascribe foreign meanings to statements of sacred Scripture, and attempt to sell their brazen errors to those involved by force. Their teachings are completely pagan, since they command men and women to doubt the grace of God. Nevertheless, they are not able to establish this most pernicious error from statements of Scripture. Explication of 2 Corinthians 4:2.[14]

Paul Presented the Truth Openly and Clearly. Wolfgang Musculus: "Commending ourselves to everyone's conscience." That is, we say what we think and present ourselves just as we are before the consciences of all people. We do not seek to hide, nor do we evade the conscience of anyone, but we teach and make known the truth of God openly and clearly before all people. This is how I understand the Greek word *synistōntes.* Interpreters translate this word "commending," lest people wonder how the apostle recommended himself to the consciences of all people by proclaiming this truth, when by it he displeased so many and pleased so very few. Paul does not say that he was seeking the favor of all through the proclamation of this truth, but he was presenting and making known to all people what he felt and taught in such a way that he proclaimed to everyone the truth of God without dissimulation.

People who act out of cunning, teach, and write in such a way that they present themselves openly to the conscience of no one. They do not proclaim the truth of God, especially in controversies when the truth is exposed to ridicule and brings danger with it. Instead, they either hide their convictions in general or they teach the truth with ambiguous words and in such a complicated fashion that no one easily understands what they think. The apostle writes that he is completely opposed to such cunning. Commentary on 2 Corinthians 4:2.[15]

Why Do So Few People Receive the Gospel? Andreas Hyperius: Now although Paul consistently proclaimed his sincerity in making known the gospel and even said previously that, through the gospel, all people with unveiled faces see the glory of God, nevertheless, some people could object, "Why is it, then, that so few people receive the gospel and for so many people the gospel is still veiled? Indeed, it seems that the gospel also has its own veil—why, then, will the law not be more excellent?" To this objection the apostle responds, "But if the gospel is not fully revealed to all people, that indeed is not because the gospel is at fault or defective. Rather, it is the fault of those who are perishing and do not wish to receive it for their salvation." And so, the fact that they do not receive the gospel and clearly see the glory of the Lord in it, Paul imputes to their wickedness and blindness. In a similar way, he argues in 1 Corinthians 1 that the word of the cross is foolishness to those who are perishing. The gospel is veiled and hidden to those who are perishing. They do not truly recognize Christ; they see nothing except the thick letter. Commentary on 2 Corinthians 4:3.[16]

Why Does Paul Say, "Our Gospel"? Wolfgang Musculus: Why is it that Paul does not say, "If the new covenant is veiled," or "if the ministry of the spirit is veiled," or "if Christ is veiled," but instead he says, "if the gospel is veiled"? And why does he not say, "If the gospel of God is veiled," but instead "if *our* gospel is veiled"? The false apostles were not seizing upon these terms "new covenant," "spirit," or "Christ" to harass Paul,

[14]Hesshus, *Explicatio Secundae Epistolae Pauli ad Corinthios,* 99v-100v.

[15]Musculus, *Commentarius . . . in posteriorem epistolam Pauli ad Corinthios,* 115.

[16]Hyperius, *Commentarii . . . in Epistolam D. Pauli ad Romanos, et Utramque ad Corinthios,* 362; citing 1 Cor 1:18.

but under the name of Paul they were attacking the term "gospel"—calling it "the gospel of Paul"—out of special contempt. Clearly, in the same way, in our own day the enemies of the doctrine of the truth of Christ have begun to call it the "gospel of Luther" by way of insult. Commentary on 2 Corinthians 4:3.[17]

People Are Lost Without the Gospel. Cyriacus Spangenberg: Now it is truly great boldness that the apostle Paul may say and maintain that all those who do not accept his gospel are lost. But, dear friends, we preachers today must be equally certain of our matters and not carry any doubt that our teaching is right, and the only teaching that makes people blessed. Therefore, I also (praise God) can say in good conscience, "Whoever does not accept by faith the gospel that I preach is certainly lost for eternity and, on the last day before God's solemn judgment seat, will be condemned to eternal damnation. This is certainly true." We render this judgment on all enemies of the Protestant [*Euangelisch*] teaching and on all opponents of our religion where they are thus stubborn and do not repent. Seventeenth Sermon.[18]

Those Who Are Perishing. Giovanni Diodati: [Paul refers to] those who have no part in eternal salvation, which includes two kinds of people: those who are without knowledge of the gospel, and those to whom it has been preached, but, being blinded by the devil who possesses their hearts, they have rejected it by their unbelief. Annotations on 2 Corinthians 4:3.[19]

4:4-6 *The Gospel of the Glory of Christ*

The Wicked Reject the Word of Truth. Menno Simons: It is well known to the honorable reader and to all who are acquainted with us that we are called seditionists and trouble-makers everywhere by the learned ones, notwithstanding that we are quiet and act decently with all people and if we now should publicly teach the Word of the Lord in the face of the revilings of the learned ones in spite of the mandate of the rulers and of the frenzy of the common people, some of them would cry, "Troublemakers," although we are, thank the Lord, clear of all rebellion and bloodshed, as has been heard. . . .

And although we do not teach at public meetings where all men meet, yet the truth is not hushed up, but is preached here and there both by day and by night, in cities and country, with tongue and pen, at the peril of life, as judges, executioners, prisons, fetters, water, fire, sword, and stake testify.

Flanders, Brabant, Holland, Gelderland . . . will have to confess at the last judgment that the Word was preached to them in power, for they on account of the preached Word have shed innocent blood like water. It is preached enough in these countries so that we may well say with the holy Paul, "If our gospel be hid, it is hid to them that are lost; in whom the god of this world has blinded the minds of those who do not believe." Reply to False Accusations.[20]

Sophists and Jews Are Blind to the Plain Truth of Scripture. Martin Luther: Christ has opened our understanding, that we might understand the Scriptures, and the gospel is preached to every creature. . . . Come forward then, you, and all the Sophists with you, and cite a single mystery which is still obscure in the Scripture. I know that to many people a great deal remains obscure; but that is due, not to any lack of clarity in Scripture, but to their own blindness and dullness, in that they make no effort to seek truth which, in itself, could not be plainer. As Paul said of the Jews in 2 Corinthians 4 . . . "If our gospel be hid to them that are lost, whose heart the god of this world has blinded." They are like people who

[17]Musculus, *Commentarius . . . in posteriorem epistolam Pauli ad Corinthios*, 116-17.
[18]C. Spangenberg, *Die ander Epistel Pauli an die Corinthier*, 72r-v.
[19]Diodati, *La Seconde Epistre de l'Apostre S. Paul aux Corinthiens*, 142; citing 2 Thess 1:8.
[20]CWMS 574*.

cover their eyes, or go from daylight into darkness, and hide there, and then blame the sun, or the darkness of the day, for their inability to see. So let the wretched abjure that blasphemous perversity which would blame the darkness of their own hearts on the plain Scriptures of God! Bondage of the Will.[21]

Guises of Satan. Simon Goulart: The prince of this world sometimes blinds the understanding of unbelievers. Sometimes he transforms himself into an angel of light, so as to pierce them under the appearance of virtue. On other occasions, he appears as covered with fire and blood to throw them into despair. For is he not called the Tempter, a word that signifies one who tests by fire? If he even dared to let fly his arrows against the blessed Son of God, the head of the church, let us not be at all astounded if he strives against the members of the church as well. Discourse Eighteen: Against One of Our Complaints.[22]

The Nature of Spiritual Blindness. Wolfgang Musculus: Paul next describes those who are perishing, from whom the gospel is veiled. If he said simply, "The god of the world has blinded their minds so that they might not see the light of the gospel," this would not completely capture the meaning. For when he says, "The god of this world has blinded the minds," and adds the phrase "of unbelievers," he clearly indicates the blindness that afflicts those that are perishing, but only if they are unbelievers. Now a person who has never heard Christ proclaimed cannot be called an unbeliever. "How can they believe in him of whom they have never heard?" Just as in the winter it is impossible to determine whether a tree is barren or fruitful, while in the summer one can discern its fruitfulness. For indeed, the time for bearing fruit is in the summer, not the winter. Just as in the dead of night, it is impossible to identify the blind when even those who have the faculty of sight can see nothing, so too it is impossible to make a judgment between faith and disbelief when the message of the Word of God does not ring forth, when the gospel is not even heard, much less either accepted by faith or rejected in unbelief. That is why Paul is careful to add the word "of unbelievers." It happens sometimes that the elect only come to faith in Christ slowly so that, having heard the Word of God, they reject it or even persecute it for some time, which is what happened in the case of the apostle himself. But that refusal cannot be called "unbelief," because it is removed by the faith that follows; in the same way, [a tree] that is slow in bearing fruit is not rightly called sterile on account of the fruitfulness that follows. Now even if people display temporary unbelief in this gospel message, they are nevertheless not subject to the blindness that so greatly affects those unbelievers who are reprobate and perishing, which is what these words of the apostle clearly teach. Commentary on 2 Corinthians 4:4.[23]

Satan Blinds Human Minds with God's Command. John Calvin: With respect to the present passage, the "blinding" is as much the work of God as of Satan, for it is in many instances attributed to God; but the power is not alike, nor is the manner the same. . . . Scripture teaches that Satan blinds human beings, not merely with God's permission, but even by his command, that he might exercise his vengeance. Thus, Ahab was deceived by Satan, but could Satan have done this by himself? By no means. But since he offered to God his services for harming, "he was sent to be a lying spirit in the mouth of all the prophets." Indeed, God is said to blind people because, after he has deprived us of right understanding of mind and the light of his Spirit, he hands us over to the devil who forcibly leads us to a reprobate mind; and God gives him the power of deception, and by so doing, inflicts just vengeance upon us by the minister of his wrath. Therefore, Paul understands

[21]Luther, *Bondage of the Will*, 72 (WA 18:607).
[22]Goulart, *Seconde partie des Discours Chrestiens*, 264.
[23]Musculus, *Commentarius . . . in posteriorem epistolam Pauli ad Corinthios*, 118; citing Rom 10:14.

that all people are possessed by the devil who do not acknowledge his doctrine to be the sure truth of God. COMMENTARY ON 2 CORINTHIANS 4:4.[24]

IT IS THE DEVIL—NOT GOD—WHO BLINDS HUMAN MINDS. CYRIACUS SPANGENBERG: In order to confront such error, the dear fathers read this text differently from us, when we read "Of whom the god of this world has blinded the mind of unbelievers." They read it thus: "of whom the God of this world has blinded the mind of unbelievers," that the meaning is "God the Lord, who is a God of heaven, earth, the whole world, has blinded," that is, "allowed to be blind or remain blind," "the mind of unbelievers." Irenaeus is of this opinion (in his book *Against Heresies*) as is Tertullian (*Against Marcion*), Hilary, Chrysostom, Theophylact, Ambrose, Augustine (*Against Faustus* and *Against the Opponents of the Law*), Theodoret, Sedulius.[†] ... And this interpretation is not so bad, but it is not St. Paul's meaning. For he is talking here not about God, the Creator of the world, but of the devil, who is the prince and god of the world, because it serves him and is under him.

Now things that people trust in are called "gods," whether it be money, goods, honor, knowledge, power, or similar things. If you trust in another person, he is your god. The rich and greedy trust in their goods. Therefore, such supply is their god, and is called "mammon." SEVENTEENTH SERMON.[25]

HUMANS ARE ATTRACTED TO THE TRICKS OF SATAN. MARTIN CHEMNITZ: The outward impulse exerted on us by the devil should not be used as a pretext or excuse for this situation, as if we were entirely unwilling and were forced into sin, and therefore we do not deserve either punishment or guilt. James puts the cause of sin at our very door. . . . Therefore, the devil casts humankind headlong into sin, not as those who are unknowing or unwilling or resisting and dragged in by the throat, but the will of humankind is attracted to the trickery of Satan, and meekly offers itself to all who lead it astray. Thus, in Ephesians, Paul writes, "He works in the children of disobedience" and "takes them captive with his snares." Thus, the cause of sin must not be placed totally outside of the will of humankind. LOCI THEOLOGICI.[26]

WHY DO WISE AND POWERFUL PEOPLE NOT UNDERSTAND THE GOSPEL? DAVID DICKSON: [Some people object,] "But how does it come to pass that your doctrine is not understood by so many wise and powerful people, if it is so clearly taught?" Paul answers that the ignorance of the gospel so plainly unfolded to them was no argument for the obscurity of his doctrine, but of the incredulity of the hearer, and his future perdition from the blindness of unbelievers, blinded by the devil, whom the world serves. For the devil further blinds the blind infidels, lest they should see God offering himself in Christ, lest they should behold Christ for their salvation, shining in the gospel, who has brought forth the invisible God to our view by his doctrine and power manifested in the flesh, so that we may behold God in Christ, the true image of God the Father. EXPOSITION OF 2 CORINTHIANS 4:4.[27]

THE GOD OF THIS WORLD. EDWARD LEIGH: Not in respect to dominion over created things, but (1) in respect to corruption, for his is the god of the evil in the world; (2) in respect to seduction; (3) in respect to opinion, or estimation, because the people of the world make the devil their god. In past times, the Marcionites and Manichaeans abused this passage to prove that there were two principles or gods, one which they

[24]CO 50:51 (CTS 40:195). 1 Kings 22:21-22.

[25]C. Spangenberg, *Die ander Epistel Pauli an die Corinthier*, 73. [†]Irenaeus, *Against Heresies* 3.7, ANF 1:420-21; Tertullian, *Against Marcion* 5.11, ANF 3:452-53; Chrysostom, *Homilies on Second Corinthians*, NPNF[1] 12:318-19; Theophylact, *Commentarius in Epistolam II ad Corinthos*, PG 124:838-39; Ambrose, *Commentaria in Epistolas B. Pauli*, PL 17:289; Augustine, *Against Faustas* 21.2, NPNF[1] 4:264-65; Theodoret, *Commentarius in omnes sancti Pauli Epistolas*, PG 82:399-402.

[26]Chemnitz, *Loci Theologici*, 1:192; citing Jas 1:14-15; Eph 2:2; 2 Tim 2:26.

[27]Dickson, *An Exposition of All St. Paul's Epistles*, 12-13*.

called good, the other evil. Annotations on 2 Corinthians 4:4.[28]

Christ's Glory Shines in Believers. Philipp Melanchthon: For Christ to be the image of God is to display the likeness of God. For Colossians 3 along with Ephesians 4 calls him the image, likeness, truth, righteousness, and holiness. And so, just as wisdom, truth, and righteousness are in God, so too they are in Christ. And with this likeness, Christ shines upon hearts, enlightens hearts, and also rules in the hearts of the saints. John 17: "The glory that you have given to me, I have given to them . . . I am in them, and you are in me." And a little earlier, Christ explains what he means by this glory, when he says: "Glorify me, father, with the glory which I had with you previously. . . ." Now faith is the knowledge of the glory of God. Annotations on 2 Corinthians 4:4.[29]

The Glory of Christ. Huldrych Zwingli: "To keep them from seeing the light of the gospel of the glory of Christ, who is the image of God." This statement is hyperbole, by which Paul describes for us the immeasurable and ineffable compassion of God the Father—as if he placed it right before our eyes. For the greatest and most excellent thing that God possessed, he gave to us, granting his Son who is the image of the Father (according to the divine nature), of one and the same nature and essence with the Father. This light—here its brilliance pours over pious minds—fills them with great joy and consolation, [but] it terrifies and blinds the eyes of the wicked. Annotations on 2 Corinthians 4:4.[30]

Christ Is the Image of God. Wolfgang Musculus: The apostle is not accustomed to stop and remain focused on Christ whenever he attributes to him those things that tend toward his glory and our salvation, but he leads the reader as if by the hand through Christ to God the Father himself. Thus, here in this passage, when he has called the gospel the light of the glory of Christ, he then adds the phrase "who is the image of God," so as to remind us that the Father should be seen and recognized in his Son. God in himself is invisible, because he does not have a physical body by which he can be seen. Whence Christ says, "No one has ever seen God." Therefore, in order to be seen and known, God sent his Word into the world, who bears his image; and this image thus illumines the minds of the elect so that in it he himself might be seen and known. In this image of God (which is Christ, the only-begotten Son of God) is not represented some corporeal likeness that is alien to God, but rather it is the splendor of his divinity, wisdom, power, will, and grace. In the flesh, a son reflects the image of his human parent. But the only-begotten Christ reflects the image of the living God, his heavenly Father, not a human parent whom he does not have. He is the splendor of God's glory and the character of his substance. . . . Whence to Philip Jesus said, "Philip, whoever sees me also sees my Father." Again, "The Father is in me and I am in the Father." And "the Father who dwells in me does the works which I do." Commentary on 2 Corinthians 4:4.[31]

Jesus Christ Is the Eternal Image of God. Tilemann Hesshus: So as to show the nature and source of that glory and majesty which the gospel announces, Paul describes the eternal divinity of Christ. The greatest glory of the church is that it knows the eternal and living God in the Son of God, and that it is renewed into the image of God through the Son, and that it is made a participant of that light and glory that shines forth in the Son of God, who is the image of the Father. The Holy Spirit calls the Son of God, our Lord Jesus Christ, "the eternal image of God" because he displays the whole Father in himself and is the splendor of God's substance. And he exhibits to

[28]Leigh, *Annotations upon all the New Testament*, 258*.
[29]*Melanchthons Werke*, 4:110; citing Col 3:12; Eph 4:24; Jn 17:22; Jn 17:5.
[30]Zwingli, *Annotatiunculae . . . ex ore Zvinglij*, 163.
[31]Musculus, *Commentarius . . . in posteriorem epistolam Pauli ad Corinthios*, 121; citing Jn 1:18; 14:9-10.

our understanding that Father God, who dwells in inaccessible light. Now, the human being Adam is also said to have been created in the image of God, but with this enormous difference: human beings are called the image of God because God has communicated to them his wisdom, righteousness, life, and freedom. But the Son of God is the image of God in his substance, born in essence as the only-begotten Son from the Father, and wholly displaying in himself the Father. "He who sees me," Jesus says, "sees the Father." Therefore, the glory of the Father shines forth in Christ, and through him we are illuminated with heavenly light so that we might know God. Athanasius elegantly stated, "And so, the Son of God, who is the image of the Father, came and was appointed to be the Mediator, so that through him the image of God, which had been undermined by our sin, might be renewed and we might recognize God again." Explication of 2 Corinthians 4:4.[32]

The Gospel Is the Face of Christ. John Donne: God . . . has not shone in people's hearts until they know the glory of God in the face of Jesus Christ, until they come to the manifestation of God in the gospel. Thus, people come short of this light when they believe in God in a general way, as an incomprehensible power, but not in Christ. So, too, people go beyond this light when they know more of God than is manifested in the gospel, which is the face of Christ Jesus. The first sort of people does not come to the light; the second goes beyond the light—and both are in blindness. Christ is the image of God, and the gospel is the face of Christ. At the present time, I do not rest in God's picture as it appears in every creature, though the image of God can be seen in every creature. I have a livelier image of God, namely, Christ. And then I do not seek [the image of] Christ's face as, according to tradition, it was sent to Agbar[†] during Christ's lifetime. Nor do I seek [the image of Christ's face] as it was imprinted in Veronica's apron,[‡] as he went to his death. . . . But I myself have the glory of God in Christ, and I have the face of Christ in the gospel. Sermon Preached at the Spittle (Easter-Monday 1622).[33]

Christ Alone Should Be Preached in Churches. Martin Luther: The church (which is a matter of the Spirit) is not born or preserved, it cannot exist, work, conquer, continue, or do any other [suitable] thing unless it is based on its foundation which is Christ alone; that is, the church must have Christ for its ruler, who rules it through faith, the Spirit, and the other gifts of his Spirit. From this it necessarily follows that [only] such preaching and teaching which are concerned exclusively with these matters and these mysteries should be done in the church; for only that should be preached in the church by which alone it is preserved and continues to exist. Therefore, one should preach Christ alone and establish him as foundation, and teach the faith and those matters which are related to the faith, as Paul has said above: "We do not preach ourselves, but Jesus Christ our Lord." Letter to Margrave Albrecht of Brandenburg.[34]

Faithful Ministers Magnify God, Not Themselves. Huldrych Zwingli: Paul subtly reproaches those apostles who strive to magnify

[32]Hesshus, *Explicatio Secundae Epistolae Pauli ad Corinthios*, 103v-104r; citing Jn 14:9. This statement captures well the central argument of St. Athanasius's *On the Incarnation* (c. 318).

[33]Donne, *Sermons of John Donne*, 4:124-25. [†]Donne is referring to two early Christian legends. According to the first legend, Abgar V king of Edessa, being afflicted with a dreadful disease, sent a letter to Jesus in which he acknowledged his divinity and requested miraculous healing. In response (according to a late variation of the legend), Jesus sent the apostle Thaddaeus to Edessa, bearing an image of Jesus that achieved the king's healing. An early version of this legend is found in Eusebius, *Ecclesiastical History* 1.13. [‡]The second legend reports that Jesus, on the road to the cross, paused to wipe the blood and sweat onto the veil of Veronica. The cloth with the imprint of the Lord's face on it was preserved, becoming a holy relic (sometimes called *volto santo*, "holy face") that was reported to perform such miracles as quenching thirst, curing blindness, and even raising the dead.

[34]LW 49:63-64 (WABR 3:216-17).

their own glory more than Christ's. Then he responds to those who were saying, "Why don't we understand what you are saying?" "We are ministers," Paul says, "not mercenaries! Therefore, as we speak so freely and with so much authority, we do so not in order to magnify ourselves, but to give glory to him whose business we execute. And it is not up to me whether those people understand the gospel which I proclaim. Rather, it is by the power of God that I preach Jesus Christ, whom no one receives or understands unless God the Father reveals him." Annotations on 2 Corinthians 4:5.[35]

Preaching Jesus Christ as Lord. Wolfgang Musculus: Paul was not simply preaching Jesus Christ, but Jesus Christ as Lord. What else is it to preach Jesus Christ as Lord than for the preacher to subject to Christ all things both in heaven and on earth, and to order everything according to him who is the one and only Savior and Redeemer? Those men who wish to rule and be considered as lords in the church are not able to do this.

Now did Paul preach Jesus Christ as Lord in the same way that he declared himself to be the servant of the Corinthians? I think not. For he was proclaiming and impressing upon everyone Jesus Christ as the universal Lord for which reason the salvation of all people is dependent upon him. But on the other hand, he was not boasting with empty words when he called himself the servant of the Corinthians, but he was displaying it in action, desiring that they might perceive it in him. Paul was serving them by preaching Christ as Lord. He was not boasting as the popes do who call themselves the "servant of all the servants." The Roman pontiffs are accustomed to call themselves by this title in all their bulls and writings, even though they conduct themselves in the church, not as servants of the faithful, but as the lords of property and bodies and souls. They proclaim that they are the "servants of all the servants," and yet they wish to be the lords of all lords. They proclaim that they are servants, yet they do not serve, because they do not preach Jesus Christ as Lord. And therefore they cannot call themselves "servants" on account of Jesus, yet in the meantime they pretend that they imitate the apostles with that empty title. Commentary on 2 Corinthians 4:5.[36]

Paul Was Not Trying to Lord Over the Corinthians. Andreas Hyperius: If the apostle discussed anything with respect to his name, he always did it to testify to the fact that he was subservient to them—not their lord—and that he wanted to benefit them "for the sake of Christ," that is, for the honor of Christ, so that the glory of God might be revealed. And here he subtly refutes the accusation of the false apostles that he was striving to be lord. Now it is clear from this that some teachers were sometimes claiming that the value of his gospel should not be considered precious. For some of them were not teaching Christ sincerely and were mixing it with traditions, laws, and so on. Moreover, they were preaching themselves more than Christ, now seeking their own glory, now striving after their own convenience. The principal matter of the gospel was disregarded because when the listeners were paying attention, the teachers were ignoring all doctrine. Moreover, some people were behaving in such a way that they did not want to have a minister, but a lord, which is a very harmful thing and alienates the souls of others from the gospel doctrine. Commentary on 2 Corinthians 4:5.[37]

God's Glory Shines Through Weak People. Jacques Lefèvre d'Étaples: "And God said, 'Let there be light, and there was light.'" God, I say, who spoke, decreed, and commanded light to arise from the darkness, also shines upon those who live on earth so that they might glorify him in the person of Christ, and for the sake of the person

[35]Zwingli, *Annotatiunculae . . . ex ore Zvinglij*, 163-64.

[36]Musculus, *Commentarius . . . in posteriorem epistolam Pauli ad Corinthios*, 123-24.

[37]Hyperius, *Commentarii . . . in Epistolam D. Pauli ad Romanos, et Utramque ad Corinthios*, 362.

of Christ, for the knowledge of the glory of God—which is the knowledge of the bright and glorious truth concerning God. They carry this treasure of divine knowledge in a fragile body, made of clay and weak flesh . . . so that the supreme excellence of this wisdom might be understood to belong to God, and not attributed to those who were manifest in a weak and mortal body. Commentary on 2 Corinthians 4:6-7.[38]

God Creates and Converts Through His Word. Martin Luther: These are difficult matters, and it is unsafe to go beyond the limit to which the Holy Spirit leads us. Let us, therefore, come to a halt with the knowledge that when the unformed heaven and the unformed earth, both of them marred by mist and darkness, had come into existence, light also came into existence out of nothing, that is, out of the very darkness. Paul cites this first work of the Creator as an extraordinary work: "Who commanded the light to shine out of darkness." "By his command," he says, "He made that light." This, therefore, is sufficient for the confirmation of our faith: that Christ is true God, who is with the Father from eternity, before the world was made, and that through him, who is the wisdom and the Word of the Father, the Father made everything. But in the passage referred to this point should also be noted: that Paul regards the conversion of the wicked—something which is also brought about by the Word—as a new work of creation. Commentary on Genesis 1:3.[39]

Christ Is the Light That Shattered Our Darkness. Huldrych Zwingli: Paul elegantly depicts that we are in darkness, in the shadow of death; we are ignorant of the light and the way of truth. But God, who is the originator of all light, had compassion on us and sent down from heaven his Son, the true light which shattered our darkness and healed all our blindness. "This light I announce, [Paul says,] and I proclaim it to everyone just as I have been commanded." Annotations on 2 Corinthians 4:6.[40]

The Light of the Knowledge of God Includes Understanding and Faith. Wolfgang Musculus: Now why is it that Paul does not say, "he has shone in our minds," but "he has shown in our hearts"? Since that light is the clarity of the knowledge of God, and knowledge pertains more to the mind than the heart, it seems that it would have been better to say, "he shone in our minds," rather than "he shone in our hearts." I answer as follows: If in this light of the knowledge of God nothing more was intended than the clarity and brightness of understanding, then it would have been far more suitable to say, "he has shone in our minds," rather than "he has shone in our hearts." But since Paul has conjoined the clarity of the knowledge of God and the zeal of faith (and faith is really not in the mind but the heart), he has rightly said that "he has shone in our hearts." Peter expressed jointly the knowledge and faith of Christ when he said in John 6, "Lord, to whom shall we go? For you have the words of eternal life, and we believe you and know that you are the Christ, the Son of the living God." And so, the light of the truth of Christ among true believers does not have clarity without burning love, nor burning love without clarity, that is, it does not have knowledge without faith, nor faith without the knowledge of God. Commentary on 2 Corinthians 4:6.[41]

The Light of the Gospel Comes from God Alone. Tilemann Hesshus: Just as Paul previously demonstrated the specific cause for the blindness and raging of the wicked, so now he teaches whence comes that true light of the godly, by which they recognize the eternal and true God who reveals himself in his Word, and by which they understand and gladly accept by faith those

[38]Lefèvre, *Commentariorum in Epistolas Beati Pauli . . . Liber Tertius*, 133; citing Gen 1:3.
[39]LW 1:17 (WA 42:13-14).
[40]Zwingli, *Annotatiunculae . . . ex ore Zvinglij*, 164.
[41]Musculus, *Commentarius . . . in posteriorem epistolam Pauli ad Corinthios*, 127; citing Jn 6:68-69.

greatest blessings of the mediator Jesus Christ. Now Paul does not want this work to be attributed to his power or effort, even though he demonstrates great fidelity to the truth of the gospel and works strenuously to make it known. Rather it is God, he says, who, in that beginning and creation of things, commanded with his Word that light should shine forth from the darkness, saying "Let there be light." God works the same way through the ministry of the gospel as it sheds rays of heavenly light into the hearts of the pious so that they might know the true God; might see God's most compassionate will concerning the redemption of humankind; might understand the reasons why the Son of God was sent into the world; might embrace with glad trust the blessings of the mediator; and might know the path that leads to eternal fellowship with God. These rays of light, which are diffused by God into our hearts through the Holy Spirit, Paul calls "knowledge of the glory of God," for this glory is truly of God, through which the eternal Father, along with the mediator-Son and Spirit are known and worshiped by us. In this gospel one sees God's infinite wisdom, eternal justice, unshakeable truth, inexhaustible goodness, and immeasurable power. Now it is quite right that we receive God's glory passively insofar as God judges true glory to be in us. Because we come to the knowledge of God's glory when we are delivered from the power of darkness, reconciled to God by the Son, given new light, admitted as children of God and coheirs of Christ. And we are called sacred temples of God. Now, this knowledge of God's glory does not happen to us unless, by true faith, we also gaze with our mind's eyes upon the dazzling and glorious face of Christ, in whom the immeasurable compassion and goodness of the Father shines forth. For all the fullness of the deity dwells bodily in Jesus Christ. And there is salvation in no one else; and there is no other name given to men and women under heaven by which they must be saved. No light of the knowledge of God manifests itself apart from Christ—without him everything is overtaken by darkness. Here we find the apostle's most weighty testimony against the supporters of synergism, since he teaches that in the conversion and regeneration of men and women, no other light than the gospel enflames our hearts (which are otherwise engulfed in darkness), and God commanded at the beginning of creation that light come forth from darkness. Therefore, since the formation of light in the first creation is the work of God alone, so the creator of all things converts men and women and shines upon them the light of the gospel without human cooperation (*synergia*). Thus, we believe that everything is given by God, and nothing comes from us. Explication of 2 Corinthians 4:6.[42]

Paul's Conversion Compared to God's Work of Creation. David Dickson: Paul here compares his conversion from Pharisaism to the creation of light out of darkness: "God, who by his omnipotent Word has produced light out of darkness, by no less efficacy has brought me, a lost sinner, out of the darkness of Pharisaism and sin, and has so powerfully enlarged my heart, illuminated by the light of Christ his glorious Son, that I cannot but communicate to others this glorious knowledge of the grace of God given to me, manifestly shining in Christ. Therefore, it is necessary for me to be faithful." Exposition of 2 Corinthians 4:6.[43]

Maturity in the Inner Person. Dirk Philips: My brotherly admonition, my friendly request, and my faithful counsel, which I give all my beloved brothers and sisters out of heartfelt love, is that you indeed exercise care over your treasures. Insofar as you have received understanding from God, insofar as Christ has come into your hearts, as much of God as has been given you through his Spirit, insofar as you have tasted of the bread of heaven and drunk of the water of life out of the fountain of salvation, that you faithfully

[42]Hesshus, *Explicatio Secundae Epistolae Pauli ad Corinthios*, 104v-106r; citing Gen 1:3; Acts 4:2.
[43]Dickson, *An Exposition of All St. Paul's Epistles*, 13*.

guard the same; progress therein, increase, and through this grow up and become strong in your inner being. Concerning the True Knowledge of Jesus Christ.[44]

Christians Bask in God's Three Lights. John Donne: Our division [of this text] must necessarily be three: there are three lights. The first shows us our creation; the second, our vocation; the third, our glorification. In the first, we who were but—but what?—but nothing were made creatures. In the second, we who were but Gentiles were made Christians. In the third, we who were but human creatures were made saints. In the first, God took us when there was no world. In the second, God sustains us in an ill world. In the third, God shall crown us in a glorious and joyful world. In the first, God made us. In the second, God mends us. In the third, God shall perfect us. First, "God commanded light out of darkness," that humans might see other creatures. Then, "he made his light shine in our hearts," that humans might see themselves. And last of all, he shall shine in "the face of Christ Jesus," so that humans might see God and live. And they shall live as long as the God of light and life shall himself live. Sermon Preached at the Spittle (Easter Monday, 1622).[45]

God's Spirit Enlightens Hearts. John Trapp: The first work of the Spirit in a person's heart is to beat out new windows there and to let in light. Commentary on 2 Corinthians 4:6.[46]

[44]CRR 6:169.
[45]Donne, *Sermons of John Donne*, 4:92-93.
[46]Trapp, *A Commentary or Exposition*, 712*.

God's Glory in the Face of Christ. Philipp Melanchthon: God's glory shines forth "in the face of Jesus Christ." For it was the glory of the letter, not the glory of God, that was shining forth in the face of Moses. For the glory which shone forth from Moses' face did not enlighten hearts with the knowledge of God. But the glory which shines in the face of Christ (that is, the power of Christ) enlightens hearts with the knowledge of God and the divine will. Annotations on 2 Corinthians 4:6.[47]

God Is Known as He Reveals Himself in Christ. John Calvin: In the same sense in which Paul had previously said that Christ is the image of the Father [in v. 4] he now says that the glory of God is revealed to us in his face. This is a remarkable passage, from which we learn that God must not be sought in his unsearchable height (for he dwells in inaccessible light), but he must be known inasmuch as he reveals himself in Christ. Hence, whatever men and women desire to know about God outside of Christ is evanescent, for they wander off the path. It is indeed true that at first God in Christ appears to be humble, but later he appears glorious to those who persevere, coming from the cross to the resurrection. Again, we see that in the word "person" there is a reference to us, because it is more useful for us to behold God as he appears in his only-begotten Son than to search out his secret essence. Commentary on 2 Corinthians 4:6.[48]

[47]*Melanchthons Werke*, 4:111.
[48]CO 50:53 (CTS 40:200); citing 1 Tim 6:16.

4:7-18 Treasures in Jars of Clay

[7]But we have this treasure in jars of clay, to show that the surpassing power belongs to God and not to us. [8]We are afflicted in every way, but not crushed; perplexed, but not driven to despair; [9]persecuted, but not forsaken; struck down, but not destroyed; [10]always carrying in the body the death of Jesus, so that the life of Jesus may also be manifested in our bodies. [11]For we who live are always being given over to death for Jesus' sake, so that the life of Jesus also may be manifested in our mortal flesh. [12]So death is at work in us, but life in you.

[13]Since we have the same spirit of faith according to what has been written, "I believed, and so I spoke," we also believe, and so we also speak, [14]knowing that he who raised the Lord Jesus will raise us also with Jesus and bring us with you into his presence. [15]For it is all for your sake, so that as grace extends to more and more people it may increase thanksgiving, to the glory of God.

[16]So we do not lose heart. Though our outer self[a] is wasting away, our inner self is being renewed day by day. [17]For this light momentary affliction is preparing for us an eternal weight of glory beyond all comparison, [18]as we look not to the things that are seen but to the things that are unseen. For the things that are seen are transient, but the things that are unseen are eternal.

a Greek *man*

Overview: Paul reminds the Corinthian believers that even though God's people will suffer many painful troubles in this life, they must not lose heart, for these "momentary afflictions" pale in comparison to the eternal glory they will one day experience in God's presence in heaven. For Protestant commentators, Paul's message provides rich, relevant insight for all Christians who struggle to reconcile their own frailty and daily sufferings, with the glorious message of God's gospel. In the mystery of his providence, God has chosen to entrust the precious "treasure" of the gospel of Jesus Christ to believers who (by the measure of the world) are frail, weak, despised, and persecuted. This was true of early Christian apostles such as John the Evangelist and Paul; it was also true of later church leaders like Athanasius and Martin Luther. Nevertheless, God never forsakes his persecuted people, and whether he rescues them *from* tribulation or preserves their faith *through* tribulation, Christians are assured that God will receive glory and praise as the gospel goes forth in power. While insisting that persecution and suffering are normative in the Christian life, Reformation commentators caution against false conclusions: persecution is not proof of gospel fidelity, and not all Christians will undergo suffering at a particular time or place. Hence, blanket judgments against believers who are suffering persecution or enjoying peace and security are unwarranted.

Reformation exegetes locate in 2 Corinthians 4:13-18 several wonderful consolations for believers facing trials and troubles in this world. Christians are promised the assistance of the Holy Spirit, who strengthens their faith, renews their minds, and restores in them the image of God. At the same time, they can anticipate the resurrection of their bodies and the immeasurable glory of living forever in God's presence. Believers, however, must receive these spiritual blessings and promises (these "unseen things") with the eyes of faith. On this point, the reformers believe that Paul's quotation of David's words from Psalm 116 is particularly significant inasmuch as Christian faith is the key that unlocks all of God's gracious promises. The fact that David was rescued from his trials through godly faith is a clear testimony that God's people in the old covenant enjoyed the same Spirit and professed the same gospel as Christians in the new covenant. Moreover, like David, Christians must make public profession of their faith rather than camouflage their convictions out of fear or embarrassment. As Calvin notes, "Faith is the mother of confession."

4:7-12 *Afflicted but Not Crushed*

A Brief Summary of Paul's Teaching. Philipp Melanchthon: This passage teaches first of all what kind of ministers of the Word it is necessary to be, namely, jars of clay; that is, "the scum and refuse of the world." Second, [this passage teaches] what effectual faith is when it quotes Psalm 116, "I believed and so I spoke." For, since faith is the light of the heart and life, the heart cannot judge otherwise than to feel, speak, and do what God's Spirit prompts it to do. As Sirach states, "The one who believes in God heeds his commandments, and those who trust in him will not be forsaken." But, on the contrary, where faith is absent, neither light, nor life, nor the Spirit is present, but instead only the ignorance of God and a disoriented spirit. Hence Psalm 77 states, "They are a generation whose heart was not upright and whose spirit did not trust in God." Third, [this passage teaches] that faith involves not only comprehending history but also the use and benefit of that history. For what is more foolish than to believe that there is a God and a Christ, and yet not to believe that he does anything! Accordingly, the apostle says, "Knowing that he who raised the Lord Jesus will also raise us." Fourth, Paul appends an epilogue when he says, "it is all for your sake," just as he stated earlier, "all things are yours, whether Paul or Apollos." . . . And so "it is all for your sake"; that is, we are your ministers (not mercenaries), and we expend our life, our soul, and all things for your sake. Fifth, Paul appends a general contrast between the exterior self and the interior self. Annotations on 2 Corinthians 4:7-18.[1]

The Devil Attacks the Treasure of God's Word. Martin Luther: [The devil] is by nature so malicious and venomous that he cannot endure anything which is good. It irks him that an apple should be growing on a tree; it pains and vexes him that you have a sound finger, and if he were able he would tear everything apart and put it out of joint. . . . And if our dear God were not guarding us through his angels and we were able to see the devil's cunning, conspiring, and lying, we should die of the sight of it alone, so many are the cannon and guns he has ranged against us. But God prevents them from striking us.

So the two heroes meet, each doing as much as possible. The devil brews one calamity after another; for he is a mighty, malicious, and turbulent spirit. So it is time that our dear God be concerned about his honor; for the Word which we wield is a weak and miserable Word, and we who have and wield it are also weak and miserable men, bearing the treasure as Paul says, in earthen vessels, which can easily be shattered and broken. Therefore, the evil spirit spares no effort and confidently lashes out to see if he can smash the little vessel; for there it is under his nose, and he cannot stand it. So the battle really begins in earnest, with water and fire to dampen and quench the little spark. Then our Lord God looks on for a while and puts us in a tight place, so that we may learn from our own experience that the small, weak, miserable Word is stronger than the devil and the gates of hell. They are to storm the castle, the devil, and his cohorts. But let them storm; they will find some there that will make them sweat, and still they will not gain it; for it is a rock, as Christ calls it, which cannot be conquered. So let us suffer what comes upon us and thus we shall learn that God will stand by us to guard and shield us against this enemy and

[1] *Melanchthons Werke*, 4:112; citing 1 Cor 4:13; Ps 116:10; Sir 32:24; Ps 77:8; 1 Cor 3:21.

all his adherents. Sermon on Cross and Suffering (1530).[2]

The Treasure Is the Knowledge of God. Huldrych Zwingli: What Paul above calls light, he now calls a treasure. This is a digression by which Paul shows that this precious treasure—namely, the knowledge of God—had been entrusted by Christ to the apostles, men in the flesh, subject to trials and weakness, so that everyone would understand that it is not by our strength, but by the authority and power of God, when we steadfastly endure the evils that afflict us and are prepared to die for Christ. And let them know that this is not from a human being, but God alone brings into the world the light of divine knowledge. Annotations on 2 Corinthians 4:7.[3]

Humans Cooperate in Preserving the Gospel Treasure. Cardinal Cajetan: We have that treasure in clay jars, or broken jars. Paul has declared that Jesus Christ is preached by ministers of the new covenant. Consequently, he declares the way that Jesus Christ is conveyed by these ministers: preaching, in fact, focuses on the words; but walking focuses on deeds. For Paul states that we not only preach the Word but also walk in the deeds of Jesus Christ. Now these deeds are expressed in fragile bodies. And to explain this, he uses the analogy of precious treasures hidden in broken jars, which are both contemptible and fragile. . . .

Paul gives the reason why a treasure so precious is kept in fragile jars, namely, so that the surpassing power for preserving the treasure among so many adverse occurrences might be of God and not from us. If the jars were impervious to change, then the power of preservation would be in the jars. But because the jars are so fragile, it is necessary that not only the power, but the surpassing power, for preserving the treasure comes from somewhere else. Now God is the "somewhere-else" proposed. And so, we have this treasure in broken jars so that the surpassing power of preserving it—which is needed for its preservation—comes from God. But Paul adds the phrase "and not from us" [*et non ex nobis*]—he does not say, "and not ours" [*et non nostra*]—so that we might understand that we also cooperate in preserving the treasure, for it is also necessary for us to preserve the treasure. However, it is not preserved through us [*ex nobis*], but by the surpassing power of God on top of our weakness and all our adversities. Commentary on 2 Corinthians 4:7.[4]

Jars of Clay Must Be Cleansed by Blood and Water. Anna Maria von Schurman: I was strengthened in this position by experience, and no one could easily persuade me, since it was truly most false, namely, that the words of life that are dead in the mouth of a dead preacher (as someone said more elegantly than accurately) bring life to dead listeners. For the preacher can indeed say the words but not grasp and give voice to the meaning and life or Spirit of Scripture; the listeners, moreover, have not the ears to hear spiritual things in a spiritual manner or grasp them inwardly. But how would the Holy Spirit attach himself to a dead person as a tool of his grace for bringing souls to life? Certainly not more, indeed less than to the crowing of the cock, which our Savior wanted to be a reminder to the turncoat Peter of his words in order to call him back from his special sin. In such a preacher the rule of sin stands in the way, but not in the cock or Balaam's ass, which accused his master of sin. For what does the light have in common with darkness, or Christ with Belial? . . . An unclean vessel cannot produce a pure drink, and the purest words and thoughts, if they flow through the unclean throats of the unregenerate (which holy Scripture compares to open graves) cannot safely be swallowed as living and pure spring water. The apostle says, "We have

[2]LW 51:206-7 (WA 32:37).
[3]Zwingli, *Annotatiunculae . . . ex ore Zvinglij*, 165.
[4]Cajetan, *In Posteriorem Pauli Epistolam ad Corinthios Commentarii*, 164.

this treasure in clay jars," but they were cleansed by the blood of Christ and the water of the Holy Spirit. For earthen vessels that were unclean and contaminated by leprosy were not even to be brought into the house of Israelites but had to be broken; much less could they be used in worship of God and in his temple to store water or blood or oil. No one calls into question that these things were types or prefigurations of the New Testament church. . . . By contrast, I have always regarded and still regard with both great honor and love as worthy teachers of the church those who have proved and continue to prove themselves faithful servants and followers of Christ not only by words and dispositions but through deeds and effects. Eukleria.[5]

Jars of Clay. Wolfgang Musculus: Paul is not speaking here about the frailty of his body, but about the humble nature of his person which the false apostles were ridiculing. He compares his person to a small clay vessel, as if he were saying, "However much your apostles condemn the humbleness of my person and express their contempt of me before everyone, nevertheless, whether they wish to or not, they abandon this treasure to me, which the Lord has found me worthy and entrusted me to carry around just as if I were a clay vessel." Now how is it that they ridicule the weakness and humble character of this vessel, and do not recognize the great heavenly treasure hidden within it? Who is so senseless that, having found a treasure in a clay vessel, they will not celebrate on account of the treasure more than be horrified on account of the humble nature of the vessel? Today, people hold in contempt the ministers of Christ because their lives are humble rather than impressive in their outer circumstances or fortune, however useful they are to the churches of Christ. And so, people do not take them seriously as if they were a treasure of gold or silver or precious stones hidden in a clay vessel . . . and they reject this treasure for themselves on account of the cheapness of the vessel, saying, "What does this little clay vessel have to do with me?" Nevertheless, on account of its humble external appearance, they reject a heavenly treasure concealed in a potter's vessel, not understanding that in this way God hides his treasure from the wise of this world and reveals it to children. Commentary on 2 Corinthians 4:7.[6]

God Works Through Poor, Small Vessels. Cyriacus Spangenberg: Those who judge the divine Word according to the appearance of people do very wrongly. If they are powerful, learned, and highly esteemed, then they think so much more of the Word. But if they are good, pious, simple, honest preachers, then people do not inquire much about their teaching. That is a perverse way and serious sin. Thus, it says, "We have such treasure in earthen vessels, so that the surpassing power may be God's, and not from us." If something good happens, if something useful is fulfilled through the preaching ministry, we must say that God has done this, whose work it is. For we are poor, small vessels, although God fulfills it through us as a means. Therefore, the honor must be given to him. Nineteenth Sermon.[7]

The Holy Spirit Empowers Suffering Christians. Martin Bucer: This Spirit . . . produces in all such a firm hope in all the grace and help of God, and in eternal life. By means of and along with these attitudes of faith, trust, and hope in God and in Christ our Lord, the Holy Spirit also produces in the children of God a deep love for God, a joyful confession and hallowing of his name in all their words and works and in the courageous acceptance of consequent sufferings and even of torments and death. A Brief Summary of Christian Doctrine.[8]

[5]Schurman, *Whether a Christian Woman Should Be Educated*, 88-89.

[6]Musculus, *Commentarius . . . in posteriorem epistolam Pauli ad Corinthios*, 129-30.

[7]C. Spangenberg, *Die ander Epistel Pauli an die Corinthier*, 77v.

[8]CPMB 80.

God Is Sovereign over Life and Death. Argula von Grumbach: I hear that some are so angry with me that they do not know how best to speed my passage from life into death. But I know for sure that they cannot harm me unless the power to do so has been given them by God. He will keep me safe, for his name's sake. Paul says in 2 Corinthians 4, "We suffer all things without complaint for the Lord's name." Psalm 3: "I will not fear a thousand"; and Isaiah 30: "One person will make a thousand tremble." Hear what the Lord says in Isaiah 43: "Do not be afraid of them, for I am with you and without me there is no salvation." An Open Letter to the Town Council of Ingolstadt.[9]

The Wicked Cannot Impede the Ministry of the Godly. Tilemann Hesshus: Paul explains the various difficulties and troubles with which the apostles were continuously afflicted, which is why he called them broken vases. But he adds that in all these things they experience God's presence and are gloriously rescued. David was burdened in various ways, but he was never reduced to such distress that he could not escape it. Thus also Paul passed through great dangers, and then experienced God's presence. . . . John the Evangelist, Athanasius, Luther, and many others suffered persecution but were not abandoned. God immediately protected them in the shadow of his hand and defended them from heaven until they finished their course. They were knocked off-balance: David was driven into exile; Jeremiah and Peter were thrown into prison; Athanasius was sometimes driven into exile by emperors; Paul was buried with rocks. They did not die, but were divinely preserved. "The Lord has disciplined me severely," David says, "but he has not given me over to death."

This is the chief point: Although apostles, bishops, and pastors endure manifold difficulties and experience various misfortunes on account of the doctrine of the gospel, nevertheless they are divinely protected, supported, and rescued with extraordinary honor, according to the promise: "I am with him in trouble; I will rescue him and honor him." But at this point, human reason objects, "What vain boasting Paul is making, because was he not overwhelmed with difficulty? Was he not abandoned? Was he not deserted? Did he not die? Did not Nero finally cut off his head? Were not Jeremiah and Stephen buried in stones? Were not both Jameses killed? Was not Lawrence[†] roasted on a grill? One can't always escape, can they?" I answer: Paul is right in boasting, since he experienced the presence of God during the whole course of his preaching ministry and was rescued from great difficulties. And he indicates here the enormous comfort that all godly pastors are protected in the shadow of the Lord's hand so that neither tyranny or human schemes can hinder the course of their ministries—indeed, not even a hair can be plucked from their head. Often, a pastor in the midst of his enemies forthrightly reproaches the wickedness of the world and refutes their errors. But truly, Isaiah, Jeremiah, [John] the Baptist, Paul, James, Stephen, when each had finally finished the course that Christ had given him, poured out his blood for the truth, and was crowned a martyr. And each of them died to the glory of God. "Precious in the sight of the Lord is the death of his saints." Explication of 2 Corinthians 4:8.[10]

The Gospel Brings Opposition. John Trapp: "We are troubled on every side." This is the world's wages to God's ministers. Truth purchases hatred. "Opposition is the patron of the gospel," Calvin once said. Truth is always accompanied with a scratched face. "We are perplexed." "Pray for me, I say, pray for me," said Latimer. "For I am sometimes so fearful that I could creep into a mouse hole; yet sometimes

[9]Grumbach, *Argula von Grumbach*, 119; citing Ps 3:6; Is 30:17; Is 43:5.

[10]Hesshus, *Explicatio Secundae Epistolae Pauli ad Corinthios*, 108v-109v; citing Ps 118:18, 91:15, 116:5. [†]St. Lawrence was a deacon in Rome who died as a martyr in 258, as he was tied atop a grill and slowly roasted to death.

God visits me again with comfort." Commentary on 2 Corinthians 4:8.[11]

The Godly Are Not Forsaken. Martin Luther: One must say with Job, "Though he slay me, yet will I trust in him," and with Paul in 2 Corinthians 4:8-9, "We are afflicted in every way, but not crushed; perplexed, but not driven to despair; persecuted but not forsaken; struck down, but not destroyed." Our life is most wretched and full of great evils and disasters, but we are not forsaken. And so the godly heart concludes, "I know that I am not confounded; my hope and my faith will not deceive me because God, the promise, the sacraments, and absolution do not deceive, inasmuch as they are of God. Accordingly, in death I shall live, and in perishing I shall be preserved." Commentary on Genesis 37:15-17.[12]

God Rescues His Ministers from All Kinds of Afflictions. Andreas Hyperius: The reason why it pleases God that ministers of the Word should be afflicted is so that he might display his power when he amazingly rescues them. If those apostles were wealthy, powerful, or noble, then the spreading of the gospel would be ascribed primarily to their authority and power. But now, since they have that treasure (or teaching office) in clay jars, and are so often afflicted and opposed, all the glory redounds to God alone, both for the spreading of the gospel and for their rescue. And the apostle clearly states here that we must look to God alone for all progress of the word and rescue from dangers and should give thanks to him alone for such progress and rescue. Now all these words are very appropriate:

"We are afflicted in every way." This universal phrase proves that there are various kinds of afflictions, and yet none of them is so great or so diverse that God does not rescue us from them all. That is clearly the reason why the apostle uses here many carefully chosen words so that he might teach the right ways to respond to any dangers [and that] the godly are never finally forsaken.

"We are afflicted in every way, but not given over to worry." . . . It is as if Paul said, "We are afflicted in every way, but not overwhelmed or pressed down; we are attacked, but not overcome."

"We are troubled, but not abandoned." . . . The Greek word *aporoumenoi* means to be driven to the greatest difficulty and rendered perplexed. But the word *exaporoumenoi* means to be conquered and demolished by evils, and to despair from weariness—such people are shown to be destitute as much of resources as of counsel.

"We are persecuted, but not forsaken." Indeed, people persecute and harm us because of the name of Christ, but God will never desert us; he will always run to help us, or rather, he will transform evil things to our good so that both we and other people are strengthened in the faith.

"We are struck down, but not destroyed." As foreigners in the world, we are thrown to the ground and trampled underfoot—as if we were soon to be destroyed—yet we are not killed but are built up and preserved in the faith. Commentary on 2 Corinthians 4:8-9.[13]

Paul's Confidence Is in God's Help. David Dickson: [Paul answers] that all his afflictions are moderated, and he himself is upheld by God in all things, that he is not destitute of the help of God, does not sink under his burden, that he does not forsake God, nor despair, is not forsaken of God, nor left or lost. Therefore, it does not matter at all how weak he is in himself. "We are afflicted," he says, "yet not distressed"; that is, on every side we are troubled with adversity, but we are not brought into such straits as to be overwhelmed, but we are preserved by the help of God in the midst of afflictions. "We are perplexed, but not in despair"; that is, we doubt sometimes what we should do in the dangers of this life, but we are not so destitute that we are void of all counsel. "We are

[11]Trapp, *A Commentary or Exposition*, 712*.
[12]LW 6:354 (WA 44:264-65); citing Job 13:15.
[13]Hyperius, *Commentarii . . . in Epistolam D. Pauli ad Romanos, et Utramque ad Corinthios*, 365.

persecuted, but not forsaken"; that is, God permits us to be vexed and treated badly by the enemies of the gospel, but he neither permits us to be slain before the time determined by him, nor does he withdraw his consolations from us. "We are cast down, but not destroyed"; that is, we sometimes seem about ready to perish, but God helping us, we are kept from perishing. Exposition of 2 Corinthians 4:8-9.[14]

Christians Are Never Forsaken by God. Wolfgang Musculus: Being afflicted by persecutions, it seemed unlikely that the fragile clay vessel would be able to endure for long. But the Lord wished that Paul should endure. Although he was unable to endure by himself, the Lord assisted him with his power and preserved him amid the persecutions, despite all expectation. That Paul was able to endure persecutions for so long, therefore, served as a proof of the divine power within him, which the false apostles pretended not to see. In the meantime, they were heaping contempt on the apostle of Christ on account of his constant persecutions.

How does one account for all the believers of Christ who willingly suffer persecution while dutifully living in this world, many of whom die from such persecutions? Is Paul also able to assert that those who suffer persecution are not forsaken? If God does not abandon them in their persecutions, why is it that Christ himself cried out from the cross, "My God, my God why have you forsaken me?" I answer that there are two kinds of forsaking: In one kind, God watches over those being persecuted in such a way that they are rescued unharmed from the hands of the wicked and they are unexpectedly preserved in this life. Thus, God rescued and delivered his apostle and many others, often by means of help at just the right moment. The other kind of forsaking is where, even in the midst of mortal danger . . . God nevertheless does not forsake them but preserves them constant in the faith. In both ways God preserved his apostle and, later on, all those believers, who were killed in those persecutions. Commentary on 2 Corinthians 4:9.[15]

The Meaning of "Death of Christ." John Calvin: Paul says here more than he said previously, for he shows that the very thing that the false apostles used as a pretext for despising the gospel, not only did not bring contempt to the gospel, but even rendered it glorious. For Paul employs the expression "death of Jesus Christ" to denote everything that rendered him contemptible before the world that was nevertheless preparing him for participation in a blessed resurrection. In the first place, the sufferings of Christ, however disgraceful they may be in the eyes of the world, nevertheless have more honor in the sight of God than all the triumphs of emperors and all the pomp of kings. . . . Thus, he elegantly reproves the folly of those who were objecting to his special fellowship with Christ. At the same time, the Corinthians are admonished to be careful lest, by contemptuously despising Paul's mean and unimpressive appearance, they do injury to Christ himself by seeking an occasion to despise him in his sufferings, which we should hold in the highest honor.

The word rendered "death" [*mortificatio*] is taken in a different sense here than in many other Scripture passages. For it often means self-denial, when we renounce the lusts of the flesh and are renewed to godly obedience. Here, however, it means the afflictions by which we are prompted to meditate on the termination of the present life. To speak more clearly, we might call the former the internal death, and the latter the external death. Both conform us to Christ, the former directly, the other indirectly, so to speak. . . . However, it is called "the death of Christ" only for believers, because the wicked—as they endure troubles in this present life—share this with Adam. But the elect participate with the Son of God, so that all those miseries that in their own nature are

[14]Dickson, *An Exposition of All St. Paul's Epistles*, 13-14*.

[15]Musculus, *Commentarius . . . in posteriorem epistolam Pauli ad Corinthios*, 133-34; citing Mt 27:46.

accursed contribute to their salvation. This indeed is common to all the children of God, that they bear the death of Christ. COMMENTARY ON 2 CORINTHIANS 4:10.[16]

BEARING THE DEATH OF CHRIST. CYRIACUS SPANGENBERG: God sends the cross to believers so that through the Holy Spirit's help they may bear and overcome it, and in this way the life of Christ may be revealed in their flesh still in this world. This then happens when Christ comforts and gives joy to hearts through the Holy Spirit, so that believers endure adversity without complaining or impatience, with a gentle spirit and a joyful disposition. We see this with the martyrs, as, comforted, they endured all kinds of punishment and finally suffered death. Thus, they bore the death of Christ in their bodies and everyone saw that Christ lived in them. In this way the life of Jesus became manifest in their bodies, so that all had to confess that the teaching for which they suffered was not vain babble or human imaginings, but the living Word of God, through which God gives new birth to people and strengthens them, so that they may bear and overcome all suffering with patience, and so that the life of Jesus is revealed in them as an example to others, so that they see this and that believers are stirred up through it to remain steadfast in this teaching, and the others are moved to accept the same. TWENTIETH SERMON.[17]

CARRYING IN OUR BODIES THE DEATH OF JESUS. ANDREAS HYPERIUS: In this final clause Paul adds this summary, as if he were saying, As foreigners in the world, we are always afflicted in our bodies and weighed down by various evils . . . because Christ suffered many troubles and died for our sake. In the same manner, we are mortified, hard-pressed, afflicted in body, even as Christ also was oppressed and afflicted. Christ has led the way; it is our responsibility to follow along that same path through tribulation, as Jesus said: "He who wishes to follow me will deny himself, take up his cross, and follow me." However, the apostle explains these matters with many words to show the different forms of rescue corresponding to the many and various dangers; and no sooner do dangers occur than God rescues us from them all. And so Paul ascribes illustrious goodness and mercy to God, and renders us more certain in faith. COMMENTARY ON 2 CORINTHIANS 4:10.[18]

THE LIFE OF JESUS REVEALED IN BELIEVERS. WOLFGANG MUSCULUS: "So that the life of Jesus is manifested in our body." Commentators explain this passage in various ways. First, it is possible to understand it in regard to the life of Jesus, in that he was preserved by God's power from all the zeal and fury of wicked men during the hour that he willingly endured the cross and gave his life for us. One finds a most excellent proof of divine power in the life of the sort of man who is preserved from every sort of peril. Such was the life of Christ; such was also the life of Paul after Christ, who manifested in his body the life of Christ.

Second, by the term "life of Jesus" it is possible to understand the life of a man living, not in peace and security, but in afflictions and under the cross. . . .

Third, Chrysostom† and after him Theophylact‡ suggest an interpretation of this sort: that since, with the mortification of the Lord Jesus, we naturally carry around afflictions and daily death in our body, what else can be expected than that his life is also manifested in our body? For who preserves us in our daily deaths except he who died, came back to life, and now lives forever? Because the Lord Jesus, for whom I die daily, is still living, his life announces that he preserves me from so continuous a mortification, against all expectation. Thus, these interpreters seek to silence those who were calling into question the belief in the resurrection of the dead.

[16]CO 50:54-55 (CTS 40:203-5).
[17]C. Spangenberg, *Die ander Epistel Pauli an die Corinthier*, 81.
[18]Hyperius, *Commentarii . . . in Epistolam D. Pauli ad Romanos, et Utramque ad Corinthios*, 365; citing Mt 10:38.

Fourth, there are some who relate this passage to the world to come, in which our bodies, which now carry around the mortification of the Lord with various kinds of trials, will be conformed to the brightness of the body of Christ. Just as our bodies here share in the image of death, so in that future world they will share in the image of life when their mortality will be swallowed up in life. Paul expresses this in 2 Timothy 2 in this fashion: "This is a trustworthy saying: If we have died with him, we shall also live with him; if we suffer, we will also reign with him."

When Paul writes, "so that the life of Jesus might also be manifested in our body," I think he is referring to that life of Jesus that is hidden in the lives of the elect and believers in the form of mortification, and it is exercised in their bodies as long as they go around in this flesh. Since this life of Jesus in them is not at all hidden in the sight of God, it will be revealed when Christ himself is revealed, a matter that Colossians 3 addresses in this fashion: "And so if you have been resurrected together with Christ, seek things that are above, where Christ is sitting at the right hand of God. Set your cares on heavenly things not on earthly things. For you have died and your life is hidden with Christ in God. When Christ who is our life will be revealed, then you also will appear with him in glory." Commentary on 2 Corinthians 4:10.[19]

Preaching the Gospel Is Dangerous. Huldrych Zwingli: To preach the gospel of Christ is nothing other than always to stand ready for battle. But by this, the life of Christ will be revealed in us, as noted in 1 Corinthians 15. Therefore, those who preach the Word not only face the danger of death but death itself threatens daily. Nevertheless, such danger encourages and comforts them, because they know that whether they are rescued from death or even killed, they will always be victorious. Indeed, in death itself they will find life. For the death of preachers produces life and fruit in their hearers. Annotations on 2 Corinthians 4:11.[20]

Dying Daily for Jesus' Sake. Tilemann Hesshus: [This verse] is not a useless repetition of his opinion, but rather is an embellishment and declaration. For he emphasizes that he is afflicted with constant troubles and continuous dangers to such an extent that every moment he keeps his eyes fixed on his death. For although Paul, as a distinguished apostle, endured more calamities and dangers than most godly people, nevertheless this situation was primarily so that the Lord might distribute the cup of salvation to everyone. Now, he shows the reason why he calls his troubles "death for Jesus' sake," namely, because it is on account of Jesus' name, which we acknowledge in the world, that all sorts of difficulties happen to us. This is just as Christ predicted: "And you will be hated by everyone on account of my name." David says exactly the same thing in Psalm 44: "Yet for your sake we are killed the whole day long; we are regarded as sheep to be slaughtered." Explication of 2 Corinthians 4:11.[21]

Paul's Meaning by "Death." Niels Hemmingsen: [This passage] is an explanation of the previous verse, for Paul explains what he means by "death" [*mortificatio*]. Now the "death of Jesus Christ" means to be given over to death, that is, to the dangers of death because of the gospel of Jesus. For in these dangers, the life of Jesus clearly manifests itself, until he rescues his servants from the dangers of death by his power. Now Paul refers to "mortal flesh," not meaning the common condition of death for all, but death through the cross, to which he had been exposed. Commentary on 2 Corinthians 4:11.[22]

Living and Dying with Jesus. John Calvin: Here is the best antidote for adversity: that

[19]Musculus, *Commentarius . . . in posteriorem epistolam Pauli ad Corinthios*, 135-36; citing 2 Tim 2:11-12; Col 3:1-4. †For Chrysostom's interpretation, see NPNF¹ 12:321. ‡For Theophylact, see PG 124:813.

[20]Zwingli, *Annotatiunculae . . . ex ore Zvinglij*, 165-66.

[21]Hesshus, *Explicatio Secundae Epistolae Pauli ad Corinthios*, 111v; citing Lk 21:17; Ps 44:22.

[22]Hemmingsen, *Commentaria in Omnes Epistolas Apostolorum*, 268.

just as Christ's death was the gateway to life, so we know that the outcome of all our miseries will be the blessed resurrection. For Christ has joined us to himself on this condition, that we will be participants of his life if, in this world, we submit to die with him. Commentary on 2 Corinthians 4:11.[23]

The Costs of Confessing Christ. Argula von Grumbach: I am called a follower of Luther, but I am not. I was baptized in the name of Christ; it is him I confess and not Luther. But I confess that Martin, too, as a faithful Christian, confesses him. God help us never to deny this, whether faced by disgrace, abuse, imprisonment, breaking on the wheel, and even death—God helping and enabling all Christians in this. Amen.

I have heard that you are reported as saying that if my own husband would not do it, some relative should act, and wall me up. But don't believe him. Alas, he is doing far too much to persecute Christ in me. In 2 Corinthians 4 Paul says, "We endure all things without complaint for the name of the Lord." So it is no difficulty for me, and I am not liable to obey him in this matter, for God says in Matthew 10 and Mark 8: "We must forsake father, mother, brother, sister, children, life and limb," and then says, "What good does it do someone to gain the whole world but ruin one's soul? With what would one repurchase one's soul?" That's the way it is; otherwise, God says, he will not confess us. But forsaking friendship, honor, property, and life does not appeal to the flesh. Letter to Adam von Thering.[24]

No Christianity Without the Cross. John Calvin: This is said ironically, because it was shameful that the Corinthians should live happily as they desired, and be carefree, while in the meantime Paul was struggling with a countless number of troubles. Such an allotment would certainly have been unfair. And it was necessary that the foolishness of the Corinthians be condemned, for they were imagining for themselves a Christianity without the cross and, not content with this, had contempt for the servants of Christ, who were not as self-indulgent as they were. Now as the term "death" denotes all afflictions, or a life of trouble, so also the term "life" denotes a condition both prosperous and pleasant. According to that maxim:[†] "Life is not to live, but to live well." Commentary on 2 Corinthians 4:12.[25]

Neither Suffering Nor Safety Are Absolute Proofs of Faithfulness. Wolfgang Musculus: I agree with those who think that Paul was reprimanding the false apostles with these words. For even as the apostle was daily disturbed in the midst of death, the false apostles were thinking that the most excellent Christians were those, like themselves, who spend their lives without any threat to their peace and safety. Observing this, therefore, Paul says, "So death is at work in us as daily we are handed over to death for the sake of Christ, but life is at work in you." . . . The false apostles were arguing two things for which Paul rightly reprimanded them. The first thing was that they were joining together circumcision and observance of the law with the gospel of Christ so as to flee persecution and the afflictions of Christ for a more peaceful and secure life. The second thing was that they were expressing contempt for the apostle Paul on account of his numerous afflictions. That is why he rightly makes this objection against them, that death is at work in him while life is at work in them. This difference frequently happens in the churches of Christ in all times, as some Christians are afflicted with death, while others experience life, peace, and safety. For is not death at work in our brothers who are in England, France, Italy, and Spain, while life is at work in those of us who live in the regions of Germany where the freedom of gospel teaching

[23]CO 50:55 (CTS 40:205).

[24]Grumbach, *Argula von Grumbach*, 144-45; citing Mt 10:21; Mk 8:36-37. Adam von Thering was the Count Palatine's administrator in Neuburg and Argula's uncle.

[25]CO 50:55-56 (CTS 40:206).[†]Calvin quotes the maxim of Martial, which appears in his *Epigrammaton libri* 6.70.

and religion is observed? Those brothers are troubled by various afflictions, and like sheep for the slaughter they are handed over to be killed on account of the gospel of Christ. [In the meantime], those of us who adhere to the same gospel live in peace and safety. Hopefully we Germans will not finally experience evil things from such a lengthy peace! The different experiences of believers in the churches can be ascribed to divine providence. But this will not excuse those people who minister the gospel of Christ in such a way that, even though they themselves are subject to no dangers in this world, they consider others to be disturbers of the peace and seditious who are afflicted because of the truth, and they condemn them even to the point of death. Similarly, we cannot approve of those people who, stirred with a fanatical spirit, disturb churches, and call the ministers of the gospel "servants of the stomach" when they are restrained by the magistrates' laws. Boasting in their sufferings, these people condemn those who are experiencing peace and quiet as if they had acquired such peace out of a zeal for corrupt doctrine rather than as a divine gift. But a quiet and secure life is not proof of corrupt doctrine any more than a life of afflictions and persecutions is proof for healthy doctrine. Commentary on 2 Corinthians 4:12.[26]

The Fruit of Gospel Ministry. Niels Hemmingsen: This brief conclusion sums up the previous verses. And this is its sense: as ministers of the Word, we are afflicted and daily exposed to the danger of death, but this death of ours works for your advantage, since through the preaching of the gospel you acquire life and salvation in Christ. Commentary on 2 Corinthians 4:12.[27]

Paul's Sufferings Strengthen the Church. The English Annotations: It is as if Paul were saying, "We die so that you may live by our death; we venture into all dangers for the building up of the church; we do not cease confirming all the believers by the examples of our patience. And you are strengthened more and more in the life of the Spirit by all our afflictions and mortal dangers. Thus, all these difficulties that we face turn to your advantage and are means to maintain the life of grace in you here and now, and further your eternal life and happiness hereafter." Annotations on 2 Corinthians 4:12.[28]

4:13-15 *Faith Cannot Remain Silent*

How the Holy Spirit Helps Us in All Troubles and Dangers. Tilemann Hesshus: Although Paul has woven a reminder of the troubles and continual dangers of the apostles and bishops, together with the sweetest consolations concerning the presence of God, freedom, and the reflection of the life of Jesus in us—for these two points of doctrine should never be separated—now nevertheless he shows with greater clarity and detail the rich source of consolation from which we can refresh and maintain ourselves in all miseries, troubles, and dangers. First, he bids us to remember the sovereign help of the Holy Spirit, who strengthens our courage in the greatest of difficulties, so that we remain unmoved by the threats of the whole world and the ragings of the devil. Second, he places before our eyes the resurrection of our bodies, in which we see that whatever tyrants may take from us in this life will be restored to us, with profit, in the next. Third, he leads us to consider our renewal, by which the gifts of God are daily augmented in us and the image of God restored to its original purity. Fourth, he compares the momentary and slight troubles of this present time with the immeasurable glory of the future life. Amid misfortunes, the Holy Spirit arouses and fortifies this great comfort, and he both demonstrates this solid comfort and gives strength of heart to those enduring all kinds of evil. Explication of 2 Corinthians 4:13-18.[29]

[26]Musculus, *Commentarius . . . in posteriorem epistolam Pauli ad Corinthios*, 138.
[27]Hemmingsen, *Commentaria in Omnes Epistolas Apostolorum*, 268.
[28]Downame, ed., *English Annotations*, FF3v*.
[29]Hesshus, *Explicatio Secundae Epistolae Pauli ad Corinthios*, 113r-v.

Like David, Christians Suffer and Live by Faith. Andreas Hyperius: Paul has explained why God determined that the godly should suffer from time to time. Now he adds what serves for consolation, namely, that the godly are always rescued after their afflictions and so should in no way forsake the truth on account of difficult situations. The first reason Paul draws from the example of David's faith who, since he was rescued through faith, it is right for other godly people also to expect deliverance through faith. Now, this subject will be even clearer if we first examine the words of David he quotes here. David, therefore, in Psalm 115,[†] gives thanks to God because he had rescued him from very serious trials, which is also clear from [vv. 16-17[‡]of] the same psalm: "You have broken my chains. To you I will offer the sacrifice of praise and call on the name of the Lord." Moreover, at the beginning of the psalm, David immediately celebrates his faith and makes a confession of his faith, for though he had been afflicted by his enemies, he had nevertheless always been rescued through his faith. Accordingly, the apostle skillfully adapts his introduction to the intention of the psalmist, saying, "Since we have the same spirit of faith, according to what has been written, 'I believed, and so I spoke.' We also believe and speak." It's as if he were saying, "Since our faith is the same as David's, and since he often suffered painful things and yet always remained constant and was rescued from dangers through faith, so let us give thanks to God when we too suffer painful things [for] we expect that, in the same way, we are going to be rescued from dangers by faith." What should be noted from this passage is this: that it is the same faith and the same Spirit working as much among the ancients under the law as all of us believers under the gospel. Whence it follows that the same church of the godly existed from the beginning of the world all the way to our own time. And so the gospel is rightly called eternal, for the fathers also had the gospel, since it was promised to Adam immediately after the fall. But this is the only difference, that their faith was focusing on those things that were going to happen in the future, which for us are present and already accomplished. Commentary on 2 Corinthians 4:13.[30]

David's Example of Faith. Heinrich Bullinger: Comfort is now drawn from the example of David, who, though he was surrounded by wicked people, did not despair, but sang Psalm 116. . . . Paul introduces these words and the consideration of David's faith by way of an example, saying, Since we have the same quality of faith that was also spoken of David, "I believed and so I spoke"—while he was experiencing misfortune and also being optimistic and giving praise to God—so it is right that we are not crushed in our misfortunes. And even if we should see that faith is scarce or nonexistent among other people, we will nevertheless rightly trust in God, whose truth and glory we celebrate so that, by doing so, we might cling to eternal life. Commentary on 2 Corinthians 4:13.[31]

The Christian's Confession. Cyriacus Spangenberg: Now as they confessed their faith, so we also confess our faith. He proves this through the witness of Scripture, from Psalm 116. There it is written, "I believe, therefore I speak." These are David's words, in which he confesses that he is keeping himself in faith in the promised Messiah and trusting in God's Word. His heart is illuminated through such faith and set on fire through the Holy Spirit to share such pure teaching with others and, in contrast, to reject false teaching and idolatry. He is persecuted and hated for this, as he himself confesses, "I am greatly afflicted." And before this he comforts himself, "Be at peace, O my soul, for the Lord does good to you. You, Lord, have snatched my soul

[30]Hyperius, *Commentarius . . . in Epistolam D. Pauli ad Romanos, et Utramque ad Corinthios*, 366-67. [†]Hyperius here is following the chapter numbering found in the Latin Vulgate (and Septuagint), which divided our (modern) Psalm 116 into two separate Psalms, Psalm 114 (vv. 1-9) and Psalm 115 (vv. 10-19). [‡]That is, Psalm 115:6-7 in the Latin Vulgate.

[31]Bullinger, *In Posteriorem D. Pauli Corinthios Epistolam Commentarius*, 283.

from death, my eyes from tears, my feet from slipping." Twentieth Sermon.[32]

Faith Is the Mother of Confession. John Calvin: Now David confesses that, when he had been reduced to the last extremity, he was so beaten down that he almost gave in, but, having soon after regained trust, he had struggled through that temptation. Accordingly, he begins the psalm like this: "I believed, therefore I will speak." For faith is the mother of confession. Paul, indeed, encouraging himself to imitate [David], exhorts the Corinthians to do the same. . . . For he only wants to say this, that believers should be brave and confident in confessing what they have believed in their heart. Let our pretended followers of Nicodemus[†] see what sort of figment their imaginations fabricate in the place of faith, when they wish faith to remain buried within them and completely silent and boast in this "wisdom"—if they say not a word of confession during their whole life. Commentary on 2 Corinthians 4:13.[33]

Faith and Speech. John Trapp: The Spirit of faith does not dwell where the door of the lips does not open in holy confession and communication. Commentary on 2 Corinthians 4:13.[34]

Hope in the Midst of Hardship. Jacques Lefèvre d'Étaples: [Paul and his colleagues] were not succumbing to or being overwhelmed by hardship, because they perceived that every day their soul was being perfected and brought closer to possessing immortality, although their body was moving toward dissolution. Now what they were suffering according to the body was light and momentary. But that which was remaining, the soul and the body restored by the resurrection (after the death of the body)—this is eternal. And so, they were focusing not on what was momentary, but on what was eternal; not on those temporary and changing things that are visible, but on those invisible things that are eternal and will never end. Christ Jesus, the eternal and invisible king, bestows all these things upon us. May all creatures, visible and invisible, praise him above all things forever! Amen. Commentary on 2 Corinthians 4:14.[35]

Christ's Resurrection Gives Us Confidence in Our Resurrection. Wolfgang Musculus: Paul does not simply say, "Knowing that God will raise us," but he says, "Knowing that he who raised the Lord Jesus, will also raise us through Jesus." Accordingly, Paul adduces the knowledge that God will raise him from the fact that God raised the Lord Jesus. Therefore, faith in the resurrection of Christ also produced a sure hope of his own resurrection. Commentary on 2 Corinthians 4:14.[36]

The Glorious Hope of the Resurrection. Tilemann Hesshus: This is the second and indeed the most precious source of consolation, namely, the resurrection from the dead. The same God who resurrected his only-begotten Son, Jesus Christ, will also resurrect us from the dead and cause us to stand in the presence of the Father. Why, therefore, are we disturbed by any injury, troubles, calamities, dangers, prisons, executions? Nothing is wasted for us, even when the world rises up against us with all its fury and violence, snatches our life and members from us, or subjects us to irons that tear our flesh or burns us with flames. For our bodies will be resurrected with great splendor, strength, brightness, and power. The body that is broken by disease, weakened with hard work, crippled by conflicts, exposed to all dangers, subservient to death will be taken away from us. On the other hand, a body free

[32]C. Spangenberg, *Die ander Epistel Pauli an die Corinthier*, 82.

[33]CO 50:57 (CTS 40:208-9). [†]Calvin wrote several treatises against so-called Nicodemites in France, who, out of fear of persecution, kept their evangelical convictions secret and continued to practice Catholic rites.

[34]Trapp, *A Commentary or Exposition*, 712*.

[35]Lefèvre, *Commentariorum in Epistolas Beati Pauli . . . Liber Tertius*, 133v.

[36]Musculus, *Commentarius . . . in posteriorem epistolam Pauli ad Corinthios*, 142.

from sorrow and trouble, firm of strength, shining with brightness, adorned with glory, spiritual in nature, and living for all eternity will be given to us. And so, what the world deems to be suffering and death works to our advantage. Therefore, in every affliction and danger, Christ's most delightful statement in John 6 should always be kept before our eyes: "This is the will of him who sent me, that everyone who looks on the Son and believes in him, should have eternal life, and I will raise him up on the last day." Explication of 2 Corinthians 4:14.[37]

Thanksgiving Glorifies God. Wolfgang Musculus: Paul again admonishes the Corinthians to be thankful for God's excellent grace and to extol God with mutual thanksgiving. Paul expressed these same things earlier in chapter 1: "so that many persons will give thanks on our behalf for the blessings granted us. . . ."

As far as this present verse is concerned, it should be noted that Paul says that expressions of thanksgiving serve to the glory of God. The kindness with which God treats us abounds to the glory of God through expressions of thanksgiving. There is no other way we can repay our beneficent God than by acknowledging from our hearts his grace and glorifying his name with expressions of thanksgiving. And this is that sacrifice of praise that the Lord established in the new covenant, where he entrusted to believers the commemoration of his death in the sacrament of his body and blood. That is why the ancients believed, quite appropriately, that the celebration of this sacrament should be called a Eucharist. Commentary on 2 Corinthians 4:15.[38]

The Benefits of Our Afflictions. Andreas Hyperius: There are two other reasons (in terms of final causes) why the godly are being rescued, namely, for the benefit of other godly people, and for increasing glory to God, which increases when many people give thanks for the rescue of the godly. He says, "It is all for your sake," because when ministers of the Word are afflicted and then are rescued from the affliction, two things happen. First, other godly people, seeing the constancy of these saints, are encouraged and strengthened in the faith, and prepared to endure troubles, having confidence that they too will be rescued. Second, glory to God also increases when, because of the rescue of many people, God is worshiped and praised by many men and women who are watching with wonder. Now, the benefit of the rescue of godly people is amplified somewhat when it is said to "overflow," that is, generously conferred without merit, and again it is said to abound, to be extended, to flow out broadly so that glory to God is rendered clearer from it. Consequently, this verse here describes for us that great benefit of affliction, but especially how we should conduct ourselves when God has given respite after our afflictions. For it is necessary that we give thanks to God, not only for the benefits that we receive from him, but also for those which other people also receive. How much greater our thanks should be when the glory of the gospel shines forth somewhere, or some other spiritual work is miraculously produced. Certainly, when we stop giving thanks, it is no wonder if God sends other calamities one after another. Commentary on 2 Corinthians 4:15.[39]

4:16-18 *The Eternal Weight of Glory*

Viewing Life with Faith-Filled Hope. Desiderius Erasmus: Indeed, the affliction of the body that we sustain for the sake of the gospel is slight and transitory. But this slight affliction produces in us no slight consequence, rather the weighty and inexpressible consequence of glory, since on account of the slight affliction sustained for the sake of Christ, we are made worthy of the

[37]Hesshus, *Explicatio Secundae Epistolae Pauli ad Corinthios*, 115v-116r; citing Jn 6:40.
[38]Musculus, *Commentarius . . . in posteriorem epistolam Pauli ad Corinthios*, 145; citing 2 Cor 1:11.
[39]Hyperius, *Commentarii . . . in Epistolam D. Pauli ad Romanos, et Utramque ad Corinthios*, 367.

supreme happiness, while a temporary death met for the sake of Christ begets for us the reward of unending immortality. Supported by this hope, we consider the life of the body worth nothing, looking not at all to such things as are seen with bodily eyes, but to those that are seen only with the eyes of faith. For the things that are perceived here, such as profit, honor, pleasure, life, loss, disgrace, suffering, death, besides the fact that they are neither real goods nor real evils, are not even of long duration. Those that are perceived with the eyes of faith, however, are as true as they are eternal. PARAPHRASES ON 2 CORINTHIANS 4.[40]

THE REMNANTS OF THE OLD MAN. MARTIN LUTHER: In every person, no matter how holy they may be, there are the remains of the old self, and of sin, and the vestige of the former Adam remains, just as the children of Israel in their day were not able to erase entirely the influence of the Jebusites, the Canaanites, and the rest of the heathen. Moreover, this old self consists of error, concupiscence, wrath, fear, apprehension, despair, evil conscience, horror of death, and so on. Those are the characteristics of the old, carnal self. They diminish, however, in the new self, but they are not extinguished until that person is extinguished by death, just as the apostle says, "Though our outer nature is wasting away, our inner nature is being renewed every day." Therefore, these evil remains of the old self are not removed by indulgences or by contrition which has begun to take place in a person. Rather the process of removal has begun, and as a person increases in spiritual health these evils are removed. This spiritual health is nothing more than faith in or love in Christ. EXPLANATION OF THE NINETY-FIVE THESES.[41]

THE DECAY OF THE OUTER SELF. JOHN CALVIN: Some interpreters improperly and ignorantly confuse the "outer person" with the "old person," for this is far different from the "old person" of which we spoke in Romans 6:6. Chrysostom[†] and others restrict it entirely to the body—which is a mistake, for the apostle wanted to express by this term everything that relates to this present life. Just as Paul here establishes two selves, so you must understand two kinds of life: the earthly and the heavenly. The "outer self" is the preservation of the earthly life, which consists not only in the blossom of one's age and in good health but also in one's wealth, honors, friendships, and other resources. Therefore, as much as we experience the lessening or loss of these blessings—which are required for maintaining the condition of our present life—so our outer self is wasting away. For when we are too much occupied with the present life and everything is going as hoped for, so the Lord takes a little away from us—things which hold us ensnared—so as to call us back to meditate on a better life. Thus, it is necessary that the condition of this present life should decay, so that the inner self might flourish, because as the earthly life declines, the heavenly life increases, at least among believers. Now the outer self of the reprobate also decays, but there is no compensation. Among the children of God, on the other hand, the corruption [of this body] is the beginning and, as it were, the cause of generation. Paul says that this happens daily, because God continually stirs us up to such meditation. Would that this were firmly seated in our minds, so that we might make steady progress amid the decay of the outer self! COMMENTARY ON 2 CORINTHIANS 4:16.[42]

THE SPIRIT MORTIFIES THE INNER PERSON DAY BY DAY. MARTIN CHEMNITZ: Baptism is called "the washing of regeneration and the renewal of the Holy Spirit"; that is, it confers two gifts: the remission of sins and the beginning of renewal which destroys the old nature of the flesh. And the remission of sins is one thing and the mortification, the purging, the destruction, or despoiling of sin is another. Remission takes away

[40]CWE 43:225-26.
[41]LW 31:124* (WA 1:554-55).

[42]CO 50:58 (CTS 40:211-12). [†]For Chrysostom's interpretation, see PG 61:461 (NPNF[1] 12:322).

the guilt of all sins, so that there is no condemnation to those who are in Christ Jesus. And this remission is full and complete. But the renewal which purges out the old leaven and despoils and destroys the body of sin is only beginning, and it is never in this life full or so perfect that none of the old nature or sin remains, because "the new self is renewed from day to day." In this way, it is easy to see the fallacy of this argument: in baptism there takes place a perfect remission of all sins; therefore in the baptized there is nothing left of sin. . . . The Pelagians once used this argument, but Augustine answered them correctly that Paul is not saying that Christ, as he perfectly cleansed his church in baptism through the remission of sins, also and immediately presented it for renewal without any spot or wrinkle. . . . But the Son of God covers the church's spots and wrinkles; and hence the Spirit mortifies, the inner self is renewed from day to day, to this end, that when God will be all in all the church may be shown forth without any wrinkle. For he is speaking of the consummated benefits of Christ which begin in this life but will be perfect and full only in the life to come. Loci Theologici.[43]

God's Consolations Come with Our Afflictions. Tilemann Hesshus: The third source of consolation is this, that those troubles, afflictions, and difficulties achieve our good and thus we consider them to be more advantages than losses. The dangers, calamities, and afflictions of our flesh are all very unpleasant and that continual training of the cross weakens our strength and crushes our nature. Whence comes Christ's complaint: "My life is spent with sorrow and my years with groaning." However, there is no danger, for the outer person—that is, the flesh infected by sin and subservient to death—is being destroyed by this process of dying. And so, we will finally strip off the old person, with its desires and passions. Thus, hatred of sin and consideration of divine judgment are stirred within us; the disgust for this life increases within us; and we are being prepared to approach death in the Lord. However, the inner person, who is born anew from the Spirit of God is being restored to the original image of God. And by means of those very disciplines of afflictions, dangers, and rescues, the inner person is being renewed and adorned from day to day, from glory to glory. Thereafter more light arises in the renewed mind, and a greater understanding of the divine Word and of the benefits of Christ are daily aroused. Thereafter, the will, which has been renewed, approaches closer to God and more readily subjects itself to his commands. The fear of God, repentance, faith in Christ, prayer, love for God, patience, thanksgiving, quickness to confess—all these things increase through those troubles. The desire for eternal life and intimacy with God are aroused. Joseph was far stronger of faith and more ardent in prayer when tormented by servitude and prison than if he had never suffered these sorts of troubles. Since the usefulness of afflictions and adversities is great, we ought to endure them with great strength of mind. Explication of 2 Corinthians 4:16.[44]

Tribulations Strengthen the Inner Person. The English Annotations: By the outward nature Paul understands our bodies, or rather our persons in the natural estate and condition of this life, which decay and are consumed by continual sufferings. By the inward nature Paul understands our souls, or persons, considered according to our spiritual estate, which cannot be discerned by the physical eye, but only by the light of the spirit. The inward nature renewed by the Spirit of God is strengthened and confirmed more and more by daily pressures and tribulations. Thus, the palm tree grows higher and flourishes more the greater the burdens that are laid upon it. In a similar way, Antaeus in his wrestling with Hercules[†] is said by the poets to have gained new strength every time

[43]Chemnitz, *Loci Theologici*, 1:305-6*; citing Titus 3:5.

[44]Hesshus, *Explicatio Secundae Epistolae Pauli ad Corinthios*, 117r-v; citing Ps 31:10; Gen 38-40.

he was thrown to the earth. Annotations on 2 Corinthians 4:16.[45]

Patience in the Face of Suffering. Dirk Philips: You may certainly rejoice in your chastising, which is a sign that you are God's friends and children. So accept it with patience, trusting that it all happens to you for good and that the Father of all mercies and the God of all grace chastises you for your need, so that you might receive his sanctification and live. And although it is somewhat difficult for the flesh, it is thus a joy for the spirit, as the apostle testified and said . . . : "We are not discouraged" (namely, in our suffering for Jesus' sake) "but even though our external passes away, so the internal is still renewed from day to day." Three Admonitions.[46]

The Godly Person's Motto. John Trapp: As he lay dying, Peter Martyr said, "My body is weak; my mind is well—well for the present, and it will be better hereafter." This is the godly person's motto. Commentary on 2 Corinthians 4:16.[47]

The Way to Glory Is by Following Christ. John Colet: Now to believe in Christ as he announces his tidings is, above all, to believe that he was the true messenger of God, and that all his message is true: part of it to be accomplished while our life is here, part to be looked for in the future. What is to be done here is a striving from love of the good to that right, devout, and just way of living which the righteous Christ showed us in himself as exemplar. And what is looked for in the future is that unending weight of glory above all measures in loftiness which such a following of Christ works in us, as we contemplate not the things that are seen but those that are not seen.

In our desire for so great and blessed a reward we ought to follow after Christ in his footsteps with breathless pace as he goes before us, so that we may arrive where he has arrived. And this we should do, it seems to me, like a four-footed beast with four swift feet: the patience, that is, of good from above; the patience of ill from beneath; the doing of good toward those above, which is called piety; the constant doing also of good toward those who are our equals and inferiors, which is called justice. For in this four-square we must press on in this life, so that we may be the more steadfastly self-consistent. By means of this armor of righteousness on the right hand and on the left, we must go on in this land of our homelessness, so that we may escape safely from the perils of injustice. First, we must go to Christ, that from him we may go to glory. Enarration on 1 Corinthians.[48]

The Excellence of the Christians' Future Hope. Wolfgang Musculus: Let us be reminded in this juxtaposition of opposites how we should console ourselves in our afflictions . . . so that we might not, out of a broken spirit, abandon the truth of God which is the only source of our salvation. Does suffering press hard upon us? Let us reflect on the future glory. Is the cross of Christ treated as shameful in this world? Its benefit will be more glorious in the future. Next, let us consider how these light afflictions bring about such a great weight of glory. Let us compare these brief moments to an eternity of glory. If our suffering is great, let us consider how excellent will be the glory of our future happiness. . . . This is certainly the most effective strategy for defeating all the things that in this world seem to gain superiority over the Lord and his believers. Is the power of caesars and kings great? Let us oppose to it the most excellent power of the one who is the supreme Lord, who sweeps away the pride of princes, and let us say, "If the Lord is for us, who can be against us?" Are those who oppose the truth

[45]Downame, ed., *English Annotations*, FF4r*. †In Greek mythology, Antaeus was a giant, the son of Poseidon and Earth, who wrestled all comers and killed those whom he defeated. That he gained strength every time he was thrown to the earth is mentioned in *Apollodorus mythographus* 2.115.

[46]CRR 6:388.

[47]Trapp, *A Commentary or Exposition*, 712*. This is a reference to the Reformed theologian Peter Martyr Vermigli, who died in 1562.

[48]Colet, *Commentary on First Corinthians* 7, 159; citing 2 Cor 6:7.

of God great in [worldly] wisdom and prudence? We have in heaven a Lord who catches the wise and prudent in their cunning and makes foolish all of their counsel. Are persecution and trouble great? Far more excellent will be the future happiness. Is the disgrace of the cross of Christ intense? The future glory is incomparably greater. In summary, whatever is judged great in this world loses its estimation of greatness when compared with heaven, which is more excellent by far. Commentary on 2 Corinthians 4:17.[49]

An Elegant Antithesis. John Trapp: "For our light affliction." Here we have an elegant antithesis, and a double hyperbole that eludes English translation. For affliction, one has glory; for light affliction, one has a weight of glory; for momentary affliction, one has eternal glory. Commentary on 2 Corinthians 4:17.[50]

Glory from Affliction. Martin Bucer: And as thou hast laid upon thy beloved Son, our Lord Jesus Christ, the afflictions, sicknesses and death deserved by us all, and hast smitten him for our sake, that we might be delivered from every affliction, death and hell, and live in him and through him, wilt thou likewise remove and repair the affliction and sickness of this our brother also, on account of the passion of thy beloved Son, so that as through this affliction he is conformed to the afflictions of thy dear Son, so he may also be conformed to his resurrection and holy and blessed life. This thy chastisement shall thus serve for the transformation and renewal of his inner self, and this temporary affliction shall bring forth for him that eternal and incomparably excellent glory which thou hast prepared for thy beloved ones. On the Visitation of the Sick.[51]

Weight of Glory. The English Annotations: The apostle seems to allude to the Hebrew word [*kabōd*] which signifies both the weight and glory. To gold and precious things, the weight adds to the value, just as the more massive and weighty the crown is, the more it is worth. And Paul implies that we shall be at the last crowned with such a crown of infinite glory, which even in this world we lively apprehend by faith, and the contemplation of it takes off all the consideration, love, and esteem of all the things in this world which are seen. And thus, our hearts are fixed on eternal things in heaven, which are not seen. Annotations on 2 Corinthians 4:17.[52]

The Eternal Weight of Glory. Edward Leigh: By "affliction," [Paul means] (1) a pressure, and that of the body only, for which believers will receive "glory" as a recompense, which includes whatsoever may make them happy, both in body and soul. (2) The kind of affliction is but some "light" thing that can be easily endured by those who are endued with a divine Spirit. But the recompense is a weight . . . which infinitely surpasses all afflictions. (3) The duration of afflictions is but for "a while," even for a moment, while the weight of glory is eternal. To show that in this contrast all degrees of comparison are exceeded, Paul adds *hyperbolē* upon *hyperbolē*, which is emphatic in Greek. Because other languages cannot express with precision this phrase, they are forced to use words or phrases which exceed all comparison, such as . . . *excellenter excellens*. Annotations on 2 Corinthians 4:17.[53]

Christians Enter Glory Through Tribulation. Cyriacus Spangenberg: A cross and suffering are indeed heavy and hard, but when we consider that in the future they will have an end and must cease, and what awaits those who believe in Christ in the hereafter, they become light and bearable. There is also no other means or medicine by which we can attain patience than by considering "that our tribulation, which here is temporary

[49]Musculus, *Commentarius . . . in posteriorem epistolam Pauli ad Corinthios*, 148; citing Rom 8:31.
[50]Trapp, *A Commentary or Exposition*, 712*.
[51]CPMB 441.
[52]Downame, ed., *English Annotations*, FF4r*.
[53]Leigh, *Annotations upon all the New Testament*, 259*.

and light, is producing eternal glory weighty beyond all measure." It is not that through a cross and suffering we earn heaven, which God gives from grace alone, but that a cross and suffering are the way and means through which believers, who have now become blessed, following the example of the one who makes them blessed and enter into glory. "For it is through much tribulation that we must enter the kingdom of God." Twentieth Sermon.[54]

Christian Hope in the Midst of Suffering. Theodore Beza: Without going further, what have we seen and continue to see happen in our day? For who has [God] raised up to oppose the great and horrible beast seated on the city of seven mountains [i.e., Rome], assisted by the strength of all the great monarchs of the earth, except people who are poor and altogether contemptible according to this world? And to summarize in a word, have not our books blunted their very sharp swords? And have not our writings extinguished all their flames wherever and as long as it has pleased and continues to please God? And if one acknowledges this, but also notes that the righteous suffer—this is very true. But let us add that everything that they suffer is nothing compared to the prize of eternal glory that will follow, though we cannot even comprehend it today. And during this trial, however harsh and long it might be (which God alone determines), it is this same great, living God who never allows his people to be tested beyond the strength with which he sustains them. Sermons on the Resurrection of Christ.[55]

Living by Faith, Not by Sight. Martin Luther: How much more correct Paul is when he says that our afflictions are temporary and light, but that the glory with which God will make up for them will have measureless significance for those who look at what is invisible, not at what is visible!

But Paul is preaching this in vain, for the world does not believe. It is wholly occupied with what is visible; it pays no attention to what is invisible and regards it as worthless. The merciful Father has given his Son, who died for our sins. He, in turn, demands of us that we confess his name before the world and also lose our life for his name's sake; and he promises that eternal rest and boundless glory will follow upon this small cross. What can be more delightful than this promise, which promises so sure a deliverance from eternal death? Besides, it is the nature of our life that eventually we must die. Why, then, do we not rather die for the sake of Christ's name? . . .

Therefore, let the list of God's blessings, physical as well as spiritual, be constantly in view, and we shall see that where there is a drop of evil, there is an ocean of God's benefits on which we should expatiate with divine rhetoric, as Paul does in an excellent manner; for with a single word he exhausts all the perils and inconveniences about which the world can complain. Commentary on Genesis 20:8.[56]

Setting Our Minds on Things Above. Niels Hemmingsen: The reason for Paul's conclusion is adduced by way of comparison. The evil things that godly people endure in this life are momentary, but the good things that they anticipate are eternal. Hence, evil things ought to be borne lightly, for eternal glory will result from them. And so, the ministry of the gospel should not fail on account of any troubles. This passage provides the greatest usefulness in all difficulties. For it reminds us to turn our eyes from those things that are visible and set our minds on things above, and to turn all our thoughts to the enjoyment of the eternal kingdom in heaven. And so, the object of the eye of faith and the inner person is far different from the eye of the flesh and the outer person. Further, when the apostle says here that patience in

[54]C. Spangenberg, *Die ander Epistel Pauli an die Corinthier*, 83v-84; citing Acts 14:22.

[55]Beza, *Sermons sur l'histoire de la resurrection* (1593), 610; citing 1 Cor 10:13.

[56]LW 3:343 (WA 43:121-22).

affliction accomplishes the weight of glory, he is not referring to the merit of glory, but of the way by which one attains to glory. So, too, he is speaking only about the afflictions of the children of God—for whom glory is their inheritance—and not the wicked, whose affliction is a prelude to eternal punishment unless they repent. Commentary on 2 Corinthians 4:17-18.[57]

Looking with the Eyes of Faith. Philipp Melanchthon: "While we look not on things seen." What Paul says here is very important, and he indicates the most profound condition of the flesh which, because it looks after its own benefit, is also ignorant of the work and wisdom of God so that whenever God accomplishes something within us against our wishes, we grumble against God's judgments. Thus, everyone is indignant about their cross and their situation, just as the sons of Israel were in the desert. And this is what Romans 12 says, "Be transformed by the renewal of your mind, so that you may prove what is the will of God, his pleasing and perfect will," that is, so that you might learn in the cross the work of God's good will. . . . And Romans 5: "suffering produces patience, and patience produces proof"—that is, the knowledge of the divine will toward us—"and proof produces hope." And this is the glory of faith: to support the works and hand of God, not to be guided by sensible things, but by the will of God gently ruling over and leading us. And so you see here again the efficacy of proclaiming faith (since Paul says this as he endures difficulties), because it does not look on fleshly things, but on the outcome of temptation. Annotations on 2 Corinthians 4:18.[58]

[57]Hemmingsen, *Commentaria in Omnes Epistolas Apostolorum*, 269.

[58]*Melanchthons Werke*, 4:113; citing Rom 12:2; 5:4.

Christians Focus on Eternal Things. Tilemann Hesshus: We Christians, Paul says, do not make a big deal about those things that are before our eyes, whether they are favorable or unfavorable to us, for the world has been crucified to us, and we to the world. All things are now perishing and will reach a successful conclusion. The troubles and sadness will not continue forever. We direct our minds to and are completely confident in those things that are not visible, but which are apprehended in the word of promise and faith, which are perpetual and eternal, namely, to heavenly intimacy with God, to the blessed life in heaven, to the joy of the Spirit, to complete restoration in God's image, to fellowship with the angels, and to the eternal kingdom of Christ, in which God will be all in all. Explication of 2 Corinthians 4:18.[59]

Living in Light of Eternity. John Trapp: "Martyrs gaze upon the crown, not the dangers. They consider the reward rather than shudder at the blows. They do not see the lictor's whipping below, but the angels cheering above." Basil[†] also tells us how martyrs that were cast out naked in the winter's night to be burned the next day, comforted themselves and one another with these words: "Sharp is the cold, but sweet is paradise. Troublesome the way, but pleasant shall be the end of our journey. Let us endure cold a little while, and the patriarchs' bosoms shall soon warm us. Let our foot burn a while, that we may dance forever with angels. Let our hand fall into the fire, that it may lay hold upon eternal life." Commentary on 2 Corinthians 4:18.[60]

[59]Hesshus, *Explicatio Secundae Epistolae Pauli ad Corinthios*, 119v.

[60]Trapp, *A Commentary or Exposition*, 713*. [†]Basil the Great was one of the three Cappadocian fathers, who played a crucial role in defending the orthodox doctrine of the Trinity during the decades after the Council of Nicaea (325).

5:1-10 OUR HEAVENLY DWELLING

For we know that if the tent that is our earthly home is destroyed, we have a building from God, a house not made with hands, eternal in the heavens. [2]For in this tent we groan, longing to put on our heavenly dwelling, [3]if indeed by putting it on[a] we may not be found naked. [4]For while we are still in this tent, we groan, being burdened—not that we would be unclothed, but that we would be further clothed, so that what is mortal may be swallowed up by life. [5]He who has prepared us for this very thing is God, who has given us the Spirit as a guarantee.

[6]So we are always of good courage. We know that while we are at home in the body we are away from the Lord, [7]for we walk by faith, not by sight. [8]Yes, we are of good courage, and we would rather be away from the body and at home with the Lord. [9]So whether we are at home or away, we make it our aim to please him. [10]For we must all appear before the judgment seat of Christ, so that each one may receive what is due for what he has done in the body, whether good or evil.

a Some manuscripts *putting it off*

Overview: Even though Paul desires to be "at home" with God in heaven, he does not lose heart or waver in well-doing as he suffers various trials and troubles, for he is confident that his mortal body will one day be resurrected as an immortal body that enjoys perfect fellowship with God forever. For Reformation commentators, these ten verses communicate the "groaning" and glorious hope experienced by all Christians. God's people on earth are like exiles or pilgrims who long for their true spiritual homeland. Though acutely aware of the frailty and corruptibility of their mortal bodies, Christian pilgrims fix their confidence on the supreme blessedness of their future resurrection when they will possess glorified bodies that are no longer afflicted with sin or death. Hence, the reformers insist, Christians should not be controlled by love of this present life nor paralyzed by fear of death—even now, by faith, Christians celebrate an everlasting Easter. And yet, Paul's statement that "while we are at home in the body we are away from the Lord," reminds our commentators that the eschatological promise has not yet been fully realized. Though God is now present with his people—and the indwelling Holy Spirit serves as the guarantee of believers' future hope—nevertheless, Christians do not yet see the Lord face-to-face or enjoy familiar conversation with him. Hence, the Christian life here and now is characterized by trusting in God's promises, pursuing personal holiness, and seeking to please the Lord through worship and good works. Protestant exegetes are especially concerned that their readers not misunderstand Paul's sober warning in 2 Corinthians 5:10 that all men and women in the final judgment will receive rewards according to their works. Paul, they insist, is not teaching that good works are salvific; rather, God has graciously determined to reward Christians in the afterlife for their good works performed by faith. The Christian life, then, must be lived in light of these two fundamental doctrines: the future resurrection and final judgment of all human beings.

Summary of Chapter 5. Tilemann Heshus: In chapter 5, Paul explains in greater detail the doctrine of consolation, which the ministry of the new covenant reveals to us. This chapter can be conveniently divided into three parts. In the first part, he explains and unfolds in greater detail that most efficacious consolation concerning the resurrection of the dead, the restoration of the image of God, the final judgment, and the immeasurable glory of the future life in which believers will be adorned in Christ. He also mentions again the consolation of the pledge of salvation, namely, the Holy Spirit. In the second part, he shows that he was not motivated by the judgment and affections of the flesh, that he did not behave in the ministry according to the old person, that he did not seek his own good, that he did not live for himself—but directing all things to the glory of God and the salvation of the church, he aimed at the Spirit's judgment and the renewal of the new self. And so, Paul returns to and repeats the third source of consolation pertaining to the renewal of the image of God. At the same time, he teaches concerning his ministry that it was not proclaimed according to the judgment of the flesh, nor was it bestowed through the passions of the flesh, but that it should be regarded as coming from the Spirit and Word of God for the renovation of men and women. In the third part, Paul summarizes again the doctrine of the gospel of reconciliation with God, through our Lord Jesus Christ, and the free remission of sins, and the office of the mediator, who was made a victim for our sins. And thus, he reveals to us a fifth most valuable consolation by showing that, with the Father now satisfied, there is free remission of sins, which the only-begotten Son of God, Jesus Christ, has procured by his intercession and sacrifice for us, and the imputation of righteousness before God. This, then, provides the greatest of all consolation in every adversity inasmuch as it brings peace to a conscience previously disturbed and bound in wickedness. Explication of 2 Corinthians 5.[1]

Five Parts to This Chapter. Niels Hemmingsen: There are five parts to this chapter. The first part is an allegorical explanation of his hope that he mentioned at the end of chapter 4. In the second part, Paul brings forward his obedience to God in ministry. For he was so enraptured by the hope of his immortality, that he had to discharge all obedience to God and do anything [commanded of him]. Paul establishes this with several reasons. In the third part, there is an appeal to the Corinthians' consciences, whereby Paul's sincerity in the ministry of the gospel is made clear. In the fourth part, Paul challenges the arrogance of the false apostles, where he adds yet more reasons for his diligence in ministry. In the fifth part, one finds the universal teaching concerning the reconciliation and benefits of Christ, a doctrine that he considers at the opportune time. For since he had said by way of confirmation that the ministry of reconciliation had been given to the apostles, it was proper to describe our reconciliation with God. Now there is a single goal to these five parts, namely, that ministers of the gospel, once they have considered the hope of immortality and the dignity of their office, should teach Christ more confidently amid the troubles of this world. Commentary on 2 Corinthians 5.[2]

5:1-5 *This Earthly Tent*

Importance of Meditating on Heaven. John Calvin: Paul has in mind to correct within us the impatience, dread, and disgust of the cross, contempt for the humble, and in short, arrogance and effeminacy. These things cannot happen unless we raise up our minds to heaven through contempt of this world. Now he advances two arguments. On the one hand, he shows the miserable condition of men and women in this life. Then he shows the supreme and perfect blessedness that awaits believers in heaven after death. For what is it that keeps people so bound to a perverse attachment to this life, except that they deceive themselves with false imaginings—thinking that they are happy living here? On the other hand, it is not enough to recognize the miseries of this life unless we become aware of the happiness and glory of the future life. Commentary on 2 Corinthians 5:1.[3]

---

[1]Hesshus, *Explicatio Secundae Epistolae Pauli ad Corinthios*, 121r-v.

[2]Hemmingsen, *Commentaria in Omnes Epistolas Apostolorum*, 269-70.

[3]CO 50:60 (CTS 40:216).

Paul's Unflagging Endurance. Wolfgang Musculus: In the same manner as other human beings, the apostle was enclosed in a weak body, corruptible and mortal, and that body was daily wasting away both from common troubles as well as from the unique and painful afflictions that he endured frequently and relentlessly for the name of Christ. Meanwhile, he was not broken of spirit, but he pressed on and endured constantly in the work of the Lord, with his eyes not on temporal things but on eternal things. The former attitude appeared astonishing, the latter almost foolish. Paul made mention of the former attitude in the previous chapter, when he said, "So we do not lose heart, but although our outer nature is wasting away, our inner nature is being renewed daily." However, he speaks about the latter attitude at the beginning of this chapter, saying, "For we know that if the tent of this our earthly home will be destroyed, we have a building from God, a dwelling not made with human hands, eternal in the heavens." Paul said that he did not focus on temporal things but eternal ones. He disciplined his mind by concentrating on this. Commentary on 2 Corinthians 5:1-5.[4]

The Body Is a Tent for the Soul. Martin Luther: This body is, as St. Paul says, only a tent of the soul, made of earth or clay, and like an old garment. But because the soul is already in a new, eternal, and heavenly life through faith, and can neither die nor be buried, we have nothing more to wait for than that this poor tabernacle may likewise be made new and incorruptible, for our better part is above and cannot leave our flesh behind. As he who is called *resurrexit* [he is risen] is risen from death and grave, so he who says, "I believe" and clings to him must also follow. For he has gone before us that we should follow, and he has begun the work in us, that through his Word and baptism we may be daily raised in him.

If you receive the Word in faith, you are given other eyes that can see through death to the resurrection and apprehend the pure thoughts and image of life. If I would judge according to my reason that I can see and understand, I should be lost. But I possess an understanding loftier than what the eyes can see and the senses feel, which faith has taught me. For there stands the text that says, *Resurrexit*, "He is risen," not for himself but for our sake, that his resurrection may be made ours, that we may also rise in him, and not remain in death and the grave, but with him may celebrate in the body an everlasting Easter. Sermons from the year 1533.[5]

Christians Await a More Glorious Home in Heaven. Huldrych Zwingli: This metaphor refers to nomads, who carry and move their tents from time to time. It alludes to the weakness, changeableness, and death of the body, that is, that although we must depart this habitation of the body, nevertheless we are surely persuaded that another more excellent home is prepared for us in heaven. Indeed, this home is not made with human hands, but is eternal. And this gives us courage to endure all of these afflictions, and even death itself, with great joy. For why should we avoid that which removes us from this "tent" that is falling apart and leads us to heavenly mansions? Annotations on 2 Corinthians 5:1.[6]

The Superiority of Our Heavenly Bodies. Wolfgang Musculus: "We have this building from God, a house not made with hands, eternal in the heavens." With these words, Paul explains why he is not bothered by the destruction of his body which does not share in the eternal blessings: namely, because it seems to him that this building is far better and the eternal happiness greater than dwelling in his earthly home. Why is that? First, he calls it *oikodomēn*, that is, a "building." There is a great difference between this and a tent. Second, he calls the building "from God" and adds by way of explanation "a house not made with hands." To be

[4]Musculus, *Commentarius . . . in posteriorem epistolam Pauli ad Corinthios*, 152; citing 2 Cor 4:16.

[5]Luther, *Day by Day We Magnify You*; citing WA 37:70.
[6]Zwingli, *Annotatiunculae . . . ex ore Zvinglij*, 167-68.

sure, our body—this earthly body that is weak, mortal, and corruptible—is built by God; it is not made with the hands of any human being. How therefore does our future body have an advantage over this present body when Paul says it will be from God and not made with human hands? In my judgment, Paul says that our future body will be from God and not made with human hands because it will be immediately perfected by divine power, without any human cooperation, which cannot be said about these earthly homes of ours which (since they are made by means of human cooperation) are said to be "made with hands." . . . Third, Paul adds the word "eternal." He compares the fragility and mortality of this earthly body, given that it is not eternal but temporary, frail, and changeable, to what we will have in the future, not a changeable body but an eternal one. And it will not be subject to time, disease, death, corruption, and so on, but set free from all these things, it will enjoy everlasting life and glory. By considering this and hoping in this, the apostle endured in the midst of suffering, and he was not so annoyed at the destruction of his body because he longed and groaned that it might be dissolved . . . and in the meantime he does not focus on what is visible and changeable, but on what is invisible and remains forever. Commentary on 2 Corinthians 5:1.[7]

Our Sure Building in Heaven. Thomas Goodwin: In this first verse of this fifth chapter, he meets with this supposition: but what if this outward self or earthly tabernacle is wholly dissolved and pulled down, what then shall become of this inner self? And he resolves it thus: "That if it is dissolved, we have a house, a building of God in the heavens." And what is the *we*, but this inner self he had spoken of, renewed souls, which dwell now in the body as in a tabernacle, as the inmates that can subsist without it? And it is as if he had said, "If this inward self is destitute of one house, we have another. God, who in this life was so careful over this inner self to renew it every day, has made another more ample provision against this great change. It is but its removing from one house to a better, which God has built." As you yourselves say in your own language, if wars should beset you, and your country house were plundered and pulled down, you would comfort yourselves with this, I have yet a city house to retire to. . . .

Nor is the phrase describing heaven as a "city house" remote either; for as Hebrews 11 states, Abraham and the patriarchs died in faith. Mark that. In faith or expectation of what? He had told us, verse 10, "He looked for a city whose builder is God." What is a city but an aggregation and heap of houses and inhabitants? Multitudes had died before Abraham and gone to heaven, from Adam, Abel, Seth, downward; and God promised him peace at his death, and to be gathered to those fathers. There was then a city built, and already replenished with inhabitants; and among others, a house provided for him, that is, his soul, built of God, and ready furnished against this removal. An Immediate State of Glory.[8]

The Nature of Our Earthly Tent. The English Annotations: St. Paul who was a tentmaker elegantly compares our body to a tent, which is appropriate in several ways. (1) A tent or tabernacle is easily raised up and as easily taken down and spoiled, just as our body is by sickness and outward violence. (2) A tent is a proper habitation for pilgrims or soldiers which do not remain in the same place. Such is also the condition of Christians while they live on the earth—they are strangers and pilgrims and soldiers fighting under Christ's banner. (3) A tent is a moveable house or habitation; so too our bodies, which are now like tents pitched upon the earth, but will hereafter be transported to heaven. (4) Tents are foul on the outside, soiled with wind and weather, but have precious things inside. So, too, the bodies and outsides of Christians are vile and contemptible, but inside they are most

[7]Musculus, *Commentarius . . . in posteriorem epistolam Pauli ad Corinthios*, 154.

[8]WTG 12:3-4*; citing Heb 11:13, 10; Gen 15:15.

beautiful and glorious with special treasures of spiritual graces, like the tents of Solomon, which were very richly furnished within. (5) A tent is not destroyed by the destruction of the parts, but by taking the parts asunder. In the same way, the death of the body is nothing but the dissolution of the parts whereof humans are composed and removing the soul from the body. Annotations on 2 Corinthians 5:1.[9]

Longing for Our Heavenly Dwelling. Cyriacus Spangenberg: Christian people today should not fear death too greatly, because it does nothing other than simply take off from us the old garment of mortality and press us out of the earthly house, so that we will be clothed with the new garment of immortality all the sooner. We should have longing and desire for this, rather than fear.

St. Cyprian[†] says, "When the walls of your house begin to become dilapidated, the beams start to creak, and here a wall falls down, there another one, and it looks as though it is about to fall into a heap, is it not true that you would not stay in it for long? And when at sea a great storm gets up around the ship to wreck it, then you would immediately bring the ship to shore. See, the world teeters and will fall into a heap, and you do not thank God or rejoice, that he presses you out of it all the sooner?"

Dear friends, we should consider that we have renounced the world and are only sojourners and strangers in it. We should therefore rejoice in the day when we are called out of this earthly house to the everlasting eternal building and dwelling. The heathen teacher Plato said as much: "We are souls, immortal creatures, enclosed within a mortal fortress or prison. Hence, departure from this life is a kind of transfer to the good life."

In order to yearn all the more for such a heavenly dwelling which is ours, we should consider more often our poor corrupt nature, our frail flesh and blood which are inclined only to sin in this life and resist God and his Word and everything good. When persons think about this, should they not yearn from the heart to cast off such wickedness? And to cry with St. Paul, "Wretched person that I am! Who will deliver me from the body of this death?" Twenty-First Sermon.[10]

Run for the Prize. Simon Goulart: Let us run with St. Paul, therefore, toward the goal of the heavenly calling, borne not with the feet of our bodies, but with holy thoughts, desires, and groans. For not only the company of angels, but even the Creator and Lord of the angels await us. It is our Father who extends his arms to us, to make us heirs and possessors of all his goods. It is the Son of God who calls us his brothers and coheirs, even to the point of giving us the fruit of his life and the price of his death. The Holy Spirit also awaits us that we might taste of his love and kindness. Because God and his angels desire our arrival, let us also desire with our whole heart to be with them. On Eternal Life.[11]

Groaning for Eternal Life. Giovanni Diodati: [Paul refers here to] the groans of burning desire, which the Holy Spirit creates within us, pushing us to aspire to eternal life. These groans are a certain proof for us that our true rest and happiness is in heaven, not on earth. Annotations on 2 Corinthians 5:2.[12]

Longing to Put on New Clothes. John Trapp: By a sudden change and not to die at all, as we see in 1 Thessalonians 4 and 1 Corinthians 15. For who wishes for death? Absolutely no one. . . . For nature abhors it, and every new self is two selves. But when Christians consider that they do not come to the narrow way except through a

[9]Downame, ed., *English Annotations*, FF4r*; citing Job 4:19; Ps 39:12; Job 7:1; Ps 45:13; Song 1:5.

[10]C. Spangenberg, *Die ander Epistel Pauli an die Corinthier*, 87v; citing Gen 8; Rom 8; 7:24. [†]St. Cyprian was the bishop of Carthage during the third century.

[11]Goulart, *XXVIII Discours Chrestien*, 327-28.

[12]Diodati, *La Seconde Epistre de l'Apostre S. Paul aux Corinthiens*, 144; citing Rom 8:23.

sacred path; that there is no passing into paradise except under the flaming sword of this angel death that stands at the entrance; that there is no coming to the city of God except through this straight and heavy lane; that there is no wiping all tears from the eyes except with the winding grave clothes—they yield to it and are not only content, but full of gladness at their departure. As in the meantime, they accept life rather than love it, they endure it rather than desire it. Commentary on 2 Corinthians 5:2.[13]

Christians Wear Garments of Righteousness Here and Now. Niels Hemmingsen: Paul confirms what he said concerning the vows and groanings of godly people. For the godly long to be clothed with their heavenly home, that is, to receive the glory of immortality, although already before in this life they are not naked but are found to be clothed. Now what is that garment with which it is necessary for us to be clothed? Paul says in Galatians 3, "As many of you as were baptized in Christ were clothed in Christ." Thus, the first garment is that, having been washed in the blood of Christ, we are clothed in his merit, by which our sins are hidden, as that verse says, "Blessed are those whose sins have been covered." Second, we are clothed in the righteousness of Christ. For just as he has expiated sin by his sacrifice, so he renders us righteous by his obedience; for as through the disobedience of one man many were judged to be sinners, so through the righteousness of one man the many were judged to be righteous. Third, we are clothed in the presence of Christ, by which he rules and comforts us. Fourth, we are clothed in the sanctification of Christ's Spirit, by which we are strengthened to be set apart to obey God. And too, it is necessary for us to be clothed with good works which, if they were absent, then all the previous garments would of necessity also be absent. For good works are the perpetual fruit of genuine faith. What is said in Matthew 22 about wedding clothes corresponds with these things. For although some people explain that wedding garment otherwise, nevertheless, [the king's] questioning and rebuke of the man who didn't have a wedding garment is applicable and clearly demonstrates that that garment is the sanctification to which we have been called. Commentary on 2 Corinthians 5:2-3.[14]

Paul Is Speaking Here Only of Believers. John Calvin: Paul restricts to believers what he has stated concerning the certainty of the future life, as it is something peculiar to them. For the wicked are also stripped of the body, but since they bear nothing in God's sight other than disgraceful nakedness, they are thus not clothed with a glorious body. Believers, on the other hand, who appear before God, clothed in Christ and adorned in his righteousness, receive the glorious garment of immortality. Now I prefer to accept this view, rather than that of Chrysostom[†] and others, who think that nothing new is said here but that Paul is only repeating what he said previously concerning putting on the eternal habitation. And so the apostle mentions here a twofold clothing whereby God clothes us with the righteousness of Christ and the sanctification of the Spirit in this life, and after death, with immortality and glory. The first is the cause of the second, because those whom God has appointed to glorify, he first justifies. Commentary on 2 Corinthians 5:3.[15]

Without Faith, We Are Naked in God's Sight. Tilemann Hesshus: Paul shows where such a great future hope rests. All men and women—as many as have lived in the world—rise again, whether they are wicked or godly, evil or good. All people, Christ says, who are in the book, will appear before the judgment seat, but they will be treated very differently: those who do

[13]Trapp, *A Commentary or Exposition*, 714*; citing 1 Thess 4:17; 1 Cor 15:51-52; Phil 1:23.

[14]Hemmingsen, *Commentaria in Omnes Epistolas Apostolorum*, 270-71; citing Gal 3:27; Mt 22:1-14; 22:12.

[15]CO 50:61 (CTS 40:218). †For Chrysostom's interpretation, see PG 61:467-68 (NPNF[1] 12:327).

good to the resurrection of life, while those who act wickedly to the resurrection of judgment. In a similar way, in this passage, the apostle restricts the glory of the future age to believers alone. It is necessary for us in this life to be covered if we wish to be clothed in the resurrection of the dead; that is, it is necessary for us in this life to be converted to God, to have embraced his Word, to be united with Christ, and received into God's covenant. For this purpose, God has appointed for us his only-begotten Son as mediator. He has announced from heaven that we should listen to him. He has established the ministry by which he calls men and women to repentance and explains to them his will. He pours out the Holy Spirit. He extends life to us and confers upon us every kind of blessing so that we might be converted to him in this life, might be received in grace, and be made sons and daughter of God. Now he adds this severe threat and judgment: he is going to throw into eternal damnation all those who were not converted in this life and had not embraced with true faith the benefits of the mediator. "Those who do not believe in the Son will not see life. But the wrath of God remains upon them." Therefore, this consolation concerning the glory of the future life is restricted to believers in Christ alone, who are clothed through Christ. Without faith in the Lord Jesus, we are completely naked in the sight of God. Explication of 2 Corinthians 5:3.[16]

The Soul Doesn't Sleep in Death. Huldrych Zwingli: Paul's sense is this: "I don't want to die so as to be completely undressed"—not because there is no other life after this life, nor because [God] punishes me for this life, but so that I might receive a better and more excellent life as this mortal life is absorbed by immortality." We see here the error of the Anabaptists, who claim that souls sleep after dying.[†] If this present life (for which death is better) is not sleep, how can that future life (which absorbs mortality) be called sleep? Annotations on 2 Corinthians 5:4.[17]

The Spirit's Groaning. Philipp Melanchthon: Paul describes the unspeakable struggle of the spirit and flesh, which he has treated in greater detail in Romans 7–8, how the spirit is carried away to spiritual things, that is, the knowledge, fear, faith, and love of God, whereas the flesh is dragged away to fleshly things and is a hindrance to the spirit. And these things should not be understood to mean that the spirit is mere knowledge, which ponders things—just as reason or conscience influences the wicked—but rather, it is the relentless restlessness of the heart, truly a grieving for the burden of bodily sin, as the apostle exclaims, "Who will liberate me from this body of death!" Annotations on 2 Corinthians 5:4.[18]

The Godly and Wicked Groan—but for Different Reasons. John Calvin: The wicked also groan because they are not content with their present situation in life. But afterward a very different disposition takes over them, that is, a clinging to life, so that they are horrified by death and do not find burdensome the long duration of their mortal life. The groaning of believers, on the other hand, arises from the fact that they know that here they are exiles from their homeland, and that they are shut up in the body as in a prison. Hence, they find burdensome this present life because in it they are not able to possess true and perfect blessedness, and because they cannot flee the bondage of sin except by death, and thus they long to be elsewhere. Commentary on 2 Corinthians 5:4.[19]

[16]Hesshus, *Explicatio Secundae Epistolae Pauli ad Corinthios*, 124r-v; citing Mt 17:5; John 3:18.

[17]Zwingli, *Annotatiunculae . . . ex ore Zvinglij*, 168. [†]The belief known as psychopannychism—that the soul goes to sleep upon physical death, to be "awakened" at the final resurrection of the body—was popular among a number of sixteenth-century Anabaptist and Radical Christians, including Michael Sattler, Gerard Westerburg, and Andreas Bodenstein von Karlstadt. One of John Calvin's first treatises, titled *Psychopannychia*, was written against this doctrine (printed in 1542). See George Hunston Williams, *The Radical Reformation*, 3rd ed. (Kirksville, MO: Sixteenth Century Journal Publishers, 1992).

[18]*Melanchthons Werke*, 4:114; citing Rom 7:24.

[19]CO 50:61-62 (CTS 40:218-19).

Two Kinds of Groaning. The English Annotations: There is a double groan, one of nature, from the apprehension and fear of death, another of grace, out of an earnest desire for eternal life, which the Spirit kindles in us. Annotations on 2 Corinthians 5:4.[20]

The Property, Not the Substance, of the Body Will Change. Wolfgang Musculus: By the term "further clothed" Paul is not saying that a new kind of body is being joined together with the old body, but rather that this body which we carry about here is being further clothed with the glory of immortality. The property of being glorified—not the substance of the new body—is what Paul compares to being newly clothed. And that is why he adds the words "so that mortality might be swallowed up by life," which perfectly explains what he means by the term "further clothed." He does not say, "so that the old, earthly, and dead body might be swallowed up by a new, heavenly, and living body," but rather that "the mortality of the earthly body might be swallowed up by life, so that death might not be tasted." Mortality is a property of the earthly body, not its substance. When mortality is swallowed up by heavenly life into life itself, which will be a sudden change that happens in a moment of time, it will not be the substance of the body that is swallowed up, but rather the property of the body, which is mortal and corruptible. Commentary on 2 Corinthians 5:4.[21]

True Life Replaces Our Dying Life. Thomas Goodwin: The fourth verse gives a genuine and sincere account of why a Christian does thus groan, and that after dissolution itself, in order to this glory, which Paul sets out with an accurate distinction of their desires of dissolution, in differences from like desires in all other people. First, negatively, not because being burdened we desire to be unclothed, or dissolved. . . . But second, positively, for this, as the top ground of that desire, that we would be clothed with that house spoken of, verse 1, and that still taken in the sense spoken of in the second verse, to the end that this mortal animal life, which the soul, though immortal in itself, now leads in the body, full of sins, clogged with a body of death and miseries, each of which has a death in it, and so it lives but a dying life. That this life may be exchanged, yes, swallowed up by that which is life indeed, the only true life, the knowing of God as we are known, and enjoying him. All which, as to our souls, is truly performed at our dissolution. An Immediate State of Glory.[22]

The Land of the Living Is in Heaven. Simon Goulart: For here, before the soul goes out of the body, we are often and long in dying, feel many assaults of death, who give us many sore blows and deadly wounds before he kills us outright. First, our infancy dies in us; next our childhood; afterward our youth or age of twenty or twenty-one grows; consequently our manly and middle age which is followed with old age, which changes both us and our affections, making us live after another manner. We shall then be in the land of the living, when we shall be the same people we seem to be, unchangeable, without grief of mind or sickness of body, not subject to any corruptions, or defilements. . . . While we live in this tabernacle of the body . . . we sigh and mourn, being heavily burdened, not that we desire to be stripped or unclothed, but to be clothed again, that that which is mortal in us may be swallowed up of life. In heaven, which indeed is the land of the living, we shall be stripped of all that is vile, contemptible, mortal, frail, and corruptible in us, and shall be clothed with a robe of glory and blessed immortality. The Wise Vieillard.[23]

Faith Will Become Sight in Eternity. Jacques Lefèvre d'Étaples: The Holy Spirit

[20]Downame, ed., *English Annotations*, FF4r*.

[21]Musculus, *Commentarius . . . in posteriorem epistolam Pauli ad Corinthios*, 159.

[22]WTG 12:4-5*.

[23]Goulart, *The Wise Vieillard*, 14-15*.

gives to holy people certain and indubitable knowledge concerning the state of the future resurrection, concerning the absence of God in this present life and his presence in the life to come. That doesn't mean that we are absent from God, either in this life nor in the future life. For in this life, God is absent from us by sight, but present to us by faith; for all things are present to God. Just as when a blind person stands looking at light, colors, and a mirror: the appearance of light, colors, and the mirror are absent to his blindness, but present through faith. For he believes with certainty that there is light, colors, and a mirror. So in the life to come, God will be present to our sight, and faith will no longer be in the shadows, but in the light. [Christians] will not only believe, but they will know and understand with perfect clarity, just as when a person who has been blind their entire life, then receives sight. Commentary on 2 Corinthians 5:5-7.[24]

The Spirit Guarantees God's Love and Our Resurrection. Tilemann Hesshus: Since the doctrine concerning the resurrection of the dead is completely contrary to human reason, which cannot comprehend how life can be drawn from death, Paul leads us to consider the promised guarantee of life. When we believe in Christ, the Son of God, we are given the Spirit of God, who is poured into our heart, as the passage says, "Now, because you are sons, God sent the Spirit of his Son shouting, 'Abba Father.'" Truly, it is a most certain guarantee of the enormous love of God toward us that he gave us his Spirit, through whom he imparts to us his heavenly gifts. The Spirit is the infallible guarantee and most obvious proof of the future resurrection. Now since the eternal Father loves us so much that he pours his Spirit into our hearts, it is certain that he will not hand us over to eternal destruction and death but will resurrect us and make us partakers of the divine nature. And since the Spirit of Christ now dwells in our mortal body, as in his temple, he prepares us daily for the glory of the future life. There is no doubt but that God, who raised the Lord Jesus and Head of the church from the dead, will also raise our mortal bodies because of the indwelling Spirit of Christ. Explication of 2 Corinthians 5:5.[25]

Christians Are Certain of Their Heavenly Home. Andreas Hyperius: Lest anyone think that what he said concerning the heavenly dwelling was uncertain or that it was doubtful that godly people were going to achieve it, Paul now adds the reason why such hope must be considered most certain, drawn from the divine promise and from the sign or guarantee already given. For a seeming difficulty could have arisen from that restatement [in v. 3] where Paul said, "If, nevertheless, in putting it on we might not be found naked." For someone could say, "Paul, how do you know what is going to happen to the body? Perhaps you will never be clothed in such glory." Therefore, Paul responds with great passion, "Yes, we really are certain," he says, "for although we are by no means acceptable in ourselves, nevertheless, God renders us acceptable and worthy. He himself is the one who has prepared us for this very thing that we might one day migrate to our heavenly home. And so that we don't doubt anything about this, God himself has already in a way given us the guarantee of the Spirit." And thus, Paul rightly says that the Spirit, or the gifts of the Spirit, are like a guarantee which makes us certain that God wishes to bring us back to himself. The Spirit here is called a guarantee (*arrabōna*), a metaphor applied to contracts, such as marriage contracts. Thus, Paul says in the first chapter of this present epistle that "the Spirit has been given to us as a guarantee." In Ephesians 1, the Spirit is called the "guarantee of our inheritance." In Romans 8, Paul says that "the Spirit bears witness together with our spirit that we are sons of God." And thus those passages certainly strengthen doubting

[24]Lefèvre, *Commentariorum in Epistolas Beati Pauli . . . Liber Tertius*, 134.

[25]Hesshus, *Explicatio Secundae Epistolae Pauli ad Corinthios*, 128v-129r; citing Gal 4:6.

consciences because they establish with certainty that those who are pleasing to God have been called to an inheritance, and they know that they have been made certain by the Spirit of God. COMMENTARY ON 2 CORINTHIANS 5:5.[26]

GOD ALONE IS THE AUTHOR OF SALVATION. HEINRICH BULLINGER: Paul now attributes all things to God, the author of everything, lest anything be ascribed to human strength. According to Ambrose,† "[Paul] says that God is going to accomplish everything in the day of judgment because he has promised his Spirit and is faithful to fulfill his pledge of this matter. For this very same Spirit is the proof of our adoption." In brief, when we obtain eternal life, it is God who brings it about. Now, he has shown what he wants to accomplish when he gave his word in the form of a guarantee. COMMENTARY ON 2 CORINTHIANS 5:5.[27]

5:6-10 *Living by Faith, Not by Sight*

CHRISTIAN CONFIDENCE IN A FOREIGN LAND. DESIDERIUS ERASMUS: So whatever storms arise, we are always confident in heart. We are quite aware of the fact that, for as long as we are at home in this habitation of the body, we are in a foreign land and separated from God. Death joins us to him more closely, not because God is not present to us in the meantime, but because he is not yet clearly perceived in the way he will be gazed upon then. For in the interim, he is in some way perceived through faith, but as if from a distance; then he will be seen close up, as he is, not through a veil. PARAPHRASES ON 2 CORINTHIANS 5.[28]

CHRISTIANS ARE EXILES AND SOJOURNERS. MARTIN LUTHER: St. Paul says in 2 Corinthians 5:6, "As long as we sojourn in the body." But if we are exiles in the body, which is ours in a very special sense, and our life in the body is nothing else than a sojourn, how much more are the things which we possess on account of the body, namely, fields, home, and money, nothing else than exiles and sojourns! The body is a gloomy prison, as it were, in which the soul is kept confined as in a prison and dungeon. Therefore, half of us is nothing, as it were, and a stinking cadaver in a grave.

Accordingly, it is sufficiently evident that the patriarchs extracted and examined the very kernel in the promises and did not cover themselves with the shell alone. Thus Abraham understood that the promise given to him included the true fatherland and the true life, namely, the future life and a life better than this one—a life which is not a servitude and captivity of the soul. COMMENTARY ON GENESIS 23:4.[29]

WE ARE ALWAYS OF GOOD COURAGE. PHILIPP MELANCHTHON: As an epilogue, Paul says to the effect: Although we are daily handed over to death, nevertheless we are of good courage, because we know that instead of this life—where we are absent from God—we will obtain a life in which we are in God's presence. The apostle does not rejoice that he lives apart from God; rather, he rejoices in this, that he is departing from the body to be with God. Accordingly, the reason for this antithesis must be very carefully considered in this speech, when he says, "We are of good courage, because though it is true we are pilgrims here, afterward we will be present with God." Moreover, these are the same things that are said in Romans 8: "The creation anxiously awaits. . . ." Again, "in hope we have been saved." ANNOTATIONS ON 2 CORINTHIANS 5:6.[30]

BEING APART FROM THE LORD. WOLFGANG MUSCULUS: Now someone will ask here whether this body of ours is so remote from the Lord that whatever actions our bodies perform thereby separate us from the Lord, and we are like aliens

[26]Hyperius, *Commentarii . . . in Epistolam D. Pauli ad Romanos, et Utramque ad Corinthios*, 370; citing 2 Cor 1:22; Eph 1:14; Rom 8:16.
[27]Bullinger, *In Posteriorem D. Pauli ad Corinthios Epistolam Commentarius*, 286. †For Ambrose's statement, see PL 17:310-11.
[28]CWE 43:228.

[29]LW 4:206 (WA 43:283-84).
[30]*Melanchthons Werke*, 4:114; citing Rom 8:19, 24.

and foreigners from him, just as the apostle's words seem to say. And how can this conclusion be reconciled with the rest of the Scriptures, where they say, "Do you not know that your bodies are members of Christ?" Or again, "Do you not know that your body is the temple of the Holy Spirit living in you, which you have from God?"

I answer: The apostle does not deny these statements. Nor do they contradict this present passage. Our bodies are not alien from Christ for they are Christ's members. And nevertheless, there is a great difference between the fellowship that unites us to Christ in this earthly life, and that fellowship that will unite us to Christ in our heavenly life when this earthly body is cast aside. Christ, departing this earth, has ascended into heaven to his celestial and eternal dwelling, and he has promised in the future to bring us also to that place, to the Father's throne as it were, to be with him forever. Since this is the situation all the way until judgment day, we are thus apart from Christ as we inhabit this present world in the body. . . . This theology is basic for Christians, though today it is mangled by quarrelsome people in a remarkable manner. The apostle addresses this when he says, "and we know that while we are in the body, we are apart from the Lord." Commentary on 2 Corinthians 5:6.[31]

God Is Always Present with His People. Tilemann Hesshus: Paul does not wish to say that our Lord Jesus Christ is far removed from the church and from every godly person. In fact, the Son of God is always present with his church—every member at every moment in every place—since he says, "I am with him in trouble, I will rescue him." And, "Where two or three are gathered in my name, I am in the midst of them." And, "I am with you always, even to the end of the age." To the patriarch Jacob, Christ says, "I will go down with you to Egypt. I will not abandon you." This is the greatest of comforts for all godly people, that Jesus Christ is present with us in every difficulty. The apostle here is not weakening this promise, but rather is speaking about the fact that we are not allowed to gaze face-to-face upon the Lord Jesus, who is our only salvation. We are not allowed to converse with him familiarly, hearing him speak and enjoying his most charming appearance. But the Son of God, who is both God and man, is present with us; he hears our prayers; he heals our wounds; he defends us; he supplies us with food; he protects us amid great dangers; and he gives to us countless blessings. Nevertheless, he does not show himself to our sight, but hides himself in those spiritual hideaways that we cannot penetrate given the dullness of our eyes. Paul calls this "to be absent from the Lord"—lacking the appearance and familiar conversation of the Lord. Explication of 2 Corinthians 5:6.[32]

Christians Are Always Confident. John Trapp: Christians are not hesitant or halting, as Adrian the emperor was, and as that man who cried out on his death bed, namely, "I have lived carefully, I die doubtfully, I do not know whither I go." That wisest of philosophers Socrates with all his skill could not answer his friends whether it were better for men and women to die or live longer. Cicero, comforting himself as well as he could by the help of philosophy against the fear of death, cried out and complained at length that the medicine was too weak for the disease. It is only true Christians who can be confident that their end shall be happy, though the beginning and middle of their lives might be troublesome. Commentary on 2 Corinthians 5:6.[33]

Christians Walk by Faith. Cardinal Cajetan: Note what Paul says concerning the body, namely, that it is corruptible, during which we walk, that is, we are sojourners. Note what he says about absence: for to walk by faith is to be

[31]Musculus, *Commentarius . . . in posteriorem epistolam Pauli ad Corinthios*, 163; citing 1 Cor 6:19.

[32]Hesshus, *Explicatio Secundae Epistolae Pauli ad Corinthios*, 130v-131r; citing Ps 91:15; Mt 18:20; Gen 46:4.

[33]Trapp, *A Commentary or Exposition*, 714-15*.

absent from the Lord—which is contrasted sharply from being present with the Lord through sight. And so, from this Paul shows that because we walk by faith (that is, we are sojourners to our heavenly fatherland) and do not see God clearly (since we are present in corruptible bodies), we are absent from the Lord. Thus, we understand "present with the Lord" to be when we will see him by sight, that is, according to the nature and beauty of God himself. This is the same thing that, in his previous epistle, Paul called "seeing face-to-face"—in both cases speaking thus directly about faith. Commentary on 2 Corinthians 5:7.[34]

We Enjoy Christ's Fellowship Though We Cannot See Him. Tilemann Hesshus: Daily we receive a great number of blessings from our Lord Jesus Christ: reconciliation with God, the gift of the Holy Spirit, nourishment, defense, teaching, counsel, direction, and he is continually present with us. "The Lord is near to all those who call upon him." Daily we address him with our prayers; we celebrate his name; we hear him prophesying and promising us eternal life. But all these things happen through the Word by faith, not by sight. That is, we do not look with our eyes upon the appearance of our Lord Jesus, for we are not yet allowed to converse face-to-face with the resurrected and glorified Lord Jesus. Explication of 2 Corinthians 5:7.[35]

Perseverance Through Faith and Hope. Andreas Hyperius: "We walk by faith," he says, "not by sight." This statement is very similar to what is said in Romans 8: "we are subjected in hope." Indeed, in this present world we are justified by faith and, having been justified through faith, we ought to walk accordingly as long as we live. But in this present life we do not possess (except by faith and hope) the eternal glory and other spiritual blessings which ought to follow justification—things which we are going to possess in the future. Therefore, having this faith or hope in the heavenly blessings to come, the saints, when they see themselves overcome with miseries in this world, should console and strengthen themselves that just as they began rightly, so they should walk and continue on. The more we are tested in this present world, the more we are encouraged in the faith, and sometimes we even want to meet our death so that we might quickly arrive at the promised glory. Commentary on 2 Corinthians 5:7.[36]

Christians Should Desire Rather Than Fear Death. John Calvin: Paul again repeats what he had said regarding the confidence of the godly—that they are so far from being crushed by the severity of the cross and from losing heart in the face of afflictions that they are made more courageous by them. For the worst of all evils is death, yet believers desire it as the beginning of perfect blessedness. . . . Observe here—what has already been stated once before—that true faith not only produces contempt for death, but even desires it, and that, on the other hand, it is a sign of disbelief when the dread of death controls us more than the joy and consolation of hope. Now, believers long for death not so that they might anticipate the Lord's day out of inappropriate desire, for they willingly keep their feet planted in their earthly post as long as it pleases the Lord, for they would prefer to live in the glory of Christ than to die to themselves and for their own advantage. For the desire that Paul is talking about comes from faith and thus it in no way disagrees with the will of God. We may also gather from these words of Paul that when souls are released from their bodies they live in the presence of God, for if being absent from the body means to have God present, then they surely live with him.

Here it is asked by some people, "How is it, then, that the holy fathers dreaded death so much, as for example David, Hezekiah, and the entire

[34]Cajetan, *In Posteriorem Pauli Epistolam ad Corinthios Commentarii*, 168-69; citing 1 Cor 13:12.

[35]Hesshus, *Explicatio Secundae Epistolae Pauli ad Corinthios*, 131; citing Ps 145:18.

[36]Hyperius, *Commentarii . . . in Epistolam D. Pauli ad Romanos, et Utramque ad Corinthios*, 370-71; citing Rom 8:20.

Israelite church, as is plain from Psalm 6, Isaiah 38, and Psalm 115?" I know how people usually answer this question—that the reason why death was so much dreaded by them was because the revelation of the future life was still so obscure, and hence the consolation weak. Now I confess that this is part but not the whole answer, for the holy fathers of the ancient church did not always tremble when forewarned about their deaths. Rather, many of them embraced death with cheerfulness and joyful hearts. For Abraham departed without regret, full of days. We do not read that Isaac avoided death. Jacob with his last breath testifies that he is anticipating the salvation of the Lord. David himself also dies peacefully without any regrets, and so too Hezekiah. Why therefore did David and Hezekiah once tearfully pray against death? The reason was because they were being punished by the Lord because of certain sins, and so they perceived the wrath of the Lord in death. This was the reason for their distress, which believers under the rule of Christ can also experience today. The desire of which Paul is speaking [in this present passage] is the disposition of a well-regulated mind. Commentary on 2 Corinthians 5:8.[37]

The Christian's Experience of Separation. Wolfgang Musculus: "To be sure, we are of good heart and would rather be separated from the body and present with the Lord." With these words, Paul lays bare the constant desire of his heart as he was eager to be relieved of this present separation to be with the Lord in heaven. He expresses the same thing elsewhere: "For I am eager to be set free to be with Christ." According to the Lord's will, Paul was enduring patiently his separation during which he was physically absent from the Lord, but in the meantime he was eager for this separation to be finished so as to be present with Lord. We see here that there are two kinds of separation that are distinguished in turn so that they cannot be at the same time but must necessarily follow one after the other. The first occurs during this present life when we are separated from the Lord; the second occurs after death, when we are separated from the body. When we are separated from the Lord, we cannot be separated from the body. When we are separated from the body, we cannot to be separated from the Lord. . . .

Let the observant reader note how Paul uses the term "separated from." For this present physical life, he employed the term "being separated from the Lord." In so doing, of course, he makes clear how brief it is. Then he uses the term "being separated from the body" to describe that period of our life that comes between the death of our body and the day of resurrection. This period is still unknown to us, for we do not gain understanding of it by our intellect, but only by experience. What therefore is the death of our body except an exchange of separations? But that second separation will not be exchanged for a third. For in the end, we will be separated neither from the Lord nor from the body but we will be in the body with the Lord forever. Commentary on 2 Corinthians 5:8.[38]

A Prayer for Perseverance. Cyriacus Spangenberg: Such comfort is not natural but the particular work of God the Holy Spirit, for which we should also ask him.

Now we ask the Holy Spirit
Above all for right belief
That he protect us at our end
When we go home from this misery.
You highest comforter in all need,
Help us to fear neither shame nor death
That our sense may not despair
When the enemy accuses our life.
Be with us in our dying need,
Guide us out of death into life.
O Lord prepare us by your power
And strengthen the weakness of our flesh
That we might contend valiantly here
Through death and life to come to you.

[37]CO 50:63-64 (CTS 40:222-24); citing Is 38:3; Ps 115:17; Gen 25:8; 35:29; 49:18; 1 Kings 2:10.

[38]Musculus, *Commentarius . . . in posteriorem epistolam Pauli ad Corinthios*, 164-65.

So it says, "We are comforted at all times and know that as long as we live in the body we are away from the Lord." That is, although God is around and near us, and also lives in us, his believers, we are nevertheless in this case still foreigners and pilgrim brothers in this world, so that we do not see him as present, as the angels see him, but we continually live away, not from ourselves but from the Lord, and we know that this sojourning, in which we do not see the Lord before our eyes, will one day have an end, when we will then truly come home and enjoy eternally the presence of our dear Lord God, with inexpressible delight and joy, and embrace, hug and kiss him as our dear Father. Twenty-Second Sermon.[39]

Christians Face the Future with Bold Confidence. The English Annotations: "We are confident." . . . We are thereby bold and live out our pilgrimage with a valiant resolution and quiet mind, so that, even though we would rather depart for home to be with the Lord (which is our great desire), nevertheless we strive to live in such a way that in our pilgrimage here we seek to please him, that at length we may be received by God into our heavenly home. Commentary on 2 Corinthians 5:8.[40]

Christians Must Strive to Please Christ. Wolfgang Musculus: Paul does not simply say, "So we desire to please him" . . . but "So we *strive* to please him." He employs the Greek word *philotimoumetha*, which means "we strive and try our hardest with great diligence." Those who strive in this way do nothing except what pleases him; they let go of everything that they think displeases the Lord, whose approval they desire in all things. This ought to be the continual practice of true Christians. And so they stand firmly on the standard of their master's word, lest, by presumptuously going beyond it . . . they should hear the Lord say, "They worship me in vain, teaching the doctrines and commands of human beings." Commentary on 2 Corinthians 5:9.[41]

Paul's Zeal to Please the Lord. Andreas Hyperius: Paul now gives the principal reason for his faith and diligence in the apostolic office, and at the same time for his perseverance and courage in enduring dangers. He also confirms what he just said, namely, that whatever happens in this life, he is zealous to please God and be present with him. Here the phrase "to be at home and to be away" simply means (without reading it tropologically[†]) "to rest at home or to make a journey abroad." Thus, Paul's meaning is this: "Whatever happens to us, whether we remain fixed to a certain place as if resting peacefully in our own home, or whether we make a journey traveling from city to city announcing the gospel everywhere, this is our concern and what we work for: that we might please the Lord." And here Paul is again commending his faith and diligence both in life and in doctrine. The phrase "we make it our aim" means to exert oneself with all effort and zeal to accomplish something. Commentary on 2 Corinthians 5:9.[42]

Christian Assurance Motivates Holy Fear. John Trapp: Our hope of heaven makes us active and abundant in God's service. The doctrine of assurance is not a doctrine of license, but the contrary. We make it our ambition, says the apostle here, to get acceptance into heaven, waiting till our Father shall call us home, and passing the time of our sojourning here in fear. The saints have their commemoration upon earth, their conversation in heaven. Commentary on 2 Corinthians 5:9.[43]

Does Paul Employ Fear to Motivate Christian Obedience? Wolfgang Musculus: You ask, "Is it appropriate to motivate

[39]C. Spangenberg, *Die ander Epistel Pauli an die Corinthier*, 92v.
[40]Downame, ed., *The English Annotations*, ff4r*.

[41]Musculus, *Commentarius . . . in posteriorem epistolam Pauli ad Corinthios*, 166; citing Mt 15:9.
[42]Hyperius, *Commentarii . . . in Epistolam D. Pauli ad Romanos, et Utramque ad Corinthios*, 371. [†]Tropology is a mode of spiritual interpretation that identifies the moral meaning of the biblical text.
[43]Trapp, *A Commentary or Exposition*, 715*; citing 1 Jn 3:3; 1 Pet 1:17.

Christians by a fear of future judgment so that they take pains to please the Lord Christ as a judge? Is it not better to encourage Christians to strive to please him as Savior and Redeemer out of feelings of love and Christian respect, which was the method that inspired the apostle himself?" I answer: It is not the intention of the apostle to plant a spirit of fear in the hearts of believers in order to induce them to religious devotion. Rather, he accommodates himself to the church of Corinth in which there were disciples of those false apostles whose hearts were not pure toward the Lord. Many of them were worldly and unrepentant people who were not at all acting in a manner pleasing to the Lord; and, as long as they paid no attention to Paul, they would have persevered in their impenitence. Wishing to strike fear into all of them, Paul makes mention of the future judgment in which everyone must appear before the judgment seat of Christ. Commentary on 2 Corinthians 5:10.[44]

All Things Will Be Brought Before Christ's Tribunal. Cardinal Cajetan: Paul says that not only those things that we did, whether morally good or morally evil, but also those sad or delightful things that happened to our body are going to be brought before Christ's tribunal. And Paul says that these things done to the body, no matter how they contributed to the moral actions we performed (either good or bad), are going to be revealed before the tribunal of Christ. And he said this both to give an explanation for what was said immediately before, namely, "we aim to please God," and at the same to give an explanation for what he said earlier, that "our present afflictions are working in us a most wonderful weight of bodily glory." For unless consideration is given before the tribunal of Christ to what happens to the body, the condition of bodily afflictions would seem irrelevant for achieving the glory of the body. From this the clear explanation of all Paul's words is gleaned, that what happens to our bodies must be judged before Christ's tribunal as either reward or punishment as well as what people did here on earth voluntarily that contributed either to good or evil. Commentary on 2 Corinthians 5:10.[45]

God Graciously Receives Our Good Work. John Calvin: Because this passage treats the rewarding of deeds, we must note briefly that just as evil deeds are punished by God, so also good deeds are rewarded, but for a different reason. For evil deeds are requited with the punishment they deserve; while God, in rewarding good deeds, does not consider merit or worthiness. For no work is so full and perfect in its particulars that it pleases him as meritorious. Moreover, there is no one whose works in themselves are pleasing to God, unless they satisfy the whole law—but no one is found who is so perfect. Hence, our only refuge is in his acceptance of us through his unmerited goodness, and that he justifies us by not imputing our sins to us. After he has received us in his favor, he also graciously and gladly receives our good works. It is on this that the reward depends. Thus, there is nothing illogical in saying that he rewards good works, as long as we understand that it in no way detracts from the fact that human beings attain eternal life by grace. On this matter I have expressed more fully in the preceding epistle, and my *Institutes* will furnish a fuller treatment of it. When Paul says, "in the body," I understand him to mean not only outward actions, but all the deeds that are done in this corporeal life. Commentary on 2 Corinthians 5:10.[46]

[44]Musculus, *Commentarius . . . in posteriorem epistolam Pauli ad Corinthios*, 167.

[45]Cajetan, *In Posteriorem Pauli Epistolam ad Corinthios Commentarii*, 169; citing 2 Cor 5:9; 4:17. Here Cajetan is pointing to the popular view among medieval Catholics that patient endurance of bodily suffering played an important role in making sinful people righteous. See Ron Rittgers, *The Reformation of Suffering: Pastoral Theology and Lay Piety in Late Medieval and Early Modern Germany* (New York: Oxford University Press, 2012), esp. 3-83.

[46]CO 50:65 (CTS 40:226). Calvin discusses this matter in greater detail in his Commentary on 1 Cor 8:13.

Jesus Christ Will Judge All Men and Women. Tilemann Hesshus: So that he might firmly establish and stimulate this fear of the Lord and earnest zeal for piety in us, Paul repeats and explains very clearly the principal point of consolation concerning the resurrection of the dead and the glory of the future age. He says not only that we are resurrected with our bodies but also that we will all stand before the tribunal of the Lord Jesus, who will judge the living and the dead. And he will reward each person for how they have lived in the body. Some will receive punishment for their wickedness; others will receive abundant rewards for their labors and good works.

In this passage, the Holy Spirit reveals an important article of our faith, namely, that our Lord Jesus Christ is not only going to resurrect the whole human race, but also that he is going to pass judgment on each and every work of men and women. Psalm 96 states, "The Lord is coming to judge the earth; he will judge the world in righteousness, and the people in his truth." And John 5 states, "The Father has given all judgment to the Son." And Acts 10 says that "Jesus was appointed by God as judge of the living and the dead." Thus, let us order our lives so that we revere from the heart this judge who accepts no one and spares no one . . . and let us keep our eyes fixed on the final judgment of Jesus Christ, the Son of God. For he says that everyone will be rewarded for how they have lived in the body, which is construed not only from the law but also from the gospel. Christ says in John 5, "Truly, truly I say to you, those who hear my words and believe him who sent me, have eternal life. He does not come into judgment but has passed from death to life." Therefore, even if those who believe in Christ are cognizant of their many sins, nevertheless, they ought not to fear, because Christ has destroyed the written charge and with his blood has cleansed us from all our sin. . . .

The godly will not only be absolved by Christ but will also receive rewards and abundant wages for their good works. "He who has given a cup of cold water will not lose his reward." But this reward is not ascribed to our merit, for our obedience is imperfect no matter how holy it might be; we never fully satisfy the spiritual law. Therefore, because God generously gives us eternal life as a free gift on account of Christ, and because he also accepts our works done in faith on account of Christ, so, contrary to what we deserve, he rewards our puny and imperfect good works out of his enormous kindness and generosity, on account of Christ, in whom all the promises of the law have been fulfilled. And truly, he crowns his gifts when he compensates our good works. Explication of 2 Corinthians 5:10.[47]

God Rewards the Workman, Not the Works. Theodore Beza: There is a great difference between giving to the worker and giving to the works. Therefore, I say well that eternal life is given to those who work, since faith is estimated by its effects, and righteousness by faith; but eternal life is not paid for their works. After this manner it is necessary to explain this passage: "Everyone must be judged according to the things which he has done in the body," and other such passages. Why so? Because good works do not justify but follow the one who believes and is already justified in Christ, just as good fruits do not make a tree good, but a tree is known to be good by its good fruits. A Little Book of Christian Questions and Responses.[48]

True Pastors Await the Judgment of Christ. Wolfgang Musculus: This sentence, "It is necessary for all of us to appear before the judgment seat of Christ," is especially useful for those times when the hypocrisy of wicked men is dominant within the church, when they try to pass themselves off for apostles of Christ, vicars, bishops, prelates, and pastors—although they are fierce wolves who do not spare the flock. In the meantime, these men condemn those who

[47]Hesshus, *Explicatio Secundae Epistolae Pauli ad Corinthios*, 133r-34v; citing Ps 96:13; Jn 5:22; Acts 10:42; Jn 5:24; Mt 10:42.
[48]Beza, *Little Book*, 60*; citing Mt 7:17, 18.

challenge them as heretics and they hand over thousands of people to death by torture and murder. The true minister of Christ, with a secure conscience, transfers his case against the false apostles and against the wicked condemnation of those men to the future tribunal of Christ, saying, "It is necessary for all of us to appear before the judgment seat of Christ." He sees those hypocritical enemies of Christ ruling in the darkness with the result that false pastors are considered to be true ones, and those true pastors are considered to be false. Knowing that these secret dark things are going to be uncovered and revealed before the judgment seat of Christ, [the true pastor] patiently endures all the injuries inflicted by wicked men and commits his cause to the day of revelation. Commentary on 2 Corinthians 5:10.[49]

In Light of God's Judgment, We Must Teach Our Children. Menno Simons: In like manner we must also do, if we rightly confess Christ, believe his Word, and with our children desire to obtain the worthy and pleasant land, and eternally to inherit it in grace, the things which he has promised his children. Therefore, let us not neglect it, but observe it well, teach our children rightly in the Word, and point out his righteous judgments—awful judgment—so that they may learn to fear the Lord with all their heart and turn from evil.

Let us also keep before them God's unfathomably great mercy, love, and the services of his grace, so that they may love him for it and walk in his statutes. Let us imprint on their hearts Jesus Christ, our only and eternal Savior, with his Holy Spirit, and example, so that they may rightly know him and follow in his footsteps. And let us set them an example in all wisdom, righteousness, and truth, with a pious and virtuous life, so that they may through the careful admonition and unblameable example of their pious parents be instructed in the kingdom of God and furnished to all manner of good works. . . .

[Christian parents] pray that their children may from their youth rightly learn to know the immortal, eternal God and Father, through Jesus Christ his beloved Son, and in truth serve him under his cross. So may they recount all the mighty works and miracles of the Lord our God; the great mercy, grace, favor, and love of his Almighty Father, his blessed Word, will, ordinance, and life, with all the merits, power, and fruit of the death and blood of Christ his blessed Son; also the goodness, wisdom, truth, and gifts of his eternal and Holy Spirit to their children and their children's children, and to all their descendants: even until the Lord Jesus Christ appears in the glorious majesty of his heavenly Father in the clouds of heaven at the final judgment, to reward everyone according to his works, be they good or evil. The True Christian Faith.[50]

All Must Appear Before God. The English Annotations: So that no one might think it of small importance what he has said regarding heavenly glory, Paul adds that everyone shall first render an account of his pilgrimage after departing from this earth. The word in the original, *phanerōthēnai*, signifies more than to appear in person, as when someone is summoned to a court. It implies that our life is laid open and scrutinized, and all our thoughts, words, and works disclosed before human beings and angels. Annotations on 2 Corinthians 5:10.[51]

[49]Musculus, *Commentarius . . . in posteriorem epistolam Pauli ad Corinthios*, 168.

[50]CWMS 388-89*.

[51]Downame, ed., *English Annotations*, FF4r*.

5:11–6:2 THE MINISTRY OF RECONCILIATION

11 Therefore, knowing the fear of the Lord, we persuade others. But what we are is known to God, and I hope it is known also to your conscience. 12 We are not commending ourselves to you again but giving you cause to boast about us, so that you may be able to answer those who boast about outward appearance and not about what is in the heart. 13 For if we are beside ourselves, it is for God; if we are in our right mind, it is for you. 14 For the love of Christ controls us, because we have concluded this: that one has died for all, therefore all have died; 15 and he died for all, that those who live might no longer live for themselves but for him who for their sake died and was raised.

16 From now on, therefore, we regard no one according to the flesh. Even though we once regarded Christ according to the flesh, we regard him thus no longer. 17 Therefore, if anyone is in Christ, he is a new creation.[a] The old has passed away; behold, the new has come. 18 All this is from God, who through Christ reconciled us to himself and gave us the ministry of reconciliation; 19 that is, in Christ God was reconciling[b] the world to himself, not counting their trespasses against them, and entrusting to us the message of reconciliation. 20 Therefore, we are ambassadors for Christ, God making his appeal through us. We implore you on behalf of Christ, be reconciled to God. 21 For our sake he made him to be sin who knew no sin, so that in him we might become the righteousness of God.

6 Working together with him, then, we appeal to you not to receive the grace of God in vain. 2 For he says,

"In a favorable time I listened to you,
and in a day of salvation I have helped you."

Behold, now is the favorable time; behold, now is the day of salvation.

a Or *creature* **b** Or *God was in Christ, reconciling*

Overview: Paul reminds the Christians at Corinth that God has entrusted him and his fellow ministers with the wonderful message of the gospel, that is, the good news that God has reconciled himself to sinners through Christ. Reformation commentators find in the concept of "reconciliation" a compelling demonstration of God's relentless love for his people, demonstrated in Christ's substitutionary death, which propitiated God's wrath, absolved sin, imputed righteousness to sinners, and brought to life those who were once spiritually dead. Having experienced God's love in Christ, Christian men and women are now compelled by a holy love to consecrate their lives to God, walk in righteousness, and submit to God's authority. Throughout this rich theological discussion, Protestant exegetes weave other themes that are immediately relevant to their contemporary readers. Paul's comparison of Christian ministers to "ambassadors" invites extensive comment on the value, nature, limitations, and legitimacy of Christian preaching. So, too, Protestant exegetes deflect the opinions of antitrinitarians such as Michael Servetus as they explain Paul's cryptic statement in 2 Corinthians 5:16 that he no longer regards Christ "in the flesh." The apostle here is not questioning the full humanity of the divine Son; rather, Paul is reminding his readers that they must no longer judge Christ from a worldly point of view. Moreover, the reformers insist, the fact that believers are reconciled to God through the gospel alone demolishes the Catholic doctrine of penance, which mandates that sins committed after baptism be expiated by works of satisfaction and the power of the papal keys. Quite the contrary: Christ's sacrificial death on the cross is a complete and sufficient atonement for the sins of all those who trust in him.

5:11-13 *Paul's Boasting*

JUDGING ON THE BASIS OF THE SPIRIT, NOT THE FLESH. TILEMANN HESSHUS: In the second part of this chapter, Paul advises the Corinthians that as they await the renewal of all things that come from Christ (through the ministry of the Spirit), they should not judge on the basis of the old flesh, but judge all things by the Spirit. And at the same time, he shows that he does not follow the passions of the flesh, nor seek his own benefit (as the world is in the habit of doing), but directs all his effort to the glory of God and the good of the church. The old flesh and its passions Paul considers as a thing dead in Christ. For he is now a new man, resurrected with Christ and born of the Spirit, a man who is guided by the command of the Holy Spirit. And after this, Paul explains the comfort coming from the renewal of God's image, and he urges the Corinthians that, having removed themselves from the passions of the flesh, they too should judge Paul's ministry according to the Spirit. Lest anyone should scoff that he is too worried about his own reputation, Paul anticipates this by saying that he so often appeals to his sincerity and good faith not to praise himself but to give his listeners an opportunity for boasting. For when faithful teachers are present, this is the pride of the church. And so it is proper for congregants to observe and celebrate the faith and sincerity of their pastors. And it is proper for us to be worried about our reputation to the extent that it benefits the church and contributes to its strengthening. It is also proper for godly congregants to refute the arrogance and scoffing of various people, by which they insult sincere pastors. EXPLICATION OF 2 CORINTHIANS 5:11-13.[1]

PAUL'S MOTIVES IN GOSPEL MINISTRY. HULDRYCH ZWINGLI: Here Paul understands fear in the sense of religious devotion, as we have learned from Genesis 31, when Jacob says, "If the fear of Isaac had not been on my side," that is, "that dread and love by which my father worshiped God." . . .

[It is as if Paul were saying,] "Since I am mindful of the religious devotion and the true faith by which I sincerely worship God, I thus exert all my energy not only to recommend the gospel of God to everyone but also (as much as lies within me) to convince them of this gospel. The God who observes all my ways has recognized this. In the meantime, I am fully confident that the consciences of all pious people will know this about me. I'm not saying this (even if it is true) so as to brag about myself, but I am speaking openly with you about the way things are, so that you might respond appropriately to those people who cause you to be hostile toward me. But if we should appear to you to violate propriety, consider the extent of the disease and the severity of the remedy; ask yourself, should we spare you by preserving propriety? Surely, all things [are done] for the glory of God and your benefit." ANNOTATIONS ON 2 CORINTHIANS 5:11.[2]

LIVING LIFE IN THE PRESENCE OF GOD. JOHN CALVIN: Two things . . . must be noted here: first, that it is not enough for people to conduct themselves honorably and actively among others unless their hearts are right before God. Second, that boasting is worthless when the evidence of the reality is missing. For none are more audacious in arrogating all things to themselves than those who have nothing. Thus, let those who wish to receive honor produce works that may give confirmation to their words. "To be known to the conscience" is more than to be known by proofs; for the conscience penetrates further than the judgment of the flesh. COMMENTARY ON 2 CORINTHIANS 5:11.[3]

PASTORS SHOULD FOCUS ON GOD'S GLORY AND THE GOOD OF THE CHURCH. TILEMANN HESSHUS: Now Paul here is considering the people's various judgments of his actions. The

[1] Hesshus, *Explicatio Secundae Epistolae Pauli ad Corinthios*, 135v-136r.

[2] Zwingli, *Annotatiunculae . . . ex ore Zvinglij*, 171-72; citing Gen 31:42.

[3] CO 50:66 (CTS 40:227).

world is full of reformers, and the church is in no way immune to them. Some people think that we should be more lenient in the ministry, to reproach sins only in general terms; to exempt and pass over in silence the sins of more honorable and powerful people; to ignore certain mistakes; to close their eyes to many sins for the sake of a few; to spare the reputation of those who are well thought of by the church. Other people want us to act more strictly. They complain that we neglect severe discipline; that we fail in our duty of reproving shameless people; that we bring contempt upon the authority of the ministry; that our moderation is untimely. Not only clear adversaries but also those who are very godly wish to be treated in this manner. They think themselves to be very wise and often judge the actions of faithful pastors, for they often follow more their own passions than the Word of God.

What then should godly people do in this? Whatever they do, they cannot satisfy the judgment of everyone. Therefore, godly people should consider the glory of God and the well-being of the church and perform their duties according to the Word of God in faith, good conscience, and not care about the various judgments of others. Explication of 2 Corinthians 5:11.[4]

Three Principles Drawn from Paul's Obedience. Niels Hemmingsen: Paul deduces from the anticipation of the Lord's judgment how intensely zealous he should be in his obedience to God in performing his ministry. Now he lists three dimensions of this obedience. First, he "persuades men and women"—this is a clear Hebraism meaning to bring people to the faith through the preaching of the gospel. . . . Second, "it is known to God," that is, it is approved by God (by way of metalepsis[†]), namely, through that faith that he had preached to others. Third, "it is known to the consciences of people," that is, people have a sure testimony of the apostolic ministry, as their conscience witnesses to his conscientiousness in performing the ministry. From this, therefore, we conclude that three principles can be established regarding the obedience of ministers, indeed, of all godly people. The first of these is drawn here from the second point, namely, piety toward God. For faith has concomitant virtues, which extend to complement godliness. The second of these, which is drawn from the third point, is that he is approved by men and women, since among them he produces a good conscience of a life well lived. The third of these, which is drawn from the first point, is his intense zeal in performing those responsibilities that pertain to his duty, because Paul here works strenuously in the gospel. And so, by his example, he exhorts other people to an intense zeal on behalf of their calling. Now Paul calls this judgment "the fear of the Lord" (by way of metonymy[‡]), and this judgment affects all those who do not obey God. Commentary on 2 Corinthians 5:11.[5]

Boasting as a Means to Defend the Truth. Cyriacus Spangenberg: In the same way after the departure of holy Luther such people also rose up in the places where he had taught and preached, who brought forth again the repudiated, inadequate talk that good works were necessary for salvation, and then gave its addendum, that without good works no one could be saved. As then St. Paul of necessity had to boast in his preaching office against those people, we also had to lift high holy Luther's teaching and defend it against these people. Twenty-Fourth Sermon.[6]

Paul's Modesty. Wolfgang Musculus: "So that you may have something against those who boast about outward appearance and not about

[4]Hesshus, *Explicatio Secundae Epistolae Pauli ad Corinthios*, 136v-137r.

[5]Hemmingsen, *Commentaria in Omnes Epistolas Apostolorum*, 272.
[†]In rhetoric, a metalepsis is "the use of one word for another which it suggests by association, as the cause for the effect, or the reverse." Charlton Lewis and Charles Short, eds., *A Latin Dictionary* (Oxford: Oxford University Press, 1991), 1139.
[‡]Metonymy is the use of an attribute or adjunct idea as a replacement for the intended word. E.g., when the word *crown* is substituted for *king*.

[6]C. Spangenberg, *Die ander Epistel Pauli an die Corinthier*, 98.

what is in the heart." Paul reprimands the false apostles who, on the basis of outward appearance, were bragging many things about themselves, although in their hearts they were very different from what they were boasting about. To boast in outward appearance and not in the heart—this means to brag publicly with human words about things that cannot be recognized in the conscience itself. Now Paul himself blunts their boasting later in chapters 10, 11, and 12.

Note here the modesty of the apostle. In the case of the Corinthians, it was plain that they had been sufficiently instructed about those matters . . . so as to silence the boasts of the false apostles and recognize Paul's good reputation. But although Paul could have criticized them for ignoring this, he said that he would give them a reason for boasting about him and furnish something against those shameless traitors, as if the Corinthians had been insufficiently instructed before now. . . . Thus he spared them, when he could have rightfully filled them with shame and scolded them sharply. Commentary on 2 Corinthians 5:12.[7]

Paul Discusses His Ministry for the Corinthians' Benefit. Giovanni Diodati: Paul gives the reason why he returns to a discussion of his ministry, namely, not to vainly boast, nor to gain gratitude and favor for himself, but for the Corinthians' own benefit, in order that, being made more certain of his faithfulness, they might recognize how blessed they were to have had him as their pastor and apostle. And hence they might hold steadfastly to him and his doctrine, in contrast to the false apostles, who were parading their zeal, holiness, and faithfulness, although guilty of the opposite vices in their consciences. Annotations on 2 Corinthians 5:12.[8]

Boasting for the Benefit of God's People. Cyriacus Spangenberg: Here we see when and why a preacher should not let his teaching and his office be despised, and when it is fitting to boast in and defend the same—namely, when it is useful for the congregation and brings about the strengthening of the teaching, and when the need to stop the mouths of the false, boastful teachers demands it, as Paul himself also says here, "so that you may be able to boast against those who boast according to appearances, and not according to the heart." Moreover, we must not be silent if we see and sense that someone, with false boasting, under the appearance of good, wants to bring in godless and impure teaching into the church of Christ. Twenty-Fourth Sermon.[9]

Paul's Sane Boasting. John Calvin: "If we are insane." This is said by way of concession. For Paul's boasting was sane or (we could call it) a most wise insanity. But since he seemed to be foolish to many people, he adopts their way of thinking. Now he asserts two things: first, that he makes no account of himself, but he has this one purpose—that he may serve God and the church. Second, that he does not at all fear the opinions of people but that he is prepared to be considered insane or sane, provided only that he faithfully performs the affairs of God and the church. The meaning, therefore, is this: "As for the fact that I announce my integrity so often, people will take this as they wish. Nevertheless, I do not do this for my own sake, but only have God and the church in view. Hence, I am prepared to be silent and to speak as much as the glory of God and the advantage of the church will require it, and I will allow the world to judge me insane, if only I am not insane in myself, but in God." This is a passage that deserves not only our notice but also our constant meditation. For unless we shall have our minds regulated in this way, the smallest occasion for offense will immediately draw us away from our duty. Commentary on 2 Corinthians 5:13.[10]

[7]Musculus, *Commentarius . . . in posteriorem epistolam Pauli ad Corinthios*, 174.
[8]Diodati, *La Seconde Epistre de l'Apostre S. Paul aux Corinthiens*, 145.
[9]C. Spangenberg, *Die ander Epistel Pauli an die Corinthier*, 99v.
[10]CO 50:67 (CTS, 40:229-30).

God's Saints Are Frequently Accused of Insanity. Andreas Hyperius: The second reason [why Paul boasts] is from usefulness. "It is useful that we do this both to make clear God's glory, and to advance your advantage and strengthen you. . . . I know that my enemies, who are nothing but most shameful, from time to time dare to accuse us and shout that we are insane. But we disregard their judgments. If we are insane—as they themselves wish to believe—we are insane to God, for the great passion with which we are eager to advance the glory of God compels us in the meantime to be more vehement beyond measure. But if we are in our senses [*sōphronoumen*]—that is, sober and sane, bearing ourselves moderately—we are sane for you so that by our modesty we might stir you to embrace and maintain the evangelical doctrine. . . ."

Now it is not new for the saints, whenever they are very vehement in either defending the cause of the gospel or correcting vices, to be accused of being insane, of being out of their mind, of speaking rudely. Thus, in Acts 26, Festus was loudly accusing Paul of insanity. So, too, it was hardly surprising that a certain uproar occurred when a single man, Elijah, dared to confront so many priests of Baal and afterward to kill all of them. Now it is certain that the saints were sometimes inspired by God's Spirit to undertake great and wondrous deeds, which seemed to call into question their sanity. Again, they knew how to behave among the obstinate and blind people; they knew what the time and place demanded, and when they should be more vehement and when more moderate. When God's glory is being protected, one ought not to guard place, time, or persons that are prohibited. But these words of Paul, and those which immediately follow, must be received since they have been expressed with great passion and some intensity. Commentary on 2 Corinthians 5:13.[11]

Two Possible Meanings. The English Annotations: Either the meaning is this: "If we are in our ecstasies and raptured, it is to God" (that is, in our private devotions when we speak to him), "but to you we always speak sober words and in a moderate temper." Or he is making reference to the commendation of his apostleship, for it so often seems to be the part of mad and foolish people to commend themselves. In this case, the meaning is this: "If we exceed at any time and are so transported in the contemplation of the dignity of our apostleship, that we seem to be besides ourselves, we do it not to boast of glory for ourselves, but to maintain the glory and honor of God. And if, on the other hand, we speak modestly of ourselves and our ministry, it is for your good, to match your modesty and to condescend to your capacity, but all means to bring you to Christ." Annotations on 2 Corinthians 5:13.[12]

Paul Loved the Christian Soul—and So Should We. John Donne: St. Paul was mad for love, and we like Paul should take into our contemplation the beauty of a Christian soul. Through the ragged apparel of the afflictions of this life, through the scars, wounds, paleness, and blemishes of sin and corruption, we can look upon the soul itself, and there see that incorruptible beauty, that white and red which the innocence and the blood of Christ has given it. And we are mad for love of this soul, ready to perform any act of danger, by way of persecution, or any act of self-abnegation, by way of humility, to stand at her door and pray and beg that she be reconciled to God. Sermon 5 Preached at St. Paul's.[13]

5:14-15 *Compelled by the Love of Christ*

Christ's Sacrificial Death Compels Us to Live for Him. Huldrych Zwingli: [It's as if Paul were saying,] "I reflect on the fact that since one man has died for the sake of all of us and, by his death, has procured life for us, therefore all of us owe him our lives, which is to say, that we should

[11]Hyperius, *Commentarii . . . in Epistolam D. Pauli ad Romanos, et Utramque ad Corinthios*, 372-73; citing Acts 26:24; 1 Kings 18.

[12]Downame, ed., *Annotations on the Second Epistle of Paul to the Corinthians*, FF4r*.

[13]Donne, *Sermons of John Donne*, 10:125.

live for him rather than for ourselves, and should be prepared even to die for him. For this reason, I easily disregard my life—clinging to no physical thing, however great it may be—but I cling to and trust in Christ alone, not according to the flesh, but according to the Spirit. For although the flesh of Christ was handed over to death for our sakes, nevertheless, we must not be so fixated on his flesh as to think that salvation is located in it, thinking that [salvation is procured] if someone sees it, touches it, and eats it." Annotations on 2 Corinthians 5:14.[14]

Paul's Burning Love for Jesus Christ. Tilemann Hesshus: Now Paul shows the source of his sincerity and faithfulness in ministry through which God has been revealed and all things directed to the glory of God and the salvation of the church, namely, that he had renounced the world and had devoted himself to Christ, through whom he had been redeemed, and by whose Spirit he had been renewed. He says, "I take off the old self with its passions. I no longer live for myself, but completely belong to Christ. I owe him my life and all things, and by his Spirit I direct all things to his glory. The love of Christ with which he most passionately loves me and by which I embrace him as my Savior—this love controls me, it seizes me and completely possesses me, so that I think about nothing, I desire nothing, I choose nothing more than Christ my Lord and Redeemer. I confess that I owe all things to Christ, and nothing whatsoever can be pleasing to me unless it serves to enlarge Christ's kingdom." The love of Christ had bound the apostle like the tightest chain, so that he couldn't help but spread the gospel in the world, even if he was sometimes treated very badly. And he knew that he would experience danger on account of the gospel. Explication of 2 Corinthians 5:14.[15]

Paul's Heart Was a Lump of Love for Jesus. John Trapp: As a reward attracts, and a punishment repulses, so love has a compulsive quality. This love of Christ had such a control on St. Paul, so hemmed him in and surrounded him, that his adversaries reported that he was a mad man (see v. 13). He erred in love toward his sweet Savior, and even exhaled his blessed soul in continual outbursts, as it were, and expressions of his dear affection to the Lord Jesus. The word he uses here suggests that he was even shut up by his love for his dear Lord, as if he were in a cage or enclosure, so that he could not get out. He had meditated so much on Christ's love . . . that his heart was turned into a lump of love. Commentary on 2 Corinthians 5:14.[16]

The Love of Christ Constrains Us. Edward Leigh: "Constrains us." Either an expression from those who are overcome by a spiritual prophecy . . . which was very powerful, so that they could not but speak; or from women in travail who cannot but cry out because of their pain. The word signifies being in a jail or enclosure, so that one cannot escape by any evasion. . . . Paul indicates, therefore, that whereas Christ had so loved him as to shed his blood for him, that very love did constrain him to refer all he could do to the honor and praise of Christ. Annotations on 2 Corinthians 5:14.[17]

The Love of Christ. Wolfgang Musculus: Paul reveals the extraordinary love of Christ, and he describes what he considers it to include. This is the love of Christ: that one man was judged worthy to die for all. No one has greater love than this that he lays down his life for his friends. But Christ did not just die for his friends, but for his enemies; he did not just die for a few people but for all people. This is the enormous breadth of divine love. . . . But we ought to beware lest we think therefore that Christ's death is for the sake of all people as if the efficacy of his death applied equally to all. Indeed,

[14]Zwingli, *Annotatiunculae . . . ex ore Zvinglij*, 172.
[15]Hesshus, *Explicatio Secundae Epistolae Pauli ad Corinthios*, 138r-v.
[16]Trapp, *A Commentary or Exposition*, 716*.
[17]Leigh, *Annotations upon all the New Testament*, 260*; citing Heb 12:15.

his death is not received by the wicked, the unbelieving, and the unrepentant, although it is sufficient in itself for the redemption of the whole human race. The salvation that comes from his death is offered to all and is sufficient for all provided that it is received by all. "For God so loved the whole world that he gave his one and only son, so that everyone who believes in him should not perish but have eternal life." In this way his death is for all (because all were dead), so that everyone who believes in him will be given life and be saved. Commentary on 2 Corinthians 5:14-15.[18]

The Whole Mystery of Christ Is Taught Here. Heinrich Bullinger: Now Paul here describes in brief the whole mystery of Christ. First, he says, "Christ died for all." Second, he infers from this, "But if he died for all, it follows that all have died." And it follows from this that in the one death of Christ there is life, for if we experienced life through any other means, Christ would have died in vain. But this should certainly be understood in terms of expiation; accordingly, salvation is in Christ alone, and his name alone has been given to all men and women, and there is no salvation in any other person. It follows from this that those who are now living do not live by their work or strength, but by the power of the living God through Christ. Whence it now happens that all who are wise and imbued with the truth have been given the whole Christ, upon whom alone they depend and to whom alone they attribute all things. In him, they live—having been dead and resurrected from the dead—because he washed away their sins with his blood and restored them to life through the resurrection. Now, these are the central truths by which we consider the divine goodness. He redeems us, not through the law or by the blood of goats or bulls, but through the blood of his only-begotten Son, apart from all sacred flesh. Commentary on 2 Corinthians 5:14-15.[19]

One Died for All. John Calvin: [Paul's] purpose must be carefully noted here—that Christ died for us so that we might die to ourselves. His explanation must also be noted—that to die to ourselves is to live to Christ; or, to put it more fully, we renounce ourselves so that we might live to Christ. For Christ redeemed us for this reason, that he might have us under his authority as his peculiar possession. Hence it follows that we are no longer our own masters. There is a similar passage in Romans 14, although here the two things are stated separately—that we are dead in Christ so that all ambition and eagerness for distinction might cease and so that we won't be annoyed to be counted as nothing; and second, that we owe to Christ our life and death, because he has completely united himself to us. Commentary on 2 Corinthians 5:15.[20]

Living for Christ. Wolfgang Musculus: What does it mean to live for Christ? It is to depend on him for all things. It is to consecrate the whole of one's life in devotion to his spirit and will. It is to subject oneself to his authority and power in all matters. Thus, it is to live the totality of one's life so that you do not model anything in life other than the spirit of Christ, and other people perceive in you nothing other than Christ in whom you live. But this kind of life is diametrically opposed to that by which we live for ourselves. That is why when Christ has established a place in our lives, he requires that we do not turn back any longer to that old way of life. For it is impossible for it to happen that we live for Christ while we continue to live for ourselves. And so Paul was right in saying, not simply "So that those who live, live in him who died for them," but he inserts the phrase "might no longer live for themselves." And not thinking this sufficient, Paul added "for him who for their sake died and was raised." Commentary on 2 Corinthians 5:15.[21]

[18]Musculus, *Commentarius . . . in posteriorem epistolam Pauli ad Corinthios*, 175, 176; citing Jn 15:13; 3:16.
[19]Bullinger, *In Posteriorem D. Pauli ad Corinthios Epistolam Commentarius*, 288-89.
[20]CO 50:68 (CTS 50:230-31); citing Rom 14:7-9.
[21]Musculus, *Commentarius . . . in posteriorem epistolam Pauli ad Corinthios*, 177.

5:16-19 *The Message of Reconciliation*

The Flesh Does Not Give Life. Philipp Melanchthon: The apostle's meaning is not that he did not know Christ according to the flesh, although at one time he came in the flesh. Rather, this is his meaning: None of the saints considers Christ according to the flesh; that is, none of the saints boasts in a fleshly way about Christ, although he certainly did appear in the flesh. This is Christ's meaning in John 6: "It is the Spirit who gives life; the flesh is of no use whatsoever." Likewise, when [Christ] says that it is necessary for him to die and ascend into heaven, because the flesh does not give life, it is the Spirit who gives life. And in John 12, where he says, "Unless a grain of wheat. . . ." And so here, Paul observes that Christ's flesh was not at all profitable, but it was necessary for him to die so that he might be made alive by the Spirit. That is why he says that "he did not know Christ according to the flesh," because he appeared in the flesh so that he might kill the flesh. Annotations on 2 Corinthians 5:16.[22]

Regarding No One According to the Flesh. Tilemann Hesshus: Because we owe all things to Christ, in him we are dead to the world and our flesh, and are now made new men and women, regenerated by the Spirit. We do not know anything according to the flesh—that is, we do not judge anyone from the vantage point of the flesh. We do not indulge our passions but we follow the judgment of the Spirit; we consider the Word; we act in the fear of the Lord in all circumstances. "It is not proper for you to evaluate my labors according to the flesh, that is with fleshly judgments and passions, nor is it proper for me to conduct my ministry labors on the basis of my flesh." For Paul, to regard someone according to the flesh is nothing other than to judge another person out of the passion of the flesh, and either to love or hate them in a carnal way. Timothy and Titus were in the flesh, and Paul had not yet put aside his flesh, and yet Paul did not know Timothy and Titus according to the flesh, but according to the Spirit and the new self. Explication of 2 Corinthians 5:16.[23]

Images Limit Christ to His Flesh. Andreas Bodenstein von Karlstadt: I cannot advise anyone who is sick unto death to cling to a carved or painted crucifix, for the simple reason that these are good for nothing, as I said, and incapable of getting the sick any further than the physical suffering of Christ, which is of no avail. As Christ himself says, "The flesh avails nothing." It does not please Paul when you know Christ in the flesh only. He therefore says, "We do not know Christ after the flesh." But those who worship images intend to make the human Christ known to laypersons. This is not good. They prefer to teach how Christ was hanging rather than why he was hanged. They teach of his body, beard, and wounds: but regarding the power of Christ, they do not teach anything. Without the power of Christ, no one will be saved: but without the physical form of Christ, many thousands shall be saved in days to come. On the Removal of Images.[24]

A New Way of Viewing Christ. Tilemann Hesshus: It's as if Paul were saying, "Previously in Judaism, before we were illuminated with the gospel and converted to Christ, we were only reasoning about Christ in a fleshly way. We were hoping that he was going to establish an earthly kingdom and share authority with us and live visibly with us. We were expecting to receive from him great wealth, illustrious honors, a pleasant life—whatever is agreeable to the flesh. We were hoping, as Cleopas and his companion said, that he was going to liberate Israel. We were insufficiently concerned about spiritual blessings, the remission of sins, the gift of the Holy Spirit, inheriting eternal life. We imagined that nothing in that

[22] *Melanchthons Werke*, 4:115; citing Jn 6:63; 12:24.

[23] Hesshus, *Explicatio Secundae Epistolae Pauli ad Corinthios*, 140r-v.

[24] CRR 8:108; citing Jn 6:27.

matter related to Christ but depended on the law. Thus, we loved Christ only in those shadows, from the flesh and in hope. But afterward he illumined us with his gospel and renewed us with his Holy Spirit, and now we do not know Christ according to the flesh. Now we perceive nothing of flesh in Christ. We do not seek riches, glory, or human favor in Christ's kingdom, but by the illumination of the Holy Spirit we see that Christ has been given to us from heaven, so that he might tear us away from the power of Satan, satisfy the wrath of God, forgive our sins, reestablish justice, bestow peace of conscience, grant the Holy Spirit, and establish us as heirs of eternal life." Explication of 2 Corinthians 5:16.[25]

Paul Acknowledges the Human Nature of Jesus. Wolfgang Musculus: "Now, nevertheless, we regard him no longer." Paul is not denying that he recognizes Christ in the flesh. Far from it. For when elsewhere he says that he knew nothing except Jesus Christ and him crucified, indeed he knew Christ in the flesh as a true man, who truly suffered and died. In saying this, therefore, Paul is not stripping from Christ his true flesh, nor the true nature of flesh, which Christ himself claimed after his resurrection when he said, "Touch and see, for a spirit does not have flesh and bones as you see that I have." But Paul denies that he any longer considers Christ according to the flesh, in the way in which it was understood in Judaism. That is why the enemies and deniers of the flesh of Christ (whether ancient or more recent) cannot claim this passage. Commentary on 2 Corinthians 5:16.[26]

This Passage Does Not Speak of the Lord's Supper. Martin Luther: The same kind of derision the devil practices also with the passage of St. Paul in 2 Corinthians 5: "We regard Christ no long according to the flesh," and "If anyone is in Christ, he is a new creation": such passages without exception force us to the conclusion that Christ's body is not in the Supper. Oh, well, we gladly submit to ridicule once more; let us see what the devil will gain by it. The fanatics should show here what St. Paul means by the expression "according to the flesh," on which the force of the argument depends. "Yes," says the devil, "I don't care about you. It is enough that my followers quote it; you must simply accept it." All right, we should like to be just as humble and point out the same. St. Paul also speaks here of slaying the old Adam and wishes to say that we must no longer live according to the flesh, but as a new creation in Christ. Hear his words yourself: "We are convinced," he says, "that if one has died for all, all have died." . . . What else can this mean than that which he says in the passage we discussed immediately above, Colossians 3, "We have died with Christ," and in Romans 6, "Our old self was crucified with Christ"? It follows here: "And he died for all, that those who live might live no longer for themselves but for him who for their sakes died and was raised." What else is this than that we must live a new life in Christ?

. . . By the expression, "according to the flesh," in this passage St. Paul means that which happens in a fleshly manner and not according to the Spirit, or in a spiritual manner, as he says in 2 Corinthians 10, "Though we walk in the flesh, we do not war according to the flesh," that is, not in a fleshly manner. . . . Therefore, the text of St. Paul irresistibly forces us to conclude that this is his meaning: Because we all have died with Christ to the world and the flesh, from now on we should no longer live or think according to the flesh, or in a fleshly manner. So we should know no one in a fleshly but only in a spiritual manner. Confession Concerning Christ's Supper.[27]

Christ Lives in a Human Body in Heaven. John Calvin: This passage is perverted by some

[25]Hesshus, *Explicatio Secundae Epistolae Pauli ad Corinthios*, 140v-141r; citing Lk 24:18.

[26]Musculus, *Commentarius . . . in posteriorem epistolam Pauli ad Corinthios*, 181; citing 1 Cor 2:2; Lk 24:39.

[27]LW 37:200-201 (WA 26:308-9); citing Col 3:3; Rom 6:6; 2 Cor 5:15; 10:3.

fanatics, such as Servetus,† for the purpose of proving that the human nature of Christ is now absorbed by the divinity. But it is not difficult to perceive how far this madness is from the apostle's intention; for he is not speaking here about the substance of his body, but of the external appearance, nor is he saying that the flesh is no longer perceived by us in Christ, but that Christ is not judged on that basis.

The whole of Scripture proclaims that Christ now lives a glorious life in our flesh as certainly as when he once suffered in it. Indeed, if this foundation is undermined, our entire faith falls to the ground. For where do we have the hope of immortality, if not from this, that we already have a display of it in Christ? For just as righteousness is restored to us in this way, that Christ, by fulfilling the law in our nature, has abolished Adam's disobedience, so also life has been restored to us in this way, that he has opened up for our nature the kingdom of God, from which it had been banished, and has given it a place in the heavenly dwelling. Therefore, unless we now recognize the flesh of Christ, we lose all confidence and comfort that we ought to have in him. COMMENTARY ON 2 CORINTHIANS 5:16.[28]

WE MUST TRUST IN CHRIST AND HIS WORD ALONE. CYRIACUS SPANGENBERG: Paul knows no one according to the flesh, neither Moses nor anyone else. He does not place his trust in anything external. In the same way, we know no one according to the flesh, be it pope or bishop, councils or church fathers, Augustine or Jerome, if they tell us to place our trust in external things and so want to bind our consciences, as is the case with forbidding people to marry or eat certain foods, monastic vows, masses, works, and so on. We know no one in this way.

Then whom do we know? We know and place our faith and trust alone in the one Lord Jesus Christ, who died for us all and rose again from the dead. In these high matters which concern the salvation of souls we must look to him alone and remove all other things from our sight.

In the same way we should not judge teaching in spiritual matters according to the flesh, that is, according to external appearance, because it does not depend on whether someone is old, wise, learned, noble, famed, eloquent, great, or lofty, but on whether they are born again through water and the Spirit, and whether they acknowledge Christ according to the Spirit, that is, according to the teaching of the Holy Spirit. Where this is not the case, we know no one and do not pay attention to their teaching, because it is all fleshly teaching. In the same way we do not know Dr. Luther according to the flesh, that is, we do not believe his teaching for the sake of his person, or because he taught it, but because it is the Word and Spirit of God. TWENTY-FIFTH SERMON.[29]

KNOWING CHRIST IN THE FLESH. JOHN TRAPP: Paul may have known Christ in the flesh, for Jesus of Nazareth was a prophet mighty in deed and word before God and all the people. Augustine wished that he might have seen three things: Rome flourishing, Paul preaching, and Christ conversing with men and women on earth. Later, Bede corrects Augustine's third wish, saying, "Yes, but let me see the king in his beauty, Christ in his heavenly kingdom." Paul was so spiritual that he took knowledge of nothing here below. He passed through the world as a man in a deep muse, or as one who is so looking for a lost jewel that he overlooks everything beside it. COMMENTARY ON 2 CORINTHIANS 5:16.[30]

SPIRITUAL AWARENESS AND TRUE VIRTUE FOLLOW REGENERATION. JACQUES LEFÈVRE D'ÉTAPLES: Come now, you ask, when did we regard Christ according to the flesh? We regarded Christ in this way, when Christ was first

[28]CO 50:68-69 (CTS 40:231-32). †Calvin maintained a lively dispute with the antitrinitarian Michael Servetus for more than a decade. In 1553, Servetus came to Geneva and was arrested, condemned by the city council, and (with Calvin's approval) executed by burning.

[29]C. Spangenberg, *Die ander Epistel Pauli an die Corinthier*, 103.
[30]Trapp, *A Commentary or Exposition*, 716*; citing Lk 24:19.

announced to us and we were living in the flesh, and not yet in the spirit. When we were catechized, we received the Word of Christ, yet we were not yet initiated into his holy nature. In other words, we regarded him according to the flesh. But when we were baptized—because we were new creatures, the old had passed away and all things had become new (since all things are made new by God)—we no longer regarded Christ according to the flesh, but according to the spirit. . . . But you might add, who was living virtuously and avoiding wickedness before regeneration? No one. For how can people live according to the spirit if they do not yet have the Spirit and have not yet received the Spirit? People receive the Spirit in regeneration. Therefore, those virtues that philosophers honor are not spiritual virtues, but rather moral and human virtues—far different than what the sacred theologians praise. By theologians, I mean Peter, Paul, John, the other apostles, their most notable disciples such as Dionysius of Hierotheus,† and others like him, who gazed upon the light of the divine Spirit and did not contemplate the light of the human spirit. For by contemplating the former, they minimized the latter. COMMENTARY ON 2 CORINTHIANS 5:16-17.[31]

CHRISTIANS ARE NEW PERSONS. MARTIN LUTHER: A Christian is a new creature, or newly created work of God who speaks, thinks, and judges all things in a different way from the world's speaking and judging. Being a new person, all things do become new, here in this life through faith, and afterward in the life to come, through openly revealing their nature. Now the world cannot do anything else but think of death according to its ancient custom and nature—that it is the most abominable and horrible thing on earth, the end of life and all joy.

But Christians, on the other hand, as new persons, are equipped with very different and even contrary thoughts, so that they can be courageous and happy, even when passing through hard times. In their hearts they remember that they possess a great treasure even though they might be poor. They are powerful princes and lords even when they are in prison, and surpassingly strong when they are weak and ill, and in highest honor when they are disdained and reviled. Similarly, they will be roused into the newness of life if they now must die. In short, they win new hearts and courage through which they make all things new here on earth. They therefore have a foretaste here of the future life, where everything will become new before their eyes and in the full light of day made new, as they now think and picture it through faith, according to their new nature. SERMON AT THE FUNERAL OF ELECTOR JOHN.[32]

CHARACTERISTICS OF A TRUE CHRISTIAN. WOLFGANG MUSCULUS: Note that while it should have been said, "If anyone is a Christian," Paul said, "If anyone is in Christ." Therefore, to be a Christian is to be in Christ. If anyone is outside of Christ, they are not a Christian. It is easy to partake of the sacraments and to be of the name and profession of Christ, but that is not what it means to be in Christ. For it entirely requires a new person. Whence Paul says, "If anyone is in Christ, they are a new creature." The largest part of Christians is still an old creature for they have not yet been regenerated and renewed by the spirit of Christ. To know a Christian, therefore, we should not so much examine their external profession, but their life. It is permissible to learn from one's life whether they are still an old creature or a new one. When the old creature is retained in substance, then they live entirely outside of the spirit of Christ. I say "in substance" so as not to condemn those delicate, young little plants still in Christ, because of the remains of the old creature. For the old creature is not stripped away in an instant; nor is the whole

[31]Lefèvre, *Commentariorum in Epistolas Beati Pauli . . . Liber Tertius*, 135. †Dionysius the Areopagite, one of Paul's converts mentioned in Acts 17:34, was believed by medieval theologians to have authored several mystical writings, including *The Celestial Hierarchy* and *The Divine Names*.

[32]LW 51:244; WA 36:255.

new creature put on suddenly. This transformation has its stages, growing in increments little by little. And in the meantime, there are indicators by which it is known, however subtle they may be. Now what it means to be in Christ, and what it means for Christ to be in us, we have treated extensively in our Commentary on John. Commentary on 2 Corinthians 5:17.[33]

A New Creature. Andreas Hyperius: If someone does not walk according to the flesh, that person we praise (as is only right) as being "in Christ" and "a new creature." So, it is seen that "to be in Christ" is the opposite of what Paul said previously, "to be according to the flesh." To be in Christ is to believe in Christ, to depend on him alone. And it happens through Christ alone that we become new persons, not from our strengths or merits. As Galatians 5 [*sic*, Galatians 6] states, In Christ Jesus, "neither circumcision counts for anything, nor uncircumcision, but only the new creation." And in Romans 6 it is called "walking in newness of life." And in Romans 7 "new way of the Spirit." And elsewhere, the term "renewal" is often used to describe the change of life for the better after one has received the Holy Spirit by faith. Commentary on 2 Corinthians 5:17.[34]

Our Need for Rebirth Proves the Doctrine of Original Sin. Martin Bucer: Although the whole of Scripture everywhere presents us with this definition [of original sin] (for surely on every page it teaches us to deny self and be transformed, that is, to repent), nevertheless it can be gathered most clearly from passages dealing with our rebirth. If indeed we cannot see the kingdom of God (become partakers of the life of God) unless we are born again, made a new creature, renewed in mind and will and our whole way of life, surely there is no doubt that we are corrupted and ruined throughout our being. On Original Sin.[35]

The New Creation. David Joris: The unchaste, old, vile being runs after and desires these [lusts or sinful desires]. But not the new creature in Christ Jesus, which is created in the image of God and is born from the Spirit and desires, seeks, and wills only that which is of a similar nature, image, or form. To these things alone does the person have great lust and desire, and they use the Spirit's will or desire in this, according to the pleasure and Word of the living God, who is an enemy of all flesh and heathendom. Pay attention. Hear, Hear, Hear.[36]

Being a New Creation in Christ. David Dickson: Paul shows the duty of the faithful who are engrafted into Christ to be this: that as new creatures they should labor for the newness of a right judgment and a holy life. And he proves from Isaiah 65:17 that those worldly things should not be so highly esteemed, for God promises an abolition of old things, and that he will make a new heaven and a new earth; that is, all things shall be new under the kingdom of Christ. From this it follows that only those things are to be esteemed among Christians that pertain to a new creature, or regeneration. For all things are made new to those that are renewed. When they are reconciled to God, they have all creatures as it were reconciled to them, and now they use them in a new way, for the glory of God and their own salvation. And they judge everything according to whether it promotes or does not promote the kingdom of God in themselves and others. Exposition of 2 Corinthians 5:17.[37]

God's Reconciliation Offered Freely to Sinners. Tilemann Hesshus: It should be noted that the apostle does not say that *we* had removed or satisfied God's wrath, but that God

[33]Musculus, *Commentarius . . . in posteriorem epistolam Pauli ad Corinthios*, 182.

[34]Hyperius, *Commentarii in Epistolam D. Pauli ad Romanos, et Utramque ad Corinthios*, 374; citing Gal 6:15; Rom 6:4; 7:6.

[35]CPMB 122.

[36]CRR 7:131-32.

[37]Dickson, *An Exposition of All St. Paul's Epistles*, 80*.

himself, being moved with mercy toward the human race, reconciled us to himself, for he himself revealed his plan of reconciliation; *he* gave his only-begotten Son; *he* established the kingdom of the Messiah; *he* voluntarily set aside his wrath out of his special goodness. And moreover, *he* accomplished that reconciliation through Jesus Christ, whom he put forward as a propitiation (*lytron*) and sacrifice for sin. This reconciliation is nothing other than this, that the eternal Father remits all of his wrath which we had provoked by our sins, for the sake of the intercession and sacrifice of his Son. He pardons all of our sins that we committed against his law. He graciously gives us back that which we lost through sin. He pronounces us righteous and makes us heirs of eternal life. With this divine comfort restored through Christ, believers are both strengthened and successfully overcome all dangers, terror of conscience, and death itself. They also rest in the propitious will of God and see that all things now work for their good; no situation is detrimental to them. Therefore, they learn that, when the soul is burdened with temptations, to look to the God who reconciles himself to us, and they seek his clear will in the Word before all things. As Ezekiel 33 states, "'As surely as I live,' says the Lord, 'I do not desire the death of sinners, but that they might be converted and live.'" And Isaiah 1: "Though your sins be as scarlet, they shall be as white as snow." In these passages, God freely offers reconciliation to us; there is therefore no reason for anyone to doubt the propitious will of God. Explication of 2 Corinthians 5:18.[38]

Reconciliation Requires the Consent of Both Parties. Wolfgang Musculus: "And he gave to us the ministry of reconciliation." The fact that the most compassionate Father reconciled us to himself through Christ his Son was not adequate for salvation unless we were given the capacity for this reconciliation. For reconciliation cannot occur between unwilling parties, but it requires the agreement and approval of both sides. As far as God is concerned, our reconciliation is accomplished through the death of Christ the mediator, the only-begotten of God. But as far as our side is concerned, reconciliation is not accomplished unless we accommodate ourselves from the heart to certain conditions so that we can have the capacity for it. These conditions are repentance and faith in Christ. Without repentance and faith, no one will be capable of this reconciliation, for the impenitent and unbelievers are excluded. Therefore, so that we might be made into partners of that reconciliation, God sent his gospel into the world through which all men and women are called to repentance and faith whereby they acquire the gift of this reconciliation. And he committed this service to the apostles as ambassadors of this reconciliation. The apostle indicates this by saying, "And he gave to us the ministry of reconciliation." He gave this ministry of reconciliation not only to Paul himself, but also to the other apostles. Even so, nothing prevents us from understanding Paul to be saying this about his own apostleship, concerning which the false apostles were wickedly stirring up controversy. And so he attributes to God not only the work of reconciliation itself, but also the administration of that ministry.

Now the attentive reader should note how elegantly the apostle apportions in turn this reconciliation of ours between God, Christ, and the apostles. He attributes the power of it to God, the accomplishment of it to Christ as mediator, who then distributes the ministry of it to the apostles, as ministers and ambassadors. God is in no way excluded for he is the source of all things; Christ did not accomplish the work of reconciliation without God; and the apostles did not undertake the administration of that ministry in the world without God. Commentary on 2 Corinthians 5:18.[39]

[38]Hesshus, *Explicatio Secundae Epistolae Pauli ad Corinthios*, 145v-146v; citing Ezek 33:11; Is 1:18.

[39]Musculus, *Commentarius . . . in posteriorem epistolam Pauli ad Corinthios*, 184-85.

The Gospel Is the Gracious Message of Reconciliation. Cyriacus Spangenberg: Although we also punish sin, and scare people with the law, our most noble task is to comfort them again and to preach reconciliation to them, namely, that all their sins have been forgiven them through Christ, and even the remaining infirmities will not be reckoned to them for death, for Christ's sake. It is a glorious title for our gospel that is, namely, a message of gracious reconciliation between God and humanity. And it is to the great praise of evangelical preachers that they do not preach damnation and death, but reconciliation and life. Twenty-Fifth Sermon.[40]

Pastors Are Ministers of Reconciliation. John Calvin: Here we have an illustrious description of the gospel as being an embassy for reconciling men and women to God. And this is also the special distinction of ministers, that they are sent to us by God with this commission, that they might be messengers—a kind of guarantor [of God's promises]. But this is not said so much to commend ministers as to provide consolation for the godly, that whenever they hear the gospel, they may know that God treats them and even pledges to return to them in grace. What could be more desirable than this blessing? Let us therefore remember that this is the chief purpose of the gospel: that although we are by nature children of wrath, we may be received by him in grace since the disagreement between God and us has been destroyed. Ministers are entrusted with this commission to deliver to us this message of such great blessing, indeed, to render us more assured of God's fatherly love toward us. To be sure, any other person can be a witness of divine grace toward us, but Paul teaches that this office is especially entrusted to ministers. When, therefore, a duly ordained minister proclaims the good news that God has been propitious to us, he should be listened to as no other than God's ambassador, bearing a public role (as they say), and endowed with legitimate authority for asserting it. Commentary on 2 Corinthians 5:18.[41]

God Was Working Through Christ. Huldrych Zwingli: This passage shows that Christ was not a mere man, but was also God, no matter how humble and despised he was during the time he lived among mortals. Thus Paul gives emphasis to this when he says that God was in Christ. Now God was not in Christ in the same way that he is in all other things, but deity dwelt corporally in Christ himself, such that Christ was truly God. For unless Christ was God, neither our salvation nor our life was possible. The one who at the same time was both Christ and God died for us. Through his death the Father reconciled the world to himself; that is, on account of Christ, he did not impute our sins to us. Annotations on 2 Corinthians 5:19.[42]

God Reconciled the World to Himself in Christ. Tilemann Hesshus: Lest we doubt the reconciliation accomplished by Christ, Paul shows who the author was of so great a work. The wondrous work of redemption and reconciliation could not have been accomplished, the power of sin and death could not have been vanquished, the kingdom of Satan could not have been demolished—unless that divine majesty was in Christ. For the human creature would not have been able to destroy sin and death and restore righteousness and life. For that reason, it was necessary that God and a human being should be our mediator. God, namely, the eternal Father, was in Christ. Deity itself performed those wondrous works in Christ. Christ says, "Those who see me see the Father. Believe me, that I am in the Father and the Father is in me." The entirety of divine majesty was in Christ; truly, the Logos was not only in Christ but is united with Christ's flesh in a personal union. Paul says that God has reconciled the world to himself in Christ, for Christ has made satisfaction

[40]C. Spangenberg, *Die ander Epistel Pauli an die Corinthier*, 105r-v.

[41]CO 50:70-71 (CTS 40:235-36).

[42]Zwingli, *Annotatiunculae . . . ex ore Zvinglij*, 173.

for the sins of the whole world. God gave his Son for the whole world. The ministry of reconciliation has been established for the whole world. In Christ Jesus, free reconciliation is offered to all people. Therefore, insofar as the majority of human beings do not participate in this reconciliation, but remain under God's wrath, these people remain guilty, because they are not grasping by faith the blessings offered to them. EXPLICATION OF 2 CORINTHIANS 5:19.[43]

THE PROMISE OF IMPUTED RIGHTEOUSNESS. MARTIN CHEMNITZ: These points are very clear from Paul: The free imputation in the article of justification is the grace of God, which for the sake of Christ does not impute against us the sins inhering in us and imputes to us (as though it actually did inhere in humankind) the perfect righteousness which does not inhere in us and which is worthy of eternal life. I am happy to use these terms of the dialecticians regarding the "basis" (*fundamentum*), the "goal" (*terminus*), and the relationship (*relatio*), because I believe this line of reasoning is more satisfactory for explaining and understanding the correct and genuine meaning of the word "imputation" in the article of justification.

There are many examples in which the word *chāshab* or *logizomai* establishes the "basis" not in the one to whom something is imputed, whether for good or for evil, but in the relationship, that is, the thinking, the judgment, and the will of the one who imputes. . . . These examples are clear, and in each of them there is the word *chāshab* or *logizomai*. Therefore, in order that the promise of imputed righteousness may be sure, its "basis" is not located in the qualities inherent in us but in the judgment and thoughts of God, which are infallibly true. LOCI THEOLOGICI.[44]

A FULLER DEFINITION OF RECONCILIATION. NIELS HEMMINGSEN: Now God has reconciled us to himself in this way: "God was in Christ, reconciling the world to himself"; that is, God the Father, who is of one essence with the Son—according to that passage "I am in the Father and the Father is in me"—has reconciled us to himself by the intercession of the Son. But if you ask, "Why is the Father not called the mediator when he was the reconciler?" I respond as follows: He has reconciled us to himself through the mediator, who is Jesus Christ alone. For even if there is an inseparable and indivisible unity of substance of the three persons—and also of their working—nevertheless, the function of the persons must not be confused and the role of the individual persons in the mystery of salvation must not be destroyed. The Father, Son, and Holy Spirit—that is, the whole Trinity—has reconciled the world to himself, but the Father sent the Son so that he might be a propitiation for sins according to the first promise, "The seed of the woman will crush the head of the serpent." Because the Son has been sent, propitiation has been accomplished. And the Holy Spirit seals this propitiation. The result of this propitiation is that God does not impute sins to those who believe in Christ, just as it is stated more broadly in Romans 3–4. Therefore, it is rightly said that the whole Trinity (with respect to agency) has reconciled us when he destroyed sins. But the Son is the only one who propitiates and fulfills obedience because by means of propitiation satisfaction was made for sins. And so Christ's obedience, by which he fulfilled the law, is imputed to believers. Whereby, men and women are reconciled to God, made acceptable to him, and considered righteous. From this we obtain a fuller definition of reconciliation, which elsewhere is called justification, namely, that for those who believe in the person of Christ, there is absolution from sin, the imputation of Christ's righteousness, and the receiving of eternal life freely on account of Christ. COMMENTARY ON 2 CORINTHIANS 5:19.[45]

---

[43]Hesshus, *Explicatio Secundae Epistolae Pauli ad Corinthios*, 147v-148r; citing Jn 14:11.

[44]Chemnitz, *Loci Theologici* 2:529; citing Num 18:26-27; Lev 17:3-4; Ps 144:3-4; Mk 15:28; Rom 2:26; 8:36; 9:8.

[45]Hemmingsen, *Commentaria in Omnes Epistolas Apostolorum*, 274; citing Gen 3:15.

God's Work of Reconciliation Through Christ. Guillaume Farel: In [Christ] is brought about and perfectly accomplished all the work of God. For by him all things are restored and made perfect in heaven and on earth because the fullness of life, of power, of virtue, of wisdom, of grace, and of justice abide in him. Becoming obedient to his Father, born of a mother, a virgin, without the seed of man, subjected to the law, Jesus never sought his glory or his will, but that of his Father. Jesus never spoke or acted to serve his own will, but always to serve that of his Father who was in him reconciling the world to himself. Summary and Brief Exposition.[46]

In What Sense Does God Reconcile the Whole World? Wolfgang Musculus: "Not imputing their sins to them." That is, forgiving their sins which were the cause of their alienation from him. For what else does the phrase "not imputing the sins of sinners" mean than "to compassionately forgive"? And what else does it mean to forgive someone than not to impute? Thus the prophet in Psalm 32 considers "forgiveness" and "the non-imputation of sins" as the same thing, saying, "Blessed is the one whose transgression is forgiven, whose sin is covered. Blessed is the one against whom the Lord does not impute sin." It was necessary for the apostle to add this clause since, with God, this reconciliation of the world could not have happened unless all of our sins were compassionately forgiven. If God had wanted to impute our sins to us, there would have been no place for reconciliation. For there was no one from the entire human race who was able to satisfy the righteousness of God for his own sin (much less for the sins of others) and, in so doing, achieve reconciliation.

Since the entire human race has been reconciled to God through Christ, are the sins of humanity thus imputed to no one? If we should interpret this passage simply, what other consequence would follow than that no one will perish, but all will be saved indiscriminately? On the basis of this and similar passages, some people in our time have attempted to renew the teaching that all people will be saved, even the wicked. It is altogether true what the apostle says: "God has reconciled the world to himself in Christ, not imputing their sins to them," as much as it relates to his work of reconciliation which is furnished and sufficient for reconciling the entire human race. But (as we said earlier) since this reconciliation cannot be valid among those who are unwilling, God himself established the ministry of reconciliation by which all people might be called and invited eagerly to accept this grace. Now if the whole world had gladly accepted this grace, then the whole world would have been reconciled and saved . . . and no human being would have perished. But since that did not happen, what other outcome was possible except that only those become participants of this general grace who, by grace, embrace it through repentance and faith? Commentary on 2 Corinthians 5:19.[47]

Reconciliation Indicates a Prior Friendship. John Donne: Reconciliation is a reintegration, a renewing of a former friendship that has been interrupted and broken. Thus, this implies a present state of enmity and hostility with God, *as well as* a former friendship with God, and also the possibility of returning to that former friendship. . . . Since enmity [between God and human beings] existed, reconciliation was required. But the fact that reconciliation occurred indicates that there was a friendship. There was a time when God and human beings were friends—God did not hate them from all eternity. God forbid! And God did not intend to break this friendship. God did not intend to fall out with human beings, for then he could never have admitted them to friendship. . . . No one can love another person as a friend this year, whom he intends to be his enemy the next year. God's foreknowledge that humans

[46] Zuidema and Van Raalte, eds., *Early French Reform*, 122.

[47] Musculus, *Commentarius . . . in posteriorem epistolam Pauli ad Corinthios*, 186; citing Ps 32:1-2.

should fall was not God's foreknowledge of what *he* intended to do, but only that human beings would become incapable of maintaining their friendship with him. Sermon 5 Preached at St. Paul's.[48]

The Sweetness of God's Majesty in Christ. John Trapp: As the salt waters of the sea, when they are strained through the earth, become sweet in the rivers, so (someone once said) the waters of majesty and justice in God, though terrible, yet once strained and derived through Christ, become sweet and delightful. Commentary on 2 Corinthians 5:19.[49]

5:20-21 *Ambassadors for Christ*

God Has Many Ambassadors. Martin Luther: If [the apostles] are all messengers of the one Lord Christ, who will be so foolish as to say that such a great Lord, who has such a great cause for the entire world, has only one messenger, and that this same messenger should then produce other messengers of his own? In that case St. Peter should not be called "one of the twelve messengers" but rather "the only messenger," and none of the others would be "one of the twelve messengers." Instead they would be "one of the eleven messengers" of St. Peter. What is the custom at the courts of the nobility? Is it not true that one lord has many messengers? Indeed, how often are many messengers sent with one message to one place, as there are now priests, bishops, archbishops, and the pope ruling over one city, not to mention some tyrants who rule in between? Christ sent all the apostles into the whole world with equal, full authority and with his word and message, as St. Paul says, "We are ambassadors for Christ," and in 1 Corinthians 3: "What then is Peter? What is Paul? Servants through whom you believed." This message means tending sheep, ruling, being bishop, and the like. But when the pope subjects all of God's messengers to himself, it is the same as if one of a prince's messengers stopped all the others and sent them wherever he pleased while he himself ran nowhere. Would this please the prince, if he found out? On the Papacy in Rome.[50]

God's Appeal Through Us. Tilemann Hesshus: Paul demonstrates the highest authority and salvific efficacy of his office. We do not proclaim our own words; we do not put forward the imaginings of our own brain. Rather, we proclaim the voice of God himself, or rather God himself preaches through us, convicts of sin, warns of his wrath, explains the benefits of his Son and offers eternal salvation. "You are not the one who is speaking," says Christ, "but it is the Spirit of your Father who is in you." Again, "Those who hear you, hear me." Therefore, let us not be annoyed that our sins in ministry are reproached; let us not despise the judgment of God; let us not delay when God encourages us to repentance; let us not doubt concerning the salvation offered to us by God; let us not doubt concerning the power of the Word that proceeds from the mouth of God himself. For certainly, the Lord Jesus Christ only desires our salvation, as Paul says: "We implore you in the name of Christ, be reconciled to God"—that is, recognize the blessings imparted by Christ. Christ has appeased the wrath of the Father by taking up our sins. The Father has voluntarily given up his wrath and offers grace. Put aside now your hostile mind against God, and repent, believe the gospel, and return to favor with God. This is the goal of all gospel ministry. Explication of 2 Corinthians 5:20.[51]

Ministry of the Word Is the Ministry of God Himself. Martin Chemnitz: Because the ministry of the Word is that of God himself, which he himself wants to carry out through ordained means and instruments in his church.

[48]Donne, *Sermons of John Donne*, 10:134, 135*.
[49]Trapp, *A Commentary or Exposition*, 716*.
[50]LW 39:74 (WA 6:300); citing 1 Cor 3:5.
[51]Hesshus, *Explicatio Secundae Epistolae Pauli ad Corinthios*, 149v-150r; citing Mt 10:20.

"We are ambassadors for Christ, as though God" (who is not far away from his ambassadors as king or ruler) "were appealing through us." Therefore, it is absolutely necessary, if you want to be a faithful pastor of the church, that you be certain that God wants to use your labors and that you are such an instrument of his. Loci Theologici.[52]

We Are Reconciled to God Through the Gospel. John Calvin: It should be noted that Paul here is addressing believers. He declares that every day he brings to them this commission. Christ, therefore, did not suffer so that our sins might be expiated only once, nor was the gospel established to pardon only those sins which we committed before baptism, but just as we sin daily, so we might also, by daily remission, be received by God in his favor. For this is a perpetual commission, which ought to be constantly sounded forth in the church until the end of the world; and the gospel cannot be preached unless the remission of sins is promised.

We have here an express and appropriate testimony for refuting the wicked opinion of the papists which tells us to seek the remission of sins after baptism from some other source than the expiation accomplished in the death of Christ. Now this doctrine is commonly taught in all the schools of the papacy, that *after* baptism we merit the remission of sins through penitence, by means of the help of the keys—as if baptism itself conferred that remission to us without penitence! By the term penitence, however, they mean [works of] satisfaction. But what does Paul say here? He calls us back to that unique expiation of Christ before baptism as well as after baptism, so that we might know that remission is always conferred to us gratuitously. Moreover, Paul passes over that distinction in silence (as if he knew nothing about it) which the papists have invented. Furthermore, all their chatter about the administration of the keys is pointless, because they imagine the keys without the gospel, when they are nothing else than a testimony of that gracious reconciliation, which is granted to us from the gospel. Commentary on 2 Corinthians 5:20.[53]

The Privileges and Duties of Christ's Ambassadors. Niels Hemmingsen: Now there are four propositions in this verse which offer us the most important doctrine and the most useful reminders. First, ministers of the Word perform an embassy on behalf of Christ. Based on this statement we can draw the following inferences: (1) Gospel ministry possesses the highest worth. (2) The greatest faithfulness is required in this embassy. (3) The ambassador is not permitted to announce anything except the words of Christ. (4) These ambassadors should be listened to as Christ himself. (5) Ministers of the gospel ought to have a legitimate calling, for it is not permissible for an ambassador to act unless they have been sent by another. (6) That person is not an ambassador of Christ, but rather a condemned trickster who announces something other than what the Lord has spoken from his mouth.

The second proposition is that God is, in a way, exhorting or preaching to those listening to the gospel—not because God actually preaches—but it's as if he were preaching in the person of ministers. Ministers of the Word are reminded by this that it is necessary to perform the embassy committed to them with resolution and courage, for they are not performing their own business, but God's. Thus, God is treated with contempt when the voice of the minister and his words are despised, as that passage says: "Those who reject you reject me." So, too, ministers of the gospel are reminded not to behave like buffoons, nor to cram foolish things into their public speeches (that is, their sermons) so as to detain their congregations longer with the people's applause. For this will certainly result in God being outraged, whose mouth ministers of the gospel are said to be. Further, those who listen are reminded to show special respect and modesty toward the ministry.

[52]Chemnitz, *Loci Theologici*, 2:699; citing Lk 1:70; Heb 1:1; 2 Cor 5:20.

[53]CO 50:73 (CTS 40:240-41).

The third proposition is that the ministers' words entreat on behalf of Christ, that is, in Christ's name, as that passage says: "Those who hear you hear me." Everything described in the first and second propositions above follow from this proposition.

The fourth proposition comprises the summary of the embassy, namely, to reconcile men and women to God. Now this exhortation is intended for all people, to those already converted as well as those not yet converted. For since we sin daily, so we need to be reconciled daily through Christ. This reconciliation, as has been stated earlier, is achieved through the justification of a person, namely, when God imputes the obedience of the Son rather than sin to persons who believe, and accepts them freely to eternal life. Therefore, the Donatists† are mistaken when they refuse pardon and restoration to grace to people who have fallen. The papists also err when they teach that men and women who have fallen after baptism merit remission of sins through penitence, thanks to the intercession of the keys. COMMENTARY ON 2 CORINTHIANS 5:20.[54]

CHRIST CONQUERED DEATH FOR US. JACQUES LEFÈVRE D'ÉTAPLES: [Paul writes,] "We pray, we ask, we beg on behalf of Christ, be reconciled to God." Oh, the immense goodness of God who was willing to recall us so affectionately and summon us so lovingly—we who, in our hostility, were perishing because of our offenses. . . . Who, then, would not run to this reconciliation? Who would disregard such great mercy? What is of greater importance than this: that God made him who knew no sin to be sin for us, and wanted sin itself to be nailed to the cross? For death was the required payment for sin. God willed, I say, to nail him to the cross (which righteousness demanded), so that we might become the righteousness of God through the one who became sin for us. We were guilty of sin. Christ, who for our sake took upon himself our sin, was bearing the weight of our sin upon his holy and innocent neck as God's judgment. He who was infinitely good exchanged his life for the death that we deserved, bearing our heavy burden and accepting our death, bestowing his life upon us, assuming our debt, and, once nailed to the cross, liberating us. To our invincible liberator, be honor, power, glory, and authority forever and ever! COMMENTARY ON 2 CORINTHIANS 5:20-21.[55]

CHRIST HAS EXPIATED HUMAN SINFULNESS. DESIDERIUS ERASMUS: We, therefore, fulfilling in the place of Christ this mission entrusted by him, beseech you in the name of Christ, as if God were exhorting you through us, to give up your old vices and be reconciled to God. For he, in order once and for all to deliver us from our sins, in some manner turned his Son into sin, although he is righteousness itself, so that girded with flesh, which in us is subject to sin, he might become an offering to expiate our crimes. Like a felon among felons, the Son was nailed to a cross so that through him God might change us, who were nothing but sin, into righteousness—not our own righteousness, nor the law's, but God's. By God's mercy, our transgressions have been forgiven so that henceforth God might regard us who have been grafted onto Christ as righteousness, just as he regarded him a sinner in our stead. PARAPHRASES OF 2 CORINTHIANS 5.[56]

THE SINS OF THE WORLD LIE ON CHRIST. MARTIN LUTHER: Therefore, Christians must adhere to this verse [i.e., John 1:29] with simplicity of heart and not let anyone rob them of it. Then they will be aware of the blindness of all heathen, of the papists, and of the godless, who themselves want to render satisfaction with pilgrimages and with good works. They make much of these and console

[54]Hemmingsen, *Commentaria in Omnes Epistolas Apostolorum*, 274-75; citing Lk 10:16. †The Donatists were an early Christian sect that refused to readmit Christians who had lapsed during times of persecution.

[55]Lefèvre, *Commentariorum in Epistolas Beati Pauli . . . Liber Tertius*, 135.

[56]CWE 43:232-33.

themselves with purgatory. But they are blind. For holy Scripture declares that the sin of the world does not lie on the world, or St. John's sin on St. John, or St. Peter's on Peter; for they are unable to bear it. The sin of the world lies on Christ, the Lamb of God. He steps forth and becomes a vile sinner, yea, sin itself, just as if he himself had committed all the sin of the world from its beginning to its end. This is to be the Lamb's office, mission, and function. Twelfth Sermon on John.[57]

The Sinless Christ Became Sin for Us. Tilemann Hesshus: Paul understands here the only-begotten Son of God—the God-man—who was free from all sin, defiled by neither original sin nor actual sin. For he was conceived by the Holy Spirit, and [named] "Jehovah is our righteousness." "He committed no sin," Peter says, "and no deceit was found in his mouth." "He knew no sin"—by this Paul indicates that he was pure from all sin. For since he was going to pay for all our sins, it was necessary that he be free from all sins. "You have loved righteousness and hated wickedness," the Holy Spirit says.

"He made sin." In this passage, Paul makes use of the prophetic expression for sin, "a guilt offering for sin," as seen in Isaiah 35 [*sic*, Isaiah 53]. . . . The eternal Father appointed his Son as a sacrificial victim whom he sacrificed for the sins of the human race to appease God's wrath and cancel the curse of the law, for it was necessary that divine justice be satisfied. Therefore, God placed upon him the sins of us all, and God pierced him for the sake of his people. Hence, Christ says, "I am laying down my life for my sheep. The Son of Man did not come into the world to be served but to serve and to lay down his life as a ransom for many." Explication of 2 Corinthians 5:21.[58]

Perpetual Doctrine of the Gospel. Martin Chemnitz: We do not ourselves devise this teaching, that Christ the mediator has fulfilled the law for us by the fullest satisfaction of the punishments and by the most perfect obedience and that this righteousness of the mediator is imputed to the believers, that by it they may be justified before God to life eternal. But this is the specific and perpetual doctrine of the gospel, of which we shall note down only a few clear statements. . . . "For our sake he made him to be sin who knew no sin, that in him we might become the righteousness of God." But how was Christ made sin? Certainly by imputation. And thus we are made the righteousness of God in him. . . . On this we should, and safely can, place our trust that we may be justified on its account, that is, that we may receive remission of sins, be absolved from the deserved sentence of damnation, be received by God into grace, be adopted as children, and finally be received to eternal life. Examination of the Council of Trent.[59]

Christ Alone Delivers Us from Sin and Death. Simon Goulart: Spiritual freedom, as opposed to bondage, is a deliverance from sin, from the wrath of God, from the curse of sin, from eternal death, and from the spirit of servitude. . . . Because, first of all, [Christ] delivers us from sin, having "been made sin for us." So, too, in his first epistle John says that "the blood of Christ cleanses you of all sin." Second, Christ delivers us from the wrath of God, because he has borne the wrath of God for us, as Paul says in 2 Corinthians 5 that "God was in Christ reconciling the world to himself, by not imputing their sins to them." And the heavenly Father himself says in Matthew 3 and Matthew 17 that Jesus Christ is his "blessed Son, in whom he is well-pleased." Third, Christ delivers us from the curse, as St. Paul says in Galatians 3: "Christ has bought us back from the curse of the law, having been made a curse for us." Fourth, it is also Christ who

[57]LW 22:168* (WA 46:682).

[58]Hesshus, *Explicatio Secundae Epistolae Pauli ad Corinthios*, 150v-151v; citing 1 Pet 2:22; Heb 1:9; Is 53:10; Mt 20:28.

[59]Chemnitz, *Examination of the Council of Trent*, 1:502, 504. In favor of the doctrine of justification by imputation, Chemnitz also cites and discusses Gal 3:13; 4:4-5; Rom 8:3-4; 1 Tim 2:6; Rom 4:23-24.

delivers us from eternal death. "He who believes in him will not perish but have eternal life." To summarize all of this in a word: by the merit of Christ's death, he abolished sin; by the merit of his obedience to the law, he brought it about that this obedience is imputed as righteousness to the believers. These benefits as a rule are included in the word "grace," especially in the writings of the apostles. On Christian Liberty.[60]

The Light of God Illumined Spiritual Darkness. John Colet: Still, that shining Wisdom of God, which no darkness could comprehend, willed to be in a manner obscured; and to commit sin for us, as it were, and to take unto itself humankind's darkness, and to become a middle ground between the shadows and the light itself, so that it might light on earth the lamp that was dead, might illumine the dark places and enlighten every person coming into this world, might give them—those who believe in his name—the power to become children of God and of the light; so that henceforth born of God, not children of humankind but through the Son of Man, they might be the children of God. Enarration on 1 Corinthians 7.[61]

The Incarnation Reveals God's Love. Menno Simons: Oh, wonderful love of God, unsearchable and past finding out! He did not send into this sad and sorrowful world an angel, a patriarch, or a prophet, but his eternal, almighty Word, his eternal Wisdom, the brightness of his glory, in the form of sinful flesh. He made him to be sin for us who knew no sin, that we might be made the righteousness of God in him. Foundation of Christian Doctrine.[62]

Christ Was Sin for Us. Cyriacus Spangenberg: Augustine[†] says, "God made him sin for us, that is, a sin offering, through which our sins are forgiven. For 'sin' means 'offering for sin,' and he is indeed offered up for our sins who was without sin, without infirmity. He alone among all human beings was such an offering, as in the Old Testament one had to select from among the cattle one that was without blemish for an offering. By this it was shown that one without sin would come, for the redemption of all sin." . . .

So Christ is made sin for us, after he agreed to endure the judgment in our place. Then God the Father accepts such an agreement by his Son and makes dear Jesus, who knew no sin, never committed any sin, who never had an evil inclination or lust, who is full of godly wisdom and righteousness—God makes him sin for us, that is, such a sin offering, which will cleanse other people from sin. He lays the punishment that should have gone out over the sin of the whole world on him, indeed lets it entirely and profusely fall on him and run over him. We hear in the passion what kind of cruel burden was laid on the Lord Christ and how severely the wrath of God pressed on him, that he sweated bloody sweat over it, and began to be sorrowful, to shake and to fear. These were sheer thunderclaps of the wrath of God which struck his body and soul. Then came the spitting, mocking, flogging, crowning, and crucifying, and the anxious cry, "My God, my God, why have you abandoned me?" This is, I believe, what it means to make Christ to be sin. Twenty-Seventh Sermon.[63]

The Christian's Alien Righteousness. Wolfgang Musculus: "So that in him we might become the righteousness of God." Paul explains for what purpose God made his innocent and righteous Son to be sin for us. He could say this because in Christ, God was expiating our sins. . . . Truly, God was pleased to make use of the antithesis of our sins and the righteousness of Christ. We were sinners; he was righteous. In order for that exchange to happen, he placed our

[60]Goulart, *Seconde partie des Discours Chrestiens*, 190-92; citing 1 Jn 5:7; Mt 3:17; 17:5; Gal 3:13; Jn 3; 5; 6.
[61]Colet, *Commentary on First Corinthians*, 155; citing Jn 1:9-13.
[62]CWMS 144.

[63]C. Spangenberg, *Die ander Epistel Pauli an die Corinthier*, 111. [†]Spangenberg here is quoting from Augustine's *Contra Pelagium & Celestium* 2:32.

sins on his righteous Son, and in turn he imparted Christ's righteousness to us sinners. Thus he has been made sin because of another's sins, and we have been made righteousness because of another's righteousness. For just as God judged him to be sin, not for his own sins, but for ours, so God has made us the righteousness of God, not by our own righteousness, but by the righteousness of Christ. . . .

Why is it that Paul does not say, "so that we might become *righteous*," but rather "so that we might become the *righteousness of God*"? In the same respect, you might ask why Paul does not say, "he who knew no sin was made a *sinner* for us," but rather "made *sin* for us"? God did not make his Son a sinner as we ourselves are sinners; but he made him sin, that is, a sacrifice of expiation for our sins. So, too, he did not make us righteous in the same way that he is righteous, because there is nothing besides sins in us . . . but he made us righteousness, that is, he imputed a righteousness to us that was not our own. There is no righteousness except that free righteousness (namely, that righteousness that he has compassionately imputed to us) which we have in his Son, not in ourselves. Therefore, the apostle does not simply say, "so that we might become righteous," but "so that in him we might become the righteousness of God." COMMENTARY ON 2 CORINTHIANS 5:21.[64]

GOD IMPUTES HIS RIGHTEOUSNESS TO US THROUGH CHRIST. TILEMANN HESSHUS: "So that we might become the righteousness of God." That is, the righteousness of God, which was demanded of us in the law, was accomplished in us through Christ, since both the punishment has been fully paid by Christ and the obedience, by which the law has been satisfied, is imputed to us by faith. Paul is not speaking about God's essential righteousness. We are not affected by the righteousness of God's essence; nor is he speaking about qualities, such as legal righteousness, infused into us. . . . Instead, he is speaking about that wondrous righteousness of God that has been revealed in the gospel, whereby the eternal Father, on the basis of the intercession and death of the Son, pardons all our sins. He imputes the obedience of his Son to us and pronounces us righteous. This righteousness is God's, not ours. It is not the righteousness by which God himself is righteous, but the righteousness by which he justifies sinners and graciously accepts them. "My mouth," Psalms 71 says, "will proclaim your righteousness, your deeds of salvation the whole day, whose number I do not know. I will come into the powerful deeds of the Lord. O Lord, I will remember your righteousness alone." Therefore, Paul names it the righteousness of God, not because it is his righteousness essentially, but because he proclaims us righteous in his Son and for the sake of his Son. And he contrasts it to our righteousness, the works of the law, and free will. That righteousness [of which Paul speaks] is not from us, nor of the law, nor of works—but is from God, who has revealed it in the gospel, provided it through a mediator, and imputed it to us by faith.

There is great importance in the phrase "so that we might become the righteousness of God." For it shows that all of our sins and filth are so hidden in Christ's shadow that the eternal Father recognizes nothing except righteousness in us, who have been engrafted into Christ by faith. For we have died with Christ, and Christ—who is Jehovah our righteousness—lives in us. In him alone, namely, in our Lord Jesus Christ, we are the righteousness of God on account of his obedience and death; that is, we are righteous before God and heirs of eternal life. EXPLICATION OF 2 CORINTHIANS 5:21.[65]

CHRIST'S SACRIFICIAL DEATH SETS US FREE. KATHARINA SCHÜTZ ZELL: O righteous Father, also help us to be strengthened and made sure by you, to break through the afflictions of this flesh and be able to enter through the narrow gate.

[64]Musculus, *Commentarius . . . in posteriorem epistolam Pauli ad Corinthios*, 191.

[65]Hesshus, *Explicatio Secundae Epistolae Pauli ad Corinthios*, 151v-152r; citing Ps 71:15-16.

Grant us your Spirit of knowledge and strength, that we may not deny you . . . because of the sin that sticks in our flesh with evil desires and unceasingly stirs it up. Therefore, the flesh struggles against the spirit and the spirit against the flesh and its evil fruits. So there is a great conflict and struggle in us: we have the will but we do not have the ability to fulfill it, yet both of these are yours. O holy Father, grant us help that in this affliction we may not be servants of sin but may overcome sin and be free children of your grace through Jesus Christ—who, being without sin, became sin for us that he might make us free. Letter to Sir Felix Armbruster.[66]

Christ Took the Punishment—but not the Demerit—of Sin. John Trapp: Someone has said that Christ loved us so much that he endured that which he most hated in order to become sin for us—he took on passive sin in himself to satisfy the active sin in us—and he endured for a time the deprivation of that which he considered more valuable than the world, namely, the sense of God's favor. . . . A reverend writer[†] once said that there are two parts to guilt: (1) What one merits or deserves. This Christ did not take. (2) The obligation to punishment. This Christ did take, and so he became sin, that is, bound to the punishment of sin. The son of a traitor loses his father's lands, not by any communion of fault, but by the communion of nature, because he is part of his father. The son is no traitor. But by his proximity to his father he is wrapped in the same punishment. And so, too, here. . . . Christ, by communion with our natures, took upon himself whatsoever was penal, that belonged to sin, though he took not nor could take the demerit of sin. Commentary on 2 Corinthians 5:21.[67]

6:1-2 *Now Is the Day of Salvation*

Paul Exhorts Corinthians to Live Profitable Lives. Wolfgang Musculus: These verses [i.e., 5:16–6:2] are closely connected with one another, whereby it seems inconvenient to divide them. In the preceding verses, the apostle has described the doctrine of our salvation that has been accomplished by God through reconciliation, by which he has reconciled to himself the human race through Jesus Christ, and he has given to the apostles the ministry of this reconciliation. Now, at the beginning of the sixth chapter that follows, he gives an exhortation where he urges the Corinthians not to receive such an extraordinary grace in vain by living unprofitable lives. Commentary on 2 Corinthians 6:1.[68]

Ministers Cooperate with God. Cardinal Cajetan: Now Paul adds the phrase "working together with him." Here we see the other part of the distinction. For first, Paul described his office to be like that of ambassadors, which is nothing more than to explain faithfully and skillfully with entreaties (or some other way) according to the purpose of an embassy. But now, Paul also describes the office of ambassadors as those who cooperate with God who sent them, and with Christ for whom they are a surrogate. And for this reason, he says, "working together with him." Commentary on 2 Corinthians 6:1.[69]

Do Not Despise the Year of Grace. Martin Luther: Therefore, I exhort you "not to receive the grace [of God] in vain," that is to say, make good use of the day that now appears, in which you can come to the knowledge of the truth. For I say that it will not remain thus; I will pass by, as the prophet [Isaiah] says, "I [God] have heard you because the year of grace is at hand; and I have

[66]Zell, *Church Mother*, 170.

[67]Trapp, *A Commentary or Exposition*, 717*. [†]The "reverend writer" to whom Trapp refers is the Puritan minister Richard Sibbes.

[68]Musculus, *Commentarius . . . in posteriorem epistolam Pauli ad Corinthios*, 192.

[69]Cajetan, *In Posteriorem Pauli Epistolam ad Corinthios Commentarii*, 172-73.

helped you because it is the year of grace." Christ says, "The darkness will come so that no one knows where he is walking; while you have the light, [believe in the light]." Therefore, be grateful, and see to it that you make use of the light while you have it. . . .

God will not tolerate it if he offers his grace to us and we despise it. Once he has departed, [it will be too late]. . . . See to it that you live your life accordingly. God offers you mercy, the remission of sins, help, and salvation. The time is at hand; use it well. If not, if it is taken away. . . . Although the monks have established a great many monasteries and the Turks have great and splendid forms of worship, they seek the Lord and yet do not find him, because their years of grace have passed. The pope and the Turk have their devotions, but not the sacrament, baptism, the Word, or the Our Father. Therefore, let us cry out to heaven while it is open to us, because later the chance will be lost. SERMON ON INVOCAVIT SUNDAY.[70]

PAUL EXTOLS THE GRACE OF GOD. PHILIPP MELANCHTHON: Thus far Paul has emphasized the antithesis between the ministry of the letter and the ministry of the spirit, interspersing along the way matters pertaining to ministers. Now he adds what we ought to do in turn. And after treating the doctrine of faith, he begins in his customary manner with exhortations. Faith is righteousness. Good morals are the fruit of faith. Furthermore, whenever he begins an exhortation, he always employs a single argument, namely, he makes mention of the greatness of God's grace. And he does this for two reasons. First, because by grace we are sure that our life is pleasing to God, and will surely accomplish what we desire and acquire the reward for our labors. This is the reasoning he employs here. Second, because in response to such great grace, we ought to repay God with gratitude. ANNOTATIONS ON 2 CORINTHIANS 6:1.[71]

THE HUMAN WILL PLAYS A ROLE IN CONVERSION. MARTIN CHEMNITZ: Concerning free will we have said elsewhere that since in conversion our will must be moved by the Word of God, this Word must certainly be heard, and since with the Word of God the Holy Spirit does his work, raising up and helping our hearts, we are to sustain ourselves with faith. Nor should we idly indulge in mistrust or other vices against conscience, nor trouble the Holy Spirit, but rather give assent to the Word of God and follow the Holy Spirit. In this spiritual struggle we feel that our will in contending against doubt and other vices is not idle. Paul instructs us about this very thing when he says in 2 Corinthians 6:1, "We entreat you not to receive the grace of God in vain." He wills that the gospel be heard. He wills that we assent to it and follow it, not indulging ourselves in wickedness contrary to our conscience. Furthermore, in Luke 11 it says, "He will give the Holy Spirit to those who ask him." It does not say, "to those who spurn him, or grieve him, or resist him." Therefore, he wills that we struggle with our infirmities. He wills that we acknowledge our sins and seek deliverance, that we do not cling to them contrary to our conscience. Thus the will is not an idle thing. LOCI THEOLOGICI.[72]

HOW CAN ONE RECEIVE GRACE IN VAIN? WOLFGANG MUSCULUS: Now if grace saves, how is it possible to receive it in vain? I answer: It is true that grace saves, but Paul is especially focusing on how it is received and employed. To hear the Word of God, that is, the word of grace, reconciliation, and salvation, is to receive the grace of God. And the fact that this grace is received in various ways is made clear from the Lord's parable in Matthew 13. Some people hear but do not understand, and therefore the evil one comes and snatches away what was sown in their hearts. Other people immediately receive it with joy but do not allow its roots to sink into their hearts, because they are fickle. And so when it happens that troubles arise

[70] LW 58:8 (WA 47:667-68); citing Is 49:8; Jn 12:35-36.
[71] *Melanchthons Werke*, 4:116.
[72] Chemnitz, *Loci Theologici*, 2:519; citing Lk 11:13.

on account of the word of grace, they are immediately disgusted and turn back. Still others receive it, but they are overwhelmed by the cares of this world and by their eagerness for deceptive riches and pleasures so that the word they have received is suffocated in their hearts and it is rendered unfruitful. Do not all these people receive the grace of God in vain, even if as soon as they heard it they received it eagerly and with joy? Are not those who receive grace profitably the people who understand what they have heard, and with sincere faith cultivate the understanding of the heart, as with good soil, and produce its fruit according to the measure of the gift of Christ, some producing a medium-sized harvest, and others a larger harvest? COMMENTARY ON 2 CORINTHIANS 6:1.[73]

PAUL IS WARNING MINISTERS—NOT HEARERS. NIELS HEMMINGSEN: The theme of this chapter is related to the previous exhortation, by which ministers of the gospel are warned not to be seen to have received the grace of God in vain, that is, the office of teaching the gospel. Chrysostom interpreted this verse as referring to the hearers [of the gospel], but the following verses indicate that the object of this present exhortation ought to be preachers, although it is of no consequence if one refers it to both—that is, ministers and hearers. But the word *synergountes*, that is, "cooperating one with another," demonstrates the shared labor of ministers. It should be noted from this example that older ministers should be reminded how to exhort others to perform their duty. COMMENTARY ON 2 CORINTHIANS 6:1.[74]

MINISTERS MUST DO MORE THAN INSTRUCT. JOHN CALVIN: Here ministers are taught that it is not enough simply to put forth doctrine. Rather, they must work hard that it may be received by the hearers, and not only once, but continually. For since they are messengers between God and human beings, their first responsibility is to offer them the grace of God, and the second is to strive with all their strength that it might not be offered in vain. COMMENTARY ON 2 CORINTHIANS 6:1.[75]

GOD'S PROMISED DAY OF SALVATION. DESIDERIUS ERASMUS: See, now is that time promised by God, the time of propitiation, in which God does not turn away the sinner who with full resolve comes to his senses and repents. See, now is that day on which we may attain salvation by living piously. There will follow that dreadful day on which reconciliation will be sought in vain. Consequently, eager to discharge our duty in this regard, we take care not to be in any respect a stumbling block for anyone, so that no failing of ours may bring censure upon the gospel of Christ, whose ministers we are. PARAPHRASES ON 2 CORINTHIANS 6.[76]

WE ARE IN THE DAY OF SALVATION. MARTIN LUTHER: Again, let this be our consolation: "Behold, now is the favorable time; I have helped you in the day of salvation." If you lack righteousness, then cry out . . . before the day of wrath comes and the grim year when there is no help. You will say, "But then I must be a pauper and a fool, condemned, forsaken." You are not therefore condemned because you undergo these things. Instead, recognize that the time of grace is at hand and that you can indeed be saved. For the most part, Paul speaks about suffering, but he also speaks about actions—of chastity or that we might make diligent use of the Word of truth. In sum: Be devout, endure evil, and think: We are in the day of salvation. SERMON ON INVOCAVIT SUNDAY.[77]

GOD'S FAVOR SEEN IN GOD'S RECONCILIATION. WOLFGANG MUSCULUS: "Behold, now is the favorable time, now is the day of salvation." You see that this present verse relates to the main point drawn from that Old Testament passage concerning the time of grace. Paul answers that it was both a

[73]Musculus, *Commentarius . . . in posteriorem epistolam Pauli ad Corinthios*, 193; citing Mt 13:1-9.
[74]Hemmingsen, *Commentaria in Omnes Epistolas Apostolorum*, 276.
[75]CO 50:75 (CTS 40:245).
[76]CWE 43:233-34.
[77]LW 58:9* (WA 47:668).

time of divine favor and the day of salvation, and also the right time in the sight of God to listen to his afflicted people crying out to him, and to liberate them from captivity. For at that time, a happiness had been granted . . . whereby God reconciled the world to himself through Christ and, through the apostles, published the word of reconciliation throughout the whole world, and summoned all people to this grace. In order to extol the happiness of his own time above that happiness concerning which the prophet prophesied to Israel, Paul does not merely say, "Now also is an acceptable time and the day of salvation," but he says emphatically, "Behold now, truly, is the acceptable time; behold now, at last, is the day of salvation." . . .

Now what else is this favor of God than that, putting aside his wrath, he had pity on the human race, and reconciled it to himself through his Son Christ, and covered it wholly with his goodwill? This favor of God brings with it all things that are in heaven and on earth. What shall I say? From the outset you gave to me this favor: the only-begotten Son of God, indeed God himself. Will there be anything in him that, at the same time, you will not bestow along with him? That is why the apostle states and asserts in Romans 8 that God is for us and that it is not possible that we be condemned by anything. Commentary on 2 Corinthians 6:2.[78]

The Favorable Day for Salvation. John Calvin: The quotation [from Isaiah 49:8] must be applied to the present subject in this way: Since God assigns a specific time to demonstrate his grace, it follows that all times are not suitable for that. Since a particular day is named "the day of salvation," it follows that the opportunity for salvation is not available every day. Now this completely depends on the providence of God, for the acceptable time is no other than what is called "the fullness of time" in Galatians 4:4. The order also must be noted. First, Paul makes mention of the time of kindness; then, the day of salvation. By this it is suggested that salvation flows to us, like a fountain, from the mercy of God alone. Therefore, we should not seek the cause in ourselves, as if we, by our works, might move God to assign his favor to us, for from whence comes the day of salvation? It comes because it is the acceptable time, that is, that time which God has ordained by his gracious favor. In the meantime, we must keep in view Paul's purpose—that we need to be prompt lest the opportunity slip away. For God is displeased when we are slow and lazy to receive the grace offered to us. Commentary on 2 Corinthians 6:2.[79]

[78]Musculus, *Commentarius . . . in posteriorem epistolam Pauli ad Corinthios*, 194-95; citing Rom 8:31.

[79]CO 50:76 (CTS 40:246-47).

6:3-13 PAUL'S HARDSHIPS

[3]We put no obstacle in anyone's way, so that no
fault may be found with our ministry, [4]but as
servants of God we commend ourselves in every
way: by great endurance, in afflictions, hardships,
calamities, [5]beatings, imprisonments, riots, labors,
sleepless nights, hunger; [6]by purity, knowledge,
patience, kindness, the Holy Spirit, genuine love;
[7]by truthful speech, and the power of God; with the
weapons of righteousness for the right hand and for
the left; [8]through honor and dishonor, through
slander and praise. We are treated as impostors,
and yet are true; [9]as unknown, and yet well known;
as dying, and behold, we live; as punished, and yet
not killed; [10]as sorrowful, yet always rejoicing; as
poor, yet making many rich; as having nothing, yet
possessing everything.

[11]We have spoken freely to you,[a] *Corinthians; our*
heart is wide open. [12]You are not restricted by us, but
you are restricted in your own affections. [13]In return
(I speak as to children) widen your hearts also.

a Greek *Our mouth is open to you*

Overview: Paul commends his apostolic ministry to the Corinthians by describing his tireless service to Christ in the face of innumerable hardships and then reminding these believers of the deep affection he has for them—encouraging them to reciprocate this affection in turn. Reformation commentators find in Paul's remarkable example a veritable gold mine of wisdom for Christian pastors and laypeople as they bear the cross of ministry and discipleship. Faithful gospel ministers must learn to endure patiently the suffering that inevitably accompanies pastoral work. In the face of hardship, they must continue to preach right doctrine, avoid scandal, pursue God's glory, guard the dignity of their office, and rely on the power and protection of the Holy Spirit. It is especially important that pastors follow Paul's example by behaving in a manner consistent with what they teach. What was said of Origen must be said of Christian ministers in general: "As was his teaching, so was his life." Throughout their treatment of these verses, Protestant exegetes are careful to counter Catholic interpretations of key words and phrases. Paul's reference in verse 5 to "hunger" and "sleepless nights" has nothing to do with prescribed Lenten fasts and Catholic vigils. So, too, the Greek word *agnotēs* in 2 Corinthians 6:6 (rendered *castitas* in the Vulgate) does not mean sexual abstinence or chastity, but rather purity of life. Protestant interpreters also insist that the list of Christian virtues that Paul here enumerates are fundamentally different from those virtues praised by pagan philosophers: Christian virtues correspond with the Word of God, are stimulated and governed by the Holy Spirit, and are directed to the glory of God. Overall, the primary thrust of Protestant comments on this passage is that Christians will inevitably suffer indignities and hardships as they follow Christ. This was true of early church fathers such as Paul, Justin Martyr, Polycarp, and Athanasius; it continues to be true in the lives of contemporary reformers such as Jan Hus and Martin Luther. Even so, the harsh reality of Christian suffering finds its most poignant and powerful expression in the poems and prayers of Anabaptist authors.

Summary of Chapters 6–7. Tilemann Hesshus: Chapters 6–7 are exhortations to persevere in piety and zeal for good works, so that in every way we might avoid scandal, adorn the profession of the gospel with honorable character, exhibit true patience in every kind of affliction, and flee the fellowship of sinful people. Then, we should also avoid wickedness of spirit and flesh, and devote ourselves to holy works in the fear of the Lord. When Paul has concluded this most passionate appeal for zeal in good works, he testifies concerning his faithfulness in ministry and goodwill toward the Corinthians, and, in turn, he counsels them to embrace the apostle with true goodwill and to interpret his fatherly correction and admonitions in good spirit. He also recalls his troubles and battles, and how he received enormous comfort from the report of Titus, who explained to him the burning zeal of the Corinthians toward Paul. Next, he alleviates the pain that they are receiving from the apostle's displeasure. He shows them that pain and sadness of this sort—which the apostles' and pastors' reproofs are causing—are beneficial if they in fact achieve repentance. And Paul states and encourages goodwill by declaring respect for the ministry of the gospel. Finally, Paul mentions that he has felt great consolation from the fact that they have kindly welcomed Titus and have demonstrated their love for preachers of the Word. This is the order that Paul adopts in this third part of the epistle and in these two chapters.

Chapter 6 is in two parts: the first part is an exhortation to be zealous for good works, to avoid scandal diligently, and to be patient in all kinds of troubles. The second part is a reminder to avoid mixing in superstition and associating with the wicked. Explication of 2 Corinthians 6 and 7.[1]

A Ministry of Affliction and Affection. Giovanni Diodati: St. Paul declares how, according to his vocation, he exhorts the Corinthians to rightfully employ the grace of God. And he conducts his ministry so as to avoid all occasion for scandal—a ministry legitimated by the sufferings of various afflictions; in the exercise of all power and gifts of the Holy Spirit among various troubles and circumstances of life. And Paul insists that he labored among them with warm affection, and he exhorts them to reciprocate this affection and to withdraw from associating with unbelievers. Annotations on 2 Corinthians 6.[2]

6:3-5 *Patience amid Suffering*

Upholding the Dignity of Ministerial Office. John Calvin: [Paul] treats three things here: First, he teaches what are the virtues by which preachers of the gospel should be esteemed. Second, he demonstrates that he himself is endowed with those virtues. Third, he admonishes the Corinthians not to acknowledge as Christ's ministers those who conduct themselves otherwise, and he will put forward here his own example. His purpose is that he may acquire authority for himself and others like him, with a view for the glory of God and the good of the church—or to restore the church once it has collapsed. His second purpose is that he may call the Corinthians back from their unreasonable enthusiasm for the false apostles, which hindered them from making as much progress in the gospel as was necessary. Ministers cause offense when, by their own misconduct, they hinder the progress of the gospel in their hearers. Paul denies doing such a thing. For he declares that he diligently avoids staining his apostleship with any mark of disgrace.

For this is Satan's cunning, to seek some misconduct in ministers which might cause disrepute to flow upon the gospel. For when he has succeeded in bringing the ministry into contempt, all hope of benefit is lost. Therefore, those who desire usefully to serve Christ must strive with all their might to maintain the honor of the ministry. The way to do this is to be careful that they are worthy of honor. For there is nothing more ridiculous than to strive to vindicate your reputation among others while you bring reproach upon yourself by your scandalous and disgraceful life. Therefore, those persons alone will be honorable

[1]Hesshus, *Explicatio Secundae Epistolae Pauli ad Corinthios*, 154v-155v.

[2]Diodati, *La Seconde Epistre de l'Apostre S. Paul aux Corinthiens*, 147.

who allow nothing that is unworthy of a minister of Christ. Commentary on 2 Corinthians 6:3.[3]

Apparel Must Not Lead Others to Stumble. Pilgram Marpeck: Our apparel is justification and chastisement; it is the grace of our heavenly Father, who does not allow his own to appear in the shame of nakedness. Therefore it behooves us to keep our priestly garments unsullied, unspotted, and clean, so that they may not be taken from us, and we be found unclothed in the shame of nakedness. All belongs to our priestly office and priesthood, and to our hearts, the temples of God. Concerning the Lowliness of Christ.[4]

A Christian Should Give Offense to No One. Martin Luther: A Christian should be careful to give no offense to anyone so that the name of God shall not be blasphemed. It is a great thing to be a Christian—that is, a new person created after God, and a true image of God in whom God himself is clearly seen. Therefore, whatever a Christian does, be it good or evil (under the name of Christian), will be counted to the honor or dishonor of the name of God. Therefore, if you follow your lusts and obey the old person within you, you do nothing but give occasion to the blasphemer and cause the name of God to be blasphemed because of you.

In this respect, Christians should take the greatest care, even if they care for nothing else, to protect and honor the name of their dear God and Savior, Jesus Christ. Sermon on the Nineteenth Sunday After Trinity (1544).[5]

The Qualities of a True Minister. Wolfgang Musculus: Knowing this, Paul himself is not only careful not to be found blameworthy, but he also requires this purity of life and ministry of all ministers of Christ so that they might be beyond reproach, as he says in 1 Timothy 3 and Titus 1. But today, few ministers are concerned about these things. It is not enough that they preach badly. . . . The majority of them also drink, gamble, conduct business, break their word, charge usury, are corrupted with hatred for their brothers, long for and secure more lucrative benefices (as they call them) out of shameless ambition. These men do not even abstain from adultery. All of them care little for how people regard their ministries, because they have little concern for the glory of Christ and the salvation of the faithful. . . .

It is not enough for the minister of Christ to avoid putting up an obstacle in anyone's way so that his ministry won't be criticized, but it is also required that he ingratiate and commend himself to all people as a minister of God, not only in one or two situations, but in all circumstances. That is, he behaves in all situations in such a way that everyone might learn the grounds for recognizing and identifying a minister of God. The [true] minister seeks God's glory rather than his own glory in all things. Imbued with the Spirit of God, he faithfully sets before all people the will of God and he encourages everyone to this through both his Word and the diligence of his life. In so doing, as the minister gives an account of his salvation, the people receive the grace of God and employ it to their benefit. For this reason, after the apostle has said, "putting no obstacle in the way of anyone," he then added, "but we commend ourselves in every way as ministers of God." Commentary on 2 Corinthians 6:3.[6]

Four Duties of a Minister. David Chytraeus: The second [part of this epistle] concerns the duties of ministers of the gospel, concerning which Paul in this passage mentions four things. First, they are God's fellow workmen, through whose preaching and ministry God offers and imparts his grace and all his benefits, as he said at the end of the previous chapter. . . . Second, they must exhort by sound doctrine, and allure and

[3]CO 50:76-77 (CTS 40:248-49).
[4]CRR 2:446; citing 1 Cor 3:16-17.
[5]Luther, *Day by Day We Magnify You*, 362 (WA 22:321).
[6]Musculus, *Commentarius . . . in posteriorem epistolam Pauli ad Corinthios*, 197; citing 1 Tim 3:1-7; Titus 1:5-16.

incite their hearers earnestly to embrace and practice the righteousness of faith and of a good conscience. . . . Third, they must be careful lest they alienate people's minds from the gospel of grace and from the ministry by giving them cause for offense in their doctrine or conversation, as Paul says here: "Giving no offense in anything, so that no fault may be found in the ministry." Fourth, that they adorn the doctrine and ministry of the gospel with all kinds of virtue, and especially with patience under the cross and steadfastness in their profession. As Paul says in this passage, "Commending yourselves in all things as God's ministers by patience." Nazianzus's[†] statement is most insightful: "They that teach well and live amiss snatch away with one hand what they offer with the other." Postil on Invocavit Sunday.[7]

Different Kinds of Scandals. The English Annotations: "Giving no offense," that is, giving no just occasion for offense or scandal. For a scandal or offense is rightly distinguished into a scandal given (*scandalum datum*) and a scandal taken (*scandalum acceptum*). A scandal taken is when a person, out of a prejudicial opinion or ill affection, willfully misconstrues a speech or action of ours and makes the worst of it. In such a case a scandal is taken, but not at all given. The giving offense, which the apostle here forbids, is when either we speak so ambiguously or do anything so indiscrete and inappropriate that a good Christian, though otherwise well-affected toward us and our ministry, cannot but be scandalized. Annotations on 2 Corinthians 6:3.[8]

Qualities of the Spiritual Life. Jacques Lefèvre d'Étaples: Is not the spiritual life different from the life of the flesh; the heavenly life different from the earthly life; the divine life from the worldly life? The spiritual, heavenly, and divine life never harms anyone. By its very nature, that life is commended before God and other people, just as light by its very nature provides benefit to the sight of everyone. The spiritual life is very patient under pressure, strong when facing privation, content in difficult circumstances, controlled when wounded, sober when imprisoned, free from quarreling, victorious over suffering, humbled by vigils and fasts, unconquerable in purity, and perceptive in acquiring knowledge. It does not pursue vengeance; it seeks the benefit of the Holy Spirit rather than itself; it reflects an attitude of flourishing but without any pretense; it is diligent in speaking the truth; it is confident in the power of God rather than itself; it is consistent in times of prosperity and adversity; it never abandons the armor of the righteousness of God; and it bestows blessing on those who are dishonored and defamed. "Blessed are you," Jesus says, "when people curse you and persecute you and speak all kinds of evil against you falsely on my account." Commentary on 2 Corinthians 6:4-8.[9]

The Cost of Godliness. Martin Luther: You will say that it costs too much to be pious, as follows in the text. But Paul says that you should not allow all these (afflictions, oppressions, and ridicule) to overwhelm you. Whoever suffers under the tyranny of the pope or the Turk fares like a brute beast. In this context belong all those things we read about here. That tyranny is already stirring up tumult against Christians, and they must nevertheless adhere to holy Scripture and to the Word of truth. . . . We do not do the things of which they accuse us, but on our account they are behaving as described in Psalm 2. We must endure it, and if they attack us, we will have to endure that as well. "Fasting" here means passive fasting, as when people are forced to endure hunger in prison. We are vilified as slanderers and deceivers. . . . They say that we are "unknown," that is, rejected before

[7]Chytraeus, *Dispositio epistolarum*, 126-27 (*A Postil of Certeine Epistles*, 95-96); citing 2 Cor 5:20. [†]Gregory of Nazianzus was one of the Cappadocian fathers, who played a strategic role in defending the orthodox doctrine of the Trinity in the years leading up to the Council of Constantinople (381).
[8]Downame, ed., *English Annotations*, FF4v.

[9]Lefèvre, *Commentariorum in Epistolas Beati Pauli . . . Liber Tertius*, 136; citing Mt 5:11.

God, because God does not know us, any more than our heart does. The devil has sent these reproaches into the world; and yet before God we are "known" and "truthful." Before the world, the devil, and our own heart, it is just the opposite. Honor on the one hand; shame, on the other. We are reviled before the world, cursed and execrated before God and his own. We must, therefore, be well armed on both sides. We are "as though slain, and yet we live." Sermon on Invocavit Sunday.[10]

The Holy Spirit Helps Christians Endure Sufferings and Death. Martin Bucer: This Spirit therefore also produces in all such a firm hope in all the grace and help of God, and in eternal life. By means of and along with these attitudes of true faith, trust, and hope in God and in Christ our Lord, the Holy Spirit also produces in the children of God a deep love for God, a joyful confession and hallowing of his name in all their words and works and in the courageous acceptance of consequent sufferings and even of torments and death. A Brief Summary of Christian Doctrine.[11]

Living What We Teach. Cyriacus Spangenberg: We preachers must direct our lives according to our teaching. For whoever does not teach himself, but himself lives differently from what he teaches, will not be able to produce much fruit or usefulness, since the two aspects belong to a teacher. First, let him faithfully present the right, true and pure teaching to his listeners. Then let him also live according to his teaching himself, so that it can be said of him, as of Origen: "As was his teaching, so was also his life." For whoever teaches good but does evil, tears down more than he builds, makes worse more than he improves, and gives the preaching office a bad name. Twenty-Eighth Sermon.[12]

Patience in Suffering. Niels Hemmingsen: What Paul stated in general terms he now explains by way of enumerating some examples or particulars so as to place more clearly before our eyes with what virtues it is necessary for genuine preachers to be endowed. Now, in this list one must distinguish between two kinds of virtues which Paul requires in gospel ministers. For some of these virtues should be permanent, while some of these virtues are not required except under certain circumstances. Labors, vigilance, integrity, knowledge, gentleness, courage, love, truthful speech, the power of God—these virtues should be permanent. However, there are virtues other than those enumerated above which do not need to be permanent. For patience is required in the face of adversities; it is an unwavering mind every time one faces suffering, hunger, imprisonment, disease, and troubles.

Let us add an explanation of some of the words from this list. Patience (*hypomonē*) is when we endure difficult circumstances with an unwavering mind and do not succumb to its weight. The source for this is spiritual regeneration, faith, knowledge of God's command, and the promise of liberation. "Blessed are those who suffer trials, since the one who is tested will receive the crown of life which God has promised to those devoted to him." This happens whether the trials oppose the body or mind and in the various ways they trouble it—many examples of which Paul recites here, such as suffering of body, poverty, want, beatings, imprisonment, troubles, exiles. Whence our apostle says, "suffering produces patience, patience character, character hope, and hope does not confound us"; that is, those who hope are not disappointed. The goal of this is that, first, we might display obedience to God in keeping with the first commandment. And second, that by maintaining our confession, we might be a good example for other people, so that they also might present themselves invincible in the face of various hardships. The difference between Christian patience and philosophical patience is drawn from the causes and the goals. Commentary on 2 Corinthians 6:4.[13]

---

[10]LW 58:8-9* (WA 47:667-68); citing Ps 2:2.

[11]CPMB 80.

[12]C. Spangenberg, *Die ander Epistel Pauli an die Corinthier*, 116.

[13]Hemmingsen, *Commentaria in Omnes Epistolas Apostolorum*, 277; citing Jas 1:12; Rom 5:3-5.

The Ways Paul's Patience Was Tested. Andreas Hyperius: Paul enumerates a heap of various kinds of trouble which tested his patience. "In afflictions," that is, when the mind is distressed and the body afflicted with pressure and they are troubled. "In hardships," namely, when grave dangers attack us or when some great need crushes us. "In distresses." Troubles of this sort are from starvation, which is a kind of misfortune. "In beatings"—for the apostle was beaten three times, as he mentions in chapter 11 below. And in Acts 16, he received many beatings in Philippi. "In imprisonment." They were often thrown into prison, as in Philippi. "In riots." Often riots were also stirred up by their enemies so that they might blame the apostles for them, just as Demetrius the silversmith, in Acts 17, provoked the crowd at Ephesus. . . . "In labors." Namely, from providing for one's daily sustenance with one's hands; also, from traveling about, and other similar things. See Acts 20; 1 Thessalonians 2; 2 Thessalonians 3. "In vigils." As Paul testifies elsewhere, he often experienced sleepless nights, never from manual labor, but sometimes from teaching, writing, and praying. Paul was praying at night in the Philippian jail, and in Acts 20, he was disputing in the middle of the night. "In hunger." Paul was frequently weakening his flesh with hunger. Now fasting is useful—as are vigils and labors—for curbing the pride of the flesh and the powerful attack of desire. In all these things enumerated hitherto, the apostle has demonstrated his exceptional endurance. Commentary on 2 Corinthians 6:4-5.[14]

Paul Endured Nine Kinds of Evils. David Dickson: [Paul] recites diverse kinds of virtues, with which his ministry is adorned, but namely, he mentions the patience with which he endured nine kinds of evils, in all of which, without murmuring, he patiently executed the offices of his ministry. For he strongly endured the troubles of his journeys with deprivation and dangers, the snares of his persecutors, prison, and tumults stirred up against him, and in preaching, his labor, watchings, and fastings. Nor did he wax faint in the work of the Lord. Exposition of 2 Corinthians 6:4-5.[15]

Financial Hardship. Wolfgang Musculus: The Greek term for "in hardships" is *en anankais*. Paul means by this the dearth of necessary things, which he addresses below in chapter 11. . . . We see today that many ministers of Christ struggle against poverty in a very unworthy manner when they fastidiously fatten their idle bellies in the churches. This is an ancient evil, to which the people of God, and even the prophets of God in the Old Testament, were susceptible, as can be seen from 2 Kings 4. Commentary on 2 Corinthians 6:4.[16]

Paul's Courage in the Face of Riots. John Calvin: The greater the gentleness and mildness of Paul's disposition, the greater was the excellence he displayed in calmly enduring riots. And he assumes praise to himself for it, for while he regarded riots with abhorrence, he nevertheless faced them bravely. And Paul should not be praised simply because he was undisturbed by riots (since this is common among all riotous persons), but because he was not fearful of riots that had been stirred up through the fault of others. And truly, two things are required of ministers of the gospel: that to the best of their ability they should be zealous to maintain the peace, and yet, on the other hand, continue undaunted in the midst of public violence, so as not to turn aside from the right course, even if heaven and earth should be upended. Commentary on 2 Corinthians 6:5.[17]

Afflictions, Hardship, and Other Difficulties. Tilemann Hesshus: Paul lists various kinds of trouble and miseries, so as to encourage us to endure patiently difficulties of

[14]Hyperius, *Commentarii . . . in Epistolam D. Pauli ad Romanos, et Utramque ad Corinthios*, 378-79.

[15]Dickson, *An Exposition of All St. Paul's Epistles*, 81-82*.

[16]Musculus, *Commentarius . . . in posteriorem epistolam Pauli ad Corinthios*, 198.

[17]CO 50:77-78 (CTS 40:250).

various sorts for the sake of Christ. The histories of Paul, [Justin] Martyr, Polycarp, Ignatius [of Antioch], Athanasius, and related accounts provide examples of various sufferings.†

"In labors and sleepless nights." Since the strength of the body is often exhausted by labors and sleeplessness, this trial must also be endured with patience. It is a great and difficult work to teach the people about God, denounce their sins, and explain the sacred Scripture. And battles and dangers often steal away sleep. So, too, pastors must often work with their hands so that they might make a living—just as Paul provided for himself the necessities of life with his hands. Our minds must remain determined in such things lest we grow faint.

"In hunger." There is need not only for temperance but also fasting so as both to control the flesh and stir the heart to ardent prayers. There is no need to impose fasts on impoverished pastors who are often lacking dry bread, if indeed hunger is often apparent in their eyes. It is clear that patience is needed in fasts of this sort. Explication of 2 Corinthians 6:5.[18]

Two Types of Vigils. Wolfgang Musculus: There are two types of vigils: the first are those employed as a good work; the second are those employed for teaching. An example of the second type of vigil is seen in Acts 20, where it is recalled how Paul devoted the entire night until daybreak teaching and exhorting the believers of Troas in the work of the Lord. . . .

It is highly unlikely that what Paul did at Troas was his usual custom, since he assembled the company of believers at night because assemblies convened during the day would have been in grave danger. It was for this reason that the practice of vigils was begun among the first Christians during times of persecution. Afterward, bishops retained the practice also during times of peace, and they appointed vigils for ordinary days, as if it was not safe to gather the church in the daytime. In the end, nothing remained of vigils except an empty name. Commentary on 2 Corinthians 6:5.[19]

Fasting That Pleases God. Guillaume Farel: The fasting which our Lord demands is to break all the ties with evil and with that with which we treat our neighbor cruelly; it is to feed those who are hungry, to house those without a home, to clothe the naked; it is to have pity on those who are like us and share the same flesh as us—the same as all the needy.

This fasting is pleasing to God and very helpful for many, actually for all. But the other type of fasting is a bodily exercise and helps only a few in comparison with the first. For the second tries to bring the flesh into servitude; it tries to mortify the flesh by taking away foods. This fasting is not in the power of any person to arrange or command of another person; those who fast can alone judge whether they have the Spirit of God. They alone can judge when and how they are to afflict their bodies, not by choice and distinction neither of foods, nor of fixed times to eat, which is useful. They should not afflict nature so much they cannot serve their neighbors. The father and mother who stay from food to the point where they are not able to provide food normally for their children do not fast, but kill their children. . . . For this reason, our Lord did not give a law or time of fasting but commanded us to live soberly in order to serve him and to help our neighbor without any distinction of foods. A Summary and Brief Exposition.[20]

Lenten Fasts Not Required. David Chytraeus: For this purpose, our ancestors appointed this epistle to be read at the beginning of Lent, because mention is made in it of the fasting, vigils, hardships, and other afflictions in

[18]Hesshus, *Explicatio Secundae Epistolae Pauli ad Corinthios*, 160v-161r. †Justin Martyr (c. 100–c. 165), Polycarp (c. 69–c. 155), and Ignatius of Antioch (d. c. 110) were all martyred for their faith, while Athanasius (c. 293–373) was exiled from Alexandria five times.

[19]Musculus, *Commentarius . . . in posteriorem epistolam Pauli ad Corinthios*, 200.

[20]Zuidema and Van Raalte, eds., *Early French Reform*, 141*.

which the godly show forth the true and earnest repentance of a sorrowful heart, and tame and subdue their flesh. And although the primitive church did not prescribe forms or laws to others regarding meat and fasting, nevertheless it was expected that during these forty days people should be more attentive to living soberly and abstain from lawful pleasures so that their minds might be better prepared and ardent in considering God's wonderful purpose concerning the passion and death of the Son of God, our Lord Jesus Christ, and also to true repentance and earnest prayer. Later on, those who were defiled with outward offenses and excommunicated—before they were absolved—would be chastised and tested with various ceremonies during Lent to determine whether they had truly repented and amended their hearts. . . . So, too, it happened that catechumens (who it appears were baptized only on Easter day and Pentecost until the time of Charlemagne), after they had given their names, were tested during the Lenten season and instructed in the true doctrine of Christ; and they were purged with fasting and other ceremonies, so that they might more worthily and reverently come to the sacrament of baptism at Easter.

Some write that fasting forty days before Easter was first established by Telesphorus who presided over the church of Rome around 130 years after Christ. But it is clear from Irenaeus[†] (who lived about 200 years after Christ's birth) that in his day people were still completely free in the matter of fasting. . .

We entreat and argue concerning the day fasts (if I may call it that), namely, when people abstain from all meat and drink, sometimes for a day or several days, or an entire day [that is, twenty-four hours], or until Vespers, that this manner of fasting was practiced even in the New Testament, but in such a way that no one prescribed the particular day or appointed which kind of meat should be abstained from. The whole matter was left free to everyone's conscience and the exigencies of the time. But afterward, there came superstitious and tyrannical laws concerning the eating of meat and fast days, and other ungodly opinions, which were condemned by the Word of God. POSTIL ON THE FIRST SUNDAY OF LENT.[21]

PAUL'S HUNGER. WOLFGANG MUSCULUS: The Greek term for "in hunger" is *en nēsteiais*. We admit that the word *nēsteiai* is frequently used for a religious fast, undertaken voluntarily. But in the story of Paul's shipwreck in Acts 27, the word is also employed for hunger endured out of necessity. . . .

Now as far as this present passage is concerned, I know that some people interpret this "hunger" as a voluntary fast, others as a fast out of necessity, and others take it in both senses. For me, it seems more correct to interpret it as hunger experienced out of necessity, which the apostle frequently endured, willingly and patiently, as a species of the sufferings of Christ. Thus, it seems right to conclude that it is beyond the purpose and intention of the apostle here to lend support to voluntary fasts, undertaken voluntarily. COMMENTARY ON 2 CORINTHIANS 6:5.[22]

6:6-10 *Trial-Tested Character*

GODLY VIRTUES. CARDINAL CAJETAN: "In purity." Understand here temperance, especially in the matter of delightful things, namely, things we adore. "In knowledge" of holy things—in which wisdom is also comprised. "In steadfastness." Understand here the virtue of hope for future eternal blessedness, anticipated over a long time. "In pleasantness," or, as some prefer, "in kindness"—each one of these activities is to be praised. And it is necessary for ministers of the new covenant to be both kind (that is, fruitful in good deeds) . . . and pleasant toward people of different groups, different ages, different sexes, different customs . . .

[21]Chytraeus, *Dispositio epistolarum*, 130-32 (*A Postil of Certeine Epistles*, 98-99, 100-101). [†]Irenaeus's comments regarding fasting in the church are found in Eusebius's *Ecclesiastical History* 5.24.12; see *The Ecclesiastical History of Eusebius*, LCL 153:509-11.

[22]Musculus, *Commentarius . . . in posteriorem epistolam Pauli ad Corinthios*, 200.

accommodating themselves to others so that they might do good to all. "In the Holy Spirit"—not according to the spirit of human reason or human understanding, but we behave according to the Holy Spirit's judgment and are instinctively directed to this end. "In genuine love." Understand here the infallible witness—indeed, the inseparable partner—of the Holy Spirit. This love is not feigned externally but is truly internal. Commentary on 2 Corinthians 6:6.[23]

Godly Character in the Face of Suffering. Andreas Hyperius: "In purity" (*en agnotēti*) which is soundness and integrity both in speech and action; and also in teaching, which Paul has boasted about elsewhere. Some people also construe it to mean purity of body or chastity, which makes us commendable to others. "In knowledge," that is, in that wisdom and prudential learning by which we guide all our actions so that we are not seen to behave rashly or foolishly. Some people interpret this as knowledge of God, without which nothing is ever done rightly. "In gentleness of mind." The Greek word *makrothymia* means steadfastness. "In kindness," that is, goodness, politeness, modesty, and radiant behavior. "In the Holy Spirit," that is, with a spirit that is not insincere or deceitful, so that one can be perceived to behave earnestly and from the heart not only according to common opinion, but also at the impulse of the Holy Spirit. "In genuine love." Hypocrites might know how to display extraordinary love in public, but it does not deserve to be called love. Commentary on 2 Corinthians 6:6.[24]

Christian Knowledge. Tilemann Hesshus: By the term "in knowledge," Paul understands that prudence which must always be applied in life and ministry lest, through our lack of wisdom, we attract to ourselves greater dangers, disturb the church with unnecessary battles, and overlook serious errors. [This prudence is necessary] so that we might remember to have no confidence in human beings, so that we might ignore various injuries, and so that we might avoid imminent dangers as much as is possible in good conscience without obscuring the truth. Explication of 2 Corinthians 6:6.[25]

Six Virtues That Characterized Paul's Patience. David Dickson: [Paul] adds six virtues of his patience, of which the first is his freedom from the pollutions of the world, while he interacted with the people of the world. Second, his discretion in handling those who listened to him. Third, his forbearance in provocations. Fourth, his gentleness in dealing with more difficult things. Fifth, his spiritual disposition in all things. Sixth, his sincere love toward all. Exposition of 2 Corinthians 6:6.[26]

All Christian Virtues Are Practiced "in the Spirit." Tilemann Hesshus: Paul wants to distinguish between the service of godly people and the virtues of the pagans. For excellent virtues such as temperance, prudence, gentleness, and kindness are discovered among the pagans, but they originate only from reason and human free will. And so, they are of the flesh, not of the Spirit; they are the letter, not life; indeed, they are mere shadows of virtues. Now, Paul calls for spiritual obedience, which has been aroused by the Spirit of God and is governed by the light of the Spirit, since it coincides with the Word of God, it is displayed in the knowledge and faithfulness of a mediator, and it is directed toward the glory of God and the salvation of the church. And so he adds, "in the Holy Spirit." The godly minister shows that he is not led by his affections nor by the wisdom of the flesh; rather he governs himself by the Holy Spirit. Explication of 2 Corinthians 6:6.[27]

[23]Cajetan, *In Posteriorem Pauli Epistolam ad Corinthios Commentarii*, 174.
[24]Hyperius, *Commentarii . . . in Epistolam D. Pauli ad Romanos, et Utramque ad Corinthios*, 379.
[25]Hesshus, *Explicatio Secundae Epistolae Pauli ad Corinthios*, 161r-v.
[26]Dickson, *An Exposition of All St. Paul's Epistles*, 82*.
[27]Hesshus, *Explicatio Secundae Epistolae Pauli ad Corinthios*, 162r.

Christian Purity Does Not Demand Celibacy. Wolfgang Musculus: The Greek for "in purity" is *en agnotāti*. The Vulgate translates it "in chastity." Paul is speaking about that purity of life that is contrasted with the impurity of lewdness and prostitution. He is not speaking about virginity or the continence of widowhood but about the purity of those who can, and should, remain in a state of marriage. When he urges his friend Timothy that he should be a model for believers in speech, in conduct, in love, in spirit, in faith, *en agneia*, that is, *in purity*, this does not mean that Timothy, by his example, should provoke everyone to virgin-like chastity, but that he should model for everyone, even for married people, a pure life free from all of the filth of prostitution and lust.

It is well-known that during the Council of Nicaea, when the bishops were wishing to introduce into the churches a new rule that would have prohibited ministers from conjugal intercourse . . . Paphnutius[†] testified eloquently that chastity included sexual intercourse of a man with his lawful wife. And on this point, the apostle also says not only that marriage should be held in honor by everyone but also that the marriage bed should remain undefiled. Commentary on 2 Corinthians 6:6.[28]

The Quality of Purity. John Trapp: "By pureness," Paul means lamb-like simplicity or sincerity. Religion loves to lie clean, a person once said. . . . No gold or precious stone is so pure as the prudent mind of a pious person, said the divine Plato. Commentary on 2 Corinthians 6:6.[29]

What Genuine Love Looks Like. Tilemann Hesshus: Paul . . . demonstrates the foundation of all true virtues and the purpose and sure standard of all action. Sincere love for neighbor is like a mother who provides godly services of every kind. Genuine love like this is absent when it is feigned, or when other good works completely vanish or degenerate into pretense. Love is feigned when people announce their duties with cheerful words . . . or discharge certain duties but do so compelled by fear or by the hope of reward or promotion. Unless they have some other motivation and acquire something advantageous to them, they will not do it. Love of this sort is not sincere and has not originated from the Holy Spirit. Genuine love considers nothing except the commandment of God and the needs of one's neighbor. It performs all things with a willing and eager heart and does good and loves no matter the time. It does not change its mind in the face of various circumstances; it does not strive for wealth or rewards. Rather, it loves and does good in the Spirit for the sake of God and awaits a reward from God. Explication of 2 Corinthians 6:6.[30]

The Virtues with Which Paul Discharged His Duty. David Dickson: [Paul] rehearses the virtues with which he discharged his duty. (1) He preached nothing besides the truth of God. (2) He demonstrated the power of the Spirit in his speech. (3) He contended against all his enemies with spiritual weapons, that is, with lawful means. Whether in prosperity, or in adversity, and with every change and vicissitude of things, he remained constant, lest he should either by enticements, or by terror, turn from the right way. Exposition of 2 Corinthians 6:7.[31]

Godly Character in the Face of Suffering. Andreas Hyperius: "In truthful speech," that is, with truthful conversation (which is a Hebraism) worthy of belief, without any deceit or lies. "In the power of God." The Greek word *dynamis* can be properly understood as the faculty of acting in any situation with authority and sovereign power in such a way that people can

[28]Musculus, *Commentarius . . . in posteriorem epistolam Pauli ad Corinthios*, 200-201; citing 1 Tim 4:12; Heb 13:4. [†]The account of Bishop Paphnutius at Nicaea is found in Socrates, *Ecclesiastical History* 1.11. See NPNF^2 2:18.

[29]Trapp, *A Commentary or Exposition*, 718*.

[30]Hesshus, *Explicatio Secundae Apostolae Pauli ad Corinthios*, 162v.

[31]Dickson, *An Exposition of All St. Paul's Epistles*, 82*.

recognize that God is presently at work and will bless with success. In this way, we read about certain [biblical figures] that God was with them in all that they did. And I think this interpretation of the passage is more correct than if we understand it to mean the power to perform miracles, since it appears that the apostle wants all these qualities to refer primarily to that what pertains to the excellence of lifestyle which can be shared by all people and are usually recommended to all people for imitation. Commentary on 2 Corinthians 6:7.[32]

Truthful Speech and God's Power. Tilemann Hesshus: "In truthful speech." This refers not only to the preaching of the gospel, but to every word spoken in the whole of life. All conversations should be true, frank, appropriate, transparent, and free from pretense, from lying, from confusion, from deception, from plotting, from melodrama, from trickery, from illusions. . . . "In the power of God." We do not behave in ministry with confidence in our individual powers, but we know that our strength comes from God, and we run to him to furnish strength. Even when we are troubled at the sight of our weakness, we should depend on him and look for strength from him. Human power is not adequate for enduring the many intense battles which a godly minister of the gospel encounters. But God supplies strength through the Holy Spirit. Paul strengthens himself in God's power when, after having been stoned at Lystra and dragged out of the city as if he were dead, the following day, brokenhearted, he teaches the gospel in Derbe and [later] he is redirected to Lystra to comfort the brothers. Explication of 2 Corinthians 6:7.[33]

Girded with the Power of God. Huldrych Zwingli: This word *dynamis* should be understood as either the miracles which God performed through Paul, or in the sense one finds above in his previous letter: "I never quit, I am strong in the power of God, and I perform strenuously my duty." The phrase "with weapons" is a metaphor drawn from a certain strong and vigorous soldier who does not give up but fights strongly and strenuously. "I fight," Paul says, "but not with weapons of the flesh, but with weapons of the spirit with which I am surrounded and guarded." Annotations on 2 Corinthians 6:7.[34]

Weapons of Righteousness. John Trapp: Against both the allurements and terrors of this world. "The Romanists have despised me, both with their applause and with their ragings," Luther stated when the pope once enticed him, and another time threatened him. When he was offered to be made a cardinal if he would be quiet, Luther replied: "No, not even if I would be made pope." When he was told that he would never find favor with the Roman Church, he said, "What will they do? Will they kill me? But can they raise me to life again, that they may kill me again? Can they kill me a second time?" Commentary on 2 Corinthians 6:7.[35]

The Christian's Warfare. Cyriacus Spangenberg: Here he calls such things weapons and armor, for God's servants must always be dressed for war, battle, and strife, since their enemy the devil is fighting against them without respite, without ceasing, and would gladly drive them from the advantage of the faith and its fruits and lead them into all unrighteousness, shame, and vice. Therefore, he attacks them in all areas. If one does not succeed, he tries the other. If he cannot make you an adulterer, he tries to see whether he can brew greed in you. If he does not succeed in that, he breathes in haughtiness and confidence in your own thinking. If that won't work, he strives to move you to anger and hatred of your neighbor. And if you defend yourself there, he has another hundred ways to get you to

[32]Hyperius, *Commentarii . . . in Epistolam D. Pauli ad Romanos, et Utramque ad Corinthios*, 379.
[33]Hesshus, *Explicatio Secundae Epistolae Pauli ad Corinthios*, 163r; citing Acts 14:19-20; 16:1-5.
[34]Zwingli, *Annotatiunculae . . . ex ore Zvinglij*, 175. Zwingli may have in mind passages such as 1 Cor 16:13.
[35]Trapp, *A Commentary or Exposition*, 718*.

irritate your neighbor either through drunkenness, or laziness, or swearing, or other incidental sins. Therefore, we must train, prove, and defend ourselves with weapons of righteousness, on the right and on the left. We must have armor on both sides. THIRTIETH SERMON.[36]

THE CHRISTIAN MINISTER'S ARMOR. NIELS HEMMINGSEN: Since sincere ministers of God have been stationed at the front of the battle line against the devil, who attempts to attack them from every side, Paul reminds them of their armor on the right and the left. That is, he wants them to be armed with the righteousness of a good conscience on the right and left so that they might be able to endure the enemy's assaults. The apostle discusses in greater detail the armor of the Christian soldier in Ephesians 6 and 1 Thessalonians 5. COMMENTARY ON 2 CORINTHIANS 6:7.[37]

THE RIGHT HAND AND THE LEFT. THE ENGLISH ANNOTATIONS: Some interpreters take the apostle's meaning to be that he himself was, and every good Christian ought to be . . . people who could use both hands alike, and lay about them, as if both were right hands. But there is no need for this explanation. For all soldiers, though they do not fight with both hands alike, yet they make use of both of them, and they have weapons and armor on both. But the greater doubt is, what does the apostle mean by the right hand and the left? The Greek commentators answer that by the right hand Paul understands honor and estimation among men and women; and by the left hand, the injuries, persecutions, and disgraces. Hence [in this view], Paul's meaning is that they are armed with righteousness or uprightness in both, in such a way that Satan cannot wound them on either side, since they are neither puffed up with honor, abundance, and prosperity, nor cast down by penury and adversity. It may be that the apostle in the metaphor of the right and left hand alludes to the words of the wise man in Proverbs 3, who speaks of blessings on the right hand and on the left. As God gives us blessings with both hands, so Christ gives us armor for both hands to defend us from Satan, the flesh, and the world, who attack us on all sides. ANNOTATIONS ON 2 CORINTHIANS 6:7.[38]

HONOR AND DISHONOR. HULDRYCH ZWINGLI: I know that a good many people view me badly, but I continue to persevere, caring not at all whether they praise me or heckle me. For I know that all those things work for the glory of God and my humiliation. ANNOTATIONS ON 2 CORINTHIANS 6:8.[39]

THE VARIOUS WAYS SATAN TEMPTS US. TILEMANN HESSHUS: Paul warns of the various ways that Satan tempts us. Sometimes he titillates pastors with honors, popular acclaim, praises, and happy success, and in this way attempts to render them contemptuous. Thus, when Nestorius† was elevated to the episcopal office of Constantinople, he was filled with stubborn pride. [So, too,] Arius‡ the lector proudly expelled the bishop of Alexandria by packing the council of bishops. But at other times, Satan brings together reproaches, insults, and calumnies so as to hurl teachers of the church completely into despair. The whole of church history teaches that Satan is in the habit of attacking faithful ministers by these kinds of reproaches. The orator Tertullus openly accused the apostle Paul of stirring up riots throughout the whole world. Athanasius was accused by the Arians‡ of adultery, murder, and inciting tyranny. Augustine was accused by the Donatists§ of distributing love potions and adultery. The lust for jeering and deceit is infinite in the world. But it is not possible for everyone to bear and put up with those abuses, for malicious accusations disturb wise men and women and crush the strength of their heart. The prophet Jeremiah was so disturbed by the great amount of jeering and false accusations that he wanted to

[36]C. Spangenberg, *Die ander Epistel Pauli an die Corinthier*, 121r.
[37]Hemmingsen, *Commentaria in Omnes Epistolas Apostolorum*, 278; citing Eph 6:10-20; 1 Thess 5:8.
[38]Downame, ed., *English Annotations*, FF4v*; citing Prov 3:16.
[39]Zwingli, *Annotatiunculae . . . ex ore Zvinglij*, 176.

abandon his teaching duties, but God restored him to the right path. And so, the mind must be strengthened in true patience. It must condemn the wicked judgments of the whole world; look to God alone for judgment and rewards; and rejoice in purity of conscience. Liars do not deceive forever. The shadows will finally give way to the light. Explication of 2 Corinthians 6:8.[40]

Receiving Praise and Enduring Insults. Wolfgang Musculus: Now after having mentioned honor and dishonor, Paul adds the words "insults and praise." For he spoke of honor and dishonor as general categories, and praise and insults as specific examples. Praise is a specific kind of honor, and an insult is a specific kind of dishonor. Thus the apostle shows that the same thing happened to him that happened to the Lord Christ, who was himself praised by some people and criticized by others. For some people were saying about him, "He is a good man," while others, on the other hand, were saying, "He is not a good man, but he seduces the crowds." And this is the common lot of all true ministers of Christ, that even as they are praised by good people, they are attacked and harshly criticized by wicked people with countless insults. For this reason, ministers must consider the fact that the disciple is not above his master, and see to it that they, along with the apostle, take up the weapons of righteousness, on both their left and right, to defend themselves from every attack, so that in both instances they might be declared true ministers of Christ. Commentary on 2 Corinthians 6:8.[41]

Bad Reports Often Result from Well-Doing. John Trapp: A martyr[†] once said, "It is written on the door of heaven, 'Do well and endure evil.'" A bad report is the ordinary reward of well doing—which caused Luther to wax proud even when he was reproached: "I am proud because I see that my reputation is growing all the worse." Jerome also wrote to Augustine: "This is my glory, that none of the heretics can give me a good word or look."[‡] It was a divine saying of Seneca: "No one sets a better rate on virtue than the one who loses a good name to keep a good conscience." Commentary on 2 Corinthians 6:8.[42]

Those the World Condemns the Spirit Approves. Tilemann Hesshus: So that we might endure and overcome jeers and malicious charges with a much stronger mind, Paul shows how different and contrary are the judgments of the world and of the Spirit. The world very wickedly and stubbornly condemns apostles and faithful bishops and pastors, for it considers them to be imposters, sons of the earth, obscure and unimportant people, fools, seditious and evil, or rather, as good as dead—for whom there was no reason in the world. Thus, the Pharisees were condemning the Christ; the pagans were condemning Polycarp and the other martyrs; the Arians were condemning Athanasius; the Nestorians were condemning Cyril; the Council of Constance was condemning Jan Hus; the Roman pope, bishops, monks, and all the universities were condemning Luther. And surely it is hard to be condemned by the judgment of the entire world, not only by the masses and the unlearned, but by priests, princes, and the most powerful part of the whole human race. But Paul commands us to be resolute and strong of spirit, since the Spirit of God judges in a different way. He does not consider us to be imposters, but witnesses of the truth. We are his friends and well-known to him. We live in him and

[40]Hesshus, *Explicatio Secundae Epistolae Pauli ad Corinthios*, 164r-v; citing Acts 24:1-8; Jer 20:7-8. [†]Nestorius, the patriarch of Constantinople, was condemned and deposed by the Council of Ephesus (431) under suspicion of teaching that there were two separate persons in the incarnate Christ. [‡]The North African priest Arius was condemned by the Council of Nicaea (325) for denying that the Son of God was coeternal and coessential with the Father. [§]Donatism was a rigorist Christian sect, then a schismatic movement in North Africa, that rejected the authority of the orthodox Catholic Church, teaching that the efficacy of the sacraments depended on the moral quality of the priest or bishop who performed them.

[41]Musculus, *Commentarius . . . in posteriorem epistolam Pauli ad Corinthios*, 204; citing Jn 7:12.

[42]Trapp, *A Commentary or Exposition*, 718*. [†]See John Foxe, *Foxe's Book of Martyrs, or The Acts and Monuments of the Christian Church* (Philadelphia: James B. Smith, 1860), fol. 1491, tome 1, oper. Lat. p. 31. [‡]Jerome, *Letter* 141, PL 22:1179-80.

serve the church with great fruitfulness. Our battles, labors, and troubles are known to him and pleasing to him; indeed, we are helped by God's Spirit. And he promises us an abundant reward in heaven. Therefore, we are not at all moved by the wicked judgment of the world. Explication of 2 Corinthians 6:8.[43]

The Trials of Honor and Disgrace. Cyriacus Spangenberg: Every servant of God should also do thus: if they are held in all esteem and honor, they shall not think too highly of themselves because of it, but say with David, "Not to us, O Lord, not to us, but to your name give honor, because of your grace and truth." Again, if one is dishonored, mistreated, and maligned by the godless, they shall not therefore become pusillanimous or impatient, nor cease nor be silent, nor abandon their office, but continue steadily, through honor and disgrace. And this is no small trial.

It is difficult and rare for someone not to think too highly of themselves because of honor bestowed. Flesh and blood do not easily accept that they should not become proud when they feel honor, and experience tells us that many people have allowed honor to deceive them and have turned away from the truth and righteousness, or at least silenced the same, and also often in religious matters, for the sake of temporal honor, have accepted something in order to please other people, or conceded, or changed.

Again, it is also difficult to put up with disgrace and dishonor, and nothing on earth hurts an honor-loving spirit as much as disgrace, especially when one comes on it through innocent things. Thirtieth Sermon.[44]

Treated as Imposters. The English Annotations: Not so in fact, but [Christians] are reputed as deceivers or adduced as such, as Christ himself was. For this, as St. Cyprian noted, has been the practice of the devil in all ages, that by his agents to cast false and foul aspersions upon the most sincere and faithful servants of Christ.[†] Annotations on 2 Corinthians 6:8.[45]

A Song for Christian Sufferers. Ursula Hellrigel:

Everlasting Father in heaven,
I call on you so ardently,
Do not let me turn from you.
Keep me in your truth
Until my final end.

O God, guard my heart and mouth,
Lord watch over me at all times,
Let nothing separate me from you,
Be it affliction, anxiety, or need,
Keep me pure in joy.

My everlasting Lord and Father,
Show and teach me,
Poor unworthy child that I am,
So that I heed your path and way.
In this lies my desire,

To walk through your power into death,
Through sorrow, torture, fear, and want.
Sustain me in this,
O God, so that I nevermore
Be separated from your love.

Many travel along this road,
The cup of suffering lies there,
And also many untrue teachings
Which try to turn us away
From Christ our Lord.

To you I raise up my soul, Lord,
I depend on you in misfortune.
Do not let me come to harm,

[43]Hesshus, *Explicatio Secundae Epistolae Pauli ad Corinthios*, 164v-165r. Polycarp of Smyrna (69-155) was martyred for his Christian faith. Athanasius of Alexandria (c. 295-373) was persecuted by the Arians for affirming the deity of the Son of God. Cyril of Alexandria (376-444) was condemned by Nestorius (c. 386-c. 450) for affirming Mary as *Theotokos*. Jan Hus (c. 1372-1415) was condemned and executed at the Council of Constance (1415) for his opposition to Roman Catholic teachings and demands for ecclesial reform.

[44]C. Spangenberg, *Die ander Epistel Pauli an die Corinthier*, 122r; citing Ps 115:1.

[45]Downame, ed., English Annotations, FF4v*; citing Mt 27:63.
[†]See Cyprian's letter to Cornelius, ANF 5:338-48.

That my enemy not stand over me
On this earth.

They have imprisoned me.
I wait, O God, with all my heart,
With very great longing,
When finally you will awake
And set your prisoners free.

O God, Father, make us like
The five virgins of your kingdom,
Who were prudently careful
To wait for the bridegroom,
With his chosen flock.

Eternal king of heaven,
Feed us and quench our thirst
In a spiritual way
With your food of truth
Which never perishes.

If you withhold your food from us
Everything is lost and useless.
Without you we bring forth nothing.
Through grace we trust in you,
It will not fail us.

I do not doubt God's power.
His judgments all are true.
He will not abandon anyone
Who stands firm in the faith,
And stays on the true paths.

Be comforted, you Christians, and rejoice,
Through Jesus Christ forevermore,
Who give us love and faith.
God comforts us through his holy Word,
On that we should rely.

I entrust myself to God and his church.
May he be my protector today,
For the sake of his name.
May this come to pass, Father mine,
Through Jesus Christ, Amen.

Epitome.[46]

[46]CRR 10:134-35.

A Prayer for Christian Sufferers.
Menno Simons:

A sad and doleful care,
This news, dear brother, share,
Which God hath now for me prepared.
A chastening he applies,
My inmost heart he tries,
My flesh in sore affliction lies.

His godly wisdom sure
That ever shall endure,
Knows perfectly
That now I lie

In anguish sore.
Help, Lord, I thee implore
That I by grace once more,
After this grievous blow
May comfort know!

The prophet has averred
With clear and clarion word
That grief is mortal man's reward;
His life ebbs fast away
Till death him low doth lay
With suffering, all the weary way.

Like to a fading flower
So is his fame and power,
Like shade of night
Man takes his flight,

Continues not
In state or constant lot
As God himself hath taught;
Now I detect that he
Deals so with me. . . .

Ah, faithful Father, Lord,
My flesh has strength no more,
This earthly house thou breakest sort.
The vile world hates me quite,
For this thy witness bright;
Thy cross I bear, with grief not light.

And yet—adversity!
Thy hand thou lay'st on me,
And presses so
My flesh lays low!

Yet rest I me
Upon thy promise free
Which ever sure shall be;
And praise thy majesty
In all eternity!

Ah, Father, God, and Lord,
Incline thy face once more
In this disease and sickness sore;
Give patience, strength, in grace
The brightness of thy face,
Mid sorrows that come on apace!

That I may constant be,
Whate'er thy way with me;
And not the last,
My soul hold fast!

Yes, Father, kind,
Preserve in pious mind
Thy sons, who sadness find,
In faith and doctrine whole,
So prays my soul!

I beg my brethren all,
Who've heard the Master's call,
My grief and pain now to recall,
And then, before God's eyes
Lay pleasant sacrifice;
Let pleasing prayer as incense rise;

That I may then again,
Delivered from this pain,
Behold thy grace,
Resume my place,

Serve Christ always,
Right well the livelong day,
This in my song I pray
With brethren everywhere,
In Word-borne prayer.

Prayer in the Hour of Affliction.[47]

The False Apostles Wrongly Accused Paul of Being Unknown. Wolfgang Musculus: [The false apostles] were saying, "This man Paul is an unknown and obscure man; we don't know who he is or where he comes from." Just as dogs bark at people they do not recognize, so those men were reviling Paul as if he were unknown. . . . If there was anyone who was well-known, it was especially Paul. For since everyone acknowledged that he was a minister of God, it was impossible that he was unknown and obscure, especially among those who had been born spiritually in Christ Jesus through his ministry. The obscurity of family and birth—which those wicked men were charging against Paul—did not at all relate to the case, and meanwhile they were shamelessly concealing the fame of Paul's name and ministry that shone forth everywhere. Indeed, Paul's fame was the very thing they were attempting to hide. But Paul defends his reputation when he says, "and yet well-known." He was not worried about the fame of his name, nevertheless he could not overlook the devilish tricks of wicked men, nor could he hide God's work in him. Commentary on 2 Corinthians 6:9.[48]

The Paradox of Christian Discipleship. Heinrich Bullinger: It is certainly necessary for those of us who want to serve God faithfully to steel our minds against all adversities. For those who run after human praise; those who are afraid of rebukes; those who love pleasure; those who hate hard work; those who buy human friendship at great expense; those who avoid persecutions as the worst of evils—that is, those who do not want to lose their souls in this world—do not belong to Christ's flock. Nevertheless, this must be carefully guarded against lest we be rightly judged as imposters. For the Lord said, "Blessed are you when others revile you and utter all sorts of evil against you on account of me. Rejoice and be glad since great is your reward in heaven." . . . Therefore, godly men and women must suffer many things on account of the truth and righteousness; however, they submit to these things with patient and

[47]CWMS 1066-68.

[48]Musculus, *Commentarius . . . in posteriorem epistolam Pauli ad Corinthios*, 204.

unwavering faith for salvation, but, in the midst of these dangers, they are not bereft of divine consolation. In fact, Paul treats the greatest consolation in these most elegant antitheses of this passage. "We die daily," he says, "but yet we live," either because the Lord rescues us from dangers, or because he amply comforts us that we might endure it, or because he gives us a better life. "We are punished"—indeed, we are scourged with various afflictions—"but not killed." We are never free from sorrow, but the Lord often comforts us so that we rejoice from the heart. From the perspective of our life situation and wealth, we are impoverished; but from the perspective of all the people we enrich through our ministry, we distribute the true and heavenly treasure of God. And these are true riches that never perish and cannot be snatched away from anyone. We possess nothing here but wander about with no certain home. Nevertheless, since we possess Christ, we have all things in him alone. Commentary on 2 Corinthians 6:9-10.[49]

Sorrowful Yet Rejoicing. Martin Luther: This is an astonishing sermon. Truly, Paul is filled with joy (and an exultant spirit)! We are poor, we possess nothing; we have no power, but our opponents do. In this world, the world is everything; we, by contrast, are nothing. But before God it is the opposite. Just as it befalls us, Paul says, the apostles and the prophets, so it befalls you, our disciples. Learn, nonetheless, that if you undergo these trials, it does not mean you are rejected by God. Even if you are nothing here, there you are everything. Christ died and was buried. The cross could be seen and death perceived clearly enough. But his resurrection was seen and perceived by no one except those to whom He chose to reveal it. Likewise, no one sees that we are righteous. . . . And yet it must be learned from the Word. Sermon on Invocavit Sunday.[50]

[49]Bullinger, *In Posteriorem D. Pauli ad Corinthios Epistolam Commentarius*, 294; citing Mt 5:11.
[50]LW 58:9* (WA 47:668).

Though Beggars, Christians Enrich the World. Martin Luther: If there were no Christians on earth, no city or country would enjoy peace; everything on earth would perish in a single day. That grain still grows in the field; that people recover from an illness; that they have their sustenance, peace, and protection—all this they owe to Christians. Indeed, we are poor beggars, yet we make many rich; although we have nothing, yet we possess everything. What kings, princes, lords, ordinary citizens, and peasants have is not theirs by reason of their golden hair but because of Christ and his Christians. Christians have the gospel, baptism, and the sacrament, by means of which they convert people, snatch souls from the clutches of the devil, wrest them from hell and death, and bring them to heaven. With these they also comfort, strengthen, and preserve poor consciences that are saddened and troubled by the devil and others. They are able to teach and instruct people in all walks of life and to help them live in a Christian and blessed way. All these are works that all kings and emperors in the world, all the mighty and the rich, all scholars and sages, are unable to do and could not purchase with all their wealth. For none of them can console and gladden a single conscience that is oppressed and aggrieved by sin. Sermons on John 14–15.[51]

Poor yet Rich. John Trapp: Godliness has a self-sufficiency. "That person who is on good terms with poverty is not poor," Seneca stated. A contented person cannot be a poor person, especially if they are a godly person. Why? The Father (that Ancient of Days) fills his memory; the Son (the wisdom of the Father) fills his understanding; the Holy Ghost (the Comforter) fills his will. And thus, he has all he needs for he has the one who has everything. Commentary on 2 Corinthians 6:10.[52]

Having Nothing, but Possessing Everything. Andreas Hyperius: The godly have

[51]LW 24:79 (WA 45:532).
[52]Trapp, *A Commentary or Exposition*, 718*; citing 1 Tim 6:6.

nothing of their own which the world would greatly admire and . . . that meager portion that they do have they don't make much of or pay much attention to. As it is said, "If your wealth increases, do not set your heart on it." And yet, since they are slaves of Christ, they have all things in Christ. Just as the more riches a greedy person has, the more they are a pauper . . . so the godly man or woman facing the most impoverished condition is nevertheless wealthy. This does not differ from what the Stoics also prescribed: "Wealth is wisdom alone."† Consequently, in a wonderful order, the apostle here enumerates all sorts of virtues, whether pertaining to righteousness, or courage, or prudence, or self-control, and it will not be difficult at all to organize each into their various classes. And the individual parts compose in themselves excellent doctrine and better philosophy than you will find in most of the philosophers' books which the pagans discuss. Commentary on 2 Corinthians 6:10.[53]

6:11-13 *Paul's Heartfelt Appeal*

Paul's Exuberance in Gospel Work. Huldrych Zwingli: Paul beautifully escapes the objection of those people who might say, "Paul, you are once again praising yourself too much." "That is true," he says, "but take it easy on me, for my heart is filled with such great joy that I am eager to burst out with an open mouth." Paul is not able to restrain himself from completely pouring himself out. Annotations on 2 Corinthians 6:11.[54]

Because Paul Loves the Corinthians, He Speaks Freely to Them. Wolfgang Musculus: Paul loved the Corinthians just as a father loves his sons, and so he spoke to them freely and confidently out of paternal affection. He acknowledges this, while at the same explaining why it is and for what occasion he finds fault with them, namely, that they don't respond with equal affection toward Paul and his companions as it was necessary for them to do so. Thus, Paul says, "Our mouth is open toward you, O Corinthians." In other words, "I am speaking freely and confidently to you, O Corinthians; I am hiding nothing; I am dissimulating nothing. Instead, I am declaring to you what I think and feel." To speak with an open mouth is nothing other than to speak without any dissimulation, to speak what is in our heart as we usually do when we are speaking to those we love or to our friends. Paul indicates, therefore, that he speaks to them as those whom he loves. . . .

Let us learn from this passage, therefore, how it is proper for a minister of Christ, when he is speaking to his brothers in the church of God, to do so freely and clearly. His mouth should not be filled with secretive or mumbling words, but he should speak openly. The wolves who have been transformed into pastors also have their mouths open toward the flock of God; but not so that they might clearly speak the things of salvation, but so that they might mangle the Lord's sheep and devour them all. Commentary on 2 Corinthians 6:11.[55]

Paul's Fatherly Affection for the Corinthians. Niels Hemmingsen: Paul turns his attention to the whole Corinthian church, to whom he shows his deepest fatherly affection. While reproaching them somewhat because they do not have similar affection for him, he urges them to repay the duty as children are supposed to do. This is the simplest sense of his words. Now Paul's discourse is symbolized in a very powerful way. The open mouth and the wide-open heart signify the passionate and truly paternal affection with which he has already embraced those Corinthians with his inmost heart. He expands upon this affection, when he adds "You are not restricted by us," that is, "I am wholeheartedly embracing you so that my

[53]Hyperius, *Commentarii . . . in Epistolam D. Pauli ad Romanos, et Utramque ad Corinthios*, 380; citing Ps 62:10; Prov 13:7. †This appears to be a version of Cicero's maxim that "the wise man alone is rich." *Paradoxa Stoicorum*, LCL 349:294-94.
[54]Zwingli, *Annotatiunculae . . . ex ore Zvinglij*, 176.

[55]Musculus, *Commentarius . . . in posteriorem epistolam Pauli ad Corinthios*, 207.

heart has been opened to receive you." "But you are restricted in your own affections," that is, "your heart has not been opened in turn to receive me and embrace me with the deepest love. That is why you, whom I call my children, should be open to and affectionately receive me so that, embracing one another, we might in turn fulfill our duty to one another and so pay back mutual love—I to you, and you to me." This passage teaches how much affection preachers of the Word and their hearers should have for one another. Commentary on 2 Corinthians 6:11-13.[56]

Return My Show of Affection! John Calvin: Paul softens his criticism both by kindly addressing them as sons and by this exhortation, by which he suggests that he still has good hopes for them. "By the same reward" Paul means "mutual duty," for there is a mutual recompense of duty between a father and his children. For just as parents have the duty to nourish their children, to instruct them, to guide them with their advice, and to defend them, so equity dictates that sons graciously provide recompense to their parents. In sum, he means what the Greeks call *antipelargian*—affection exercised in return. "I bear parental affection toward you," Paul says. "Show yourselves to be my sons by your devotion and respect in return." Commentary on 2 Corinthians 6:13.[57]

Preachers Are Like Fathers to Their People. Cyriacus Spangenberg: The pious apostle considered that they would be sincerely sorry for their misdeeds and failings (for which he had punished them so severely). Therefore, he also comforts them with such friendly and loving words. And preachers and servants of the church must also follow this example when they have punished the sins of the people severely and earnestly and then see that they are sincerely sorry for the same and that they truly repent of them. They shall drop their harshness and comfort again their troubled hearts with tenderness. For the gospel is this type of teaching which does not break completely the bruised reed, but lifts it up again, which does not put out completely the smoldering wick, but lights it again. So the Son of God did not come to destroy, but to save what was lost. For preachers and their listeners must behave toward one another as parents and children. Parents must provide for children, teach, rule, warn, chastise, and protect them. Preachers also owe all things to their listeners in spiritual matters. In contrast, children must be obedient to their parents, receive in goodness all chastisement and punishment, improve themselves, gladly follow, and, wherever they can, honor and give joy to their parents. Listeners must also show themselves to be such toward their preachers. And this is the comfort that Paul gives to his Corinthians, along with teaching about how they in turn must behave toward him as their father. Thirty-First Sermon.[58]

[56]Hemmingsen, *Commentaria in Omnes Epistolas Apostolorum*, 279.
[57]CO 50:80 (CTS 40:256).
[58]C. Spangenberg, *Die ander Epistel Pauli an die Corinthier*, 126r; citing Mt 12:20; 18:11.

6:14–7:1 The Temple of the Living God

[14]*Do not be unequally yoked with unbelievers. For what partnership has righteousness with lawlessness? Or what fellowship has light with darkness?* [15]*What accord has Christ with Belial?*[a] *Or what portion does a believer share with an unbeliever?* [16]*What agreement has the temple of God with idols? For we are the temple of the living God; as God said,*

"I will make my dwelling among them and walk among them,
and I will be their God,
and they shall be my people.
[17]*Therefore go out from their midst,*
and be separate from them, says the Lord,
and touch no unclean thing;
then I will welcome you,
[18]*and I will be a father to you,*
and you shall be sons and daughters to me,
says the Lord Almighty."

7 *Since we have these promises, beloved, let us cleanse ourselves from every defilement of body*[b] *and spirit, bringing holiness to completion in the fear of God.*

a Greek *Beliar* b Greek *flesh*

Overview: Recognizing Christian believers to be God's temple, Paul warns the Corinthians to avoid being allied with unbelievers and exhorts them to cleanse themselves from every defilement. Reformation exegetes discuss at length the nature and purpose of biblical separation. For some, Paul's injunction against being "unequally yoked" relates primarily, or even exclusively, to contracting marriages to partners who have disavowed Christ (i.e., Muslims or Jews). Many Protestant reformers extend the term "unbeliever" to include Roman Catholics and other self-professed Christians who are mired in superstition, idolatry, and wickedness. Anabaptist commentators extend Paul's standard of separation even further to encompass Roman Catholics and Protestants who practice infant baptism, attend worldly sermons, frequent taverns, sing songs about sex, and practice religious coercion. For Anabaptist authors, the world is like ancient Babylon, from which God's people must flee, for "the only thing to be learned from the world is evil." But separation from wickedness is only half of the story. Reformation commentators of all confessions are quick to remind their readers that, thanks to divine regeneration, Christian are now sacred temples in whom God dwells through his Holy Spirit. God is not simply near his people; he actually lives within their hearts, a holy presence that transforms, refreshes, nourishes, protects, and comforts them. Indeed, as Wolfgang Musculus and Tilemann Hesshus observe, the closer the union we have with God, the greater our happiness, joy, and righteousness. At the same time, most Protestant commentators reject the idea of Christian perfection on this earth: while spiritual regeneration occurs once and is definitive, sanctification remains a lifelong pursuit.

6:14-15 *Do Not Be Yoked with Unbelievers*

Christians Have No Partnership with Unrighteousness. Desiderius Erasmus: For you Christ is abundantly rich, abundantly glorious, abundantly powerful, abundantly fortunate. Let him alone suffice for you; embrace him with your whole heart; recognize your greatness; recognize your felicity; consider yourselves too great to have fellowship with the unbelieving. The difference between you is too great to allow you to be joined by the same yoke. For what partnership at all does righteousness have with unrighteousness? Or what communion does light have with darkness? Or what harmony does Christ have with Belial? Conflicting deities, conflicting religion, conflicting morals, conflicting hope. What agreement is there between the temple of God and profane images? For you are the temple of the living God. Paraphrase on 2 Corinthians 6.[1]

Do Not Be United with Wickedness. Huldrych Zwingli: From his discussion of plenty and scarcity, Paul now digresses to discuss the yoke of unbelievers. Now it is obvious that believers should not attempt to contract marriages with unbelievers. This discussion was prompted, no doubt, by those matters that Paul discussed in 1 Corinthians 7 regarding unequal marriages, although Paul's words regarding a marriage already contracted should not be applied to the contracting of marriages. Therefore, Paul discourages them from joining themselves to wicked people and unbelievers, because there should be no fellowship or agreement between righteousness and wickedness. "As I said earlier, you are the righteousness of God through Christ. Why, therefore, do you unite yourself with wickedness? You are a light in the Lord. Why do you commune with the darkness? Again, as you yourselves said, God's temple should have no fellowship with idols. For just as there are no idols in God's external temple (even though the Gentiles have them in the temples of their gods), so you also, who are God's true and holy temple, must have no dealing with idols and idolaters." Annotations on 2 Corinthians 6:14-16.[2]

The Dangers of Being Unequally Yoked. Niels Hemmingsen: This is an exhortation by which Paul encourages the Corinthians not to pollute themselves with the customs and works of unbelievers. For those who touch pitch will be defiled by it. Now the apostle uses a very elegant metaphor here, alluding to the law of Moses in Deuteronomy 22, where it was commanded not to hitch an ox and ass under the same yoke. For Paul says that you should not be *heterozygountēs* with unbelievers; that is, you should not be unequally yoked with unbelievers. But people are called "unequally yoked" when, as they experience various situations, they cooperate together in the same work, as when a believer marries an unbelieving wife (or vice versa), or when a believer dines at a table of demons, or, finally, when a believer has dealings with an unbeliever in some other affair. . . . This exhortation is observed in Paul's words at Ephesians 5: "Have nothing to do with the unfruitful works of darkness, but instead expose them." Now, since this exhortation of Paul is universal, it can be appropriately applied also to an ill-matched marriage, lest a faithful man or woman be joined to an unbelieving spouse. Commentary on 2 Corinthians 6:14.[3]

Why Separation Is Sometimes Necessary. Hans Denck: Hearts which hold high this wondrous deed of God through Christ and walk in his steps delight me. I love them to the extent that I am able to recognize them. I cannot, on the other hand, have a great deal of fellowship with those who refuse to hear me yet will not be silent on controversial issues, for I cannot detect the spirit of Christ in them. Rather, they seem to have a perverse spirit that seeks to force me away from my belief to theirs (God beware), be it right or wrong. Even if this spirit were right and the zeal laudable, it is certainly used unwisely. For a person ought to know that in matters of faith, things should be voluntary and without coercion. Thus I separate myself from some, not because I consider myself better or more just than they, but because I find a great deal lacking in them in such matters and I prefer to seek the precious stone free and without obstruction, and, having found it, I seek to keep peace with everyone (as far as lies in me). From others again, persecutions and such like fears have separated me. My heart, however, is not turned away from them, especially not if they are

[1]CWE 43:238.
[2]Zwingli, *Annotatiunculae . . . ex ore Zvinglij*, 177.
[3]Hemmingsen, *Commentaria in Omnes Epistolas Apostolorum*, 279; citing Deut 22:10; 1 Cor 10:21; Eph 5:11.

God-fearing. By God's grace, I do not wish to have anything to do with error and unrighteousness, as much as I am able to discern these, nor do I want to have fellowship, even though I am among sinners and those who err. Recantation.[4]

Who Are These "Unbelievers"? Wolfgang Musculus: Now Paul does not simply employ the word *apistous*, that is, "unbelievers," to describe all those who do not possess faith in the heart, as is the case with many people in Christian churches. These people are not to be considered "unbelievers" since they have been baptized, profess with their mouths the Christian faith, and participate outwardly in the sacraments of Christ along with other believers. Rather, Paul considers "unbelievers" to be those who do not profess the Christian faith, who are alien from Christ and the church of Christ, such as the Turks and Jews are today. Paul does not want the Corinthians to be yoked with people like that. Hence, this passage is abused by all those who shout that fellowship must be broken when there is any sort of disagreement and when people have different interpretations of a particular passage of Scripture. These people cry out, "The apostle is warning us not to be yoked with unbelievers," as if someone is an "unbeliever" as soon as they do not agree with us in everything and through everything. Those who think this way are unhealthy of mind. In our opinion, Anabaptists are this sort of people in our day, who condemn others as "unbelievers" whenever they refuse to subscribe to their sect. Why do I mention the Anabaptists? This evil has disturbed churches from the times of the apostles to our own day. Commentary on 2 Corinthians 6:14.[5]

Unbelievers Are Not Neighbors. Andreas Bodenstein von Karlstadt: We should observe diligently how God commanded love of neighbor and how it resembles love of God and love of self. We should also know who our neighbor is, for Christ, our example, did not say in vain, "Love your neighbor." To the brood of vipers, he says, "You look for a sign, but you will see none other than that of the prophet Jonah." To the Pharisees and hypocrites, Christ said, "Those who are well do not need a physician." He also forbade us to throw pearls before swine and said, "Let go of the blind leaders," and "Beware of the sourdough of the Pharisees." Paul too forbade us to have fellowship with those who teach and live contrary to God. Another apostle says, "Do not invite to your house nor greet those who do not bring the teaching of Christ."

Now if we are not to have a friendly chat with, greet them, or invite to our homes those who do not have Christ's teaching, then we are also not allowed to love such people as our neighbors. Similarly, if I am not to feed or provide with drink anyone who strives against Christ, that person cannot be my neighbor. And if I am not to throw the little pearl before the swine, it must follow that all animals that have a human skin and the form of a human being must not be regarded as my neighbor, but as swine to whom I must not extend the good works due to a neighbor. One must therefore carefully consider who the neighbor is who we are to love as ourselves, so that we do not act contrary to God's love at the very moment when we intensively practice the love of neighbor. For we would only create a love of neighbor which is more unlike the love of God than a beam is unlike a human being. Regarding the Two Greatest Commandments.[6]

What Does It Mean to Be Unequally Yoked? Wolfgang Musculus: What does it mean to be yoked with unbelievers? There are some people who refer it to an ill-matched marriage when Christians marry unbelievers. . . . Others stretch the sense of this passage too far,

[4] Denck, *Selected Writings*, 127.

[5] Musculus, *Commentarius . . . in posteriorem epistolam Pauli ad Corinthios*, 209-10.

[6] CRR 8:242-43*; citing Mt 19:19; 12:39; Lk 5:39; Mt 7:6; 15:14; 16:6; 2 Jn 10.

referring it also to matters that concern the interactions of people in social relationships. In our view, the apostle is speaking here about those interactions that can corrupt the purity of religion, either those things that pertain to religion immediately (for example, that the Corinthians were eating food offered to idols with unbelievers in their temples and at their sacrifices) or some other way that the Corinthians were corrupting the purity of religion which Paul had heard about: that they were sitting with the rabble of unbelievers at theatrical spectacles; that they were marrying unbelievers; and that, in trivial and unnecessary court cases, they were running after the judgment of unbelievers. Commentary on 2 Corinthians 6:14.[7]

The Dangers of Being Unequally Yoked. Edward Leigh: This verse condemns an unequal yoking of believers with infidels, whether in familiar society (thus, Calvin) . . . or rather in marriage, as other interpreters take it. (1) Because of the inequality of such yoking. (2) Because of the unavoidable peril of contagion. Annotations on 2 Corinthians 6:14.[8]

True Christians Must Separate Themselves from Idolaters. Dirk Philips: Finally, we could not refrain from asking all God-fruitful ones, all lovers of the truth through the mercy of God to pray, to admonish, and to warn them that they be careful, and that they have nothing to do with impurity just as Paul wrote to the Corinthians and thus admonishes us. . . .

It is plain from these words that one must separate himself from the unclean, apostate, and idolaters so that one does not participate in their sin. For although a person himself is innocent of any misdeed, he can thereby dirty and soil himself through fellowship and consenting to it. Of this we have sufficient clear examples and witnesses in the Scripture, as also the express word of the apostle which says, "A little leaven sours the whole dough." The Frisian-Flemish Division.[9]

Catholics Misapply This Verse. John Trapp: A wise person once said, "Do not dare to yoke yourself with any untamed heifer that bears not Christ's yoke." Here, the apostle seems to allude to the Jewish law that states that an ox and an ass cannot be coupled together. The Catholic doctors at Douay, commenting on Leviticus 19:19, state, "Here all participation with heretics and schismatics is forbidden." King Philip II of Spain[†] stated that he would rather have no subjects than subjects of different religions. Commentary on 2 Corinthians 6:14.[10]

The Meaning of Lawlessness. Martin Chemnitz: *Anomia* [lawlessness] is used in opposition to righteousness in Hebrews 1:9 and 2 Corinthians 6:14. Therefore, just as righteousness is conformity with the law of God, so *anomia* is depravity or an action which is in conflict with the law of God. Loci Theologici.[11]

The Dangers of Associating with the Wicked. Tilemann Hesshus: This exhortation of the apostle is very serious, by which he warns the Corinthians that they should abstain from dealing with wicked people and avoid the confusion of superstition. Gentile idolators who had not yet accepted the doctrine of the gospel, when they were sacrificing to their idols, were inviting their acquaintances and friends who had converted [to Christianity] to banquets and public sacrifices, as if it didn't matter which religion a person embraced. And so believers were entwined in idolatry. Immediately afterward, Satan attempts to mix religious

[7]Musculus, *Commentarius . . . in posteriorem epistolam Pauli ad Corinthios*, 210.
[8]Leigh, *Annotations upon all the New Testament*, 261*.
[9]CRR 6:539-40; citing 2 Cor 6:14-18; 1 Cor 5:6; Gal 5:9.
[10]Trapp, *A Commentary or Exposition*, 719*. [†]King Philp II (1527–1598) ruled the Catholic empire of Spain during the Spanish Golden Age. He saw himself as a defender of Catholic Europe and was famously responsible for sending the Spanish Armada against England after the Protestant Elizabeth Tudor I took the throne after Philip's wife Mary Tudor died.
[11]Chemnitz, *Loci Theologici*, 1:267.

ceremonies so that he might cloak his blasphemy and abomination within this covering as well as instill in Christian believers little by little a contempt for the gospel and true worship of God. . . . Thus, there are many people in our times who are not ignorant of the doctrine of the gospel, nay rather, they profess it, who join themselves with the popes—whom they know worship idols and defend foul errors. They listen to idolatrous masses. They partake of the Sacrament under one species,† contrary to the words of institution of the Son of God. They are present at prayers for the dead. They participate in religious pilgrimages and processions adoring the host. They feast with monks and canons. They devote their service to popes and bishops, either to avoid danger, or for advantage and gain, or in hopes of promotion to greater honor. And so, by their collusion with the clear enemies of the truth, such Belials are pleased with themselves, as if they are free from all guilt. . . . But if there are people who are terrified by the fear of God and indebted of heart to the truth; who detest idols and blasphemies; who avoid the ceremonies and feasts of the wicked; who benefit consistently from the truth—those persons are like prodigies in the world who bring upon themselves the hatred of their friends. They are considered disturbers of the peace in the republic and expose themselves to various dangers in the world. . . . Therefore, Paul urges the Corinthians to guard themselves from such satanic plots and demonstrate sincere faith with true godliness. Explication of 2 Corinthians 6:14-15.[12]

Christ and Belial. John Calvin: As to the etymology of the word *Belial*, there is not agreement even among the Hebrews. The meaning, however, is not in doubt. For Moses takes the word or idea of Belial to mean a wicked and foul thought, and in various places those who are wicked and abandoned to iniquity are called people or sons of Belial. Hence it is that Paul has employed the word here to mean the devil, the head of all wicked persons. For by means of similitude, he applies what is true of the head to the members, as if he were to say, "Just as there is an irreconcilable difference between Christ and Satan, so also we must remain aloof from partnership with the wicked." When, however, Paul refuses to the Christian any portion with an unbeliever, he is not referring to food, clothing, estates, the sun, air, as I mentioned above, but to those things which are peculiar to unbelievers, from which the Lord has separated us. Commentary on 2 Corinthians 6:15.[13]

"Belial" Sounds Like the Hebrew Words "Without Yoke." Wolfgang Musculus: Now the word "Belial," which is found nowhere else in the New Testament, Paul took from the Old Testament Scriptures. In the Old Testament, people who are wicked, sinners, rash and not subject to discipline are called the "sons of Belial," as is seen in 1 Samuel 25 concerning Nabal, 1 Samuel 2 concerning the sons of Samuel, and 1 Kings 21 concerning the two false witnesses. Now they are called the sons of Belial because they are without a yoke. For the Hebrew word *Belial* sounds the same as the two Hebrew words "without yoke." . . . Whence Jerome,† in his translation of chapter 19 of the book of Judges, when the text read "Behold, the men of the city, men of the son of Belial," added the phrase, "that is, without a yoke." Why Paul calls Satan "Belial" is not for us to ask. For he is the most wicked of all creatures. He is the author of all sinners. Commentary on 2 Corinthians 6:15.[14]

Belial and Christ Can't Be Lords of the Same House. Martin Luther: We do not accept that addition of the papists who cry out,

[12]Hesshus, *Explicatio Secundae Epistolae Pauli ad Corinthios*, 169r-170r. †This refers to the prohibition in Catholicism that prevented laity from receiving the wine in the Eucharist; they received the bread while the wine was reserved for priests.

[13]CO 50:51 (CTS 40:258-59).

[14]Musculus, *Commentarius . . . in posteriorem epistolam Pauli ad Corinthios*, 211; citing 1 Sam 25:17, 25; 2 Sam 2:12; 1 Kings 21:10. †The relevant portion of Jerome's translation of Judges 19:22 reads, "venerunt viri civitatis illius, filii Belial (id est, absque jugo)."

"You have the keys from us, the sacrament of the altar, the calling, and the ministry, which are the marks of the true church. But one thing is lacking, namely, that you refuse to acknowledge that the pope and the cardinals are the church." With regard to this, therefore, there is a conflict between us and the papists. We refuse to admit the enemy along with the Head of the household, for Christ and Satan cannot rule the same house at the same time. For "What accord has Christ with Belial?" Accordingly, if the pope should be honored, it is necessary for us to deny Christ. For he does not allow Satan to reign in his house. If we want to have a church, it must not be polluted and commingled with any satanic doctrine. But the papal traditions are godless and in conflict with the Word of God, and it is for the sake of this Word alone that God wants to make his abode with us. Therefore, those traditions must be shunned, for Belial and Christ cannot be lords or heads of one house. Commentary on Genesis 28:17.[15]

6:16–7:1 *Temples of God*

Four Reasons Why Believers Should Not Associate with Wicked People. David Dickson: [Paul exhorts] that they abstain from all unlawful society with unbelievers who may hinder them from serving God, or cause them to be alienated from true religion, or in any way pollute them by their association. . . . The arguments Paul gives for this exhortation are four.

Argument 1: Your condition and profession as Christians on the one hand, and the sins of idolatry which are openly professed on the other hand, are no less opposed to one another than righteousness is to iniquity, light to darkness, Christ to the devil, faith to infidelity, the temple of God to the temple of idols, among which there can be no communion. Therefore, Christians ought to have no communion with unbelievers in idolatry, or in any other sins that unbelievers openly profess. . . . [But] Paul did not forbid them from inhabiting the same city with unbelievers, nor from negotiating or eating meat with them, if they should be invited to dinner or supper. . . .

Argument 2 [v. 16]: You are the holy temple of God, which Paul proves by the testimony of Moses from Leviticus 26 and Ezekiel 37. Therefore, it is not lawful for you to pollute yourselves by associating with unbelievers. . . .

Argument 3 [vv. 17-18]: God commands you to separate from idolaters, and the pollutions of the world, and not to touch them: Therefore, you ought to beware of them.

Argument 4: God makes this promise to those who keep themselves pure from the defilements of the world and who do not participate with other people's sins: God will be a Father to them, that is, he will make amends for all their hurts and provide full consolation against all evils, which they, looking to themselves, may suffer due to other people's sins. God will truly communicate himself to them and will manifest his paternal affection toward them. Exposition of 2 Corinthians 6:15-18.[16]

Paul Was a True Prophet. Jacques Lefèvre d'Étaples: Now when Paul says, "as God said," he demonstrates that he is a prophet and that God is speaking a prophetic oracle through his mouth. It is not necessary to always demand that what is spoken by way of prophecy come from someone other than Paul. For Paul himself was a prophet, and through him the Holy Spirit spoke more intimately than to other prophets. Wasn't Paul prophesying when he said somewhere, "Now the Spirit expressly says . . ."—identifying his prophecy with the "last days"? If you demand that this prophecy [i.e., from 1 Tim 4:1] came from someone other than Paul, you are wasting your time. Therefore, there is no need to struggle to identify the prophet who spoke this present prophecy, even if the prophet Isaiah spoke something similar to it, when it reveals the mysteries of Christ, the Gospel

[15]LW 5:245-46* (WA 43:598).

[16]Dickson, *An Exposition of All St. Paul's Epistles*, 82*; citing Lev 26:12; Ezek 37:27.

writers, and the apostles. Commentary on 2 Corinthians 6:16.[17]

God Dwells in His People's Hearts. John Calvin: Paul proves that we are the temples of God from that which God once promised to the people of Israel: that he would dwell among them. First, God cannot dwell among us unless he dwells within each one of us, for in this passage he promises this as a singular privilege: "I will dwell in the midst of you." Nor does this "dwelling" or presence consist merely in earthly blessings, but it must be understood chiefly of spiritual grace. Hence, the passage does not simply mean that God is near us, as though he were in the air, flying around us, but it means rather that he has his residence in our hearts. Commentary on 2 Corinthians 6:16.[18]

God Is Near to His People. Heinrich Bullinger: The gift of an explanation is added. Paul had spoken about the temple; now he adds who should be called a temple, namely, the man or woman in whom God lives by his Spirit, grace, and power. Now, truly, since idols have no reality, believers have no business with them because they have God in their hearts. And this reasoning is valid not only against idolatrous Gentiles but also against some Christians who are also addicted to worshiping idols. Now Paul has not simply called it the "temple of our God," but "the temple of the living God." All those material things are changeable and material; only God is present to his creatures without form or change. And so, also, his name is presented in Scripture. For just as the name Jehovah (*Yahweh*) concerns his life and essence, so his presence is spoken of with [the names] *Eloah*, *El*, or *Elohim*. Many people interpret this name to mean "strength," but it actually speaks of his presence. For the word *El* signifies "at," and the relative *he* (□) is added which refers to itself and is everywhere among all creatures. . . . And thus God himself testifies in the prophets and says, "I am a God who is near, and not far off." Commentary on 2 Corinthians 6:16.[19]

The Happiness of Being God's People. Wolfgang Musculus: "And I will be their God, and they shall be my people." God explains here to what end he wishes to dwell with them and walk with them: namely, so that he might be their God, and guide and protect them as his own people. For to be the God of someone is to be their savior. And to be the people of God is to be bound to him in faith and obedience, and to be sanctified by his name. No one can ever fully fathom the happiness that comes from being the people of God. Reflecting on this, the prophet said, "Blessed are the people whose God is the Lord"—and so it is in fact. The closer the union we have with God, the greater our happiness. Outside of God, everything that this foolish world most eagerly runs after vanishes. Commentary on 2 Corinthians 6:16.[20]

Temples of the Living God. Tilemann Hesshus: The greatest glory and happiness of the pious man or woman is that they are called the temple of God. For the Scripture indicates that the faithful have been rescued from the tyranny of Satan and, once reconciled to God, have been cleansed from all their sin and born anew as sons and daughters of God. And God the Father, Son, and Holy Spirit live in their heart and is always present with them so that upon them he shines new light, imparts comfort, gives peace, utters groans, creates life, pours forth joyfulness, brings forth gifts, and makes them participants of all celestial benefits. Now God does not inhabit them as an indifferent host, but he disseminates in the soul of men and women rays of his wisdom, righteousness, truth, joyfulness, life, and happiness.

[17]Lefèvre, *Commentariorum in Epistolas Beati Pauli . . . Liber Tertius*, 136r-v; citing 1 Tim 4:1.
[18]CO 50:82 (CTS 40:260-61).
[19]Bullinger, *In Posteriorem D. Pauli ad Corinthios Epistolam Commentarius*, 297; citing Jer 23:13.
[20]Musculus, *Commentarius . . . in posteriorem epistolam Pauli ad Corinthios*, 215; citing Ps 144:15.

And he governs, protects, and sustains men and women, even as he adorns them as his home. Therefore, no greater glory, no greater happiness can be experienced by men and women than to be the temple of God. To be sure, God is everywhere and his presence fills heaven and earth; but he does not live everywhere. He is said to live in godly people to whom he imparts the rays of his light and makes participants of life. Explication of 2 Corinthians 6:16.[21]

Go Out from Them! Huldrych Zwingli: How will they preach to unbelievers if they are commanded to go out from—not remain with—them? The word "go out" in this passage means to keep oneself from the pollution of those with whom you live. And if there is no hope of them repenting, to also go out from them, as Christ commands in Matthew 10. Now Paul explains this when he says, "Do not touch an unclean thing." If they are so impure and defiled that there is no hope [for their correction], leave them and do not cohabit with the wicked. Now Paul explains elsewhere with an allegory what God wills by this command when he forbade the Jews from touching any unclean thing. Annotations on 2 Corinthians 6:17.[22]

Christians Should Avoid Wickedness, Not Unbelievers. Wolfgang Musculus: "Therefore, go out from the midst of them." You will say, "Believers, therefore, should withdraw from all places in which unbelievers live, and so they must abandon the whole world. For the believers living in the world are very few in number." I answer: the apostle did not require that believers abandon the dwelling places of unbelievers, whence there is no contamination, but rather to separate themselves from the customs and practices of those who were impious and those who were shameful and wicked. In the meantime, he does not dissolve all social interactions, which are necessary for believers as much as unbelievers. Yes, indeed, he did not even condemn sharing a meal with a profane person, as we see in 1 Corinthians 10. That is why Paul's statement "go out from the midst of them and be separate from them" relates to the specific matter which the apostle is discussing and should not be employed for a purpose beyond this. And so we today, when we urge all believers to abandon Babylon in accordance with that passage from Revelation 18, "Fallen, fallen the great Babylon. . . . Come out of her, my people, lest you participate in her sins and share in her plagues," we do not require a physical separation (except when Babylon threatens conscience or life), but a separation from the corruption of impious worship and adulterous teaching. Commentary on 2 Corinthians 6:17.[23]

Separate from the World and Its Abominations! Michael Sattler: Concerning separation, we have agreed that a separation should take place from the evil which the devil has planted in the world. We simply will not have fellowship with evil people, nor associate with them, nor participate with them in their abominations. That is, all who have not submitted themselves to the obedience of faith and have not united themselves to God so that they want to do his will are a great abomination before God. Since this is so, nothing but abominable things can issue from them. For there has never been anything in the world and among all creatures except good and evil, believing and unbelieving, darkness and light, the world and those who are out of the world, God's temple and idols, Christ and Belial, and neither may have anything to do with the other. And the commandment of the Lord is evident—he tells us to become separated from evil. In this way he wants to be our God, and we will be his sons and daughters. Further, he also admonishes us to withdraw from Babylon and worldly Egypt so that we will not participate

[21]Hesshus, *Explicatio Secundae Epistolae Pauli ad Corinthios*, 175r-v.
[22]Zwingli, *Annotatiunculae . . . ex ore Zvinglij*, 177; citing Mt 10:14.
[23]Musculus, *Commentarius . . . in posteriorem epistolam Pauli ad Corinthios*, 215; citing 1 Cor 10:27; Rev 18:2, 4.

in the suffering which the Lord will inflict upon them. The Schleitheim Articles.[24]

Have No Fellowship with the Wicked. Menno Simons: Do not have anything to do, as the holy Paul has taught and commanded, and do not eat, with people who being of age and driven by the Spirit were baptized into the body of Jesus Christ with us, that is, the church, but afterward, whether through false doctrine or a vain and carnal life, reject and separate themselves from the body and fellowship of Christ, no matter whether it be father or mother, sister or brother, man or wife, son or daughter, no matter who he be, for God's Word applies to all alike and there is no respect of persons with God. We say, avoid them if they reject the admonition of their brethren, done in sighing, tears, and a spirit of compassion and of great love, and if they nevertheless continue in their Jewish doctrine of sword, kingdom, polygamy, and similar deceptions . . . [and] all fellowship with evil work such as attending the preaching of worldly preachers, infant baptism, worldly Lord's Supper, and similar abominations, as also drunkenness, avarice, fornication, adultery, unseemly conversation. Admonition on Church Discipline.[25]

Christians Must Separate Themselves from the Wicked World. Anabaptists of Trieste: Concerning the separation from the world, Christ commanded us to have no fellowship with evil and wickedness and the unfruitful works of darkness, which the devil has planted in the world. . . . Therefore, following Scripture and the command of God we have separated ourselves from all the unfruitful works of darkness, all popish and worldly wickedness with their idolatry, attending the liturgy, taverns, the singing of songs about sex, citizens' commitments, worldly obligations, and other similar evils. These are considered important in the world but are nevertheless kept contrary to God and his command since those are the places at which God is most egregiously blasphemed. . . . We avoid all appearance of evil and hypocrisy. Because the world lies in wickedness . . . with so much evil living before God, the only thing to be learned from the world is evil. But since by the grace of God we have seen this wickedness, we have gone out from her according to the command of God, that is, we have separated ourselves from all unrighteousness. We cannot serve two masters. Whoever desires to be a friend of the world will be God's enemy. This is our position on separation from all unrighteousness according to God's command. Confession.[26]

Protestants Justified Separating from Rome. John Trapp: For gross idolatry and for fundamental errors alone must we separate. Corruptions grew so great in the Church of Rome that it justly occasioned first the separation of the Greek churches from the Latin churches, and then of the Reformed churches from the Roman. Machiavelli[†] observed that after the first Christian millennium, there was nowhere less piety than in those that lived nearest to Rome. And Cardinal Bellarmine[‡] bewails that ever since we [Protestants] accused the pope of being the antichrist, his kingdom has not only not increased, but has greatly decreased. Commentary on 2 Corinthians 6:17.[27]

No Unclean Thing. Edward Leigh: This exhortation is taken from Isaiah 52. To "touch an unclean thing" is no longer used in figurative speech; but the apostle employs a plainer phrase when he says, "have no fellowship with the unfruitful works of darkness," that is, do not associate with a person in bad action. The unclean thing not to be touched is not the person with

[24]Baylor, ed., *The Radical Reformation*, 175; citing 2 Cor 6:17.
[25]CWMS 412.

[26]CRR 10:268; citing Eph 5:11; 2 Cor 6; 7.
[27]Trapp, *A Commentary or Exposition*, 719*. [†]Niccolò Machiavelli (1469–1527) was a Florentine diplomat, historian, and political philosopher who was especially critical of the immorality of the papal church. [‡]Cardinal Robert Bellarmine (1542–1621) was a Jesuit theologian and church leader whose theological writings were especially important in responding to the Protestant attacks.

whom we associate in any action, but the action itself in which we associate with them. Annotation on 2 Corinthians 6:17.[28]

Accepted as Sons and Daughters. Cardinal Cajetan: The all-powerful God promises two things. First, he promises to welcome them. "I have said, 'Come out and be separate': I do not want you to wander; rather, having come out and separated from them, I will accept you into my spiritual house here, and finally into heaven in eternity." For the all-powerful Lord says, "I will be to you a father, and you will be my sons and daughters." The second thing he promises is divine adoption. [He says,] "not only do I accept you into my house, but I take upon myself the responsibility to be your father, loving you, providing for you, taking care of you. . . . And for your part, you will exercise toward me the responsibilities of sons and daughters, loving me, revering me, obeying me." Commentary on 2 Corinthians 6:18.[29]

God's Burning Love for His Sons and Daughters. Tilemann Hesshus: Just as in his voice as God, he has promised blessings to all people everywhere—blessings both spiritual and bodily, heavenly and earthly, eternal and temporal—so in his voice as Father he has provided to us, as his sons and daughters, all the blessings of the kingdom of Christ, namely, freedom from sin and death; the restraint of Satan; the remission of sins; the imputation of righteousness; the giving of the Holy Spirit; guidance; comfort; nourishment; protection; friendship; assistance in calling; length of days; and inheritance to eternal life. Now the Father's love that embraces his sons and daughters is a burning love that refreshes, feeds, and comforts them. He is present with his children to pardon their sins, appease his wrath, bless them continually. He gives them all necessary things and bequeaths to them a large inheritance. Interpreters believe that these words are taken from Jeremiah 31, where God says, "I will lead them in blessings, for I have become a father to Israel and Ephraim is my firstborn." But I am confident that Paul was looking back to all of God's promises which he revealed through the Spirit, if they have understanding, that God wishes to be our father, and to receive us as his sons and daughters by faith. This is the source of his greatest and sweetest promise, that the eternal Father pronounced by [the prophet] Nathan concerning the Messiah, 1 Samuel 7 [*sic*, 2 Samuel 7]: "I will be to him a Father and he will be to me a son," as the eternal God testifies that he is the father of the Messiah. And so, too, he promises that he will be the gentlest father to all who believe in Christ and will count us among his sons and daughters.

In this regard, Christ says, "I ascend to my God and your God, to my Father and your Father." So, too, God says in Isaiah 43, "Bring my sons from far away, and my daughters from the ends of the earth." And in Isaiah chapter 56: "I will give to them in my house and within my walls an inheritance and name better than sons and daughters." Whence also John says in chapter 1: "He gave to them the power to become children of God." Explication of 2 Corinthians 6:18.[30]

Let Us Cleanse Ourselves! Huldrych Zwingli: "Let us cleanse ourselves." Here Paul, by means of anagogy,[†] ascends higher, that is, "I not only want you to avoid having fellowship with unbelievers, but to be careful in all your affairs and in every action to be pure and clean, and this by his grace that has purified us." Now by the word "spirit," understand the soul or mind of a human being. We should be pure also of mind, for the entirety of a human being—both in body and soul—is impure, namely, in the flesh; and the Spirit of God is not able to be impure. For it is not enough for the body to be pure through washing, while the mind remains contaminated in its thoughts and

[28]Leigh, *Annotations upon all the New Testament*, 261*; citing Is 52:11.

[29]Cajetan, *In Posteriorem Pauli Epistolam ad Corinthios Commentarii*, 177.

[30]Hesshus, *Explicatio Secundae Epistolae Pauli ad Corinthios*, 178r-179r; citing Jer 31:9; 2 Sam 7:14; Jn 20:17; Is 43:6; 56:5; Jn 1:12.

depraved desires. Nay, rather, the mind of a Christian man and woman becomes accustomed to holy and pure thoughts. Annotations on 2 Corinthians 7:1.[31]

Defilements of Body and Spirit. Martin Luther: Here a theological question arises. How can we become "purer than snow" even though the remnants of sin always cling to us? I answer: I have always said that human beings are divided into spirit and flesh. Therefore, as far as the total person is concerned, there remain remnants of sin or, as Paul calls them, "defilements of body and spirit." Defilements of the spirit are doubts about grace, imperfect faith, murmurings against God, impatience, imperfect knowledge of the will of God, and the like. Defilements of the flesh are adultery, lusts, murder, brawls, and the like. The defilements of the spirit are increased in the world through heretics, the defilements of the spirit through other offenses, so that both spirit and body are polluted. Because of these defilements we are never as pure and holy as we really should be. Still, we have obtained baptism, which is most pure; we have obtained the Word, which is most pure; and in the Word and Baptism we have by faith obtained the blood of Christ, which is surely most pure. According to this purity, which in spirit and faith we have from Christ and from the sacraments that he instituted, the Christian is rightly said to be purer than snow, purer than the sun and the stars, even though the defilements of spirit and flesh cling to him. These are concealed and covered by the cleanness and purity of Christ, which we obtain by hearing the Word and by faith. Commentary on Psalm 51:8.[32]

Purity Is Required of Both Soul and Body. John Calvin. Since Paul has already showed that we have been called to purity, he now adds that it should be conspicuous in the body as well as in the soul. For it is clear that the term "flesh" here refers to the body just as the term "spirit" refers to the soul, since if the term "spirit" signified the gift of regeneration, Paul's statement concerning the defilement of the spirit would be absurd. Therefore, he would have us be pure of defilement not only inwardly but also externally, as is subject to human observation. It's as if he were to say, "Let us not only have consciences that are pure before God, but let us also consecrate to him our whole body and its members, so that no impurity may be seen in any part of us."

Now if we consider what point he is making, we will easily see that people act very shamelessly who excuse external idolatry with I don't know what excuses. . . . Hence, they have no basis for thinking that they have rendered satisfaction to God [by maintaining a pure conscience]. For those persons who show any appearance or sign of idolatry whatsoever or take part in any wicked or superstitious rites—even if they were completely pure in their minds (which isn't possible)—would nevertheless not escape the guilt of pollution of their bodies. Commentary on 2 Corinthians 7:1.[33]

The Reality of God's Promises Is Enjoyed Now. Wolfgang Musculus: Promises are considered to be of two sorts. The first type of promise is the hope of future benefit. Thus, we have the promise of possessing future resurrection, eternal life and glory with Christ in eternity. This excellent promise has not yet been realized, but we anticipate it with faith and hope. Second, we have certain kinds of promises where we also obtain what is promised. The promises that the apostle mentions here ought to be attributed to this second category. For surely these promises are received in this present life by faith and relate to the present grace by which God counted them worthy to be his elect and believers, and thereafter made them recipients of his calling and justification. Hence, it is more agreeable to interpret the passage in this manner: "Since we have these

[31]Zwingli, *Annotatiunculae . . . ex ore Zvinglij*, 177-78. †Anagogy is a mode of spiritual interpretation that identifies allusions to the afterlife in the biblical text.

[32]LW 12:366-67; citing 2 Cor 7:1; Ps 51:8.

[33]CO 50:83-84 (CTS 40:263-64).

promises," that is, "since we have obtained and possess these promises." It is as if Paul were saying, "Since, therefore, we are now the temple of God, God himself is our father who lives and walks with us, and we are his people, his sons and daughters." Commentary on 2 Corinthians 7:1.[34]

It Is God's Spirit That Purifies Us. Cyriacus Spangenberg: My dear friends, we must take this to heart and diligently keep ourselves from all sin and all godlessness. Earnest prayer will be necessary for this, that God will purify and sanctify us through his Holy Spirit and keep us through the same in such purity and holiness, or when we fall short of it, that he will bring us back to it, for the sake of his beloved son Jesus Christ. In other words, "there is nothing in a man or woman without your light." And as Christ says, "Without me you can do nothing." Thirty-Second Sermon.[35]

The Corinthians Must Beware of Idolatry and Inner Defilement. David Dickson: The first verse of this chapter belongs to the preceding chapter, wherein from the former promises Paul draws an exhortation, that they should not only beware of idolatry and its outward appearance, but also from all defilements of spirit and body, that is, from sins which either pollute the soul within or defile the body. And desiring the perfecting of holiness, Paul exhorts that in the future they proceed in the fear of God. He uses a single argument for this: the promises that God has made to you [in chapter 6] rightfully require this of you, that you apply yourselves diligently to these duties. Exposition of 2 Corinthians 7:1.[36]

Christians Must Grow in Sanctification. The English Annotations: "Perfecting holiness," or . . . finishing the work of sanctification, begun in our regeneration. For although regeneration (as well as generation) occurs once, yet sanctification is achieved in us by degrees and every good Christian must profit in Christ's school and grow continually both in knowledge as well as grace until we arrive at such perfection as we are capable in this life. As St. Augustine notes, this is but an imperfect perfection at best; a perfection of parts, but no way of degrees. Annotations on 2 Corinthians 7:1.[37]

---

[34]Musculus, *Commentarius . . . in posteriorem epistolam Pauli ad Corinthios*, 217-18.

[35]C. Spangenberg, *Die ander Epistel Pauli an die Corinthier*, 131; citing Jn 15:5.

[36]Dickson, *An Exposition of All St. Paul's Epistles*, 83*.

[37]Downame, ed., *English Annotations*, GG1r; citing 2 Pet 3:18.

7:2-16 PAUL'S JOY

[2]Make room in your hearts[a] *for us. We have wronged no one, we have corrupted no one, we have taken advantage of no one. [3]I do not say this to condemn you, for I said before that you are in our hearts, to die together and to live together. [4]I am acting with great boldness toward you; I have great pride in you; I am filled with comfort. In all our affliction, I am overflowing with joy.*

[5]For even when we came into Macedonia, our bodies had no rest, but we were afflicted at every turn—fighting without and fear within. [6]But God, who comforts the downcast, comforted us by the coming of Titus, [7]and not only by his coming but also by the comfort with which he was comforted by you, as he told us of your longing, your mourning, your zeal for me, so that I rejoiced still more. [8]For even if I made you grieve with my letter, I do not regret it—though I did regret it, for I see that that letter grieved you, though only for a while. [9]As it is, I rejoice, not because you were grieved, but because you were grieved into repenting. For you felt a godly grief, so that you suffered no loss through us.

[10]For godly grief produces a repentance that leads to salvation without regret, whereas worldly grief produces death. [11]For see what earnestness this godly grief has produced in you, but also what eagerness to clear yourselves, what indignation, what fear, what longing, what zeal, what punishment! At every point you have proved yourselves innocent in the matter. [12]So although I wrote to you, it was not for the sake of the one who did the wrong, nor for the sake of the one who suffered the wrong, but in order that your earnestness for us might be revealed to you in the sight of God. [13]Therefore we are comforted.

And besides our own comfort, we rejoiced still more at the joy of Titus, because his spirit has been refreshed by you all. [14]For whatever boasts I made to him about you, I was not put to shame. But just as everything we said to you was true, so also our boasting before Titus has proved true. [15]And his affection for you is even greater, as he remembers the obedience of you all, how you received him with fear and trembling. [16]I rejoice, because I have complete confidence in you.

a Greek lacks *in your hearts*

Overview: Thanks to Titus's favorable report, Paul now expresses his joy that the Corinthians have experienced heartfelt repentance and have once again received him and his message with goodwill. Reformation commentators believe that the apostle's transparent love and compassion for the Corinthian believers serves as a salutary guide for all gospel ministers. Pastors must be prepared to live and die for their people. They must faithfully proclaim the gospel message and show their people the way of salvation. They experience deep joy, not in banquets, lavish clothes, or the applause of the crowd, but when their people submit to God's Word and discipline, and when sinners come to repentance and experience spiritual restoration. At the same time, faithful ministers must expect to face the fierce attacks of Satan, both external and internal, whether in the form of exiles, persecutions, lies, temptations, doubts, or tormented consciences. This was true of the prophet Jeremiah and the apostle Paul, and it was also the case for Athanasius and Martin Luther. Finally, the distinction that Paul makes between worldly and godly grief in 2 Corinthians 7:10 invites extensive discussion among early Protestant exegetes as they seek to explain the nature and fruit of Christian repentance. Godly repentance has nothing to do with the Catholic sacrament of penance or works of satisfaction. Rather, the biblical concept of repentance involves heartfelt sorrow and turning away from sin. This kind of repentance produces a harvest of excellent fruit such as holy indignation, ardent love for God, desire for holiness, renewed commitment to obedience, and fear of dishonoring God.

7:2-4 *Paul's Pastoral Instincts*

Paul Wronged No One. Huldrych Zwingli: Someone might say, "What? Are you completely perfect? Are you completely holy?" Now Paul, by way of excuse, is standing his ground against his opponents who were falsely accusing him of boasting. He responds, therefore, to the objection by way of antipophora:[†] "I am not boasting of holiness or perfection. Nevertheless, I know this, that I have harmed no one and corrupted no one, but have preached for the purpose of edification. And I have corrupted neither the life nor customs of anyone, nor have I cheated anyone. I do not say this so as to criticize or condemn you, or to belittle what is in your heart. For, as I said to you previously, it is my heartfelt desire to live and die for you. Your life is my life; your death is my death. . . . Now it is so far from my purpose to condemn you, because I boast everywhere about your faith and perseverance, and I draw a lot of comfort from you. In all my affliction and tribulation, you are my joy and consolation." Annotations on 2 Corinthians 7:2.[1]

Distinguishing True Apostles from False Ones. Wolfgang Musculus: Let us observe here the difference between true and false apostles. True apostles have nothing to do with dominating others with false doctrine and with a zealous greed for profit. Indeed, they bring harm to no one, they corrupt no one, they exploit no one. But how greatly false apostles are infected by the spirit of domination, false doctrine, and greediness for profit! Thus, they afflict harm upon those whom they dominate; they corrupt those whom they teach; they cheat vulnerable people out of any wealth they can. Take a close look at the Roman Church and see how you should judge that office which they defend as the apostolic seat. If you find that it is free from domination, free from the corruption of false doctrine, free from insatiable greed for profit so that it can be said that it afflicts harm on no one, corrupts no one, cheats no one with false bargains, then fine and good—recognize there an imitation of apostolic purity. But if you detect a dominator, a corruptor, and a cheat, recognize it as the seat of the antichrist and the accursed imposter of Satan, ruling in the church under the pretext of being the apostolic seat. Commentary on 2 Corinthians 7:2.[2]

Paul's Example of Love and Kindness. Tilemann Hesshus: It's as if Paul were saying, "Embrace me with your soul, with true and sincere goodwill, so that I might embrace you." He says to the Galatians, "Become as I am for I have become as you are"; that is, you should be in your soul toward me as I am toward you. Look closely at my sincere goodwill and show that same love toward me in turn. Convince yourselves that I most passionately love you Corinthians as sons. "We have wronged no one; we have corrupted no one; we have defrauded no one." He shows the Corinthians that they have no reason to have a mindset that is hostile toward the apostle Paul, since he has in no way harmed them. Rather, by preaching the truth of the gospel, he has all the more faithfully served them. And he has bestowed great kindness on them by showing them the way to eternal salvation. Pastors cause injury when they abuse their authority and office. And they exercise cruel tyranny when they bring sadness to those whom they should comfort, binding up those whose sins they should absolve. Under the appearance of ministry, they either torture good souls or banish men and women from good

[1]Zwingli, *Annotatiunculae . . . ex ore Zvinglij*, 179-80. [†]Antipophora is a rhetorical figure in which the speaker poses a question and then answers it.

[2]Musculus, *Commentarius . . . in posteriorem epistolam Pauli ad Corinthios*, 221.

company by unfair excommunications. . . . They corrupt their hearers by spreading false teachings whereby faith is extinguished and impiety is instilled in their minds. Under the pretext of ministry, they cheat their hearers by gaping after their possessions and thinking up clever ways to satisfy their desires. Paul teaches that such endeavors must be avoided. Explication of 2 Corinthians 7:2.[3]

Paul Insists on His Innocence. John Trapp: "We have wronged no one." Ministers must live in such a way that, if necessary, they may boast in their innocence and integrity, as did Moses, Samuel, Paul, and Philipp Melanchthon. "We have corrupted no one." That is, as the false apostles had done with their leaven of false doctrine, which eats like a cancer or gangrene, that in due time reaches every part of the body and even infects the brain. In one of Plato's dialogues, Protagoras boasted that during the sixty years he had lived, he had spent forty years in corrupting the youth.[†] "We have defrauded no one." We have cunningly exploited no one—as those former imposters did who made prize of their prisoners. Commentary on 2 Corinthians 7:2.[4]

Paul's Love for the Corinthians. Cyriacus Spangenberg: He demonstrates how much he loves them in various ways and says first, "You are in our hearts such that we die with you or live with you. Neither death nor anything else will separate the love that I bear for you. For I am willing, not just to live with you, but also to go with you to death. And nothing must seem so important to me that I would give up for it the love that I have for you." This is a fine example of how a pastor or preacher must be disposed toward his listeners and spiritual children. If it goes ill with you (he wants to say), it is my death. If it goes well with you, it is my joy and life. From my heart I delight in your welfare, and your mishap is sorrow for my heart. Thirty-Second Sermon.[5]

Perfect Friendship. Giovanni Diodati: The term "to die" signifies a perfect friendship and union. It is as if two friends pledged to one another never to abandon the other, either in life or death; or, as if they were living one and the same life. Annotations on 2 Corinthians 7:3.[6]

Titus's Visit Has Consoled Paul's Mind. John Calvin: Now, since Paul had attained the openness of heart that he had desired among the Corinthians, he leaves off complaining and cheerfully pours out his heart. It's as if he had said, "What need is there that I should expend so much effort in a matter that is already accomplished? For it seems to me that I now have what I was seeking. For the things that Titus has reported to me concerning you are not only sufficient for calming my mind, but also give me reason for boasting about you. Indeed, they have even dispelled the grief that I experienced due to my many and great afflictions." Paul proceeds, step by step, to develop this thought further, for glorying is more than being of an easy and calm mind; and being freed from that grief caused by many afflictions is greater than either of these. Chrysostom[†] explains this confidence somewhat differently, in this way: "The reason I deal with you more freely is because, having confidence in your goodwill toward me, I think I can have all the more freedom with you." I have stated, however, what seems more probable to me, namely, that the report given by Titus had erased the unfavorable impression that had previously tormented his mind. Commentary on 2 Corinthians 7:4.[7]

Paul's Commendations of the Corinthians. Cardinal Cajetan: "I have great

[3]Hesshus, *Explicatio Secundae Epistolae Pauli ad Corinthios*, 182v-183v.

[4]Trapp, *A Commentary or Exposition*, 720*; citing 2 Tim 2:17; 2 Pet 2:3. [†]The dialogue in view is Plato's *Protagoras*.

[5]C. Spangenberg, *Die ander Epistel Pauli an die Corinthier*, 132v.

[6]Diodati, *La Seconde Epistre de l'Apostre S. Paul aux Corinthiens*, 149.

[7]CO 50:86 (CTS 40:267-68). [†]For Chrysostom's interpretation, see PG 62:577-78 (NPNF[1] 12:400).

confidence in you." Determined to show his great love for them, Paul here begins to discuss a different subject, which connects very well with the previous warning. He intends, in fact, to discuss the matter that was so successfully addressed in his first letter to the Corinthians. And quite appropriately, he moderates the rebuke of his previous warning in this ensuing commendation of them because, having obeyed this aforesaid warning, they have been convincingly restored. And so, Paul sets forth four commendations concerning the Corinthians. The first is that his confidence in them abounds. Second, "I boast greatly on account of you"; that is, "there are many reasons at hand for me to be proud of you." And the third: "I am filled with comfort." And the fourth: "I am abounding with joy in all our tribulation." However, the statement "in all our tribulation" refers also to the third commendation, for the sense is that "among all our tribulations, I have been filled with comfort, in addition to abounding in joy"—that is, because joy overcomes tribulations. Commentary on 2 Corinthians 7:4.[8]

Overflowing with Joy. John Trapp: The Greek reads "I do over-abound exceedingly with joy." Others may revel, but the godly only rejoice. They have an exuberance of joy, such as no good can match or evil conquer. Consider the martyrs both ancient and modern. "Oh, how my heart leaps for joy," one of them said, "that I am so near the apprehension of eternal bliss! God, forgive my ingratitude and unworthiness of so great a glory. In all the days of my life I was never so merry as I am now in this dark dungeon."[†] Believe me, there is no such joy in the world as the people of Christ have under the cross. Commentary on 2 Corinthians 7:4.[9]

7:5-9 The Corinthians' Grief Has Led to Repentance

Daily Fears Are Necessary. Martin Luther: We should pray . . . that in our last hour we may not experience this terror and fear, even though we are unable to endure death without a murmur. Paul reminds us: "Fighting without and fear within." But in our daily life these fears are necessary. They enable us to mortify our old selves and to awaken them lest they snore in perfect smugness.

Therefore, just as boys whom the rod cannot reform must be reformed with a club, so these people, whom physical punishments do not improve and who do not learn the fear of God from such punishments, must be humbled with the fire of hell and with an experience of God's wrath, that they might not remain utterly insensate. Commentary on Psalm 90:7.[10]

Fighting Without, Terror Within. Philipp Melanchthon: Just as he said in his previous letter, "Daily I die on account of your glory." Again: "In fear and much trembling I lived among you." Where those terrors come from is indicated below: "Who is weak and I am not weak." For it is impossible to proclaim the gospel without suffering the cross from the right hand and left. . . . Now this is a figure of the statement received from Deuteronomy 32: "Outdoors the sword will devastate, and indoors terror." Annotations on 2 Corinthians 7:5.[11]

Paul's Troubles and Worries. Wolfgang Musculus: Paul now gives a brief explanation of what he said [in the previous verse], "in all our troubles." . . . What is mentioned here in these verses happened to Paul after the conversion of the Corinthians and Ephesians, when he revisited Macedonia for the sake of strengthening them, the

[8]Cajetan, *In Posteriorem Pauli Epistolam ad Corinthios Commentarii*, 178.

[9]Trapp, *A Commentary or Exposition*, 720*. [†]John Foxe, *Foxe's Book of Martyrs, or The Acts and Monuments of the Christian Church* (Philadelphia: James B. Smith, 1860), fols. 1668-70.

[10]LW 13:115-16 (WA 40/3:550); citing 2 Cor 7:5.

[11]*Melanchthons Werke*, 4:118; citing 1 Cor 15:31; 2:3; 2 Cor 11:29; Deut 32:25.

account of which is found in Acts 19–20, and in 2 Corinthians 1 above. And so, when he says, "for when we came into Macedonia," Paul is not speaking about his first visit with them, but his second. During this latter visit he was weighed down with troubles. Although he does not give specific examples, nevertheless he does describe these troubles in general terms, saying "This flesh of ours had no rest, but we were afflicted at every turn." By the word "flesh" Paul means the outer, physical body, exhausted by countless labors and, at the same time, afflicted by the insults of wicked people so that it experienced no rest. To be sure, he was harassed not only by troubles but also by fears. Thus, he says, "conflicts on the outside, fears within." Externally, Paul was attacked by enemies who did not believe him, who were contradicting the truth of Christ and persecuting his servants. Internally, Paul was tormented by worries, fearing that weak persons would be seduced by the false apostles or diverted by persecution from their profession of the name of Christ. Thus, Paul, both externally and internally was afflicted in every way so that his physical body experienced no rest. Commentary on 2 Corinthians 7:5.[12]

Satan's Manifold Attacks. Tilemann Hesshus: Satan attempts to crush us and throw our faith off balance and deter us from the works of our calling. For that reason, he attacks us with every kind of temptation. He not only incites and equips external enemies against us who assault us with lies, exiles, and persecutions in cruel and various ways, but he also disturbs our souls with temptations and internal distresses. He barrages us with dread. He shrouds our minds in a fog so that we are less attentive to the greatness of [God's] promises. He instills doubt concerning the kind will of God toward us. He pressures our conscience to dispute with him regarding our assurance. He often attempts to transfer the imperfections of the disordered church to us. He often attempts to persuade us that God himself is our adversary. And he ransacks every corner of our conscience to stir up terrors and dreads in it and cause burdensome difficulties. For this battle in the mind is much more difficult and sorrowful than what is endured with external enemies. Thus Moses, David, Jeremiah, Paul, Athanasius, and Luther were often, in the midst of great terrors, disputing with Satan regarding the basis of their assurance. But they encouraged themselves with the Word and conquered their fears. Others experience the anxious fears that are felt from the internal vices of the church. For evils close to home (which are manifold in the church) sting most bitterly. Paul endured both these things at the same time. Now Paul is speaking about all evils that produce anxiety. But there is no doubt that he especially understood those spiritual and internal temptations with which Satan afflicts faithful teachers. There are certainly many things that torture the godly breast of those who teach, both external and domestic: the betrayal of friends, the secret machinations of hypocrites, the treachery of false brothers, the failure of colleagues, schisms borne from unimportant matters, the confusion of simple people, and innumerable other things. But God demonstrates that the most oppressive thing that burdens the mind of pastors is when their conscience is embattled, when their conscience becomes a terror to them. For this reason, Jeremiah prays, "Be not a terror to me; you are my refuge in the day of disaster." Explication of 2 Corinthians 7:5.[13]

God Comforts the Humble. Wolfgang Musculus: Insofar as he had said, "I have been filled with comfort and very great joy," Paul now proceeds to explain what he means. He says two things: first, who comforts him, and second, whence he is comforted. The first he attributes to God; the second he attributes to the coming of Titus. "But God," he says, "has comforted us."

[12]Musculus, *Commentarius . . . in posteriorem epistolam Pauli ad Corinthios*, 224.

[13]Hesshus, *Explicatio Secundae Epistolae Pauli ad Corinthios*, 185r-186r; citing Jer 17:17.

The comfort that Paul mentioned at the outset of his letter, by which he was restored in the midst of troubles, he continues to ascribe to God in the course of his letter. Now Paul does not simply say, "God has comforted us," but he prefaces it with the words "he who comforts the humble." Thus, he expresses the character and nature of God, who so desires good things for the humble that, with singular zeal, he runs to help those who are troubled, but detests the proud so much that he opposes them to their loss. Now, Paul is not speaking about people whose mindset is humble and modest, but those who are downcast and oppressed. . . .

[Next] Paul remembers whence God has comforted him, namely, through the coming of Titus. Paul sent Titus to Corinth along with some other brothers (as he says in the next chapter), and when Paul had . . . come to Troas, and when he did not discover Titus there as he had hoped, he was troubled in his spirit and so he left Troas and departed for Macedonia, all the while eagerly anticipating his coming. Since, therefore, he was very troubled for some time, God's favor brought it about that he was refreshed and thrilled when Titus arrived. Thus, Paul says: "God comforted us by the coming of Titus." This man was very pleasing to Paul because he was a dependable partner in all his labors, and Paul endured his absence with difficulty; for that reason, Paul rejoiced greatly when he received Titus back safe. Paul had few faithful colleagues in the work of the Lord. For many people were seeking their own concerns, not the Lord's concerns, and thus Paul was justified in his concern for the sake of Titus himself, and he received great comfort and joy from his return. Commentary on 2 Corinthians 7:6.[14]

God Loves to Comfort His People. John Trapp: This is one of God's sweetest attributes that we can profitably plead for and produce through prayer. He loves to comfort those that are forsaken of their hopes. He will not crush, but rather cherish, that worm Jacob. "He will not break the bruised reed." [This is seen in] the coming of Titus, who came very opportunely, even while Paul was writing this epistle. God's comforts are therefore sweet, because seasonable. He never comes too soon, nor stays for too long. He waits to be gracious, though being a God of judgment. Commentary on 2 Corinthians 7:6.[15]

The Corinthians' Good Report. Andreas Hyperius: Paul mentions a twofold reason for his comfort: first, the coming of Titus, and second, Titus's report regarding the happy condition of the Corinthian church. And so it seems that that prior reason [for comfort] is mentioned to make the latter reason appear all the more excellent by comparison. An emphasis is placed on "your longing, your tears, and your zeal for me." All these things testified that the Corinthians had nothing but goodwill for Paul and greatly desired his presence; that they had been moved to heartfelt repentance and were thinking well of his letter of rebuke; and, moreover, that they were very concerned about his health. When Paul heard of these things, not only was his distress alleviated but he also derived enormous joy from them. For previously, he was constantly dreading that the false apostles would seduce them, and, with excesses and vices increasing little by little, the gospel doctrine would be obscured and finally lost. But when Paul learned that all things were safe and that many people were persisting in right doctrine, and also that those who were sinning had been called back to the right path, he derived enormous joy from this. Thus, indeed, apostolic people ought to rejoice whenever they hear about the happy advance of the gospel, the progress of God's people in spiritual matters, and the repentance of those who have fallen. Commentary on 2 Corinthians 7:6-7.[16]

[14]Musculus, *Commentarius . . . in posteriorem epistolam Pauli ad Corinthios*, 225; citing 2 Cor 1:4.

[15]Trapp, *A Commentary or Exposition*, 721*; citing Mt 12:20.

[16]Hyperius, *Commentarii . . . in Epistolam D. Pauli ad Romanos, et Utramque ad Corinthios*, 386.

Paul Finds Joy Even in Sorrow. Jacques Lefèvre d'Étaples: Wherever the apostles traveled, they faced spiteful machinations, hardships, and innumerable tribulations so that, with their bodies wracked by these hardships, they might give up announcing the gospel. But the indomitable spirit which dwelt within them made them superior to all these hardships, victors of all these attacks. So in the face of many hardships, they experienced many consolations, sometimes the assistance coming from God above, sometime the assistance coming from believers down below. Paul does not deny what happened to him. Rather, this holy life is so full of joy and consolation that Paul finds joy and consolation even from his sorrow—not from any sort of sorrow, but from that sorrow which turns to God. For those who repent, who turn themselves from sin to God, convert to God by turning away from themselves. Therefore, the sorrow that leads to conversion is holy and comes from God; it rightly brings about spiritual joy not only in human beings, but even among God's angels (who reveal the Savior). Commentary on 2 Corinthians 7:6-7.[17]

Grief Born of Piety Is Fruitful. Desiderius Erasmus: This world has its own grief—but a fruitless and harmful one—when people feel tortured in their minds because of diminution of wealth or loss of pleasures, or because of anger or jealousy. Piety also has its own grief, but it is a fruitful and indeed salvific grief. By it you have been touched in such a way that, so far from experiencing any detriment from me, you have gained a good conscience. For the person who grieves because they have offended God provides proof of a conscience set straight, and sorrow leads to repentance in such a way that it does not allow a person to slip back into former transgressions. On the other hand, the grief born of worldly desires brings death; it is harmful equally to body and soul. Paraphrases on 2 Corinthians 7.[18]

Paul Deals Gently with Those Who Have Repented. Martin Luther: [The Corinthians] wanted to be [considered] Christians and boasted and bragged that the gospel had been preached to them by the great apostles. This is why St. Paul had to write to them so harshly and scold them as he did nowhere else, so that it even seems too much to write this way to Christians; weak, fearful consciences could certainly have been affected more than they could endure. Afterward, in his second epistle, when he sees that they were somewhat distressed at his stern writing, he softens it and deals gently with those who have now been moved to repentance. Postil for the Ninth Sunday After Trinity.[19]

Paul Did Not Regret the Corinthians' Sorrow. Wolfgang Musculus: Paul explains what he had said concerning the sorrow of the Corinthians, indicating that he was speaking about the grief that had been brought on by his first letter. Now Paul was experiencing pain because he had grieved those whom he loved. And he would have certainly regretted it except that he understood that their sadness was profitable for their salvation. Thus, he says, "For even if I caused you grief by our letter, I do not regret it." He goes on to explain why he did not regret it. . . . He was finding no pleasure from their sadness, and so he did not write to grieve them but to demonstrate his concern for them and his longing for their salvation. And yet, he recognized that his letter would cause them to be aggrieved, which he now says he does not at all regret. Commentary on 2 Corinthians 7:8.[20]

A Rebuke That Produces Fruit. Tilemann Hesshus: Paul's sense is this: "I clearly see that my letter of rebuke cast you into sorrow, even if that

[17]Lefèvre, *Commentariorum in Epistolas Beati Pauli . . . Liber Tertius*, 136r-137r.

[18]CWE 43:241-42.

[19]LW 78:307 (WA 22:157).

[20]Musculus, *Commentarius . . . in posteriorem epistolam Pauli ad Corinthios*, 227.

sorrow was momentary. Though your repentance soon brought about comfort, nevertheless I do not regret—rather I rejoice—that I wrote sternly, not that I delight in your sorrow, but in the usefulness which that sorrow brought about, namely, life-giving repentance." For the Word of God does not sadden a person constantly, but only momentarily, for God does not seek that a person perish, but that repentance should be followed by salvation. Therefore, in that very severe rebuke, God's most merciful will always shines forth, which most ardently longs for our salvation.

The Canaanite woman was most deeply saddened when she heard Christ say, "I was not sent, except to the lost sheep of the house of Israel." Again, "It is not good to take the children's food and give it to the dogs." But that sadness lasted only a moment, for he soon said, "Oh woman you have great faith; let it be to you as you wish." David was deeply saddened when he heard the rebuke of Nathan: "You are that man, guilty of death." But that sorrow lasted only for a time, for he encouraged himself with the comforting words, "The Lord has absolved your sin." Therefore, when the Corinthians were repenting due to Paul's rebuke, they were greatly saddened for having offended God by committing incest and deforming the church, Paul rejoiced in that fruit of his letter. EXPLICATION OF 2 CORINTHIANS 7:8.[21]

THE MEANING OF TRUE REPENTANCE. WOLFGANG MUSCULUS: "Because you were grieved to repentance." The Greek for this is *eis metanoian,* that is, "to repentance." The meaning of the word *metanoia* is not adequately translated by the Latin word *poenitentia,* although Erasmus† tried mightily to ascribe the same meaning to them since he reckoned that the Latin word *poenitere* was derived from the roots *pone* and *tenere,* that is, "to recognize after the deed." More correctly, Lorenzo Valla‡ states that "the two Greek nouns *metanoia* and *metamelia* have a different meaning than our Latin noun *poenitentia.* For the noun *poenitentia* is related to the Latin verb *poenitet,* which means 'it irks' or 'it annoys.' But the Greek words *metanoia* and *metamelia* are related in their meaning to 'pulling back' and 'concern to change for the better.' . . . And so, our Latin word *poenitentia* signifies 'to become sorrowful,' while the Greek word *metanoia* signifies 'a change of mind.'" . . . And so, rather than rendering this passage with the Latin phrase *ad poenitentiam,* I prefer to render it *ad resipiscentiam* [to repent; to change one's mind], according to the meaning of the Greek word *metanoia.* Now Paul will remind the Corinthians shortly that this sorrow had produced this sort of repentance. We have taught somewhere above that the apostles were not like the Pharisees who were more concerned that those who sinned experienced sorrow than true repentance. The apostle indicates here in an eloquent fashion that he was not delighted by the sorrow of the Corinthians, but by their repentance. COMMENTARY ON 2 CORINTHIANS 7:9.[22]

WOUNDS THAT BRING HEALING. THE ENGLISH ANNOTATIONS: Just as a good physician does not rejoice because he has administered a bitter potion to his patient, but because the potion has procured the patient's comfort; just as a surgeon who lances a wound is not glad that he has caused pain to the injured parts, but because healing has been achieved through this pain—so the apostle does not rejoice because he has made the Corinthians sorrowful, but because by their sorrow they have gained health for their souls and many spiritual graces, as he mentions in verse 11. ANNOTATIONS ON 2 CORINTHIANS 7:9.[23]

TRUE REPENTANCE LEADS TO A NEW LIFE. JOHN TRAPP: The Greek means a thorough change of both the mind and behavior. Luther says, "The best and most appropriate repentance is a new life."

[21]Hesshus, *Explicatio Secundae Epistolae Pauli ad Corinthios,* 187-88. See Mt 15:21-28; 2 Sam 12:1-14.

[22]Musculus, *Commentarius . . . in posteriorem epistolam Pauli ad Corinthios,* 229. †Musculus here is challenging the decision of Erasmus in his *Annotations* (1521) to translate the Greek word *metanoia* with the Latin word *poenitentia.* See Erasmus, *Opera Omnia* 6.3:388. ‡Lorenzo Valla, *De Collatione Novi Testamenti,* Amsterdam: Henricum Laurentium, 1630, 152r-v.

[23]Downame, ed., *English Annotations,* GG1r.

This statement, though condemned by Pope Leo X, is certainly an excellent one. Repentance for sin is worth nothing without repentance from sin. "If you repent with a contradiction," says Tertullian, "God will pardon you with a contradiction. You repent, and yet continue in your sin. God will pardon you, and yet send you to hell." Such is the case of a pardon with contradiction. COMMENTARY ON 2 CORINTHIANS 7:9.[24]

WORLDLY SORROW AND GODLY SORROW. JACQUES LEFÈVRE D'ÉTAPLES: Those who would heal a wounded person must induce them to grief. . . . And this is the sort of godly sorrow that leads to salvation. But the grief that leads to death (and thus to ruin) is compared to worldly sorrow, which leads to death. A person has squandered his riches through his avarice: he is sorrowful; he grieves; he seeks a remedy; he is angry at heaven and accuses God. This is worldly sorrow and brings forth death. Another person solicits a bishopric (I'm imagining this), not for the sake of the ministry, but to gain a lofty reputation and temporal goods (which are like shadows, and ought to be accompanied by spiritual goods): he is disappointed; he misses his hoped-for ambitions; he is sad; he mourns inconsolably; with a wounded conscience, he is deprived of the comfort of friends; he is cursed by enemies and shunned by friends. This is worldly sorrow, and it announces a future death which is eternal. But if this person comes to his senses, and grieves for possessing such foolish concupiscence, and if, falling to his knees, he prays for forgiveness in tears, and if he chooses to lead the life of a pauper, without status or greed, so that he might not again offend God in so perilous a fashion . . . this is truly godly sorrow, and almost certainly announces eternal life. COMMENTARY ON 2 CORINTHIANS 7:9-10.[25]

[24]Trapp, *A Commentary or Exposition*, 721*. A similar statement appears in Luther's Ninety-Five Theses: "When our Lord and Master Jesus Christ, said 'Repent,' he called for the entire life of believers to be one of penitence" (thesis 1).

[25]Lefèvre, *Commentariorum in Epistolas Beati Pauli . . . Liber Tertius*, 137.

7:10-12 *The Nature of Godly Grief*

GODLY AND WORLDLY SORROW. PHILIPP MELANCHTHON: There is no difference between sorrow according to the world and sorrow according to God except this, that those who are sorrowful according to God recognize their sins and confess that they are rightly afflicted, offering a sacrifice to the God of justice, since he punishes justly. As it says in Daniel, "Everything that you did to us, truly you did with right judgment." And Daniel 9, "To us belongs shame, but to you our Lord belongs mercy and forgiveness." And to those who willingly endure the hand of God and await redemption, Lamentations 3 says, "It is good to wait silently for the salvation of God." . . . And so, Paul here speaks of repentance—not doing penance—in the same way as the Lord in the gospel: "My yoke is easy and my burden is light." For truly the love of the cross is not a cross. Those who are sorrowful according to the world are outraged by God's judgment, as Jeremiah 2 says: "I am innocent, without sin." So, too, those who do not recognize their sin and do not confess are justly afflicted, and so they have no hope of being redeemed. ANNOTATIONS ON 2 CORINTHIANS 7:10.[26]

FOUR KINDS OF GODLY SORROW. WOLFGANG MUSCULUS: It is clear that everyone who experiences godly sorrow, in the end, is also gladdened by God. Now there are four kinds of godly sorrow that occur at the present time. The first kind is that which the apostle is thinking of here in this passage. And this sort alone, he says, is adequate to produce repentance. The second kind is where a godly person experiences sadness because of disgrace for the sake of God's name. People suffer this kind of sorrow every day who either live as exiles because of their faith in God, or live among false Christians, idolaters, and enemies of the Word of God. Thus were those people who, though they were godly,

[26]*Melanchthons Werke*, 4:118-19; citing Dan 3:30; 9:8-9; Lam 3:26; Mt 11:30; Jer 2:35.

lived amid the people of God in Jerusalem itself and groaned and mourned over the detestable practices that were happening there, as one can read in Ezekiel 9. . . . The third kind of godly sorrow is experienced by all who suffer injuries, jeers, and persecutions because of the name of God. The passage 1 Peter 2 pertains to this, where it says, "For this is a gracious thing, when mindful of God, a person endures sorrows while suffering unjustly." The fourth kind of godly sorrow is born out of a desire to appear in God's presence, when the spirits of faithful people who love God experience sorrow on account of the length of their pilgrimages. An example of this happened to David when he was in exile. He makes mention of this in Psalm 42 when he says, "As the deer pants for springs of water, so my soul pants for you, O God." That this longing was accompanied by sadness is clearly seen when David goes on to say, "My tears have been my bread day and night." Again, "Why are you sad, O my soul, and why are you in turmoil within me?" The apostle Paul experienced this same emotion . . . for he says, "I desire to be released and be with Christ." These are the kinds of sorrow that are "godly sorrows." More could be added to this list, but I think these are sufficient for the present. And if only they would be applicable to us! COMMENTARY ON 2 CORINTHIANS 7:10.[27]

GRIEF IN THE LIVES OF PETER AND JUDAS. MARTIN LUTHER: Judas had a heavier load on his back than Peter. Therefore, he fell into despair, thinking there would never be any help or consolation. So out of woe and sorrow he went away and hanged himself, poor man! But why? Because he had been slothful in hearing the Word of God. He despised it and never bettered himself by it. Thus, when he needed consolation and had the Word no longer, it was impossible for him to find help.

Peter also wept bitterly. He was anxious and worried because of his sins, but he had been more diligent in listening to the Word of his Lord Christ, and he had engraved it on his mind. Therefore now, in the hour of his need, he seized on it and held fast to it, comforted himself with it, and hoped that God would be gracious to him. That is the one true help in such a need, and the hapless Judas lacked it. But that Peter held firmly to the Word and grace of God, the Lord himself testifies when he says, "I have prayed for you, that your own faith may not fail."

Therefore, learn here what is true repentance. Peter weeps bitterly, that is the beginning of repentance, that the heart acknowledges sin and is grieved for it, that it has no love for it or desire to continue in it but is saddened that it has not kept God's will and has fallen into sin. But we cannot do that by ourselves; the Lord must look upon us as he looked upon Peter. SERMON FROM THE YEAR 1545.[28]

GODLY SORROW. CYRIACUS SPANGENBERG: Godly sorrow is when one is sad, distressed, and troubled because of sins committed, by which one has angered God. Then one actually feels how fiercely our Lord God is angry because of sin, and one recognizes how rightly he punishes us for the same, and yet one does not lose heart or despair or grumble against God because of this. Instead, one acknowledges that he punishes us rightly, and therefore patiently bears the punishment or chastisement, and in such pain and sadness holds on to faith in God's inexpressible and great mercy, entrusts oneself to it completely and calls on God from the heart through Jesus Christ and asks for the forgiveness of sins. And because God has certainly promised us the same, one grasps it also by faith and therefore puts one's heart at peace and rejoices again in Christ Jesus. Thus, one is rid of sorrow again, and love follows, and the fear of God, patience and hope together with a new obedience, with all the fruits of righteous repentance. THIRTY-THIRD SERMON.[29]

[27]Musculus, *Commentarius . . . in posteriorem epistolam Pauli ad Corinthios*, 231-32; citing 1 Pet 2:19; Ps 42:1, 3, 11; Phil 1:23.

[28]Luther, *Day by Day We Magnify You*, 162 (WA 52:768); citing Lk 22:32.

[29]C. Spangenberg, *Die ander Epistel Pauli an die Corinthier*, 136r.

Repentance Is Not the Cause of Salvation. John Calvin: Paul seems to make repentance the cause of salvation. If this were true, it would follow that we are justified by works. I respond that we must note what Paul is discussing here. For he is not inquiring about the cause of salvation, but simply commending repentance from the fruit it produces—he says that it is like a way by which we are brought to salvation. And rightly so, for Christ freely calls us, but it is to repentance. God freely pardons our sins, but only when we renounce them. Indeed, God accomplishes in us two things at one and the same time: that being renewed by repentance, we might be liberated from the bondage of our sins; and that being justified by faith we might be liberated also from the curse of our sins. Therefore, these are inseparable graces, and on account of their indivisible connection, repentance can appropriately and properly be called an introduction to salvation, though in this way: that it be represented more as an effect than a cause. These are not proofs for the sake of avoiding [the truth], but a true and simple solution, for while the Scripture teaches us that we never obtain remission of sins without repentance, at the same time, it establishes in a variety of passages that it is the mercy of God that is the grounds or cause for obtaining it. Commentary on 2 Corinthians 7:10.[30]

Godly and Worldly Sorrow. The English Annotations: Godly sorrow [is] a sorrow according to God, a sorrow coming from God that is pleasing to God and brings the sinner to God. It is then that sinners' hearts are truly rent for having offended God by their sins, and they have become confident of the forgiveness of Jesus Christ and fully and steadfastly resolved (as far as God enables them) to shun and avoid all sin in the future. As St. Ambrose† put it, "One truly bewails that which they have done who never does afterward that which they have bewailed." . . .

By worldly sorrow Paul means that grief that is experienced by people of the world who are not regenerated by the Spirit of God, whose grief and sorrow is nothing else than the bitter smart of their misery without any serious and sincere repentance. Or else, it is the remorse and pricking of their consciences for their sins, but without faith and without intention of amendment, and without conversion to God. Hence, all this grief and sorrow of theirs is nothing but a preparation for eternal death and a kind of beginning of the same. This was what Nero experienced; after he had put both the apostles Peter and Paul to death, it is said that he felt the torments of hell in his conscience, and ran about crying, "Have I no friend or enemy that will kill me and rid me of my pain?"‡ Or again, worldly sorrow means a sorrow only for the loss of worldly things, or a sorrow only caused by the fear of God's judgment in unbelievers, whereupon there commonly follows hardness of heart and a reprobate sense, and ultimately, despair and damnation itself. Annotations on 2 Corinthians 7:10.[31]

Church Discipline Abets True Repentance. Martin Bucer: The ancient and apostolic churches demonstrated the same severity against all serious misconduct, in order that they might move those who sinned to that godly sorrow which leads to repentance and which no one regrets, and that in the congregation there might be maintained and increased that fear, as well as zeal and enthusiasm to live a Christian life, together with anger and hatred against vices, as testified by the holy apostle in 2 Corinthians 7.

This is where we find the origin of the public confession and penance of which we read in Tertullian, Cyprian, Ambrose, and all the ancient holy fathers. When any of the Christians had in some way fallen into serious and public sin, through which others were offended, they were not

[30]CO 50:90 (CTS 40:274-75).

[31]Downame, ed., *English Annotations*, GG1v. †For Ambrose's statement, see PL 17:323. ‡John Foxe refers to a similar statement from Nero: *Acts and Monuments* (1570) 1:63.

admitted to the fellowship of Christ's table until they had given the church a clear and satisfactory indication of their repentance and reformation and had done enough to prove that they were truly sorry for their sins and had given themselves with all their hearts to reformation of their ways. True Care of Souls.[32]

Seven Fruits of Repentance. Wolfgang Musculus: Paul declares the nature of godly sorrow; he has said that repentance produces salvation. Now he enumerates the fruits that sorrow and repentance have produced for the Corinthians. He counts seven fruits, namely, anxiety, reparation, indignation, fear, desire, zeal, and punishment. He says, "See what this godly sorrow has produced." He is not fully capable of expressing how much the Corinthians owe to the sorrow that they received from his first letter. . . . It is as if he should say, "That sorrow of yours, which seemed distressing and bitter not only for you but also for me, see how useful it was for you and what exceptional fruit of true repentance it has produced in you." Commentary on 2 Corinthians 7:11.[33]

Seeking to Clear Oneself. John Calvin: Because Erasmus rendered this word "satisfaction," ignorant persons were misled by the ambiguity of the term and applied it to popish *satisfactions*, whereas Paul employs the Greek word *apologia* (defense). This is the reason why I have preferred to retain the Latin word *defensionem* (defense), which the Old Interpreter [i.e., Jerome] had made use of. But it must be noted that this indicates here a kind of defense that consists more in the supplication for pardon than in averting sins. Just as a son who desires to clear himself to his father does not undertake a formal pleading of his case, but rather acknowledges his guilt, more than confidently excusing himself. For hypocrites excuse themselves—indeed, they arrogantly defend themselves—more like those who dispute with God than those who give thanks to him. Commentary on 2 Corinthians 7:11.[34]

Indignation, Fear, Longing, Zeal, and Punishment. Tilemann Hesshus: "What indignation." This passion usually follows the recognition of sin and sorrow in relation to God. When we recognize that we have offended God and provoked his wrath, we detest our sin and we get angry with ourselves somewhat for having acted foolishly. With good reason, the Corinthians were indignant for the incest which deformed the whole church and incited the wrath of God against the church. And so, they were rightly enraged at those other fornicators, troublemakers, and profaners of the Lord's Supper.

"What fear." The repentant Corinthians feared lest the apostle Paul should be more hostile toward them and lest, like the apostle, something more serious should be decided against them. They were also fearing the wrath of God, lest he should kindle a more severe punishment against them, once again removing his word from them, or sending some other very serious calamity. This sort of godly fear is a clear sign of true and serious repentance, for sin is recognized and God's judgment against sin is considered. Thus, David was fearing the wrath of God in Psalm 51: "Deliver me from bloodguiltiness, O God, the God of my salvation." And Psalm 28: "Do not drag me off with the wicked, with the workers of evil, who speak peace with their neighbors while evil is in their hearts."

"What longing." The wicked also experience fear, a deluge of calamities, and God pouring out his judgment against their sin. But they do not long for salvation, but rather they grumble against God. However, because pious people encourage themselves by faith, even as they experience fear, they long for and desire consolation. The Corinthians were longing to see and embrace Paul to prove their repentance to him, and, after such weighty rebukes,

[32]Bucer, *Concerning the True Care of Souls*, 104-5 (*Von der waren Seelsorge*, 162).
[33]Musculus, *Commentarius . . . in posteriorem epistolam Pauli ad Corinthios*, 233.
[34]CO 50:90-91 (CTS 40:275-76).

to hear words of comfort from him. Even this was a clear sign of their earnest improvement.

"What zeal." Zeal is the ardent love of God that is born from faith and the consideration of God's benefits, aroused in the heart by the Holy Spirit, because the pious mind tries to protect the glory of God and the truth of the gospel. The Corinthians were showing that they burned with this zeal as they were protecting the glory of God and his holy name, and lest the gospel of Jesus Christ be held in poor esteem, they excommunicated that incestuous person. Pious people are zealous for these things and they live in a manner consistent with that saying, "Zeal for your house has consumed me."

"What punishment." Paul speaks of punishment because the Corinthians, having been admonished by Paul's letter, excommunicated the incestuous person and rebuked those contentious people and those who profaned the Lord's Supper, and they removed from the fellowship those who were participating in sacrifices to idols. For by their severity they had protected the glory of God, the holy name of the church, the truth of the gospel, and the authority of the apostle Paul. Explication of 2 Corinthians 7:11.[35]

Indignation and Repentance. John Calvin: This mindset also accompanies sacred sorrow, that sinners are very angry against their vices, and even against themselves—just as all those who are animated by a right zeal as often as they see God offended. This mindset, however, is more intense than mere sorrow. For the first step is that evil be displeasing to us. The second is that, being inflamed with anger, we press hard upon ourselves so that our consciences might feel real grief. Now it could be that the indignation mentioned here is that with which the Corinthians burned against the wrongdoing of the one or the few, whom they were previously indulging. Thus, they were repenting of their previous support of the wrongdoing or with disregarding it. Commentary on 2 Corinthians 7:11.[36]

Sinners Mortify Themselves for Their Sin. John Trapp: Out of the deepest self-abhorrence, the buffeting of the flesh and giving it a black eye—the cross of mortification—as St. Paul once did. Thus, the women parted with their mirrors. Mary Magdalene wiped Christ's feet with her hair, with which she had formerly made nets by which to catch fools. Thomas Cranmer[†] burned his right hand first—the hand with which he had [recanted of the Protestant faith], and often repeated in the flames, "This unworthy right hand," for as long as his voice allowed him. The person who is truly repentant penalizes himself and withholds from his flesh some lawful comforts, or even forfeits everything. These seven signs of godly sorrow are to be seen in the repenting church described in Canticles chapter 5, as a worthy example or emblem. "I sleep," there is indignation, "but my heart awakens," there's apology. "I arose to open . . . ," there's study or care or diligence. "My soul failed," there's her zeal. "I sought him, I called on him," there's her vehement desire. "The watchmen found me, they struck me. . . ." There's her revenge, while she shrank not from any danger, but followed Christ through thick and thin in the night. And all this shows her fear of being again overtaken with drowsiness. Commentary on 2 Corinthians 7:11[37]

Seven Signs of Godly Sorrow. Edward Leigh: The Holy Ghost has set down seven fruits or signs of godly sorrow. . . . (1) *Care* to leave all our sins. (2) *Apology*, whereby persons are moved to accuse and condemn themselves for their past sins, both before God and human beings. (3) *Indignation*, whereby persons are exceedingly angry with themselves for their offenses. (4) *Fear*, lest they

[35]Hesshus, *Explicatio Secundae Epistolae Pauli ad Corinthios*, 194v-195v; citing Ps 51:14; 28:3; 69:9.

[36]CO 50:91 (CTS 40:276).

[37]Trapp, *A Commentary or Exposition*, 722*; citing Ex 38:3; Lk 7:36-38. [†]Thomas Cranmer's martyrdom—including his burning of the hand that signed the recantation—is found in John Foxe, *Foxe's Book of Martyrs, or The Acts and Monuments of the Christian Church* (Philadelphia: James B. Smith, 1860), 393-94.

should fall into former sins again. (5) *Desire*, whereby they crave for strength and assistance against sin. (6) *Zeal* in the performance of all good duties, contrary to their special sins. (7) *Revenge*, whereby they subdue their bodies, that they may not be an instrument of sin. Annotations on 2 Corinthians 7:11.[38]

The Corinthian's Zeal for the Right. Cardinal Cajetan: "So although I wrote to you, it was not for the sake of him who caused the injury"—namely, the incestuous son—"nor for the sake of the one who suffered"—namely, the father and husband who suffered the injury and adultery. You should not think that these denials represent Paul's intention, but relate to the benefit that resulted to these Corinthians. For the sense here is not that "I wrote on account of the one who caused the injury and he who suffered the wrong"—though Paul had expressly written for the sake of his correction. Rather, the sense is "Even if the outcome of my letter had not been the correction of the incestuous man and the revenge of the father who had suffered the injury, nevertheless that related outcome did result. . . . Even if no other fruit had resulted from our letter, this one thing did follow: namely, that your zeal, which you have for us in the presence of God, was made clear to you yourselves." And so, by excommunicating that man, it was made clear to the Corinthians that they themselves were zealous for their particular church. But not whatever kind of church: rather, that church which they had in the name, authority, and position of Paul. Their actions was not according to human emotions, but before the eyes of divine majesty. That is, they had acted according to the profound truth which God takes into consideration, which is pleasing to God. Commentary on 2 Corinthians 7:12.[39]

Scandal to the Gospel. The English Annotations: "That which moved me to write unto you so sharply," Paul states, "was not the injury either offered by the son, or suffered by the father, but the public scandal of the church." . . . Though the sin was only in the incestuous person, and the particular wrong done to his father, yet in regard that this incestuous contract was tolerated among the Corinthians, and no censure inflicted upon the delinquent, the whole church received a wound in it. And the enemies of the truth took occasion to blaspheme the holy name and profession of Christians, as if such foul acts as this were fruits of Christian liberty, or practices allowed by the doctrine of the gospel. Annotations on 2 Corinthians 7:12.[40]

7:13-16 *Paul's Confidence in the Corinthians*

Paul's Recommendations Were Not in Vain. Desiderius Erasmus: Since this affair has resulted in consolation for you . . . I too personally rejoice on account of your joy. But the joy of Titus has increased this pleasure of ours. He was welcomed among you on my recommendation in such a way that his spirit was refreshed by all, when he saw that my authority carried so much weight with you. As a result, if I have boasted at all in his presence about your uprightness and obedience, I have not been put to shame. For this is a risk a person takes when he recommends anyone. I had commended him to you, you to him. On both sides it has turned out well: for just as you have found that Titus, in every circumstance, was the sort of person I told you he was, so he has found that whatever boasts I made about you in his presence are true. Accordingly, neither before you nor before him am I ashamed of empty claims. Although even before this he esteemed you, still now, after experiencing your devotion, he has been powerfully drawn to you, in his inmost being, while he ponders and reconsiders in his own mind the great alacrity with which you all obeyed our will when he conveyed it, and the great reverence

[38]Leigh, *Annotations upon all the New Testament*, 262*.
[39]Cajetan, *In Posteriorem Pauli Epistolam ad Corinthios Commentarii*, 179.
[40]Downame, ed., *Annotations on the Second Epistle of Paul to the Corinthians*, GG1v*.

and fear with which you welcomed him at his coming. Paraphrases of 2 Corinthians 7.[41]

The Comfort and Refreshment Derived from Ministry. Wolfgang Musculus: Paul returns to the subject he began to discuss earlier [in v. 6], when he said, "But God, who comforts the humble, comforted us by the coming of Titus. . . ." Up to this point he has explained and expanded upon this comfort that he received from them through Titus. Now, repeating this, Paul turns his attention to that comfort with which they refreshed Titus himself and Paul mentions how much joy it brought him. For that reason, Paul says, "we received comfort from your comfort." . . .

Note the comfort and refreshment that is experienced by a true minister of Christ when he undertakes his labors in ministry, if he keeps the people committed to the cause of piety, displeased with their sins, fearing God, devoted and obedient toward himself. I do not doubt that comfort of this sort, when it proceeds from faithful people, consoled the labors and afflictions of the apostle, and today it also consoles the faithful minister of Christ who seeks nothing other in his ministry than to produce much fruit for his Lord. Those people are motivated otherwise who are concerned with stuffing either their stomachs or their pockets. Commentary on 2 Corinthians 7:13.[42]

Paul's Newfound Joy Because of the Corinthians. Tilemann Hesshus: The apostle attempts to remove every doubt from the Corinthians and persuade them that their church has completely satisfied him, that nothing more of the offense remains in his mind, but that he rejoices greatly from that consolation of the church, for it has once again been confirmed by Titus's report that the church has repented. Likewise, he shows his burning love for the Corinthian church since he acknowledges that he has also been filled with joy and consolation from the consolation of the church. This response ought always to be evident in godly pastors: that they should be concerned about the salvation and well-being of the church as if it were their own. He also shows the many ways that he had been refreshed by them when he learned that Titus's joy and spirit had been revived by the Corinthians. . . . In this way God also confirms the souls of godly pastors—in other respects pitifully vexed with constant concerns, dangers, and temptations—when he reveals to them the unanimity of godly servants, their eagerness, their fruitful labor, their salvation, and the benefit of the godly. And so it makes them always more eager for new labors. Explication of 2 Corinthians 7:13.[43]

Paul Was Truthful in Doctrine and Action. Andreas Hyperius: Paul reports the other reason why he was comforted and greatly pleased concerning the Corinthians—namely, because Titus had discovered all things true among the Corinthians which Paul had previously boasted to him about before departing for Achaia. And thus he was not ashamed. And Paul here gives splendid praise and testimony regarding the Corinthians because he had great confidence in their goodness and obedience, when he was writing his first epistle. Moreover, the apostle praises the Corinthians here, not as flatterers usually do, but as good teachers are accustomed to do when extolling their diligent disciples. The apostle seems to allude here to the fact that people are usually ashamed who are blamed falsely by the reports of others. There is, however, a certain comparison being strongly made when Paul says that that report which he recounted to Titus was no less true than all the doctrine which he had previously taught them. Thus, Paul commends here the truth, both in his teaching and in all speech and action. Commentary on 2 Corinthians 7:14.[44]

[41]CWE 43:244.

[42]Musculus, *Commentarius . . . in posteriorem epistolam Pauli ad Corinthios*, 237-38.

[43]Hesshus, *Explicatio Secundae Epistolae Pauli ad Corinthios*, 198v-199r.

[44]Hyperius, *Commentarii . . . in Epistolam D. Pauli ad Romanos, et Utramque ad Corinthios*, 389.

THE MINISTER'S LOVE FOR HIS PEOPLE SHOULD GROW. WOLFGANG MUSCULUS: "And his affection for you is even greater." Paul speaks of Titus's "affection" [*viscera*]. By "affection," we should understand the emotion of love, which the Greeks call *storgēn*, which has its habitation in the deepest recesses of the heart. . . . A lot of play-acting in words and deeds takes place when humans express love for one another, whereby nothing is expressed from the recesses of the heart. These cases do not deserve the term "affection"; rather, the term "affection" is appropriate only when there is true love, when there is no place for play-acting. In order to commend this in Titus, Paul does not say, "He boasts a lot about you and says many splendid things about you," but, "And his affection for you is even greater."

The Greek term for "even greater" is *perissoterōs*, that is, "more abundant." Paul says this because, not only does Titus still have affection for them, but his affection for the Corinthians is even greater than it was before. . . . The minister of Christ loves the believers whom he governs by the Word: first, because they belong to Christ; second, because they have been committed to his care and trust, quite apart from the fact that they are partners of the same faith and salvation. But this love commonly allows for growth, and the minister's affection is even greater if the people, because of their piety, demonstrate themselves obedient and teachable in everything, just as a father loves his sons, first on account of the fact that they are his children, and then his love for them grows even greater when he sees that they are respectful, obedient, and compliant toward him in all things. This is what happened to Titus—and what needs to happen to all ministers of the Word, when they have sincere concern for Christ and his church. COMMENTARY ON 2 CORINTHIANS 7:15.[45]

WITH FEAR AND TREMBLING. JOHN CALVIN: By these two words Paul sometimes expresses simply respect, and this meaning perhaps fits this passage—although I would have no objection to view the "trembling" to mean explicitly, that, being conscious of their wrongdoing, they were afraid to face him. Indeed, even those who are resolute in their wickedness panic at the sight of the judge, but voluntarily trembling (which comes from their natural sense of shame) is a sign of repentance. Whichever explanation you choose, this passage teaches what is the right reception of ministers of Christ. Certainly, it is not sumptuous banquets, nor splendid apparel, nor flattering and honorable salutations, nor the plaudits of the multitude that gratify an upright and faithful pastor. Instead, he experiences the fullness of joy when the doctrine of salvation is received reverently from his mouth, when he possesses the authority that belongs to him for the edification of the church, when the people devote themselves to his discipline to be regulated by his ministry under Christ's authority. An example of this we see here in Titus. And finally, in conclusion, Paul confirms again what he said previously: that he had never been offended to such a degree that he entirely despaired of the Corinthians. COMMENTARY ON 2 CORINTHIANS 7:15-16.[46]

[45]Musculus, *Commentarius . . . in posteriorem epistolam Pauli ad Corinthios*, 240.
[46]CO 50:94 (CTS 40:282).

8:1-15 ENCOURAGEMENT TO GIVE GENEROUSLY

We want you to know, brothers,[a] *about the grace of*
God that has been given among the churches of
Macedonia, [2]for in a severe test of affliction, their
abundance of joy and their extreme poverty have
overflowed in a wealth of generosity on their part.
[3]For they gave according to their means, as I can
testify, and beyond their means, of their own accord,
[4]begging us earnestly for the favor[b] *of taking part in*
the relief of the saints— [5]and this, not as we expected,
but they gave themselves first to the Lord and then by
the will of God to us. [6]Accordingly, we urged Titus
that as he had started, so he should complete among
you this act of grace. [7]But as you excel in everything—
in faith, in speech, in knowledge, in all earnestness,
and in our love for you[c]*—see that you excel in this act*
of grace also.
[8]I say this not as a command, but to prove by the
earnestness of others that your love also is genuine.
[9]For you know the grace of our Lord Jesus Christ,
that though he was rich, yet for your sake he became
poor, so that you by his poverty might become rich.
[10]And in this matter I give my judgment: this
benefits you, who a year ago started not only to do
this work but also to desire to do it. [11]So now finish
doing it as well, so that your readiness in desiring it
may be matched by your completing it out of what
you have. [12]For if the readiness is there, it is accept-
able according to what a person has, not according to
what he does not have. [13]For I do not mean that
others should be eased and you burdened, but that as
a matter of fairness [14]your abundance at the present
time should supply their need, so that their abun-
dance may supply your need, that there may be
fairness. [15]As it is written, "Whoever gathered much
had nothing left over, and whoever gathered little
had no lack."

a Or *brothers and sisters* **b** The Greek word *charis* can mean *favor* or *grace* or *thanks*, depending on the context **c** Some manuscripts *in your love for us*

Overview: In 2 Corinthians 8, the apostle Paul shifts his attention to the Corinthians' financial collection on behalf of the Jerusalem church, pointing to the lavish gifts of the Macedonian believers and the extravagant self-giving love of Jesus Christ to motivate the Corinthians to generous giving. Not surprisingly, Reformation commentators find in these verses important lessons regarding private and public charity relevant to their own age. Almsgiving that pleases God is spontaneous and sacrificial; it issues from a simple and sincere heart; it is marked by joy, eagerness, prayerfulness, and a generous spirit. More important than the amount given is the goodwill displayed, for when Christians contribute to the needs of brothers and sisters in financial distress, they give to the Lord. At the same time, several Protestant interpreters launch pointed criticisms against perceived errors related to charity and almsgiving found among their Catholic and Anabaptist opponents. Charitable giving is not a good work that merits salvation, but a fruit of Christian obedience and genuine faith. Financial provision should be given to the deserving poor, not to fake beggars, lazy mendicant monks, and avaricious Catholic priests. Several commentators also discuss and condemn Anabaptist groups like the Hutterites that interpret Paul's words in 2 Corinthians 8 to abolish private property and establish a communal ownership of goods. For most of the reformers, Christian love requires generosity, not economic equality. But the greatest concern of Reformation interpreters centers on Paul's profound description of Jesus Christ in 2 Corinthians 8:14: the Son of God humbled himself, living and dying in abject physical poverty, so that his blood-bought people might experience the riches of heaven. The Christian's final hope is found, not in an abundance of material goods, but in the spiritual riches that come from Jesus Christ, which are (as Calvin notes) one hundred times more precious than all the treasures of the world.

Summary of Chapters 8–9. John Calvin: Now, after clearing away all reason for offense and regaining favor for his ministry, Paul commends to them the believers in Jerusalem, that the Corinthians might provide support to them in their need. He would not have been successful had he attempted this at the beginning of his epistle. Hence, he has prudently deferred it until he had prepared their minds for it. And so, he takes up in this chapter and the next nothing other than to exhort the Corinthians to be active and diligent in collecting alms to be delivered to Jerusalem for relieving the poverty of the brothers and sisters there. For they were afflicted with a great famine, so that they could scarcely support life without being assisted by other churches. The apostles had commended this matter to Paul, and he had promised to take care of it, and had already done so in part, as we have seen in the previous epistle. Now, however, he urges them on again. Commentary on 2 Corinthians 8.[1]

Paul Motivates the Corinthians to Give. Tilemann Hesshus: This is the fourth part of this epistle, in which the apostle Paul discretely asks the Corinthians to use their material resources to assist the saints in Jerusalem. These saints were afflicted with great poverty due to the famine, which was spreading throughout the world during the imperial reign of Claudius, and due to the very severe persecutions that they, as Jews who were professing the name of Christ, were enduring at the hands of the raging of the Jews. The other apostles had entreated Paul to perform this duty, as he himself testifies in Galatians. And so Paul diligently collected alms throughout the church for Christian Jews in Jerusalem and in Palestine. Since Paul is recommending to many other Macedonian churches promptness in contributing alms, he attempts to stir them up by the example of others (rather than by an argument) so that these Corinthians also might demonstrate their gratitude to God and kindness toward impoverished Christians in Judea. For rivalry to perform good deeds is a sacred thing when a person, goaded by piety and goodness of others, regrets that they are seriously wanting in the performance of his duty, and thereafter attempts either to imitate or surpass the zeal and piety of other people. . . .

Pastors learn from this passage in large part how to apply the care of the poor to their ministries: namely, that they should stir up their congregations by diligently exhorting them to alleviate the needs of the poor and that, by this act of charity, they might demonstrate the sincerity of their faith. Their congregations also learn from this passage that God no doubt demands this charity from them so that they might not neglect those struggling with poverty, but contribute alms with a simple and eager heart, bring help to the poverty of the saints, and assist them with all kindness. "Give," the Son of God says, "and it will be given to you." And Solomon, in Proverbs 4 [*sic*, Proverbs 5] states, "Let your springs be diverted to outsiders; you, O Lord, will pour it out on them." Moreover, when the apostle urges the saints in the Corinthian church to contribute alms according to their capacity, he approves the ownership of these things and teaches that it is permitted for godly people to hold property. For if Paul had desired all things to be held in common, he would have commanded that all material goods should be gathered into a single pot. But instead, he exhorts and asks that each person bestow freely something of small measure from their possessions. Therefore, this proves the ownership of material goods and teaches that it is permissible for people to possess things, as is also made clear from the seventh commandment: "You shall not steal." Explication of 2 Corinthians 8.[2]

[1]CO 50:95 (CTS 40:283-84).

[2]Hesshus, *Explicatio Secundae Epistolae Pauli ad Corinthios*, 201r-v, 202v-203r; citing Gal 2:20; Prov 5:16; Lk 6:38; Ex 20:15.

8:1-7 *The Macedonians' Extravagant Generosity*

Paul Praises the Macedonians' Example. Jacques Lefèvre d'Étaples: Paul has commended the Corinthians for that sorrow which they experienced that led to repentance and many beneficial changes. Now he praises the Macedonians for their generosity and for promoting works of charity for the saints, so that by their example, he might provoke the Corinthians to employ a similar goodness—just as when a father sets before the eyes of his sons an important example for them to imitate in order to depict the life which they ought to esteem and admire. Commentary on 2 Corinthians 8:1-5.[3]

Motivating Generosity Within the Church. Wolfgang Musculus: The grace of God takes many shapes and is also dispensed in many ways, especially among the churches of God, according to the measure of the Spirit's administration. We see here that grace had been bestowed to the churches of Macedonia that had not yet been given to the believers of the church of the Corinthians, so that the apostle considered it necessary to write them about it so as to provoke them to emulation. And thus it is with vigilant ministers of Christ, that if a special gift of God has been given to some church that is committed to their care . . . they should congratulate the brothers and sisters and give thanks to the Lord, and humbly entreat a similar kind of gift from them. Commentary on 2 Corinthians 8:1.[4]

Nine Reasons Why Paul Commends the Generosity of the Macedonians. David Dickson: Paul commends the liberality of the Macedonian churches for nine reasons: Reason 1: Because it was the gift of God's grace that they contributed anything for the use of the poor Jews [v. 1]. Reason 2: Because they gave alms at a time when they suffered heavy afflictions [v. 2]. Reason 3: Because they contributed with joy [v. 2]. Reason 4: Because in poverty they were generous [v. 2]. Reason 5: Because they were willing to give more bountifully than they were able [v. 3]. Reason 6: Because they offered freely. They were not provoked by the example of others, but rather they were leaders to others, lest they should neglect this duty of charity [v. 4]. Reason 7: Because they were constantly praying that what they gave might be received. Reason 8: Because they entreated the apostle, that he together with others would take responsibility for gathering and dispensing that which they and others were about to give. Reason 9: Because beyond the apostle's expectation, they consecrated themselves and all their possessions to God. And they also committed themselves to the apostle, that they might be ruled by him in all things, according to the will of God [v. 5]. Exposition of 2 Corinthians 8:1-5.[5]

The Mysterious Dispensation of God's Grace. Wolfgang Musculus: It ought to be noted that this grace was given not only to one or two churches but to the churches of Macedonia in general. And this also was an example of God's special graciousness, that this grace was bestowed in common among all the churches of the province. Frequently in secular affairs, geographical proximity and common background are the most important factors contributing to a similar experience. But when speaking of the gifts of God, if there is any similar experience found among the churches of a single province, it ought to be attributed more (indeed, especially) to the special dispensation of God—and this explanation we should not question nor can it be refuted. If you ask why it is that God has given to the churches of Germany this exceptional grace of being renewed and restored according to the doctrine of Christ when the churches of other provinces do not yet possess this same freedom, we can attribute it to nothing other than the special

[3]Lefèvre, *Commentariorum in Epistolas Beati Pauli . . . Liber Tertius*, 137v.
[4]Musculus, *Commentarius . . . in posteriorem epistolam Pauli ad Corinthios*, 243.
[5]Dickson, *An Exposition of All St. Paul's Epistles*, 84*.

wisdom of God, by which he dispenses his gifts as he wishes. Nevertheless, we cannot deny that God also uses . . . the power of a neighbor's example as well as the earnestness of faithful ministers. Commentary on 2 Corinthians 8:1.[6]

God Gives So That We Might Give. The English Annotations: The bounty of the Macedonians he calls *charin*, either from *chairō* or from *charizōmai*, either as the word is derived from a verb signifying "to rejoice," because what they bestowed upon the saints at Jerusalem they did it most willingly and cheerfully. Or as the word is derived from a verb signifying "to freely give," thereby intimating that that charity whereby we freely give to others is a free gift of God to us. "Give to us, not only because we give, but also so that we might give." Annotations on 2 Corinthians 8:1.[7]

The Generosity of the Macedonians. Wolfgang Musculus: Even though the Macedonians are being tested by many afflictions and suffering extreme poverty due to the deprivation of their goods, nevertheless, because they are filled with an abundance of joy, they are overflowing in their generosity to the saints because they have given lavishly. Therefore, Paul does not simply tell the Corinthians about the financial contribution of the Macedonians, but he adds the circumstances surrounding it. Paul mentions that they have given with joy (that is, cheerfully and eager to give) so that the Corinthians might also understand what it is to give with joy. For God loves a cheerful giver. Second, the Macedonians demonstrated eagerness in giving this contribution while enduring many afflictions. Third, the joy that they had was not small but abundant and overflowing. Fourth, they gave while still impoverished. Fifth, they did not give with stinginess, but generously and lavishly. Thus, Paul honors, respects, and commends the contribution of the Macedonians so as to make clear the singular grace that God had given them, and also to propose, by way of example, the sort of gift suitable for all of the churches. Commentary on 2 Corinthians 8:2.[8]

The Macedonians Display Two Great Virtues. Niels Hemmingsen: Paul commends the Macedonians for two great virtues. First, that in the midst of the greatest afflictions, the Spirit has produced joy in them. Second, that in their profound poverty, they have been generous toward poor saints. These words of commendation are directed toward this outcome, that the Corinthians, who abound in material resources, might be inspired to generosity. For, if the Macedonians—who were afflicted with poverty—were so generous, what should the Corinthians do, who abound with so many resources? This especially ought to be noted, that the apostle ascribes to the "grace of God" two kinds of virtue, namely, patience under the cross, and generosity toward the saints. For God is both the author of comfort and joy under the cross (and thus God is called our "comfort"), and he himself inspires a generous disposition of heart toward the needy, contrary to our fleshly judgment. The more persons determine to renounce the flesh, the more they contribute to other people. Second, since Paul calls the "grace of God" that openness and generosity toward the poor, we know that when we are generous toward the poor, the favor of God comes to each one of us—provided that our alms are not corrupted by the yeast of the Pharisees. And so, Paul calls that generosity the wealth of simplicity because he wants it to originate from a simple and sincere heart of charity, and to result in the glory of God and in the support of the poor. Commentary on 2 Corinthians 8:1-2.[9]

Joy in Great Trial. John Calvin: "In much trial," that is, while they were tried with

[6]Musculus, *Commentarius . . . in posteriorem epistolam Pauli ad Corinthios*, 244.
[7]Downame, ed., *English Annotations*, GG1v*.
[8]Musculus, *Commentarius . . . in posteriorem epistolam Pauli ad Corinthios*, 244-45.
[9]Hemmingsen, *Commentaria in Omnes Epistolas Apostolorum*, 285.

adversity, they nevertheless did not stop rejoicing in the Lord. . . . By the word "joy," Paul means that spiritual consolation by which believers sustain themselves under their afflictions. For the wicked either delude themselves with empty thoughts by avoiding the perception of the evil, and amusing themselves with inane comforts, or they almost entirely succumb to grief and allow themselves to be overwhelmed by it. But the faithful seek an opportunity for joy in the affliction itself, as is seen in Romans 8. COMMENTARY ON 2 CORINTHIANS 8:2.[10]

AFFLICTION AND GENEROSITY. THE ENGLISH ANNOTATIONS: "In a great trial of affliction." Those manifold afflictions with which the Lord tried them did not only not slacken their joyful readiness, but also made it much more excellent and famous. Afflictions are like a file, whereby God brightens the graces of the Spirit in his children. "And their deep poverty." As a dark soil forms an oriental diamond, so the great afflictions of the churches of Macedonia set off their spiritual joy, and their extreme poverty produced their rich liberality. "Their liberality." The original Greek word *aplotētos*, which though it is sometimes taken for "liberality" (as in Romans 12), yet properly signifies "simplicity," that which Clement of Alexandria terms . . . "singleness of heart."[†] This is a virtue whereby a person is inclined to do works of mercy and generosity freely and absolutely, without any dark motives to gain anything for themselves. . . . The one who contributes to the needs of the poor, simply to relieve them, and in obedience to God's command, without any other motive or inducement, deserves that commendation that the apostle here gives to the Macedonians "wealth of generosity." ANNOTATIONS ON 2 CORINTHIANS 8:2.[11]

THE MACEDONIANS' EXTREME POVERTY. JOHN TRAPP: Their poverty being now at the very bottom and having little left beside hope, they were even exhausted and yet gave liberally. Giles of Brussels,[†] martyr, gave to the poor whatsoever he had, that necessity could spare, and only lived by his science, which was of a cutler. Some he refreshed with his meat, some with his clothes, some with his household stuff. One poor woman there was brought to bed and had no bed to lie in; to whom he brought his own bed, himself content to lie in the straw. COMMENTARY ON 2 CORINTHIANS 8:2.[12]

THE GRACIOUS GIFT OF THE MACEDONIANS. ANDREAS HYPERIUS: Here we have the proof that as their poverty abounded, their capacity for giving freely and generously greatly increased, with each member supplying their small part. "I testify," Paul says—which is a way of saying, "I am in no way lying." "They gave, not only according to their means, but above their means." What more can he say? Who would not be amazed that such goodwill could be generated? Where do you now find such things? The one who has much owes much—but not beyond their means. Nevertheless, it is possible for a person to give out of an abundance of generosity, as the apostle himself did, who worked with his hands, not only so that he might provide sustenance for himself, but also for others with whom he could share something. This was, in fact, giving beyond one's means. But what is more, Paul adds "they were begging us earnestly" for the grace to take part in the ministry among the saints from this public collection. The translator [Jerome] very appropriately employs the Latin word *beneficium* for the Greek word *charis*. Whereas the Greek reads *koinōnian*, and the interpreter translates it as *societatem* (fellowship), we more properly called it a *communicationem* (sharing) or *participationem* (participation), namely, when physical resources were being distributed in common. How else the interpreter translates the word *koinōnias* is seen in various passages.

[10]CO 50:95-96 (CTS 50:284-85).

[11]Downame, ed., *English Annotations*, GG1v*. [†]Clement of Alexandria, *The Instructor* 3.12, ANF 2:294.

[12]Trapp, *A Commentary or Exposition*, 723*. [†]The martyrdom of Giles Tilleman, a cutler of Brussels, is found in John Foxe, *Foxe's Book of Martyrs, or The Acts and Monuments of the Christian Church* (Philadelphia: James B. Smith, 1860), 609.

In general terms, Paul calls "saints" those people who believe in Christ and, having been baptized, are consistently living in a godly manner. Now, this is an important thing: the Macedonians did not make their contribution because of some external appeal, but they asked themselves how their alms might be received. And they made the most of that particular situation to stir up the Corinthians so that it might rightly cause them shame if, having heard such things about the Macedonians, they themselves did nothing. But Paul expands further upon their kindness in what follows. Commentary on 2 Corinthians 8:3-4.[13]

The Nature of True Generosity. Cyriacus Spangenberg: Here we learn how someone in the greatest poverty may be rich and give richly, namely, when someone is generous [*einfaltig*] and compassionate with the poor and shares as much with them as they can. What is then lacking in the coffers, he has so much more richly in simplicity [*einfaltigkeit*] of soul. Chrysostom:[†] "Generosity is judged not by the amount given, but in the goodwill displayed." There are many hindrances to this kind of generosity, like if we think about what we will have left after we give from what is there to the poor, or what kind of trouble could present itself in times to come for which we also might need money. Again, how much we ourselves must still need before we have enough for the year. Again, what we want to put aside as a reserve for the children. Or again, how small the reserve might become if we tapped into it in this way. Such thoughts prevent us from arriving at generosity, and moreover, the poor Lazarus is then forgotten about. But whoever relies on God's blessing and waits for their calling in simplicity is not tied by such bonds, but their hands remain free to give alms to the needy. Thirty-Fourth Sermon.[14]

The Meaning of *Koinōnia*. Huldrych Zwingli: The word *koinōnia*, which the interpreter Jerome translates as "sharing" [*communicatio*] and "participation" [*participatio*] in 1 Corinthians 10 is here translated with the word "fellowship" [*societas*]. For the word "participation" [*participatio*] is better suited for that earlier passage, while the word "fellowship" [*societas*] is better suited here. Annotations on 2 Corinthians 8:4.[15]

Examples of Caring for the Poor. Cyriacus Spangenberg: This custom of collecting alms in the congregation thus remained a long time in Christendom. When people came together for preaching or to take the sacrament, they brought together food and money and then distributed them to the poor (1 Corinthians 11). This lasted until the time of Emperor Maurice (AD 580) when Gregory, bishop of Rome, a great lover of the poor, died. When a great famine came over Italy, the poor ran to Pope Sabinian (as they had been used to doing) wanting help from the common coffers. But there was no comfort there. The pope said that Gregory had shamefully exhausted all the church's goods. Then he seized and burned all his books and was thus the first to completely take away from the poor the church's goods and diverted everything from the common coffers only to the religious and to church construction. But the pious bishops Paulinus, Ambrose, and Exupery melted down chalices in time of need so that they could help the poor. And St. Dominic is said to have sold himself into slavery several times and to have helped the poor with such money.

[13]Hyperius, *Commentarii . . . in Epistolam D. Pauli ad Romanos, et Utramque ad Corinthios*, 391.

[14]C. Spangenberg, *Die ander Epistel Pauli an die Corinthier*, 141v-142r; citing Lk 16:19-31. The terms *einfaltig* and *einfaltigkeit* mean "simple" and "simplicity" respectively. The first is used to translate *aplous* in Mt 6:22. The notion of "simplicity" is extended to include "generosity." [†]For Chrysostom's interpretation, see PG 61:571 (NPNF[1] 12:395).

[15]Zwingli, *Annotatiunculae . . . ex ore Zwinglii*, 182; citing 1 Cor 10:16. Zwingli is here entering the debate over the best way to translate the Greek word *koinonia*. In the Vulgate translation of 1 Cor 10:16, two different Latin words (*communicatio* and *participatio*) were employed to translate the two occurrences of the word *koinonia* in that single verse—an interpretive decision that Erasmus criticized in his *Annotations*. See Anne Reeve and M. A. Screech, eds., *Erasmus' Annotations on the New Testament*, facsimile edition (Leiden: Brill, 1990), 488.

Afterward the rich created fiefdoms and benefices from their goods, so that the religious should help the poor with what was left over. But that all ended up with either idle monks and priests devouring it with dogs, whores, and horses, or great lords, nobility, the bourgeois, and farmers taking it for themselves, and letting the servants of the church along with the poor suffer hunger. God must punish this in the end. Thirty-Fourth Sermon.[16]

True Apostles Are Concerned for the Needs of the Church. Philipp Melanchthon: The apostles want the church to give itself to the Lord and then to themselves by the will of God; that is, not from a carnal disposition, but that they might heed the apostles' word and devote themselves to the needs of the church through love. By contrast, the false apostles want the church to be subservient to themselves, as Galatians states: "They want you to be circumcised, so that in your flesh." Annotations on 2 Corinthians 8:5.[17]

True Piety Begets Generosity and Obedience. Wolfgang Musculus: "But they gave themselves first to the Lord, and then also to me." Now Paul added this statement for emphasis, expressing in a beautiful way the most important elements that complement true piety, namely, generosity and kindness in supporting the needs of the saints. Paul preached this, and the Macedonians had done more than the apostle could have hoped for. The fullness of piety is comprised in these three parts: First, that we give ourselves first and foremost to the Lord. Second, that we give ourselves also to those who are ministers of the Lord by the will of God. Third, that we love the brothers and sisters, and support them in their needs with all our strength. . . .

God has established this as his perpetual will lasting to the end of the world that Christians should obey those true ministers of Christ by whom they have been established in faith and true piety. They should obey, I say, not everything, but that which concerns the teaching of their ministry and Christ, and their salvation. Those people who are in the papacy, obey in a servile fashion the false apostles and false pastors, all of whom are as much tyrants as imposters. And even the greater part of those who boast about the gospel of Christ have not given themselves to the Lord or to their ministers but indulge their own wills in all things. Commentary on 2 Corinthians 8:5.[18]

Love of God Is Evident in Love for His Ministers. Tilemann Hesshus: "Then also to us." Unless people first dedicate themselves to the Lord, they will never undergo dangers for the sake of God's ministers. For, when faith in Christ is so genuine that a man or woman dares to put at risk their life and all their fortune for the sake of the name of Christ, there is no doubt that they will also give to God's ministers and endure with them jealousy and every other kind of danger for the sake of their common salvation. For truly, those who love the Lord also love his ministers. If a person forsakes God's faithful ministers during times of persecution out of fear that he might draw powerful hatred and dangers upon himself, and so flees from associating with them, that person shows that he is foreign to them. No matter how much a person might boast that he will devote everything for the sake of Christ's name, nevertheless, it is certain that it is nothing but mere pretense. For, as a person abandons Christ's ministers, so too in times of danger, he will abandon the Son of God himself. Explication of 2 Corinthians 8:5.[19]

Paul Possessed God's Authority. John Calvin: Paul says, "They gave themselves first to God, and then to us." One might ask whether their giving themselves to God was different from their

[16] C. Spangenberg, *Die ander Epistel Pauli an die Corinthier*, 142v.
[17] *Melanchthons Werke*, 4:122; citing Gal 6:13.

[18] Musculus, *Commentarius . . . in posteriorem epistolam Pauli ad Corinthios*, 249, 250.
[19] Hesshus, *Explicatio Secundae Epistolae Pauli ad Corinthios*, 203v-204r.

giving themselves to Paul. It is well-known that when God charges or commands by means of another person, he associates the minister with himself, both in authority to command and in obedience to be rendered. "It seemed good to the Holy Spirit and us," the apostles say, even though, as instruments, they were only announcing what was revealed and enjoined by the Spirit. Again, "The people believed the Lord and his servant Moses," even though Moses had nothing apart from God. And this is indicated by the clause which thereafter follows—"by the will of God." For since they were being obedient to God, the Corinthians (who had committed themselves to his ministry and agreed to be regulated by his counsel) were following this principle, that they were listening to Paul speaking as from the mouth of God. Commentary on 2 Corinthians 8:5.[20]

First to God, Then to His Ministers. Niels Hemmingsen: This is the sense: "They far exceeded our expectation, for they were ready not only to contribute their offering but even to give their very selves to the Lord and to us. Hence, we encouraged Titus that just as he had started, so he should strenuously complete this gift among you, exhorting you to be generous toward those in need." Now, when Paul said that they had given themselves first to the Lord and then to him, this is a testimony both of the Macedonians' piety toward God, and their respect toward the apostle according to the will of God, who wishes us to obey the ministry. Commentary on 2 Corinthians 8:5-6.[21]

Titus's Charge. Tilemann Hesshus: "When I witnessed so great an eagerness among the Macedonians, I urged Titus that, just as he had begun to collect alms in Macedonia on behalf of the church, so he should continue to complete this grace among the Corinthians." Paul adds this reference to Titus so that the Corinthians might know that Titus was chosen for this office by the authority and request of the apostle and the church. In truth, all things were arranged so that they might promote the Macedonians' extraordinary eagerness for contributing their alms. Hence, with this commendation, Paul is trying to stimulate the Corinthian church to emulate their example. Explication of 2 Corinthians 8:6.[22]

True Christian Fruit. Wolfgang Musculus: When rightly considered, the force of Paul's exhortation holds a lot of weight. Those to whom much is given much is required. The Lord had given a lot to the Corinthians, so that they excelled other churches in faith, speech, knowledge, diligence—to say nothing of their other spiritual gifts. It was reasonable, therefore, that great eagerness for true piety should also be expected of them. The more carefully a vine is cultivated, the more fruit is expected of it. Faith, speech, knowledge, and other kinds of gifts—these are a reflection of having been cultivated. Now, generosity of various sorts is a fruit that proceeds from true love. Hence, one should not ask, "Why is it necessary for the Corinthians to excel in generosity?" Or, "Isn't it sufficient that they excel in faith, speech, and knowledge?" Or, "Does the nature of Christians require that those who excel in one thing must excel in all gifts?" We must distinguish between those things that are necessary for all Christians . . . such as the zeal of love, and those things that are not deemed essential, such as those qualities that Paul ascribed as excellent among the Corinthians. That is not to say that these qualities are of no use (since, as we said, they are the reflection of having been cultivated, whence the fruit of true piety increases), but no Christian is judged according to the measure of these qualities to be great or small, or more or less pious in the sight of God. The Macedonians, though they did not excel as much as the Corinthians in some of these qualities (as I noted), were excelling in the works of love, just as when we judge a tree healthy

[20]CO 50:97 (CTS 40:287-88); citing Acts 15:28; Ex 14:31.
[21]Hemmingsen, *Commentaria in Omnes Epistolas Apostolorum*, 286.
[22]Hesshus, *Explicatio Secundae Epistolae Pauli ad Corinthios*, 204v.

because of its true fruit. Commentary on 2 Corinthians 8:7.[23]

The Many Gifts of the Corinthian Church. Tilemann Hesshus: Paul very gently urges the Corinthians to be prompt in contributing their alms. So he advises that they should take counsel among themselves. Since they excel in all things, it is only right that, in this virtue as well, they should also outdo them and take the lead over others. The apostle shows here that the Corinthian church was adorned with exceptional gifts of the Holy Spirit. They were demonstrating their faith because they had embraced Paul's teaching concerning the crucifixion and resurrection of Christ. They were displaying their speech because there were many among them trained in the Word of God and capable of teaching it. They were also strong in knowledge, that is, in the use and experience of things and in spiritual wisdom. Their zeal for cleansing and building up the church, for proclaiming the gospel, for worshiping the divine name, and for comforting the afflicted was also exceptional. The burning love that the Corinthians had for Paul was evident from their repentance and sadness, and the zeal expressed toward the incestuous man. Here we see God's enormous goodness, that he had established a church in that place adorned with so many excellent gifts, when it was a horrible cesspool and dregs of all wickedness. Paul now urges the church to stay the course and surpass others in generously helping the poor. The Greek word in this passage does not signify the unmerited favor or mercy of God; rather, it is that virtue of generosity, the prompt contribution of alms, which was aroused among the saints by the grace of God. Explication of 2 Corinthians 8:7.[24]

8:8-9 *Christ Became Poor for Our Sake*

The Riches of Christ's Divinity Received from His Poverty. Desiderius Erasmus: Not that I demand this from you, but I mention the readiness of the Macedonians for this reason that, challenged by their example, you might of your own accord make evident the sincerity of your love, in this way too emulating the Lord Jesus Christ to the best of your ability. Although he was rich and the Lord of all, nevertheless in order to benefit us, of his own accord he made himself poor. He became man, his power concealed, in order that you might grow rich through his poverty, as if an exchange of properties occurred, so that by this exchange, when the poverty of humanity was taken up into himself, he might impart to us the riches of his divinity. Paraphrases of 2 Corinthians 8.[25]

Is Generosity Prescribed or Advised? Philipp Melanchthon: Because the apostle says here, "I say this not as a command," and again, "I give my advice in this matter," certain people conclude that sharing of goods is not prescribed but only offered as advice. However, the sharing of goods is prescribed in Deuteronomy 15. This is clear when the Lord says, "I command you to open wide your hand to your brothers and sisters who are destitute and poor." So too in Isaiah 58: "Share your bread with the hungry. . . . Then, your light will break forth as with the dawn." Yet if there is no light when they demand compensation from their debtors, as it is clear in that passage of Isaiah, then the sharing of goods is prescribed. And in 1 John 3 we read, "Those who have the wealth of this world and see their brothers and sisters in need, and close their hearts to them, how does God's love abide in them" who do not share their goods? Therefore, the sharing of goods is prescribed. This same thing is asserted in Luke 6: "Give to everyone who asks of you." And, "Whatever you wish that others would do to you, do also to them." . . . Now how does this relate to this passage of Paul? I answer: Paul

[23]Musculus, *Commentarius . . . in posteriorem epistolam Pauli ad Corinthios*, 252-53.
[24]Hesshus, *Explicatio Secundae Epistolae Pauli ad Corinthios*, 205r-v.
[25]CWE 43:247.

himself infers that he does not require anything from people who are not affluent; therefore, he does not command because he does not know the extent of the Corinthians' material resources, and so he requires nothing. As he makes clear from this statement: "Complete in that matter what you can. . . ." Now Paul indicates that people are required by their wealth, when he says, "Wishing the genuineness of your love to be proved," indicating that it is not genuine love unless those who have resources share them with others. And a little later, Paul says: "It is necessary for there to be fairness. . . ." Again, in the final chapter of 1 Timothy, "Teach those who are rich in this present age." Annotations on 2 Corinthians 8:8.[26]

The Rule of Charity. John Calvin: But if anyone might ask—"Was it not permissible for Paul to prescribe what he had received as a commandment of the Lord?" The answer is easy—that God, indeed, everywhere commands that we assist our brothers and sisters in need, but he never specifies the amount, that after making a calculation we might divide between ourselves and the poor. He never binds us to the circumstances of times, persons, or places, but he calls us take the rule of charity as our guide. Commentary on 2 Corinthians 8:8.[27]

Paul Chooses Not to Command. Wolfgang Musculus: We are not disputing here whether Paul had the power to command them. In this matter that he is talking about, he decided not to make a command. For Paul is looking for a giver who is not forced or reluctant, but who is spontaneous and cheerful. He gives great praise for the contribution of the Macedonians, because, without even an exhortation, much less a command from the apostle, they spontaneously made such a generous contribution. It is for this same reason, therefore, that Paul not only commands nothing in this matter to the Corinthians but also shows clearly that he does not speak these things as a command. Commentary on 2 Corinthians 8:8.[28]

Gifts Given Freely Are More Precious. The English Annotations: The apostle might have laid his command upon the Corinthians in this matter, since charity is a duty required of all Christians and all should contribute to the needs of the saints according to their ability. Nevertheless, Paul commends this duty to them rather than commands it because the more willing and free our charitable contributions are, the more acceptable they are to God and human beings. As Pliny† once stated, "Myrrh that runs out of the tree of its own accord is far more precious than the myrrh that runs out after the tree has been cut." Annotations on 2 Corinthians 8:8.[29]

Genuine Generosity. John Trapp: The Greek word *gnēsion* means sincere, natural, genuine, as opposed to bastardly. Our present age abounds with "mouth-mercy" which is good and cheap, like the rotting fruit that is found growing in every hedge. Only a small amount in the hands is worth more than a great many mouthfuls. . . . St. James tells of some people in his time that would feed their poor brothers and sisters with good words and good wishes, as if they had been a sort of chameleon, who, like Ephraim, feeds on the wind. Note what a poor man once said to a cardinal who refused him a penny for which he begged and offered him instead a blessing, for which he had not begged. "If your blessing had been worth a penny, I would not have wanted it. Keep it for yourself." Commentary on 2 Corinthians 8:8.[30]

The Poverty of Christ. Wolfgang Musculus: "Though he was rich, for your sake he became

[26]*Melanchthons Werke*, 4:1; citing Deut 5:11; Is 58:78; 1 Jn 3:17; Lk 6:30, 31; 1 Cor 8:8; 1 Tim 6:17.
[27]CO 50:93 (CTS 40:289-90).

[28]Musculus, *Commentarius . . . in posteriorem epistolam Pauli ad Corinthios*, 171.
[29]Downame, ed., *English Annotations*, GG1v*; citing Philem 8-9. †See Pliny the Elder, *Natural History* 12.35.
[30]Trapp, *A Commentary or Exposition*, 724*; citing Jas 2:15, 16; Hos 12:1.

poor, so that you, by his poverty, might become rich." This is the grace of our Lord Jesus Christ, which, if the Corinthians had examined it closely, they would not have needed the apostolic admonition. Paul says three things: First, that Christ became poor when he was rich. Second, for whom he did this. Third, for what reason he did this. Christ became poor, Paul says, though he was rich. As the only-begotten Son of God and heir of all things, Christ was rich. He became poor, not by giving up his divine nature, but by not using it. Although he was the Lord of all, he became the servant of all, coming into the world, not so that it might serve him, but so that he himself might serve all things. Although he had the right over all things in heaven and on earth, he refrained for a time from possessing and employing it to such an extent that he possessed less than foxes on earth and birds in heaven. Thus, in Matthew 8, it says, "Foxes have holes, and the birds of the air have nests, but the Son of Man has nowhere to lay his head." The lowliness of his parents, his birth, his education, and his life situation demonstrated his abject poverty. Thus, he emptied himself, taking the form of a servant, along with the greatest humility and poverty. . . . For whose sake did he become poor? "For your sake," Paul says. Why did he not say more generally, "on account of all of us"? Did he become poor exclusively for the sake of the Corinthians? While Paul applies this general grace specifically to the Corinthians, he does not intend by this to remove it from other believers. But he applies it to the Corinthians alone because it serves the purposes that he has in mind. Paul is firm in his insistence that, if the grace of Christ is examined, it has not been conferred on all people in general but has been conferred on us specifically. If you hear the words "for God loved the world so much that he gave his only-begotten Son," though you might not feel your soul being moved with its effect, even so, you will experience it if, without any doubt, you confess with the apostle concerning the benefit of Christ, "who loved me and gave himself for me." It was for this reason that the apostle preferred to say here that "he became poor for our sake," rather than "he became poor for all of us," so that by contemplating this costly grace, the Corinthians might be more effectively encouraged to imitate him. Commentary on 2 Corinthians 8:9.[31]

Christ Did Not Shrink from His Human Status. Martin Chemnitz: The Scriptures proclaim to us Immanuel, God made man and made a participant in flesh and blood; and they affirm that the Word of the Father was made flesh, not through change, but by the ineffable power of the union. . . . Paul says, "Though he was rich, yet for our sake he became poor." Now, the manhood assumed by God (as Nestorius[†] would have it) was not made poor, for it was assumed unto riches, even unto glory. Therefore, it remains to be said that he who is rich was made as God, not through change, for he remained what he was, namely, God. Therefore, in what did the abject state of poverty consist? The Nestorians say, in the fact that he assumed someone like us. But in no way is God violated. Therefore, how is he made poor, since he is by nature God? He who was in the form of God was born of the seed of David according to the flesh and took on the condition of a servant. Moreover, having been made a man, he did not shrink from the status of humanity. But if we remove him from the conditions and words of humankind, if we strip away his flesh, we also destroy the salvation of the world. Loci Theologici.[32]

Christ's Humility and Poverty. Menno Simons: Worthy men, do learn to know what God's own and eternal Son, Christ Jesus, suffered upon earth, what he taught, and what example he

[31]Musculus, *Commentarius . . . in posteriorem epistolam Pauli ad Corinthios*, 256; citing Mt 8:20; Jn 3:16; Gal 2:20.

[32]Chemnitz, *Loci Theologici*, 1:123. [†]Nestorius (d. 450), patriarch of Constantinople, was deposed as a heretic by church councils in part because he distinguished too greatly between the two natures of Christ, seemingly denying a substantial union of the human and divine natures in the person of Christ. Like Nestorius, other Antiochene exegetes were condemned for attributing portions of Jesus' story (i.e., his hunger or conversely his divine knowledge) to one or the other of his natures.

left you. He sought his Father's glory and the salvation of our poor souls. His doctrine was his Father's Word, and his progress a sure way to the kingdom of God. Who, being in the form of God, says Paul, thought it not robbery to be equal with God: but made himself of no reputation, and took upon him the form of a servant; and came into this sorrowful world, poor and miserable. There was no room for him in the inn when he was born; nothing whereon to lay his head during his ministry; nor in his death wherewith to quench his thirst. Yet he was the one through whom the almighty, all-bountiful Father provides for all his created beings, place of dwelling, cover, meat, and drink, as Paul says: "For ye know the grace of our Lord Jesus Christ, that though he was rich, yet for your sakes he became poor, that ye through his poverty might be rich." Foundations of Christian Doctrine.[33]

Becoming Poor for One's Neighbor. Peter Walpot: "For you know the grace of our Lord Jesus Christ, that though he was rich, yet for your sake he became poor, so that you through his poverty might become rich." Paul is here wanting that we would gladly also become poor for the sake of others, to love each other as Christ has loved us. This would do if we put on Christ and put off the old human nature. Christian Community of Goods.[34]

This Passage Does Not Promise Earthly Riches. Wolfgang Musculus: Spiritual poverty cannot be applied to Christ. If he had been spiritually poor, absolutely no one would have become spiritually rich. But he experienced earthly poverty, which does not exclude spiritual riches. On the other hand, he did not earn, nor did he provide, earthly riches for believers when he took on earthly poverty, because these earthly riches are not worthy of heavenly grace and calling, and they do not render people happy. But spiritual riches, by which people are made rich in happiness, last forever. That is why those works of popes, bishops, cardinals, and other prelates have no part in the poverty of Christ, even though they think that this passage of the apostle relates to them most directly, as if Christ became poor for their sake so that they might abound in earthly accomplishments of kings and princes in the present age. These things cannot be said about Christ without greatly insulting him, no less than if one said, "Christ became humble for us, so that we might be exalted and proud in this present age. Christ became subject to the law, so that we might live any way we pleased without the law. Christ became obedient to God his Father for our sake, so that we do not have to obey God or human beings. Christ endured all manner of afflictions and temptations for us, so that we might enjoy all kinds of sensual pleasures and delights." The [papists] should also add this statement: "Christ ascended to heaven for us, so that we might descend into the fires of hell." Commentary on 2 Corinthians 8:9.[35]

We Are Made Rich in Christ's Poverty. Cyriacus Spangenberg: Christ Jesus our Lord is rich, for everything is his. Heaven and earth are his creation, and everything in them belongs to him as the only and eternal Son of the Father. He is Almighty God over all, and after he took our flesh and blood to himself and became human, "the Father made him heir over all." "And he gave him the nations as an inheritance and all the ends of the world as his possession." "And he thus made him Lord over all the works of his hands, and put all things under his feet." Although he is rich, "and was in the form of God, he did not consider it as plunder to be equal with God, but emptied himself and took the form of a servant." And he became so poor that "foxes have their holes, and the birds under heaven have their nests, but the Son of Man does not have anywhere to lay his head."

[33]CWMS 209; citing Phil 2:6, 7.

[34]Liechty, ed., *Early Anabaptist Spirituality*, 167-68; citing Eph 4:17-32.

[35]Musculus, *Commentarius . . . in posteriorem epistolam Pauli ad Corinthios*, 257.

And when he died, he did not even have as his own possession on the whole earth (although he himself had created it) a place where they could bury him, but another had to lend him his tomb. That is what "becoming poor" means. It is not that such riches were stolen from him against his will, but that he emptied himself of and abstained from the same, as though they were not his, as though he had no right to them, as the story of the Lord Christ demonstrates the kind of poverty and indigence he suffered from his mother's womb until his death.

But he did all this, says the apostle, and "became so poor for your sake, so that you through his poverty might become rich." This is the noble and worthy exchange: Christ is born indigent and poor in this world so that we may be born rich and blessed in heaven. He becomes ill and weak for a time so that we may become healthy and strong for eternity. He becomes a sinner and a fool before the world so that we may become holy, righteous, and wise before God. He dies an ignominious death so that we might receive a glorious life. In summary, he gives us his piety for our evilness, his innocence for our sin, his righteousness for our wickedness, his life for our death, his heaven for our hell. This is what Paul means by the words, "Although Christ is rich, he becomes poor for your sake, so that you through his poverty may become rich." But his riches do not leave him, although he empties himself of them. Therefore, the apostle does not say, "He was rich," but "He is and remains rich." Although he became poor for a time for our sake, he proves his riches in spiritual matters, and suffers alongside this great poverty on earth in the temporal realm. Thirty-Fifth Sermon.[36]

8:10-15 *Finish the Good Work*

The Generous Person Gives to the Lord. John Calvin: Now this "benefit" is not perceived according to the flesh; for where is the person who is persuaded that it is beneficial to deprive himself of something so as to help others? Indeed, it is the saying of a pagan author:[†] "What you have given away is the only riches that you will always have"—but the reason is that "whatever is given to friends is placed beyond all risk." However, the Lord does not want us to be influenced by the hope of a reward, or of any compensation in return, but, on the contrary, even if people should be ungrateful so that it seems we have lost what we have given away, nevertheless, he wants us to persevere in doing good. For the benefit comes from this, that "the person who gives to the poor lends to the Lord" (as Solomon states in Proverbs 19). And the Lord's blessing alone should be regarded as a hundred times more precious than all the treasures of the world. Commentary on 2 Corinthians 8:10.[37]

Paul Is Advising, Not Commanding. Heinrich Bullinger: Paul urges the Corinthians based on what is beneficial to them. "This matter," he says, "which I'm pestering you about is neither burdensome nor difficult. That which you already began, or rather, have almost acquitted—that is what I am urging you to complete." For he also mentions the collection in chapter 16 of his previous letter. This is the reason for the conjecture that this second epistle was written a year after the previous one. The paraphraser [Erasmus][†] correctly interprets the sense of this passage in this manner: "Just as in the previous letter I did not require celibacy of you, but advocated it, thinking of your welfare, so too in this matter I am advising, not commanding, and I am advising for this reason, because I think it will turn out to your advantage, especially seeing that what I am now advocating, you, yourselves, without my persuasion, have begun not only to do, but even to will of your own accord. Now, therefore, it remains for you to bring to completion what you have begun to do on your own accord. Just as you long since willingly

[36]C. Spangenberg, *Die ander Epistel Pauli an die Corinthier*, 145v-146r; citing Heb 1:2; Ps 2:8, 8:6; Phil 2:6-7; Mt 8:20.

[37]CO 50:99 (CTS 40:291-92); citing Prov 19:17. [†]The reference is to Martial, *Epistle* 5.39-42.

adopted that intent, so after the example of the Macedonians you should carry it through, not beyond your ability as they did, but in accordance with each person's means." COMMENTARY ON 2 CORINTHIANS 8:10-11.[38]

CHRISTIANS MUST GIVE ACCORDING TO THEIR ABILITY. JOHN CALVIN: It is very likely that the ardor of the Corinthians had quickly cooled, otherwise they would have completed without any delay that which they had undertaken to do. But the apostle, as if no fault had yet been committed, gently admonishes them to complete that which they had begun well.

When Paul adds the phrase "out of what you have," he anticipates an objection; for the flesh is always ingenious in inventing subterfuges. Some people give the excuse that they have families, whom it would be inhuman to neglect. Others, since they are unable to give very much, use this as a pretext for giving nothing. "Could I give such a small amount?" Paul removes all excuses of this nature when he commands everyone to contribute in proportion to their ability. He also adds the reason, because God looks at the heart, not at the amount given. For when he says that readiness of mind is acceptable to God, according to the individual's ability, he means this: "If you contribute a small amount from your limited resources, your disposition is judged in the sight of God as no less than when a rich person contributes a great sum out of his abundance. For the disposition is not evaluated by what you don't have; that is, God by no means requires that you contribute more than your resources allow." In this way, no one is excused; for the rich, on the one hand, owe to God a larger offering, and the poor, on the other hand, ought not be ashamed of their limited resources. COMMENTARY ON 2 CORINTHIANS 8:11-12.[39]

THE NATURE OF TRUE ALMSGIVING. WOLFGANG MUSCULUS: This is the sense of the passage: Where a willingness of heart is displayed . . . such willingness is acceptable and pleasing. A person is responsible according to what they have; nothing more is required of them. Thus, three elements are required in giving alms: the first is desire; the second is ability; and the third is giving. Without the second element, the third is not required; without the first element, the third is not approved. The first element is approved without the third, and it is sufficient if the second element is lacking. The size of the third element depends on the second. See the wisdom of the apostle! Although the completion of the contribution requires nothing beyond the Corinthians' resources, it does require a generous payment from their resources. Nevertheless, Paul makes no mention concerning this latter point, since it would have been annoying and viewed with unfavorable suspicion, but he impressed upon them what was more acceptable, not requiring more than they were able to perform. COMMENTARY ON 2 CORINTHIANS 8:12.[40]

THE LAW OF NEIGHBORLY LOVE. MARTIN CHEMNITZ: We must not love only those who are near to us whom we want to help, but those whom God for whatever reason puts before us, these we must recognize as our neighbors. Furthermore, love for our neighbor has degrees or order, as is clear from Scripture. . . . Therefore, we should maintain this rule: (1) that we acknowledge as our neighbors those whom God has placed next to us; (2) that we show them willingly our works of love. For "persons are accepted by God according to what they have and not what they do not have." LOCI THEOLOGICI.[41]

ACCEPTABLE ALMS. JOHN TRAPP: Noah's sacrifice could not have been very large, yet it was greatly accepted. Jacob bade his sons to take a

[38]Bullinger, *In Posteriorem D. Pauli ad Corinthios Epistolam Commentarius*, 305. †For the citation of Erasmus, see CWE 43:247-48.
[39]CO 50:100 (CTS 40:292-93).

[40]Musculus, *Commentarius . . . in posteriorem epistolam Pauli ad Corinthios*, 261.
[41]Chemnitz, *Loci Theologici*, 2:410.

little of every good thing and carry it for a present to the lord of Egypt. Saul and his servant presented Samuel with the fourth part of a shekel, around the value of our five pence. These people learned that thankfulness was not measured by God and good people by its weight, but by the will of the giver. God calls for that which a person's heart inclines them to do, be it more or less; so low does his Highness stoop to our meanness! God prefers the willingness of the mind before the worthiness of the work. The poor widow's mite was beyond the magnificence of the rich because it came out of a richer mind. Commentary on 2 Corinthians 8:12.[42]

Deserving and Undeserving Poor. Martin Luther: [A Christian] should be willing to lend and give to everyone who asks him. Yet if he knows that he is a scoundrel, he is not obliged to give it to him. Christ is not telling me to give what I have to any scoundrel that comes along and to deprive my family of it or others who may need it and whom I am obliged to help, and then to suffer want myself and become a burden to others. . . . Therefore, it is important to be careful here and to ascertain what sort of people there may be in a city, who there is poor and badly off and who is not, rather than let in any vagrant or tramp who is not in need and could very well support himself. There are plenty of such people roaming around the country nowadays, whom I would call Squire Filth. They would like to take advantage of this teaching and use it to have a good time with other people's possessions until they are all used up, wandering around from one place to another. Such people should be turned over to the police and taught something different, instead of deceiving pious folk with their mischief.

This is what St. Paul teaches in 2 Corinthians 8:13: He is asking the Corinthians for a contribution to the poor Christians in the famine, but he does not mean that on account of it "others should be eased and you burdened," that is, that they should have toil and trouble and be in want themselves in order to let their possessions make the other people happy. Sermon on Matthew 5:38-49.[43]

God's Order Allows for Private Property. Cyriacus Spangenberg: From this saying of Paul the Anabaptists want to conclude that Christians may not have property, but that all goods must be common to them all and that anybody may use another's money, bread, and wine as they themselves wish, as the Lacedemonians once used to do. Plato also prescribed this kind of regime, which is wrong and unrighteous.[†] For if it were contrary to God that people have something as property, he could not have given the command "You shall not steal." For if everything belongs to one as much as to the other, no one can steal, whatever they might want to take. But since God forbids stealing, it follows that people may have property in accordance with God's order. Thirty-Fifth Sermon.[44]

The Principle of Equality. Jacques Lefèvre d'Étaples: At that time, of course, there were poor saints who lived in Jerusalem who were poor in an earthly sense but rich in a spiritual sense. By contrast there were those who abounded in riches but were poor in a spiritual sense. Both groups abounded in one thing and were poor in the other. Each group, in turn, was addressing the poverty of the other, and supplying what was missing—and this equality was pleasing to God. Paul demonstrated this by an example that is read in Exodus: When they were collecting manna, "those who gathered much did not have too much; those who gathered little, did not have less than

[42]Trapp, *A Commentary or Exposition*, 724*; citing Gen 8:20-21; 43:11-12; 1 Sam 9:7-9.

[43]LW 21:117 (WA 32:396-97).

[44]C. Spangenberg, *Die ander Epistel Pauli an die Corinthier*, 148v; citing Ex 20:15. [†]The idea of Spartan economic egalitarianism has a long history, though the reality is more complex. For a detailed discussion, see Stephen Hodkinson, *Property and Wealth in Classical Sparta* (London: Duckworth, 2000). Plato argues that to serve the common interest, the common ownership of property is necessary: *Republic* 5.462b-c, LCL 237:494-97.

those who gathered much." It is proper for the saints, therefore, and those who are truly fed on the same manna (which is the body of Christ), to be zealous for a reputation of showing equality, for in this way those who are superior fulfill their duty to those who are inferior, and those who are inferior repay the superior with obedience. Commentary on 2 Corinthians 8:14-15.[45]

The Nature of Christian Giving. Wolfgang Musculus: Paul does not simply say, "You should supply them," but, "so that your abundance should supply their need," by which he makes two points. First, he stipulates that the future contribution should not seem burdensome, because the phrase "out of their abundance" indicates something that ought to be given. For the person who gives out of his abundance in no way threatens the necessities of his life, because he has given nothing of those things he needs. . . .

Second, in reminding them of the needs of the saints, which the abundance of the Corinthians ought to supply, Paul indicates the reason why this required contribution is urgent, namely, the poverty of the needy saints, whom the Corinthians ought to be moved out of compassion to support as brothers and sisters. Let us remind ourselves on whom our generosity should be bountifully conferred: namely, on poor and needy brothers and sisters. Paul indicates that it is poverty—not the purity and merits of holy people—that should be eagerly supplied with alms. Thereafter, fakes and beggars began to conceal themselves in the sanctity of monks and nuns and religious men, so that they were called spiritual ones (a title which belongs to the living God alone) in a world of dead people, performing their vigils, prayers, and psalm singing for the salvation of everyone. And under this pretext, they have devoured a vast quantity of riches so that one cannot say that the poverty of such people is being assisted, but rather that support is being provided for their luxury and laziness. Commentary on 2 Corinthians 8:14.[46]

Paul's Prescription for Financial Anxiety. Philipp Melanchthon: There is a very good reason why Paul cites the passage regarding manna in Exodus 16, if you consider the spiritual sense. First, the warning about manna forbids people from being worried about their sustenance, and at the same time warns them, as Deuteronomy 8 says, "He afflicted you with hunger and gave you manna from heaven . . . , to show you that humans do not live on bread alone." With this same passage the Lord also wishes to strengthen us in the gospel against this weakness and foolish worry. And the apostle here rehearses this biblical story as if to say: Perhaps you are worried about your livelihood so that you have become weary of generosity. But what is it that you are worried about? The Lord will shepherd you just as he did Israel in the desert, as Psalm 147 says: "He gives food to the beasts and to the black ravens that cry."

Second, Paul restrains humans' desire to heap up riches for themselves, because he says, "Whoever gathered much had nothing left over." For this indicates that the outcome is not in our hands however much we wildly try to increase our possessions. Ecclesiastes 9: "there is no bread to the wise." And Proverbs 20: "An inheritance which is gained quickly at first, will in the end be without blessing." . . . Third, Paul commands fairness, because God's intention is to distribute resources in such a way that those who collect much do not have too much, and those who collect little do not have too little. Therefore, this is his will that they bestow their wealth on the needy. Annotations on 2 Corinthians 8:15.[47]

Paul Appeals to Old Testament Example. Wolfgang Musculus: Paul cites this passage from the story of the manna in Exodus 16, which reads as

[45]Lefèvre, *Commentariorum in Epistolas Beati Pauli . . . Liber Tertius*, 138; citing Ex 16:18.

[46]Musculus, *Commentarius . . . in posteriorem epistolam Pauli ad Corinthios*, 262-63.

[47]*Melanchthons Werke*, 4:123-24; citing Ex 16:4; Deut 8:3; Ps 147:9; Ex 16:18; Eccles 9:11; Prov 20:21.

follows: "This is the word that the Lord has commanded you. 'Gather it, each one of you, as much as one needs to eat. Each person should take an omer, according to the number of souls that live in his tent.' And the sons of Israel did this, some gathering more and others less. And when they measured it according to the measure of the omer . . . those who had gathered much did not have too much, and those who gathered little suffered no want. Each of them gathered as much as was needed to eat."

The apostle introduces this story and applies its lesson to show how the Lord is pleased by the equality of necessary provisions among his people. For the Lord himself furnishes these provisions out of his goodness. By contrast, he is displeased by the greediness of those who accumulate for themselves more than necessary use requires, since by exceeding the standard of necessity they cause harm to their neighbors. The principle of equality is expressed in Moses' statement: "those who had gathered much did not have too much, and those who gathered little suffered no need." . . .

But it is deplorable that even among us, people of the new covenant, love, and the mutual sharing that comes from love, has grown cold. As a result, there are many people who argue that equality of this sort in food and clothing should now come from heaven, just as it happened in the desert. . . . Others think that we should not wait until the end of the world for such equality, since we might acquire it in this age at an opportune time. Commentary on 2 Corinthians 8:15.[48]

Neither Surplus Nor Want. The English Annotations: Though the children of Israel in the wilderness, according to God's command, gathered manna—some more, some less—yet when they measured it with an omer, those who gathered much had nothing left over, and those who gathered less had no lack. The apostle elegantly applies this history to the dispensation of Christian bounty and charity, which ought to be so ordered by the discretion of the governors of the church so that those who receive more may have no surplus, and those who receive less may not experience want. In the same way that all the Israelites had a sufficient amount according to their appetite and the size of their family, so here [Paul intends that] all be sufficiently provided for through a careful distribution, with an eye to the various needs of those that are to be relieved. Annotations on 2 Corinthians 8:15.[49]

Equality in the Christian Community. Peter Walpot: "Those who gathered much did not have too much, and those who gathered little did not have too little." Here the apostle desires that the rich have no more than the poor and the poor no more than the rich. Rather, there should be Christian community and equality. . . . Therefore, out of Christian love, we also should hold all goods which God has bestowed upon us in common enjoyment with our neighbors, brothers and families and not hold them as private. For now is an even more glorious nuptial feast proclaiming the year of redemption than it was in the Old Testament. Yes! It is the year of grace! Christian Community of Goods.[50]

[48]Musculus, *Commentarius . . . in posteriorem epistolam Pauli ad Corinthios*, 265-66, 267; citing Ex 16:16-18.

[49]Downame, ed., *English Annotations*, GG1v*.

[50]Liechty, ed., *Early Anabaptist Spirituality*, 168, 139*; citing Lev 25:1-22.

8:16-24 COMMENDATION OF TITUS

[16]But thanks be to God, who put into the heart of Titus the same earnest care I have for you. [17]For he not only accepted our appeal, but being himself very earnest he is going[a] to you of his own accord. [18]With him we are sending[b] the brother who is famous among all the churches for his preaching of the gospel. [19]And not only that, but he has been appointed by the churches to travel with us as we carry out this act of grace that is being ministered by us, for the glory of the Lord himself and to show our good will. [20]We take this course so that no one should blame us about this generous gift that is being administered by us, [21]for we aim at what is honorable not only in the Lord's sight but also in the sight of man. [22]And with them we are sending our brother whom we have often tested and found earnest in many matters, but who is now more earnest than ever because of his great confidence in you. [23]As for Titus, he is my partner and fellow worker for your benefit. And as for our brothers, they are messengers[c] of the churches, the glory of Christ. [24]So give proof before the churches of your love and of our boasting about you to these men.

a Or *he went* **b** Or *we sent*; also verse 22 **c** Greek *apostles*

OVERVIEW: In the second half of 2 Corinthians 8, the apostle Paul continues to discuss the collection for the Jerusalem church, while giving special commendation to Titus and his unnamed traveling companions. For Reformation commentators, the example of Titus demonstrates that God is the ultimate source of all physical and spiritual provision as well as the origin of every godly impulse toward generosity and faithful service. Neither pastor nor preacher can adequately fulfill their office unless God enables them through the Holy Spirit. Reformation exegetes also find in Paul's example important lessons for pastors and laypeople as they administer the church's resources: they must strive for a good conscience before God and a good reputation before their neighbors; they must avoid every appearance of evil; they must be zealous for God's glory as the highest goal of their service. Even so, those who administer church funds should not be surprised when they face a barrage of calumnies and slander from wicked people, for even Jesus Christ himself endured false accusations from his enemies. An additional concern of early modern commentators is to identify the two companions who were appointed to accompany Titus on his mission. Proposed candidates include Barnabas, Luke, Silas, and Apollos. Regardless of who they might have been, the fact that Paul calls them "the glory of Christ" (2 Cor 8:23) speaks volumes of the value of diligent and faithful Christian ministers.

8:16-21 *Aiming at What Is Honorable*

BUT THANKS BE TO GOD! JOHN TRAPP: *Deo gratia* was always in Paul's mouth and in Augustine's, and should be in ours. COMMENTARY ON 2 CORINTHIANS 8:16.[1]

GOD PROVIDES PHYSICAL AND SPIRITUAL NOURISHMENT TO HIS PEOPLE. JOHN CALVIN: So as to leave the Corinthians without excuse. Paul now finally adds that God had given them strong motivators who would attend to the matter. And in the first place, he names Titus, who, he says, had been divinely raised up. This was of great importance in the present case. For Titus's mission would be all the more effective if the Corinthians recognized him to have come to them at God's initiative. Now, from this passage,

[1]Trapp, *A Commentary or Exposition*, 725*.

as from innumerable others, we gather that there are no godly affections that do not proceed from God's Spirit. And furthermore, that it is a testimony of divine concern for his people when he raises up ministers and guardians who are eager to relieve their needs. But if the providence of God is seen in caring for bodily provision, how much more will he be concerned that his people not be lacking spiritual nourishment? Hence, it is his special and peculiar work to raise up pastors.

"Accepting our appeal"—indicates that Titus had undertaken this business at Paul's urging. This he corrects afterward, saying that Titus had not so much been influenced by the advice of others, as motivated spontaneously out of his own concern. Commentary on 2 Corinthians 8:16-17.[2]

Titus's Eager Heart. Niels Hemmingsen: Commending those whom he was going to send to Corinth, Paul first remembers Titus, whom he mentions not so much by way of recommendation and encouragement, as to recognize the special eagerness of his heart in the matter of collecting alms from the Corinthians. When Paul gives thanks to God for this, he indicates not only that all godly impulses in humans are stimulated by God's Spirit but also that this work is very pleasing to God, so that those needy persons might be helped by the brothers. Commentary on 2 Corinthians 8:16.[3]

Exhortations and Prayers Accomplish Great Things. Heinrich Bullinger: "I wasn't the only one who wished to do this," Paul says. "Titus acted the same way before me when he came to you of his own accord and encouraged you to give generously." Paul is speaking here about Titus's first visit to the Corinthians. For Titus had come to Paul after visiting these churches in Macedonia (as we demonstrated a little earlier). Now, our prayers and exhortations affect great things, and should be highly valued. And subtle proof is found in this passage when Paul gives thanks to God. Commentary on 2 Corinthians 8:16-17.[4]

God Works Through His Ministers. Cyriacus Spangenberg: Paul rightly says, "Thanks be to God, who put such concern for you into Titus's heart," that Titus loves you so much, carries such good hope for you, and cares so faithfully for you, that you may thus have praise with God and human beings (for which he also persists, praises, extols, urges, and spurs you and us on). He does not do this from himself, nor did another human being put this in him at some point, but it comes from God. He did not put in him a small, mean concern for you, but such a great and earnest concern, not into his mouth but into his heart. So this is a divine work, and what Titus does and seeks after that, God himself does. Therefore, you should allow yourselves to be loved by him in this manner, and not despise his concern in any way.

From this we should now learn, first, that when our preachers and pastoral caregivers are diligent with and for us in teaching, comforting, disciplining, warning, and so on, this is not a human work but God's own work, which God is doing in us and demonstrating to us through his servants. Next, we should learn from this that no preacher can fulfill his office diligently and beneficially, indeed no human being can think or do anything good, unless God himself works it in him through his Holy Spirit. Third, we should also strengthen our faith from this and trust God all the more firmly, because as God puts such diligence and concern into the hearts of his servants for physical needs he will truly also much less allow his faithful to suffer lack of any spiritual goods. If he awakens the hearts of his upright pastoral caregivers to take on the temporal poverty of their hearers, he will much more direct them to consider the spiritual needs of the poor, and in order that the same may

[2]CO 50:102-3 (CTS 40:297-98).
[3]Hemmingsen, *Commentaria in Omnes Epistolas Apostolorum*, 287.
[4]Bullinger, *In Posteriorem D. Pauli ad Corinthios Epistolam Commentarius*, 308.

be met, to be diligent and concerned. Thirty-Sixth Sermon.[5]

Paul Probably Referring to Luke in This Passage. Martin Luther: Luke, . . . who wrote later [than Matthew or Mark], declares that one of his motives is to write in historical order, since many others had disregarded the sequence of this history. Hence many are of the opinion, and it is quite credible, that St. Paul had St. Luke in mind when he declares, commending him to the Corinthians, "With him we are sending the brother who is famous among all Christians for his preaching of the gospel." Confession Concerning Christ's Supper.[6]

Paul Probably Referring to Barnabas in This Passage. John Calvin: The fact that three people are sent is evidence of the high expectations that were held for the Corinthians, and that it was necessary for them to be all the more attentive lest they disappoint the hopes of the churches. However, it is uncertain who the second person was, although some people conjecture that it was Luke, others that it was Barnabas. Chrysostom[†] prefers Barnabas—and I agree with him, because it is known that, by the decision of the churches, he had been appointed as Paul's companion. As, however, it is almost universally agreed that Luke was one of those who delivered this epistle [to the Corinthians], I have no objection that he be considered the third person mentioned [in verse 22].

Now Paul honors the second person (whoever he might be) with an illustrious commendation, that he had conducted himself in the gospel in a praiseworthy manner; that is, he deserved praise for promoting the gospel. For although Barnabas deferred to Paul in the office of preaching, nevertheless they shared the same ministry together. He adds further that this colleague had received praise, not simply from one person, or from one church, but from all the churches. To this general testimony Paul joins a specific one that is relevant to the present subject, namely, that he had been chosen for this duty by the agreement of the churches. Now, it is unlikely that this honor would have been conferred upon him unless he was long known to be qualified for it. We must note, however, the manner of election that was customary among the Greeks—a show of hands (*cheirotonia*), in which the nobles took the lead by virtue of their authority and wise deliberation, while the common people signaled their approval. Commentary on 2 Corinthians 8:18.[7]

Titus's Traveling Companion Was Probably Luke. Wolfgang Musculus: That Paul did not send Titus alone, but sent two brothers with him did not happen without consultation, as we will soon see below. Now there is a difference of opinion regarding the identity of this brother who was praised by all the churches for his preaching and who was Paul's chosen companion on his missionary journey. Some people understand this companion to be Luke, and others Barnabas. Chrysostom[†] took this brother to be Barnabas because he was a companion with Paul in his missionary journey and because of his clear preaching of the gospel. A number of recent interpreters have agreed with this interpretation. Sophronius, however, writes that this present passage refers to Luke. . . . And Jerome agrees with him.[‡] This, of course corresponds to what we learn about Luke in the Acts of the Apostles, because he was a companion in Paul's missionary journeys. No doubt he received a lot of praise among all the churches, especially the Gentile churches, because he wrote the evangelical history with exceptional conscientiousness and diligence in the Greek language. . . . Given these conjectures, I think that those people are probably correct who interpret this passage to refer to Luke rather than to Barnabas.

[5]C. Spangenberg, *Die ander Epistel Pauli an die Corinthier*, 151.
[6]LW 37:316 (WA 6:461).

[7]CO 50:103-4 (CTS 40:299-300). [†]For Chrysostom's interpretation, see PG 62:523 (NPNF[1] 12:363-64).

Here is my opinion on the matter. Paul says here that this brother was the one whom he sent to Corinth together with Titus, and that this brother was the companion chosen by the churches for his missionary journey. Thus, we should not understand this missionary journey to refer to all of Paul's travels in general, but only to that journey that Paul organized to bring the collection of the Gentile churches back to Jerusalem. Several brothers, who had been appointed by the churches to accomplish this task, were sent out together with Paul. It seems to me very unlikely that Barnabas was among these men. For after Barnabas separated from Paul due to their difference regarding Mark's coming on the missionary journey, nothing more is read about their collaboration. We read about their separation in Acts 15, at which time neither the Corinthians nor the Macedonians had been converted, since the conversion of the Macedonians followed afterward, as is seen in Acts 16, and the conversion of the Corinthians after that, as Acts 18 has it. Therefore, since this embassy to the Corinthians had not occurred before their conversion but a long time after, and since Barnabas had separated from Paul before the Corinthians were converted and there is no report that they joined together thereafter, how could Paul have finally sent Barnabas along with Titus to Corinth for the sake of the administration of this matter at the beginning of Acts 19? But it is abundantly clear to all from the narration of his departure that Luke left with Paul on that journey to Jerusalem. Hence, those who think that the apostle's words here refer to Barnabas do not seem to have sufficiently examined this matter. Commentary on 2 Corinthians 8:18.[8]

The Gospel Does Not Change Regardless of Who Declares It. Martin Luther: "The gospel" is not only what Matthew, Mark, Luke, and John have written. . . . No matter who writes and teaches it, whether Matthew or Thomas, and no matter in what words or tongues, it is the same gospel of God. It does not make any difference how many books and writers teach it, because it is all the same thing that all are teaching. Therefore, the remarks of the apostle concerning a certain disciple, "whose praise is in the gospel through all the churches," are not necessarily to be interpreted as referring to the Gospel of St. Luke but rather in this way, that his reputation was in the proclamation of the gospel, that is, the Word of God. Thus also Apollos and others were esteemed in a similar way, that is, because they knew how to proclaim Christ in eloquent and thoughtful words. Commentary on Romans 1:3-4.[9]

The Gospel Written or the Gospel Preached? The English Annotations: The brother "whose praise is in the gospel." That is, either in the Gospel "written by him" (if one translates this passage following St. Jerome), by which he means St. Luke the Evangelist; or, in the gospel "preached by him," by which he means someone else, such as Barnabas and Apollos, who were praised in all the churches for their excellent gifts of preaching the gospel. Annotation on 2 Corinthians 8:18.[10]

The Unnamed Brother. Edward Leigh: Henri Estienne says [this brother] was Silas. Jerome, Cajetan, Grotius, Bilson, and some others say Luke the Evangelist. Others such as Chrysostom, Calvin, Dr. Hall think it was someone else, whether Barnabas or Apollos. . . . À Lapide in one passage says it was Barnabas, because he was by the vote of the church made Paul's companion.[†] Annotations on 2 Corinthians 8:18.[11]

[8]Musculus, *Commentarius . . . in posteriorem epistolam Pauli ad Corinthios*, 269-70.[†]For Chrysostom's interpretation, see PG 62:523 (NPNF[1] 12:363-64). The reference to Sophronius most likely refers to the Christian leader and patriarch of Jerusalem who negotiated the surrender of Jerusalem to the Arabs in the early seventh century. [‡]Jerome, *Lives of Illustrious Men*. NPNF[2] 3:363.

[9]LW 25:148-49* (WA 56:169-70).

[10]Downame, ed., *English Annotations*, GG1v*.

[11]Leigh, *Annotations upon all the New Testament*, 262*. [†]Jerome, *Letter to Paulinus*, NPNF[2] 6:102; Cardinal Cajetan (Thomas de Vio), *In omnes D. Pauli et aliorum apostolorum epistolas*

THE GENEROSITY OF GOD'S PEOPLE BRINGS GLORY TO GOD. TILEMANN HESSHUS: Paul says that he is administering the kindness and generosity, as well as the eagerness, of the saints for the glory of the Lord. For praise is ascribed to Christ when bold generosity is observed among the faithful. For in this way the doctrine of Christ and the power of the Spirit are known in this world, when the faithful of Christ are adorned with extraordinary virtues. Paul wants the eagerness of the saints to become known to everyone so that others might be encouraged to embrace the gospel with praise. EXPLICATION OF 2 CORINTHIANS 8:19.[12]

THE PURPOSE OF ADMINISTERING ALMS. ANDREAS HYPERIUS: That is, "since this responsibility has been assigned to him, he should collect alms in the same way that we administer and dispense the ministry of the gospel, but also for the glory of God and for testifying to the eagerness of your goodwill." Thus, with these words are described the greatest proof of gospel ministers, namely, that wherever they dispense alms, they do so as faithful and honest ministers. And second, that they administer these same alms not for their own private benefit, nor to secure for themselves some glory thereby, but only for bringing glory to God and to display the goodwill of those who have eagerly contributed the alms. Likewise, it is possible here to see what kinds of persons ought to be chosen to be entrusted with alms: it is necessary that they appear trustworthy. So, too, alms ought also to be distributed for their ultimate purpose, namely, for the glory of God and to testify to the eagerness of others. COMMENTARY ON 2 CORINTHIANS 8:19.[13]

PAUL WISHES TO AVOID ALL SUSPICION. HULDRYCH ZWINGLI: The reason we did not entrust this gift to one person was so that we might deprive calumniators of every evil suspicion. For although Titus is such an excellent man that this entire business could have been entrusted to him alone, nevertheless we did not want to commit it to him lest there be some opportunity for accusation. For we want to be honorable not only before God, but also before other people. ANNOTATIONS ON 2 CORINTHIANS 8:20.[14]

A GOOD CONSCIENCE BEFORE GOD AND PEOPLE. NIELS HEMMINGSEN: Paul explains the reason why he sends other people, namely, so that there would be no malicious person who would say that Paul was concerned for his own personal advantage rather than the needs of the poor (because no one is immune from Satan's vicious attacks). Therefore, Paul, that honorable and holy man, says that he is concerned not only to have a good conscience before God but also to be free from any false accusations of people. Whence, Augustine states, "The one who neglects their own reputation is cruel, because it is no less necessary to have a good conscience before our neighbor as before God."[†] We know that Paul's example here is intended not only for ministers of the Word, but also for all godly people. COMMENTARY ON 2 CORINTHIANS 8:20-21.[15]

PAUL SOUGHT TO AVOID FALSE ACCUSATIONS. TILEMANN HESSHUS: The Greek word *stellomenoi* is a metaphor taken from sailing, where sailors avoid rocks or danger by changing direction. "I exercise self-restraint," Paul says, "and I avoid all things which are able to come under suspicion, so that I might give no occasion to anyone to disfigure my ministry with a false accusation." It was not sufficient for Paul to live a holy life before God and

commentarii (Lyon: Iacobi & Petri Prost, 1639), 183; Hugo Grotius, *Aentekeningen over de brieven van den apostel Paulus* (Amsterdam: Albert en Barent Visscher, 1693), 407; Chrysostom, *Homilies on First and Second Corinthians*, NPNF[1] 12:363-64; John Calvin, *Commentary on Second Corinthians*, CTS 40:299-300; Cornelius à Lapide, *Commentaria In Omnes D. Pauli Epistolas* (Antverpiae: Martin Nutius and John Meursium, 1614), NN1r.

[12]Hesshus, *Explicatio Secundae Epistolae Pauli ad Corinthios*, 212v.

[13]Hyperius, *Commentarii . . . in Epistolam D. Pauli ad Romanos, et Utramque ad Corinthios*, 395-96.

[14]Zwingli, *Annotatiunculae . . . ex ore Zvinglij*, 183.

[15]Hemmingsen, *Commentaria in Omnes Epistolas Apostolorum*, 288. [†]Augustine, *First Sermon on the Way of Life of His Clergy*, in *Sermons*, trans. Edmund Hill, The Works of Saint Augustine III/10 (New York: New City Press, 1995), 165.

protect his conscience unharmed. He also attempted to anticipate every occasion for false accusation. Now, the administration of public monies and large financial gifts certainly exposed him to the accusations of wicked people. Indeed, the maliciousness of the world is so great that it does not spare even the most generous benefactor, nor persons who live in a most holy fashion and diligently avoid all injustice. Not even Christ was immune from false accusations, and the world spared neither the apostles nor the prophets. Therefore, one must act both cautiously and carefully, especially in handling business matters that invite scandal so that, as much as it is possible, we might escape all occasion for spiteful accusations. At the same time, we ought to prepare our minds in such a way that, if we are exposed to slander and attacked with calumnies—even after we have taught faithfully, lived in a holy manner, administered our affairs in the fear of the Lord, and cautiously avoided all appearance of evil—we will not flag in our zeal for virtue, but even perform this obedience to God, so that we might not only live in a holy manner but also bear patiently the calumnies of wicked people with innocence and for the glory of God. Certainly, when it is possible for us to do so, we should try our hardest to avoid all slanders, affronts, and disparagements. For we need to have a good conscience before God and a good reputation before our neighbor. And so, Paul states, "We aim at what's honorable, not only in God's sight, but also in the sight of other people." Explication of 2 Corinthians 8:20-21.[16]

Avoiding the Appearance of Evil. Wolfgang Musculus: Paul explains here how he avoids the perverse suspicions and accusations of evil men concerning his ministry, saying that he is "aiming at what is honorable." The Greek is *pronooumeni*, that is, "exercising foresight." He indicates that he does not undertake the administration of these funds in a careless fashion, nor in a suspicious manner, but honorably and faithfully. And therefore he did not send some ordinary person who was poorly known, nor did he send Titus by himself, however esteemed he was of men and well known by them, but he sent other men along with Titus who were honorable and approved of faith, lest he give to anyone the occasion to blame him in this affair. This passage should be carefully noted by those who minister in the church of God in any fashion, especially in matters relating to money, that they might imitate the sincerity, trustworthiness, and caution of the apostle. In the first place, we see here that Paul was not indifferent to what other people were saying and thinking about him, whether blaming or praising him. "Taking this course," he says, "lest anyone should blame us about this generous gift that is being administered by us." He recognized that this generous gift, which he had been chosen to administer, was a lot of money. He considered how easy it would be for him to be viewed with perverse suspicion on account of it, how shameful for his apostolic office this type of suspicion would be, and how harmful it would be for the future cause of Christ and the impoverished saints. And so, he was very careful to take these precautions. Today, there is not even a crumb of this kind of concern in the minds of the Roman pontiffs, who boast in their succession from Peter and Paul. . . . So then, how does one take precautions to avoid being blamed by people in the administration of such a great quantity of money? Not by laws, threats, and oaths, as the pontiffs are accustomed to do. How then? I answer: in a manner altogether apostolic and effective. Paul lays down this twofold strategy. First . . . the apostle was committed to avoiding being butchered by the accusations and attacks of wicked men. Second . . . he was anxious to exercise precaution by aiming at what was honorable. How? "Not only before the Lord," he says, "but also before men"; that is, he lived in a truthful manner that was known to God, but he also sought the appearance of what was truthful and honorable to satisfy the consciences of other people. In 1 Thessalonians 5 we are commanded

[16]Hesshus, *Explicatio Secundae Epistolae Pauli ad Corinthios*, 212v-213v.

not only to avoid evil itself but also the appearance of evil. COMMENTARY ON 2 CORINTHIANS 8:21.[17]

BEWARE OF AMBITION! JOHN CALVIN: Certainly, nothing is worse than ambition, which corrupts the best things in the world, disfigures, I say, the most respectable things and renders the sacrifices of the sweetest smell an offensive odor before the Lord. That is why this passage is slippery, and people must be careful lest they pretend to desire a good reputation along with Paul, when they are (in fact) very far from Paul's devotion. For, Paul here was concerned to live honorably before men and women so that no one might stumble by his example, but rather all might be edified. Hence, we must take care not to seek a good name for our own benefit if we desire to be like him. "The one who is unconcerned about their reputation is cruel," Augustine states, "because it is no less necessary to have a good conscience before our neighbor as before God."[†] This is true, provided you consider the welfare of your brothers and sisters with a view toward the glory of God, and in the meantime are prepared to endure abuse and disgrace in place of praise, if the Lord should so will it. Let the Christian man or woman, however, always take care to frame their lives for the edification of their neighbors, and pay diligent attention, so that the ministers of Satan have no pretext for reviling them, to the dishonor of God and the offense of the good. COMMENTARY ON 2 CORINTHIANS 8:21.[18]

PAUL WAS CONCERNED ABOUT HIS REPUTATION. DAVID DICKSON: Paul gives the reason why he joined to himself traveling companions who had the reputation for faithfulness in the administration of this financial collection, gathered for the use of the church of Jerusalem, namely, that he might remove the opportunity for his adversaries to spread bad reports and calumniate him, accusing him of helping himself to some of the money collected. In addition, he did this so as to confirm his reputation among all people, as he guarded his conscience before God, that he might be kept in the holy purpose of his integrity in this business. EXPOSITION OF 2 CORINTHIANS 8:21.[19]

8:22-24 *Partners and Coworkers in Christ*

TITUS'S TRAVELING COMPANION WAS PROBABLY SYLVANUS. JACQUES LEFÈVRE D'ÉTAPLES: It is very likely Sylvanus who is the third brother whom Paul commends here and who served as Titus's companion and colleague. But since Paul does not name him expressly, his identity is not known with certainty. Nevertheless, these men were honored among the churches and viewed as apostles—not those first apostles who were companions of Christ and appointed as leaders over all the earth, but those second apostles who were appointed apostles of the churches. Even so, they were brightly shining forth the glory of Christ. COMMENTARY ON 2 CORINTHIANS 8:22-23.[20]

PAUL'S RECOMMENDATION OF A THIRD COLLEAGUE. DESIDERIUS ERASMUS: To these two individuals, highly regarded by you, we have added also a third, a brother of ours. Even if he is not as thoroughly known to you, still, we personally have found him diligent and trustworthy time and again in many circumstances, but more diligent in this work than in the other matters. As a result, I am entirely confident that you will not hesitate to entrust to them even a sizable amount of money, whether you have in view Titus, my colleague and a sharer in the labors that I am undertaking for your sake, or the others joined to him, who, besides the fact that they are our brothers, have been chosen by the decision of the

[17]Musculus, *Commentarius . . . in posteriorem epistolam Pauli ad Corinthios*, 273; citing 1 Thess 5:22.
[18]CO 50:104-5 (CTS 40:302-3). [†]Augustine, *First Sermon on the Way of Life of His Clergy*, in *Sermons*, trans. Edmund Hill, The Works of Saint Augustine III/10 (New York: New City Press, 1995), 165.

[19]Dickson, *An Exposition of All St. Paul's Epistles*, 85*.
[20]Lefèvre, *Commentariorum in Epistolas Beati Pauli . . . Liber Tertius*, 138.

churches for this responsibility. Through them the gospel has been made so illustrious that with good reason they could be called not only apostles, but even the glory of Christ. Paraphrases of 2 Corinthians 8:22-23.[21]

Paul's Endorsement of Titus and His Colleagues. Heinrich Bullinger: Paul adds a third brother—perhaps Silvanus (who is also called Silas) or someone else. Next, he commends all these men to the Corinthians with great enthusiasm. Summing up the preceding statement, Paul's sense is as follows: "We sent Titus, Barnabas, and Silas to you because we had great confidence in all of you, since I supposed you would receive them as the worthy men they are. Titus is my colleague and partner in all my labors; in the same way you kindly welcomed me, please also kindly receive this colleague in my name. As far as those other two men are concerned, they are brothers and representatives of the churches; indeed, the glory of Christ, and the honor and ornaments of the gospel." We learn thus how and in what ways ministers of the Word, churches, and good people should be commended. Commentary on 2 Corinthians 8:22-23.[22]

Paul Calls Titus His Partner. Wolfgang Musculus: Titus was the apostle's disciple, and yet Paul calls him his partner. Why is that? Because he was his fellow helper. Therefore, Titus was a partner of his labors, not of his apostolate; and he did not have apostolic authority. In this way, we see the modesty of the apostle, because he called his disciple simply as his partner. Commentary on 2 Corinthians 8:23.[23]

Illustrious Descriptions of the Church. John Trapp: So the church is called the glory, God's glory, a crown of glory and a royal diadem in the hand of Jehovah, the throne of God, the throne of glory, the ornament of God, indeed, the beauty of his ornament, set in majesty. As someone commented, "There is not so much of the glory of God in all his works of creation and providence as in one gracious action that a Christian performs." Commentary on 2 Corinthians 8:23.[24]

Ministers Should Be the Glory of Christ. Wolfgang Musculus: Paul calls the "glory of Christ" either the two brothers, or one of the brothers and Titus. From this, we should carefully note the kind of ministers we should hold in high esteem in the church, accepting them with love and respect, namely, those who serve diligently and faithfully, who live in such a manner that they are not the disgrace, but the glory of Christ their Lord. Those who act differently, who serve their stomachs rather than Christ, who run after profit in the church, who destroy rather than feed the sheep of Christ, and at the same time live shamelessly—they are not the glory of Christ but bring dishonor to his name. And so, they are not to be respected, but, as tasteless salt, they should be regarded with contempt and thrown away. Commentary on 2 Corinthians 8:23.[25]

Let Us Honor Christ! Cyriacus Spangenberg: For whoever hears the faith, teaching, and confession of the Christian faithful, and sees alongside these their good works, is moved by this to honor and praise the Lord Christ, whose teaching this is and who has commanded them to live this way. Oh, my dear friends, let us also be an honor to Christ! He will certainly in turn richly honor and adorn us with eternal glory and all kinds of blessing. Moreover, it is a glorious comfort to all upright teachers and preachers that they bear such a splendid title, that the Holy Spirit calls them an honor to Christ. For all that they teach leads to the honoring of Christ, and what people

[21]CWE 43:251-52*.

[22]Bullinger, *In Posteriorem D. Pauli ad Corinthios Epistolam Commentarius*, 309.

[23]Musculus, *Commentarius . . . in posteriorem epistolam Pauli ad Corinthios*, 275.

[24]Trapp, *A Commentary or Exposition*, 725*; citing Is 4:5; 46:13; 62:3; Ex 17:6; Jer 4:21; Ezek 7:20.

[25]Musculus, *Commentarius . . . in posteriorem epistolam Pauli ad Corinthios*, 275.

do according to their teaching, and the goodness they show them in return, all happens to the honor of Christ. Thirty-Sixth Sermon.[26]

Paul's Arguments for Generous Giving. Andreas Hyperius: After having affirmed his confidence in those men and explained their situation and mission, Paul now urges the Corinthians to diligently complete the work begun and to warmly welcome those commended brothers in every way possible. Now there are in this conclusion several different convincing arguments. The first argument relates to the effect of love. It is as if Paul were saying, "You should serve them well so as to demonstrate that you have been endowed with true love." The second argument relates to Paul's previous opinion and boasting concerning them. It is as if he were saying, "I have boasted a lot regarding your goodness and generosity toward other people. Therefore, be careful so that it does not seem that I have boasted about you in vain." For, not only now, as he was sending Titus along with the two other colleagues, but also many other times previously, the apostle had boasted about the goodness of the Corinthians, as he stated a little earlier in the preceding chapter. In the third argument, Paul sharply urges them to a greater degree of generosity by pointing to the judgment and praise of other churches. It is as if he were saying, "Deal with them just as you would want other churches to judge you and receive praise from them." Lavish praise that is destined for others greatly excites the mind. Thus, according to Ovid:† "The growth of praise and virtue serves as an immense stimulus." Commentary on 2 Corinthians 8:24.[27]

[26]C. Spangenberg, *Die ander Epistel Pauli an die Corinthier*, 152v.

[27]Hyperius, *Commentarii . . . in Epistolam D. Pauli ad Romanos, et Utramque ad Corinthios*, 397. †The quotation from Ovid is found in his *Epistolae ex Ponto* 4.2.36.

9:1-5 THE COLLECTION FOR CHRISTIANS IN JERUSALEM

Now it is superfluous for me to write to you about the ministry for the saints, [2]for I know your readiness, of which I boast about you to the people of Macedonia, saying that Achaia has been ready since last year. And your zeal has stirred up most of them. [3]But I am sending[a] the brothers so that our boasting about you may not prove empty in this matter, so that you may be ready, as I said you would be. [4]Otherwise, if some Macedonians come with me and find that you are not ready, we would be humiliated—to say nothing of you—for being so confident. [5]So I thought it necessary to urge the brothers to go on ahead to you and arrange in advance for the gift[b] you have promised, so that it may be ready as a willing gift, not as an exaction.[c]

a Or *I have sent* **b** Greek *blessing;* twice in this verse **c** Or *a gift expecting something in return;* Greek *greed*

Overview: In this brief pericope, Paul encourages the Corinthian believers to fulfill their stated intentions and give a liberal financial contribution to the Jerusalem church, thereby justifying Paul's confident boasts of their generosity. Reformation interpreters address a conundrum at the heart of this passage: if Paul is so confident that the Corinthians will give their promised contribution, why does he exhort them to generosity and send Titus and his companions to them to ensure the collection? Paul is not being duplicitous; rather, he recognizes how easy it is to turn aside from good intentions. As Tilemann Hesshus notes, love and generosity quickly evaporate unless stimulated by the commands of God, the promises of the Holy Spirit, the example of the saints, and the exhortations of faithful pastors. Reformation commentators note several other principles related to benevolence in these verses: the generosity of one person can easily stimulate the giving of others; true benevolence rests in action, not simply good intentions; miserliness is a condition that can affect not only the giver but also the recipient of alms. Finally, the extraordinary effort Paul takes to ensure that the Jerusalem collection takes place free of shame or offense reflects his greater concern for the spread of Christ's kingdom, the edification of the churches, and the honor of the ministry of the Word.

Summary of Chapter. David Dickson: Paul continues to speak concerning the collection. There are two parts to this chapter. In the first part (to v. 6), Paul gives the reasons why he sent to them the three assigned brothers. At the same time, he interjects some arguments to persuade them to hasten the collection. In the second part of the chapter, Paul adds more arguments to move the Corinthians to give generously, as is becoming of the saints. Exposition of 2 Corinthians 9.[1]

Organization of This Chapter. Niels Hemmingsen: There are four parts to this chapter. First, there is an emphasis that the alms that the Achaeans had for some time should be made ready. Second, Paul explains clearly why he was sending Titus and others to the Corinthians. Third, he exhorts them to a form of generosity that is free from sadness and not at all compelled. Fourth is a brief concluding declaration of thanksgiving on account of the inexpressible gift of God. Commentary on 2 Corinthians 9.[2]

Is Paul Being Genuine Here? John Calvin: Someone . . . may possibly suspect that Paul here feigns something he does not really think (which is

[1]Dickson, *An Exposition of All St. Paul's Epistles*, 85*.
[2]Hemmingsen, *Commentaria in Omnes Epistolas Apostolorum*, 289.

very absurd). For, if he believes them to be sufficiently prepared to do their duty, why does he so earnestly set about to admonish them? And on the other hand, if he doubts their willingness, why does he declare that it is unnecessary to admonish them? Love brings with it these two things: good hope and anxious concern. Paul would never have given such a testimony regarding the Corinthians if he had not been persuaded of what he said. He had seen a happy beginning, and he hoped that further progress would be no different. But because he was well aware of the unsteadiness of human nature, he could not be too careful to keep them from turning aside from their godly intention. Commentary on 2 Corinthians 9.[3]

9:1-4 *Completing Details for the Collection*

Paul Hopes to Use the Corinthians as a Positive Example. Huldrych Zwingli: Paul exhorts and stimulates the Corinthians to generosity toward the saints who were living in Jerusalem, seizing this opportunity in order that their eagerness might be boasted among the Macedonians and that their zeal might motivate many others. Annotations on 2 Corinthians 9:1.[4]

Paul's Rhetorical Strategy. Andreas Hyperius: Paul proceeds further to add persuasive arguments, since in the preceding verses he had requested only that they demonstrate charity toward those whom he sent and mentioned nothing about the public collection of alms. And so, he skillfully adds necessary instruction regarding the collection of alms (though he touches on this matter only lightly by way of a rhetorical preterition), saying that it was not at all necessary to speak more explicitly about this matter—indicating sufficiently, nevertheless, what he most wanted to accomplish. And this is his purpose: "This is what I most ask of you, that you welcome most humanely those whom I am now sending to you. For as far as alms are concerned—how many or what sort are collected—there is no need for me to prescribe or regulate anything." For the apostle no doubt supposes that if it happens that those men are received kindly, the situation with the poor [in Jerusalem] would be carefully addressed at the same time. And he speaks frankly with the Corinthians so that they might decide this matter for themselves out of their free will. Commentary on 2 Corinthians 9:1.[5]

Motivating Christians to Give Generously. Tilemann Hesshus: The apostle continues to exhort the Corinthians to contribute alms so as to demonstrate by this diligence his extraordinary concern for the needs of the saints. For the apostle was very much aware of the many weaknesses of the saints. Even if the minds of godly people are sometimes inclined to assist others, nevertheless, very quickly, they are either delayed, or called back from their original intention, or their love begins to grow cold, unless they are constantly inspired, encouraged, and stimulated by the command of God, the promises of the Holy Spirit, the examples of the saints, and the exhortation of pastors. The reason that Paul says it is superfluous to write to them concerning the contribution of alms is because he wishes to commend the Corinthians' knowledge and readiness of mind—for it is a mistake to stimulate those who already have a ready inclination in themselves. Therefore, Paul shows how much godliness and generosity he attributes to the Corinthians, which is so evident that he can boast about it to the Macedonians and which has excited many people to show generosity toward the saints. Explication of 2 Corinthians 9:1-2.[6]

The Location of Achaia. The English Annotations: Achaia is the country in which the city of Corinth was situated, and sometimes the

[3]CO 50:106 (CTS 40:305).
[4]Zwingli, *Annotatiunculae . . . ex ore Zvinglij*, 183.
[5]Hyperius, *Commentarii . . . in Epistolam D. Pauli ad Romanos, et Utramque ad Corinthios*, 397.
[6]Hesshus, *Explicatio Secundae Epistolae Pauli ad Corinthios*, 216v-217r.

word is taken generally for all of Greece, sometimes particularly for a part of Peloponnesus, known by that name. ANNOTATIONS ON 2 CORINTHIANS 9:2.[7]

ZEAL IS INFECTIOUS. JACQUES LEFÈVRE D'ÉTAPLES: Achaia is the region where Corinth is located, bordered on one side by the Ionian Sea, and on the other side by the Aegean Sea. The apostle adds the reason why the brothers had been sent to them: namely, to make sure it did not happen that, should the Corinthians be unprepared and remiss in their pious duty, the Macedonians, who had been inspired to this virtuous work by their example, might also become remiss. For zeal works this way, that if zeal is magnified in one person, it is also magnified in another; [but] if it becomes slack in one person, it also slackens a little in another. This is seen among those who zealously compete for victory, whether in music, wrestling, jumping, and similar kinds of competition, where intense zeal is praised among those competing, and slackness results in blame, even when the goal is empty glory. How much more for that zeal, then, when one competes for perfect glory concerning holy virtue? COMMENTARY ON 2 CORINTHIANS 9:2.[8]

THE READINESS OF THE CORINTHIANS. WOLFGANG MUSCULUS: "For I know the readiness of your mind." How did Paul know this? In the previous chapter above, he said, "who not only began to do this work a year ago, but also wishes to do it now." But in the meantime, they could have changed ten times over, with their readiness ending in repentance, which we see happen daily in human affairs. For what happened to the Galatians could also have happened to the Corinthians. But Paul had greater hope for the quality of their love, believing that they would still possess the same readiness in this matter that they had exemplified the previous year. Therefore, he said that he knew the readiness of their mind because he did not know anything different in this affair. COMMENTARY ON 2 CORINTHIANS 9:2.[9]

THE RICH LANGUAGE OF GENEROSITY. THE ENGLISH ANNOTATIONS: The apostle in this chapter describes the bountiful contributions of the Corinthians to the saints with the name of various virtues: zeal, simplicity, grace, benediction, and righteousness. Zeal, because it proceeded out of fervent love, and so much tended to God's glory; simplicity, because they did it out of a free mind and singleness of heart, without any sinister intention or expecting any retribution; grace, because it was the gift of God proceeding from his grace; benediction or blessing, because God's blessing enables them to do it, and the poor saints bless God for this supply of their wants; last, righteousness, either because pious bounty is a part of that righteousness, or justice in general, which comprises all the virtues . . . or because we are not lords of the goods of this life, but stewards only, and he is an unjust steward who holds that wholly in his own hands, for his own advantage, which by order from his Master he ought to dispense to others for their relief and sustenance. ANNOTATIONS ON 2 CORINTHIANS 9:2.[10]

PAUL ANSWERS THE UNSPOKEN QUESTION. CARDINAL CAJETAN: Paul is answering this unspoken question: "If you are so confident in our willingness, why did you send us these distinguished men to accomplish this work?" He explains the reason why he sent these distinguished brothers in this way: "Not so that we might boast [in ourselves], but so that our boasting about you in this matter might not be in vain." And Paul adds this explanation, "so that you would be prepared just as I told the Macedonians you would be prepared." And thus, the reason Paul sent the

[7]Downame, ed., *English Annotations*, GG2r*.
[8]Lefèvre, *Commentariorum in Epistolas Beati Pauli . . . Liber Tertius*, 138v.
[9]Musculus, *Commentarius . . . in posteriorem epistolam Pauli ad Corinthios*, 278, citing 2 Cor 8:10.
[10]Downame, ed., *English Annotations*, GG2r*.

brothers was so that [the Corinthians] might be prepared—not so that they might be eager to give, but so that money might be found ready. COMMENTARY ON 2 CORINTHIANS 9:3.[11]

PAUL WISHES TO AVOID VAIN BOASTING. WOLFGANG MUSCULUS: Paul explains in greater detail for what purpose he had sent those brothers. The most important reason was that he feared, if the Corinthians were found to be unprepared, he would be exposed to shame along with them, seeing that he had expected to boast in them. Paul indicates this when he says: "so that our boasting about you (meaning: what had been prepared in Achaia) may not prove vain." Now "to prove vain" is that which is forsaken. Therefore, it is the truth alone that renders everything we do and say as genuine; and so, without the truth, everything is altogether vain. Great is the boast of truth. But when the whole person is a liar, what else follows than that the whole person is vain and empty since they are void of the truth? That is why if we are to flee the disgrace of boasting, we must be eager for the truth. COMMENTARY ON 2 CORINTHIANS 9:3.[12]

PAUL'S STRATEGY TO ELICIT THE CORINTHIANS' GENEROSITY. NIELS HEMMINGSEN: Paul explains openly the reason why he sent Titus, along with those other two brothers, to Corinth, namely, so that alms designated for the poor might be ready when the apostle and the Macedonians came. He presses for this outcome with many words, namely, "so that our boasting might not be empty," "so that you might be ready," "so that we might not be humiliated in our confident boasting," "so that I must be silent for the moment," "so that you might not be embarrassed when the Macedonians come." For we blush all the more when we commit a sin in the sight of many people. With these copious and embellished words, Paul urges the Corinthians to do their duty. The word *hypostasis*, by which Paul means "confident," is the same in this passage as that Hebrew word *tocheles*, which the Septuagint interprets as *hypostasis* in Psalm 39; that is, that hope or expectation or assurance which is the firm confidence of the mind. COMMENTARY ON 2 CORINTHIANS 9:3-4.[13]

THE CORINTHIANS MUST BE PREPARED TO GIVE. HULDRYCH ZWINGLI: It is possible for a person who commends another to be mistaken. But the person who is praised—if he fails—has greater guilt and greater shame. It is as if Paul were saying, "This proof of boasting relates more to you than to me; therefore, be careful lest they discover you to be unprepared." ANNOTATIONS ON 2 CORINTHIANS 9:4.[14]

PAUL'S CONFIDENCE IN THE CORINTHIANS. JOHN CALVIN: Since the Greek word here is *hypostasis*, the Old Interpreter [Jerome] rendered it substance [*substantia*]. Erasmus renders it subject matter [*argumentum*], but neither is suitable. Now Budé† observes that this word is sometimes taken to mean boldness or confidence, as it is in Polybius, when he states, "It was not so much his bodily strength, as his *boldness* [*hypostasin*] and courage that proved confounding to the enemy." Therefore, the Greek word *hypostatikos* sometimes means one who is bold and confident. Now, everyone must see how fitting this accords with Paul's argument. Hence it appears that other interpreters have unwittingly been mistaken. COMMENTARY ON 2 CORINTHIANS 9:4.[15]

THE GROUND OF PAUL'S CONFIDENCE. THE ENGLISH ANNOTATIONS: Greek "in the substance," or "foundations of this boasting." The word in the original is *hypostasis*, which can signify one of two things: either a steadfastness and steadiness of

[11]Cajetan, *In Posteriorem Pauli Epistolam ad Corinthios Commentarii*, 184.

[12]Musculus, *Commentarius . . . in posteriorem epistolam Pauli ad Corinthios*, 280.

[13]Hemmingsen, *Commentaria in Omnes Epistolas Apostolorum*, 289.

[14]Zwingli, *Annotatiunculae . . . ex ore Zvinglij*, 183-84.

[15]CO 50:107 (CTS 40:306-7). †The Catholic humanist Guillaume Budé (1468–1540) was a prominent philologist and Hellenist in Paris in the first half of the sixteenth century.

mind which cannot be moved by any terror or fear, and so it shows the assured confidence St. Paul had in them—that they would make good what he had promised on their behalf. Or it may signify a ground or foundation, and so the meaning is that he would not be ashamed of his boasting to others of their readiness, because there was a good ground and foundation for it; either the public faith of the Corinthians who engaged themselves to contribute generously to the saints, or some present pledge which he saw from them, namely, some remarkable sums collected a year before. ANNOTATIONS ON 2 CORINTHIANS 9:4.[16]

9:5 *Greed and Generosity*

PAUL PROTECTED THE REPUTATION OF HIS MINISTRY. WOLFGANG MUSCULUS: "So I thought it necessary to urge the brothers to go on ahead to you." Why was this necessary? And why was it necessary, if the Macedonians came, for the apostle to guard against the possibility that they would be offended by the lack of preparation of the Corinthians and that he would be humiliated along with them? Paul thought about it this way, and so he was motivated accordingly. Today, nothing seems to be less important than to avoid humiliation and shame so that the ministry of the Word may not be disgraced. But this is exactly what the apostle was concerned about most of all, namely, the edification of the churches and the propagation of the kingdom of Christ, and just as he promoted these things, so he also zealously commanded them. . . . Hence, the only reason that Paul thought it necessary to send the brothers to Corinth was to avoid offense. And this should still be the concern of those who care for the church. COMMENTARY ON 2 CORINTHIANS 9:5.[17]

THE BLESSING OF GIVING ALMS. TILEMANN HESSHUS: Because Paul did not want his boasting to be in vain or to prove worthless, he exhorted not only the Corinthians but also the brothers he sent (who previously came from Corinth) to prepare the collection of alms before the Macedonians came so that the truth might match Paul's boasting. The word "blessing" [*benediction*] is written here to connote an extreme kindness [*beneficentia*]. When God blesses us, at the same time he also shows us kindness and effectively gives us all things. This meaning is here applied also to human beings, though in a less appropriate manner, for humans do not quickly perform acts of kindness nor do they assist others as effectively as they might intend. Nevertheless, by the use of this expression Paul wishes to indicate not only good intentions, but also helping one's neighbor in deed and action. Now alms are called a blessing [*benediction*] because there is no loss, nay rather, it is completely given back to us and blesses us if we give anything to poor people with a pure heart.

The Greek word *pleonexia* here is interpreted as "miserliness," as it clearly relates to what follows. For those of us who have received rich blessings from God and who place all our security not in the abundance of riches but in the Lord, we should give alms, not sparingly, or grudgingly, nor with a closed fist, but liberally and generously. EXPLICATION OF 2 CORINTHIANS 9:5.[18]

THE WARNING AGAINST GREED APPLIES TO THE CORINTHIANS. WOLFGANG MUSCULUS: The Greek for the phrase "not as defrauding" is *kai mē hōsper pleonexian*. The Vulgate version renders it "not as greed." The Greek word *pleonexia* means that very great desire where we long to have more than is right. As a result, the old interpreters translated this word into Latin as "greed" [*avaritia*]. But it is not entirely clear whether this passage is speaking about the desire of the Corinthians or the desire of those brothers whom the apostle sent to them. To be sure, it is possible to sin in both ways, as much in giving as in receiving: persons

[16]Downame, ed., *English Annotations*, GG24*.
[17]Musculus, *Commentarius . . . in posteriorem epistolam Pauli ad Corinthios*, 282.
[18]Hesshus, *Explicatio Secundae Epistolae Pauli ad Corinthios*, 217v-218r.

who give, if they give rather stingily, are guilty of this vice of *pleonexia*; persons who receive, if they receive something greedily by hungering for more than is appropriate, are also guilty of this same *pleonexia*. Therefore, I think that the apostle is warning the Corinthians that their financial contribution, promised for the needs of the saints, when it is finally prepared and ready, should not be given frugally or stingily, but lavishly as is befitting of praise. And the flow of the passage favors this interpretation. COMMENTARY ON 2 CORINTHIANS 9:5.[19]

THE FRUIT OF COVETOUSNESS. JOHN TRAPP: "Not as something extorted," says Piscator,[†] "or something given stingily." Not like a gift wrung or squeezed out of you, like sour juices squeezed out of crabapples. Covetous people part from their money as with the blood out of their hearts. . . . God will set off all hearts from such misers, who, in their miserliness, are so unreasonably merciless. Bounty or blessing (for this is what the Greek word signifies) is here appropriately opposed to covetousness. And St. Paul concludes that when church contributions are not free and generous, covetousness is the cause. COMMENTARY ON 2 CORINTHIANS 9:5.[20]

[19]Musculus, *Commentarius . . . in posteriorem epistolam Pauli ad Corinthios*, 283.

[20]Trapp, *A Commentary or Exposition*, 726*. [†]Johannes Piscator (1546–1624) was a German Reformed theologian and biblical scholar who published expansive commentaries on both the Old and New Testaments.

9:6-15 THE CHEERFUL GIVER

[6]The point is this: whoever sows sparingly will also reap sparingly, and whoever sows bountifully[a] will also reap bountifully. [7]Each one must give as he has decided in his heart, not reluctantly or under compulsion, for God loves a cheerful giver. [8]And God is able to make all grace abound to you, so that having all sufficiency[b] in all things at all times, you may abound in every good work. [9]As it is written,

"He has distributed freely, he has given to the poor;
his righteousness endures forever."

[10]He who supplies seed to the sower and bread for food will supply and multiply your seed for sowing and increase the harvest of your righteousness. [11]You will be enriched in every way to be generous in every way, which through us will produce thanksgiving to God. [12]For the ministry of this service is not only supplying the needs of the saints but is also overflowing in many thanksgivings to God. [13]By their approval of this service, they[c] will glorify God because of your submission that comes from your confession of the gospel of Christ, and the generosity of your contribution for them and for all others, [14]while they long for you and pray for you, because of the surpassing grace of God upon you. [15]Thanks be to God for his inexpressible gift!

a Greek *with blessings*; twice in this verse **b** Or *all contentment* **c** Or *you*

Overview: In this passage, Paul concludes his discussion of the Jerusalem collection (begun in 8:1) by employing the analogy of sowing seeds to demonstrate that God multiplies the fruitfulness of Christian generosity in a variety of unexpected ways. Reformation commentators are especially impressed by Paul's image of the diligent farmer, who gladly plants seed in expectation of reaping an abundant harvest. In a similar way, Christians are encouraged to give alms voluntarily, cheerfully, and sacrificially, confident that God will one day produce a bountiful harvest of spiritual and physical blessings: the poor will be nourished, Christians will rejoice, and God will be praised. Scripture also indicates that God frequently compensates generous benefactors with still more riches to share. Cheerful generosity should thus be the spiritual posture of all believers, for it reminds them that every necessity of life comes from God's generous provision. Despite overall agreement on the importance of charitable giving, Reformation commentators identify points of disagreement in the application of these principles. The Catholic exegete Cardinal Cajetan emphasizes the cooperative role that men and women play in bearing spiritual fruit. The Reformed commentator Wolfgang Musculus criticizes Roman Catholics who contribute alms on behalf of dead saints rather than living ones. The Anabaptist minister Balthasar Hubmaier finds the doctrine of human free will in Paul's command that Christians give cheerfully. Commentators also differ over the identity of the "inexpressible gift" for which Paul gives exuberant thanks in 2 Corinthians 9:15, with some believing it refers to Christ, others to the gospel, and still others to God's extraordinary grace that has stimulated the Corinthians' act of generosity.

9:6-10 *A Bountiful Harvest of Generosity*

Giving Under Compulsion Is Not True Generosity. Desiderius Erasmus: It is with good reason that in Greek we call this contribution *eulogia*, that is, "a blessing," because a benefit ought to be given and received, not grudgingly, nor with murmuring, but with good wishes; otherwise, it will seem an extortion, not a collection. Let each one contribute voluntarily if they want to, and as much as they wish.

But we remind you of this: the more generously each one contributes, the richer is the reward they will bring back. The person who does their sowing sparingly likewise will reap sparingly; the one who sows eagerly and with high expectations will in equal measure reap what they have sown, not as though on my bidding, but as each has voluntarily determined in their own heart. For a person gives more generously and more gladly who gives voluntarily. That one gives quite resentfully who gives with a gloomy spirit, as if compelled. But God loves a cheerful giver. Indeed, in God's eyes a person who does their duty under compulsion does not do his duty. Paraphrases on 2 Corinthians 9.[1]

The Analogy of Sowing and Reaping. Wolfgang Musculus: Paul could have explained this matter simply, but he preferred to use an analogy that was well-known and very agreeable to everyone, drawn from those who plant seed in the earth and gather from it food to sustain their lives. Paul suggests that the same condition applies to giving alms that exists for planting seed. For when a person plants, part of the grain they have previously received from the Lord's blessing they devote to domestic use, the other part they set aside to plant in the earth. Now they do this, not with sorrowful groans, but with cheerful optimism. They cast the seed in the open field, not with a tight-fisted hand, but with an open hand. . . . And they not only throw the seed, but they work hard to break up the soil as they bury the seed in the heart of the earth whereby their effort bears fruit. And they commit to the Lord its growth and anticipates fruit from his generosity. In a similar way, the person who gives alms does not give anything except that which they have previously received from the hand of God's blessing (with the exception of those things obtained in a wicked fashion). And some of this wealth they apply to their own personal needs, and some they set aside for the poor. And when they share with the poor, they do so not groaning sorrowfully, nor sparingly, but with a generous hand. And just as with seed planted in an open field, so they cast their alms upon the poor hungry person, and commend it wholly to the grace of God, knowing that what is planted in the heart of the poor will not perish. The person who thus sows alms generously will receive in turn a generous harvest of divine reward. Commentary on 2 Corinthians 9:6.[2]

The Generous Reap Both Heavenly and Earthly Blessings. Tilemann Hesshus: Although Paul does not doubt that the intention of the Corinthians is to help the poor people, and thus he says that he is going to refrain from a more detailed exhortation, nevertheless he intersperses admonitions and promises because there are various groups in the church: some do their duty voluntarily, others need to be spurred on to do so. And however eager the saints might be, nevertheless, they must be instructed according to the will of God and encouraged by the divine promises. Here, Paul elegantly compares giving alms to sowing. The person who sows throws the seed by hand and scatters it upon the earth, where it rots and dies, so that it seems to have perished and there appears no hope of fruit. But when the time comes for the harvest, then it returns to us a great profit, and we see the abundant produce of the sowing. The process of almsgiving is a lot like this, while we bequeath alms to the poor, distributing them by hand, showing kindness now to this person, now to that person. That which we distribute seems to us to have perished; no fruit is apparent. But we must anticipate the time of harvest, for in due time the Lord pays back to us with a vast and abundant profit whatever we have given in turn to that poor person. Now Paul adds a reminder: those who are spare in sowing will also reap sparingly. That is, those who bequeath in a miserly fashion will gather

[1]CWE 43:253-54*.

[2]Musculus, *Commentarius . . . in posteriorem epistolam Pauli ad Corinthios*, 283-84.

little fruit from their effort. But those who sow generously and copiously will harvest God's abundant blessing. Therefore, those who are furnished with the resources of this world should be rich in good works, for this promise of Christ is most certain: "Give and it will be given to you." They will harvest blessings—that is, copiously—and reap in abundance the fruit of their alms. Now, we ought to understand that this refers not only to spiritual and heavenly blessing but also earthly and bodily blessings. For the good deeds of the saints, apart from the fact that they receive an abundant reward laid up in heaven, are also compensated in this life with physical blessings from God. Psalm 41 reads, "Blessed is the one who considers the poor! In the day of trouble the Lord will deliver them. The Lord protects them and keeps them alive. . . . The Lord will restore them from their sickbed." Explication of 2 Corinthians 9:6.[3]

Alms Produce a Bountiful Heavenly Crop. The English Annotations: Alms must be given neither stingily nor unwillingly, but frankly and freely, since it is the sowing of that seed that will bring us a plentiful harvest both here and hereafter. With other kinds of seed that we sow, we also reap an increase; but with this sort of seed here, we not only reap a plentiful crop on the earth, but a much more plentiful harvest in heaven. Annotations on 2 Corinthians 9:6.[4]

Rewards and Punishments Will Be Unequal in the Afterlife. Theodore Beza: Question: Therefore, you say that there will be unequal punishments of the damned? Answer: Although one must inquire concerning this thing very soberly, still I do not say it timidly. For besides that the very rationale of justice requires that since all sins are not equal among themselves, except inasmuch as they match in general; the one who sins more grievously will be punished more grievously. . . . Question: Therefore, unequal also will be the glories of those who will be saved? Answer: Altogether, for the rationale of contraries requires it. And what the apostle said, that those who have sown sparingly will reap sparingly, does not seem to refer to temporal blessings only. Question and Responses.[5]

God Praises Generous People. Jacques Lefèvre d'Étaples: Paul urges [the Corinthians] to be very diligent in performing the good work that they have decided in their hearts. How greedy and far from God's will are those people who decide to give nothing, or who are slow and slack in giving, or who give with sorrowful hearts. They deny providence and do not imitate the blessing of God; rather, they imitate the cursing of the world. And those who give out of their poverty, that is, from those resources which would otherwise curb their need and poverty, usually do so with sorrowful hearts, and therefore do not follow Paul's command, but abandon their sufficiency for poverty. Nevertheless, if there are any people so perfect that they, for the sake of Christ, joyfully and freely give gifts from their scarce resources to those saints more impoverished than them, they will not lack a reward from God, who praised the widow more than others because, in her poverty, she gave two small copper coins. As Jesus said, "Truly, I say to you, that this poor widow gave more than all the others. For they all gave gifts to God out of their abundance; but she, out of her poverty, gave all she had to live on."

What if some people are poor not because of indigence, but because of their need for pleasure? Such persons are not truly poor, but overly affluent. If you contribute to the needs of a pleasure monger, you lose virtue and grace. But if you contribute to the needs of a generous person, you procure virtue and will attain grace and blessing from God. Commentary on 2 Corinthians 9:7.[6]

[3]Hesshus, *Explicatio Secundae Epistolae Pauli ad Corinthios*, 218r-219r; citing Lk 6:38; Ps 41:1-2, 3.
[4]Downame, ed., *English Annotations*, GG2r*.
[5]Beza, *A Little Book of Christian Questions and Responses*, 62*.
[6]Lefèvre, *Commentariorum in Epistolas Beati Pauli . . . Liber Tertius*, 139; citing Mk 12:43-44.

Generous Obedience of Children. John Calvin: Because Paul has commanded that they should give liberally, this also needed to be added: that generosity is judged by God not so much from the amount given, as from the disposition of the heart. It is true that he wanted to induce them to give a lot, so that the brothers might be more abundantly helped; but he had no desire to extort anything from them against their will. Therefore, he commands them to give willingly whatever they should be able to give. . . . "[For God loves] a cheerful giver. . . ." Paul calls us back to God, as I said earlier, for alms are a sacrifice. Now, no sacrifice is pleasing to God unless it is given voluntarily. For when Paul teaches that "God loves a cheerful giver," he indicates (on the other hand) that those who are stingy and hypocritical are rejected by him. For God does not wish to lord it over us in the manner of a tyrant, but as he acts toward us like a father, so he requires from us the generous obedience of children. Commentary on 2 Corinthians 9:7.[7]

Now Is the Time to Sow. Peter Walpot: It is as when, through Moses, the Lord commanded Israel to bring gifts for work on the ark of the covenant, that each should bring to the Lord gifts with a willing heart, of gold, silver, bronze, colored silks, and the like. Therefore, let us sow while there is yet time for harvest, for the winter will come. Then it will be too late to sow; the time to sow is now. When this time is over comes the harvest and cutting time. The one who does not sow in summer, but waits until the harvest time to sow, is foolish. Now is the seeding time, not time to harvest but to sow and scatter about. The seeding time calls us to scatter and not to gather, to give out and not to hold back, and in no way to be stingy with temporal goods, so that we will later reap a hundredfold. But whoever will not sow and in this way prepare for the harvest must go away empty-handed from the community. Christian Community of Goods.[8]

Generous Giving Is an Act of Free Will. Balthasar Hubmaier: If now almsgiving is not out of necessity or out of pity, but out of joy, then not all things must happen out of necessity. For a forced and a joyful giver do not fit together. Freedom of the Will.[9]

God Loves a Cheerful Giver. Wolfgang Musculus: Paul gives the reason why alms should not be given sorrowfully or out of compulsion, namely, because God is not pleased with those sorrowful and reluctant people who give, but he loves a cheerful giver. Now the reason is evident why God loves a cheerful giver. God observes the gift itself as well as the heart of the giver. For cheerfulness of heart in the act of giving is more precious than gold. And so, the generosity of people is measured more by their kindness in giving than in the size of their gift. Paul has little enthusiasm for a gift when it is given with sorrow, a point he also makes in Romans 12, saying, "Persons who act mercifully, let them do so with cheerfulness." Commentary on 2 Corinthians 9:7.[10]

A Free and Enthusiastic Giver. Andreas von Bodenstein Karlstadt: If it is true that God, who is merciful in forgiving, wants prompt punishment, how much more true is it that the one who is lazy in producing works which occur for the betterment of their neighbor is damned, and is an abomination before God. God wants a person to be a free, enthusiastic giver, who gives quickly and willingly. A ready and willing mind, inclined to action, pleases God. Whether One Should Proceed Slowly.[11]

Liberality Implies Liberty. The English Annotations: People do not properly give what is extorted from them, for liberality implies liberty, and [the command to give] and liberty cannot well stand together. God loves cheerful givers, who first

[7]CO 50:108 (CTS 40:309-10).
[8]Liechty, ed., *Early Anabaptist Spirituality*, 168-69; citing Ex 25:1-7.
[9]CRR 5:463.
[10]Musculus, *Commentarius . . . in posteriorem epistolam Pauli ad Corinthios*, 286; citing Rom 12:8.
[11]Baylor, ed., *The Radical Reformation*, 60.

give their hearts to God before they give their alms to the poor. And the more they give with a cheerful countenance, the more they comfort the receiver, giving hope of future bounty, for what people do cheerfully they will do again upon a similar occasion. . . . It is most certain that God esteems no offering of ours which is not given freely with liberality, according to our ability. Annotations on 2 Corinthians 9:7.[12]

Not Everything Occurs by Necessity. Balthasar Hubmaier: Since God created reasonable beings, in heaven as angels and on earth as humankind, he desired to be supremely honored and praised by them. Now, there is no greater honor that a person can render to God than to praise, honor, and magnify him without compulsion and unforced, because God loves the cheerful givers (and not those who give by compulsion). He therefore gave both kinds of beings a free and unforced will, as the Scriptures testify and say, "In the beginning, God placed humankind (in paradise) and left them free to make their own decisions; he gave them his commandments and law saying, 'If you keep the commandments, they will preserve you and eternally keep your faith.' He has set before you fire and water; reach out and take which you choose; before a person are life and death, good and evil, and whichever they prefer is theirs." Here we see clearly in the first place that God made humanity that he could and should, without compulsion and without force, honor and praise him and keep his commandments; God gave a person this choice and entrusted to them the power to choose water or fire, good or evil, life or death. . . . [A] person can choose, will, and work, not only before the fall but also since the fall on the authority of the divine Word in which God gives to those who will and believe the power and might to do and accomplish what he has commanded them to do. Apologia.[13]

God Gives Far More Than What We Ask. Martin Luther: But the apostle wants to point out this, which he also does elsewhere, namely, that God gives to those who call upon him even more than they request, so that, just as the request in comparison with the gift is poor and modest, so the one who makes the request could not even have contemplated such great gifts, to say nothing of requesting them. Thus, we read in Ephesians 3, "He is able to do far more abundantly than all that we ask or think," and above in Romans 8, "We do not know how to pray as we ought," and in 2 Corinthians 9, "God is able to make all grace abound in you." God, therefore, is rich as he hears us, but we are poor as we pray; he is powerful in his fulfilling, while we are weak and fearful in our asking. For we do not ask as much as he is willing and able to give; that is, we do not ask according to his power but far beneath his power and in accordance with our own infirmity. But he cannot give except in accord with his power. Lectures on Romans 10:12.[14]

Sufficiency in All Things. Philipp Melanchthon: Paul promises abundance in two ways. First, they will experience a sufficiency of temporal resources. As Proverbs states, "Whoever gives to the poor will not want" and "Whoever is prone to mercy will be blessed, for he shares his bread with the poor." Second, they will experience a lavish store of spiritual resources, both sufficient and abundant. Hence, in Proverbs 19 we read, "Whoever is generous to the poor lends to the Lord." And later, Paul cites Psalm 112, which says, "His righteousness remains forever because he disperses his goods to the poor." So, too, the Lord states in the Gospel, "Whoever gives a cup of water to one of these little ones of mine. . . ." And again, Matthew 25, "I was hungry, and you gave me something to eat." You might ask, "Are we then saved by works rather than faith?" I respond, "That's correct!" For faith justifies us—it doesn't

[12]Downame, ed., *English Annotations*, GG2r*.
[13]CRR 5:532-33*; citing Sir 15:14-17.
[14]LW 25:412* (WA 56:420); citing Rom 10:12; Eph 3:20; Rom 8:26; 2 Cor 9:8.

save us. Now it saves us when it bears fruit. And Scripture speaks about the fruit of faith, as is clear in that very same psalm that the apostle cites: "Their heart is firm, trusting in the Lord." Annotations on 2 Corinthians 9:8.[15]

God Promises to Provide Sufficiently for His Generous People. Wolfgang Musculus: Paul explains how God makes all grace abound to those who hasten to the aid of the poor. "So that having all sufficiency in all things," he says, "you may abound in all good works." He is still employing the analogy of a farmer who, because he has planted, reaps an abundant harvest by the Lord's blessing and gathers it into his barn. He experiences the blessing of the Lord in two ways, first in that he receives from his harvest a sufficient amount on which to live, and second, in that he receives beyond what is sufficient so that he might plant [a new crop] and also share with poor people. . . . The word "sufficiency" [*autarkeian*] must be carefully examined in this passage. Godly people are promised, not what pertains to luxury and pleasures, but what is sufficient for their basic needs, which yields contentment. Those who exceed these limits fall into the vice of greed and become ensnared in innumerable temptations; in short, they produce barren and unfruitful works in place of good works. Hence, the apostle with very good reason joins the phrase "abounding in every good work" with the word *autarkeia*, that is, sufficiency. Commentary on 2 Corinthians 9:8.[16]

God Blesses Those Who Are Generous. Edward Leigh: Paul prevents a secret objection of those who might fear poverty for themselves, if they should give abundantly. And he shows that whatever they give will return to them with surplus. The apostle in the original is emphatic, stating this three times. First, not in one but in every necessity. Second, not sometimes, but at every time. Third, not some sufficiency, but a sufficiency of every grace. Annotations on 2 Corinthians 9:8.[17]

God's Power Defies the Imaginings of the Flesh. Niels Hemmingsen: Paul gives an argument based on the power of God in contrast to the imagining of the flesh. The flesh thinks to itself, "whatever is given to the poor is lost to me." But Paul says that the power of God works in such a way that not only do all the benefits of those gifts overflow upon [the poor] so that they lack nothing with respect to the sustaining of this present life, but they also stimulate others to good works. And so, God compensates duty with benefit, and adorns and rewards virtue with goodness. If wealthy people considered these things, not so many poor people would perish due to hunger and indifference and they would want poor people to be reckoned among the members of God's household. Commentary on 2 Corinthians 9:8.[18]

Generosity Is Characteristic of Righteous People. David Dickson: Paul confirms his argument [why the Corinthians should give generously] out of Psalm 112, where it is written that righteous people distribute their goods and give to the poor, and their righteousness remains forever. Hence, this argument is suggested: That it is characteristic of righteous people to distribute their goods and give to the poor, and that the ordinary blessing of God is upon them so that they might have even more to bestow. Therefore, show yourselves righteous by giving liberally. Exposition of 2 Corinthians 9:9.[19]

God Rewards the Generous with Other Divine Gifts. Niels Hemmingsen: Paul proves that God is accustomed to see to it that those who are generous toward poor people abound in every good work by appealing to Psalm 112, where David identifies the blessed person by

[15]*Melanchthons Werke*, 4:124-25; citing Prov 28:27; 22:9; 19:17; Ps 112:9; Mt 10:42; 25:35; Ps 112:7.
[16]Musculus, *Commentarius . . . in posteriorem epistolam Pauli ad Corinthios*, 287-88.
[17]Leigh, *Annotations upon all the New Testament*, 263*.
[18]Hemmingsen, *Commentaria in Omnes Epistolas Apostolorum*, 290.
[19]Dickson, *An Exposition of All St. Paul's Epistles*, 86*; citing Ps 112:9.

their fear of God and other virtues. Among these virtues he mentions [in verse 9] generosity toward poor people: the blessed person "has distributed [their goods]," David writes, and "has given to the poor." In Hebrew, this word means "they have broken into pieces" (namely, "bread")—a word that indicates eagerness and an act of generosity. Then David adds, "their righteousness endures forever." This indicates that God is accustomed to compensating those who are compassionate toward the poor with other divine benefits, and especially that they are preserved in righteousness and godliness. For piety is magnified when it is practiced in this particular way, and so it is preserved. Commentary on 2 Corinthians 9:9.[20]

An Apt Allegory from Agriculture. Tilemann Hesshus: With a zealous imprecation and prayer, Paul affirms the Corinthians all the more in their generosity and teaches them not to diminish their charitable giving, but to increase it all the more and at the same time to obtain a generous increase of spiritual gifts. Now Paul's meaning is understood rightly to refer first to the goods of this life, and then to spiritual goods. The farmer does not have seed for planting the field by his own effort, but by the kindness and goodness of God. And in the same way, God also most generously supplies bread for food: "For your Father, who is in heaven, knows that you need all these things," Christ says in Matthew 6. And Psalm 147 states, "He gives to the beasts their food and to the young ravens that cry." And Psalm 104: "All things look to you for their food in its time." There is no reason to despair when the seed is thrown into the earth. For the same God who supplies the seed for sowing, will also supply bread for food. Psalm 34: "Fear the Lord all you his saints, for those who fear him lack nothing."

The entire process of agriculture teaches us splendidly that all things happen to us by the divine goodness and compassion. When the farmer turns over the earth several times with his plow and waters it, he spreads seed, some of which can live in the earth. The seed dies in the earth, and endures various storms, rain, snow, hail, wind. No farmer can do anything to help or protect or increase what he has cast into the earth; rather, he must wait for the blessing and generosity of God. When the dead seed is brought to life by God it bears an abundant produce, some thirtyfold, others sixtyfold, and others one-hundred-fold. This is a most obvious demonstration that our life is sustained, not by our industry, or our diligence, or our labor, but by God's kindest generosity. Therefore, there is no reason for us to fear that we will lack life's necessities when we bequeath alms, but we must always look to God who gives with an open hand and fills all with his goodness.

Paul then applies this allegory from agriculture to spiritual gifts. "The Lord," he says, "will increase the harvest of your righteousness." When we live in the fear of the Lord and are submissive to him, not only does God supply us with the necessary things of this life, but he also endows us with spiritual gifts and gives them increase. He calls generosity and all types of liberality "righteousness," for true righteousness is not only not defrauding anyone but also much more than that: it is doing good to everyone with the greatest of zeal and drawing out from the font of generosity. The harvest of this righteousness is enlarged by God inasmuch as true piety is established in human beings. The mind is greatly illumined in the knowledge of God and the understanding of the divine Word. The heart is greatly fortified in faith. Love toward God and neighbor becomes more passionate. Confidence in prayer, patience in affliction, exuberance in thanksgiving, diligence in the work of one's calling—each of these is greatly strengthened. Explication of 2 Corinthians 9:10.[21]

The God Who Gives Seed Will Multiply It. Cyriacus Spangenberg: A sower, although

[20]Hemmingsen, *Commentaria in Omnes Epistolas Apostolorum*, 290-91.

[21]Hesshus, *Explicatio Secundae Epistolae Pauli ad Corinthios*, 221r-222v; citing Mt 6:32; Ps 147:9; 104:27; 34:9.

he does not have much seed, does not think, "See, you must keep your seed, so that you can eat of it. If you sowed it, you might die of hunger." By no means. Rather he thinks, "The one who gives seed will also certainly be able to give bread. You will sow and wait for God's blessing." We should also think like this. The God who has given so much that I can give a poor person a coin, a piece of bread, and so on will also be able to give more. I will give in the name of the Lord and help because I can. "What one gives to the poor is sown in a fertile field," says St. Augustine.†

We read about Emperor Tiberius, who began to reign in AD 577, that when he was told by the empress and others that he should not give out so very many and such large alms, he answered, "Because one gives alms to the poor, there will be no lack of money in the imperial treasury." God also ordained it that he found the great and mighty buried treasures of Emperor Justinian in Constantinople and of Narses in Italy. The prophet Haggai says in turn that God closes the heavens and withholds rain and dew because one is so unmerciful toward the poor.

Paul took this saying from the thirtieth chapter of Isaiah: "The Lord will give rain to your seed that you have sown in your field, and bread from the income from the field, and full sufficiency from the same." In summary, "The one who gives seed to the sower will also give bread for food," that is, for need, for what else could be more useful? THIRTY-SEVENTH SERMON.[22]

GOD SUPPLIES ALL THE NECESSITIES OF LIFE. ANDREAS HYPERIUS: The apostle expresses this argument in the form of a pious prayer in which he very clearly states—as if placing it before the eyes—what spiritual benefits are to be received from giving generously to poor people, and he extols them with suitable words as if they had already done so. Of course, he does this so that the Corinthians might be persuaded all the more to give generously by the consideration of these matters. He continues to delight in using allegories—or metaphors—related to sowing and reaping. "I pray," he says, "to the one who supplies seed for sowing." This is a remarkable circumlocution describing God, in which is signified the sum of his goodness toward us. If he supplies seed—and, indeed, from a single seed there is always a multiplication—he will also always be able to supply you with the necessities of life, so that you never need to fear anything in the future when you give anything to the poor. And so, by this circumlocution, the power of God is proved. Now there follows Paul's prayer, or that which he prays about them.

"And he will supply bread for food." Not only does God supply new seed, but also bread. Now by the term "bread" it is proper to understand all necessary sustenance as it is often described in the Scriptures. As Saul said in 1 Samuel 4 [*sic*, 1 Samuel 14], "Cursed be anyone who eats bread until this evening, and I am avenged on my enemies." What ought to be clear is that he meant by this food in general, because afterward it was required that Jonathan be punished for violating this command, who nevertheless did not taste bread, but only honey.

"And will multiple your seed." That is, God sees to it that your wealth, with which you deprive yourself in order to share with the poor, is multiplied and increased, just as seed that is sown is multiplied. He sees to it that your kindness abounds to you.

"And he increases the harvest of your righteousness." . . . Paul says that he hopes that the righteousness of the Corinthians might increase into a great harvest, that is, that they might always advance more and more in every kind of virtue. Now these words which Paul here employs must be noted, namely, "he will multiply," "he will increase the harvest," "you will be enriched," which certainly should be applied when praying for them, that all things might be most bountiful, most productive, and the greatest. COMMENTARY ON 2 CORINTHIANS 9:10.[23]

[22]C. Spangenberg, *Die ander Epistel Pauli an die Corinthier*, 157v-158r; citing Is 30:23. †Augustine, *Sermon 367 on Luke's Gospel, 16:19-31*, in *Sermons*, trans. Edmund Hill, The Works of Saint Augustine III/10 (New York: New City Press, 1995), 297.

[23]Hyperius, *Commentarii . . . in Epistolam D. Pauli ad Romanos, et Utramque ad Corinthios*, 400; citing 1 Sam 14:24.

God and Humans Cooperate in Sowing. Cardinal Cajetan: Having declared the power of divine love and declared from the authority of Scripture the supreme reward awaiting the future life, Paul now declares the efficacy of divine love in this life—specifically, what God produces in this life through cheerful givers. Now, Paul declares this efficacy briefly according to an analogy proportional to the efficacy of God in natural things. And he intends to teach that just as God works together with human beings in sowing natural things, so, proportionally, God also works together with human beings in sowing spiritual things. . . . For a cheerful giver is like the act of sowing; and those alms are like a seed planted for bearing manifold fruit. For the sower recognizes the power of sowing to produce much fruit. And the person who gives alms ought to give as one sowing, that is, looking ahead to the future harvest. Now, just as God supplies seed to the person sowing, and even furnishes strength to the young plant (since God himself is the author of nature), so he furnishes strength to make the alms fruitful. And just as God does not abandon sowing to the natural actions of the seed, so he does not abandon the sowing of alms to the gratuitous actions according to the order of the gift of alms. Commentary on 2 Corinthians 9:10.[24]

9:11-15 *True Generosity Produces Thankfulness and Praise*

The Believer's True Riches. John Calvin: Paul again makes use of the word "bountifulness" to express the nature of true liberality—when our care has been cast on God, we cheerfully lay out our possessions for whatever purpose he directs. He teaches that these are the true riches of believers, when, relying on God's providence for the sufficiency of their livelihood, they are not by distrust held back from doing good. Nor is it without good reason that he describes with the title "wealth" the abundance of a mind that is simple and contented with moderate provision. For no one is more hungry or famished than those who disbelieve, who are tormented with worry to possess things. Commentary on 2 Corinthians 9:11.[25]

God Is Praised Through Our Generosity. Andreas Hyperius: "That you will be enriched in every way in all bountifulness." That is, "I pray that every day your giving might become more blessed to you so that you are always able to be generous with the same generosity of mind toward others." For I think that what is signified here is what was previously said, that "being supplied with all things, you might abound in every good work." And the word "bountifulness" here is to be taken for "bountifulness in giving," which we spoke about earlier, and the apostle himself will soon explain, when he talks about bountifulness of sharing.

"Which through us will produce thanksgiving to God." Paul says, "Because of what your bountifulness of giving produces through us (who distribute your alms in good faith), God is praised and honored by those people, namely, the poor saints, who realize that they have been helped by your generosity." Therefore, since it makes a difference to exhibit diligently such generosity to all so that God might be praised, and God is praised by the saints who have received the alms, it is reasonable that they should generously give their wealth to poor believers. And let us consider here how those who are generously provided for by others in times of need should not only give thanks to people but especially to God. Inasmuch as it is God who always provides for and feeds the godly (and even the wicked, the birds, and the wild animals), he moves the wealthy heart to give, and by these riches, their wealth is increased and expanded. Commentary on 2 Corinthians 9:11.[26]

Expressing Generosity to Living Saints, Not Dead Ones. Wolfgang Musculus: The

[24]Cajetan, *In Posteriorem Pauli Epistolam ad Corinthios Commentarii*, 185.

[25]CO 50:110-11 (CTS 40:314).

[26]Hyperius, *Commentarii . . . in Epistolam D. Pauli ad Romanos, et Utramque ad Corinthios*, 400-401.

believers' generous gift provides these two benefits for those who are supported by them (if they are saints, that is, Christians and pious people), namely, the support of the poor saints and the praise of God. Concerning the first benefit, Paul says, "not only supplying the needs of the saints." As they pass through this life, the saints lack many things both in body and soul which brotherly love is able to supply. But papal superstition turns the ignorant people of Christ away from the living saints and their many needs to revering dead people, whom it would be impossible to satisfy even if they did have needs. They have become accustomed to pay out the greatest expenses for those saints who are dead, while in the meantime they neglect the pressing needs of the saints who are still living. These blind people do not recognize what a godly work it is to satisfy the needs of the saints. As long as we are in this life, we are subject to the common condition that we lack many things, which we are unable to supply through our own capacity. No mortal human being is sufficient in himself for all things; everyone needs assistance from others. In this way divine providence has established and arranged human affairs so that we are necessarily joined and united together, bound as with a chain, and mutual need conjoins even those who are not united by mutual love. Therefore, those who are so inclined that they delight to provide for the needs of their brothers and sisters, these people are certainly partakers of the divine nature inasmuch as they are led by the divine spirit of love.

As far as the second benefit is concerned, Paul says, "but also it abounds in many thanksgivings to God." In this we see the gratitude of the saints, in that they give thanks to God for bodily provision and nourishment, recognizing that it is his goodness and providence that prompts the brothers and sisters to meet their needs. Those who are wealthy in this age, abounding in pleasures and luxuries, do not recognize it as such. Commentary on 2 Corinthians 9:12.[27]

What Paul Means by "Service." John Calvin: By the term "ministry," he means what he had undertaken at the request of the churches. Now what we translate as "service" is in Greek *leitourgia*—a term that sometimes means "sacrifice," and sometimes any office that is publicly assigned. Both of these meanings fit well this present passage. For, on the one hand, it is common for alms to be called sacrifices. On the other hand, as when duties are distributed among the citizens, no one refuses to undertake the office assigned to him, so, in the church, sharing [with others] ought to be judged a necessary duty. Therefore, the Corinthians and others, by assisting the brothers and sisters in Jerusalem, were offering to God a sacrifice, or they were discharging a service that was proper and duty-bound to fulfill. Paul was the minister of that sacrifice, but the term ministry or service can also refer to the Corinthians. But [which interpretation one chooses] matters little. Commentary on 2 Corinthians 9:12.[28]

God Is Praised Through Generous Giving. Cyriacus Spangenberg: God is praised and exalted by many, as Paul goes on to say here. For this aid, this contribution, the service of bringing alms as a sacrifice and collecting them for the poor and then giving them to them, does not only fulfill the needs of the saints but also overflows, such that many thank God for this our faithful service, and praise God. If the congregation gives generously and the leaders distribute it faithfully, the poor have cause to thank God, that he has moved the hearts of the congregation to such generosity and has then given them such pious, kindhearted, faithful leaders, who are so diligent and meticulous about how they can well use the alms, so that the poor may enjoy them better and all the more richly. Thirty-Seventh Sermon.[29]

Submission to the Gospel Brings Glory to God. Wolfgang Musculus: Let us observe

[27]Musculus, *Commentarius . . . in posteriorem epistolam Pauli ad Corinthios*, 292.

[28]CO 50:111 (CTS 40:314-15).

[29]C. Spangenberg, *Die ander Epistel an die Corinthier*, 158v.

in this passage that when we recognize the gospel of Christ it results in the glory of God. "They will glorify God," he says, "because of your obedience (or your submission) coming from your agreement in the gospel of Christ, and because of the generosity of your gift for them and for all others." Therefore, when with harmonious submission we agree in the gospel, that is, in the doctrine of the gospel of Christ, presenting ourselves together as people yielded and responsive to its apostles and ministers, and out of love share our goods with needy brothers and sisters—it is exactly then that we give people a reason to glorify God on account of us. Those who devote themselves in this fashion to the gospel of Christ—they are the true evangelicals, since God is rightly glorified by all pious people. Commentary on 2 Corinthians 9:13.[30]

Reasons for Thanksgiving. Niels Hemmingsen: Paul has said that their generosity toward the poor resulted in many giving thanks to God, and now he lists four reasons for this. First of all, because that generosity gave certain proof of the Corinthians' experience of faith. Second, because it testified concerning their unanimous obedience to the gospel of Christ. Third, because their bountifulness, that is, their generosity and kindness toward the poor, has been manifested. Fourth, because they have so united their minds with the destitute people of Jerusalem that they both pray and long for them from the heart and have deep affection for them on account of this eminent grace, that is, the great generosity they feel toward them. These advantages should also move us to showing liberality toward poor people. Commentary on 2 Corinthians 9:13-14.[31]

Jesus Is the Gift of God to Sinners. Martin Luther: Who, I ask, could do justice to these great blessings and miracles in thought or word? Then why do we not exclaim with the apostle in 2 Corinthians 9:14 [*sic*, 2 Corinthians 9:15]: "Thanks be to God for his inexpressible gift!" For is it not a wonderful thing that a man in all respects like myself gives me eternal life and takes away death, sin, damnation, the tyranny of the devil, and the poison of the sin left in the flesh? Lectures on Genesis 48:20.[32]

Reasons to Motivate Giving. John Calvin: Paul omits no advantage that might be effective for influencing the Corinthians. First, he has made mention of the comfort that believers would experience. Second, he has mentioned the thanksgiving by means of which God has been glorified. And too, this would be a confession that would give testimony to everyone of their complete unanimity in faith and godly obedience. Now he adds the reward that the Corinthians would receive from the saints, namely, goodwill, springing from gratitude and intercessions. "They will have mutual recompense," he says, "because they will regard you with love as they ought and will be careful to commend you to God in their prayers." Commentary on 2 Corinthians 9:14.[33]

The Gospel Is a Most Precious Gift. Martin Luther: No preaching is greater than that about grace and the forgiveness of sins; yet we are such wicked people that when anyone has heard or read it once, they know it and are immediately a master and a doctor. Then they seek something higher, as if they had accomplished everything, and produce new factions and divisions.

I myself have now been learning this for so many years and worked at it with all diligence (more than any of those who imagine that they know it) in preaching, writing, reading, and so on. Yet I cannot brag about any mastery but must be happy that I remain a student with those who are just beginning to learn. This is why I must admonish and warn all who want to be Christians, both teachers and students, to be on their guard

[30]Musculus, *Commentarius . . . in posteriorem epistolam Pauli ad Corinthios*, 293.
[31]Hemmingsen, *Commentaria in Omnes Epistolas Apostolorum*, 291.
[32]LW 8:184 (WA 44:713).
[33]CO 50:111 (CTS 40:315-16).

against this shameful delusion and boredom and to know that this is the highest and most difficult skill that can be found on earth. Even St. Paul has to confess and say that it is "an inexpressible gift"; that is, how high and precious it is in itself cannot be impressed on people with words. Postil for the Nineteenth Sunday After Trinity.[34]

God's Indescribable Gift. Wolfgang Musculus: "Thanks be to God for his indescribable gift!" These words are made as an exclamation, for when Paul considers the extraordinary grace of God and how much the Corinthians have promised to the saints in Judea, he breaks out in praise [*doxologian*] and concludes the topic he has been treating in chapters 8 and 9. And so, he not only shows his affection toward both the church of Jerusalem and the church of Corinth, but he also provokes the minds of the Corinthians to magnify, along with him, the special and superior grace of God. Indeed, he says that the gift of God is "indescribable," that is, that no one is fully able to explain and fathom it. . . . Now Paul calls "the indescribable gifts of God" those fruits which he reminds them to provide from the church collection both for giving and receiving. Commentary on 2 Corinthians 9:15.[35]

No Tongue Can Recount the Grace of God. Niels Hemmingsen: The goal of this striking statement of thanksgiving is so that the Corinthians, who had heard his preaching, might not be praised. For by this exclamation Paul reminds them that the basis for boasting does not come from us, but from God. We learn three things from this striking sentence: First, that in all things, we should express thanks to God. Second, that both willing the good and doing the good are gifts of God. Third, that no one can fully proclaim the benefits and gifts of God, for the human tongue is not able to recount such things. Commentary on 2 Corinthians 9:15.[36]

The Corinthians Were Conduits of God's Generosity. The English Annotations: So that the Corinthians will not be puffed up by his rich commendation and praise of their pious generosity, Paul concludes his exhortation with this passionate exclamation, in which he ascribes the glory and thanksgiving, not to the Corinthians who were but conduits of God's bounty, but to God himself, who is the fountain of all goodness and who both inclined their hearts and furnished them with the means to supply so liberally the needs of the saints. Some understand Christ himself to be this "unspeakable gift," since he is called the "gift of God" in John 4. Others understand this gift to be the gospel, which is also an "unspeakable gift." But the context of this passage seems to refer instead to the unsurpassing grace of God upon the Corinthians mentioned in the previous verse. So, the plain meaning is, "Thanks be to God for his unspeakable gift, which he has bestowed upon you in filling you with his grace, and stirring up your hearts in so liberal a manner to relieve the saints in Jerusalem, whereby so much glory redounded to God, and honor to our holy profession." Annotations on 2 Corinthians 9:15.[37]

The Indescribable Gift Is Christ. John Trapp: This passage refers to Christ (according to Theophylact,† whom Piscator‡ follows), who is called the "gift" in John 4 by virtue of his excellence, and the "benefit" in 2 Timothy 6 [*sic*, 1 Timothy 6]. Commentary on 2 Corinthians 9:15.[38]

[34]LW 79:195 (WA 22:322).
[35]Musculus, *Commentarius . . . in posteriorem epistolam Pauli ad Corinthios*, 295.

[36]Hemmingsen, *Commentaria in Omnes Epistolas Apostolorum*, 291.
[37]Downame, ed., *English Annotations*, GG2r*; citing Jn 4:10.
[38]Trapp, *A Commentary or Exposition*, 727*; citing Jn 4:10; 1 Tim 6:2. †For the interpretation of Theophylact, see PG 124:898. ‡Johannes Piscator (1546–1624) was a German Reformed theologian and biblical scholar who published expansive commentaries on both the Old and New Testaments.

10:1-18 PAUL DEFENDS HIS MINISTRY

I, Paul, myself entreat you, by the meekness and gentleness of Christ—I who am humble when face to face with you, but bold toward you when I am away!— [2]I beg of you that when I am present I may not have to show boldness with such confidence as I count on showing against some who suspect us of walking according to the flesh. [3]For though we walk in the flesh, we are not waging war according to the flesh. [4]For the weapons of our warfare are not of the flesh but have divine power to destroy strongholds. [5]We destroy arguments and every lofty opinion raised against the knowledge of God, and take every thought captive to obey Christ, [6]being ready to punish every disobedience, when your obedience is complete.

[7]Look at what is before your eyes. If anyone is confident that he is Christ's, let him remind himself that just as he is Christ's, so also are we. [8]For even if I boast a little too much of our authority, which the Lord gave for building you up and not for destroying you, I will not be ashamed. [9]I do not want to appear to be frightening you with my letters. [10]For they say, "His letters are weighty and strong, but his bodily presence is weak, and his speech of no account." [11]Let such a person understand that what we say by letter when absent, we do when present. [12]Not that we dare to classify or compare ourselves with some of those who are commending themselves. But when they measure themselves by one another and compare themselves with one another, they are without understanding.

[13]But we will not boast beyond limits, but will boast only with regard to the area of influence God assigned to us, to reach even to you. [14]For we are not overextending ourselves, as though we did not reach you. For we were the first to come all the way to you with the gospel of Christ. [15]We do not boast beyond limit in the labors of others. But our hope is that as your faith increases, our area of influence among you may be greatly enlarged, [16]so that we may preach the gospel in lands beyond you, without boasting of work already done in another's area of influence. [17]"Let the one who boasts, boast in the Lord." [18]For it is not the one who commends himself who is approved, but the one whom the Lord commends.

Overview: After an interlude of several chapters, Paul returns in 2 Corinthians 10 to the defense of his apostleship, arguing that his ministry is waged with divine weapons, that he has exercised his apostolic authority with integrity, and that his boasting in the Lord is fully justified. Paul's vigorous self-defense is in response to the relentless accusations and attacks of the false apostles, which invites Reformation commentators to explore in detail the striking differences between faithful and fraudulent Christian ministers. The false apostles (and their sixteenth-century equivalents) live carnal lives; they boast in their religious conquests; they exalt themselves rather than Christ and his gospel. By contrast, Paul and other legitimate ministers renounce fleshly wisdom and employ the weapons of the Spirit in their ministries—an arsenal that includes the divine Word, zealous faith, burning love, and patience in affliction. While some Anabaptists argue that Paul's reference to spiritual weapons is an indirect prohibition of all forms of physical coercion or violence, the majority of Protestant interpreters think the apostle is speaking specifically about the spiritual nature of Christian ministry. Several commentators take this opportunity to castigate Roman Catholic bishops for using fleshly weapons such as the hangman's noose, fire, water, and prison to punish religious dissenters. In this passage Paul strikes the perfect balance by demonstrating humility and gentleness in his approach to the Corinthians (2 Cor 10:1), while at the same time exercising the spiritual power of the keys (Mt 16:19) as he teaches God's truth, censures hardened sinners, and declares forgiveness for the repentant (2 Cor 10:6). Good ministers must be ambidextrous as they wield the weapon of God's Word: with one hand they destroy Satan's dominion and with the other hand they encourage believers and build up Christ's church.

Paul's confident boasting of his ministry among the Corinthians elicits a great deal of discussion among sixteenth-century commentators. Surely, the false apostles and their early-modern counterparts are blameworthy for incessant boasting of their eloquence, their education, their academic degrees, and (as with the Jesuits) their far-flung missionary travels. But what is to be made of Paul's boasting? Reformation authors insist that Paul's boasting is legitimate because it was truthful, it was measured by his vocation, it defended his apostolic authority, and (most important of all) its purpose was to demonstrate God's grace and goodness among the Corinthians. Indeed, all Christians should celebrate the gifts, ministry opportunities, and fruitfulness that God gives them. As Tilemann Hesshus notes, even if we are not Athanasius, Augustine, or Martin Luther, we should serve faithfully and joyfully in the vocation assigned to us.

The Climax of Paul's Letter. Philipp Melanchthon: The final part of this epistle is a kind of climax in which Paul, with great vehemence, makes various warnings. First, the Corinthians must beware of the false apostles who were teaching carnal works and ceremonies, and they must guard against being pulled away from the simplicity of the gospel which they had embraced. In the same way are those who introduce us to satisfactions, Masses, and carnal righteousness, who pull us away from the simplicity of the Word of God, and also those philosophies that regard the gospel as a Jewish fiction or trickery. Second, Paul warns about personal behavior, as is seen in chapter 13. For this is the sum of the Christian life: faith and behavior—which is the fruit of faith. Annotations on 2 Corinthians 10:1.[1]

Summary of Chapter 10. John Calvin: In the tenth chapter, Paul begins to defend himself and his apostolic office from the calumnies with which the wicked harassed him. First, he shows that he is splendidly equipped with the armor that is required for fighting in Christ's army. Next, he declares that the authority which he had exercised in the previous epistle was grounded on the confidence of a good conscience. And he shows them that he had no less power in his actions when present, than authority in his words when absent. Last, by comparing himself with them, he shows how vain their boasting is. Commentary on 2 Corinthians.[2]

Paul's Defense of His Apostolic Authority. Niels Hemmingsen: There are three principal sections to this chapter. The first section is the introduction, in which by means of a solemn appeal he requests fairness and gentleness from the Corinthians. In the second section, Paul gives a defense of his apostolic authority against those Corinthians who were disparaging it. In this section there are three parts: First, because they were attacking the humility and meanness of his person, Paul first responds by way of concession, and then alleges his apostolic authority by which he shows that their accusations are not valid. Second, because some among them were boasting that they were ministers of Christ and holding Paul in contempt, he also responds that he is in no way inferior to them in this regard; rather, that he can boast more than them on account of his power. Third, because they were maliciously attacking his previous letter as far too harsh, saying that when he is present he is weak and his words contemptible—Paul responds that he said nothing in his letter that he would not also do in their presence. Then, praising them in an ironical fashion, he

[1] *Melanchthons Werke*, 4:125.
[2] CO 50:7 (CTS 40:106-7).

compares himself to them and shows how he was a minister faithful to the gospel work committed to him. The third section contains the standard by which Paul wants each person to examine himself to know when he can rightly boast. Commentary on 2 Corinthians 10.[3]

10:1-6 *Weapons of Divine Power*

Paul Returns to a Topic Treated Earlier. Wolfgang Musculus: We said at the beginning of chapter 8 that the topic of making a contribution to the saints had been inserted into the middle of the epistle so that, by this somewhat more tolerable interlude, as it were, Paul's discussion concerning the sincerity of his apostleship (which he had treated previously, and now will treat hereafter) might be made more acceptable. Now, having finished this interlude, Paul promptly returns to that topic that he had touched upon somewhat in the previous eight chapters pertaining to the defense of his apostleship. For he was of the opinion that this situation had not yet been fully resolved, because it was extremely important and necessary for him to resist the wickedness of the false apostles, and he was forced to defend the authority of his apostleship. With his authority undermined, it would necessarily follow that all the fruit of his ministry already harvested, and still to be produced, would be lost. Commentary on 2 Corinthians 10:1.[4]

Paul Imitates God's Preference for Mercy over Punishment. Jacques Lefèvre d'Étaples: The apostle Peter, with only a word spoken to Ananias and his wife Saphira, punished their lie with death, for the edification of the church. In Paphos, Paul by his word afflicted Elymas (who was fighting against the way of the Lord) with blindness for a time for the edification of Sergius Paulus. Paul also handed over the adulterer to be physically tormented by Satan, so that his spirit might be saved on the day of the Lord. The apostles did not do these things out of human power, but by the power of the Spirit, who sees all things and has all power at his disposal. For this reason, their weapons came from God, not from other humans, and their weapons were not only more powerful than human beings, but of all spiritual powers. Nevertheless, because God is kind and compassionate, showing mercy to the wicked and bestowing grace rather than punishment, Paul (being driven by the Spirit of God and imitating divine compassion) prefers to exercise compassion rather than punishment against certain people who were false apostles among the Corinthians. These false apostles were announcing false teaching that was not according to the truth of Christ and contrary to the way of the Lord. They were leading people into false doctrines against the true traditions of the apostles. Paul wishes, I say, to show mercy, if they repent. And so that they might repent, he frequently entreats them, that if they are enduring divine chastisement, they should understand that it is due to their own faults rather than Paul's malevolence and harshness. For when God punishes, when he demonstrates his severity, he does it with no malevolence, for he is both benevolent and a benefactor of all; rather, he punishes only their faults. And for this reason, God uses fear to deter us and wins us over by promises so that we do not sin, for he does not want to punish us but to show us mercy, always winning us over to the good by using fear to deter us, threaten us, and coax us. . . . In this way, Paul imitates the good God by aiming at compassion and not punishment. Commentary on 2 Corinthians 10:1.[5]

Christian Leaders Must Be Gentle and Friendly. Cyriacus Spangenberg: He wants to give an example to all bishops and teachers, that when they want to punish and warn the people

[3]Hemmingsen, *Commentaria in Omnes Epistolas Apostolorum*, 292.
[4]Musculus, *Commentarius . . . in posteriorem epistolam Pauli ad Corinthios*, 296.
[5]Lefèvre, *Commentariorum in Epistolas Beati Pauli . . . Liber Tertius*, 139v; citing Acts 5:1-11; Acts 13:8-12; 1 Cor 5:1-5.

they should do this with gentleness and friendliness, not with excommunicating, cursing, strangling, burning, drowning, and so on, as happens in the papacy. For Christ wants his apostles, bishops, and preachers to have a gentle heart and a will inclined to friendliness toward their people, not tyrannical, murderous behavior. Paul demonstrates this here with his own example and asks his listeners to consider their own salvation and blessedness and not despise such great patience and longanimity of God. For where this happens, we would need to fear that a terrible punishment would follow it. Thirty-Eighth Sermon.[6]

Emulating the Gentleness of Christ. Martin Luther: The Evangelists everywhere describe the dear Lord as friendly and most gracious, able to overlook much that his people do. St. Paul calls this *philanthropia* (kindness) in Titus 3 and *epieikeia* (gentleness) in 2 Corinthians 10. For *epieikeia* means that a person is able to be lenient and does not act harshly but bears and endures. On the other hand, when the Pharisees and the proud saints come before him, he is not at all the same man as before and is plenty self-willed, stubborn, and unfriendly. Sermon on Matthew 20:20-28.[7]

The Gentleness of Christ Should Serve as a Model for Our Ministries. Wolfgang Musculus: The Lord Christ preferred to use mildness and gentleness, rather than severity, toward sinners. Hence, in all his words and deeds he appeared mild and gentle. People broken of conscience by their sense of sin require this kind of a physician. For nothing is less suitable for healing such wounds than pharisaical severity, because rather than curing evil it makes it worse. Knowing this, the apostle had imitated the example of the Lord, and by his gentleness and mildness he was winning many people. Paul also admonished Timothy about this, saying: "It is necessary that the servant of the Lord not be violent, but gentle toward all, apt to teach, enduring evil with gentleness." . . . Therefore, since there is nothing more pleasing and needful for sinners than this gentleness and mildness of Christ, we must not despise it in our ministries, but on account of the Lord's example and our own needs, we should embrace it eagerly and have nothing to do with the approach of the Pharisees and the self-righteous who are more inclined to severity and condemning sins than the Lord's gentleness. For the Lord was so gentle and kind toward sinners that he even shared table fellowship with them. Now the gentleness of the Lord should not only elicit our approval but also lead us to holy wonder and fear so that we might turn those who have been admonished to repentance, warning them about the wrath and righteous judgment of God as well as hell itself. Commentary on 2 Corinthians 10:1.[8]

Accusations of the False Prophets. Tilemann Hesshus: "The false apostles ascribe vehemence and boldness to me, but I am meek and gentle, as Christ taught us to behave toward the church." The gentleness of Christ is the virtue that is aroused by the Holy Spirit, by which, mindful of human weakness, we put aside all rigor and act gently with those who are weaker and carefully endure the infirmities of others. Paul distinguishes between the gentleness of Christ and that of the world. Scipio, Laelius, Scaevola, Fabius Maximus, Atticus† were all gentle, but their gentleness was only governed by the judgment of reason and was only a shadow of true virtue. But the gentleness of Christ is governed by the Word of God and the Holy Spirit, and thus it is not only purer, but also stronger. . . . Paul teaches here, therefore, that it is wrong to accuse him of pride since he always has the virtues of Christ in his sight.

"I who am humble before you." This was the harsh accusation of the false apostles, that Paul

[6] C. Spangenberg, *Die ander Epistel Pauli an die Corinthier*, 160r-v.
[7] LW 68:65* (WA 47:365-66); citing Titus 3:4; 2 Cor 10:1.
[8] Musculus, *Commentarius . . . in posteriorem epistolam Pauli ad Corinthios*, 297; citing 1 Tim 3:3.

had displayed humility and debased himself when he was present in Corinth. But now that he was absent, he was proud and severe and wrote bitter censures. Paul therefore responds that he does not want it to be necessary to use those bold and severe words that he had considered employing against certain carnal persons. He shows that he is willing to rebuke sinners harshly in person. Nevertheless, he will not descend to this severity and boldness unless forced to do so. Explication of 2 Corinthians 10:1.[9]

Paul Waged Spiritual Warfare. Huldrych Zwingli: Even though I have a body of flesh, nevertheless, I do not walk according to the flesh, nor do I wage war for fleshly things (especially in this matter), but I wage war for the glory of God. However much the false apostles regard us with contempt, we are not cowardly and weak in this battle, but we are strong and equipped with weapons—not of iron—but of the spirit. With these weapons, we demolish whatever vaunts itself against God, and by them we subjugate many people to our commander. I do not worry about those who boldly reproach me; on the contrary, I am prompted to boast when I gain ultimate vengeance over defiant and rebellious people. I do this not only for my own boasting, but also for the common good of all of you "when your obedience is complete." Annotations on 2 Corinthians 10:2-6.[10]

Gentleness—Not Cowardly Negligence. John Calvin: "I beg of you that when I am present." Some think that Paul's oration here is defective, and that he does not explain the matter of his request. I think rather that what was absent from the previous clause is here completed, so that it is a general exhortation. "Show yourself teachable and compliant toward me, so that I won't be forced to be more severe." It is the duty of a good pastor to win over his sheep peacefully and kindly, so that they might allow themselves to be governed, rather than constrained by violence. I confess that severity is sometimes necessary, but we must always begin with gentleness, and persevere in it, as long as the hearer shows himself to be teachable. Severity must be the last resort. "We must," he says, "try every option before rushing to harshness, or rather, we must never be severe unless forced to it." Meanwhile, as to their judgment that Paul was puny and timid when he was opposed by others close at hand, he intimates that they were mistaken in this when he announces that he will strongly resist the defiant to their faces. "They despise me," he says, "as if I were a puny person, but they will find me braver and more courageous than they would have wished when they engage me seriously in hand-to-hand combat." . . . Here is the best middle way: as much as possible, we must seek to draw rather than push people away. But when mildness has no effect in dealing with callous and obstinate people, then exercising rigor becomes necessary. Otherwise, it will be neither moderation nor impartiality, but cowardly negligence. Commentary on 2 Corinthians 10:2.[11]

God's People Are Frequently Accused of "Walking in the Flesh." Wolfgang Musculus: I ask you, if Paul seemed in the eyes of the false apostles to walk according to the flesh—the very one who, in speaking and living, gave forth the aroma of Christ—what person will now follow after him in spiritual matters that wicked people will not accuse of walking according to the flesh? No minister of Christ escapes the slanderous mouth of the wicked, since not even Christ himself was able to escape from accusations that he was a seducer, a glutton, a drunkard, a friend of prostitutes, and a companion of sinners. And so today, very filthy men defame married

[9]Hesshus, *Explicatio Secundae Epistolae Pauli ad Corinthios*, 227v-228r. [†]Scipio Africanus, Gaius Laelius, and Quintus Fabius Maximus Verrucosus were Roman statesmen and generals. Quintus Mucius Scaevola was a prominent Roman jurist. Titus Pomponius Atticus was a wealthy Roman patriciate and correspondent with Cicero.
[10]Zwingli, *Annotatiunculae . . . ex ore Zvinglij*, 185.

[11]CO 50:113* (CTS 40:319).

ministers of Christ as "customers of prostitutes," "adulterers," "incestuous men," and "men enflamed with wicked lusts" . . . and they describe the state of marriage as "walking according to the flesh." The minister of Christ should regard these accusations as no better than the barking of dogs, and this type of slanderer as comparable to dogs, since he does not know how to speak well about good and honorable things. Commentary on 2 Corinthians 10:2.[12]

The Christian Life Is Perpetual Spiritual Warfare. Tilemann Hesshus: Paul is addressing not only the false apostles but also those who have been disturbed by the false apostles, who have interpreted the actions of Paul according to the judgment of the flesh, as if Paul mixes those carnal affections with the ministry. They are people who walk according to the flesh, who employ carnal judgment and wisdom, or cunning. They disregard the Word of God and the judgment of the Spirit; they do everything for the sake of their own profit and glory. The Corinthians, along with some other people, had such impressions also about Paul, judging him very badly. But Paul vehemently refutes these accusations: although he walks in the flesh, nevertheless, he does not wage war according to the flesh. To walk in the flesh is to delight in the natural life and still be clothed in the flesh. But to wage war according to the flesh is to use the judgments and wisdom of the flesh, to accommodate oneself to the world, to avoid the dangers of [religious] confession, to bend doctrine to rational judgment, and pursue human freedom and the advantages of this life. And nothing is accepted—even if you have the express commandment of God—unless you are completely protected by human defenses. Paul denies that he does such things. Rather, he uses spiritual weapons and thus his warfare is spiritual. The Christian profession is nothing other than perpetual warfare, because we have given the first place to Christ and we follow his standard. Satan, along with his entire kingdom, rises up against us. He attempts to separate us from Christ with every kind of weapon. He continually fights against us. He plots various traps. He harasses us with troubles and frightens us with various apparitions. He especially attacks ministers of the Word as leaders of the army. Therefore, our hearts must be prepared and fortified so that we can endure and overcome the continual assaults of Satan, the world, and the flesh. Explication of 2 Corinthians 10:3.[13]

Walking in the Flesh, but Not According to the Flesh. Wolfgang Musculus: Let us note here that Paul confesses that he walks "in the flesh," namely, in flesh that is humble and weak, but then he denies that he walks "according to the flesh." Therefore, it is one thing to live in the flesh and another to live according to the flesh; it is one thing to walk in the flesh and another to walk according to the flesh. Christ himself lived and walked in the flesh as a true man who was living among and interacting with people, eating, drinking, sleeping, and everything else that pertains to sustaining the weakness of the flesh. Nevertheless, he neither lived nor walked according to the flesh. For to live and walk according to the flesh is to do all things according to the desires, counsel, and corrupt longings of the flesh—such things had no place in Christ. If the Corinthians had not repressed in themselves the spirit of Christ, they would have been able to see that same quality in the apostle. Commentary on 2 Corinthians 10:3.[14]

Ministry as Warfare. John Trapp: the ministry is a kind of militia. Christ rides on ministers, as his white horses, conquering and seeking to conquer. Commentary on 2 Corinthians 10:3.[15]

[12]Musculus, *Commentarius . . . in posteriorem epistolam Pauli ad Corinthios*, 299.

[13]Hesshus, *Explicatio Secundae Epistolae Pauli ad Corinthios*, 228r-229r.

[14]Musculus, *Commentarius . . . in posteriorem epistolam Pauli ad Corinthios*, 300.

[15]Trapp, *A Commentary or Exposition*, 727*; citing 1 Tim 1:18; Rev 6:2.

Spiritual Weapons Destroy Human Wisdom. Desiderius Erasmus: The arms of our warfare, which is spiritual, are not powerful in the human way with iron or bronze, but they are powerful through the inbreathing of God for demolishing whatever defense seems to have been set up against him. With them we demolish and overturn clever counsels and all the lofty pretentiousness of the ungodly, which is erected and elevated on the bulwarks of human wisdom, in opposition to the knowledge of God, which we profess through the gospel. We not only cast down but also subdue and take captive all human thinking, so that henceforth it may obey Christ against whom previously it was in rebellion. Paraphrases on 2 Corinthians 10.[16]

Divine Power That Destroys Strongholds. Philipp Melanchthon: "For the weapons of our warfare are not of the flesh." There is a striking antithesis in this passage between the wisdom of the flesh and the wisdom of the spirit. Now, you must understand this conflict between the wisdom of the flesh and the wisdom of the spirit so that you might know not only how to wage war with the world, but also with your own heart—and, what is far more dangerous, with the spirits. And this passage here is the most spiritual of all Paul's passages that I know of. The first antithesis is this: "the weapons of our warfare are not of the flesh but have power." The fact that power (instead of spirit) is contrasted to the flesh indicates that there is no power, pride, wisdom, or righteousness of the flesh. Isaiah 40 states, "All their pride is like the flowers of the field," and, on the other hand, "the Word of the Lord endures forever"—that is, the conscience which has been fortified by the Word of God cannot be confounded by any creature. And so, Paul adds here the word "divine," that is, this power comes through God, which indicates that there is no creaturely power whatsoever that is superior to the power of God. Micah 5 states: "He shall stand and shepherd his flock in the strength of the Lord."

The second antithesis is this: "to destroy strongholds." By "stronghold" Paul means the confidence of creatures whereby they naturally search for their salvation in the strongholds of wisdom, material possessions, and so on. As Obadiah states, "You who say in your heart, 'Who will bring me down to the earth?'" And Ezekiel 28: "You have said, 'I am a god.'" These fleshly strongholds will be destroyed by the spirit of the mouth of God, as Psalm 33 states: "He will not be saved in the abundance of his power." And by way of summary, this is the power of the Word of God: to pull us away from creaturely things and show us God, so that we might fear and trust in him alone. Annotations on 2 Corinthians 10:4.[17]

Weapons of the Spirit. Wolfgang Musculus: The weapons of the flesh are not only iron, wood, bronze, and stone, but also such weapons as carnal wisdom, prudence, reason, and knowledge that are used by philosophers, the wise, the learned, and the eloquent when they are fighting. In sum, all the armor of the flesh is weak, whereas the armor of the Spirit of God is powerful. For the Spirit arms his people with divine strength, with the word of life, with truth, with zealous faith, with burning love, with patience in afflictions, and with an unassailable constancy of spirit. Outfitted with these weapons, and especially with the sword of the Word of God, bishops once battled all sorts of heresies. But now, having thrown them aside, bishops make use of the weapons of the flesh—swords, the hangman's noose, fire, water, prisons, and so on—and they think that they have been equipped with these weapons chiefly for extirpating gospel doctrine. But, in fact, they find out that the more they attempt to destroy the truth, the weaker are the weapons of the flesh. Commentary on 2 Corinthians 10:4.[18]

---

[16]CWE 43:258-59.

[17]*Melanchthons Werke*, 4:126; citing Is 40:6, 8; Mic 5:4; Obad 3; Ezek 28:2; Ps 33:16.

[18]Musculus, *Commentarius . . . in posteriorem epistolam Pauli ad Corinthios*, 301-2.

Faithful Ministers Have the Devil as Their Enemy. Cyriacus Spangenberg: Whoever has once sworn under our Lord Jesus Christ's holy standard and has so entered into the battle array must not think that for one second that they will have rest from the devil. Therefore, it will be necessary to pay good attention and have good armor, especially for preachers and teachers, who stand at the forefront and must keep watch day and night, and whom the devil is in the habit of afflicting the most fiercely. Because in such an office, good days and much rest are not to be sought, whoever does not want to fight and contend should rather stay away. For whoever wants to preach the gospel must preach it purely and rightly. If someone does this, they certainly have the devil for an enemy, who cannot and does not like to stand it. Because it does to him as much as hot oil or pitch does to the bare skin of one of us. He becomes so angry about it that he uses all his guile and power against us. Thirty-Eighth Sermon.[19]

Paul Avoided Carnal Strategies. David Dickson: [It is as if Paul were saying,] I have no need to use carnal weapons by subtly changing my behavior, sometimes flattering, sometimes boasting, or using any other similar evil devices, but my spiritual weapons (such as they are) were sufficiency in the truth, boldness in the exercising of ecclesiastical discipline, zeal, patience, Christian fortitude, and other virtues, wherewith being armed, I do wage my warfare. Therefore, I am not to be condemned. Exposition of 2 Corinthians 10:4.[20]

We Must Overcome Devil, Reason, and Flesh. Andreas Bodenstein von Karlstadt: One must be well versed in suffering and know and understand the truth and love of God. For this reason, St. Paul teaches us that we must be equipped with the truth in order to overcome the devil. The weapons of our knighthood with which to destroy the fortification are not carnal, but mighty before God. Through them we overcome all attacks and all obstacles which rise up against the knowledge of God. We hold captive all reason in the obedience of Christ, and we must overcome devil, reason, and flesh through the truth which we know, and we must suffer tribulation in love and understanding, otherwise suffering is of no use to righteousness. Where this skill does not exist, there the flesh and devil are victorious. Several Main Points of Christian Teaching.[21]

Christians' Weapons Are Not Carnal. The English Annotations: "The weapons of our warfare . . . are not carnal," that is, the weapons that people naturally utilize so as to gain authority and do great things, such as riches, friends, honors, eloquence, the favor of princes, and the like. We do not conquer our enemies by any of these weapons, but rather by the contrary: poverty, weakness, infamy, rudeness, plain speech, and foolishness in the world's eyes. These weapons are made mighty through God's power who especially shines forth his glory by confounding glory with infamy; who shows his power by confounding power with weakness; who demonstrates his wisdom by confounding wisdom with what the world considers foolishness. Annotations on 2 Corinthians 10:4.[22]

Two Kinds of Swords. Balthasar Hubmaier: The brothers run to and fro, crying overly loud: "Here you see what the Christian breastplate and defense should be, not made of iron or long wood, but of the gospel, the gospel. The faith, the faith. The Word of God, the Word of God should be our sword and weapon. Truly Paul tells us to polish the breastplate and to clean our Christian weapons well for the other weapons are all from the devil." Answer: Stop running about, dear brothers, and note what I want to say to you in good peace. . . .

[19]C. Spangenberg, *Die ander Epistel Pauli an die Corinthier*, 161v.
[20]Dickson, *An Exposition of All St. Paul's Epistles*, 86*.
[21]CRR 8:367*; citing Eph 6; 1 Cor 13; 15; Is 5; 11; 27.
[22]Downame, ed., *English Annotations*, GG2v*.

There are two kinds of swords in Scripture. There is a spiritual one that is used against the treacherous attacks of the devil, such as Christ used against Satan. And that is the Word of God. Indeed, Paul speaks here to the Ephesians and the Corinthians about this sword concerning which Christ also says, "I have not come to bring peace but the sword." In addition to that there is also an external sword that one uses for the protection of the righteous and for the terror of evil persons here on earth. That is given to the government in order to maintain a common territorial peace with it. It is also called a spiritual sword, when one uses it according to the will of God. These two swords are not in opposition to each other. On the Sword.[23]

The Christian's True Weapons. Menno Simons: No, beloved sirs, no! [Weapons] will not deliver you in the day of the righteousness of God. I tell you the truth in Christ, the rightly baptized disciples of Christ, note well, they who are baptized inwardly with Spirit and fire, and externally with water, according to the Word of the Lord, have no weapons except patience, hope, silence, and God's Word. The weapons of our warfare, says Paul, are not carnal, but mighty through God to the pulling down of strongholds. . . .

Our weapons are not weapons with which cities and countries may be destroyed, walls and gates broken down, and human bloodshed in torrents like water. But they are weapons with which the spiritual kingdom of the devil is destroyed and the wicked principle in humanity's soul is broken down, flinty hearts broken, hearts that have never been sprinkled with the heavenly dew of the holy Word. We have and know no other weapons besides this, the Lord knows, even if we should be torn into a thousand pieces, and if as many false witnesses rose up against us as there are spears of grass in the fields, and grains of sand upon the seashore.

Once more, Christ is our fortress; patience our weapon of defense; the Word of God our sword; and our victory a courageous, firm, unfeigned faith in Jesus Christ. And iron and metal spears and swords we leave to those who, alas, regard human blood and swine's blood about alike. Those who are wise let them judge what I am saying. Foundation of Christian Doctrine.[24]

Our Hearts Must Cling to God's Word. Martin Luther: There is no other advice for resisting the devil and remaining undevoured by him than through firm faith. . . . This means that the heart which clings to God's Word must lay hold of it completely and regard it as true, for faith cannot be or remain without the Word, and it cannot listen to or lay hold of anything else. This is why we must separate the Word far from all reason and wisdom, and place it far above them, so that they are simply nothing, even dead, in matters which concern God's governance, such as how we are to escape from sin and eternal death. Reason must keep silent and give God's Word alone the honor of being true. St. Paul says about the preaching office of the gospel: "We take all reason captive under the obedience of Christ." Postil for the Third Sunday After Trinity.[25]

Preaching Destroys the Stronghold of Satan. Wolfgang Musculus: Paul explains the power and efficacy of his warfare, ascribing to it the overthrow of the kingdom of Satan and the captivity of the mind to the obedience of Christ, and finally also the vengeance against all disobedience. We fight, he says, to destroy strongholds. He is speaking with an analogy drawn from the military world, in which the strongholds of the enemy are overthrown and destroyed, and those captives who were seized are rescued. Now concerning these strongholds about which Paul speaks, he connects it with what follows, saying "overthrowing reasoning." The Greek word *logismous* is translated with the Latin word *consilium*. That word means the exercise of

[23]CRR 5:508-10*; citing Eph 6:14; Mt 4:1-11, 10:34.

[24]CWMS 198*.

[25]LW 78:119 (WA 22:42-43).

reasoning powers. Paul intends here the wisdom of human reasoning that is impure and corrupt, through which Satan especially rules over humankind. . . . Such strongholds of Gentile philosophy and wisdom are destroyed by the power of the spirit of Christ through the preaching of the gospel in the hearts of people. . . . Therefore, ministers of the gospel fight, not with flesh and blood, nor with fortifications and towers of stone, but with wisdom, glory, righteousness, and power against those fighters who have been blinded by the kingdom of Satan. And they do not use carnal weapons against them, but they preach and declare to the world only the truth of God, for it is with this armor alone that they gain the victory against the gates of hell. Commentary on 2 Corinthians 10:4-5.[26]

Christians Must Be Made Subject to Christ. John Calvin: It is my view that, having previously spoken more particularly about the conflict of spiritual armor, along with impediments that rise up against the gospel of Christ, Paul now speaks of the ordinary preparation by which men and women must be brought into his obedience. For as long as we rest in our own judgment and are wise in our own eyes, we are far from having made any progress toward the doctrine of Christ. This is why we must start with this, that the person who is wise must become a fool; that is, we must give up our own understanding, and renounce the wisdom of the flesh, and so present our minds to Christ empty so that he might fill them. Now the form of speech must be noted when he says that he "brings every thought into captivity," for it is as if he wished to say that the liberty of the human mind must be restrained and bridled, lest it be wise apart from the doctrine of Christ; and further, that its audacity cannot be restrained by any other means than as one taken captive. Now it is by the guidance of the Spirit that the mind is brought into line where it remains in voluntary captivity. Commentary on 2 Corinthians 10:5.[27]

The Power of the Gospel. Andreas Hyperius: Paul adds by way of expansion that not only do we demolish arguments and every lofty opinion, but further (still retaining the allegory) we take every thought captive to obey Christ. Now by this Paul indicates how great is the efficaciousness of evangelical doctrine, handed down from the apostles, that human hearts—reluctantly and unwilling—are drawn to agree with the gospel and submit themselves to Christ. Paul makes reference to this in Romans 1: "We have received grace and apostleship to bring about obedience of faith among all the Gentiles." In the same passage, the gospel is called the "power of God." And in 1 Corinthians 1 the gospel is described as the "power of God" by which the wisdom of the wisest person is overturned. Therefore, Paul's commendation here of the power of the Word of God as well as his commendation of the ministry of the Word is noteworthy. And it must be observed that Paul says men and women are drawn to obedience *to Christ*. He does not say obedience *to ourselves*—for this would be arrogant and not far removed from tyranny. Whatever the apostle did, he always directed to the glory of God; he was never seeking his own private benefit, just as soldiers assault fortresses and cities for their commanding officer. Commentary on 2 Corinthians 10:5.[28]

Bring into Captivity. John Trapp: See here the process of St. Paul's ministry. He overthrows, captures, subdues to the obedience of the Lord Christ. See a similar passage in Jeremiah 1. Osroes I,[†] king of Parthia, was so thoroughly defeated by the Romans that he made a law that none of his successors should ever wage war with

[26]Musculus, *Commentarius . . . in posteriorem epistolam Pauli ad Corinthios*, 302.

[27]CO 50:115-16 (CTS 40:324); citing 1 Cor 3:18.

[28]Hyperius, *Commentarii . . . in Epistolam D. Pauli ad Romanos, et Utramque ad Corinthios*, 405; citing Rom 1:5, 6; 1 Cor 1:24.

them again. So too here. Commentary on 2 Corinthians 10:5.[29]

Human Reason Must Be Crushed. Pilgram Marpeck: The law and the commands of God will stand eternally as a means of distinguishing good and evil, and in this knowledge of good and evil is the root and beginning of sin. From thence, the law emerged, along with sin, and was to be a verdict and condemnation of the knowledge and understanding of our devastated reason, which is the head of the serpent. The judgment of Christ acts as the stern righteousness of God, for he has given all judgment to the Son. The head of the serpent, that is, our reason, must be crushed, either through faith, or through vengeance and punishment in unbelief. The law is spiritual, but we are carnal. To be spiritually minded is life, to be carnally minded is death. Similarly, the serpent head of our reason must, and will be crushed, either by the preaching of faith, which takes all reason captive, or by the law in unbelief, which results in eternal destruction. Judgment and Decision.[30]

Heretic Valentinus Did Not Take Every Thought Captive to Faith. Martin Chemnitz: In the times of Antoninus Pius there was a certain Valentinus who was an expert in the teachings of Plato. He was converted to Christianity, and since he surpassed his coworkers in wit and eloquence, he aspired to become a bishop. But when another man, because of his constancy of confession, was preferred above him in the election, he became angry and began to think how he might take revenge for what he interpreted as an injury inflicted upon him. Thus, he got the idea of reviving many of the enormous errors which had been both attacked and refuted by Irenaeus and Tertullian[†] and other ancient writers. . . . And to embarrass the catholic faith, Valentinus not only dreamed up many gods but also suggested the most incredible names for them. If anyone wants to read them, they can find the long list in Irenaeus, Tertullian, and Epiphanius.[‡]

But because this corruption was an attempt to reconcile the philosophy of Plato with the doctrine of the church, it greatly disturbed the church because those who had come into the church from the schools of the philosophers had not yet "brought into captivity every thought to the obedience of faith," eagerly laid hold on these ideas and defended and spread abroad this raving of Valentinus.[§] . . . As a result of all this, with less elegance than truth, Tertullian wrote, "Philosophers are the patriarchs of heretics."[◊] Loci Theologici.[31]

The Twofold Power of the Keys. Andreas Hyperius: The apostle again adds by way of extension something that is important, and he presents in precise order these clauses using the image of war. For, in the first place, they demolish the fortifications. Then, from the fortifications, they bring out the captives who were defeated and force them to submit. Now if they finally do not want to submit, but continue to resist, then a more severe form of punishment is exercised against them. "In addition to right teaching," Paul says, "we have yet another kind of punishment, namely, a spiritual one, which, when there is need, we exercise against those who do not want to submit to Christ, and we exercise it in such a way that they are brought back to obedience." Now Paul understood by this the power of the keys, by which they have power to excommunicate or hand over to Satan those who do not wish to obey Christ and his sacred gospel—Paul himself exercised this

[29]Trapp, *A Commentary or Exposition*, 727*; citing Jer 1:10. [†]Osroes I ruled over the western portion of the Parthian Empire from AD 109 to 129. His rule was temporarily interrupted in 116, when the Roman emperor Trajan defeated his armies.
[30]CRR 2:316; citing Jn 5:22; Rom 8:6.

[31]Chemnitz, *Loci Theologici*, 1:63. [†]Tertullian's statement is found in *De anima* 3 (ANF 3:183). [‡]Irenaeus, *Against Heresies* 1.1, ANF 1:316-17; Tertullian, *Against the Valentinians* 1.7, ANF 3:506-7; Epiphanus, *Against Heresies* 1.2.31, PG 41:474-78. [§]For more on the Gnostic leader Valentinus, see W. H. C. Frend, *The Rise of Christianity* (Philadelphia: Fortress, 1984), 207-8. [◊]Tertullian, *On the Soul* 3, ANF 3:183.

power when he handed the incestuous man over to Satan. And so, Paul describes here briefly a twofold power of the keys: the first is one of teaching which he explained in his previous statements regarding the power of gospel doctrine. The second one is related to jurisdiction, by which sins are bound and the repentant absolved—this, therefore, is the spiritual power which the apostle claims for himself against the false apostles, who were always attempting to disparage his authority. And the apostle was rightly using this power. For he never wanted to employ for himself that carnal power in which both the hypocrites and tyrants delighted. Commentary on 2 Corinthians 10:6.[32]

Binding Sins and the Wrath of God. Tilemann Hesshus: Paul asserts that he is equipped not only with weapons for rescuing men and women from Satan's kingdom and turning their minds to Christ but also for avenging and punishing disobedience. "For the gospel of Christ is a life-giving aroma of life to those who are being saved, but a deadly aroma of death to those who are perishing." Some interpreters understand by this the external vengeance and punishment imposed on the wicked, as in 1 Corinthians 5, where Paul handed the incestuous man over to Satan; and where he struck the sorcerer Elymas with sudden blindness; and where Peter killed with a word Ananias and Sapphira. But the use of this kind of power to strike terror in the wicked is only exceedingly rare. Therefore, it is more correct for us to understand this to be the general power of the ministry, for Christ has furnished ministers with the power now to bind, now to pardon sins. When, therefore, the apostle binds the sins of unbelievers with the word of law, threatening them with the wrath of God, it is then that he punishes their disobedience. But no one should think that terrifying threats are unprofitable for holding back sins and proclaiming divine wrath. For even if vengeance or some corporal punishment does not immediately follow, nevertheless, since the Son of God affirms that he is going to confirm in heaven whatever pastors bind on earth, there is no doubt that their condition is most wretched whose disobedience is punished by the ministry and whose sins are bound. They have been excluded from the society of the church; they have no part in the kingdom of Christ; they are not protected from the severe wrath of God; they are strangers to life in God; they are daily more likely to be overwhelmed with terrible wickedness; they are also more likely to be struck down by blindness and insanity. Every single moment they are exposed to the plots and violence of Satan. Access to God is not available to them when they seek his counsel and need his assistance. And generally speaking, while they remain unrepentant, the wrath of God suddenly overthrows and plunges them into eternal destruction. Explication of 2 Corinthians 10:6.[33]

The Power of God's Word to Punish. John Trapp: Vengeance is every bit as ready in God's hand as in the minister's mouth. See Matthew 16 and 18. [The prophet] Elisha has his sword as well as [kings] Jehu and Hazael. God hews people by his prophets and flays them by the words of his mouth. By preaching, Christ many times smites the earth. His word lays hold on them, and that which they have counted wind, has become fire to devour them. Commentary on 2 Corinthians 10:6.[34]

10:7-12 *Paul Is Not Ashamed of His Authority*

Paul's Spiritual Union with Christ. Desiderius Erasmus: Do you still judge an apostle from things that are seen, as the common crowd judges a prince from his retinue, or from the ostentatious fanfare of fortune? I shall not say

[32]Hyperius, *Commentarii . . . in Epistolam D. Pauli ad Romanos, et Utramque ad Corinthios*, 405.

[33]Hesshus, *Explicatio Secundae Epistolae Pauli ad Corinthios*, 234r-235r; citing 2 Cor 2:15; Acts 13:8-12; 5:1-11.

[34]Trapp, *A Commentary or Exposition*, 727*; citing Mt 16:19; 18:18; 1 Kings 19:17; Hos 6:5; Is 11:4; Zech 1:6; Jer 5:13-14.

anything, for the moment, about false apostles, but this I shall say in general: if anyone has confidence in themselves on account of their belonging to Christ, either because they saw him as a mortal, or because they were related to him by blood, let them ponder carefully the fact that, just as they belong to Christ, so also do we belong to Christ. In this respect we are equals; they have no grounds for despising us, while flattering themselves. For it is not a relationship of the flesh that joins us more closely with Christ, but rather the Spirit. Paraphrases on 2 Corinthians 10.[35]

Paul Defends His Authority. Philipp Melanchthon: There is less danger when one struggles against external enemies, but the dangers of fighting against spiritual enemies are even worse when they are pretentiously fought in the name of Christ. Thus, the false apostles, deceptively treating the Word of God, were fighting and attacking Paul's godly example by means of the examples of holy men, because the entire church in Judea was subservient to the law. And so, he says: "If anyone is confident that they are of Christ, let them recognize that we also are of Christ." It's as if he were saying, "I will allow no one to undermine my authority. I have been called. I teach the Word of God. Whether I am opposed by holy men or angels, this is nothing to me. I myself am a holy man. If anyone's authority is strong, I put my authority up against their authority." In a similar way today, the examples of the saints is held up in defense of Masses and prayers, but one can say to them: "If you are confident that you are of Christ, you should recognize that we also are of Christ." Annotations on 2 Corinthians 10:7.[36]

The Corinthians Are Judging by False Appearance. John Calvin: The clause "according to appearance" can be taken in two ways: either the visible and manifest reality itself; or an outward mask that deceives us. The sentence too can be read either interrogatively or affirmatively. In fact, the verb *blepete* can be taken either in the imperative mood, or in the subjunctive mood. Nevertheless, I think Paul is scolding and reproving the Corinthians here because they allowed their eyes to be dazzled with empty pretense. It's as if he were saying: "You make much of other people who are swollen with their own self-importance, while you look down on me because I don't show off and brag about myself." Now, Christ also contrasts the judgment that is according to appearance and right judgment. Hence, Paul rebukes the Corinthians because, being content with show or appearance, they did not carefully investigate what kind of persons should be considered servants of Christ. Commentary on 2 Corinthians 10:7.[37]

Boasting the Name "Christian" Is Not Enough. Cyriacus Spangenberg: Let whoever among us claiming to be a Christian and boasting that they belong to Christ also behave according to Christ's word, so that they do not bear this title in vain or be more of a shame to the Lord Christ than an honor. It is easy to say, "I am a Christian." See to it also that is actually true.

Many boast about the Christian name who are not actually Christians but apostles of the devil, false prophets, teachers of works, preachers of dreams, babblers, sophists, papists, Epicureans, and wicked Christians. They may well bring forth the holy Scripture under the title and name of Christ. Indeed, they boast about Christian leaders and teachers and claim that the heavens would have fallen in long ago and the world would have sunk if it were not for them. Now it requires art to be careful of such beautiful devils and not be deceived.

The apostle intends here to warn faithfully all preachers of the gospel not to quarrel among themselves because of gifts, nor to despise one another as was happening in Corinth, where one called himself Apollish, the second Peterish, the third Paulish. And in our day, one despises another because they had a learned teacher, or spent longer

[35]CWE 43:259-60.
[36]*Melanchthons Werke*, 4:127.
[37]CO 50:117 (CTS 40:326-27).

in the university or school, or has a higher degree than another. Nothing good can come from this. Thirty-Ninth Sermon.[38]

Paul Was Duty-Bound to Rebuke Wickedness. Huldrych Zwingli: "If you belong to Christ, recognize that it is my duty to sharply rebuke and reprove wickedness, for I am also a minister of Christ. And I have been called to this: to demolish whatever is erected against God. Therefore, if you are endowed with the Spirit of God, you will easily see that our boasting is neither excessive nor groundless. For I do everything for your edification, while others in the meantime destroy and corrupt you with their various teachings." Annotations on 2 Corinthians 10:7-8.[39]

True Authority from the Lord. Wolfgang Musculus: Paul does not say simply "our authority," but he adds the phrase "which the Lord gave to us." He does not defend his apostleship recklessly, with the rashness of human presumption (as the false apostles were doing), but with the legitimate authority received from Christ himself. And the demonstration of this authority was seen in clear effects, so that he was not ashamed to boast about it. Today, people who boast in the apostolic authority prove that the Lord has given it to them when they are able to demonstrate it by its effects, and thus they are not ashamed to boast about it. They show the truth of their boasting through the accomplishment of the Lord's work. The Lord does not allow the authority that he gives to be vain and ineffective, but he establishes it and fortifies it by the power of the Spirit.

Paul then adds "for building you up and not for destroying you," by which he expressed the function and goal of his authority. When he says, "not for destroying you," he is not contradicting what he has said earlier, that the weapons of his warfare were the power of God for destroying strongholds. He has received with his apostleship these two things from God, namely, power [*potentia*] and authority [*potestas*]. The Greeks call the former *dynamin*, the latter *exousian*. He employs the word "power" to describe warfare, and he attributes to it the function of destroying the strongholds and pride of Satan's kingdom and leading captive minds into the obedience of Christ, as he has described in the preceding verses. He employs the word "authority" to describe the building up of believers, which he is thinking of in this passage. . . . Both of these functions also pertain in our own day to all those who are appointed ministers of the Word in the church. For if they wish to perform faithfully their ministries, they will have to endure the intense hostility of popes, bishops, and all those who are devoted to the Roman tyranny, who cannot bear to see the destruction of wickedness, superstition, and their own power, nor can they bear to see the building up of believers. For [true ministers] will be concerned not only boldly to destroy the enemy's strength by the power of the Word but also to use their power wisely to build up the believers. Thus, ministers need to be ambidextrous: with one hand they demolish those who destroy the church, and with the other hand they build up those who edify the church. Commentary on 2 Corinthians 10:8.[40]

The Limits of Episcopal Authority. Philipp Melanchthon: In this verse, you will particularly note the extent of episcopal authority, namely, "for building up, not destroying." From this we see first that bishops do not have the right to enact and draft laws, because consciences are not edified by human laws; at most, they do not oppose or harm spiritual things. Second, to the extent that bishops decide anything, certainly this passage establishes that the punishment of mortal sins cannot be imposed by virtue of

[38]C. Spangenberg, *Die ander Epistel Pauli an die Corinthier*, 165v-166r.
[39]Zwingli, *Annotatiunculae . . . ex ore Zvinglij*, 185-86.
[40]Musculus, *Commentarius . . . in posteriorem epistolam Pauli ad Corinthios*, 308, 9.

human traditions, for bishops possess no power for destruction—and it is a form of extreme destruction to impose the punishment of mortal sin. But just as those bishops destroy who impose the yoke and law, so too they destroy by breaking the laws, causing scandal to the weak, as Matthew 9 states: "the skins burst and the wine pours out." And so too Romans 14: "[Let us pursue] what is for edification." Annotations on 2 Corinthians 10:8.[41]

The Right Use of Spiritual Power. Cyriacus Spangenberg: Still today upright bishops, pastors, and superintendents have great power from God in that they can excommunicate stiff-necked and coarse sinners. But this does not occur with the intention that they should be eternally cut off and lost from God's assembly, but rather much more for their improvement so that they, being ashamed and frightened, may improve themselves. And as Paul says in 1 Corinthians 5: we give them over to Satan for the perishing of the flesh, so that the spirit will be saved on the day of the Lord Jesus. When that happens, the body of such a penitent sinner must indeed be lost.

Thus, we have here a fine regulation for how the church's power is to be used, namely, for improvement and not for perdition. If this has happened in the papacy it is due to their having made a law: A pope has such great power and authority from God, that even if he erred and led many thousands of souls into error and eternal perdition, no one should be so bold as to tell him, "You are doing wrong." Paul is not here thinking of such tyrannical, diabolical power, but says that power has been given to him from the Lord in order to improve. And if he boasted of the same power, he would not thereby be put to shame, but prove it and remain standing with all honor. Thirty-Ninth Sermon.[42]

Ministers Given Authority to Build Up the Church. Martin Bucer: Certainly, all who teach or issue ordinances or make regulations in the church are Christ's ministers and envoys, and must teach, ordain, and regulate only as Christ has decreed. They have no power to act against the truth but only on behalf of the truth, and their entire authority had been given them for building up, not for destroying, the church. On Faith.[43]

Church Authority Both Destroys and Edifies. The English Annotations: The authority of the church proves to be destructive for some people, namely, for those whom the church's censures do not bring to repentance and a humble confession of their sins and to submission to the governors of the church but who remain steadfast in their obstinacy. For [by this censure], they are cut off from Christ's mystical body, and from the means of grace and the communion of the saints. Yet at the same time the church's authority was also given for edification which occurs when scandals are removed, and those people cut off from the congregation who would otherwise infect it with heresy, schism, or scandalous behavior. Annotations on 2 Corinthians 10:8.[44]

Ecclesiastical Power Must Edify the Church. Niels Hemmingsen: Although the apostle was modest (because he ascribed to himself a rank among other inferior ministers), nevertheless, for the sake of defending his authority, he commended his dignified position. And lest anyone ascribe it to arrogance, he claims that it is wholly acceptable to God, when he states: "The authority which the Lord has given to me is not for your destruction but for your edification. Do not suppose that what I am boasting about are empty words to terrify you." It should be noted here that the goal of ecclesiastical power is the edification of the church. Thus, whosoever destroys the church through doctrine, action, or

[41]*Melanchthons Werke*, 4:128-29; citing Mt 9:17; Rom 14:19.
[42]C. Spangenberg, *Die ander Epistel Pauli an die Corinthier*, 166v-167r; citing 1 Cor 5:5.
[43]CPMB 184.
[44]Downame, ed., *English Annotations*, GG2v*.

life—that person boasts in vain that he is the vicar or servant of Christ. Commentary on 2 Corinthians 10:8-9.[45]

Paul Speaks with the Authority of Christ. Tilemann Hesshus: Paul does not throw empty terrors at them (as the arrogant and brash are accustomed to do), but he uses the authority given to him by the Lord, and so he wishes them to receive his correction as if it proceeded from none other than the Lord Jesus himself. Explication of 10:9.[46]

Hypocrites Attack the Rigor of Godly Leaders. Wolfgang Musculus: See the perversity of those people! They criticize the gravity of Paul's letters, as if he were feigning this intensity out of false zeal, when in fact they had given him good reason for writing in this fashion. In a very similar way in our day, people condemn Luther's writings of being too caustic. These are the same people who, out of their stubborn malice, give Luther just cause to rail against them, for they attack the teaching of the truth not only in their very malicious books but also with their edicts and bulls, and they mercilessly persecute the faithful with fire, sword, and noose. They are the worst kind of people: they find fault with the rigor of anyone who responds with harshness to their malice. Commentary on 2 Corinthians 10:10.[47]

Paul Defends His Integrity. Niels Hemmingsen: This is an objection and accusation of the false apostles that Paul acted one way in his letters, when he was absent, and a different way when he was present. "When he is absent," they say, "his letters are weighty and powerful, but when he is present with us, not only is he weak but his speech is also contemptible." From this it appears that Paul's enemies were bragging greatly of the severity of his person and the strangeness of his vague, ostentatious, and lofty words. . . . Paul responds to this accusation as if he were saying: "To the person who charges that I am bold in my letters when absent and cower when I am speaking in person to those who despise me, I wish to make this response: 'I behave the same whether present or absent; I shall say nothing more.'" Commentary on 2 Corinthians 10:10-11.[48]

Self-Flattery Leads to Shame and Foolishness. John Calvin: Here Paul points out their folly. The one-eyed person among the blind sees keenly. The person who is hard of hearing hears clearly among those who are completely deaf. Such were those that were satisfied with themselves and promoting themselves among others, simply because they did not consider anyone superior to themselves. Now, if they had compared themselves to Paul, or someone like him, they would have been forced to put aside that stupid belief immediately and would have turned their bragging into shame.

For an explanation of this passage, one needs to look no further than to the monks, for although almost all of them are as ignorant as asses, yet they are supposed to be learned on account of their long robe and hood. If anyone has even a tiny taste of elegant literature, he proudly spreads out his feathers like a peacock, becomes extraordinarily famous, and is adored among his companions. But if the mask of his hood were laid aside, and a thorough examination be made, his vanity would be detected. Why so? The old proverb is indeed true: Ignorance is bold. But that excessively insolent arrogance of the monks proceeds especially from this—that they measure themselves by themselves, for since there is nothing in their cloisters other than barbarism, it is not surprising if the one-eyed person rules among the blind.

Such were Paul's rivals, for inwardly they were flattering themselves, not considering what virtues

[45]Hemmingsen, *Commentaria in Omnes Epistolas Apostolorum*, 294.
[46]Hesshus, *Explicatio Secundae Epistolae Pauli ad Corinthios*, 238v.
[47]Musculus, *Commentarius . . . in posteriorem epistolam Pauli ad Corinthios*, 310.
[48]Hemmingsen, *Commentaria in Omnes Epistolas Apostolorum*, 294.

entitled a person to true praise, and how far short they came from the excellence of Paul and others like him. And indeed, this one consideration should rightly have infused them with shame. But it is the just punishment of the ambitious that in their foolishness they become ridiculous (which they desperately want to avoid), and in place of the glory which they especially desire, they incur disgrace. Commentary on 2 Corinthians 10:12.[49]

The Folly of the False Apostles. Tilemann Hesshus: Paul shows that he does not want to imitate the vanity of the false apostles who made themselves great and commended themselves. For Paul states that true and genuine boasting is that which is from the Lord, not from an empty shadow. Next, he severely reprimands the false apostles because they measure themselves by themselves and foolishly compare themselves to themselves. In other words, the false apostles were so pleased with themselves that they judged no one equal to themselves; they were not awaiting the judgment of other people, but only pushed themselves forward. And so, they alone wished to be seen as wise, eloquent, well-educated, and endowed with great gifts. Truly, this was great foolishness. For when we are pleased with ourselves more than is right, and admire our gifts more than is justified, then no one is more inept at judging ourselves than we ourselves. Whence Solomon in Proverbs 27 states: "Let another praise you, not your own mouth; a stranger, and not your own lips." Truly, praise of oneself is worthless. Therefore, the false apostles were acting very foolishly because they were thinking to exalt themselves by their own judgment, and arrogantly promoting themselves. Nevertheless, they were demonstrating that what they were was not what they wanted others to think of them, neither in faith, ministry, doctrine, or life. Explication of 2 Corinthians 10:12.[50]

Beware of Self-Exaltation! John Trapp: Turning to the other end of the perspective, [the false apostles] see themselves as larger, and others lesser than they are. Their soul is like a bladder that is so filled with earthly vanities—though these are but wind—that it grows great and swells with pride. O pray to be saved from this perilous pinnacle of self-exaltation. Look into the perfect law of liberty and draw near to God. The nearer we come to God, the more rottenness we find in our bones. The more men and women look into the brilliance of the sun, the less they see when they look away from it. Commentary on 2 Corinthians 10:12.[51]

Scripture Is the Measure of Truth. Dirk Philips: One reads holy Scripture and observes therein the signs by which the congregation is purified and set before our eyes, measure ourselves according to this true plumb line, and test ourselves with this touchstone. Then it shall be discovered whether we or our opponents are closer to the truth. Yes, if we then, or they, shall be held as the Christian congregation. If the kingdom of God were to exist in high sounding words, in false idle boasting, and not in power and truth, in righteousness, peace, and joy in the Holy Spirit, then the false prophets and false Christians would always have won the game. The Enchiridion.[52]

10:13-18 *Boasting in the Lord*

Legitimate Boasting. Wolfgang Musculus: Let us note that Paul does not say, "we will not boast," but "we will not boast beyond limits." Thus, he does not claim to eschew all boasting in general. From this we rightfully infer that boasting is not always unlawful for the saints. Certainly, it is unlawful and blameworthy for a person to boast falsely rather than truthfully, to boast about things in which there is no truth, or in what someone else has done, or immoderately, or beyond the limits

[49]CO 50:120 (CTS 40:332-33).
[50]Hesshus, *Explicatio Secundae Epistolae Pauli ad Corinthios*, 239r-v; citing Prov 27:2.
[51]Trapp, *A Commentary or Exposition*, 728*.
[52]CRR 6:178; citing 1 Cor 4:20.

acceptable to the Lord, or for reasons that are empty and groundless rather than certain and useful, or in one's own flesh or the flesh of another rather than in the Lord. Nothing of this sort is seen in the boastings of the saints, who boast truthfully, about their own affairs, with moderation and full understanding, and in the Lord.

Next, let us observe that Paul says, "but according to the measure (*tōn kanonos*)," that is, the rule, "by which God has apportioned the measure to us." . . . You see here that God has given not only those things that are good . . . but he also distributes his measure to each person, to some more, to others less; no one receives nothing, no one receives everything. In this, you see the rule for assigning this distribution. . . . Paul does not explain what this rule is by which God apportions his gifts to each person according to his measure. And it is not possible to explain it with certainty. Because it corresponds to the secret of divine providence that God distributes wisely, usefully, sufficiently to each person all things that are necessary for either sustaining life or undertaking ministry. Commentary on 2 Corinthians 10:13.[53]

Paul's Boasting Was Measured by God's Calling. Cardinal Cajetan: Paul employs the metaphor of a measuring cord, which builders use as a rule for their work of construction. For the master builder marks off the parts of the project with a measuring cord (which is called a *regula*) when directing the whole work of construction, or of cultivating the earth, or of building a rampart, and the purpose of the rule is to measure each part of the project. Paul uses this metaphor to indicate that the source for his boasting was measured by the extent of the territory in which he had up till then preached according to the limit [*regula*], determined not by himself, nor by the apostles, but by God. Now the extent of Paul's territory at that time reached all the way to Corinth. Read the Acts of the Apostles and you will find that Paul was frequently led by the Holy Spirit where he should preach and discuss things with the people. Understand that God assigned to Paul the places where he should preach. At the same time, let the wise reader recognize that Paul was not only preaching by divine appointment, but he was also preaching in a territory according to the limit [*regula*] assigned to him by God and so he went to some places and not to others. That is why the boasting of Paul rested not on himself but was assigned to Paul according to the divine measure [*regula*] and why those rivals were praising themselves as universal teachers, as if they were running throughout all regions. This was the reason for their great boasting. For even if they were boasting about the immense extent of the territory they covered, Paul had not claimed anything from their region. Commentary on 2 Corinthians 10:13.[54]

God Gives Different People Different Vocations. Tilemann Hesshus: After Paul has touched upon the false apostles' empty boasting, now, in turn, he demonstrates with apostolic modesty the extent to which it is permissible for us to boast, namely, according to the limits that the Lord has given to us and no more than that. People who boast beyond limits and measure are those who wish to attribute to themselves what God has not given them and who thrust themselves into someone else's calling. Arius boasted beyond limits when he attributed to himself greater gifts than he had and strained to expel another from his office. The Roman pontiff wishes to be called "the universal bishop of the whole world" and "head of the church"—authority he has certainly not received from God but has taken up for himself. Therefore, he is praising himself and boasting beyond limit. But the apostle Paul lived within the proper boundaries and was mindful of the limits which the Lord was placing on him.

Here the apostle is warning most gravely that we must diligently consider the limit that the Lord

[53]Musculus, *Commentarius . . . in posteriorem epistolam Pauli ad Corinthios*, 315.

[54]Cajetan, *In Posteriorem Pauli Epistolam ad Corinthios Commentarii*, 189.

has imparted to us, that is, the work to which the Lord has called us and the gifts with which he has equipped us. For a man or woman cannot assume for themselves anything except what is given them from above. No labor or work is blessed if the Lord has not commanded and motivated it. . . . God does not distribute equal measure to every person. He establishes some to be apostles, others prophets, others teachers, others pastors, and others rulers. He gives some people the gift of healing, others the faculty of performing miracles—all according to his kindest will. The vocation of Moses was of one sort, whom God established as a "god" to Pharaoh and led God's people. Aaron had a different calling. Elijah led the church for twenty years, Elisha for seventy years. Jonah was sent to Nineveh in the kingdom of Assyria, the prophet Micah only preached in the kingdom of Israel. Isaiah instructed the church for eighty years, Jeremiah for only forty years. Isaiah advised that Jerusalem not be handed over to Sennacherib; Jeremiah, from the command of God, taught that the city should be handed over to Nebuchadnezzar. John the Baptist performed his ministry for barely two years; John the Evangelist presided over the church in doctrine and authority for almost eighty years. Hence, the Lord distributes different limits to his servants, and he lays upon them various struggles and afflictions. We must consider carefully, therefore, the limit the Lord has given to us. And even if you are not Athanasius, Augustine, or Luther, you should nevertheless serve faithfully in your position, according to the limit which the Lord has apportioned to you. Explication of 2 Corinthians 10:13.[55]

The Apostles Honored Their Divinely Set Boundaries. The English Annotations: For the apostles, their dioceses encompassed the whole world, and they were commissioned to preach to all nations. Yet their journeys took them to different regions as God directed their paths, and they were careful not to interrupt or hinder one another so as to avoid interfering in the labor of another. By contrast, the false apostles traveled wherever they might gain an advantage and arrogated to themselves the conversion of those countries where the true apostles had already planted the faith. Annotations on 2 Corinthians 10:13.[56]

Paul Brought the Gospel to the Corinthians. John Calvin: "For we are not overextending." Paul alludes to persons who either forcibly stretch out their hands or raise themselves up on their feet when they want to snatch what they do not have in hand, for such is the greedy desire for glory—indeed, it is often more disgusting than that. For ambitious persons not only stretch out their hands and lift up their feet, but they throw themselves headlong to obtain some pretext for glory. Paul indicates that his rivals were like that. He afterward declares the reasons he had come to the Corinthians, namely, because he had founded their church by his ministry. And so he says "in the gospel of Christ," for he had not come to them empty-handed, but had been the first to bring to them the gospel. Commentary on 2 Corinthians 10:14.[57]

Paul Is Celebrating God's Grace Among the Corinthians. Tilemann Hesshus: Paul shows that he is not boasting in vain, for indeed, the Corinthians were competent witnesses that Paul was appointed a teacher of the Gentiles, and that God was present in his calling and conferred a blessed outcome. Already in his ministry Paul had established many churches in Asia, Macedonia, and Achaia; but because his authority was disparaged among the Corinthians, he only appeals to their testimony. "You Corinthians," he says, "were previously idolaters, ignorant of God, strangers from [spiritual] life; none of you made any mention of the kingdom of Christ and his blessings. And then, God gave to me this measure or limit, that I might extend the gospel of Christ to

[55]Hesshus, *Explicatio Secundae Epistolae Pauli ad Corinthios*, 239r-v.

[56]Downame, ed., *English Annotations*, GG2v*.

[57]CO 50:121 (CTS 40:335).

you and admit you to the fellowship of the church. It is only right and with good reason that I boast concerning you, because I was profitable to you in the Lord. You are my crown, my glory, and my joy."

This boasting of the apostle is moderate in that he is not proclaiming their works but rather is celebrating the kindness of God, who had granted a blessed outcome to Paul's ministry as he also converted the Corinthians to faith in Christ. He cautiously admonishes the Corinthians not quickly to forget the greatest benefits of God which they received from the words and preaching of Paul concerning the knowledge of the true God and the mediator Jesus Christ. These things were intended not only to be heard by the false apostles, but also to refute them. Explication of 2 Corinthians 10:14.[58]

Weak Faith Slows the Advance of the Gospel. John Calvin: Paul again indirectly reproves the Corinthians because they had been an obstacle to his making greater progress in advancing the gospel. For when he says that he hopes that, with their faith growing, the boundaries of his boasting will be enlarged, he intimates that the weakness of their faith, with which they were struggling, was the reason why his progress [in proclaiming the gospel] was somewhat hindered. It is as if he were saying, "I should now have been occupied in gaining new churches—and that with your assistance, if you had made the progress that you should have—but now you delay me by your weakness. Nevertheless, I hope that the Lord will enable you to make more progress in the future, and in this way the glory of my ministry will increase according to the limit of my divine calling." Commentary on 2 Corinthians 10:15.[59]

Paul Boasts in Those Whom He's Discipled. Niels Hemmingsen: With this comparison by antithesis, Paul gravely rebukes the false apostles who were boasting in the labors of others and beyond the limit assigned to them. It's as if he were saying: "Those people boast outside their limits, but I boast according to the measure [set by God], and so I hope that, with your faith maturing, I will be magnified in you as your progress in faith shows itself all the more. For the boasting of teachers is in the progress of their students. And I do not hope for just this, but much more, namely, that I might extend my sphere of influence well beyond you, to those who have not yet heard the gospel, lest I should boast in those who have been prepared through the influence of others—that is, lest I claim for myself what the Lord has measured out to others. That is just what your false apostles are doing; but since I boast in my sphere of influence, I will evangelize among those who have not yet heard the gospel." Commentary on 2 Corinthians 10:15.[60]

Not Boasting in the Labors of Others. Andreas Hyperius: A certain enlargement of his boasting would seem to be from his hope of obtaining more boasting in the future. It is as if he were saying: "Not only can we rightly boast about you, but I hope soon in the future to boast also in other neighboring regions where I have decided to announce the gospel. And then, indeed, I will not be boasting about someone else's limit (i.e., area of influence), nor will I claim for myself praise for someone else's labor, but I will be boasting according to my personal limit and from my own labor and according to those things that I myself have acquired by my own effort." And here he is still reproaching the false apostles for foolishly claiming the right to boast in someone else's labor. Paul uses an elegant metaphor when he speaks of faith "growing up," that is, increasing or becoming larger. For he was hoping that, in the future, the faith of the Corinthians might increase greatly, so that his boasting in them might be magnified in abundance, that is, it might grow up in a wonderful way—yet still remaining within its limits, that is, without going to excess and within the measure

[58]Hesshus, *Explicatio Secundae Epistolae Pauli ad Corinthios*, 241v-242r.

[59]CO 50:121-22 (CTS 40:336).

[60]Hemmingsen, *Commentaria in Omnes Epistolas Apostolorum*, 295.

prescribed by God. Now this would especially occur when their neighbors will be encouraged to embrace the gospel since it was customary for neighboring regions to leave behind their customs and manners when Paul taught them. Then, truly, he might boast rightly concerning these things that had been prepared for him, that is, which had been accomplished by his own labor. And he would not boast in someone else's area of influence, nor would he exceed his own limit and seize anything for himself from another person's boasting. Commentary on 2 Corinthians 10:15-16.[61]

Paul's Expansive Missionary Travels. Wolfgang Musculus: "So that we might preach the gospel also in those regions beyond you." Paul does not specify those regions beyond Corinth where he was hoping to preach the gospel. . . . If you consider the route by which he traveled from Jerusalem all the way to Corinth, beyond Corinth there was especially Macedonia, where nevertheless he had preached Christ before he had come to Corinth. As a matter of fact, in Romans 15, Paul boasts that he had proclaimed the gospel of Christ all the way to Illyricum, which is on the far end of Macedonia. Finally, Paul also traveled all the way to Rome, though as a prisoner, and he evangelized there for two years. Commentary on 2 Corinthians 10:16.[62]

Paul Planted Many Notable Churches. Tilemann Hesshus: Paul had been commissioned by God to gather the church from the whole world through the ministry of the gospel. And he established very notable churches in many places: Ephesus, Philippi, Thessalonica, Iconium, Derbe, Lystra, Antioch, Pisidia, and in many other places. And finally, he brought the light of the gospel to the imperial palace in Rome. Thus, Paul's boasting was not limited to Corinth, but extended itself also to other churches. And indeed, in many places, Paul gathered a church in which the message of the gospel had not been heard previously. Therefore, he was not boasting in the labor of others or in fields harvested by others, but he was rejoicing in those regions where the Lord had worked through him. Explication of 2 Corinthians 10:16.[63]

Empty Boasts of Visiting Foreign Fields. John Trapp: "In the regions beyond you." This was part of the braggadocio of the false apostles. And it is also now seen among the Jesuits, those peddlers and wandering beggars [*Agyrtae*], who cross sea and land, proud of the conversions that they have achieved in India and Africa, and like Dampadius, they become upset whenever people don't commend them every time they spit on the ground. The emperor Caius was ready to destroy the whole Senate because they did not deify him for marching with his whole army to the ocean to fetch a few oyster shells. Commentary on 2 Corinthians 10:16.[64]

Paul Does Not Intrude in Other People's Labors. The English Annotations: "Not boasting in another person's rule." A metaphor taken from builders who stretch out their line where they mean to build. And the apostle's meaning is that he would not intrude into any other person's work, nor desire to sow the seed of the Word in those regions and countries which other people had prepared and husbanded with the preaching of the gospel. Annotations on 2 Corinthians 10:16.[65]

Paul's Primary Objectives. David Dickson: [It is as if Paul were saying,] We do not boast in the labors of other people, as if we had converted to the Christian faith those whom we never did, which is what these Pretenders do when they boast in you Corinthians, whom they did not convert. But we hope that, after you are further established in the faith, you may be confident and seek to

[61]Hyperius, *Commentarii . . . in Epistolam D. Pauli ad Romanos, et Utramque ad Corinthios*, 408.
[62]Musculus, *Commentarius . . . in posteriorem epistolam Pauli ad Corinthios*, 318; citing Rom 15:19.
[63]Hesshus, *Explicatio Secundae Epistolae Pauli ad Corinthios*, 243r-v.
[64]Trapp, *A Commentary or Exposition*, 728*.
[65]Downame, ed., *English Annotations*, GG2v*.

propagate our gospel and share with your neighbors so that they may also hear my preaching. For truly, I hope that the borders of our ministry through you will be greatly enlarged in accordance with the purpose of my calling, to whom God committed the apostleship to the Gentiles. I hope, I say, that it will come to pass that we have the opportunity to preach the gospel also in those regions that are beyond us. In so doing, I will not need to boast in another's harvest, prepared by the efforts of other people, as the false apostles are now doing as they boast about you Corinthians, whom I converted to salvation, not them. Exposition of 2 Corinthians 10:16.[66]

We Should Boast in God Alone. Huldrych Zwingli: In all these things, may all of us seek the glory of God alone, whose work we are performing. And truly, whoever wishes to boast, let them boast in the name of God, who makes his grace known to the world through us, as his ministers. Annotations on 2 Corinthians 10:17.[67]

The Nature of Boasting. Wolfgang Musculus: Paul intends this general advice to pertain to all people commonly. For he says, "Whoever it is who boasts, and whatever he boasts about," from such a person it is required that "they should boast in the Lord." In the first chapter of 1 Corinthians, Paul attributed this same advice to Scripture, saying, "As it is written, 'Let the one who boasts, boast in the Lord'"—referring back, I think, to Jeremiah 9. For to boast in the Lord, is not to boast about all those things we ascribe to our own strength, wisdom, or righteousness, but, rather, we attribute all things to divine providence and seek to boast about that rather than our own glory. People who are thus inclined cannot boast according to the flesh, and therefore they do not boast beyond their own capacity, or about what is false, or about what someone else has done—which is the very thing the false apostles were doing who, since they were zealous for vainglory, could not boast in the Lord.

Anyone who boasts, boasts about these three things: First, a person finds delight and exults within themselves concerning what they are boasting about. None of us boast about the disagreeable things that grieve us, but we boast about things that are auspicious, good, and excellent. (I am speaking here about the hearts of honorable people; for carnal people rejoice in carnal things, and wicked people rejoice in wicked things.) Thus, Proverbs 2 says, "[Evil people] rejoice in doing evil and delight in the perverseness of evil." Second, people do not confine their gladness to the secret place of their consciences, but they discuss it and proclaim it among other people. . . . And they do not make their boasts mildly but brashly, not every now and again but frequently. This is especially true of those who boast about things that are false and useless. Third, by their bragging they seek praise and glory. . . . And here the zeal of the godly is distinguished from the zeal of the wicked. For godly persons do not seek to glorify themselves but seek the glory of God, even as they delight in him; and they do not proclaim their own virtues but proclaim God's grace and goodness and thus they boast in the Lord rather than in themselves. But when wicked people boast, they hunt after glory and praise for themselves, and commend themselves rather than God. Commentary on 2 Corinthians 10:17.[68]

God Alone Commends. Heinrich Bullinger: Paul now breaks off this discussion and says, "Unlike those [false apostles] who have left the truth, we seek all the glory for God alone, whose affairs we undertake." "Let the one who boasts, boast in the Lord." Paul also quotes this statement in 1 Corinthians 1. Moreover, he adds a general statement, by which he teaches that the only person approved is the one whom God commends as holy and virtuous—not that person who extols himself and trumpets self-praise. We also read in

[66]Dickson, *An Exposition of All St. Paul's Epistles*, 87*.
[67]Zwingli, *Annotatiunculae . . . ex ore Zvinglij*, 186.
[68]Musculus, *Commentarius . . . in posteriorem epistolam Pauli ad Corinthios*, 319; citing 1 Cor 1:31; Prov 2:14.

Proverbs 27, "Let another person praise you, and not your own mouth; a stranger, and not your own lips." Commentary on 2 Corinthians 10:17-18.[69]

The Central Principle of Boasting. Niels Hemmingsen: Paul is thinking here of both himself and the false apostles as he appropriately passes on this principle which is necessary for all godly people to follow in their actions: "Those who boast must boast in the Lord," that is, with deeds both honorable and noble. First, he assumes that all boasting before God is genuine. Second, that whoever has received the grace of God should give back boasts to God. In the first principle he has in mind pride, in the second greed—two vices which horribly defile the otherwise excellent gifts of God. Paul adds the reason for the principle by comparing their causes: one of them causes ruin, the other is productive. Persons who commend themselves to others, become filthy and deserve contempt, for their commendation is not true. But those whom God commends are approved by God and other people. But who is commendable to God? Those persons who test and examine that all things are rightly done according to Paul's principle. Commentary on 2 Corinthians 10:17-18.[70]

True Evidence of the Lord's Commendation. Wolfgang Musculus: Paul does not say, "the one whom other people commend," but "the one whom the Lord commends." Human commendation does not render a person approved. The false apostles were being commended by letters of recommendation from other people, as we saw in chapter 4 above, and yet nevertheless they were not approved [by God] but were rather condemned as imposters. . . . Now when the Lord commends someone, he does not make a mistake, nor does he mislead anyone—that is why it is necessary that a person should be approved by him. The Lord's commendation is not like that of human beings . . . for he does not commend with words, but with clear evidence, namely, with his works and gifts, by which he gives to each person what he wishes them to possess. Thus, the Lord was commending Paul as an exceptional apostle, and declared him approved through the great power of his apostleship. The false apostles did not possess this kind of commendation, so why was it that they seemed approved? They were showing off their great reservoir of knowledge, wisdom, and eloquence, and they were snubbing Paul as humble and ignorant in speech, considering themselves superior to him. Let us draw the conclusion from this rule of divine commendation whether or not ministers of Christ have been approved. If they have been equipped for the ministry with the necessary gifts of God, and have demonstrated it with clear evidence, we recognize in them the commendation of God and we hold them in high esteem as approved. No tree is judged to be good from the commendation of words, but it is judged by the abundance of its good fruit. So too when judging and testing ministers, we are able to recognize the tree by its fruit. Commentary on 2 Corinthians 10:18.[71]

[69]Bullinger, *In Posteriorem D. Pauli ad Corinthios . . . Commentarius*, 318; citing 1 Cor 1:31; Prov 27:2.

[70]Hemmingsen, *Commentaria in Omnes Epistolas Apostolorum*, 295.

[71]Musculus, *Commentarius . . . in posteriorem epistolam Pauli ad Corinthios*, 321, 322.

11:1-15 PAUL AND THE FALSE APOSTLES

I wish you would bear with me in a little foolishness. Do bear with me! [2]For I feel a divine jealousy for you, since I betrothed you to one husband, to present you as a pure virgin to Christ. [3]But I am afraid that as the serpent deceived Eve by his cunning, your thoughts will be led astray from a sincere and pure devotion to Christ. [4]For if someone comes and proclaims another Jesus than the one we proclaimed, or if you receive a different spirit from the one you received, or if you accept a different gospel from the one you accepted, you put up with it readily enough. [5]Indeed, I consider that I am not in the least inferior to these super-apostles. [6]Even if I am unskilled in speaking, I am not so in knowledge; indeed, in every way we have made this plain to you in all things.

[7]Or did I commit a sin in humbling myself so that you might be exalted, because I preached God's gospel to you free of charge? [8]I robbed other churches by accepting support from them in order to serve you. [9]And when I was with you and was in need, I did not burden anyone, for the brothers who came from Macedonia supplied my need. So I refrained and will refrain from burdening you in any way. [10]As the truth of Christ is in me, this boasting of mine will not be silenced in the regions of Achaia. [11]And why? Because I do not love you? God knows I do!

[12]And what I am doing I will continue to do, in order to undermine the claim of those who would like to claim that in their boasted mission they work on the same terms as we do. [13]For such men are false apostles, deceitful workmen, disguising themselves as apostles of Christ. [14]And no wonder, for even Satan disguises himself as an angel of light. [15]So it is no surprise if his servants, also, disguise themselves as servants of righteousness. Their end will correspond to their deeds.

OVERVIEW: In this pericope, Paul boasts in his apostleship in order to warn the Corinthian church against the deception of the false apostles, who continue to undermine Paul's message by ridiculing his simple speech, condemning his homely appearance, and misconstruing his decision to preach the gospel free of charge in Corinth. Once again, Reformation commentators find good reasons to commend Paul for boasting in his ministry, for the false apostles are leading God's people away from the one true gospel by their pompous words, their pretense of holiness, their feigned zeal, and their fake wisdom. The exegetes call special attention to Paul's burning jealousy to present the Corinthian church as a pure and beautiful bride to her bridegroom Christ—this driving passion for the spiritual fidelity of Christ's church should characterize all faithful gospel ministers. The sharp contrast between Paul and the false apostles raises other lessons for church life and ministry. Reformation commentators exhort their readers to emulate Paul's spiritual eloquence rather than the contrived rhetoric of false teachers that lacks substance. They also applaud Paul's humility and generous spirit in preaching the gospel free of charge, although they make clear that, under normal circumstances, it is permissible for ministers to receive wages for their service. Several Protestant commentators also call attention to Paul's use of sacred oaths (in 2 Cor 11:10-11) in order to rebut the Anabaptists, who reject all oath-giving. Finally, the deceptive character of the false apostles—who promote themselves as "apostles of Christ" and "servants of righteousness"—sheds important light on Satan and his evil designs. Reformation commentators are convinced that this same satanic spirit of deception has seeped into their contemporary church, although they sharply disagree on the identity of these false teachers. Most Protestant interpreters associate these "ministers of Satan" with the pope and the Roman

Catholic clergy; by contrast, Anabaptist and Radical leaders suggest that Satan's servants include reformers such as Martin Luther, whose perceived hypocrisy and ungodliness undermine true piety and new life in Christ.

Summary of Chapter. John Calvin: In the eleventh chapter, Paul calls upon the Corinthians to renounce those depraved inclinations with which they had been corrupted, reminding them that nothing is more dangerous than to be seduced from the simplicity of the gospel. Now, the reason that he began to be somewhat despised among them—while they received other people with greater favor—happened not because he was guilty of any fault, but due to their arrogance and delighting in pleasures. But those other people had brought them nothing better or more excellent. Now Paul was contemptible to them for no other reason than because he did not ingratiate himself with elegant speech or because, by voluntary submission, he had given up his just claim so as to humor their weakness. This irony contains an indirect reproach of their ingratitude, for where was the fairness of esteeming him less when he had accommodated himself to them? He shows, however, that the reason why he did not take the wages that were due him was not because he loved the Corinthians less, but so that the false apostles (whom Paul saw were devising traps by this strategy) might not in any way be judged superior.

After Paul rebukes the unfair and malicious judgment of the Corinthians, he praises himself with pious boasting—mentioning how magnificently he could boast, were he so inclined—stating, however, that it is for their sake that he plays the fool in proclaiming his own praises. Finally, checking himself as it were in the middle of the course, he states that his chief ground for boasting is that humility which was despised by the proud, for he had been admonished by the Lord not to boast in anything other than his weaknesses. Commentary on 2 Corinthians.[1]

[1]CO 50:8 (CTS 40:107-8).

Paul's Superiority to the False Apostles. Niels Hemmingsen: The apostle exhorts the Corinthians not to be deceived by the false apostles and be led away from their fiancé Christ. And demonstrating that the reasons which the false apostles were alleging to despise him were not at all just, Paul clearly shows with many arguments that he is not only their equal but is far superior to them.

Paul is skillful in the wonderful way that he organizes this chapter. For the apostle seeks to persuade the Corinthians (who were despising him) not to cling to the false apostles, and, given that their souls were in clear danger, he considers it necessary to show the various ways he is superior to those false apostles. Now, with this very suitable introduction, he makes an appropriate wish. For he desires to indulge in a little foolishness—for they were singing their own praises—so that once they are duly corrected, he might explain his great fear that they are allowing themselves to be deceived by the false apostles. Whence, Paul indicates the chief argument of this chapter, namely, that they should avoid being seduced by the false apostles but should instead attach themselves to him. Having established this argument, Paul responds briefly to the calumnies of the false apostles who were bringing up the simplicity of Paul's speech, his contemptible appearance, and his refusal to accept remuneration as a sign that he had hostile feelings toward the Corinthians—accusations that fall apart in his description of the false apostles. And he shows how deceptively they are acting under the pretext of godliness and that they are acting by satanic example, whose servants they are. Then, so that he might bring the false apostles into line, he again asks and prays that they might endure his foolishness so that by this means he might prove to the Corinthians how slavishly they are subjecting themselves to the false apostles. Then he suggests that he also is able and wishes to boast and sets up a comparison between himself and the false apostles, in which he shows the many ways that he is not only equal but even superior to them. COMMENTARY ON 2 CORINTHIANS 11.[2]

11:1-6 *Paul's Divine Jealousy for the Corinthians*

THE NATURE OF PAUL'S FOOLISHNESS. JACQUES LEFÈVRE D'ÉTAPLES: Those deceivers were not only disparaging Paul before the Corinthians, saying, "When he is physically present, he is feeble and his speech is contemptible," but they were also calling him foolish, considering to be insufficient what was preeminent. Oh owl, how you judge day to be night! For as the wisdom of this world is foolishness before God (a foolishness due to insufficient wisdom), so the wisdom of God is foolishness to the world (a foolishness due to preeminent wisdom and surpassing perfection). And what is light to people who are partially blind, are shadows to those of keener sight (shadows due to insufficient sight). On the other hand, what is light to those who see clearly are shadows to those who are partially blind (but shadows due to preeminence and perfection). And thus, the foolishness of Paul is light to those spiritual people who see clearly, but they are shadows to those who are partially blind and carnal. And Paul wished in the same fashion that the Corinthians, in a spirit of goodwill, would be capable [to discern] the preeminence of his foolishness. . . . And in this sense, Paul desires that "you would bear with me a little in foolishness." COMMENTARY ON 2 CORINTHIANS 11:1.[3]

THE LIMITS OF TOLERANCE. WOLFGANG MUSCULUS: Without such mutual tolerance, the conduct of human life cannot occur either in the profane or sacred spheres, inasmuch as there is no one (however superior or lowly he may be) who is so wise, so good, so constant and complete in the good that he does not occasionally fall into error and act foolishly. Paul was not acting foolishly here, but he makes use of concession in this passage, and likewise he requests tolerance, which they owe to him even if, in fact, he is occasionally acting silly. Nevertheless, we must not allow this passage to be used as a defense by those false teachers who repress the people of Christ under the servitude of the antichrist and argue in the following fashion: "Even if the apostolic see errs and acts somewhat foolishly in matters related to the church, one should not thereby desert it, but rather, it should be tolerated with obedience and reverence as the mother of the churches, and whatever foolishness it might display should be attributed to old age." We answer: Those things we condemn in the Roman Church are neither trivial nor the foolish things of old age, but we condemn the enormous abominations in worship, the introduction of shameful morals, and the wicked dominion and antichristian tyranny found in the most depraved government of all. If she were a mother (and not the Babylonian harlot), and if she were a little silly, we would easily tolerate this. . . . We should be tolerant when it does not undermine the glory of God, the purity of our faith, or the salvation of anyone's soul. COMMENTARY ON 2 CORINTHIANS 11:1.[4]

PAUL HAS A PURPOSE IN HIS FOOLISHNESS. TILEMANN HESSHUS: Paul, showing with what great vanity the false apostles are boasting about themselves, stoops to their approach to also boast about carnal and outward things; or rather, he demonstrates that he has no less reason for praising and promoting himself on account of the flesh than the false apostles did. But he teaches that such boasting is connected with foolishness, and that the Corinthians should patiently tolerate and properly interpret this foolishness of Paul's—and, indeed, should receive it as wisdom—so that, by his example, he might restrain the empty boasting of the false apostles. And this also gives evidence of

[2]Hemmingsen, *Commentaria in Omnes Epistolas Apostolorum*, 295-96.
[3]Lefèvre, *Commentariorum in Epistolas Beati Pauli . . . Liber Tertius*, 140v.
[4]Musculus, *Commentarius . . . in posteriorem epistolam Pauli ad Corinthios*, 322-23.

his love and concern for them. Explication of 2 Corinthians 11:1.[5]

Paul's Boasting Was Justified. The English Annotations: Paul grants that, in a sense, he may deserve to be censured as a fool, but he adds therewith that he boasts against his will for the Corinthians' benefit, because he sees them deceived by certain cunning people through the craft and subtlety of Satan. For persons to commend themselves—even if it is based on truth—seems to savor of foolishness and vainglory. Yet in St. Paul's case, his decision to speak the truth concerning the infallible testimonies of his apostleship and to stop the mouths of the false apostles who degraded his person and vilified his ministry, by means of sweet rhetorical insinuation and craving pardon, was part of godly wisdom. Annotations on 2 Corinthians 11:1.[6]

Paul Faithfully Delivered the Virgin Church to Christ. Desiderius Erasmus: By a spiritual union I have joined you, as a chaste and undefiled virgin, to him, as though to your only husband so that from him you may never be separated. Nothing of yours do I claim for myself. He is the spouse. I have merely played the role of "bridesman." I handed over to him a bride chaste and pure, but I am afraid that somehow, just as long ago the serpent's wiles seduced the simple mind of Eve, vitiating the purity in which she had been created, so you too, likewise, in your simplicity may be seduced through the cunning of false apostles, and you may deviate from the purity which, thus far, you have practiced toward your spouse, Christ Jesus. Both he and you were alike pure when you received him through us. Paraphrases on 2 Corinthians 11.[7]

Paul's Godly Jealousy. Tilemann Hesshus: It is as if Paul were saying: "I am not being motivated by perverse affections, nor am I being moved by rivalry, expecting you to reject all other teachers and accept me alone. I am not demanding those things that are rightfully mine, nor am I chasing after power or glory; rather, I am inflamed with a pure and divine zeal as in the sight of God. I am burning with indignation because false teachers are attempting to lead you away from the path of truth. I am fearful for your salvation, which I imparted to you by the preaching of the gospel. I ardently desire to strengthen your faith against the traps and insults of Satan. It is right, therefore, that you gladly receive those things that I am offering to you." Explication of 2 Corinthians 11:2.[8]

The Marriage of Christ and the Church. Philipp Melanchthon: Paul has often spoken elsewhere concerning the marriage of Christ and the church, in which you will observe the most profound union of all things good and evil. That is, our evil is transferred to him, his goodness to us, so that we are one flesh, with our flesh made holy by his flesh. Now these things become ours, just as he himself becomes ours, not by works but by faith. It is like in a civil marriage, where there is no obligation between the man and woman except by a mutual promise [*fide*] that all things might be shared. The apostles have the role of both helping arrange and witnessing to these marriages. And so he says, "I am jealous for you, but not for my own sake, but for the one to whom you were promised in marriage." Annotations on 2 Corinthians 11:2.[9]

Paul Betrothed the Corinthians to Christ. Huldrych Zwingli: Out of parental concern, Paul interjects this statement "I betrothed you to one husband" (which extends until the passage [in v. 4] where he says, "For if someone . . .") by adducing a metaphor from marriage. . . . Christ is the groom to whom the souls of believers are united, having been

[5]Hesshus, *Explicatio Secundae Epistolae Pauli ad Corinthios*, 246v-247r.
[6]Downame, ed., *English Annotations*, GG2v*.
[7]CWE 43:264.
[8]Hesshus, *Explicatio Secundae Epistolae Pauli ad Corinthios*, 247r.
[9]*Melanchthons Werke*, 4:129.

betrothed by faith, and they promise that they will not tear themselves from his embrace. Since Paul saw the harm that the false apostles were inflicting among the Corinthians through their cunning, he bluntly calls for faith in Christ (which was being corrupted and ruined by human teachings); in so doing, he pursued the Corinthians with the impatience of a lover, warning them not to depart from the faith by which they were first joined to Christ. ANNOTATIONS ON 2 CORINTHIANS 11:2.[10]

TRUE MINISTERS ARE FRIENDS OF THE BRIDEGROOM. JOHN CALVIN: Paul proves from the goal of his preaching the nature of his zeal, for its tendency was to join them to Christ in marriage and retain them in this union. Here, however, he portrays for us in his own person a picture of a good minister, since there is only one bridegroom of the church, the Son of God. All ministers are friends of the bridegroom, just as John the Baptist testified concerning himself in John 3. Thus, all ought to be concerned that the fidelity of this sacred marriage should remain safe and inviolable. This they cannot do unless they are endued with the affection of the bridegroom, so that every one of them may be as concerned with the purity of the church as a husband is for the chastity of his wife. Away then with coldness and laziness in this matter, for the person who is cold will never be qualified for this office. But let them in the meantime be careful not to pursue their own interests rather than those of Christ, nor to thrust themselves in his place, lest while they claim themselves to be friends of the bridegroom, they turn out to be in reality adulterers, by alluring the bride to love themselves. COMMENTARY ON 2 CORINTHIANS 11:2.[11]

THE CHURCH HAS ONE HUSBAND. WOLFGANG MUSCULUS: "For I betrothed you to one husband." Paul says this so that the minister of Christ, who has been ordained to the ministry of reconciliation, might lead everyone through the preaching of the gospel to faith in Christ and might unite them to Christ as though he were betrothing them. Now he does not simply say, "I presented you to the knowledge and faith of Christ," which nevertheless he certainly could have said, but he says something even more, "I joined you," or "I betrothed you," as the ancients have it, "to one husband so that I might present or offer a chaste virgin to Christ." Both the knowledge of Christ and faith in Christ hold out the promise for eternal life, but this betrothal by which we are united with Christ in the same way that newlyweds are secretly united as one flesh communicates a far greater status to the human race, greater in distinction, honor, and happiness. Paul could have said, "I subjected you to one lord so that you might obey him and serve him faithfully." But this way of speaking would not have expressed the dignity and happiness of that excellent union of ours with Christ. Note, likewise, how Paul adorns the exceptional dignity of his apostleship, when he describes himself not simply as a minister, but also as a groomsman of Christ. It is not in the role of a servant that he betroths a certain virgin to his king, but rather, the king gives him this commission on account of his unique trust and close friendship. Paul also indicates that this trust in him is justified, when he says, "So that I might present a chaste virgin to Christ." He was not satisfied with any sort of betrothal, but he was taking pains to present to Christ a true virgin rather than a woman already married to another man; indeed, he wishes to present to Christ a virgin who has not been polluted and corrupted by illicit love, but completely chaste. COMMENTARY ON 2 CORINTHIANS 11:2.[12]

PREACHERS ARE THE LORD'S GROOMSMEN. CYRIACUS SPANGENBERG: "I am jealous for you (he says) with godly jealousy. For I promised you to one husband, that I would present to Christ a pure

[10] Zwingli, *Annotatiunculae . . . ex ore Zvinglij*, 187.
[11] CO 50:123-24 (CTS 40:349-40); citing Jn 3:29.
[12] Musculus, *Commentarius . . . in posteriorem epistolam Pauli ad Corinthios*, 324.

virgin." Here we hear clearly how great a benefit and service we have from preachers of the divine Word. They are our Lord Christ's envoys and groomsmen, sent out by him in order to court us poor, miserable, impoverished, and sinful people for such a rich, glorious, mighty, and holy bridegroom, and to lead us and betroth us to the same for eternal benefit. Oh, whoever thinks rightly of this would certainly love and honor his preacher most highly! But the world values such a heavenly, divine wedding as nothing. It is also for this reason that few rejoice over the same, and this is an especially great negligence.

But much more scandalous is this great ingratitude: one does not only despise the servants of God, who gladly release us from the devil and want to lead us and betroth us to the Lord Christ, but also hates and persecutes them, and one does this most of all when these servants of God most receive us and are jealous for us with a godly jealousy. They teach, preach, admonish, discipline, and warn not with the intention of betraying us or otherwise bringing us into danger or wanting to set us on an unstable seesaw, but in order to betroth us to Christ and to place our faithful hand into his faithful protection, not to put us on human comfort, but to confidently put, present, attach, and unite us to his (as the eternal truth) belief and trust, not to an aloof, unknown or mere friend or imperious Lord, but as to our loving bridegroom and friendly, kindly husband, who as a pious bridegroom and a pious husband wants to demonstrate love, provision, protection, and all faithfulness. This is especially comforting. Woe to the one who does not rejoice in such a comfort or use it. Fortieth Sermon.[13]

The Consolation of Having Christ as Our Bridegroom. Johann Spangenberg: God the Father prepared a great, magnificent wedding feast for his Son Christ Jesus, the heavenly Bridegroom, and has invited every person in the world to this feast through the spoken Word of the preaching of the gospel. Now that person who believes the words of the apostles or any other devout preacher and messenger of Christ will be led to Christ as a pure virgin, so that the entire Christian church in general, as well as each and every believing soul, becomes first and foremost the Lord Christ's delightful and dear bride and wife. . . .

This is indeed a magnificent consolation! Christ is not only our Father, Brother, and Friend, but he even calls himself with the most friendly name on earth—our Bridegroom. That is the great mystery of which Paul boasts so highly in Ephesians 5. For how could a person experience greater joy than to be able to boast freely and say: "Christ is my Bridegroom—one body, one heart, one Spirit with me. He tore me—poor, miserable creature, conceived and born in sin, filled with every unrighteousness and crime—out of God's wrath and the devil's jaws. For my sake he bought me with his precious blood and through baptism purified me from sin. And still to this day he lets his holy Word be preached through which he leads me into full relationship with God. All heavenly goods, grace, and gifts are richly shared, so that he brings me out of this miserable, wretched existence and life into his glory, into his heavenly chamber—into eternal life." Postil for the Feast of the Virgins.[14]

Paul Longs for a Pure Church. Menno Simons: The church of Christ is the bride of Christ, and Christ does not want his bride to conceive except of the incorruptible seed. As Paul says, "I have espoused you to one husband, that I may present you as a chaste virgin to Christ." Yes, so pure Paul wanted the church to be that if there were any who caused divisions and offenses contrary to the doctrine which he had taught, they should be avoided. Yes, if they had any in the church that were drunkards, covetous, fornicators, idolatrous, or proud, they should avoid them and not eat with them. . . . How then could they have

[13]C. Spangenberg, *Die ander Epistel Pauli an die Corinthier*, 171v.

[14]J. Spangenberg, *Postilla Teütsch*, 6:128r-v, 129v-130v; citing Eph 5:22-33.

such people as preachers? Admonition to the Amsterdam Melchiorites.[15]

The Cunning of Satan. Wolfgang Musculus: Now what tricks did Satan employ to deceive Eve? First, Satan attacked Eve rather than Adam since as a woman she was weaker and more inclined to curiosity and credulity. This is his custom today as well. He tempts weaker people before others. Paul says elsewhere that Adam was not seduced. Why? Because Adam did not believe the serpent's words that Satan set before Eve, but he yielded to his wife's seduction. Therefore, he was not clever, but was attacked by the temptation of Eve. . . . Second, Satan also acted cleverly because he attacked Eve when she was alone, absent from Adam. For he was fearful that he would tempt her in vain if he did it in the presence of her husband. Third, he made a cunning plan to employ the assistance of a bewitched serpent so that there would seem to be less danger. Fourth, in a cunning fashion he pretended kindness as if he was sincerely eager for the honor and happiness of the first human beings. Fifth, Satan tempted Eve on an issue of no minor importance, but if he won, he would hurl the whole human race into destruction. Sixth, he was employing urgings and promises that seemed lovely to inquisitive flesh. Seventh, Satan also disparaged the Word of God. Finally, Satan led her away from faith and obedience. Paul wants us to consider all these things when he says that Eve was deceived by the cunning of the serpent. And was Satan not doing the same thing in the church of the Corinthians when, with similar cunning through the instrumentality of the bewitched apostles, he was corrupting and ruining simple people who had been deceived by his lying words and, in the absence of the apostle, was leading them away from pure doctrine and faith in which our salvation exists? Such cunning of Satan, which remains effective to this present day, ought to be recognized by all believers, especially by ministers of Christ. Commentary on 2 Corinthians 11:3.[16]

Eve, the Serpent, and the False Apostles. Niels Hemmingsen: Paul explains how much he fears for the Corinthians, namely, that he is fearful that, being seduced by the false apostles, they might fall away from the salvation that they had received through Christ. Now there is here a twofold comparison: one is of Eve and the church, the other is of the serpent (that is, the devil) and the false apostles. Now, as Eve before the fall was a type of the church, so, in the same way, after the fall, she is a figure of falling away from grace through disobedience. Therefore, the salvation of Eve was based on her obedience to the simplicity of the Word of God, and her fall existed from the corruption of the word and her disobedience. So, too, the salvation of the church of Christ is founded upon the simplicity of the gospel and in its faith and obedience, and the destruction of the church is in its defection from the simplicity of the gospel.

The second comparison is between the serpent and the false apostles, which is constructed this way: Just as the serpent, with his pretended zeal for the first parents, deceived Eve by pointing out the fruit of paradise (fruit that Eve, when she listened to the serpent, saw was suitable for eating, desirable to the eyes, and desirable for conferring wisdom), so the false apostles in their cunning were endeavoring to lead the church away from the simplicity of the gospel of Christ, and thus to sell them into eternal punishment—giving as a pretext the outward appearance of things, pompous words, the pretense of holiness, feigned zeal, and the impression of wisdom. Here it should be noted first of all how great is the kindness of Christ, who, when we were ruined by our sin and subject to damnation, restored us to salvation by his gospel. Second, we should note how great is the worth and importance of the ministry of the Word and what honor

[15]CWMS 1023; citing 1 Pet 1:23.

[16]Musculus, *Commentarius . . . in posteriorem epistolam Pauli ad Corinthios*, 327-28; citing 1 Tim 2:13-14.

sincere ministers of the gospel deserve from the church—men who teach and model true godliness both in word and deed. And by contrast, we should consider how great a plague on the church are false teachers, who lead men and women from the simplicity of the gospel to human corruption and so throw themselves headlong into certain damnation. Moreover, Paul's statement insinuates the proposition he has made previously, namely, that the Corinthians should be careful not to be deceived by the false prophets. For he considers that the clear outcome of the proposition will lead to danger and sure damnation—just as Eve fell away from grace and salvation. COMMENTARY ON 2 CORINTHIANS 11:3.[17]

PURE DEVOTION IN CHRIST. JOHN CALVIN: Now Paul says that he is concerned lest the minds of the Corinthians be corrupted from the simplicity that is "in Christ." It is true that, in Greek, Paul states *eis Christon*, which Erasmus renders as "toward Christ." But the Old Interpreter [Jerome] has come closer (in my opinion) to the mind of Paul because the simplicity which is said to be "in Christ" comprises the genuine and pure doctrine of the gospel and allows for no foreign corruption. By this, Paul intimates that people's minds are adulterated as soon as they turn away, even a little bit, from the pure doctrine of Christ. And rightly so, for who would not condemn a married woman of impurity as soon as she lends her ear to a pimp? So too when we listen to wicked and false teachers, who are Satan's pimps, we show by clear betrayal that we do not maintain conjugal fidelity toward Christ. And let us note the word *simplicity*, for Paul's fear was not that the Corinthians would soon openly and completely abandon Christ, but that, deviating little by little from that simplicity (which they had been taught) toward profane and foreign contrivances, they would finally be disgraced. COMMENTARY ON 2 CORINTHIANS 11:3.[18]

CHRIST ALONE HAS JUSTIFIED THE CHRISTIAN. PHILIPP MELANCHTHON: "Now if someone comes and preaches another Jesus." Why is it that the apostle maintains in Galatians: "Let those who are teaching any gospel other than [my] own be anathema," and here he says that the apostles were preaching another gospel? I answer: both passages have the same purpose. For the force of his argument is this: If Christ, whom I preached, did not justify you, then you are right to allow for another; but if he did justify you, why then do you seek another? We will reply to our [present-day] false apostles in exactly the same way: If Christ justifies, why then do you seek justification by means of works? ANNOTATIONS ON 2 CORINTHIANS 11:4.[19]

THERE IS ONLY ONE GOSPEL, ONE CHRIST, ONE SPIRIT. HEINRICH BULLINGER: Thus far, Paul has explained why he wanted the mind of the Corinthians to be bound to him alone, namely, because he was zealous for the name of Christ and was concerned that they might be perverted by the cunning of the false apostles. This also pertains to what now follows. Paul's sense is this: "It is not that you are enjoying companionship with some new teachers after me. But you would welcome other apostles even if they preach a different Christ and a different gospel to you. . . . This is altogether certain: either those apostles of yours preach the same thing that we preach to you, or they preach a different message. If they preach the same message, why do you despise us? Why do you prefer those apostles to us? If they preach a different message, they are actually imposters and good-for-nothings. Why do you have confidence in imposters while condemning faithful teachers? There is no other gospel than the one we preached to you. There is no other Christ and Spirit of God than the ones we taught, and which you received. Likewise, if anyone has proclaimed a gospel to you other than the one you received, let him be cursed!"

[17]Hemmingsen, *Commentaria in Omnes Epistolas Apostolorum*, 296-97.
[18]CO 50:124 (CTS 40:341-42).
[19]*Melanchthons Werke*, 4:130; citing Gal 1:9.

It is evident that this passage is against the papists who assert in the pope's name that not all things handed down for our salvation come from the apostles, so that they might more easily impose on men and women (who are persuaded and trapped by this sacrilege) these lies which they dignify and embellish with the title of apostolic tradition. Woe to these worthless imposters! There is one gospel; one Lord Christ; one Spirit and down payment for the faithful. Commentary on 2 Corinthians 11:4.[20]

Paul Rejects a False Gospel of Good Works. Cyriacus Spangenberg: Against this, St. Paul's opponents also taught about Jesus that one is saved through him, but only insofar as one is also circumcised and keeps the works of the law. This was another and not the true Jesus, "who came into the world to save sinners." The true Jesus is the only mediator between God and humankind and has made satisfaction for the sins of the whole world, and "has gone once into the sanctuary and has accomplished an eternal redemption."

From this it is now easy to judge whether they preach the true Jesus, who teach and write that good works are necessary for salvation, and therefore necessarily that without good works no one can be saved, and also that without the same no one has ever been saved. Also, those who write about the conversion and justification of humanity, and also in part free will and the remaining capacities of humanity, and alongside this always take the name of Jesus on their lips at the same time yet deny his power by their appended imaginings of reason and philosophy. Truly Paul did not teach such a half and incomplete Jesus who in his own enjoined work would need our cooperation and help and without the same could not achieve anything virtuous, as all his epistles prove. Forty-First Sermon.[21]

[20]Bullinger, *In Posteriorem . . . ad Corinthios Epistolam Commentarius*, 320.

[21]C. Spangenberg, *Die ander Epistel Pauli an die Corinthier*, 174; citing 1 Tim 1:15; Heb 9:12.

The Corinthians Too Quickly Disparage Paul and His Ministry. Tilemann Hesshus: Certainly, if anyone preaches another Christ, another Spirit, or another gospel, that person should under no circumstances be listened to. Why, then, does Paul say that their devotion was approved, if they were listening to another gospel? Paul's statement to the Galatians ought to be noted: "If anyone has taught another gospel, let them be anathema!" Therefore, this present passage should be taken otherwise, because when Paul says, "another Jesus, another Spirit," he means it no doubt in this sense: "If these new teachers announce something about our Lord Jesus Christ that is more fruitful than our message; if they explain the benefits of the mediator in a more illustrious fashion; if they propose a more excellent teaching of the Holy Spirit and bestow on you more splendid gifts by the laying on of hands; if they offer a clearer and more vigorous promise of the gospel—far be it from me to criticize your passion for learning, for that is something of which I would greatly approve. For nothing would please me more than to see you making great progress in the knowledge of God and the benefits of Christ. But in truth, I am not inferior to the greatest of the apostles, for I received my gospel by the revelation of Jesus Christ. I was in the third heaven and paradise. I have been instructed in the heavenly school. I have been endowed with no fewer gifts than the other apostles—who are considered to be pillars of the church—in the understanding of Scripture, the knowledge of tongues, and the faculty for performing miracles by the Holy Spirit. It is a sure fact that those new teachers are not able to convey more fruitful doctrine and a greater understanding of Christ's kingdom than what I imparted to you. Therefore, you Corinthians have acted imprudently when you have so quickly admired the new teachers and listened to the calumnies they have lodged against me. The rich and fruitful doctrine that I have passed on to you by the apostolic spirit, and the immense good that you have received from my ministry of the Holy Spirit, should rightly call you back from making any disparaging comments against me." Explication of 2 Corinthians 11:4-5.[22]

Paul's Ministry Reflects God's Favor. John Calvin: Paul now convicts them of ingratitude by removing the only thing that could serve as an excuse for them, for he demonstrates that he was on equal footing with those super apostles. The Corinthians were ungrateful, therefore, for not esteeming the apostle more highly, whom they had experienced as such. For the authority they rightly owed to Paul they transferred to men of no value. For the sake of modesty, nevertheless, Paul says that he "considers" to be the case, what was abundantly evident to everyone, for he recognizes that God had adorned his apostleship with no lesser marks of favor than John or Peter. Now the person who despises the gifts of God which God himself recognizes cannot clear himself of the charge of being spiteful and ungrateful. Therefore, whenever you see the gifts of God, you must reverence God himself there. Commentary on 2 Corinthians 11:5.[23]

Paul Again Appeals to His Authority. Andreas Hyperius: The proof of the preceding argument (namely, why they ought constantly to cling to Christ and the pure doctrine once for all handed down) comes from Paul's authority, which he wanted to be recognized from the comparison of his person to those other super apostles. Now he approaches and begins his case by announcing his authority a second time. For it is likely that the false apostles were advertising themselves as super apostles, or at least, they were boasting that they had been sent first by James and Peter, whereas Paul had not been sent by them. Wherefore, Paul wishes that his life and doctrine be compared with the life and doctrine of those other apostles, for he does not doubt that he would be found their equal, or at least not inferior to them (as he very modestly states). Now Paul does not say this to insult those other apostles, but more to convey the certainty of his authority. He freely submits his authority also to the others, but nevertheless, he does not want to be treated with contempt as his enemies were alleging and trying to prove to everyone. We learn from this that when someone is praised, or when someone boasts concerning their own virtues and deeds, nothing should be done in this to the prejudice of other people. For the gifts with which God endows them are also possessed by others, and just as no one has all the gifts, so few people are destitute of all gifts. Commentary on 2 Corinthians 11:5.[24]

Despite His Detractors, Paul Was Skilled as an Orator. Jacques Lefèvre d'Étaples: Paul concedes to his detractors that he is unskilled in speech, for they were mindful of human eloquence and knew only a single language. They considered Paul unskilled, ignorant, and inarticulate, though he knew all languages. But Paul's "lack of skill and ignorance" was abounding in knowledge. For because Paul knew all languages [*omnilinguis*], he frequently mixed in his discourse words that belonged to other languages—and because of this some people considered him uneducated and ignorant of speech, though this resulted not from ignorance but from the knowledge of manifold languages. . . . Now if someone who is Latin, and at the same time Greek, were to print [a book] in the language of Greco-Latin, a person who is Latin alone would consider this ignorant and unskilled writing. But, truly, a person who knows both languages would say that what seemed to be unskillful writing abounds in knowledge. And this is surely what happened to Paul, who does not seem to follow the customary pattern of speaking. . . .

Indeed, I believe if Paul had desired to follow the pure pattern of speaking, characteristic of Demosthenes or some other very well-spoken

[22]Hesshus, *Explicatio Secundae Epistolae Pauli ad Corinthios*, 249v-250v; citing Gal 1:9.
[23]CO 50:125 (CTS 40:343-44).

[24]Hyperius, *Commentarii . . . in Epistolam D. Pauli ad Romanos, et Utramque ad Corinthios*, 411.

person, he could have surpassed the orator in such eloquence. Even [Lorenzo] Valla,† known as the most perceptive critic of languages, . . . observed the charge against Paul concerning improper word usage: "You do not take into consideration true Greek," he says, "the language which Paul spoke accurately. He surpassed no less than Demosthenes himself in presenting the majesty of subjects with words both appropriate and elegant." Thus Valla's statement. Likewise, Eusebius‡ says, "Paul was considered the most eloquent among all the apostles and was very powerful in his words and expression." COMMENTARY ON 2 CORINTHIANS 11:6.[25]

TRUE KNOWLEDGE IS FOUNDED ON THE CROSS. PHILIPP MELANCHTHON: "Although I am unskilled in speech, nevertheless I am not so in knowledge." Just as in 1 Corinthians Paul says, "Not with the wisdom of words, so that the cross of Christ will not be emptied," so here he says that he is unskilled in speech; that is, he does not contend by means of natural judgment or reason. I call natural judgment that understanding of sacred matters which is only literal, not spiritual. But true knowledge is the experience of spiritual things, or the knowledge of the cross of Christ. Again, as he says: "I knew nothing except Jesus and him crucified!" Moreover, the knowledge of the cross is the knowledge of sin and righteousness. ANNOTATIONS ON 2 CORINTHIANS 11:6.[26]

KNOWLEDGE IS MORE IMPORTANT THAN ELOQUENCE. WOLFGANG MUSCULUS: Paul does not say that he is unskilled in speaking—for that was not the case. Rather, speaking concessively, he says "*even if* I am unskilled in speaking, which is the claim those people are throwing at me." Elsewhere, in Acts 14, we read that Paul was a master of words to such an extent that the Gentiles mistook him for Mercury. And nevertheless, the apostle is not proudly arguing about who uses more elegant words, which the false apostles were making much of. For it is not as important in the church of Christ that the minister employs splendid rhetoric than that he possesses a knowledge of divine things and proclaims seriously and faithfully indispensable knowledge with intelligible words. Some people strive after worldly eloquence, while others employ such worldly eloquence unprofitably in the church. The story of the philosopher is well known who, after engaging in a long disputation with well-educated bishops that accomplished nothing, then listened to a certain godly and unskilled old man make a simple speech, delivered reverently from the heart, which won over his conscience. The philosopher said: "When you were interacting with me with words, I was repaying your words with words, and what you were saying was undermined by the art of speaking. But when, instead of words, power came forth from the mouth of the person speaking, no words were able to resist this power. For a human cannot fight against God."† . . . Nevertheless, I do not wish to be a defender of those who, for this reason, belittle the purity of speech and are distinguished for their ignorance. COMMENTARY ON 2 CORINTHIANS 11:6.[27]

PAUL'S ELOQUENCE. THE ENGLISH ANNOTATIONS: St. Paul did not lack the sort of eloquence that was appropriate for an apostle of Christ and the gospel, but he willingly avoided that kind of painted speech and those rhetorical strains about which the false apostles bragged so much. Although St. Jerome in his third letter to the Ephesians notes certain solecisms, hyperboles, and deficiencies in St. Paul's manner of expressing himself, yet St. Augustine† in *De doctrina Christiana* and St. Chrysostom‡ in his comments, and even Jerome in his *Epistles*,§ highly extol St. Paul's

[25]Lefèvre, *Commentariorum in Epistolas Beati Pauli . . . Liber Tertius*, 140v-141r. †Lorenzo Valla (1407–1457) was one of the most important humanists and biblical scholars of his day. ‡The fourth-century church historian Eusebius praises Paul's eloquence in his *Ecclesiastical History*.

[26]*Melanchthons Werke*, 4:130-31; citing 1 Cor 1:17; 2:2.

[27]Musculus, *Commentarius . . . in posteriorem epistolam Pauli ad Corinthios*, 332; citing Acts 14:12. †This story comes from Rufinus, *Ecclesiastical History* 1.3.

eloquence. In fact, few if any have ever attained the level of Paul's eloquence, which proceeded not from the study of rhetoric, nor was learned in the schools, but was given him by the Spirit. Annotations on 2 Corinthians 11:6.[28]

Paul Accommodated His Speech to His Audience. John Trapp: "Even if I am rude in speech." The Greek word is *idiot*, a person who speaks in a plain, forthright, homespun and homely manner. Ancient Christians busied themselves (says Cyril) "not with contrived and newly devised language, but with solid demonstrations drawn out of holy Scriptures."[†] Jerome reports of Didymus that he was an apostle-like writer, as you might easily gather from his style, for "his substance was as lofty as his language was low and ordinary."[‡] Jerome himself is commended greatly by learned people . . . though he is not always so curious and careful in his choice of words. But I do not see the reason why Jerome censures St. Paul as sharply as he does "for his intricate sense, his dark elocution, and his unskillfulness in the grammatical arts." It is true that Paul was a plain preacher, as he here acknowledges. The reason why he affects this plain style, he tells us in 1 Corinthians 1, was to accommodate himself to the capacities of simple people. But Acts 17:22 and Acts 26 show that he could also assume the role of an orator when he wanted to. And in Acts 14, the Lycaonians called him Mercury because he was a master of speech. And as for his epistles, there is as good a rhetoric found in them as in any heathen orator. Demosthenes is but dull when compared to him. And Augustine's wish was to see "Paul preaching," which he would have considered to be a great happiness. Commentary on 2 Corinthians 11:6.[29]

11:7-11 *Paul Preached the Gospel Free of Charge*

Paul's Humility. Tilemann Hesshus: The world is accustomed to hold in contempt people who behave modestly and do not preach themselves with splendid words. So, too, the world is suspicious of those who do not try to promote themselves and it admires those who magnify themselves to first place, for it loves display and ostentation. Now, the same thing was also happening among the Corinthians, where the false apostles, who were snobbishly boasting about themselves, were held in high esteem and recognized as such. Now Paul was humbling himself so that he might instruct the Corinthians by his example how one should live in Christ's kingdom—and for that very fact the false apostles condemned him, since Paul's humility (as a virtue most worthy of praise) might be responsible for arousing the Corinthians to a burning love for the apostle. For humility elicits extraordinary favor among men and women, as long as it is from the heart, without pretense or a desire for profit, nor thrusting itself forward. And indeed, Paul humbled himself to the advantage of the Corinthians, no doubt so that he himself might be lifted up—that is, so that the Corinthians might perceive fully his pious teaching and might be more blessed imitating the modesty of Paul and closer to the kingdom of Christ. Explication of 2 Corinthians 11:7.[30]

People Despise Free Gifts. Wolfgang Musculus: Now Paul is seen here explaining how he humiliated himself so that the Corinthians might be exalted, namely, by preaching the gospel without charge. . . . Nothing can ever be received in this world both more useful and precious, which is worthy of greater honor, than what the apostle had given to the Corinthians free of charge. But this humility had produced contempt, not only of his

[28]Downame, ed., *English Annotations*, GG2v-GG3r*. [†]See Augustine, *On Christian Doctrine* 4.7 (NPNF[1] 2:577-78). [‡]Chrysostom, *Homilies on 2 Corinthians* (NPNF[1] 12:385-86). [§]Jerome seems to more often complain about Paul's Greek. For example, in *Against Rufinus*, Jerome says Paul "showed contempt for Greek eloquence, or at least kept quiet about it because of his humility" (NPNF[1] 12:385).

[29]Trapp, *A Commentary or Exposition*, 729-30*; citing 1 Cor 1:17; Acts 17:22-31; 26:2; 14:12. [†]Cyril of Jerusalem expresses this sentiment in his catechetical lectures. See lecture 12.16, NPNF[2] 7:76. [‡]Jerome, *Preface to Didymus on the Holy Spirit*, NPNF[2] 3:470.

[30]Hesshus, *Explicatio Secundae Epistolae Pauli ad Corinthios*, 252r-v.

person but also of the gospel of God which he had preached without charge. This same thing happens today in evangelical churches where, though it costs very little, the entire ministry of the gospel is shown little esteem. Such trifles (as we perceived them) were given generously to the papacy when it wasn't reformed. Such is the perversity of our flesh. Heaven itself becomes worthless if it is offered free of charge, and it is thought that God is not generous unless he sells his good gifts or imparts only what is well-deserved. Commentary on 2 Corinthians 11:7.[31]

The Reason Paul Preached Free of Charge. Huldrych Zwingli: Paul proclaimed the gospel to the Corinthians free and without cost for a clear reason, namely, so that he might remove from the false apostles any opportunity for accusation. For since they were preaching only for the sake of their stomachs, they did not dare to make a lot of noise concerning their wicked wages that they were receiving from it. Annotations on 2 Corinthians 11:7.[32]

The Unreasonableness of the False Apostles' Accusations. Niels Hemmingsen: By means of a question and a statement of surprise, Paul sets forth two accusations that the false apostles were making. First, they objected (when he was absent) to the contemptible nature of the apostle's person, namely, because he made himself too familiar with everyone and he even submitted himself to the least important people so as to exalt them, that is, so that he might lead them to knowledge in Christ. Second, because he preached the gospel free of charge when others received remuneration. He shows how unfair both of these accusations were. He asks, "Does a person sin who humbles himself so that he might exalt others? Is a person blameworthy who preaches the gospel free of charge so as to avoid scandal?" Both of these, of course, are an obligation of the office. Why is it necessary for a person, who is both wicked and spiteful, to seek an opportunity to slander? Paul is by no means laying down a law for ministers of the Word by his example of abstaining from remuneration—except for those facing a similar situation to his. And the papists do not rightly construct from this example works of supererogation, since Paul did nothing other than what his duty required. For all ministers of God should avoid scandals as much as possible so that the edification of the church might not be hampered by them. Commentary on 2 Corinthians 11:7.[33]

Ministers Must Have an Honorable Profession. John Trapp: "I have preached to you freely." Because Paul earns his living from his hands so that he might preach free of charge, [the Corinthians] despised him as a lowly manual laborer. This is the world's wages: Nothing is as unhappy as poverty. . . . Ministers must have an honorable profession (and not be forced to weave for a living, as Musculus[†] did, or to serve as a mason, as another great scholar) or else they will be viewed shamefully. Commentary on 2 Corinthians 11:7.[34]

Spoils of Spiritual Victory. John Calvin: "I robbed other churches." I think that Paul has intentionally used an offensive term to express better the indignity of being condemned by the Corinthians. He says, "I have obtained payment from the spoils of others so that I might serve you. Since I have spared you the expense, how shameful it is that you pay me back so badly!" Now, this is a metaphor taken from what is customary among soldiers; for as conquerors seize spoils from the nations they have conquered, so everything Paul took from the churches that he had won to Christ

[31]Musculus, *Commentarius . . . in posteriorem epistolam Pauli ad Corinthios*, 335.
[32]Zwingli, *Annotatiunculae . . . ex ore Zvinglij*, 188.

[33]Hemmingsen, *Commentaria in Omnes Epistolas Apostolorum*, 298.
[34]Trapp, *A Commentary or Exposition*, 730*. [†]After arriving in Strasbourg as a religious refugee in 1527, the reformer and biblical scholar Wolfgang Musculus supported his family for a time by working as a weaver.

were like spoils of his victory—although he would never have taken it against their will, but what they freely gave was in a sense due by right of spiritual warfare. COMMENTARY ON 2 CORINTHIANS 11:8.[35]

THE GENEROSITY OF THE MACEDONIAN CHURCHES. NIELS HEMMINGSEN: Paul recognizes that the Macedonian churches, which were experiencing poverty, were also more generous toward ministers of the gospel. Now, when he says that he has robbed the churches, it ought to be understood in this way: whatever godly people freely contribute to the sustenance of gospel ministers is like a debt that is rightly owed for spiritual warfare. For those who proclaim the Word liberate men and women by preaching the gospel and spiritual warfare, and they subject to Christ those who were previously subject to Satan. With these words, Paul is also somewhat critical of the ingratitude of the Corinthians who allowed that he should receive financial support from other churches even though he was serving them. Many people imitate their example today, who, experiencing severe poverty like the Macedonians, give generous support to ministers serving other churches. COMMENTARY ON 2 CORINTHIANS 11:8.[36]

PAUL'S GOOD WORK OF SUPEREROGATION. CARDINAL CAJETAN: This clause ought to be read in light of the same question: "Did I sin because I plundered other churches, receiving remuneration from them, so that I might minister among you?" Paul is heaping up objections that even his rivals were not making, for they would hardly make the accusation against Paul that he was evangelizing the Corinthians without financial support, because they demanded such support for themselves. Now Paul not only reports that his action is free from sin (rather it is a supererogatory good work), but he adds how zealous he was concerning this that he received financial support from foreign churches when he came to the Corinthians. And he speaks of "plundering" the foreign churches not only for their benefit, but for the benefit of the Corinthians who were receiving from them. And he said this to blunt the distraction of rivalry from every side. Now, if in fact, the false apostles were slandering Paul for proclaiming the gospel to the Corinthians without remuneration, they would be twisting the facts to denigrate Paul's authority, claiming he has no power to exact remuneration. Paul refutes this argument by adding that he received support from foreign churches not only when he was preaching to those churches, but also when he was preaching to the Corinthians—which indicated greater authority. COMMENTARY ON 2 CORINTHIANS 11:8.[37]

PAUL "ROBBED" POORER CHURCHES. THE ENGLISH ANNOTATIONS: It was lawful for St. Paul to receive a stipend for his labors in the ministry, yet because, when he preached in Corinth, he received wages to defray his necessary expenses from other poor churches, he calls this (by way of metaphor) "robbing them," for he received from these other churches what they could not easily spare. This support he should have instead received from the Corinthians with whom he resided and among whom he then exercised his ministry—they should have supplied his needs. ANNOTATIONS ON 2 CORINTHIANS 11:8.[38]

TOO FEW MACEDONIANS TODAY! JOHN CALVIN: Observe, however, that he says that he had suffered poverty, for he would never have been a burden to them had he not been forced by poverty. Nevertheless, in the meantime, he labored with his hands, as we have seen before. But as the manual labor was not sufficient to sustain his life, something additional was contributed by the Macedonians. Additionally, he does not say that the means of his livelihood was supplied by the

[35]CO 50:127 (CTS 40:347).
[36]Hemmingsen, *Commentaria in Omnes Epistolas Apostolorum*, 298.
[37]Cajetan, *In Posteriorem Pauli Epistolam ad Corinthios Commentarii*, 191-92.
[38]Downame, ed., *English Annotations*, GG34*.

Macedonians, but only that they supplied what was lacking. We have spoken elsewhere about the holy apostle's prudence and diligence in guarding against dangers. Here, we must note the godly zeal of the Macedonians who did not hesitate to contribute from their resources for his support, so that the gospel might be proclaimed to others—even those wealthier than they were. Oh, how few Macedonians there are today, and how many Corinthians are found everywhere! Commentary on 2 Corinthians 11:9.[39]

Paul Indirectly Reprimands the False Apostles. Niels Hemmingsen: That which Paul said briefly he repeats in greater detail here, and he adds two things. First, that the reason for his inactivity was not due to his condition and apathy toward others; rather, he did not want to be a burden to those Corinthians. By this statement, Paul was reprimanding somewhat the false apostles who (since their appetites were listless) were living freely off other people's resources. Second, he says that in the future he will do nothing to be a burden to the Corinthians—which he also said with respect to the false apostles, who could perhaps misrepresent the things he was saying, as if Paul were enraged at the Corinthians for not contributing support, or at least provoking them to greater generosity. Commentary on 2 Corinthians 11:9.[40]

The Corinthians' Miserliness Did Not Slacken Paul's Zeal. The English Annotations: The Greek commentator asserts that word in the original, *katenarkēsa*, signifies a fainting or slackness, coldness, or numbness. And the apostle's meaning is this, that though he was in great need when he preached to the Corinthians, and was not supplied by them, yet his zeal was in no way cooled, nor did his industry slacken. In no way did he flag in his ministry, nor did he solicit or pressure the Corinthians to give him financial assistance, though they withheld their bounty from him. Annotations on 2 Corinthians 11:9.[41]

The Truth of Christ Was in Paul. Wolfgang Musculus: The truth of Christ was in the apostle in a number of ways. First, inasmuch as the Spirit of Christ (who is the Spirit of truth) was in Paul, he could not be defeated by the world. Second, Paul possessed the knowledge and understanding of the mystery of Christ, by which the truth of Christ is known. Third, Paul loved the knowledge of the truth and did a great number of things out of the feeling of his heart. Fourth, the truth of Christ was in his mouth through the ministry of the Word because he was preaching Christ. The first three of these are common to all believers; the fourth applies specifically to the ministry of the Word. Even so the fourth is not completely foreign to believers, who also have the truth of Christ in their mouths when they exalt with praises and proclaim the grace and truth acquired from Christ. Commentary on 2 Corinthians 11:10.[42]

Paul Seeks to Distance His Ministry from the False Apostles. Tilemann Hesshus: It is a kind of oath-giving when says: "The truth of Christ is in me," that is, "I want you to believe me that the truth of Christ is in me, so that no doubts concerning my situation will be published about me that might impair or silence my boasting in the regions of Achaia." For he once again announced among them that he did not want to take any remuneration from the Corinthians so that he might be able to boast that he was serving the Corinthians and the churches in Achaia without cost. Now, lest anyone suspect that Paul did not want to receive any remuneration from the Corinthians out of his contempt or hatred for them, Paul explains that the reason underlying his decision is far different. He gives witness to God of

[39]CO 50:127 (CTS 40:348).
[40]Hemmingsen, *Commentaria in Omnes Epistolas Apostolorum*, 298.
[41]Downame, ed., *English Annotations*, GG3r*.
[42]Musculus, *Commentarius . . . in posteriorem epistolam Pauli ad Corinthios*, 340.

his love toward the Corinthians. He says that the reason for his decision to accept no remuneration from the Corinthians was so that all occasion for boasting might be cut off from the false apostles, as if they were equal in ministry with Paul—for Paul knew that the false apostles would not abstain from remuneration. Therefore, Paul preaches the gospel to the Corinthians free of charge so that he might demonstrate his burning zeal for them. He advises that it is proper for faithful ministers to remain focused on advancing the course of the gospel, adorning their ministries, and refuting false teachers, so that they might never neglect any opportunity to build up the church. Explication of 2 Corinthians 11:10.[43]

Paul's Careful Response to His Enemies. Andreas Hyperius: The reason why Paul does not accept the slanders of his enemies is included for close scrutiny. Paul's enemies were slandering him harshly because (as we suggested earlier) some people did not want to accept the apostle because he did not love them from the heart. For we accept things reluctantly from those whom we do not love. Therefore, he exposes this slander by close examination, saying, "But why do we accept nothing from you? Is it because" (as his enemies claim) "we do not love you?" Paul responds by adding an explanation: "Nothing of the sort! Certainly, we love you intensely, as God himself, who sees the heart, very well knows." Then, in the words that follow, Paul at last explains why he accepted nothing from them. Commentary on 2 Corinthians 11:11.[44]

Paul Swears of His Love for the Corinthians. John Calvin: We treat with greater familiarity those whom we love. Lest the Corinthians, therefore, should take it as an insult that he refused their generosity while he allowed himself to be supported by the Macedonians—and even uttered an oath that he would do so in the future—he anticipates that suspicion also. And employing the rhetorical figure of *anthypophora*,[†] he asks (as if employing their voice) whether this was an indication of a hostile mind? Paul does not respond directly to this question, but his indirect response has far more weight, inasmuch as he calls God to be a witness of his good will toward them. You see here that these three verses contain two oaths, but they are lawful and holy because they have a good end in view and a legitimate reason is involved. Therefore, to condemn indiscriminately all oaths is to play the part of fanatics,[‡] who make no distinction between white and black. Commentary on 2 Corinthians 11:11.[45]

The Minister's Love Must Be Known. John Trapp: "Because I love you not?" It should be a minister's concern to preserve in the hearts of his people the recognition that he loves them. For if they once conceive an incurable prejudice against him, thinking he hates them or some such thing, there's no good that will come of it. Commentary on 2 Corinthians 11:11.[46]

11:12-15 *False Apostles Masquerade as Angels of Light*

The False Apostles Are Dangerous Imposters. Desiderius Erasmus: As a matter of fact, these men do not preach the gospel sincerely, but for their own profit and pride. Moreover, although they have not been sent by Christ, and do not do his work, nevertheless they falsely claim for themselves the honor of the name "apostle." They pretend that they have been hired for the Lord's vineyard, to undertake his cause through their own efforts, although they obstruct his work,

[43] Hesshus, *Explicatio Secundae Epistolae Pauli ad Corinthios*, 254r-v. [44] Hyperius, *Commentarii . . . in Epistolam D. Pauli ad Romanos, et Utramque ad Corinthios*, 410-11.

[45] CO 50:128 (CTS 40:348-49). [†] According to Charlton Lewis and Charles Short, ed., *A Latin Dictionary* (Oxford: Oxford University Press, 1991), 131, *antypophora* is a "rhetorical figure in which one anticipates the arguments of his antagonist and refutes them." [‡] This is an allusion to Anabaptists, many of whom refused to participate in oaths of any kind for any reason. [46] Trapp, *A Commentary or Exposition*, 730*.

and attend to the affairs of their belly under pretext of gospel teaching, while foisting in certain dogmas of their own. They are just like people who mix deadly poison with the most exquisite wine, in order the more effectively to deceive. Meanwhile, masquerading as apostles—the better to impose upon the naive, under the pretext of authority and the shadow of a great name—they are actors more truly than apostles. This, however, is the most pernicious kind of imposture: under the pretense of piety, to implant the poison of impiety. Paraphrases on 2 Corinthians 11.[47]

The Reasons Paul Rejects Financial Provision. Heinrich Bullinger: Paul explains in greater clarity how he excels those other apostles in these matters, and at the same time, he answers why he does not accept any wage or remuneration from the Corinthians. He says that it is not because he hates their gifts, but because he wants to snatch every opportunity away from the false apostles lest they claim to be equal to Paul and boast that they are similar to him. Now in this passage, Paul employs a tedious form of speech [*macrologia*] which makes its meaning less clear. And he strengthens his argument by appealing to all the things that the Corinthians consider most weighty. It is possible to understand these words in this sense: "I am accepting nothing from you so that the false apostles won't consider themselves to surpass us. For if they were preaching free of charge (with their resources being fully furnished by other people) this would show that they surpassed us. Now, because they are boasting about this, I wish that they might receive nothing from you . . . nay rather, that they might be like us also, who are receiving nothing from them." But this interpretation is at variance with that which soon follows: "You put up with it if someone plunges you into servitude, if someone preys on you, if someone takes from you." For this reason, Ambrose[†] does not interpret Paul carelessly when he states that Paul refuses the offer of financial provision for two reasons. First, so that he would not be thought similar to the false apostles, who were preaching, not for God's glory, but for their own benefit, so that the Corinthians might not have any chance for being robbed. The second reason for not accepting [remuneration] is that no one can demand a lot without their vigor of gospel power becoming listless. For the person who receives [gifts] from sinners loses authority to denounce their wrongdoing. Therefore, people are to be praised when they do not accept so much from others that, once corrected, they can be raised up from death to life. Thus, the first interpretation seems to be more accurate. Commentary on 2 Corinthians 11:12.[48]

In Every Way, Paul Surpasses the False Apostles. Andreas Hyperius: Paul explains the reason why he wished to receive no remuneration, namely, lest his opponents, who were seeking an opportunity to seize and snatch glory for themselves, might seem to have surpassed him in some matters, or at least to be his equal. Certainly, in this matter they were not equals to Paul, nor could they boast against him, because he was receiving nothing. And the fact that Paul was receiving absolutely nothing, and that those opponents were always voraciously collecting a lot from various people, is stated more clearly a little later. And Paul very modestly says, "that they may be discovered to be as we are." He does not say, "that they may be discovered to be inferior to us," but "to be as we are"—that is, not at all superior—since Paul, actually, would leave them far behind, not only in this matter of not accepting remuneration but also in all other matters. Commentary on 2 Corinthians 11:12.[49]

Satan Sends Deceitful Workers. Wolfgang Musculus: We should hardly be surprised

[47]CWE 43:267-68.

[48]Bullinger, *In Posteriorem D. Pauli Corinthios Epistolam Commentarius*, 323. [†]For Ambrose's interpretation, see PL 17:341-42.

[49]Hyperius, *Commentarii . . . in Epistolam D. Pauli ad Romanos, et Utramque ad Corinthios*, 411.

if the false apostles, these deceitful workers, were dressed in the appearance of the apostles of Christ, since Satan himself is disguised as an angel of light. It is not a great thing, therefore, if the ministers of Satan also copy his example, feigning that they are ministers of righteousness. Their end will correspond to their deeds. Now Paul first expresses who it is who desires the opportunity [to be considered equal to him], namely, the false apostles. "For such men are false apostles," he says. Second, Paul gives the reason why he is eager to remove from them the opportunity they are seeking: "Because they are deceitful workers," he says. Third, Paul explains the nature of their deceit, saying that they "disguise themselves as apostles of Christ and ministers of righteousness." Fourth, Paul says that, as the ministers of Satan, they imitate his clever devices. Fifth, Paul threatens them with the destruction they deserve. Commentary on 2 Corinthians 11:13-15.[50]

The Satanic Wiles of the False Apostles. David Dickson: Paul here shows the necessity of his boasting because the wickedness of these pretenders forced him to this boasting. For they pretended that they were apostles of Christ and workers in the vineyard of God, when in fact they only cared about their own business, not God's. They preached the gospel for profit's sake and for their own honor. They pretended that they were ministers of Christ, when in fact they were only like stage actors. And this should not surprise us, seeing that these deceivers were apostles of Satan, imitating the devil (who sometimes assumes the form of a celestial angel, that under the pretense of zeal and piety he might beguile people) whose conduct these pretenders emulated. They talked about the glory of Christ, when in fact they sacrificed all their effort to their belly, to their purse, to their honor, caring nothing for what happened to the apostles or the churches but only about their own desires. That is why the apostle threatens them with eternal death, which is what they deserved. Exposition of 2 Corinthians 11:13-15.[51]

Satan's Schemes Against the Church. Tilemann Hesshus: So that the Corinthians might be all the more diligent in guarding themselves against the false apostles, Paul describes their schemes and tricks. Believers are very secure; as long as they have the ministry of the Spirit, and hear godly sermons, they should recognize there is no danger. And certainly, there is great happiness being a member of the true church and to hear God speaking in the ministry of the Spirit. But their minds must always be on the alert to avoid the traps of Satan, for he is not inactive. The more vigorous they are with enthusiasm for right doctrine, the more energetically Satan works to disturb that enthusiasm, or he uses clever devices to insult God. The more the condition of the church flourishes somewhat, the more Satan plots clever tricks and employs fanatical spirits who cause dissension. Therefore, we must pay careful attention to how we hear and be vigilant lest, by our recklessness, we are subverted by imposters.

Paul calls the false apostles deceitful workers, who apply themselves entirely to distress the church with their deceits. They do not serve in good faith to illuminate the glory of God and build up the church, but they always seek their own good and disparage the authority of faithful teachers. They alone wish to be admired by everyone and held in high esteem. Their lips are softer than butter, yet nevertheless they plot warfare in their heart. They display great godliness before others, while they haughtily despise the judgments and commandments of God and condemn his supreme authority. They pretend that they have a burning zeal to liberate men and women from wicked errors, while in the meantime they attempt to seduce them from the truth and imbue them with false opinions. . . . Such was Eusebius of Nicomedia,† the court preacher of Arianism. Such was

[50]Musculus, *Commentarius . . . in posteriorem epistolam Pauli ad Corinthios*, 345.

[51]Dickson, *An Exposition of All St. Paul's Epistles*, 88*.

Severian,[‡] the deacon of Chrysostom. Such was the monk Pelagius.[§] And nearly all heretics have this spirit as well. Thus, they cannot be recognized immediately on first appearance. Christ himself teaches in Matthew 7 in what way and by what tricks false teachers transform themselves into apostles of Christ: "They come to you," he says, "in sheep's clothing but inwardly they are ravenous wolves." Explication of 2 Corinthians 11:13.[52]

External Appearances Often Deceive. Niels Hemmingsen: Paul demonstrates by the false apostles' innate character the clever devices they employed to appear like true apostles. For he says that they are workers, to be sure, but the sort who employ all kinds of deceit. And thus, if one only considers their external appearance, they would seem to be most certainly apostles of Christ. For hypocrites make their external appearances look attractive, when, in the meantime, their minds lie cloaked in various opinions and their affections are enslaved to ungodliness. Now, "to transfigure" or "to transform" is nothing other than to make one's outer appearance attractive, so that what a person seems on the outside is different than what is within the heart. We should be warned, therefore, not to allow ourselves to be deceived by external masks of this sort. Commentary on 2 Corinthians 11:13.[53]

False Teachers Disguise Themselves with Lofty Titles. John Trapp: The Manichees[†] derived their name from *manna*, because they held that whatsoever they taught was to be received as food from heaven. Montanus[‡] said that he was the Comforter. . . . Novatus[§] called himself Moses, and claimed one of his brothers was Aaron. The Family of Love set[◊] out their Kingdom of the Gospel. The Swenckfeldians[Δ] (Luther called them *Stinckfeldians* because of his bad opinion of them) called themselves by that glorious name, the Confessors of the Glory of Christ. Commentary on 2 Corinthians 11:13.[54]

Satan Cloaks Himself as an Angel of Light. Jacques Lefèvre d'Étaples: When the spirit of darkness deceives curious people, he calls himself an angel of light and a good spirit of God. And the person deceived by this spirit, even if they should acknowledge openly that they have an evil spirit, will be trusted as a good angel by those who have a python spirit (which is the worst form of idolatry). Yes, they pretend that they are angels of light, that is, that they are transforming themselves into angels of light. So also those who are workers of wickedness, who misuse exorcisms, consecrations, hymns, and incense, and who profane the divine names—these people consider themselves to be good angels who are able to summon celestial powers. Nevertheless, all of these people are soldiers fighting on behalf of the prince of this world and under the ruler of darkness. Commentary on 2 Corinthians 11:14.[55]

---

[52]Hesshus, *Explicatio Secundae Epistolae Pauli ad Corinthios*, 255r-256r; citing Mt 7:15. [†]Eusebius of Nicomedia was a leader of the Arian group in the fourth century who baptized Emperor Constantine on his deathbed in AD 337. [‡]Severian of Gabala was a popular preacher in Constantinople around 400 who opposed Chrysostom. [§]Pelagius (born c. 360) was a British monk who was confronted by Augustine and condemned by the Synod of Carthage (418) for rejecting the doctrine of original sin and affirming instead that human beings possess unhindered free will and are able to achieve salvation without God's grace.

[53]Hemmingsen, *Commentaria in Omnes Epistolas Apostolorum*, 299.

[54]Trapp, *A Commentary or Exposition*, 730*. [†]Manichaeism (founded by the prophet Mani in the third century) was a religious movement that rejected the unique claims of Christianity and posited a dualistic cosmology that posited a good spirit world and evil material world. [‡]Montanus was a second-century Christian prophet who founded a sectarian community in Asia Minor characterized by asceticism, apocalyptic expectation, and spiritual gifts. [§]Novatian (c. 200–258) was a Roman presbyter whose rigorist attitude toward Christians who had lapsed during persecution led to his excommunication and the formation of a sectarian church named after him. [◊]The Family of Love was a sixteenth-century mystical sect, founded by Henry Nicholis, that rejected infant baptism and the orthodox doctrine of the Trinity. [Δ]Caspar Schwenckfeld (1490–1561) was a Silesian mystic and theologian who parted company from the magisterial Protestant reformers in his rejection of infant baptism, oath-taking, and the visible institutional church, as well as his teaching of the deification of Christ's humanity.

[55]Lefèvre, *Commentariorum in Epistolas Beati Pauli . . . Liber Tertius*, 141r-141v.

True Angels. Wolfgang Musculus: Paul does not simply say, "he disguises himself as an angel," but "he disguises himself as an angel of light." Satan is by nature a spirit just as are the angels of light. Angels are those creatures sent from God to undertake some task of his, for the word *angel* means "messenger." That evil spirit was an angel who was sent to deceive the wicked king Ahab to be a lying spirit in the mouth of all of Ahab's prophets. The mission was what made him an angel, but he was not an angel of light but of darkness and error. An angel of light is a minister of truth and a messenger of the grace of God. That is what Gabriel was, who was sent to the Blessed Virgin; we read the same thing about the angels who proclaimed the gospel to the shepherds. In a similar fashion, angels were sent to announce the resurrection to the women, and they appeared to the patriarchs and prophets, to Christ and the apostles. Though Satan can disguise himself, he cannot transform himself into an angel of this sort. Thus, the deceiving spirit that God used to punish Ahab disguised himself as an angel of light, as if he was a spirit of truth. Through these disguises, Satan has attacked the churches with all kinds of errors, ungodliness, superstitions, false worship, and idolatry. Commentary on 2 Corinthians 11:14.[56]

Satan's Work Is Discerned by Its Fruit. Pilgram Marpeck: Whoever therefore establishes, commands, prohibits, coerces, punishes, or judges before the time the good or evil fruit is revealed lays claim to the authority, power, and office of the Holy Spirit of the Lord Jesus Christ and, contrary to love, goodness, and grace runs ahead of Christ Jesus. For the Son of God himself has committed this office and work to the Holy Spirit of God, and the office is to be carried out after his earthly, human life has ended. With reference to this work he says, "The Holy Spirit will come and judge because of sin, judgment, and righteousness," judging and searching hearts, for the Holy Spirit works good fruits in the children of light to reveal them before all. Similarly, the spirit of wickedness, who often and in many ways disguises himself as the spirit of light, has his work in the children of darkness. These too are driven by the Holy Spirit to do their own deeds in order that by the power and finger of God they may be known and revealed by their fruits. Concerning Hasty Judgments and Verdicts.[57]

Ministers of Christ and Ministers of Satan. Niels Hemmingsen: In a similar fashion, Paul demonstrates with a suitable example that the false apostles are transforming themselves into apostles of Christ. This is clear in the case of Satan, who not only destroyed our first parents under the appearance of holiness and friendship, but also, in every age thereafter, brought in idolatry to the ruin of humankind. If he would have immediately dissuaded men and women from every religion, there would have been those who recognized his horns (as it is customary to say). But now, Satan seems to be very enthusiastic about the salvation of men and women and, as an angel of light, he establishes various religions. But in the meantime, he kills men and women by trickery and deception. The account of Pope Gregory[†] is well known, to whom Satan offered visions of the dead so that he might institute that horrible and blasphemous Mass for the dead. . . . Thereafter, Satan contrived many other things in the kingdom of the antichrist, by which the kingdom of Christ was secretly and deceptively attacked. The ministers of Satan are not that dissimilar from those of Christ's. They want to be called priests of God, a servant of servants, successors of the apostles, pillars of the church, instruments of the Holy Spirit—so that whatever they say is considered to be an article of faith. Therefore, being warned by this statement of Paul's, let us learn to distinguish rightly between true ministers and those who falsely usurp this title for themselves and wish to be seen as ministers of

[56]Musculus, *Commentarius . . . in posteriorem epistolam Pauli ad Corinthios*, 347; citing 1 Kings 22:21-22; Lk 1:26-38; 2:8-14; 24:1-7.

[57]CRR 12:153; citing Jn 10:8.

Christ, even though they are false apostles. For false apostles are those who feign that they are apostles when they are not, even as the false Christ is the one who fakes that he is Christ and Messiah, when he is not. Commentary on 2 Corinthians 11:14-15.[58]

Antidote to Satan's Schemes. Martin Chemnitz: So that the devil may have no excuse to seek us out, the Scripture gives us two remedies. For Satan goes after us in two ways; either through tricks or traps, like "an angel of light," or through the use of raw power. An antidote to the first method is what Paul says in 2 Corinthians 2, 1 Timothy 6, and 2 Timothy 2. Believers must recover their senses, return to a sober life, be brought back to a sound mind; or as Luther renders it in his Bible, [*nüchtern warden*] be made sober, freed from the devil's harness, that is, that we may throw off our bonds. Loci Theologici.[59]

Satan as an Angel of Light. The English Annotations: An "angel of light" is a good and holy one, partaking of the brightness of celestial glory, living and dwelling in that same glory, whereas the evil angels are confined to everlasting darkness. Now Satan may be said to transform himself into an angel of light, either when he assumes for himself a luminous body (as if he were an angel of heaven), or when he suggests things that seem to favor piety, zeal, and holiness—thereby giving the impression that these things proceed from a holy and blessed angel. Whereas in truth, these things that Satan suggests lead instead to the dishonor of God and the ruin of people's souls. Annotations on 2 Corinthians 11:14.[60]

Beware of Satan's Messengers! Dirk Philips: Loving brothers and sisters in the Lord! In our time there are many people who claim the new birth. They prattle on about the new creature and Paul's statement, "[In Christ] neither circumcision nor uncircumcision means anything; what counts is a new creation." But in very few are found the true rebirth and the character of the new creature. What is found is the guile and deception of Satan, who "masquerades as an angel of light." He shows himself in great power in his servants, who make a fine show of themselves and speak with elevated and arrogant words concerning godly and spiritual things (though it is all hypocrisy). They speak glowingly of the new birth and the new creature and the true inner self. Indeed, some people are dazzled by this display, for they enchant them and blind their eyes with fine and affected language and a beautiful appearance of false piety.

Therefore, out of Christian love I must warn you against such false Christians and messengers of Satan. Through the grace of God, I write for you this short admonition concerning the new birth and the new creature. I want to show that not everyone who claims the new birth and prattles on about the new creature is in fact a person reborn from God. It is only the person who has taken on a godly character and the nature of Jesus Christ, who has part in the power and character of the Holy Spirit, is conformed to the image of Jesus Christ and serves God in submission, obedience, and righteousness. In short, a true Christian is a new person and a new creation in Jesus Christ. Concerning the New Birth.[61]

Satan's Tricks. Argula von Grumbach: A disputation is easily won when one argues with force, not Scripture. As far as I can see, that means that the hangman is accounted most learned. It's easy to see, though, that the devil has helped to arrange this fine hullabaloo. God will not put up

[58]Hemmingsen, *Commentaria in Omnes Epistolas Apostolorum*, 299. †Gregory the Great (590–604) was the first Roman pope to sanction the practice of reciting Masses for the souls of deceased persons.

[59]Chemnitz, *Loci Theologici*, 178; citing 2 Cor 2:11; 1 Tim 6:9; 2 Tim 2:26.

[60]Downame, ed., *English Annotations*, GG3r; citing Col 1:13; 2 Pet 2:4; Jude 6.

[61]Liechty, ed., *Early Anabaptist Spirituality*, 200-201; citing Gal 6:15.

with your ways much longer. In 2 Corinthians 11:14 Paul says: "The devil turns himself into an angel of light." So it is no wonder that confident tricksters turn themselves into apostles of Christ. An Account of a Christian Woman.[62]

Satan's Wiles. Dirk Philips: This is the nature, character, and skill of Satan, that he transforms himself into an angel of light. Therewith he hides his guile and hypocrisy, disguises and conceals his ministers, and sets them before the world in a beautiful appearance of piety. The Sending of Preachers.[63]

Luther Condemns the True Prophetic Word. Thomas Müntzer: I speak of the divine word with its manifold treasures. . . . But you deny the true word and hold before the world only an outward appearance of it. You turn yourself most powerfully into an arch-devil since, from the text of Isaiah, and contrary to reason, you make God the cause of evil. Is not the most terrible punishment of God on you? You are deluded, and nevertheless you want to be a leader of the blind for the world. You want to make God responsible for the fact that you are a poor sinner and a venomous little worm with your worthless humility. You have done this with your fantastic reasoning, which you have concocted out of your Augustine. It is truly a blasphemy impudently to despise humankind, concerning the freedom of the will.

You say that I want my teaching believed right away and forced on others, and that I do not want to give anyone time to reflect. I say, with Christ, "The one who is of God hears his word." Are you of God? Why do you not hear it? Why do you mock it and condemn what you have not experienced? Are you still trying to work out what you should teach others? You should much more truly be called a crook than a judge. It will become evident to poor Christendom how your carnal reason has indeed acted against the undeceivable spirit of God. Let Paul render judgment on you. A Highly Provoked Defense.[64]

The Need for Discernment and Courage. John Calvin: If anyone should now ask, "Should we then be suspicious of everyone?" I answer that the apostle did not at all intend this. But there are marks of discretion that would be stupid—not wise—for us to overlook. Paul only wishes to arouse our attention, lest we judge a lion too hastily by its hide. For if we are not precipitous in forming a judgment, the Lord will see to it that its ears are conspicuous soon enough. Further, Paul wishes in a similar way to admonish us, when we are evaluating a servant of Christ, not to look at the mask, but to seek after what is most important. The phrase "servant of righteousness" is a Hebraism for faithful and honest people.

"Whose end will be." Paul adds this for the consolation of godly people. For it is a statement of a courageous person who despises the foolish judgments of others and patiently awaits the day of the Lord. In the meantime, he demonstrates a singular confidence of conscience which does not shrink from the judgment of God. Commentary on 2 Corinthians 11:14-15.[65]

Judgment According to Their Deeds. Andreas Hyperius: [Here we have] a curse of the false apostles—in the form of a threat about the disastrous and horrible end that awaits them for their guilt. For this is the meaning of the clause "according to their deeds." For when their deeds are evil, it necessarily happens that the worst possible outcome occurs. Thus, Philippians 3 states that "their end is their destruction." And 2 Peter 2 says that false prophets and false teachers are going to bring upon themselves swift destruction. That is why [the Corinthians] must beware of both themselves and their works, and especially their false teaching, if they do not want to experience a similar end to that of the false

[62]Grumbach, *Argula von Grumbach*, 84.
[63]CRR 6:198-99.
[64]Baylor, ed., *The Radical Reformation*, 90; citing Is 40:2, 6; Jn 8:47.*
[65]CO 50:129 (CTS 40:351-52).

apostles. And as for Paul, he has behaved himself with such great humility and has preached the gospel without charge. Commentary on 2 Corinthians 11:15.[66]

The Elect Sometimes Wounded by Satan's Arrows. Simon Goulart: Now ordinarily the wicked are used as instruments and arrows of Satan when they encounter [the righteous]. On the other hand, it also happens that the elect of God, surprised by the weakness of their faith, or having fallen into some unpremeditated sin, or shaken by too great a fear of people, or carried away by deceit, against their will and thought, wound themselves and others in the volley of flaming arrows, having been overcome by a strange and marvelous trick of Satan. The Second Part of Christian Speeches.[67]

[66]Hyperius, *Commentarii . . . in Epistolam D. Pauli ad Romanos, et Utramque ad Corinthios*, 414; citing Phil 3:19; 2 Pet 2:1.

[67]Goulart, *Seconde partie des Discours Chrestiens*, 267.

11:16-33 Paul's Suffering as an Apostle

I repeat, let no one think me foolish. But even if you do, accept me as a fool, so that I too may boast a little. 17What I am saying with this boastful confidence, I say not as the Lord would[a] but as a fool. 18Since many boast according to the flesh, I too will boast. 19For you gladly bear with fools, being wise yourselves! 20For you bear it if someone makes slaves of you, or devours you, or takes advantage of you, or puts on airs, or strikes you in the face. 21To my shame, I must say, we were too weak for that!

But whatever anyone else dares to boast of—I am speaking as a fool—I also dare to boast of that. 22Are they Hebrews? So am I. Are they Israelites? So am I. Are they offspring of Abraham? So am I. 23Are they servants of Christ? I am a better one—I am talking like a madman—with far greater labors, far more imprisonments, with countless beatings, and often near death. 24Five times I received at the hands of the Jews the forty lashes less one. 25Three times I was beaten with rods. Once I was stoned. Three times I was shipwrecked; a night and a day I was adrift at sea; 26on frequent journeys, in danger from rivers, danger from robbers, danger from my own people, danger from Gentiles, danger in the city, danger in the wilderness, danger at sea, danger from false brothers; 27in toil and hardship, through many a sleepless night, in hunger and thirst, often without food,[b] in cold and exposure. 28And, apart from other things, there is the daily pressure on me of my anxiety for all the churches. 29Who is weak, and I am not weak? Who is made to fall, and I am not indignant?

30If I must boast, I will boast of the things that show my weakness. 31The God and Father of the Lord Jesus, he who is blessed forever, knows that I am not lying. 32At Damascus, the governor under King Aretas was guarding the city of Damascus in order to seize me, 33but I was let down in a basket through a window in the wall and escaped his hands.

a Greek *not according to the Lord* **b** Or *often in fasting*

Overview: In this section, Paul continues his "fool's speech" in which he defends his ministry and refutes the arrogance of the false apostles by boasting in the numerous trials and suffering he has endured as a faithful servant of Christ. Reformation commentators insist that Paul, in assuming the guise of a boasting "fool," does not wish the Corinthians to emulate his boasting but rather, paradoxically, is warning against such braggadocio. Indeed, there is nothing more toxic in Christian ministry than vainglory and arrogant boasting! The reformers see special significance in the fact that the apostle vindicates his ministry, not by trumpeting his various achievements, but by enumerating the many troubles and dangers he has experienced. The long list of the hardships and persecutions Paul faced—both at sea and on land, both in cities and in the countryside, at the hands of both Jews and Gentiles—should cause Christian men and women to give up their dreams of living peaceful and secure lives free from trouble. Rather, the Christian life is one of perpetual spiritual conflict, often accompanied by physical danger and suffering. Especially troubling are those "false brothers" who corrupt the church by their wicked example and teaching. Like Paul, faithful ministers must remain eager for the welfare of God's people, leaving no stone unturned in protecting the weak of conscience, refuting false teachers, and instructing the faithful in biblical doctrine. Finally, the narrative of Paul's precipitous flight from Damascus in 2 Corinthians 11:32-33 invites extensive discussion among Reformation exegetes as to whether and when it is permissible for Christian leaders to flee persecution. The general consensus is that fleeing danger is justified, if it can be done in good conscience, with the approval of the church, and without violating one's appointed vocation.

11:16-21a *Paul Indulges in More Boasting*

Paul's Strategy for Boasting. John Calvin: "I repeat." The apostle has a twofold strategy. In part, he wishes to refute the disgusting vanity of the false apostles, inasmuch as they were such annoying trumpeters of their own praise. And second, he wants to lodge a complaint with the Corinthians because they imposed upon him the necessity of boasting, contrary to the intention of his mind. Paul states, "again I say." For previously, he had made it abundantly clear that there was no reason why he should be despised. At the same time, he had also shown that he was very different from those other men, and thus should not be required to regulate his boasting according to their measure. And so, he shows them again for what reason he had hitherto boasted, namely, so that he might vindicate his apostleship from contempt, for if the Corinthians had done their duty, he would have said not a word about this matter. Commentary on 2 Corinthians 11:16.[1]

Paul Is Counteracting the Boasts of the False Apostles. Cyriacus Spangenberg: What people say in the proverb "Self-praise stinks" is well spoken. And it is therefore a foolish thing in itself for people to boast about themselves, what they have done and achieved. But, dear God, when one also sees and hears that the false teachers falsely brag and boast about ten things of which not even one is true and moreover do such things with great dishonor for God's truth and for the suppression of the same, and again in this boasting they put forward as nothing but the pure Word of God their own opinions, human dreams and distortion of the teaching, and thus with Sirens' sweet song and fair and friendly sugarcoated words lead people astray. It is certainly not becoming for any faithful pastor or worker in the Lord's vineyard to be silent about this or to let others cause his work and faithfulness to be despised or treated with suspicion.

Therefore, when Paul sees how the new teachers in Corinth were bragging, as if they only had got it right and Paul's teaching and preaching were simple child's play and silliness, he does right in acting and working against it, freely confessing before the whole world, so that no damage may come to the gospel by an unforeseen thing through such a cunning attack of Satan. Forty-Third Sermon.[2]

Paul Seeks to Silence the False Apostles' Boasting. Tilemann Hesshus: So that Paul might weaken the pride and empty boasting of the false apostles, and so that he might refute the Corinthians' shallowness who, like outward masks, were boasting only according to the flesh, Paul shows that he is in no way inferior to the false apostles. Now he reminds them of this so that they would not appear to take Paul for a fool, since he was not only comparing himself to the false apostles, but even claiming to surpass them. And he did it only for this reason: that he might tamp down and confound their groundless boasting.

When Paul says that he speaks not according to the Lord, but as a fool, he signals that he does not intend the Corinthians to imitate him in this way, unless the need for teaching forces them to do so. In general, Paul is not teaching how one should boast in the flesh, but rather that people should avoid all boasting. Paul wishes the Corinthians to consider the reason why he has lowered himself to that foolishness: not because he wishes to make himself great according to fleshly standards, but only so as to weaken the false apostles' empty boasting by his own counter-boasting. And Paul teaches the Corinthians that this approach is very different from the way the faith of godly teachers ought to be ascertained. The Greek phrase

[1] CO 50:130 (CTS 40: 352-53).

[2] C. Spangenberg, *Die ander Epistel Pauli an die Corinthier*, 182v-183r.

hypostasin kaukēseōs Paul calls confidence and a firm mind in boasting, which does not waver with doubt. Commentary on 2 Corinthians 11:16-17.[3]

Paul's Boasting Is in Response to the False Apostles. Niels Hemmingsen: This little introduction prepares the way for the comparison that follows, and Paul anticipates an objection by means of prolepsis.[†] It is foolish to praise oneself, and truly (as Paul says) it is foolish to boast before the Lord, since everyone sees how great their weakness is. That is why Paul says he is doing this with respect to the boasting of others, and he asks that they think well of this foolishness, especially since the opportunity and confidence for his boasting is so great. Commentary on 2 Corinthians 11:16-17.[4]

Paul Here Speaks as a Private Person. Giovanni Diodati: I am not speaking in this matter in my role as a public person, that is, as an apostle, who should never proclaim himself, nor seek his own glory, but only that of Christ. Rather, I present myself here as a private person, imitating the vanity of my opponents in order to exalt myself. The false apostles boast so as to dazzle and seduce you. As for me, I boast to beat back their tricks and remove from your eyes the blindfold of admiration you have for their persons, so that you might see that (with respect to any commendable quality) they do not have a single advantage over me for exalting themselves by my diminution. Annotations on 2 Corinthians 11:17.[5]

Paul's Words Are Inspired by God. The English Annotations: Whatever St. Paul wrote in his epistles, he wrote by divine inspiration. Yet, when he delivers something that is not an express commandment from God, he states that he speaks by permission, and not by command, as seen in 1 Corinthians 7: "to the rest I say; I, not the Lord." And so too in this passage: because the Spirit of God in Scripture nowhere advises us to commend ourselves or boast in our gifts, but rather the contrary, Paul says that he is not speaking according to the Lord, but, as it were, by way of folly—not folly in fact, but in a manner that seemed foolish. Annotations on 2 Corinthians 11:17.[6]

The Danger of Vainglory Among Preachers. Martin Luther: Paul was not greatly concerned when his person was regarded as insignificant and the false apostles were regarded as great, but he could not tolerate the gospel being wrecked and the Christians he had converted in Corinth being led astray. For that reason, he did everything he could, even becoming a fool and bragging. However, through his rich spirit he uses boasting in a masterly way and beautifully spoils and destroys the boasting of the false apostles. . . .

The summary of this [passage] is that there is no more harmful or poisonous vice in a preacher or a teacher than vainglory—though greed is also an evil in them, and the two commonly go together. For the sake of their own profit, so they can gain all the more, they want to be something high, special, and great. Whatever has no value is worth nothing; whatever does not bear gives nothing. All other vices are more bearable in a preacher—though none are good, and he should by rights be irreproachable and perfect, as St. Paul teaches in Titus 1. That is unsurprising, for the two vices are naturally and directly opposed to the nature of the preaching office. The preaching office was appointed to seek God's glory and to believe with its whole heart, as the psalmist says, "The heavens declare the glory of God," and yet it must endure insult and shame, as Jeremiah laments and says, "The Word of the Lord is for me a reproach and derision daily." The world does not suffer; for that reason, it is impossible for the one who seeks his own glory to remain on the right path and to

[3]Hesshus, *Explicatio Secundae Epistolae Pauli ad Corinthios*, 258v-259r.

[4]Hemmingsen, *Commentaria in Omnes Epistolas Apostolorum*, 299.

[†]Prolepsis is a rhetorical strategy in which a speaker anticipates and answers possible objections.

[5]Diodati, *La Seconde Epistre de l'Apostre S. Paul aux Corinthiens*, 161.

[6]Downame, ed., *English Annotations*, GG3r*; citing 1 Cor 7:6, 12.

preach the pure Word of God. He flees reproach and derision, and so also flees from seeking God's glory; he must preach what pleases the people and honors himself, so that his skill and understanding are praised. POSTIL ON SEXAGESIMA SUNDAY.[7]

WORLDLY BOASTING. DAVID CHYTRAEUS: To boast according to the flesh: that is, to speak about fleshly, outward, and vain things, such as the nobility of one's own country or household, of one's own wisdom and virtues, of ceremonies, and especially to vaunt and prefer oneself before others like a Thrasos.[†] . . . Plutarch[‡] says most appropriately that it is a very pleasant thing for us to hear ourselves praised by others, but it is a most irksome thing to hear other people praising themselves. POSTIL ON SEXAGESIMA SUNDAY.[8]

TWO KINDS OF BOASTING: HUMAN AND DIVINE. JOHANN SPANGENBERG: From these words we discern that there are two kinds of boasting: human boasting and divine boasting. What is human boasting? Human boasting is whenever human beings pride themselves on account of their goods, money, power, honor, knowledge, work, or merit. This boasting is transitory; it soon ends. For as the foundation is, so too is the building.

What is divine boasting? Divine boasting is a living confession of Christians—that they have a merciful God. And such boasting is a special praise and thanksgiving for divine goodness and kindness. A special consolation for him during times of cross-bearing and suffering through which his heart becomes joyful, his courage plucks up, and his conscience is brought to a peaceful state, scorning everything that might be against him. POSTIL ON SEXAGESIMA SUNDAY.[9]

BOASTING ACCORDING TO THE LORD IS VALID. CARDINAL CAJETAN: Consider the reason [for boasting], which is normally not "according to the Lord," but reflects foolishness. From this passage, we see that, although some people boast according to their carnal affections, we who are spiritual should not be provoked to praise ourselves, since such provocation is not normally "according to God," but according to foolishness. Now since the reason that provoked Paul was to constrain boasting, he calls his approach "boasting."

Along with these things, it should be noted that although the reason for boasting should normally be rejected as not "according to God," if, nevertheless, that same reason is connected to something "according to God," the person who wisely uses that reason should prove how it relates to it. This is what is happening in this present passage. For the kind of boasting practiced by the false apostles was connected to the danger of corrupting the Corinthians, and for that reason Paul was wisely provoked thereafter to boasting. Hence, Paul does not say, "I too will boast according to the flesh" (which would be to imitate sin), but "I will boast" (which indicates he was provoked to boasting, but not to the effect of boasting). COMMENTARY ON 2 CORINTHIANS 11:18.[10]

PAUL APPEALS TO THE CORINTHIANS' WISDOM AND PATIENCE. ANDREAS HYPERIUS: Paul again modestly and politely intimates the reason for boasting in this way and excuses himself of all guilt. Now he assures them that he ought to be patiently listened to for two reasons (taken from previous proofs), the one based on their wisdom, the other based on their patience. This second argument is drawn from the greater to the lesser, by which he indirectly rebukes the false apostles' arrogance, greed, and ill-temper—although in this latter argument he uses sarcasm to cloak subtly his reproach and rebuke of the Corinthians' foolish patience and their receptiveness to many teachings from the false apostles. Now this is Paul's meaning:

[7]LW 76:320, 321 (WA 17.2:143-44); citing Titus 1:6-9; Ps 19:1; Jer 20:8.
[8]Chytraeus, *A Postil of Certeine Epistles*, 81*. †In Greek mythology, Thrasos was the personification of rashness, insolence, and excessive boldness. ‡Plutarch was a first-century Greek philosopher, historian, and biographer who wrote an essay on self-praise entitled *Moralia: De se ipsum laudando*. See LCL 405:109-68.
[9]J. Spangenberg, *Postilla Teütsch*, 4:120v-121r.
[10]Cajetan, *In Posteriorem Pauli Epistolam ad Corinthios Commentarii*, 193.

"I am confident that you will listen patiently when we are forced by the occasion to be foolish and to announce our praises of these things. The first reason is this: you have been endowed with sufficient wisdom to be able to learn from foolish speaking. For a wise person does not find it a burden to listen to all things, even if they approve the statements of only a few people." The second reason has to do with their patience—from the greater to the lesser. "You show patience on many other matters even more serious and troubling. That is why I am confident that you will listen patiently to this matter." Paul states that "they bear it if someone makes them a slave"—meaning that they would become complete slaves if they submitted themselves to the false apostles' authority. Commentary on 2 Corinthians 11:19-20.[11]

The Tyranny of the False Apostles. Wolfgang Musculus: The Corinthians would hardly have endured all these things from the false apostles if they had known that they were fools. Note the ways that they were foolish. Paul attributes to the false apostles' tyrannical dominion, voraciousness, greed, arrogance, and abusive behavior. The false apostles would not have been able to exercise such abuse against the Corinthians if they had not been very cunning and deceptive, which is why Paul earlier called them "deceitful workers." This type of fool we Germans call "evil fools" (*böse Narren*). . . .

Paul scolds the Corinthians for their absurd tolerance. They should not have put up with such things from true apostles, much less false ones. The tolerance of false bishops in the churches is like this and has been like this now for many centuries, for no matter how wicked was the thing that the bishops were imagining, the majority of all our people were shamefully enduring it and continue also to endure it today. It is not that we are not warned about this since it is very clear to everyone. Commentary on 2 Corinthians 11:20.[12]

False Teachers Still Afflict the Church. Tilemann Hesshus: This is irony and a grave rebuke. The Corinthians were truly foolish, for they were enduring the capricious commands, the exorbitant fees, the pride, and ill-temper of the false apostles, while at the same time enduring Paul's serious reminders with less patience. Thus, the apostle indirectly rebukes them and commands them henceforth to use greater wisdom. The same is also evident when people, endowed with wicked judgment, seize the affections of the crowds; or when false teachers and authors of corruption are treated more kindly, supported more lavishly, and tolerated with greater moderation than godly, sincere, and faithful pastors. If the imposters act more tyrannically, the people endure it; if, with ill-temper, they demand wages, their hearers grant them freely; if any accusations are made against their behavior, their hearers zealously excuse them; if they are very negligent in their duties, the people are not troubled by this. Even if these false teachers reproach vices harshly; even if they arrogantly attack political authorities; even if they place burdens on their hearers—nevertheless, the people endure all these things. How overbearing and tyrannically the bishops, abbots, monks, and priests completely dominate the church! The popes and bishops pronounce the most severe sentence of excommunication against emperors and kings for frivolous reasons. . . . Many priests, canons, and monks defile the wives and daughters of honorable citizens. Bishops and canons are gluttons for the church's alms. Although monks have more than enough income, even so they swindle money by begging and can never be satisfied. Still, neither bishops nor canons nor monks teach anything sound about the knowledge of the true God, the benefits of the mediator, faith in Jesus Christ, the way to obtain eternal life. Explication of 2 Corinthians 11:20.[13]

Christians Often Refuse to Submit to Faithful Pastors. Martin Bucer: It has

[11]Hyperius, *Commentarii . . . in Epistolam D. Pauli ad Romanos, et Utramque ad Corinthios*, 414-15.
[12]Musculus, *Commentarius . . . in posteriorem epistolam Pauli ad Corinthios*, 352.
[13]Hesshus, *Explicatio Secundae Epistolae Pauli ad Corinthios*, 259r-260r.

always turned out that the more faithful those who care for souls have been in the exercise of their pastoral ministry, the more Satan has aroused disobedience against them, not only in the goats, but also among the immature sheep. And on the other hand, Satan arranges for the foolish sheep then to commit themselves entirely and completely to unfaithful and false shepherds, and to suffer and tolerate from them whatever they ask of them. This is what befell even the clever and spiritually rich Corinthians, so that dear Paul writes to them in 2 Corinthians 11: "You even put up with anyone who enslaves you or exploits you or takes advantage of you or defiles you or slaps you in the face."

At this time, too, how many there are who want to be counted as excellent Christians who will not tolerate any punishment or discipline in the Lord at the hands of their faithful ministers of the gospel but are quick to submit themselves to the leaders of sects and accept all manner of violence and sheer tyranny at their hands, out of the Lord. TRUE CARE OF SOULS.[14]

CHARACTERISTICS OF THE FALSE TEACHERS. TILEMANN HESSHUS: [First], they are tyrannical and attempt to reduce the church into servitude. They prescribe laws to enforce their power, and they assume for themselves more authority than the Lord has given to them. Whence, in Psalm 12 we read: "We will magnify our tongue; our lips are our own. Who is Lord over us?" It's as if one said, "The power to teach and to judge belongs to us. We do not want laws to be prescribed for us." . . . Second, they devour the people, just as it is said in Psalm 14: "They work evil and devour my people, they devour them like bread." Christ also said this to the Pharisees in Luke 20: "Because they devour the house of the widow." The defenders of corruption can never be satisfied. . . . Third, they are haughty. They insolently promote themselves, as it says in Psalm 37 [*sic*, Psalm 73]: "Pride is their necklace; violence covers them like a garment. Their eyes swell through fatness; they walk according to the deliberation of their hearts. They scoff and speak wickedness; they loftily speak malicious words. They set up their mouth against the heavens and their tongue passes over the earth." . . . Fourth, they strike your face, that is, they boldly bring insults against them. They treat them disgracefully and consider them to be their possession alone. EXPLICATION OF 2 CORINTHIANS 11:20.[15]

THE CORINTHIANS ARE VICTIMS OF THE FALSE APOSTLES' ABUSE. DAVID DICKSON: [It is as if Paul were saying to the Corinthians,] "It is clear that you are enduring harsher things than this foolishness of my boasting. For first, you endure those importunate people who bring you into bondage." Such were the false apostles, who exercised their power over them, dividing the church of Corinth into factions, and setting themselves up as captains and lords over their followers among the Corinthians, treating them as if they were soldiers and servants. "Second, you endure those who are devouring you." Such were the false apostles who were eating up the resources of the Corinthians through their stately banquets. "Third, you endure spoilers." Such also were the false apostles who, though they did not collect wages, nevertheless coveted gifts and found ways to weasel them from the Corinthians. "Fourth, you endure those who condemn you." Such were the false apostles, who because they were of the Jewish nation and had some exceptional gifts of the Spirit that others in the church of Corinth did not have, exalted themselves above the Corinthians who were drawn from the illiterate and ignoble Gentiles. "Fifth, you endure those that hit you in the face or heap reproaches on you. Why therefore should you not endure my justified boasts?" EXPOSITION OF 2 CORINTHIANS 11:20.[16]

[14]Bucer, *Concerning the True Care of Souls*, 194-95 (*Von der waren Seelsorge*, 228).

[15]Hesshus, *Explicatio Secundae Epistolae Pauli ad Corinthios*, 260v-261r; citing Ps 12:4; 14:4; Lk 20:47; Ps 73:6-8.

[16]Dickson, *An Exposition of All St. Paul's Epistles*, 88*.

Immature Christians Accept Abuse from False Teachers. John Trapp: "For you suffer. . . ." Like the papal penitentiaries, those miserably misled and muzzled creatures. They write of our King Henry II,[†] that going to Canterbury to visit the sepulcher of his own martyr Thomas Becket, once he was within sight of the church, he alighted and went three miles on his bare feet so that the hard stones yielded bloody tokens of his devotion on the way. Pope Clement V[‡] caused Dandalus, the Venetian ambassador, to come before him tied in chains and to wallow under his table with the dogs, while his holiness sat at supper. The pope[§] whipped Henry IV of France (in the person of his ambassador at Rome) after the singing of every verse of *Misere*, until the whole psalm was completed. Commentary on 2 Corinthians 11:20.[17]

11:21b-29 *Paul's Many Hardships for the Gospel*

Paul Takes on the Persona of a Foolish Person. Niels Hemmingsen: I consider this to be a confirmation of the consequence of the preceding argument, as if Paul were saying: "This abuse would be deserved if you did not receive me as your apostle, since you have endured so much from those ambitious men. Nevertheless, since I am able to boast no less than them—or rather, more than them—it is permissible for me to assume, at least a little, the persona of a foolish person." Now, a comparison follows in which he explains what he holds in common with the false apostles and what basis he has for boasting his preeminence over them. Commentary on 2 Corinthians 11:21.[18]

Paul Is a More Faithful Gospel Minister Than the False Apostles. Tilemann Hesshus: It is possible to gather from the epistle to the Philippians (in which the same words are found) that it was common for the false apostles to show off their noble background and the prerogative of the flesh. Therefore, Paul demonstrates that he is not at all inferior to them. And being unaccustomed to boast in this way among the Gentiles, he promptly repeats that he is speaking in a foolish manner in order to warn them not to imitate this kind of boasting—for he has been forced to do it against his will. He does not speak in this way for his own sake, but to refute the false apostles. Paul does not grant that the false apostles were Christ's ministers, for earlier he called them ministers of Satan and deceitful workers. But because they no doubt wanted to be considered ministers of Christ, Paul concedes this temporarily; nevertheless, he proves that they are not equal to him, since he discharged the ministry with far more zeal, with more burning affection, and firmer patience. When Paul says that he is greater, he does not mean it is unimportant to be a minister of Christ, for this honor is far greater and far more important than for someone to be the king or queen of the world. Explication of 2 Corinthians 11:21.[19]

Christ Is the True Offspring of Abraham. Heinrich Bullinger: An encomium follows in which Paul argues in the order his rivals were accustomed to boasting. Now they were boasting concerning the antiquity of their lineage as well as their ancestors and illustrious race. . . . Now Israel is the same person as Jacob, the father of Judah, whence the Jews derived their name, just as the Israelites derived their name from their father Israel. He was superior in every kind of virtue and famous in the whole of canonical Scripture. And the promise was given to Abraham, the father of believers, and he received circumcision, was justified by faith, and was called the friend of God. The inheritance of a son was promised to Abraham, though he was without offspring; and so

[17]Trapp, *A Commentary of Exposition*, 731*. [†]King Henry II's penitence for the murder of Thomas Becket occurred in 1170. [‡]Pope Clement V was the pontiff from 1305 to 1313. [§]The pope who oversaw King Henry IV's conversion to the Roman Catholic faith in 1593 was Clement VIII.

[18]Hemmingsen, *Commentaria in Omnes Epistolas Apostolorum*, 300.

[19]Hesshus, *Explicatio Secundae Epistolae Pauli ad Corinthios*, 261v-262r.

the offspring of Abraham was greatest both in speech and in reality. Everyone knows how much the Jews were boasting of the name of Abraham, as seen in John 8 and the false apostles in the same way were glorying in the flesh and boasting that they were Hebrews, Israelites, and the offspring of Abraham. Therefore, Paul adds this: "If there is anything of value among you, I also can boast concerning all these things. However, from God's perspective, that person is a true Israelite and offspring of Abraham who believes that Christ alone is the true seed of Abraham sent from God and imitates the example of Abraham with his holy life." Now the context of this passage depends on what has come before. "Although I am thought of as nothing and considered to have nothing to boast about (as the false apostles think), nevertheless, even if another person thinks himself superior, I myself believe that I excel them." Now Paul inserts here by way of a parenthesis, "I am speaking as a fool," for earlier he stated, "I do not speak according to the Lord, but as a fool." Finally, Paul continues to sing his own praise. And those things he makes mention of here, he treats in greater detail in Acts 22 and Philippians 3. To be sure, it is very disgraceful to boast concerning the virtues of our ancestors—but let me respond to this briefly. Truly it is a beautiful thing to be well-born of a noble race with noble virtues. Marius's[†] elegant speech on this topic in the presence of Sallust during the Numidian war stands out: "Surely, antiquity recognized no nobility except that which was acquired by excellent virtues and splendid deeds." Commentary on 2 Corinthians 11:22.[20]

Paul Was in No Way Inferior to the False Apostles. Wolfgang Musculus: It is customary for people to reward those who are bolder and prouder with special privileges. Now the false apostles were considering the excellence of their lineage—because they were Jews, Israelites, and of the seed of Abraham—worthy of special privilege and, due to this background, they were becoming so puffed up among the Greeks that they were plunging into servitude all of the believers and treating them very abusively. Paul is going to make light of their boldness and pride when he says, "Are they so proud because they are Hebrews? But I too am a Hebrew. Because they are Israelites? I too am an Israelite. Because they are from the seed of Abraham? I too am of the seed of Abraham. Therefore, they can boast of no title by which they are superior to me or I am inferior to them. Indeed, I myself could boast in the flesh, if it were appropriate for an apostle of Christ boldly to boast about such things." Paul makes a similar statement against the false apostles in Philippians 3, saying: "Look out for the dogs, look out for the evil doers, look out for the circumcisers. For we are the real circumcision who worship God in the spirit and boast in Christ Jesus and put no confidence in the flesh—though I myself have reason for confidence in the flesh. If other people think they have confidence in the flesh, I have more: circumcised on the eighth day, of the people of Israel, from the tribe of Benjamin, a Hebrew of Hebrews, as to the law a Pharisee; as to zeal, persecuting the church; as to righteousness, under the law blameless." Commentary on 2 Corinthians 11:22.[21]

The Jews' False Confidence in Their Ancestry. Andreas Hyperius: "Are they Hebrews? So am I." This praise is based on an argument from people or nation. Now, all the Jews began to be called Hebrews, from Eber, the son of Shelah, the father of Peleg in Genesis 11. On this matter, see our commentary on Hebrews. "Are they Israelites? So am I. Are they offspring of Abraham? So am I." Praise based on an argument from the greater. It is known how much Abraham and Jacob (also called Israel, from which is derived the name of the Israelites) are celebrated throughout

[20]Bullinger, *In Posteriorem . . . ad Corinthios Epistolam Commentarius*, 325-26; citing Jn 8:39-47. [†]Gaius Marius was the Roman general who commanded the armies during the Numidian War, a seven-year conflict (112–105 BC) between the Roman Republic and King Jugurthine of Numidia.

[21]Musculus, *Commentarius . . . in posteriorem epistolam Pauli ad Corinthios*, 356-57; citing Phil 3:2-6.

Scripture. And so, many Jews were commending themselves based on the fact that they had descended from such important ancestors. Now, Christ teaches elsewhere that this boasting was meaningless (that is, bragging that one was born from illustrious ancestors) given that the Jews had greatly degenerated from the virtues of [Abraham and Jacob]; and that their superiority would not matter unless the Jews were resembling the virtues of their ancestors: "You reproach the Jews because they do not do the works of Abraham," and "God is able to raise up from these stones sons of Abraham." The apostle also states in Philippians 3: "All these things which seemed to be profit and gain I counted as loss for the sake of Christ." Commentary on 2 Corinthians 11:22.[22]

Paul, a Superior Jew. David Dickson: The second sign of Paul's dignity he lays down specifically: that he is worthy to be compared to the false apostles in the nobility of his lineage. For if he had sought to boast in a holy nation, he had sprung from a family that had not mixed itself with the Gentiles. He was a Hebrew, born of Hebrew parents. If he would boast in the nobility of his race, he had sprung from the more noble Israelites, because he came from the tribe of Benjamin, who was the son of Rachel, a freeborn woman—while some of the tribes had their origin from bondmaids. If the false apostles took pride in the antiquity of religion, that they remained in the covenant as true descendants of Abraham, here also Paul was equal to any of them. Exposition of 2 Corinthians 11:22.[23]

Paul Outshines the False Apostles in Hardships. Desiderius Erasmus: Even in regard to those things that truly do contribute to apostolic glory, we outshine them. They are ministers of Christ—let us grant it—but I am more so (to speak foolishly, but to speak the truth nonetheless). I have shown that this is so, not through arrogance, nor by taking gifts, nor by boasting of family origin, but by the very proofs that truly attest an apostolic heart. I have endured more labors than they; far more grievously have I felt the lash; more often have I been cast into prison; more frequently have I run the risk of death. But if you wish some instances to be recounted in detail: five times I received forty lashes less one, when I was beaten by the Jews; three times I was beaten with lictors' rods; once I was stoned; three times I was shipwrecked; I spent an entire night and day on the high sea in the greatest despair of my life. But why should I go on enumerating individual instances, since frequently, for the sake of the gospel, I was in danger, not only in sailing, but also in journeys on land? Repeatedly I encountered dangers from rivers, dangers from brigands, dangers from the persecution of the Jews, dangers from the violence of the Gentiles, dangers springing up in the city, dangers in the desert, dangers in the sea when I came close to being slaughtered by the sailors, dangers from these falsely called Christians who were resisting our gospel. Not to recall, for the moment, the constant labors and hardships undertaken for the sake of the gospel; the frequent nights without sleep, the hunger and thirst endured times without number, the frequent times without food, the hardships of cold and nakedness endured. But what I have recounted thus far pertains only to the affliction of my body. Paraphrases on 2 Corinthians 11.[24]

Paul Is a Servant of Christ. John Calvin: "Are they ministers of Christ?" Now since he is treating matters worthy of true praise, Paul is no longer satisfied to lower himself to an equal position [with the false apostles], but rather exalts himself above them. For Paul scatters their carnal boastings just as puff of wind disperses smoke, by comparing those things they had in common. But because the false apostles had nothing of substance

[22]Hyperius, *Commentarii . . . in Epistolam D. Pauli ad Romanos, et Utramque ad Corinthios*, 415; citing Gen 11:16; Lk 3:8; Phil 3:7.
[23]Dickson, *An Exposition of All St. Paul's Epistles*, 89*.
[24]CWE 43:270-72.

in their ministries, he with good reason dissociates himself from their rank when boasting in all sincerity. For to be a servant of Christ is far more honorable and illustrious than to be the firstborn son from among all the firstborn sons of Abraham's posterity. Once again, however, so as to anticipate calumnies, Paul prefaces his comments by saying that he speaks as a fool. "Imagine this," he says, "this boasting of mine is foolish—but it is nevertheless true." Commentary on 2 Corinthians 11:23.[25]

Paul's Unwavering Service to Christ. Martin Luther: Here conditions were even more difficult and terrible when the devil directed all his hellish quivers and cannons against the apostle. These Paul had to endure perpetually, as he states very clearly in 2 Corinthians 11. And yet he remained in his office without wavering, regarding no danger and no suffering so great as to impel him to desist from his preaching. But who would want to live in constant expectation of all this if he were not as sure of this article [regarding the resurrection] as he is of his own life? Indeed, I can say for myself, if I knew that no more than honor and goods were at stake here and I could earn the whole world's possessions three times over with this, the world could still not induce me to deliver a single sermon. I would rather crawl nine yards down into the ground than be exposed to such danger. But there is something else in store for us than we may seek and acquire here, something which easily compensates for suffering and misery. Compared with this, as St. Paul declares in Romans 8:18, all else is to be accounted as nothing. Here we may eat and drink and accept what we obtain, although the world begrudges us that, but it is not for this that we are Christians or that we believe. No, we are awaiting something loftier, something better—an inexpressible, eternal treasure. Commentary on 1 Corinthians 15:31.[26]

Paul an Untiring Servant of God. John Trapp: Chrysostom called Paul *Insatiabilem Dei cultorem*, that is, an untiring servant of God. Commentary on 2 Corinthians 11:23.[27]

Paul's Tireless Labors on Behalf of the Gospel. Tilemann Hesshus: "With far greater labors." Not only did the apostle Paul work much harder than the false apostles—who were deceptively attempting to transfer to themselves the works of others—but he also worked harder than those from among the true apostles of Christ, as mentioned in 1 Corinthians 15. Paul taught and established many churches in Antioch Pisidia, Lystra, Derbe, Iconium, Berea, Tarsus, Salamis, Paphos, Ephesus, Troas, Thessalonica, Philippi, Corinth, Athens, and Rome. And as he writes to the Romans: "He brought the gospel from Jerusalem all the way to Illyricum," so that the whole of Cilicia, Asia Minor, Pontus, Bithynia, Cappadocia, Thrace, Macedonia, Achaia, Syria, Arabia, and Phoenicia was illuminated by Paul's teaching. This would not have been possible without tireless and enormous labor. Therefore, the false apostles were stupid in trying to compare themselves to Paul. Explication of 2 Corinthians 11:23.[28]

How Suffering Proves Excellence in Ministry. Wolfgang Musculus: When Paul said that he was a better minister of Christ, lest it seem that he said this rashly, he proves it through a clear and distinct argument, namely, through all kinds of manifold and painful troubles and dangers that he was suffering for the sake of Christ, some of which he now enumerates: labors, beatings, imprisonments, near-death experiences, being stoned, shipwrecks, and other various dangers. Someone may ask: "Is the person who endures more troubles and dangers therefore the better minister of Christ?" . . . I answer: Just as suffering does not make a person a martyr of Christ, but one

[25]CO 50:133 (CTS 40:358).
[26]LW 28:153-54 (WA 36:609); citing 2 Cor 11:23-29; Rom 8:18.
[27]Trapp, *A Commentary or Exposition*, 731*.
[28]Hesshus, *Explicatio Secundae Epistolae Pauli ad Corinthios*, 263v-264r; citing 1 Cor 15:10; Rom 15:19.

must rather consider the cause of the suffering, so also, dangers by themselves do not demonstrate that a person is a minister of Christ, but rather dangers prove it when they are faithfully endured for the sake of the gospel of Christ proclaimed with righteous zeal. The apostle does not vindicate his ministry by the excellence of its reputation and appearance; rather he establishes the proof of it through the multitude of troubles and dangers. This is the fate of those who sincerely and faithfully proclaim the gospel in this world because it renders the minister of Christ subject to all kinds of troubles, afflictions, and dangers. Indeed, the more zeal with which a person proclaims Christ, the more numerous and harsher the dangers he will encounter. By this proof one can verify excellence in the ministry of Christ. Commentary on 2 Corinthians 11:23.[29]

Paul's Courage in Proclaiming the Gospel. Tilemann Hesshus: It is clear that Paul was endowed with great strength of spirit so that neither scourging, nor adversities, nor dangers were able to deter him from the ministry of teaching. Having been badly treated in Antioch, he nevertheless soon taught the gospel at Iconium. He was almost killed by stoning in Lystra; when he picked himself up, he returned to the work of teaching in Derbe. Having been thrown into prison in Philippi, as soon as he was liberated, he proclaimed the gospel to the Thessalonians with the same enthusiasm as before. And so on and on, through repeated afflictions and dangers, Paul's faithfulness in ministry and his constant love toward Christ shone forth. Paul demonstrated through these battles that he was not seeking his own good, but that which would benefit Jesus Christ, and that he would not hesitate to expose his life to extreme dangers for the sake of the glory of Christ and the salvation of the church. The false apostles, in the meantime, because they were looking after their own safety, cunningly avoided dangers and instead taught those things that would gratify obstinate Jews. Explication of 2 Corinthians 11:23.[30]

Paul's Faithfulness in Ministry. Niels Hemmingsen: This list of the apostle's labors and persecutions demonstrates how far Paul surpassed the false apostles in ministry. For these men were running after soft leisure, while Paul regarded with contempt all difficulties, labors, and dangers in order to propagate the kingdom of Christ. Second, this passage commends to us Paul's faithfulness in ministry, who, despite all his miseries, did not give up his confession or ministry. Third, this example is put forward to be imitated by all ministers of the Word as well as all godly people, so that, whatever injury they suffer, they too may not despair of their confession or ministry. Regarding the forty lashes, see Deuteronomy 25. Commentary on 2 Corinthians 11:23.[31]

A Summary of Paul's Suffering. Tilemann Hesshus: Luke the Evangelist gave to us Paul's history in the book of Acts, and he also diligently recorded the sermons that Paul preached, but he did not report all the battles Paul endured—he passed over most of them in silence, and only marked out the main points. This is clear from the present passage. For Luke makes mention of only one stoning, which happened at Lystra, and one scourging, which happened in Philippi, and one shipwreck. Therefore, we do not possess Paul's entire history, of which Paul himself provides a quick summary here. Now the apostle teaches us by this recollection of his troubles and dangers that we are nowhere safe in this world, for indiscriminately and everywhere the impure spirit schemes to trap us. He desires to turn all the elements of this world to our destruction if he can. Therefore, if we are faithful ministers of Christ, we will have no hope for any security in any place. In the palaces of

[29]Musculus, *Commentarius . . . in posteriorem epistolam Pauli ad Corinthios*, 358.

[30]Hesshus, *Explicatio Secundae Epistolae Pauli ad Corinthios*, 264r-v.

[31]Hemmingsen, *Commentaria in Omnes Epistolas Apostolorum*, 300; citing Deut 25:3.

princes, in cities, in academies, in the countryside, and whatever place godly and faithful pastors serve, they are constantly in great dangers. Hence, we must consider in whom we have believed. And in the first place, we must constantly pray that God's Son might compassionately protect us with the shadow of his hand as we live in the midst of wolves and that he might reign in us by his Spirit so that we might not fall into the traps of the enemy. Paul recounts the dangers from false brothers among the various and multiple dangers that encircle godly teachers. For this grim plague rages against the church since many people pretend godliness, friendship, and fellowship when they fiercely hate us, and they desire nothing more than to be accepted among us. These people often hurl the most bitter griefs against us and produce the most horrible dangers for us. Explication of 2 Corinthians 11:23-26.[32]

Flogged, Beaten, and Stoned. Andreas Hyperius: Paul mentions as the first thing that he had been beaten five times, and one of those times he had received forty lashes minus one. For this was the way the law in Deuteronomy 25 prescribed a person to be flogged: "If a person has sinned and seems to deserve a beating, let them force the offender to lie down in public to be flogged. The beating should be commensurate with the sin, not excessive, so that the number should not exceed forty lashes, lest the flogged brother go away disgraced before your eyes." And so it appears that the Jews—pretending to be kind—did not wish to inflict forty lashes. Consequently, the apostle, judged by the Jews to be wicked and worthy of a flogging, had been beaten on five occasions in this way on account of his zeal for the gospel. Moreover, that Paul was also beaten with rods by Gentile judges according to the Roman custom is made clear in Acts 16, where it is reported that he was beaten with rods in Philippi. The apostle says here that this happened to him three times. "Once I was stoned." How frequently Paul faced death; that is, how often and in how many places he was in danger of losing his life! One time he was stoned in the Lycaonian city of Lystra, as described in Acts 14. Commentary on 2 Corinthians 11:24-25.[33]

Paul Did Not Employ Force Against His Enemies. Paul Glock: How plainly the apostle speaks of the suffering which he endured for the sake of Christ. It was inflicted by those who did not believe him. He suffered lashes five times, was beaten with rods, and was stoned once. All that, he says, he suffered. But nowhere is it written that he even once defended himself or that he forced these same rogues and knaves to his faith and to what he preached, neither with hangmen nor with bailiffs. For he says: "Do not avenge yourselves, my dearest ones, but yield place to anger." Thus, it is manifest that neither Christ nor the apostles used force or violence to force people to their teaching, preaching, or their church. First Defense.[34]

Paul Adrift at Sea. Martin Luther: Among the other external, physical points about which St. Paul boasts (in which he surpasses the false apostles, who suffer nothing for the sake of the Word or of souls but only boast about their name and person), he says that he spent day and night in the depth of the sea. Some apply that to the voyage about which Luke writes, when for fourteen days they did not eat or see the stars, but always, day and night, were among the waves and billows of the sea. Others think that he was personally submerged in the deep sea and, like Jonah the prophet, remained under the sea, but only for a day and a night. The text almost reads that way, though some understand jail or prison, because in the Greek nothing is said about the sea but only about the deep. Postil on Sexagesima Sunday.[35]

[32]Hesshus, *Explicatio Secundae Epistolae Pauli ad Corinthios*, 264v-265v; citing Acts 14; 16; 27.

[33]Hyperius, *Commentarii . . . in Epistolam D. Pauli ad Romanos, et Utramque ad Corinthios*, 416; citing Deut 25:1-3; Acts 16:23; 14:19.

[34]CRR 10:319; citing 2 Cor 11:25; Rom 12:19.

[35]LW 76:327 (WA 35:609); citing Acts 27:13-38; Jn 1:17.

Paul Sank to the Depths. The English Annotations: Some interpreters understand "I have been in the deep" to mean a deep dungeon, whose name was Bythos, where St. Paul lay hidden for a time in Lystra. A more probable explanation is that the term "deep" means the sea in which he floated or swam after his shipwreck. . . . The epistle of Sulpicius Severus† states: "It seem likely to me that the preacher to the Gentiles was engulfed by waves and after remaining at sea for three days, he was drawn out of the depths and rescued at night." Annotations on 2 Corinthians 11:25.[36]

The Dangers of Sea Voyages. Andreas Hyperius: Often, for the sake of proclaiming the gospel, Paul was forced to sail across various seas, such as the Aegean or Syrian seas, when he was traveling from Asia to Greece or vice versa. It is possible from the book of Acts to list several voyages where repeated dangers occurred that seemed to threaten life even for those who knew the ferocity of the sea. It comes to mind that Plato somewhere designated sailors neither among the living nor among the dead because they could never be certain of life. Commentary on 2 Corinthians 11:25.[37]

Paul's Constant Dangers. Wolfgang Musculus: "In danger from rivers." Paul has mentioned earlier the dangers from the sea. He now mentions those many serious dangers that he frequently encountered on his journeys. Flowing rivers could hardly be crossed without peril. Paul often experienced dangers of this kind. "Danger from robbers." Robbers especially bothered travelers and the unarmed. This probably happened more than once to Paul. "Dangers from my own people." That is, the Jews, from whose lineage he was born. We read in Acts about the plots and attacks that the Jews employed to crush Paul. "Dangers from the Gentiles." Namely, those to whom Paul was preaching and whose false worship he was rejecting. We read about this in Acts. The Jews were persecuting Paul as a rebel against the law and the people of God. But the Gentiles were persecuting him as an opponent and enemy of their gods. Thus, Paul was exposed to the hatred and treachery of everyone, both the Jews and Gentiles. "Danger in the city." Ambrosiaster† understands this city to be Damascus. . . . Chrysostom‡ rightly understands this as referring to more than one city. For Paul was endangered not only in Damascus but also in many other cities. Now I think Paul is especially thinking of those riots that wicked citizens, both Jews and Gentiles alike, stirred up against him. "Danger in the wilderness." The dangers of the wilderness, in addition to robbers, are wandering, hunger, thirst, being buffeted by sandstorms (in which a great number of travelers are covered and buried in great piles of sand), and the attack of wild beasts which are numerous in solitary places. "Danger at sea." In addition to shipwrecks and violent storms, ships sailing in open seas are subject to many other dangers including pirates, sea fish, Charybdis and Scylla, sandbanks, and cliffs. "Danger from false brothers." The less people are able to guard against a brother because of familiarity, the more dangerous they become. Now Paul is speaking chiefly of those people who were from the circumcision party who were pursuing him with hatred because of obedience to the law of Moses; even so these people also wanted to be considered as Christians. We see very clearly today what happens to godly people at the hands of false brothers. Concerning false brothers, see Galatians 2. Commentary on 2 Corinthians 11:26.[38]

Paul's Opponents Were Everywhere. John Calvin: By the phrase "dangers from

[36]Downame, ed., *English Annotations*, GG3r*. †Sulpicius Severus was a Christian writer and chronicler from Aquitania (modern-day France) who lived in the fourth and early fifth centuries.

[37]Hyperius, *Commentarii . . . in Epistolam D. Pauli ad Romanos, et Utramque ad Corinthios*, 416.

[38]Musculus, *Commentarius . . . in posteriorem epistolam Pauli ad Corinthios*, 361-62. †For Ambrosiaster's interpretation, see PL 17:315. ‡For Chrysostom's interpretation, see PG 62:571 (NPNF[1] 12:395).

people" Paul means those dangers that came from his own descendants, because of that burning hatred all the Jews had for him. Second, he faced the hostility of the Gentiles. And third, the traps of the false brothers were threatening him. And thus, it happened that he was hated by all for the name of Christ. I take Paul to mean "a voluntary fast," since he has previously spoken about hunger and poverty. These were the marks (*insignia*) with which he proved himself to be (and for good reason) an eminent servant of Christ. For how better may we know a servant of Christ than by so many, so various, and so important proofs? On the other hand, those dainty braggarts had done nothing and suffered nothing for Christ—nevertheless, they foolishly praised themselves. Commentary on 2 Corinthians 11:26.[39]

Constant Dangers, Constant Difficulties. Andreas Hyperius: Dangers threatened Paul everywhere he went on account of the gospel. In the cities he was often threatened with death, mistreated, and expelled, as is seen in Acts. When he either fled to the wilderness or journeyed through it, dangers threatened from wild animals, robbers, and other things. Nor was he safe at sea from enemies and evil men, for often they were sailing in the same boat with him.

"Danger from false brothers." What is far more distressing is when we are confronted by those fake brothers who seem to be going to help us. The Psalm writer also indicates this when he writes in Psalm 55, "If it had been my enemy that taunted me, I would have endured it, but it was you, a man close to my heart, my guide and friend." Paul, in another passage, complains about false brothers. And today, there is no more serious danger that threatens godly people than false brothers who go throughout the world and spread in the Lord's field the seed of wicked doctrine, and then, if they can, once they have received payment, they betray and entirely sell the godly.

"In toil and hardships . . ." Paul brings up other common troubles and hardships—all of which must be endured in ministry and borne for the sake of the gospel. Now if he had wished to abandon his office and renounce the gospel of Christ, he would have been able to live splendidly and at peace among those Jews. And thus, he was often afflicted by a shortage of necessary resources, lacking food, clothing, and those sorts of things, and as a consequence, he labored with his hands days, and sometimes nights, to provide for himself. And he often taught and disputed late into the night, as is seen in Acts 20. Hunger differs from fasting, because it arises out of need; the latter is voluntary for governing the uncontrolled impulse of the flesh. Commentary on 2 Corinthians 11:26-27.[40]

The Many Trials of Christian Ministers. Tilemann Hesshus: The whole life of the apostle was full of worries and sorrow, concerns, and troubles. For in this way God demonstrates to the world that the apostles were not seeking their own kingdom, nor were they zealous for their own advantage and desires, but, out of their love for the truth and their zeal for extending the light of the gospel, they renounced the world and made little of their lives. Now for this reason, Satan throws every kind of trouble against the apostles and never grants them any peace and quiet in order to exhaust them and break down their spirits. And if he is not able to completely deter them from professing the gospel, he can at least hold them back. And so, he throws one trouble after another, hunger, thirst, cold, nakedness, exile, diseases, the treachery of false brothers, the betrayal of friends, the false accusations of sycophants, and whatever else people find unpleasant. Truly, for the apostles . . . the whole of their life was full of misery, as in a tragedy. Now, while mentioning these things, the apostle teaches what attitude is necessary for us to have in ministry. We must entirely give up dreams

[39]CO 50:134 (CTS 40:360-61).

[40]Hyperius, *Commentarii . . . in Epistolam D. Pauli ad Romanos, et Utramque ad Corinthios*, 416-17; citing Ps 55:12-13; Acts 20:7-12.

of a peaceful life. Instead, the mind must be prepared and fortified so as to yield to no adversities. Instead, with cheerfulness and constancy let us continue in our ministry, and let us refresh ourselves in this, that with our words we are rescuing souls from the jaws of Satan and winning them for our Lord Jesus Christ. Explication of 2 Corinthians 11:27.[41]

Do All Servants of Christ Suffer Hardships? John Calvin: Now it is asked whether anyone can be a servant of Christ who has not been troubled by so many evils, dangers, and troubles. I answer that not all things are necessarily required for all people, but where these things are seen, a more certain and illustrious testimony is conspicuous. That person, therefore, who will be distinguished by so many marks of distinction, will not despise others who are less illustrious and less thoroughly tested, nor will he be puffed up with pride. But, nevertheless, whenever there is need for it, that person will be prepared (following Paul's example) to exult with a holy boasting against deceitful and worthless persons, as long as they remain focused, not on themselves, but on Christ only—for nothing but pride or ambition could corrupt and deform all these praises. For the chief thing is that we serve Christ with a pure conscience. All other things are, as it were, additional. Commentary on 2 Corinthians 11:27.[42]

Paul's Concern for the Churches. Cyriacus Spangenberg: The pious apostle carried a constant concern in his heart for all the churches. Anyone who cares for a church learns to a good extent what a load it is and can easily measure what kind of burden it was for Paul to care daily for all the churches. This truly exhausted his strength and left him little rest, for he had to worry about many things, that tyrants not destroy the newly created churches or that the false teachers not do damage [them], indeed that none of the new Christians bring trouble on themselves. Today comes this rumor, tomorrow another word which increased the apostle's concern; now came letters, then messengers, and then he had to write or send faithful brothers or go himself, and he truly had much trouble because of this.

Indeed, there is no office that gives greater cause for concern than the preaching office, and whoever has this office will receive enough causes for concern. The devil will not stop giving cause for all kinds of concern everywhere. So that one will not be able to be secure in much, such concerns seek an upright home, more than the work itself. For who can stop being concerned for the churches that are dear to him? Especially when he sees how badly things are going and the manifold punishments of God that the great horde causes in the whole church under the cover of the gospel. Forty-Fourth Sermon.[43]

Paul's Anxiety for the Churches. Niels Hemmingsen: Paul recounts that he daily remembers the assembly of the churches and the concern that he has for all of them. Paul was distinguishing these matters from those extraneous things since what needed to be preserved related to the substance of the church itself. For many people fall into doubts; many poor people complain; the church is often attacked by enemies. In these and similar difficulties the churches were looking to the apostle for help as to their highest governor and it was extremely burdensome to respond to all these difficulties. The ministers of the churches were learning from him how to do their duty, how to cure those who were erring in conscience and doubting, and how to care not only for the entire body of believers, but also the individual members. Commentary on 2 Corinthians 11:28.[44]

---

[41]Hesshus, *Explicatio Secundae Epistolae Pauli ad Corinthios*, 266v-267r.

[42]CO 50:134 (CTS 40:361).

[43]C. Spangenberg, *Die ander Epistel Pauli an die Corinthier*, 189v-190r.

[44]Hemmingsen, *Commentaria in Omnes Epistolas Apostolorum*, 300.

Paul's Fervent Care for the Churches. Tilemann Hesshus: With his apostolic spirit, Paul clearly testifies that he is anxious on behalf of all the churches. His desire is that the churches everywhere should be rightly established and thoroughly strengthened against imposters. He desires that the churches everywhere should be built up in tranquility and all those converted to God should walk in a manner worthy of the Lord, in justice, holiness, and true righteousness. Paul does not aspire to absolute authority in all the churches, as does the Roman antichrist, who, although he promotes himself as the vicar of Christ and the visible head of the entire church, and the universal pastor, nevertheless does not really undertake any care for the church. He is not concerned for the church to be instructed in piety; he does not explain the benefits of the mediator; he does not refute and restrain the errors that everywhere increase. Instead, he acts so that he might be adored as the only divine authority in the world and he devastates the vineyard of the Lord. How far different was the attitude of the apostle Paul who undertook the care of all the churches! How diligently he repressed and refuted the fanatical spirits! In his writings, he encouraged the godly in right judgment and prayed fervently to God each day for the growth of all the churches. Commentary on 2 Corinthians 11:28.[45]

Christian Ministry Involves Spiritual Warfare. John Calvin: Now what a picture we have here of a complete minister, concerned not just with one, or ten, or thirty churches, but all of them together, as he teaches some, encourages some, exhorts some, gives counsel to some, a cure for the diseases to others. Now, from Paul's words, we can gather that no one can have a heartfelt concern for the churches without being pressured by many difficulties, for the government of the church is not a delightful occupation in which we spend our time pleasantly and experience delight of heart, but it is a hard and severe warfare (as has been mentioned previously), with Satan now and then giving us as much trouble as he can, and leaving no stone unturned to disturb us. Commentary on 2 Corinthians 11:28.[46]

Concern for the Churches. John Trapp: [Theodore] Beza states that Calvin[†] was not otherwise affected toward churches, even those far away, than if he had borne them upon his own shoulders. Calvin often sighed, "How long, Lord," over the poor afflicted churches of Christ, and he was much more affected by their miseries than with any of his own personal miseries. Emperor Theodosius said of Ambrose,[‡] "I could not but love the man for, while he lived and when he died, he took more care for the church than for himself." Commentary on 2 Corinthians 11:28.[47]

Paul's Ardent Love for God's People. Martin Luther: Among the outward points (that is, those that did not concern his own person but hurt and injured others), he lists these two: that he is weak and indignant when anyone is weak or made to fall. In that way he abundantly shows what an ardent heart he had and how full of love he was, so that the fault and injury of another hurt him as if it were his own injury. I think that with "weakness" he does not mean physical weakness or sickness, but spiritual [weakness] in the faith. He means those who are still young in faith, have a timid, weak conscience, and so are still green and weak in faith. . . .

So also [he says] that he "burns"; that is, it greatly grieves and torments him when anyone is made to fall, that is, when anyone through dangerous doctrine or example falls away from faith in any point. He says much about this

[45]Hesshus, *Explicatio Secundae Epistolae Pauli ad Corinthios*, 267v-268r.

[46]CO 50:134 (CTS 40:362).

[47]Trapp, *A Commentary or Exposition*, 732*. [†]See Theodore Beza's *The Life of John Calvin* (Darlington, UK: Evangelical Press, 1997), 99. [‡]The relationship between Emperor Theodosius I and Ambrose the bishop of Milan was not always this cordial, as when the bishop excommunicated Theodosius for his sanction of the massacre of seven thousand people in Thessalonica in 390.

offense to faith in Romans 14. But because he cannot be offended with those who are offended, as he became weak with the weak, he says, "I burn and have sorrow of heart about this." Postil on Sexagesima Sunday.[48]

Paul Was Concerned for All Sorts of People. Wolfgang Musculus: Paul indicates that he holds in love all Christians equally, and does not distinguish between the rich and poor, between the noble and common, between the well-educated and the ignorant, but he is concerned for the salvation of all people equally. It is as if Paul said, "Now who is so contemptible that I do not have compassion on his weakness? And who falls away and I am not troubled by it?" People who associate only with the powerful, the noble, the wealthy, the well-educated, and the like are not inclined in this way and are careful to avoid offending those sorts of people; thus, they bear no concern for the common people, the poor and the ignorant and they are not at all concerned about their salvation, because they are treacherously seeking their own benefit rather than faithfully seeking Christ and Christ's sheep. Commentary on 2 Corinthians 11:29.[49]

Paul's Tormented Spirit. Tilemann Hesshus: "Who is weak?" That is, "if I have perceived someone becoming weak or exhausted in the ministry"—as happened to so many when persecutions were breaking out during the time of the apostles—"I am distressed and my spirit is tormented, I feel grief in my soul for that person and I attempt to encourage and strengthen him in every way possible. If someone is caused to stumble into error or into serious sin, I notice they have fallen; I completely burn with sorrow, knowing that Satan inflicts bitter wounds on all the churches through a single scandal." When David committed adultery and murder, the prophets Nathan, Gad, and Asaph experienced the most severe pain by this scandal, because they saw that a long sequence of evils would follow thereafter. For that reason, Paul says that he "burns," that is, that he is beaten down with enormous sorrow whenever scandals are reported to him. Explication of 2 Corinthians 11:29.[50]

11:30-33 *To Flee or Not to Flee?*

Paul Boasts in His Suffering and Weakness. John Calvin: This is the conclusion of all that has come before—that Paul is more inclined to boast of those things that are related to his weakness, that is, those things which, in the opinion of the world, might more bring him contempt than glory. These things include hunger, thirst, imprisonments, stonings, floggings, and the like—things which, in truth, we are generally ashamed of and consider most disgraceful. Commentary on 2 Corinthians 11:30.[51]

Should A Christian Flee a Plague? Martin Luther: To begin with, some people are of the firm opinion that one need not and should not run away from a deadly plague. Rather, since death is God's punishment, which he sends upon us for our sins, we must submit to God and with a true and firm faith patiently await our punishment. They look upon running away as an outright wrong and as lack of belief in God. Others take the position that one may properly flee, particularly if one holds no public office.

I cannot censure the former for their excellent decision. They uphold a good cause, namely, a strong faith in God, and deserve commendation because they desire every Christian to hold to a strong, firm faith. It takes more than a milk faith to await a death before which most of the saints themselves have been and still are in dread. Who would not acclaim these earnest people to whom death is a little thing? They willingly accept God's

[48]LW 76:327, 328 (WA 17.2:149-50).
[49]Musculus, *Commentarius . . . in posteriorem epistolam Pauli ad Corinthios*, 364.
[50]Hesshus, *Explicatio Secundae Epistolae Pauli ad Corinthios*, 268r.
[51]CO 50:135 (CTS 40:363).

chastisement, doing so without tempting God, as we shall hear later on. . . .

Those who are engaged in a spiritual ministry such as preachers and pastors must likewise remain steadfast before the peril of death. We have a plain command from Christ: "A good shepherd lays down his life for the sheep but the hireling sees the wolf coming and flees." For when people are dying, they most need a spiritual ministry which strengthens and comforts their consciences by word and sacrament and in faith overcomes death. However, where enough preachers are available in one locality and they agree to encourage the other clergy to leave in order not to expose themselves needlessly to danger, I do not consider such conduct sinful because spiritual services are provided for and because they would have been ready and willing to stay if it had been necessary. We read that St. Athanasius fled from his church that his life might be spared because many others were there to administer his office.[†] . . .

Accordingly, all those in public office such as mayors, judges, and the like are under obligation to remain. This, too, is God's word, which institutes secular authority and commands that town and country be ruled, protected, and preserved, as St. Paul teaches in Romans 13: "The governing authorities are God's ministers for your own good." To abandon an entire community which one has been called to govern and to leave it without official or government, exposed to all kinds of danger such as fires, murder, riots, and every imaginable disaster is a great sin. It is the kind of disaster the devil would like to instigate wherever there is no law and order. St. Paul says, "Anyone who does not provide for his own family denies the faith and is worse than an unbeliever." On the other hand, if in great weakness they flee but provide capable substitutes to make sure that the community is well governed and protected, as we previously indicated, and if they continually and carefully supervise them [i.e., the substitutes], all that would be proper.

What applies to these two offices [church and state] should also apply to persons who stand in a relationship of service or duty toward one another. . . .

Where no such emergency exists and where enough people are available for nursing and taking care of the sick, and where, voluntarily or by orders, those who are weak in faith make provision so that there is no need for additional helpers, or where the sick do not want them and have refused their services, I judge that they have an equal choice either to flee or to remain. . . .

It is not forbidden but rather commanded that by the sweat of our brow we should seek our daily food, clothing, and all we need and avoid destruction and disaster whenever we can, as long as we do so without detracting from our love and duty toward our neighbor. How much more appropriate it is therefore to seek to preserve life and avoid death if this can be done without harm to our neighbor, inasmuch as life is more than food and clothing, as Christ himself says in Matthew 6. If someone is so strong in faith, however, that he can willingly suffer nakedness, hunger, and want without tempting God and not trying to escape, although he could do so, let him continue that way, but let him not condemn those who will not or cannot do the same. Whether One May Flee From a Deadly Plague.[52]

Should a Christian Use Medicine to Avoid a Plague? Martin Luther: If one makes no use of intelligence or medicine when they could do so without detriment to their neighbor, such a person injures their body and must beware lest they become a suicide in God's eyes. By the same reasoning a person might forego eating and drinking, clothing and shelter, and boldly proclaim their faith that if God wanted to preserve them from starvation and cold, he could do so without food and clothing. Actually that would be suicide. It is even more shameful for a person to pay no heed to their own body and to fail to protect it against the plague the best they are able, and then to infect and poison others who might have remained alive if they had taken care of

[52]LW 43:120-23*; citing 1 Cor 3:2; Jn 10:11; Rom 13:4; 1 Tim 5:8; Mt 6:25. [†]Augustine, *Letter* 228, PL 33:1017.

their body as they should have. They are thus responsible before God for their neighbor's death and are a murderer many times over. Indeed, such people behave as though a house were burning in the city and nobody was trying to put the fire out. Instead they give leeway to the flames so that the whole city is consumed, saying that if God so willed, he could save the city without water to quench the fire. Whether One May Flee From a Deadly Plague.[53]

Paul Argues from His Suffering. The English Annotations: "If I must boast." Paul turns against his adversaries their objections against him, as if he should say: "They point to the calamities I face in order to take my authority away from me. But if I would boast in myself, I would make no better argument than to boast in my sufferings for the gospel; and God is my witness that I have devised and invented nothing." Annotations on 2 Corinthians 11:30.[54]

Fleeing Persecution and Faithfulness. Niels Hemmingsen: So that the Corinthians might have greater confidence in him, Paul calls on God as the witness of his narrative. For since God knows all things fully, he is able to provide wise testimony. This account is also reported by Luke in Acts 9, which occurred when the apostle returned to Damascus a second time. For, after he was divinely converted along the road and baptized in Damascus by Ananias, he went into Arabia to proclaim the Word of God. When he returned to Damascus a second time, with the whole city aroused against him, he escaped the hand of the governor of Aretas, king of Arabia, and thence departed for Jerusalem. Now, Paul's decision to flee does not at all support the frivolity of people who flee for any possible reason—whether they change their post because of a very light insult or because they are concerned about their leisure or stomach—but only those who are forced by a necessity similar to that of Paul's, and, like him, are able to glorify the Lord, because God only grants strength of spirit to people so that they might strongly despise all dangers. On the other hand, Paul's decision also warns people not to throw themselves into the hands of their enemies, instead of fleeing, when it is possible for them to preserve their godliness. Now it is clear from this that the zeal of many martyrs, who freely handed themselves over for slaughter, was unhealthy and not at all according to knowledge. But this weakness and foolish zeal, the Lord has no doubt considered good on account of the faith of Christ. Commentary on 2 Corinthians 11:31-33.[55]

Paul's Account Does Not Contradict Luke's. Wolfgang Musculus: Luke reports this event in Acts 9. . . . His account seems to differ from Paul's descriptions which ascribes the plot against him to the governor of King Aretas who was guarding the city, while Luke ascribes the plot to the Jews living in Damascus and makes no mention of this governor. But there is no true discrepancy here. Luke casts all the blame on the Jews because they had initiated this plan to kill Paul and were the chief authors of this evil. But Paul reckoned that it was the governor of the king who, at the urging of the Jews, had closed up the city and had applied his authority as the guardian of the gate to arrest and kill him. . . . Josephus in book 18 chapters 9 and 11 of his *Jewish Antiquities* gives information about who King Aretas was. Commentary on 2 Corinthians 11:32.[56]

Fleeing Persecution Is Permissible. Tilemann Hesshus: Luke describes this history in Acts 9. When Paul was converted to the knowledge of the Son of God, he thereafter brought testimonies from the sacred Scripture into the synagogues of Damascus, and he demonstrated constantly and with great zeal that Jesus Christ

[53]LW 43:131.

[54]Downame, ed., *English Annotations*, GG3r*.

[55]Hemmingsen, *Commentaria in Omnes Epistolas Apostolorum*, 301; citing Acts 9:23-25.

[56]Musculus, *Commentarius . . . in posteriorem epistolam Pauli ad Corinthios*, 366, 367.

was the living Son of God. He stirred up so much a Jewish rabbi against himself that, at the instigation of the Jews, the governor closed the city gates and had them guarded day and night so that Paul might not escape and they might kill him. But the believers, after placing Paul in a basket, lowered him through a window in the wall and so he escaped the hand of tyranny.

And so, from the very beginning of Paul's ministry, Satan demonstrated how great a furor he would press against Paul, and that he should expect this from then on. Paul recalls these events as he now mentions the false apostles, who, although they wanted to be considered the greatest of teachers and to have exceeded Paul in all things, yet they tasted no dangers but cunningly avoided them. Here one often debates whether it is permissible for a teacher of the church to flee danger. The response of our Lord Jesus Christ is very clear in Matthew 10: "If they are going to persecute you in one city, flee to another." Since the Son of God, the head of the church and teacher of righteousness, both advises and teaches us to flee when persecution arises, we do not need to fear at all that we will wound our conscience by fleeing. It is permissible to flee and withdraw oneself from the furies of men when tyrants make extreme threats or when the people are stirred up to sedition, or even when the plague grows—especially, with the urging of the church, to spare ourselves and the church by withdrawing for a time. Thus, Paul acted rightly by fleeing from the Jewish rabbi in Damascus, and also when he withdrew from the riots and seditions in Ephesus. So, too, Athanasius acted rightly when he withdrew from the furies of the Arians and withdrew himself from the threats of the tyrant Julian. When the Pharisees were breathing threats against Christ, he departed Judea and went to Galilee. EXPLICATION OF 2 CORINTHIANS 11:30-33.[57]

BUT WE SHOULD NOT ALWAYS FLEE PERSECUTION. TILEMANN HESSHUS: But, in fact, Paul is right to call [fleeing persecution] a "weakness." For, in addition to our weakness, the fear of the flesh enters into us. Whether we flee or endure extreme danger, our faith is not so strong that it is not mixed with the flesh, shrinking back from the danger of confession and weakness. Paul frankly admits these things since the false apostles were loudly trumpeting only their virtues. Another example is found in Christ our Lord. For though fleeing out of his boundless wisdom, nevertheless he did not swerve from perfect obedience. Cases can occur where it is not permissible immediately to run away from our enemies, especially when the church suggests and asks that we remain and when extreme danger is not yet imminent. . . . Thus, Nehemiah acted strongly and wisely when he did not withdraw due to the threats of the sycophants, for he understood that their advice and warnings were not from God. And the circumstances of the season and especially the Spirit of Christ (who must be diligently petitioned in times of need) will teach the godly mind when it must stand in battle against the enemy, and when it is permissible to flee to preserve life. Just as the same emperor is skilled and brave to know when he must begin fighting with the enemy, and again, when he must avoid fighting with the enemy. Christian men and women avoid that crazy recklessness which blindly throws itself into danger without need. They also avoid that deception and simulation whereby we abandon the necessary responsibilities of our office on account of the dread and fear of sycophants and tyrants. "The way of the righteous is level and unobstructed," says Solomon in the Proverbs. He easily sees what is pleasing to God and beneficial for the church, and what can be done without harming the conscience. EXPLICATION OF 2 CORINTHIANS 11:30-33.[58]

PAUL JUSTIFIED IN CLIMBING DOWN THE WALLS. JOHN CALVIN: Some people may ask . . . whether it was lawful when Paul climbed down the city walls—since this was a capital offense. I

[57]Hesshus, *Explicatio Secundae Epistolae Pauli ad Corinthios*, 268v-269v; citing Mt 10:23.

[58]Hesshus, *Explicatio Secundae Epistolae Pauli ad Corinthios*, 269v-270r; citing Neh 4:15-23; Prov 15:19; Is 26:7.

answer, first, that it is not known whether that punishment was sanctioned by law in the East. Second, even if it was, Paul nevertheless was guilty of nothing, because he neither did it out of hostility nor for sport, but out of necessity. The law would not punish a person who jumps from the walls to save his life from fire, and what difference is there between a fire and the savagery of robbers? In matters of law, we must always consider reason and equity. This consideration will exempt Paul from any guilt. Commentary on 2 Corinthians 11:33.[59]

[59]CO 50:135* (CTS 40:364).

Paul Escaped Out a Window. John Trapp: This was an honest trick, even though it was against Roman law to leap over walls. Cicero[†] says that "the laws ought always to be bent toward equity." The sense of the law is the law itself, and not always the letter of the law. Commentary on 2 Corinthians 11:33.[60]

[60]Trapp, *A Commentary or Exposition*, 732*. [†]Calvin also quotes this passage from Cicero in his *Commentary on Acts 9:25* (CO 48:212).

12:1-10 Paul's Vision and His Thorn

I must go on boasting. Though there is nothing to be
gained by it, I will go on to visions and revelations of
the Lord. [2]I know a man in Christ who fourteen
years ago was caught up to the third heaven—
whether in the body or out of the body I do not know,
God knows. [3]And I know that this man was caught
up into paradise—whether in the body or out of the
body I do not know, God knows— [4]and he heard
things that cannot be told, which man may not utter.
[5]On behalf of this man I will boast, but on my own
behalf I will not boast, except of my weaknesses—
[6]though if I should wish to boast, I would not be a fool,
for I would be speaking the truth; but I refrain from it,
so that no one may think more of me than he sees in
me or hears from me. [7]So to keep me from becoming
conceited because of the surpassing greatness of the
revelations,[a] a thorn was given me in the flesh, a
messenger of Satan to harass me, to keep me from
becoming conceited. [8]Three times I pleaded with the
Lord about this, that it should leave me. [9]But he said
to me, "My grace is sufficient for you, for my power is
made perfect in weakness." Therefore I will boast all
the more gladly of my weaknesses, so that the power
of Christ may rest upon me. [10]For the sake of Christ,
then, I am content with weaknesses, insults, hardships,
persecutions, and calamities. For when I am weak,
then I am strong.

a Or *hears from me, even because of the surpassing greatness of the revelations. So to keep me from becoming conceited*

Overview: Compelled by the false apostles' reckless boasts, Paul in these verses continues to defend his apostolic credentials, which are attested, not only by a heavenly vision, but also by a "thorn in the flesh" that serves as a constant reminder of Christ's power and his weakness. Reformation commentators encounter in this pericope a quiver full of perplexing questions: What is the difference between visions and revelations? Did Paul's rapture in 2 Corinthians 12:2 entail the actual removal of his body from this world? What is the third heaven, and how is it related to paradise? And of course, the greatest mystery of all: What was Paul's thorn in the flesh? On this latter question, early modern commentators offer a long list of suggestions, including frequent headaches, stomach disease, human adversaries such as Hymenaeus and Alexander (1 Tim 1:20), Satanic attacks, a speech impediment, terrors of demons, and even lust. Whatever their nature, God uses thorns like these in believers' lives to vitiate their pride, teach them humility, and strengthen their faith. The fact that the apostle prayed three times to be relieved of his thorn, but without success, raises the further question of why God failed to answer Paul's ardent prayer. On this final question, commentators agree that, from a larger perspective, God *did* respond to Paul's prayer by giving strength through the Holy Spirit so that he might endure Satan's attacks. This passage, then, offers enormous comfort to Christians as they suffer, for they are assured of God's sustaining grace and power even as they experience physical weakness. Indeed, the cross that godly people endure is not a sign of an angry judge, but the testimony of a loving Father.

Paul Continues to Refute the False Apostles. Tilemann Hesshus: In this chapter the apostle continues his refutation of the arrogance of the false apostles, and he suggests that, even if he freely boasts, he has far more just and illustrious reasons to do so. And as one example, Paul mentions the heavenly revelation so that he might suppress their frivolous boasting and, moreover, by exalting himself, he might far surpass the false apostles in the excellence of his revelations.

Now he reports that he had been caught up all the way to the third heaven and into paradise, where he had heard ineffable words. Of course, our Lord Jesus Christ had often appeared to Paul (as one sees from the Acts of the Apostles), but he controlled himself and did not recount everything, for he considered it sufficient to have blunted the foolishness of the false apostles. And Paul frankly admits that God had given to him a thorn in his flesh so that he would not become arrogant on account of the prominence of his gifts and revelations. And so, he prefers to boast concerning his weakness and troubles so that the power and glory of Jesus Christ might become more conspicuous.

Next, Paul blames the Corinthians for forcing him to descend to this kind of writing, for it would have been proper for them to defend Paul's apostolic authority and discredit the foolish boasting of the false apostles. For in nothing were they inferior to the other churches that the apostle had established. Paul had brilliantly taught them the doctrine of Christ's spiritual kingdom and had confirmed it with apostolic miracles. Hence, the Corinthians had no reason for bending their ears so readily to the false apostles who were attempting to disparage Paul's authority. So as not to be a burden to them, Paul received no remuneration from the Corinthians, and he commanded no penance from them. . . . And not only was Paul not a burden to the Corinthians, but neither was Titus, whom Paul had sent to them.

Finally, Paul solemnly affirms that he is saying these things in the sight of God in Christ Jesus and for the edification of the Corinthian church. And he is deeply concerned lest the Corinthians should fail in godliness and become more listless and fall back into quarrels, rivalries, disputes, and other such vices. Thus, the apostle Paul clearly demonstrates that he labors not to promote his own reputation; rather, it is confirmed that he is anxious that the Corinthian church make progress in piety and become pure in the faith. Explication of 2 Corinthians 12.[1]

Summary of the Chapter. Niels Hemmingsen: These are the parts of this chapter: First, there is an exposition of Paul's rapture into the third heaven. Second, he provides a statement of the purpose of his temptations, namely, so that he won't be praised on account of the revelations. Third, he mentions his delight in being persecuted for Christ. Fourth, he provides a statement of the reason for his boastings since they vindicate his apostolic authority. Fifth, the apostle makes mention of his coming to the Corinthians and the concerns he has for them. Commentary on 2 Corinthians 12.[2]

Paul's Holy Boasting. David Dickson: Paul continues in his holy boasting. There are three parts to this chapter. In the first part (through v. 11), he explains the heavenly vision he received, together with the events surrounding it. In the second part (through v. 19), he proves that the Corinthians ought to have freed him from the need to boast or defended him. In the third part he describes the causes of his troubles. Exposition of 2 Corinthians 12.[3]

12:1-6 *Paul's Heavenly Vision*

Timeless Benefits of Paul's Heavenly Visions. Moïse Amyraut: What benefit do we derive from the apostle's words here? Surely, my brothers, he illustrates the glory of the holy gospel! For what sect of philosophers from among those that have been the most famous in all the centuries can claim to be confirmed by similar visions? What religion—regardless of who established it—has received such a magnificent and authentic seal of the divinity of its revelation? Certainly, Moses climbed to the top of the mountain and had very intimate communications with God there. But Mount Sinai is one thing, the third heaven is another! The commandments that Moses received, which constituted the body of the law—that is one

[1]Hesshus, *Explicatio Secundae Epistolae Pauli ad Corinthios*, 271v-272v.

[2]Hemmingsen, *Commentaria in Omnes Epistolas Apostolorum*, 301.

[3]Dickson, *An Exposition of All St. Paul's Epistles*, 89*.

thing; but Paul's unutterable words are quite another! Besides this, these experiences establish the apostleship of this great servant of God and make him (I do not know how) even more effective in comforting and edifying the Gentiles, to whom our Lord had especially destined him to employ his ministry. And it is important that he should be worthy of our respect, and it should be clear to all that our ancestors were converted by a man that God raised up in such a wonderful fashion and allowed to participate in things beyond comprehension, conversing together in his presence in his sanctuary on high. Finally, although this happened to Paul alone, and we do not see any other examples, even so he does not fail to provide an opportunity for us to reflect on these things and on the foretastes that God gives us in this life of the heavenly delight to which we aspire. He does not catch us up to heaven in reality, but he does send heaven into our hearts through foretastes of his eternal delight and assurances of our blessed adoption, which he imprints on our consciences. Just as St. Paul boasted in God for being so kind to take him up to paradise, let us also boast in him for being so kind to place paradise in our souls. But as Paul was boasting in God alone, in the same manner let us give glory alone to our Redeemer for our consolation and our hope. Four Sermons.[4]

The Proper Use of God's Gifts. John Calvin: Now as if in the middle of his course, Paul restrains himself from going further, and in this way he most appropriately calls attention to the impudence of his rivals, and he testifies that he engages in this kind of contest with them only reluctantly. For how shameful they were to solicit, or rather, to beg for praise from every quarter so that they might seem equal to such a great man! As to the latter, he admonishes them by his own example that the more numerous and the more illustrious the graces with which anyone of us abounds, the less ought that person think of their own excellences. Thinking like this is exceedingly dangerous, for, as when entering a labyrinth, that person is soon dazzled so as to be too keen in discerning his gifts while being ignorant of himself. Paul is fearful lest this should happen to him. Indeed, God's gifts should be recognized so that we might be aroused, first, to show gratitude and, second, to use them rightly. But to appropriate them for the purpose of boasting—that cannot be done without great danger.

This is the difference between visions and revelations: A revelation often happens either in a dream or by an oracle in which nothing appears to the eyes, while a vision is almost never given without a revelation—that is, without God disclosing what he wishes by it. Commentary on 2 Corinthians 12:1.[5]

The Difference Between Visions and Revelations. Wolfgang Musculus: Several interpreters have described what the difference is between visions and revelations. Augustine defined three kinds of visions, namely, physical visions, spiritual visions, and mental visions. See Augustine's comments on Genesis 11, where he has a long and involved discussion concerning visions in which he treats this present passage. It is possible for there to be spiritual as well as physical visions in which there is no revelation unless it happens separately. An example of a physical vision is in Daniel 5, when Balthasar saw a hand writing words on the wall, and nevertheless he did not understand what he saw, because the vision was not accompanied by a revelation, which was provided afterward by Daniel. The visions which the eunuchs, who were in the service of Pharaoh, saw in Genesis 40 and which pharaoh saw in Genesis 41 were spiritual visions which did not include a revelation, until it was given by Joseph. [By contrast], the spiritual vision that Daniel saw in Daniel 7 was joined with a revelation. And very often revelations occur without visions, through the inner inspiration of the Holy Spirit. Now the apostle is speaking here about these kinds of

[4]Amyraut, *Le Ravissement de Saint Paul*, 36-38.

[5]CO 50:136 (CTS 40:365-66).

visions and revelations when he says, "I will come to visions and revelations of the Lord." Commentary on 2 Corinthians 12:1.[6]

Visions and Revelations. The English Annotations: Some interpreters distinguish between visions and revelations in this manner: a vision, they say, is when something is supernaturally represented to the sight, of which the party does not know the meaning and significance. Such was the vision of pharaoh and Nebuchadnezzar. A revelation, they say, is when something is supernaturally represented to the sight, and the meaning and significance is made known to the party who received the vision. Such were the visions of the prophets. But because it is not probable that St. Paul here had any vision whose meaning Christ did not reveal to him, other interpreters more convincingly distinguish visions from revelations in this fashion: visions may occur without ecstasy, as when the women saw the angels at the grave and were frightened, but not in a state of ecstasy; but revelations, such as Paul speaks about here, were apparitions experienced in a state of ecstasy. Such was the case with Peter in Acts 10 and St. John in Revelation 1. Annotations on 2 Corinthians 12:1.[7]

Some Anabaptists Claim They Have Had Heavenly Visions Like Paul. Sebastian Franck: Some [Anabaptists] tell of new commands of God revealed daily to evangelize both their brothers as well as strangers. Some go into a trance, distort their faces, and lie prone up to an hour. Some shake, some lie still, some as much as two or three days. Afterward, when they again come to themselves, they prophesy and tell of wonders as though they had been in a different world. They think they have this in common with Paul . . . who was caught up into the third heaven. Many cannot tell the mysteries which they saw in this trance. To some this trance comes often, to some seldom, to others not at all. Many of them make much of visions and dreams, some nothing. On the Anabaptists.[8]

Paul Refers to Himself in the Third Person. Moïse Amyraut: It is certain here that Paul is speaking about himself, and yet he did it as if he were speaking about a third person. . . . In this, as in all other things, Paul is imitating our Lord. For, although often in the Gospel [Jesus] speaks about himself in the first person, it also often happens that he expresses himself in the third person. In the Gospel of Matthew alone, there are twenty-five or thirty places where [Jesus], in place of saying "I" or "me," says instead "the Son of Man," and attributes to a third person that which one would normally say in the first person. . . .

When Paul states that "he knows a man in Christ," he is saying nothing more than that he knows a Christian man. For in the New Testament, it is the same thing to be in Christ and to have believed in him and embraced his gospel. And our apostle expresses himself in this way for a specific reason, because he could have said "I know an apostle of Christ." If he had wanted to glorify himself, he could have expressed himself in this fashion: "I know one who has received election, a man set apart from his mother's womb to preach the gospel among the nations, a person called of God to this role by miracles and the revelations of Christ, to be an illustrious instrument of the Redeemer's grace, who has enriched and ennobled thousands with beautiful knowledge." But besides the fact that it was far from his natural inclination to parade his titles and qualities, this would have given his enemies just the opening that they hoped for, namely, to insult him for what they called his arrogance. Thus, Paul takes for himself only the quality of a Christian, which is sovereignly glorious in truth; but, because it was shared by any number of other people, and even his enemies (though they were false teachers), by

[6]Musculus, *Commentarius . . . in posteriorem epistolam Pauli ad Corinthios*, 368.
[7]Downame, ed., *English Annotations*, GG3r*; citing Gen 41; Dan 2; Lk 24:1-5; Acts 10:17; Rev 1:10.
[8]CRR 10:236.

attributing it to himself, he was not afraid that they would take this opportunity to accuse him of vainglory. Four Sermons.[9]

I Knew a Man in Christ. The English Annotations: The meaning is either this: "'I speak this in Christ,' that is, it is spoken without vainglory, for I am seeking nothing but Christ Jesus alone." Or this: "'I knew a man in Christ,' that is, a Christian and believer, a man—even myself—who for all that is nothing other than a man, no god or angel." In this latter case he speaks of himself in the third person as a token of his humility. . . . The words "in Christ" may also carry the form of an oath as in Romans 9:1. Annotations on 2 Corinthians 12:2.[10]

Paul's Revelation Occurred Long After His Conversion. Andreas Hyperius: If we pay careful attention, Paul was not only "caught up" in Damascus when he was first called to the gospel and neither drank nor ate for three days (as many want to interpret this passage) but also at another time long afterward. For it is clear that this present vision occurred at some time other than during his first conversion since he had preached the gospel for seventeen years before he, together with Barnabas, went up to Jerusalem (as he himself reports in Galatians 1 and 2), and not until after that time did he come to Corinth. And it is not absurd to say that the Lord illumined and confirmed that chosen vessel (I mean Paul) with new and extraordinary visions at various times. Commentary on 2 Corinthians 12:2.[11]

Fourteen Years Ago. David Chytraeus: This epistle was written to the Corinthians twenty-two years after Paul's conversion, which was sixty-five years after Christ's birth. It was then that this vision was shown to Paul—not as he journeyed to Damascus, but about eight or nine years after his conversion. Postil for Sexagesima Sunday.[12]

Paul Was Actually Caught Up to Heaven. Moïse Amyraut: The apostle says that he was "caught up"—and this term deserves our consideration. For, in our French version, we sometimes use it to signify what we otherwise mean by the term "to be in ecstasy," when there is a separation of the soul from all external senses, so that they no longer perform their function, and, meanwhile, being overcome by this vision (which is an interior sense), one sees extraordinary and miraculous things. Thus it is said of St. Peter, in Acts 10, that being in the city of Joppa, and having gone up on the housetop around the sixth hour for prayer, he experienced an ecstasy of the spirit, that is, his soul was transported so that it abandoned its external senses. . . . I see that some who interpret the account that St. Paul reports in this present passage do so as if it were a question of this kind of ecstatic experience. . . .

I will only say that the word which the apostle inserts in the original, "caught up," has a particular emphasis. Because it signifies an actual transport of something from one place to another, being done with some kind of violence or with some great speed. The word is used this way in the book of Acts, where it is reported that the captain of the Jerusalem fortress, fearing that Paul would be torn to pieces by the Jews, commanded that the soldiers go down and "snatch him up" from the midst of them and bring him to the fortress. . . . This is also how the word is taken in that passage in the Gospel where it is said that the troops wanted to "catch up" our Lord to make him king—and there are many other similar passages. Thus, if it happens only in this sort of vision, where the soul

[9]Amyraut, *Le Ravissement de Saint Paul*, 11-14.
[10]Downame, ed., *English Annotations*, GG3r*.
[11]Hyperius, *Commentarii . . . in Epistolam D. Pauli ad Romanos, et Utramque ad Corinthios*, 419 ; citing Gal 1:18; 2:1-2.

[12]Chytraeus, *A Postil of Certeine Epistles*, 84*. Recent biblical scholars do not agree with Chytraeus's chronology. F. F. Bruce has established that Paul was converted to Christianity around the year 33, and that he wrote the Corinthian correspondence in 55–56—not in the year 65 as Chytraeus indicates. See Bruce, *Paul, Apostle of the Heart Set Free* (Grand Rapids: Eerdmans, 1977), 475.

is not at all actually separated from the body, but only caught up in ecstasy, at least it must be that the apostle St. Paul believed to have seen God transporting him on high into heaven, to hear there the unutterable words that he reports to us. . . . [Thus], it seems that he wanted us to understand that this experience of being "caught up" was an actual removal [from this world] into heaven, either of his soul or of his entire person. Four Sermons.[13]

We Don't Know Whether Paul's Soul Was Separated from His Body. The English Annotations: Paul's words could mean "Whether God allowed this to happen by framing in my soul some representation of those heavenly things without an actual separation of the soul from the body, or whether my soul was actually separated for a while from my body and transported to heaven to contemplate there these marvelous things—I do not know—but I am sure that I actually beheld these things." Or Paul's words could also mean, "Whether I was caught up into heaven with body and soul together, or with the soul only, is unknown to me." Thomas Aquinas and other schoolmen argue that St. Paul was only in an ecstasy, and for a time beside himself, and that his soul was not actually separated from his body because then he would have been dead, and that afterward, when he came to himself, he would have been raised from the dead. But this does not follow. For according to the opinion of philosophers and some theologians who distinguish the spirit or reasonable soul from the vegetative and sensory soul, the reasonable soul of St. Paul might actually have been severed from his body for a time, without Paul's death and with his sensory soul remaining in his body. All who attempt to explain that which the apostle himself could not understand are nothing but presumptuous. St. Augustine[†] rightly censures as impudent and rash those who offer such explanations, no matter how likely they might appear. Annotations on 2 Corinthians 12:2-3.[14]

Three Levels of Heaven. Cardinal Cajetan: Now Paul called that highest place the "third heaven," for three heavens are mentioned in sacred Scripture. The lowest is the airy heaven, according to that passage: "the birds of heaven." The middle is that starry heaven, which is mentioned in the beginning of Genesis: "And God set them in the expanse of heaven." The third and highest is "all the waters that are above the heavens," which Scripture mentions frequently. Now this we call the watery heaven, but philosophers call it the Prime Mover; indeed, a later tradition calls it the highest heaven, though nothing of the sort is found in Scripture. Now Paul mentions his being "caught up" to indicate that this raising up of his inner self happened by the strength of the one raising him up, not by any participating force of nature. Commentary on 2 Corinthians 12:2.[15]

Paul Raptured into the Third Heaven. Martin Luther: Many have written about the rapture of St. Paul into the third heaven and to paradise—and have fretted about what the first, second, third heaven, and paradise are. But since St. Paul, who was there and himself does not say and cannot say—he says, "Man may not utter, for he heard unspeakable words"—we will have to submit and confess that we do not know. That is unimportant, for he boasts about this not so that we would know or be raptured according to his example, but so that he could shut the mouths of fanatics and demonstrate how insignificant their boasting was compared to his. But it is certain that he was raptured out of this life into an inexpressible life—otherwise it would not be called "raptured." Postil for Sexagesima Sunday.[16]

[13]Amyraut, *Le Ravissement de Saint Paul*, 16-20; citing Acts 10:9-11; 22:24; Jn 6:15.

[14]Downame, ed., *English Annotations*, GG3r-v*. [†]See Augustine, *De Genesi ad litteram liber* 12.3 (PL 34:456).

[15]Cajetan, *In Posteriorem Pauli Epistolam ad Corinthios Commentarii*, 195; citing Gen 1:17, 7.

[16]LW 76:328 (WA 17/2:150-51).

The Third Heaven Is Ineffable. Philipp Melanchthon: Many people say many things about the third heaven. Since a special revelation is a unique gift, who are we to judge what kind it is? Those who dwell on this passage unnecessarily are guilty of impious curiosity. And thus, Paul denies that this revelation of his can be explained with words, just as no spiritual experiences can be explained with words. Now, because Christ wished to be understood, it is necessary that everyone be God-taught [*theodidactos*]; the hearts of the saints must be touched by the Spirit of God. I am of the opinion that the third heaven should be understood as some level of knowledge of the Trinity. Annotations on 2 Corinthians 12:2.[17]

Paul Tasted the Sublime Mysteries of Heaven. Wolfgang Musculus: By the "third heaven," I do not doubt that the apostle wished to signify that he, in his inner person, had been caught up into the most secret and sublime mysteries of heaven. That is why we should not be anxious to argue about the number of the heavens. It is known, of course, that there are many levels of the one heaven that are called by the name "heaven" in the Scriptures. Thus, the sky where birds fly is called "heaven." . . . So, too, "heaven" is the celestial expanse where one finds the sun, moon, and stars. Moreover, "heaven" is that crystalline and fiery realm. . . . Someday, we will be able to understand heaven better than we do now on earth. In my opinion, the careful examination of the heavens ought to be postponed until we are enjoying that condition of felicity. . . .

Augustine examines whether the phrase "into paradise" in verse 3 should be understood as the same as "to the third heaven." Nicholas of Lyra† argues that they are the same, which is also the view of a number of more recent interpreters. But Paul has distinguished two separate experiences of being caught up. . . . When he was caught up to the third heaven, he was seeing the glory of God and the glory of Christ reigning in heaven. But "paradise" refers to the residence of the blessed saints, the patriarchs, and the prophets, where Paul not only saw what he himself would become after the dissolution of his body, but also heard certain secrets which rendered him better instructed in his apostolic office. Commentary on 2 Corinthians 12:2-3.[18]

The Third Heaven and Paradise. Niels Hemmingsen: Now as for the way he was "caught up," since the apostle states that he does not know whether it was in the body or outside the body, it is not for us scrupulously to inquire, because this was unknown to the apostle himself. Moreover, since he understands the third heaven and paradise to be the same thing, and the third heaven is no doubt the place of the blessed spirits, where the divine majesty reveals himself all the more glorious to the angels and the souls of the saints, and where Christ with his glorified body is worshiped by the angels and the souls of the saints, it is proved that paradise here does not signify the place in which the first human parents were placed by God. For paradise was on the earth which afterward, in the universal flood, was destroyed by the inundation of water. And it was a type of this paradise that Christ mentioned as did Paul in this present passage. Now when Paul here calls the third heaven (that is, the place of the blessed) paradise, he indicates that believing in Christ ought not only to restore the position of honor in which the first parents lived before the fall, but also that the future happiness in the heavenly paradise is much greater than it would have been on the earth. Now if anyone asks: Why is it here called the third heaven, why not the first, or the second? Moreover, are there more heavens than three? We can respond to this question in this fashion. First, Scripture mentions an "airy heaven," in which birds fly. Then, another region, which borders the airy heaven is called "the heavens" in

[17]*Melanchthons Werke*, 4:131.

[18]Musculus, *Commentarius . . . in posteriorem epistolam Pauli ad Corinthios*, 370. †Nicholas of Lyra (1270–1349) was a Franciscan teacher and one of the foremost biblical exegetes of the Middle Ages.

which are located all the visible celestial bodies, such as planets and, fixed above them, the stars. Now, beyond this is the third heaven, which the apostle mentions here. The first and second heavens humans can ascend with their mathematical speculations. For the third heaven, Jesus Christ is the only teacher, who established Paul in the gospel ministry lest he seem inferior to the other apostles who conversed with the Lord bodily on the earth. Now when the apostle says that he heard unutterable things which no mortal is able to comprehend, he reminds us to desire that heavenly school in which, although now we see only in a mirror dimly, we will see face-to-face, contemplating the glory of the Lord. Therefore, let our citizenship be in heaven, where Christ our savior sits in the glory of the Father. Commentary on 2 Corinthians 12:2-3.[19]

Paul's Ecstatic Revelation. Huldrych Zwingli: "This pertains to the revelations—not to the life—of that man: namely, that I was so overwhelmed by heavenly splendor and ineffable joy that I did not fully know whether I was in the body or outside the body, for I was in a state of ecstasy and seized with ineffable joy, and I was filled with insatiable pleasure when so many and such great things were revealed to me, which I am not at all able to capture with words."

Paradeisos is a garden and place full of delights. However, here it is employed as a synecdoche[†] for the exceptional pleasure and charm which so captivated Paul's mind that he was not able to tear himself away from it—a pleasure so pure that Paul thought that he was already then in heaven. We read a similar sort of thing in Matthew 17 when Christ displayed his glory to his [disciples]. By the phrase "the third heaven," I think Paul simply means by way of a strong hyperbole something that is surpassing and ravishing. Annotations on 2 Corinthians 12:2-3.[20]

Paradise Denotes Celestial Glory. John Calvin: Since a region especially pleasant and delightful is called in Scripture "the garden of God," it became common among the Greeks to use the term *paradise* to denote celestial glory, even before Christ's advent, as it appears in Sirach 40. It is also used this way in Luke's Gospel, when Christ responds to the thief: "Today you will be with me in paradise"—that is, you will delight in the presence of God, in the condition and life of the blessed. Commentary on 2 Corinthians 12:3.[21]

The Meaning of "Paradise." Moïse Amyraut: Jesus Christ and the apostles employ this term "paradise" to indicate the place of heavenly delight where the spirits of believers are gathered after death. For you know that our Lord speaks in this way to the thief who was converted beside him as he hung on the cross: "Today, you will be with me in paradise." And in Revelation 2, he says "to the one who overcomes, I will give to him to eat from the tree of life, which is in the middle of the paradise of my God." And St. Paul, as you see here, after having said that he was "caught up into the third heaven"—which is no doubt the place of glory and delight—added that he was "caught up into paradise" to signify the same thing. Four Sermons.[22]

Paradise and Its Delights. Andreas Hyperius: Now it is known that paradise was a garden, which the Lord planted for a garden in Eden, perhaps not far from the city of Edenna or Edessa in Mesopotamia. And so it seems that the memory of the name was preserved when the place itself was abandoned. For the memory of this name see Ezekiel 27 [*sic*, Ezekiel 28] and Isaiah 37. Now the first human beings were placed in that most fertile and pleasant garden so that they might abound there in delights. But with their fall, the dignity of the place was also destroyed—as no

[19]Hemmingsen, *Commentaria in Omnes Epistolas Apostolorum*, 302.
[20]Zwingli, *Annotatiunculae . . . ex ore Zvinglij*, 189; citing Mt 17:1-3.
[†]A synecdoche is a figure of speech in which the part is used for the whole.

[21]CO 50:137 (CTS 40:368-69); citing Sir 40:17, 28; Lk 23:43.
[22]Amyraut, *Le Ravissement de Saint Paul*, 25-26; citing Lk 23:43; Rev 2:7.

doubt the sin of our first parents deserved. Hence, this word *paradise* began to be employed metaphorically of any charming place. . . . Thus, in Genesis 13, considering the plane of Sodom, it is said that it was like paradise or the garden of the Lord. But heaven, the seat of the blessed, also began to be called by the name "paradise" on account of its supreme dignity; for this reason, the Lord said to the thief: "Today you will be with me in paradise," that is, in the celestial kingdom, just as that thief prayed that he would be brought into the kingdom of the Messiah. Consequently, when Paul here says that he was caught up into the third heaven, or into paradise, it seems to me that this hyperbolic way of speaking does not express the excellence of his vision and the miraculous ecstasies he experienced, so that, even if he were transported into heaven itself (as we might say) and placed outside himself, it would nevertheless be impossible for him to behold things more marvelous and more thrilling to the whole soul. This seems to be the simplest and most reasonable interpretation. Commentary on 2 Corinthians 12:3.[23]

God's Perfect Knowledge. Moïse Amyraut: Certainly, my brothers, neither the Corinthians nor anyone else can doubt that God knew exactly how all of this took place. Things of old, things present, things to come—all of these are laid bare and uncovered before his eyes. God's knowledge is not limited even to these things. He even knows all things that are possible, even though they do not and never will have any actual existence. How, therefore, would God ignore the things that he himself has done, and which are executed by the power of his hand? But that also is not what the apostle St. Paul wishes to say. He means that it is God alone who knows him, and that if we want to know about it, it is necessary for us to make our request to God. Four Sermons.[24]

Paul's Ecstatic Vision Caused Him to Forget Himself. John Trapp: So far did Paul forget and neglect his own body, which is so dear and near in comparison to the incomparable delight he then took in the Lord. "O that joy! O my God, when shall I be with thee?" These were the dying words of the last Lord Harrington, right before he passed into heaven. "O the joys, the joys, the unspeakable joys that I feel in my soul!" said another person that was entering into heaven and had a foretaste of eternal life. Peter in the transfiguration was so enraptured, that he never thought about constructing a tabernacle for himself in Matthew 17—he didn't care if he lay out of doors, so that he might longer enjoy that glimpse of heaven's glory. Commentary on 2 Corinthians 12:3.[25]

Words That Cannot Be Uttered. Jacques Lefèvre d'Étaples: Why is it that Paul said that he heard unutterable words of which human beings cannot speak? I certainly think this: that those words were so great and the measure of them so immense that no human being could express such great things to another mortal. And if Paul disclosed anything from those words, he revealed them not in the unutterable form that he heard them, but with utterable words according to human fashion. In a similar way, the disciple whom God loved wrote down the holy apocalypse, not as he heard it (for what he heard could not be spoken to human beings), but with utterable words and in a form that was possible to speak and describe. Whenever angels present themselves to people shaking with fear and reveal secrets to their minds, it is impossible to speak to other human beings in this fashion, for angelic speech is not the same as human speech. Therefore, those things were unutterable which it was not at all permitted nor possible to speak to a human being. Paul was able, in a human fashion, to write and report to the Corinthians what he heard and saw. But he held back, lest the

[23]Hyperius, *Commentarii . . . in Epistolam D. Pauli ad Romanos, et Utramque ad Corinthios*, 409-10; citing Ezek 28:13; Is 37:12; Gen 13:10; Lk 23:43.
[24]Amyraut, *Le Ravissement de Saint Paul*, 106-7.
[25]Trapp, *A Commentary or Exposition*, 732*; citing Mt 17:4.

Corinthians attribute more wisdom to a mortal human being than was right, and lest they focus more on him and less on God than was proper. Commentary on 2 Corinthians 12:4.[26]

The Limits of Human Knowledge. John Calvin: From this we may gather a most useful warning regarding setting boundaries to knowledge. We are naturally inclined to curiosity. Hence, having abandoned altogether or tasting lightly and despising that doctrine which is effective for edification, we are driven to frivolous questions. Then, there follows recklessness and rashness so that we do not hesitate to judge on matters unknown and hidden. From these two sources has arisen a great part of scholastic theology, and everything that babbler Dionysius[†] dared to fabricate concerning *Celestial Hierarchies*. It is important for us to be all the more sensible so as not to know anything except what the Lord wishes to reveal to his church. Let this be the limit of our knowledge. Commentary on 2 Corinthians 12:4.[27]

Paul's Unspeakable Words. Wolfgang Musculus: Paul employs the Greek phrase *arrēta rēmata*, that is, words which cannot or ought not to be spoken, either because they are shameful and disgraceful, or mystical and thus a hidden mystery, or wicked, or prohibited. We think that these words were not *unspeakable* per se, but that Paul judged it as inappropriate that they be spoken by a human being to other humans outside of heaven. That is why he adds the phrase "of which it is not permissible for human beings to speak." Saying this, Paul cuts off all the curiosity we have to learn about it. Commentary on 2 Corinthians 12:4.[28]

[26]Lefèvre, *Commentariorum in Epistolas Beati Pauli . . . Liber Tertius*, 142v.

[27]CO 50:138 (CTS 40:370-371). [†]Dionysius the Pseudo-Areopagite was a sixth-century mystical theologian who presented a Platonic vision of Christianity in his most influential writings, including the *Celestial Hierarchy*, *Divine Names*, and *Mystical Theology*.

[28]Musculus, *Commentarius . . . in posteriorem apostolam Pauli Corinthiorum*, 371.

Words Unutterable. Moïse Amyraut: First, it is necessary to note that this word "unutterable" and the phrase "what is impossible for anyone to recount" only signify the same thing—the latter has been added to serve as a commentary and explanation of the former. . . . One can take the words of St. Paul here in two ways, and in fact, interpreters render them in different ways. For some people translate it as . . . "it is not *possible* for a man to recount," and others render it thus: "it is not *permissible* or allowable for a man to recount." . . . Those who consider the word "unutterable" in the usage of good Greek authors (since, I believe, this is the only place where one encounters this word in the New Testament), will find that it is most ordinarily employed to indicate those things that one is not permitted to say—things which, even though one could express them with words, ought nevertheless to be kept hidden in sacred silence. Four Sermons.[29]

The Flesh Grumbles Against the Cross. Philipp Melanchthon: "On behalf of this man I will boast, but I will not boast concerning myself. . . ." It should be noted generally how often Paul says that he boasts in the cross, so that we might learn from this that the cross brings salvation. This doctrine cannot persuade the flesh, which grumbles against the judgment of God, just as the children of Israel grumbled constantly in the desert (which is a most grievous sin). As Numbers 14 states: "How long will this people despise me?" Annotations on 2 Corinthians 12:5.[30]

Godly Boasting. Niels Hemmingsen: Paul had been forced by the slanderous words of the false apostles to show that he was not inferior to the other apostles. Now he splendidly shows within what boundaries he will confine that holy boasting. First, he rejects the opportunity to boast in himself and he directs the focus of boasting to God. Second, he excludes boasting in the flesh.

[29]Amyraut, *Le Ravissement de Saint Paul*, 52-53, 54, 64.

[30]*Melanchthons Werke*, 4:131; citing Num 14:11.

Third, he imposes a bridle on himself by considering his weakness lest he step outside the goal. Therefore, we also learn here seven things that ought to be included in Christian boasting. First, since we are compelled to tell of the blessings of God toward us, we will recognize him as their author and not proclaim ourselves, but God alone. Second, we will avoid that selfishness which is accustomed to force us to attribute even a tiny bit of praise to ourselves. Third, we will place a yoke on our flesh; we will consider how great is our weakness when we are left to ourselves [and] how much we are stimulated thinking about the power of God, who strengthens our weakness with his power. Commentary on 2 Corinthians 12:5-6.[31]

Paul Boasts in God's Goodness. Tilemann Hesshus: Paul shows that he has good reasons for boasting, for he is not trumpeting his own virtues or good works but is celebrating the immense goodness of God toward him. He had obtained from God the privilege to spread abroad such a lofty revelation by no merits of his own. Rather God, who out of his immense goodness had called Paul to the apostolic office and established him as a teacher of the Gentiles, had translated him into heaven out of his great mercy so that he might be rendered more confident in so glorious a revelation. Therefore, Paul proclaimed the infinite goodness of God toward him when he boasted concerning these revelations. And he could boast about many things, not because he was foolish (as was the case with the false apostles), but because he was speaking the truth. Now he held himself back and showed that he was reluctant to have this remembrance dragged from him. For Paul feared lest more things be attributed to him than was right, for hearers are inclined either to hold their teachers with less reverence than they should, or to attribute to them more things and hold them in a more exalted position than is proper. Now, although it was a serious sin not to imitate the apostle in love and service as was appropriate, nevertheless it was much more serious to be guilty of too much reverence rather than too little. For there was danger lest they worship the apostle instead of the mediator, and to depend entirely on his authority. John the Baptist reprimanded his disciples when they would have willingly imposed on him the title Messiah. And the people of Lystra would have sacrificed to Paul and Barnabas because of the healing of the lame man, had not Paul prohibited it. Truly, when people make more of an apostle or anyone else than is proper, then Christ—who is the only foundation of our salvation—is diminished. Therefore, so that the Corinthians or others might not be taken over by such madness, Paul preferred to pass over his revelations in silence, for he considered it sufficient to receive the authority of an apostle and faithful minister of Christ among his hearers. Explication of 2 Corinthians 12:5-6.[32]

Paul's Restraint and Humility. Niels Hemmingsen: Paul here is anticipating [his opponents' argument]. For, to the false apostles who might be able to object, "He has now described everything about which he can boast," Paul responds and affirms that he has many other things for which he could truly boast about in the Lord. But he restrains himself in this matter, lest someone ascribes more to him than what should be observed in his apostleship. For Paul is content to be satisfied with that role that God has assigned to him. Consider here the contrast: the false apostles were boasting about many things for which the Corinthians had no experience. But Paul was boasting only about those things which were known to the Corinthians' experience. Thus, he quietly and subtly rebukes the false apostles who were proudly boasting and, in the meantime, were vane liars. For, it is altogether foolish to boast when there is no truth present. Commentary on 2 Corinthians 12:6.[33]

[31]Hemmingsen, *Commentaria in Omnes Epistolas Apostolorum*, 392.

[32]Hesshus, *Explicatio Secundae Epistolae Pauli ad Corinthios*, 277r-278r.

[33]Hemmingsen, *Commentaria in Omnes Epistolas Apostolorum*, 302-3.

Being Viewed Realistically. John Trapp: "Let no one," said Gregory, "desire to seem more than they are, so that they may be more than they seem." "It does not please me," said Augustine,† "that I am thought by many people to be that which I am not. For truly they love not me, but another for me." Commentary on 2 Corinthians 12:6.[34]

12:7-10 *Paul's Thorn in the Flesh*

God's Strength and Human Frailty. Desiderius Erasmus: So that I might not be too exalted by the loftiness of the revelations, or more highly regarded among people than is good, the gracious will of God permitted a goad and affliction of the body to be given to me. Its purpose is both to remind me forcibly of myself and to prove to all that I am mortal, subject to ills we all share. Moreover, to afflict me as I do Christ's work, a messenger and servant of Satan was given, in order to hinder my gospel and to harass me with the most savage persecutions, just as if, hurling me down and pressing upon me, he were to beat me on the head, so that I should not be unduly elated. Since the situation was fiercely annoying for me, three times I asked the Lord to free me from this affliction.

But he, having my interest at heart more than I myself, responded after this fashion: "Paul, be content with my kindness toward you; you are not to press your demands any further. The fact that you are being pummeled by afflictions pertains, at the same time, both to making my glory illustrious—for while you are safe under my protection you cannot be conquered, no matter how great the storms—and to your salvation, inasmuch as the more you are afflicted by the evils of the body, the richer you grow in the goods of the spirit." Thus it happens that God's strength finds its true end in human frailty, and weakness completes power. Paraphrases on 2 Corinthians 12.[35]

Paul's Thorn Was Persecution and Suffering. Martin Luther: Dear God, if temptation must still cling to such a great man so that he does not boast about his great revelations, then how are others and we who are weak to be free from boasting? Many teachers in the past have explained that this thorn was a temptation of the flesh in St. Paul. That [explanation] was caused by the Latin text, which reads *stimulus carnis*, "a stake or goad of the flesh." But that cannot be, for he does not call fleshly temptation a "goad," since a goad is rather something bad and painful, and the goad of the flesh here is not something with which the flesh pierces, but rather by which it is pierced. Moreover, the Greek text has "a thorn for the flesh," or a thorn on or in the flesh. This is very close to the German proverb, as we say, "The club is tied to the dog's neck." It is as if he would say: "Just as you use a club on a dog, a ring on a bear's nose, a bit in a horse's mouth, or a gag in a pig's jaw so that they do not run or bite or act mischievously, so it also happens that I have a thorn, that is, a large club, on my body so that I do not boast."

He himself explains what that thorn or club is when he says, "the angel of Satan," that is, the devil who hits him with his fists, that is, confidently thrashes and pounds him. Therefore, it cannot be a fleshly temptation. I am not displeased to think that this thrashing and pounding from the devil, who is his club, means all the persecution and suffering which he listed above. . . .

Yet it seems from the text that it was something special that the devil himself forced on St. Paul's body, because it says that the thorn or club was Satan's angel with which Satan pounded on his body—also because he so diligently asked three times that it leave him, but that was not granted. I do not think that he would have asked that persecution leave him, as if he did not want to endure any persecution. Because he himself does not inform us what it was, we must let it remain a secret suffering, which no one other than St. Paul knew. What we do know is enough, namely, that just as God had given him great revelations, which no one can know, on the other hand he also used

[34]Trapp, *A Commentary or Exposition*, 733*. †Augustine's statement is found in *S. Aureli Augustini Operum Sectio II, Epistolae* (Leipzig; G. Freytag, 1904), 44:252.
[35]CWE 43:274-75.

such a club on him and sent such a thorn upon his body to restrain him from being elated. No one knew, other than he alone, how that thorn or club beat him black and blue and thrashed him. Postil on Sexagesima Sunday.[36]

Paul's Thorn Was Various Temptations. John Calvin: Now it is asked what that thorn was. Those people are ridiculous who think that Paul was tempted by lust—hence, that interpretation must be rejected. Others think that Paul was afflicted with frequent headaches. Chrysostom[†] is more inclined to think that the reference is to Hymenaeus and Alexander and the like, who were causing many troubles for Paul at the instigation of the devil. My opinion is that, under this term is comprehended every kind of temptation with which Paul was afflicted. For the word "flesh" here, in my judgment, signifies not the body but that part of the soul that has not yet been regenerated. Thus, this would be the sense: "A thorn was given to me so that my flesh might be stabbed by it, for I am not yet so spiritual that I am not exposed to temptations according to the flesh."

Moreover, he calls [this thorn] a messenger of Satan for this reason: since all temptations are sent by Satan, whenever they attack us, they warn us that Satan is near. Hence, whenever we are aware of temptation, it is important for us to arouse ourselves and quickly arm ourselves to repel Satan's assaults. Commentary on 2 Corinthians 12:7.[37]

Paul's Thorn Was the Adversities He Faced. Heinrich Bullinger: Now Paul was given a thorn in the flesh. . . . Theophylact[†] understood the term "thorn in the flesh" as lustful temptation to which he was especially exposed. But the dangers, vigils, imprisonments, chains, journeys, and labors would not have allowed licentiousness to run riot in Paul's most sacred body. St. Jerome's commentary on Paul's epistle to the Galatians reports that some people were of the opinion that this thorn was poor physical health and that Paul was often afflicted with headaches.[‡] There are others, whose number includes Aquinas and Erasmus's *Annotations*, of the opinion that Paul suffered from a stomach disease. In reality, the word "thorn" means a sharpened stake; thus, we take it here as a metaphor for the adversity that was torturing the flesh and whole body of the apostles from time to time. Now, this follows naturally from the interpretation of "angel of Satan." For an "angel" signifies a messenger, almost a minister, and the word "Satan" means adversary. Thus, the apostle establishes a kind of classification, either of persons (as one might understand a troop of adversaries, the false apostles, and persecutors of the Word of the Lord), or all the kinds of adverse things that afflicted Paul's body. St. Ambrose also explains it this way.[§] Commentary on 2 Corinthians 12:7.[38]

Paul's Thorn Was a Human Opponent. Wolfgang Musculus: The Latin word "goad" (*stimulus*) translates the Greek *skolops*, a word that means "stake," "peg," and "spike," namely, a piece of wood that is sharp and pointed at the tip. A goad was used among the ancients and is still used among a great many nations in various ways. Some use goads to prod and drive cattle; others use them as spears in military conflicts; others use them to make enclosures and ramparts; still others use them to torture criminals. Here, the apostle is using this word in a metaphorical rather than a specific sense. He indicates what he means by it when he adds the phrase "messenger of Satan." People have different opinions about the specific identity of Paul's goad. Some people think it refers to the headaches that Paul frequently suffered; others to the suffering of colic; others to the stirrings of carnal lust; others to the terrors of Satan; others to all kinds of

[36]LW 76:328-29 (WA 17.2:151-52).

[37]CO 50:139 (CTS 40:373-74); citing 1 Tim 1:20. [†]For Chrysostom's interpretation, see PG 61:577-78 (NPNF[1] 12:400).

[38]Bullinger, *In Posteriorem . . . ad Corinthios Epistolam Commentarius*, 331. [†]For Theophylact's interpretation, see PG 124:931, 934. [‡]Jerome, *Commentary on Galatians*, PG 26:381. [§]For Ambrose's statement, see PL 17:349-50.

temptations; others to some demons. But Chrysostom† is much closer to the true sense of the apostle, in my judgment, when he interprets the word "goad" as relating to Paul's enemies who were inflicting him with numerous injuries, insults, and persecutions, among whom he lists by name Alexander the coppersmith, Hymenaeus, and Philetus. Certainly, Paul especially complains about Alexander in 2 Timothy 4 because he caused Paul great harm and strongly resisted Paul's message. Nevertheless, I think that the apostle is speaking in this passage about one specific and especially wicked adversary, whom he particularly calls an angel of Satan. Alexander was like this; he was troublesome for Paul not only in one place but opposed him most irrationally wherever he went. Paul compares him to a spike and peg because just as a very sharp spike injures the flesh by stabbing it, so the attacks of Alexander were like stab wounds. Commentary on 2 Corinthians 12:7.[39]

Paul's Thorn to Be Taken Metaphorically. David Chytraeus: The Greek word *skolops* signifies a sharp stake; whereupon, the verb *anaskolopizein* signifies to be stabbed with a stake. Consequently, Lucian ridiculed Christ by calling him the wizard of Palestine who was stabbed on a post. But in this passage of St. Paul, it seems that the word should be taken metaphorically to refer to singular torments or sharp griefs both of body and mind, or all kinds of adversities, slanders, backbitings, reproaches, deprivations, persecutions, and such struggles of faith as are described in Psalms 69 and 38 and elsewhere. These and other similar torments remind us of the humility and obedience we owe to God, and of God's power working salvation to everyone who believes through weak and miserable instruments. Postil on Sexagesima Sunday.[40]

Paul's Thorn Was Residual Sin. David Dickson: The source of his humiliation had something to do with the relics of sin in his flesh or his corrupt nature that was not yet abolished (namely, some motion of concupiscence) that tempted him to sin further. He compares this motion to a thorn left in lopped wood, because it was as troublesome to him as a thorn that has attached itself to the foot of a traveler. . . .

This temptation sent from the devil solicited him to sin with such intensity that he was forced to call out for divine assistance, lest he should be overcome by it. The intensity of this temptation will be clear to the person who reads Romans 7. Thus, this thorn was a most effective means for humbling the apostle. For Paul, who courageously endured all troubles and battles with both his physical and spiritual enemies, is heard howling and crying out in his battle with the flesh, "O wretched man that I am, who shall deliver me?" Exposition of 2 Corinthians 12:7.[41]

The Thorn Was Spiritual Affliction. The English Annotations: By this "thorn in the flesh" some interpreters understand concupiscence. But the words that follow, which the apostle adds by way of explanation, namely, "the messenger of Satan to buffet me," do not agree well with concupiscence. Nor is it likely that St. Paul, who spent all his time in travel and toilsome labor, watching and fasting, should have been troubled with fleshly lust, and if he had been, no doubt he would have used that remedy which he prescribed to others affected by a similar affliction. Other interpreters, therefore, understand this phrase to refer to Alexander the Coppersmith, or some other instrument of Satan, who treated harshly the apostle and was a thorn in his side; or even Satan himself, who, through God's permission, had power to punish the apostle in his body, as he did Job and St. Jerome and other saints (if we believe the ecclesiastical histories). But since the remedy

[39]Musculus, *Commentarius . . . in posteriorem epistolam Pauli ad Corinthios*, 375; citing 2 Tim 4:14-15. †For Chrysostom's interpretation, see PG 577-78 (NPNF[1] 12:400).
[40]Chytraeus, *A Postil of Certeine Epistles*, 85-86.

[41]Dickson, *An Exposition of All St. Paul's Epistles*, 91*; citing Rom 7:24.

mentioned in verse 9 was spiritual, it is not likely that the malady was corporal. It seems, therefore, that because the apostle was exalted by visions and angelic apparitions, it pleased God to humble him to a similar extent, by allowing Satan (who transforms himself into an angel of light) to set upon the apostle in such a furious fashion, attacking both his faith and his sincerity, that the apostle was thereby greatly disheartened. This frightening assault and face-to-face reproach was a kind of brow-beating or buffeting; and because it somewhat hindered Paul in carrying out his business with a cheerful spirit, it is not inappropriately compared to a thorn in the foot, which causes one who is afflicted to limp about and walk only with very great pain. Annotations on 2 Corinthians 12:7.[42]

Paul's Thorn Was a Constant Torment. Edward Leigh: Some have interpreted [the thorn in the flesh] to be original corruption sent by the devil; others interpret it to be a spiritual wound, the sting of conscience pressing down to the lowest hell his senses that had previously been taken up to the highest heavens. Others say that Paul was unable to do any good, praying or preaching, for God had tamed and prevented his pride by eclipsing his gifts and spirit—for Paul repeats twice in this verse, as a thing worthy of our notice, "lest he should be exalted above measure." Some interpreters understand this prick in the flesh as a bodily disease, such as a headache or the Iliac Passion;[†] others believe it to be blasphemous thoughts that darted into his mind with violence. Some say Paul was much reproached by the false apostles, as a man of modest presence, and perhaps there was some imperfection in his speech. Some may have charged that he lived on the people's bounty or misled them. It is certain that, whatever it was, [this thorn in the flesh] was a constant and impetuous torment. Annotation on 2 Corinthians 12:7.[43]

God Humbles His People Through Their Thorns. John Calvin: Now Paul adds the phrase "which strikes a blow at me," by which expression he elegantly expresses the idea that he has been brought under control. For to be struck with a blow is a horrible kind of indignity. Accordingly, if anyone's face has been beaten black and blue, they do not dare to appear in the sight of others on account of shame. In a similar manner, whatever infirmity we struggle with, let us remember that we are, as it were, struck by the Lord with the view of attacking our pride so that we might learn humility. Let those people who possess illustrious virtues especially keep this in mind: if they have any mixture of vices; if they are attacked by anyone with hatred; if they are bruised by anyone with insults—these things are not merely rods of the heavenly Master but blows to instill them with shame and beat back their pride. Now let all godly people take notice of how great is the poison of pride, just as Augustine says in in his third sermon "On the Words of the Apostle," that "it cannot to be cured except by poison."[†] And certainly, as it was the cause of the ruin of humanity, so it is the last vice with which we must contend. Commentary on 2 Corinthians 12:7.[44]

Our Afflictions Direct Us to God and His Will. Johann Spangenberg: St. Paul says, "So that I would not exalt myself because of these great revelations, a thorn was given to me, in my flesh, namely, Satan's angel who beats me with his fists so that I do not exalt myself." It's as if he wanted to say: "Just as we bind a collar on a dog's neck, place a bridle in the horse's mouth, a ring in the bear's nose, a gag in the pig's throat, so that they do not run too fast, bite, and become boisterous, so also God gave me a thorn, binding a large collar onto my body, placing hidden suffering and special affliction, so that I would not exalt myself rather than the great mercy of God, but instead would

[42]Downame, ed., *English Annotations*, GG3v*; citing 1 Cor 7:9; Job 1-2.

[43]Leigh, *Annotations upon all the New Testament*, 264-65*. [†]A serious medical condition, iliac passion is the failure of the forward movement of the bowels.

[44]CO 50:139-40 (40:374-35). [†]Calvin may be referring to Augustine's *Sermon* 163 on Gal 5:16-21. See Augustine, *Sermons*, trans. Edmund Hill, The Works of Saint Augustine III/5 (New York: New City Press, 1992), 173.

remain humble. And I have pleaded with the Lord three times, that Satan would leave me. The Lord said to me: 'Let my grace be sufficient for you. My power is mighty in the weak.'"

In this we see the benefit of afflictions, namely, that they drive us to call on God for help. Christ cannot be mighty in us—nor even his Word and faith—if our bodies are not thrust into afflictions and weakness. For if human power and creaturely aid and consolation is present, God cannot do his work in us. However, if we instead allow God to work in us, then our weakness becomes eternal strength, our suffering eternal joy, and our temporal death eternal life. Amen. Postil for Sexagesima Sunday.[45]

Paul's Elevation and Humiliation. Moïse Amyraut: If you regard the apostle from one side, that he had received such wonderful revelations, he no doubt had good reasons to be triumphant; but if you consider him from the other side, where he is exposed to the harassment of a demon, this causes one to be horrified. But if you join these two things together, they make an excellent combination, where the reason for boasting and the reason for humiliation are remarkably balanced. And the resulting effect deserves to be carefully considered. For, first of all, this serves as a counterbalance in the soul of St. Paul between elevation and humiliation and prevents his spirit from being carried away beyond its limits. Because, if God had not made such a counterweight to continually warn this great servant of God of the infirmity of his nature and the fragility of his humanity—regardless of what sanctification was in him—he would never have been able to cease having too glorified of a view of himself and of transgressing the bounds of Christian humility. Furthermore, it also serves to curb the spirit of other believers who, when they consider St. Paul, stop themselves from having too high an opinion of themselves. Four Sermons.[46]

[45]J. Spangenberg, *Postilla Teütsch*, 4:124v-125r.
[46]Amyraut, *Le Ravissement de Saint Paul*, 155-56.

God Uses Temptations in Christians' Lives. Simon Goulart: Because this great man has patiently endured the blows of Satan, he also endures the burden that God gives him to carry. [In the same way] let us soften our afflictions with the hope of eternal life. In conclusion, let us add some comments of the ancient fathers. St. Augustine once said that by temptation people learn to know themselves.[†] Again, he said that God allows us to be tempted as much as it is profitable for us. Again, he commented that during our earthly pilgrimage, our life is not immune from sin and temptation, which work together for our advancement. And no one is discovered to have faith that has not first been tempted; nor can a person be crowned until after the victory; nor can he be victorious if he has not been in battle; nor can a person fight, if he has not faced enemies and temptations. . . . And St. Ambrose said that God, who is the governor and Lord of all things, together with all the armies of angels, watches your combat against the devil and prepares for you the eternal crown.[‡] The Second Part of Christian Speeches.[47]

The Goad Was God's Gift to Paul. Wolfgang Musculus: Paul does not simply say that he suffered from a goad, but that the goad was given to him by none other than God himself, and that it was intended to protect him rather than punish him. It was like an antidote that a doctor gives to counteract the danger of disease. That is why it seems to me that those who interpret the Greek word *edothē* as "God *permitted* Satan to afflict me with the goad" do not fully consider Paul's zeal for God. Chrysostom,[†] perhaps out of reverence, does not attribute anything of evil to God. . . . But the apostle here does not use a word "permitting" but he clearly says, "God has given me a goad." Thus, he indicates that he believed that God had given the goad to him as a special gift. We

[47]Goulart, *Seconde Partie des Discours Chrestiens*, 310-11. [†]Augustine, *Sermons*, trans. Edmund Hill, The Works of Saint Augustine III/1 (New York: New City Press, 1990), 178. [‡]Ambrose, *De Sacramentis* 1.2.4, PL 16:419.

should avoid this manner of explaining the sacred Scriptures, where words attributed to God such as giving, delivering, hardening, blinding, killing, destroying, and so on are explained by the word "permitting." In my judgment this approach does not satisfy the intention of the Holy Spirit. COMMENTARY ON 2 CORINTHIANS 12:7.[48]

ADVERSITY STRENGTHENS CHRISTIAN FAITH. CYRIACUS SPANGENBERG: Here we are clearly shown that our dear Lord God also sends to his most beloved and greatest saints adversity and temptation, not so that they will perish, but in order to stave off a trouble, namely, presumption or spiritual pride. The beloved prophets Isaiah, Jeremiah, King David, and the apostle Paul had excellent, great, exalted gifts which were lacking in others. God also achieved great things through them. Now they could easily have taken credit for such things and become proud. Therefore, God allows a bitter wind to blow under their eyes from time to time and them to be well purified, from the outside with persecution and adversity, from the inside through the recognition of their failings, weakness, and sins, so that through this they might be caused not to boast in themselves or their works, but to give God the glory as Isaiah does in chapter 26: "Lord, everything that we achieve, you have given us." And Jeremiah in chapter 10: "I know, Lord, that a man's action does not stand in his power, and it stands in no one's might how he walks or goes his way. Discipline me Lord, but with measure and not in your anger, so that you will not destroy me." And Jonah in chapter 2: "You, Lord, have brought my life out of perishing, Lord my God." And David in Psalm 130: "Lord, if you will reckon sins, Lord who will stand? But with you is forgiveness, so that people will fear you." And Paul to the Romans in chapter 7: "I know that nothing good dwells in me, that is in my flesh. Miserable man that I am, who will redeem me from the body of this death? I thank God through Jesus Christ our Lord." God wants to have this kind of confession from his own, therefore he now brings them through various kinds of adversity. FORTY-SIXTH SERMON.[49]

GOD PERMITS SATAN TO TEMPT CHRISTIANS. DIRK PHILIPS: Christians also have thus to fight against besetting sins, against the world, against Satan, and his ministers. Of this warfare Paul writes to the Ephesians, as everyone may read. Paul also had such warfare, for he said that a thorn of the flesh was given him as a messenger of Satan, who beat him with fists so that he should not exalt himself on account of the greater revelations which were shown him by God. And when he prayed to the Lord three times that Satan might go away from him, the Lord answered him, "Be content with my grace, for my power becomes stronger through weakness."

In these words of the apostle, we observe how God allows his saints to be tempted by Satan for the reason that they should learn to know their human weakness, humble themselves under the mighty hand of God, and rely upon the Lord's grace. And they then will be strengthened by the Lord with his grace, and all the temptations of Satan will not harm them. Yes, Jesus Christ, our Lord and Savior, blessed in eternity, has himself striven with Satan and overcome him. For when he was baptized of John the Baptist, he was led of the Spirit into the wilderness in order to be tempted of Satan; Satan came to him and tested him with three temptations. But the Lord Jesus Christ overcame all the temptations and cunning of Satan with the sword of the spirit. TABERNACLE OF MOSES.[50]

SATAN'S MESSENGERS INCLUDE ADVERSITIES AND DANGERS. HULDRYCH ZWINGLI: Paul stated above that Satan often transforms himself

[48]Musculus, *Commentarius . . . in posteriorem epistolam Pauli ad Corinthios*, 376. †For Chrysostom's interpretation, see PG 61:578 (NPNF[1] 12:400).

[49]C. Spangenberg, *Die ander Epistel Pauli an die Corinthier*, 197v; citing Is 26:12; Jer 10:23-24; Jn 2:6; Ps 130:3-4; Rom 7:24-25.
[50]CRR 6:279; citing Heb 12:1; Eph 6:10-20; 1 Pet 5:6; Mt 4:1-10.

into an angel of light, that is, putting on the appearance of feigned piety, as [he said in] Genesis 3, "you will be as gods." Here, Paul understands the phrase "messenger [lit. *angel*] of Satan" . . . to refer to all the adversities and evil that happen to us, which follow no doubt as the common experience of human beings. Whatever adversities or dangers they endure, these they either call "the devil" or judge to come from the devil. Annotations 2 Corinthians 12:7.[51]

God Is Always Faithful in Answering Prayer. John Calvin: Now it may seem to follow from this Paul in no way prayed in faith, unless we want to consider all God's promises null and void. For we read everywhere in Scripture that whatever we ask for in faith will be given to us. Yet Paul prays, and does not receive. I answer: as there are different ways of asking, so there are different ways of receiving. We ask in simple terms for those things for which we have an express promise, such as the perfecting of the kingdom of God and the hallowing of his name, the remission of our sins, and whatever works toward our salvation. But when we consider that the kingdom of God can, or rather must, be advanced in this or that particular way; and when we consider that this or that is necessary for the hallowing of his name—we are often mistaken in our opinion. In a similar fashion, we often fall into error as to what tends toward our salvation. Therefore, we ask confidently and without exception for those prior things, while it is not left to us to prescribe the means. But if we specify the means, there is always an unstated condition implied. Now Paul was not so ignorant as not to know this. Hence, as to the object of his praying, there is no doubt that he was heard, even if he experienced a refusal as to its exact form. From this we are admonished not to become despondent as if praying were wasted effort when God does not satisfy or comply with our wishes. But let us be satisfied with his grace, that is, that we are not being forsaken by him. For this is the reason why he sometimes mercifully denies to his people what he grants (out of his wrath) to the wicked: because he foresees better what is good for us than our minds can comprehend. Commentary on 2 Corinthians 12:8.[52]

Paul's Most Important Prayers Were Answered. Tilemann Hesshus: We must flee to the Lord with ardent prayer both in every tribulation and when we face serious affliction of various sorts and are tormented because the minister of Satan, as it were, pierces us with a stake and strikes us with blows. For the Lord has destroyed the power of Satan and exercises control over all creatures. When his Word is unleashed, it drives away every kind of disease, it heals all wounds, it conquers all terrors, and rescues us from all temptations. "Believe in me," [Jesus] says, "for I have overcome the world." And Psalm 91: "I am with him in trouble, I will deliver him and honor him." And the Lord himself says: "Call on me in trouble, and I will deliver you and you shall glorify me." Therefore, we will not find a safer or stronger defense against Satan and his harassments anywhere than in the Lord Jesus Christ, to whom we must continually flee with serious and ardent prayer.

But Paul asked the Lord three times and yet he did not obtain freedom from the messenger of Satan: was his prayer therefore ineffective? Not at all. Rather, Paul obtained the most important thing for which he asked, for his soul was strengthened in the power of the Holy Spirit so that he might patiently endure those blows of Satan. And because he witnessed Christ's power and glory shining forth in his weakness, he rejoiced even in this affliction of his flesh. And because he was preserved in humility, the Lord compensated with great spiritual good the refusal of bodily liberation. Explication of 2 Corinthians 12:8.[53]

---

[51]Zwingli, *Annotatiunculae . . . ex ore Zvinglij*, 190; citing 2 Cor 11:14; Gen 3:5.

[52]CO 50:140-41 (CTS 40:376-77); citing Mt 6:9.

[53]Hesshus, *Explicatio Secundae Epistolae Pauli ad Corinthios*, 279v-280r; citing Jn 16:33; Ps 91:15; 50:15.

The Power of Prayer in the Face of Temptations. Niels Hemmingsen: The apostle mentions that he prayed to the Lord three times (that is, often) that the messenger of Satan might depart from him (that is, that he would be liberated from his bitter temptation). From this, we learn two things: First, that when we face temptations, we should not give into them but should immediately take up weapons and run for help to our strongest defense, the name of the Lord. Second, that the Lord alone is able to delivers us from temptation—which Paul teaches by this prayer of his. Commentary on 2 Corinthians 12:8.[54]

Paul's Fervent Prayer. John Trapp. "I sought the Lord three times," that is, frequently and fervently. God respects not the arithmetic of our prayers, how many there are; nor the rhetoric of our prayers, how neat they are; nor the geometry of our prayers, how long they are; nor the music of our prayers, how melodious they are; nor the logic of our prayers, how methodical they are; but the divinity of our prayers, how heart-sprung they are. Not gifts, but graces prevail in prayer. Commentary on 2 Corinthians 12:8.[55]

God's Grace Is Sufficient. John Calvin: "He said to me." It is uncertain whether Paul had this answer by special revelation, nor is it of great importance. For God answers us when he strengthens us inwardly by the Spirit and sustains us by his comfort, so that we do not give up hope and patience. He commands Paul to be content with his grace and, in the meantime, not refuse his chastisement. Therefore, we must endure evil however long it might last, because it will go very well with us when we have the grace of God to support us. The word "grace" here does not mean God's favor (as it does elsewhere), but by metonymy,[†] it signifies the assistance of the Holy Spirit, which comes to us by the unmerited favor of God. Now this ought to be sufficient for godly people because it is a firm and invincible support against their ever falling back. Commentary on 2 Corinthians 12:9.[56]

Christ Is Powerful in His People. Martin Luther: It is an amazing kind of power which becomes stronger through being weak. Who has ever heard that power is weak? Or [who has ever heard] that power, because it is weak, becomes still stronger? In that way he separates human power and divine power. Human power becomes stronger as it increases and weaker as it decreases. But God's power—that is, his Word in us—rises the more it is suppressed. That is because God as Creator makes everything out of nothing, and then again makes everything into nothing. Human power cannot do that. That is the true palm tree wood which rises up the more it is burdened and weighed down.

Here you see that "weakness" must be understood not as spiritual weakness, as above, but as external weakness—that is, not only as sickness, but as every kind of evil, misfortune, suffering, and persecution by which the body is beaten black and blue and humbled. He contrasts this weakness with the power of Christ, which cannot tolerate any spiritual weakness, and says, "So that the power of Christ may rest upon me, I will boast gladly in my weakness," that is . . . in "insults, hardships, persecutions, and calamities." So in summary, Christ is not mighty in us, and his Word and faith cannot be strong in us, unless our body is pierced with weaknesses. The false apostles especially guarded themselves against this. Postil for Sexagesima Sunday.[57]

The Power of God's Grace. Philipp Melanchthon: In this passage one finds the richest comfort and a commendation of the magnitude of grace. Therefore, while not

[54]Hemmingsen, *Commentaria in Omnes Epistolas Apostolorum*, 303.
[55]Trapp, *A Commentary or Exposition*, 733*.
[56]CO 50:141 (CTS 40:377). [†]Metonymy is the use of an attribute or adjunct idea as a replacement for the intended word. E.g., when the word *crown* is substituted for *king*.
[57]LW 76:329-30 (WA 17.2:152-53).

removing our sins, he saves us and declares himself to be more powerful than sins. Just as Romans 5 says, "If death reigned through one man's trespass, how much more will life reign by grace," that is, if sin was powerful, how much more will grace be powerful. And as Romans 4 states, "in hope against hope," and Romans 8: "If God is for us, who can be against us?" Annotations on 2 Corinthians 12:9.[58]

God's Strength Made Perfect in Weakness. Martin Luther: My dear Urbanus [Rhegius]: Your report that you are buffeted by a messenger of Satan and are suffering from a thorn in the flesh does not distress me too much, for I recognize in this that you are conformed to the image of God's Son and all the saints. I believe that this trial comes to you, as it does to other brethren who occupy high stations, in order that we may be humbled. Therefore, be of good courage, let your heart be comforted, and wait on the Lord, who said to St. Paul, "My strength is made perfect in weakness." God is faithful. By him we were called. He will perform a good work in us until the day of Jesus Christ. Amen. This Lord have I heard, and by him have I been comforted as much as the Lord has given it to me to be.

I have told you to be confident and to know that you are not alone when you are occasionally afflicted, for "the same afflictions are accomplished in your brethren that are in the world." We must support one another and be supported. Even so, Christ supports all of us from the beginning of the world unto the end. We cannot always be strong and healthy, nor always weak and infirm. Our condition depends upon him who blows where he wishes. By these vicissitudes he teaches us not to be arrogant, as we might be if we were always strong, and not to despair, as we might if we were always infirm. "He knows our frame," said David; "he remembers that we are dust." We are best off when we ourselves acknowledge that we are framed of dust and are mere dust.

Buy why should I write all this to you, who are Christ's? Only because a brother must speak to his brother, and each must give the other his hand in this vale of tears, until that day comes for which we long. Letter to Urbanus Rhegius.[59]

God Works in Our Weakness. Wolfgang Musculus: The Greek is not *dia astheneias*, that is, "by weakness," but *en astheneia*, that is, "in weakness." The power of God was *illustrated* by the weakness of the apostle, but it was not made perfect by it, but by the Spirit of God in his weakness. This is the reason, or rather this explains better how God's grace was sufficient in Paul. For, God says . . . "My power, by which I work through your apostleship and preserve you from all sorts of dangers, is made perfect in your great weakness rather than in your strength. For if you choose to bear all things through your own strength and are sufficient to preserve yourself, then there is no room for my power. Moreover, the more your are weak and at the mercy of many dangers, the more there is room for my power to work in you and to preserve you lest, being buried beneath so many dangers, you should perish. That is why when that messenger of Satan pommels you, and your plea that he depart from you effects nothing, nay rather, he rages all the more, this serves as a greater opportunity for showing forth my power, in the same way that the more serious a disease is, the more renown is ascribed to the doctor's skill." Commentary on 2 Corinthians 12:9.[60]

God's Strength Cannot Be Conquered. The English Annotations: The strength or power of God can neither be increased nor diminished. Yet it is said to be perfected when it manifests itself to the full and demonstrates that

[58]*Melanchthons Werke*, 4:131-32; citing Rom 5:17; 4:18; 8:31.

[59]Tappert, *Luther: Letters of Spiritual Counsel*, 41 (WABR 7:147-48); citing Rom 8:29; 2 Cor 12:9; Phil 1:6; 1 Pet 5:9; Jn 3:8; Ps 103:14. Urbanus Rhegius (1489–1541) was a Lutheran reformer who served as the city preacher of Augsburg and, later, as the superintendent of the church in Lüneburg.

[60]Musculus, *Commentarius . . . in posteriorem epistolam Pauli ad Corinthios*, 378.

nothing can overcome or conquer it. The greater the infirmities that people experience, the stronger and more perfect is God's power in supporting them in all assaults of temptation. Annotations on 2 Corinthians 12:9.[61]

In What Should Christians Boast? Johann Spangenberg: First, in the grace of God, that they have a merciful Father who has graciously adopted them as his children out of pure grace and kindness and has called them to eternal life. Second, in their cross-bearing and suffering, for in this they have sure signs of divine favor, kindness, grace, and lovingkindness. Third, on account of their office that they have from God, like St. Paul has here. Postil on Sexagesima Sunday.[62]

The Cross Makes God's People Invincible. Niels Hemmingsen: Paul here concludes why he wishes to boast in his weaknesses more than in great revelations. For, on the cross, Christ demonstrates to men and women the greatness of his presence and power, while he renders them invincible by the strength of his Spirit. Note well that what is seen as shameful to the world is glorious to servants of Christ. For the cross that godly people experience is not a sign of an angry judge, but a testimony of the Father's love. He disciplines them with the rod of the cross so that they might not run wild indulging the flesh against God, and finally perish in their guilt. Note also here the testimony concerning the divinity of Christ. Commentary on 2 Corinthians 12:9.[63]

Paul Is Content with His Weakness. Tilemann Hesshus: After Paul understood from Christ's answer that Christ's power was illuminated and became more visible by his weakness, Paul not only reconciles himself to patience, but also boasts in his afflictions and weaknesses. For he has this one desire, that Jesus Christ might be worshiped in the world as extensively as possible—Paul is not concerned with his own honor. Now, he sees that Christ attains the greatest honor in this way: if Christ's power lives in him. He extensively employs the word "weakness," and also mentions the insults, hardships, persecutions, and calamities in which our weakness is easily seen. For we are anxious of spirit and afraid of these things. But Christ, who is with us in tribulation, demonstrates his power at that moment, not only to defend us and deliver us from hardships, but also, in the midst of so many difficulties and dangers, to extend his kingdom through our weaknesses, and bring about the salvation of many people and convict and confound the ragings of the world.

He says, "When I am weak" (namely, in myself), "then I am strong" (but, in Christ). These words contain enormous comfort that ought to encourage and strengthen us. For we should not be alarmed by our internal weaknesses, nor should we be disturbed by external difficulties thrown against us in ministry, if indeed it is pleasing to Christ to make his power evident in our weakness. It is our responsibility to labor faithfully and pray fervently. The rest we entrust to Christ, that he will build his church, set in place the heavens, and establish the earth—even if the whole world growls. Explication of 2 Corinthians 12:10.[64]

How Can a Person Be Weak and Strong at the Same Time? Wolfgang Musculus: In fact, there seems to be a paradox in what Paul says. For first, was he not weak from the sheer fact of being a human being? Humans are always weak. Moreover, the apostle was a human being always exposed to weakness. Therefore, he was always weak. What, then, does he mean when he says, "When I am weak, therefore I am strong"? Therefore, he was always strong. Second, when he is weak, on the contrary he is strong—these conditions, at that same time, are at variance with one another. For those who are weak are thus not

[61]Downame, ed., *English Annotations*, GG3v*.

[62]J. Spangenberg, *Postilla Teütsch*, 4:121r-v.

[63]Hemmingsen, *Commentaria in Omnes Epistolas Apostolorum*, 304.

[64]Hesshus, *Explicatio Secundae Epistolae Pauli ad Corinthios*, 283r-284r.

strong because they are weak. And those who are powerful are not weak because they are strong. Thus, there seems to be a contradiction in these words: "For when I am weak, then I am strong."

I respond to the first objection this way: just as Paul calls his weaknesses the insults, deprivations, persecutions, and worries borne for the sake of Christ, so then he says that he is weak when he is afflicted by insults, deprivations, persecutions, and worries. That is why what he says should not be ascribed to the general weakness of human nature. To the second objection, I answer: the apostle speaks truthfully in sayings at the same time that he is both weak and strong. He says that he is weak in respect to the evil things that he was suffering at the hands of wicked people. But he says that he is strong with respect to the power of Christ through which he was strengthened and preserved in his weaknesses. He was made weak because of Christ, and he was made strong because of that same Christ. That is why there is no contradiction in these words of his: "When I am weak, then I am strong." In a similar fashion, the Christian will rightly say: When I am foolish, then I am wise. When I am a sinner, then I am righteous. When I am wretched, then I am happy. When I am inconspicuous, then I am illustrious. When I am killed, then I am alive. Commentary on 2 Corinthians 12:10.[65]

Two Kinds of Crosses. Niels Hemmingsen: Paul repeats the same sentence for the purpose of amplification and distinction. He says, "when I am weak," namely, with respect to my strength when I am weighed down by the cross; "then I am strong," namely, in the protection of Christ, who strengthens me so that I do not give in. Now, further, there are two kinds of crosses: The first is imposed on us because of the truth and is not related to our personal guilt. The second we have brought upon ourselves because of our guilt. We need to know that repentance and acting in obedience is a sacrifice acceptable to God for both kinds of crosses. Commentary on 2 Corinthians 12:10.[66]

Paul Was Victorious in His Afflictions. David Dickson: Paul had now learned not only to bear all afflictions courageously for the gospel, which helped make him more humble, but out of them to take much pleasure. Because when he perceived himself the weakest, flying to Christ, he experienced his more powerful presence that sustained and comforted him, and likewise, made him victorious. Exposition of 2 Corinthians 12:10.[67]

Paul's Life Illustrates the Truth of This Verse. The English Annotations: When I am weak in myself, I am strong in Christ; or, when I am weak in the flesh, I am strong in the Spirit. When Paul was cast into prison and his feet held fast in the stocks, he by his prayer caused the foundation of the prison to be shaken. When after Paul had suffered shipwreck, and was cast onto a barbarous island, and there a viper attached itself to his finger and the islanders considered him as good as dead, he not only shook the viper off without injury, but also gained great favor from the chief man of the island by curing his father of a fever and a flow of blood. And when Paul was brought before Nero, and everyone abandoned him, yet even there (as a forlorn prisoner) he got the better of his powerful adversaries and was delivered out of the mouth of lions. Thus, God strengthened Paul in his greatest infirmities and distresses, and delivered him, so that the account of Paul's life confirmed what he here stated regarding himself. Annotations on 2 Corinthians 12:10.[68]

The Holy Spirit Strengthens Weak, Persecuted Christians. Leonhard Schiemer: The Scriptures tell us in many places, especially in the Psalms, the prophets, in Isaiah,

[65]Musculus, *Commentarius . . . in posteriorem epistolam Pauli ad Corinthios*, 380-81.

[66]Hemmingsen, *Commentaria in Omnes Epistolas Apostolorum*, 304.

[67]Dickson, *An Exposition of All St. Paul's Epistles*, 91*.

[68]Downame, ed., *English Annotations*, GG3v*; citing Acts 16:25-26; 28:3-10.

and the Lamentations of Jeremiah that the whole strength of Christians consists of being still. It is in not giving up in discouragement, but to be patient and thus to await the comfort of the Holy Spirit amid the greatest desolation and misery. This is the true infirmity about which Scripture and especially Paul writes: "When I am weak, then I am strong." He also says that even as the suffering of Christ flows over us so does the comfort through Christ. . . . The life of the world has a happy beginning and an eternal mournful end. Our life has a mournful beginning, but then the Holy Spirit comes soon and anoints us with the oil of joy unspeakable. It is not a matter of solitary waiting for the comfort of God, but a Christian should and is able to encourage others and give comfort in tribulation. LETTER TO THE CHURCH OF GOD AT RATTENBERG.[69]

[69]CRR 10:80.

12:11-21 Concern for the Corinthian Church

11 I have been a fool! You forced me to it, for I ought to have been commended by you. For I was not at all inferior to these super-apostles, even though I am nothing. 12 The signs of a true apostle were performed among you with utmost patience, with signs and wonders and mighty works. 13 For in what were you less favored than the rest of the churches, except that I myself did not burden you? Forgive me this wrong!

14 Here for the third time I am ready to come to you. And I will not be a burden, for I seek not what is yours but you. For children are not obligated to save up for their parents, but parents for their children. 15 I will most gladly spend and be spent for your souls. If I love you more, am I to be loved less? 16 But granting that I myself did not burden you, I was crafty, you say, and got the better of you by deceit. 17 Did I take advantage of you through any of those whom I sent to you? 18 I urged Titus to go, and sent the brother with him. Did Titus take advantage of you? Did we not act in the same spirit? Did we not take the same steps?

19 Have you been thinking all along that we have been defending ourselves to you? It is in the sight of God that we have been speaking in Christ, and all for your upbuilding, beloved. 20 For I fear that perhaps when I come I may find you not as I wish, and that you may find me not as you wish—that perhaps there may be quarreling, jealousy, anger, hostility, slander, gossip, conceit, and disorder. 21 I fear that when I come again my God may humble me before you, and I may have to mourn over many of those who sinned earlier and have not repented of the impurity, sexual immorality, and sensuality that they have practiced.

Overview: After recounting the exhilarating experience of being caught up into the third heaven earlier in this chapter, the apostle Paul now "returns to earth" once more to answer his critics and defend his apostolic authority as he prepares to come to Corinth for a third visit. Reformation commentators observe that Paul is more forceful here than elsewhere in leveling blame against the Corinthians: rather than standing up for Paul, they have believed the lies of the false apostles who have accused him of greed, pride, deception, and pastoral indifference. Nothing could be further from the truth! Paul spent more time in Corinth than most other mission stations; he served without remuneration and humbly endured suffering; he performed signs and wonders to testify to the glory of the gospel; he worked tirelessly to build up the believers in steadfast faith and true godliness. As any good pastor, Paul is tormented by the lack of spiritual improvement among the Corinthians and deeply concerned that his next visit will require painful confrontations and sharp rebukes. Once again, Reformation interpreters believe that Paul's pastoral example invites a variety of contemporary applications. Like loving parents, ministers must care deeply for their spiritual children. Their driving concern must be for their people's salvation, not their material affluence. Faithful shepherds of God's flock do not seek the wool and milk of the sheep, but the sheep themselves. Moreover, as in the case of Paul and Titus, wise pastors must choose their assistants carefully, especially when fiduciary responsibility is at stake. The prudent pastor closes every loophole for misunderstanding and slander. The apostle's example also reminds contemporary ministers that before rebuking sinners, they must first grieve deeply over their people's sins and do everything to foster repentance. Church discipline may become necessary, but it must be employed in a spirit of gentleness so as to correct the fault. Finally, the apostle Paul's tireless labors on behalf of the Corinthian church offer an important reminder that gospel ministers must not grow discouraged by their people's apathy, contentiousness, and ingratitude, but look to the Son of God for their certain reward. God's approval must be the minister's ultimate goal and consolation.

12:11-13 *Signs of an Apostle*

PAUL NOW PLACES BLAME ON THE CORINTHIANS. JOHN CALVIN: Up till now, with various apologies, Paul had begged their forgiveness for having proclaimed his own glory contrary to his own custom and intention, and contrary also to propriety and what was due to his apostolic office. Now, instead of begging for forgiveness, Paul throws blame back onto the Corinthians who should have beaten back these vices. For when the false apostles were slandering Paul, the Corinthians should have strenuously opposed them and faithfully rendered testimony to his virtue as he deserved. Indeed, he quickly scolds them, lest those who were unfavorably disposed toward them might put a wrong construction upon the defense that he had brought forward . . . or persist in slandering him. COMMENTARY ON 2 CORINTHIANS 12:11.[1]

PAUL'S OFFICE AND PAUL'S PERSON. NIELS HEMMINGSEN: Paul excuses his boasting and shows to what end he has undertaken it, namely, so that he might vindicate his apostolic authority to the Corinthians, who, having spurned him, had begun to align themselves with the false apostles. One must note here that Paul distinguishes between his office and his person. He defends his office, for he was practicing it to defend the truth of the gospel. As for his person, he recognizes that it is nothing, and he did not wish to follow the example of the false apostles in boasting of their gifts. Godly ministers of the Word should imitate both of these things: they should strenuously defend their office and judge themselves with humility. COMMENTARY ON 2 CORINTHIANS 12:11.[2]

THE CORINTHIANS FAILED TO SUPPORT PAUL'S AUTHORITY. THE ENGLISH ANNOTATIONS: "You ought to have maintained the authority of my ministry and given a testimony to the truth, how innocently I and my fellow workers carried ourselves among you." Here again Paul appeals to the consciences of the Corinthians and makes them witnesses of those things, whereby God had sealed his apostleship among them. And again, he declares by certain arguments how far he is from all covetousness, and how tenderly and affectionately he loves them in Christ. ANNOTATION ON 2 CORINTHIANS 12:11.[3]

WICKED PEOPLE HAVE ALWAYS QUESTIONED PAUL'S AUTHORITY. JOHN TRAPP: "I was not at all inferior." And yet there was a group of silly souls (that thought themselves to be jolly fellows) in the days of Zwingli, in the year 1519, who talked this way at Zurich: . . . "What was Paul, but a man? He was an apostle, but of an inferior rank. He was not one of the twelve. He did not converse with Christ. He composed none of the twelve articles of the creed. We would as soon believe Thomas or Scotus, as Paul." . . . St. Paul says here: "I am as much of an apostle as they are, who are more than super apostles" (for so the Greek reads). But Paul cannot be heard, for "there is no remedy against the vicious attacks of sycophants." COMMENTARY ON 2 CORINTHIANS 12:11.[4]

PAUL AND THE "SUPER APOSTLES." JOHN CALVIN: By the term "super apostles" some understand Paul's rivals, who were arrogating themselves to first place. But I understand it to mean those who were chief among the twelve. It is as if Paul were to say: "Let me be compared to any of the apostles; I have no fear of being found inferior." For although Paul was on the best of terms with all the apostles so that he was prepared to praise them above himself, nevertheless he contended against their names when falsely

[1]CO 50:143 (CTS 40:381).
[2]Hemmingsen, *Commentaria in Omnes Epistolas Apostolorum*, 304.
[3]Downame, ed., *English Annotations*, GG3v*.
[4]Trapp, *A Commentary or Exposition*, 734*.

assumed. For the false apostles were abusing by means of this pretext, that they had been in the company of the twelve, that they held all their views, that they were acquainted with all their plans, and similar such things. Thus, seeing that they were taking false pride in these masks and counterfeit titles and that they were making progress among the ignorant people, Paul considered it necessary to lower himself to this comparison. Commentary on 2 Corinthians 12:11.[5]

Even Though I Am Nothing. Cardinal Cajetan: [Paul is saying] that he did not have lesser divine gifts than Peter, James, and John had, who were the "supreme apostles." And he said this because the false apostles were saying that Paul was not equal to the apostles, who were with Christ in the flesh. The clause "even though I am nothing" is joined with the preceding phrase, so that he might temper what he had said. Indeed, Paul elsewhere states, "I am the least of the apostles, unworthy to be called an apostle"—and in this way he tempers his words with the same humility. For Paul states that he possessed equal gifts of God, even if there is nothing that is lower than to be the least of the apostles. And hence, he says "I am nothing, as far as it concerns me, but I am equal to the supreme apostles with regard to the gifts of God." Commentary on 2 Corinthians 12:11.[6]

Signs of a True Apostle. Wolfgang Musculus: Paul provides two kinds of signs by which his apostleship was signified and proclaimed among the Corinthians as in other places. The first is his endurance of all kinds of suffering, which he calls here "utmost endurance." This is the patience by which he endured with constancy every adversity for the sake of Christ. Previously, in chapter 6 above, Paul has enumerated those things that he endured, by which he was commending himself in every way as a minister of Christ, saying: "But as ministers of God we commend ourselves in every way by great endurance, in afflictions. . . ." It is a sign of a true apostle not simply to endure evil, but to endure those evils suffered for the sake of Christ with a cheerful spirit. Satan and his martyrs do otherwise. Paul ascribes the second sign of his apostleship to those signs, wonders, and mighty works, which he had performed among the Corinthians by the power and agency of the Spirit of Christ. By "signs" here he means miracles, such as the healing of people with diseases, the blind, the lame and lepers, the casting out of demons, and the raising of the dead. Paul means the same thing with the Greek words *terata* and *dynameis*, that is, wonders and mighty works, or powers. Those miracles that were performed by the apostles through divine agency were called "signs" because they were signifying that the message of the gospel, to which they were attached, was from heaven and had been sent from God into the world; so, too, by their nature, these miracles were warning everyone that this message had been sent for the salvation of humankind. These miracles are called *terata*, that is, wonders and portents, because their occurrence was beyond the normal order of nature and their appearance was wondrous. These miracles are also called *dynameis*, because they were performed by nothing but the singular power of God. Thus in different ways, Paul calls these same miracles signs, wonders, and mighty works. Commentary on 2 Corinthians 12:12.[7]

Four Signs of Paul's Apostleship. Niels Hemmingsen: Paul proves that he was not inferior to the other apostles and enumerates four proofs from his own apostleship: endurance, signs, wonders, and powers. Endurance is that strength of soul that keeps us from becoming disheartened of spirit in difficult times and from abandoning our [Christian] confession due to the tedium of the work—as many people once did, and many do so today to the assured

[5]CO 50:143 (CTS 40:381-82).

[6]Cajetan, *In Posteriorem Pauli Epistolam ad Corinthios Commentarii*, 196-97; citing 1 Cor 15:9.

[7]Musculus, *Commentarius . . . in posteriorem epistolam Pauli ad Corinthios*, 383-84; citing 2 Cor 6:4.

destruction of their souls. Such endurance should be common among all ministers of the Word. Now the three proofs that follow are particular signs of the apostolic office, which the apostle to the Hebrews divides into two sorts. . . . For the Lord saw fit to confirm his doctrine (as if with some sacred seals) by means of miracles for healing human sickness and the infirmities of the human mind. The apostle enumerates those miracles by which the truth of the gospel was sealed for most people. Now, a miracle by definition is an extraordinary and unusual work of God that leads human minds to wonder. Now *sēmeia*, that is, "signs," are so named because they stir the human mind to consider something more than what appears on the surface. Christ, by means of his voice alone, heals the deaf and dumb. This sign excites the minds of onlookers to think about something higher, namely, that Christ has been endowed with divine power and that he is the true Messiah, even if this is not apparent from the outside. Second, Paul lists wonders, which are so-called because they contain something new and unusual, as was the case when Christ raised a man from the dead with his voice alone. . . . In the third place, Paul adds strength or powers, which the epistle to the Hebrews adds are distributed by the Holy Spirit. Now the strength or powers are those by which the efficacious Lord demonstrates his peculiar strength to godly people in ways the devil cannot at all imitate with his tricks. The Lord sealed his gospel with an authentic seal through the distribution of the Holy Spirit, not only on the day of Pentecost, but also more frequently in the apostolic church with the prayers of the apostles and the laying on of hands. These miraculous signs of God's truth should always be in our sight, for their general usefulness will endure in the church, and no other is legitimate and true than this sign of celestial doctrine. And although signs of this sort do not continue today, nevertheless, we must perpetually gaze upon that miracle previously performed, which, once the gospel was confirmed throughout the world, had to cease—not indeed in usefulness, but in fact. Commentary on 2 Corinthians 12:12.[8]

Paul Did Not Burden the Church. Heinrich Bullinger: Paul proves that he is an apostle by another argument. "There are others edifying the churches," he says, "whom we think worthy of the title of apostles, and by this name they proved themselves to be apostles of the Lord. Yes, and you who were edified by us were in no way inferior to those churches, for nothing was bestowed to the churches by the super apostles that was not also bestowed by me on your church. Therefore, you should want to acknowledge that you were not pressured to acknowledge that I was a true apostle of the Lord." Now, by way of irony, Paul adds what follows, "except that I myself was not a burden to you. Forgive me this wrong!" Paul mentioned the benefit that he did not impose any harm. Hence, in this way also (as we indicated in chapter 11) he wanted to surpass all the other apostles, rather than acknowledging wrongdoing. And thus he employs irony to acknowledge the awkwardness of this kind of speaking. Further, since the Corinthian church had been properly instituted by Paul, and since it was in no way inferior to those churches established by the super apostles, thus it was free from those institutions about which the popes boast today. It is certain that those things established by the popes do not belong to the constitution of a well-founded and true church. Commentary on 2 Corinthians 12:13.[9]

The Corinthians Had Received from Paul Many Favors. Tilemann Hesshus: The apostle Paul mentions briefly to the Corinthians that in no way were they inferior to the other churches, for they had heard from Paul's mouth many very fruitful sermons concerning the benefits of the mediator. Paul stayed among the Corinthians longer than in other places. He performed

[8]Hemmingsen, *Commentaria in Omnes Epistolas Apostolorum*, 304-5; citing Heb 2:2-4.

[9]Bullinger, *In Posteriorem . . . ad Corinthios Epistolam Commentarius*, 333-34.

among them apostolic signs and miracles. He displayed apostolic patience and humility. Nevertheless, they did not match other churches in zeal of piety and love toward the apostle. To be sure, Paul honors the Philippians and Ephesians with far more praise than the Corinthians. Therefore, he encourages [the Corinthians] to imitate the piety and zeal and reverence of the other churches toward the apostle Paul. Lest they be able to rush maliciously into slander because he did not accept payment from the Corinthians, Paul reports that he had well-founded reasons for sparing them this. Speaking ironically, he calls a "wrong" that which was a proven benefit to signify that they were very much assigning unjust actions to Paul. For this reason, they should have understood that Paul was not zealous for his own profit, but eager to serve God's glory and build up the church with an illustrious faith. Explication of 2 Corinthians 12:13.[10]

Forgive Me This Wrong! John Calvin: "Forgive me this wrong," he says. For [the Corinthians] were ungrateful in two ways, since they not only condemned the person by whose kindness they were placed under obligation but were even turning his liberality toward them into a reason for reproach. Chrysostom[†] thinks that no irony is implied here, but rather this is a statement of apology. But if anyone examines the entire context more closely, they will easily see that this gloss is foreign to Paul's intention. Commentary on 2 Corinthians 12:13.[11]

12:14-18 *Paul Like a Parent of the Corinthians*

Paul Has Expended Himself for the Corinthians. Desiderius Erasmus: Now I have been with you twice, and I have not been troublesome to anyone. And see, my intention is to visit you a third time; however, I shall not be a burden for anyone, any more than I was before. I am not doing this rashly (although I am not yet bringing forward my earnest reason), but whatever the reason for my action, I am serving your interests and playing the part of a true father. For offspring are not obligated to heap up riches for their parents, but on the contrary, parents for their offspring. The affection of parents has this characteristic: that they not only spend their hard-earned resources, but they spend themselves also for their children. Well then, far from extorting anything from you, I am ready and most willing to spend my possessions for you, and even myself in addition, if that is what the welfare of your soul requires. It is enough for me to make this provision as a father for his children, even though I am quite aware that I am finding in you the same thing parents generally find in their children, namely, that although I love you very dearly, I am not equally loved by you in return, but am ranked behind those who are not as well disposed to you as I. Annotations on 2 Corinthians 12.[12]

Paul's Affection for the Corinthians. Jacques Lefèvre d'Étaples: Now the statement that Paul adds demonstrates his fatherly affection for the Corinthians and his desire to emulate Christ who said: "No one has greater love than the one who gives his life for his friends." Paul was not seeking the Corinthians' possessions, but the Corinthians themselves; in the same way, Christ came into the world not seeking the possessions of dying men and women, but those men and women themselves, so that he might save them and give them immortality. Fathers save up treasure for their children, not vice versa. So, too, Paul wishes to save up treasure for the Corinthians, not vice versa. Having already come to them on two occasions, Paul paid his own expenses so that he might save them. He is prepared a third time to pay his own expenses for their salvation; and not only to pay his own expenses but also to lay aside his expenses and

[10]Hesshus, *Explicatio Secundae Epistolae Pauli ad Corinthios*, 286r-v.
[11]CO 50:144 (CTS 40:384). [†]For Chrysostom's interpretation, see PG 61:585-86 (NPNF[1] 12:404-5).

[12]CWE 43:277.

sacrifice himself for their souls. What could be greater than this love? For what the father experiences his children also experience. When the father is generous, the child is affected by this generosity. Commentary on 2 Corinthians 12:14.[13]

Paul's Three Intended Visits. Andreas Hyperius: For the sake of amplification, Paul adds that in the past he did not want to accept anything from them. He states that he now wishes to come to them a third time. For the first time he was among them was when he was first planting the gospel. He also arranged to come a second time, as promised in his first epistle. And in this second epistle, he apologized for a visit that he did not perform. As far as the visit promised here, Paul discharged it when he subsequently set sail as written in Acts 20, he went to Macedonia, then into Greece, and afterward set sail for Syria. For it is reported there how he came to Troas, then to Assos, then to Mitylene. . . . And at that time—although Luke does not report it—from Macedonia he came into Achaia, and then also visited Corinth, receiving the financial collection to deliver it to Jerusalem. Commentary on 2 Corinthians 12:14.[14]

Paul Was Pursuing the Corinthians in Love. Wolfgang Musculus: In the previous chapter above, Paul has given the reason why he did not at all wish to be a burden to the Corinthians, namely, so that he might remove the opportunity from those false apostles who were desiring to appear like Paul and boast about it. Now here Paul lays down an additional reason, saying, "For I seek not what is yours, but you." It is not unusual for a person to do the same thing for a variety of reasons. The first reason concerned the false apostles; this second reason expresses the affection of parental love with which Paul was pursuing the Corinthians. For it was Paul's nature, like a father, to care more for the advantage of his children than for his own profit. And that is why he seeks, not what they possess, but the Corinthians themselves. Love does not long after the things of the beloved; it loves the beloved, not her possessions. People pursue what they love with singular concern, and desire it to be safe. Thus, out of his concern for the Corinthians, Paul was not wishing to be burdensome to them, because he was not seeking their possessions, but the Corinthians themselves. As a true apostle of Christ, called to be a fisher of men and women, he was seeking the Corinthians, not their money. And he was seeking them not in order to subject them to himself, as the false apostles were doing and still do today, but so that he might lead them to Christ, and once they were in Christ, to preserve them in his grace and in true salvation. Commentary on 2 Corinthians 12:14.[15]

Preachers Must Be Primarily Concerned with People's Souls. Cyriacus Spangenberg: With this Paul gives a lesson to all preachers and gives himself as an example, that although a servant of the gospel may have and take his living from the gospel, he should not look primarily to it, but should be most preoccupied with the salvation of people's souls, that in truth they are well taught and led to righteousness through God's Word. We should not be concerned with the wool and the milk of the little sheep, but with the little sheep themselves, to pasture them well and to bring them to Christ. In popedom they have truly not kept to this rule, since they have only sought temporal goods and all things that the people owned, completely unconcerned whether they were going to God or to the devil. To this end they have silenced the Word of God and preached vain human teaching, lies, and fables, to the perishing and disadvantage of many thousands of souls. Nor may they boast that they are disciples of St. Paul, with the truth that has come to light. Forty-Seventh Sermon.[16]

[13]Lefèvre, *Commentariorum in Epistolas Beati Pauli . . . Liber Tertius*, 143; citing Jn 15:13.
[14]Hyperius, *Commentarii . . . in Epistolam D. Pauli ad Romanos, et Utramque ad Corinthios*, 423; citing Acts 20:1-16.
[15]Musculus, *Commentarius . . . in posteriorem epistolam Pauli ad Corinthios*, 386; citing 2 Cor 11:12.
[16]C. Spangenberg, *Die ander Epistel Pauli an die Corinthier*, 204v.

THE DUTIES OF PARENTHOOD. MARTIN CHEMNITZ: Paul in Ephesians 6 describes the duties of parents under three headings: (1) The upbringing [of children], which includes both their nurture and their protection. In 2 Corinthians 12, "Parents should accumulate wealth for their children." (2) Disciplining them, which includes directing their morals, and this is done by training, instructing, and chastening. . . . (3) The instruction of the Lord. For because people are born in order that the knowledge of God might be spread and celebrated, therefore not only must the bodies of those who are born be nourished, not only must their financial welfare be regarded, but particularly we must take care that they be instructed in the teaching which has been given by God, and he calls it an admonition, because he wills that this commandment be given to parents, so that their children may live in prayer and the other practices of godliness. LOCI THEOLOGICI.[17]

CARING FOR—NOT SHEARING—GOD'S FLOCK. JOHN TRAPP: "I seek not your possessions." Not the fleece, but the flock. Paul did not have those instruments of a foolish shepherd . . . the shears and milk pail, and so on. "The whole senate can witness," Beza[†] said, "that whereas Calvin had a very small stipend, yet he was so far from being discontent with it, that when a more ample allowance was freely offered to him, he obstinately refused it. All the goods that he left behind him when he died (his library also being sold for a great expense) came scarcely to three hundred French crowns." "I never sought riches, pleasures, or preferments," Melanchthon said. "I do ingenuously profess," said Mr. Rollock, "that of all my stipends I have not saved two pence, for I never cared for the things of this world."[‡] Luther never found himself once tempted to covetousness.[§] And in this way, I wish we were all Lutherans. COMMENTARY ON 2 CORINTHIANS 12:14.[18]

PAUL'S UNREQUITED LOVE. WOLFGANG MUSCULUS: Paul says three things here. First, that he loves them *perissoterōs*, that is, copiously and abundantly. This depicts a fountain of abundant love with which he was affectionate toward them. Second, that the Corinthians loved him less. Paul complains about this with sorrow. But that is the costly fate of lovers: the more they love, the less they are loved. Lovers have this in common with God who, despite his incomparable love for us, is loved less by us. . . . Third, that Paul is nevertheless not hindered from all the more freely expending his whole self for the Corinthians, speaking of that abundant love by which he was pursuing them. So great is the power of love that it conquers everything, it consumes and devours everything when one would expect it to be destroyed. Thus, that saying is not without merit, "Love conquers all. Truly, as soon as it does this it conquers itself." COMMENTARY ON 2 CORINTHIANS 12:15.[19]

CHRIST WILL REPAY MINISTERS' SACRIFICES AND SUFFERING. TILEMANN HESSHUS: Not only had Paul not demanded payment from the Corinthians, but he was even prepared to pay out of his own resources for their use—and not only to pay this expense for them, but also to pour out his life for them. Thus, the greater Paul's burning love for the Corinthian church, the less they were sincerely loving Paul; his love was a very severe reproof for their apathy, carelessness, and ingratitude. Therefore, Paul exhorts them to pay a

[17]Chemnitz, *Loci Theologici*, 2:400; citing Eph 6:4; Prov 23:13; Heb 12:7.

[18]Trapp, *A Commentary or Exposition*, 734*. [†]Beza's statement regarding Calvin's modesty and the value of the reformer's estate is found in his *The Life of John Calvin* (Darlington, UK: Evangelical Press, 1997), 132-33. [‡]Melanchthon expresses this sentiment in a letter to Aquila, dated August 29, 1547; see CR 6:649-50. Henry Charteris (1565–1628), Rollock's successor and biographer, recounts Rollock making this statement to city magistrates on his deathbed, asking them to continue to care for the University of Edinburgh. Charteris, "Vitae et Obitus D. Roberti Rolloci, Scoti," in *Select Works of Robert Rollock*, ed. William Gunn (Edinburgh: Wodrow Society, 1849), lii, lxxxii. [§]John Foxe attributes this statement about Luther to Hieronymous Weller: John Foxe, *Foxe's Book of Martyrs, or The Acts and Monuments of the Christian Church* (Philadelphia: James B. Smith, 1860), 7.11, 861.

[19]Musculus, *Commentarius . . . in posteriorem epistolam Pauli ad Corinthios*, 388-89.

recompense and show the same affection toward him that he himself had toward the Corinthians. Now, Paul provides for us an example of patience. If, when we face suffering, troubles, and battles, our hearers do not respond in a kind and respectful fashion, we should not be annoyed and grow weary and disheartened in ministry because of their ingratitude, but we should look to the Son of God for our reward, who will very justly judge our battles and abundantly compensate our sufferings. Explication of 2 Corinthians 12:15.[20]

Degrees of Paul's Love for the Corinthians. The English Annotations: That is, "I will not only bestow my pains and my estate, but also my body, and lay down my life for you." Here the Greek commentator notes seven steps or degrees in the apostle's love. First, that he could have received maintenance from them (since Christ commanded that ministers of the gospel should live by the gospel) but he would not. Second, that though he was in need, yet he would not charge them in any way to relieve him. Third, he preached constantly to them, though they gave him nothing for his efforts. Fourth, he was at great expense with them. Fifth, he not only gladly bestowed what he had among them but was willing to be bestowed, and he sacrificed his life for them. Sixth, he did all this for people who treated him coldly. Seventh, though they in no way answered him in his love, but as his love for them grew still hotter, theirs grew colder for him, yet in no way diminished in his love or care for them. Annotations on 2 Corinthians 12:15.[21]

Spend and Be Spent. John Trapp: If like clouds we sweat ourselves to death, so if souls may be brought home to God, it would be a blessed way of dying. Mr. Samuel Crooke's[†] motto was *Impendam & expandar*: "I will spend and be spent." This he cheerfully verified. Commentary on 2 Corinthians 12:15.[22]

The Deceptive Strategies of Paul's Opponents. Wolfgang Musculus: When Paul says, "I myself was not burdensome to you," he expresses the concession of the false apostles, who were acknowledging what they could not deny. But they were making him offensive by adding this perverse explanation, saying, "It is true that he was not at all burdensome to you, but he did this out of deceit so that, by cunning, he might trick you and later conquer you." This is how malicious people usually argue. What they cannot deny, they maliciously suppress with perverse explanations. This very frequently happens to those who are likened to "Spiritualists." So, too, when the Pharisees could not bear the glory and light of Christ's deeds, although they were unable to deny them without manifest shame, they scoffed his deeds with a perverse explanation, saying that he did them through Beelzebub, the prince of demons. In our own day, it is possible to see countless examples of this sort of malice expressed toward those who turn to the truth of the gospel of Christ. But no one should be surprised by this. For if Satan attempted to maliciously impugn not only the work of Paul, but even of Christ, it ought not seem unusual if he pours out his venom on us as well. Commentary on 2 Corinthians 12:16.[23]

Paul Sharply Warns the Corinthians. Jacques Lefèvre d'Étaples: But Paul foresees what the detractors and calumniators of the good were going to say, namely, they would allege that Paul was making an excuse through cunning and sly tricks to receive financial support and make a public collection among the Corinthians. Those who do this are directed by the spirit of the world,

[20]Hesshus, *Explicatio Secundae Epistolae Pauli ad Corinthios*, 287v-288r.
[21]Downame, ed., *English Annotations*, GG3v*.
[22]Trapp, *A Commentary or Exposition*, 734*. [†]Samuel Crooke was a prominent minister and author in seventeenth-century England, who sided with the Parliamentary cause during the English Civil War.
[23]Musculus, *Commentarius . . . in posteriorem epistolam Pauli ad Corinthios*, 389; citing Lk 11:15-19.

not the Spirit of God. Those who do this are concerned with their own well-being, not the public good, nor the good of others and the perfecting of virtue. Yes, and Paul sent Titus and a brother with him, whoever he was, whether Luke or Sylvanus or someone else. They were walking in the Spirit of God, concerned with the public good, not their own advantage, and seeking the edification of others. But, because there were some among the Corinthians such as detractors who were thinking neither about God nor the Spirit, but only about those passible and fleshly things, and calumniators of good people, and those fomenters of sedition and factions—for that reason Paul warned them and others who had sinned gravely against discipline that, before his third coming they should repent and do penance (for that is what is meant by repentance), lest in his coming God might take vengeance on them. For Paul himself was not the punisher nor was he the avenger, but God was the one who would punish. Knowing, therefore, that unless they repented, God would punish them when Paul came, he warns and exhorts them to repent. Commentary on 2 Corinthians 12:16-18.[24]

Avoiding All Appearance of Evil. John Calvin: "But granting that"—these words indicate that Paul had been accused by wicked people of having swindled with the help of hired persons what he had refused to accept in person. He had done no such thing, but (as it is said) "they measure by their own measuring stick."[†] For it is customary for the wicked to shamelessly impute to the servants of God whatever they themselves would do if they were given the opportunity. Hence, Paul is forced to defend the integrity of those whom he sent so as to defend himself from a charge shamefully fabricated, for if they had sinned in any way it would have been imputed to him. Now, who would be surprised that Paul was so cautious in the matter of almsgiving when he had been harassed by so many unfair judgments after having taken so many precautions? However, let his case be an example for us not to look upon it as a thing new and intolerable if sometimes we have to respond to similar calumnies. But let this especially be a warning for us to use godly caution lest we provide any opportunity for revilers. For we see that it is not enough for us to give evidence of our own integrity if those assisting us are not also perceived as being such. Hence our choice of those who will help us is neither unimportant or perfunctory, but must be made with great care and diligence. Commentary on 2 Corinthians 12:16-17.[25]

Paul's Integrity Was Above Reproach. Tilemann Hesshus: Not only did Paul, when he was teaching among the Corinthians, carefully avoid the appearance that he was doing it for the sake of payment, so also he took pains lest it appear that he was scheming to get their riches. And so, Paul had no doubt instructed Titus that he should not seek any financial support from the Corinthians, so that they might not be suspicious that Paul had personally received something and that he was only pretending to be free from greed. . . . And so, by his integrity, he closed all loopholes for slander. Even so, he was not able to win the favor of the Corinthians. The false apostles, with their clever cunning, were no doubt accusing Paul of deceitfully seeking to cover up his greed and extort through other people what he did not dare demand for himself. Therefore, Paul appeals to the conscience of the Corinthians and brings up the example of Titus, whom he sent to the Corinthians. For Paul had extorted nothing through Titus, whence that slander against Paul was seen to be clearly unjust and that Paul was a complete stranger to this sort of deception. The fact that Titus was walking in that same spirit and was following in the footsteps of Paul greatly

[24]Lefèvre, *Commentariorum in Epistolas Beati Pauli . . . Liber Tertius*, 143v.

[25]CO 50:145-46 (CTS 40:386-87). [†]The quotation is probably a paraphrase of Horace's words: "Metiri se quenquam suo modulo ac pede erum est." In Horace *Epistles* 1.7.98.

recommended Paul's doctrine and teaching. Explication of 2 Corinthians 12:16-18.[26]

Important Lessons from Paul's Example. Andreas Hyperius: Paul repeats by means of close attention or imitation what his adversaries were slandering him about, namely, that he deceptively did not want to accept any payment so that, by this strategy, he might place them completely under obligation to him, so that afterward he might cunningly swindle them, if not in person, at least through others. He refutes this slanderous accusation, therefore, by clearly showing that the Corinthians had not been extorted, neither by him nor by anyone else. Now he makes a very forceful and sharp complaint to dissuade them from wanting to make such an argument. And let us note here the strategy of those people who, although they do not do something openly by themselves, nevertheless accomplish it secretly through other people. For, the more they insidiously induce others to perform such pestilential practices both in churches and in the political sphere, the more secretly they commit their frauds. And this also should be noted, that those who were sent out by the apostle were walking in his same spirit and footsteps, that is, they demonstrated the greatest harmony in doctrine and life. The phrase "to walk in the same spirit" is a Hebraism for living and acting in the same manner, for it is proper to be taught by the same spirit. Accordingly, such agreement befits all ministers in the church. If only all ministers had been walking in the same footsteps from the apostle's day to our own time and there would not be so many wicked doctrines and idolatrous practices sneaking into the church of God! Commentary on 2 Corinthians 12:16-18.[27]

Titus Fulfilled Paul's Godly Intentions. Wolfgang Musculus: "Did Titus take advantage of you?" Paul sent Titus for the purpose of collecting the money from the Corinthians. But he collected it not for Paul, nor for himself, but for the benefit of the saints. Further, he did not collect it by force but voluntarily, not out of greed but out of praise. That is why nothing that Titus had done was contrary to Paul's intention. Commentary on 2 Corinthians 12:18.[28]

Titus Did Not Take Advantage of the Corinthians Either. David Dickson: Paul here avoids an objection. Some people might say, "Although you yourself did not receive wages from them, perhaps you gleaned some of the profits from those companions you sent to them." Paul answers that the companions and ambassadors whom he had sent to them had been careful not to burden the Corinthians. Thus, he checks his adversaries, while at the same time clearing himself from the strategies that those crafty workers used who, though they seemed to receive nothing for themselves, enlisted others to receive for their use whatsoever they could squeeze from the Corinthians. Therefore, the Corinthians ought to defend Paul and silence his accusers in his absence. Exposition of 2 Corinthians 12:18.[29]

12:19-21 *Paul's Fear for a Future Visit*

Paul Was Speaking in the Sight of God. Wolfgang Musculus: The sense here is this: "We are in no way feigning so as to give an excuse for ourselves, but we are speaking those things that are true." He indicates this by saying that he speaks in the sight of God in Christ. For here there is no place for guile. To speak in the sight of God is to speak with a reverent awareness of God even as if one were speaking in the presence of the divine majesty. Paul adds the words "in Christ" which can be interpreted to mean either "for the sake of Christ" (that is, concerning Christ), or "in the spirit of

[26]Hesshus, *Explicatio Secundae Epistolae Pauli ad Corinthios*, 288r-v.
[27]Hyperius, *Commentarii . . . in Epistolam D. Pauli ad Romanos, et Utramque ad Corinthios*, 424.
[28]Musculus, *Commentarius . . . in posteriorem epistolam Pauli ad Corinthios*, 391.
[29]Dickson, *An Exposition of All St. Paul's Epistles*, 92*.

Christ," or "according to the testimony of Christ." Now we should not interpret this phrase to apply only to this specific case but more generally, regarding all the things that Paul was speaking in Christ. It is as if he were saying: "It is not my habit to make excuses like those who are accustomed to concoct false arguments, but I have been appointed so that whatever I speak, especially for the sake of Christ, I will not speak rashly or lightly, but with great reverence, as if I were in the presence of God." . . .

Paul wrote many things in this letter, some of which seemed to have to do with himself, inasmuch as he was fighting against enemies, boasting about many things, asserting his apostolic authority, and defending his own innocence, and so on. But in all that he wrote, he was in no way seeking his own benefit; rather, he directed all things to this goal, that the Corinthians might be built up in faith and sincerity toward Christ and in true godliness. He indicates this when he says, "all for your edification, beloved." Commentary on 2 Corinthians 12:19.[30]

Reasons Why Paul's Apology Was Necessary. David Dickson: Some might say, Why does Paul write these things? Why is he defending himself? Is he sensitive about some evil? Or does he want us to praise him? Paul answers by giving five reasons explaining why he was so concerned in this manner.

Reason 1. I have not written these things so as to clear myself among you, or to excuse myself, as if I were guilty of some evil or desired glory. Rather, I have written out of my love for you, that I might promote your edification and salvation, lest you, thinking little of my apostleship, should be diverted from the simplicity of the gospel by the false apostles. I call upon God (who knows my mind) and Christ (whose business I do) to serve as witnesses of the truth of my assertions. . . .

Reason 2. I am afraid that if the false apostles diminish my authority and doctrine among you, when I come I shall find you in a bad condition, that is, infected with those evils which come from schisms, such as arguments or contentions; copying or envying one another concerning the gifts of God; wrath or anger from mutual injuries; brawling or mutual provocations; backbiting and whispering, by which people both in public and private try to defame one another; puffing up of the mind out of pride; and last, tumultuous seditions. . . .

Reason 3. I am afraid that you will find me more severe than I would wish, unless you correct your errors by admonitions and submit to my doctrine and authority in the Lord. . . .

Reason 4. I am afraid that if my authority is despised among you, many among you will not repent but continue in their defilement, fornications, and other such sins that I reproved in my former epistle. . . .

Reason 5. I am afraid that the Lord will afflict me when I come to you, that is, that your sins will create shame, sadness, and mourning within me, and offenses among you. For you are my glory and joy if you behave yourselves as children should; but you will cause me shame and sadness if you do otherwise.

It was necessary for Paul to maintain his authority as an apostle and his apostolic doctrine in order to prevent these evils and take away the scandals arising among them. It was for this reason that the apostle's apology was necessary. Exposition of 2 Corinthians 12:19-21.[31]

Fear, Love, and Kindness. John Calvin: "I fear," he says. This fear proceeded from love, for if he had not been concerned for their salvation, he would have altogether overlooked this matter from which he was gaining no personal advantage. For otherwise a person is afraid to offend when he foresees that it will be hurtful to himself. "And I shall be found by you." Here is a second reason for Paul's fear, lest he be forced to act with greater severity. Now it is a mark not only of love but even

[30]Musculus, *Commentarius . . . in posteriorem epistolam Pauli ad Corinthios*, 392-93.

[31]Dickson, *An Exposition of all St. Paul's Epistles*, 92*.

of kindness, to avoid severity and to pursue milder remedies. . . . Therefore, Paul teaches by his own example that pastors must always seek out milder remedies for the correction of faults, before they have recourse to extreme severity; and, at the same time, we must, by admonitions and rebukes, prevent the need to use extreme rigor. Commentary on 2 Corinthians 12:20.[32]

Contention, Jealousy, Slander, Gossip, Conceit, Disorder. Tilemann Hesshus: The apostle demonstrates his paternal concern for the Corinthians because they were listening so easily to the false apostles and were permitting Paul to be slandered among them. For good reason, then, the apostle was fearful that the Corinthians were walking according to the flesh. For when slanderous words are spread by false teachers, first they throw the listeners into doubt; and they soon banish a sense of security, which then generates contentions, squabbles, detractions, and confusion. Paul therefore was afraid that when he came to Corinth he might find them to have degenerated from true piety, and that he would be forced, on the basis of his office, to use sharp reproofs among them, when he would have preferred to praise their piety, faith, modesty, love, and liberality. Contentions are squabbles concerning unnecessary things, they are disputes about words (*logomachiai*), wrangling concerning donkey's shadows, when people defend their opinions doggedly (which is the fruit of ambition) and, at last, such contentions break out into wrangling, hatred, and confusion. There was nothing but contention over the question of the freedom of good works—agreement between the factions would have been possible if they had moderated their passions. For both things that were asserted were very true: that the good works of the saints are necessary because they are divinely mandated; and that the good works of the saints are bestowed freely by the Spirit, not by cooperating with the law. Rivalry occurs when one person is envious of the virtue and honor of someone else and tries to prefer himself to the other. Theodoret,[†] bishop of Cyrrhus, depending on his own erudition, was envious of Cyril, bishop of Alexandria, and was grieved that he had greater authority in the church. And so, he opposed himself to Cyril and excited an uproar in the church, causing great scandal among the godly. It usually happens that wrath is born from envy and contention, which impede our prayers and often create hideous scandals.

The word "jealousy" indicates almost the same meaning as "contentions," except that it appears to be a more moderate word. Now the apostle warns that even mild jealousies are not proper for Christians because they are a sign of fleshly security and spring up from the well of ambition.

"Slandering" is the act of degrading other people that originates from envy and jealousy, not so that we might improve our neighbors or draw them back to the right path, but so that we might totally crush them. Doeg, one of Saul's servants, was a slanderer when he reported to the king that Ahimelech had given to David bread and Goliath's sword; this report greatly inflamed the heart of the king to distrust David and pursue him anew. The court preacher Eusebius of Nicomedia[†] was guilty of slandering Athanasius, that sure and steadfast defender of the truth, and betrayed him before Emperor Constantine as if he were the author and ringleader of all the controversies in the church. . . .

"Murmurers" are those who tell gossip: when unreliable people spread among the ordinary people whatever futile things they have heard, and they weary themselves with their lying reports. . . . Now contentions, hatred, suspicions, and uproars are all stirred up by gossipers, and they are often the cause of great tumults.

Conceit is indicative of pride and arrogance, which inflates its own self-worth, as seen in the fox in Aesop's Fable. John of Antioch was conceited and arrogant in the controversy surrounding Nestorius when he proudly opposed Cyril, who was defending the orthodox view. Paul of Samosata[§] was also conceited and arrogant, as the *Ecclesiastical History* shows. . . .

[32]CO 50:146 (CTS 40:388).

"Seditious people." Careless and restless people often stir up confusion and seditions in the church. For Satan often induces careless and restless minds to disturb the peace of the church. A number of different Arians stirred up seditions and uproars in Alexandria, Milan, and other churches. Therefore, the apostle was fearful lest disagreements should arise among the godly in Corinth, and that uproars should be stirred up. He takes notice that many people were living carelessly and giving an opportunity to Satan's traps. Explication of 2 Corinthians 12:20.[33]

Paul's Fears and Self-Justification. Andreas Hyperius: Paul explains how he fears that when he comes it will be different than desirable. Now, the phrase "I fear" is repeated by way of the grammatical figure zeugma,[†] as in the following sense: "I fear that there might be contentions among you . . . , and that when I come again, I will be afflicted of soul and distressed on account of those people for whom my teaching (which was delivered under the greatest of hardships) accomplished nothing and whom I ought to bring to repentance by the more strict discipline of the church." Paul then enumerates some of the vices which were especially prevalent among the Corinthians, but besides those things he explained previously, let us understand the following. He especially notes those vices that he criticized in his first letter, such as disagreements and the creation of factions, and Paul encouraged them to regain harmony among themselves, for all these things were related to this same issue and were recognized among them.

An antithesis is hidden in these words: "I fear that when I come God may humble me before you." For Paul's adversaries were concluding that he was doing everything from pride and arrogance to shamefully take their possessions. But he, on the contrary, recognized that he was doing everything with the greatest humility and anguish of soul. He explained this to them again with the words appended, saying that he was mourning and grieving because of those people who had not repented of their wicked life of the past. Thus, Samuel mourned throughout his life for Saul. In fact, godly ministers of the Word cannot help but mourn when they consider the fact that, although they taught with the greatest diligence, nevertheless men and women were in no way made better, but rather became worse and daily fell headlong into more serious vices. Now Paul lists in the second place impurity and lust, sins which the Corinthians committed frequently and with impunity, which are treated in 1 Corinthians 6. Commentary on 2 Corinthians 12:20-21.[34]

Hostility and Slander Are Kinds of Murder. Martin Chemnitz: The second point to consider is what is meant by the killing prohibited in the fifth commandment. The word "kill" of itself means to destroy, to snuff out, or to cut off the life of a person. But Christ in his interpretation in Matthew 5 shows that to kill under the fifth commandment refers not only to the act itself but also to the inner attitudes of the heart, to our deeds and to our words. . . . Christ lists four kinds of homicide, and a more proper catalog of sins that are in conflict with this precept cannot be drawn up. Indeed, from this list we must draw the rule that in the case of each of the individual commandments four kinds of sin are to be noted: (1) the inner emotions of the heart or mind; (2) sins of gesture; (3) sins of words; (4) sins of deeds. . . .

---

[33]Hesshus, *Explicatio Secundae Epistolae Pauli ad Corinthios*, 289v-291r; citing 1 Sam 22:9. [†]The conflict between Theodoret and Cyril, which raged during the 430s, was over Theodoret and John of Antioch's opposition to Cyril's uncompromising condemnation of Nestorius. Theodoret was condemned and excommunicated by the Second Council of Ephesus in 449. [‡]Eusebius of Nicomedia (d. c. 342) was the Arian bishop of Nicomedia, who opposed Athanasius (c. 293-373), the homoousian bishop of Alexandria. [§]Paul of Samosata, the onetime bishop of Antioch, was deposed by the Synod of Antioch in 269 for teaching that Jesus, having been born a mere man, was later infused with the divine Logos.

[34]Hyperius, *Commentarii . . . in Epistolam D. Pauli ad Romanos, et Utramque ad Corinthios*, 425. [†]A zeugma is a grammatical figure, "according to which two nouns or two infinitives are united to a verb which is applicable to only one of them." See Charlton Lewis and Charles Short, eds., *A Latin Dictionary* (Oxford: Oxford University Press, 1991), 2018.

The fourth [*sic*, third] kind of murder is committed by the tongue, as when a person says, "you fool," out of anger, evil intent, or with the intention of doing him harm. Paul adds many terms to this list: "contentions," "quarrels," "disputing," and in 2 Corinthians 12 he refers to strife, contentions, and seditions. Loci Theologici.[35]

Paul Grieves Over the Sins of the Corinthians. Tilemann Hesshus: When the apostle writes to the Philippians, he calls the church there his crown and joy, as the church is growing in the knowledge of God, and is persisting in constancy of faith, and is patiently enduring suffering, and is producing an abundant harvest of good works. By contrast, here he calls the [Corinthian] church his humiliation and grief, since he recognizes that the church that he had established was degenerating from its original godliness and had lapsed into carelessness. Now if a church grows in faith and godliness, and brings forth the fruit of good works, then it is adorned and magnified and decreed by God worthy of praise. For nothing is more pleasing to an apostle or godly pastor than when he sees his hearers making progress in godliness, and when, by his labor, numerous people are gathered into Christ's church. Moreover, God strengthens us in a remarkable way in the labor of our calling; he comforts us amid the dangers and troubles which we endure for the sake of the ministry. And finally, he also causes the glory of the church to overflow among those of us who faithfully serve him by the Word.

On the other hand, when we watch our hearers abandon godliness, waver in their confession, or retreat into carnal carelessness, this causes the greatest sadness for faithful pastors. For they fear that their strenuous labors might be for nothing; they fear that they might be blameworthy for having (perhaps) overlooked necessary correction, or not to have provided adequate reproofs. And so, Paul is also worried here that, when he comes to Corinth, God might humble him with grief and force him to lament because of the carelessness and impenitence of many of them. Paul shows here that many of them judge too rigidly the teachers of the church—those people, of course, who have previously defiled themselves with wickedness, lusts, and other vices. They do not seriously repent; they are never truly sorry for having allowed sins, but they have joined themselves to the church with a pretended faith. These people, then, are the most reckless "reformers" of their teachers and pastors. Now those who seriously repent and embrace the benefits of the mediator with sincere faith—those are the people who customarily respect the ministry and think modestly and honorably about their pastors. Therefore, Paul warns the Corinthians that they should be provoked to serious repentance for having permitted this foul and lustful behavior. Explication of 2 Corinthians 12:21.[36]

Though Accused of Pride, Paul Was Truly Humble. Huldrych Zwingli: There is a beautiful antithesis here, for the person they were despising for being humble they were falsely accusing as proud. It is as if Paul were saying: "Your so-called apostles accuse me of being proud. If I discover, therefore, such shameful things still among you when I come to you, then I will be completely humiliated." For even though Paul taught faithfully, he was despised and did not see the Corinthians' behavior corrected, which he desired so intensely that his soul was tormented. Annotations on 2 Corinthians 12:21.[37]

Guidelines for Excommunication. Wolfgang Musculus: First, note that Paul does not say, "and I may condemn," or "and I may excommunicate," but he says, "and I may mourn." It is easy to reproach and excommunicate sinners, especially when one employs the justice and power of the

[35]Chemnitz, *Loci Theologici*, 2:405-6, 407; citing Mt 5:21-26; 2 Tim 2:14; Titus 3:2; Phil 2:14.

[36]Hesshus, *Explicatio Secundae Epistolae Pauli ad Corinthios*, 291v-292v.

[37]Zwingli, *Annotatiunculae . . . ex ore Zvinglij*, 191.

magistrate. But it is not so with mourning. For only those who love, mourn, and parental affection is expressed even toward delinquent children. I see some people today who are not so much committed to mourning as they are to excommunicating people. And they use excommunication not so much for gathering sinners as for excluding them. They cite the example of Paul, but they do not share the emotions of his heart. We more quickly chase after excommunication than mourning.

Second, what great mourning is necessary when not just a single person is unrepentant, but a great many people are equally unrepentant, as we read in 1 Corinthians 5. Is it appropriate then to excommunicate those persons, to remove that yeast [from the dough] so that they do not corrupt the entire lump? Clearly, for the wise pastor, excommunication should not be rashly employed on everyone, but one must consider very carefully whether or not it will work for the edification and restoration of evildoers. Now we act with dangerous presumption when we excommunicate a great multitude of people for some common vice, instead of one or two people who are guilty of some enormous and detestable sin that everyone finds shameful, such as when a man fornicates. . . . For in doing this there is danger that the multitude might create a schism in the church and, rather than emending their evil, only change them for the worse. Fearing this, the apostle did not say, "When you are gathered together and in my spirit, excommunicate many of those people who have previously sinned," but he says, "and I may mourn over many of those."

Third, the purpose of excommunication is not only to reform sinners who have offended the church with their enormous sin and refuse to change but also to make the rest of the congregation more cautious. We see that this did not happen in the church of the Corinthians. For even though the church had excommunicated that fornicator by the command of the apostle, there were still many people in that church who did not have any repentance for these sins and who were not especially induced to repentance by the example of the excommunicated person and the fear of excommunication.

Fourth, Paul does not simply say, "those who have sinned earlier," but he adds, "and have not repented of the impurity." . . . Therefore, Paul mourns, not so much because of the sin as because the sinners have not been brought to repentance. The repentance of a sinner is not the occasion for grief, but rather for rejoicing, as Luke 15 tells us happens in heaven among the angels. From this we can see both what great benefit there is in repentance, and what great evil there is when people do not repent. Commentary on 2 Corinthians 12:21.[38]

Paul's Fear and Affection. Niels Hemmingsen: This is a declaration of what Paul had said in general. For he explains that he is afraid of what state he will find them in and, likewise, what state they will find him in if, having spurned him, they listen to the false apostles. He enumerates several vices that are well known and which do not require our interpretation as much as our serious renunciation of them, if we want only to glorify Christ. Paul humbly expresses his grief on behalf of those Corinthians (who had been seduced by the false apostles and were troubled by so many vices) so that ministers of the Word might try to imitate that affection of the apostle. Commentary on 2 Corinthians 12:21.[39]

Repentance and Recovery. John Trapp: Impenitence makes sin mortal, says St. John in 1 John 5, or rather immortal, as Paul states in Romans 2. It is not the falling into the water that drowns, but lying in it. God's people may sink once and again to the bottom, but the third time they rise and recover by means of repentance. Commentary on 2 Corinthians 12:21.[40]

[38]Musculus, *Commentarius . . . in posteriorem epistolam Pauli ad Corinthios*, 397-98; citing Lk 15:7.

[39]Hemmingsen, *Commentaria in Omnes Epistolas Apostolorum*, 306.

[40]Trapp, *A Commentary or Exposition*, 735*; citing 1 Jn 5:16; Rom 2:5.

Pastors Hold God's People in Their Hearts. John Calvin: Meanwhile, Paul describes the disposition of a true and genuine pastor when he says that he will look upon the sins of others with grief. And surely, the right way of acting is like this: that every pastor should have his church enclosed in his heart, and be affected by its maladies, sympathize with its troubles, and lament its sins—just as if they were his own. We see how Jeremiah petitions to be given "a fountain of tears" that he might weep bitterly for the calamity of his people. We see that godly kings and prophets, to whom the governance of the people was committed, were affected with similar feelings. It is, indeed, the common experience of all godly people to be grieved in every case where God is offended, and to mourn the ruin of brothers and sisters . . . but it is especially required of pastors. Furthermore, Paul enumerates here a second list of vices, which, however, belong to one principal point, namely, unchastity. Commentary on 2 Corinthians 12:21.[41]

[41]CO 50:147 (CTS 40:389-90); citing Jer 9:1.

13:1-10 FINAL WARNINGS

This is the third time I am coming to you. Every charge must be established by the evidence of two or three witnesses. [2]I warned those who sinned before and all the others, and I warn them now while absent, as I did when present on my second visit, that if I come again I will not spare them— [3]since you seek proof that Christ is speaking in me. He is not weak in dealing with you, but is powerful among you. [4]For he was crucified in weakness, but lives by the power of God. For we also are weak in him, but in dealing with you we will live with him by the power of God.

[5]Examine yourselves, to see whether you are in the faith. Test yourselves. Or do you not realize this about yourselves, that Jesus Christ is in you?—unless indeed you fail to meet the test! [6]I hope you will find out that we have not failed the test. [7]But we pray to God that you may not do wrong—not that we may appear to have met the test, but that you may do what is right, though we may seem to have failed. [8]For we cannot do anything against the truth, but only for the truth. [9]For we are glad when we are weak and you are strong. Your restoration is what we pray for. [10]For this reason I write these things while I am away from you, that when I come I may not have to be severe in my use of the authority that the Lord has given me for building up and not for tearing down.

OVERVIEW: As Paul prepares to conclude his letter, he once again defends his apostolic authority and warns the most obstinate members of the Corinthian congregation to examine themselves and repent so that there will be no need for harsh rebukes when he pays a third visit to Corinth. Throughout this passage, Reformation commentators identify important insights regarding the nature and proper expression of ecclesiastical authority. Spiritual authority is not based on boastful claims, extraordinary gifts, or an attractive physical appearance. Rather, the authority of Christian ministry is always derived from the truths of Scripture, and it is through faithful exposition of God's Word that Jesus Christ works most powerfully in his church. To be sure, like Paul, Christian ministers often appear weak and unimpressive, and they are prone to suffering; but even in their abject weakness, the resurrected Christ works in power to humble the proud, rescue the penitent, and build up his church. Importantly, Paul's authority is spiritual, not civil—a fact that Protestant interpreters leverage to criticize the medieval church's practice of wielding its power over the political states of Europe. For the reformers, then, both false apostles and modern-day heretics completely misconstrue the dynamics of true spiritual authority.

Protestant exegetes also make much of Paul's statement in 2 Corinthians 13:5, "Examine yourselves to see whether you are in the faith," believing that this passage provides clear proof that faithful Christians can expect to experience assurance of their salvation—a doctrine the Council of Trent expressly rejects in its Statement on Justification (1547). But how can a believer find such assurance? Although suggestions vary, a number of Protestant exegetes indicate that personal assurance is found through inner and external proofs: the inner witness of the Holy Spirit who testifies to a Christian's adoption; and external attitudes such as humility, godliness, holiness, and a penitent heart. Finally, as frequently noted elsewhere, Reformation commentators lift up Paul's example as a worthy model for Christian ministers and laypeople. He cares more for the well-being of the Corinthian church than his own reputation. He is willing to become weak and humble, so that they may be strong in the faith. His deep love for the Corinthians spills out in fervent prayers for their spiritual growth and restoration. In this passage, Paul prays before he speaks—a practice that all Christian workers should emulate.

Summary of Chapter. John Calvin: In the thirteenth chapter, by warning such persons that he will treat them more severely, he exhorts all in general to recognize his apostleship, as it will be to their benefit to do so. Since it would be ruinous for them to despise the one whom they had found by experience to be a trustworthy and faithful ambassador from the Lord. Commentary on 2 Corinthians.[1]

Paul's Argument. Tilemann Hesshus: In this chapter, Paul shows that he is going to deal (with considerably greater severity) with those careless and refractory persons who were not at all affected by the apostle's very gentle and paternal admonitions. Now he addresses them in a more direct fashion—and especially that person who was guilty of this dissension. He points out that abuse and contempt overflow onto Christ himself, who has given Paul his ministry. Neither his weakness nor his humility is an impediment to Christ demonstrating his power in these things. He exhorts the Corinthians to examine themselves carefully whether sincere faith is conspicuous in them, whether Christ indwells them, and whether God's Spirit is directing them—or, by contrast, whether they are foreigners from Christ and led by their human desires. Paul testifies to his love for the Corinthians, even as he wishes them to be sincere and approved in the faith and to shine before God in zeal for good works, committing no evil thing. And he testifies that he has written his letter for this purpose, that they might be pure in godliness. Finally, he exhorts them to rejoice, to be blameless, and to experience comfort and unity, living in peace with one another. Explication of 2 Corinthians 13.[2]

Structure of Chapter 13. Niels Hemmingsen: This chapter constitutes the epilogue of the entire epistle, except that it does not expressly mention almsgiving. In the first part he mentions his coming. In the second part he threatens punishment to those who were defiant. In the third part, Paul defends the authority of his apostleship. In the fourth part, he discourages their vices and exhorts them to virtue. In the fifth part, he demands in his own name that the Corinthians greet one another and he prays with joy for them. Commentary on 2 Corinthians 13.[3]

13:1-4 *Paul's Anticipated Third Visit*

Three Visits and Three Witnesses. John Calvin: Paul continues to reprove the brashness of those of whom he has been speaking. Some of them are living carelessly and licentiously, others, stirring up contentions and strife among themselves, cared nothing for his rebukes. Now, his speech did not apply to the body of the whole church, but only certain members that were diseased and half rotten. Hence, he now indulges more freely in sharp rebukes because his concern is with particular people, not the entire church. Moreover, he perceived that with persons of this sort, he would do them no good by kindness and mild remedies. After having spent a year and a half among them, he had visited them a second time. Now he forewarns them that he is going to come a third time, and he says that his three visits to them will be in place of three witnesses. He quotes the law concerning the authority of witnesses; not in the natural and literal sense (as it is called), but by means of anagogy or similitude, accommodating it to its particular purpose. "The declaration of the law," he says, "must be established on the testimony of two or three people for settling disputes." (For the word *established* means that a decision is pronounced so that a quarrel may cease.) "Indeed, I am but one person; but in my three visits, I will have the authority of three witnesses, or my three visits are in place of three testimonies." For the threefold effort that Paul made for their welfare, on three different occasions, which proved his

[1]CO 50:8 (CTS 40:108).

[2]Hesshus, *Explicatio Secundae Epistolae Pauli ad Corinthios*, 293v-294r.

[3]Hemmingsen, *Commentaria in Omnes Epistolas Apostolorum*, 306.

perseverance, could with good reason represent three persons. Commentary on 2 Corinthians 13:1.[4]

Paul Will Give the Corinthians Three Warnings. Wolfgang Musculus: Paul cites this passage from Deuteronomy 19: "Only on the evidence of two witnesses or of three witnesses will a charge be established." Now to establish a charge is the same as substantiating a case by means of testimony, which was confirmed by two or three witnesses of the fact. Paul applies this law with his quotation. It is as if he were saying: "Very soon I will come to you for a third time and will reprove you for your lack of repentance." That is why they will have no excuse in the future if they disregard this third reproof, for just as a matter is established by the evidence of two or three witnesses according to the law, and is judged as final, so it will be with this third admonition that, having been sufficiently warned, they will rightly be condemned. And so, if they will not repent with this third reproof, it will be clear that they are guilty of continuing stubbornly in their impenitence. Christ says a similar thing in Matthew 18, when he limits a sufficient rebuke to a threefold warning, saying, "If your brother has sinned against you, go and tell him his fault, between you and him alone. If he listens to you, you have gained your brother. But if he does not listen to you, take one or two others along with you, so that every charge will be established by the evidence of two or three witnesses. If he refuses to listen to them, then tell it to the church. And if he refuses to listen to the church, then let him be to you as a Gentile and tax collector." In the same way a person is condemned as defiant in a judicial forum if he does not appear after the third legitimate summons. Commentary on 2 Corinthians 13:1.[5]

Three Warnings Before Conviction. Giovanni Diodati: "Must be established." The sense is this: "These three warnings of my coming will serve as a kind of testimony for you, by which, if you refuse to amend yourselves, you will be convicted of incorrigible rebellion sufficient to advance to immediate sentencing." Now this warning is addressed, not to the entire body of the church, to which Paul had already rendered a better testimony in the beginning [of the epistle], but to the corrupted part of the church. Annotations on 2 Corinthians 13:1.[6]

Gentle and Harsh Rebukes. Tilemann Hesshus: There is always a great difference between citizens in the church: among some there is more light, among others there is less light. Some people are more affected by the threats of their pastors, other people less so. Some people always fear God, repenting seriously of their sins; other people fiercely reject threats, living carefree lives. Now the faithful minister must provide care for all members, treating gently those who are remediable, and fiercely reproaching those who are more uncontrolled.

Therefore, just as Paul in the previous two chapters has gently corrected the remediable group and admonished them to do their duty with very kind words, so in this present chapter, he treats the obstinate and careless with considerably greater harshness and severity. When he quotes the law of Moses concerning calling two or three witnesses, he clearly demonstrates that he will do nothing in a suspicious fashion or based on false accusation or rash prejudice. For those people had no reason to fear Paul who, conscious of their sin, offered true and serious repentance to him. But for those who were impenitent and presumptuous, he sternly threatened not to spare them. And there is no doubt how he would give notice of their punishment: of course, he would threaten to excommunicate those people who were previously polluting themselves with their lusts, and obscene morals, and other wicked deeds. For, in truth, those people

[4]CO 50:147-48 (CTS 40:390-91); citing Deut 19:15.
[5]Musculus, *Commentarius . . . in posteriorem epistolam Pauli ad Corinthios*, 399-400.

[6]Diodati, *La Seconde Epistre de l'Apostre S. Paul aux Corinthiens*, 167; citing 2 Cor 10:6.

were not serious in repentance and were still indulging in their carnal desires, quarrels, accusations, and rebellions. Paul would not have descended to such bitter threats if he had not determined that there were those in the assembly of the Corinthians who required stronger remedies and would not make way for more milder threats. Explication of 2 Corinthians 13:1.[7]

Paul's Candid Warnings to the Corinthians. Andreas Hyperius: Paul states candidly that those people among the Corinthians who had been lawfully convicted should be severely punished and that he was not relaxing any of the authority that he had previously used and threatened he was going to use in the previous epistle. All these things he pronounced with the weightiest of words. First, he wants no one to doubt his upcoming visit. Second, in order to make clear that he will judge all things properly, he mentions the testimony of Scripture from Deuteronomy 17 concerning the procedure for investigating and pronouncing judgment against offenders. Third, he repeats and wants them to remember that when he was present among them he had spoken the same thing he had also written in his first letter, that if he did not find them reformed, he would spare none of them. Such a serious threat of this sort is in no way a disgrace for a minister of the Word. Commentary on 2 Corinthians 13:1-2.[8]

Paul Is Behaving Like a Prophet. Jacques Lefèvre d'Étaples: Paul is speaking here like the prophets who were making threats—not prophesying absolutely what will come to pass (for they did not prophesy absolutely), but unless the people change their behavior and propitiate God for those things which have been mentioned to them. And Paul says that what will happen is not slight: for it is not Paul, but Christ who is in him, who will punish them. Paul himself is an instrument [of punishment], just as he is an instrument of [God's] power and miracles. This was the reason that faithlessness was applied to their sins: they did not believe that Christ had entrusted Paul with his power to punish those who did not believe. . . . Now the Corinthians were saying: "It is true that Christ is powerful. But this man is weak in person, though in his writing he can boast of the power of Christ." Yes, followers of Christ are weak in the flesh for the sake of imitating the sufferings of Christ, but they are strong in the power of God, by which they live with him and are spiritually powerful. Although Elijah was weak in body and in human strength, he was spiritually strong in the power and strength of God. By such power, he was able, with a speech, to summon fire from heaven and, with a word, to shut up the heavens [from giving rain]. It was not that his speech or word summoned fire from heaven or shut up the heavens for three and a half years; rather, the fire summoned from heaven and the heavens shut up were signs of the divine power in him. It is the same with both Paul and followers of Christ: they are powerful in Christ. Commentary on 2 Corinthians 13:2-3.[9]

Paul's Godly Severity. Niels Hemmingsen: The sense of Paul's threat is as follows: "As I mentioned in my previous epistle when I warned that I would be present with you a second time, now I write again to those who were sinning previously and I warn all the rest of you who are indulging in vices, that when I come I will use my authority and will draw the sword of the Spirit against those who have been convicted of some crime. And I will not spare anyone." Ministers of the Word should piously and prudently imitate this example of severity for the purpose of edification. Commentary on 2 Corinthians 13:2.[10]

Testing the Spirits. John Calvin: Someone will object: What? Will a person who boasts that

[7]Hesshus, *Explicatio Secundae Epistolae Pauli ad Corinthios*, 294r-295r.
[8]Hyperius, *Commentarii . . . in Epistolam D. Pauli ad Romanos, et Utramque ad Corinthios*, 416; citing Deut 17:1-7.
[9]Lefèvre, *Commentariorum in Epistolas Beati Pauli . . . Liber Tertius*, 145; citing 1 Kings 18–19.
[10]Hemmingsen, *Commentaria in Omnes Epistolas Apostolorum*, 307.

he has Christ for his authority be exempt from all investigation of his doctrine? What false prophet will not boast in this way? How, then, will one distinguish between truth and falsehood, and what, then, will become of that command: "Test the spirits, whether they are from God"? Paul anticipates all objections of this sort when he says that Christ has worked powerfully in them by his ministry. For these two clauses "Christ speaking in me," and "who is powerful in you, not weak" must be read together, in this sense: "Christ, by exercising his power toward you in my doctrine, has testified that he is speaking by my mouth, so that you have no excuse on the ground of ignorance."

We see that Paul not only boasts with words but also proves in reality that Christ is speaking in him, and he convinces the Corinthians before expecting them to trust him. Whoever, then, will speak in the church—whatever title they will claim for themselves—it will be permissible to inquire of their doctrine, until Christ has manifested himself in them, lest a judgment be formed about Christ rather than human beings. But when it is clear that it is the Word of God that is advanced, what Paul says in this regard is valid: that it is God himself who is not believed. With this same confidence, Moses stated: "What are we—I and Aaron? You are tempting God!" In a similar way, Isaiah asks, "Is it too small a thing that you grieve men, unless you also grieve my God?" For no more place for evasion remains when it is apparent that it is a minister of God who is speaking, and that he is faithfully discharging his office. Commentary on 2 Corinthians 13:3.[11]

Christ Works Powerfully in His Ministers. Andreas Hyperius: The meaning is as follows: "You want to attack us and judge us for the mildness and modesty that you have always seen in us at other times and for not being very bold. But I say this to you: if you want to attack and test us for our boldness against sinners in the name and power of Christ, I promise this, that just as Christ, when he was crucified, appeared weak but afterward was proved to be very powerful, so also, although now we have been humbled and weak in the manner of Christ, nevertheless, when there is need, we will exercise extraordinary power and strength in his name." And so, Paul rebukes them for falsely accusing him for not being at all bold against sinners. Now, the fact that Paul can act powerfully, even though he seems weak, he proves by way of comparison from the example of Christ, who, even though he appeared weak, nevertheless afterward displayed extraordinary power. Moreover, underlying this statement "who is not weak in dealing with you" there is an argument from what's possible and what's equal. It's as if he were saying: "Christ is powerful in you. Therefore, he will also be powerful in me." Hence, it is clear from this that Christ is actively working in ministers of the Word, and what they do when they rightly exercise ecclesiastical power toward those who sin publicly should thus be received as being done by Christ himself. For all the things they do come from the power of God. Whence, in 1 Corinthians 5, Paul passes sentence against the incestuous man in this way: "In the name of our Lord Jesus Christ, when you are assembled in the name of our Lord Jesus Christ and my spirit is present, together with the power of our Lord Jesus Christ, you are to deliver this man to Satan for the destruction of the flesh, so that his spirit may be saved in the day of the Lord Jesus." Commentary on 2 Corinthians 13:3.[12]

Paul's Work Has Been Christ's Work. The English Annotations: Paul here gives a sharp rebuke [to the Corinthians] for when they despise the apostle's admonitions, they tempt Christ's own patience, and when they condemn Paul as a miserable man, they lay nothing against him which is not common to him with Christ. "If you seek a proof that Christ is speaking in me, look to yourselves, who derived all your soundness from

[11]CO 50:149 (CTS 40:394-95); citing Num 16:11; Is 7:13.

[12]Hyperius, *Commentarii . . . in Epistolam D. Pauli ad Romanos, et Utramque ad Corinthios*, 416; citing 1 Cor 5:4-5.

my ministry—if you have any." Annotations on 2 Corinthians 13:3.[13]

Paul Vindicates His Authority. David Dickson: Paul here gives reasons for his severe threatening of divine vengeance: because they tempted Christ and the apostle, doubting whether Christ spoke in the apostle, or the apostle from the authority of Christ. And he also adds a further argument to vindicate his authority. "Christ has powerfully manifested himself among you by my ministry," Paul suggests, "partly by the grace given to sinners, partly by the gifts of the Spirit conferred upon the presbyters, and others, partly by miracles done among you, partly by the correcting of stubborn sinners. Therefore, fear!" Exposition of 2 Corinthians 13:3.[14]

Like Christ, the Apostles Are Empowered by God. Desiderius Erasmus: [Christ] was not weak in regard to you, even if he was once weak before the Jews and Pilate. On the contrary, he proved himself powerful among you: at his name you have seen the dead come to life again, demons flee, the sick healed. For although once, because of the weakness of the nature he had taken on, he willed to be fixed to the cross, nevertheless he ought not on that account to be considered weak. He died through the infirmity of the body he had assumed, but he lives through the strength of God the Father. Likewise, we apostles, who follow in the footsteps of Christ our teacher, although we may be feeble to the unbelieving, as we are beaten by them, cast into prison, and abused with insults, still, through the strength of God, we shall with him be powerful toward you, if your stubbornness overcomes our gentleness. Paraphrases on 2 Corinthians 13.[15]

Did Christ Suffer Weakness by Necessity or Choice? John Calvin: Here . . . a question arises—whether Christ endured such weakness because he was subjected to it by necessity, and not freely. For what we suffer from weakness, we suffer from constraint and not from free choice. When the Arians once were abusing this pretext to oppose the divinity of Christ, the orthodox fathers gave this explanation of it—that it happened by appointment, inasmuch as Christ willed it, not because he was constrained by any necessity. This response is true, provided it be properly understood. There are some, however, who wrongly extend this appointment to Christ's human will, as if it were not the condition of his nature, but a permission contrary to his nature. For example: "The fact that he died," they say, "did not happen because his humanity was (strictly speaking) subservient to death, but by appointment, because he chose to die." I grant, indeed, that he died because he chose to do so. But where did this choosing come from, except that he had clothed himself freely in a mortal nature? For if we make Christ's human nature so different than our own, we will overturn the chief foundation of our faith. That is why we should understand it in this way—that Christ suffered by appointment, not by constraint, because although he was in the form of God and could have removed himself from necessity, nonetheless he suffered from weakness because he emptied himself. Commentary on 2 Corinthians 13:4.[16]

The Nature of Christ's Weakness. The English Annotations: "In weakness . . ." St. Hilary[†] in his book *De Trinitate* expounds this passage as follows: "Through the weakness of his flesh which was subject to all human infirmities, with the exception of sin; or, relating to the vile form of a servant, which he took upon himself when he humiliated himself." . . . Christ was subject to painful infirmities during his state of humiliation here upon the earth, but none of these infirmities were sinful. Annotations on 2 Corinthians 13:4.[17]

[13]Downame, ed., *English Annotations*, GG4r*.
[14]Dickson, *An Exposition of All St. Paul's Epistles*, 92*.
[15]CWE 43:279-81.
[16]CO 50:149-50 (CTS 40:394-95); citing Phil 2:6.
[17]Downame, ed., *English Annotations*, GG4r*. †See Hilary of Poitiers, *De Trinitate* 9.13 (NPNF[2] 9:159).

Christ Is Alive and Powerful. Wolfgang Musculus: Paul defends the glory of the power of Christ against the contempt of the cross. Since he was preaching Christ crucified, it appeared that he was preaching a Christ who was weak rather than powerful, a man who could be despised without danger. Paul does not deny, indeed he acknowledges, the manifest weakness of Christ's flesh in his crucifixion and death. But he hurries on to declare that the living Christ is no longer subject to weakness as before, but is glorified by virtue of his divine nature, and thus Paul is able to declare that Christ is free from all contempt. It is as if Paul were saying: "Therefore, do you despise Christ speaking in me because he died through the weakness of his flesh? Indeed, he died in weakness, but he is no longer dead for he lives by the power of God, having been raised from the dead. And because he is now alive, he is no longer weak, but endowed with the power of God. And I have amply declared the power of Christ among you, by which you are able to recognize that we have a Christ who is neither dead nor weak, but living and powerful." Commentary on 2 Corinthians 13:4.[18]

Do Not Be Offended by External Appearances! Tilemann Hesshus: Paul warns that it is very unsuitable for believers to be offended by the external weakness, undistinguished appearance, and the distressful suffering of their teachers. For the Son of God also took upon himself weakness for the sake of our salvation and, in his weakness, was crucified, so that nothing can be considered more weak, more vile, or more despicable in the eyes of the world. Nevertheless, it is not right to despise Christ on account of his physical frailty, for he was not permanently clothed in this weakness, but, by the power of God raising him from the dead, he put aside all weakness and now lives in power and the fullness of majesty as the head of the whole church and the Lord of all creation, who sits at the right hand of the eternal Father, and has dominion over all things in heaven and on earth. Those who carefully consider the majesty and divine power of Christ will not be offended by the weakness with which he was crucified, because from that source one will experience powerful consolation. And with burning hearts, they will give thanks to Christ for having lowered himself from that sublime majesty to such great weakness for the sake of our salvation. And so, it was not right for the apostle's godly listeners to be offended by his weakness, troubles, and vile appearance since they were living and powerfully ruling with Christ. . . .

When Paul says that he is living with Christ by the power of God, he is not only speaking about the glory of the future life, but is indicating that, having been crucified and raised with Christ, he has now been given life and power in ministry for the salvation of many people—which is what the particle "toward you" suggests. "And so, my weakness, which some among you greatly exaggerated, was not an obstacle for me; in fact, God himself established many churches through me and the kingdom of his Son was extended far and wide, and even you were affected by my ministry." Therefore, those Corinthians were able to testify that Christ was powerful in Paul. Once more here, Paul warns the whole church that it should not seek external pomp in ministers, nor should it be offended by the outward appearance or weakness of ministers. But they should reflect on this, that Christ Jesus is acting and speaking through them, for he is visible from their doctrine, life, and faith in ministry. Explication of 2 Corinthians 13:4.[19]

Paul's Comfort for Pastors and Preachers. Cyriacus Spangenberg: Because the world remains the world and does not inquire as to what one can say or boast about the preaching office from God's Word, but rather slanders the office together with the people who hold it, and yet

[18]Musculus, *Commentarius . . . in posteriorem epistolam Pauli ad Corinthios*, 404.

[19]Hesshus, *Explicatio Secundae Epistolae Pauli ad Corinthios*, 296r-297r.

because preachers and pastors are also people and can easily become discouraged, St. Paul comforts them here, not with a human, fleshly, worldly, temporal, or temporary comfort, but with a godly, spiritual, heavenly, eternal, and enduring comfort, and thus says, "Although Christ was crucified in weakness, he lives in God's power. And although we also are weak in him, we also live with him in God's power among you."

Here he sets the Master and the disciples, the Lord and the servants, next to one another, and makes them the same in weakness and glory. This is a great honor for all those who are faithful servants of Christ and perform their office diligently according to Christ's command, and it is also a great comfort to them that Christ wants to be powerful in them against all those who oppose the preaching office. So now he says first of our head and Lord Christ, if he showed himself lowly and weak for a time such that he also died, so now he lives in might and authority in divine power. Although he is crucified (he says) in weakness, according to his human nature which was willing to die there, so he lives in the power of God. This is also what he writes elsewhere, Phil. 2, "Jesus Christ, although he was in the form of God . . ." Forty-Eighth Sermon.[20]

13:5-8 *Test Yourselves!*

The Corinthians' Consciences. Wolfgang Musculus: "Examine yourselves to prove whether you are in the faith." Paul here shifts the grounds of his argument to their consciences. It is as if he were saying: "But if you do not acknowledge the power of Christ living in me, at least acknowledge that it lives in you. Consider carefully and show whether the power of Christ has been disclosed to you. If that power is discovered in you, then why do you not recognize it in me, through whom you received it?" This is a summary of the present passage. . . . Some people interpret the clause "that Jesus Christ is in you" to relate to the grace of Christ, by which believers are being regenerated and made righteous, and their consciences granted peace. But their interpretation differs from the focus of the argument with which the apostle is concerned. For he is not dealing with justifying grace in this passage and those spiritual gifts which accompany it, but with the power of Christ, that through the fear of it the unrepentant Corinthians might be called back to repentance.

Nevertheless, I acknowledge that it is appropriate to apply this passage as a specific warning to examine whether we have faith in Christ and whether or not Christ dwells in us by faith. For there are certain tests of faith by which we recognize whether or not Christ is in our hearts by his Spirit seeing that the slothful are incapable of being true believers in Christ. Commentary on 2 Corinthians 13:5.[21]

Corinthians Must Examine Both Their Faith and Behavior. Cardinal Cajetan: Paul previously stated, "not as I wish" and explained right behavior. Now he explains the same thing regarding faith. Now whether this word refers to the faith that is necessary for salvation, or whether it is the faith that is freely and graciously given (namely by a miracle) is not entirely clear. "Test yourselves." Unless this is an intensification [of what was said previously], he is referring here to behavior and so he is warning them to examine themselves both in faith and in behavior. "Do you not realize this about yourselves that Jesus Christ is in you?" It is as if he were saying: "It is certain that you recognize yourselves in this respect, that Jesus Christ is in you." This can be understood of Christ being in them by faith, or by the gift of tongues and prophecy, or by the evident punishment which they had experienced in the incestuous person (of which the Corinthians were in the middle). Commentary on 2 Corinthians 13:5.[22]

[20]C. Spangenberg, *Die ander Epistel Pauli ad die Corinthier*, 211r-v; citing Phil 2:6.

[21]Musculus, *Commentarius . . . in posteriorem epistolam Pauli ad Corinthios*, 406, 407.

[22]Cajetan, *In Posteriorem Pauli Epistolam ad Corinthios Commentarii*, 198-99; citing 2 Cor 12:20.

The Need to Examine Our Consciences. Tilemann Hesshus: After Paul adequately refuted the false apostles and reproved the rashness of the Corinthians, he finally sends them back to examine their own consciences. And thus, by doing this, they can learn with whom Paul acts more leniently and whom he reproves more harshly. "Prove for yourselves," he says, "if you are in the faith. You do not need to fear my threat. For, if you recognize your presumption and impenitence, should you not wonder at the severity of my reprimand, and, considering it, to repent quickly?" Truly, such a proof and examination of conscience should often be undertaken by godly people lest they clothe themselves in an empty appearance of piety. Indeed, it is necessary to practice self-examination in such a way that we diligently consider whether we have embraced the gospel from the heart and have a burning love and zeal for heavenly doctrine. Now those who despise the divine word or pretend to be zealous for heavenly doctrine—this is the clearest proof of presumption and ungodliness. David says, "Salvation is far from the wicked, for they do not seek your statutes." And Christ says in John 14, "Whoever does not love my word does not keep it." On the other hand, if anyone notices within themselves a serious zeal for heavenly doctrine, they can conclude from this that they are being led by the Spirit of God. David says, "I have considered my ways"—which is to say, "I have examined my way and myself, and I have turned my steps to your testimony. . . .

Second, the conscience must be examined whether we have repented with all sincerity and from the heart. Truly, we should be terrified by God's wrath and our hearts should grieve that we provoke his wrath. Then, both examining and stimulating our faith, we should find rest from our terrified conscience in the promise of the gospel concerning the benefits of the mediator. When we observe these things within ourselves, we are able to establish with certainty that we are led by the Spirit of God, for serious and eager repentance is not a work of the flesh. And a sincere faith in the mediator does not result from human's free will, but it is a most certain fruit of the Holy Spirit, persuading men and women to fear God. Explication of 2 Corinthians 13:5.[23]

Testing Examines Deeds, Not Words. Margaret Fell: [Hope in Christ] is a mystery to all you carnal professors, who are yet in your sins and your uncleanness, and yet will tell of faith, and hope, and God, and Christ. But your root is rottenness, your ground is corrupt, and your chaff is to be burned; the fire is kindled, which cannot be quenched. They day of the Lord is come, which burns as an oven, and all your corrupt profession and deceitful hypocrisy shall be as stubble. . . . Your profession of God and Christ in words (when in works you deny him) will not serve you; the Lord abhors all your vain profession and hypocrisy. Therefore, give over your deceitful dissembling, and turn to that which rips you up, and lays you naked and bare before the Lord God, from whom you cannot hide yourselves. . . . Give over deceiving of your souls, for those who do righteousness are righteous, even as they are righteous; and all sin and uncleanness the light condemns, and if your hearts condemn you, God is greater, and knows all things. Therefore do not deceive yourselves but search and try your own selves, for if you know not how that Christ is in you, you are reprobates. And so all you formal professors, try your own selves, and to the Light come to be tried, and there you will see your rotten profession will be too light. And do not deceive your souls, but now ye have time, prize it, while it is called today. To All the Professors in the World.[24]

Paul Defends Assurance of Faith. John Calvin: This passage is worth our careful attention for two reasons. First, it shows the relationship that exists between the faith of the people and of the preaching of their minister, namely, that one is the mother that produces and

[23]Hesshus, *Explicatio Secundae Epistolae Pauli ad Corinthios*, 297v-298r; citing Ps 119:155; Jn 14:24; Ps 119:59.

[24]Fell, *Women's Speaking Justified*, 78-79*; citing Is 5:24; Lk 3:17; Mal 4:1; Ezek 23:29; 1 Jn 3:7; Lam 3:40.

brings forth, and the other is the daughter, that must not forget her origin. Second, this passage proves the assurance of faith, which the sophists at the Sorbonne undermine, or rather, almost entirely banish from the minds of men and women. For they condemn the "rashness" of everyone who is persuaded that they are members of Christ and have him dwelling in them. For they command us to be content with what they call a "moral inference"—that is, sheer conjecture—so that our consciences remain constantly in suspense and confused. But what does Paul say here? He declares that all people who doubt whether they possess Christ and are a part of his body are reprobates. Therefore, let us hold this alone to be right faith, which causes us to rest safely in God's grace, with no wavering opinion, but with a firm and constant assurance. Commentary on 2 Corinthians 13:5.[25]

Absolute Assurance of Salvation Not to Be Expected. Council of Trent: As no pious person ought to doubt the mercy of God, the merit of Christ, and the virtue and efficacy of the sacraments, so each one, when considering themselves and their own weakness and indisposition, may have fear and apprehension concerning their own grace, since no one can know with the certainty of faith, which cannot be subject to error, that they have obtained the grace of God. . . .

Canon 15: If anyone says that a person who is born again and justified is bound *ex fide* to believe that they are certainly in the number of the predestined, let them be anathema. Canon 16: If anyone says that they will for certain, with an absolute and infallible certainty, have that great gift of perseverance even to the end, unless they shall have learned this by a special revelation, let them be anathema. Decree Concerning Justification.[26]

Christians Can Have a Certain Faith. Cyriacus Spangenberg: The Council of Trent has also concluded that one should consider as reckless and unchristian people those who dare say that they are certainly members of Christ, children of God, and heirs of eternal life, and that one should have a good hope of this but not conclude it completely, for such would be great presumptuousness and make people secure, as Cardinal Hosius[†] writes in his heretical books.

Against such false, cursed, and damned diabolical teaching of the papists, Paul puts right here the contrast and wants everyone to be certain of his faith. And he therefore says, "Test yourselves, whether you are in the faith," and he writes right away against the Council of Trent and the pope's teaching when he says in Romans 8: "I am certain of this, that neither death nor life, neither angels nor principalities, neither power, either present or future, or high or low, nor any other creature may separate us from the love of God, which is in Christ Jesus our Lord." And 2 Timothy 1: "I know in whom I believe and am certain that he can keep my deposit until that day." We should also follow this example of Paul's and be certain of our faith's religion and salvation and rest in the certain grace of God, firm and without doubt. For God has no desire or pleasure in doubters. Forty-Ninth Sermon.[27]

Christ in You. Tilemann Hesshus: Not only does Paul want us to be certain about the faith, but he also wants us to be certain that Jesus Christ dwells within us, which is known by the same process of examination. There can be no more effective way for us to discover this, which draws us away from false security and pride, than if we consider that we are temples of God and that Christ Jesus lives in our hearts. For Christ testifies that the whole divinity of the eternal Father, Son, and Holy Spirit lives in the hearts of believers, those who have embraced with a genuine love the Word of God. "If anyone loves me, they will obey my word, and my Father will love them, and we

[25]CO 50:151 (CTS 40:396-97).

[26]Schroeder, *Canons and Decrees of the Council of Trent*, 35, 44.

[27]C. Spangenberg, *Die ander Epistel Pauli an die Corinthier*, 213r-v; citing Rom 8:38-39; 2 Tim 1:12. [†]Cardinal Stanislaus Hosius was a leading Catholic apologist and papal legate to the Council of Trent in 1562–1563.

will come to him and make our home with them." What immeasurable benefit, glory, and happiness that the divine majesty lowered himself to such an extent that he did not hesitate to choose to seat himself in our hearts, as in a sacred temple—a dwelling which cannot but be fruitful—so that the eternal Father, on account of his Son, the mediator, through the Holy Spirit imparts divine light and imputes righteousness to us! He renews us in his image; he rescues lost people; he equips the will with power; he bends the heart to love the truth; he adorns us with heavenly gifts; and, subsequently, he governs and defends us. Because of this, then, godly people should examine whether they have God dwelling in them, who will always call them back from false security. Explication of 2 Corinthians 13:5.[28]

Believers and Reprobates. Niels Hemmingsen: Paul appeals to the testimony of the Corinthians. He has stated that the power of Christ was effective in his ministry, and now he confirms it by their example. The answer to this dilemma can be resolved in this way: "Either you feel that Christ dwells within you by faith, or you are altogether condemned—choose your side. If Christ dwells within you, then the purpose for the ministry was effective through the power of Christ. If, however, he does not dwell in you, you are really condemned. But, because you do not want to believe such a thing, you must confess that my ministry was equipped by the power of Christ." Note here immediately the opposition of contrary things, namely, the believer and the reprobate. For if someone is a believer, they cannot be called reprobate; and, by contrast, the person who is reprobate will never be called a believer without confusing opposite things. But how would the Corinthians be able to test and examine whether they were in the faith? There is a twofold way for proving this, namely, an interior proof and an exterior proof. The interior proof is the Holy Spirit, who bears witness to our spirit that we are the sons and daughters of God. For when the Holy Spirit effects faith in us through the preaching of the Word and true repentance occurs through the knowledge of Jesus Christ, and, correspondingly, when the Spirit stirs in our heart new passion for the law of God—this is called "bearing witness to our spirit." The exterior proof is a life that is innocent, godly, and holy, which displays a good conscience and a kind of perpetual repentance. Because the first and interior proof is hidden, it requires external testimony. For the person who is without the exterior proof should not boast that they have the interior proof. Commentary on 2 Corinthians 13:5.[29]

The Corinthians' Higher Duty. John Calvin: Now Paul urges them all the more vehemently, even as he remains confident that he will not be rejected by the Corinthians. One of two things was necessary—that they would either assign to Paul the honor due to an apostle or condemn themselves as unbelievers and acknowledge that there was no church in their midst. Paul however softens the severity of his statement by using the expression "I hope." But he does this in such a way as to remind them of their higher duty, for it is very cruel to disappoint the hopes that have been entertained as to our integrity. "I hope," he says, "that you will know when you have been restored to a right mind." Now he wisely says nothing about himself in this second clause, calling them to remember the benefits of God with which they have been adorned; or rather, he substitutes their salvation in place of his authority. Commentary on 2 Corinthians 13:6.[30]

Ministers and Their Hearers. Wolfgang Musculus: Here is Paul's sense in this passage: "Even if there are many among you who are wicked and hostile to Christ, I nevertheless hope that

[28]Hesshus, *Explicatio Secundae Epistolae Pauli ad Corinthios*, 300r-301r; citing Jn 14:23.

[29]Hemmingsen, *Commentaria in Omnes Epistolas Apostolorum*, 307-8.

[30]CO 50:151-52 (CTS 40:398).

when I come to you in the power and spirit of Christ that you will have a clear proof of Christ speaking in me, as you seek, so that you will recognize that I am not at all a false apostle of Christ, but a true one."

It is possible for a man to be a true and genuine minister in the church of God even if his hearers are wicked. Now it is the concern of ministers of Christ to have this objective, that when those who listen to them are finally judged, they might be approved by God and recognized as such. And they can accomplish this if they attend to all of those duties that concern a faithful minister, so that all the guilt rests upon the hearers, just as with barren trees that are unable to produce fruit despite careful tending. Now it sometimes happens that the diligence of ministers serves as proof that the souls of their hearers are ignoble and wicked when they labor in vain to cultivate them [in godliness]. On the other hand, we see that it frequently happens that the barrenness of the hearers serves as proof of the carelessness of the ministers. But that church is certainly blessed where the spiritual progress of the hearers recommends the faith, concern, and diligence of the true minister of Christ. Commentary on 2 Corinthians 13:6.[31]

Paul's Righteous Intentions. Heinrich Bullinger: You come across a kind of person that allows entire kingdoms and cities to be destroyed provided that it be said that he acted prudently and conquered them. But Paul was furnished with a different disposition because he said that if anything should be pointed out about the Corinthians' guilt, he would count himself among the reprobate lest it seem that he was too concerned for his own glory. He then adds by way of anticipation: "I do not speak in this fashion in order to allege my goodness at the expense of your innocence. For I would gladly suffer being known by the title of 'reprobate' as long as you would not be rejected. Therefore, all our boasting about our authority relates to this, that you should be considered honorable." Now Paul defends this with two statements. First, "No power that we exercised was against anything just and true, but only against lies and wickedness," as was said in chapter 10. Second, "Far be it that I should be eager to be praised at the expense of your name because it is my joy to be weakened so that you might be perfected. I entreat you to read these things and impress them on your heart, for you are God's special people or the Lord's flock." Commentary on 2 Corinthians 13:7-8.[32]

Paul's Ministry of Prayer. Wolfgang Musculus: Paul was not only writing and sending brothers to bring the Corinthians back to the right path, but he was also praying to God for them—and with good reason. For he knew that his efforts to plant and water would accomplish nothing unless God gave the growth and the fruitfulness. As Augustine somewhere wisely said concerning the minister of the word: "He should be one who prays before he speaks."† Ministers of Christ should pray to God not only for the gift of understanding and speech, but also for fruitful growth [in their hearers]. They should pray not only in church with the congregation of the faithful in the customary fashion, but also in the privacy of their own homes out of their burning zeal, praying that they might also speak in church more passionately and powerfully. The mouth of the person who instructs is cold and lifeless whose heart has not first warmed the sermon with the spirit and ardor of prayer. Prayer also enables the mind to teach zealously as well as listen carefully. Commentary on 2 Corinthians 13:7.[33]

False Apostles Often Condemn Godly People. Niels Hemmingsen: Since outward

[31]Musculus, *Commentarius . . . in posteriorem epistolam Pauli ad Corinthios*, 408.

[32]Bullinger, *In Posteriorem . . . ad Corinthios Epistolam Commentarius*, 336-37.

[33]Musculus, *Commentarius . . . in posteriorem epistolam Pauli ad Corinthios*, 408-9. †Augustine, *On Christian Doctrine* 4.2, NPNF[1] 2:584-85.

honesty, good morals, and restraint from all injury provide testimony of the inner godliness of men and women, Paul prays that they will abstain from all wrong. Now although the false apostles did not understand this, even so Paul was praying for it so that the effectiveness of his ministry might be demonstrated from the Corinthians' testimony. He states that he is not praying for this for his own sake, but instead for the sake of their salvation. In the meantime, he has nothing to say if he seems to be rejected by the judgment of the false apostles. For it often happens that those who are truly godly are considered to be reprobate by false apostles. Paul's example here should be imitated by the minister of the word. Commentary on 2 Corinthians 13:7.[34]

The Church Has Priority Over Paul's Reputation. Tilemann Hesshus: "I pray to God that you may not do wrong." [Paul is saying,] "I am not worried about my reputation, but what I am writing is for the sake of your salvation. I am afraid that you have carelessly abandoned God, for despising the apostolic office is a step toward blatant ungodliness. Hence, I am praying that you are blameless and pure before God so that nothing shameful might reside in you and you will not sin against your conscience but shine forth in every form of godliness. I am not praying to compel you to approve my authority toward you—this has been given to me by the Lord Jesus."

"Though we seem to have failed." The apostle's intention is not that he is worried about his salvation. Rather, as he says in 1 Corinthians 9, he exerts the greatest effort lest, having preached to others, he himself should be rejected. Therefore, with this resolve in view, Paul does not at all labor for himself, but only for the church to be safely established and appear blameless in the sight of God. And even if people judge Paul to be reprobate, nevertheless, he will not be condemned by God's judgment later on. Now, men and women judge according to outward appearances and are hindered by their perverse affections. But the Lord looks upon the heart; when he will be judged, the Lord will not condemn him. . . . The judgment of God is far different from the judgment of human beings. Paul teaches us here that we ought not to be overly worried about our reputation, but only that nothing harmful should happen to the church. Our only concern should be that we defend and spread far and wide the glory of Christ. Indeed, we are to present the church holy and blameless before Christ—even at the sacrifice of our reputation, our good name, and our life. Our reputation must not be entirely disregarded for the sake of our neighbor, but we should find it preferable to build up, teach, advance, and provide care for the church. Explication of 2 Corinthians 13:7.[35]

Paul's Extraordinary Love for the Corinthians. Andreas Hyperius: Lest it seem that Paul, with a tyrannical disposition, desired to rage against the Corinthians or to boast proudly, or that he, as one approved, was looking down upon them as reprobates, Paul explains in detail how he was speaking from the heart, and the reasons and affections that motivated him. And so he says, "I speak in this way so that you may not do wrong. And I desire this, that you might be approved, but we are the one who is rejected (that is, being weak and empty), having no reason for criticizing you." He says that this was his greatest prayer and that all his effort was inclined toward this one thing, that they might always act in an honorable fashion, and he was prepared even to be considered rejected, provided that they might be approved. . . .This quality of breathing out extraordinary affection and amazing love with which Paul was endowed befits all ministers of the church. And he does not simply want to be considered rejected, but to be viewed as a reprobate, that is, as one condemned, reviled, and considered a liar in the eyes of the world—taken for a reprobate and vain person—while the virtue and

[34]Hemmingsen, *Commentaria in Omnes Epistolas Apostolorum*, 308.

[35]Hesshus, *Explicatio Secundae Epistolae Pauli ad Corinthios*, 301v-302r; citing 1 Cor 9:27.

goodness of the Corinthians might become known before God and other people. Now when Paul said that he prays to God, it seems that he is calling God as a witness, that he was truly feeling this in his heart, and thus he desired that his feelings should be considered as ratified by all. Commentary on 2 Corinthians 13:7.[36]

Self-Abasement to Glorify God. John Trapp: "Though we be like a reprobate," namely, in your esteem. The good heart is content to vilify, even nullify, itself so that God may be glorified and his people edified. Let [the godly person] be a footstool, or whatever else, to help Christ onto his throne. As Luther[†] stated: "Let Luther be called Satan so that Christ might live and reign. Amen." Commentary on 2 Corinthians 13:7.[37]

The Word of Truth Is More Important Than Unity. Martin Luther: This is so great a good that no human heart can grasp it (therefore it necessitates such a great and hard fight). It must not be treated lightly, as the world maintains and many people who do not understand, saying we should not fight so hard about an article and thus trample on Christian love. They say that although we err on one small point, if we agree on everything else, we should give in and overlook the difference in order to preserve Christian unity and fellowship.

No, my good person, do not recommend to me peace and unity when God's Word is lost thereby, for then eternal life and everything else would be lost. In this matter there can be no yielding nor giving way, no, not for love of you or any other person, but everything must yield to the Word, whether it be friend or foe. The Word was given to us for eternal life and not to further outward peace and unity. The Word and doctrine will create Christian unity or fellowship. Where they reign, all else will follow. Where they are not, no concord will ever abide. Therefore, do not talk to me about love and friendship, if that means breaking with the Word, or the faith, for the gospel does not say that love brings eternal life, God's grace, and all heavenly treasures, but that these come from the Word. Sermons from the Year 1531.[38]

Paul Was Speaking the Truth to the Corinthians. Wolfgang Musculus: The word "truth" covers a wide range of things, which Pilate also realized when he said to the Lord, "What is truth?" But I think it is employed here to mean the truth of Christ and the truth of the Christian's profession to which it pertains, so that those who are Christians might abstain from all evil and do what is good and honorable. For those who are foreign to the truth of Christ act in a very different manner. Therefore, when Paul said that he was praying to God for the Corinthians that they might not do evil, he was not doing this so that he himself might appear good, but so that they might do what was honorable. And consequently, he added these words "for we cannot do anything against the truth of God" to indicate that, if they were blameless in their zeal for the truth of Christ, he could have nothing against them . . . but rather he would be on their side so as to build them up and strengthen them more and more. Paul speaks as an apostle of Christ, assuming nothing for himself except what was according to the power received from God. Commentary on 2 Corinthians 13:8.[39]

Paul's Authority Seeks to Defend the Truth. Tilemann Hesshus: That is, "I am not desiring to praise myself or increase my authority in whatever way, whether it happens when I am boasting about the truth or correcting the church—whereas the false apostles have no concerns either to advance or impede the truth, but only to push

[36]Hyperius, *Commentarii . . . in Epistolam D. Pauli ad Romanos, et Utramque ad Corinthios*, 417.

[37]Trapp, *A Commentary or Exposition*, 736*. [†]Luther's statement is found in a letter to George Spalatin, dated June 12, 1527. See WABR 6:62.

[38]Luther, *Day by Day We Magnify You*, 379 (WA 34/2:387).

[39]Musculus, *Commentarius . . . in posteriorem epistolam Pauli ad Corinthios*, 413; citing Jn 18:38.

themselves forward and to be considered great. Or rather, they do not want to be outdone, even if they recognize that the truth would be concealed and the church destroyed by dissention." This attitude is not in Paul, who considers nothing except the ancient truth and the salvation of the church. For he does not desire any authority or power to be attributed to him that might obscure or harm the truth. And if he should either boast or take anything for himself, or attempt anything against the truth, he knows that he can not stand but will soon be thrown down because God is the protector and most zealous defender of the truth.

Paul says these things for the sake of the godly, lest they fear him because of this threat of the apostle. For godly people fear him, even when they are living holy lives. But the wicked are presumptuous and defiant, even when they are polluting themselves with wicked deed. Thus, Paul commands the godly and innocent people to be of good heart, because none of his authority or power is against truth and innocence, but is only for the truth, that is, to demonstrate and propagate the truth. Explication of 2 Corinthians 13:8.[40]

Christian Leaders Must Be Subject to the Truth. John Calvin: This passage here must be carefully observed because it defines the boundaries of the power that pastors of the church should have, namely, that they should be ministers of the truth. The papists shout that it is written in Scripture, "The person who hears you, hears me; the person who despises you, despises me." Again, "Obey those who are set over you." And so, under this pretext, they appropriate for themselves every liberty for usurping unbounded dominion, while, at the same time, they are professed and sworn enemies of the truth, and strain for its destruction with all their strength. In order to expose such impudence, this one statement of Paul will suffice, which declares that they must themselves be subject to the truth. Commentary on 2 Corinthians 13:8.[41]

The Minister's Authority Confirms Christ's Truth. Niels Hemmingsen: The reason Paul speaks about his own apostolic authority: "The power which we apostles have received from Christ is not to display our glory, but it pertains to confirming the truth of Christ. For just as the proofs of our apostleship are attributed only to the certainty of the gospel, so we are the preachers of its power, not its authors." But those who attempt something against the truth of the gospel, and those who want to exalt themselves by another's authority, are not rightly using the power of Christ, but rather, are obeying Satan. Note as well that this extends all the way to ecclesiastical power—which is not bound to human beings, but to the ministry as Christ works through weak and powerless people. Commentary on 2 Corinthians 13:8.[42]

Paul Is Speaking of the Truth of Innocence and Piety. The English Annotations: Although it is a true axiom that . . . "the truth is strongest and cannot be subverted," yet it seems here that the apostle does not so much mean the truth of doctrine, but the truth of life, sincerity, and true piety. For Paul threatens to use his apostolic power in punishing the Corinthians, which is the reason he prays in verse 7 that they might escape evil. And this exhortation he establishes upon this reason: "For we cannot do anything against the truth," that is, if you are innocent and walk in the truth, you do not need to fear anathema or church censure, for the power which the Lord has given us, is to support the church and not destroy it, to uphold and maintain innocence and righteousness, true religion, and virtue, while suppressing the contrary. Annotations on 2 Corinthians 13:8.[43]

Apostasy Is a Dangerous Precipice. John Trapp: "For we cannot do anything against the truth." A person who temporarily professes Christ

[40]Hesshus, *Explicatio Secundae Epistolae Pauli ad Corinthios*, 302r-v.
[41]CO 50:152 (CTS 40:399); citing Lk 10:16; Heb 13:17.
[42]Hemmingsen, *Commentaria in Omnes Epistolas Apostolorum*, 308.
[43]Downame, ed., *English Annotations*, GG4r*.

may fall away in such a way as to persecute the truth that they once professed and the ministry that they once admired. A saint, even in their greatest lapses, never falls as far as that. Bishop Latimer† tells of a man who fell from the known truth and began to mock and scorn it—yet was afterward touched in his conscience for it. "Beware of this sin," he says, "for I have known none except this one man that repented. It is a very dangerous precipice." COMMENTARY ON 2 CORINTHIANS 13:8.[44]

13:9-10 *Paul Seeks to Build Up, Not Tear Down*

CHRIST ACCOMPLISHES GREAT THINGS THROUGH OUR WEAKNESS. TILEMANN HESSHUS: Paul here calls weakness a disgrace and regards himself with contempt, as he also does above. His intention is this: "I do not refuse to be weak, that is, overlooked and despised, if only you might be strong in the Lord, pure in the knowledge of God, strong in the faith, and steadfast in love." He says that he is glad when he is weak, that is, when he was treated as shameful by the world and considered contemptible, for this condition of ministers keeps them within the bounds of humility and modesty, lest they should become haughty. Now, Paul encourages them with great hope, because an abundant reward has been stored up for them in heaven. But this disgrace and contempt must not arise from the church, lest it be charged with presumption and ungodliness. On the other hand, nothing can be done when the world is so hostile toward apostles and faithful pastors—but let it not impede our ministry or salvation as both advance more and more. Christ accomplishes remarkable things through our weakness and disgrace, for he wishes the church to be strong, that is, established in faith, burning in love, and illustrious in the praise of good works. EXPLICATION OF 2 CORINTHIANS 13:9.[45]

PAUL'S PASSION FOR THE CORINTHIANS' PROGRESS. ANDREAS HYPERIUS: Paul repeats the reason for his previously stated feeling, as if to make it clearer. "If we were weak (as if having no power), you indeed would be strong (thus, living), because you would have concern about nothing nor would you deserve criticism. And we are certainly glad and rejoice on account of this." Just as teachers rejoice if their students make progress, because there is no need for severe and loud exhortations or whippings, so the apostle would rejoice if those Corinthians were behaving so well that he did not need to use his authority. . . . "Your soundness or wholeness is what we pray for." Paul repeats again his prayer, or his highest concern, as if desiring that these two reasons might be firmly impressed on their minds. Wholeness is the consummation of virtues, as in common parlance we speak of a complete and perfect person, in whom nothing—or almost nothing—is lacking. COMMENTARY ON 2 CORINTHIANS 13:9.[46]

PAUL DESIRED SPIRITUAL HEALTH AMONG THE CORINTHIANS. GIOVANNI DIODATI: Paul proves that he is in no way abusing his power, especially since he does not imitate the tyrants of the world who keep their people cowering in fear, so as to always exercise absolute power. Paul, on the contrary, loved nothing more than to see the believers strong and vigorous in the works of the spiritual life, that he might have the opportunity to approach them with kindness and humility as being disarmed of this formidable power. ANNOTATIONS ON 2 CORINTHIANS 13:9.[47]

THE CORINTHIANS' RESTORATION. TILEMANN HESSHUS: The Greek word *katartizein* signifies

[44]Trapp, *A Commentary or Exposition*, 736*. †Hugh Latimer was an English reformer and preacher who died a martyr's death in 1555 during the reign of Queen Mary.

[45]Hesshus, *Explicatio Secundae Epistolae Pauli ad Corinthios*, 303r-v.

[46]Hyperius, *Commentarii . . . in Epistolam D. Pauli ad Romanos, et Utramque ad Corinthios*, 417.

[47]Diodati, *Le Seconde Epistre de l'Apostre S. Pauli aux Corinthiens*, 167.

when a dislocated member [of the body] is put back into place. And in the case of the word *katartisis*, it signifies wholeness, when all the members have been put in place, fully agreeing among themselves and fulfilling their duty. Therefore, Paul indicates that some of the members of the Corinthian church, through the deceit of the false apostles and the Corinthians' presumption, were in a sense dislocated, causing serious pain to the body of Christ. Therefore, Paul has this one prayer—not that he himself will be exalted, but that each member of the body of Christ, with proper symmetry, might agree with one another, being strong in the right, and doing their duty. Wholeness is also this, the complete perfection of the members of the body of Christ, which cannot exist unless they are in Christ Jesus, in whom all things must be joined and rightly ordered. Explication of 2 Corinthians 13:9.[48]

God's Restoration Needed. John Trapp: "Your restoration," or "jointing again." Beza says that the meaning is this: That whereas the members of this church were all, as it were, dislocated and out of joint, they should now again be joined together in love, and they should endeavor to amend what was wrong among them, either in faith or manners. Commentary on 2 Corinthians 13:9.[49]

Paul's Reason for Writing This Letter. Wolfgang Musculus: As Paul concludes his letter, he explains the reason and intention why, while absent from them, he wished to write the Corinthians before he finally came to them. The false apostles were saying: "His letters are weighty, but he is feeble in his physical presence," that is, "When he is present with us he cannot do those things that he threatens in his letters. He thunders so much in what he writes so that he might keep under his power those who are terrified by his letters." Against this, Paul says: "This is the reason I am writing these things while I am away from you, not because I am incapable of being severe toward those who are disobedient . . . but so that I might not be severe," that is, "so that I might not be forced to employ harshness according to the power which the Lord has given me. . . ." It was because of his mercy that Paul was not acting in a severe manner—but the false apostles said it was because he lacked the power to do so. Therefore, Paul warns them that, in the future, if they do not follow the rules that he has set down in his letter, he will no longer show mercy but act severely in their presence. Commentary on 2 Corinthians 13:10.[50]

Paul's Authority Was Spiritual, Not Civil. Tilemann Hesshus: In the way of all fathers, Paul demonstrates his love toward the Corinthians and directs all things for their benefit. He testifies that what he has written somewhat harshly in this letter, he has written for this reason, that those who were aware of their wickedness might in the meantime repent, lay aside their presumption, and return to earnest zeal for godliness, so that they might deliver Paul from all need to establish a harsh example among them. He shows that he is reluctant to use harshness against the impenitent unless he is forced to do so. He prefers that all would repent so that there would be no need for an example of severity. But lest the defiant and proud suppose that Paul's violent threats (when he is absent) are empty threats, he repeats what he also stated earlier: apostolic authority had been given to him from our Lord Jesus Christ for severely punishing the defiant and even hurling the thunderbolt of excommunication on the obstinate.

That authority is not an external or civil power or dominion. But it is a spiritual ministry which is articulated in these words: "Those whose sins you release will be released. And those whose sins you retain will be retained. And I give to you the keys of the kingdom of heaven." Here, Christ does not

[48]Hesshus, *Explicatio Secundae Epistolae Pauli ad Corinthios*, 303v.
[49]Trapp, *A Commentary or Exposition*, 736*.
[50]Musculus, *Commentarius . . . in posteriorem epistolam Pauli ad Corinthios*, 415.

arm his apostles with any civil power for transferring kingdoms, absolving subjects from their oaths (for which magistrates are responsible), usurping the power of the sword, or establishing hierarchy. Instead, Christ has established them ministers of the Word so that they might explain the will of God to men and women, announce God's favor to those who repent and the promise of grace to those who embrace him by faith. . . . But ministers place before the eyes of the presumptuous, the obstinate, and the impenitent the serious wrath of God and impending eternal destruction. This is truly the greatest of all powers, for nothing is more beneficial, and nothing can be spoken or thought more magnificent than a man having the power to pardon human sins. And nothing more useful can be desired than the pardon of sins and reconciliation with God. Explication of 2 Corinthians 13:10.[51]

Church Discipline Is for Edification. Niels Hemmingsen: The Corinthians have this threat of punishment unless they repent. It is as if Paul should say: "I do not want to use my power freely to punish you. For that reason, I am writing these things so that you might reform yourselves and be restored to wholeness. If not, when I come to you, I will be forced to use my severity." It should be noted that this more severe ecclesiastical jurisdiction concerns the edification of both the whole body of the church, and those who are rebuked. Commentary on 2 Corinthians 13:10.[52]

The Purpose for Punishment Is to Accomplish Spiritual Good. Cardinal Cajetan: He repeats that his use of power is so that the Corinthians might correct themselves and that there would be no need for Paul to use his power, for this power has been given by God, not for harming, but for building up, not for producing evil things, but for accomplishing good spiritual things. For the judgments of this present life are not for punishing (for this is reserved for the judgment of the future life) but for accomplishing spiritual good, either in the one who is punished or in the church. Commentary on 2 Corinthians 13:10.[53]

Church Order Must Build Up, Not Destroy. Martin Bucer: The power of the church in fact lies in the institution of discipline and order, but it is a power to be used only for building up, not for destroying, to the end that everything pertaining to Christ's discipline may be more perfectly and reverently administered. On the Church.[54]

[51]Hesshus, *Explicatio Secundae Epistolae Pauli ad Corinthios*, 304r-305r; citing Mt 16:19.

[52]Hemmingsen, *Commentaria in Omnes Epistolas Apostolorum*, 308.

[53]Cajetan, *In Posteriorem Pauli Epistolam ad Corinthios Commentarii*, 199.

[54]CPMB 221.

13:11-14 Final Greetings

11 Finally, brothers,[a] rejoice. Aim for restoration, comfort one another,[b] agree with one another, live in peace; and the God of love and peace will be with you. 12 Greet one another with a holy kiss. 13 All the saints greet you.

14 The grace of the Lord Jesus Christ and the love of God and the fellowship of the Holy Spirit be with you all.

a Or *brothers and sisters* **b** Or *listen to my appeal*

Overview: Paul concludes his second letter to the Corinthian church by making a final exhortation, offering a final promise, and extending a final benediction of praise to the triune God. Several Reformation commentators believe that Paul, in his exhortation, is effectively summarizing the fundamental message of the entire epistle: the Corinthians must grow in godliness, comfort one another, be united in doctrine, and seek peace and tranquility. If they pursue these Christian virtues, a promise awaits them: the God of love and peace will be with them. Reformation exegetes are especially impressed by the beautiful trinitarian benediction with which Paul concludes his epistle, for here one finds the pinnacle of evangelical doctrine, that the Father loves the world; the Son achieves salvation for sinners through his gracious death and resurrection; and the Holy Spirit unites pardoned sinners to Christ, enflames their hearts with love, and illumines their minds with understanding. The fact that Paul here mentions the name of Jesus Christ before the name of God the Father is of no concern, since (as Martin Chemnitz points out) the apostle is often indifferent to the precise order by which he enumerates the persons of the Trinity. What is crucial is this: that all of Scripture testifies to the fact that the three persons of the Godhead, Father, Son, and Holy Spirit, are the one true God, and that each person is in all respects that one true God. His glorious name is to be forever praised, both by the Christians in Corinth, and by believers in every age.

13:11-13 *Instructions for the Church*

God Is the Author of Love and Peace. Desiderius Erasmus: Be of the same mind, and do not contend with one another by reason of differing opinions. Let there be peace among you and mutual charity. If you do this, God, the author of charity and peace, will be present to favor and befriend you. Greet one another with a holy kiss, not the sort the common crowd gives, but one that is from the heart. All the saints who are here greet you. Paraphrases on 2 Corinthians 13.[1]

Advice for Troubled Times. Andreas Hyperius: This is a brief conclusion to the entire epistle, packed with wholesome exhortations, which treats some of the fundamental parts of the entire epistle. He wishes them to be well and in good health. Likewise, he desires them to be blameless, zealous in pursuing pure doctrine and a holy life. He tells them to "take comfort" and not to fear abandoning the gospel due to any evil, either against themselves or against the apostle himself. "Agree with one another, live in peace." This statement seems to be for abolishing divisions and overturning the sects that had arisen in the church, which he discussed in greater detail in his first epistle. "And the God of love and peace will be with you." A promise by which they are encouraged to live in peace. God is called the "God of love and peace" because he alone is the true author and the one who bestows true love and peace. In the same

[1] CWE 43:282.

way, at the beginning of this epistle, he is called "the God of all consolation." Accordingly, we should receive these things as if they were being said to us, that we might diligently cultivate love and peace, especially in these most distressing times, when love and peace are found neither in churches nor in states. Commentary on 2 Corinthians 13:11.[2]

An Exhortation and Promise. Niels Hemmingsen: A farewell with an exhortation and a promise. The exhortation contains a summary of whatever was disputed earlier in the epistle, namely, that they should pursue growth of godliness; that they should mutually comfort one another, which is love; that they should agree in doctrine, and should love peace and tranquility, by whose power the kingdom of Christ is known in this life. The promise is that the God of peace and love will be with them. It is as if Paul were to say: "Since God loves peace and love, in like manner, he will fulfill his promise to the peacemakers and give mutual love to those who love." Commentary on 2 Corinthians 13:11.[3]

Paul's Final Farewell. David Dickson: Paul concludes his epistle with a very appropriate exhortation, which is sixfold. (1) That they may rejoice in obeying his admonitions with real joy. (2) That they may be perfect, or spiritually healthy, and, having laid aside their factionalism, they may be joined one to another. (3) That they may have comfort by obeying him. (4) That in their beliefs they may agree among themselves. (5) That they may follow the way of peace with united affections. Paul confirms these exhortations by promising the divine presence in the fuller gifts of his grace, which God, who delights in peace and love, desires to give to those that strive after peace and love. . . . (6) That they would show toward one another the signs of mutual love without dissimulation, as is becoming of saints. Exposition of 2 Corinthians 13:11-12.[4]

Paul's Exhortation for Peace and Unity. John Calvin: "Finally brothers." Paul tempers whatever there was of harshness in the rest of the epistle because he does not want to leave their minds in an exasperated state, but rather to calm them. For only then are rebukes beneficial, when they are seasoned, as it were, with honey so that the hearer may receive them in an agreeable spirit (if indeed that is possible). However, it seems that Paul is turning from the few sick persons to the entire church. And so, he declares that he is thinking about its wholeness and desiring its consolation. "Being of one mind" and "living in peace" have different meanings, because the one proceeds from the other. The former pertains to agreement of opinion, while the second indicates goodwill and union of hearts.

"And the God of peace." He adds this phrase so that his exhortation might have a greater impact among them. But, at the same time, he intimates that God will be with us if we cultivate peace among ourselves—but that those who are alienated from one another are also alienated from him. For where there are discords and arguments, there, it is certain, the devil reigns. "Now what agreement is there between light and darkness?" Paul calls him the God of peace and love, who has commended peace and love to us, because God loves them and is their creator. We have spoken concerning the "kiss" in the two previous epistles. Commentary on 2 Corinthians 13:11.[5]

God Is the Source of Love and Peace. Wolfgang Musculus: "And the God of love and peace will be with you." Thus far, Paul has delivered an exhortation, to which he now adjoins a promise of divine favor if they experience and are eager for peace. "God," he says, "will be with you," that is, he will not leave you destitute of his grace and help but will support you with the assistance of his powerful Spirit. And Paul does not simply say, "God will be with you," but "the God of love and peace will be with you." Why? Because, God is

[2]Hyperius, *Commentarii . . . in Epistolam D. Pauli ad Romanos, et Utramque ad Corinthios*, 418.
[3]Hemmingsen, *Commentaria in Omnes Epistolas Apostolorum*, 308.
[4]Dickson, *An Exposition of All St. Paul's Epistles*, 93*.

[5]CO 50:154 (CTS 40:402-3); citing 2 Cor 6:14.

not a being of hatred and dissension, but of love and peace, that is, he both loves and is the author of love and peace, and so he cannot abandon his zeal for love and peace. . . .

God himself comes to us with his Spirit of grace, and he fills our hearts with an eager desire for love and peace, and then in his love he embraces more and more those who have been transformed by his love. "If anyone loves me," Christ says, "he will keep my word, and my father will love him, and we will come to him and make our home with him." Now how is it that a person loves Christ and keeps his word unless, by grace, we are loved by God? God loves first. And to make it possible for us also to love, he pours his Spirit into our hearts. And after he has brought them to new birth, he embraces more tightly and tenderly those who love him by his grace. This is not surprising, for God is love, as John testifies in one of his epistles: "and so those who remain in love, remain in God, and God remains in them." Commentary on 2 Corinthians 13:11.[6]

Three Remedies for Three Maladies. The English Annotations: Paul applies three remedies to the three principal maladies that afflicted the Corinthians, namely, ignorance, cowardliness, and schism. To the first malady he applies growth in grace, the knowledge of Christ, and a striving for perfection, saying "be perfect." To the second malady he applies spiritual courage, saying "be of good comfort." To the third malady he applies unity, saying "be of one mind, live in peace." Annotations on 2 Corinthians 13:11.[7]

Resting in God's Peace and Joy. John Donne: This is the sum and end of all, that when God sends humble and hard-working pastors to teachable and responsive congregations, that we pray, and you receive us in Christ's stead, we shall not only find rest in God, but . . . God shall find the savor of rest in us. God shall find a Sabbath to himself in us, and rest from his jealousies and anger toward us. And we shall have a Sabbath life here in the rest and peace of conscience, and a life of one everlasting Sabbath hereafter, where to our rest there shall be added joy, and to our joy glory, and this rest, and joy, and glory super-invested with that which crowns them all, namely, eternity. Sermon Number 5 Preached at St. Paul's.[8]

The Holy Kiss. John Calvin: The custom of kissing was very common among the Jews, as is clear from Scripture. In Greece, though, it was not so common and popular—but it was not unknown. It is probable that Paul is speaking here about a solemn kiss, by which people greeted one another in their sacred assemblies. For I could easily believe that a kiss was used in connection with the Lord's Supper already during the age of the apostles—in place of which, in certain countries that were somewhat averse to the custom of kissing, the practice of kissing the patina crept in. Whatever the case, since this was a symbol of mutual love, I have no doubt that Paul meant to encourage them to cultivate goodwill among themselves—not only in their hearts and as they performed necessary duties but also with the sign of a kiss, as long as it was "holy," that is, not immodest or deceptive, though it is possible to make the word "holy" in the sense of "sacred." Commentary on 1 Corinthians 16:20.[9]

A Sign of Affection and Goodwill. Tilemann Hesshus: "Greet one another with a holy kiss." Not only among the Jews, but also among the Greeks and other nations, the custom of giving a kiss was used for showing goodwill, as is shown both in the sacred scriptures as well as from the histories. Alexander [the Great] refused to kiss the Callisthenes as a sign of his anger when they did not worship him. But Paul no doubt wants

[6]Musculus, *Commentarius . . . in posteriorem epistolam Pauli ad Corinthios*, 417; citing Jn 14:23; 1 Jn 4:16.
[7]Downame, ed., *English Annotations*, GG4r*.
[8]Donne, *Sermons of John Donne*, 10:139*.
[9]CO 49:572 (CTS 40:79-80). The *patina* is the dish used to serve the consecrated bread during the Catholic Mass.

godly people to embrace one another with a holy kiss because it is a sign that a person is free from all evil affections and has sincere (and not disguised) goodwill. Explication of 2 Corinthians 13:12.[10]

Passing the Peace. Cardinal Cajetan: "Greet one another with a holy kiss." This ancient custom of the church is related to giving the peace in the sacred observance of the Mass. "The saints greet you"—meaning, "those who are with me." Commentary on 2 Corinthians 13:12-13.[11]

13:14 *A Trinitarian Benediction*

Paul Concludes by Invoking the Trinity. Jacques Lefèvre d'Étaples: Paul concludes his letter by mentioning the mystery of the most-divine Trinity, attributing love to the Father, grace to the Son, and fellowship to the Holy Spirit. For "the Father loved the world so much that he gave his only-begotten Son." And concerning the Son, it is said: "grace and truth have come through Jesus Christ." And concerning the Holy Spirit, it is said: "For by one Spirit we have all been baptized into one body." The love of the Father makes us his children. The grace of the Son justifies us. The unity of the Holy Spirit makes us one. The love of the Father has drawn us. The grace of the Son has adorned us. The unity of the Holy Spirit has joined us and engrafted us to God. Therefore, to the greatest Father, the greatest Son, and the greatest Holy Spirit, the one, greatest, and most-divine God, be the highest honor, the highest of all thanks and praise, the highest concord and unity, for ever and ever. Amen. Commentary on 2 Corinthians 13:14.[12]

The Holy Trinity and Church Unity. John Calvin: Paul concludes his epistle with a prayer, which contains three clauses, in which the sum of our salvation consists. First, he desires for them the grace of Christ, second, the love of God, and third, the communion of the Holy Spirit. The word "grace" here does not mean unmerited favor but is a metonymy[†] that denotes the whole benefit of redemption. But it seems here that the order is reversed, because the "love of God" is placed second, which is nevertheless the cause of that grace; and hence it is first in order. I answer that the arrangement of words in Scripture are not always exact; nevertheless, this present order also corresponds with the common form of teaching that is used in Scripture, for "when we were enemies of God, were reconciled by the death of his Son," although the Scripture is accustomed to speak of this in two ways. For it sometimes states what I have already cited from Paul, that there was hostility between us and God before we were reconciled through Christ. On the other hand, we hear what John says in John 3, "For God loved the world so much that he gave his only begotten Son, etc." The statements appear to be opposite; but it is easy to reconcile them. For in one case, we look to God and in the other case we look to ourselves. For God, as to himself, loved us before the creation of the world, and redeemed us for no other reason than because he loved us. As for us, when we see nothing in us except an occasion for wrath, that is, sin, we cannot perceive any love for God toward us without a mediator. . . . "The fellowship of the Holy Spirit" is added because it is only under his guidance that we come to possess Christ and all his benefits. Paul seems, nevertheless, at the same time to allude to the variety of gifts that he mentions elsewhere, because God does not bestow the Spirit to everyone separately but distributes to each according to the measure of grace, so that the members of the church, by mutually communing with one another, may cherish unity. Commentary on 2 Corinthians 13:14.[13]

---

[10]Hesshus, *Explicatio Secundae Epistolae Pauli ad Corinthios*, 308v.

[11]Cajetan, *In Posteriorem Pauli Epistolam ad Corinthios Commentarii*, 199.

[12]Lefèvre, *Commentariorum in Epistolas Beati Pauli . . . Liber Tertius*, 145v; citing Jn 3:16; 1:17; 1 Cor 12:13.

[13]CO 50:154-56 (CTS 40:403-4); citing Rom 5:10; Jn 3:16.

[†]Metonymy is the use of an attribute or adjunct idea as a replacement for the intended word. E.g., when the word *crown* is substituted for *king*.

THREE PERSONS IN ONE GODHEAD. CYRIACUS SPANGENBERG: The great, comforting, and holy apostle finally concludes this letter with Christian, Spirit-filled well-wishes, just as he had begun the epistle with a similar wish. . . . Here he touches the lofty article of the three who are differentiated in the one Godhead. He thinks of God the Father when he says, "the love of God," and of God the Son when he says, "the grace of our Lord Jesus Christ," and of the Holy Spirit when he says, "the fellowship of the Holy Spirit be with you all." He does not keep the order which we otherwise use in describing the persons of the Holy Trinity, when we name the Father first, then the Son, and finally the Holy Spirit. Instead, he names first the Son, then the Father, and then the Holy Spirit, and he does this for this reason: he wants thereby to show that "among these three persons none is the first, none is the last, none is the greatest, none is the least. Rather all three persons are equally eternal with one another, equally great, so that three persons may be honored in one Godhead, and one God in three persons," as St. Athanasius[†] says about this in his creed. FIFTIETH SERMON.[14]

THE TRINITARIAN PATTERN IN PAUL'S LETTERS. MARTIN CHEMNITZ: Gregory of Nazianzus notes that sometimes Scripture mentions the three persons, as "in the name of the Father, and of the Son, and of the Holy Spirit," and at other times two persons, as in the exordia of the epistles, "Grace be unto you and peace from God our Father and the Lord Jesus Christ," and at still other times one person, as at the close of the Pauline epistles, "The grace of our Lord Jesus Christ be with you." This way of speaking at times preserves the order of the persons, as in the preceding examples, and at other times is indifferent to the order, as when, the name of the Son is placed ahead of the name of the Father in 2 Corinthians 13:14, "the grace of the Lord Jesus Christ, the love of God, and the communion of the Holy Spirit be with you all." Likewise, when the name of the Holy Spirit is placed ahead of the name of the Son, as in Ephesians 3, "that you may be strengthened in the Spirit, so that Christ may dwell in our hearts by faith." That is to say, Scripture bears witness that the three persons and the entire Trinity are the one true God, and that each person is perfectly and in all respects that one true God. LOCI THEOLOGICI.[15]

THE PINNACLE OF EVANGELICAL DOCTRINE. NIELS HEMMINGSEN: This auspicious prayer contains the pinnacle of evangelical doctrine and expressly acknowledges the Trinity of persons. Then it also shows the specific actions of the persons in the process of salvation. It is the pinnacle of doctrine that we are saved by the grace of Christ, for this grace is opposed to the wrath of God and damnation. The Trinity of persons, Father, Son, and Holy Spirit, is expressed, who is one God in essence, and triune in persons. The actions of each person in the process of salvation is also distinguished. The Father loves. The Son embraces us with his grace, covering our sins and imputing his obedience to us. This greatest of all blessings is communicated and sealed to us when faith is formed in us through the preaching of the Word, and our heart is enflamed with new light, which is the work of the Holy Spirit. COMMENTARY ON 2 CORINTHIANS 13:14.[16]

A FINAL PRAYER. TILEMANN HESSHUS: To you, eternal Father of our Lord Jesus Christ, and to you, our Lord Jesus Christ, the crucified and resurrected Son of God, and to you the life-giving Holy Spirit, I give thanks with my whole heart for your enormous blessings. For, in the beginning, you provided efficacious consolation through the light of your Word when you kindly

[14]C. Spangenberg, *Die ander Epistel Pauli an die Corinthier*, 220r.
[†]For the Athanasian Creed, see Philip Schaff, *The Creeds of Christendom*, vol. 2, 6th ed. (Grand Rapids, MI: Baker, 1985).

[15]Chemnitz, *Loci Theologici*, 1:74-75; citing Eph 3:16-17.
[16]Hemmingsen, *Commentaria in Omnes Epistolas Apostolorum*, 309; citing Jn 3:16.

rescued me from every temptation. O holy and all-powerful God, increase within me the knowledge of you and of your will; strengthen my faith; inflame my heart with love for Jesus Christ our Redeemer; show to me your saving plans; direct me by your Word and your Spirit in all my activity; allow me to be a useful instrument in your church. Grant me a happy and peaceful end to this life, in faith and invocation of Jesus Christ, so that I might worship you, eternal Father, you, only-begotten Son, and you, Holy Spirit for all eternity. Amen. Explication of 2 Corinthians 13:14.[17]

[17]Hesshus, *Explicatio Secundae Epistolae Pauli ad Corinthios*, 309v-310r.

Map of Europe at the Time of the Reformation

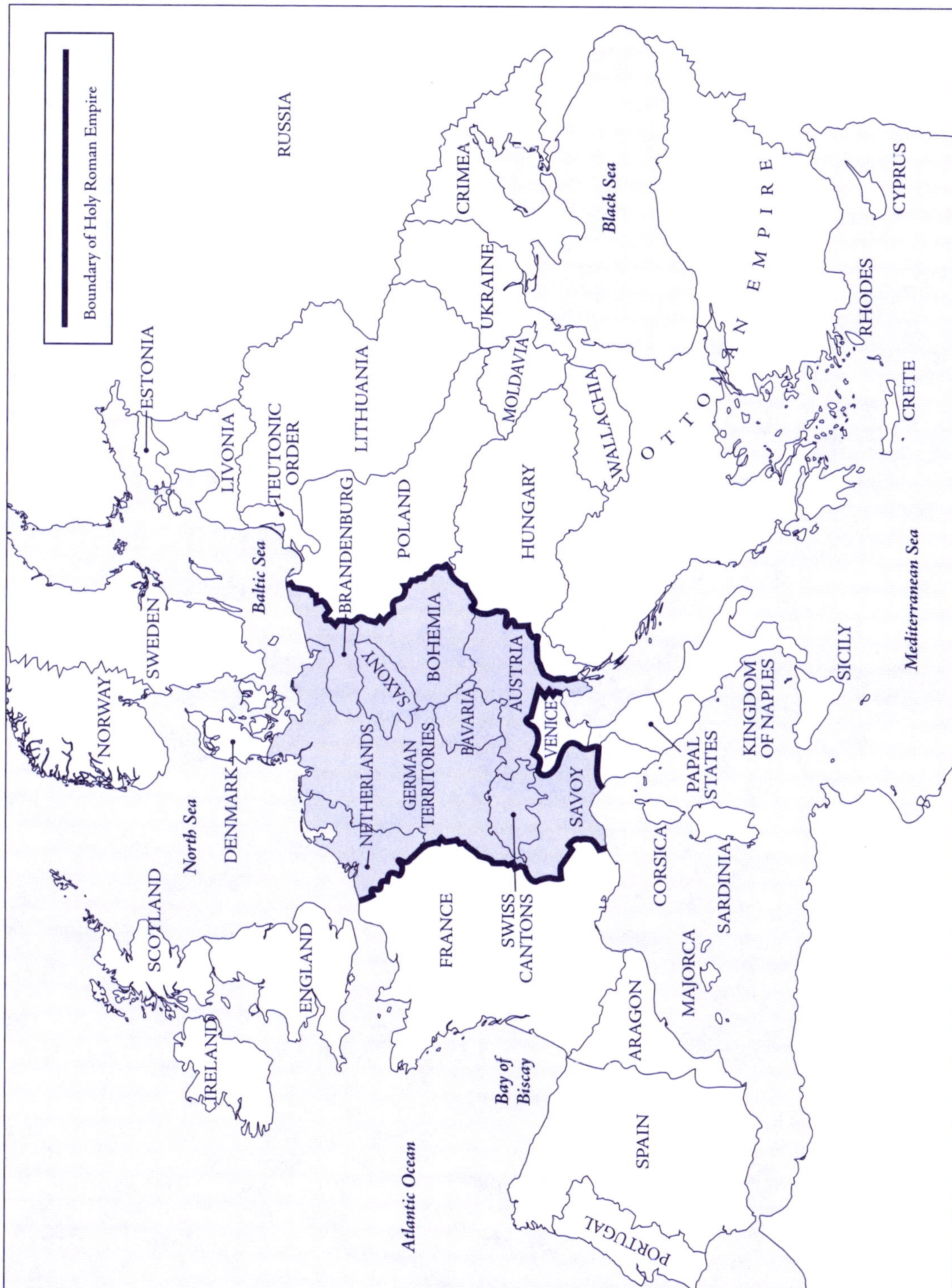

Timeline of the Reformation

	German Territories	France	Spain	Italy	Switzerland	Netherlands	British Isles
1309–1377		Babylonian Captivity of the Papacy					
1337–1453		d. Nicholas of Lyra Hundred Years' War	b. Paul of Burgos (Solomon ha-Levi)(d. 1435) Alonso Tostado (1400–1455)				Hundred Years' War
1378–1415		Western Schism (Avignon Papacy)		Western Schism			
1384							d. John Wycliffe
1414–1418					Council of Basel (1431–1437)		
1415				Council of Constance; d. Jan Hus; Martin V (r. 1417–1431); Council of Florence (1438–1445)			
1450	Invention of printing press						
1452				b. Leonardo da Vinci (d. 1519)			
1453				Fall of Constantinople			
1455–1485	b. Johannes Reuchlin (d. 1522)						War of Roses; rise of House of Tudor
1456	Gutenberg Bible						
1460				Pope Pius II issued *Execrabilis*			
1466		b. Jacques Lefèvre d'Étaples (d. 1536)					
1467						b. Desiderius Erasmus (d. 1536)	b. John Colet (d. 1519)
1469	b. Antoius Broickwy von Königstein (d. 541)						
1470				b. Santes Pagninus (d. 1541)			b. John (Mair) Major (d. 1550)
1475				b. Michelangelo (d. 1564)			
1478	b. Wolfgang Capito (d. 1541)		Ferdinand and Isabella	b. Jacopo Sadoleto (d. 1547)			b. Thomas More (d. 1535)

	German Territories	France	Spain	Italy	Switzerland	Netherlands	British Isles
1480	b. Balthasar Hubmaier (d. 1528); b. Andreas Bodenstein von Karlstadt (d. 1541)						
1481–1530			Spanish Inquisition				
1482					b. Johannes Oecolampadius (d. 1531)		
1483	b. Martin Luther (d. 1546)						
1484	b. Johann Spangenberg (d. 1550)				b. Huldrych Zwingli (d. 1531)		
1485	b. Johannes Bugenhagen (d. 1554)						b. Hugh Latimer (d. 1555)
1486	r. Frederick the Wise, Elector (d. 1525); b. Johann Eck (d. 1543)						
1488	b. Otto Brunfels (d. 1534)						b. Miles Coverdale (d. 1568)
1489	b. Thomas Müntzer (d. 1525); b. Kaspar von Schwenckfeld (d. 1561)						b. Thomas Cranmer (d. 1556)
1491	b. Martin Bucer (d. 1551)		b. Ignatius Loyola (d. 1556)				
1492			Defeat of Moors in Grenada; Columbus discovers America; expulsion of Jews from Spain	Alexander VI (r. 1492–1503)			
1493	b. Justus Jonas (d. 1555)						
1494							b. William Tyndale (d. 1536)
1496	b. Andreas Osiander (d. 1552)					b. Menno Simons (d. 1561)	
1497	b. Philipp Melanchthon (d. 1560); b. Wolfgang Musculus (d. 1563) b. Johannes (Ferus) Wild (d. 1554)						

	German Territories	France	Spain	Italy	Switzerland	Netherlands	British Isles
1498				d. Girolamo Savonarola	b. Conrad Grebel (d. 1526)		
1499	b. Johannes Brenz (d. 1570) b. Justus Menius (d. 1558)			b. Peter Martyr Vermigli (d. 1562)			
1500			b. Charles V (–1558)				
1501	b. Erasmus Sarcerius (d. 1559)						
1502	Founding of University of Wittenberg			Julius II (r. 1503–1513)		b. Frans Titelmans (d. 1537)	
1504					b. Heinrich Bullinger (d. 1575)		
1505	Luther joins Augustinian Order			b. Benedict Aretius (d. 1574)			
1506		b. Augustin Marlorat (d. 1562)		Restoration of St. Peter's begins			
1507				Sale of indulgences approved to fund building			
1508	b. Lucas Lossius (d. 1582)						
1509		b. John Calvin (d. 1564)					r. Henry VIII (–1547)
1510	Luther moves to Rome			b. Immanuel Tremellius (d. 1580)			b. Nicholas Ridley (d. 1555)
1511	Luther moves to Wittenberg						
1512				Sistine Chapel completed			
1512–1517				Fifth Lateran Council; rejection of conciliarism			
1513	Luther lectures on Psalms			r. Pope Leo X (–1521)			b. John Knox (d. 1572)
1515	Luther lectures on Romans	r. Francis I (–1547); b. Peter Ramus (d. 1572)					
1516		Est. French National Church (via Concordat of Bologna)		Concordat of Bologna		Publication of Erasmus's Greek New Testament	
1517	Tetzel sells indulgences in Saxony; Luther's Ninety-five Theses						

	German Territories	France	Spain	Italy	Switzerland	Netherlands	British Isles
1518	Heidelberg Disputation; Luther examined by Cajetan at Diet of Augsburg			Diet of Augsburg			
1519	Leipzig Disputation	b. Theodore Beza (d. 1605)	Cortés conquers Aztecs; Portuguese sailor Magellan circumnavigates the globe		Zwingli appointed pastor of Grossmünster in Zurich; b. Rudolf Gwalther (d. 1586)		
1520	Publication of Luther's "Three Treatises"; burning of papal bull in Wittenberg		Coronation of Charles V	Papal Bull v. Luther: *Exsurge Domine*			
1521	Luther excommunicated; Diet/Edict of Worms—Luther condemned; Luther in hiding; Melanchthon's *Loci communes*	French-Spanish War (–1526)	French-Spanish War; Loyola converts	Papal excommunication of Luther			Henry VIII publishes *Affirmation of the Seven Sacraments* against Luther; awarded title "Defender of the Faith" by Pope
1521–1522	Disorder in Wittenberg; Luther translates New Testament						
1521–1525		First and Second Habsburg–Valois War					
1522	Luther returns to Wittenberg; Luther's NT published; criticizes Zwickau prophets; b. Martin Chemnitz (d. 1586)		Publication of Complutensian Polyglot Bible under Cisneros		Sausage Affair and reform begins in Zurich under Zwingli		b. John Jewel (d. 1571)
1523	Knight's Revolt	Bucer begins ministry in Strasbourg	Loyola writes Spiritual Exercises	r. Pope Clement VII (–1534)	Iconoclasm in Zurich		
1524	Luther criticizes peasants; d. Johann von Staupitz					Erasmus's disputation on free will	
1524–1526	Peasants' War						
1525	Luther marries; execution of Thomas Müntzer; publication of Luther's *Bondage of the Will*				Abolition of mass in Zurich; disputation on baptism; first believers' baptism performed in Zurich		

	German Territories	France	Spain	Italy	Switzerland	Netherlands	British Isles
1526					Zurich council mandates capital punishment of Anabaptists	Publication of Tyndale's English translation of NT	
1527	d. Hans Denck (b. c. 1500) d. Hans Hut (b. 1490) b. Tilemann Hesshus (d. 1588)			Sack of Rome by mutinous troops of Charles V	First Anabaptist executed in Zurich; drafting of Schleitheim Confession		
1528	Execution of Hubmaier						
1529	Second Diet of Speyer; evangelical "protest"; publication of Luther's catechisms; Marburg Colloquy; siege of Vienna by Turkish forces	Abolition of mass in Strasbourg			d. Georg Blaurock (b. 1492)		Thomas More appointed chancellor to Henry VIII
1530	Diet of Augsburg; Confession of Augsburg	d. Francois Lambert (Lambert of Avignon) (b. 1487)	Charles V crowned Holy Roman Emperor				
1531	Formation of Schmalkaldic League				d. H. Zwingli; succeeded by H. Bullinger		
1532		Publication of Calvin's commentary on Seneca; conversion of Calvin	b. Francisco de Toledo (d. 1596)				
1533	b. Valentein Weigel (d. 1588)	Nicholas Cop addresses University of Paris; Cop and Calvin implicated as "Lutheran" sympathizers	b. Juan de Maldonado (d. 1583)				Thomas Cranmer appointed as Archbishop of Canterbury; Henry VIII divorces
1534	First edition of Luther's Bible published	Affair of the Placards; Calvin flees d. Guillame Briçonnet (b. 1470)		Jesuits founded; d. Cardinal Cajetan (Thomas de Vio) (b. 1469)			Act of Supremacy; English church breaks with Rome
1535	Bohemian Confession of 1535; Anabaptist theocracy at Münster collapses after eighteen months				b. Lambert Daneau (d. 1595)		d. Thomas More; d. John Fisher

	German Territories	**France**	**Spain**	**Italy**	**Switzerland**	**Netherlands**	**British Isles**
1536	Wittenberg Concord; b. Kaspar Olevianus (d. 1587)				First edition of Calvin's *Institutes* published; Calvin arrives in Geneva (–1538); First Helvetic Confession	Publication of Tyndale's translation of NT; d. W. Tyndale	d. A. Boleyn; Henry VIII dissolves monasteries (–1541)
1537					Calvin presents ecclesiastical ordinances to Genevan Council		
1538					Calvin exiled from Geneva; arrives in Strasbourg (–1541)		
1539		Calvin publishes second edition of *Institutes* in Strasbourg		d. Felix Pratensis			Statute of Six Articles; publication of Coverdale's Great Bible
1540				Papal approval of Jesuit order			d. Thomas Cromwell
1541	Colloquy of Regensburg	French translation of Calvin's *Institutes* published	d. Juan de Valdés (b. 1500/1510)		d. A. Karlstadt; Calvin returns to Geneva (–1564)		
1542	d. Sebastian Franck (b. 1499)			Institution of Roman Inquisition			War between England and Scotland; James V of Scotland defeated; Ireland declared sovereign kingdom
1543	Copernicus publishes *On the Revolutions of the Heavenly Spheres*; d. Johann Eck (Johann Maier of Eck) (b. 1486)						
1545–1547	Schmalkaldic Wars; d. Martin Luther			First session of Council of Trent			b. Richard Bancroft (d. 1610)
1546	b. Johannes Piscator (d. 1625)						
1547	Defeat of Protestants at Mühlberg	d. Francis I; r. Henri II (–1559)					d. Henry VIII; r. Edward VI (–1553)
1548	Augsburg Interim (–1552) d. Caspar Cruciger (b. 1504) b. David Pareus (d. 1622)						

	German Territories	France	Spain	Italy	Switzerland	Netherlands	British Isles
1549	d. Paul Fagius (b. 1504)	d. Marguerite d'Angoulême (b. 1492)			Consensus Tigurinus between Calvin and Bullinger		First Book of Common Prayer published
1550	b. Aegidius Hunnius (d. 1603)						
1551–1552				Second session of Council of Trent			
1552	d. Sebastian Münster (b. 1488) d. Friedrich Nausea (b. c. 1496)						Book of Common Prayer revised
1553	d. Johannes Aepinus (b. 1449)				Michael Servetus executed in Geneva		Cranmer's Forty-Two Articles; d. Edward VI; r. Mary I (d. 1558)
1554							Richard Hooker (d. 1600)
1555	Diet of Augsburg; Peace of Augsburg establishes legal territorial existence of Lutheranism and Catholicism b. Johann Arndt (d. 1621)	First mission of French pastors trained in Geneva				b. Sibbrandus Lubbertus (d. 1625)	b. Lancelot Andrewes (d. 1626) b. Robert Rollock (d. 1599); d. Hugh Latimer; d. Nicholas Ridley d. John Hooper
1556	d. Pilgram Marpeck (b. 1495) d. Konrad Pellikan (b. 1478) d. Peter Riedemann (b. 1506)		Charles V resigns			d. David Joris (b. c. 1501)	d. Thomas Cranmer
1557							Alliance with Spain in war against France
1558			d. Charles V				b. William Perkins (d. 1602); d. Mary I; r. Elizabeth I (–1603)
1559		d. Henry II; r. Francis II (–1560); first national synod of French reformed churches (1559) in Paris; Gallic Confession		First index of prohibited books issued	Final edition of Calvin's *Institutes*; founding of Genevan Academy	b. Jacobus Arminius (d. 1609)	Elizabethan Settlement

	German Territories	France	Spain	Italy	Switzerland	Netherlands	British Isles
1560	d. P. Melanchthon	d. Francis II; r. Charles IX (1574); Edict of Toleration created peace with Huguenots	d. Domingo de Soto (b. 1494)		Geneva Bible		Kirk of Scotland established; Scottish Confession
1561-1563				Third session of Council of Trent			
1561						Belgic Confession	
1562	d. Katharina Schütz Zell (b. 1497/98)	Massacre of Huguenots begins French Wars of Religion (–1598)					The Articles of Religion—in Elizabethan "final" form (1562/71); publication of Latin edition of Jewel's *Apology*
1563	Heidelberg Catechism						
1564				b. Galileo (d. 1642)	d. J. Calvin		b. William Shakespeare (d. 1616); publication of Lady Ann Bacon's English translation of Jewel's *Apology*
1566	d. Johann Agricola (b. 1494)			Roman Catechism	Second Helvetic Confession		
1567						Spanish occupation	Abdication of Scottish throne by Mary Stuart; r. James VI (1603–1625)
1568						d. Dirk Phillips (b. 1504) Dutch movement for liberation (–1645)	*Bishops' Bible*
1570		d. Johannes Mercerus (Jean Mercier)		Papal Bull *Regnans in Excelsis* excommunicates Elizabeth I			Elizabeth I excommunicated
1571	b. Johannes Kepler (d. 1630)		Spain defeats Ottoman navy at Battle of Lepanto				b. John Downame (d. 1652)
1572		Massacre of Huguenots on St. Bartholomew's Day		r. Pope Gregory XIII (1583–1585)		William of Orange invades	b. John Donne (d. 1631)
1574		d. Charles IX; r. Henri III (d. 1589)					

	German Territories	France	Spain	Italy	Switzerland	Netherlands	British Isles
1575	d. Georg Major (b. 1502); Bohemian Confession of 1575						
1576		Declaration of Toleration; formation of Catholic League		b. Giovanni Diodati (d. 1649)		Sack of Antwerp; Pacification of Ghent	
1577	Lutheran Formula of Concord						England allies with Netherlands against Spain
1578	Swiss Brethren Confession of Hesse d. Peter Walpot		Truce with Ottomans				Sir Francis Drake circumnavigates the globe
1579			Expeditions to Ireland			Division of Dutch provinces	
1580	Lutheran Book of Concord						
1581			d. Teresa of Avila				Anti-Catholic statutes passed
1582				Gregorian Reform of calendar			
1583							b. David Dickson (d. 1663)
1584		Treaty of Joinville with Spain	Treaty of Joinville; Spain inducted into Catholic League; defeats Dutch at Antwerp			Fall of Antwerp; d. William of Orange	
1585	d. Josua Opitz (b. c. 1542)	Henri of Navarre excommunicated		r. Pope Sixtus V (–1590)			
1586							Sir Francis Drake's expedition to West Indies; Sir Walter Raleigh in Roanoke
1587	d. Johann Wigand (b. 1523)	Henri of Navarre defeats royal army					d. Mary Stuart of Scotland
1588		Henri of Navarre drives Henri III from Paris; assassination of Catholic League Leaders	Armada destroyed				English Navy defeats Spanish Armada
1589		d. Henri III; r. Henri (of Navarre) IV (–1610)	Victory over England at Lisbon				Defeated by Spain in Lisbon
1590		Henri IV's siege of Paris		d. Girolamo Zanchi (b. 1516)			Alliance with Henri IV

	German Territories	France	Spain	Italy	Switzerland	Netherlands	British Isles
1592	d. Nikolaus Selnecker (b. 1530)						
1593		Henri IV converts to Catholicism					Books I-IV of Hooker's *Laws of Ecclesiastical Polity* published
1594		Henri grants toleration to Huguenots					
1595		Henri IV declares war on Spain; received into Catholic Church		Pope Sixtus accepts Henri IV into Church			Alliance with France
1596		b. René Descartes (d. 1650) b. Moïse Amyraut (d. 1664)					
1597							Book V of Hooker's *Laws of Ecclesiastical Polity* published
1598		Edict of Nantes; toleration of Huguenots; peace with Spain	Treaty of Vervins; peace with France				
1600	d. David Chytraeus (b. 1531)						
1601							b. John Trapp (d. 1669)
1602					d. Daniel Toussain (b. 1541)		
1603							d. Elizabeth I; r. James I (James VI of Scotland) (–1625)
1604	d. Cyriacus Spangenberg (b. 1528)						d. John Whitgift (b. 1530)
1605						b. Rembrandt (d. 1669)	Guy Fawkes and gunpowder plot
1606							Jamestown Settlement
1607							b. John Milton (d. 1674)
1608							
1610		d. Henri IV; r. Louis XIII (–1643)	d. Benedict Pererius (b. 1535)			The Remonstrance; Short Confession	

	German Territories	France	Spain	Italy	Switzerland	Netherlands	British Isles
1611							Publication of Authorized English Translation of Bible (AV/KJV); George Abbot becomes Archbishop of Canterbury (–1633)
1612							b. Richard Crashaw (d. 1649)
1616							b. John Owen (d. 1683)
1617							b. Ralph Cudworth (d. 1689)
1618–1619						Synod of Dordrecht	
1618–1648	Thirty Years' War						
1620							English Sepratists land in Plymouth, Massachusetts
1621							d. Andrew Willet (b. 1562)
1628							Puritans establish Massachusetts Bay colony
1633	d. Christoph Pelargus (b. 1565)						Laud becomes Archbishop of Canterbury
1637	d. Johann Gerhard (b. 1582)					*Statenvertaling*	
1638							d. Joseph Mede (b. 1638)
1640				Diodati's Italian translation of Bible published			
1642–1649							English civil wars; d. Charles I; r. Oliver Cromwell (1660)
1643		d. Louis XIII; r. Louis XIV (–1715)					
1643–1649							Westminster Assembly
1645							d. William Laud (b. 1573)

	German Territories	France	Spain	Italy	Switzerland	Netherlands	British Isles
1648		Treaty of Westphalia ends Thirty Years' War					Books VI and VIII of Hooker's *Laws of Ecclesiastical Polity* posthumously published
1656	d. Georg Calixtus (b. 1586)						
1658							d. Oliver Cromwell
1659							Richard Cromwell resigns
1660							English Restoration; r. Charles II (–1685)
1662							Act of Uniformity; Book VII of Hooker's *Laws of Ecclesiastical Polity* posthumously published
1664						d. Thieleman Jans van Braght (b. 1625)	d. John Mayer (b. 1583)
1671							d. William Greenhill (b. 1591)
1677							d. Thomas Manton (b. 1620)
1678						d. Anna Maria von Schurman (b. 1607)	
1688							Glorious Revolution; r. William and Mary (-1702); d. John Bunyan (b. 1628)
1691							d. Richard Baxter (b. 1615)

BIOGRAPHICAL SKETCHES OF REFORMATION-ERA FIGURES AND WORKS

This list is cumulative, including all the authors cited in the Reformation Commentary on Scripture to date as well as other people relevant to the Reformation and Reformation-era exegesis. For works consulted, see "Sources for Biographical Sketches," p. 477.

Cornelius À Lapide (1567–1637). Flemish Catholic biblical exegete. A Jesuit, Lapide served as professor of Holy Scripture and Hebrew at Louvain for twenty years before taking a similar role in Rome, where he taught until his death. He is best known for his extensive commentaries on the Scriptures. Encompassing all books of the Bible except Job and the Psalms, his work employs a fourfold hermeneutic and draws heavily on the work of patristic and medieval exegetes.

Thomas Adams (1583–1653). Anglican minister and author. He attended the University of Cambridge where he received his BA in 1601 and his MA in 1606. Following his ordination in 1604, Adams served as curate at Northill in Bedfordshire. In 1611, he became vicar of Willmington. Three years later he served the parish of Wingrave, Buckinghamshire, where he remained until 1618. From 1618 to 1623 Adams was preacher at St. Gregory by St. Paul's. He also served as chaplain to Henry Montague, First Earl of Manchester, and Lord Chief Justice of England. Among his most important works are the *Happiness of the Church* (1618) and an extensive commentary on 2 Peter (1638).

Johannes Aepinus (1499–1553). German Lutheran preacher and theologian. Aepinus studied under Martin Luther,* Philipp Melanchthon* and Johannes Bugenhagen* in Wittenberg. Because of his Lutheran beliefs, Aepinus lost his first teaching position in Brandenburg. He fled north to Stralsund and became a preacher and superintendent at Saint Peter's Church in Hamburg. In 1534, he made a diplomatic visit to England but could not convince Henry VIII* to embrace the Augsburg Confession.* His works include sermons and theological writings. Aepinus became best known as leader of the Infernalists, who believed that Christ underwent torment in hell after his crucifixion.

Johann Agricola (c. 1494–1566). German Lutheran pastor and theologian. An early student of Martin Luther,* Agricola eventually began a controversy over the role of the law, first with Melanchthon* and then with Luther himself. Agricola claimed to defend Luther's true position, asserting that only the gospel of the crucified Christ calls Christians to truly good works, not the fear of the law. After this first controversy, Agricola seems to have radicalized his views to the point that he eliminated Luther's *simul iustus et peccator* ("at the same time righteous and sinful") paradox of the Christian life, emphasizing instead that believers have no need for the law once they are united with Christ through faith. Luther responded by writing anonymous pamphlets against antinomianism. Agricola later published a recantation of his views, hoping to assuage relations with Luther, although they were never personally reconciled. He published a commentary on Luke, a series of sermons on Colossians, and a massive collection of German proverbs.

Henry Ainsworth (1571–1622/1623). English Puritan Hebraist. In 1593, under threat of persecution, Ainsworth relocated to Amsterdam, where he served as a teacher in an English congregation. He composed a confession of faith for the community and a number of polemical and exegetical works, including annotations on the Pentateuch, the Psalms and Song of Songs.

Henry Airay (c. 1560–1616). English Puritan professor and pastor. He was especially noted for his preaching, a blend of hostility toward Catholicism and articulate exposition of English Calvinism. He was promoted to provost of Queen's College Oxford (1598) and then to vice chancellor of the university in 1606. He disputed with William Laud* concerning Laud's putative Catholicization of the Church of England, particularly over the practice of genuflection, which Airay vehemently opposed. He also opposed fellow Puritans who wished to separate from the Church of England. His lectures on Philippians were his only work published during his lifetime.

Albert the Great (1201–1280). German theologian, philosopher, scientist, and ecclesiastic. Albert was born in Lauingen, located in the Bavarian-Swabian region. After completing his studies at Padua, Albert joined the Dominicans in 1220s. Upon finishing further theological studies at Cologne, Albert became a conventual lecturer during the 1230s at Hildesheim, Freiberg (Saxony), Regensburg, and Strasbourg. In the early 1240s, Albert was sent to Paris where he became a master of theology, and regent of the university in 1245. He served as regent until 1248. While at Paris, Albert commenced his paraphrases of Aristotle's works. Furthermore, Albert authored a systematic theology, and lectured on the four Gospels and nine books of the Old Testament. Albert is best known for having taught Thomas Aquinas,* who, as his assistant, transcribed his course on the works of Dionysius and Aristotle's *Nicomachean Ethics*.

Alexander (Ales) Alesius (1500–1565). Scottish Lutheran theologian. Following the martyrdom of his theological adversary Patrick Hamilton (c. 1504–1528), Alesius converted to the Reformation and fled to Germany. In 1535 Martin Luther* and Philipp Melanchthon* sent him as an emissary to Henry VIII* and Thomas Cranmer.* He taught briefly at Cambridge, but after the Act of Six Articles reasserted Catholic sacramental theology he returned to Germany, where he lectured at Frankfurt an der Oder and Leipzig. Alesius composed many exegetical, theological and polemical works, including commentaries on John, Romans, 1–2 Timothy, Titus and the Psalms.

Robert Allen (fl. 1596–1612). English Protestant clergyman and writer. Allen is known only by his writings, which reveal few biographical details except that he was a minister and he wrote from London and Suffolk. His works include a theological summary of Proverbs and Ecclesiastes, an exposition of the Gospel, and a catechism.

Andreas Althamer (c. 1500–1539). German Lutheran humanist and pastor. Forced from the chaplaincy at Schwäbisch-Gmünd for teaching evangelical ideas, Althamer studied theology at Wittenberg before serving as a pastor in Eltersdorf, Nuremberg, and Ansbach. A staunch Lutheran, he contended against Reformed theologians at the 1528 disputation at Bern and delivered numerous polemics against Anabaptism. He also composed an early Lutheran catechism, published at Nuremberg in 1528.

William Ames (1576–1633). English Puritan theologian. Heavily influenced by William Perkins* while at Cambridge, Ames was unable to find employment in the English church due to his Puritan commitments. Most of his life was spent in exile in the Netherlands, where he served as chaplain to English forces at The Hague and was the pastor of a small congregation. Best known as a controversialist during his early career, Ames was the theological advisor to the president of the Synod of Dort (1618–1619) and was later installed as chair of theology at the University of Franeker in Friesland. *The Marrow of Theology* (1627) is viewed as a model of seventeenth-century Puritan theology.

Moïse Amyraut (1596–1664). French Reformed pastor and professor. Originally intending to be a lawyer, Amyraut turned to theology after an encounter with several Huguenot pastors and having read Calvin's* *Institutes*. After a brief stint as a parish pastor, Amyraut spent the majority of his career at the Saumur Academy. He was well known for his irenicism and ecumenicism (for example, in advocating intercommunion with Lutherans). Certain aspects of his writings on justification, faith, the covenants and especially predestination proved controversial among the Reformed. His doctrine of election is often called hypothetical universalism or Amyraldianism, stating that Christ's atoning work was intended by God for all human beings indiscriminately, although its effectiveness for salvation depends on faith, which is a free gift of God given only to those whom God has chosen from eternity. Amyraut was charged with grave doctrinal error three times before the National Synod but was acquitted each time. Aside from his theological treatises, Amyraut published paraphrases of almost the entire New Testament and the Psalms, as well as many sermons.

Anabaptists of Trieste (1539). Following a meeting between Swiss Brethren and the Hutterites at Steinabrunn on December 6, 1536, around 140 radicals were arrested and imprisoned in Falkenstein Castle. After six weeks in captivity, the ninety men of the group were forced to march to Trieste to be sold as galley slaves. Twelve days after arrival, all but twelve prisoners managed to escape and return to Moravia, where they published a confession of their beliefs.

Jakob Andreae (1528–1590). German Lutheran theologian. Andreae studied at the University of

Tübingen before being called to the diaconate in Stuttgart in 1546. He was appointed ecclesiastical superintendent of Göppingen in 1553 and supported Johannes Brenz's* proposal to place the church under civil administrative control. An ecclesial diplomat for the duke of Württemberg, Andreae debated eucharistic theology, the use of images, and predestination with Theodore Beza* at the Colloquy of Montbéliard (1586) to determine whether French Reformed exiles would be required to submit to the Formula of Concord.* Andreae coauthored the Formula of Concord. He and his wife had eighteen children.

Lancelot Andrewes (1555–1626). Anglican bishop. A scholar, pastor and preacher, Andrews prominently shaped a distinctly Anglican identity between the poles of Puritanism and Catholicism. He oversaw the translation of Genesis to 2 Kings for the Authorized Version.* His eight-volume collected works—primarily devotional tracts and sermons—are marked by his fluency in Scripture, the Christian tradition and classical literature.

Thomas Aquinas (1225–1274). Dominican medieval theologian. Thomas Aquinas was born into a noble family in Rocasecca, Italy. In 1230 Thomas's father sent him to the abbey at Monte Casino as a child oblate. When, at age fourteen, Thomas was given the choice between taking his final vows and leaving, he chose to go to Naples to study at the school recently founded by the Holy Roman Emperor. While studying at Naples, Thomas came into contact with the Dominicans, and joined this order in 1244. Although his family objected to his decision at first, to the point of actually imprisoning Thomas, they came to accept his decision the following year. Afterwards, Aquinas traveled to Paris where he began his formal studies under Albert the Great (1200–1280). Aquinas followed his teacher to Cologne in 1248 where he was ordained a priest, and completed his course in theology. Four years later, he was appointed a bachelor in the Dominican convent in Paris where he lectured on Peter Lombard's (1096–1160)* *Sentences*. In 1256, Thomas was incepted as a master of the sacred page, and he taught in Paris until 1259. In 1261, he was appointed lecturer at a school in Orvieto. Four years later, Aquinas was transferred to Rome, and in 1268 returned to Paris. In 1272, the Dominican order appointed Aquinas to start a new school in Naples. A mystical experience reportedly caused Aquinas to abruptly cease his writing. Aquinas died at a monastery in Fossanova. In addition to his major works, *Summa Theologia* and *Summa Contra Gentiles*, Aquinas's voluminous corpus includes extensive commentaries on Jeremiah, Lamentations, Isaiah, Job, and an incomplete one on the Psalms. Aquinas also wrote commentaries on the Gospels of Matthew and John as well as the Pauline Epistles. Furthermore, at the request of the pope, Aquinas produced the *Catena Aurea*, a commentary on the four Gospels consisting of exegetical statements by the Latin and Greek fathers. One of the most significant features of Aquinas's biblical commentaries is his emphasis on the literal meaning of a Scriptural text. As a representation of medieval Catholic theology, Aquinas's theology was regularly challenged by the Protestant reformers.

Benedict Aretius (d. 1574). Swiss Reformed professor. Trained at the universities of Bern, Strasbourg and Marburg, Aretius taught logic and philosophy as well as the biblical languages and theology. He advocated for stronger unity and peace between the Lutheran and Reformed churches. Aretius joined others in denouncing the antitrinitarian Giovanni Valentino Gentile (d. 1566). He published commentaries on the New Testament, as well as various works on astronomy, botany and medicine.

Aristotle (388–322 BC). Ancient Greek philosopher and scientist. Aristotle was born in Stagira, Chalkdice, northern Greece. He is considered the "Father of Western Philosophy" along with his teacher, Plato, because his teaching produced the bases for almost every discipline studied in the Western world. After his father's death while he was still a child, Aristotle was raised by his guardian, Proxenus of Atarneus. At the age of about eighteen, Aristotle joined Plato's Academy in Athens, where he remained until his was thirty-seven. Aristotle's writings cover a wide range of subjects: physics, biology, zoology, metaphysics, logic, ethics, aesthetics, poetry, theater, music, rhetoric, psychology, linguistics, and politics. Shortly after Plato's death, King Philip II of Macedonia requested his services as a tutor to his son, Alexander the Great. Aristotle began tutoring the young prince in 343 BC. While teaching Alexander, Aristotle was able to acquire hundreds of books for the library of what would become his Lyceum. Aristotle's work profoundly shaped scholarship during the Middle Ages and early modern period as his logic was employed in the exegesis of Scripture and formation of theology. Among the major theologians who incorporated Aristotle's methods into their theological systems was Thomas Aquinas.* Aristotle's methods and categories would also be utilized by many Protestant theologians throughout the sixteenth and seventeenth centuries.

Jacobus Arminius (1559–1609). Dutch Remonstrant pastor and theologian. Arminius was a vocal critic of high

Calvinist scholasticism, whose views were repudiated by the Synod of Dordrecht. Arminius was a student of Theodore Beza* at the academy of Geneva. He served as a pastor in Amsterdam and later joined the faculty of theology at the university in Leiden, where his lectures on predestination were popular and controversial. Predestination, as Arminius understood it, was the decree of God determined on the basis of divine foreknowledge of faith or rejection by humans who are the recipients of prevenient, but resistible, grace.

Johann Arndt (1555–1621). German Lutheran pastor and theologian. After a brief time teaching, Arndt pastored in Badeborn (Anhalt) until 1590, when Prince Johann Georg von Anhalt (1567–1618) began introducing Reformed ecclesial policies. Arndt ministered in Quedlinberg, Brunswick, Eisleben and Celle. Heavily influenced by medieval mysticism, Arndt centered his theology on Christ's mystical union with the believer, out of which flows love of God and neighbor. He is best known for his *True Christianity* (1605–1609), which greatly influenced Philipp Jakob Spener (1635–1705) and later Pietists.

John Arrowsmith (1602–1659). English Puritan theologian. Arrowsmith participated in the Westminster Assembly, and later taught at Cambridge. His works, all published posthumously, include three sermons preached to Parliament and an unfinished catechism.

Articles of Religion (1562; revised 1571). The Articles underwent a long editorial process that drew from the influence of Continental confessions in England, resulting in a uniquely Anglican blend of Protestantism and Catholicism. In their final form, they were reduced from Thomas Cranmer's* Forty-two Articles (1539) to the Elizabethan Thirty-Nine Articles (1571), excising polemical articles against the Anabaptists and Millenarians as well as adding articles on the Holy Spirit, good works and Communion. Originating in a 1535 meeting with Lutherans, the Articles retained a minor influence from the Augsburg Confession* and Württemberg Confession (1552), but showed significant revision in accordance with Genevan theology, as well as the Second Helvetic Confession.*

Anne Askew (1521–1546). English Protestant martyr. Askew was forced to marry her deceased sister's intended husband, who later expelled Askew from his house—after the birth of two children—on account of her religious views. After unsuccessfully seeking a divorce in Lincoln, Askew moved to London, where she met other Protestants and began to preach. In 1546, she was arrested, imprisoned and convicted of heresy for denying the doctrine of transubstantiation. Under torture in the Tower of London she refused to name any other Protestants. On July 16, 1546, she was burned at the stake. Askew is best known through her accounts of her arrests and examinations. John Bale (1495–1563), a bishop, historian and playwright, published these manuscripts. Later John Foxe (1516–1587) included them in his *Acts and Monuments*, presenting her as a role model for other pious Protestant women.

Mary Astell (1666–1731). English writer and philosopher. Astell received an informal education from her uncle, a clergyman. Left almost penniless after the death of her parents, she settled in London, where she made her career as a writer. She is best known for her proto-feminist works, including *A Serious Proposal to the Ladies* (1694, 1697), *Some Reflections on Marriage* (1700), and *The Christian Religion, as Professed by a Daughter of the Church of England* (1705). In these works she argues for the moral and intellectual equality of the sexes and the need for women to receive a similar education to men so that they can navigate the world by themselves. Retiring from writing, Astell spent her final decades organizing a charity school for girls in Chelsea backed by the Society for the Propagation of Christian Knowledge.

Augsburg Confession (1530). In the wake of Luther's* stand against ecclesial authorities at the Diet of Worms (1521), the Holy Roman Empire splintered along theological lines. Emperor Charles V sought to ameliorate this—while also hoping to secure a united European front against Turkish invasion—by calling together another imperial diet in Augsburg in 1530. The Evangelical party was cast in a strongly heretical light at the diet by Johann Eck.* For this reason, Philipp Melanchthon* and Justus Jonas* thought it best to strike a conciliatory tone (Luther, as an official outlaw, did not attend), submitting a confession rather than a defense. The resulting Augsburg Confession was approved by many of the rulers of the northeastern Empire; however, due to differences in eucharistic theology, Martin Bucer* and the representatives of Strasbourg, Constance, Lindau and Memmingen drafted a separate confession (the Tetrapolitan Confession). Charles V accepted neither confession, demanding that the Evangelicals accept the Catholic rebuttal instead. In 1531, along with the publication of the Augsburg Confession itself, Melanchthon released a defense of the confession that responded to the Catholic confutation and expanded on the original articles. Most subsequent Protestant confessions followed the general structure of the Augsburg Confession.

Augustine of Hippo (354–430 AD). North African bishop and theologian. Augustine was born in Thagaste

(Ahras, Algeria), a small town in the Roman province to Numidia, the son of a Christian mother, Monica, and a non-Christian father, Patricius, a local official of modest means. Enabled by local patronage, Augustine received a classical education, which afforded him the opportunity to pursue advanced training in rhetoric at Carthage. Upon completing his education at Carthage, Augustine taught rhetoric there as well as in Rome and Milan, where he was appointed official rhetorician of that city. Inspired by his reading of Cicero's *Hortensius*, Augustine embarked upon a quest for wisdom. While in Carthage, Augustine was repulsed by the seemingly simplistic Christianity he encountered, and therefore joined the Manicheans. Having become disillusioned by the Manichaeans' failure to lead him to the wisdom they promised, Augustine was eventually drawn to orthodox Christianity by the preaching of Ambrose (340–397) and his reading of the Neo-Platonist philosopher Plotinus (204–270). As a result of his conversion in 386, Augustine abandoned his secular ambitions in favor of a celibate life fully committed to intellectual and spiritual devotion to God. Towards this end, Augustine returned to north Africa to establish a semi–monastic community. However, in 391, while visiting Hippo Regius, he was forcibly ordained into the priesthood, and made bishop of that church in 396. In addition to his many duties as a bishop, Augustine engaged in controversies against the Manicheans, Donatists, and Pelagians, which took up the remainder of his life and career. He died in 430 while the Vandals besieged Hippo. Among his many works, Augustine devoted several to exegesis. He outlines exegetical principles in his *De Doctrina Christiana* ("On Christian Doctrine"), and he authored extensive series of homilies on most of the books of the New Testament as well as the Old Testament books of Psalms and Genesis (incomplete). During the Reformation era, both Catholic and Protestant theologians appealed to and engaged with Augustine's theology, especially his emphases upon original sin and humanity's need for God's grace.

Authorized Version (1611). In 1604 King James I* commissioned this new translation—popularly remembered as the King James Version—for uniform use in the public worship of the Church of England. The Bible and the Apocrypha was divided into six portions and assigned to six companies of nine scholars—both Anglicans and Puritans—centered at Cambridge, Oxford and Westminster. Richard Bancroft, the general editor of the Authorized Version, composed fifteen rules to guide the translators and to guard against overly partisan decisions. Rather than offer an entirely fresh English translation, the companies were to follow the Bishops' Bible* as closely as possible. "Truly (good Christian Reader)," the preface states, "we neuer thought from the beginning that we should need to make a new Translation, nor yet to make of a bad one a good one . . . but make a good one better, or out of many good ones, one principall good one, not iustly to be excepted against: that hath bene our endeauour, that our mark." Other rules standardized spelling, dictated traditional ecclesial terms (e.g., *church, baptize* and *bishop*), and allowed only for linguistic marginal notes and cross-references. Each book of the Bible went through a rigorous revision process: first, each person in a company made an initial draft, then the company put together a composite draft, then a supercommittee composed of representatives from each company reviewed these drafts, and finally two bishops and Bancroft scrutinized the final edits. The text and translation process of the Authorized Version have widely influenced biblical translations ever since.

Gervase Babington (1549/1550–1610). English Anglican bishop. Born into an influential family, Babington studied at Cambridge and spent time as a preacher at the university and as prebendary of Hereford Cathedral before serving, in turn, as bishop of Llandaff, Exeter, and Worcester. He published a number of sermons, expositions of the Ten Commandments and Lord's Prayer, and notes on Genesis, Exodus, and Leviticus.

Robert Bagnall (b. 1559 or 1560). English Protestant minister. Bagnall authored *The Steward's Last Account* (1622), a collection of five sermons on Luke 16.

Friedrich Balduin (1575–1627). German Lutheran theologian. After spending time in the pastorate at Freiberg and Oelsnitz, Balduin was appointed professor of theology at Wittenberg in 1604, where he remained until the end of his life. He also served as head of the theology faculty, superintendent of churches, and assessor of the consistory. Known for his commitment to Lutheran orthodoxy, Balduin's major works include a commentary on the Pauline letters and writings on exegesis, homiletics, and casuistry.

John Ball (1585–1640). English Puritan theologian. Ball was a respected educator. He briefly held a church office until he was removed on account of his Puritanism. He composed popular catechisms and tracts on faith, the church and the covenant of grace.

John Barlow (1580/1581?–1629/1630). English Protestant minister. Educated at Oxford, Barlow ministered in Plymouth, Halifax, and Chester. A number of his sermons have been preserved, including his teachings on 2 Timothy 1 and 1 Thessalonians 4:18.

Thomas Bastard (c. 1565–1618). English Protestant minister and poet. Educated at Winchester and New College, Oxford, Bastard published numerous works, including collections of poems and sermons; his most famous title is *Chrestoleros* (1598), a collection of epigrams. Bastard was alleged to be the author of an anonymous work, *An Admonition to the City of Oxford*, which revealed the carnal vices of many clergy and scholars in Oxford; despite denying authorship, he was dismissed from Oxford in 1591. Bastard was recognized as a skilled classical scholar and preacher. He died impoverished in a debtor's prison in Dorchester.

Jeremias Bastingius (1551–1595). Dutch Reformed theologian. Educated in Heidelberg and Geneva, Bastingius pastored the Reformed church in Antwerp for nearly a decade until the Spanish overran the city in 1585; he later settled in Dordrecht. He spent the last few years of his life in Leiden on the university's board of regents. He wrote an influential commentary on the Heidelberg Catechism that was translated into English, Dutch, German and Flemish.

Johann (Pomarius) Baumgart (1514–1578). Lutheran pastor and amateur playwright. Baumgart studied under Georg Major,* Martin Luther* and Philipp Melanchthon* at the University of Wittenberg. Before becoming pastor of the Church of the Holy Spirit in 1540, Baumgart taught secondary school. He authored catechetical and polemical works, a postil for the Gospel readings throughout the church year, numerous hymns and a didactic play (*Juditium Salomonis*).

Richard Baxter (1615–1691). English Puritan minister. Baxter was a leading Puritan pastor, evangelist and theologian, known throughout England for his landmark ministry in Kidderminster and a prodigious literary output, producing 135 books in just over forty years. Baxter came to faith through reading William Perkins,* Richard Sibbes* and other early Puritan writers and was the first cleric to decline the terms of ministry in the national English church imposed by the 1662 Act of Uniformity; Baxter wrote on behalf of the more than 1700 who shared ejection from the national church. He hoped for restoration to national church ministry, or toleration, that would allow lawful preaching and pastoring. Baxter sought unity in theological, ecclesiastical, sociopolitical and personal terms and is regarded as a forerunner of Noncomformist ecumenicity, though he was defeated in his efforts at the 1661 Savoy Conference to take seriously Puritan objections to the revision of the 1604 Prayer Book. Baxter's views on church ministry were considerably hybrid: he was a paedo-baptist, Nonconformist minister who approved of synodical Episcopal government and fixed liturgy. He is most known for his classic writings on the Christian life, such as *The Saints' Everlasting Rest* and *A Christian Directory*, and pastoral ministry, such as *The Reformed Pastor*. He also produced *Catholick Theology*, a large volume squaring current Reformed, Lutheran, Arminian and Roman Catholic systems with each other.

Thomas Becon (1511/1512–1567). English Puritan preacher. Becon was a friend of Hugh Latimer,* and for several years chaplain to Archbishop Thomas Cranmer.* Becon was sent to the Tower of London by Mary I and then exiled for his controversial preaching at the English royal court. He returned to England upon Elizabeth I's* accession. Becon was one of the most widely read popular preachers in England during the Reformation. He published many of his sermons, including a postil, or collection of sermon helps for undertrained or inexperienced preachers.

Belgic Confession (1561). Written by Guy de Brès (1523–1567), this statement of Dutch Reformed faith was heavily reliant on the Gallic Confession,* although more detailed, especially in how strongly it distances the Reformed from Roman Catholics and Anabaptists. The Confession first appeared in French in 1561 and was translated to Dutch in 1562. It was presented to Philip II (1527–1598) in the hope that he would grant toleration to the Reformed, to no avail. At the Synod of Dordrecht* the Confession was revised, clarifying and strengthening the article on election as well as sharpening the distinctives of Reformed theology against the Anabaptists, thus situating the Dutch Reformed more closely to the international Calvinist movement. The Belgic Confession in conjunction with the Heidelberg Catechism* and the Canons of Dordrecht were granted official status as the confessional standards (the Three Forms of Unity) of the Dutch Reformed Church.

Robert Bellarmine (1542–1621). Italian Catholic cardinal. A Jesuit, Bellarmine first taught at Louvain before being appointed chair of polemical theology at the Roman College. Much of Bellarmine's career was devoted to the refutation of Protestant teachings, and his three volume work, the *Controversies* (1586–93), was widely disseminated in the post-Tridentine era as the foremost refutation of the evangelical message. He was influential in the official revision of the Vulgate* text during the reign of Pope Clement VIII (1536–1605), with the resulting version, the Sixto-Clementine Vulgate, providing the basic biblical text for Catholics until Vatican II. Bellarmine is also a controversial figure in the history of science. Appointed to the Holy Office, also known as the

Inquisition, by Pope Paul V (1550–1621), it was he who examined Galileo Galilei (1564–1642) and ordered him to treat heliocentrism as a hypothesis rather than a reality, believing the evidentiary threshold had not yet been met. Later in his career, Bellarmine's attention turned to works on devotion and piety, and include his extensive commentary on the Psalms (1611).

Bernard of Clairvaux (1090–1153). French abbot and theologian. Born the son of a Bugundian knight, Bernard became interested in the new reforming movement at Citeaux, and thus abandoned his preparation for a secular career in favor of monastic life there. Towards this end, Bernard persuaded thirty-one of his friends and relatives to follow him to Citeaux, and join the Cistercian order. Among this group were four of Bernard's brothers. In 1115, Bernard went with others of his order to found a Cistercian monastery at Claivaux. Bernard's austere approach to the monastic life attracted many followers to the point that by the time of his death there were sixty-eight Cistercian houses. Throughout his career, Bernard preached, mediated theological disputes, and advised. Bernard is best known for having preached the Second Crusade (1147–1150) as well as advising his former student, Pope Eugenius III (r. 1145–1153), and engaging in theological controversies with Peter Abelard (1079–1142) and Gilbert of Poitiers (1085–1154). One of the distinguishing characteristics of Bernard's theology is his Christocentric mysticism. Among Bernard's most important works are his treatises *On Consideration* and *On Loving God* along with his *Sermons on the Song of Songs* as well as many other sermons on the liturgical year and other subject. Many of the reformers in the sixteenth century cited Bernard extensively, especially Martin Luther* and John Calvin*.

Richard Bernard (1568–1641). English Puritan minister. A moderate Puritan, Bernard eschewed separation from the Church of England, spending the majority of his career in parish ministry at Batcombe, Somerset. Many of his works, including a handbook for pastors and a household catechism, were well received and printed numerous times during his lifetime.

Theodore Beza (1519–1605). French Reformed pastor and professor. Beza was compatriot and successor to John Calvin* as moderator of the Company of Pastors in Geneva during the second half of the sixteenth century. He was a noteworthy New Testament scholar whose *Codex Bezae* formed the basis of the New Testament section of later English translations. A leader in the academy and the church, Beza served as professor of Greek at the Lausanne Academy until 1558, at which time he moved to Geneva to become the rector of the newly founded Genevan Academy. He enjoyed an international reputation through his correspondence with key European leaders. Beza developed and extended Calvin's doctrinal thought on several important themes such as the nature of predestination and the real spiritual presence of Christ in the Eucharist.

Theodor Bibliander (1504?–1564). Swiss Reformed Hebraist and theologian. Professor of Old Testament at the Zurich Academy from 1531, Bibliander published two Hebrew grammars, a collection of letters by Zwingli* and Oecolampadius*, commentaries on Isaiah, Ezekiel, and Nahum, a Latin translation of the Qur'an, and a tract warning Christians against the threat of Islam. He taught a universalist view of predestination, arguing that God saved all people unless they rejected divine grace. Following a dispute with double-predestinarian Peter Martyr Vermigli*, he was forced into retirement in 1560.

Thomas Bilson (1546/1547?–1616). English Anglican Bishop and theologian. A celebrated preacher and theologian, Bilson served as canon of Winchester Cathedral and warden of Winchester College before becoming bishop of Worcester. He held this position for only one year, however, before his appointment to the wealthier see of Winchester. As an advisor to King James I,* he preached at his coronation, and he was involved with the publication of the 1611 Authorized Version,* being part of the Cambridge company responsible for translating the Apocrypha, the author of part of the front matter, and one of the text's final editors. His extant writings defend the episcopacy against Erastianism, condemn rebellion, and argue for a literal understanding of Christ's descent into hell.

Hugh Binning (1627–1653). Scottish Presbyterian theologian. At the age of eighteen, Binning became a professor of philosophy at the University of Glasgow. In his early twenties he left this post for parish ministry, and died of consumption a few years later. His commentary on the Westminster Confession and a selection of his sermons were published after his death.

Samuel Bird (d. 1604). Anglican minister and author. A native of Essex, Bird matriculated at Queen's College, Cambridge, where he received his BA in 1570 and his MA in 1573, at which time he was also elected a fellow of Corpus Christi College, Cambridge. For reasons unknown, Bird resigned his fellowship sometime in 1576. He spent nearly the entirety of his post-university career as rector of St. Peter's in Ipswich until his death in 1604. Among Bird's major works are *A Friendlie Communication or Dialogue Betweene Paule and Demas, wherein is Disputed*

How We are to Use the Pleasures of This Life (1580), *Lectures upon the 11. Chapter of Hebrews and upon the 38. Psalme* (1598), and *Lectures upon the 8 and 9 Chapters of the Second Epistle to the Corinthians* (1598).

Bishops' Bible (1568). Anglicans were polarized by the two most recent English translations of the Bible: the Great Bible (1539) relied too heavily on the Vulgate* and was thus perceived as too Catholic, while the Geneva Bible's* marginal notes were too Calvinist for many Anglicans. So Archbishop Matthew Parker (1504–1575) commissioned a new translation of Scripture from the original languages with marginal annotations (many of which, ironically, were from the Geneva Bible). Published under royal warrant, the Bishops' Bible became the official translation for the Church of England. The 1602 edition provided the basis for the King James Bible (1611).

Christopher Blackwood (1607/1608–1670). English Baptist pastor. Initially an Anglican priest, Blackwood served at the parishes of Stockbury and Rye until Puritan sympathies led him to migrate to New England. Returning to England, he pastored briefly at Cranbrook until Baptist preaching caused him to leave the established church, be rebaptized, and serve as a pastor of a General Baptist congregation in Staplehurst. Joining the Parliamentary Army in their goal to evangelize Ireland, he helped plant a number of Baptist churches and pastored at Wexford, Kilkenny, and Dublin. His numerous writings include treatises on baptism and repentance, a catechism, and a commentary on the first ten chapters of Matthew.

Georg Blaurock (1492–1529). Swiss Anabaptist. Blaurock (a nickname meaning "blue coat," because of his preference for this garment) was one of the first leaders of Switzerland's radical reform movement. In the first public disputations on baptism in Zurich, he argued for believer's baptism and was the first person to receive adult believers' baptism there, having been baptized by Conrad Grebel* in 1525. Blaurock was arrested several times for performing mass adult baptisms and engaging in social disobedience by disrupting worship services. He was eventually expelled from Zurich but continued preaching and baptizing in various Swiss cantons until his execution.

Bohemian Confession (1535). Bohemian Christianity was subdivided between traditional Catholics, Utraquists (who demanded Communion in both kinds) and the *Unitas Fratrum*, who were not Protestants but whose theology bore strong affinities to the Waldensians and the Reformed. The 1535 Latin edition of this confession—an earlier Czech edition had already been drafted—was an attempt to clarify and redefine the beliefs of the *Unitas Fratrum*. This confession purged all earlier openness to rebaptism and inched toward Luther's* eucharistic theology. Jan Augusta (c. 1500–1572) and Jan Roh (also Johannes Horn; c. 1490–1547) presented the confession to King Ferdinand I (1503–1564) in Vienna, but the king would not print it. The *Unitas Fratrum* sought, and with slight amendments eventually obtained, Luther's advocacy of the confession. It generally follows the structure of the Augsburg Confession.*

Bohemian Confession (1575). This confession was an attempt to shield Bohemian Christian minorities—the Utraquists and the *Unitas Fratrum*—from the Counter-Reformation and Habsburg insistence on uniformity. The hope was that this umbrella consensus would ensure peace in the midst of Christian diversity; anyone who affirmed the 1575 Confession, passed by the Bohemian legislature, would be tolerated. This confession was, like the Bohemian Confession of 1535, patterned after the Augsburg Confession.* It emphasizes both justification by faith alone and good works as the fruit of salvation. Baptism and the Eucharist are the focus of the sacramental section, although the five traditional Catholic sacraments are also listed for the Utraquists. Though it was eventually accepted in 1609 by Rudolf II (1552–1612), the Thirty Years' War (1618–1648) rendered the confession moot.

Samuel Bolton (1606–1654). English Anglican minister. Bolton served a number of parishes in London before being elected to the Westminster Assembly. He spent the remainder of his career as master of Christ's College, Cambridge. A number of his writings were published, including works on sin, the sacraments, and Christian freedom.

Book of Common Prayer (1549; 1552). After the Church of England's break with Rome, it needed a liturgical manual to distinguish its theology and practice from that of Catholicism. Thomas Cranmer* drafted the Book of Common Prayer based on the medieval Roman Missal, under the dual influence of the revised Lutheran Mass and the reforms of the Spanish Cardinal Quiñones. This manual details the eucharistic service, as well as services for rites such as baptism, confirmation, marriage and funerals. It includes a matrix of the epistle and Gospel readings and the appropriate collect for each Sunday and feast day of the church year. The 1548 Act of Uniformity established the Book of Common Prayer as *the* authoritative liturgical manual for the Church of England, to be implemented everywhere by Pentecost 1549. After its 1552 revision, Queen Mary I banned it; Elizabeth I* reestablished it in 1559, although it was rejected by Puritans and Catholics alike.

The Book of Homilies (1547; 1563; 1570). This collection of approved sermons, published in three parts during the reigns of Edward VI and Elizabeth I,* was intended to inculcate Anglican theological distinctives and mitigate the problems raised by the lack of educated preachers. Addressing doctrinal and practical topics, Thomas Cranmer* likely wrote the majority of the first twelve sermons, published in 1547; John Jewel* added another twenty sermons in 1563. A final sermon, *A Homily Against Disobedience*, was appended to the canon in 1570. Reprinted regularly, the *Book of Homilies* was an important resource in Anglican preaching until at least the end of the seventeenth century.

Martin (Cellarius) Borrhaus (1499–1564). German Reformed theologian. After a dispute with his mentor Johann Eck,* Borrhaus settled in Wittenberg, where he was influenced by the radical Zwickau Prophets. He travelled extensively, and finally settled in Basel to teach philosophy and Old Testament. Despite his objections, many accused Borrhaus of Anabaptism; he argued that baptism was a matter of conscience. On account of his association with Sebastian Castellio (1515–1563) and Michael Servetus (1511–1553), some scholars posit that Borrhaus was an antitrinitarian. His writings include a treatise on the Trinity and commentaries on the Torah, historical books, Ecclesiastes and Isaiah.

Sigmund Bosch (unknown). German Anabaptist hymn writer. An elder in the Swiss and South German Anabaptist churches, Bosch collaborated with Pilgram Marpeck* in his ministry. He is known to have composed three hymns and a letter on the end times, which he addressed to the congregation in Austerlitz.

John Bourchier (d. 1660). English Puritan parliamentarian. Bourchier served as a justice of the peace in Yorkshire until imprisoned at the outbreak of the English Civil War. After his release, he was elected as the member of parliament for Ripon, and in this capacity he served as a judge at the trial of Charles I and signed the king's death warrant. Deemed too ill for trial with the other regicides, he died soon after the Restoration of the monarchy under Charles II.

John Bowle (d. 1637). Anglican pastor. After matriculating from Cambridge, Bowle was household pastor to Sir Robert Cecil (1563–1612) and held a pastorate at Tilehurst in Berkshire. He was appointed dean of Salisbury in 1620 and bishop of Rochester in 1629.

John Boys (1571–1625). Anglican priest and theologian. Before doctoral work at Cambridge, Boys pastored several parishes in Kent; after completing his studies he was appointed to more prominent positions, culminating in his 1619 appointment as the Dean of Canterbury by James I.* Boys published a popular four-volume postil of the Gospel and epistle readings for the church year, as well as a companion volume for the Psalms.

John Bradford (1510–1555). English Reformer, prebendary of St. Paul's, and martyr. Bradford was born in Blackley, Manchester, to an affluent family. After grammar school, Bradford at first began legal studies at the Inner Temple in London. However, while there, he heard the preaching of a fellow student, and thus converted to an evangelical faith. This conversion caused Bradford to abandon his study of law and enroll at St. Catherine's Hall, Cambridge, to study theology. He completed his MA in 1549, and in the same year, received an appointment of fellow at Pembroke Hall, Cambridge. In August, 1550, Bishop Nicholas Ridley ordained Bradford a deacon, and appointed him his personal chaplain. Bradford's exceptional preaching moved King Edward VI to select him as his chaplain and prebendary at St. Paul's Cathedral. After Mary Tudor succeeded her half-brother to throne, Bradford was tried and convicted of heresy on January 31, 1555. He was executed at the stake on July 1 of the same year.

Anne Bradstreet (1612–1672). English-American Puritan poet. Born in Northampton, Bradstreet married at sixteen and emigrated to the Massachusetts Bay Colony, of which both her father and husband would serve as governors. Mother to eight children, Bradstreet also wrote poetry. Much of her verse reflects on marriage, children, and her Puritan faith. While her writing received a mixed reception from contemporaries, many of whom viewed poetry as outside a woman's purview, she is today celebrated as the most significant early English poet in North America.

Thieleman Jans van Braght (1625–1664). Dutch Radical preacher. After demonstrating great ability with languages, this cloth merchant was made preacher in his hometown of Dordrecht in 1648. He served in this office for the next sixteen years, until his death. This celebrated preacher had a reputation for engaging in debate wherever an opportunity presented itself, particularly concerning infant baptism. The publication of his book of martyrs, *Het Bloedigh Tooneel of Martelaersspiegel* (1660; *Martyrs' Mirror*), proved to be his lasting contribution to the Mennonite tradition. *Martyrs' Mirror* is heavily indebted to the earlier martyr book *Offer des Heeren* (1562), to which Braght added many early church martyrs who rejected infant baptism, as well as over 800 contemporary martyrs.

David Bramley (unknown). English lay preacher. Two works by Bramley survive, an exposition of Matthew 11:25 and a treatise arguing for the acceptance of lay preachers without university training like himself. On both tracts, he is identified simply as a "Preacher of the Gospel."

Johannes Brenz (1499–1570). German Lutheran theologian and pastor. Brenz was converted to the reformation cause after hearing Martin Luther* speak; later, Brenz became a student of Johannes Oecolampadius.* His central achievement lay in his talent for organization. As city preacher in Schwäbisch-Hall and afterward in Württemberg and Tübingen, he oversaw the introduction of reform measures and doctrines and new governing structures for ecclesial and educational communities. Brenz also helped establish Lutheran orthodoxy through treatises, commentaries and catechisms. He defended Luther's position on eucharistic presence against Huldrych Zwingli* and opposed the death penalty for religious dissenters.

Guillaume Briçonnet (1470–1534). French Catholic abbot and bishop. Briçonnet created a short-lived circle of reformist-minded humanists in his diocese under the sponsorship of Marguerite d'Angoulême. His desire for ecclesial reform developed throughout his prestigious career (including positions as royal chaplain to the queen, abbot at Saint-Germain-des-Prés and bishop of Meaux), influenced by Jacques Lefèvre d'Étaples.* Briçonnet encouraged reform through ministerial visitation, Scripture and preaching in the vernacular and active study of the Bible. When this triggered the ire of the theology faculty at the Sorbonne in Paris, Briçonnet quelled the activity and departed, envisioning an ecclesial reform that proceeded hierarchically.

William Bridge (1600?–1670). English Puritan minister. Bridge ministered in Norfolk and Essex until excommunicated as a Nonconformist and exiled, leading him to Rotterdam, where he copastored a church with Jeremiah Burroughs.* Returning to England, he was a member of the Westminster Assembly and pastored at Great Yarmouth until ejected from the ministry by the Act of Uniformity (1662). Many of Bridge's sermons were published during his life, and he also composed a number of works designed to encourage struggling believers.

Walter Bridges (unknown). English Anglican minister. Three works are attributed to Bridges. Two were published anonymously, a sermon on Joab before the House of Commons and a catechism for those taking the Eucharist, while a third, a sermon on unity given before the Lord Mayor and Aldermen of London, names him and his position as preacher at St. Dunstans-in-the-East, London.

Thomas Brightman (1562–1607). English Puritan pastor and exegete. Under alleged divine inspiration, Brightman wrote a well known commentary on Revelation, influenced by Joachim of Fiore (d. 1202). In contrast to the putatively true churches of Geneva and Scotland, he depicted the Church of England as a type of the lukewarm Laodicean church. He believed that the Reformation would result in the defeat of the Vatican and the Ottoman Empire and that all humanity would be regenerated through the spread of the gospel before Christ's final return and judgment.

Hugh Broughton (1549–1612). English Puritan Hebraist and theologian. Following his time as a student and fellow at Cambridge, Broughton established himself as a scholar and preacher in London. His first work, *A Concent of Scripture* (1588), an attempt to harmonize the chronology of Scripture, caused significant controversy and led him to spend much of the next two decades traveling throughout Europe. On the Continent, he built a reputation in disputes with numerous Jewish, Catholic, and Protestant scholars and helped to plant an English Reformed church in Amsterdam, a congregation he may also have pastored for a time. Broughton's extensive writings include comments on numerous aspects of the Old Testament and New Testaments, a genealogy of Christ, and an explication of Christ's descent into hell.

Robert Browne (c. 1550–1633). English Nonconformist minister. While drawn to Puritan teachings, Browne began his career within the Church of England, ministering in London and Cambridge. Convinced that more radical reformation was needed outside the constraints of the state, Browne is recognized as the first to found a separatist church, establishing a congregation in Norwich, with those who followed him becoming known as Brownists. After a brief imprisonment, he left for Middelburg in the Netherlands, gathering a church based on the principles he espoused in his two most important works, *A Treatise of Reformation Without Tarrying* (1582) and *The Life and Manners of All True Christians* (1582), which set forth the foundations of congregationalist church government. Browne did not remain a separatist, however, and after a few years returned to England and reentered the Church of England, serving as a school headmaster and pastoring in Northamptonshire.

Otto Brunfels (c. 1488–1534). German Lutheran botanist, teacher and physician. Brunfels joined the Carthusian order, where he developed interests in the natural sciences and became involved with a humanist circle associated with Ulrich von Hutten and Wolfgang Capito.* In 1521, after coming into contact with Luther's* teaching, Brunfels abandoned the monastic life, traveling and spending time in botanical research and pastoral care. He received a medical degree in Basel and was appointed city physician of Bern in 1534. Brunfels penned defenses of Luther and Hutten, devotional biographies of biblical figures, a prayer book, and annotations on the Gospels and the Acts of the Apostles. His most influential contribution, however, is as a Renaissance botanist.

Martin Bucer (1491–1551). German Reformed theologian and pastor. A Dominican friar, Bucer was influenced by Desiderius Erasmus* during his doctoral studies at the University of Heidelberg, where he began corresponding with Martin Luther.* After advocating reform in Alsace, Bucer was excommunicated and fled to Strasbourg, where he became a leader in the city's Reformed ecclesial and educational communities. Bucer sought concord between Lutherans and Zwinglians and Protestants and Catholics. He emigrated to England, becoming a professor at Cambridge. Bucer's greatest theological concern was the centrality of Christ's sacrificial death, which achieved justification and sanctification and orients Christian community.

Johannes Bugenhagen (1485–1558). German Lutheran pastor and professor. Bugenhagen, a priest and lecturer at a Premonstratensian monastery, became a city preacher in Wittenberg during the reform efforts of Martin Luther* and Philipp Melanchthon.* Initially influenced by his reading of Desiderius Erasmus,* Bugenhagen grew in evangelical orientation through Luther's works; later, he studied under Melanchthon at the University of Wittenberg, eventually serving as rector and faculty member there. Bugenhagen was a versatile commentator, exegete and lecturer on Scripture. Through these roles and his development of lectionary and devotional material, Bugenhagen facilitated rapid establishment of church order throughout many German provinces.

Henry Bull (d. 1575?). English Protestant theologian and martyrologist. Little is known about Bull's circumstances after he was expelled from Magdalen College, Oxford, for snatching the censer from the hand of a priest officiating Mass. A committed reformer, he edited, translated, compiled, and published a number of Protestant works, including a book of prayers and meditations and writings by John Hooper* and Martin Luther.* He also worked alongside John Foxe* in the compilation of *Acts and Monuments*, while Miles Coverdale's* *The Letters of the Martyrs* is largely Bull's work.

Heinrich Bullinger (1504–1575). Swiss Reformed pastor and theologian. Bullinger succeeded Huldrych Zwingli* as minister and leader in Zurich. The primary author of the First and Second Helvetic Confessions,* Bullinger was drawn toward reform through the works of Martin Luther* and Philipp Melanchthon.* After Zwingli died, Bullinger was vital in maintaining adherence to the cause of reform; he oversaw the expansion of the Zurich synodal system while preaching, teaching and writing extensively. One of Bullinger's lasting legacies was the development of a federal view of the divine covenant with humanity, making baptism and the Eucharist covenantal signs.

Heinrich Bünting (1545–1606). Lutheran theologian and pastor. Bünting was born in Hanover, Germany, and studied theology at the University of Wittenberg, where he graduated in 1569. Upon finishing his studies at Wittenberg, Bünting became a pastor at Lemgo, where he was dismissed in 1575. Afterward he moved to Gronau an der Leine, where he served until his appointment as superintendent in Goslar. However, due to controversy over some of his teachings, Bünting was relieved of his position in 1600, retiring thereafter to Hanover, where he lived the remainder of his life. Bünting's most notable work is his *Itinerarium Sacrae Scripturae* (1581), a summary of biblical geography. Throughout this treatise, Bünting follows the travels of various major biblical figures, highlighting their theological as well as exegetical importance. When published, the *Itinerarium Sacrae Scripturae* was the most complete summary of biblical geography. Among the work's distinctive features is its collection of maps.

John Bunyan (1628–1688). English Puritan preacher and writer. His *Pilgrim's Progress* is one of the best-selling English-language titles in history. Born to a working-class family, Bunyan was largely unschooled, gaining literacy (and entering the faith) through reading the Bible and such early Puritan devotional works as *The Plain Man's Pathway to Heaven* and *The Practice of Piety*. Following a short stint in Oliver Cromwell's parliamentary army, in which Bunyan narrowly escaped death in combat, he turned to a preaching ministry, succeeding John Gifford as pastor at the Congregational church in Bedford. A noted preacher, Bunyan drew large crowds in itinerant appearances and it was in the sermonic form that Bunyan developed his theological outlook, which was an Augustinian-inflected Calvinism. Bunyan's opposition to the Book of Common Prayer and refusal of official ecclesiastical licensure led to multiple imprisonments, where he wrote many of his famous allegorical works, including *Pilgrim's Progress, The Holy City, Prison Meditations* and *Holy War*.

Michelangelo Buonarroti (1475–1564). Italian Catholic artist and poet. Michelangelo was born in Florence but spent the majority of his career in Rome, completing artworks commissioned by the popes of the early sixteenth century. One of the most recognized artists of all time, his artworks include the *Pietà* (1499), *David* (1501–1504), the ceiling of the Sistine Chapel (1508–1512), *Moses* (1515), and the *Last Judgment* (1536–1541), which remain famous and have done much to shape Western aesthetics. Toward the end of his life, his interests shifted toward architecture, culminating with his contributions to the designs of St. Peter's Basilica in Rome. Michelangelo is thought to have been devoutly Catholic throughout his life, but recent scholarship has considered the complexity of his relationship with the Catholic Reformation and the Protestant movement.

Jeremiah Burroughs (c. 1600–1646). English Puritan pastor and delegate to the Westminster Assembly. Burroughs left Cambridge, as well as a rectorate in Norfolk, because of his nonconformity. After returning to England from pastoring an English congregation in Rotterdam for several years (1637–1641), he became one of only a few dissenters from the official presbyterianism of the Assembly in favor of a congregationalist polity. Nevertheless, he was well known and respected by presbyterian colleagues such as Richard Baxter* for his irenic tone and conciliatory manner. The vast majority of Burroughs's corpus was published posthumously, although during his lifetime he published annotations on Hosea and several polemical works.

William Burton (d. 1616). English Puritan minister. Burton first ministered in Norwich, where he was present for the burning of Francis Kett (d. 1589) for Arianism. He later pastored in Bristol, Reading, and London. Throughout his life, he published a number of his sermons and treatises as well as a brief catechism.

Anthony Cade (d. 1641). Anglican pastor. Cade served as tutor and chaplain to George Villiers, First Duke of Buckingham (1592–1628), a close confidante of King James I* before holding a number of pastoral positions in Leicestershire and Northamptonshire.

Cardinal Cajetan (Thomas de Vio) (1469–1534). Italian Catholic cardinal, professor, theologian and biblical exegete. This Dominican monk was the leading Thomist theologian and one of the most important Catholic exegetes of the sixteenth century. Cajetan is best-known for his interview with Martin Luther* at the Diet of Augsburg (1518). Among his many works are polemical treatises, extensive biblical commentaries and most importantly a four-volume commentary (1508–1523) on the *Summa Theologiae* of Thomas Aquinas.*

Georg Calixtus (1586–1656). German Lutheran theologian. Calixtus studied at the University of Helmstedt where he developed regard for Philipp Melanchthon.* Between his time as a student and later as a professor at Helmstedt, Calixtus traveled through Europe seeking a way to unite and reconcile Lutherans, Calvinists and Catholics. He attempted to fuse these denominations through use of the Scriptures, the Apostles' Creed, and the first five centuries, interpreted by the Vincentian canon. Calixtus's position was stamped as syncretist and yielded further debate even after his death.

John Calvin (1509–1564). French Reformed pastor and theologian. John Calvin was born in Noyon, France. After receiving his primary education in the aristocratic family of Charles de Hangest, he attended the University of Paris to prepare for further study of theology. However, after completing his BA degree, as per his father's instructions, Calvin proceeded to the study of the law at Orleans of Bourges. While at Orleans, Calvin's interests in Greek and Latin literature were reawakened. Upon his father's death, Calvin resumed his study of classical literature at the newly founded College of Royal Readers in Paris under the direction of Guillaume Bude. The product of these studies was his commentary on Seneca's *De Clementia* (1532). Sometime between 1533 and 1534 Calvin experienced a "sudden conversion" due largely to the influence to Martin Luther's 1520 treatises. Calvin's embracing of an evangelical faith forced him to flee France. From there he went to Basel, where he wrote the first edition of his *Institutes of the Christian Religion* in 1536. The *Institutes* became a theological dogmatics for the Reformed churches. Calvin spent most of his career in Geneva (excepting a three-year ministry in Strasbourg with Martin Bucer*). In Geneva, Calvin reorganized the structure and governance of the church and established an academy that became an international center for theological education. He was a tireless writer, revising his *Institutes* several times, and authoring theological treatises as well as biblical commentaries. Calvin is also known for his debates with his contemporaries, including Michael Servetus, whose anti-Trinitarian views led to his execution in Geneva in 1553. Calvin also maintained friendly correspondence with many reformers, including Melanchthon* and Bullinger*, the latter of whom he was able to come to an agreement with regarding the presence of Christ in the Lord's Supper with the signing of the *Consensus Tigurinus* in 1551, which brought a degree of unity between Geneva and Zurich and to the Reformed tradition. One of the foremost figures during the Reformation period, Calvin has an extensive exegetical and theological legacy.

Wolfgang Capito (1478?–1541). German Reformed humanist and theologian. Capito, a Hebrew scholar, produced a Hebrew grammar and published several Latin commentaries on books of the Hebrew Scriptures. He corresponded with Desiderius Erasmus* and fellow humanists. Capito translated Martin Luther's* early works into Latin for the printer Johann Froben. On meeting Luther, Capito was converted to Luther's vision, left Mainz and settled in Strasbourg, where he lectured on Luther's theology to the city clergy. With Martin Bucer,* Capito reformed liturgy, ecclesial life and teachings, education, welfare, and government. Capito worked for the theological unification of the Swiss cantons with Strasbourg.

Pietro Carnesecchi (1508–1567). Italian humanist. Carnesecchi rose in the papal bureaucracy under Medici patronage, but after the death of Clement VII* he began to deviate from Catholic orthodoxy, aligning himself with Juan de Valdés.* While he retained relations with the established church, he also read Protestant works by theologians such as Luther,* Calvin,* and Bucer,* and his only extant doctrinal writing defends Bucer's view of the Eucharist over that of Zwingli.* Carnesecchi was able to avoid arrest by the Inquisition for a time, and his condemnation to death in absentia was pardoned under Pope Pius IV (1499–1565). However, Pius V (1504–1572) was a longtime opponent of Carnesecchi, and upon his election to the papal office, reopened the case and those of a number of others suspected of Protestant leanings. While seeking refuge in Florence, Carnesecchi was betrayed to the Inquisition by Cosimo I de' Medici, and following trial he was beheaded.

François Carrière (d. 1665). French Catholic theologian. A Franciscan doctor of theology, Carrière composed a commentary on the whole Bible, a summary of Catholic doctrine, and a history of the papacy.

John Carter (1554–1635). English Puritan minister. After graduating from Cambridge, Carter served as vicar at Bramford, Suffolk, until disputes over his Puritanism within the congregation led him to be moved to the nearby parish of Belstead.

Thomas Cartwright (1535–1606). English Puritan preacher and professor. Cartwright was educated at St. John's College, Cambridge, although as an influential leader of the Presbyterian party in the Church of England he was continually at odds with the Anglican party, especially John Whitgift.* Cartwright spent some time as an exile in Geneva and Heidelberg as well as in Antwerp, where he pastored an English church. In 1585, Cartwright was arrested and eventually jailed for trying to return to England despite Elizabeth I's* refusal of his request. Many acknowledged him to be learned but also quite cantankerous. His publications include commentaries on Colossians, Ecclesiastes, Proverbs and the Gospels, as well as a dispute against Whitgift on church discipline.

Mathew Caylie (unknown). English Protestant minister. Caylie authored *The Cleansing of the Ten Lepers* (1623), an exposition of Luke 17:14-18.

Jan Cents (Unknown). Dutch Anabaptist. Believed to be a leader of the Anabaptist congregation in Amsterdam, Cents was the first signer and possibly author of a confession intended to unite Frisian and High German Mennonites.

John Chardon (d. 1601). Irish Anglican bishop. Chardon was educated at Oxford. He advocated Reformed doctrine in his preaching, yet opposed those Puritans who rejected Anglican church order. He published several sermons.

Christian Chemnitz (1615–1666). German Lutheran theologian. Grandnephew of Martin Chemnitz,* Christian Chemnitz was principal at the high school in Jena before serving the church as a deacon and archdeacon in Weimer and Braunschweig then as superintendent in Eisenach. Returning to Jena, he received his doctorate and replaced John Major as professor of theology, also serving as dean of the theology faculty and rector of the university. He wrote on numerous biblical, pastoral, and controversial topics, with his works including a defense of Lutheranism, instructions for young ministers, and a series of sermons on judgement.

Martin Chemnitz (1522–1586). German Lutheran theologian. A leading figure in establishing Lutheran orthodoxy, Chemnitz studied theology and patristics at the University of Wittenburg, later becoming a defender of Philipp Melanchthon's* interpretation of the doctrine of justification. Chemnitz drafted a compendium of doctrine and reorganized the structure of the church in Wolfenbüttel; later, he led efforts to reconcile divisions within Lutheranism, culminating in the Formula of Concord*. One of his chief theological accomplishments was a modification of the christological doctrine of the *communicatio idiomatium*, which provided a Lutheran platform for understanding the sacramental presence of Christ's humanity in the Eucharist.

David Chytraeus (1531–1600). German Lutheran professor, theologian and biblical exegete. At the age of eight Chytraeus was admitted to the University of Tübingen. There he studied law, philology, philosophy, and theology, finally receiving his master's degree in 1546. Chytraeus befriended Philipp Melanchthon* while sojourning in Wittenberg, where he taught the *Loci communes*. While teaching exegesis at the University of Rostock Chytraeus became acquainted with Tilemann Heshusius,* who strongly influenced Chytraeus away from Philippist theology. As a defender of Gnesio-Lutheran theology Chytraeus helped organize churches throughout Austria in accordance with the Augsburg Confession.* Chytraeus coauthored the Formula of Concord* with Martin Chemnitz,* Andreas Musculus (1514–1581), Nikolaus Selnecker* and Jakob Andreae.* He wrote commentaries on most of the Bible, as well as a devotional work titled *Regula vitae* (1555) that described the Christian virtues.

David Clarkson (1622–1686). English Puritan theologian. After his dismissal from the pastorate on account of the Act of Uniformity (1662), little is known about Clarkson. At the end of his life he ministered with John Owen* in London.

Robert Cleaver (1571–1613). English Puritan pastor. Cleaver served as rector at Drayton in Oxfordshire until silenced by Archbishop Richard Bancroft for advocating Nonconformity. Despite opposition from ecclesiastical authorities, Cleaver enjoyed a reputation as an excellent preacher. His published works include sermons on Hebrews 4 and Song of Songs 2 as well as one on the last chapter of Proverbs. Cleaver also authored *The Parsimony of Christian Children*, which contained a defense of infant baptism against Baptist criticisms.

George Close (unknown). English Protestant preacher. A series of Close's sermons on Matthew 16 were copied and published while he served as a reader at St. Antholin, London.

Michael Cobabus (d. 1686). German Lutheran theologian and mathematician. Trained in philosophy, mathematics, and theology at the University of Rostock, Cobabus remained in the city, serving as rector of the city school until appointed professor of mathematics at the university. He later received a doctorate in theology from the University of Griefswald and exchanged his position in the Rostock mathematics faculty for a professorship in theology.

Johannes Cocceius (1603–1669). German Reformed theologian. Cocceius first served as professor of biblical philology in his hometown of Bremen before moving to Franeker, where he taught Hebrew and theology, and finally to Leiden, where he spent the majority of his career as professor of theology. Cocceius is perhaps best remembered for his exposition of Reformed federal theology, defining the relationship between humanity and God in terms of progressive covenants. His critics, chief among them Gisbertus Voetius (1589–1676), argued that Cocceius's view of salvation history ignored the unity of the Scriptures and spiritualized the Old Testament. His other writings are extensive, including commentaries on all the books of the Bible, an influential Hebrew and Aramaic lexicon, and numerous works on theology, ethics, and philology.

John Colet (1467–1519). English Catholic priest, preacher and educator. Colet, appointed dean of Saint Paul's Cathedral by Henry VII, was a friend of Desiderius Erasmus,* on whose classical ideals Colet reconstructed the curriculum of Saint Paul's school. Colet was convinced that the foundation of moral reform lay in the education of children. Though an ardent advocate of reform, Colet, like Erasmus, remained loyal to the Catholic Church throughout his life. Colet's agenda of reform was oriented around spiritual and ethical themes, demonstrated in his commentaries on select books of the New Testament and the writings of Pseudo-Dionysius the Areopagite.

Vittoria Colonna (1490–1547). Italian Renaissance poet. Born into a noble family, Colonna was betrothed at three years of age to Fernando d'Ávalos (1489–1525), and they married in 1509. D'Ávalos was largely absent on military campaigns during their marriage, while she exercised his governorship of Benvenuto and became involved in the literary circles of Rome and Naples. One of the most important writers of her age, her friends included Pietro Bembo (1470–1547), Marguerite de Navarre,* and Michelangelo Buonarroti.* Writing primarily in the Petrarchan style, Colonna's reputation as a poet grew after the death of her husband, and much of her poetry was dedicated to his memory. Spiritual concerns form a major element of Colonna's writings, promoting contemplation and the ascetic life. While denied her desire to take holy orders in widowhood, Colonna spent much of her life residing in religious communities, and she was actively involved in movements seeking their improvement, collaborating with reformers such as Reginald Pole,* Juan de Valdés,* and Bernardo Ochino.*

Gasparo Contarini (1483–1542). Italian statesman, theologian and reform-minded cardinal. Contarini was an able negotiator and graceful compromiser. Charles V requested Contarini as the papal legate for the Colloquy of Regensburg (1541), where Contarini reached agreement with Melanchthon* on the doctrine of justification (although neither the pope nor Luther* ratified the agreement). He had come to a similar belief in the priority of faith in the work of Christ rather than works as the basis for Christian life in 1511, though unlike Luther, he never left the papal church over the issue; instead he remainied within it to try to seek gentle reform, and he adhered to papal sacramental teaching. Contarini was an important voice for reform within the Catholic Church, always seeking reconciliation rather than confrontation with Protestant reformers. He wrote many works, including a treatise detailing the ideal bishop, a manual for lay church leaders, a political text on right governance and brief commentaries on the Pauline letters.

Christoph Corner (1518–1594). German Lutheran theologian. Professor of philosophy, rhetoric, and theology at the University of Frankfurt, Corner participated in the drafting of the Formula of Concord.* He also served as superintendent of churches in Mark Brandenberg.

Antonio del Corro (1527–1591). Spanish Reformed pastor and theologian. After encountering the ideas of Martin Luther* and other reformers, Corro abandoned the Hieronymite order. Leaving Spain to avoid charges of heresy, he traveled through Europe, spending time in Geneva and Lausanne before pastoring churches in France and the Low Countries. The arrival of Spanish armies in the Netherlands saw Corro and his family relocate to England, where he pastored a church of Spanish exiles in London and taught at Temple Church and Oxford. Corro courted controversy throughout his career, entering into debates with a wide array of Protestant theologians. In England, he was suspended from his pastorate for slander and examined a number of times for heresy, with some finding suggestions of Arianism in his Christology. Although these charges were never upheld, they clouded his later career and legacy.

Antonius Corvinus (1501–1553). German Lutheran theologian and administrator. After meeting Luther* and Melanchthon,* Corvinus left the humanist circle of Erasmus* to serve as a pastor in cities including Goslar, Witzenhausen, and Pattensen. A signatory of the Schmalkald Articles,* much of his career was devoted to constructing the organizational apparatus of the Lutheran church, and he established disciplinary procedures and church orders for numerous cities in northern Germany. His expository postils on the Gospels, Epistles, Psalms, and Genesis were also distributed widely in order to aid preachers of the region.

John Cosin (1594–1672). Anglican preacher and bishop. Early in his career Cosin was the vice chancellor of Cambridge and canon at the Durham cathedral. But as a friend of William Laud* and an advocate for "Laudian" changes, he was suspected of being a crypto-Catholic. In 1640 during the Long Parliament a Puritan lodged a complaint with the House of Commons concerning Cosin's "popish innovations." Cosin was promptly removed from office. During the turmoil of the English Civil Wars, Cosin sojourned in Paris among English nobility but struggled financially. Cosin returned to England after the Restoration in 1660 to be consecrated as the bishop of Durham. He published annotations on the Book of Common Prayer* and a history of the canon.

John Cotton (1584–1652). New England Puritan minister. Cotton was born to Puritan parents in Derby, England. He entered Trinity College, Cambridge, graduating with his bachelor's degree in 1603. Afterward, Cotton became a fellow at Emmanuel College, Cambridge, which at the time was heavily influenced by Puritanism. There, Cotton finished his master's degree in 1606. Cotton then served as head lecturer, dean, and catechist for the college. It was in this period that he heard the preaching of Richard Sibbes,* which proved instrumental in Cotton's personal conversion. Cotton received a bachelor of divinity in 1610 from Cambridge and was shortly thereafter ordained into the priesthood of the Church of England. However, Cotton's increasing nonconformity brought him into conflict with episcopal authorities, which prompted him to move to the colony of Massachusetts in July 1633. Upon his arrival, he immediately assumed a position of leadership as the teacher of the First Church of Boston. Throughout his tenure, Cotton exerted significant influence in the civic and ecclesiastical affairs of the colony. He continued in his ministry at First Church until his death on December 23, 1652. Over the course of his ministry, Cotton wrote nearly forty works. Among these were the *Keys of the Kingdom of Heaven, and the Power Thereof* (1644) and *Exposition upon the Thirteenth Chapter of Revelation* (1655).

Council of Constance (1414–1418). Convened to resolve the Western Schism, root out heresy and reform the church in head and members, the council asserted in *Sacrosancta* (1415) the immediate authority of ecumenical councils assembled in the Holy Spirit under Christ—even over the pope. Martin V was elected pope in 1417 after the three papal claimants were deposed; thus, the council ended the schism. The council condemned Jan Hus,* Jerome of Prague (c. 1365–1416) and, posthumously, John Wycliffe. Hus and Jerome, despite letters of safe conduct, were burned at the stake. Their deaths ignited the Hussite Wars, which ended as a result of the Council of Basel's concessions to the Bohemian church. The council fathers sought to reform the church through the regular convocation of councils (*Frequens*; 1417). Martin V begrudgingly complied by calling the required councils, then immediately disbanding them. Pius II (r. 1458–1464) reasserted papal dominance through *Execrabilis* (1460), which condemned any appeal to a future council apart from the pope's authority.

Council of Trent (1545–1563) Convoked by Pope Paul III (r. 1534–1549) with the support of Charles V*, the nineteenth ecumenical council was convened in the northern Italian city of Trent. Attended primarily by Italian clerics, it met in three distinct phases. Beginning in December 1545, during its first eight sessions, the council issued doctrinal decrees, asserting the authority of tradition alongside Scripture, the authenticity of the Vulgate, the prerogative of the church in interpretation, and the necessity of human cooperation in the work of salvation. Ecclesial abuses were also addressed, as attempts were made to eliminate absenteeism and pluralism and devolve power from Rome to bishoprics and parishes. The council was suspended following the outbreak of the plague in Trent in March 1547. A number of Protestant delegates were present during the second phase of the council, which met between May 1551 and April 1552 under the supervision of Pope Julius III (r. 1550–1555). The primary achievement of this period of the council was the clarification of teachings on the seven sacraments, with transubstantiation, the objective efficacy of the Eucharist, and the necessity of auricular confession confirmed as dogma. Reconvened by Pope Pius IV (r. 1559–1565) in 1561, the third phase of the council addressed the relationship between bishops and Rome, resulting in affirmations of the divine appointment of the church hierarchy and the obligation of bishops to reside in their dioceses. Clerical education, the regulation of marriage, and teachings on purgatory, indulgences, the use of images, and the saints were also addressed.

Miles Coverdale (1488–1568). Anglican bishop. Coverdale is known for his translations of the Bible into English, completing William Tyndale's* efforts and later producing the Great Bible commissioned by Henry VIII* (1539). A former friar, Coverdale was among the Cambridge scholars who met at the White Horse Tavern to discuss Martin Luther's* ideas. During Coverdale's three terms of exile in Europe, he undertook various translations, including the Geneva Bible*. He was appointed bishop of Exeter by Thomas Cranmer* and served as chaplain to Edward VI. Coverdale contributed to Cranmer's first edition of the Book of Common Prayer.*

William Cowper (Couper) (1568–1619). Scottish Puritan bishop. After graduating from the University of St. Andrews, Cowper worked in parish ministry for twenty-five years before becoming bishop. As a zealous Puritan and advocate of regular preaching and rigorous discipline, Cowper championed Presbyterian polity and lay participation in church government. Cowper published devotional works, sermon collections and a commentary on Revelation.

Benjamin Coxe (fl. 1646). English Baptist minister. Coxe began his career in the Church of England, ministering at parishes in Devonshire, Bedford, and Coventry. After preaching against infant baptism, he was challenged to a public debate by Richard Baxter.* Coxe lost and was briefly arrested after refusing to leave the city. Following his release, he joined a congregation of Anabaptists in London.

Walter Cradock (1606–1659). Welsh Anglican minister. Cradock was born in Llangwm, Monmouthshire, Wales. After completing his education at the University of Oxford, Cradock assumed his first position as curate at Peterson-super-Ely, Glamorgan. In 1633, Cradock, along with some other Welsh ministers, was reported to Archbishop William Laud* and the Court of High Commission for preaching nonconformity and for refusing the *Book of Sports*. In 1634 Cradock traveled throughout Wexham and Herefordshire encouraging the establishment of Welsh Nonconformist congregations. Cradock later became pastor of an Independent congregation at Llanfair Waterdine in 1639. When the English Civil War began, Cradock and his conventicle moved to Bristol, but when Royalist forces came to occupy the city, he and some of his group departed for All-Hallows-the-Great, where he preached regularly with Henry Jessey (1603–1663). In 1641, Cradock was among the group of preachers for Wales commissioned by the Long Parliament. Later, he served as regular preacher for the Barebones Parliament. Throughout this period, Cradock was an ardent supporter of Oliver Cromwell. Cradock lived the remainder of his life quietly while ministering to a congregation at Llangwm. Throughout his career, Cradock authored a number of devotional works, among which were *Gospel Liberty* (1648) and *Gospel Holiness* (1655).

Thomas Cranmer (1489–1556). Anglican archbishop and theologian. Cranmer supervised church reform and produced the first two editions of the Book of Common Prayer.* As a doctoral student at Cambridge, he was involved in the discussions at the White Horse Tavern. Cranmer contributed to a religious defense of Henry VIII's* divorce; Henry then appointed him Archbishop of Canterbury. Cranmer cautiously steered the course of reform, accelerating under Edward VI. After supporting the attempted coup to prevent Mary's assuming the throne, Cranmer was convicted of treason and burned at the stake. Cranmer's legacy is the splendid English of his liturgy and prayer books.

Richard Crashaw (1612–1649). English Catholic poet. Educated at Cambridge, Crashaw was fluent in Hebrew, Greek and Latin. His first volume of poetry was *Epigrammatum sacrorum liber* (1634). Despite being born into a Puritan family, Crashaw was attracted to Catholicism, finally converting in 1644 after he was forced to resign his fellowship for not signing the Solemn League and Covenant (1643). In 1649, he was made a subcanon of Our Lady of Loretto by Cardinal Palotta.

Herbert Croft (1603–1691). Anglican bishop. As a boy Croft converted to Catholicism; he returned to the Church of England during his studies at Oxford. Before the English Civil Wars, he served as chaplain to Charles I. After the Restoration, Charles II appointed him as bishop. Croft ardently opposed Catholicism in his later years.

John Crompe (d. 1661). Anglican priest. Educated at Cambridge, Crompe published a commentary on the Apostles' Creed, a sermon on Psalm 21:3 and an exposition of Christ's passion.

Oliver Cromwell (1599–1658). Commander of the Parliamentary forces during the English Civil War. Lord Protector of the Commonwealth of England, Scotland, and Ireland. Cromwell was born in Huntingdon, East Anglia, the only surviving son of Robert Cromwell. In 1616, he enrolled at the University of Cambridge as a fellow commoner. However, he withdrew from the university the following year due to his father's death. He represented Huntingdon in Parliament in 1628, and later Cambridge in the Short and Long Parliaments. During the Civil War, he commanded the Parliamentary forces, which he led to victory at the Battles of Marston Moor (1644) and Naseby (1645). After the execution of King Charles I in 1649, he became a member of the Council of State. It was at this time that the monarchy was abolished. In 1653, he was elevated to the position of Lord Protector of the Commonwealth. He declined the crown, though it was offered him in 1657. As Lord Protector, he endeavored to lead the postwar recovery, suppress military resistance, and advance British influence throughout Europe and the world. Moreover, he promoted a limited religious toleration in the kingdoms of England, Scotland, and Ireland. After his death in 1658, his son Richard (1626–1712) succeeded him as Lord Protector. However, due to incompetence, Richard was forced to resign, which paved the way for the Restoration of the monarchy in 1660 with the ascension of Charles II (1630–1685) to the throne. One year after the Restoration, Oliver Cromwell's body was disinterred from Westminster Abbey, hung on the gallows at Tyburn, and cast into an unmarked grave.

Caspar Cruciger (1504–1548). German Lutheran theologian. Recognized for his alignment with the theological views of Philipp Melanchthon,* Cruciger was a scholar respected among both Protestants and Catholics. In 1521, Cruciger came Wittenberg to study Hebrew and remained there most of his life. He became a valuable partner for Martin Luther* in translating the Old Testament and served as teacher, delegate to major theological colloquies and rector. Cruciger was an agent of reform in his birthplace of Leipzig, where at the age of fifteen he had observed the disputation between Luther and Johann Eck.*

Elisabeth Cruciger (c. 1500–1535). German Lutheran hymnist. Following her conversion to Lutheranism, Cruciger left the Praemonstratensian order and relocated to Wittenberg, where she married Caspar Cruciger.* While her authorship has been contested, recent scholarship has assigned Cruciger the place of the first female Lutheran hymnist for her composition of "Lord Christ is the Only Son of God" (Herr Christ der einig Gotts Sohn) (1524).

Ralph Cudworth (d. 1624) English Protestant minister. Father of noted Cambridge Platonist Ralph Cudworth (1617–1688), the elder Cudworth was a fellow of Emanuel College, Cambridge and rector of Aller in Somersetshire.

Marguerite d'Angoulême (1492–1549). French Catholic noblewoman. The elder sister of King Francis I of France, Marguerite was the Queen of Navarre and Duchess of Alençon and Berry. She was a poet and author of the French Renaissance. She composed *The Mirror of a Sinful Soul* (1531)—condemned by the theologians of the Sorbonne for containing Lutheran ideas—and an unfinished collection of short stories, the Heptaméron (1558). A leading figure in the French Reformation, Marguerite was at the center of a network of reform-minded individuals that included Guillame Briçonnet,* Jacques Lefèvre d'Etaples,* Gérard Roussel (1500–1550) and Guillame Farel (1489–1565).

Jakob Dachser (1486–1567). German Anabaptist theologian and hymnist. Dachser served as a Catholic priest in Vienna until he was imprisoned and then exiled for defending the Lutheran understanding of the Mass and fasting. Hans Hut* rebaptized him in Augsburg, where Dachser was appointed as a leader of the Anabaptist congregation. Lutheran authorities imprisoned him for nearly four years. In 1531 he recanted his Radical beliefs and began to catechize children with the permission of the city council. Dachser was expelled from

Augsburg as a possible insurrectionist in 1552 and relocated to Pfalz-Neuberg. He published a number of poems, hymns and mystical works, and he versified several psalms.

Jean Daillé (1594–1670). French Reformed pastor. Born into a devout Reformed family, Daillé studied theology and philosophy at Saumur under the most influential contemporary lay leader in French Protestantism, Philippe Duplessis-Mornay (1549–1623). Daillé held to Amyraldianism—the belief that Christ died for all humanity inclusively, not particularly for the elect who would inherit salvation (though only the elect are in fact saved). He wrote a controversial treatise on the church fathers that aggravated many Catholic and Anglican scholars because of Daillé's apparent demotion of patristic authority in matters of faith.

Lambert Daneau (1530?–1595). French Reformed pastor and theologian. After a decade of pastoring in France, following the St. Bartholomew's Day Massacre, Daneau fled to Geneva to teach theology at the Academy. He later taught in the Low Countries, finishing his career in southern France. Daneau's diverse works include tracts on science, ethics and morality as well as numerous theological and exegetical works.

John Davenant (1576–1641). Anglican bishop and professor. Davenant attended Queen's College, Cambridge, where he received his doctorate and was appointed professor of divinity. During the Remonstrant controversy, James I* sent Davenant as one of the four representatives for the Church of England to the Synod of Dordrecht.* Following James's instructions, Davenant advocated a *via media* between the Calvinists and the Remonstrants, although in later years he defended against the rise of Arminianism in England. In 1621, Davenant was promoted to the bishopric of Salisbury, where he was generally receptive to Laudian reforms. Davenant's lectures on Colossians are his best-known work.

William Day (1605–1684). Anglican theologian. Born and raised in Windsor, Berkshire, Day received his early education from Eton College. Afterward, he matriculated at King's College, Cambridge, where he was elected a fellow in 1624. Day received his BA in 1629, and MA in 1632. In 1635, Day was incorporated MA at Oxford and in 1637 became vicar of Mapledurham, Oxfordshire. Throughout his long career, Day conformed to all the ecclesiastical changes dictated by the government through the Restoration, during which he retained his vicarage. Finally, Day was made divinity reader at the King's Chapel, Windsor Chapel. He published two commentaries, *An Exposition of the Book of the Prophet Isaiah* (1654) and *A Paraphrase and Commentary upon the Epistle of St. Paul to the Romans* (1666).

Defense of the Augsburg Confession (1531). See *Augsburg Confession.*

Hans Denck (c. 1500–1527). German Radical theologian. Denck, a crucial early figure of the German Anabaptist movement, combined medieval German mysticism with the radical sacramental theology of Andreas Bodenstein von Karlstadt* and Thomas Müntzer.* Denck argued that the exterior forms of Scripture and sacrament are symbolic witnesses secondary to the internally revealed truth of the Sprit in the human soul. This view led to his expulsion from Nuremberg in 1525; he spent the next two years in various centers of reform in the German territories. At the time of his death, violent persecution against Anabaptists was on the rise throughout northern Europe.

Stephen Denison (unknown). English Puritan pastor. Denison received the post of curate at St. Katherine Cree in London sometime in the 1610s, where he ministered until his ejection from office in 1635. During his career at St. Katherine Cree, Denison waded into controversy with both Puritans (over the doctrine of predestination) and Anglicans (over concerns about liturgical ceremonies). He approached both altercations with rancor and rigidity, although he seems to have been quite popular and beloved by most of his congregation. In 1631, William Laud* consecrated the newly renovated St. Katherine Cree, and as part of the festivities Denison offered a sermon on Luke 19:27 in which he publicly rebuked Laud for fashioning the Lord's house into a "den of robbers." Aside from the record of his quarrels, very little is known about Denison. In addition to *The White Wolf* (a 1627 sermon against another opponent), he published a catechism for children (1621), a treatise on the sacraments (1621) and a commentary on 2 Peter 1 (1622).

Arthur Dent (d. 1607). English Puritan preacher. Ordained in the Church of England, Dent ministered in Essex, where he made his Puritan sympathies clear and was disciplined for refusing to wear a surplice and make the sign of the cross. He published a number of works, including an exposition of the Articles of Faith and an exposition of Revelation targeted against the Roman Catholic Church.

Marie Dentière (1495–1561). Belgian Reformed theologian. Dentière relinquished her monastic vows and married Simon Robert (d.1533), a former priest, in Strasbourg. After Robert died, she married Antoine Froment (1508–1581), a reformer in Geneva, and became involved in the reform of that city. Her best-known writings are a tract addressed to Marguerite d'Angoulême,* the *Very Useful Epistle* (1539), in which she espoused the evangelical faith and the right of women to interpret and teach scripture, and a preface to Calvin's sermon on 1 Timothy 2:8-12. Dentière is the only woman to have her name inscribed on the International Monument to the Reformation in Geneva.

Edward Dering (c. 1540–1576). English Puritan preacher. An early Puritan, Dering's prospects of advancement in the Elizabethan church were effectively ended after a sermon in front of the Queen in which he described her as an "untamed and unruly heifer" while criticizing the state of the church and clergy. While continuing with intemperate and critical attacks throughout his career, Dering established himself as a preacher at St. Paul's Cathedral in London, where he became known for his pastoral concern and desire to teach the assurance of salvation.

Jean D'Espagne (1591–1659). French Independent pastor. After leading churches at Orange and the Hague, D'Espagne departed under accusations of immorality and settled in London, where he pastored a French congregation. A fractious figure, he led a group that separated from the established French congregation and entered into numerous controversies. Many of his extant writings are targeted toward errors he perceived in the theology and practice of others.

David Dickson (1583?–1663). Scottish Reformed pastor, preacher, professor and theologian. Dickson defended the Presbyterian form of ecclesial reformation in Scotland and was recognized for his iteration of Calvinist federal theology and expository biblical commentaries. Dickson served for over twenty years as professor of philosophy at the University of Glasgow before being appointed professor of divinity. He opposed the imposition of Episcopalian measures on the church in Scotland and was active in political and ecclesial venues to protest and prohibit such influences. Dickson was removed from his academic post following his refusal of the oath of supremacy during the Restoration era.

Veit Dietrich (1506–1549). German Lutheran preacher and theologian. Dietrich intended to study medicine at the University of Wittenberg, but Martin Luther* and Philipp Melanchthon* convinced him to study theology instead. Dietrich developed a strong relationship with Luther, accompanying him to the Marburg Colloquy (1529) and to Coburg Castle during the Diet of Augsburg (1530). After graduating, Dietrich taught on the arts faculty, eventually becoming dean. In 1535 he returned to his hometown, Nuremberg, to pastor. Later in life, Dietrich worked with Melanchthon to reform the church in Regensburg. In 1547, when Charles V arrived in Nuremberg, Dietrich was suspended from the pastorate; he resisted the imposition of the Augsburg Interim to no avail. In addition to transcribing some of Luther's lectures, portions of the Table Talk and the very popular *Hauspostille* (1544), Dietrich published his own sermons for children, a manual for pastors and a summary of the Bible.

Louis de Dieu (1590–1642). Dutch Reformed pastor and linguist. Committed to his pastoral and teaching ministry in Leiden, Dieu turned down the opportunity to teach theology and Old Testament at the University of Utrecht. He published grammars of Hebrew (1626) and Persian (1639); a comparative grammar of Hebrew, Aramaic, and Syriac (1628); and a collection of writings on the New Testament text.

Giovanni Diodati (1576–1649). Italian Reformed theologian. Diodati was from an Italian banking family who fled for religious reasons to Geneva. There he trained under Theodore Beza;* on completion of his doctoral degree, Diodati became professor of Hebrew at the academy. He was an ecclesiastical representative of the church in Geneva (for whom he was a delegate at the Synod of Dordrecht*) and an advocate for reform in Venice. Diodati's chief contribution to the Italian reform movement was a translation of the Bible into Italian (1640–1641), which remains the standard translation in Italian Protestantism.

John Dod (c. 1549–1645). English Puritan pastor. Over the course of his lengthy pastoral career (spanning roughly sixty years), Dod was twice suspended for nonconformity and twice reinstated. A popular preacher, he published many sermons as well as commentaries on the Ten Commandments and the Lord's Prayer; collections of his sayings and anecdotes were compiled after his death.

John Donne (1572–1631). Anglican poet and preacher. Donne was born into a strong Catholic family. However, sometime between his brother's death from the plague while in prison in 1593 and the publication of his *Pseudo-Martyr* in 1610, Donne joined the Church of England. Ordained to the Anglican priesthood in 1615 and already widely recognized for his verse, Donne quickly rose to prominence as a preacher—some have deemed him the best of his era. His textual corpus is an amalgam of erotic *and* divine poetry (e.g., "Batter My Heart"), as well as a great number of sermons.

Dordrecht Confession (1632). Dutch Mennonite confession. Adriaan Cornelisz (1581–1632) wrote the Dordrecht Confession to unify Dutch Mennonites. This basic statement of Mennonite belief and practice affirms distinctive doctrines such as nonresistance, shunning, footwashing, and the refusal to swear oaths. Most continental Mennonites subscribed to this confession during the second half of the seventeenth century.

Johann George Dorsche (1597–1659). German Lutheran theologian. Dorsche pastored briefly at Entzheim before being called to Strasbourg, where he earned his doctorate, was appointed professor of theology, and served as a preacher at the cathedral. He spent the last five years of his life as professor of theology at the University of Rostock. Dorsche published a number of theological works as well as commentaries on the Gospels and Hebrews.

John Downame (c. 1571–1652). English Puritan pastor and theologian. See *English Annotations.*

Charles Drelincourt (1595–1669). French Reformed pastor, theologian and controversialist. After studying at Saumur Academy, Drelincourt pastored the Reformed Church in Paris for nearly fifty years. He was well known for his ministry to the sick. In addition to polemical works against Catholicism, he published numerous pastoral resources: catechisms, three volumes of sermons and a five-volume series on consolation for the suffering.

The Dutch Annotations (1657). See *Statenvertaling.*

Daniel Dyke (d. 1614). English Puritan preacher. Born of nonconformist stock, Dyke championed a more thorough reformation of church practice in England. After the promulgation of John Whitgift's* articles in 1583, Dyke refused to accept what he saw as remnants of Catholicism, bringing him into conflict with the bishop of London. Despite the petitions of his congregation and some politicians, the bishop of London suspended Dyke from his ministry for refusing priestly ordination and conformity to the Book of Common Prayer.* All of his work was published posthumously; it is mostly focused on biblical interpretation.

John Eachard (unknown). English Anglican minister. After graduating with his master of arts from Trinity College, Cambridge, Eachard was the vicar at Darsham in Suffolk. At least two of his sermons, one on Matthew 3:10 and another on Revelation 12:11, were published in his lifetime.

Johann Eck (Johann Maier of Eck) (1486–1543). German Catholic theologian. Though Eck was not an antagonist of Martin Luther* until the dispute over indulgences, Luther's Ninety-five Theses (1517) sealed the two as adversaries. After their debate at the Leipzig Disputation (1519), Eck participated in the writing of the papal bull that led to Luther's excommunication. Much of Eck's work was written to oppose Protestantism or to defend Catholic doctrine and the papacy; his *Enchiridion* was a manual written to counter Protestant doctrine. However, Eck was also deeply invested in the status of parish preaching, publishing a five-volume set of postils. He participated in the assemblies at Regensburg and Augsburg and led the Catholics in their rejection of the Augsburg Confession.

Edward VI of England (1537–1553). English monarch. Son of Henry VIII* and Jane Seymour (1508–1537), Edward ascended to the throne as a minor, leaving the practical power of the monarchy in the hands of those appointed by the Regency council as Lord Protector of the Realm, first, his uncle, Edward Seymour, duke of Somerset (1500–1552), and afterwards, John Dudley, duke of Northumberland (1504–1553). Under Somerset and Northumberland, and with Thomas Cranmer* installed as Archbishop of Canterbury, the eclectic reforms made during the reign of Henry VIII were drawn into the service of a thoroughly Protestant transformation. During the reign of Edward, communion in two kinds was instituted, all services were held in the vernacular, and a series of ecclesiastical visitations oversaw the suppression of Catholic religion. Alongside the flood of Protestant refugees from the continent that sheltered in the kingdom, the publication of the revised Book of Common Prayer*, the Book of Homilies* and the Forty–Two Articles (1553) helped establish the future direction of Anglicanism.

Elizabeth I of England (1533–1603) English monarch. The daughter of Henry VIII* (r. 1509–1547) and Anne Boleyn (c. 1501–1536), Elizabeth outwardly conformed to Catholicism during the reign of her sister Mary I (r. 1553–1558), but her Protestant upbringing encouraged the hopes of many reformers upon her accession in 1558. With the 1559 Elizabethan Settlement, Elizabeth redefined England as a Protestant country, with the Act of Supremacy asserting the monarch as the head of the English church, and the Act of Uniformity establishing the 1559 *Book of Common Prayer** as the valid order of service within the realm. However, Elizabeth resisted the aggressive persecution of Catholics for political reasons, while also allowing some traditional vestments, furniture and ceremonies to be retained. Her moderate and pragmatic reforms frustrated many who wished for more thorough change and led to the emergence of the Puritan movement. Elizabeth faced numerous threats during her reign, including the machinations of Scottish Catholics and claims to the throne of Mary Stuart (1542–1547), leading to her rival's imprisonment and execution in 1587; the attempted invasion of England by Spain, which culminated in the celebrated defeat of the Spanish Armada in 1588; and a Catholic rebellion in Ireland that was suppressed during the Nine Years War (1594–1603). Elizabeth never married, and was succeeded on the throne by James I* following her death in 1603.

Edward Elton (1569–1624). Puritan minister. Elton served as pastor of St. Mary Magdalen's Church in Bermondsey, Surrey. Richard Baxter* praised him for his exegetical works, among which were *Three Excellent Pious Treatises in Sundry Sermons upon the Whole Seventh, Eighth, and Ninth Chapters of the Epistle to the Romans* and *An Exposition of the Epistle of St. Paul to the Colossians.*

English Annotations (1645; 1651; 1657). Under a commission from the Westminster Assembly, the editors of the English Annotations—John Downame* along with unnamed colleagues—translated, collated and digested in a compact and accessible format several significant Continental biblical resources, including Calvin's* commentaries, Beza's* *Annotationes majores* and Diodati's* *Annotations.*

Desiderius Erasmus (1466–1536). Dutch Catholic humanist and pedagogue. Erasmus, a celebrated humanist scholar, was recognized for translations of ancient texts, reform of education according to classical studies, moral and spiritual writings and the first printed edition of the Greek New Testament. A former Augustinian who never left the Catholic Church, Erasmus addressed deficiencies he saw in the church and society, challenging numerous prevailing doctrines but advocating reform. He envisioned a simple, spiritual Christian life shaped by the teachings of Jesus and ancient wisdom. He was often accused of collusion with Martin Luther* on account of some resonance of their ideas but hotly debated Luther on human will.

George Estey (c. 1560–1601). English Anglican priest. After graduating from Cambridge, Estey was ordained in the Church of England and served as vicar of St. Mary in Bury St. Edmunds, Suffolk.

Paul Fagius (1504–1549). German Reformed Hebraist and pastor. After studying at the University of Heidelberg, Fagius went to Strasbourg where he perfected his Hebrew under Wolfgang Capito.* In Isny im Allgäu (Baden-Württemberg) he met the great Jewish grammarian Elias Levita (1469–1549), with whom he established a Hebrew printing press. In 1544 Fagius returned to Strasbourg, succeeding Capito as preacher and Old Testament lecturer. During the Augsburg Interim, Fagius (with Martin Bucer*) accepted Thomas Cranmer's* invitation to translate and interpret the Bible at Cambridge. However, Fagius died before he could begin any of the work. Fagius wrote commentaries on the first four chapters of Genesis and the deutero-canonical books of Sirach and Tobit.

Guillaume Farel (1489–1565) French Reformed preacher and theologian. At the vanguard of the French Reformation, Farel was a student of Jacques Lefèvre d'Étaples* and member of Archbishop Briçonnet's* circle in Meaux until his desire for more rapid change saw him depart in 1523 to preach the Protestant message in Basel, Montbéliard, Strasbourg, Bern, and Aigle. During this period of his ministry, he composed the first French Protestant book, an evangelical commentary on the Lord's Prayer and the Apostle's Creed, as well as the first French Confession of Faith. A catalyst in Geneva's acceptance of the Reformation in 1536, it was Farel who persuaded Calvin* to settle in the city. After he and Calvin were banished from Geneva in 1538, Farel accepted the pastorate in Neuchâtel, a position he held until his death while continuing to travel and support the Reformation in the French-speaking lands.

John Fary (unknown). English Puritan pastor. Fary authored *God's Severity on Man's Sterility* (1645), a sermon on the fruitless fig tree in Luke 13:6-9.

Margaret Fell (1614–1702). English Quaker. Known as the "Mother of Quakerism," Fell was born at Dalton-in-Furness in northern England. The daughter of a local judge, she married Thomas Fell, who was a judge as well as a member of Parliament, representing Lancashire. In 1652, under the preaching of George Fox (1624–1691), Fell and her daughters became members of the Society of Friends (the Quakers). From that time onward, she became a pivotal figure in the subsequent development of the Quaker movement. Throughout her extensive correspondence to powerful members of the nobility, including King Charles II (r. 1660–1685), she pleaded for the release of imprisoned Quakers. Fell was arrested in 1664 for leading Quaker meetings and for her refusal to swear the Oath of Obedience, and she was sentenced to four and a half years imprisonment. After her release, she married George Fox in 1669, her first husband having died eleven years earlier. In addition to her advocacy for incarcerated Quakers, Fell enhanced the work of the Quaker Women's Meeting, which consisted of caring for the sick and elderly as well as orphans and prisoners. Her exegetical works include *For Mannaseth Ben Israel* and *A Loving Salutation to the Seed of Abraham,* both published in 1656, and translated into Hebrew (the latter believed to have been translated by the Jewish philosopher Benedict Spinoza). Moreover during her imprisonment, she authored her most famous treatise, *Women's Speaking Justified, Proved and Allowed of by the Scriptures.*

William Fenner (1600–1640). English Puritan pastor. After studying at Cambridge and Oxford, Fenner ministered at Sedgley and Rochford. Fenner's extant writings, which primarily deal with practical and devotional topics, demonstrate a zealous Puritan piety and a keen interest in Scripture and theology.

Charles Ferme (1566–1617). Scottish Reformed pastor and educator. After studying and teaching at the University of Edinburgh, Ferme pastored in Philorth, where he later served as the principal of a newly chartered university. The reconstitution of the episcopacy brought challenges for Ferme, and his resistance saw him imprisoned a number of times, including a three-year incarceration on the Isle of Bute. His only extant writing is a logical analysis of Romans.

Henry Ferne (1602–1662). English Protestant minister. Ferne ministered at a number of parishes in the north of England before serving as an extraordinary chaplain to Charles I* after earning his doctorate of divinity. A committed Royalist, he left official ministry during the Civil War (1642–1651), though he often preached, wrote a number of theological treatises against the Roman Catholics, and accompanied the king on a number of occasions. After the Restoration, Ferne served as master at Trinity College, Cambridge, and dean of Ely Cathedral before becoming bishop of Chester.

Richard Ferrers (Unknown). English poet. Ferrers is remembered for his poem *The Worth of Woman* (1622), defending the equality and value of women.

First Helvetic Confession (1536). Anticipating the planned church council at Mantua (1537, but delayed until 1545 at Trent), Reformed theologians of the Swiss cantons drafted a confession to distinguish themselves from both Catholics and the churches of the Augsburg Confession.* Heinrich Bullinger* led the discussion and wrote the confession itself; Leo Jud, Oswald Myconius, Simon Grynaeus and others were part of the assembly. Martin Bucer* and Wolfgang Capito* had desired to draw the Lutheran and Reformed communions closer together through this document, but Luther* proved unwilling after Bullinger refused to accept the Wittenberg Concord (1536). This confession was largely eclipsed by Bullinger's Second Helvetic Confession.*

John Fisher (1469–1535). English Catholic bishop and theologian. This reputed preacher defended Catholic orthodoxy and strove to reform abuses in the church. In 1521 Henry VIII* honored Fisher with the title *Fidei Defensor* ("defender of the faith"). Nevertheless, Fisher opposed the king's divorce of Catherine of Aragon (1485–1536) and the independent establishment of the Church of England; he was convicted for treason and executed. Most of Fisher's works are polemical and occasional (e.g., on transubstantiation, against Martin Luther*); however, he also published a series of sermons on the seven penitential psalms. In addition to his episcopal duties, Fisher was the chancellor of Cambridge from 1504 until his death.

Matthias Flacius (1520–1575). Lutheran theologian. A native of Croatia, Matthias Flacius commenced his studies at the University of Tubingen, and completed them at Wittenberg, where through Luther's influence, he embraced the university's evangelical theology. Flacius began his career as instructor of Hebrew at the University of Wittenberg in 1544, and remained in this post until 1549. As a devoted follower of Luther's teachings, Flacius sought to defend them in their purity which drove him and Nikolaus von Amsdorf as leaders of the Gnesio-Lutherans to oppose the more moderate positions of Philipp Melanchthon and his sympathizers, the Philippists, in several controversies concerning the role of free will and good works in justification as well as relations with Calvinism. After serving as a professor at the University of Jena (1557–1561), Flacius spent the remainder of his life as an independent scholar, frequently moving from one city to another to escape persecution. Flacius died in Frankfurt am Main in 1575. His important exegetical works are *De vocabula Dei* (1549), *Clavis Scripturae Sacrae* (1567), and *Glossa Novi Testamenti* (1570). Flacius also published two historical works, *Catalogus Testium Veritatis* (1556) and the *Magdeburg Centuries*.

Marcantonio Flaminio (1498–1550). Italian humanist and poet. Flaminio was dependent on patronage, and he spent much of his life in the houses of noble benefactors in Bologna, Genoa, and Verona. While he never left the Roman church, he was drawn to intellectual currents that sought reform. In Naples, he participated in an intellectual circle that included Juan de Valdés* and Pietro Carnesecchi* before joining the house of Cardinal Pole* in Viterbo. Alongside his poetry and humanistic writings, Flaminio also edited one of the most significant Italian texts of the Reformation, Benedetto de Mantova's* *The Benefit of Christ* (1543).

John Flavel (c. 1630–1691). English Puritan pastor. Trained at Oxford, Flavel ministered in southwest England from 1650 until the Act of Uniformity in 1662, which reaffirmed the compulsory use of the Book of Common Prayer. Flavel preached unofficially for many years, until his congregation was eventually allowed to build a meeting place in 1687. His works were numerous, varied and popular.

Giovanni Battista Folengo (1490–1559). Italian Catholic exegete. In 1528 Folengo left the Benedictine order, questioning the validity of monastic vows; he returned to the monastic life in 1534. During this hiatus Folengo came into contact with the Neapolitan reform-minded circle founded by Juan de Valdés.* Folengo published commentaries on the Psalms, John, 1–2 Peter and James. Augustin Marlorat* included Folengo's comment in his anthology of exegesis on the Psalms. In 1580 Folengo's Psalms commentary was added to the Index of Prohibited Books.

John Forbes (1568?–1634). Scottish Reformed pastor. While minister at Alford in Aberdeenshire, Forbes was appointed moderator of the Presbyterian Aberdeen Assembly, which met against the orders of King James I.* Refusing to accept the monarch's jurisdiction, he was exiled to the Continent and settled in the Netherlands, where he pastored English congregations at Middleburg and Delft until forced out under the reforms of Archbishop Laud.*

Formula of Concord (1577). After Luther's* death, intra-Lutheran controversies between the Gnesio-Lutherans (partisans of Luther) and the Philippists (partisans of Melanchthon*) threatened to cause a split among those who had subscribed to the Augsburg Confession.* In 1576, Jakob Andreae,* Martin Chemnitz,* Nikolaus Selnecker,* David Chytraeus* and Andreas Musculus (1514–1581) met with the intent of resolving the controversies, which mainly regarded the relationship between good works and salvation, the third use of the law, and the role of the human will in accepting God's grace. In 1580, celebrating the fiftieth anniversary of the presentation of the Augsburg Confession to Charles V (1500–1558), the *Book of Concord* was printed as the authoritative interpretation of the Augsburg Confession; it included the three ancient creeds, the Augsburg Confession, its Apology (1531), the Schmalkald Articles,* Luther's *Treatise on the Power and Primacy of the Pope* (1537) and both his Small and Large Catechisms (1529).

John Foxe (1516–1587). English Protestant martryrologist, historian. John Foxe was born in Boston, Lincolnshire. After completing his early education, Foxe became a fellow at Magdalen College, Oxford, where he completed his BA degree in 1537, and MA in 1543. Also he was lecturer in logic from 1539 to 1540. However, in 1545, Foxe was forced to resign from Magdalen because he had adopted Protestant beliefs. After leaving Oxford, Foxe became tutor to the children of the Earl of Surrey. During this time Foxe made the acquaintance of John Bale (1495–1562) who fostered his interest in history. When Mary Tudor ascended the throne of England in 1553, Foxe fled to the continent. While there, Foxe traveled to Frankfurt, where in 1555 he met Edmund Grindal (1519–1583), who had been composing accounts of Protestant martyrs. Foxe later joined Grindal in Basel, where he translated his narratives into Latin. Foxe published the book resulting from his labors in Basel in 1559. After Elizabeth I* succeeded to the throne in the same year, Foxe returned to England. Upon his return he began working with the printer, John Day, who published the first English edition of Foxe's work. This voluminous work, *The Acts and Monuments*, underwent four editions during the remainder of the author's lifetime. *The Acts and Monuments* contributed significantly to the development of the national identity and piety of Elizabethan England. Shorter versions of this work are known simply as *Foxe's Book of Martyrs*.

Francis I of France (1494–1547). French monarch. Francis ascended to the French throne following the death of Louis XII (1462–1515), who was both his cousin and father-in-law. Much of Francis's reign was dominated by warfare. In Italy, victory over the Swiss allowed him to assert his dynastic claim to the Duchy of Milan, and extract liberties for the French church from Pope Leo X* through the Concordat of Bologna. His campaign against Charles V* was less successful, however, as Milan was lost and following defeat at the Battle of Pavia, Francis was taken prisoner. His release was negotiated by his sister, Marguerite d'Angouleme*, though he reneged in its terms once reaching safety, ensuring continued conflict with the Holy Roman Emperor throughout his reign. Francis fostered humanistic learning within his kingdom, and while he resisted Lutheran and other evangelical thought, he gave some space for its expression, giving protection to scholars such as those gathered around his sister and Bishop Guillaume Briçonnet* at Meaux. His desire for social order saw him take increasingly strident steps against the Reformation, however, particularly after his bedchamber was pamphleted during the Affair of the Placards, and the final years of his reign saw a significant increase in attempts to reassert Catholic doctrine and stamp out Protestantism with persecution.

Sebastian Franck (1499–1542). German Radical theologian. Franck became a Lutheran in 1525, but by 1529 he began to develop ideas that distanced him from Protestants and Catholics. Expelled from Strasbourg and later Ulm due to his controversial writings, Franck spent the end of his life in Basel. Franck emphasized God's word as a divine internal spark that cannot be adequately expressed in outward forms. Thus he criticized religious institutions and dogmas. His work consists mostly of commentaries, compilations and translations. In his sweeping historical *Chronica* (1531), Franck supported numerous heretics condemned by the Catholic Church and criticized political and church authorities.

Leonhard Frick (d. 1528). Austrian Radical martyr. See *Kunstbuch*.

John Frith (1503–1533). English reformer, author, and martyr. Frith was born in Westerham, Kent. He was the son of Richard Frith, the innkeeper of the White Horse Inn. After receiving his earlier education at Sevenoaks Grammar School and Eton College, Frith matriculated at Queen's College, Cambridge, where Stephen Gardiner (1497–1555), future bishop of Winchester, and opponent of the English Reformation, was his tutor. Frith graduated with his BA degree in 1525, having obtained proficiency in Latin and mathematics. While still a student, Frith met Thomas Bilney (1495–1531), who most likely introduced him to evangelical faith. After graduating, Frith became a junior canon at Christ Church, Oxford. However, while at Oxford, Frith along with nine others was imprisoned in a fish cellar for possessing what ecclesiastical authorities considered "heretical books." Upon his release, Frith traveled to the Continent, where he assisted William Tyndale* with his translation work. Also while on the Continent, Frith translated some antipapal polemical works, and authored *A Disputation of Purgatory*. Upon Frith's return to England in 1532, he was arrested and imprisoned several times for publicly preaching against transubstantiation and purgatory. Eventually, Frith was imprisoned in the Tower of London, and later transferred to Newgate Prison. He was burned at the stake on July 4, 1533.

Libert Froidmont (1587–1653). Belgian philosopher, scientist, and theologian. A childhood friend of Cornelius Jansen (1585–1638), Froidmont entered the Society of Jesus and his early career was focused on philosophy and the sciences, teaching at Antwerp, Saint-Michel, and Louvain. Drawn to the rigorous but controversial Augustinianism of Jansen, Froidmont earned his doctorate in theology in 1628 and succeeded Jansen as chair of theology at Louvain. While publishing a number of theological and exegetical works, including a commentary on Paul's letters, Froidmont was also active in the scientific and philosophical debates of his era. He published against Nicolas Copernicus (1473–1543) and Galileo Galilei (1564–1642), whom he argued were wrong but not heretical, and was one of the first to engage with the thought of René Descartes (1596–1650).

William Fulke (1538–1589). English Protestant theologian. Responsible for preaching and lecturing on Old Testament and other subjects, William Fulke courted controversy during his tenure as fellow at Cambridge. He was briefly expelled for his advocacy of Vestarians and later resigned until acquitted of being in an incestuous marriage. He left Cambridge to serve as chaplain to Robert Dudley, Earl of Leicester (1532–1588), returning almost a decade later as master of Pembroke College. He is best remembered as a controversialist and was the author of numerous anti-Catholic tracts.

Thomas Fuller (1608–1661). English Protestant minister. Fuller, the son of a minister, graduated from Cambridge, and his early career was overseen by his uncle John Davenant,* who secured his nephew a number of pastoral positions. Known for his wit and moderation, Fuller was a chaplain in the Royal army during the Civil War (1642–1651), and he served as an extraordinary chaplain to King Charles II (1630–1685) after the Restoration. He composed a number of exegetical and pastoral works, but he is primarily remembered for his historical writings. These include histories of the Crusades and the church in England as well as a biographical dictionary, the *History of the Worthies of England* (1622).

Gallic Confession (1559). This confession was accepted at the first National Synod of the Reformed Churches of France (1559). It was intended to be a touchstone of Reformed faith but also to show to the people of France that the Huguenots—who faced persecution—were not seditious. The French Reformed Church presented this confession to Francis II (1544–1560) in 1560, and to his successor, Charles IX (1550–1574), in 1561. The later Genevan draft, likely written by Calvin,* Beza* and Pierre Viret (1511–1571), was received as the true Reformed confession at the seventh National Synod in La Rochelle (1571).

Geneva Bible (originally printed 1560). During Mary I's reign many English Protestants sought safety abroad in Reformed territories of the Empire and the Swiss Cantons, especially in Calvin's* Geneva. A team of English exiles in Geneva led by William Whittingham (c. 1524–1579) brought this complete translation to press in the course of two years. Notable for several innovations—Roman type, verse numbers, italics indicating English idiom and not literal phrasing of the original languages, even variant readings in the Gospels and Acts—this translation is most well known for its marginal notes, which reflect a strongly Calvinist theology. The notes explained Scripture in an accessible way for the laity, also giving unlearned clergy a new sermon resource. Although controversial because of its implicit critique of royal power, this translation was wildly popular; even after the publication of the Authorized Version (1611) and James I's* 1616 ban on its printing, the Geneva Bible continued to be the most popular English translation until after the English Civil Wars.

Johann Gerhard (1582–1637). German Lutheran theologian, professor and superintendent. Gerhard is considered one of the most eminent Lutheran theologians, after Martin Luther* and Martin Chemnitz.* After studying patristics and Hebrew at Wittenberg, Jena and Marburg, Gerhard was appointed superintendent at the age of twenty-four. In 1616 he was appointed to a post at the University of Jena, where he reintroduced Aristotelian metaphysics to theology and gained widespread fame. His most important work was the nine-volume *Loci Theologici* (1610–1625). He also expanded Chemnitz's harmony of the Gospels *(Harmonia Evangelicae)*, which was finally published by Polykarp Leyser (1552–1610) in 1593. Gerhard was well-known for an irenic spirit and an ability to communicate clearly.

George Gifford (c. 1548–1600). English Puritan pastor. Gifford was suspended for nonconformity in 1584. With private support, however, he was able to continue his ministry. Through his published works he wanted to help develop lay piety and biblical literacy.

George Gifford (d. 1620). English Puritan minister. A celebrated preacher in Maldon, Essex, Gifford was removed from the pulpit when he refused to subscribe to Articles of Conformity drawn up by Archbishop John Whitgift.* Allowed to continue ministry in the office of lecturer, he also served as a representative for Essex at Puritan synods. He published numerous works, including a primer for common Christians, a dialogue between a Catholic and a Protestant, and two works on witchcraft.

Anthony Gilby (c. 1510–1585). English Puritan translator. During Mary I's reign, Gilby fled to Geneva, where he assisted William Whittingham (c. 1524–1579) with the Geneva Bible.* He returned to England to pastor after Elizabeth I's* accession. In addition to translating numerous continental Reformed works into English—especially those of John Calvin* and Theodore Beza*—Gilby also wrote commentaries on Micah and Malachi.

Bernard Gilpin (1517–1583). Anglican theologian and priest. In public disputations, Gilpin defended Roman Catholic theology against John Hooper (c. 1495–1555) and Peter Martyr Vermigli.* These debates caused Gilpin to reexamine his faith. Upon Mary I's accession, Gilpin resigned his benefice. He sojourned in Belgium and France, returning to pastoral ministry in England in 1556. Gilpin dedicated himself to a preaching circuit in northern England, thus earning the moniker "the Apostle to the North." His zealous preaching and almsgiving roused royal opposition and a warrant for his arrest. On his way to the queen's commission, Gilpin fractured his leg, delaying his arrival in London until after Mary's death and thus likely saving his life. His only extant writing is a sermon on Luke 2 confronting clerical abuses.

Paul Glock (c. 1530–1585). German Radical preacher. A teenage convert to Hutterite Anabaptism, Glock spent nineteen years imprisoned at Hohenwittlingen, unwilling to recant. While incarcerated, he wrote hymns, a confession and defense of his beliefs, and numerous letters that proved influential in the development of Anabaptist thought. After helping extinguish a fire at the prison in 1576, Glock was freed and settled with the Brethren in Moravia.

Glossa ordinaria. This standard collection of biblical commentaries consists of interlinear and marginal notes drawn from patristic and Carolingian exegesis appended to the Vulgate*; later editions also include Nicholas of Lyra's* *Postilla*. The *Glossa ordinaria* and the *Sentences* of Peter Lombard (c. 1100–1160) were essential resources for all late medieval and early modern commentators.

Franciscus Gomarus (1563–1641). Dutch Reformed theologian and pastor. A religious refugee at an early age, Gomarus's family was forced to leave Bruges for the Palatinate, with Gomarus receiving a Reformed education at Strasbourg, Neustadt, Oxford, Cambridge, and Heidelberg. He pastored at Frankfurt am Main until becoming professor of theology at the University of Leiden, where he came into extended conflict with colleague Jacobus Arminius* over predestination. Gomarus left Leiden in protest when Conradus Vorstius,* a follower of Arminius with Socinian tendencies, was appointed over his objections. Gomarus then pastored briefly at Middelburg before teaching at the Reformed academy at Saumur and the University of Groningen. Representing the university at the Synod of Dordrecht,* Gomarus was a leading opponent of Remonstrant theology and a key figure in ensuring their censure.

Robert Gomersall (1602–1646?). English Protestant minister and dramatist. Little is known of Gomersall's life beyond his graduation from Oxford and entrance into the ministry. He published a number of poetic and dramatic works, including a tragedy on the life of Italian prince

Ludovicio Sforza (1452–1508) and a poetic meditation on Judges 19–20.

Thomas Goodwin (1600–1679). Puritan minister. Goodwin was born October 5, 1600, in Norfolk. After receiving his early education from local schools, Goodwin matriculated at Christ College, Cambridge, which was a prime center of Puritan influence. He graduated with the BA degree in 1616 and MA in 1620. Upon receiving his MA, Goodwin became a fellow and lecturer at the university. In October 1620, Goodwin experienced a profound conversion on his twentieth birthday. After his conversion, Goodwin joined the Puritan party at Cambridge. He was licensed to preach in the Church of England in 1625. Three years later, Goodwin became lecturer at Trinity Church. He served as vicar of this church from 1632 to 1634. Unwilling to comply with Archbishop William Laud's* directives for conformity, Goodwin was forced to resign all of his ecclesiastical and academic positions, and leave Cambridge. During the remainder of the 1630s, due to John Cotton's* influence, Goodwin came to adopt the principles of Independency. In 1639, in order to escape the increasing restrictions of unauthorized preachers, Goodwin fled to the Netherlands, where he worked with other English Independent exiles. In 1641, Goodwin returned to England per Parliament's request, and preached before it on April 27, 1642. Goodwin was later appointed a delegate to the Westminster Assembly. In the Assembly, Goodwin proved himself to be one of the foremost advocates of Independency. After the Westminster Assembly adjourned, Goodwin was appointed a lecturer at Oxford, and a year later became president of Magdalen College. Furthermore, Goodwin served as an advisor to Oliver Cromwell (1599–1658) and as the Lord Protector's Oxford commissioner. Goodwin also tended to Cromwell on his deathbed. In addition to his university and advisory duties, Goodwin pastored an Independent church at Oxford. Notably, Goodwin was one of the primary authors of the Savoy Declaration of Faith (1658), which served as the confession of faith for the Independent/Congregational churches. When Charles II ascended to the throne of England in 1660, Goodwin withdrew from Oxford to London, where he pastored an Independent congregation until his death at the age of eighty. Throughout his career, Goodwin produced an enormous literary corpus, which includes many exegetical works. Best known among these are his expositions of Ephesians and Revelation.

Marie le Jars de Gournay (1565–1645). French Catholic writer and editor. Born into the minor nobility, the early death of Gournay's father led her family to relocate to their estate in Picardy, where she taught herself Latin and Greek. After reading the *Essais* (1580) of Michel de Montaigne (1533–1592), she committed herself to a life of literature and became active in the intellectual circles of Paris. While she translated many classical writings, she is best known for her editorial work on Montaigne's essays and her advocacy for the rights of women, laid out in a number of writings including *The Equality of Men and Women* (1622) and *The Ladies' Grievance* (1626).

Simon Goulart (1543–1628) French Reformed pastor, translator, and theologian. Goulart spent most of his career as a pastor in Geneva and its surrounds, particularly at the city parish of St. Gervais, and was the leader of the Company of Pastors during the last decades of his life. A prolific translator, he published numerous French editions of classical, patristic, and contemporary works from diverse authors including Plutarch, Seneca, Chrysostom, Cyprian, Tertullian, Beza*, Perkins* and Vermigli*. He also composed numerous devotional writings, important histories of early French Protestantism, and polemical treatises supporting the Huguenot cause.

Conrad Grebel (c. 1498–1526). Swiss Radical theologian. Grebel, considered the father of the Anabaptist movement, was one of the first defenders and performers of believers' baptism, for which he was eventually imprisoned in Zurich. One of Huldrych Zwingli's* early compatriots, Grebel advocated rapid, radical reform, clashing publicly with the civil authorities and Zwingli. Grebel's views, particularly on baptism, were influenced by Andreas Bodenstein von Karlstadt* and Thomas Müntzer.* Grebel advocated elimination of magisterial involvement in governing the church; instead, he envisioned the church as lay Christians determining their own affairs with strict adherence to the biblical text, and unified in volitional baptism.

William Greenhill (1591–1671). English Puritan pastor. Greenhill attended and worked at Magdalen College. He ministered in the diocese of Norwich but soon left for London, where he preached at Stepney. Greenhill was a member of the Westminster Assembly of Divines and was appointed the parliament chaplain by the children of Charles I. Oliver Cromwell included him among the preachers who helped draw up the Savoy Declaration. Greenhill was evicted from his post following the Restoration, after which he pastored independently. Among Greenhill's most significant contributions to church history was his *Exposition of the Prophet of Ezekiel.*

Catharina Regina von Greiffenberg (1633–1694). Austrian Lutheran poet. Upon her adulthood her guardian (and half uncle) sought to marry her; despite her protests of their consanguinity and her desire to remain celibate, she relented in 1664. After the deaths of her mother and husband, Greiffenberg abandoned her home to debtors and joined her friends Susanne Popp (d. 1683) and Sigmund von Birken (1626–1681) in Nuremberg. During her final years she dedicated herself to studying the biblical languages and to writing meditations on Jesus' death and resurrection, which she never completed. One of the most important and learned Austrian poets of the Baroque period, Greiffenberg published a collection of sonnets, songs and poems (1662) as well as three sets of mystical meditations on Jesus' life, suffering and death (1672; 1683; 1693). She participated in a society of poets called the Ister Gesellschaft.

Lady Jane Grey (1537–1554). English Protestant monarch, sometimes known as "the Nine Days Queen." The eldest daughter of Henry Grey and Frances Brandon, the daughter of Henry VIII's* younger sister Mary, Jane received an extensive Protestant and humanist education. She married Lord Guildford Dudley (c. 1535–1554), son of Edward VI's* chief minister John Dudley, Duke of Northumberland (1504–1553). Seeking to avoid succession by Edward's Catholic half-sister Mary I, Edward and Northumberland conspired to alter the order of succession, naming Jane as heir in the king's will. Following Edward's death, Jane reluctantly took the crown on July 9, 1553, but Northumberland and other Protestants were unable to raise adequate support for her claim and the Privy Council proclaimed Mary queen on July 19. Upon Mary's accession, Jane was imprisoned in the Tower of London and after trial was executed alongside her husband for treason. A handful of her writings exist demonstrating her religious affections, while the story of her martyrdom is prominent in John Foxe's *Acts and Monuments*.

Edmund Grindal (c. 1519–1583). English Anglican archbishop. Grindal began his career in the church as chaplain to Nicholas Ridley* and King Edward VI* until forced to exile in Strasbourg during the reign of Mary I.* Returning to England upon the accession of Elizabeth I,* Grindal helped set the direction for the Church of England, participating in the 1559 Westminster Conference and serving as a member of the committee revising the liturgy. A moderate reformer, he reluctantly became bishop of London despite concerns over continuing Roman practices such as the wearing of vestments and the use of wafer bread for communion. His tenure as archbishop of York was marked by disputes with Presbyterians who wished to abolish the episcopacy and prayer book. Grindal was appointed Archbishop of Canterbury in 1575, but a conflict with Queen Elizabeth I hampered his ability to make change. He refused her request to suppress the "prophesyings" of Puritan clergy and meetings for theological discussion and sermon preparation. After addressing a remonstrance to the queen, he refused to resign, and he was stripped of the administrative power of his position until his death.

Hugo Grotius (1583–1645). Dutch lawyer, statesman, and humanist. Grotius began practicing law at The Hague in 1599, was appointed Advocate-General of the Fisc for the provinces of Holland, Zeeland, and West Friesland in 1607 and in 1613 became pensionary of Rotterdam. As debates between Calvinists and Arminians came to national significance, Grotius sided with the Remonstrants, especially in his rejection of Reformed arguments for the independence of the church, defending the right of the state to appoint ministers and adjudicate over matters of doctrine. Following the victory of Maurice of Orange (1567–1635) over Grotius's patron Johan van Oldenbarnevelt (1547–1619) and the condemnation of Arminianism at the Synod of Dordrecht* (1618–1619), Grotius was imprisoned, though only briefly, as he escaped in a book chest and fled to Paris. Unable to secure return from exile, Grotius became a Swedish ambassador to France while seeking religious toleration and the establishment of a Christian republic. A number of his works from this period, in particular *De Jure Belli ac Pacis* (On the law of war and peace, 1625) made a significant contribution to the establishment of international law.

Argula von Grumbach (c. 1490–c. 1564) German Lutheran noblewoman. Grumbach, an attendant of Queen Kunigunde of Austria (1465–1520), was one of the first women to publish in support of the Reformation. She is best known for letters from 1523 and 1524 written in defense of Arsacius Seehofer (1503–1545), a lecturer at the university of Ingolstadt accused of Lutheranism. For unknown reasons, Grumberg ceased to publish after 1524, although her private correspondence after this time demonstrates a continued effort to support evangelical reform.

Johann Jacob Grynaeus (1540–1617). Swiss Reformed theologian. Raised Lutheran, Grynaeus replaced his father as pastor at Rotelen. After becoming professor of Old Testament at Basel, however, Grynaeus caused conflict by embracing Reformed theology. He avoided controversy by spending two years at the University of Heidelberg. Upon his return to Basel, his opponents had largely died, and he was made superintendent of the church in the city and professor of New Testament.

Grynaeus aligned the Basel church with his Reformed convictions and reorganized the city's educational system while preaching regularly and composing numerous theological, exegetical, and practical works.

William Guild (1586–1657). Scottish Reformed minister and theologian. Guild was born in Aberdeen and educated at Marischal College. He was licensed to preach in 1605 and ordained to serve as minister of the parish of King Edward in 1608. In 1617, Guild joined the protest for the liberties of the Scottish national church. While in Edinburgh, Guild met the acquaintance of Bishop Lancelot Andrewes,* who was accompanying King James VI/I* on his royal visit to the city. Moreover, Guild dedicated his best-known work, *Moses Unveiled* (1620), to both Andrewes and the king. He was later appointed chaplain to Charles I, and shortly thereafter received the degree of doctor of divinity. In 1631, Guild was given his second charge in Aberdeen. When he assumed this charge, Guild expressed his support for episcopacy. He signed the National Covenant in 1638 with some conditions. However, when in 1640 an army came to Aberdeen to enforce full subscription to the Covenant, Guild fled to the Netherlands. After returning to Scotland later that year, he was appointed Guild Principal for King's College Aberdeen, but was deprived of this post by Oliver Cromwell's (1599–1658) military commissioners in 1651. Following his deprivation, Guild lived in retirement until his death in Aberdeen.

Rudolf Gwalther (1519–1586). Swiss Reformed preacher. Gwalther was a consummate servant of the Reformed church in Zurich, its chief religious officer and preacher, a responsibility fulfilled previously by Huldrych Zwingli* and Heinrich Bullinger.* Gwalther provided sermons and commentaries and translated the works of Zwingli into Latin. He worked for many years alongside Bullinger in structuring and governing the church in Zurich. Gwalther also strove to strengthen the connections to the Reformed churches on the Continent and England: he was a participant in the Colloquy of Regensburg (1541) and an opponent of the Formula of Concord.*

Matthias Hafenreffer (1561–1619). German Lutheran theologian. After holding pastoral positions in Herenberg, Ehingen, and Stuttgart, Hafenreffer was appointed professor of theology at Tübingen, a position he held for more than twenty-five years. He composed exegetical works on Nahum, Habakkuk, and Ezekiel, a number of polemical works, and a theological *loci communes* that served as a common textbook within the Lutheran churches for much of the seventeenth century.

Henry Hall (unknown). English Protestant preacher. A fellow of Trinity College, Cambridge, Hall preached and published a sermon given before the House of Commons in 1644 on Matthew 11:12.

Joseph Hall (1574–1656). English Anglican bishop and controversialist. After studying at Cambridge, Hall courted controversy with a series of satires before entering the ministry of the Church of England. As a pastor, Hall served parishes in Suffolk and Essex and was chosen by James I* as an English delegate at the Synod of Dordrecht.* Upon his return, Hall was appointed bishop of Exeter and later transferred to the see of Norwich, where, despite his low-church preferences, his defense of the episcopacy saw him convicted of praemunire by the Puritan parliament and imprisoned in the Tower of London for a short time with a number of other bishops. Hall's literary output was extensive and included controversial tracts against the Brownists and Arminians, treatises on virtue and union with Christ, and numerous devotional works.

Hans Has von Hallstatt (d. 1527). Austrian Reformed pastor. See *Kunstbuch*.

Henry Hammond (1605–1660). Anglican priest. After completing his studies at Oxford, Hammond was ordained in 1629. A Royalist, Hammond helped recruit soldiers for the king; he was chaplain to Charles I. During the king's captivity, Hammond was imprisoned for not submitting to Parliament. Later he was allowed to pastor again, until his death. Hammond published a catechism, numerous polemical sermons and treatises as well as his *Paraphrase and Annotations on the New Testament* (1653).

Jörg Haug (Unknown) German Anabaptist leader. Haug was a radical preacher during the 1525 Peasant's Revolt and composed a tract entitled *A Christian Order of a True Christian* (1524) enumerating seven degrees of faith reached by Christians.

Peter Hausted (d. 1645). Anglican priest and playwright. Educated at Cambridge and Oxford, Hausted ministered in a number of parishes and preached adamantly and vehemently against Puritanism. He is best known for his play *The Rival Friends*, which is filled with invective against the Puritans; during a performance before the king and queen, a riot nearly broke out. Haustead died during the siege of Banbury Castle.

Erhart Hegenwald (Unknown). Swiss Protestant teacher and doctor. A teacher at the Pfäffen Monastery in St. Gallen and at the Schola Carolina in Zurich, Hegenwald recorded the minutes of Zwingli's* First Zurich Disputation in 1523. Correspondence demonstrates he remained in contact with the Zurich reformers while he studied medicine at Wittenberg, and after graduating in 1526, he may have practiced as a physician in Frankfurt.

Heidelberg Catechism (1563). This German Reformed catechism was commissioned by the elector of the Palatinate, Frederick III (1515–1576) for pastors and teachers in his territories to use in instructing children and new believers in the faith. It was written by theologian Zacharias Ursinus (1534–1583) in consultation with Frederick's court preacher Kaspar Olevianus* and the entire theology faculty at the University of Heidelberg. The Heidelberg Catechism was accepted as one of the Dutch Reformed Church's Three Forms of Unity—along with the Belgic Confession* and the Canons of Dordrecht—at the Synod of Dordrecht,* and became widely popular among other Reformed confessional traditions throughout Europe.

Ursula Hellrigel (b. c. 1521). Austrian Anabaptist. Imprisoned for her heterodox beliefs at 17, authorities sought Hellrigel's recantation, but she refused to acquiesce. After five years she was released from prison and exiled from the Tyrol. The thirty-sixth hymn in the first known Anabaptist hymnal, the *Ausbund* (1654), is commonly attributed to her.

Niels Hemmingsen (1513–1600). Danish Lutheran theologian. Hemmingsen studied at the University of Wittenberg, where he befriended Philipp Melanchthon.* In 1542, Hemmingsen returned to Denmark to pastor and to teach Greek, dialectics and theology at the University of Copenhagen. Foremost of the Danish theologians, Hemmingsen oversaw the preparation and publication of the first Danish Bible (1550). Later in his career he became embroiled in controversies because of his Philippist theology, especially regarding the Eucharist. Due to rising tensions with Lutheran nobles outside of Denmark, King Frederick II (1534–1588) dismissed Hemmingsen from his university post in 1579, transferring him to a prominent but less internationally visible Cathedral outside of Copenhagen. Hemmingsen was a prolific author, writing commentaries on the New Testament and Psalms, sermon collections and several methodological, theological and pastoral handbooks.

Henry IV of France (1553–1610). French monarch. Son of Jeanne of Navarre* and Antoine de Bourbon (1518–1562), Henry's religious loyalties wavered throughout his life. Raised Protestant at the behest of his mother, he practiced Catholicism while attending the Valois court. After his mother's death in 1572, Henry succeeded her as King of Navarre and soon afterwards married Margaret of Valois (1553–1615), the daughter of Henry II of France (1519–1559) and Catherine de' Medici (1519–1589). Their wedding provided the occasion for the St. Bartholomew's Day Massacre, when Catholic forces seized the opportunity to decimate the Huguenot leadership gathered to celebrate the nuptials in Paris, leading to an outbreak of mob violence that devastated the Huguenot movement. A great proportion of the Protestants in France were killed in the weeks that followed the wedding, while many others, including Henry, reconverted to Catholicism. In 1576, Henry escaped the influence of the Valois court, returned his allegiance to Protestantism and took a leadership role amongst the Huguenots. Following the assassination of Henry III of France (1551–1589), Henry was the presumptive heir, but French Catholics were unwilling to accept his rule and Henry was unable to assert his prerogative outside Huguenot strongholds. In 1593, therefore, Henry converted again to Catholicism, with legend claiming he justified his decision with the phrase "Paris is worth a mass." Over the following years, Henry established his authority throughout his kingdom, and while remaining Catholic, provided some relief to Protestants, particularly through the Edict of Nantes (1598), essentially ending the Religious Wars. Henry's pragmatic reign ended with his assassination by a Radical Catholic in 1610.

King Henry VIII of England (1491–1547). English monarch. The second son of Henry VII (r. 1485–1509) and Elizabeth of York (1466–1503), Henry VIII succeeded his father to the English throne, his elder brother Edward having died in 1502. Soon after accession, he married his brother's widow, Catherine of Aragon (1485–1536). Following several stillbirths and the birth of a daughter, Mary, Henry, who was desperate for a male heir to head off dynastic challenges, wished separation from Catherine in order to marry Anne Boleyn (c. 1501–1536). Believing his marriage cursed as it transgressed the commands in Leviticus against marrying a brother's widow, Henry sought dispensation from the church for his annulment and remarriage. While the case was first heard by a papal legate in England, it was transferred to Rome upon the order of Pope Clement VII*, who wished to placate Charles V, Catherine's nephew, whose troops had recently sacked Rome and held the pope under house arrest. Henry asserted praemunire, arguing that as king, he was supreme in his own kingdom. With the formation of the Reformation Parliament in 1529, the legislative process to disentangle the English Church from the Roman was begun. The issue of Henry's divorce was finalized in 1533, after Thomas Cranmer* became Archbishop of Canterbury and declared his marriage to Catherine invalid. While Henry's divorce, assertion of royal supremacy, and subversion of Catholic institutions gave impetus to English Protestantism, Henry's beliefs remained essentially Catholic, and these continued to be enforced by law. He ultimately married six times, and was succeeded by Edward VI*, his son by his third wife, Jane Seymour (1508–1537). Elizabeth I*, Henry's daughter by Anne Boleyn, later became Queen and with the Elizabethan Settlement in 1559, redefined England as a Protestant country.

George Herbert (1593–1633). Anglican minister, theologian, and poet. Herbert was born in Montgomery Powys, Wales, on April 3, 1593, to a noble family. After completing his early education at Westminster School, Herbert matriculated at Trinity College, Cambridge, in 1609. He graduated with both his bachelor's and master's degrees. Shortly thereafter Herbert was elected a fellow of the college, and then became Reader of Rhetoric. From 1620 to 1627, Herbert was Public Orator for the University of Cambridge. In 1624, Herbert was elected to Parliament. However, after the death of King James I,* and of his other major patrons, Herbert withdrew from politics to pursue a career in the church. Toward this end, Herbert was ordained to the priesthood of the Church of England in 1630, and appointed rector of Fugglestone St. Peter and later Bemerton St. Andrews in Wiltshire near Salisbury. While at St. Andrews, Herbert composed his collection of poems titled *The Temple* and his guide for rural ministers, *A Priest to the Temple, or The Country Parson: His Character and Rule of Holy Life*. Twice a week Herbert traveled to Salisbury, where he attended services at Salisbury Cathedral. Following the services, Herbert would compose music with the cathedral musicians. Herbert died of consumption in 1633.

Tilemann Hesshus (1527–1588). German Lutheran theologian and pastor. Hesshus studied under Philipp Melanchthon* but was a staunch Gnesio-Lutheran. With great hesitation—and later regret—he affirmed the Formula of Concord.* Heshuss ardently advocated for church discipline, considering obedience a mark of the church. Unwilling to compromise his strong convictions, especially regarding matters of discipline, Hesshus was regularly embroiled in controversy. He was expelled or pressed to leave Goslar, Rostock, Heidelberg, Bremen, Magdeburg, Wesel, Königsberg and Samland before settling in Helmstedt, where he remained until his death. He wrote numerous polemical tracts concerning ecclesiology, justification, the sacraments and original sin, as well as commentaries on Psalms, Romans, 1–2 Corinthians, Galatians, Colossians and 1–2 Timothy, and a postil collection.

Edo Hilderich (1533–1599). German Lutheran historian and theologian. Hilderich (also named Hildericus) was born to a noble family in Frisia. After attending a local school, Hilderich went on to the University of Wittenberg, where he received the degree of master of philosophy in 1556. Among his teachers was Philipp Melanchthon.* In 1559, Hilderich was appointed to the Faculty of Arts at Wittenberg. He also served as professor of mathematics at the University of Jena from 1564 until 1567, when he resigned the post in order to return to the arts faculty at Wittenberg, of which he became dean in 1570. Three years later he became rector of the academy in Magdeburg, and went from there to the University of Frankfurt in 1575. In 1577, Hilderich became professor of history and Hebrew at Frankfurt. Following the expulsion of the Reformed theologians from the University of Heidelberg in 1578, he went there to be the second professor of theology and Hebrew language. He received his doctorate at Heidelberg a year later. However, Hilderich's refusal to sign the Formula of Concord resulted in removal from his post. On June 3, 1581, he accepted the professorship of theology at the University of Altdorf, where he later became rector in 1582, and professor of Hebrew in 1584. Hilderich's most important exegetical work is his *Oratio de politia et hierarchia populi Iudaici*, published in 1570, in which he traces the history of ancient Israel's government.

Samuel Hieron (1576?–1617). English Puritan minister. After graduating from Cambridge, Hieron became a minister in the Church of England and gained a reputation as a popular preacher in London before becoming the vicar at Modbury in Devonshire. Many of his sermons were published during his lifetime, and he also composed treatises on prayer and the value of Scripture.

Cornelis Hoen (c. 1460–1524). Dutch humanist, jurist, and theologian. A lawyer at the Court of Holland at the Hague, Hoen was prosecuted in 1523 over his sympathy for the evangelical message. He proposed a symbolic interpretation of Christ's presence in the Eucharist justified with reference to Matthew 24:23 in an influential, posthumously-published treatise.

Melchior Hoffman (1495?–1543). German Anabaptist preacher. First appearing as a Lutheran lay preacher in Livonia in 1523, Hoffman's claim to direct revelation, his perfectionist teachings and his announcements that the end of the world would occur in 1533 saw him alienated from both Lutheran and Reformed circles. After converting to Anabaptism in Strasbourg in 1530, a city he claimed would rise as the spiritual Jerusalem, Hoffman escaped brief arrest and fled to the Netherlands, where his preaching made him the first to bring the radical faith to the Low Countries. Believing himself to be Elijah, Hoffman gathered numerous followers, including future Anabaptist leaders Obbe Philips* and Jan Mathijs (d. 1534), until his arrest in Strasbourg in 1533, whereupon he was imprisoned for the final decade of his life. A tendency toward mystical allegory and apocalyptic exegesis supported by direct revelation is found in his writings, which include commentaries on Romans, Revelation, and Daniel 12 alongside numerous tracts, pamphlets, and letters.

Nathaniel Holmes (1599–1678). English Puritan theologian. Educated at Oxford, Holmes was a preacher in the Anglican Church until his millenarian views led him to establish an independent congregation. His publications include defenses of infant baptism and exclusive psalmody; treatises against witchcraft, usury, and astrology; and a commentary on the Song of Solomon.

Christopher Hooke (unknown). English Puritan physician and pastor. Hooke published a treatise promoting the joys and blessings of childbirth (1590) and a sermon on Hebrews 12:11-12. To support the poor, Hooke proposed a bank funded by voluntary investment of wealthy households.

Richard Hooker (c. 1553–1600). Anglican priest. Shortly after graduating from Corpus Christi College Oxford, Hooker took holy orders as a priest in 1581. After his marriage, he struggled to find work and temporarily tended sheep until Archbishop John Whitgift* appointed him to the Temple Church in London. Hooker's primary work is *The Laws of Ecclesiastical Polity* (1593), in which he sought to establish a philosophical and logical foundation for the highly controversial Elizabethan Religious Settlement (1559). The Elizabethan Settlement, through the Act of Supremacy, reasserted the Church of England's independence from the Church of Rome, and, through the Act of Uniformity, constructed a common church structure based on the reinstitution of the Book of Common Prayer.* Hooker's argumentation strongly emphasizes natural law and anticipates the social contract theory of John Locke (1632–1704).

Thomas Hooker (1586–1647). English-American Puritan Preacher. Hooker ministered at churches in Surrey and Essex and established a school to teach pastors until threatened with arrest as Archbishop Laud* worked to suppress Puritanism. Fleeing to Holland and then New England, he pastored a church in New Town (later Cambridge), Massachusetts before playing an important role in the foundation of Hartford, Connecticut and assisting with the composition of the state constitution.

John Hooper (d. 1555). English Protestant bishop and martyr. Impressed by the works of Huldrych Zwingli* and Heinrich Bullinger,* Hooper joined the Protestant movement in England. However, after the Act of Six Articles was passed, he fled to Zurich, where he spent ten years. He returned to England in 1549 and was appointed as a bishop. He stoutly advocated a Zwinglian reform agenda, arguing against the use of vestments and for a less "popish" Book of Common Prayer.* Condemned as a heretic for denying transubstantiation, Hooper was burned at the stake during Mary I's reign.

John Hoskin (unknown). English Protestant preacher. Hoskin published a sermon on Matthew 18:23 in 1610 in which he is identified as a minister of God's Word and student of divinity.

Rudolf Hospinian (Wirth) (1547–1626). Swiss Reformed theologian and minister. After studying theology at Marburg and Heidelberg, Hospinian pastored in rural parishes around Zurich and taught secondary school. In 1588, he transferred to Zurich, ministering at Grossmünster and Fraumünster. A keen student of church history, Hospinian wanted to show the differences between early church doctrine and contemporary Catholic teaching, particularly with regard to sacramental theology. He also criticized Lutheran dogma and the Formula of Concord*. Most of Hospinian's corpus consists of polemical treatises; he also published a series of sermons on the Magnificat.

Hans Hotz (dates unknown). Swiss Anabaptist leader. Born in Grüningen, near Zurich, Hotz was an associate of Georg Blaurock.* He defended Anabaptism as spokesman for the Swiss Brethren at disputations in Zofingen (1532) and Bern (1538).

John Howson (1557?–1632). English Anglican bishop. Howson held a number of pastoral positions in Oxfordshire before becoming vice chancellor of Oxford University. An opponent of Puritanism, he was appointed bishop of Oxford in 1619, and then to the bishopric of Durham in 1628, where he was an advocate for the reform program of Archbishop Laud.*

Caspar Huberinus (1500–1553). German Lutheran theologian and pastor. After studying theology at Wittenberg, Huberinus moved to Augsburg to serve as Urbanus Rhegius's* assistant. Huberinus represented Augsburg at the Bern Disputation (1528) on the Eucharist and images. In 1551, along with the nobility, Huberinus supported the Augsburg Interim, so long as communion of both kinds and regular preaching were allowed. Nevertheless the people viewed him as a traitor because of his official participation in the Interim, nicknaming him "Buberinus" (i.e., scoundrel). He wrote a number of popular devotional works as well as tracts defending Lutheran eucharistic theology against Zwinglian and Anabaptist detractions.

Balthasar Hubmaier (1480/5–1528). German Radical theologian. Hubmaier, a former priest who studied under Johann Eck,* is identified with his leadership in the peasants' uprising at Waldshut. Hubmaier served as the cathedral preacher in Regensberg, where he became involved in a series of anti-Semitic attacks. He was drawn to reform through the early works of Martin Luther*; his contact with Huldrych Zwingli* made Hubmaier a defender of more radical reform, including believers' baptism and a memorialist account of the Eucharist. His involvement in the Peasants' War led to his extradition and execution by the Austrians.

Aegidius Hunnius (1550–1603). German Lutheran theologian and preacher. Educated at Tübingen by Jakob Andreae (1528–1590) and Johannes Brenz,* Hunnius bolstered and advanced early Lutheran orthodoxy. After his crusade to root out all "crypto-Calvinism" divided Hesse into Lutheran and Reformed regions, Hunnius joined the Wittenberg theological faculty, where with Polykarp Leyser (1552–1610) he helped shape the university into an orthodox stronghold. Passionately confessional, Hunnius developed and nuanced the orthodox doctrines of predestination, Scripture, the church and Christology (more explicitly Chalcedonian), reflecting their codification in the Formula of Concord.* He was unafraid to engage in confessional polemics from the pulpit. In addition to his many treatises (most notably *De persona Christi*, in which he defended Christ's ubiquity), Hunnius published commentaries on Matthew, John, Ephesians and Colossians; his notes on Galatians, Philemon and 1 Corinthians were published posthumously.

Jan Hus (d. 1415). Bohemian reformer and martyr. This popular preacher strove for reform in the church, moral improvement in society, and an end to clerical abuses and popular religious superstition. He was branded a heretic for his alleged affinity for John Wycliffe's writings; however, while he agreed that a priest in mortal sin rendered the sacraments inefficacious, he affirmed the doctrine of transubstantiation. The Council of Constance* convicted Hus of heresy, banned his books and teaching, and, despite a letter of safe conduct, burned him at the stake.

Hans Hut (1490–1527). German Radical leader. Hut was an early leader of a mystical, apocalyptic strand of Anabaptist radical reform. His theological views were shaped by Andreas Bodenstein von Karlstadt,* Thomas Müntzer* and Hans Denck,* by whom Hut had been baptized. Hut rejected society and the established church and heralded the imminent end of days, which he perceived in the Peasants' War. Eventually arrested for practicing believers' baptism and participating in the Peasants' War, Hut was tortured and died accidentally in a fire in the Augsburg prison. The next day, the authorities sentenced his corpse to death and burned him.

George Hutcheson (1615–1674). Scottish Puritan pastor. Hutcheson, a pastor in Edinburgh, published commentaries on Job, John and the Minor Prophets, as well as sermons on Psalm 130.

Roger Hutchinson (d. 1555). English reformer. Little is known about Hutchinson except for his controversies. He disputed against the Mass while at Cambridge and debated with Joan Bocher (d. 1550), who affirmed the doctrine of the celestial flesh. During the Marian Restoration he was deprived of his fellowship at Eton because he was married.

Andreas Hyperius (1511–1564). Dutch Protestant theologian. After a peripatetic humanist education that encompassed studies in theology, canon law, and medicine, Hyperius became professor of theology at Marburg in 1541 and held this position until his death. Often viewed as mediating between Lutheran and Reformed thought, Hyperius was particularly concerned with the practical application of theology, demonstrated in his composition of the first Protestant text on homiletic method.

Abraham Ibn Ezra (1089–c. 1167). Spanish Jewish rabbi, exegete and poet. In 1140 Ibn Ezra fled his native Spain to escape persecution by the Almohad Caliphate. He spent the rest of his life as an exile, traveling through Europe, North Africa and the Middle East. His corpus consists of works on poetry, exegesis, grammar, philosophy, mathematics and astrology. In his commentaries on the Old Testament, Ibn Ezra restricts himself to *peshat* (see *quadriga*).

Valentin Ickelshamer (c. 1500–1547). German Radical teacher. After time at Erfurt, he studied under Luther,* Melanchthon,* Bugenhagen* and Karlstadt* in Wittenberg. He sided with Karlstadt against Luther, writing a treatise in Karlstadt's defense. Ickelshamer also represented the Wittenberg guilds in opposition to the city council. This guild committee allied with the peasants in 1525, leading to Ickelshamer's eventual exile. His poem in the Marpeck Circle's *Kunstbuch** is an expansion of a similar poem by Sebastian Franck.*

Arthur Jackson (1593?–1666). English Presbyterian minister. Known for his pastoral concern, Jackson served at a number of parishes in London. Imprisoned briefly for his support of the Royalist cause, after the Restoration, he was ejected from ministry following the 1662 Act of Uniformity. Jackson's primary works are a series of annotations of many books of the Old Testament.

Thomas Jackson (1579–1640). Anglican theologian and priest. Before serving as the president of Corpus Christi College at Oxford for the final decade of his life, Jackson was a parish priest and chaplain to the king. His best known work is a twelve-volume commentary on the Apostles' Creed.

King James I of England (VI of Scotland) (1566–1625). English monarch. The son of Mary, Queen of Scots, James ascended to the Scottish throne in 1567 following his mother's abdication. In the Union of the Crowns (1603), he took the English and Irish thrones after the death of his cousin, Elizabeth I.* James's reign was tumultuous and tense: Parliament and the nobility often opposed him, church factions squabbled over worship forms and ecclesiology, climaxing in the Gunpowder Plot. James wrote treatises on the divine right of kings, law, the evils of smoking tobacco and demonology. His religious writings include a versification of the Psalms, a paraphrase of Revelation and meditations on the Lord's Prayer and passages from Chronicles, Matthew and Revelation. He also sponsored the translation of the Authorized Version*—popularly remembered as the King James Version.

Cornelius Jansen (1585–1638). Dutch Catholic bishop and theologian. Jansen studied and taught in France and Holland, joining the theological faculty of the University of Leuven after receiving his doctorate. He later became bishop of Ypres. An ardent Augustinian, his posthumously published work *Augustinus* (1640) caused great controversy by advocating for the utterly gratuitous character of God's grace in opposition to the teachings of Jesuit Luis de Molina (1536–1609), which put greater emphasis on human choice. Due to its perceived Protestant leanings, *Augustinus* was judged heretical, and Jansen's followers, known as Jansenists, took up his cause in a series of conflicts that carried on into the eighteenth century.

Jeanne of Navarre (1528–1572) French Reformed noblewoman. Daughter of Henry II, King of Navarre (1503–1555) and Marguerite d'Angoulême*, Jeanne was forced into a strategic marriage at age 12 by her uncle, Francis I* to William, Duke of Cleves (1516–1592). Shifting political alignments allowed her an annulment after four years and in 1548 she wed the first Prince of the Blood, Antoine de Bourbon (1518–1562). Jeanne took the throne of her father, and after making a public announcement of her conversion to the evangelical faith, established a Reformed community at Béarn. A regular correspondent of reformers such as Calvin* and Beza* and an advocate for the reformation of her lands, Jeanne nevertheless remained largely neutral and advocated tolerance during the first years of religious war. At the outbreak of the Third War of Religion (1569–1570), however, she recognized her moderate position was untenable, and from the Protestant stronghold of La Rochelle served as political head for the Huguenot cause alongside Gaspard de Coligny (1519–1572), commander of the Huguenot armed forces.

John Jewel (1522–1571). Anglican theologian and bishop. Jewel studied at Oxford where he met Peter Martyr Vermigli.* After graduating in 1552, Jewel was appointed to his first vicarage and became the orator for the university. Upon Mary I's accession, Jewel lost his post as orator because of his Protestant views. After the trials of Thomas Cranmer* and Nicholas Ridley,* Jewel affirmed Catholic teaching to avoid their fate. Still he had to flee to the continent. Confronted by John Knox,* Jewel publicly repented of his cowardice before the English congregation in Frankfurt, then reunited with Vermigli in Strasbourg. After Mary I's death, Jewel returned to England and was consecrated bishop in 1560. He advocated low-church ecclesiology, but supported the Elizabethan Settlement against Catholics and Puritans. In response to the Council of Trent, he published the *Apoligia ecclesiae Anglicanae* (1562), which established him as the apostle for Anglicanism and incited numerous controversies.

St. John of the Cross (Juan de Yepes y Álvarez) (1542–1591). Spanish Catholic mystic. Born into poverty, Álvarez entered the Carmelite order in Medina del Campo, where, after studying theology at Salamanca, he met the famed mystic Teresa of Ávila (1515–1582). Drawn to her vision of the contemplative life, with two others, he established the first house of Discalced (barefoot) Carmelite Friars and became a leader in the Catholic reform movement. An exceptional administrator and spiritual leader, for more than twenty years, John of the Cross sought to return his order to its original vision of asceticism and prayer while establishing many new reformed Carmelite houses. He encountered significant resistance in his work for renewal, however, and spent nine months imprisoned and tortured by his Carmelite superiors. Considered among the foremost poets in Spanish literary history, his poems, including *The Spiritual Canticle*, *Ascent of Mount Carmel*, and *The Dark Night of the Soul* demonstrate his overriding desire for spiritual growth and closeness to God.

Francis Johnson (1562–1618). English Brownist pastor. A popular Puritan preacher at Cambridge, Johnson was arrested for slander and factitiousness after a sermon criticizing the ecclesiastical hierarchy and the comfortable lives of the ministers at the school. Retracting some of his statements, he was released and expelled from Cambridge. While pastoring an English church in the Netherlands, he came across writings from followers of Robert Browne* and became convinced of the need to separate from the established church and commit to congregational church polity, but his attempts to institute these changes in the church led to his firing. Returning to England, Johnson became pastor of the Brownist church in London, for which he was arrested numerous times until he convinced the Privy Council to allow him to found a Brownist church in Newfoundland. The expedition was canceled, however, and he returned to the Netherlands, where he pastored separatist churches, some alongside Henry Ainsworth* and John Smyth,* until his death.

Justus Jonas (1493–1555). German Lutheran theologian, pastor and administrator. Jonas studied law at Erfurt, where he befriended the poet Eobanus Hessus (1488–1540), whom Luther* dubbed "king of the poets"; later, under the influence of the humanist Konrad Muth, Jonas focused on theology. In 1516 he was ordained as a priest, and in 1518 he became a doctor of theology and law. After witnessing the Leipzig Disputation, Jonas was converted to Luther's* cause. While traveling with Luther to the Diet of Worms, Jonas was appointed professor of canon law at Wittenberg. Later he became its dean of theology, lecturing on Romans, Acts and the Psalms. Jonas was also instrumental for reform in Halle. He preached Luther's funeral sermon but had a falling-out with Melanchthon* over the Leipzig Interim. Jonas's most influential contribution was translating Luther's *The Bondage of the Will* and Melanchthon's *Loci communes* into German.

Robert Jones. A pseudonym; see Thomas Lushington.

William Jones (1561–1636). Anglican minister and theologian. After teaching at Cambridge, Jones ministered at East Bergholt in Suffolk for forty-four years, publishing a commentary on Philemon and Hebrews and tracts on suffering, the nativity, and arrangements to be made before one's death.

David Joris (c. 1501–1556). Dutch Radical pastor and hymnist. This former glass painter was one of the leading Dutch Anabaptist leaders after the fall of Münster (1535), although due to his increasingly radical ideas his influence waned in the early 1540s. Joris came to see himself as a "third David," a Spirit-anointed prophet ordained to proclaim the coming third kingdom of God, which would be established in the Netherlands with Dutch as its *lingua franca*. Joris's interpretation of Scripture, with his heavy emphasis on personal mystical experience, led to a very public dispute with Menno Simons* whom Joris considered a teacher of the "dead letter." In 1544 Joris and about one hundred followers moved to Basel, conforming outwardly to the teaching of the Reformed church there. Today 240 of Joris's books are extant, the most important of which is his *Twonder Boek* (1542/43).

Jörg Haugk von Jüchsen (unknown). German Radical preacher. Nothing is known of Haugk's life except that during the 1524–1525 Peasants' War in Thuringia, he was elected as a preacher by the insurrectionists in his district. He composed one extant tract, titled *A Christian Order of a True Christian: Giving an Account of the Origin of His Faith*, published in 1526 but likely written before the Peasants' War. While lacking reference to most distinctive Anabaptist doctrines, this pamphlet became popular among radicals as it set out the stages of Christian growth toward perfection.

Andreas Bodenstein von Karlstadt (Carlstadt) (1486–1541). German Radical theologian. Karlstadt, an early associate of Martin Luther* and Philipp Melanchthon* at the University of Wittenberg, participated alongside Luther in the dispute at Leipzig with Johann Eck.* He also influenced the configuration of the Old Testament canon in Protestantism. During Luther's captivity in Wartburg Castle in Eisenach, Karlstadt oversaw reform in Wittenberg. His acceleration of the pace of reform brought conflict with Luther, so Karlstadt left Wittenberg, eventually settling at the University of Basel as professor of Old Testament (after a sojourn in Zurich with Huldrych Zwingli*). During his time in Switzerland, Karlstadt opposed infant baptism and repudiated Luther's doctrine of Christ's real presence in the Eucharist.

Edward Kellett (d. 1641). Anglican theologian and priest. Kellett published a sermon concerning the reconversion of an Englishman from Islam, a tract on the soul, and a discourse on the Lord's Supper in connection with Passover.

David Kimchi (Radak) (1160–1235). French Jewish rabbi, exegete and philosopher. Kimchi wrote an important Hebrew grammar and dictionary, as well as commentaries on Genesis, 1–2 Chronicles, the Psalms and the Prophets. He focused on *peshat* (see *quadriga*). In his Psalms commentary he attacks Christian interpretation as forced, irrational and inadmissible. While Sebastian Münster* censors and condemns these arguments in his *Miqdaš YHWH* (1534–1535), he and many other Christian commentators valued Kimchi's work as a grammatical resource.

Moses Kimchi (Remak) (1127–1190). French Jewish rabbi and exegete. He was David Kimchi's* brother. He wrote commentaries on Proverbs and Ezra-Nehemiah. Sebastian Münster* translated Kimchi's concise Hebrew grammar into Latin; many sixteenth-century Christian exegetes used this resource.

Andreas Knöpken (c. 1468–1539). German Lutheran pastor. Knöpken worked in Pomerania as assistant to Johannes Bugenhagen* before relocating to Riga. Here he served as pastor of St. Peter's, and after a brief setback that saw him return to his previous position, he returned and won a disputation before the authorities, which allowed him to undertake the evangelical reform of the city. Knöpken oversaw the reorganization of the churches and schools, composed the church order, wrote a commentary on Romans, and arranged a number of hymns based on the Psalms.

John Knox (1513–1572). Scottish Reformed preacher. Knox, a fiery preacher to monarchs and zealous defender of high Calvinism, was a leading figure of reform in Scotland. Following imprisonment in the French galleys, Knox went to England, where he became a royal chaplain to Edward VI. At the accession of Mary, Knox fled to Geneva, studying under John Calvin* and serving as a pastor. Knox returned to Scotland after Mary's death and became a chief architect of the reform of the Scottish church (Presbyterian), serving as one of the authors of the Book of Discipline and writing many pamphlets and sermons.

Antonius Broickwy von Königstein (1470–1541). German Catholic preacher. Very little is known about this important cathedral preacher in Cologne. Strongly opposed to evangelicals, he sought to develop robust resources for Catholic homilies. His postils were bestsellers, and his biblical concordance helped Catholic preachers to construct doctrinal loci from Scripture itself.

Kunstbuch. In 1956, two German students rediscovered this unique collection of Anabaptist works. Four hundred years earlier, a friend of the recently deceased Pilgram Marpeck*—the painter Jörg Probst—had entrusted this collection of letters, tracts and poetry to a Zurich bindery; today only half of it remains. Probst's redaction arranges various compositions from the Marpeck Circle into a devotional anthology focused on the theme of the church as Christ incarnate (cf. Gal 2:20).

Osmund Lake (c. 1543–1621). English Pastor who ministered at Ringwood in Hampshire.

Thomas Lamb (d. 1686). English Nonconformist minister. Lamb earned a living as a soap boiler while serving as a teaching elder and occasional preacher at a congregational church in London. Convicted of the necessity of adult baptism and the invalidity of infant baptism, he formed a Particular Baptist congregation and led this church for four years before rejoining the Church of England as a layman, retracting his former teachings and becoming a vocal opponent of separatism. Toward the end of his life, he turned to philanthropy, seeking to improve the lives of the poor and prisoners and to further the religious education of children.

François Lambert (Lambert of Avignon) (1487–1530). French Reformed theologian. In 1522, after becoming drawn to the writings of Martin Luther* and meeting Huldrych Zwingli,* Lambert left the Franciscan order. He spent time in Wittenberg, Strasbourg, and Hesse, where Lambert took a leading role at the Homberg Synod (1526) and in creating a biblically based plan for church reform. He served as professor of theology at Marburg University from 1527 to his death. After the Marburg Colloquy (1529), Lambert accepted Zwingli's symbolic view of the Eucharist. Lambert produced nineteen books, mostly biblical commentaries that favored spiritual interpretations; his unfinished work of comprehensive theology was published posthumously.

Eitelhans Langenmantel (d. 1528). German Radical writer. The son of the mayor of Augsburg, Langenmantel was converted to Anabaptism and was rebaptized by Hans Hut* in 1527. Arrested for his heterodox views later that year, he was freed after accepting the validity of infant baptism during a debate, but after renouncing his recantation in 1528, he was rearrested and beheaded. Seven tracts he composed during 1526 and 1527 survive, focusing on the Lord's Supper and the moral life.

Emilia Lanier (1569–1645). English poet. The daughter of a musician at the court of Elizabeth I,* she received a humanist education at the home of Susan Bertie, Countess of Kent (b. 1554). Following a long affair with Henry Carey (1526–1596), Lord Chamberlain to the queen, and after conceiving a child, she married a distant cousin, Alfonso Lanier (unknown). She is best known for a book of poetry written in the hope of securing a patron, *Salve Deus Rex Judaeorum* (1611), which contains a number of protofeminist themes. Modern scholars have also suggested she may be the "Dark Lady" who appears in a number of William Shakespeare's (1564–1616) sonnets.

Hugh Latimer (c. 1485–1555). Anglican bishop and preacher. Latimer was celebrated for his sermons critiquing the idolatrous nature of Catholic practices and the social injustices visited on the underclass by the aristocracy and the individualism of Protestant government. After his support for Henry's petition of divorce he served as a court preacher under Henry VIII* and Edward VI. Latimer became a proponent of reform following his education at Cambridge University and received license as a preacher. Following Edward's death, Latimer was tried for heresy, perishing at the stake with Nicholas Ridley* and Thomas Cranmer.*

William Laud (1573–1645). Anglican archbishop, one of the most pivotal and controversial figures in Anglican church history. Early in his career, Laud offended many with his highly traditional, anti-Puritan approach to ecclesial policies. After his election as Archbishop of Canterbury in 1633, Laud continued to strive against the Puritans, demanding the eastward placement of the Communion altar (affirming the religious centrality of the Eucharist), the use of clerical garments, the reintroduction of stained-glass windows, and the uniform use of the Book of Common Prayer.* Laud was accused of being a crypto-Catholic—an ominous accusation during the protracted threat of invasion by the Spanish Armada. In 1640 the Long Parliament met, quickly impeached Laud on charges of treason, and placed him in jail for several years before his execution.

Ludwig Lavater (1527–1586). Swiss Reformed pastor and theologian. Under his father-in-law Heinrich Bullinger,* Lavater became an archdeacon in Zurich. In 1585 he succeeded Rudolf Gwalther* as the city's Antistes. He authored a widely disseminated book on demonology, commentaries on Chronicles, Proverbs, Ecclesiastes, Nehemiah and Ezekiel, theological works, and biographies of Bullinger and Konrad Pellikan.*

Laws and Liberties of the Inhabitants of Massachusetts (1647). North American colonial constitution. The first printed set of laws in the American colonies, the 1647 *Laws and Liberties of the Inhabitants of Massachusetts* was a revision of the *Massachusetts Body of Liberties* (1641), a legal code collected by Puritan minister Nathaniel Ward (1578–1652). The *Laws and Liberties* codified Puritan expectations of doctrine and morality, and included provision for the punishment for heresy, stipulating banishment for Anabaptism. The majority of the document consists of practical clauses addressing general and specific aspects of communal and commercial life.

John Lawson (unknown). Seventeenth-century English Puritan. Lawson wrote *Gleanings and Expositions of Some of Scripture* (1646) and a treatise on the sabbath in the New Testament.

Jacques Lefèvre d'Étaples (Faber Stapulensis) (1460?–1536). French Catholic humanist, publisher and translator. Lefèvre d'Étaples studied classical literature and philosophy, as well as patristic and medieval mysticism. He advocated the principle of *ad fontes*, issuing a full-scale annotation on the corpus of Aristotle, publishing the writings of key Christian mystics, and contributing to efforts at biblical translation and commentary. Although he never broke with the Catholic Church, his views prefigured those of Martin Luther,* for which he was condemned by the University of Sorbonne in Paris. He then found refuge in the court of Marguerite d'Angoulême, where he met John Calvin* and Martin Bucer.*

Edward Leigh (1602–1671). English Puritan biblical critic, historian and politician. Educated at Oxford, Leigh's public career included appointments as a Justice of the Peace, an officer in the parliamentary army during the English Civil Wars and a member of Parliament. Although never ordained, Leigh devoted himself to the study of theology and Scripture; he participated in the Westminster Assembly. Leigh published a diverse corpus, including lexicons of Greek, Hebrew and juristic terms, and histories of Roman, Greek and English rulers. His most important theological work is *A Systeme or Body of Divinity* (1662).

John Lightfoot (1602–1675). Anglican priest and biblical scholar. After graduating from Cambridge, Lightfoot was ordained and pastored at several small parishes. He continued to study classics under the support of the politician Rowland Cotton (1581–1634). Siding with the Parliamentarians during the English Civil Wars, Lightfoot relocated to London in 1643. He was one of the original members of the Westminster Assembly, where he defended a moderate Presbyterianism. His best-known work is the six-volume *Horae Hebraicae et Talmudicae* (1658–1677), a verse-by-verse commentary illumined by Hebrew customs, language and the Jewish interpretive tradition.

Wenceslaus Linck (1482–1547). German Lutheran theologian and preacher. As dean of the theology faculty at the University of Wittenberg and successor to Johannes von Staupitz* as the prior of the Augustinian Monastery, Linck worked closely with Martin Luther* and attended the Heidelberg Disputation with him. He replaced Staupitz as vicar-general of the Augustinian order in 1520 in Germany, a capacity in which he pronounced all members free from their vows before renouncing the order himself. After periods of ministry in Munich and Altenburg, Linck settled in Nuremberg, where he became known as an exemplary preacher and an advisor to cities undertaking Protestant reform. He published a significant number of sermons and practical tracts as well as a paraphrase and annotations on the Old Testament.

Peter Lombard (1095–1160). Scholastic theologian, bishop of Paris. Though little is known about his life, some records indicate that Lombard came from the region of Novara in Lombardy. Bernard of Clairvaux* patronized his studies at Reims, and later recommended him for further study at St. Victor in Paris. In 1144, Lombard participated in an examination of the writings of Gilbert of Poitiers for heresy. Lombard became a canon at Notre Dame in 1145, and an archdeacon there in 1156. Meanwhile he spent a year and a half in Rome as an assistant to Theobald, bishop of Paris. Lombard was elected bishop of Paris in 1159. He died less than a year later. Lombard's most important work was the *Four Books of the Sentences*, which served as the standard textbook for theology throughout the remainder of the Middle Ages, and at the beginning of the early modern period. Additionally, Lombard produced commentaries on the Psalms and Pauline epistles.

Johannes Lonicer (1499–1569). German Lutheran theologian and linguist. After studying in Erfurt and Wittenberg, Lonicer renounced his Augustinian vows. He briefly taught Hebrew at the University of Freiburg, but controversy saw him flee to Strasburg, where he worked with a printer, translating some early Lutheran vernacular works into Latin. At the opening of the University of Marburg, Lonicer was appointed to teach Greek and Hebrew, and he later also served as professor of theology.

Lucas Lossius (1508–1582). German Lutheran teacher and musician. While a student at Leipzig and Wittenberg, Lossius was deeply influenced by Melanchthon* and Luther,* who found work for him as Urbanus Rhegius's* secretary. Soon after going to work for Rhegius, Lossius began teaching at a local gymnasium (or secondary school), *Das Johanneum*, eventually becoming its headmaster. Lossius remained at *Das Johanneum* until his death, even turning down appointments to university professorships. A man of varied interests, he wrote on dialectics, music and church history, as well as publishing a postil and a five-volume set of annotations on the New Testament.

Sibrandus Lubbertus (c. 1555–1625). Dutch Reformed theologian. Lubbertis, a key figure in the establishment of orthodox Calvinism in Frisia, studied theology at Wittenburg and Geneva (under Theodore Beza*) before his appointment as professor of theology at the University of Franeker. Throughout his career, Lubbertis advocated for high Calvinist theology, defending it in disputes with representatives of Socinianism, Arminianism and Roman Catholicism. Lubbertis criticized the Catholic theologian Robert Bellarmine and fellow Dutch reformer Jacobus Arminius*; the views of the latter he opposed as a prominent participant in the Synod of Dordrecht.*

Thomas Lushington (1590–1661). English Anglican minister. Best known as the tutor of polymath Sir Thomas Browne (1605–1682), Lushington also served as a chaplain to Richard Corbet, bishop of Oxford. Committed to the program of Archbishop Laud,* he lost his position during the English Civil Wars and retired to write. Most of his works were published anonymously or pseudonymously, including a translation of a commentary on Hebrews by Polish theologian Johannes Crellius (1590–1633) as G. W. and a series of sermons given at Oxford as Robert Jones.

Martin Luther (1483–1546). German Lutheran priest, professor, and theologian. Martin Luther was born in Eisleben, Saxony, to an entrepreneurial minor. Upon completing his earlier education at Eisenach, Luther matriculated at the University of Erfurt where he completed his BA in 1502, and MA in 1505. While at Erfurt, Luther studied the philosophy of William of Ockham (1285–1347), and his disciple, Gabriel Biel (1420–1495). After receiving his MA, Luther proceeded to the study of law. However, a number of events culminating in his promise to St. Anne (the patron saint of minors) to become a monk compelled Luther to withdraw from law school and join the Augustinian monastery at Erfurt in 1505. At this monastery, Luther was ordained a priest. Later, the Augustinians sent Luther to the University of Wittenberg to study theology. In 1512, Luther received his doctorate, and took up the post of lecturer in Bible at Wittenberg, a position he would hold the rest of his life. While a professor at this university, Luther reinterpreted the doctrine of justification. Convinced that righteousness comes only from God's grace, he disputed the sale of indulgences with his *Ninety–Five Theses*, which he reportedly posted to the door of All Saints' Church in Wittenberg on October 31, 1517. Luther's positions brought conflict with Rome. He challenged the Mass, transubstantiation, and communion in one kind, and his denial of papal authority led to excommunication. Though Luther was condemned by the Diet of Worms, Frederick III, the Elector of Saxony, provided him safe haven. Luther later returned to Wittenberg with public order collapsing under Andreas

Bodenstein von Karlstadt* and steered a more cautious path of reform. Among his most influential works are three treatises published in 1520: *To the Christian Nobility of the German Nation, On the Babylonian Captivity of the Church*, and *On the Freedom of a Christian*. His rendering of the Bible and liturgy in the vernacular, as well as his hymns and sermons, proved extensively influential.

Georg Major (1502–1574). German Lutheran theologian. Major was on the theological faculty of the University of Wittenberg, succeeding as dean Johannes Bugenhagen* and Philipp Melanchthon.* One of the chief editors on the Wittenberg edition of Luther's works, Major is most identified with the controversy bearing his name, in which he stated that good works are necessary to salvation. Major qualified his statement, which was in reference to the totality of the Christian life. The Formula of Concord* rejected the statement, ending the controversy. As a theologian, Major further refined Lutheran views of the inspiration of Scripture and the doctrine of the Trinity.

John (Mair) Major (1467–1550). Scottish Catholic philosopher. Major taught logic and theology at the universities of Paris (his alma mater), Glasgow and St Andrews. His broad interests and impressive work drew students from all over Europe. While disapproving of evangelicals (though he did teach John Knox*), Major advocated reform programs for Rome. He supported collegial episcopacy and even challenged the curia's teaching on sexuality. Still he was a nominalist who was critical of humanist approaches to biblical exegesis. His best-known publication is *A History of Greater Britain, Both England and Scotland* (1521), which promoted the union of the kingdoms. He also published a commentary on Peter Lombard's *Sentences* and the Gospel of John.

Juan de Maldonado (1533–1583). Spanish Catholic biblical scholar. A student of Francisco de Toledo,* Maldonado taught philosophy and theology at the universities of Paris and Salamanca. Ordained to the priesthood in Rome, he revised the Septuagint under papal appointment. While Maldonado vehemently criticized Protestants, he asserted that Reformed baptism was valid and that mixed confessional marriages were acceptable. His views on Mary's immaculate conception proved controversial among many Catholics who conflated his statement that it was not an article of faith with its denial. He was intrigued by demonology (blaming demonic influence for the Reformation). All his work was published posthumously; his Gospel commentaries were highly valued and important.

Thomas Manton (1620–1677). English Puritan minister. Manton, educated at Oxford, served for a time as lecturer at Westminster Abbey and rector of St. Paul's, Covent Garden, and was a strong advocate of Presbyterianism. He was known as a rigorous evangelical Calvinist who preached long expository sermons. At different times in his ecclesial career he worked side-by-side with Richard Baxter* and John Owen.* In his later life, Manton's Nonconformist position led to his ejection as a clergyman from the Church of England (1662) and eventual imprisonment (1670). Although a voluminous writer, Manton was best known for his preaching. At his funeral in 1677, he was dubbed "the king of preachers."

Benedetto da Mantova (c. 1495–c. 1556). Italian Catholic monk. Benedetto entered the Benedictine order in Mantua and served as dean at San Giorgio Maggiore in Venice. At San Nicolò l'Arena on Mt. Etna, he became acquainted with Waldensian and Protestant thought, which influenced his composition of *The Benefit of Christ*, one of the most significant Italian writings of the Reformation. Marcantonio Flaminio* was asked to rewrite the text in more elegant prose before its anonymous publication in 1543, and although the work drew the ire of the Inquisition, Benedetto's authorship was not uncovered during his lifetime. His increasingly radical spiritualism saw him arrested in Padua, though nothing of his later life is known.

Felix Mantz (d. 1527). Swiss Anabaptist Leader. An early supporter of Zwingli* in Zurich, Mantz's frustration with the pace of the magisterial Reformation led him to found an independent congregation, the Swiss Brethren, with Conrad Grebel,* Georg Blaurock,* and others. Mantz and Grebel represented the Brethren in two disputations with Zwingli over infant baptism in 1525. Defeated, the Brethren refused to cease meeting and rebaptizing adults, which they considered a first baptism, leading to suppression by the Zurich authorities. Mantz was able to spread his message for a time, traveling through a number of Swiss regions despite several arrests. Imprisoned by the Zurich authorities in March 1526 with Grebel and Blaurock, he briefly escaped, but having returned to his practice of believers' baptism, he was executed by drowning, the punishment for Anabaptism, in January 1527.

Lucrezia Marinella (1571–1653). Venetian poet and writer. While famous for her writings, very little is known of Marinella's personal life. As was expected of a women of her class, she spent most of her life in seclusion, and she did not participate in public life. She married a physician, but the fact that she had two children is only known from her will. Marinella's writings spanned a number of subjects, including, philosophy, religious poetry, and proto-feminist texts on the abilities of women and their place in society. Perhaps her best-known work is *The Nobility and Excellence of Women and the Defects and Vices of Men* (1600), in which she argues for the moral and intellectual superiority of women.

Augustin Marlorat (c. 1506–1562). French Reformed pastor. Committed by his family to a monastery at the age of eight, Marlorat was also ordained into the priesthood at an early age in 1524. He fled to Geneva in 1535, where he pastored until the Genevan Company of Pastors sent him to France to shepherd the nascent evangelical congregations. His petition to the young Charles IX (1550–1574) for the right to public evangelical worship was denied. In response to a massacre of evangelicals in Vassy (over sixty dead, many more wounded), Marlorat's congregation planned to overtake Rouen. After the crown captured Rouen, Marlorat was arrested and executed three days later for treason. His principle published work was an anthology of New Testament comment modeled after Thomas Aquinas's* *Catena aurea in quatuor Evangelia*. Marlorat harmonized Reformed and Lutheran comment with the church fathers, interspersed with his own brief comments. He also wrote such anthologies for Genesis, Job, the Psalms, Song of Songs and Isaiah.

Pilgram Marpeck (c. 1495–1556). Austrian Radical elder and theologian. During a brief sojourn in Strasbourg, Marpeck debated with Martin Bucer* before the city council; Bucer was declared the winner, and Marpeck was asked to leave Strasbourg for his views concerning paedobaptism (which he compared to a sacrifice to Moloch). After his time in Strasbourg, Marpeck traveled throughout southern Germany and western Austria, planting Anabaptist congregations. Marpeck criticized the strict use of the ban, however, particularly among the Swiss brethren. He also engaged in a christological controversy with Kaspar von Schwenckfeld.*

Stephen Marshall (c. 1594–1655). English Presbyterian minister. Known for his Nonconformist preaching, Marshall pastored in Essex before appearing on the national stage prior to the Civil War (1642–1651). An advocate of armed rebellion against a lawful sovereign over religious matters, he preached before Parliament a number of times, was a member of the Westminster Assembly, and served as lecturer at St. Margaret's, Westminster. He also ministered to Archbishop Laud* and Charles I* before their executions.

Gregory Martin (1542?–1582). English Catholic priest and translator. After studying at Oxford, Martin tutored the sons of the Duke of Norfolk until leaving for the college of Douai, where he received his doctorate. He taught for two years at the English college in Rome before returning to the college of Douai, which was temporarily based at Rheims. While he composed a number of polemical writings, he is best known as the primary translator of the Douai-Rheims Bible, an English translation of the Vulgate with commentary and notes intended to provide a Catholic alternative to the influx of Protestant annotated English Bibles. The New Testament was published at Douai in 1582 and the Old Testament at Rheims in 1609–1610.

Mary I of England (1516–1558). English monarch. Daughter of Henry VIII* and his first wife Catherine of Aragon (1509–1553), Mary was raised in the strict Catholicism of her mother. Her succession of Edward VI, her half-brother, was briefly contested by Lady Jane Grey*, daughter of Henry VIII's younger sister, in whom Protestants placed their hopes, but unable to raise adequate support, this challenge was quickly dismissed. Upon her ascent, Mary set about the task of restoring the Catholic religion, a reversal of royal policy that was positively received by much of the populace. While able to reestablish relations with the Pope and reassert the mass and other aspects of Catholicism, the impoverishment of the church following the dissolution of the monasteries and the closure of the chantries was difficult to overcome. Other aspects of popular piety, including the cult of the saints, pilgrimages, and the doctrine of purgatory, were not restored during her reign. Mary looms large in the Protestant imagination, and her persecution of evangelicals led to the moniker "Bloody Mary." The accounts of martyrs such as Thomas Cranmer*, Hugh Latimer*, and Nicholas Ridley* were immortalized in John Foxe's (1516–1587) *Acts and Monuments** and became a mainstay of Protestant propaganda.

Johannes Mathesius (1504–1565). German Lutheran theologian and pastor. After reading Martin Luther's* *On Good Works*, Mathesius left his teaching post in Ingolstadt and traveled to Wittenberg to study theology. Mathesius was an important agent of reform in the Bohemian town of Jáchymov, where he pastored, preached and taught. Over one thousand of Mathesius's sermons are extant, including numerous wedding and funeral sermons as well as a series on Luther's life. Mathesius also transcribed portions of Luther's Table Talk.

Anthony Maxey (d. 1618). Anglican minister. Maxey was born in Essex and educated at Westminster School. After completing his early education at Westminster, Maxey matriculated at Trinity College, Cambridge, in 1578. Maxey graduated Cambridge with the BA (1581), MA

(1585), BD (1594), and DD (1608) degrees. However, he was unable to obtain a fellowship at Trinity. King James I* appointed Maxey as his chaplain and dean of Windsor on June 21, 1612. Maxey was also inducted into the Order of the Garter. He died on May 3, 1618. Maxey's published works consist of three sermons: *The Churches Sleep*; *The Golden Chain of Man's Salvation*; and *The Fearful Point of Hardening*.

John Mayer (1583–1664). Anglican priest and biblical exegete. Mayer dedicated much of his life to biblical exegesis, writing a seven-volume commentary on the entire Bible (1627–1653). Styled after Philipp Melanchthon's* *locus* method, Mayer's work avoided running commentary, focusing instead on textual and theological problems. He was a parish priest for fifty-five years. In the office of priest Mayer also wrote a popular catechism, *The English Catechisme, or a Commentarie on the Short Catechisme* (1621), which went through twelve editions in his lifetime.

Joseph Mede (1586–1638). Anglican biblical scholar, Hebraist and Greek lecturer. A man of encyclopedic knowledge, Mede was interested in numerous fields, varying from philology and history to mathematics and physics, although millennial thought and apocalyptic prophesy were clearly his chief interests. Mede's most important work was his *Clavis Apocalyptica* (1627, later translated into English as *The Key of the Revelation*). This work examined the structure of Revelation as the key to its interpretation. Mede saw the visions as a connected and chronological sequence hinging around Revelation 17:18. He is remembered as an important figure in the history of millenarian theology. He was respected as a mild-mannered and generous scholar who avoided controversy and debate, but who had many original thoughts.

Philipp Melanchthon (1497–1560). German Lutheran educator, reformer, and theologian. Philipp Melanchthon was born in the Palatinate, the son of an armorer. He attended the Latin school in Pforzheim, where he lived with the sister of Johannes Reuchlin* to whom he was related by marriage. Having completed his early education, Melanchthon went on to attend the University of Heidelberg, where he received his BA in 1511. Afterwards, he earned his MA from the University of Tubingen in 1514. In 1518, Reuchlin recommended Melanchthon for the new professorship of Greek at the University of Wittenberg, where he remained for the rest of his life. There, Melanchthon taught Greek, rhetoric, and logic. Melanchthon is known as the partner and successor to Martin Luther* in reform in Germany and for his pioneering *Loci Communes*, which served as a theological textbook. Melanchthon participated with Luther in the Leipzig disputation, helped implement reform in Wittenberg, and was a chief architect of the Augsburg Confession.* Later, Melanchthon and Martin Bucer* worked for union between reformed and Catholic churches. On account of Melanchthon's ecumenical disposition and his modification of several of Luther's doctrines, he was held in suspicion by some.

Andrew Melville (1545–1622). Scottish Reformed theologian. Melville was born at Baldovie on August 1, 1545, to an evangelical family. After finishing his early education at Montrose Grammar School, he matriculated at St. Mary's College, St. Andrews, in 1559. Melville graduated St. Andrews in 1564, after which he traveled to Paris, where he studied Greek, Hebrew, mathematics, and other languages. While in Paris, Melville came under the influence of Petrus Ramus,* whose pedagogical methods he would later utilize in Scotland. From there, he proceeded to Poitiers to study law. There, he became regent of the College of St. Marceon. However, when Poitiers came under siege, Melville departed the city for Geneva, where Theodore Beza* warmly received him. Shortly after Melville's arrival in Geneva, he assumed the chair of humanities at the academy. Melville remained in this position at the academy until 1573, when he returned to Scotland. In 1574, Melville was appointed principal of the College of Glasgow. While in this post, Melville led in the reform of the college's curriculum, and engaged in ecclesiastical controversy. He served on the committee that drafted the Second Book of Discipline, and was elected moderator of the General Assembly in 1578. In 1580, Melville became principal of St. Mary's College, St. Andrews, where he initiated the same types of reform as he did at Glasgow. Throughout his career, Melville denounced royal ecclesiastical supremacy, arguing strongly for the autonomy of the national church. For this he was summoned to the Privy Council in Edinburgh in 1584 on the possible charge of treason for his resistance to royal ecclesiastical authority. Though they could not charge Melville with sedition, the Privy Council still determined to consign him to trial, but Melville managed to escape to England. While in England, he visited Puritan leaders at Oxford and Cambridge. He also lectured on Genesis in London. Melville returned to Scotland in 1585, and became rector of the University of St. Andrews in 1590. He was eventually deprived of this rectorship in 1587 for his opposition to episcopacy. In 1606, along with several ministers, he was summoned to appear before Hampton Court, where he gave some uncompromising speeches.

These speeches resulted in Melville's imprisonment in several places, including the Tower of London. Melville was released from the Tower on April 19, 1611, and from there traveled to France. Having arrived in France, Melville proceeded through Paris and Rouen to Sedan, where he assumed the chair of theology. He remained in Sedan until his death in 1622. Melville authored an extensive literary corpus, which includes a commentary on Romans.

Justus Menius (1499–1558). German Lutheran pastor and theologian. Menius was a prominent reformer in Thuringia. He participated in the Marburg Colloquy and, with others, helped Martin Luther* compose the Schmalkald Articles.* Throughout his career Menius entered into numerous controversies with Anabaptists and even fellow Lutherans. He rejected Andreas Osiander's (d. 1552) doctrine of justification—that the indwelling of Christ's divine nature justifies, rather than the imputed alien righteousness of Christ's person, declared through God's mercy. Against Nikolaus von Amsdorf (1483–1565) and Matthias Flacius (1520–1575), Menius agreed with Georg Major* that good works are necessary to salvation. Osiander's view of justification was censored in Article 3 of the Formula of Concord*; Menius's understanding of the relationship between good works and salvation was rejected in Article 4. Menius translated many of Luther's Latin works into German. He also composed a handbook for Christian households and an influential commentary on 1 Samuel.

Johannes Mercerus (Jean Mercier) (d. 1570). French Hebraist. Mercerus studied under the first Hebrew chair at the Collège Royal de Paris, François Vatable (d. 1547), whom he succeeded in 1546. John Calvin* tried to recruit Mercerus to the Genevan Academy as professor of Hebrew, once in 1558 and again in 1563; he refused both times. During his lifetime Mercerus published grammatical helps for Hebrew and Chaldean, an aid to the Masoretic symbols in the Hebrew text, and translated the commentaries and grammars of several medieval rabbis. He himself wrote commentaries on Genesis, the wisdom books, and most of the Minor Prophets. These commentaries—most of them only published after his death—were philologically focused and interacted with the work of Jerome, Nicholas of Lyra,* notable rabbis and Johannes Oecolampadius.*

Thomas Mocket (1602–1670?). British Puritan minister. Mocket ministered in Wales and England, publishing numerous works, including a catechism, a tract on the duties of Christians, and an excursus on the celebration of Christmas.

Peter Moffett (d. 1617). English Protestant clergyman. Rector at Fobbing, Essex, Moffett published a commentary on the Song of Solomon and a sermon on 1 Timothy 1:16.

Ambrose Moibanus (1494–1554). German Lutheran bishop and theologian. Moibanus helped reform the church of Breslau (modern Wroclaw, Poland). He revised the Mass, bolstered pastoral care and welfare for the poor, and wrote a new evangelical catechism.

Olympia Morata (1526/27–1555). Italian Protestant humanist and theologian. Daughter of a humanist scholar, her father taught in the court of Ferrara, and she was raised alongside Anna d'Este (1531–1607), daughter of Protestant Renée of France (1510–1574) and later wife of Francis, Duke of Guise (1519–1563), a central antagonist in the St. Bartholomew's Day Massacre. A precocious scholar, Morata's classical, humanist, and biblical studies drew her toward the evangelical currents of the court, but these Protestant leanings also raised the constant suspicion of the Inquisition. In 1550, Morata married Andreas Grundler (unknown), a German Protestant doctor, and moved to his native Schweinfurt, where, facing limited opportunities due to her gender, she continued her studies and privately tutored in Greek and the classics. She developed an extensive correspondence with friends, especially noblewomen she had met at court, and Protestant leaders including Luther*, Melanchthon* and Matthias Flacius (1520–1575), whom she asked to translate some of Luther's work into Italian. Most of Morata's writings were destroyed during the siege of Schweinfurt in 1553–1554, and while she was able to resettle in Frankfurt, she died of tuberculosis soon afterwards. In her writings that survived the siege, her scholarly erudition is clear, and her letters demonstrate a ministerial care for her correspondents and desire for the spread of the Reformation message.

Thomas More (1478–1535). English Catholic lawyer, politician, humanist and martyr. More briefly studied at Oxford, but completed his legal studies in London. After contemplating the priesthood for four years, he opted for politics and was elected a member of Parliament in 1504. A devout Catholic, More worked with church leaders in England to root out heresy while he also confronted Lutheran teachings in writing. After four years as Lord Chancellor, More resigned due to heightened tensions with Henry VIII* over papal supremacy (which More supported and Henry did not). Tensions did not abate. More's steadfast refusal to accept the Act of Supremacy

(1534)—which declared the King of England to be the supreme ecclesial primate not the pope—resulted in his arrest and trial for high treason. He was found guilty and beheaded with John Fisher (1469–1535). Friends with John Colet* and Desiderius Erasmus,* More was a widely respected humanist in England as well as on the continent. Well-known for his novel *Utopia* (1516), More also penned several religious treatises on Christ's passion and suffering during his imprisonment in the Tower of London, which were published posthumously.

Henry Morley (d. 1616). English Protestant preacher. Morley published a sermon of the cleansing of the leper given at St. Paul's Cathedral in London during an outbreak of the plague in 1603.

Sebastian Münster (1488–1552). German Reformed Hebraist, exegete, printer, and geographer. After converting to the Reformation in 1524, Münster taught Hebrew at the universities of Heidelberg and Basel. During his lengthy tenure in Basel he published more than seventy books, including Hebrew dictionaries and rabbinic commentaries. He also produced an evangelistic work for Jews titled *Vikuach* (1539). Münster's *Torat ha-Maschiach* (1537), the Gospel of Matthew, was the first published Hebrew translation of any portion of the New Testament. Despite his massive contribution to contemporary understanding of the Hebrew language, Münster was criticized by many of the reformers as a Judaizer.

Thomas Müntzer (c. 1489–1525). German Radical preacher. As a preacher in the town of Zwickau, Müntzer was influenced by German mysticism and, growing convinced that Martin Luther* had not carried through reform properly, sought to restore the pure apostolic church of the New Testament. Müntzer's radical ideas led to expulsions from various cities; he developed a highly apocalyptic theology, in which he heralded the last days that would establish the pure community out of suffering, prompting Müntzer's proactive role in the Peasants' War, which he perceived as a crucial apocalyptic event. Six thousand of Müntzer's followers were annihilated by magisterial troops; Müntzer was executed.

John Murcot (1625–1654). English Puritan pastor. After completing his bachelor's at Oxford in 1647, Murcot was ordained as a pastor, transferring to several parishes until in 1651 he moved to Dublin. All his works were published posthumously.

Simon Musaeus (1521–1582). German Lutheran theologian. After studying at the universities of Frankfurt an der Oder and Wittenberg, Musaeus began teaching Greek at the Cathedral school in Nuremberg and was ordained. Having returned to Wittenberg to complete a doctoral degree, Musaeus spent the rest of his career in numerous ecclesial and academic administrative posts. He opposed Matthias Flacius's (1505–1575) view of original sin—that the formal essence of human beings is marred by original sin—even calling the pro-Flacian faculty at Wittenberg "the devil's latrine." Musaeus published a disputation on original sin and a postil.

Wolfgang Musculus (1497–1563). German Reformed pastor and theologian. Musculus produced translations, biblical commentaries and an influential theological text, *Loci communes Sacrae Theologiae* (*Commonplaces of Sacred Theology*), outlining a Zwinglian theology. Musculus began to study theology while at a Benedictine monastery; he departed in 1527 and became secretary to Martin Bucer* in Strasbourg. He was later installed as a pastor in Augsburg, eventually performing the first evangelical liturgy in the city's cathedral. Displaced by the Augsburg Interim, Musculus ended his career as professor of theology at Bern. Though Musculus was active in the pursuit of the reform agenda, he was also concerned for ecumenism, participating in the Wittenberg Concord (1536) and discussions between Lutherans and Catholics.

Georg Mylius (1548–1607). German Lutheran pastor and theologian. Mylius began his career as a preacher in Augsburg, rising to superintendent of the churches in the city after receiving his doctorate in theology. He was arrested and ejected from the city by the Catholic-dominated council for his opposition to the Gregorian calendar, returning briefly to learn of the death of his pregnant wife and child. After grieving in Ulm, Mylius spend the remainder of his career as a preacher and professor of theology at Wittenberg, with a brief hiatus teaching at Jena.

Hans Nadler (unknown). German Radical layperson. An uneducated and illiterate needle salesman, after receiving baptism from Hans Hut* in 1527, Nadler sought to share the faith with those he met during his extensive travels. He is remembered through the records of his arrest and examination, recorded by a court reporter, which give insight into his beliefs and activities as a committed Anabaptist layperson, whereby he affirmed believer's baptism, the spiritual reception of the Eucharist, and nonresistance.

Friedrich Nausea (c. 1496–1552). German Catholic bishop and preacher. After completing his studies at Leipzig, this famed preacher was appointed priest in Frankfurt but was run out of town by his congregants during his first sermon. He transferred to Mainz as cathedral preacher. Nausea was well connected through the German papal hierarchy and traveled widely to preach to influential ecclesial and secular courts. Court preacher for Ferdinand I (1503–1564), his reform tendencies fit well with royal Austrian theological leanings, and he was enthroned as the bishop of Vienna. Nausea thought that rather than endless colloquies only a council could settle reform. Unfortunately he could not participate in the first session of Trent due to insufficient funding, but he arrived for the second session. Nausea defended the laity's reception of the cup and stressed the importance of promulgating official Catholic teaching in the vernacular.

Melchior Neukirch (1540–1597). German Lutheran pastor and playwright. Neukirch's pastoral career spanned more than thirty years in several northern German parishes. Neukirch published a history of the Braunschweig church since the Reformation and a dramatization of Acts 4–7. He died of the plague.

Nicholas of Lyra (1270–1349). French Catholic biblical exegete. Very little is known about this influential medieval theologian of the Sorbonne aside from the works he published, particularly the *Postilla litteralis super totam Bibliam* (1322–1333). With the advent of the printing press this work was regularly published alongside the Latin Vulgate and the *Glossa ordinaria*. In this running commentary on the Bible Nicholas promoted literal interpretation as the basis for theology. Despite his preference for literal interpretation, Nicholas also published a companion volume, the *Postilla moralis super totam Bibliam* (1339), a commentary on the spiritual meaning of the biblical text. Nicholas was a major conversation partner for many reformers though many of them rejected his exegesis as too literal and too "Jewish" (not concerned enough with the Bible's fulfillment in Jesus Christ).

John Norden (1547–1625). English devotional writer. Norden was born at Somerset, and in 1564 entered Hart Hall, Oxford where he graduated with his BA in 1568, and MA in 1573. Norden spent most of his life Middlesex, moving later to St. Giles in the Fields in 1619, where he remained until his death in 1625. Throughout his life, Norden distinguished himself also as a cartographer, chorographer, and antiquarian. His best known devotional work was his Progress of Piety (1596).

Alexander Nowell (1517–1602). Anglican theologian. Born in Lancashire, Nowell was educated at Brasenose College, Oxford where he shared a room with the future martyrologist John Foxe. Nowell was elected a fellow at the same college, where he spent thirteen years. In 1543, he was appointed master of Westminster School, and in December, 1551, a prebendary of Westminster Abbey. Though elected to the House of Commons in 1553, Nowell was permitted to assume his seat because as a prebendary, he had a seat in Convocation. Because of his evangelical convictions, Nowell lost prebendary in 1554, after which he fled to the Continent, traveling first to Strasbourg, and then to Frankfurt. When Elizabeth I ascended the throne, Nowell returned to England where he afterwards served as chaplain to Edmund Grindal. In 1561 Nowell became Dean of St. Paul's Cathedral, a post which he held until his death. Nowell's best known work was his Catechism originally written in Latin (1563), and translated into English by Thomas Norton in 1570.

Bernardino Ochino (1487–1564). Italian Reformed theologian. After serving as vicar general of the Franciscan order, Ochino left the foundation of the Capuchins, where he assisted in the composition of their constitution and served as vicar general. A famed preacher, his teaching came to the attention of the Inquisition as it began to reflect the thought of Juan de Valdés. Summoned to Rome in 1542, he fled to Geneva with Peter Martyr Vermigli* where his Reformed orthodoxy, tinged with Franciscan mysticism, was brought into the open. Following his flight, Ochino led an unstable life, with brief stays in Basel, Strasbourg, and Augsburg before moving to England with Vermigli in 1548 where he was able to compose a significant treatise against the Roman church. His doctrinal orthodoxy was questioned by the pastor of the Italian congregation in London, but his case left unresolved when he departed for Geneva, then Basel and Zurich, at the accession of Mary*. As pastor of a congregation of Italian refugees in Zurich, Ochino courted considerable controversy. He refused to have his works approved by the city magistrates before publication, and his opponents alleged that his Dialogi XXX (1563) included questionable teachings on the Trinity and divorce while seeming to advocate polygamy. Expelled from Zurich in 1563, he died in Moravia the following year.

Charles Odingsells (d. 1637). English Protestant preacher. Odingsells published two sermons on prophesying and miracles from Matthew 7 given at Langar in Nottinghamshire.

Johannes Oecolampadius (Johannes Huszgen) (1482–1531). Swiss-German Reformed humanist, reformer and theologian. Oecolampadius (an assumed name meaning "house light") assisted with Desiderius Erasmus's* Greek New Testament, lectured on biblical languages and exegesis and completed an influential Greek grammar. After joining the evangelical cause through studying patristics and the work of Martin Luther,* Oecolampadius went to Basel, where he lectured on biblical exegesis and participated in ecclesial reform. On account of Oecolampadius's effort, the city council passed legislation restricting preaching to the gospel and releasing the city from compulsory Mass. Oecolampadius was a chief ally of Huldrych Zwingli,* whom he supported at the Marburg Colloquy (1529).

Kaspar Olevianus (1536–1587). German Reformed theologian. Olevianus is celebrated for composing the Heidelberg Catechism and producing a critical edition of Calvin's *Institutes* in German. Olevianus studied theology with many, including John Calvin,* Theodore Beza,* Heinrich Bullinger* and Peter Martyr Vermigli.* As an advocate of Reformed doctrine, Olevianus oversaw the shift from Lutheranism to Calvinism throughout Heidelberg, organizing the city's churches after Calvin's Geneva. The Calvinist ecclesial vision of Olevianus entangled him in a dispute with another Heidelberg reformer over the rights of ecclesiastical discipline, which Olevianus felt belonged to the council of clergy and elders rather than civil magistrates.

Josua Opitz (c. 1542–1585). German Lutheran pastor. After a brief stint as superintendent in Regensburg, Opitz, a longtime preacher, was dismissed for his support of Matthias Flacius's (1520–1575) view of original sin. (Using Aristotelian categories, Flacius argued that the formal essence of human beings is marred by original sin, forming sinners into the image of Satan; his views were officially rejected in Article 1 of the Formula of Concord.*) Hans Wilhelm Roggendorf (1533–1591) invited Opitz to lower Austria as part of his Lutheranizing program. Unfortunately Roggendorf and Opitz never succeed in getting Lutheranism legal recognition, perhaps in large part due to Opitz's staunch criticism of Catholics, which resulted in his exile. He died of plague.

Lucas Osiander (1534–1604). German Lutheran pastor. For three decades, Osiander—son of the controversial Nuremberg reformer Andreas Osiander (d. 1552)—served as pastor and court preacher in Stuttgart, until he fell out of favor with the duke in 1598. Osiander produced numerous theological and exegetical works, as well as an influential hymnal.

John Owen (1616–1683). English Puritan theologian. Owen trained at Oxford University, where he was later appointed dean of Christ Church and vice chancellor of the university, following his service as chaplain to Oliver Cromwell. Although Owen began his career as a Presbyterian minister, he eventually departed to the party of Independents. Owen composed many sermons, biblical commentaries (including seven volumes on the book of Hebrews), theological treatises and controversial monographs (including disputations with Arminians, Anglicans, Catholics and Socinians).

Ephraim Pagitt (1575–1647). English Protestant minister. Pagitt ministered at St. Edmunds in London until forced into retirement for his Royalist tendencies during the Civil War (1642–1646). Some of his later writings demonstrate sympathy for Presbyterian theology, and he became an opponent of Baptists and other sectarians. His most popular writing was *Heresiography* (1662), in which he set out to catalog the heretics he identified within the church.

Santes Pagninus (c. 1470–1541). Italian Catholic biblical scholar. Pagninus studied under Girolamo Savonarola* and later taught in Rome, Avignon and Lyons. He translated the Old Testament into Latin according to a tight, almost wooden, adherence to the Hebrew. This translation and his Hebrew lexicon *Thesaurus linguae sanctae* (1529) were important resources for translators and commentators.

Johann Pappus (1549–1610). German Lutheran theologian. After a decade as a teacher of Hebrew and professor of theology at the Strasbourg academy, Pappus was appointed president of the city's company of pastors. Despite resistance from the Reformed theologian Johann Sturm (1507–1589), he led the city away from its Swiss Reformed alliances and toward subscription to the Lutheran Formula of Concord. A talented humanist, Pappus published more than thirty works on controversial, theological, historical, and exegetical subjects.

David (Wängler) Pareus (1548–1622). German Reformed pastor and theologian. Born at Frankenstein in Lower Silesia, Pareus studied theology at Heidelberg under Zacharias Ursinus (1534–1583), the principal author of the Heidelberg Catechism.* After reforming several churches, Pareus returned to Heidelberg to teach at the Reformed seminary. He then joined the theological faculty at the University of Heidelberg, first as a professor of Old Testament and later as a professor of New Testament. Pareus edited the *Neustadter Bibel* (1587), a publication of Martin Luther's* German translation with Reformed annotations—which was strongly denounced by Lutherans, especially Jakob Andreae* and Johann Georg Sigwart (1554–1618). In an extended debate, Pareus defended the orthodoxy of Calvin's exegesis against Aegidius Hunnius,* who accused Calvin of "judaizing" by rejecting many traditional Christological interpretations of Old Testament passages. Towards the end of his career, Pareus wrote commentaries on Genesis, Hosea, Matthew, Romans, 1 Corinthians, Galatians, Hebrews and Revelation.

Catherine Parr (1512–1548). The last of King Henry VIII's* six wives, Catherine Parr was Queen Consort to Henry from 1543 until his death in 1547. She enjoyed a close relationship with two of her step children, Elizabeth and Edward (the future Queen Elizabeth I* and King Edward VI), involving herself extensively in their education. Having married three more times after the death of Henry VIII, Catherine died in 1548. Her published works are *Psalms or Prayers* (1543) and a *Lamentation of a Sinner* (1548).

Paul of Burgos (Solomon ha-Levi) (c. 1351–1435). Spanish Catholic archbishop. In 1391 Solomon ha-Levi, a rabbi and Talmudic scholar, converted to Christianity, receiving baptism with his entire family (except for his wife). He changed his name to Paul de Santa Maria. Some have suggested that he converted to avoid persecution; he himself stated that Thomas Aquinas's* work persuaded him of the truth of Christian faith. After studying theology in Paris, he was ordained bishop in 1403. He actively and ardently persecuted Jews, trying to compel them to convert. In order to convince Jews that Christians correctly interpret the Hebrew Scriptures, Paul wrote *Dialogus Pauli et Sauli contra Judaeos, sive Scrutinium Scripturarum* (1434), a book filled with vile language toward the Jews. He also wrote a series of controversial marginal notes and comments on Nicholas of Lyra's* *Postilla*, many of which criticized Nicholas's use of Jewish scholarship.

Christoph Pelargus (1565–1633). German Lutheran pastor, theologian, professor and superintendent. Pelargus studied philosophy and theology at the University of Frankfurt an der Oder, in Brandenburg. This irenic Philippist was appointed as the superintendent of Brandenburg and later became a pastor in Frankfurt, although the local authorities first required him to condemn Calvinist theology, because several years earlier he had been called before the consistory in Berlin under suspicion of being a crypto-Calvinist. Among his most important works were a four-volume commentary on *De orthodoxa fide* by John of Damascus (d. 749), a treatise defending the breaking of the bread during communion, and a volume of funeral sermons. He also published commentaries on the Pentateuch, the Psalms, Matthew, John and Acts.

Konrad Pellikan (1478–1556). German Reformed Hebraist and theologian. Pellikan attended the University of Heidelberg, where he mastered Hebrew under Johannes Reuchlin. In 1504 Pellikan published one of the first Hebrew grammars that was not merely a translation of the work of medieval rabbis. While living in Basel, Pellikan assisted the printer Johannes Amerbach, with whom he published some of Luther's* early writings. He also worked with Sebastian Münster* and Wolfgang Capito* on a Hebrew Psalter (1516). In 1526, after teaching theology for three years at the University of Basel, Huldrych Zwingli* brought Pellikan to Zurich to chair the faculty of Old Testament. Pellikan's magnum opus is a seven-volume commentary on the entire Bible (except Revelation) and the Apocrypha; it is often heavily dependent upon the work of others (esp. Desiderius Erasmus* and Johannes Oecolampadius*).

William Pemble (1591–1623). Puritan theologian and author. Pemble was born in Egerton, Kent. He was educated at Magdalen College, Oxford, where he graduated with his BA degree in 1614. Afterward he moved to Magdalen Hall, where he became a reader and tutor in divinity. He received his MA in 1618. Primarily a Hebrew scholar, Pemble authored commentaries on Ecclesiastes (1629), the first nine chapters of Zechariah (1629), and portions of Ezra, Nehemiah, and Daniel. Pemble also wrote *An Introduction to the Worthy Receiving the Sacrament* (1628), as well as treatises on predestination and justification. He died of a fever on April 14, 1623.

Benedict Pererius (1535–1610). Spanish Catholic theologian, philosopher and exegete. Pererius entered the Society of Jesus in 1552. He taught philosophy, theology, and exegesis at the Roman College of the Jesuits. Early in his career he warned against neo-Platonism and astrology in his *De principiis* (1576). Pererius wrote a lengthy commentary on Daniel, and five volumes of exegetical theses on Exodus, Romans, Revelation and part of the Gospel of John (chs. 1–14). His four-volume commentary on Genesis (1591–1599) was lauded by Protestants and Catholics alike.

William Perkins (1558–1602). English Puritan preacher and theologian. Perkins was a highly regarded Puritan Presbyterian preacher and biblical commentator in the Elizabethan era. He studied at Cambridge University and later became a fellow of Christ's Church college as a preacher and professor, receiving acclaim for his sermons and lectures. Even more, Perkins gained an esteemed reputation for his ardent exposition of Calvinist reformed doctrine in the style of Petrus Ramus,* becoming one of the first English reformed theologians to achieve international recognition. Perkins influenced the federal Calvinist shape of Puritan theology and the vision of logical, practical expository preaching.

François Perrault (1577–1657). French Reformed pastor for over fifty years. His book on demonology was prominent, perhaps because of the intrigue at his home in

1612. According to his account, a poltergeist made a commotion and argued points of theology; a few months later Perrault's parishioners slew a large snake slithering out of his house.

Dirk Philips (1504–1568). Dutch Radical elder and theologian. This former Franciscan monk, known for being severe and obstinate, was a leading theologian of the sixteenth-century Anabaptist movement. Despite the fame of Menno Simons* and his own older brother Obbe, Philips wielded great influence over Anabaptists in the Netherlands and northern Germany where he ministered. As a result of Philips's understanding of the apostolic church as radically separated from the children of the world, he advocated a very strict interpretation of the ban, including formal shunning. His writings were collected and published near the end of his life as *Enchiridion oft Hantboecxken van de Christelijcke Leere* (1564).

Obbe Philips (1500–1568). Dutch radical leader. Trained as a physician, Philips was drawn to mystical Anabaptism, as taught by Melchior Hoffman (1495–1543) in his hometown of Leewarden. After adult rebaptism and ordination, he preached in Amsterdam, Delft, Appingedam, and Grongen, and he ordained other leaders including his brother Dirk Philips*, David Joris*, and Menno Simmons*. Disillusioned with the growth of revolutionary, enthusiastic, and apocalyptic elements within Anabaptism and unable to reconcile any visible church with the church of God, Philips withdrew from the radical movement in 1540, after which nothing is known of his life. His only extant writing, entitled *The Confession of Obbe Philips*, was published after his death and recounts elements of the history of the Anabaptist movement and defends his departure from the movement.

James Pilkington (1520-1576). Protestant bishop of Durham and Elizabethan author. Born in Lancashire, Pilkington received his early education at Manchester Grammar School. Afterwards, he entered Pembroke College, Cambridge, and later transferred to St. John's College, Cambridge, from where he graduated with his BA degree in 1539, and MA in 1542. Pilkington was appointed vicar of Kendal in 1545, but resigned this position shortly thereafter in order to return to Cambridge. While there, Pilkington was granted a license to preach, and was awarded the degree of Bachelor of Theology in 1551. In this same year, Pilkington became president of the college. When Mary Tudor succeeded her half-brother, Edward VI, in 1553, Pilkington fled to the Continent where he traveled to Zurich, Geneva, Frankfurt, and Strasbourg. He returned to England in 1559 when Elizabeth I ascended the throne of England. After returning to England, Pilkington became Regius Professor of Divinity at Cambridge and after, bishop of Durham in 1560. Pilkington's major work was his voluminous commentary on the Prophet Haggai.

Charles Pinner (Unknown). English Protestant pastor. Pinner studied at New College, Oxford, and served as rector at Wootton Bassett in Wiltshire. His extant writings include two sermons on 1 Timothy and two on 1 Peter.

Hector Pinto (c. 1528–1584). Portuguese Catholic theologian and exegete. A member of the order of Saint Jerome, Pinto taught theology and Scripture at the Universities of Sigüenza and Coimbra. A respected theologian and exegete, he published commentaries on Daniel, Nahum, Jeremiah, and Isaiah and an influential devotional work, *The Image of the Christian Life*.

Caritas Pirckheimer (1466–1532). German Catholic nun. Sister of famed humanist Wilibald Pirckheimer (1470–1530), Caritas received a humanistic education before entering the Franciscan convent at Nuremberg. Extolled by Erasmus* as one of the most learned women in Europe, Pirckheimer served as abbess at the advent of the Reformation, and her experiences are recorded in a journal covering the pivotal years of 1524–1528. While Nuremberg accepted Lutheran theology under the leadership of the city council and preachers such as Andreas Osiander (1498–1552), Pirckheimer defended the right of her order to continue in their vocation. She ultimately won a concession after a visit from Philipp Melanchthon* in 1525, who recommended that the council allow those who wished to remain in the cloister to live out their vows in peace.

Johannes Piscator (1546–1625). German Reformed theologian. Educated at Tübingen (though he wanted to study at Wittenberg), Piscator taught at the universities of Strasbourg and Heidelberg, as well as academies in Neustadt and Herborn. His commentaries on both the Old and New Testaments involve a tripartite analysis of a given passage's argument, of scholia on the text and of doctrinal loci. Some consider Piscator's method to be a full flowering of Beza's* "logical" scriptural analysis, focused on the text's meaning and its relationship to the pericopes around it.

Amandus Polanus von Polansdorf (1561–1610). German Reformed educator and theologian. Polanus spent his career as an educator, serving as a tutor for noble families and a teacher at the Bohemian Brethren school in Moravia before earning his doctorate and becoming professor of Old Testament and later dean of the theological faculty at the University of Basel. His best-known work is the *Syntagma theologiae christianae* (1609), a compendium of Reformed dogmatics.

Constantino Ponce de la Fuente (1502–1559). Spanish Protestant theologian and preacher. A priest in Seville, Ponce de la Fuente was a critic of the established church and associated with the evangelical circle in the city. A popular preacher, he authored a catechism and a number of books on doctrine and the Christian life that focused on the work of Christ. Charged with heresy by the Inquisition, he admitted to the authorship of a number of heretical writings and died in prison awaiting trial while his works were added to the Index of Prohibited Books.

Matthew Poole (1624–1679). English Nonconformist minister. Having made known his preference for simplicity in worship, Matthew Poole was rector of St Michael-le-Querne until the passing of the 1662 Act of Uniformity led him to resign. Living off his inheritance, he preached occasionally and composed some brief tracts but devoted much of his effort to the compilation of Latin biblical commentary in the *Synopsis criticorum* (1669) and the composition of his own annotations on Scripture. He died in Amsterdam, having fled London during the Popish Plot (1678–1681). He believed his life was in danger for his anti-Catholic writings as part of a Catholic conspiracy to kill Charles II, which was ultimately revealed as a fiction concocted by Titus Oates (1649–1705).

Thomas Porter (d. 1667). English Anglican minister. A graduate of Christ's College, Cambridge, Porter ministered in Flintshire in Cheshire and at Whitchurch in Shropshire. Among his published works are a sermon on Matthew 5:13 and a response to antitrinitarian John Knowles (fl. 1646–1668).

Gabriel Powell (1575–1611). Puritan minister. Powell was born at Ruabon in Denbigshire in 1575. Having completed his studies at Jesus College, Oxford, Powell became master of the free-school in Ruthen. During his tenure at Ruthen, Powell closely studied the writings of the church fathers as well as philosophy, and afterward endeavored to publish several works based on this research. Finding his present location to be a hinderance to his literary objectives, Powell relocated to Oxford, entering St. Mary's Hall, where he finished his anticipated projects. Powell is chiefly known for his literary debate with Thomas Bilson (1547–1619) concerning Christ's descent into hell. Later, Richard Vaughan (1550–1607), bishop of London, appointed Powell his domestic chaplain. Powell died on December 31, 1611. In addition to many controversial and polemical works, Powell wrote a commentary on Romans 1.

Vavasor Powell (1617–1670). Welsh Puritan minister and author. Powell was born at Knucklas, Radnorshire, Wales. After completing his education at Jesus College, Oxford, Powell returned to Wales to assume the position of a local schoolmaster. During this time, Powell came under the influence of Walter Cradock's* preaching as well as the writings of Richard Sibbes* and William Perkins,* resulting in his conversion to Puritanism. Soon thereafter he became an itinerant preacher, traveling throughout Wales. He was arrested twice for nonconformity. During the Civil War, Powell first preached in London, and shortly thereafter pastored an Independent congregation in Wales. On December 26, 1641, Royalist forces arrested and imprisoned Powell. In 1646, as victory for the Puritans appeared inevitable, Powell was released, and allowed to return to Wales, having received a letter of endorsement from the Westminster Assembly. Back in Wales, Powell played a prominent role in the Westminster Assembly's 1650 commission for the better propagation of the gospel throughout Wales. In 1653, Powell returned to London, where he preached at St. Ann Blackfriars. It was at this time that Powell denounced Oliver Cromwell (1599–1658) for assuming the position of Lord Protector. For this reason, he was arrested and imprisoned. At the Restoration in 1660, Powell was again arrested and imprisoned for unauthorized preaching for seven years. Though released in 1667, Powell was once more arrested and incarcerated. He remained in custody until his death on October 27, 1660. Powell authored many poems and a concordance to the Bible.

Felix Pratensis (d. 1539). Italian Catholic Hebraist. Pratensis, the son of a rabbi, converted to Christianity and entered the Augustinian Hermits around the turn of the sixteenth century. In 1515, with papal permission, Pratensis published a new translation of the Psalms based on the Hebrew text. His *Biblia Rabbinica* (1517–1518), printed in Jewish and Christian editions, included text-critical notes in the margins as well as the Targum and rabbinic commentaries on each book (e.g., Rashi* on the Pentateuch and David Kimchi* on the Prophets). Many of the reformers consulted this valuable resource as they labored on their own translations and expositions of the Old Testament.

John Preston (1587–1628). Puritan minister and author. Preston was born at Upper Heyford, Northamptonshire, on October 27, 1587. He studied philosophy at King's College and Queen's College, Cambridge, earning his bachelor's degree in 1607. He became a fellow at Queen's in 1609, and a prebendary at Lincoln Cathedral a year later. During this period, Preston studied medicine and astronomy. In 1611, he received the MA degree. Sometime afterward, he experienced a conversion under the preaching of John Cotton.* After his conversion, Preston went on to study theology, concentrating mainly on Thomas Aquinas,* Duns Scotus, and William of Ockham. From there, he proceeded to the reformers, especially John Calvin.* Preston was appointed court chaplain in 1615. In this position he was influential in the promotion of Puritans to high civil office. Preston later assumed the positions of dean and catechist at Queen's College, Cambridge, where he distinguished himself by preaching a series of sermons that formed the basis of his body of divinity. In 1622, he received the degree of bachelor of divinity, becoming thereafter master of Emmanuel College, Cambridge. While at Emmanuel, Preston participated in the conflict between Calvinism and Arminianism. Moreover, in the same year, Preston succeeded John Donne* as preacher at Lincoln's Inn. Two years later, Preston accepted the lectureship at Trinity Church. He died at the age of forty in 1628. Throughout his prodigious career, Preston authored a sizable corpus, which includes published sermons on Romans.

Quadriga. The *quadriga*, or four senses of Scripture, grew out of the exegetical legacy of Paul's dichotomy of letter and spirit (2 Cor 3:6), as well as church fathers like Origen (c. 185–254), Jerome (c. 347–420) and Augustine* (354–430). Advocates for this method—the primary framework for biblical exegesis during the medieval era—assumed the necessity of the gift of faith under the guidance of the Holy Spirit. The literal-historical meaning of the text served as the foundation for the fuller perception of Scripture's meaning in the three spiritual senses, accessible only through faith: the allegorical sense taught what should be believed, the tropological or moral sense taught what should be done, and the anagogical or eschatological sense taught what should be hoped for. Medieval Jewish exegesis also had a fourfold interpretive method—not necessarily related to the *quadriga*—called *pardes* ("grove"): *peshat*, the simple, literal sense of the text according to grammar; *remez*, the allegorical sense; *derash*, the moral sense; and *sod*, the mystic sense related to Kabbalah. Scholars hotly dispute the precise use and meaning of these terms.

Edward Rainbow[e] (1608–1684). Anglican minister, scholar, and bishop. Rainbow was born at Lincolnshire on April 20, 1608. After completing his education, Rainbow matriculated at Corpus Christi College, and later transferred to Magdalene College, Cambridge, where he graduated with the BA (1627), MA (1630), BD (1637), and DD (1643). He was elected a fellow at Magdalene in 1633 and a master there in 1642. In 1630, Rainbow accepted the mastership of the Kirton-in-Lindsey but shortly afterward moved to London. In 1632, Rainbow took holy orders and preached his first sermon in April of that year. His first appointment was that of curate of Savoy Hospital. Rainbow was recalled to Cambridge in 1633 and elected a fellow. Four years later he became dean of Magdalene and master of the same college in 1642. Though dismissed from his mastership by Parliament in 1650, Rainbow was restored to it in the year of the Restoration (1660). At the same time, he was appointed chaplain to the king. In 1661, Rainbow became dean of Peterborough, and appointed vice chancellor of Cambridge a year later. Rainbow was elected bishop of Carlisle in 1664. As bishop, Rainbow led in the systemic reform of his diocese. Rainbow died March 26, 1684. His published works consist of three published sermons and an incomplete treatise, *Verba Christi*.

Petrus Ramus (1515–1572). French Reformed humanist philosopher. Ramus was an influential professor of philosophy and logic at the French royal college in Paris; he converted to Protestantism and left France for Germany, where he came under the influence of Calvinist thought. Ramus was a trenchant critic of Aristotle and noted for his method of classification based on a deductive movement from universals to particulars, the latter becoming branching divisions that provided a visual chart of the parts to the whole. His system profoundly influenced Puritan theology and preaching. After returning to Paris, Ramus died in the Saint Bartholomew's Day Massacre.

Rashi (Shlomo Yitzchaki) (1040–1105). French Jewish rabbi and exegete. After completing his studies, Rashi founded a yeshiva in Troyes. He composed the first comprehensive commentary on the Talmud, as well as commentaries on the entire Old Testament except for 1–2 Chronicles. These works remain influential within orthodox Judaism. Late medieval and early modern Christian scholars valued his exegesis, characterized by his preference for peshat (see quadriga).

Reformatio Legum Ecclesiasticarum (1552). Under the leadership of Archbishop of Canterbury Thomas Cranmer,* Edward VI* established a committee of thirty-two bishops, theologians, and lawyers including Nicholas Ridley,* John Hooper,* Peter Martyr Vermigli,* Matthew Parker (1504–1575), and William Cecil (1520–1598) to align the laws of the English church with Reformed theology and English civil law. Completed in 1552, it touched on diverse topics, including church organization, doctrine and heresy, qualifications for ministry, and marriage and divorce. It was brought before

Parliament in 1553, where it was blocked by John Dudley, Duke of Northumberland (1504–1553), who wished to decrease church powers, and then dropped upon the accession of Mary I. A manuscript of the proposal revised by John Foxe (1516/1517–1587) was published in 1671, and while some elements of the Reformatio Legum Ecclesiasticarum were adopted under Elizabeth I, thoroughgoing reform of ecclesiastical law was not brought about until the *Book of Canons* (1604).

Remonstrance (1610). See *Synod of Dordrecht.*

Johannes Reuchlin (1455–1522). German Catholic lawyer, humanist and Hebraist. Reuchlin held judicial appointments for the dukes of Württemberg, the Supreme Court in Speyer and the imperial court of the Swabian League. He pioneered the study of Hebrew among Christians in Germany, standing against those who, like Johannes Pfefferkorn (1469–1523), wanted to destroy Jewish literature. Among his many works he published a Latin dictionary, an introductory Greek grammar, the most important early modern Hebrew grammar and dictionary (*De rudimentis hebraicis*; 1506), and a commentary on the penitential psalms.

Edward Reynolds (1599–1676). Anglican bishop. Reynolds succeeded John Donne* as the preacher at Lincoln's Inn before entering parish ministry in Northamptonshire. During the English Civil Wars, he supported the Puritans because of his sympathy toward their simplicity and piety—despite believing that Scripture demanded no particular form of government; later he refused to support the abolition of the monarchy. Until the Restoration he ministered in London; afterward he became the bishop of Norwich. He wrote the general thanksgiving prayer which is part of the morning office in the *Book of Common Prayer.**

Urbanus Rhegius (1489–1541). German Lutheran pastor. Rhegius, who was likely the son of a priest, studied under the humanists at Freiburg and Ingolstadt. After a brief stint as a foot soldier, he received ordination in 1519 and was made cathedral preacher in Augsburg. During his time in Augsburg he closely read Luther's* works, becoming an enthusiastic follower. Despite his close friendship with Zwingli* and Oecolampadius,* Rhegius supported Luther in the eucharistic debates, later playing a major role in the Wittenberg Concord (1536). He advocated for peace during the Peasants' War and had extended interactions with the Anabaptists in Augsburg. Later in his career he concerned himself with the training of pastors, writing a pastoral guide and two catechisms. About one hundred of his writings were published posthumously.

Lancelot Ridley (d. 1576). Anglican preacher. Ridley was the first cousin of Nicholas Ridley,* the bishop of London who was martyred during the Marian persecutions. By Cranmer's* recommendation, Ridley became one of the six Canterbury Cathedral preachers. Upon Mary I's accession in 1553, Ridley was defrocked (as a married priest). Ridley returned to Canterbury Cathedral after Mary's death. He wrote commentaries on Jude, Ephesians, Philippians and Colossians.

Nicholas Ridley (c. 1502–1555). Anglican bishop. Ridley was a student and fellow at Cambridge University who was appointed chaplain to Archbishop Thomas Cranmer* and is thought to be partially responsible for Cranmer's shift to a symbolic view of the Eucharist. Cranmer promoted Ridley twice: as bishop of Rochester, where he openly advocated Reformed theological views, and, later, as bishop of London. Ridley assisted Cranmer in the revisions of the Book of Common Prayer.* Ridley's support of Lady Jane Grey against the claims of Mary to the throne led to his arrest; he was tried for heresy and burned at the stake with Hugh Latimer.*

Peter Riedemann (1506–1556). German Radical elder, theologian and hymnist. While traveling as a Silesian cobbler, Riedemann came into contact with Anabaptist teachings and joined a congregation in Linz. In 1529 he was called to be a minister, only to be imprisoned soon after as part of Archduke Ferdinand's efforts to suppress heterodoxy in his realm. Once he was released, he moved to Moravia in 1532 where he was elected as a minister and missionary of the Hutterite community there. His *Account of Our Religion, Doctrine and Faith* (1542), with its more than two thousand biblical references, is Riedemann's most important work and is still used by Hutterites today.

John Robinson (1576–1625). English Puritan pastor. After his suspension for nonconformity, Robinson fled to the Netherlands with his congregation, eventually settling in Leiden in 1609. Robinson entered into controversies over Arminianism, separation and congregationalism. Most of his healthy congregants immigrated to Plymouth in 1620; Robinson remained in Leiden with those unable to travel.

John Rogers (1505–1555). English Protestant Bible translator. Rogers was born in Deritend, Birmingham. After receiving his early education at the Guild School of St. John the Baptist, Rogers matriculated at Pembroke Hall, Cambridge, where he graduated with the BA degree in 1526. He served as rector of Holy Trinity the Less in London from 1532 to 1534, when he left for the Continent to serve as chaplain to the English merchants of the Company of the Merchant Adventurers. It was at this time that he met William Tyndale,* under whose influence he came to embrace an evangelical faith. After Tyndale's death, Rogers completed his late colleague's translation of the Old Testament, which had ended with 2 Chronicles, by adding Miles Coverdale's translation of the remainder, including the Apocrypha. The resulting work, known as the "Matthew Bible" (Rogers published it under the pseudonym "Thomas Matthew") was published in 1537. It has the distinction of being the first complete English Bible translated essentially from the original languages to be printed. "Matthew's Bible" served as the basis for the Great Bible (1540), which in turn was used by those who prepared the Bishops' Bible (1568), on which later the King James Version (1611) was produced. In 1540, Rogers enrolled at the University of Wittenberg, where he became close friends with Philipp Melanchthon.* During his three years at Wittenberg, Rogers was a superintendent of the Lutheran Church in northern Germany. When Rogers returned to England in 1548, he published a translation of Melanchthon's *Considerations of the Augsburg Interim*, and later served in a variety of ecclesiastical roles. Rogers was burned at the stake for heresy during the reign of Mary Tudor on February 4, 1555.

Nehemiah Rogers (1593–1660). Anglican priest. After studying at Cambridge, Rogers ministered at numerous parishes during his more than forty-year career. In 1643, he seems to have been forced out of a parish on account of being a Royalist and friend of William Laud.* Rogers published a number of sermons and tracts, including a series of expositions on Jesus' parables in the Gospels.

Richard Rogers (1550?–1618). English Presbyterian minister. Rogers spent much of his career as lecturer at Wethersfield, Essex, where he was well-known as a Nonconformist. His writings, which include an introduction to the Christian life and a commentary on the book of Judges, demonstrate his Puritan leanings.

Thomas Rogers (d. 1616). Anglican theologian and translator. Rogers attended Christ Church, Oxford, where he completed his BA degree in 1573 and MA in 1576. Later he served as rector of Horrigner in Suffolk, and chaplain to Archbishop of Canterbury, Richard Bancroft. He died at Horringer and was buried in his church. Among his many works were an exposition of the Thirty-Nine Articles as well as a paraphrase of the Psalms and a translation of Niels Hemmingsen's commentary on Psalm 84.

Robert Rollock (c. 1555–1599). Scottish Reformed pastor, educator and theologian. Rollock was deeply influenced by Petrus Ramus's* system of logic, which he implemented as a tutor and (later) principal of Edinburgh University and in his expositions of the Bible. Rollock, as a divinity professor and theologian, was instrumental in diffusing a federalist Calvinism in the Scottish church; he lectured on theology using the texts of Theodore Beza* and articulated a highly covenantal interpretation of the biblical narratives. He was a prolific writer of sermons, expositions, commentaries, lectures and occasional treatises.

David Runge (1564–1604). German Lutheran theologian. First appointed professor of Hebrew at the University of Greifswald, Runge supported and later replaced his father in teaching philosophy and theology. After receiving his doctorate, he was named to the theological faculty at Wittenberg, where he also served as dean and rector of the university.

Johann Rurer (1480–1542). German Lutheran pastor. Rurer was court chaplain to Margrave Casimir of Brandenberg–Kulmbach (1481–1527), and the first Protestant pastor in Ansbach. Conflict over church order and his desire for reform led to his expulsion, but he was recalled after Casimir's death by his successor, George (1484–1543), who sought a throughgoing Lutheran reformation of the town and appointed Rurer preacher at the collegiate church.

Samuel Rutherford (1600–1661). Scottish Reformed theologian. Rutherford was born in Nisbet, Roxburghshire. After completing his early education at Jedborough, Rutherford enrolled at the University of Edinburgh, where he received his MA degree in 1621. In 1623, Rutherford was appointed professor of humanities at Edinburgh. Two years later, he was dismissed from his position on account of misbehavior with the woman who would later be his wife. Sometime after this incident, he underwent a spiritual conversion. In 1625, Rutherford commenced the study of theology at Edinburgh. Upon finishing his studies, Rutherford was called to pastor a church in Antwoth by Solway in Kirkcudbrightshire. Throughout his ministry, Rutherford proved to be an ardent opponent to episcopacy. For this, he was summoned to appear before the Court of High Commission in 1630. Despite the court's warnings to cease and desist, Rutherford continued his nonconformity. Rutherford also participated extensively in the Arminian controversy, writing treatises against Arminius as well as the Jesuits. Since Rutherford's virulent opposition to Arminianism placed him in direct opposition with the English episcopacy, he was once again summoned by the Court of High Commission in 1636. After a three-day trial, Rutherford was deprived of his ministerial office and ordered not to preach anywhere in Scotland. Meanwhile he was confined to Aberdeen. In 1638, when the National Covenant was signed and Presbyterianism restored in Scotland, Rutherford left Aberdeen and assumed the post of professor of theology at St. Mary's College, St. Andrews. Later, Rutherford served as a commissioner to the Westminster Assembly, where he contributed to the discussions related to the Shorter Catechism. In 1647, Rutherford returned to Scotland, where he was appointed principal of St. Mary's College, and rector of the university in 1651. After the monarchy was restored, Rutherford was charged with treason, and deprived of all his ecclesiastical and university positions. He died on March 30, 1661. Throughout his career, Rutherford published many sermons and theological works, most famous of which is *Lex Rex* (The law is king), a treatise arguing against the divine right of kings.

Jacopo Sadoleto (1477–1547). Italian Catholic Cardinal. Sadoleto, attaché to Leo X's court, was appointed bishop in 1517, cardinal in 1536. He participated in the reform commission led by Gasparo Contarini.* However, he tried to reconcile with Protestants apart from the commission, sending several letters to Protestant leaders in addition to his famous letter to the city of Geneva, which John Calvin* pointedly answered. Sadoleto published a commentary on Romans that was censored as semi-Pelagian. His insufficient treatment of prevenient grace left him vulnerable to this charge. Sadoleto emphasized grammar as the rule and norm of exegesis.

Alfonso Salmerón (1515–1585). Spanish Catholic exegete and theologian. While studying at the Sorbonne, Salmerón met Ignatius Loyola (1491–1556) and, with five others, took a vow of poverty and service to church and pope. After ministering in France, the group traveled to Rome, where they were given papal approval to form the Society of Jesus. Salmerón helped write the constitutions of the order, and following the priorities of the Jesuits, spent much of his career focused on education. He lectured throughout Italy, served briefly on the faculty of the University of Ingolstadt, and, in Naples, founded one of the first Jesuit colleges. He also undertook a number of missions as a papal emissary and served as a papal theologian at all three meetings of the Council of Trent. His primary works are his commentaries on the New Testament, which cover the Gospels, Acts, and Paul's letters.

Heinrich Salmuth (1522–1576). German Lutheran theologian. After earning his doctorate from the University of Leipzig, Salmuth served in several coterminous pastoral and academic positions. He was integral to the reorganization of the University of Jena. Except for a few disputations, all of Salmuth's works—mostly sermons—were published posthumously by his son.

Robert Sanderson (1587–1663). Anglican bishop and philosopher. Before his appointment as professor of divinity at Oxford in 1642, Sanderson pastored in several parishes. Because of his loyalty to the Crown during the English Civil Wars, the Parliamentarians stripped Sanderson of his post at Oxford. After the Restoration he was reinstated at Oxford and consecrated bishop. He wrote an influential textbook on logic.

Edwin Sandys (1519–1588). Anglican bishop. During his doctoral studies at Cambridge, Sandys befriended Martin Bucer.* Having supported the Protestant Lady Jane Grey's claim to the throne, Sandys resigned his post at Cambridge upon Mary I's accession. He was then arrested and imprisoned in the Tower of London. Released in 1554, he sojourned on the continent until Mary's death. On his return to England he was appointed to revise the liturgy and was consecrated bishop. Many of his sermons were published, but his most significant literary legacy is his work as a translator of the Bishop's Bible (1568), which served as the foundational English text for the translators of the King James Bible (1611).

Erasmus Sarcerius (1501–1559). German Lutheran superintendent, educator and pastor. Sarcerius served as educational superintendent, court preacher and pastor in Nassau and, later, in Leipzig. The hallmark of Sarcerius's reputation was his ethical emphasis as exercised through ecclesial oversight and family structure; he also drafted disciplinary codes for regional churches in Germany. Sarcerius served with Philipp Melanchthon* as Protestant delegates at the Council of Trent, though both withdrew prior to the dismissal of the session; he eventually became an opponent of Melanchthon, contesting the latter's understanding of the Eucharist at a colloquy in Worms in 1557.

Michael Sattler (c. 1490–1527). Swiss Radical leader. Sattler was a Benedictine monk who abandoned the monastic life during the upheavals of the Peasants' War. He took up the trade of weaving under the guidance of an outspoken Anabaptist. It seems that Sattler did not openly join the Anabaptist movement until after the suppression of the Peasants' War in 1526. Sattler interceded with Martin Bucer* and Wolfgang Capito* for imprisoned Anabaptists in Strasbourg. Shortly before he was convicted of heresy and executed, he wrote the definitive expression of Anabaptist theology, the Schleitheim Articles.*

Girolamo Savonarola (1452–1498). Italian Catholic preacher and martyr. Outraged by clerical corruption and the neglect of the poor, Savonarola traveled to preach against these abuses and to prophesy impending judgment—a mighty king would scourge and reform the church. Savonarola thought that the French invasion of Italy in 1494 confirmed his apocalyptic visions. Thus he pressed to purge Florence of vice and institute public welfare, in order to usher in a new age of Christianity. Florence's refusal to join papal resistance against the French enraged Alexander VI (r. 1492–1503). He blamed Savonarola, promptly excommunicating him and threatening Florence with an interdict. After an ordeal by fire turned into a riot, Savonarola was arrested. Under torture he admitted to charges of conspiracy and false prophecy; he was hanged and burned. In addition to numerous sermons and letters, he wrote meditations on Psalms 31 and 51 as well as *The Triumph of the Cross* (1497).

Leupold Scharnschlager (d. 1563). Austrian Radical elder. See *Kunstbuch.*

Leonhard Schiemer (d. 1528) Austrian radical martyr. Troubled by the hypocrisies he experienced, Scheimer left the Franciscan order and spent a period of time wandering. Attracted to the teachings of Hans Hut* after hearing him debate Balthasar Hubmaier* in Moravia, he was rebaptized and traveled widely throughout Austria and Southern Germany, spreading the Anabaptist message until he was arrested in Rattenberg, where he was condemned to death and beheaded. A number of his essays and hymns survive, dispersed among the *Kunstbuch** and other collections of radical writings.

Hans Schlaffer (c. 1490–1528). Austrian Radical martyr. Drawn by Luther's theology, Schlaffer resigned his priesthood in 1526 only to turn to Anabaptism soon afterward. While contemporaries recognized his ability as a preacher, he never settled in a ministry position. He spent time among Radical congregations in Freistadt, Nicholsburg, Augsburg, Nuremberg, and Regensburg before his arrest in Schatz, where he was executed. Nine writings by Schlaffer remain, most of which were composed during his imprisonment. They include confessions of his beliefs and devotional works, which have been preserved among Hutterite churches.

Schleitheim Articles (1527). After the death of Conrad Grebel* in 1526 and the execution of Felix Manz (born c. 1498) in early 1527, the young Swiss Anabaptist movement was in need of unity and direction. A synod convened at Schleitheim under the chairmanship of Michael Sattler,* which passed seven articles of Anabaptist distinctives—likely defined against both magisterial reformers and other Anabaptists with less orthodox and more militant views (e.g., Balthasar Hubmaier*). Unlike most confessions, these articles do not explicitly address traditional creedal interests; they explicate instead the Anabaptist view of the sacraments, church discipline, separatism, the role of ministers, pacifism and oaths. Throughout the document there is a resolute focus on Christ's example. Also referred to as the Schleitheim Confession and the Schleitheim Brotherly Union, the Schleitheim Articles are considered the definitive statement of Anabaptist theology, particularly regarding separatism.

Schmalkald Articles (1537). In response to Pope Paul III's (1468–1549) 1536 decree ordering a general church council to solve the Protestant crisis, Elector John Frederick (1503–1554) commissioned Martin Luther* to draft the sum of his teaching. Intended by Luther as a last will and testament—and composed with advice from well-known colleagues Justus Jonas,* Johann Bugenhagen,* Caspar Cruciger,* Nikolaus von Amsdorf (1483–1565), Georg Spalatin (1484–1545), Philipp Melanchthon* and Johann Agricola*—these articles provide perhaps the briefest and most systematic summary of Luther's teaching. The document was not adopted formally by the Lutheran Schmalkald League, as was hoped, and the general church council was postponed for several years (until convening at Trent in 1545). Only in 1580 were the articles officially received, by being incorporated into the *Book of Concord* defining orthodox Lutheranism.

Sebastian Schmidt (1617–1696). German Lutheran theologian. After serving as pastor in Entzheim and rector of the high school in Lindau, Schmidt became professor of theology at Strasbourg. His body of writings is extensive and includes commentaries on many of the Pauline letters, Hebrews, John, and Jeremiah.

Dietrich Schnepff (1525–1586). German Lutheran pastor and theologian. Schnepff taught briefly at the city school in Tübingen while working toward his theological doctorate before taking pastorates in Derendingen and Nürtingen. Returning to Tübingen as professor of theology, Schnepff also took on additional roles as rector of the university and pastor of the Collegiate Church.

Anna Maria van Schurman (1607–1678). Dutch Reformed polymath. Van Schurman cultivated talents in art, poetry, botany, linguistics and theology. She mastered most contemporary European languages, in addition to Latin, Greek, Hebrew, Arabic, Farsi and Ethiopian. With the encouragement of leading Reformed theologian Gisbertus Voetius (1589–1676), van Schurman attended lectures at the University of Utrecht—although she was required to sit behind a wooden screen so that the male students could not see her. In 1638 van Schurman published her famous treatise advocating female scholarship, *Amica dissertatio . . . de capacitate ingenii muliebris ad scientias*. In addition to these more polemical works, van Schurman also wrote hymns and poems, including a paraphrase of Genesis 1–3. Later in life she became a devotee of Jean de Labadie (1610–1674), a former Jesuit who was also expelled from the Reformed church for his separatist leanings. Her *Eucleria* (1673) is the most well known defense of Labadie's theology.

Kaspar von Schwenckfeld (1489–1561). German Radical reformer. Schwenckfeld was a Silesian nobleman who encountered Luther's* works in 1521. He traveled to Wittenberg twice: first to meet Luther and Karlstadt,* and a second time to convince Luther of his doctrine of the "internal word"—emphasizing inner revelation so strongly that he did not see church meetings or the sacraments as necessary—after which Luther considered him heterodox. Schwenckfeld won his native territory to the Reformation in 1524 and later lived in Strasbourg for five years until Bucer* sought to purify the city of less traditional theologies. Schwenckfeld wrote numerous polemical and exegetical tracts.

Scots Confession (1560). In 1560, the Scottish Parliament undertook to reform the Church of Scotland and to commission a Reformed confession of faith. In the course of four days, a committee—which included John Knox*—wrote this confession, largely based on Calvin's* work, the Confession of the English Congregation in Geneva (1556) and the Gallic Confession.* The articles were not ratified until 1567 and were displaced by the Westminster Confession (1646), adopted by the Scottish in 1647.

Abraham Scultetus (1566–1625). Silesian Reformed theologian. Scultetus spent the majority of his career in service of the Palatinate, holding a number of pastoral roles before becoming court preacher to Elector Frederic V (1596–1632). Appointed professor of theology at Heidelberg in 1618, he represented the Palatinate at the Synod of Dordrecht* (1618–1619), where he opposed the theology of the Remonstrants. Scultetus is often vilified for encouraging Reformed Frederic V to take the crown of Lutheran Bohemia, an act that led to war and the defeat of Frederic V, but his exegetical, historical, and pastoral teachings nevertheless garnered significant respect from his contemporaries.

Second Helvetic Confession (1566). Believing he would soon die, Heinrich Bullinger* penned a personal statement of his Reformed faith in 1561 as a theological will. In 1563, Bullinger sent a copy of this confession, which blended Zwingli's and Calvin's theology, to the elector of the Palatinate, Frederick III (1515–1576), who had asked for a complete explication of the Reformed faith in order to defend himself against aggressive Lutheran attacks after printing the Heidelberg Confession.* Although not published until 1566, the Second Helvetic Confession became the definitive sixteenth-century Reformed statement of faith. Theodore Beza* used it as the organizing confession for his *Harmonia Confessionum* (1581), which sought to emphasize the unity of the Reformed churches. Bullinger's personal confession was adopted by the Reformed churches of Scotland (1566), Hungary (1567), France (1571) and Poland (1571).

Obadiah Sedgwick (c. 1600–1658). English Puritan minister. Educated at Oxford, Sedgwick pastored in London and participated in the Westminster Assembly. An ardent Puritan, Sedgwick was appointed by Oliver Cromwell (1599–1658) to examine clerical candidates. Sedgwick published a catechism, several sermons and a treatise on how to deal with doubt.

Nikolaus Selnecker (1530–1592). German Lutheran theologian, preacher, pastor and hymnist. Selnecker taught in Wittenberg, Jena and Leipzig, preached in Dresden and Wolfenbüttel, and pastored in Leipzig. He was forced out of his post at Jena because of suspicions that he was a crypto-Calvinist. He sought refuge in Wolfenbüttel, where he met Martin Chemnitz* and Jakob Andreae.* Under their influence Selnecker was drawn away from Philippist theology. Selnecker's shift in theology can be seen in his *Institutio religionis christianae* (1573). Selnecker coauthored the Formula of Concord* with Chemnitz, Andreae, Andreas Musculus (1514–1581), and David Chytraeus.* Selnecker also published lectures on Genesis, the Psalms, and the New Testament epistles, as well as composing over a hundred hymn tunes and texts.

Short Confession (1610). In response to some of William Laud's* reforms in the Church of England—particularly a law stating that ministers who refused to comply with the Book of Common Prayer* would lose their ordination—a group of English Puritans immigrated to the Netherlands in protest, where they eventually embraced the practice of believer's baptism. The resulting Short Confession was an attempt at union between these Puritans and local Dutch Anabaptists ("Waterlanders"). The document highlights the importance of love in the church and reflects optimism regarding the freedom of the will while explicitly rejecting double predestination.

Richard Sibbes (1577–1635). English Puritan preacher. Sibbes was educated at St. John's College, Cambridge, where he was converted to reforming views and became a popular preacher. As a moderate Puritan emphasizing interior piety and brotherly love, Sibbes always remained within the established Church of England, though opposed to some of its liturgical ceremonies. His collected sermons constitute his main literary legacy.

Menno Simons (c. 1496–1561). Dutch Radical leader. Simons led a separatist Anabaptist group in the Netherlands that would later be called Mennonites, known for nonviolence and renunciation of the world. A former priest, Simons rejected Catholicism through the influence of Anabaptist disciples of Melchior Hoffmann and based on his study of Scripture, in which he found no support for transubstantiation or infant baptism. Following the sack of Anabaptists at Münster, Simons committed to a nonviolent way of life. Simons proclaimed a message of radical discipleship of obedience and inner purity, marked by voluntary adult baptism and communal discipline.

Henry Smith (c. 1550–1591). English Puritan minister. Smith stridently opposed the Book of Common Prayer* and refused to subscribe to the Articles of Religion,* thus limiting his pastoral opportunities. Nevertheless he gained a reputation as an eloquent preacher in London. He published sermon collections as well as several treatises.

John Smyth (d. 1612). English Baptist minister. Ordained as an Anglican clergyman, Smyth served as a lecturer in Lincoln, but left the established church for a separatist congregation in Gainsborough. Moving to Amsterdam, he began to follow the teachings of Jacobus Arminius* and led a group to break away from the English Reformed congregation, undertake rebaptism, and form their own church. He soon decided he did not have the authority to establish a church and baptize, but trying to lead his congregation on another course saw him excommunicated with a number of his close followers. This smaller group was rejected when they attempted to join a Mennonite congregation, and so were forced to form another congregation, which dissolved after Smyth's death. Smyth wrote a number of the earliest English treatises expressing Baptist principles including *The Differences of the Churches of the Separation* (1608) and *The Character of the Beast* (1609). He also wrote a reflection on the Lord's Prayer, *A Paterne of True Prayer* (1605).

Domingo de Soto (1494–1560). Spanish Catholic theologian. Soto taught philosophy for four years at the University in Alcalá before entering the Dominican order. In 1532 he became chair of theology at the University of Salamanca; Soto sought to reintroduce Aristotle in the curriculum. He served as confessor and spiritual advisor to Charles V, who enlisted Soto as imperial theologian for the Council of Trent. Alongside commentaries on the works of Aristotle and Peter Lombard (c. 1100–1160), Soto commented on Romans and wrote an influential treatise on nature and grace.

Fausto Sozzini (1539–1604). Italian theologian. Without a formal education, Sozzini used his inherited wealth to travel widely throughout Europe after his family came under the suspicion of the Inquisition for Lutheranism. Spending time in Lyons, Zurich, and Geneva, he published his first work, an explanation of the prologue to John's Gospel, claiming Christ was not divine, but a human worthy of respect due his divinely appointed office. Returning to Italy, Sozzini served at the Florentine court of Isabella de Medici (1542–1576) for more than a decade, departing for Basel, then Transylvania and Poland after her death. His thoroughgoing rationalism saw him elevate human reason over divine revelation and traditional doctrine. He rejected the doctrine of the Trinity and Nicene orthodoxy, instead arguing that Christ was not divine and did not make atonement for humanity, but rather served as a model of victory over death for all people.

Cyriacus Spangenberg (1528–1604). German Lutheran pastor, preacher and theologian. Spangenberg was a staunch, often acerbic, Gnesio-Lutheran. He rejected the Formula of Concord* because of concerns about the princely control of the church, as well as its rejection of Flacian language of original sin (as constituting the "substance" of human nature after the fall). He published many commentaries and sermons, most famously seventy wedding sermons (*Ehespiegel* [1561]), his sermons on Luther* (*Theander Luther* [1562–1571]) and Luther's hymns (*Cithara Lutheri* [1569–1570]). He also published an analysis of the Old Testament (though he only got as far as Job), based on a methodology that anticipated the logical bifurcations of Peter Ramus.*

Johann Spangenberg (1484–1550). German Lutheran pastor and catechist. Spangenberg studied at the University of Erfurt, where he was welcomed into a group of humanists associated with Konrad Muth (1470–1526). There he met the reformer Justus Jonas,* and Eobanus Hessius (1488–1540), whom Luther* dubbed "king of the poets." Spangenberg served at parishes in Stolberg (1520–1524), Nordhausen (1524–1546) and, by Luther's recommendation, Eisleben (1546–1550). Spangenberg published one of the best-selling postils of the sixteenth century, the *Postilla Teütsch*, a six-volume work meant to prepare children to understand the lectionary readings. It borrowed the question-answer form of Luther's *Small Catechism* and was so popular that a monk, Johannes Craendonch, purged overt anti-Catholic statements from it and republished it under his own name. Among Spangenberg's other pastoral works are *ars moriendi* ("the art of dying") booklets, a postil for the Acts of the Apostles and a question-answer version of Luther's *Large Catechism*. In addition to preaching and pastoring, Spangenberg wrote pamphlets on controversial topics such as purgatory, as well as textbooks on music, mathematics and grammar.

John Spilsbury (1593–1668). English Baptist pastor. A cobbler by trade, Spilsbury left congregationalism to found the first Particular Baptist church in London, teaching a theology that attempted to fuse Reformed teachings on the covenant and particular atonement with the Anabaptist demand for adult baptism upon confession of faith. He composed a number of works on baptism and may have been an author of the 1644 London Baptist Confession of Faith.

Georg Spindler (1525–1605). German Reformed theologian and pastor. After studying theology under Caspar Cruciger* and Philipp Melanchthon,* Spindler accepted a pastorate in Bohemia. A well-respected preacher, Spindler published postils in 1576 which some of his peers viewed as crypto-Calvinist. To investigate this allegation Spindler read John Calvin's* *Institutes*, and subsequently converted to the Reformed faith. After years of travel, he settled in the Palatinate and pastored there until his death. In addition to his Lutheran postils, Spindler also published Reformed postils in 1594 as well as several treatises on the Lord's Supper and predestination.

Statenvertaling (1637). The Synod of Dordrecht* commissioned this new Dutch translation of the Bible ("State's Translation"). The six theologians who undertook this translation also wrote prefaces for each biblical book, annotated obscure words and difficult passages, and provided cross-references; they even explained certain significant translation decisions. At the request of the Westminster Assembly, Theodore Haak (1605–1690) translated the *Statenvertaling* into English as *The Dutch Annotations Upon the Whole Bible* (1657).

John Stalham (d. 1681). English Puritan minister. Stalham likely ministered in Edinburgh before becoming vicar of Terling in Essex. An opponent of Quakerism who sought to remove disreputable ministers from their pulpits, Stalham himself lost his position with the 1662 Act of Uniformity, leading him to found a congregational church in the same village.

Johann von Staupitz (d. 1524). German Catholic theologian, professor and preacher. Frederick the Wise summoned this Augustinian monk to serve as professor of Bible and first dean of the theology faculty at the University of Wittenberg. As Vicar-General of the Reformed Augustinian Hermits in Germany, Staupitz sought to reform the order and attempted unsuccessfully to reunite with the conventional Augustinians. While in Wittenberg, Staupitz was Martin Luther's* teacher, confessor and spiritual father. He supported Luther in the early controversies over indulgences, but after releasing Luther from his monastic vows (to protect him), he distanced himself from the conflict. He relocated to Salzburg, where he was court preacher to Cardinal Matthäus Lang von Wellenburg (d. 1540) and abbot of the Benedictine monastery. Staupitz wrote treatises on predestination, faith and the love of God. Many of his sermons were collected and published during his lifetime.

Peter Sterry (d. 1672). English Puritan theologian. Associated with the Cambridge Platonists, Sterry was closely aligned with the Parliamentarians during the English Civil War, serving as chaplain to Robert Greville (1607–1643) and Oliver Cromwell.* After the execution of Charles I, he was appointed preacher to the Council of State and asked to examine its ministers. Cast out from influence after Cromwell's death, Sperry spent the last years of his career writing and tutoring private students.

Petrus Stevartius (1549–1624). German Catholic theologian. A Jesuit, Stevartius spent most of his career as professor of exegesis at the University of Ingolstadt, also serving as rector and procurator. He also established a library for the school and an orphanage in the city. His writings include commentaries on most Pauline letters and James and a defense of the Jesuits.

Michael Stifel (1486–1567). German Lutheran mathematician, theologian and pastor. An Augustinian monk, Stifel's interest in mysticism, apocalypticism and numerology led him to identify Pope Leo X as the antichrist. Stifel soon joined the reform movement, writing a 1522 pamphlet in support of Martin Luther's* theology. After Luther quelled the fallout of Stifel's failed prediction of the Apocalypse—October 19, 1533 at 8 a.m.—Stifel focused more on mathematics and his pastoral duties. He was the first professor of mathematics at the University of Jena. He published several numerological interpretations of texts from the Gospels, Daniel and Revelation. However, Stifel's most important work is his *Arithmetica Integra* (1544), in which he standardized the approach to quadratic equations. He also developed notations for exponents and radicals.

John Stoughton (1593?–1639). English Puritan minister. Stoughton pastored at Aller in Somerset and St. Mary Aldermanbury in the city of London. A Puritan, he was briefly arrested by Archbishop Laud, accused of financially supporting the Puritan cause. A collection of his sermons and other writings was published after his death.

Viktorin Strigel (1524–1569). German Lutheran theologian. Strigel taught at Wittenberg, Erfurt, Jena, Leipzig and Heidelberg. During his time in Jena he disputed with Matthias Flacius (1520–1575) over the human will's autonomy. Following Philipp Melanchthon,* Strigel asserted that in conversion the human will obediently cooperates with the divine will through the Holy Spirit and the Word of God. In the Weimar Disputation (1560), Strigel elicited Flacius's opinion that sin is a substance that mars the formal essence of human beings. Flacius's views were officially rejected in Article 1 of the Formula of Concord*; Strigel's, in Article 2. In 1567 the University of Leipzig suspended Strigel from teaching on account of suspicions that he affirmed Reformed Eucharistic theology; he acknowledged that he did and joined the Reformed confession on the faculty of the University of Heidelberg. In addition to controversial tracts, Strigel published commentaries on the entire Bible (except Lamentations) and the Apocrypha.
William Strode (1602–1645). English Anglican minister, dramatist, and poet. A Royalist and an opponent of Puritanism, Strode spent most of his life around Oxford, where he studied and then served as a public orator and canon of Christ Church. A popular poet, he also preached a number of times before the king and had a number of his plays performed at court.
William Strong (d. 1654). English Independent minister. Forced to leave his ministry in Dorset by Royalists during the Civil War, Strong built a reputation as a preacher in London, ministering to an independent congregation at St. Dunstan's-in-the-West. Many of his sermons were published, as well as treatises on communion with God and the covenants.
Johann Sutell (1504–1575). German Lutheran pastor. After studying at the University of Wittenberg, Sutell received a call to a pastorate in Göttingen, where he eventually became superintendent. He wrote new church orders for Göttingen (1531) and Schweinfurt (1543), and expanded two sermons for publication, *The Dreadful Destruction of Jerusalem* (1539) and *History of Lazarus* (1543).
Swiss Brethren Confession of Hesse (1578). Anabaptist leader Hans Pauly Kuchenbecker penned this confession after a 1577 interrogation by Lutheran authorities. This confession was unusually amenable to Lutheran views—there is no mention of pacifism or rejection of oath taking.
Synod of Dordrecht (1618–1619). This large Dutch Reformed Church council—also attended by English, German and Swiss delegates—met to settle the theological issues raised by the followers of Jacobus Arminius.* Arminius's theological disagreements with mainstream Reformed teaching erupted into open conflict with the publication of the *Remonstrance* (1610). This "protest" was based on five points: that election is based on foreseen faith or unbelief; that Christ died indiscriminately for all people (although only believers receive salvation); that people are thoroughly sinful by nature apart from the prevenient grace of God that enables their free will to embrace or reject the gospel; that humans are able to resist the working of God's grace; and that it is possible for true believers to fall away from faith completely. The Synod ruled in favor of the Contra-Remonstrants, its Canons often remembered with a TULIP acrostic—total depravity, unconditional election, limited atonement, irresistible grace, perseverance of the saints—each letter countering one of the five Remonstrant articles. The Synod also officially accepted the Belgic Confession,* Heidelberg Catechism* and the Canons of Dordrecht as standards of the Dutch Reformed Church.
Arcangela Tarabotti (1604–1652). Italian Catholic nun. At the age of eleven, Tarabotti entered a Benedictine convent as a student-boarder; three years later her father forced her to take monastic vows. The dignity of women and their treatment in the male-controlled institutions of early modern Venice concerned Tarabotti deeply. She protested forced cloistering, the denial of education to women, the exclusion of women from public life and the double standards by which men and women were judged. Tarbotti authored numerous polemical works and an extensive correspondence.
Johannes Tauler (c. 1300–1361). German mystical theologian. A Dominican friar and disciple of Meister Eckhart (c. 1260–c. 1328), Tauler spent most of his career as a mendicant preacher in Strasburg and Basel. Known through a collection of about eighty German sermons, Tauler taught a practical spirituality, accessible to those outside the cloister and intended to draw his audience to deeper contemplation of the divine nature.
Richard Taverner (1505–1575). English Puritan humanist and translator. After graduating from Oxford, Taverner briefly studied abroad. When he returned to England, he joined Thomas Cromwell's (1485–1540) circle. After Cromwell's beheading, Taverner escaped severe punishment and retired from public life during Mary I's reign. Under Elizabeth I,* Taverner served as justice of the peace, sheriff and a licensed lay preacher. Taverner translated many important continental Reformation works into English, most notably the Augsburg Confession* and several of Desiderius Erasmus's* works. Some of these translations—John Calvin's* 1536 catechism, Wolfgang Capito's* work on

the Psalms and probably Erasmus Sarcerius's* postils—he presented as his own work. Underwritten by Cromwell, Taverner also published an edited version of the Matthew Bible (1537).

Jeremy Taylor (1613–1667). Anglican theologian, preacher, and author. Son of a barber, Taylor studied at Cambridge before the patronage of Archbishop Laud* drew him into the work of the English church. After serving as chaplain to Laud and King Charles I (1600–1649), he entered parish ministry. Following the outbreak of the Civil War (1642–51), his commitment to the Royalist cause saw him imprisoned at least three times. Withdrawing to Wales, he ran a school preparing students for university while serving as chaplain to the earl of Carbery. Known for his skill as a writer, it was here that Taylor composed many of his best known works, including his popular devotional manuals, *The Rules and Exercises of Holy Living* (1650), and *The Rules and Exercises of Holy Dying* (1651). After the Restoration, Taylor was made Bishop of Down and Connor in Ireland and served as vice-chancellor of the University of Dublin.

Thomas Taylor (1576–1633). English Puritan pastor. Taylor ministered in Watford and Reading before becoming minister at St. Mary Aldermanbury in the city of London. He wrote more than fifty works on diverse topics, including a commentary on Titus, a response to the Gunpowder Plot, and an explanation of the role of the law under the gospel.

Thomas Taylor (1576–1632). Puritan minister and commentator. Taylor was born in Richmond, Yorkshire. He was educated at Christ's College, Cambridge, where he earned the degrees of Bachelor of Arts (1595) and Master of Arts (1598). Prior to entering pastoral ministry, Taylor served as a fellow and lecturer in Hebrew at the university. Throughout his academic career, Taylor was significantly influenced by the writings of William Perkins.* At the age of twenty-five, Taylor preached a virulent sermon against the papacy before Queen Elizabeth I.* As a Puritan, Taylor denounced the ecclesiastical policies of Archbishop Richard Bancroft.* In 1612, Taylor became minister of a church in Watford, Hertfordshire. While serving this charge, Taylor preached regularly in Berkshire and Reading. Moreover, Taylor formed and led a Puritan seminary, where he personally trained Nonconformist preachers. In the early 1620s, Taylor served as a chaplain to Edward Conway (1564–1631), secretary of state under James VI/I* (1566–1625). In 1625, Taylor was called to be curate and lecturer at St. Aldermanbury, London. While there, he organized and ran another Puritan seminary. Two years later, Taylor joined several other Puritans' efforts to send relief to oppressed Reformed ministers on the Continent. Taylor retired from his labors in 1630 due to ill health. He died of pleurisy in 1632. His main works include *Christ Revealed; or The Old Testament Explained* and *An Exposition of Titus*.

Teresa of Ávila (1515–1582). Spanish monastic reformer and mystical theologian. Born into a wealthy merchant family, Teresa entered the Carmelite order at Ávila in 1535. While Teresa initially enjoyed the lax practices of the convent, reading devotional literature caused her to deepen her spirituality, and in 1555 she began to have visions of God and claimed to have mystical union with him. Convinced the monastic life required complete withdrawal, Teresa could no longer tolerate the practices of her Carmelite cloister and founded the Discalced Carmelites with John of the Cross* (1542–1591) in 1562, which was committed to enclosure and strict asceticism. By her death, she had personally founded fourteen houses for her new order despite significant resistance from Carmelite leaders. She also wrote extensively. Her best-known works are *The Way of Perfection* (1577), a method for the contemplative life, and *The Interior Castle* (1577), a manual for spiritual growth.

Thirty-Nine Articles. See *Articles of Religion*.

Thomas Thorowgood (1595–1669). English Puritan pastor. Thorowgood was a Puritan minister in Norfolk and the chief financier of John Eliot (1604–1690), a Puritan missionary among the Native American tribes in Massachusetts. In 1650, under the title *Jews in America, or, Probabilities that Americans be of that Race*, Thorowgood became one of the first to put forward the thesis that Native Americans were actually the ten lost tribes of Israel.

John Tillinghast (1604–1655). English Puritan minister. Tillinghast began his ministry in the Church of England, pastoring two congregations in Sussex until he moved to London and became an independent, leading him to pastor Puritan congregations in Suffolk and Norfolk. He was a member of the Fifth Monarchists, a millenarian Puritan sect that believed the political upheaval of their time was ushering in the kingdom of Christ.

Frans Titelmans (1502–1537). Belgian Catholic philosopher. Titelmans studied at the University of Leuven, where he was influenced by Petrus Ramus.* After first joining a Franciscan monastery, Titelmans realigned with the stricter Capuchins and moved to Italy. He is best known for his advocacy for the Vulgate and his debates with Desiderius Erasmus* over Pauline theology (1527–1530)—he was deeply suspicious of the fruits of humanism, especially regarding biblical studies. His work was published posthumously by his brother, Pieter Titelmans (1501–1572).

Francisco de Toledo (1532–1596). Spanish Catholic theologian. This important Jesuit taught philosophy at the universities of Salamanca and Rome. He published works on Aristotelian philosophy and a commentary on Thomas Aquinas's* work, as well as biblical commentaries on John, Romans and the first half of Luke. He was also the general editor for the Clementine Vulgate (1598).
John Tombes (1603–1676). English Baptist pastor. After leaving Oxford, Tombes held many pastoral positions in Anglican churches throughout the Midlands until founding a Baptist church in Bewdley, Worcestershire. He left this congregation following a debate with Richard Baxter,* leading him to take on a number of pastoral positions in Herefordshire while continuing to seek public debates and writing against Quakerism and Roman Catholicism.
Laurence Tomson (1539–1608). English Reformed politician and translator. Tomson was born in Northhamptonshire and educated at Magdalen College, Oxford. He graduated with his BA degree (1559) and MA degree (1564). Tomson was a fellow at Magdalen until he resigned in 1569. Prior to this resignation, Tomson was part of a diplomatic delegation to France. From 1575 to 1587, Tomson served in the House of Commons and attended the royal court at Windsor in 1582. He went on further embassies throughout Europe, where he occasionally lectured on Hebrew. Tomson died on March 29, 1608. Tomson's chief exegetical contribution was his revised text and annotations of the New Testament of the Geneva Bible.
Edward Topsell (d. 1638?). English Protestant minister. Topsell held a number of pastoral posts in Sussex, Dorset, and the Midlands before being appointed perpetual curate of St. Botolph's, Aldersgate, in the city of London. While he composed a number of religious works, including his lectures on Ruth, which were so popular they appeared in three editions, he is primarily remembered for his two illustrated works on natural history, which cataloged four-footed animals and serpents.
Alonso Tostado (1400–1455). Spanish Catholic bishop and exegete. Tostado lectured on theology, law and philosophy at the University of Salamanca, in addition to ministering in a local parish. Tostado entered into disputes over papal supremacy and the date of Christ's birth. Tostado's thirteen-volume collected works include commentaries on the historical books of the Old Testament and the Gospel of Matthew.
Daniel Toussain (1541–1602). Swiss Reformed pastor and professor. Toussain became pastor at Orléans after attending college in Basel. After the third War of Religion, Toussain was exiled, eventually returning to Montbéliard, his birthplace. In 1571, he faced opposition there from the strict Lutheran rulers and was eventually exiled due to his influence over the clergy. He returned to Orléans but fled following the Saint Bartholomew's Day Massacre (1572), eventually becoming pastor in Basel. He relocated to Heidelberg in 1583 as pastor to the new regent, becoming professor of theology at the university, and he remained there until his death.
John Trapp (1601–1669). Anglican biblical exegete. After studying at Oxford, Trapp entered the pastorate in 1636. During the English Civil Wars he sided with Parliament, which later made it difficult for him to collect tithes from a congregation whose royalist pastor had been evicted. Trapp published commentaries on all the books of the Bible from 1646 to 1656.
Immanuel Tremellius (1510–1580). Italian Reformed Hebraist. Around 1540, Tremellius received baptism by Cardinal Reginald Pole (1500–1558) and converted from Judaism to Christianity; he affiliated with evangelicals the next year. On account of the political and religious upheaval, Tremellius relocated often, teaching Hebrew in Lucca; Strasbourg, fleeing the Inquisition; Cambridge, displaced by the Schmalkaldic War; Heidelberg, escaping Mary I's persecutions; and Sedan, expelled by the new Lutheran Elector of the Palatine. Many considered Tremellius's translation of the Old Testament as the most accurate available. He also published a Hebrew grammar and translated John Calvin's* catechism into Hebrew.
Richard Turnbull (d. 1593). English minister. A preacher in London, Richard Turnbull published sermons on James, Jude, and Psalm 15.
William Tyndale (Hychyns) (1494–1536). English reformer, theologian and translator. Tyndale was educated at Oxford University, where he was influenced by the writings of humanist thinkers. Believing that piety is fostered through personal encounter with the Bible, he asked to translate the Bible into English; denied permission, Tyndale left for the Continent to complete the task. His New Testament was the equivalent of a modern-day bestseller in England but was banned and ordered burned. Tyndale's theology was oriented around justification, the authority of Scripture and Christian obedience; Tyndale emphasized the ethical as a concomitant reality of justification. He was martyred in Brussels before completing his English translation of the Old Testament, which Miles Coverdale* finished.
John Udall (1560?–1592). English Puritan pastor. Udall began his pastoral career in the Anglican parish of Kingston-upon-Thames, becoming known for his preaching and Puritan convictions, particularly his

rejection of the episcopacy. While facing discipline for his views, he published anonymous and pseudonymous pamphlets critical of the established church alone and with friends, leading to his losing his position in London and relocating to Newcastle, where he continued in ministry and criticism. Udall was arrested under suspicion of complicity in publishing the critical tracts and, unwilling to deny that he wrote them, was convicted and sentenced to death. The death sentence was not carried out, however, and he remained in prison almost two years until pardoned, but died soon after release.

Guillaume du Vair (1556–1621). French Catholic priest, lawyer, and writer. While du Vair took holy orders in his youth, much of his life was spent serving the state as a counselor of the parliament of Paris, a representative of King Henry IV both in France and abroad, and as Keeper of the Seals, the highest legal office in the country. The last four years of his life were spent as the bishop of Lisieux. His studies on Epictetus and the Stoics, and attempts to relate Stoicism to the Christian faith, were influential in the dissemination of this philosophy during the seventeenth and eighteenth centuries. He also wrote significant works on politics, the moral life, prayer, and the use and abuse of the French language.

Juan de Valdés (1500/10–1541). Spanish Catholic theologian and writer. Although Valdés adopted an evangelical doctrine, had Erasmian affiliations and published works that were listed on the Index of Prohibited Books, Valdés rebuked the reformers for creating disunity and never left the Catholic Church. His writings included translations of the Hebrew Psalter and various biblical books, a work on the Spanish language and several commentaries. Valdés fled to Rome in 1531 to escape the Spanish Inquisition and worked in the court of Clement VII in Bologna until the pope's death in 1534. Valdés subsequently returned to Naples, where he led the reform- and revival-minded Valdesian circle.

Henry Vaughan (1617/1618–1661). English Protestant preacher. Possibly a student at Christ's College, Cambridge, Vaughan published a sermon on Matthew 5:20 given to the House of Commons.

Thomas Venatorius (c. 1490–1551). German Lutheran theologian, mathematician, and humanist. Following a humanistic education, Venatorius spent the majority of his career in Nuremberg, where he advocated for reform as the head of the city's school system and as a preacher and pastor in the city's churches. His theological and pastoral works include one of the first Protestant works on ethics, a short catechism, and a commentary on 1 Timothy. He also edited the first Greek edition of Archimedes's writings and translated Aristophanes's *Plutus*.

Peter Martyr Vermigli (1499–1562). Italian Reformed humanist and theologian. Vermigli was one of the most influential theologians of the era, held in common regard with such figures as Martin Luther* and John Calvin.* In Italy, Vermigli was a distinguished theologian, preacher and advocate for moral reform; however, during the reinstitution of the Roman Inquisition Vermigli fled to Protestant regions in northern Europe. He was eventually appointed professor of divinity at Oxford University, where Vermigli delivered acclaimed disputations on the Eucharist. Vermigli was widely noted for his deeply integrated biblical commentaries and theological treatises.

Matthieu Virel (fl. 1561–1595). French Reformed pastor and theologian. Only two episodes from Virel's life are known: he preached the reformation message at Namur in 1561, and sixteen years later he pastored a French congregation in Basel. He published two known works: an excursus on the calendar and a brief summary of the Christian religion.

Pierre Viret (1511–1571). Swiss Reformed pastor and teacher. Converted to Protestantism at the University of Paris, Viret returned to his hometown, Orbe, where Guillaume Farel* brought him into ministry. Preaching also at Payerne and Neuchâtel, Viret's success in spreading the Reformed faith led to an assassination attempt before he and Farel sought to reform Geneva. Soon after the Genevan Assembly voted to accept the Reformation, Viret relocated to Lausanne, where he established the Reformed faith, served as chief pastor, and founded a Reformed academy. After almost twenty-five years, he was exiled from the city, spending a short time pastoring and teaching in Geneva until establishing himself in southern France, where he brought the evangelical faith to Lyons, pastored, and served as an advisor to Jeanne d'Albret, the queen of Navarre (1528–1572).

Juan Luis Vives (1492?–1540). Spanish Catholic humanist. Born into a Jewish family but baptized Catholic, Vives spent most of his life outside Spain following the persecution of his family by the Inquisition. After studying in Paris, he lived in Bruges, where he became part of the intellectual circle around Erasmus,* and taught at Oxford toward the end of his life. Vives largely avoided entering into religious controversies, and his works received a mixed reception from both Catholics and Protestants. He is best known for his educational and social writings, including an influential Latin primer, works on pedagogy and women's education, and arguments for pacifism and poor relief.

Gisbertus Voetius (1589–1676). Dutch Reformed theologian. Voetius pastored at Vlijmen and Heusden and served as the youngest delegate at the Synod of Dordrecht* before becoming professor of theology and Oriental languages at the University of Utrecht. While Voetius's writings demonstrate concern for missions, practical piety, and personal purity, he also entered into numerous theological controversies during his career. His Reformed commitments led to ongoing conflicts with Arminians and Catholics, and he sought to uphold the importance of the Old Testament against Johannes Cocceius's (1603–1669) formulation of the covenants. He also entered into debate with René Descartes (1596–1650) and his followers, arguing from an Aristotelian perspective that to accept Cartesian skepticism was to reject biblical truth and the Christian tradition.

Conradus Vorstius (1569–1622). Dutch Arminian-Socinian theologian. A student of David Paraeus* and Johannes Piscator,* Vorstius's Socinian tendencies emerged during his tenure as professor of theology at Steinfurt. After an apology and examination, he was allowed to replace Arminius* as professor of theology at Leiden though never permitted to teach, as his questioning of the doctrine of atonement and the eternity, foreknowledge, and omnipresence of God drew wide censure, ultimately from King James I of England.* Exiled to Gouda and deposed at the Synod of Dordrecht,* Vorstius published numerous theological works and a commentary on the Pauline letters.

Vulgate. In 382 Pope Damasus I (c. 300–384) commissioned Jerome (c. 347–420) to translate the four Gospels into Latin based on Old Latin and Greek manuscripts. Jerome completed the translation of the Gospels and the Old Testament around 405. It is widely debated how much of the rest of the New Testament was translated by Jerome. During the Middle Ages, the Vulgate became the Catholic Church's standard Latin translation. The Council of Trent recognized it as the official text of Scripture.

George Walker (1581–1651). Puritan minister. Walker was born at Hawkshead, Lancashire, and educated at St. John's College, Cambridge. After graduating Cambridge, Walker moved to London, where he became rector of St. John the Evangelist on Watling Street in 1614. He served this parish for nearly forty years. Throughout his ministry, Walker showed himself to be an ardent opponent of the papacy and practices within the Church of England that he deemed not sufficiently reformed. Toward this end, Walker engaged numerous disputations and literary debates with both conformists and Catholics. For his sermons that were critical of the Church of England, he was summoned to appear before Archbishop Laud in 1635 and the Star Chamber in 1638, which fined and imprisoned him for twelve weeks. On another occasion, Walker was incarcerated for as long as two years for his nonconformity until released by the Long Parliament. In 1643, Walker was selected to serve in the Westminster Assembly and to participate in the trial of Laud. Walker died in London. Among his many published sermons and polemical works is a treatise on justification.

Thomas Walkington (d. 1621). Anglican minister and author. Born in Lincoln, he was educated at Cambridge, graduating with his BA in 1597 and his MA in 1600. Walkington was elected a fellow at St. John's College, Cambridge, in 1602. Later, he received a BD from Oxford and a DD from Cambridge. He served as rector of parishes in Northamptonshire, Lincolnshire, and Middlesex. A prolific author, Walkington published works on diverse subjects. Among his biblical works are *An Exposition of the First Two Verses of the Sixth Chapter to the Hebrews in form of a Dialogue* (1609) and *Theologicall Rules to Guide Us in the Understanding and Practice of Holy Scripture* (1615).

Peter Walpot (d. 1578). Moravian Radical pastor and bishop. Walpot was a bishop of the Hutterite community after Jakob Hutter, Peter Riedemann* and Leonhard Lanzenstiel. Riedemann's *Confession of Faith* (1545; 1565) became a vital authority for Hutterite exegesis, theology and morals. Walpot added his own *Great Article Book* (1577), which collates primary biblical passages on baptism, communion, the community of goods, the sword and divorce. In keeping with Hutterite theology, Walpot defended the community of goods as a mark of the true church.

Richard Ward (c. 1601–1684). English Anglican pastor. Educated at Cambridge and St. Andrews, Ward pastored in London and Essex. His published writings include a commentary on Matthew and an explanation of the Solemn League and Covenant (1643), which allied Scottish Covenanters and English Parliamentarians during the First English Civil War (1642–1646).

Thomas Watson (d. 1686). English Puritan pastor. After graduating from Cambridge, Watson became pastor of St. Stephen Walbrook in the city of London, a pulpit he served for twenty years, though he was imprisoned for a year for his part in the plot of Christopher Love (1618–1651) to restore Charles II to the throne. A well-respected preacher, Watson was expelled from official ministry by the 1662 Act of Uniformity, though he continued to preach in private until his retirement. While Watson published many sermons and devotional works, he is perhaps best known for *A Body of Divinity* (1692), a series of sermon on the Westminster Catechism.

Valentin Weigel (1533–1588). German Lutheran pastor. Weigel studied at Leipzig and Wittenberg, entering the pastorate in 1567. Despite a strong anti-institutional bias, he was recognized by the church hierarchy as a talented preacher and compassionate minister of mercy to the poor. Although he signed the Formula of Concord,* Weigel's orthodoxy was questioned so openly that he had to publish a defense. He appears to have tried to synthesize several medieval mystics with the ideas of Sebastian Franck,* Thomas Müntzer* and others. His posthumously published works have led some recent scholars to suggest that Weigel's works may have deeply influenced later Pietism.

Hieronymus Weller von Molsdorf (1499–1572). German Lutheran theologian. Originally intending to study law, Weller devoted himself to theology after hearing one of Martin Luther's* sermons on the catechism. He boarded with Luther and tutored Luther's son. In 1539 he moved to Freiburg, where he lectured on the Bible and held theological disputations at the Latin school. In addition to hymns, works of practical theology and a postil set, Weller published commentaries on Genesis, 1–2 Samuel, 1–2 Kings, Job, the Psalms, Christ's passion, Ephesians, Philippians, 1–2 Thessalonians and 1–2 Peter.

Westminster Assembly (1643–1652). English church council. Called by English Parliament to advise on church reform, the Westminster Assembly was made up of more than 120 clergymen, thirty parliamentary observers, and a delegation from the Church of Scotland. Beginning with a review of the Articles of Religion,* the most heated debates were undertaken over ecclesiology, as factions argued for presbyterianism, congregationalism, Erastianism, and episcopalianism, with the council ultimately recommending presbyterianism to the parliament. Much of the legacy of the assembly is held in the major documents it produced, the *Directory for Public Worship* (1644), *The Form of Presbyterial Church Government* (1645), the *Westminster Confession of Faith* (1646), the *Shorter Catechism* (1647), and the *Larger Catechism* (1648), which became foundational for the English and Scottish churches and many of the Reformed denominations.

John Whitgift (1530–1604). Anglican archbishop. Though Whitgift shared much theological common ground with Puritans, after his election as Archbishop of Canterbury (1583) he moved decisively to squelch the political and ecclesiastical threat they posed during Elizabeth I's* reign. Whitgift enforced strict compliance to the Book of Common Prayer,* the Act of Uniformity (1559) and the Articles of Religion.* Whitgift's policies led to a large migration of Puritans to Holland. The bulk of Whitgift's published corpus is the fruit of a lengthy public disputation with Thomas Cartwright,* in which Whitgift defines Anglican doctrine against Cartwright's staunch Puritanism.

Johann Wigand (1523–1587). German Lutheran theologian. Wigand is most noted as one of the compilers of the *Magdeburg Centuries*, a German ecclesiastical history of the first thirteen centuries of the church. He was a student of Philipp Melanchthon* at the University of Wittenburg and became a significant figure in the controversies dividing Lutheranism. Strongly opposed to Roman Catholicism, Wigand lobbied against innovations in Lutheran theology that appeared sympathetic to Catholic thought. In the later debates, Wigand's support for Gnesio-Lutheranism established his role in the development of confessional Lutheranism. Wigand was appointed bishop of Pomerania after serving academic posts at the universities in Jena and Königsburg.

Thomas Wilcox (c. 1549–1608). English Puritan theologian. In 1572, Wilcox objected to Parliament against the episcopacy and the Book of Common Prayer,* advocating for presbyterian church governance. He was imprisoned for sedition. After his release, he preached itinerantly. He was brought before the courts twice more for his continued protest against the Church of England's episcopal structure. He translated some of Theodore Beza* and John Calvin's* sermons into English, and he wrote polemical and occasional works as well as commentaries on the Psalms and Song of Songs.

Johann (Ferus) Wild (1495–1554). German Catholic pastor. After studying at Heidelberg and teaching at Tübingen, this Franciscan was appointed as lector in the Mainz cathedral, eventually being promoted to cathedral preacher—a post for which he became widely popular but also controversial. Wild strongly identified as Catholic but was not unwilling to criticize the curia. Known for an irenic spirit—criticized in fact as *too* kind—he was troubled by the polemics between all parties of the Reformation. He preached with great lucidity, integrating the liturgy, Scripture and doctrine to exposit Catholic worship and teaching for common people. His sermons on John were pirated for publication without his knowledge; the Sorbonne banned them as heretical. Despite his popularity among clergy, the majority of his works were on the Roman Index until 1900.

Andrew Willet (1562–1621). Anglican priest, professor, and biblical expositor. Willet was a gifted biblical expositor and powerful preacher. He walked away from a promising university career in 1588 when he was ordained a priest in the Church of England. For the next thirty-three years he served as a parish priest. Willet's commentaries summarized the present state of discussion while also offering practical applications for preachers. They have been cited as some of the most technical commentaries of the early seventeenth century. His most important publication was *Synopsis Papismi, or a General View of Papistrie* (1594), in which he responded to many of Robert Bellarmine's critiques. After years of royal favor, Willet was imprisoned in 1618 for a month after presenting to King James I* his opposition to the "Spanish Match" of Prince Charles to the Infanta Maria. While serving as a parish priest, he wrote forty-two works, most of which were either commentaries on books of the Bible or controversial works against Catholics.

Thomas Wilson (d. 1586). English Anglican priest. A fellow of St John's, Cambridge, Wilson fled to Frankfurt to escape the Marian Persecution. After his return to England, he served as a canon and Dean of Worcester.

George Wither (1588–1667). English poet, satirist, and hymn writer. Wither was born in Bentworth, Hampshire. After finishing his early education under the tutelage of a local minister, Wither continued his studies at Magdalen College, Oxford. Afterward, he studied law at the Inns of Chancery. Wither commenced his literary career with the publication of an elegy on the occasion of the death of Henry Frederick, Prince of Wales (1594–1612). Most of Wither's literary works consist of satirical pamphlets for which he was regularly arrested, imprisoned, and released. He fought in the Parliamentary Army during the Civil War. A conforming Anglican, Wither composed numerous hymns as well as translations of the Psalms. Two of Wither's major works are *Preparation to the Psalter* (1619), in which he explores various literary aspects of the Bible, and *Hymns and Songs of the Church* (1622/1623). He died in London.

John Woolton (c. 1535–1594). Anglican bishop. After graduating from Oxford, Woolton lived in Germany until the accession of Elizabeth I.* He was ordained as a priest in 1560 and as a bishop in 1578. Woolton published many theological, devotional and practical works, including a treatise on the immortality of the soul, a discourse on conscience and a manual for Christian living.

John Wycliffe (c. 1330–1384). English theologian, philosopher, and reformer known as "the Morning Star of the Reformation." While holding benefices from a number of parishes, Wycliffe spent the majority of his career at Oxford, where he studied, taught, and served as head of Balliol College. His early work focused on logic and metaphysics, but after entering into the service of John of Gaunt, Duke of Lancaster (1340–1399) and serving as a royal envoy to discuss taxes with papal representatives, Wycliffe turned his attention to more practical concerns. His criticism of papal power and wealth drew initially civil and ecclesiastical approval, but application of his principle that any headship profiting the governor rather than the governed is illegitimate to the English church brought controversy and censure. This criticism increased as he rejected transubstantiation, criticized monasticism, argued along Augustinian lines that only the invisible body of the elect constituted the true church, that Scripture belongs to the body of the elect rather than the institutional church, and that as many leaders of the visible church were likely reprobate, their offices and sacraments were invalid. While dismissed from Oxford in 1381, powerful defenders protected Wycliffe from further consequences during his lifetime, but he was condemned as a heretic at the Council of Constance (1515), whence he was exhumed and his remains burned. While largely condemned by contemporaries, Wycliffe, and his followers, the Lollards, are often viewed as forerunners of the Reformation who prepared the way for the tumult of the sixteenth century.

Girolamo Zanchi (1516–1590). Italian Reformed theologian and pastor. Zanchi joined an Augustinian monastery at the age of fifteen, where he studied Greek and Latin, the church fathers and the works of Aristotle and Thomas Aquinas.* Under the influence of his prior, Peter Martyr Vermigli,* Zanchi also imbibed the writings of the Swiss and German reformers. To avoid the Inquisition, Zanchi fled to Geneva where he was strongly attracted to the preaching and teaching of John Calvin.* Zanchi taught biblical theology and the *locus* method at academies in Strasbourg, Heidelberg, and Neustadt. He also served as pastor of an Italian refugee congregation. Zanchi's theological works, *De tribus Elohim* (1572) and *De natura Dei* (1577), have received more attention than his commentaries. His commentaries comprise about a quarter of his literary output, however, and display a strong typological and christological interpretation in conversation with the church fathers, medieval exegetes, and other reformers.

Katharina Schütz Zell (1497/98–1562). German Reformed writer. Zell became infamous in Strasbourg and the Empire when in 1523 she married the priest

Matthias Zell, and then published an apology defending her husband against charges of impiety and libertinism. Longing for a united church, she called for toleration of Catholics and Anabaptists, famously writing to Martin Luther* after the failed Marburg Colloquy of 1529 to exhort him to check his hostility and to be ruled instead by Christian charity. Much to the chagrin of her contemporaries, Zell published diverse works, ranging from polemical treatises on marriage to letters of consolation, as well as editing a hymnal and penning an exposition of Psalm 51.

Martha Elizabeth Zitter (Unknown). German Catholic nun. Zitter entered the Ursuline convent in Erfurt during her teenage years. Most of what is known about her is drawn from a letter she composed to her mother, explaining her decision to leave the order and become Lutheran, which focuses on aspects of her vows and Roman Catholic piety she believes to be unbiblical. Despite this public departure from the Roman church, however, Zitter returned toward the end of her life.

Ulrich Zwingli (1484–1531). Swiss Reformed humanist, preacher and theologian. Zwingli studied at the University of Vienna, and afterwards the University of Basel, where he received his BA and MA in 1504 and 1506. Ordained in September 1506, Zwingli became priest of the church in Glarus where he taught himself Greek, and read deeply in the church fathers. During this period, Zwingli was also greatly impacted by the writings of Desiderius Erasmus*. In 1516, Zwingli accepted the position of priest at the Benedictine Abbey at Einsiedeln in Schwyz, where he intently studied the Greek New Testament, and learned Hebrew. When he became a preacher in the city cathedral at Zurich, Zwingli enacted reform through sermons, public disputations, and conciliation with the town council, abolishing the Mass and images in the church. Zwingli broke with the lectionary preaching tradition, instead preaching serial expository biblical sermons. He later was embroiled in controversy with Anabaptists over infant baptism and with Martin Luther* at the Marburg Colloquy (1529) over their differing views of the Eucharist. Zwingli, serving as chaplain to Zurich's military, was killed in the Second Battle of Kappel.

SOURCES FOR BIOGRAPHICAL SKETCHES

General Reference Works

Allgemeine Deutsche Biographie. 56 vols. Leipzig: Duncker & Humblot, 1875–1912; reprint, 1967–1971. Accessible online via deutsche-biographie.de/index.html.

Baskin, Judith R., ed. *The Cambridge Dictionary of Judaism and Jewish Culture*. New York: Cambridge University Press, 2011.

Benedetto, Robert, ed. *The New Westminster Dictionary of Church History*. Vol. 1. Louisville: Westminster John Knox Press, 2008.

Bettenson, Henry and Chris Maunder, eds. *Documents of the Christian Church*. 3rd ed. Oxford: Oxford University Press, 1999.

Betz, Hans Dieter, Don Browning, Bernd Janowski and Eberhard Jüngel, eds. *Religion Past & Present: Encyclopedia of Theology and Relgion*. 13 vols. Leiden: Brill, 2007–2013.

Bremer, Francis J. and Tom Webster, eds. *Puritans and Puritanism in Europe and America: A Comprehensive Encyclopedia*. 2 vols. Santa Barbara, CA: ABC-CLIO, 2006.

Gritsch, Eric W. *A History of Lutheranism*. Minneapolis: Fortress Press, 2002.

Haag, Eugene and Émile Haag. *La France protestante ou vies des protestants français*. 2nd ed. 6 vols. Paris: Sandoz & Fischbacher, 1877–1888.

Hillerbrand, Hans J., ed. *Oxford Encyclopedia of the Reformation*. 4 vols. New York: Oxford University Press, 1996.

Kolb, Robert, and Timothy J. Wengert, eds. *The Book of Concord: The Confessions of the Evangelical Lutheran Church*. Translated by Charles Arand et al. Minneapolis: Fortress, 2000.

McKim, Donald K., ed. *Dictionary of Major Biblical Interpreters*. Downers Grove, IL: InterVarsity Press, 2007.

Müller, Gerhard, et al., ed. *Theologische Realenzyklopädie*. Berlin: Walter de Gruyter, 1994.

Neue Deutsche Biographie. 28 vols. projected. Berlin: Duncker & Humblot, 1953–. Accessible online via deutsche-biographie.de/index.html.

New Catholic Encyclopedia. 15 vols. New York: McGraw-Hill, 1967; 2nd ed., Detroit: Thomson-Gale, 2002.

Oxford Dictionary of National Biography. 60 vols. Oxford: Oxford University Press, 2004.

Pelikan, Jaroslav. *The Christian Tradition*. 5 vols. Chicago: University of Chicago Press, 1971–1989.

Stephen, Leslie, and Sidney Lee, eds. *Dictionary of National Biography*. 63 vols. London: Smith, Elder and Co., 1885–1900.

Terry, Michael, ed. *Reader's Guide to Judaism*. New York: Routledge, 2000.

Wordsworth, Christopher, ed. *Lives of Eminent Men connected with the History of Religion in England*. 4 vols. London: J. G. & F. Rivington, 1839.

Additional Works for Individual Sketches

Akin, Daniel L. "An Expositional Analysis of the Schleitheim Confession." *Criswell Theological Review* 2 (1988): 345-70.

Astell, Mary. *The Christian Religion, as Professed by a Daughter of the Church of England*. Edited by Jacqueline Broad. Toronto: Iter Inc and the Center for Reformation and Renaissance Studies, 2013.

Bald, R. C. *John Donne: A Life*. Oxford: Oxford University Press, 1970.

Beeke, Joel, and Randall J. Pederson. *Meet the Puritans*. Grand Rapids: Reformation Heritage Books, 2006.

Bireley, Robert, *The Refashioning of Catholicism, 1450–1700*, Washington, DC: Catholic University of America Press, 1999.

Blok, P. J., and P. C. Molhuysen, eds. *Nieuw Nederlandsch Biografisch Woordenboek*. 10 vols.

Brackney, William H. *A Genetic History of Baptist Thought: With Special Reference to Baptists in Britain and North America*. Atlanta: Mercer University Press, 2004.

———. *Historical Dictionary of the Baptists*. 2nd ed. Lanham, MD: Scarecrow, 2009.

Brook, Benjamin. *The Lives of the Puritans.* 3 vols. London: James Black, 1813. Reprint, Pittsburgh, PA: Soli Deo Gloria, 1994.

Brown, Peter. *Augustine of Hippo: A Biography.* Berkeley & Los Angeles, CA: University of California Press, 1967.

Burke, David G. "The Enduring Significance of the KJV." *Word and World* 31, no. 3 (2011): 229-44.

Campbell, Gordon. *Bible: The Story of the King James Version, 1611–2011.* Oxford: Oxford University Press, 2010.

Cathcart, William. *The Baptist Encyclopaedia.* 3 vols. Philadelphia: Louis H. Everts, 1881.

Charles, Amy. *A Life of George Herbert.* Ithaca, NY: Cornell University Press, 1977.

Christian, Jacob. *The Sovereign Map: Theoretical Approaches to Cartography Throughout History.* Chicago: University of Chicago Press, 2006.

Coffey, John. *Politics, Religion, and the British Revolutions: The Thought of Samuel Rutherford.* Cambridge: Cambridge University Press, 1997.

Colish, Marcia. *Peter Lombard,* 2 vols. Leiden, Netherlands: Brill, 1993.

Culpepper, Scott. *Francis Johnson and the English Separatist Influence: The Bishop of Brownism's Life, Writings, and Controversies.* Macon, GA: Mercer University Press, 2011.

Doornkaat Koolman, J ten. "The First Edition of Peter Riedemann's 'Rechenschaft.'" *Mennonite Quarterly Review* 36, no. 2 (1962): 169-70.

Emerson, Everett H. *John Cotton.* New York: Twayne, 1990.

Fischlin, Daniel and Mark Fortier, eds. *Royal Subjects: Essays on the Writings of James VI and I.* Detroit: Wayne State University Press, 2002.

Fishbane, Michael A. "Teacher and the Hermeneutical Task: A Reinterpretation of Medieval Exegesis." *Journal of the American Academy of Religion* 43, no. 4 (1975): 709-21.

Friedmann, Robert. "Second Generation Anabaptism as Illustrated by the Walpot Era of the Hutterites." *Mennonite Quarterly* 44, no. 4 (1970): 390-93.

Frymire, John M. *The Primacy of the Postils: Catholics, Protestants, and the Dissemination of Ideas in Early Modern Germany.* Leiden: Brill, 2010.

Furcha, Edward J. "Key Concepts in Caspar von Schwenckfeld's Thought, Regeneration and the New Life." *Church History* 37, no. 2 (1968): 160-73.

Gordon, Bruce, *The Swiss Reformation.* Manchester: Manchester University Press, 2002.

Greaves, Richard L. *Society and Religion in Elizabethan England.* Minneapolis: University of Minnesota, 1981.

Greiffenberg, Catharina Regina von. *Meditations on the Incarnation, Passion, and Death of Jesus Christ.* Edited and translated by Lynne Tatlock. The Other Voice in Early Modern Europe. Chicago: University of Chicago Press, 2009.

Grendler, Paul. "Italian biblical humanism and the papacy, 1515-1535." In *Biblical Humanism and Scholasticism in the Age of Erasmus.* Edited by Erika Rummel, 225-76. Leiden: Brill, 2008.

Haemig, Mary Jane. "Elisabeth Cruciger (1500?–1535): The Case of the Disappearing Hymn Writer." *Sixteenth Century Journal* 32, no. 1 (2001): 21-44.

Harpley, W., ed. *Report and Transactions of the Devonshire Association for the Advancement of Science, Literature and Art* 24 (July 1882). Plymouth: William Brendon and Son, 1892.

Heiden, Albert van der. "Pardes: Methodological Reflections on the Theory of the Four Senses." *Journal of Jewish Studies* 34, no. 2 (1983): 147-59.

Hendrix, Scott H., ed. and trans. *Early Protestant Spirituality.* New York: Paulist Press, 2009.

Hvolbek, Russell H. "Being and Knowing: Spiritualist Epistelmology and Anthropology from Schwenckfeld to Böhme." *Sixteenth Century Journal* 22, no. 1 (1991): 97-110.

Kahle, Paul. "Felix Pratensis—a Prato, Felix. Der Herausgeber der Ersten Rabbinerbibel, Venedig 1516/7." *Die Welt des Orients* 1, no. 1 (1947): 32-36.

Kelly, Joseph Francis. *The Ecumenical Councils of the Catholic Church: A History.* Collegeville, MN: Liturgical Press, 2009.

Koop, Karl, ed. *Confessions of Faith in the Anabaptist Tradition 1527–1660.* Translated by Cornelius J. Dyck et al. CRR 11. Kitchener, ON: Pandora Press, 2006.

Lake, Peter. *The Boxmaker's Revenge: "Orthodoxy", "Heterodox" and the Politics of the Parish in Early Stuart London.* Stanford, CA: Stanford University Press, 2001.

Lane, Anthony N. S. *Calvin and Bernard of Clairvaux.* Princeton, NJ: Princeton Theological Seminary, 1996.

Lane, Belden C. *Ravished by Beauty: The Surprising Legacy of Reformed Spirituality.* Oxford: Oxford University Press, 2011.

Lee, Jason K. *The Theology of John Smyth* (Macon, GA: Mercer University Press, 2003).

Lockhart, Paul Douglas. *Frederick II and the Protestant Cause: Denmark's Role in the Wars of Religion, 1559–1596.* Leiden: Brill, 2004.

Lubac, Henri de. *Medieval Exegesis: The Four Senses of Scripture*. 3 vols. Translated by Mark Sebanc and E. M. Macierowski. Grand Rapids: Eerdmans, 1998–2009.

Manetsch, Scott, *Calvin's Company of Pastors: Pastoral Care and the Emerging Reformed Church, 1536–1609*. Oxford: Oxford University Press, 2013.

Manschereck, Clyde Leonard. *Melanchthon, the Quiet Reformer*. New York: Abingdon, 1958.

Marinella, Lucrezia. *The Nobility and Excellence of Women and the Defects and Vices of Men*. Edited and translated by Anne Dunhill. Chicago: University of Chicago Press, 1999.

Matheson, Peter, *Argula von Grumbach: A Woman's Voice in the Reformation*. Edinburgh: T&T Clark, 1995.

McGuire, Daniel Patrick. *The Difficult Saint: Bernard of Clairvaux and his Tradition*. Collegeville, MN: Cistercian Publication, 1991.

McKinley, Mary B. "Volume Editor's Introduction." In *Epistle to Marguerite of Navarre and Preface to a Sermon by John Calvin*, edited and translated by Mary B. McKiney. Chicago: University of Chicago Press, 2004.

M'Crie, Thomas. *The Life of Andrew Melville*. 2 vols. Edinburgh: William Blackwood, 1819.

Norton, David. *A Textual History of the King James Bible*. New York: Cambridge University Press, 2005

Nuttall, Geoffrey. *The Welsh Saints, 1640–1660: Walter Cradock, Vavasor Powell, Morgan Llwyd*. Cardiff: University of Wales Press, 1957.

Oberman, Heiko A. *Luther: Man Between God and the Devil*. New York, NY: Doubleday, 1989.

O'Meara, Thomas F. *Albert the Great: Theologian and Scientist*. Chicago: New Priory Press, 2013.

Packull, Werner O. "The Origins of Peter Riedemann's Account of Our Faith." *Sixteenth Century Journal* 30, no. 1 (1999): 61-69.

Papazian, Mary Arshagouni, ed. *John Donne and the Protestant Reformation: New Perspectives*. Detroit: Wayne State University Press, 2003.

Paulicelli, Eugenia. "Sister Arcangela Tarabotti: Hair, Wigs and Other Vices." In *Writing Fashion in Early Modern Italy: From Sprezzatura to Satire*, by idem, 177-204. Farnham, Surrey, UK: Ashgate, 2014.

Pragman, James H. "The Augsburg Confession in the English Reformation: Richard Taverner's Contribution." *Sixteenth Century Journal* 11, no. 3 (1980): 75-85.

Rashi. *Rashi's Commentary on Psalms*. Translated by Mayer I. Gruber. Atlanta: Scholars Press, 1998.

Raynor, Brian. *John Frith: Scholar and Martyr*. Kent, UK: Pond View Books, 2000.

Reid, Jonathan A. *King's Sister—Queen of Dissent: Marguerite of Navarre (1492–1549) and her Evangelical Network*. Leiden: Brill, 2009.

Schmidt, Josef, "Introduction" in Johannes Tauler, *Sermons*. New York: Paulist Press, 1985, 1-34.

Smith, Hannah. "Mary Astell, *A Serious Proposal to the Ladies* (1694), and the Anglican Reformation of Manners in Late-Seventeenth-Century England." In *Mary Astell: Reason, Gender, Faith*, edited by William Kolbrenner and Michal Michelson, 31-48. New York: Routledge, 2007.

Spinka, Matthew. *John Hus: A Biography*. Princeton, NJ: Princeton University Press, 1968.

———. *John Hus at the Council of Constance*. New York: Columbia University Press, 1968.

———. *John Hus and the Czech Reform*. Hamden, CT: Archon Books, 1966.

Steinmetz, David C. *Reformers in the Wings: From Geiler von Kayserberg to Theodore Beza*. Oxford: Oxford University Press, 2000.

———. "The Superiority of Pre-Critical Exegesis." *Theology Today* 37, no. 1 (1980): 27-38.

Stjerna, Kirsi. *Women of the Reformation*. Malden, MA: Blackwell Publishing, 2009.

Synder, C. Arnold. "The Confession of the Swiss Brethren in Hesse, 1578." In *Anabaptism Revisited: Essays on Anabaptist/Mennonite Studies in Honor of C. J. Dyck*. Edited by Walter Klaassen, 29-49. Waterloo, ON; Scottdale, PA: Herald Press, 1992.

———. "The Schleitheim Articles in Light of the Revolution of the Common Man: Continuation or Departure?" *Sixteenth Century Journal* 16, no. 4 (1985): 419-30.

Thornton, Wallace. *John Foxe and His Monument: A Theological-Historical Perspective*. Birmingham, AL: Aldersgate Heritage Press, 2013.

Todd, Margo. "Bishops in the Kirk: William Cowper of Galloway and the Puritan Episcopacy of Scotland." *Scottish Journal of Theology*, 57 (2004): 300-312.

Tschackert, Paul. "Varel, Edo Hilderich of." In *General German Biography* (ADB). Volume 39. Leipzig: Duncker & Humblot, 1895.

Van Liere, Frans. *An Introduction to the Medieval Bible*. New York: Cambridge University Press, 2014.

Voogt, Gerrit. "Remonstrant-Counter-Remonstrant Debates: Crafting a Principled Defense of Toleration after the Synod of Dordrecht (1619–1650)." *Church History and Religious Culture* 89, no. 4 (2009): 489-524.

Wabuda, Susan. "Henry Bull, Miles Coverdale, and the Making of *Foxe's Book of Martyrs*." In *Martyrs and Martyrologies: Papers Read at the 1992 Summer Meeting and the 1993 Winter Meeting of the Ecclesiastical History Society*, edited by Diana Wood, 245-58. Oxford: Blackwell, 1993.

Wallace, Dewey D. Jr. "George Gifford, Puritan Propaganda and Popular Religion in Elizabethan England." *Sixteenth Century Journal* 9, no. 1 (1978): 27-49.

Wawrykow, Joseph P. *The Westminster Handbook to Thomas Aquinas*. Louisville, KY: Westminster John Knox, 2005.

Wendel, Francois. *Calvin: The Origins and Development of His Religious Thought*. New York: Harper & Row, 1963.

Wengert, Timothy J. "'Fear and Love' in the Ten Commandments." *Concordia Journal* 21, no. 1 (1995): 14-27.

Wiesner-Hanks, Merry, ed. *Convents Confront the Reformation: Catholic and Protestant Nuns in Germany*. Translated by Joan Skocir and Merry Wiesner-Hanks. Milwaukee: Marquette University Press, 1996.

———. "Philip Melanchthon and John Calvin against Andreas Osiander: Coming to Terms with Forensic Justification." In *Calvin and Luther: The Continuing Relationship*, edited by R. Ward Holder, 63-87. Göttingen: Vandenhoeck & Ruprecht, 2013.

Wilkinson, Robert J. *Tetragrammaton: Western Christians and the Hebrew Name of God*. Leiden: Brill, 2015.

Yarnell, Malcolm. "Christopher Blackwood: Exemplar of the Seventeenth-Century Particular Baptists." *Southwestern Journal of Theology* 57, no 2 (Spring 2015): 181-205.

BIBLIOGRAPHY

Primary Sources and Translations Used in the Volume

Amyraut, Moïse. *Le Ravissement de Saint Paul Explique en Quatre Sermons*. Saumur: Antoine Rousselet, 1660.

Baylor, Michael, ed. *The Radical Reformation*. Cambridge Texts in the History of Political Thought. New York: Cambridge University Press, 1995.

Beza, Theodore. *The Life of John Calvin*. Darlington, UK: Evangelical Press, 1997.

———. *A Little Book of Christian Questions and Responses*. Translated by Kirk M. Summers. Allison Park, PA: Pickwick, 1986.

———. *Sermons sur l'histoire de la resurrection de nostre Seigneur Iésus Christ*. Geneva: Jean Le Preux, 1593.

Bromiley, G. W., ed. and trans. *Zwingli and Bullinger*. LCC 24. Philadelphia, PA: Westminster, 1953.

Bucer, Martin. *Common Places of Martin Bucer*. Edited by David F. Wright. The Courtenay Library of Reformation Classics 4. Berkshire, UK: Sutton Courtenay Press, 1972.

———. *Concerning the True Care of Souls*. Translated by Peter Beale. Edinburgh: Banner of Truth Trust, 2009.

Bullinger, Heinrich. *The Decades of Henry Bullinger*. Edited by Thomas Harding. 2 vols. Grand Rapids, MI: Reformation Heritage Books, 2004.

———. *In Posteriorem D. Pauli ad Corinthios epistolam Heinrychi Bullingeri commentarius*. Zurich: Christoffel Froschouer, 1535.

Cajetan, Cardinal (Thomas de Vio). *In Posteriorem Pauli Epistolam ad Corinthios Commentarii*. In *Opera omnia quotquot in Sacrae Scripturae expositionem reperiuntur*. 5 vols. Lyon: Jean & Pierre Prost, 1639. Digital copy online at books.google.com.

Calvin, John. *Commentaries on the Epistles of Paul the Apostle to the Corinthians*. Translated and edited by John Pringle. 2 vols. CTS 39-40. Edinburgh: Calvin Translation Society, 1848–1849. Digital copy online at archive.org.

———. *Institutes of the Christian Religion* (1559). Edited by John T. McNeill. Translated by Ford Lewis Battles. LCC 20-21. Philadelphia: Westminster, 1960. Latin text available in CO 2 (1864).

———. *Ioannis Calvini Operae quae supersunt omnia*. 59 vols. Corpus Reformatorum 29-88. Edited by G. Baum, E. Cunitz, and E. Reuss. Brunswick and Berlin: C. A. Schwetschke, 1863–1900. Digital copy online at archive-ouverte.unige.ch/unige:650.

Chemnitz, Martin. *Examination of the Council of Trent*. Translated by Fred Kramer. 4 vols. St. Louis: Concordia Publishing House, 1971–1986.

———. *Loci Theologici*. Translated by J. A. O. Preus. 2 vols. St. Louis: Concordia Publishing House, 1989.

Chytraeus, David. *Dispositio epistolarum, quae diebus dominicis et aliis in ecclesia usitate populo proponi solent*. Wittenberg: Johannes Crato, 1563. Digital copy online at www.gateway-bayerne.de.

———. *A Postil or Orderly Disposing of Certeine Epistles Usually Red in the Church of God, uppon the Sundayes and Holydayes Throughout the Whole Yeere*. London: Henrie Bynneman, for Lucas Harrison and George Bishop, 1579. Digital copy online at EEBO.

Colet, John. *John Colet's Commentary on First Corinthians.* Edited and translated by Bernard O'Kelly and Catherine A.L. Jarrott. Medieval and Renaissance Texts and Studies. Binghamton, NY: Center for Medieval and Early Renaissance Studies, 1985.

Denck, Hans. *Selected Writings of Hans Denck, 1500–1527.* Edited and translated by Edward J. Furcha. Texts and Studies in Religion Series. Lewiston, NY: Edwin Mellen, 1989.

Dickson, David. *An Exposition of All St. Paul's Epistles, together with an Explanation of those other Epistles . . . Wherein the sense of every Chapter and Verse is Analytically unfolded.* London: Eglesfield, 1659. Digital copy online at EEBO.

Diodati, Giovanni. *Pious Annotations Upon the Holy Bible.* London: Nicolas Fussel, 1651. Digital copy online at EEBO.

———. *La Seconde Epistre de . . . S. Paul aux Corinthiens.* In *Les Epistres des Saints Apostres.* Amsterdam: Pierre Le Grand, 1667.

Donne, John. *The Sermons of John Donne.* Edited by George R. Potter and Evelyn M. Simpson. 10 vols. Berkeley: University of California Press, 1953–1962.

Downame, John, ed. *The English Annotations.* 2nd ed. London: John Legatt, 1651. Digital copy online at EEBO.

Erasmus, Desiderius. *Erasmus' Annotations on the New Testament. Acts—Romans—1 and 2 Corinthians.* Edited by Anne Reeve and M. A. Screech. Leiden: Brill, 1990.

———. *Paraphrases on the Epistles to the Corinthians, the Epistles to the Ephesians, Philippians, Colossians, and Thessalonians.* Collected Works of Erasmus 43. Edited by Robert D. Sider. Translated and annotated by Mechtilde O'Mara and Edward A. Phillips, Jr. Toronto: University of Toronto Press, 2009.

Fell, Margaret. *Women's Speaking Justified and Other Pamphlets.* Edited by Jane Donawerth and Rebecca M. Lush. Toronto: Iter Press, 2018.

Goodwin, Thomas. *The Works of Thomas Goodwin.* 12 vols. Edinburgh: James Nichol, 1861–1866.

Goulart, Simon. *XXVIII Discours Chrestiens. Touchant l'estat du Monde & de l'Eglise de Dieu. Nouvellement mis en lumiere, pour l'instruction & consolation des fideles affligez, & qui aspirant à la vie eternelle.* Geneva: Iacob Stoer, 1591. Digital copy online at www.e-rara.ch.

———. *Seconde partie des Discours Chrestiens. Contentant XX. Traitez divers, pour l'instruction & consolation des fideles.* Geneva: Iacob Stoer, 1595. Digital copy online at www.e-rara.ch.

———. *The Wise Vieillard or Old Man.* London: John Dawson, 1621. Digital copy online at EEBO.

Grumbach, Argula von. *Argula von Grumbach. A Woman's Voice in the Reformation.* Edited by Peter Matheson. Edinburgh: T&T Clark, 1995.

Hemmingsen, Niels. *Commentaria in Omnes Epistolas Apostolorum, Pauli, Petri, Iudae, Iohannis, Iacobi, et ineam quae ad Hebraeos.* Frankfurt am Main, 1579. Digital copy online at prdl.org.

Hesshus, Tilemann. *Explicatio Secundae Epistolae Pauli ad Corinthios.* Helmstadt: Jacob Lucius, 1580. Digital copy online at prdl.org.

Hubmaier, Balthasar. *Balthasar Hubmaier: Theologian of Anabaptism.* Edited and translated by H. Wayne Pipkin and John H. Yoder. CRR 5. Scottdale, PA: Herald, 1989.

Hyperius, Andreas. *Commentarii D. Andreae Hyperii, Doctissimi ac Clarissimi Theologi, In Epistolam D. Pauli ad Romanos, et utramque ad Corinthios.* Zurich: Froschauer, 1583.

Joris, David. *The Anabaptist Writings of David Joris, 1535–1543.* Edited and translated by Gary K. Waite. CRR 7. Scottdale, PA: Herald, 1994.

Karlstadt, Andreas Bodenstein von. *The Essential Carlstadt.* CRR 8. Edited by Edward J. Furcha. Walden, NY: Plough Publishing, 2019.

———. *The Eucharistic Pamphlets of Andreas Bodenstein von Karlstadt.* Translated and edited by Amy Nelson Burnett. Early Modern Studies 6. Kirksville, MO: Truman State University Press, 2011.

Kolb, Robert, and Timothy J. Wengert, eds. *The Book of Concord: The Confessions of the Evangelical Lutheran Church.* Translated by Charles Arand, Etic Gritsch, Robert Kolb, William Russell, James Schaff, Jane Stohl, and Timothy Wengert. Minneapolis: Fortress, 2000.

Lefèvre d'Étaples, Jacques. *Jacobi Fabri Stapulensis in omnes D. Pauli epistolas commentariorum libri XIII. Commentariorum in Epistolas Beati Pauli . . . Liber Tertius.* Cologne: Eucharii, 1531. Digital copy online at www.gateway-bayern.de.

Leigh, Edward. *Annotations upon all the New Testament philologicall and theologicall wherein the emphasis and elegancie of the Greek is observed . . .* London: W. W. and E. G. for William Lee, 1650. Available at downloads.it.ox.ac.uk/ota-public/tcp/Texts-HTML.

Liechty, Daniel, ed. *Early Anabaptist Spirituality: Selected Writings.* Classics of Western Spirituality. Mahwah, NJ: Paulist Press, 1994.

Luther, Martin. *Bondage of the Will.* Translated by J. I. Packer and O. R. Johnston. New York: Fleming H. Revell, 1957.

———. *D. Martin Luthers Werke, Kritische Gesamtausgabe. Briefwechsel.* 18 vols. Weimar, 1930–1985.

———. *D. Martin Luthers Werke, Kritische Gesamtausgabe: [Schriften].* 73 vols. Weimar: Hermann Böhlaus Nachfolger, 1883–2009. Digital copy online at archive.org.

———. *Day by Day We Magnify You: Daily Readings for the Entire Year.* Edited by Marshall D. Johnson. Rev. ed. Minneapolis: Augsburg, 2008.

———. *Luther on Women: A Sourcebook.* Edited by Susan Karant-Nunn and Merry Wiesner-Hanks. Cambridge: Cambridge University Press, 2003.

———. *Luther's Works* [American Edition]. 82 vols. Planned. St. Louis: Concordia; Philadelphia, PA: Fortress, 1955–1986, 2009–.

———. *Martin Luther's Basic Theological Writings.* 2nd ed. Edited by Timothy F. Lull. Minneapolis: Fortress, 2005.

———. *The Sermons of Martin Luther.* Edited and translated by John Lenker. 8 vols. Grand Rapids, MI: Baker, 1983.

———. *The Works of Martin Luther.* The Philadelphia Edition. Philadelphia: Muhlenberg, 1932.

Melanchthon, Philipp. *Melanchthons Werke in Auswahl.* Edited by Peter F. Barton. 7 vols. Gütersloh: Gerd Mohn, 1951–1963.

Musculus, Wolfgang. *Commentarius . . . in posteriorem epistolam Pauli ad Corinthios.* In *In Ambas Apostoli Pauli ad Corinthios Epistolas Commentarii.* Basel: Johannes Herwagen, 1566. Digital copy online at www.gateway-bayerne.de.

Oberman, Heiko A. *Forerunners of the Reformation: The Shape of Late Medieval Thought Illustrated by Key Documents.* Philadelphia: Fortress, 1981.

Perkins, William. *The Work of William Perkins.* Edited by Ian Breward. Appleford, UK: Sutton Courtenay Press, 1970.

Philips, Dirk. *Writings of Dirk Philips.* Edited and translated by Cornelius J. Dyck, William E. Keeney, and Alvin J. Beachy. CRR 6. Scottdale, PA: Herald, 1994.

Schaff, Philip, ed. *The Creeds of Christendom: With a Critical History and Notes.* 3 vols. New York: Harper & Row, 1877. Reprint, Grand Rapids, MI: Baker, 1985. Digital copy online at ccel.org.

Schroeder, H. J. *Canons and Decrees of the Council of Trent.* St. Louis: Herder, 1955.

Schurman, Anna Maria Van. *Whether A Christian Woman Should Be Educated and Other Writings from Her Intellectual Circle.* Edited and Translated by Joyce L Irwin. Chicago: University of Chicago Press, 1998.

Sibbes, Richard. *The Complete Works of Richard Sibbes*. Edited by Alexander B. Grosart. 7 vols. Edinburgh: James Nichol, 1862–1864.

Simons, Menno. *The Complete Writings of Menno Simons, c. 1496–1561*. Edited by J. C. Wenger. Scottdale, PA: Herald, 1984.

Snyder, Arnold C., ed. *Sources of South German / Austrian Anabaptism*. Translated by Walter Klaassen, Franck Friesen, and Werner O. Packull. CRR 10. Kitchener, ON: Pandora, 2001.

Spangenberg, Cyriacus. *Die ander Epistel Pauli an die Corinthier*. Strasburg: Samuel Emmel, 1563. Digital copy online at books.google.com.

Spangenberg, Johann. *Postilla Teütsch: Auslegung der Episteln, so auff die Sonntage vom Advent biß auff Ostern in der Kirchen gelesen warden*. Postilla Teütsch 4. Magdeburg: Michael Lotter, 1544. Digital copy online at www.gateway-bayerne.de.

Tanner, Norman P., ed. *Decrees of the Ecumenical Councils*. 2 vols. Washington, DC: Georgetown University Press, 1990.

Thysell, Carol. *The Pleasure of Discernment: Marguerite de Navarre as Theologian*. New York: Oxford University Press, 2000.

Trapp, John. *A Commentary or Exposition upon All the Books of the New Testament*. London: Ekins, 1656. Digital copy online at EEBO.

Weigel, Valentin. *Valentin Weigel Sämtliche Schriften*. 14 vols. Stuttgart-Bad Constatt: Frommann-Holzboog, 1996–.

Zell, Katharina Schütz. *Church Mother: The Writings of a Protestant Reformer in Sixteenth-Century Germany*. Edited and translated by Elsie McKee. Chicago: University of Chicago Press, 2006.

Zuidema, Jason, and Theodore Van Raalte. *Early French Reform: The Theology and Spirituality of Guillaume Farel*. St. Andrews Studies in Reformation History. Burlington, VT: Ashgate, 2011.

Zwingli, Huldrych. *Annotatiunculae per Leonem, ex ore Zwinglii in utraque Pauli ad Corinthios Epistolam publice exponentis conceptae*. Zurich: Christoph Froschauer, 1528. Digital copy online at www.e-rara.ch.

———. *Early Writings*. Edited by Samuel Macauley Jackson. Durham, NC: Labyrinth, 1987.

Other Works Consulted

Augustijn, Cornelis. *Erasmus: His Life, Works, and Influence*. Translated by J. C. Grayson. Toronto: University of Toronto Press, 1991.

Barrett, C. K. *A Commentary on the Second Epistle to the Corinthians*. New York: Harper & Row, 1973.

Bettenson, Henry, and Chris Maunder, eds. *Documents of the Christian Church*. 4th ed. New York: Oxford University Press, 2011.

Black, M. H. "The Printed Bible." In *The Cambridge History of the Bible*, vol. 3, *The West from the Reformation to the Present Day*, edited by S. L. Greenslade, 408-75. Cambridge: Cambridge University Press, 1963,

Bray, Gerald, ed. *1–2 Corinthians*. ACCS NT 7. Downers Grove, IL: IVP Academic, 1999.

Brecht, Martin. *Martin Luther, Shaping and Defining the Reformation, 1521–1532*. 3 vols. Translated by James Schaaf. Minneapolis: Fortress, 1985–1993.

Bruce, F. F. *Paul, Apostle of the Heart Set Free*. Grand Rapids, MI: Eerdmans, 1977.

Chambers, Bettye Thomas. *Bibliography of French Bibles*. Vol. 1, *Fifteenth- and Sixteenth-Century French-Language Editions of the Scriptures*. Geneva: Droz, 1983.

Lewis, Charlton, and Charles Short, eds. *A Latin Dictionary*. Oxford: Oxford University Press, 1991.

Croce, Benedetto. *Galéas Caracciolo, Marquis de Vico*. Geneva: Droz, 1965.

Cross, F. L., and E. A. Livingstone. *The Oxford Dictionary of the Christian Church*. 3rd ed. New York: Oxford University Press, 2005.

Duffy, Eamon. *Saints and Sinners: A History of the Popes*. New Haven, CT: Yale University Press, 1997.

Eusebius of Caesarea. *Ecclesiastical History: Popular Edition*. Grand Rapids, MI: Baker, 1981.

Farmer, Craig S. *The Gospel of John in the Sixteenth Century: The Johannine Exegesis of Wolfgang Musculus*. Oxford Studies in Historical Theology. New York: Oxford University Press, 1997.

Fee, Gordon. *The First Epistle to the Corinthians*. New International Commentary on the New Testament. Grand Rapids, MI: Eerdmans, 1987.

Foxe, John. *Foxe's Book of Martyrs, or, The Acts and Monuments of the Christian Church*. Philadelphia: James B. Smith, 1860.

Frend, W. H. C. *The Rise of Christianity*. Philadelphia: Fortress, 1984.

Frymire, John. *The Primacy of the Postils: Catholics, Protestants, and the Dissemination of Ideas in Early Modern Germany*. Leiden: Brill, 2010.

George, Timothy. *Reading the Scripture with the Reformers*. Downers Grove, IL: IVP Academic, 2011.

———. *Theology of the Reformers*. Rev. ed. Nashville: B&H Academic, 2013.

Gordon, Bruce. *Calvin*. New Haven, CT: Yale University Press, 2009.

Greschat, Martin. *Martin Bucer: A Reformer and His Times*. Translated by Stephen E. Buckwalter. Louisville, KY: Westminster John Knox, 2004.

Hagen, Kenneth. "What Did the Term *Commentarius* Mean to Sixteenth-Century Theologians?" In *Théorie et pratique de l'exégèse: Actes du troisième colloque international sur l'histoire de l'exégèse biblique au XVI siècle*, edited by Irena Backus and Francis Higman, 13-38. Geneva: Droz, 1990.

Hains, Todd R. "Luther and the Bound Conscience in His German Church Postils." MA thesis, Trinity Evangelical Divinity School, 2007.

Hammond, N. G. L., and H. H. Scullard, eds. *Oxford Classical Dictionary*. 2nd ed. Oxford: Clarendon, 1970.

Hillerbrand, Hans, ed. *The Oxford Encyclopedia of the Reformation*. 4 vols. New York: Oxford University Press, 1996.

Holder, R. Ward, ed. *Companion to Paul in the Reformation*. Leiden: Brill, 2009.

Hughes, Philip E. *Paul's Second Epistle to the Corinthians*. New International Commentary on the New Testament. Grand Rapids, MI: Eerdmans, 1973.

Kingdon, Robert M. *Adultery and Divorce in Calvin's Geneva*. Cambridge, MA: Harvard University Press, 1995.

Krans, Jan. *Beyond What Is Written: Erasmus and Beza as Conjectural Critics of the New Testament*. Leiden: Brill, 2006.

Kruse, Colin. *2 Corinthians*. Tyndale New Testament Commentary. Grand Rapids, MI: Eerdmans, 1997.

Kuhl, Sigrun. "The Religious Roots of Modern Poverty Policy: Catholics, Lutheran, and Reformed Protestant Traditions Compared." *European Journal of Sociology* 46 (2005): 91-126.

Lindberg, Carter. *Beyond Charity: Reformation Initiatives for the Poor*. Minneapolis: Fortress, 1993.

Manetsch, Scott M. *1 Corinthians*. RCS NT 9a. Downers Grove, IL: IVP Academic, 2017.

———. *Calvin's Company of Pastors: Pastoral Care and the Emerging Reformed Church, 1536–1609*. New York: Oxford University Press, 2013.

———. "(Re)construction the Pastoral Office: Wolfgang Musculus's Commentaries on 1 and 2 Corinthians." In *On the Writing of New Testament Commentaries*, edited by Stanley Porter and Eckhard Schnabel, 253-66. Leiden: Brill, 2013.

McIndoe, John. "John Calvin: Preface to the Homilies of Chrysostom." *Hartford Quarterly* 5 (1965): 19-26.

McKim, Donald K., ed. *The Cambridge Companion to John Calvin*. Cambridge: Cambridge University Press, 2004.

———, ed. *Dictionary of Major Biblical Interpreters*. Downers Grove, IL: IVP Academic, 2007.

Meylan, Henri. "Professeurs et Étudiants, Question d'Horaires et de Leçons." In *La Réforme et l'éducation*, edited by Jean Boisset, 67-85. Toulouse: Privat, 1974.

Morris, Leon. *1 Corinthians*. Tyndale New Testament Commentaries. Grand Rapids, MI: Eerdmans, 1998.

Muller, Richard A. *Dictionary of Latin and Greek Theological Terms: Drawn Principally from Protestant Scholastic Theology*. Grand Rapids, MI: Baker, 1985.

Muller, Richard A., and John L. Thompson, eds. *Biblical Interpretation in the Era of the Reformation: Essays Presented to David C. Steinmetz in Honor of His Sixtieth Birthday*. Grand Rapids, MI: Eerdmans, 1996.

Olin, John, ed. *A Reformation Debate: John Calvin and Jacopo Sadoleto*. Reprint, Grand Rapids, MI: Baker, 1987.

Ozment, Steven. *Protestants: The Birth of a Revolution*. New York: Doubleday, 1993.

Parker, T. H. L. *Calvin's New Testament Commentaries*. Louisville, KY: Westminster John Knox, 1993.

Pelikan, Jaroslav. *The Reformation of the Bible, the Bible of the Reformation*. New Haven, CT: Yale University Press, 1996.

Plass, Ewald M., ed. *What Luther Says: A Practical In-Home Anthology for the Active Christian*. St. Louis: Concordia, 1959.

Puyroche, M. "La bibliothèque d'un Pasteur à la fin du XVI siècle." *Bulletin de la société de l'histoire du Protestantisme français* 21 (1872): 327-37.

Rittgers, Ronald. *The Reformation of Suffering: Pastoral Theology and Lay Piety in Late Medieval and Early Modern Germany*. New York: Oxford University Press, 2012.

Schilling, Heinz. "Confessional Europe." In *Handbook of European History 1400–1600*, edited by Thomas Brady, Heiko A. Oberman, and James Tracy, 2:641-82. Leiden: Brill, 1994.

Stephens, W. P. *The Theology of Huldrych Zwingli*. Oxford: Oxford University Press, 1986.

———. *Zwingli: An Introduction to His Thought*. Oxford: Oxford University Press, 2001.

Strauss, Gerald. "The Mental World of a Saxon Pastor." In *Reformation Principle and Practice: Essays in Honour of Arthur Geoffrey Dickens*, edited by Peter Newman Brooks, 161-70. London: Scholar Press, 1980.

Thompson, John L. "Calvin as a Biblical Interpreter." In *The Cambridge Companion to John Calvin*, edited by Donald McKim, 58-73. Cambridge: Cambridge University Press, 2004.

———. *Reading the Bible with the Dead: What You Can Learn from the History of Exegesis That You Can't Learn from Exegesis Alone*. Grand Rapids, MI: Eerdmans, 2007.

Thompson, Mark. *A Sure Ground on Which to Stand: The Relation of Authority and Interpretive Method in Luther's Approach to Scripture*. Eugene, OR: Wipf & Stock, 2006.

Vogler, Bernard. *Le Clergé Protestant Rhénan au Siècle de la Réforme, 1555–1619*. Paris: Éditions Ophrys, 1976.

Wengert, Timothy J., ed. *Dictionary of Luther and the Lutheran Traditions*. Grand Rapids, MI: Baker Academic, 2017.

———. "The Rhetorical Paul: Philip Melanchthon's Interpretation of the Pauline Epistles." In *A Companion to Paul in the Reformation*, edited by R. Ward Holder, 129-64. Leiden: Brill, 2009.

Williams, George Hunston. *The Radical Reformation*. 3rd ed. Kirksville, MO: Sixteenth Century Journal Publishers, 1992.

Author and Writings Index

Subject Index

Scripture Index